e Zambezi River a...st
here came to be a new people
...a name. This tribe had been
of various people fleeing from
each other: "We are fleeing the
...,...and we are fleeing the East
e and put a stop to our flight."
e area did not see things the
nameless ones seek their own
corner of earth around which
atchtowers manned by archers.
e Zambezi River and the vast
here came to be a new people
a name. This tribe had been

IN PRAISE OF BLACK WOMEN
1

IN PRAISE OF BLACK WOMEN

1

Ancient African Queens

Simone Schwarz-Bart
with André Schwarz-Bart

Translated by
Rose-Myriam Réjouis and Val Vinokurov

With a foreword by
Howard Dodson

The University of Wisconsin Press
Modus Vivendi Publications

The University of Wisconsin Press
2537 Daniels Street
Madison, Wisconsin 53718

Modus Vivendi Publications
The Galleria
P.O. Box 460091
Houston, Texas 77056-8091

Copyright © 2001
Modus Vivendi Publications
All rights reserved

5   4   3   2   1

Printed in Hong Kong

Library of Congress Cataloging-in-Publication Data
Schwarz-Bart, Simone.
    [Hommage à la femme noire. English]
    In praise of black women /
  Simone Schwarz-Bart, with André Schwarz-Bart ; translated by Rose-Myriam Réjouis and Val Vinokurov ; with a foreword by Howard Dodson.
    448 pp.   cm.
    Translation of: Hommage à la femme noire.
    ISBN 0-299-17250-3
    1. Women, Black—Biography. 2. Afro-American women—Biography.
  I. Schwarz-Bart, André, 1928- II. Title.
HQ1123 .S379   2001
305.48'896'00922—dc2   00-012316

This second edition is published under the auspices of the United Nations Educational, Scientific and Cultural Organization.

CONTENTS

Foreword vii

Acknowledgments: The Eye Of Love viii

Black Eve 2

Black Women Ten Thousand Years Ago 16

Ahmose Nofretari 28

Hatshepsut 42

Tiye 52

The Candaces 62

Makeda 74

Daurama 84

Yennenga 100

Sogolon Konté 118

Amina Kulibali 130

Amina of Zaria 148

Heleni 162

Ana de Sousa Nzinga 174

Mentowah 188

Beatrice Kimpa Vita 202

Queen Poku 220

Sogané Touré 230

The Story of Nandi 242

Tata Ajeché 258

Modjadji I 270

Ranavalona I 284

N'Daté Yalla 296

Nongqawuse 308

Sarraounia 320

The Story of Naga 336

Manta Tisi 350

Taitu Bethel 362

Ranavalona III 378

Mamochisane 394

Principal Works Consulted 405

Sources of Texts Cited 412

List of Illustrations 419

FOREWORD

Until the mid-1960s, black women the world over were doubly victimized by what historian Gerder Lerner termed "scholarly neglect and racist assumptions." As a consequence they (and we) were denied knowledge of their unique pasts as well as access to their thoughts, visions, aspirations, and perspectives. Wherever one looked for documented evidence of their historical and cultural roles, be it in textbooks, in academic disciplines, in grade school and high school classes, or the public media, black women were invisible beings, voiceless beings.

Anyone who has ever lived among women of African descent knows that it is inconceivable to even imagine invisible or voiceless black women. Wherever one looks in the black world, one finds in black women a living, working, struggling, nurturing presence—the primary source of life itself. And their voices—their prodding, probing, commanding, caressing, captivating, caring, melodic, and melancholy voices are omnipresent realities in black families and communities everywhere. By the 1970s, fueled by the global movements for political, economic, and social change of which they were so much a vital part, black women began to emerge as major figures in local, national, and international affairs.

Of course black women have been central to the development of humankind since its inception. Whether one traces humanity's origins back to the biblical Eve or anthropological Lucy, the roots of human existence lead back to Africa and to African women. Despite this fact, black women have either been completely written out of history or have had their roles so trivialized as to make them appear to be insignificant. Fortunately, over the last three decades these errors of commission and omission have begun to be corrected. This series of volumes is an important part of that corrective action.

When Simone Schwarz-Bart visited the Schomburg Center in the mid-1980s to conduct research for this project, we were in the midst of conducting a symposium on the history of black women in the Americas. As she described her project to me, I was impressed by both its geographic and historical scope. Her goal was to rescue and reconstruct the lives of black women worldwide dating back to Eve and Lucy and to trace their diverse roles in human history down through the end of the twentieth century.

This series of volumes first published in French in 1988 did just that—textually and in vivid color images. I am delighted that she has found the wherewithal to make it available in this English language edition. I'm certain you will find these books interesting, informative, uplifting, and inspiring!

Howard Dodson

THE EYE OF LOVE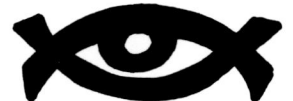

I would like to thank all those who offered their energy, resources and good spirit to help me make *Hommage à la Femme Noire* by Simone Schwarz-Bart available to the English-Speaking world. All played very different, albeit crucial roles in this adventure. For their unshakable support and belief I would like to thank. . .

Thierry Pélage, my husband, who pushed me to start this entire journey, encouraged me through the darkest moments and didn't hesitate to adjust his career and change continents to help me achieve this particular dream . . .

Sharon Byfield and Margrette Francisco, who encouraged me at moments when starting this project seemed impossible . . .

David Ashton, my British lawyer, who brought home to me the necessity of starting any project on the right legal foot and without whom this book wouldn't exist . . .

Neslyn Watson-Druée, my business angel, who believed in me and displayed unusual patience to see me achieve this wonderful but arduous goal and Yvonne Thompson who introduced her to me . . .

Danielle Marcelline, my French lawyer and friend, who guided me graciously towards the acquisition of the English language rights . . .

Robert Baensch, Director of the Center for Publishing at New York University, my mentor, who helped my metamorphosis from a Cosmetics Sales and Marketing Director into a real Publisher . . .

Rose-Myriam Réjouis and Val Vinokurov, the translators, for their work, total dedication and sustained encouragements . . .

Neil Gantcher, my New York lawyer, and not my agent, who, would you believe, graciously introduced me to my co-publishing partner . . .

Dr. Robert Mandel, Director of the University of Wisconsin Press, my co-publishing partner, who immediately understood the importance of this project and supported my efforts towards its materialization . . .

The entire team at the University of Wisconsin Press, who have shown enormous good will and adjusted considerably to fit this project into their tight schedule . . .

Alexandra Legendri, Flore Monthieux, Monique Monthieux, Chantal Claverie, members of my family, who supported my efforts and often prayed for the success of this project . . .

Paul Bates, Huguette Bessard, Alain and Marie-Aline Monthieux, Sophie Moreau, Juliette Kabondo Shirley for donating air miles or providing accommodations when necessary during the development phase or the promotional tour of *In Praise of Black Women* . . .

Cedric Cooper, Ginny Fowler and Daniel Rios for their help and words of wisdom . . .

I dedicate all my efforts to Simone Schwarz-Bart, who believed in me always to reach my goal, my son Alexenri Monthieux Pélage and to my grandmother, Odette Monthieux . . .

Sandrah Monthieux Pélage

Publisher
Modus Vivendi Publications

IN PRAISE OF BLACK WOMEN
1

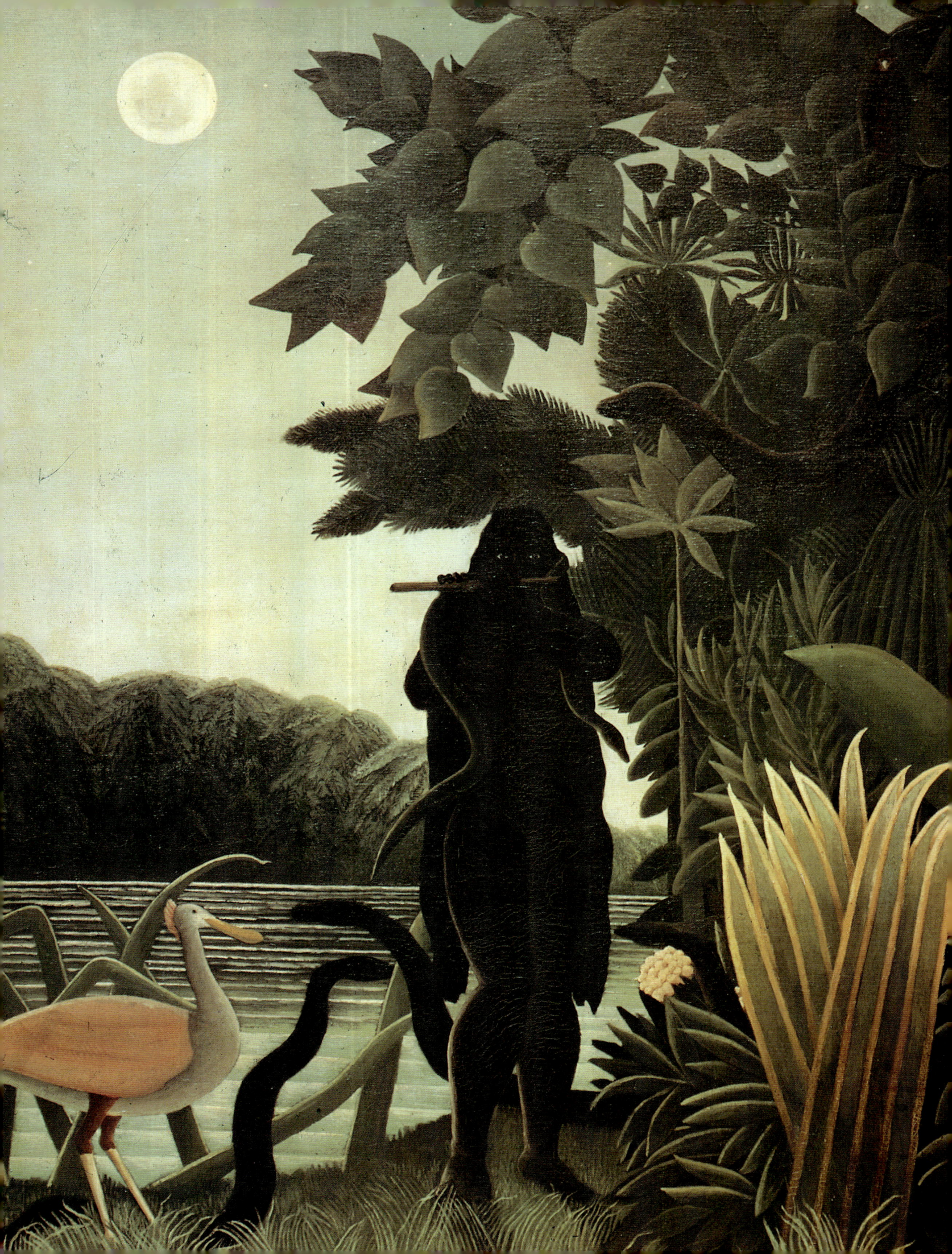

BLACK EVE

THE FIRST WOMAN

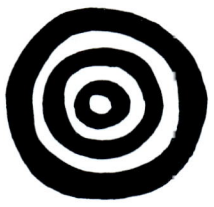

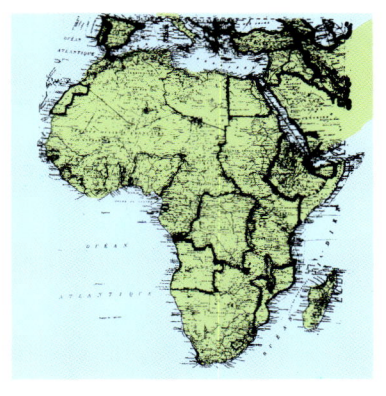

Lucy, the young African, is the grandmother of us all, black and white, red and yellow alike. She is the womb from which all of humanity came...

PEOPLE OF THE BOOK, THOSE ADHERING TO THE THREE GREAT RELIGIONS OF THE BOOK, SEE IN THE BIBLICAL STORY OF CREATION A HOLY STORY; OTHER PEOPLE SEE IT AS AN OLD TALE, AN ILLUMINATED PICTURE WITH COLORS MORE OR LESS faded. For both of them, the story of Adam bears no relation to today.

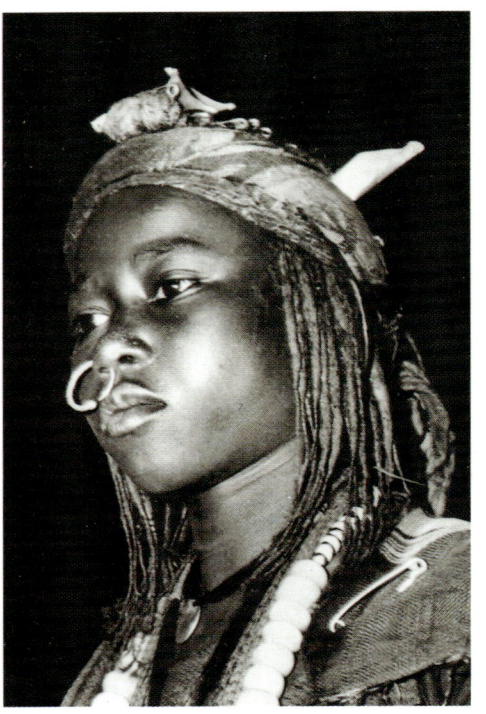

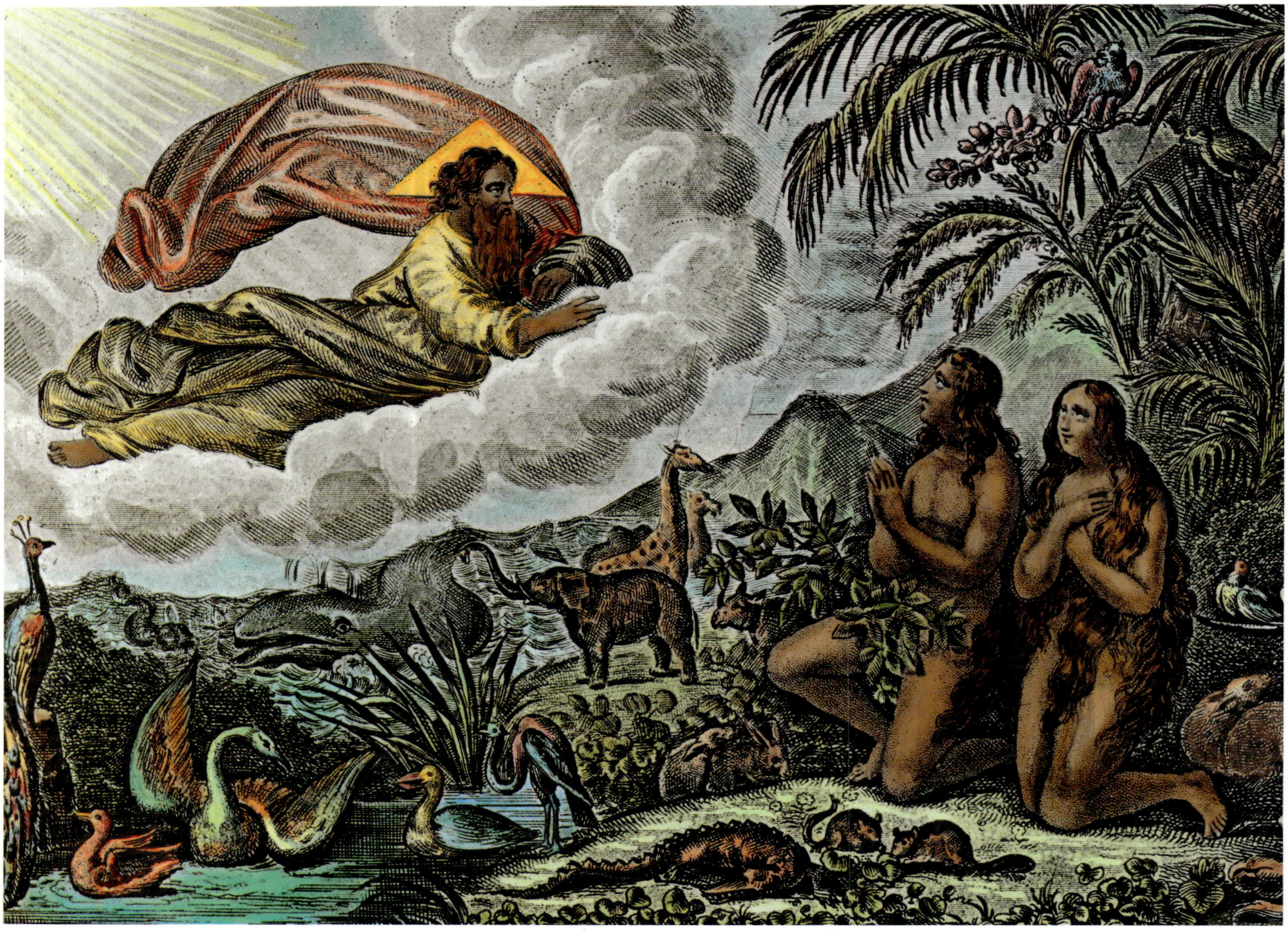

THE BIBLICAL STORY AS A HOLY STORY OR AN ILLUMINATION

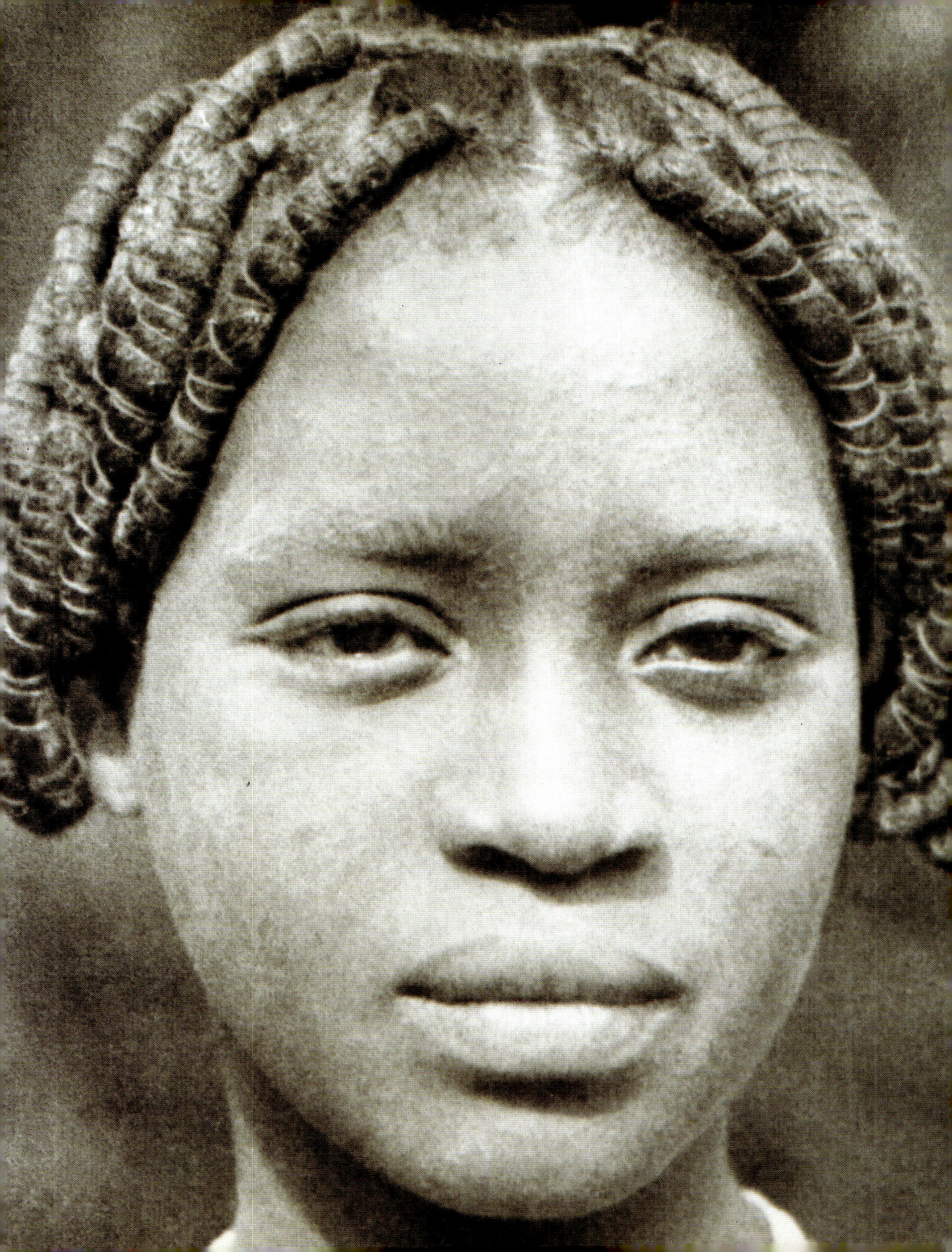

But if you think about it, that primeval couple placed at the origin of all humanity tells us a story that hasn't aged a bit for six thousand years.

As one ancient commentary puts it so well: "if God at first created a single man, a single woman, it is so that we may all have the same ancestors and so that no one may ever be able to say to another: 'I am better than you by birth.'"

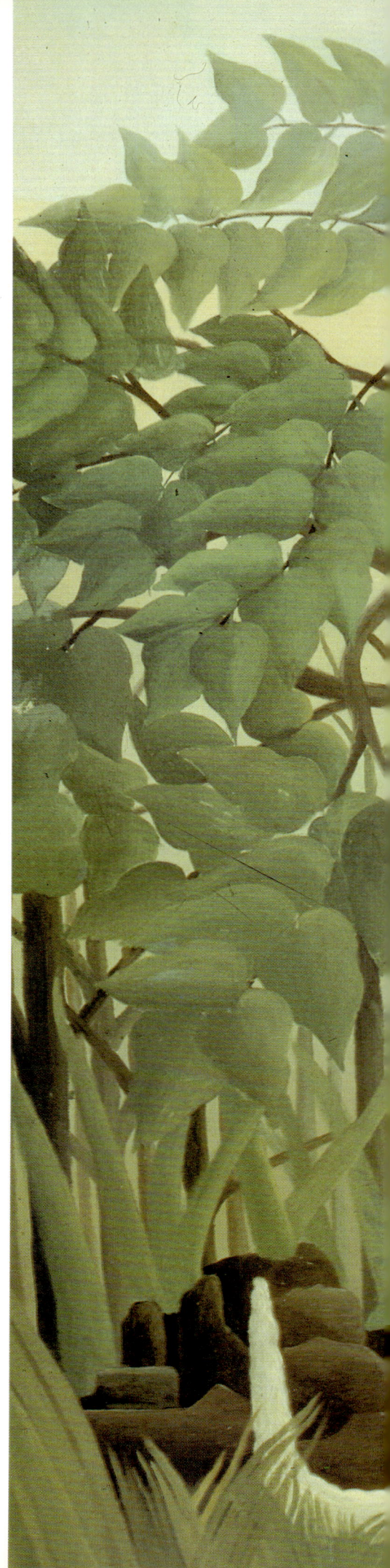

An old legend points out that Adam's very body was made with clay from the four corners of the earth, so that, in the infinite string of centuries to come, no nation could ever claim: *our* country is favored above all others, humanity arose from *our* soil and only afterwards did it spread over the rest of the planet.

This legend tells us that there never was an afterwards, that no people arose early or late, that there is no place, no face, above all others: all were born on the same day, of the same blood.

This idea of a single human family has not always included men and women of black skin.

To justify slavery and the slave trade, some divided the human species into unequal races. And then, using science as a pretext, they went looking for "proofs" of this inequality down to the most deeply buried fossils in the earth's belly.

A zealous few have even advanced the theory that blacks don't belong to humankind, that, in the great Tree of Life, they represent a different branch, one closer to primates than *Homo sapiens*.

Far be it from me, today, to try to reverse the roles and assert the superiority of the black race; this would be unworthy of our past, our sufferings and struggles.

But it is at least pleasant to note that after having tried to put us among the ranks of baboons (haven't some claimed that, under certain hot and humid conditions, a monkey and a black woman could mate?), Western science is forced to recognize that all of humanity was born on this old continent, so covered with spite: Africa, Black Africa, to be precise.

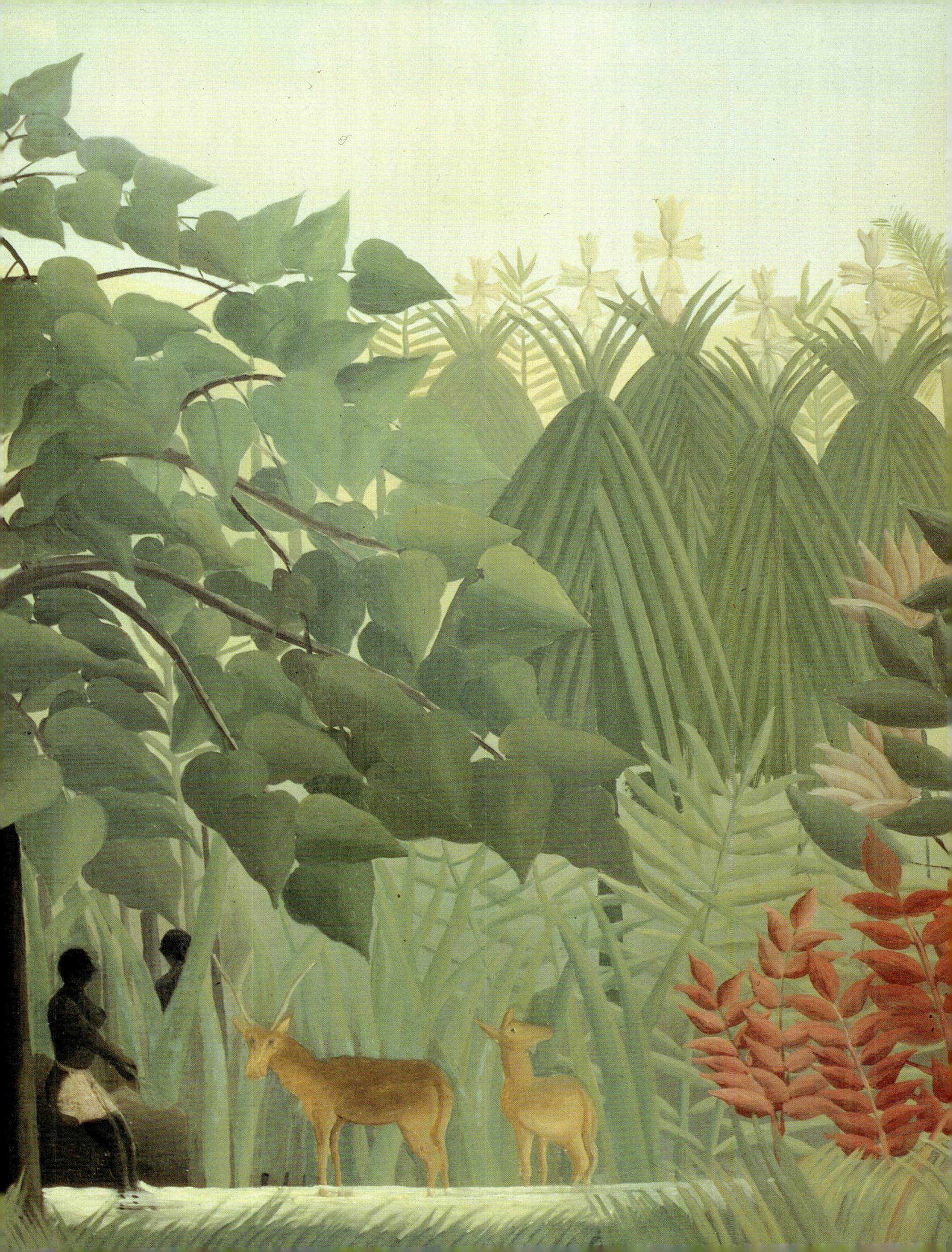

The Mother of Humankind

Three men go one after another to Ouendé's to make their needs known to him. One of them says: "I want a horse." Another says: "I want dogs so I can go hunting in the bush." The third says: "I want a woman to quench my thirst."

And Ouendé gives them everything: a horse to the first, dogs to the second, a woman to the third.

The three men leave. But then the rain comes, confining them to the bush; the woman cooks for them, for all three of them. The men say: "Let's go back to Ouendé's." And so they go.

All of them then ask for women. And Ouendé is willing to change the horse into a woman, and the dogs into women as well.

The men leave. But the woman who was the horse turns out greedy. The women who used to be dogs are mean; but the first woman, the one Ouendé gave to the first man, she is good: she is the mother of humankind.

The Legend of Creation

When things were not yet things, Mébère the Creator made man out of clay. He took the clay and shaped it into man. And so man got his beginnings, but he began life as a lizard. Mébère then put this lizard into a basin of seawater. For five days. The lizard spent five days in the basin. Then seven days. Seven days did he spend in the basin. On the eighth day, Mébère looked at him. The lizard came out of the basin, but he was a man now. And he said to the Creator, "Thank you."

Why the World Was Peopled

Abasi got up, sat there, made all the big things, all the little things, the water, the forest, the river, the streams, the beasts of the forest; he made all of the various things that now exist in the world. He did not make man. All the men lived above, with Abasi. At that time, no man lived down below in the world; there were only the beasts in the forest, the fish in the waters, the birds that we see in the air, and many other countless beings. But man did not exist in the world. All men were in exile, they lived with Abasi in his village. When Abasi sat down to eat, they would join him and Altan.

In the end, Altan called, Abasi answered and she said to him: "The situation, as it stands, is just no good. You own the land up here, you own the sky in which they live here, but down below you have created a whole place to live, and now if you don't put the men there, it's all no good. Think of a way to put the men on earth so that they'll stay there and light fires and thus warm up the sky; because it's quite cold up here since there's no fire on earth."

This discovery is relatively recent: in 1959 two paleontologists, Louis and Mary Leakey, dug up the skull of a humanoid that was 1.75 million years old. The place of discovery: the Olduvai Gorge in East Africa, where the fault in the ground lets one read the whole story of life like a book, each page a distinct geological layer. Scientists have little doubt: we stand before the cradle of humankind.

And so the two links come together: the scientific narrative meets up with the old story of creation.

Earthly paradise did exist: in Africa.

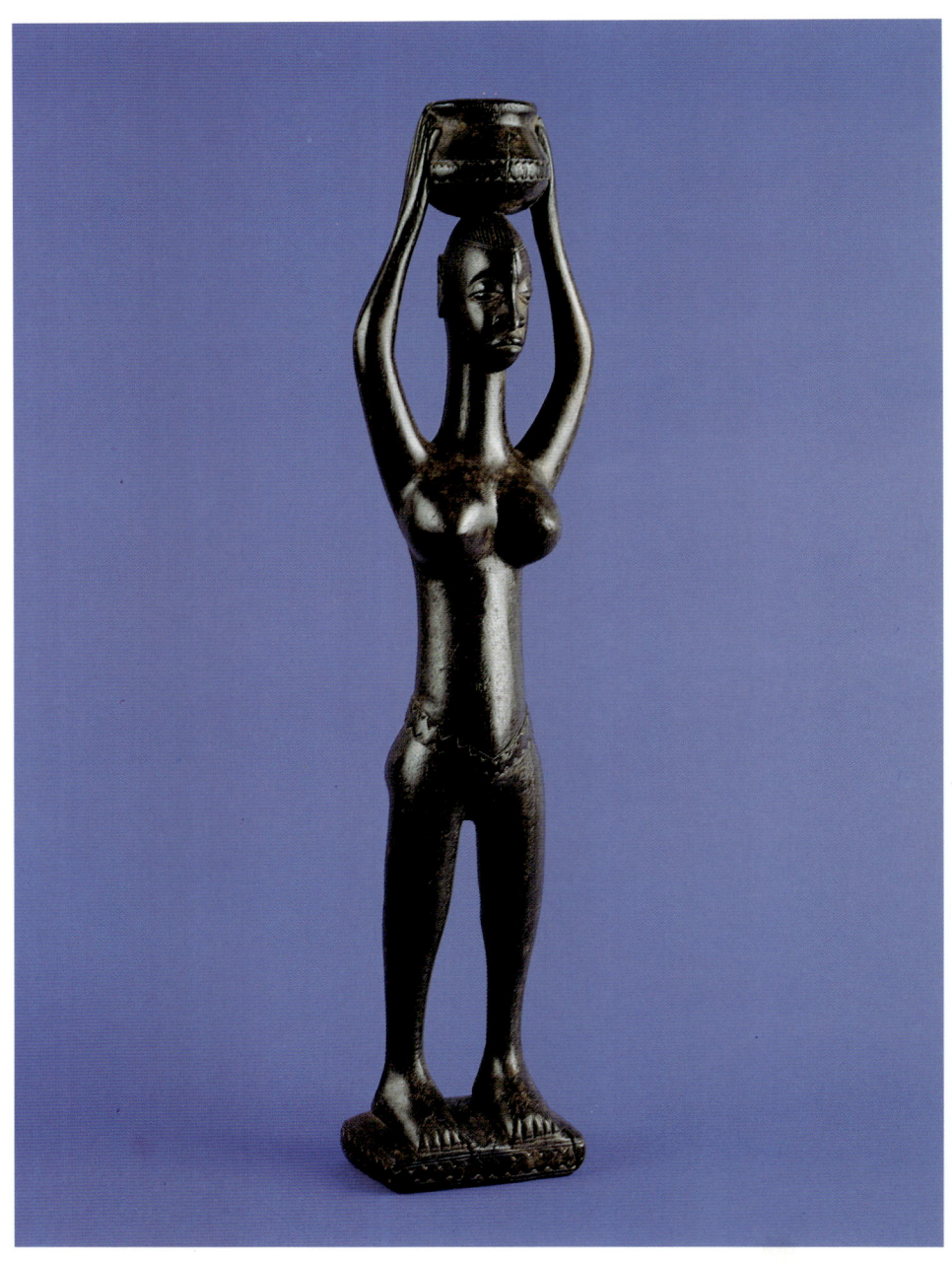

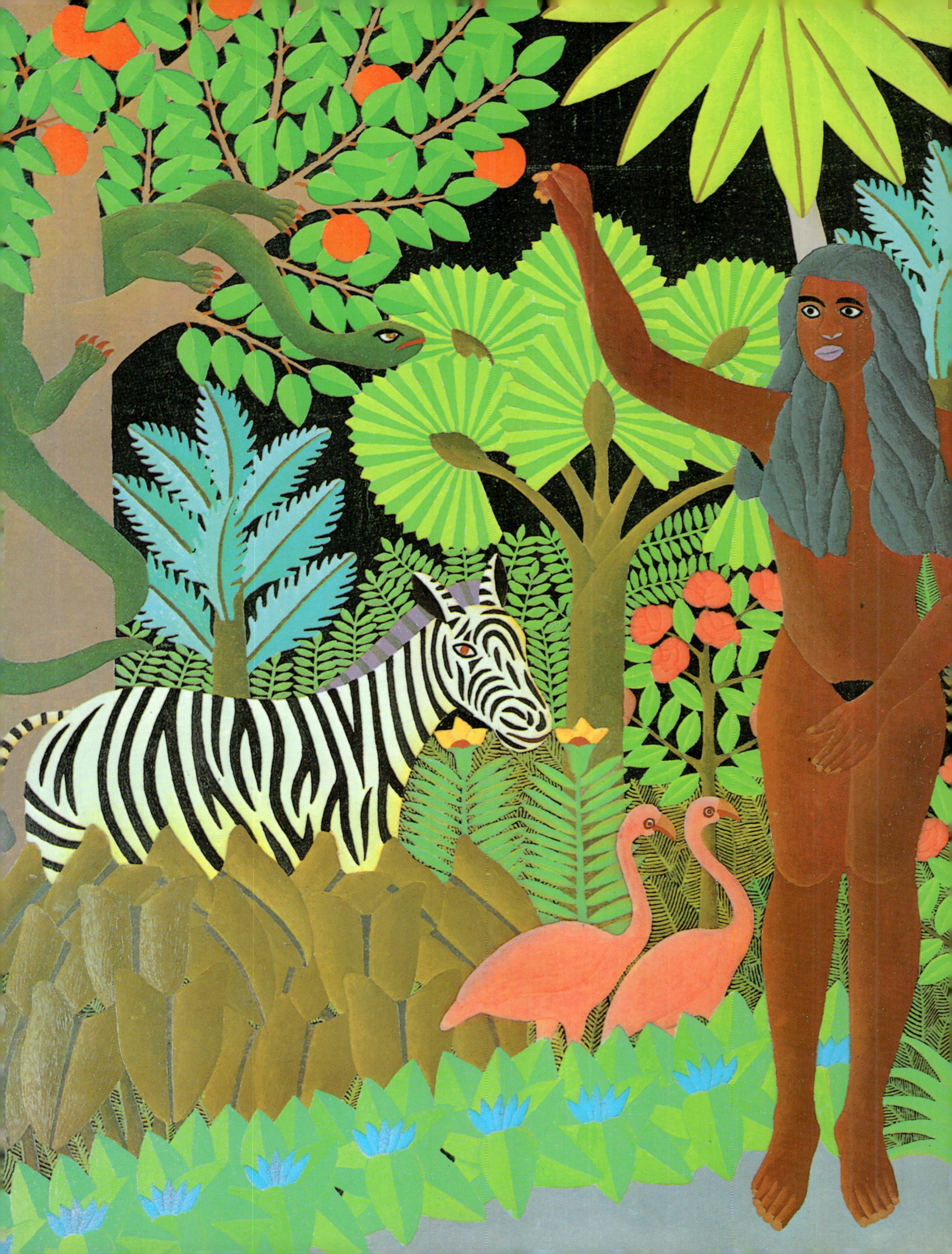

Black Eve, the Mother of Humankind, Unifying the Human Race

For the hundreds of thousands of years that went by between the appearance of man in Africa and his settlement of Europe in the north and Asia in the east, Africa remained the most important theater for the drama of human evolution.

The unity of the human race is a given from which no one can be excepted. People have developed not only their knowledge, but also their superstitions, philosophies, and religions, without ever severing their common ties, physical as well as spiritual, without ever ceasing to be members of the human race.

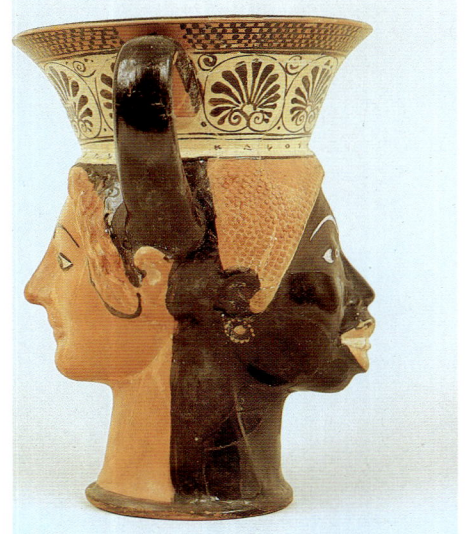

AN IMAGE OF BEAUTY AS SEEN BY THE GREEKS, 2,500 YEARS AGO

Black Eve, an Additional, Genetic Proof

Human mitochondria are transmitted only through women.

The study of mitochondrial DNA continues to astonish the world. In examining these little fragments of DNA belonging to the placenta cells of 147 women of different ethnicities, Prof. Wilson and six of his colleagues discovered that the foremother of us all had first seen the light of day somewhere in Africa. Why? Because the mitochondria of Black, European, Asian, and Australian and New Guinean Aboriginal women all contained genes found only in African women.

Furthermore, we know that the mutation rate of this DNA is 2 to 4% per million years. So it was easy to go back in time and figure out the date at which all the now different varieties of mitochondria were still one strain, belonging to a single woman who begat the human race.

It is no less curious to note that the first man was a woman, so to speak.

Indeed, since the Leakeys' discovery, we have been witness to a veritable stampede of paleontologists to the fault at Olduvai, that Garden of Eden in present-day imagination, to extract thousands of flint and bone fragments. And so it was that, on November 30th, 1974, there appeared a strange fossil, three-and-a-half million years old, the humble remains of a small woman, whom, out of friendship, the scientists baptized Lucy.

More recent tests show that Lucy, the young African, is the grandmother of us all, blacks and whites, yellows, reds, people of the sea and dwellers of the steppe, those who live with the sun or with the polar cold. She is the one womb from which all of humanity came.

No doubt we would have trouble seeing our common ancestor in her: we'll never know what features covered the splintered bones buried in the sands of Olduvai. But before commencing with this work, devoted to heroines often little known, forgotten, I wanted to salute the woman I like to call Black Eve.

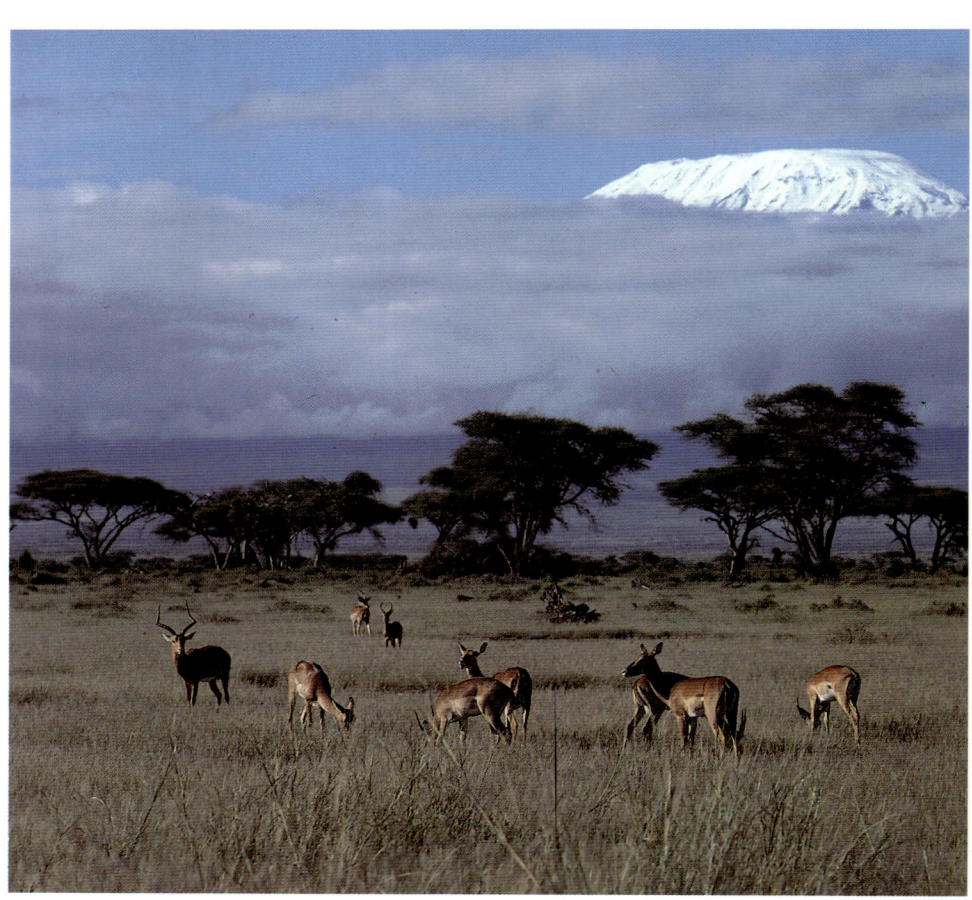

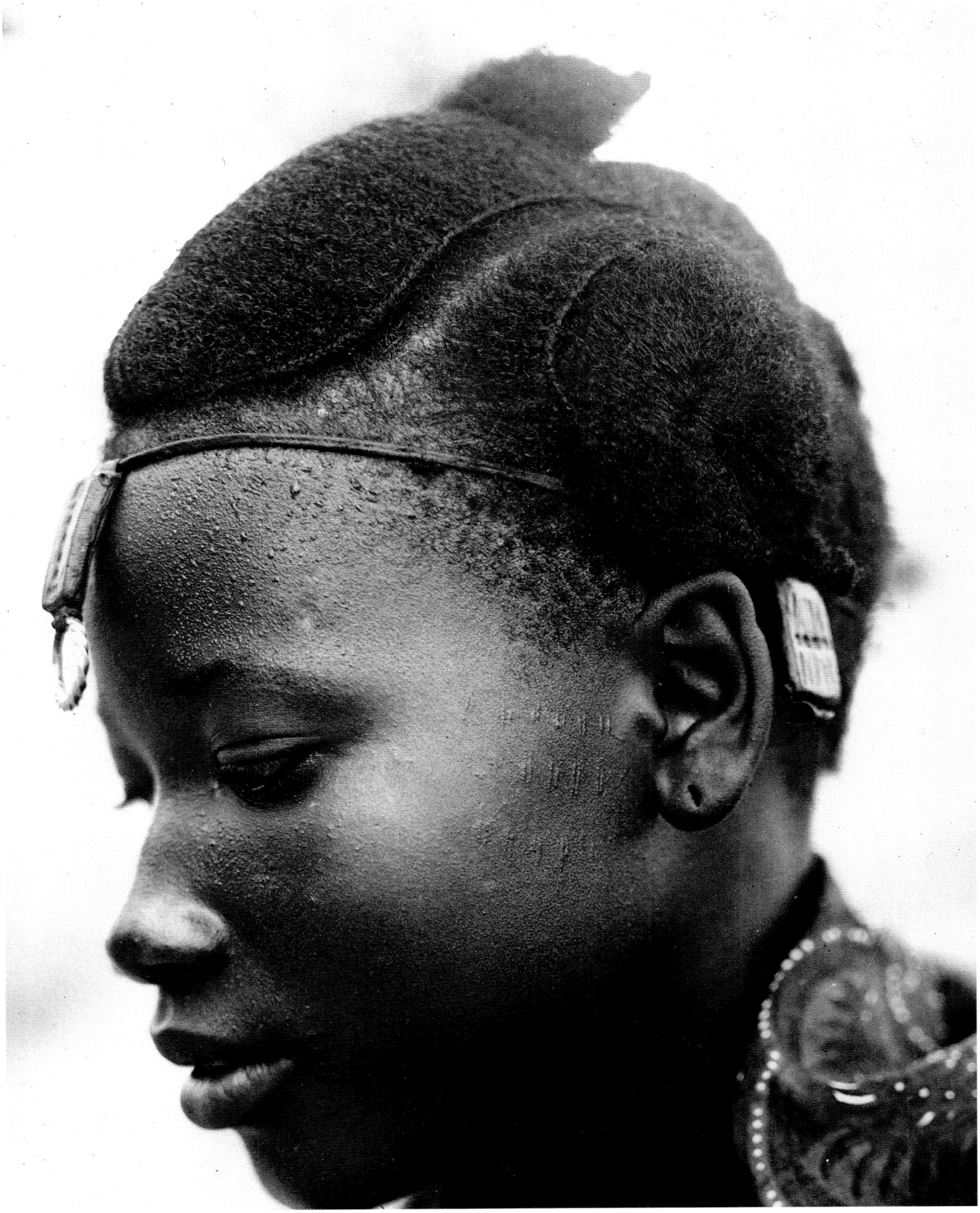

BLACK EVE

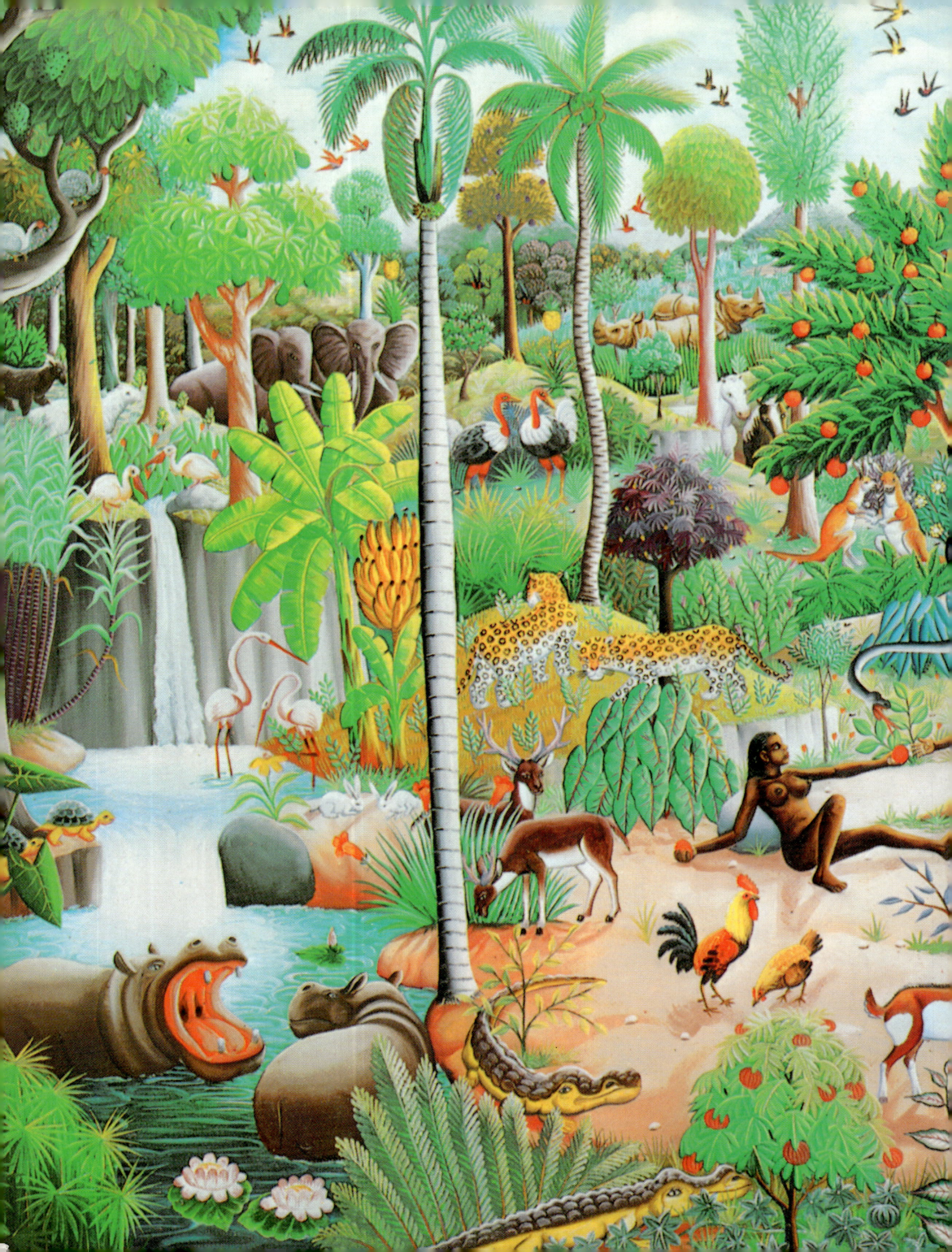

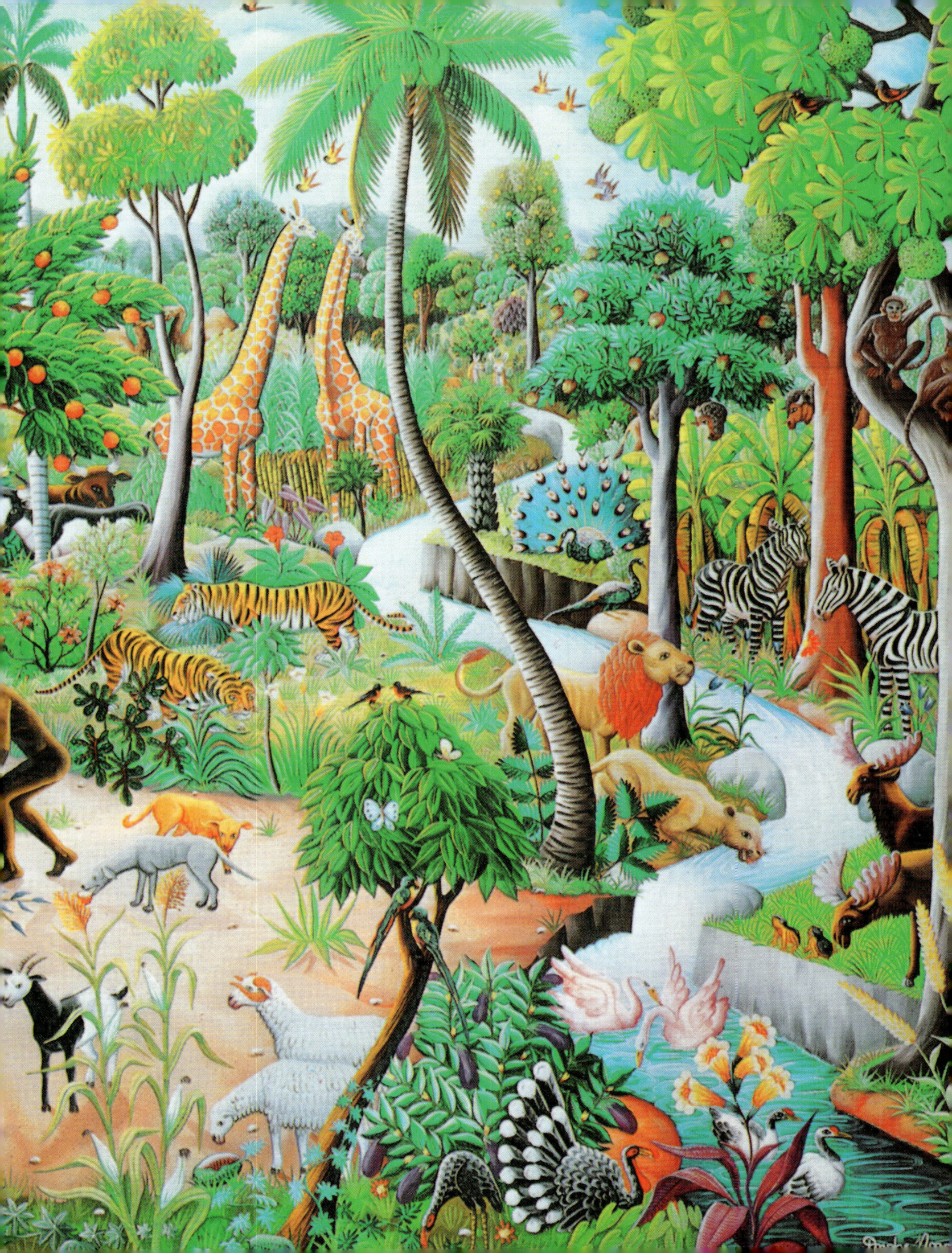

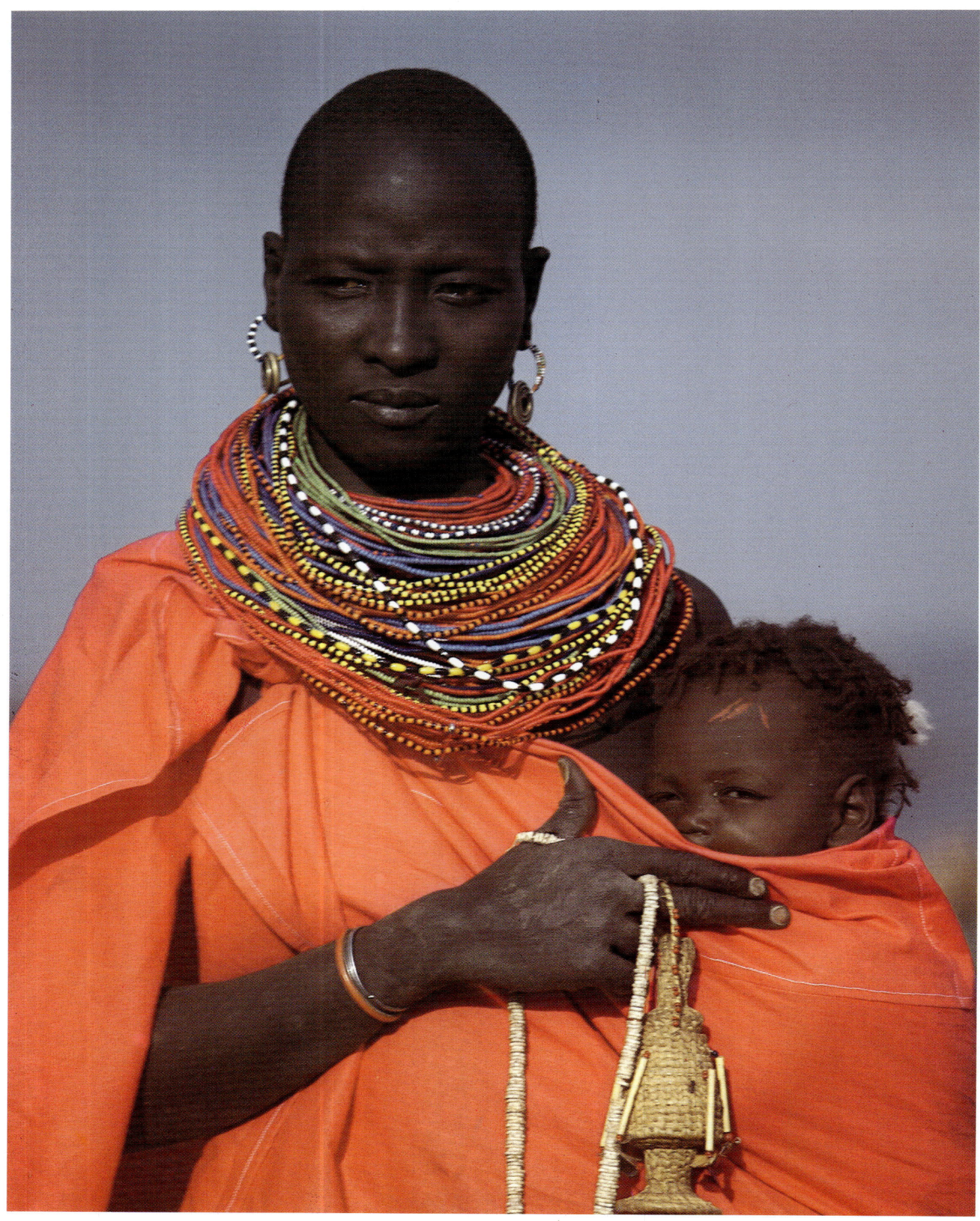

WORDS
OF AN ORDINARY WOMAN

The heart is the person. Because everything belongs to the heart. Everything depends on the heart.

To the heart belong desire, love, hatred. Everything. Because the heart is the person.

Hear our proverb. We say: "Don't stand before the eyes of someone handing things out, stand before his heart!" You are close to someone only when you are close to his heart.

Whoever is close to someone's heart is worth more than the one who is close to her eyes.

If I am far from your eyes and you wish to give me something, you will always remember me through your heart. But if I am far from your heart, you will forget me, even if I am here in front of your eyes.

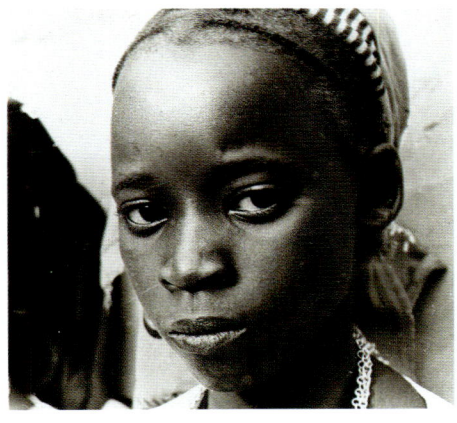

What is big in every human being is the heart.

When you look at someone, you can see the eyes completely. You can measure someone's eyes. But you'll never manage to measure someone's heart. Only God can say He knows someone's heart.

The heart is worth more than the eye. We express this in a proverb: "The eye is narrow, the heart is broad." If you are far from your friend, your heart sees him, but your eyes cannot. If you miss your country, your heart can see all of its hills, all of its trees, all of the settlements you have left behind there. Your heart remembers, and in remembering sees all of these things. But the eyes can't see any of that.

Distance can't stop the heart from seeing. But it can stop the eyes.

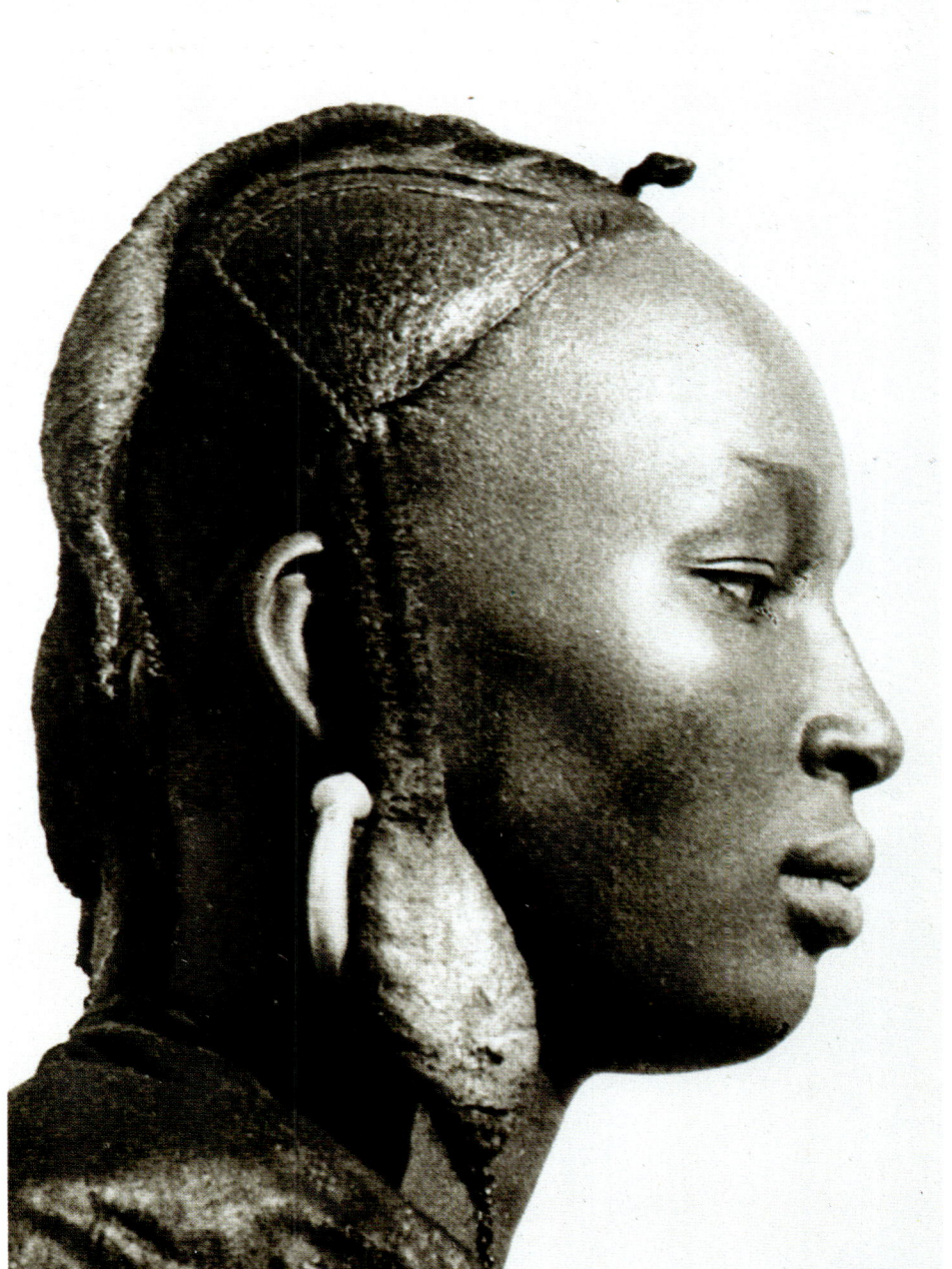

The heart is the person. It's the heart that loves. It's the heart that hates. It's the heart that suffers. And it's the heart that remembers things and people. If you forget someone's name, you'll say: "I'm heartless, I have forgotten!"

The heart is the person. The heart is the body. A body with no heart has no life. Disease or health in a body depend on the heart: the heart is what beats and flutters, the heart brings on nausea.

The heart is the person. Because the heart is personality, moods, goodness, meanness. It is courage or fear. Anger, too. I tell you again, for us, the heart is everything.

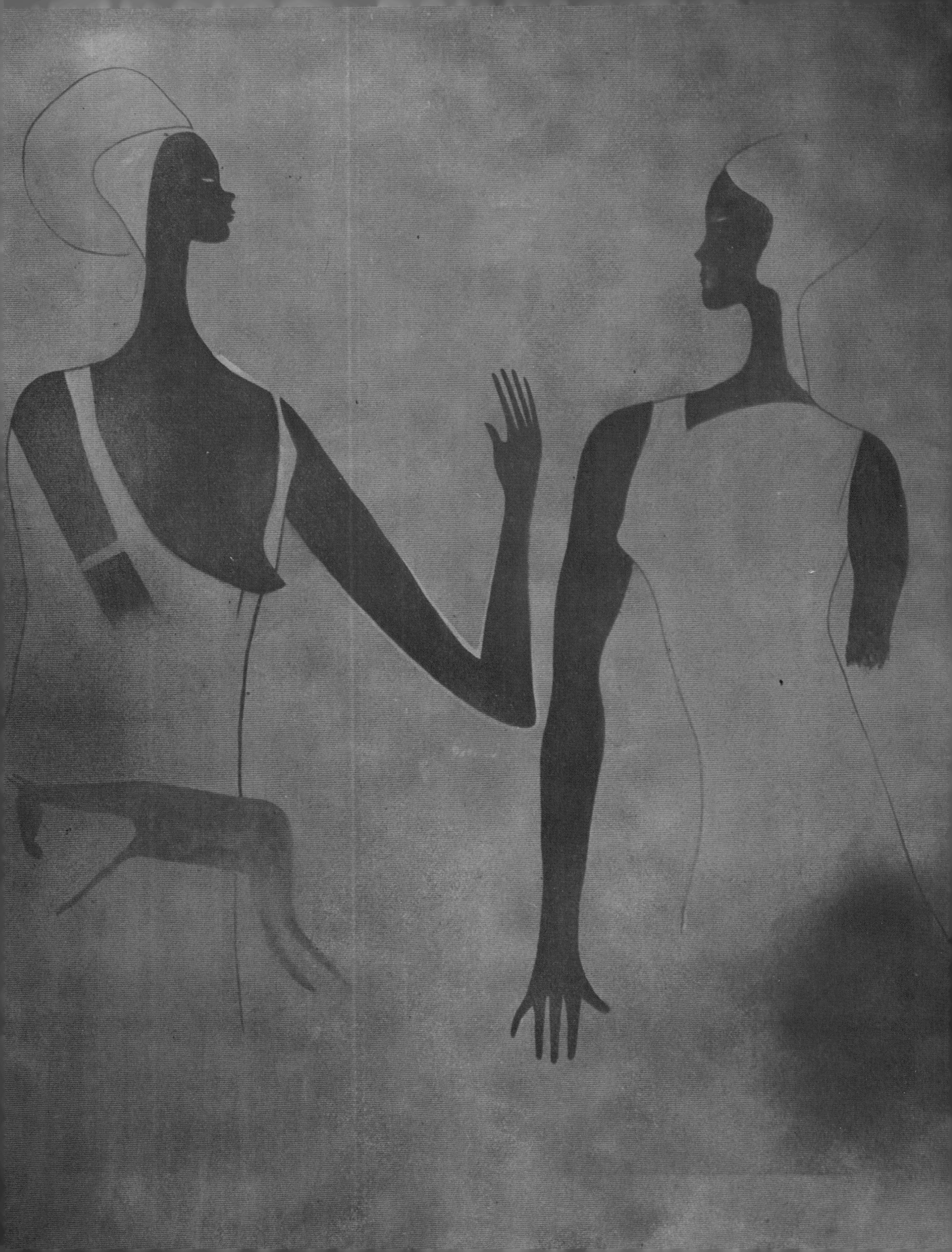

BLACK WOMEN

TEN THOUSAND YEARS AGO

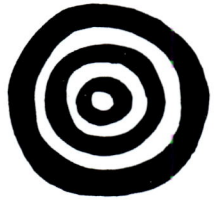

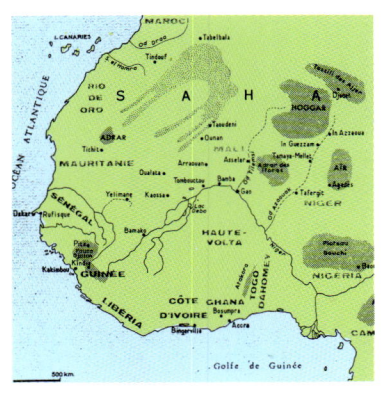

Born ten thousand years ago, these ancient inhabitants of the Sahara, captured here, in the course of their daily lives, on the walls of the Tassili caves seem to come right out of the twentieth century...

A LONG TIME AGO, ABOUT TEN THOUSAND YEARS AGO, THE SAHARA WAS ONE OF THE GREENEST AND MOST FERTILE AREAS ON EARTH. IMMENSE LAKES AND TUMULTUOUS STREAMS SHELTERED RICH AQUATIC FAUNA: FISH OF ALL KINDS, GIANT LIZARDS, oversized hippopotamuses whose remains still break through the sand here and there.

As in the rest of Africa, the men were hunters, fishermen, and farmers. We can still find their tools in the soil today. Bone harpoons, hooks, spikes, arrows, axes, and adzes made of polished stone.

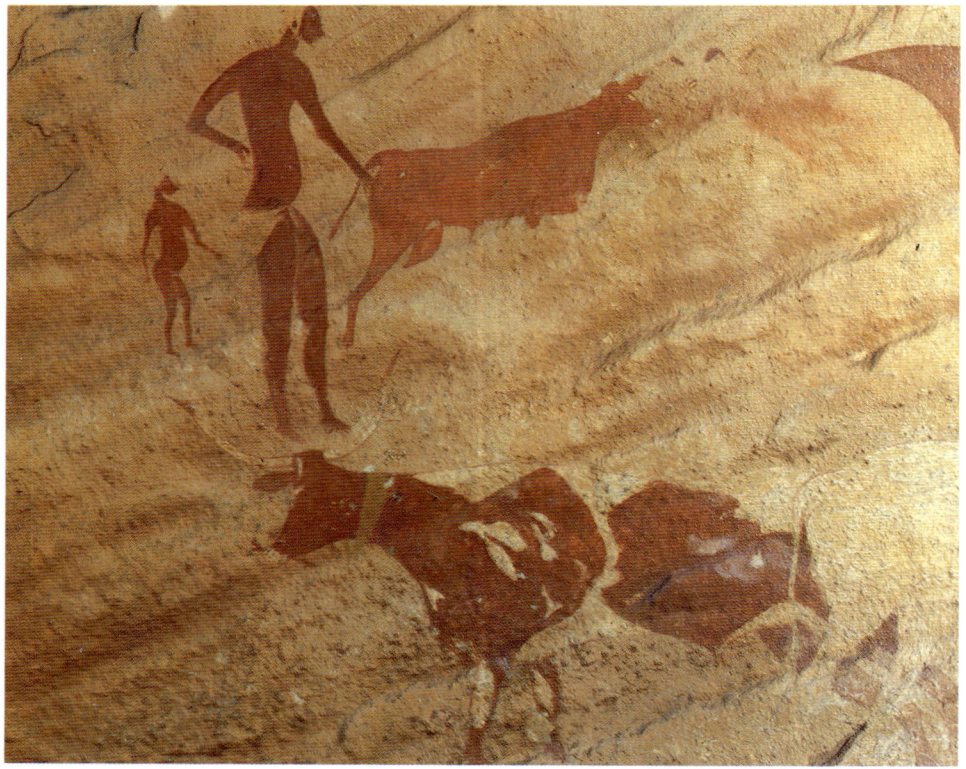

The ancient inhabitants of the Sahara are known to us by way of remarkable frescoes, painted right on the walls of the Tassili caves. They have portrayed themselves so faithfully that we can imagine them in their daily lives, as if a lens had captured them on the spot ten thousand years ago.

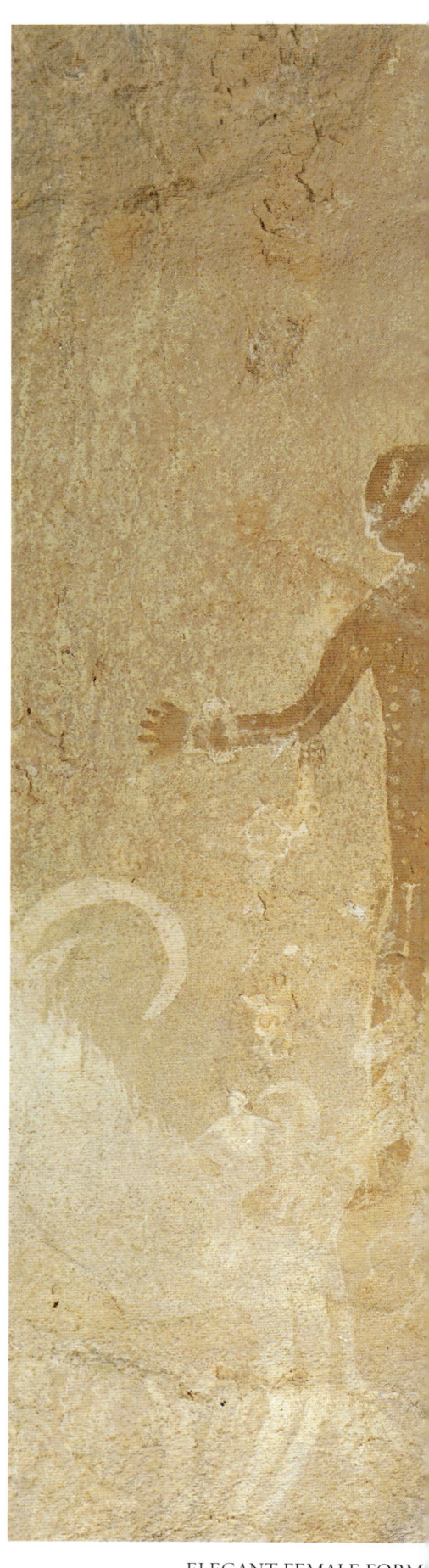

ELEGANT FEMALE FORM

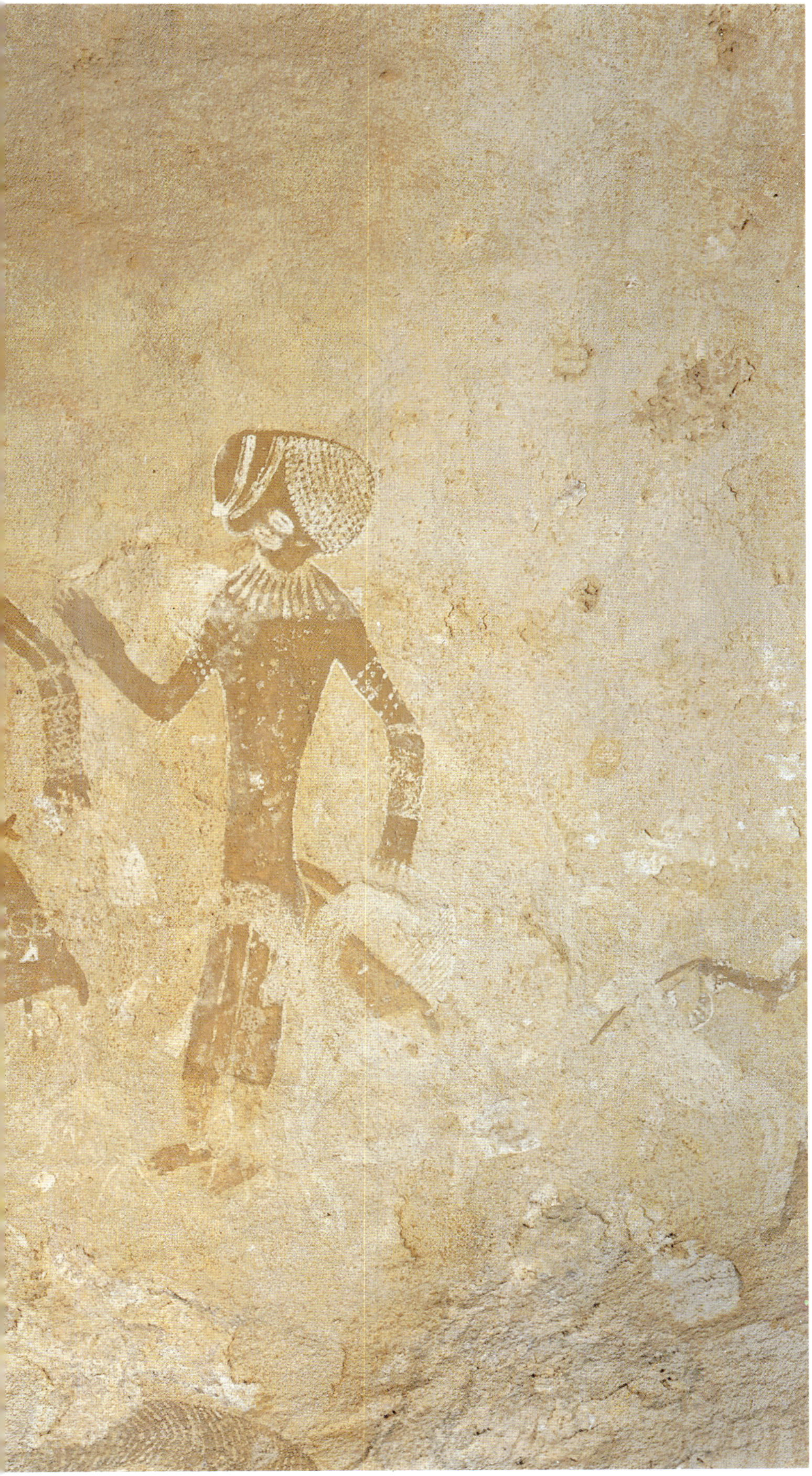

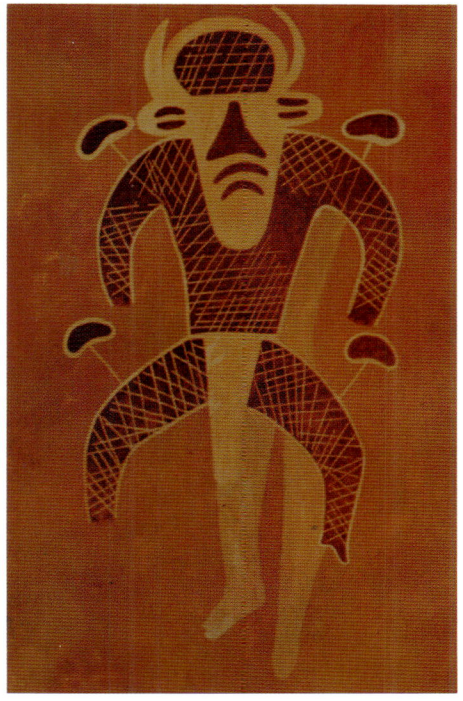

This fresco was painted in the center of a deep and rather obscure shelter, whose layout indicates a sanctuary. The pose of the man with the mask evokes that of someone astride a horse. One will note that the hands and feet have not been represented. The only clothing is a triangle-shaped loincloth tied around the waist with a rope. The mask, oval-shaped and adorned with horns, is of the same style as certain masks still used in West Africa. Indeed, the Senufo of Ivory Coast still possess a similar kind of initiation mask, with its horns turned outward.

Art

Early art, without neglecting human representation, was above all an animalist art. Man is interested in animal behavior. His sketches caught them in familiar poses: on the lookout, playing, fighting, mating, or running away, seized with fear. In general, the species most portrayed were those whose flesh was most prized.

A Discovery

One finds the image under the shelter of an isolated rock. Water, once more, produces its magical effect.
On the wet rock, the graceful silhouette of a woman taking long strides. One of her legs, slightly curved, has just touched the ground, while the other is bent just above it. Fine fringes hang from the knees, the spread-out arms, and the belt.

GRACE THE WET ROCK

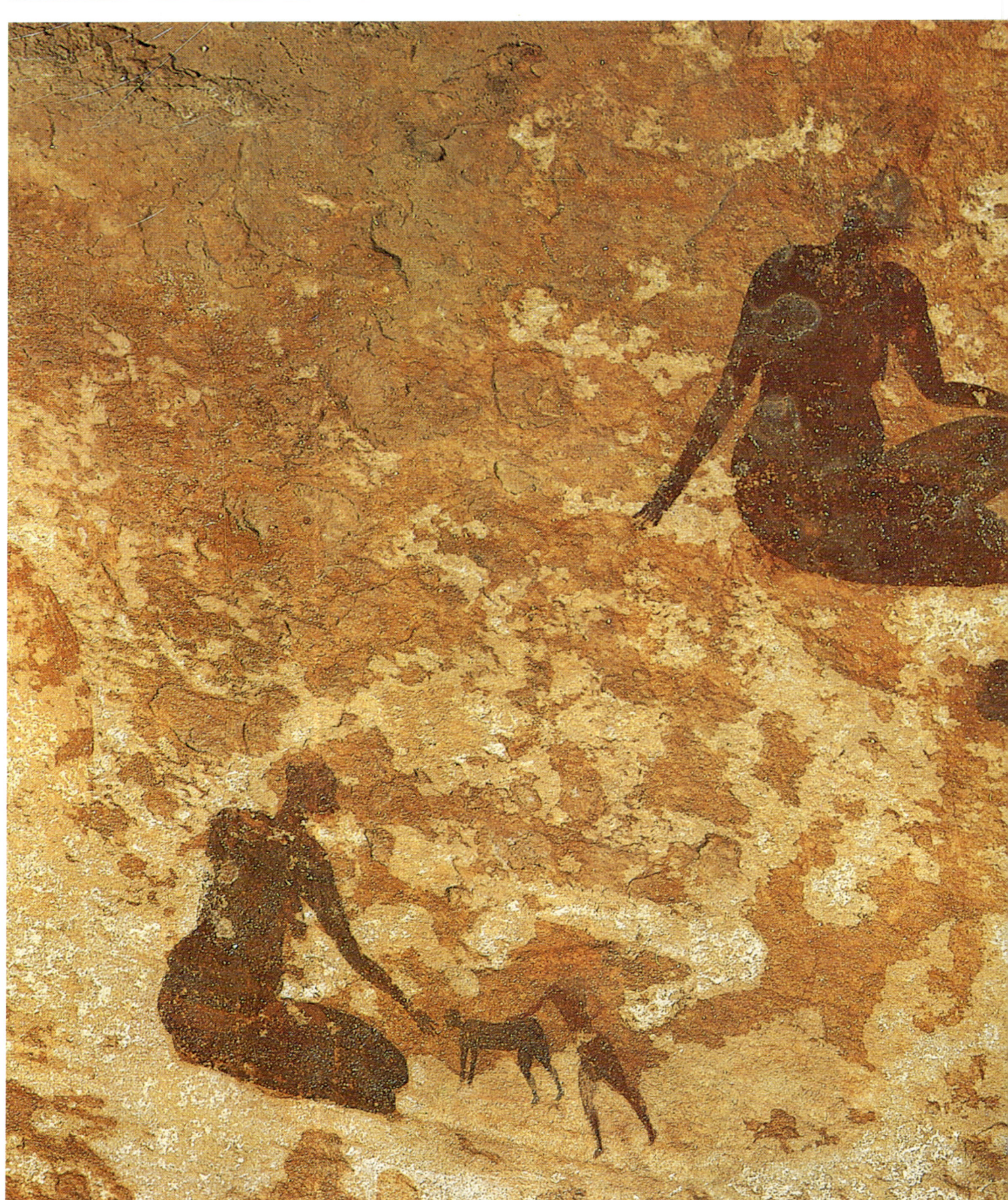

A FAMILY SCENE

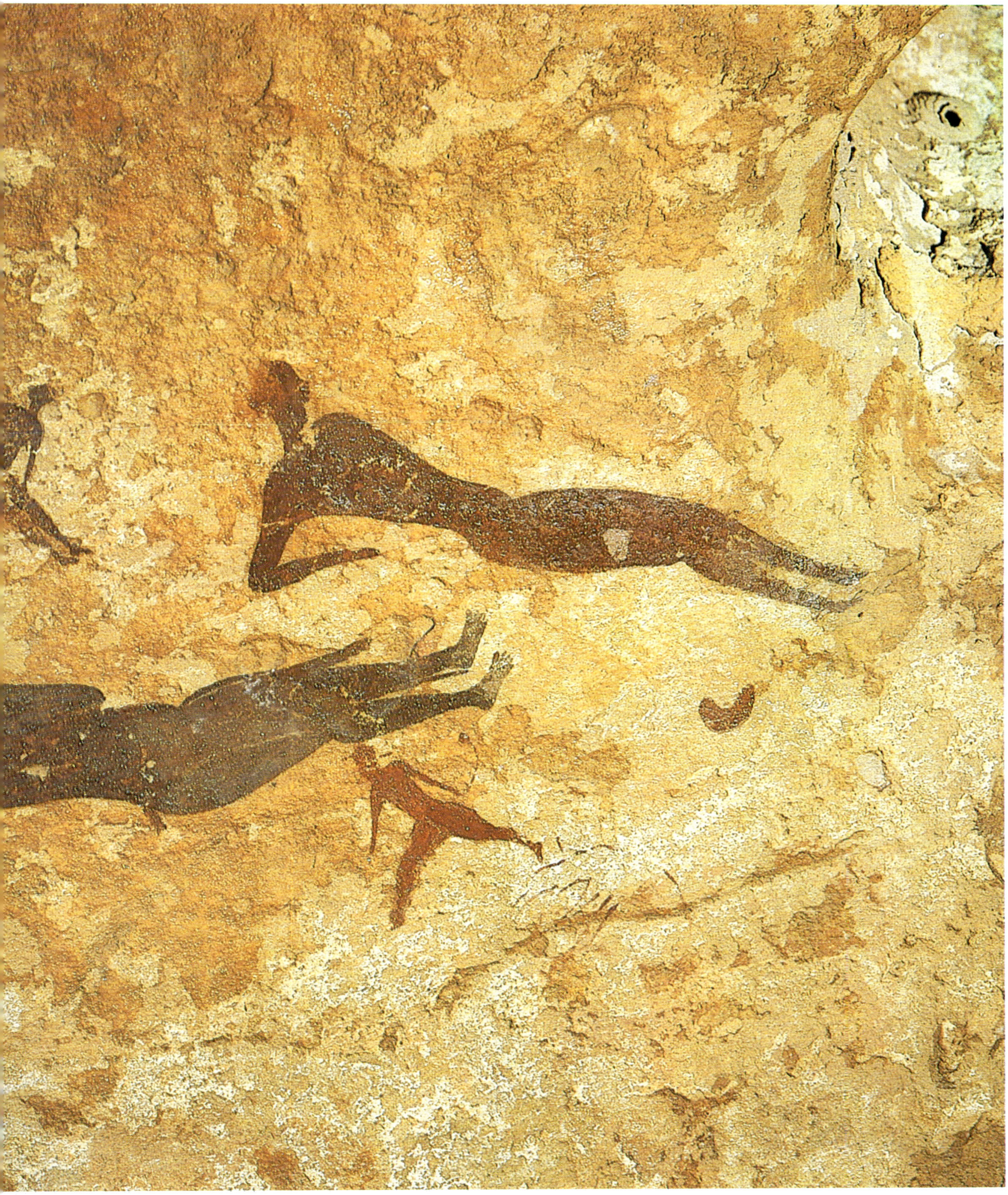

BLACK WOMEN, TEN THOUSAND YEARS AGO

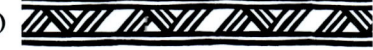

TEN THOUSAND YEARS AGO

Their instruments, ornaments, and hair styles can still be seen today in certain parts of Africa. Thus, for example, many masks represented on these frescoes are analogous to those used by the Senufo of Ivory Coast.

As for the silhouettes of these Black women, they seem as though they could have been traced today.

One can find them here and there in the world, identical, from the shores of Senegal to the edges of the Zambezi River, from the hills of the Caribbean and the streets of Harlem to the favellas dotting Rio's skyline.

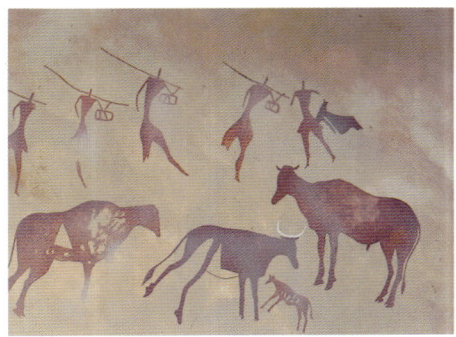

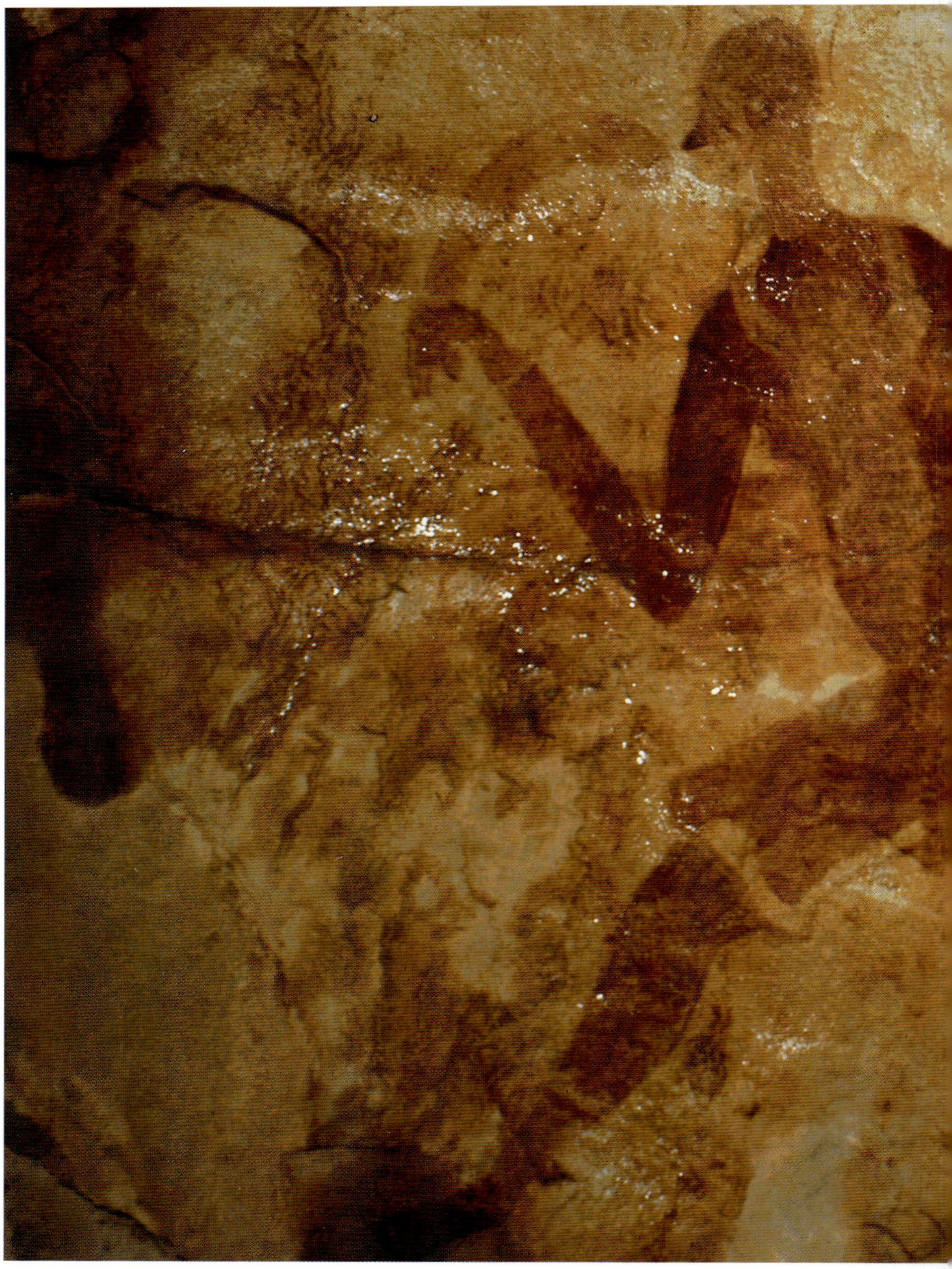

The Three Styles of Rock Art

From 7000 until at least 1000 B.C.E., there was the monumental art of the "Hunters" or "Bubalus" period, depicting the great wild animals in scenes of capture, pursuit, or mating. The hunters, wearing animal-shaped masks, reveal hunting techniques still used in the forests.

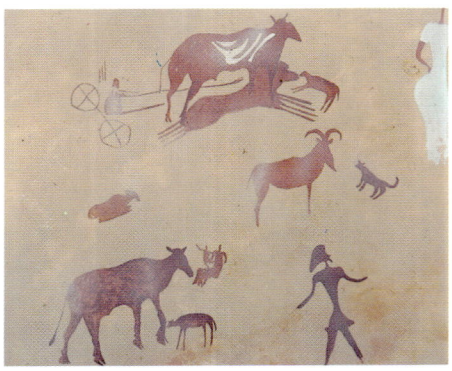

A more exuberant and supple style develops in the "Herders" or "Cattle" period, which lasts from 5000 to 2500 B.C.E. Alongside the persistence of hunting, the domestication of animals is confirmed by these naturalistic portrayals, which depict the lives of creatures that have been subdued and become submissive to the breeder who cares for them.

The "Horse" or "Caballine" style succeeds the Cattle period by the end of the Saharan neolithic period, around 2000 B.C.E. The galloping horses are represented in the momentum of a swift and unfettered leap. The legs are drawn horizontally, in a lanky and geometric stylization that suggests such speed that they hardly touch the ground.

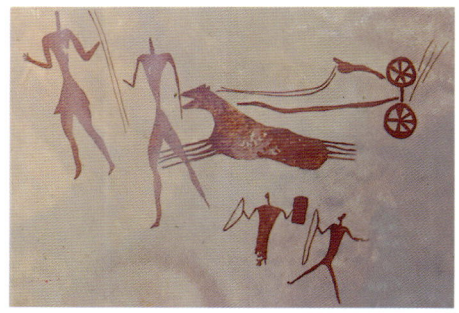

SILHOUETTES FOREVER

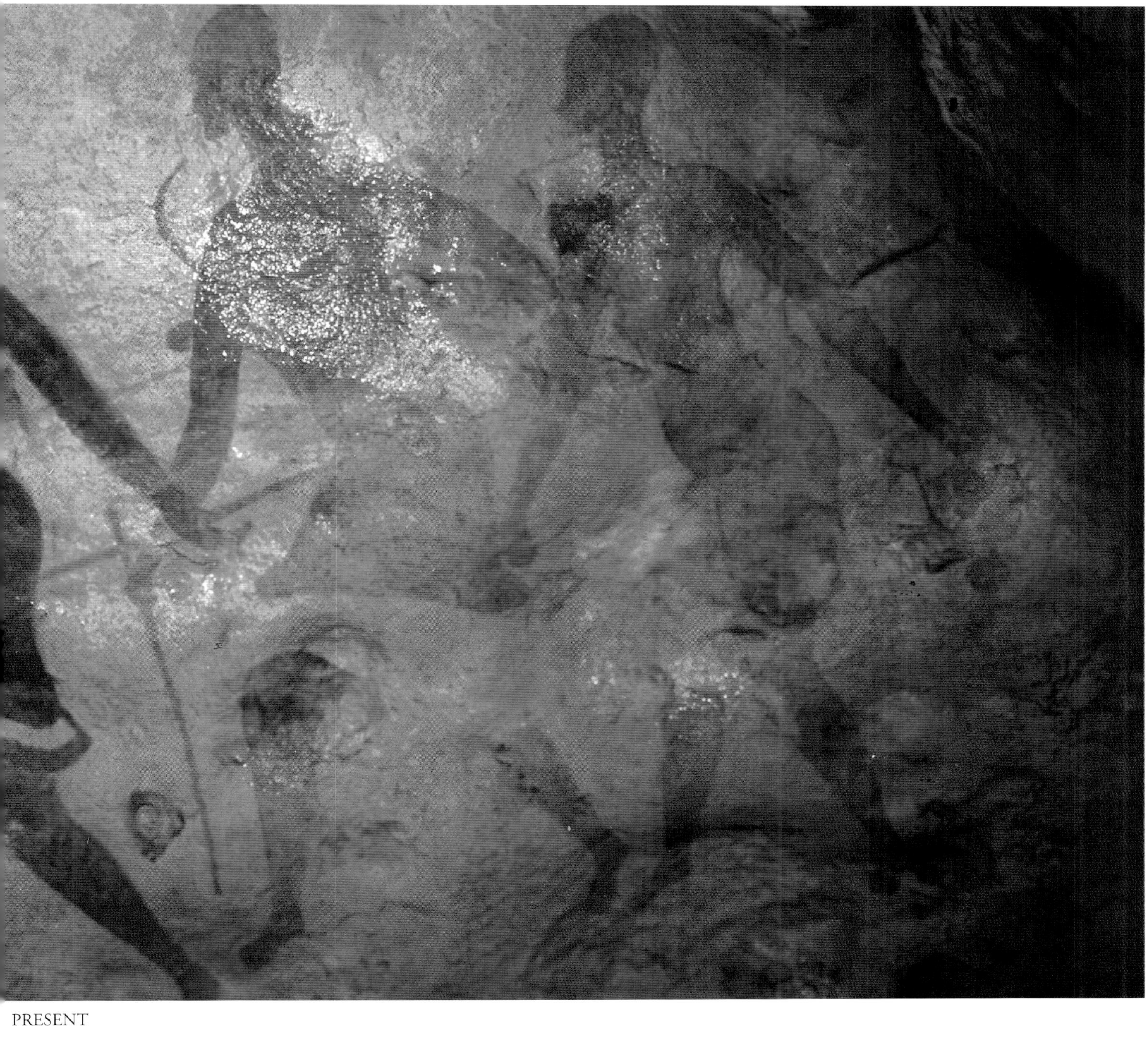

BLACK WOMEN, TEN THOUSAND YEARS AGO

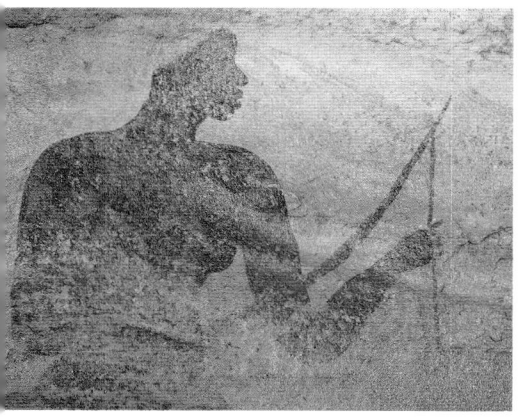
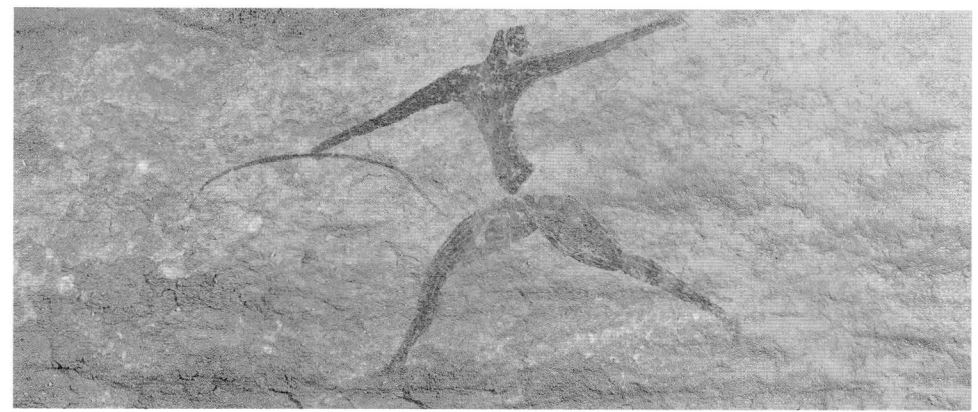

The Desert

Some time before the fourth millennium B.C.E., the Sahara began to lose its green fertility. Its great streams that flowed south towards the Niger and east toward the Nile, and whose dry beds can still be traced, started to wither and perish; its populations migrated. There are many testimonies to this long and disastrous change. These paleolithic Blacks of Khartoum—who laid the foundations of a large part of the Nile civilization and who were able to make ceramics even before they were made in Jericho, the oldest city known to the world—lived on the edges of a stream whose waters would rise up to four, or sometimes ten yards above flood level. They used barbed and bone spearheads, replaced later by harpoons that were incredibly precise, with three or more barbs and a serrated edge; the models which bear the most similarity to such harpoons of the Nile Valley can be found in Wadi Azaouak, about 1864 miles west across the wild Sahara we know today.

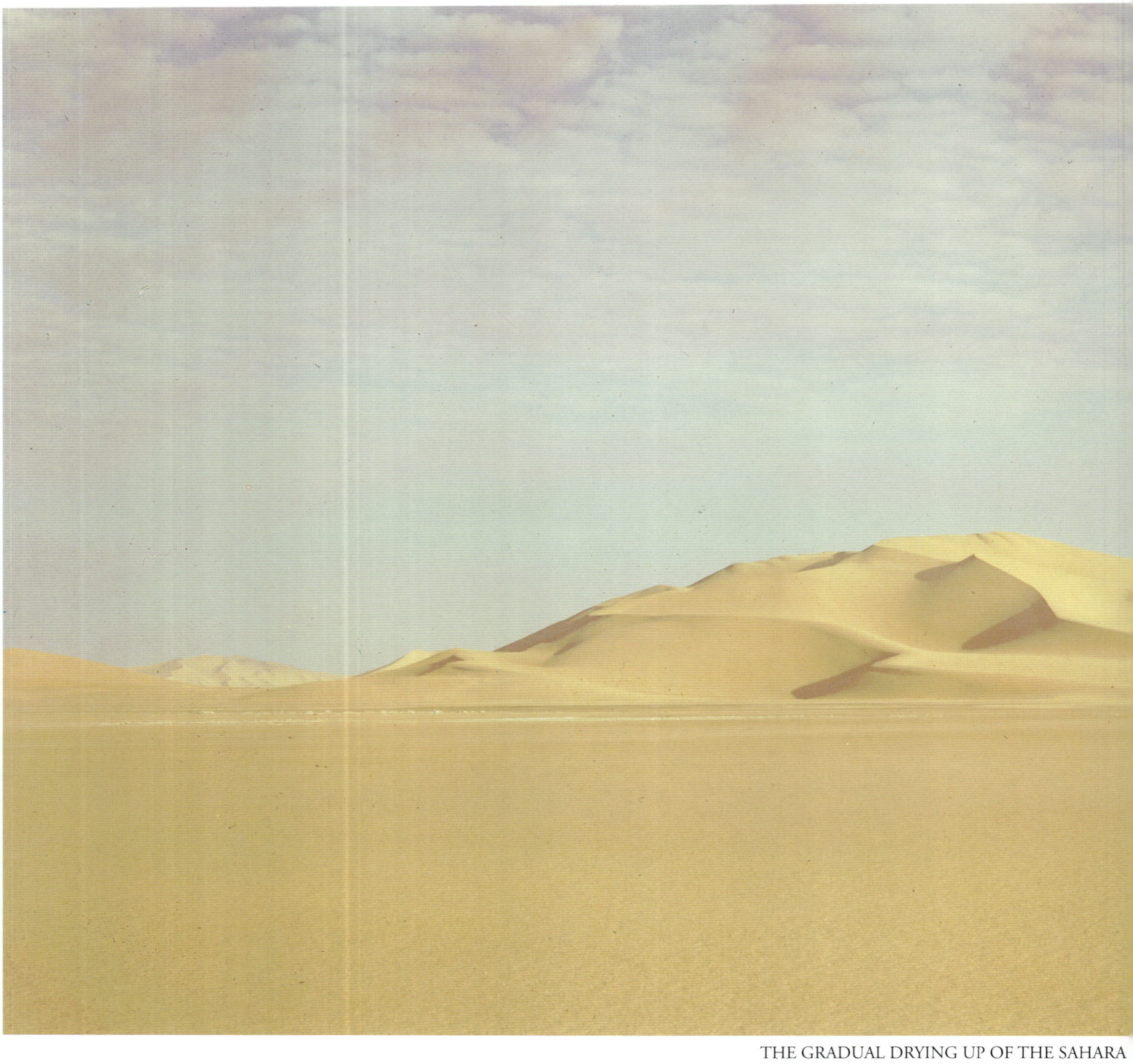

THE GRADUAL DRYING UP OF THE SAHARA

BLACK WOMEN, TEN THOUSAND YEARS AGO

The progressive drying up of the Sahara forced all these people into exile. But the frescoes they left behind, painted in the mists of time, have retained an astonishing freshness. They used natural pigments ground fine in mortars, then kneaded into melted animal grease or cooked bone marrow.

The technique of oil painting as we know it today was already around back then.

The History of How Africa Came To Be Inhabited

Africa has 350 million inhabitants, of whom a third are whites, generally living in the north, and two thirds blacks, living south of the Sahara. All scientists today recognize that Africa is the cradle of humanity because this is where the oldest traces of human beings have been found: tools of the Australopithecus in Tanzania and, more recently, those found in the Omo Valley in Ethiopia, go back two to three million years.

In a time long past, blacks lived in a Sahara still humid and covered with savanna; Pygmies occupied the greater part of the continent's interior. With the drying of the Sahara (fourth to third millennium B.C.E.), the black farmers and shepherds went down into the Nile Valley in Egypt and Nubia where they formed the first known civilizations, then toward the south where they pushed the Pygmies back into the forested areas. Endless migrations resulted in intermingling, exchanges, the domination of certain people over others. Most West Africans believe themselves to be originally from the east: such is the case for the Hausa, the Mossi, the Songhai.

The most typical case is that of the Bantus of Central and South Africa, characterized by their linguistic unity, who would have lived in the area between Chad, Cameroon, and Nigeria. Beginning at the end of the first millennium, they reached Kongo, Angola, Rhodesia, where they founded powerful states based on agriculture and metallurgy. In the sixteenth century, they arrived in South Africa where they pushed back the Bushmen and the Hottentots into the Kalahari. In the nineteenth century, they came up against the Dutch, who were being pushed inland by the English on the coast.

Through the centuries Africa has welcomed waves of foreign migrants. The Arabs settled in the north and in the Nile Valley; the Chinese, the Indians, and especially the Malays landed on the eastern coast and Madagascar; the Europeans chose southern Africa.

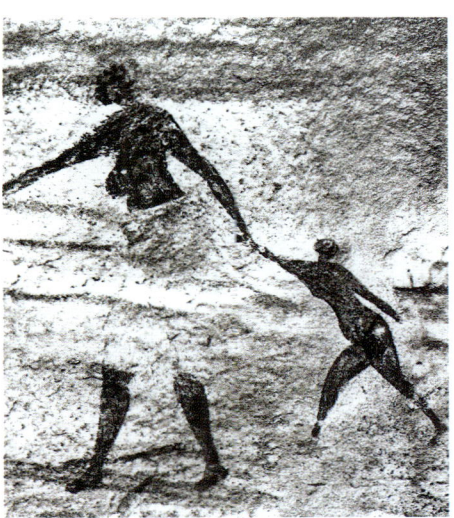

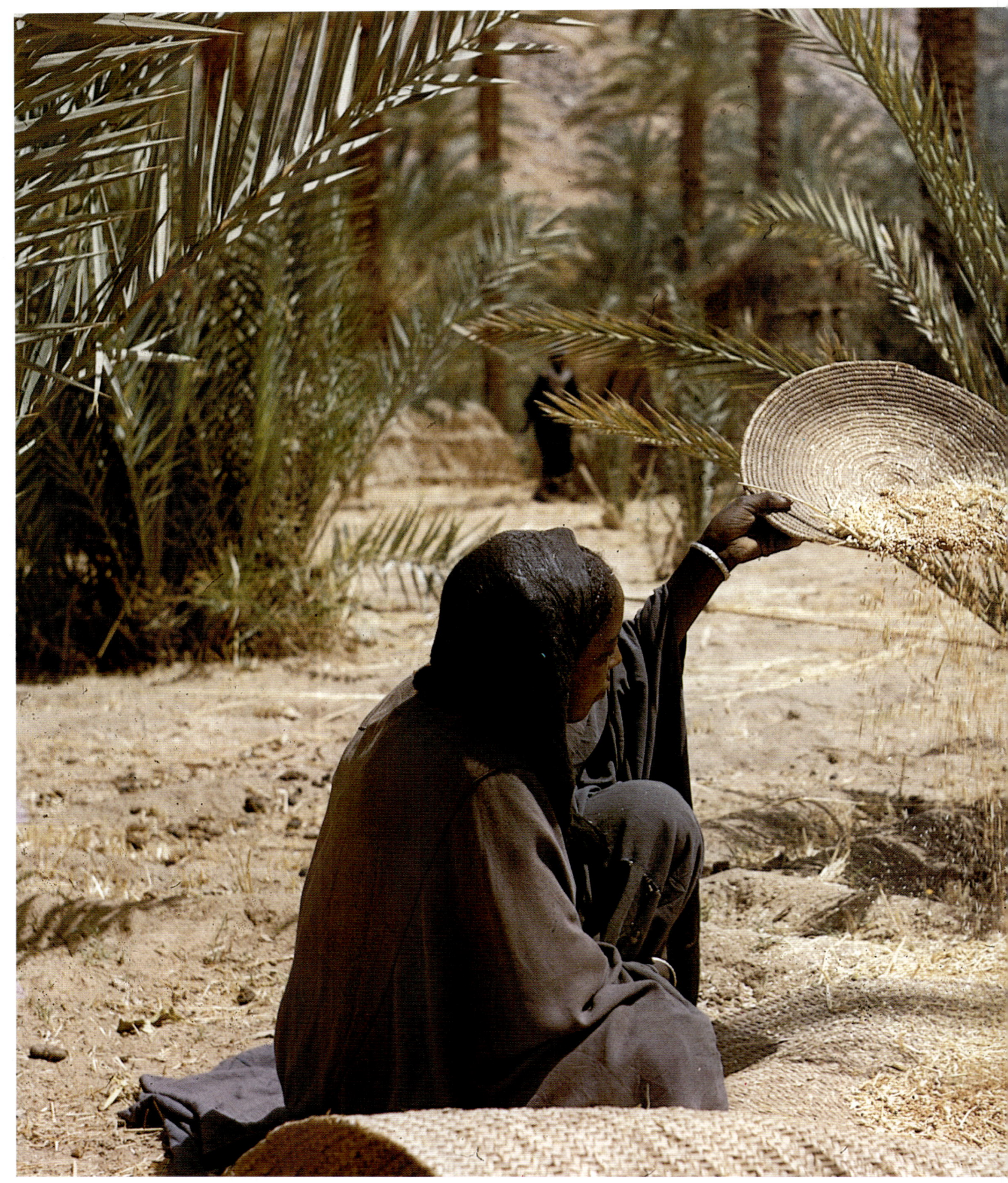

WOMEN OF TASSILI TODAY

WORDS
OF AN ORDINARY WOMAN

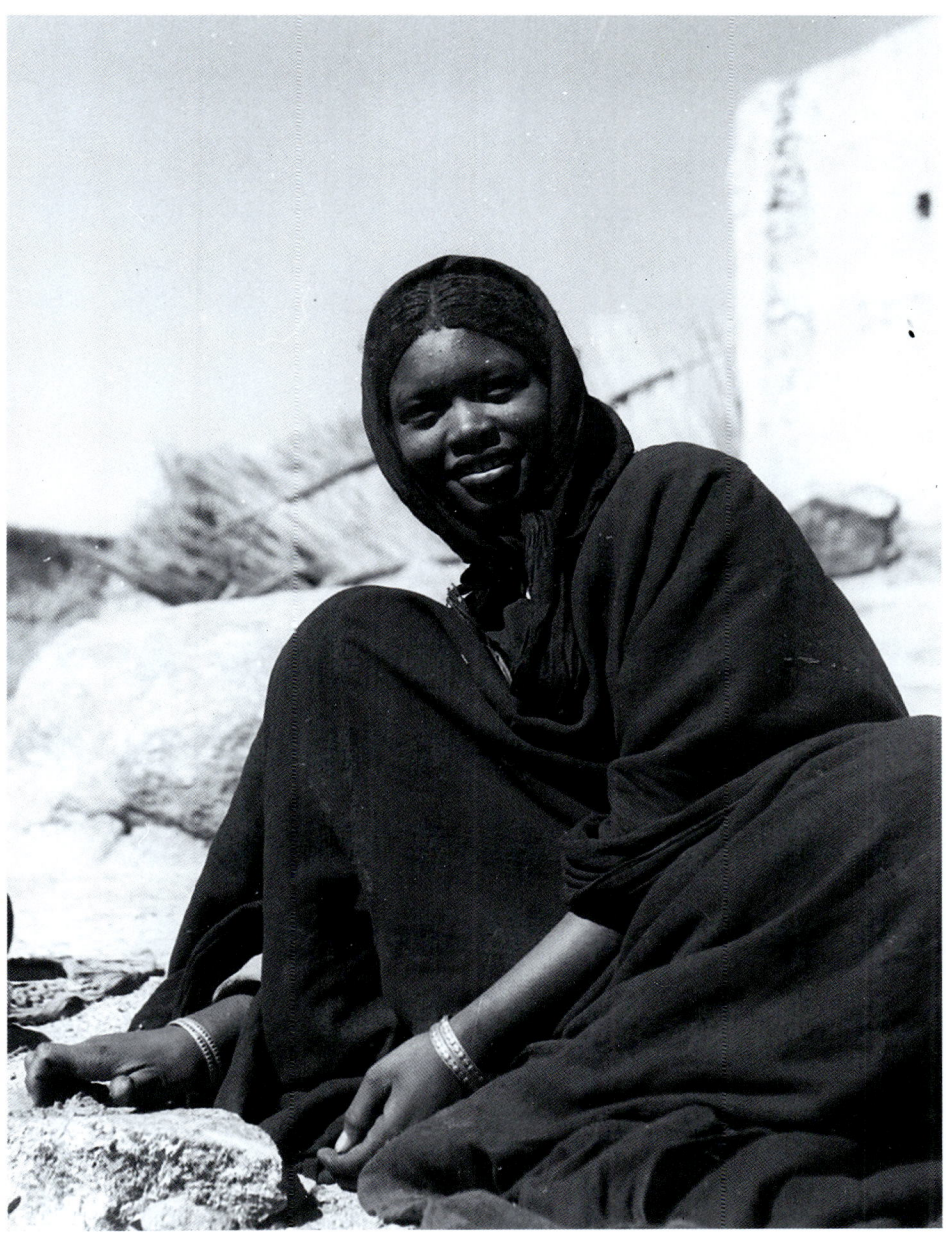

We always want to live with others. If we can't always do that, it is because of dire need: because of the breeding, because of the herd. We have to accept living in isolation, so that our animals may find happiness in good grazing.

But in the wet season, it's different. In the wet season, no one has the right to live alone. In the wet season, one cannot live outside of the clan.

The months of the wet season are the most beautiful of the year. Especially for us women. In the dry season, we meet almost no one. We stay at home and the settlements are far from each other. The men can always meet by the well. But us, we wait with impatience for the coming of the first rains that will bring the clan together.

Then, we move every day, looking for water and fresh grass. It is the season of much milk, the season of feasts, the season of the ingathering of the whole clan. The wet season is truly the time of happiness.

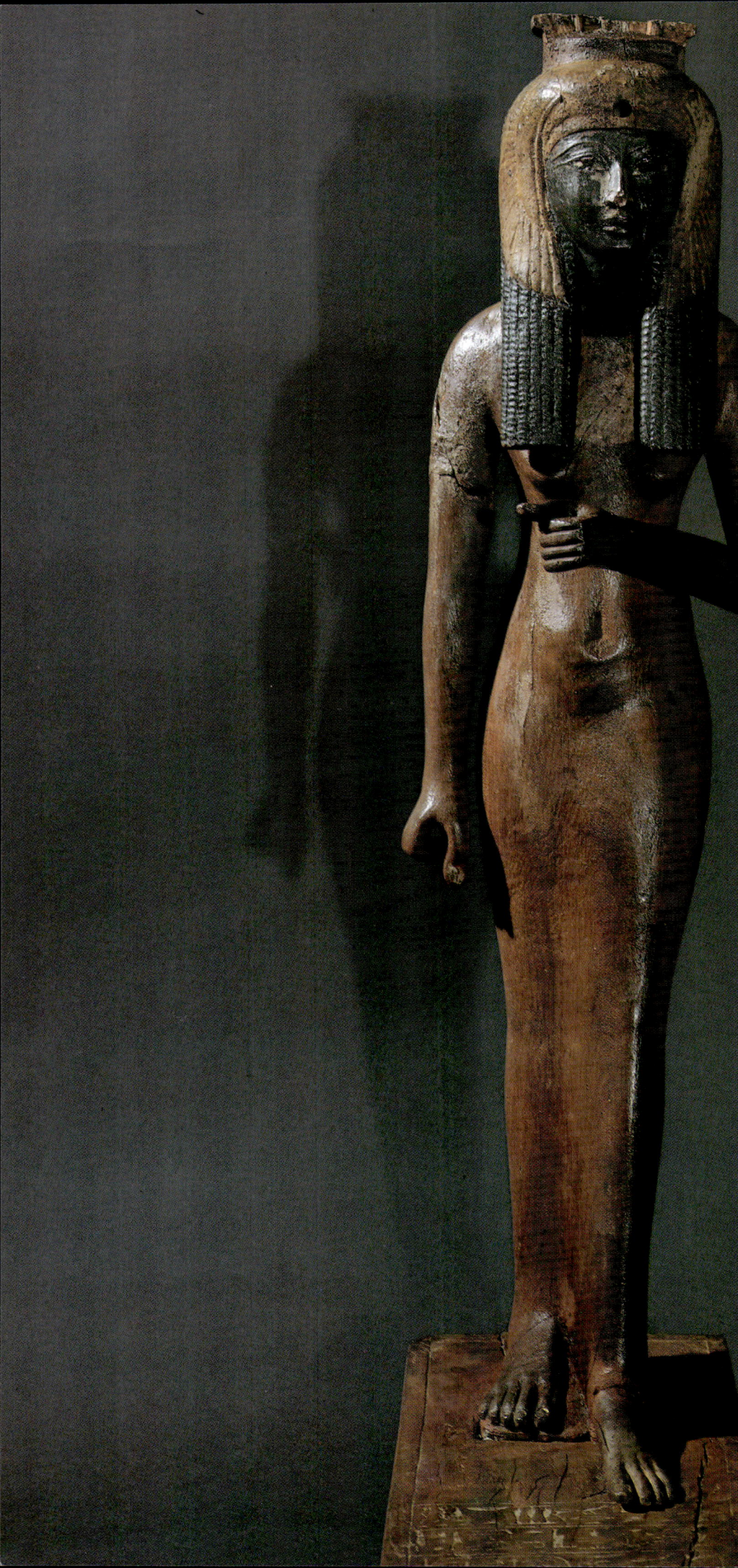

AHMOSE-NOFRETARI

THE WOMAN WHO BECAME DIVINE

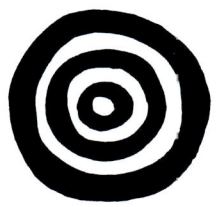

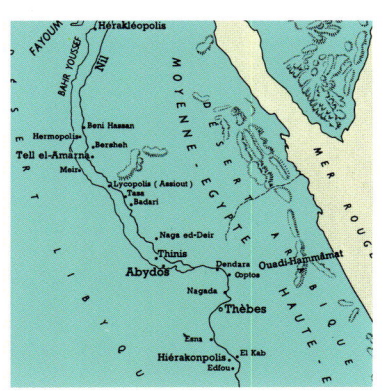

Liberator of the kingdom alongside her brother Ahmose, she was the first queen to share the bed of the god Amon...

EGYPT IS DAUGHTER OF THE
NILE, AS THE GREEKS WOULD SAY. IN THE BEGINNING, SHE WAS BUT A BROAD EXPANSE OF SALTY WATER; THEN HER ALLUVIA, WHICH CAME FROM THE LAKES OF CENTRAL AFRICA, BUILT UP THE LAND HIDDEN UNDER THE BLUE WAVES OF the Mediterranean.

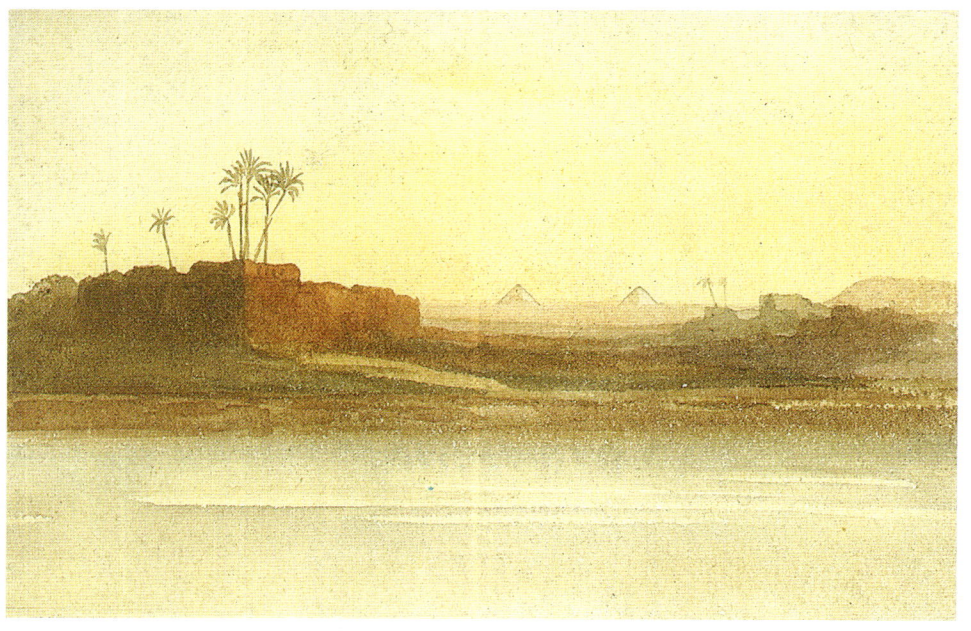

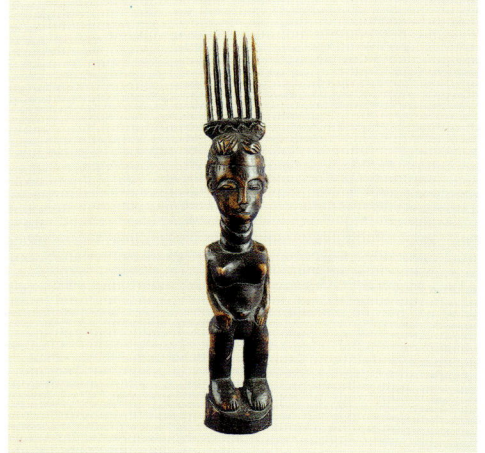

THE IMPRINT OF AFRICA

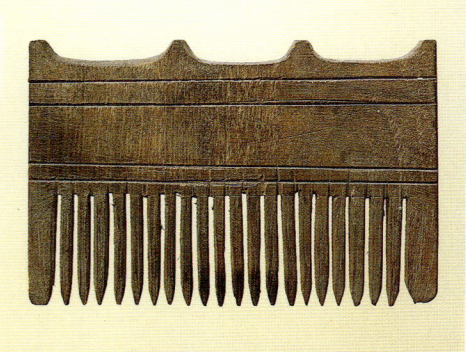

ON ARTIFACTS AND CUSTOMS

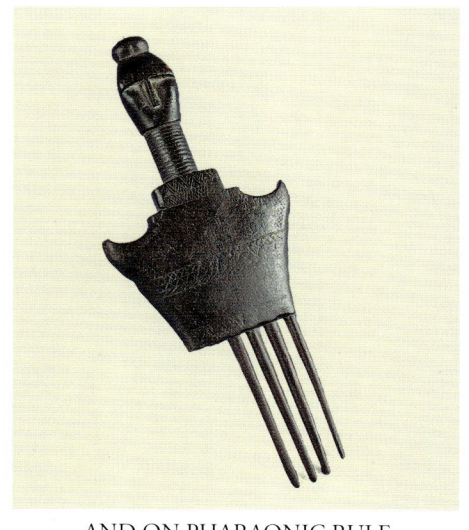

AND ON PHARAONIC RULE

After the drying of the Sahara, its inhabitants also followed the course of the alluvia, running into other races settled in the areas around the Mediterranean. The place where they met is called ancient Egypt. For the 4,500 years of her existence, she's remained faithful to her source. Her customs and her gods have retained the imprint of Mother Africa, which the ancient Egyptians recognized as their original country: she was for them the country of the spirits, of God, the mysterious land they evoked in the Book of the Dead.

In many ways, the pharaohs resembled the absolute monarch in traditional Africa, who was pivotal to his kingdom and responsible for the rising sun; and their wives ruled on earth as in the heavens, where they made love to the gods.

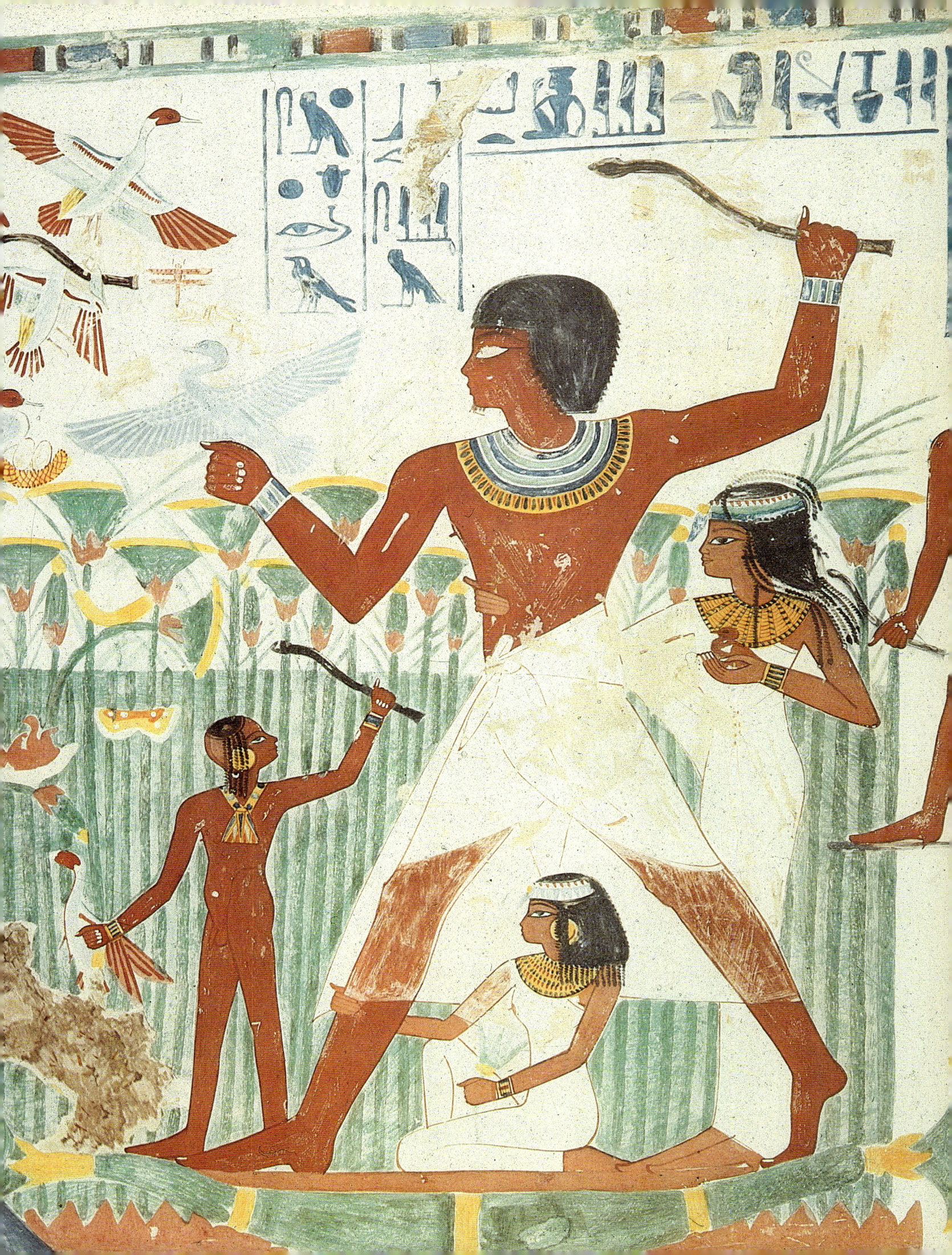

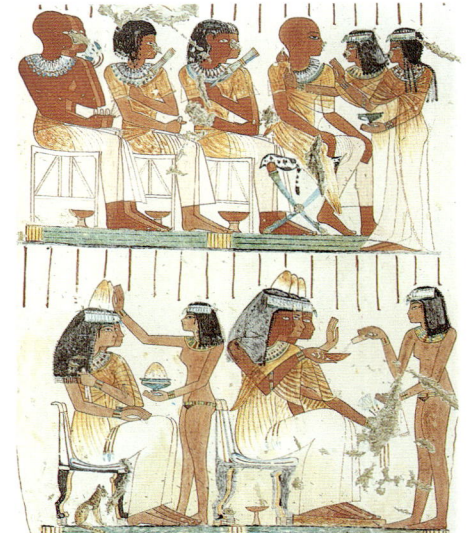

Love Scenes

Manethon, who wrote at the beginning of the Common Era, divides the vast history of Egypt into thirty chapters, thirty dynasties stretching from Pharaoh Menes to poor Cleopatra, who committed suicide in 33 C.E., marking the last period of the final chapter.

As far as we know, the relationship of love and intimate sensuality between queens and gods has not always existed: priestesses, young women chosen for their grace and beauty, were the first to unite with the god Amon in the vast stone alcoves. Then came Ahmose-Nofretari, liberator of the kingdom alongside her brother Ahmose, and first queen to share the god Amon's bed.

Among the most beautiful and carnal of all feminine representations, the god's wives are frequently depicted in the company of Amon, during the Ethiopian period. Often facing his wife, the god presents the ankh, the sign of life, while expressing his bliss to "the one who fills the shrine with the scent of her perfume." Next to the characters one reads: "My heart is greatly satisfied." In the north of the great Temple of Karnak, in the region where several chapels were erected to Amon, one of the more suggestive scenes once again shows the god's wife, tightly embracing her demiurge, chest to chest, and holding him by the shoulder. Elsewhere, she wraps her arms around the neck of the god, her nervous thigh boldly brushing against Amon's. Furthermore, a group fragment, preserved at the Cairo Museum, materializes the mystical union of this couple (where Amon embraces the god's wife Amonirdis, who is sitting on his knees), an unusually intimate image. The languorous attributes bestowed upon the god's wives during the New Empire are still used. Moreover, these love scenes include captions supposedly etched by the god himself: "She who delights the god's flesh, who makes love with the god, she who is fulfilled when she sees Amon...." She is also sometimes confused with his daughter: "The daughter of Amon, of his flesh, the daughter he loves."

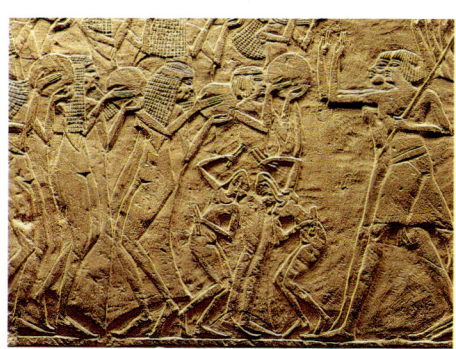

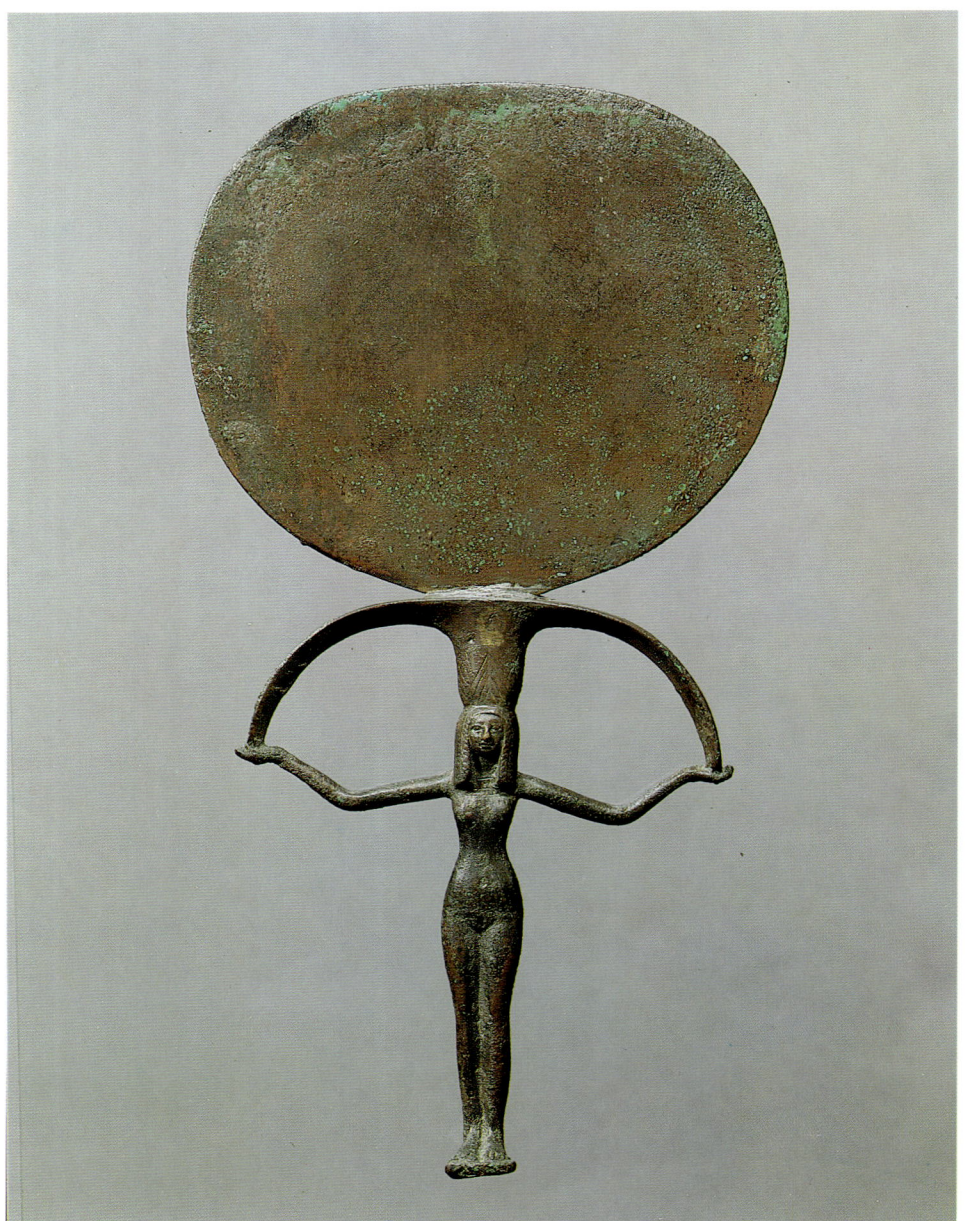

"PRIESTESSES WERE THE FIRST ONES TO UNITE WITH THE GOD AMON"

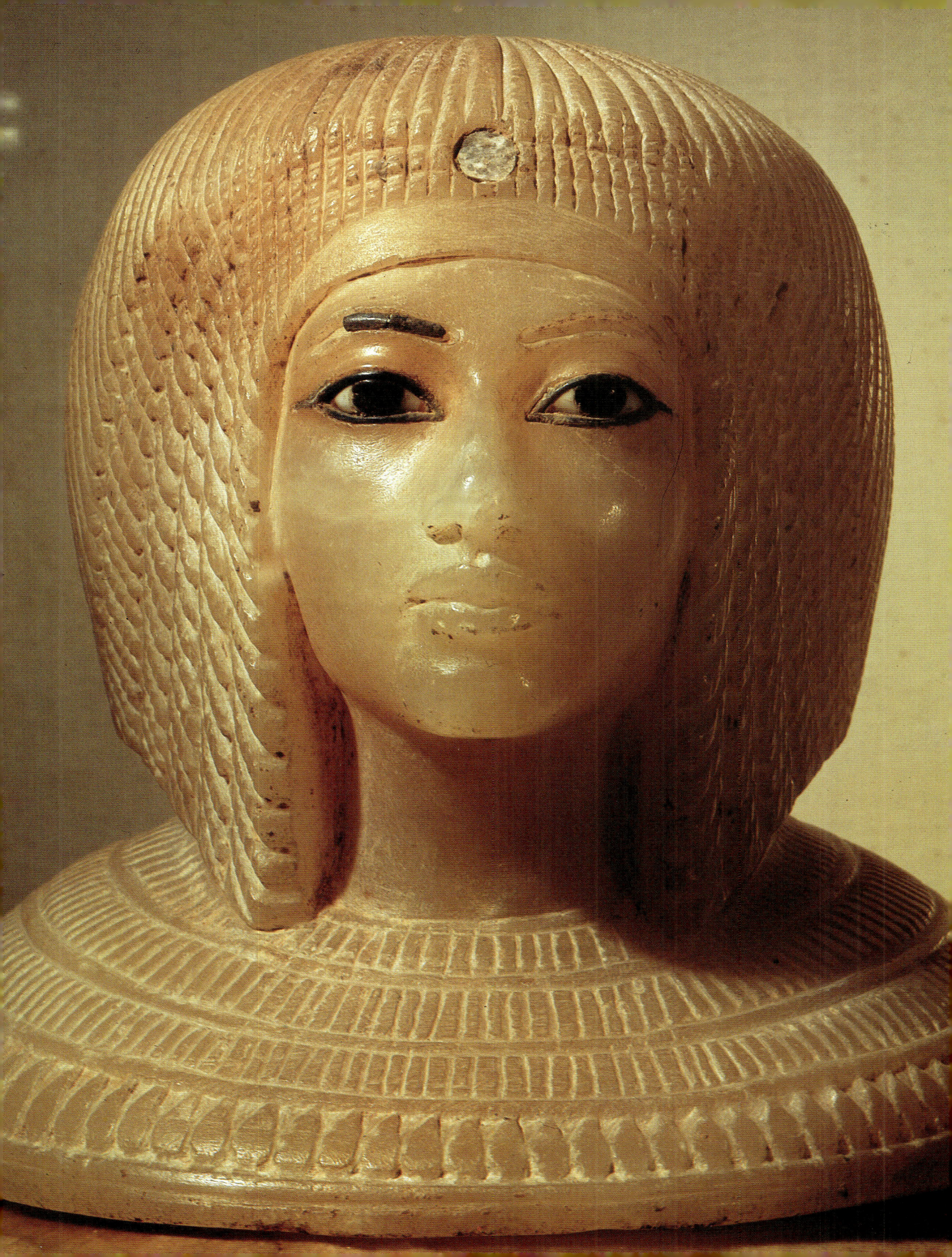

Other women would follow her example, but no human wife would ever be so close to the god: so much so that she herself came to be regarded as a goddess, becoming the object of a cult that lasted many centuries after her death.

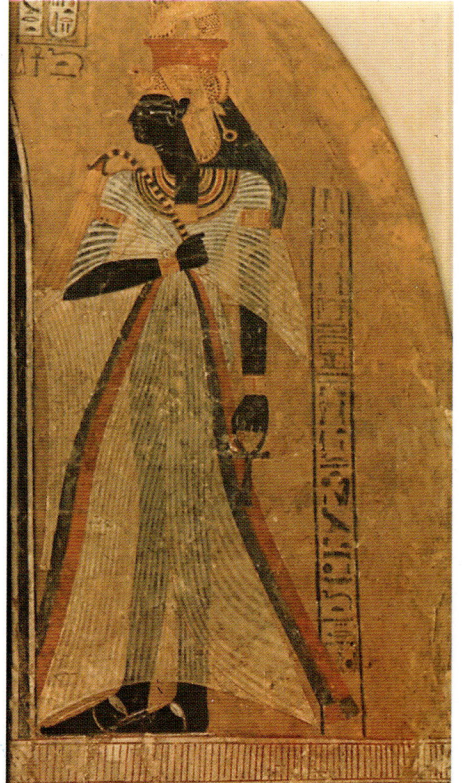

Ahhotep

The great Ahhotep died at a very old age, perhaps over eighty-four years. She assumed the regency of her second heir, Ahmose, who was then very young. After having unified most of the country, she was able to sway those opposed to her.

The opinions of Egyptologists vary about one point concerning her: did this loyal, energetic, diplomatic, and organized woman go so far as to rally Egyptian soldiers to stop an uprising?

One can be easily convinced that she did, given the praise Ahmose lavishes on his mother, exhorting his subjects to honor her:

Praise the lady of the country,
the ruler of the shores of distant realms,
Whose name soars
in the highlands
Who takes the people's fate in hand,
Wife of the king, sister of a sovereign,
life, health, strength!
Royal daughter, venerable mother of the king,
Who still watches over things,
who unifies Egypt.
She has assembled its notables,
whose unity she has insured;
She brought in its fugitives,
she has gathered its dissidents;
She has pacified Egypt,
she has pushed back its rebels;
Life to Ahhotep, royal wife!

This regent, whose conduct was so decisive when destiny unexpectedly compelled her to take over for three pharaohs, was, no doubt, one of the few women ever to receive a military decoration.

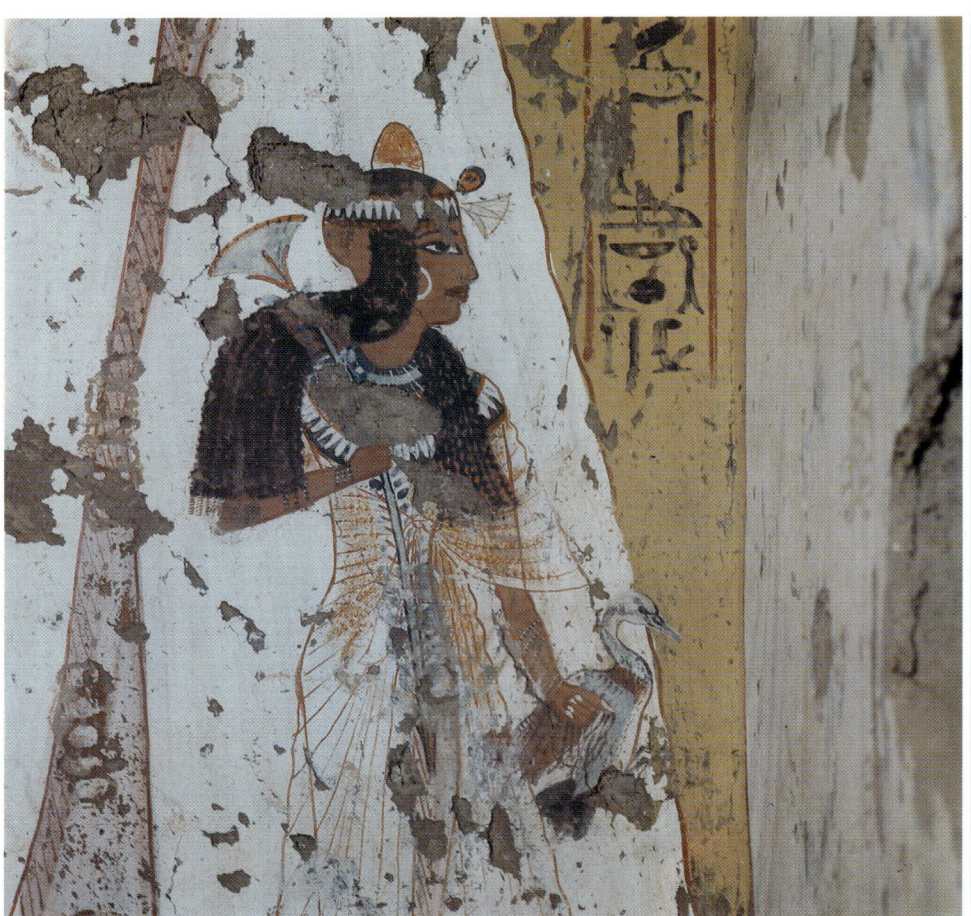

There are many representations of Ahmose-Nofretari, but she most often appears in her funerary temple, the "million year castle," as the faithful of that time used to say.

One can often see her at the head of the other deified pharaohs, the "masters of eternity" who followed or preceded her: Ramses II, Sitr I, Ohremheb, Tuthmosis IV, Tuthmosis III, Muntuhotep, and Snefru; though she is at the head, she is still the only woman, because she was the only woman ever to reach the status of a goddess in the long history of Egypt.

There are many Egyptian figures that have become unrecognizable, their images destroyed by posterity's strange posthumous revenge.

But the veneration which surrounds Ahmose-Nofretari has left her image intact, and one can see it evolve into stone and wood, as well as mural frescoes, "black skin, beautiful face, elegant, her hair crowned with feathers."

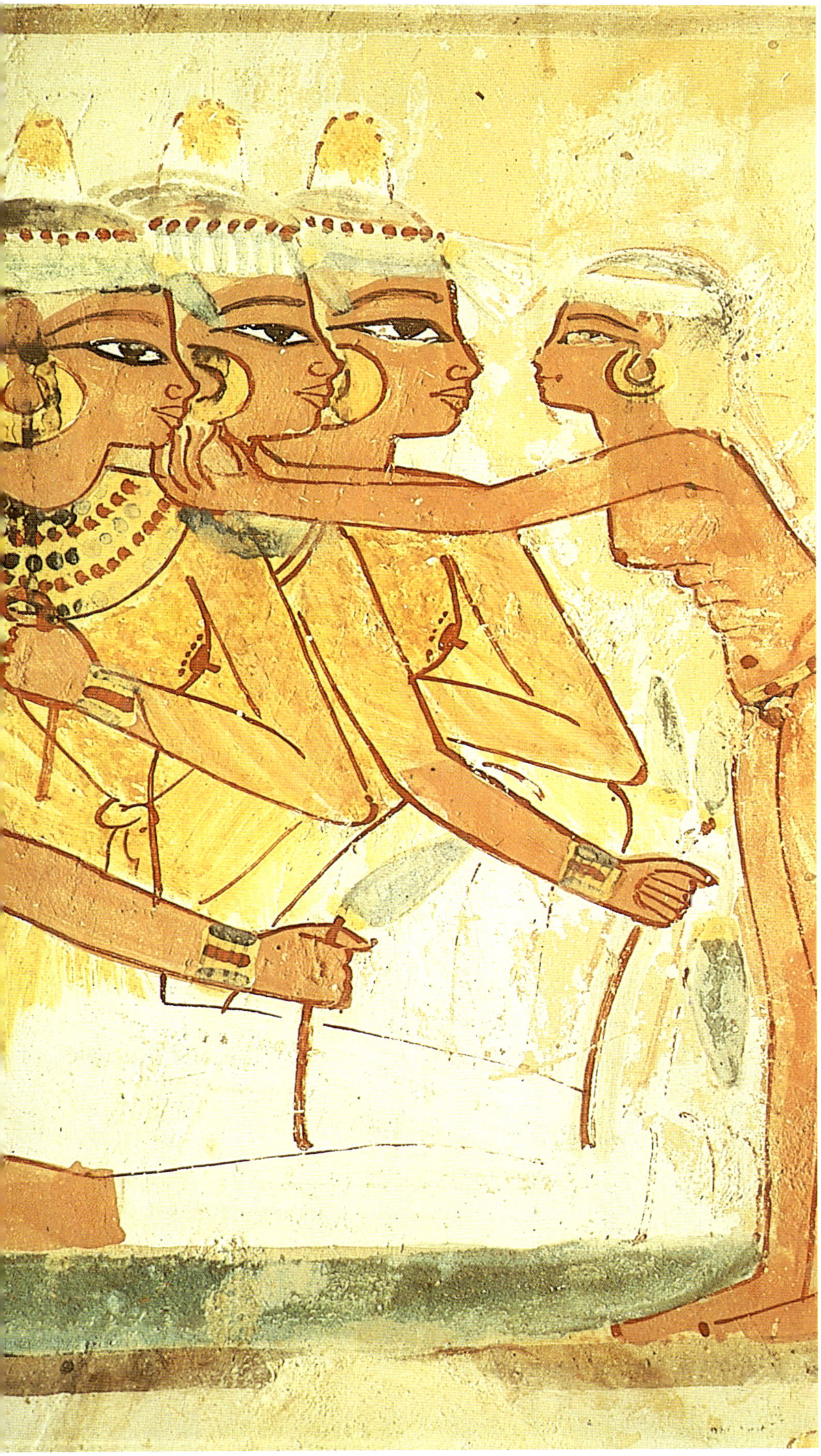

AHMOSE NEFRETARI

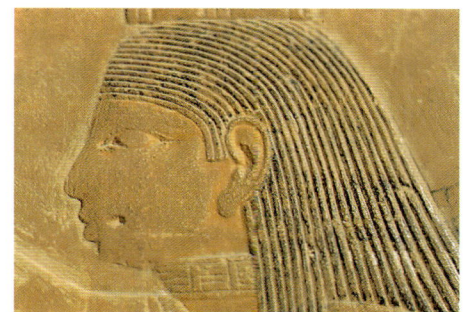

A Lady's Appearance

The appearance of an affluent lady, like that of her husband, was an important matter. A bas-relief depicts a royal favorite in all her stylishness. She rests on a comfortable sofa. In her hand she holds a disk-shaped mirror made of polished silver, with a column-shaped handle of ebony and gold. The hair-dresser has not remained idle. With her long fingers, she has artfully produced a length of small braids. With an ivory pin, she pins up the hair she has not gotten to yet. This work will take time. To bolster her patience, a servant has brought her a goblet. He pours the contents of a vial into it. "To your health!" he says, as the mistress brings the goblet to her lips. The more modest wife of Anapu, a minor landowner, takes care of her own hair while her husband and brother-in-law are in the fields. She does not like to be bothered. If she were to get up, she would lose the thread of her hairdo and would have to start all over.

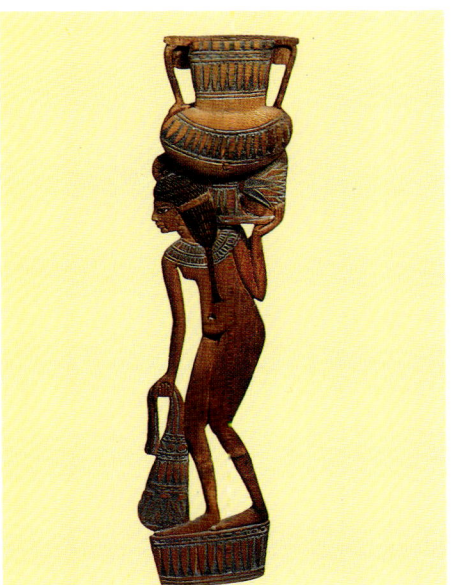

Song of Love

Your love is in my skin
like a reed in the arms of the wind.
You fulfill,
and one need not ever eat,
You intoxicate, and one need not drink.

A LADY'S APPEARANCE

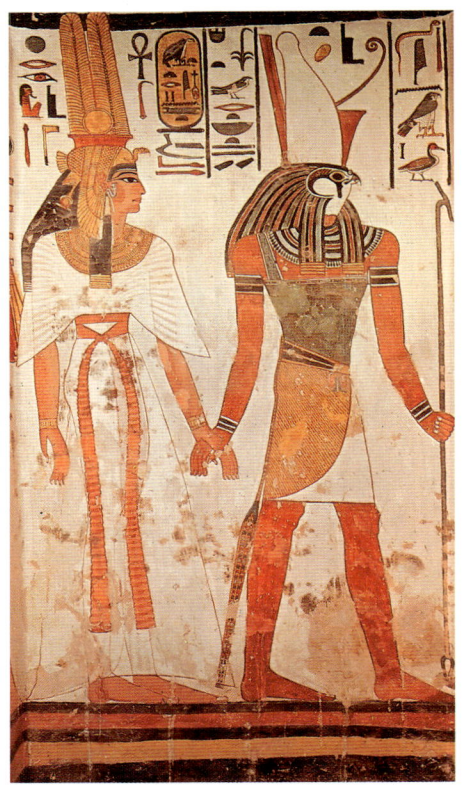

The Lovely Hour

What a lovely hour this is!
How it stretches into eternity.
Since I have slept by your side,
You have lifted my heart.

When I kiss her
And her lips are half-opened
I feel drunk
Without having drunk mead.

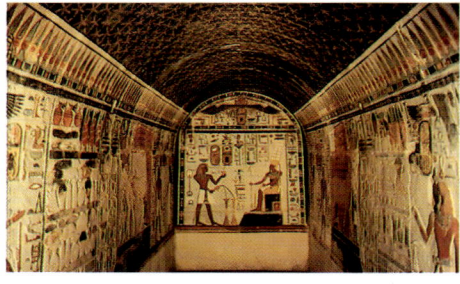

Intoxication

The beloved and her friend
Stroll under the shades,
Intoxicated by wine and sorbet
Perfumed with oil and unguent.

Truth

Doesn't Truth, too, itself desire
a drunken heart?

Proverb

"There is myrrh on the dark hair of Truth."

Even her mummy has been found, remarkably preserved. The anthropologist Ernest Chantre describes her: "... long face, the little mouth, and the little thick lips, the small ears near the head, the straight nose, short but not flat, with prominent nostrils."

A stroke of the magic wand takes her from another time, and voilà: we stand before a contemporary Wolof or Fulani girl, treading along the coast of Senegal or the Niger River, a heavy wig of sisal falling in silky waves down to her shoulders.

Ahmose-Nofretari was born at the end of the occupation by the Hyksos, invaders from the east who controlled Egypt for more than two centuries.

Her father, King Seqenenre Tao, played a large role in the national war against the Hyksos; but history has remembered her mother, the famous Queen Ahhotep, one of the most remarkable women Egypt has known.

Ahhotep's husband Seqenenre had been killed in a battle against the Hyksos; today we possess his mummy riddled with wounds.

Without the intervention of Ahhotep, the death of the king on the battlefield would have signaled the end of the struggle and a centuries-long return of the Hyksos invaders: she mustered the troops in his name, breathing courage into deserters, and pursued the liberation of the realm.

A stela found in the Temple of Karnak declares:

"Praise the mistress of the kingdom, the august woman, who has reunited Egypt, taken care of its army and protected it. May she, the royal wife, Ahhotep, live forever."

Ahmose-Nofretari is a very young woman when her father dies. The very gods of the kingdom have been wounded by his death: when the cult has been so degraded, disorder rules in the heavens as on earth; and it even seems that one has descended into primordial chaos, the beginning of time, when the sky itself has not yet taken shape.

But Ahmose-Nofretari is never far from the gods, even in the most desperate hour; she welcomes all events with a serenity worthy of the pious, of those who are priestesses in their own souls before they assume the spiritual leadership of others. Her brother Ahmose has taken the title of pharaoh of the Two Lands and then chases out the Hyksos from the Sinai Desert, even beyond the mountains of Canaan.

Ahmose-Nofretari accompanies him in all his battles and lends a helping hand. The day after his victory she and her brother marry, as did their parents, and as generations of "sister-wives," for whom royal incest is both a duty and a privilege, will do thereafter.

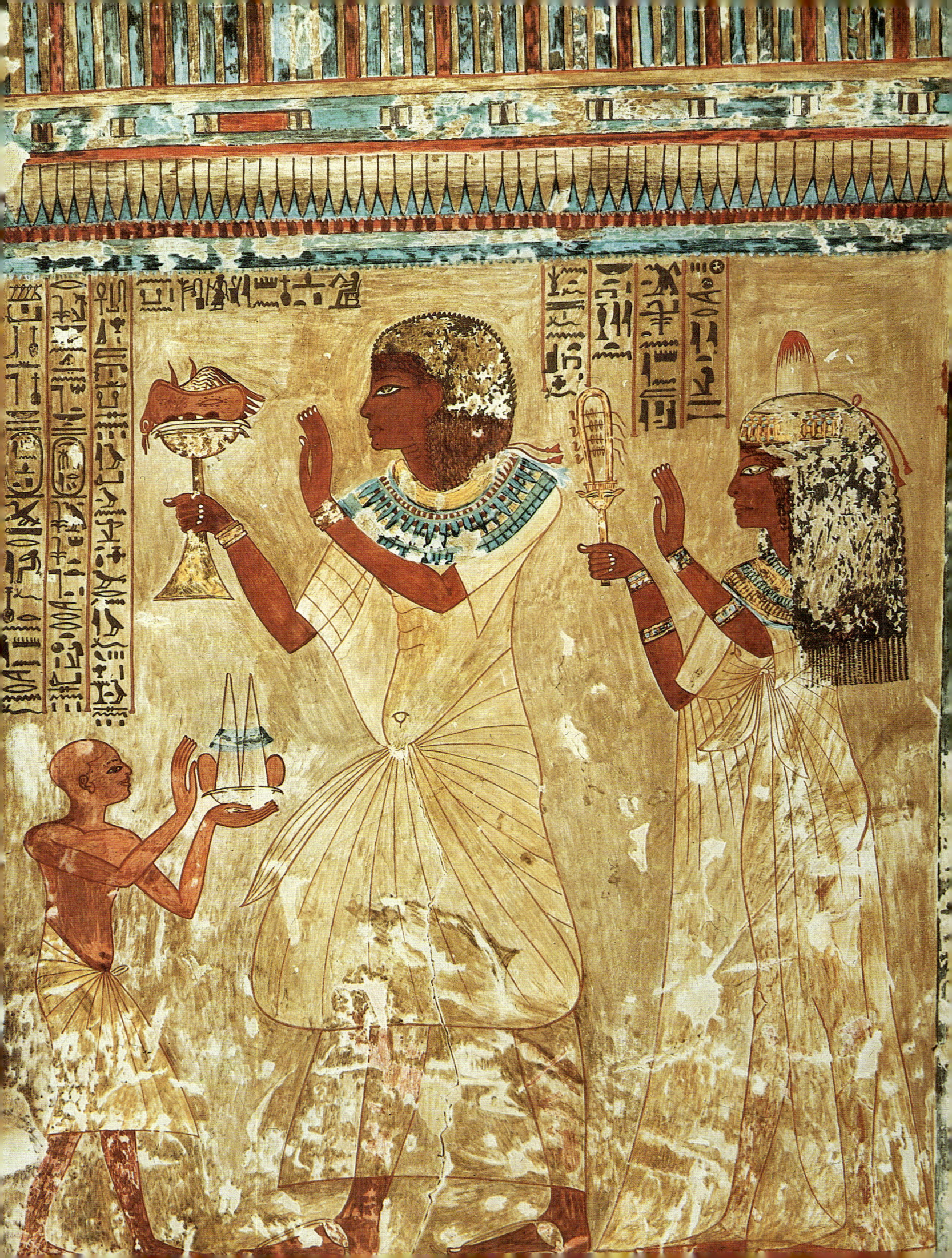

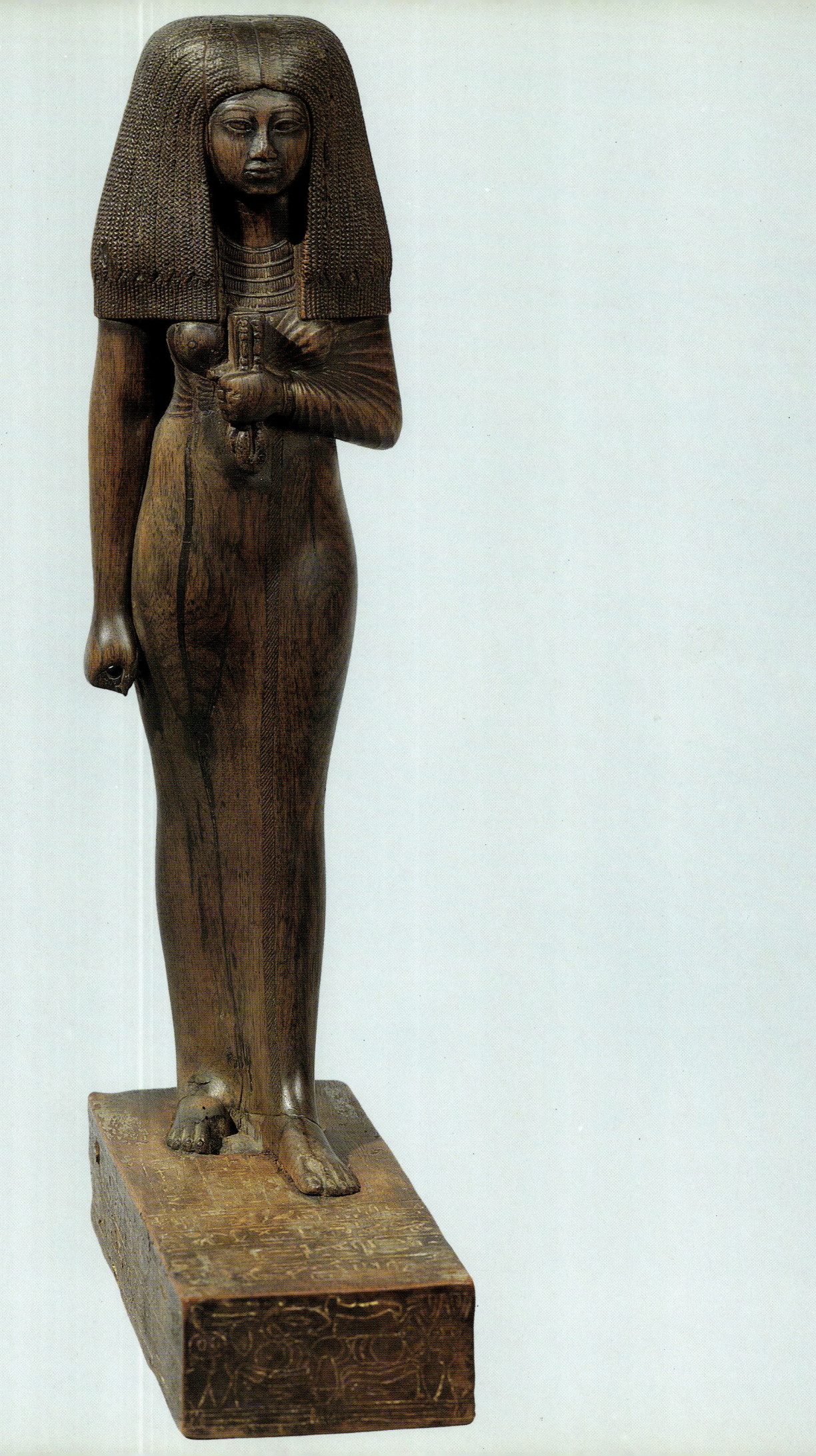

AHMOSE NEFRETARI

She ensures that the temples are raised again, that the old customs are reestablished down to the last detail.

She is particularly attentive to the cult of the god Amon, of whom the pharaoh Ahmose, her brother-husband, is the earthly representative: every morning, as did his ancestors, Ahmose walks around the palace so that the sun may complete its circle in the sky.

Soon, Ahmose-Nofretari is invested with the title of prophet of Amon. And her piety is so ardent, her beauty is so strange, so clearly supernatural, that a halo of legends surrounds her name in the sacred shade of the temples of the Upper Nile. People say that the god Amon visits her regularly, that he lives in her body and strokes her breasts, and never tires of contemplating her face; and those who come near her at the temple in Thebes whisper that a spark of peaceful, blissful, truly divine sensuality shows in her gaze.

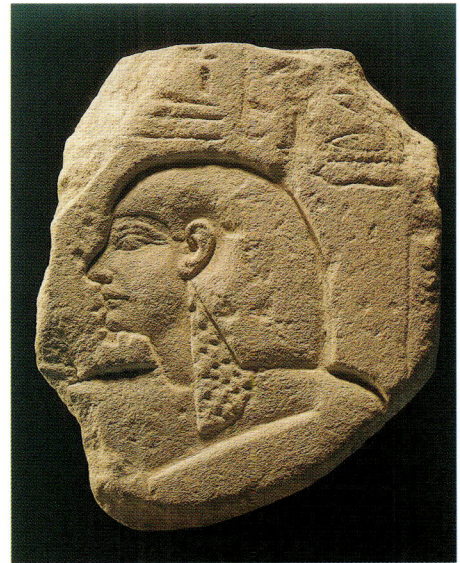

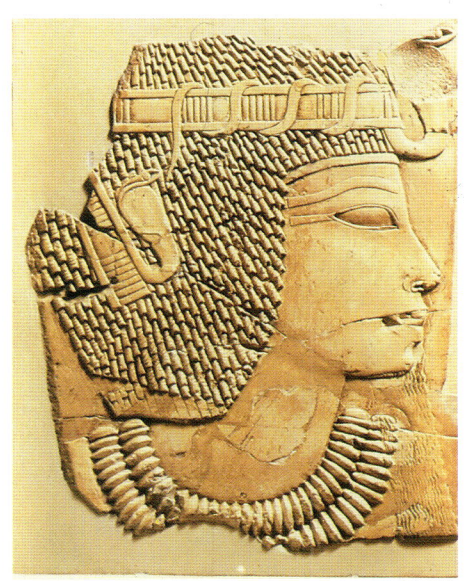

Music

Egyptians have always loved music. They loved it even before the invention of any instrument, as they clapped their hands to accompany the voice. The flute, the oboe, the harp were already around in the days of the pyramids.

It was appropriate to thank the gods, but no one ever forgot that we have only a short time on Earth to enjoy their gifts. One should always take advantage of any beautiful day when the clemency of the gods and the generosity of the host complement each other so well. The harpist Neferhotep repeated these truths at a banquet:

"Bodies have relinquished themselves since the day the gods were born, and younger generations take their place. As long as Ra rises every morning and Tup sleeps at Manu, then males will engender and women will conceive, noses will breathe, but whatever is born will one day return to its place. Make this day happy, oh priest. May we offer up perfumes of the best quality, essences to please your nose, and garlands and lilies for your shoulders and for the neck of your beloved sister."

She is in her forties when her husband-brother Ahmose dies, when she is officially invested with the title of spouse of god.

And then she rules alongside her son Amenophis I, controls the material and spiritual life of the kingdom, and, together with the new pharaoh, conducts the famous ritual of the divine cult which will rule daily life in Egypt for centuries.

From now on, she wears her hair in the fashion of the goddess Mut, the god Amon's wife in heaven: a helmet with two long feathers, above which shines a golden sun surrounded by the horns of the god Sothis. And everyone will sing the praises of the sweet-voiced spouse with her animated hands and beautiful face, elegant with her double feather: "She is the great queen of love, the mistress of charm whose beauty fulfills the god."

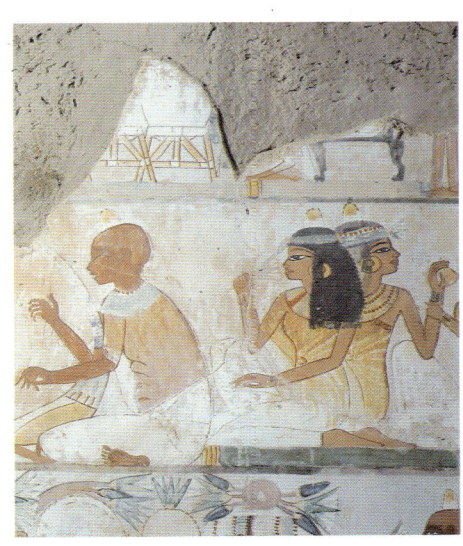

Musicians and Dancers

Music and dance companies hired out their services and sometimes went from town to town, along with acrobats, to perform for private functions and weddings, but also for certain large-scale religious festivals.

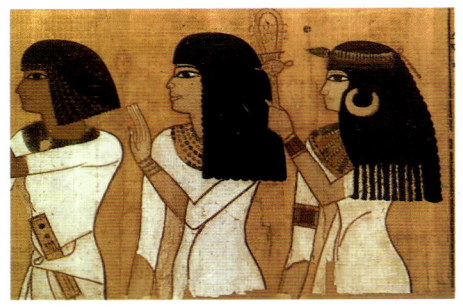

She dances and plays the sistrum in the temple of Amon, sings hymns for him; she is depicted with her arms wrapped around the god, hugging him, chest to chest, and holding him by the shoulder, while Amon holds out the letter of life, the "ankh," to her, by which he says: my heart is most satisfied.

People also say that she is the protector of the poor, listening to the most modest of prayers; and perhaps it is this tenderness that will make her the object of a cult that lasts for over five hundred years.

And so, she who had chased out the invader will continue to extend her protection over the kingdom; she who had reestablished the temples, who had brought back the people to their gods, has herself entered the temples as a goddess, an object of special adoration in the history of Egypt.

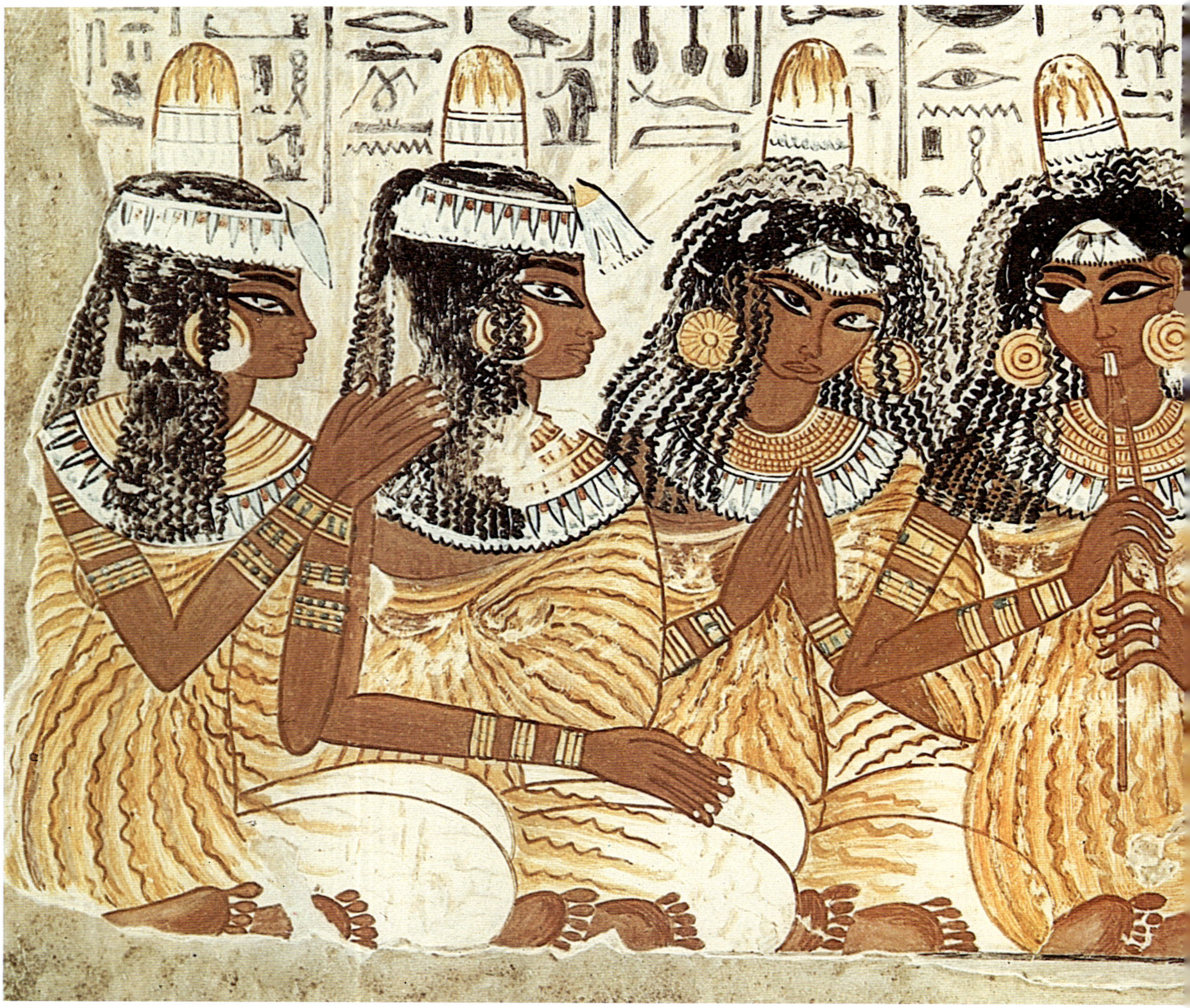

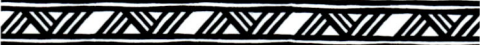 AHMOSE NEFRETARI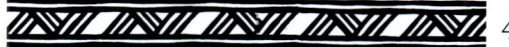

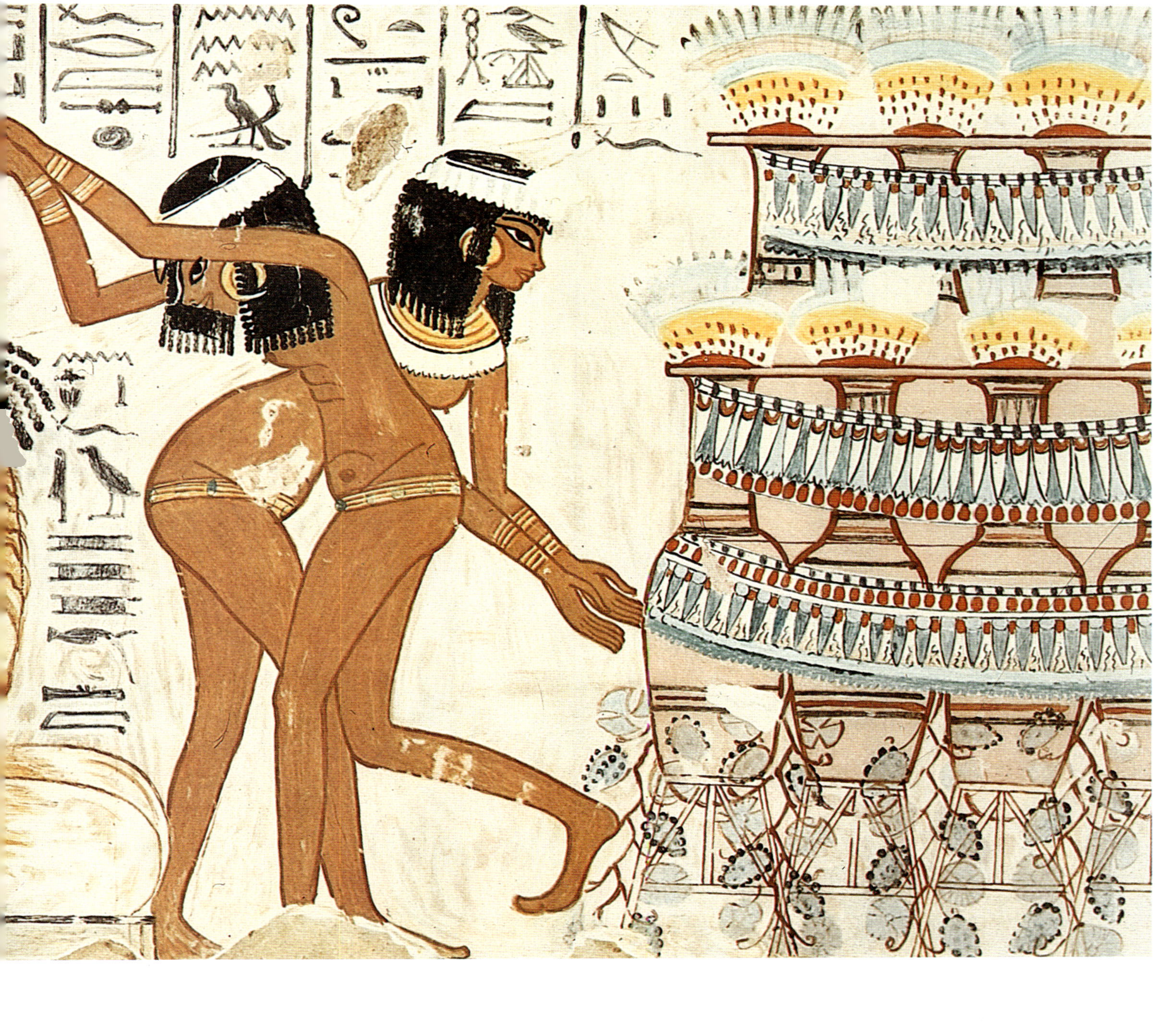

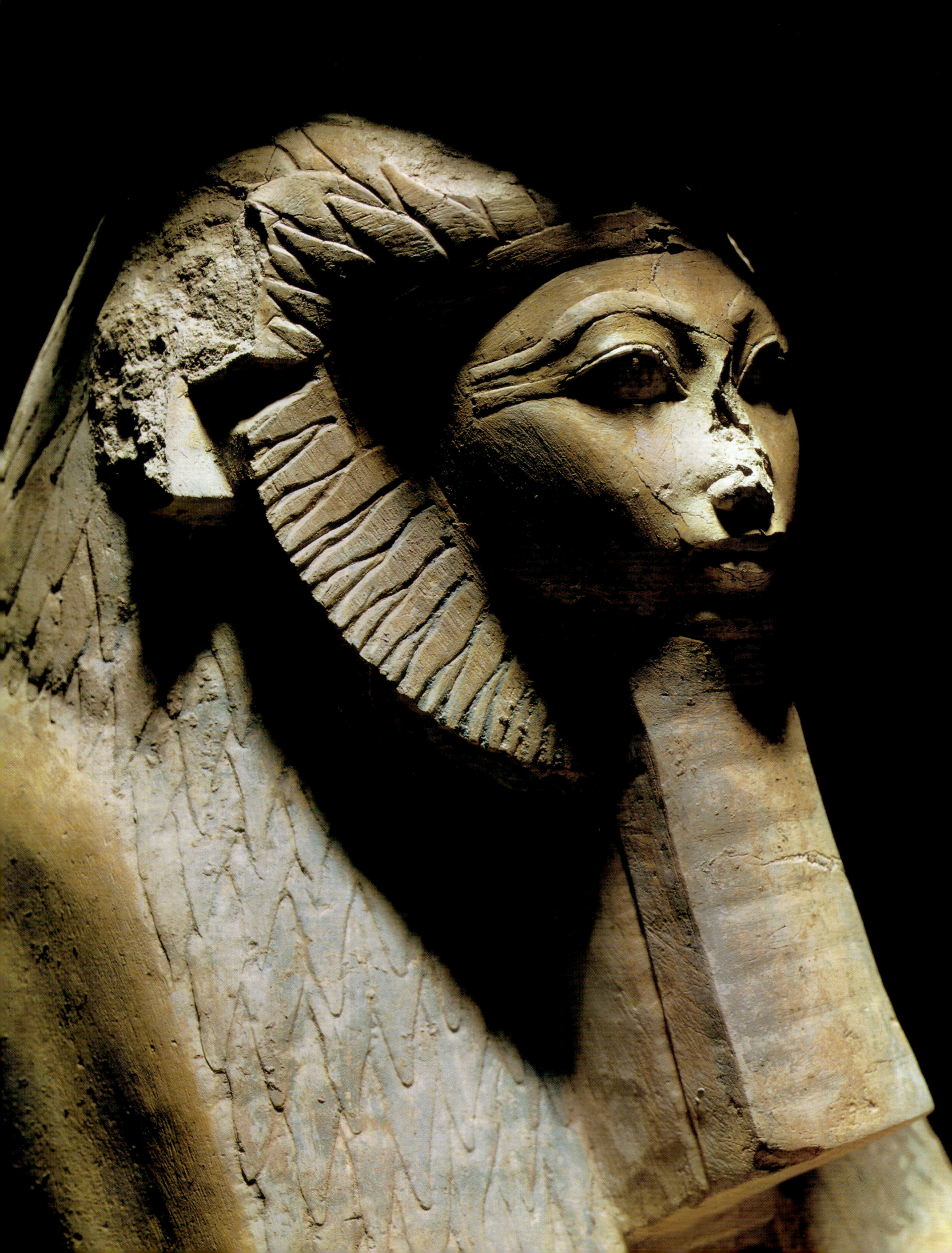

HATSHEPSUT

DAUGHTER OF THE GOD AMON

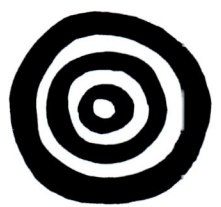

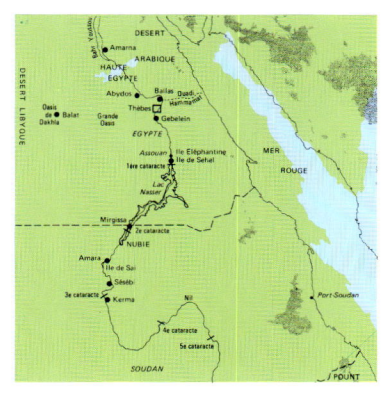

She was born out of the love of a queen and a god, and her name means "she of noble bearing"...

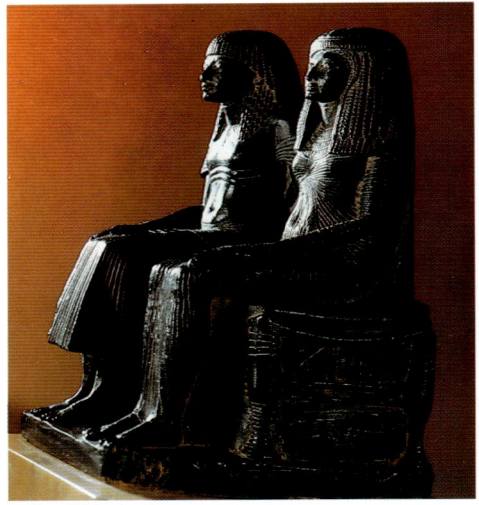

GREAT ROYAL SPOUSE

THE QUEEN HATSHEPSUT IS THE DIRECT DESCENDANT OF AHMOSE-NOFRETARI: THROUGH ROYAL INCEST, THE SAME BLOOD FLOWS THROUGH THEIR VEINS. HER BIRTH IS THE SUBJECT OF A LEGEND IN WHICH SOME SEE ONE OF THE SOURCES OF CHRISTIANITY: THE MOTHER OF HATSHEPSUT IS SO beautiful that the god Amon becomes lovesick over her; dying from desire, the god leaves his home in the skies one night and infuses her with his divine substance.

This is how the story goes, as recounted in a bas relief of the period:

"She woke up amid the scent of the god, and she made sure that he was satisfied thanks to her. Then she said to him: 'Great is your power; after you have been with me in all your splendor, while your dew still covers all my body, to see your flesh is a precious thing.' And then, the god Amon once more took his pleasure with her."

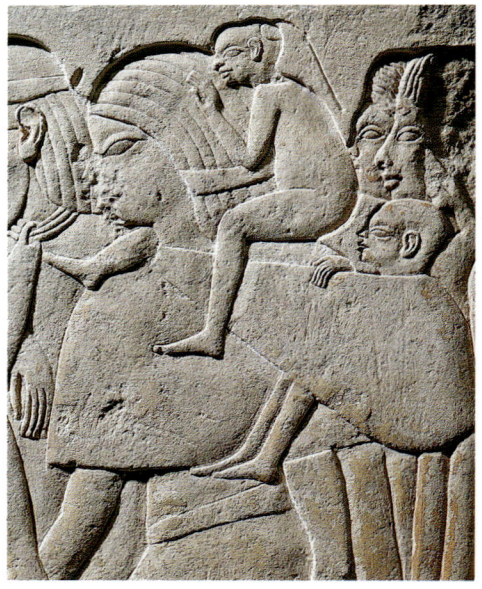

THE GOD COMES DOWN ONE NIGHT

Hatshepsut was born of the love of the queen and the god Amon. Her name means "she of the noble bearing."

Princess Hatshepsut is often described as "a serenely beautiful young woman in bloom."

Upon the death of her father Tuthmose I, she is married to her half-brother Tuthmose II and becomes the great royal spouse, the first lady of the Two Lands. Her husband dies from a skin disease, and she then serves as the crown regent until her child, Tuthmose III, comes of age.

A supernatural daughter of Amon, she does not wish to rule as a mere regent and soon crowns herself pharaoh.

She then sheds her feminine appearance; and the images found in the temple at Dayr al-Bahri show her wearing the symbolic beard and loincloth of a pharaoh.

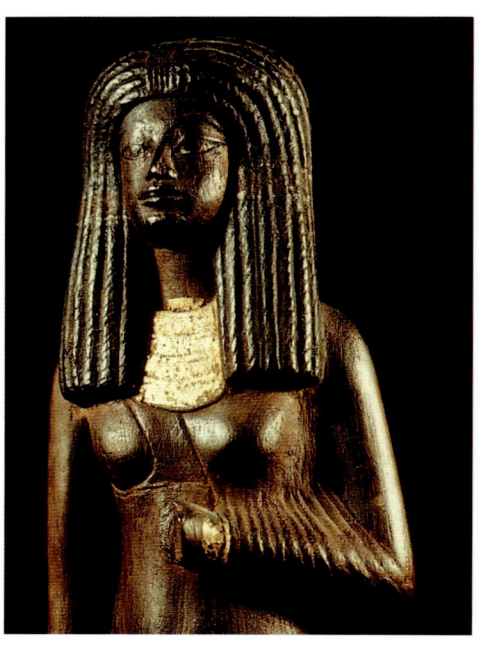

THE FIRST LADY OF THE TWO LANDS

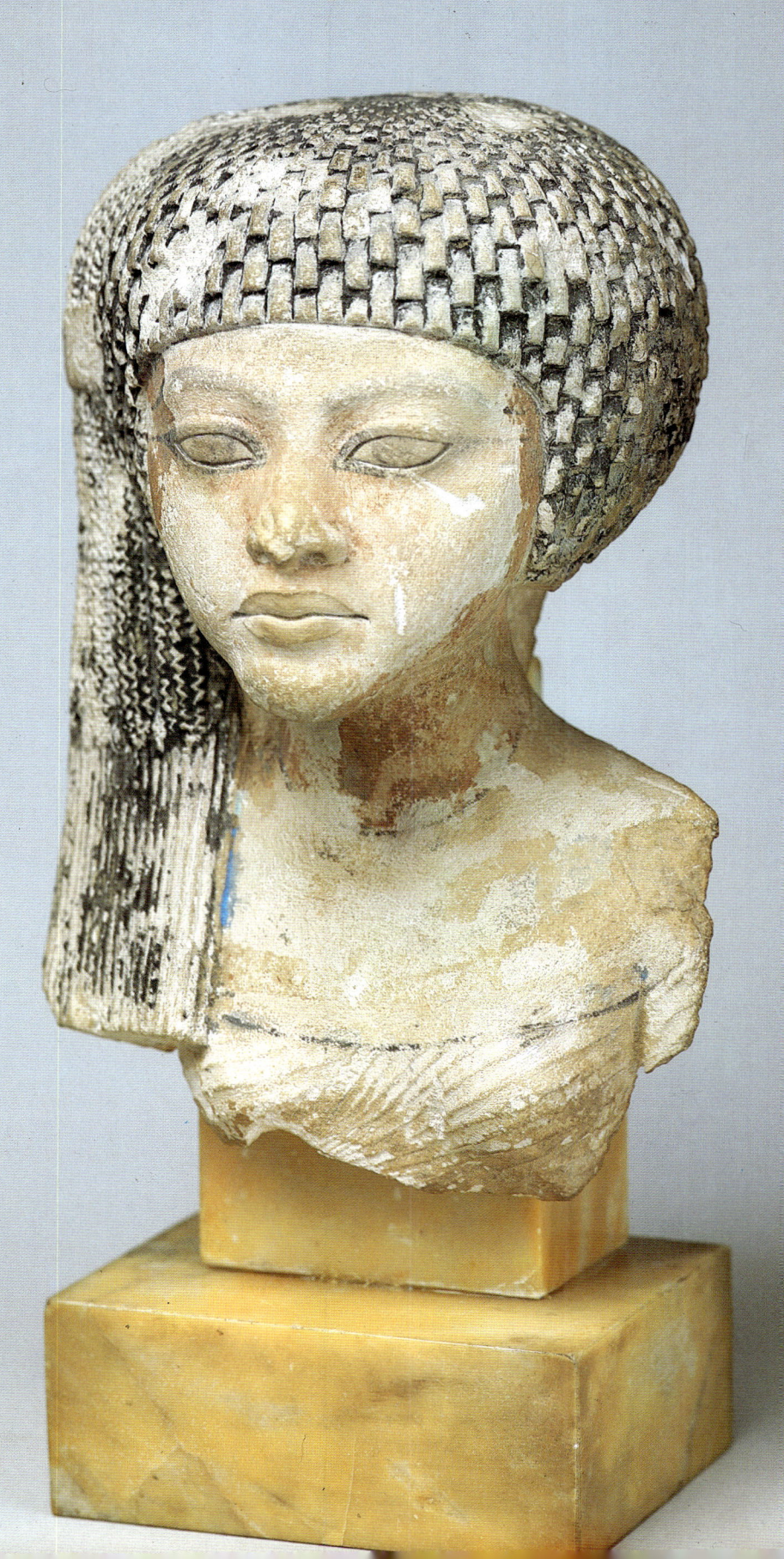

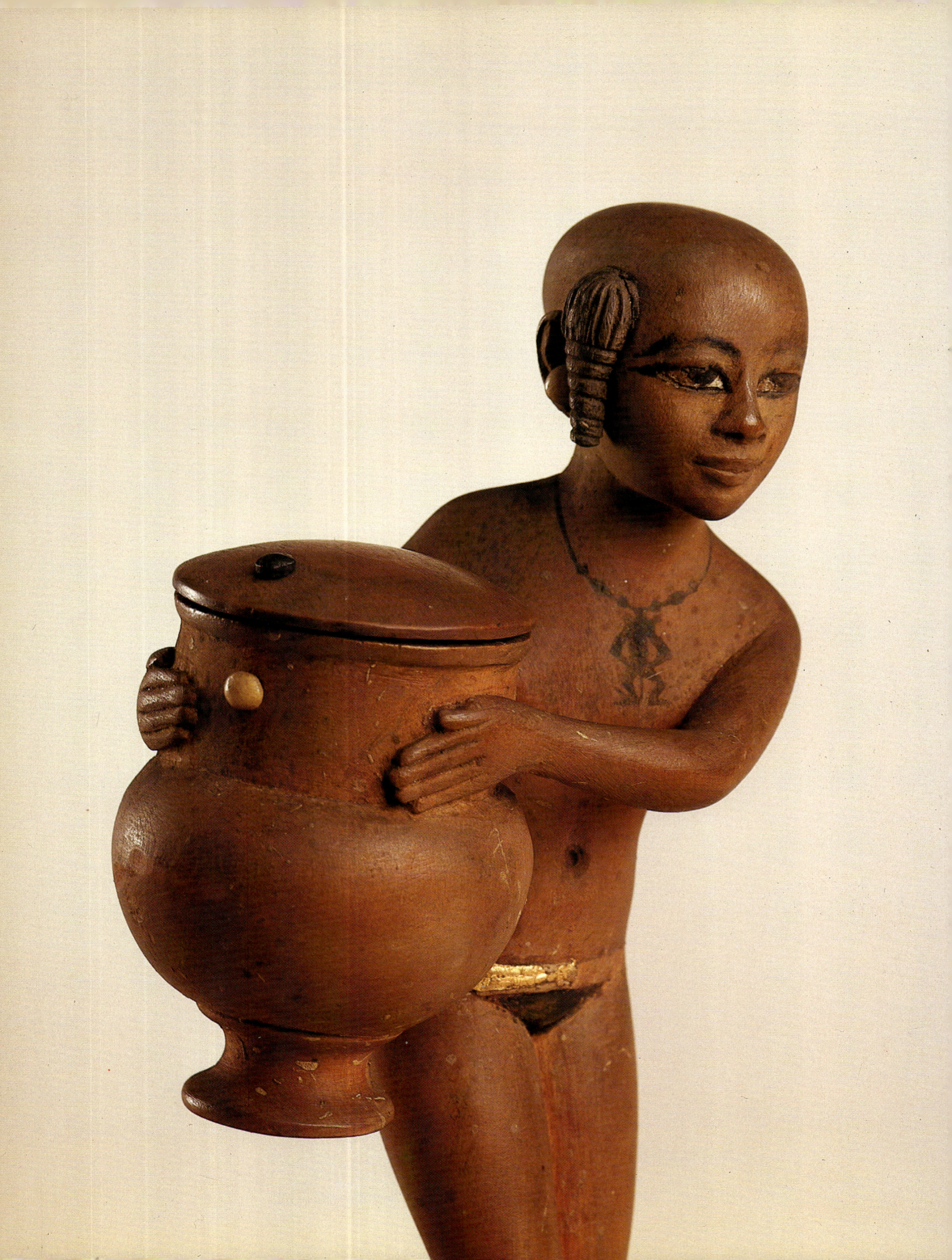

HATSHEPSUT

Her rule is an oasis of peace, a calm in the storm. Her predecessors had been busy fighting the Hyksos, and her successors would in their turn become conquerors. Hatshepsut, on the other hand, thinks only of the prosperity of the kingdom; and she manages her wealth so skillfully, displaying her strength and her desire for peace, that no war clouds her reign.

Art in this period reaches a summit of purity. Hatshepsut's face, with its large almond-shaped eyes and its triangular, hieratic line brightened by a extraordinary spark of mischief and intelligence, perfectly symbolizes a renewed and vibrant classicism.

Trade is established with the peoples to the east and with the inhabitants of the Greek Isles.

Turquoise mines are opened in the Sinai at Serapit El Khadim and Maghara. But the queen will never send slaves there and exhaust them with cruel labor. At her request, Egyptian volunteers are directed to the harvest of the blue stone, and Bedouins already in the desert are called upon as well. These are the same Bedouins to whom we owe the spread of hieroglyphs beyond Egypt, hieroglyphs that will be transformed, little by little, into the script of the Phoenicians and then the Greeks, who invented our alphabet.

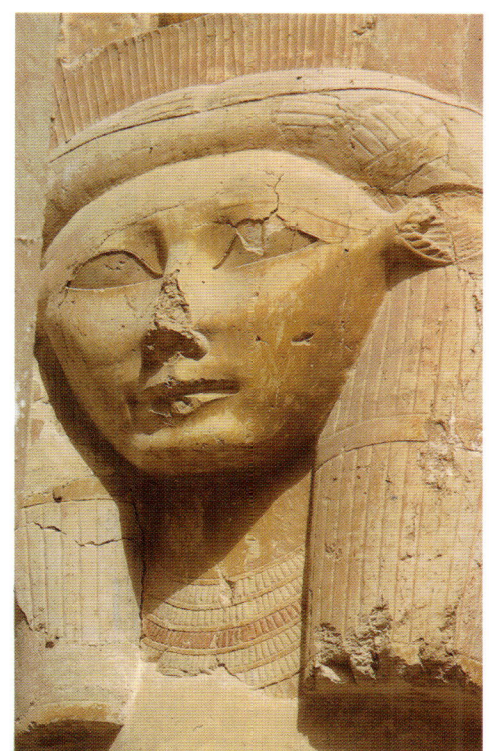

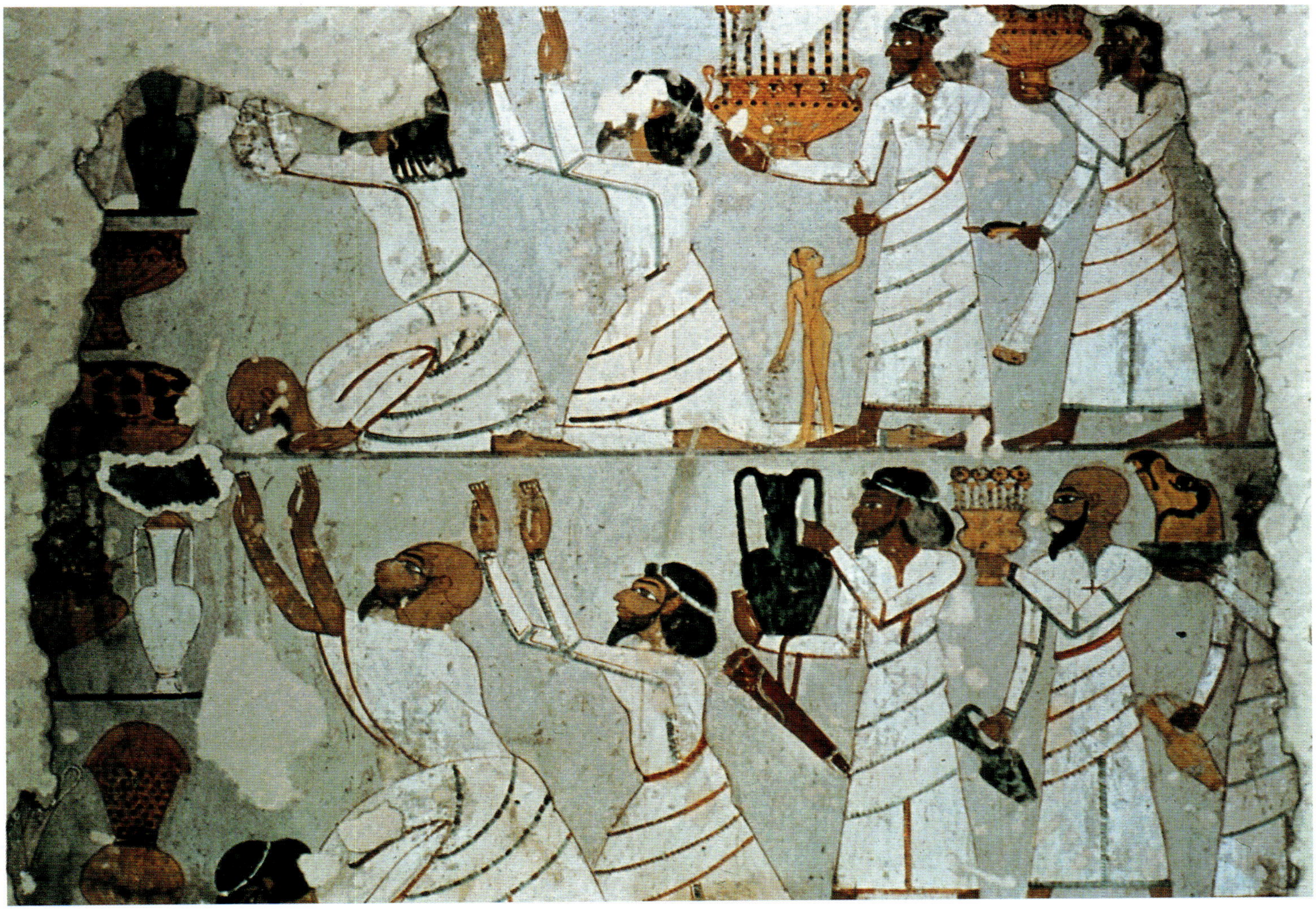

ART REACHES A SUMMIT OF PURITY

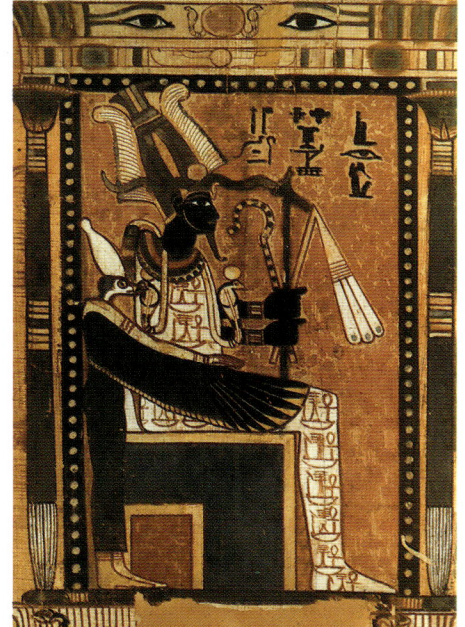

THE GREAT GODDESS

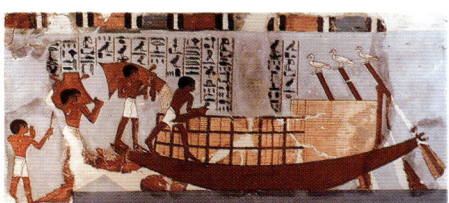

The Flood and the Tears of Isis

Whenever the Nile begins to swell, at the same time there always occurs an event that might have guided the creators of the calendar. The star Sirius (Sopdet is its Egyptian name), which no one had seen for some time, appears for a brief moment in the west right before sunrise. The Egyptians did not fail to associate the two phenomena. They attributed the flood to the tears of Isis.

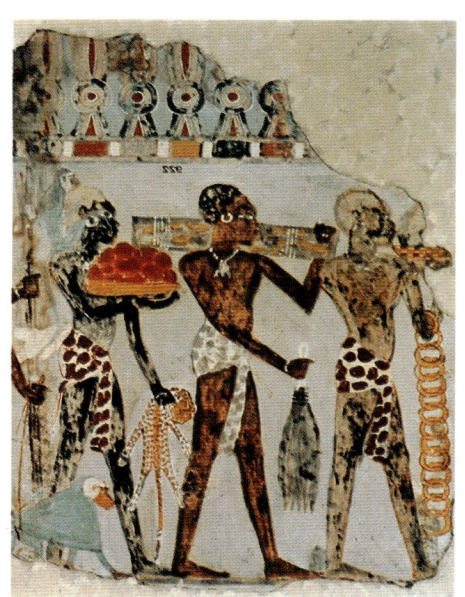

THE EXPEDITION RETURNS

Hatshepsut sent caravans deep into Asia and ships to the ports of the Mediterranean; but the greatest enterprise of her reign was the expedition to the kingdom of Punt, which occurred around the year 1495 B.C.E.

The official purpose of the Punt expedition was the quest for resins and spices, for trees that produced incense that was in great demand in the temples, and the engineers probably wanted to discover the sources of the Nile, to understand the ebbs and flows on which the great body of Egypt depended; but deeper motives can be discerned. The Egyptians had always seen Punt as the country of the ancestors, cradle of the Egyptian race and civilization. It is the place from which the great goddess Hathor, ruler of the sky and of all the gods, comes. And this fascination exerted itself, above all, on Queen Hatshepsut, who remembered her Nubian origins, and whose prime minister and confidant, the official architect of the kingdom, as well as her secret lover, was a black man named Senenmut.

Five vessels leave from Thebes and go up the Nile until they reach the waterfalls, where towpaths allow them to go around these natural obstacles; one of these towpaths has recently been discovered near the citadel of Mirgissa, which overhangs the second waterfall.

The scene of the arrival in Punt has been painted on the walls of Hatshepsut's temple in Dayr al-Bahri: the inhabitants of Punt, some Ethiopian, others Bantu, live in huts on stilts, similar to those that can be seen today among people who dwell along the Nile; the landscape, dominated by gingerbread palms, is that of present-day Nubia. Elephant tusks, animal skins, as well as malachite, spices, and cinnamon bark fill the vessels. And of course the wonder of all wonders: thirty-one incense trees, roots clinging to blocks of soil, are the objects of almost maternal care.

Another scene shows them upon their return from the expedition: a crowd of priests and sailors, preceded by a drummer, advances alongside the temple of Karnak; further off, the delegates from Punt hold the leashes of monkeys and a giraffe, an elephant, as well as two panthers that will humbly follow Queen Hatshepsut. Heaps of incense trees lie at the queen's feet, ready to be transplanted in Egyptian soil. This is the expedition's most important achievement: henceforth, the ceremonies will be conducted with pure, freshly harvested, living incense. Hatshepsut is full of joy. She takes a few drops of incense elixir in her hands and spreads it on her face and on all her limbs: "As soon as she did that," the hieroglyphs say, "her own smell mingled with that of Punt, and her face began to shine like a golden leaf."

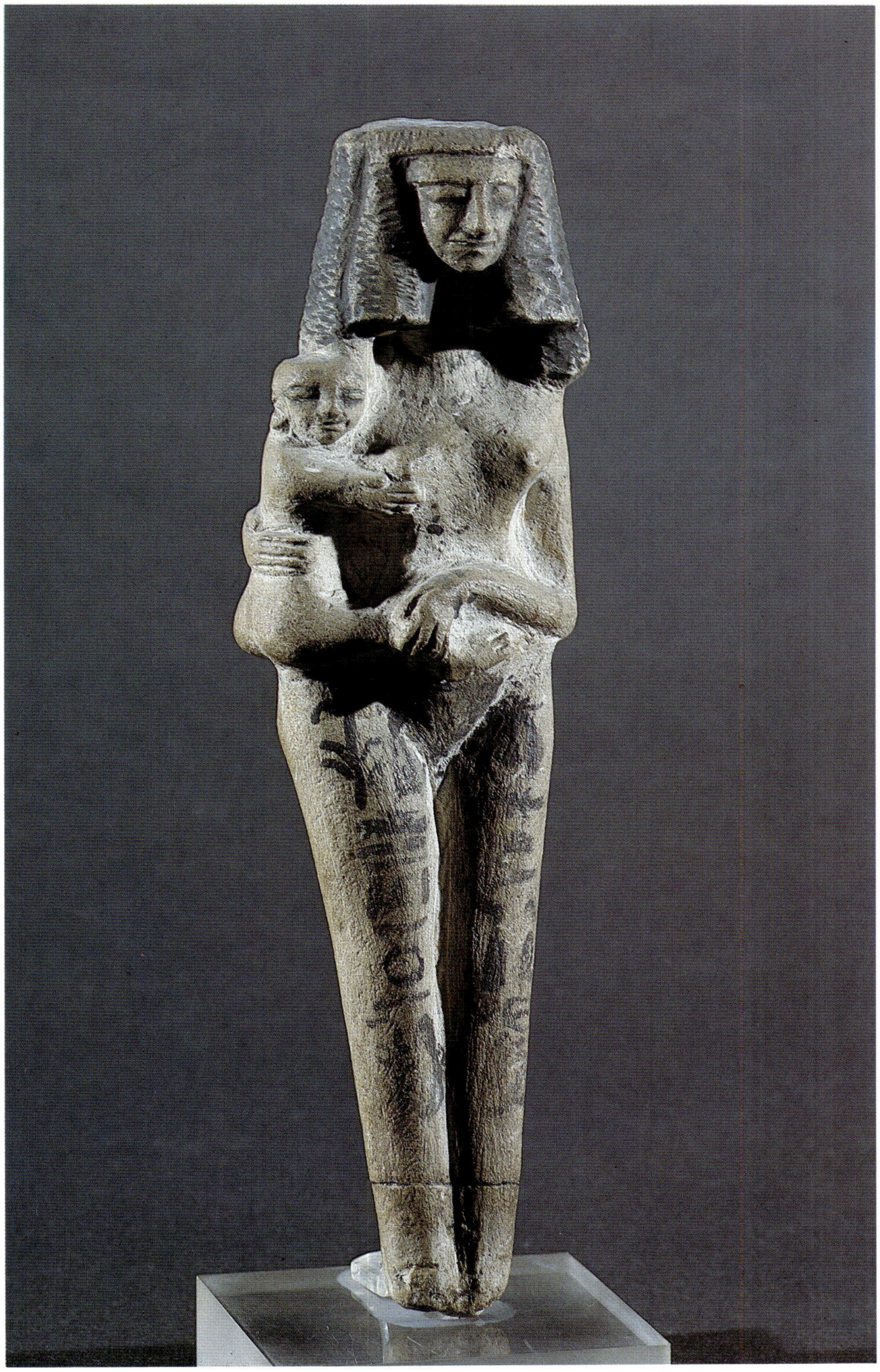

HATSHEPSUT

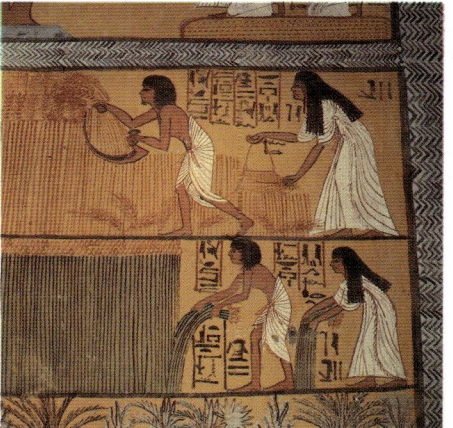

She is a Fertile Field

*If you are wise, build a house
and make a home.
Love your wife as you should.
Fill your belly and cover your back.
Unguent is what cures her body.
Bring joy to her heart
as long as you live,
For she will be a fertile field for her master.*

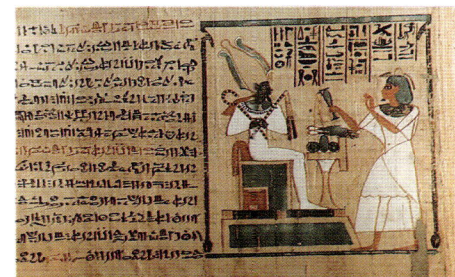

Husband and Wife

*I break him who breaks the hours
And he who breaks the hours breaks me.
He must not live, the god who planned
to separate husband and wife.*

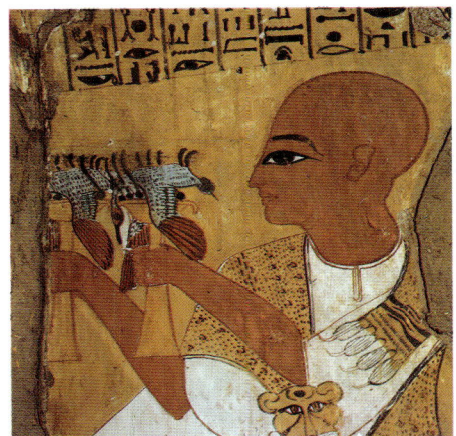

A Son's Letter to His Mother

The following must bring back to your memory what you have told your son: "Bring me quails, I would like to eat some." See, your son has brought you seven quails and you have eaten them.

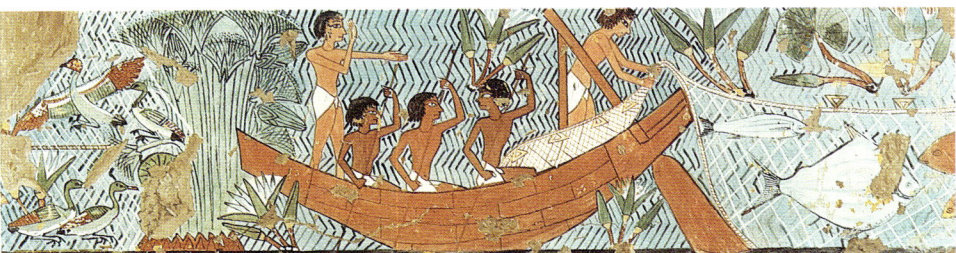

"FIVE VESSELS GOING UP THE NILE ..."

Senenmut

Steward and tutor to the royal daughter and governor of the royal house, for more than fifteen of the first years of Hatshepsut's reign, he functioned as the second-in-command in the country.

His faithfulness seems to have been absolute. Attached to all of her achievements, he displayed his respect and devotion to her.

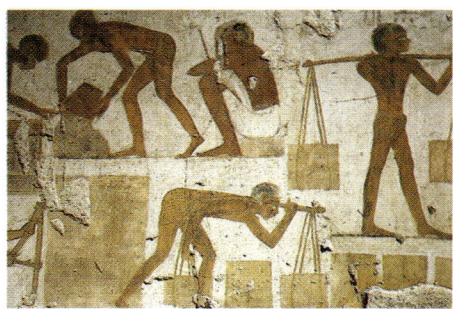

He profusely repeated the name of his queen on his own monuments, even tracing it in code, in cryptography, not only to protect her from any possible magic assault, but also to provoke the curiosity and attention of readers. His creative imagination rose to the occasion of every critical moment of the reign, and his activities along the course of his rise were completely linked to the queen's endeavors.

From this situation it is very tempting to imagine yet another degree of intimacy between the two protagonists of this story, and to lend the queen—whose gender evidently forbade her from choosing a great royal spouse, as a male pharaoh could, though this enforced her celibacy—tender feelings towards that most faithful of her faithful, the talented partisan who enlisted himself in the work-in-progress and took care to see all the projects through.

The reign of Hatshepsut would probably never have reached such splendor without the collaboration of the black man Senenmut, who was to her what Colbert was to Louis XIV, what Disraeli was to Queen Victoria.

The number and the importance of the tasks he assumed are astonishing. High priest, steward of the royal house, he was also the architect of the Temple of Dayr al-Bahri, a wonder of wonders. He stands throughout the reign of Hatshepsut as the second-in-command. He was her vassal, the most faithful of the faithful, skilled in realizing the queen's grandest projects as well as her most ordinary and daily wishes. He was also a scientist, a mind filled with knowledge, with all the astronomical science of his times: the vault of his tomb is a remarkably precise and detailed outline of the vault of the sky as it appeared over the temple while he lived—something that gives one pause.

Counselor, protector of the crown, artist and scientist, this man of many talents also played a more secret role by the queen's side.

More than a century ago, the excavations of the Valley of the Kings uncovered a mummy that some believe to have been the child of Hatshepsut and Senenmut. The papyrus that came with it shows us a young black-skinned man, truly ebony, with the small wig worn by people from the south; on the shroud we find the tablet and insignia of the queen-pharaoh, Hatshepsut, ruler of the Two Lands.

This papyrus can be seen on the first floor of the Cairo Museum, unrolled at the end of the main wall like a flag, a banner carrying the greatest secret of Hatshepsut: her greatest joy, and her greatest pain.

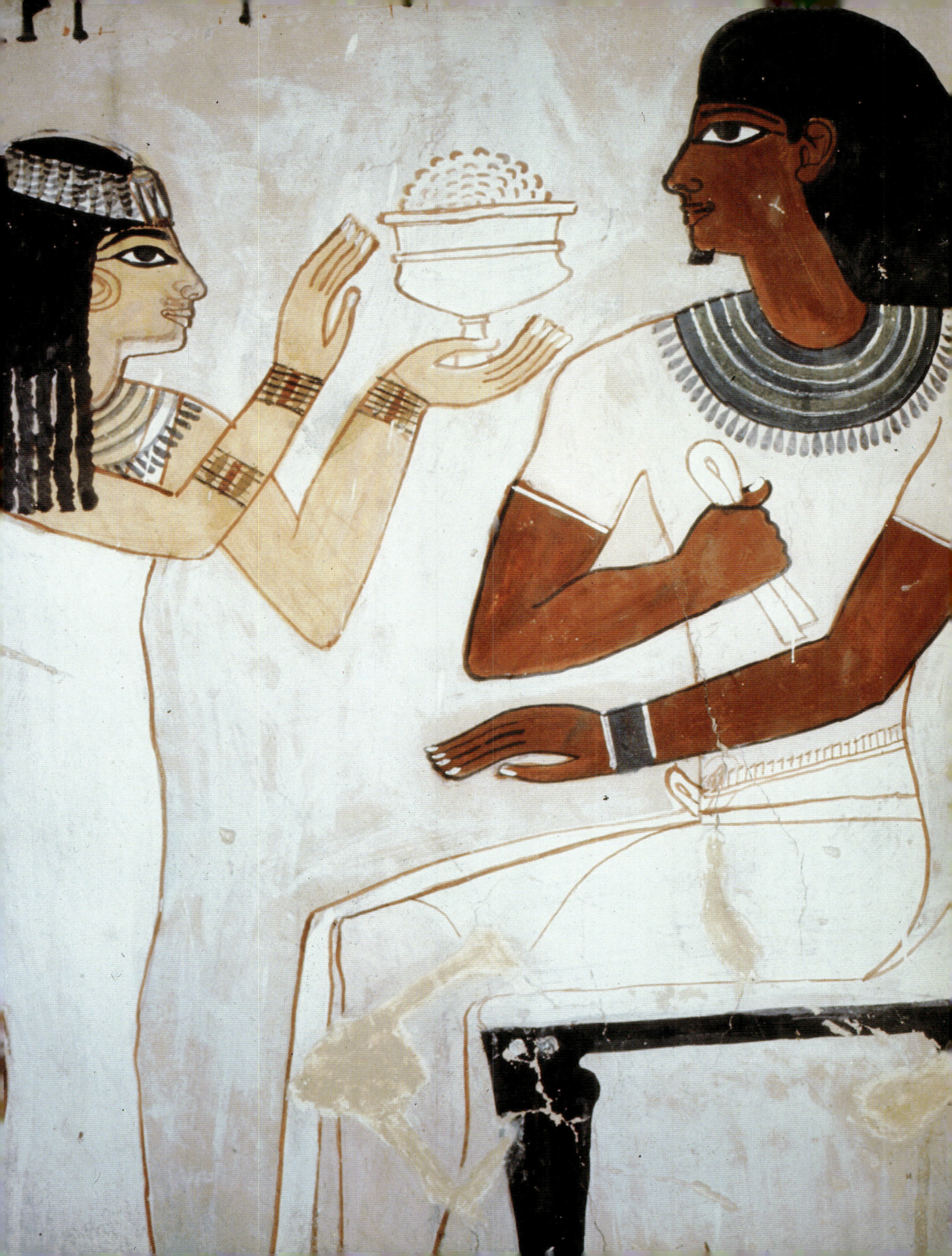

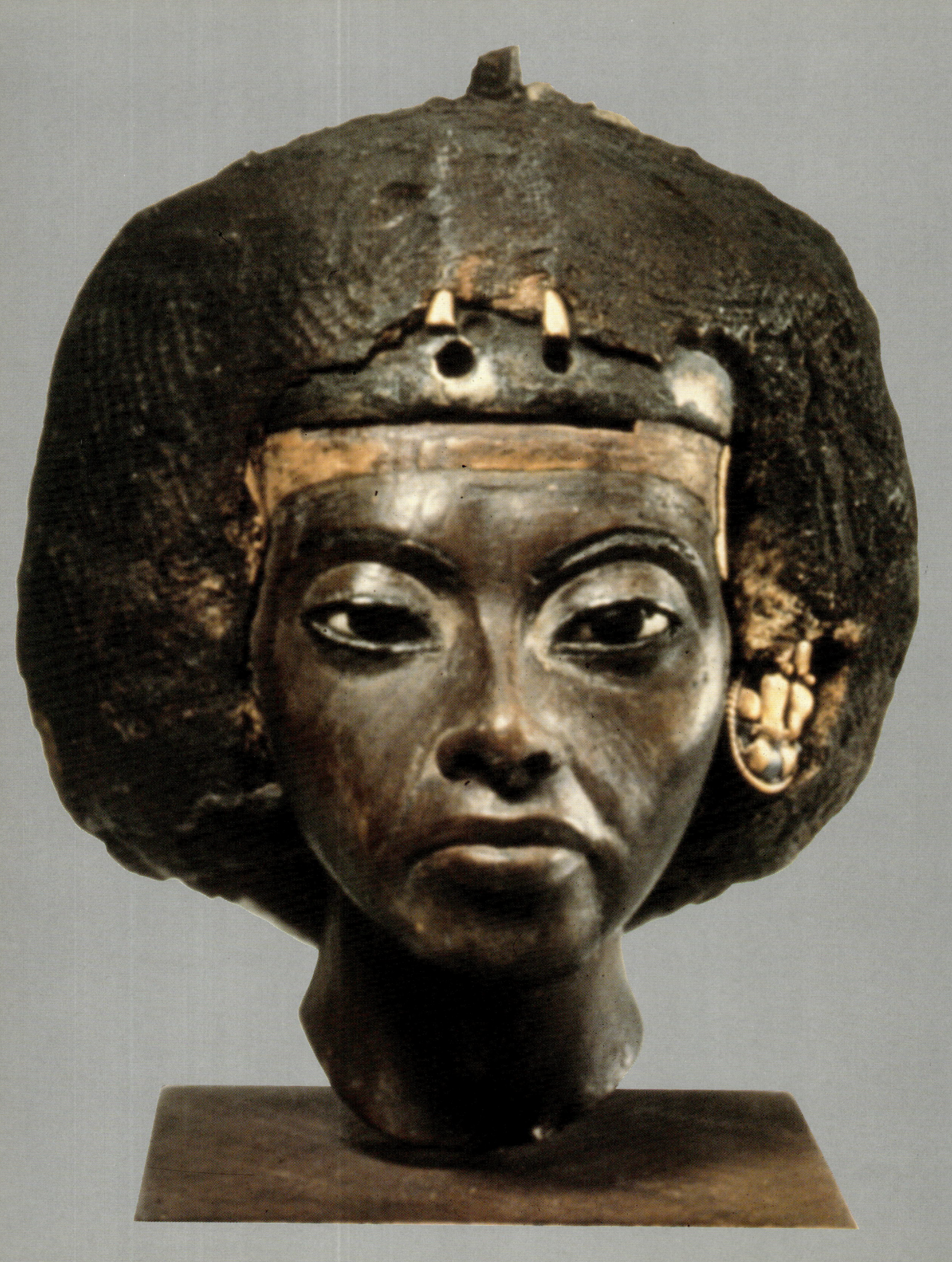

TIYE

QUEEN OF EGYPT

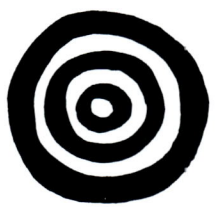

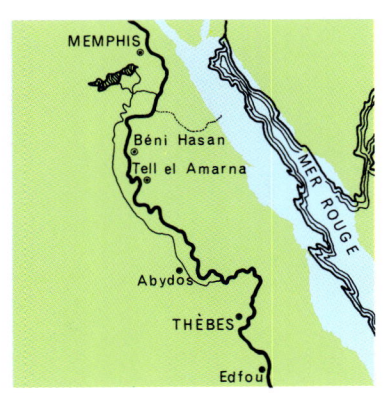

Little known today since she was black, Queen Tiye is nonetheless among the women who have most marked human history. . . .

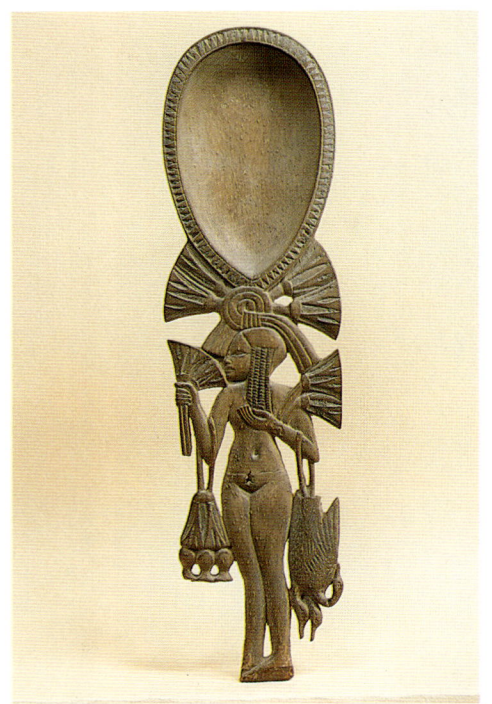

LITTLE KNOWN SINCE SHE WAS BLACK, SELDOM STUDIED BY EGYPTOLOGISTS, QUEEN TIYE IS NONETHELESS AMONG THE WOMEN WHO HAVE MOST MARKED HUMAN HISTORY. THOUGH OF HUMBLE ORIGIN, SHE WAS THE PHARAOH AMENHOTEP III'S GREAT royal spouse, about 3,500 years ago. And her power stretched throughout the empire, from the furthest tip of the Near East to the kingdom of Napata in present-day Sudan.

Her beauty was legendary, but it was her personality that especially illuminated the reign of Amenhotep III.

For her, the pharaoh built a new palace west of Thebes, in a place now called Malkata. Also for her pleasure, he had an immense lake dug in the desert, measuring 3,500 by 700 cubits.

Little by little, Tiye became the arbiter of taste in her day. And the revolution in Egyptian art, which had then been in serious decline, dates back to her rule.

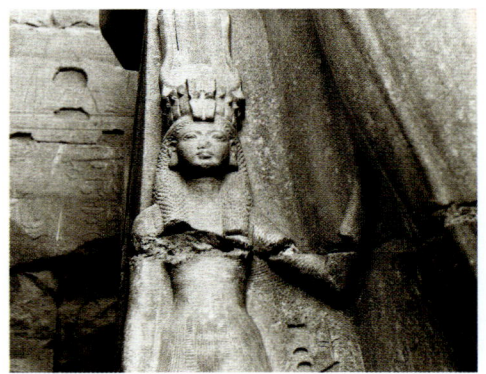

A SCULPTORS' WORKSHOP

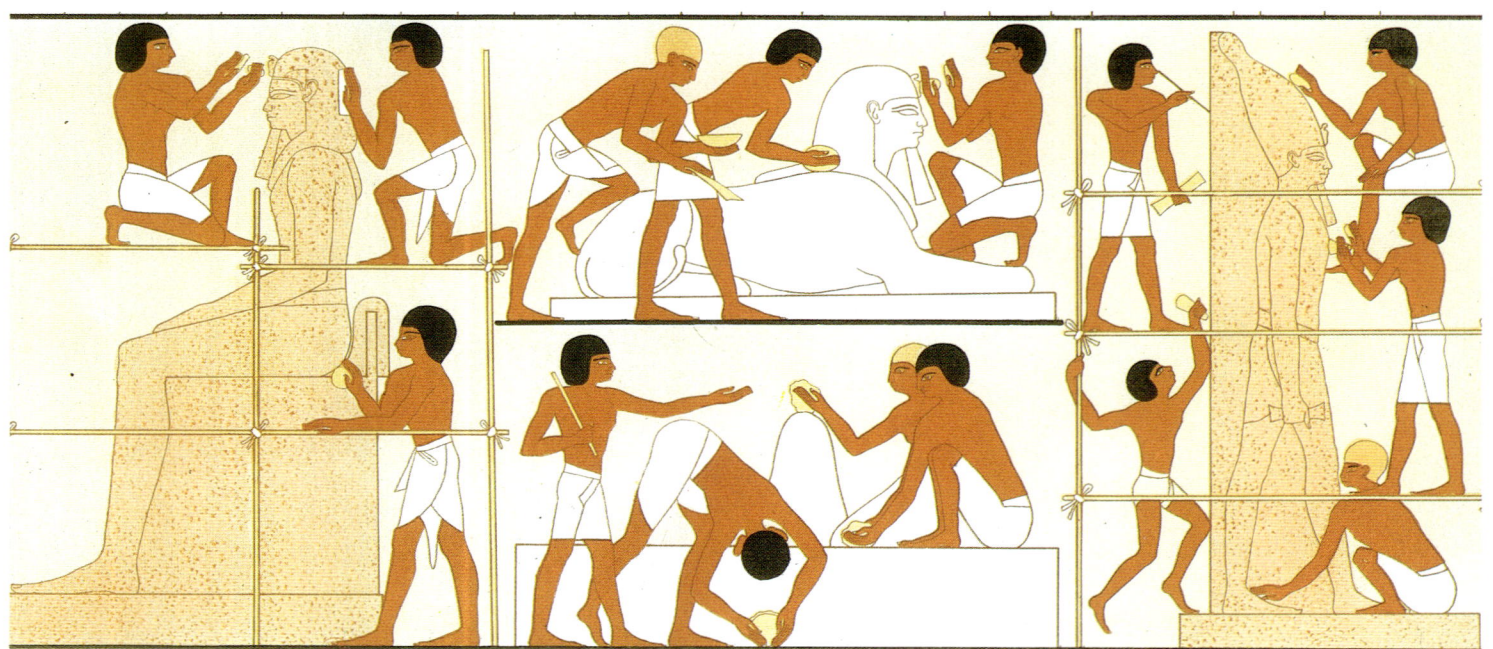

HER BEAUTY WAS LEGENDARY

TIYE

Celebrating the Day

*Turn the day into a glorious feast,
Put together before you
unguent and perfume,
Place wreaths of lotus and poppies
around your neck,
While the one who is in your heart
is sitting beside you.*

*Don't allow your heart to sink
no matter what happens
Urge others to sing and dance
before you,
Recall not the evil
so hated by the god,
Think of happiness, dear man,
The true measure of moderation.*

*Honest, peaceful man
of even temper
Who laughs and never speaks ill,
Give drink to your heart each day,
Until the day comes
when you must climb into the ship of death.*

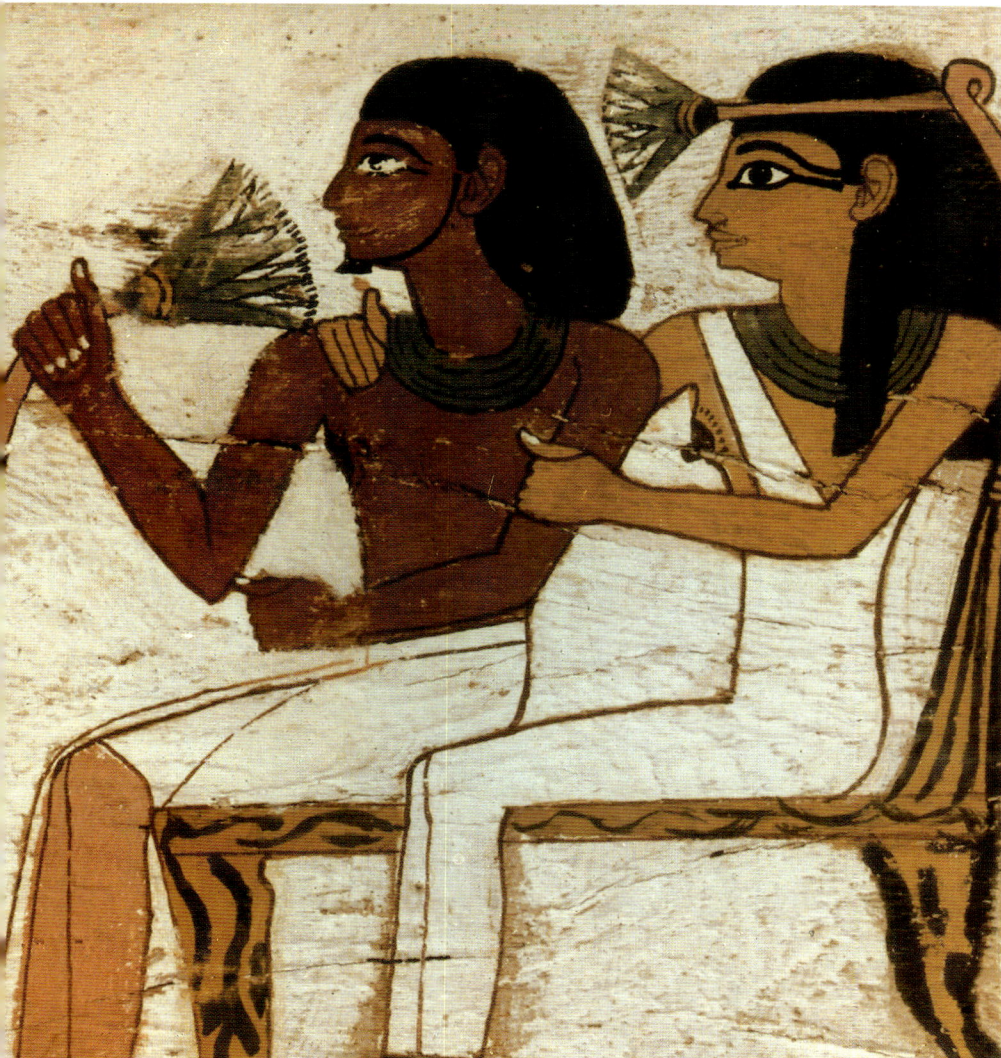

"THE ONE WHO IS IN YOUR HEART IS SITTING BESIDE YOU"

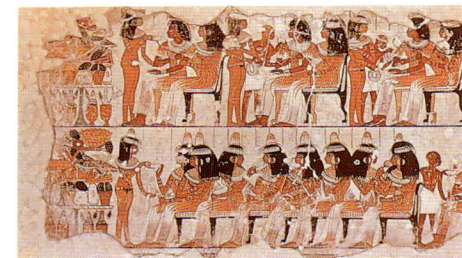

The Feasts

Egyptians eagerly abandoned their tasks for the sake of a party and jumped on their boats: women with castanets and men with flutes. Until they docked, they would dance and sing, or gibe at the people they met along their way. During the feast, more wine was drunk, it was said, than during the rest of the year. The feast of *tekhi*, a word meaning "intoxication," which was celebrated the first of the second month, was not one to be missed.

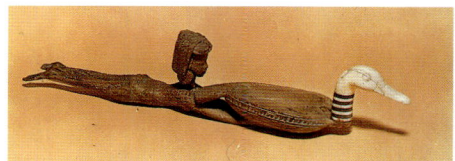

Names of Women

She loves life.
Who is she? What is her fate?
She's our sister.
The one who is loved like the Nile.
The bright one.
Egypt's desire.
Intoxication.
The daughter of intoxication.
The star of men.
The moor's abode.
Queen of eternity.

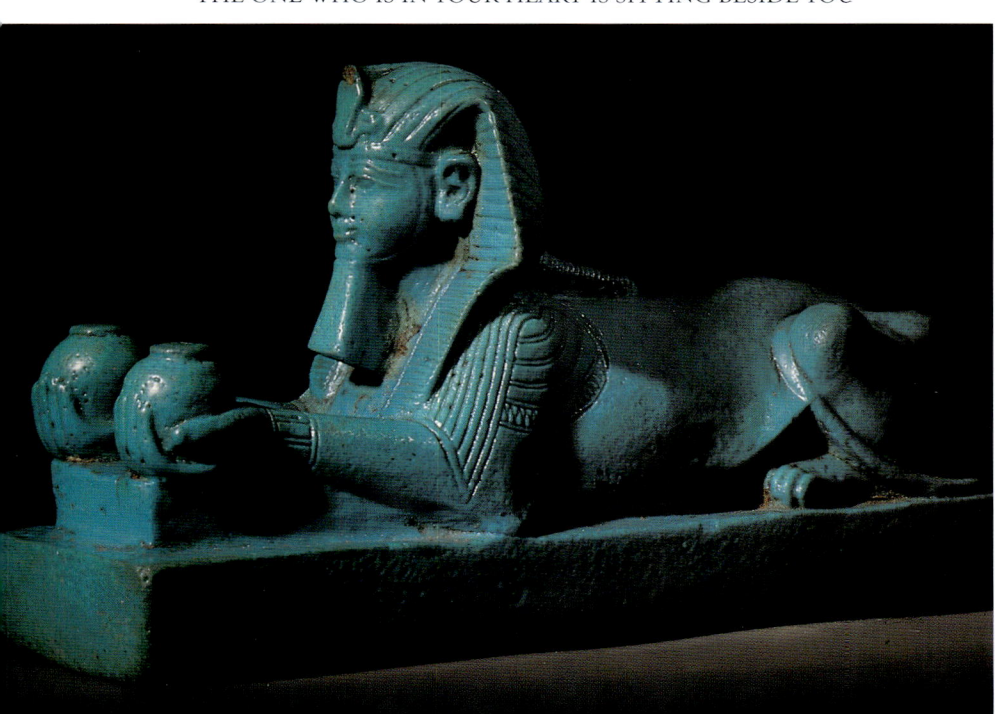

AMENHOTEP III

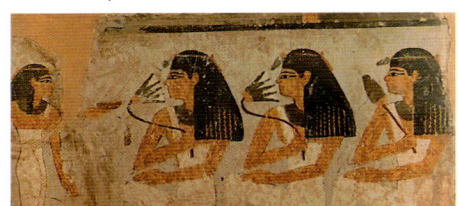

The Divine Votaries

The elder princesses of royal blood, to strengthen their hold on the country through the cult, were destined to form a new religious order. These "divine votaries" had the legal and civil status of wives of the god Amon; in other words, they could not enter into any marriage contract with a mortal. The first Theban to be thus pledged to Amon was Amonirdis, the daughter of the Ethiopian king Kashta. The Theban matriarchal order continues with Chapenapet, the daughter of Piye, likewise destined to these divine wedding vows. Then, under Taharqa, it was Chapenapet II, the daughter of Amonirdis I. Under the control of the pharaohs, the divine votaries were aided, in an effort to bolster the government, by a group of notables, Egyptian priests, and Ethiopian warriors whose tasks were to counsel and to look to the execution of decisions made. There could only be one divine votary in power at any one time. The transmission of the title and of the function took place through adoption; and while a votary was alive, no other princess could aspire to the same role. Every votary designated her own successor.

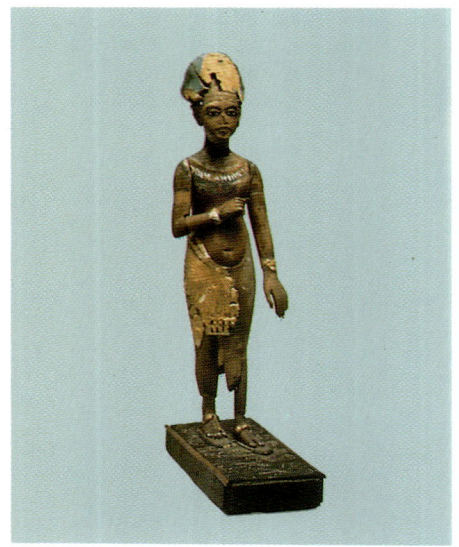

The One and Only

*Her heart was sharper
than those of a million men,
She was more eminent
than a thousand gods.*

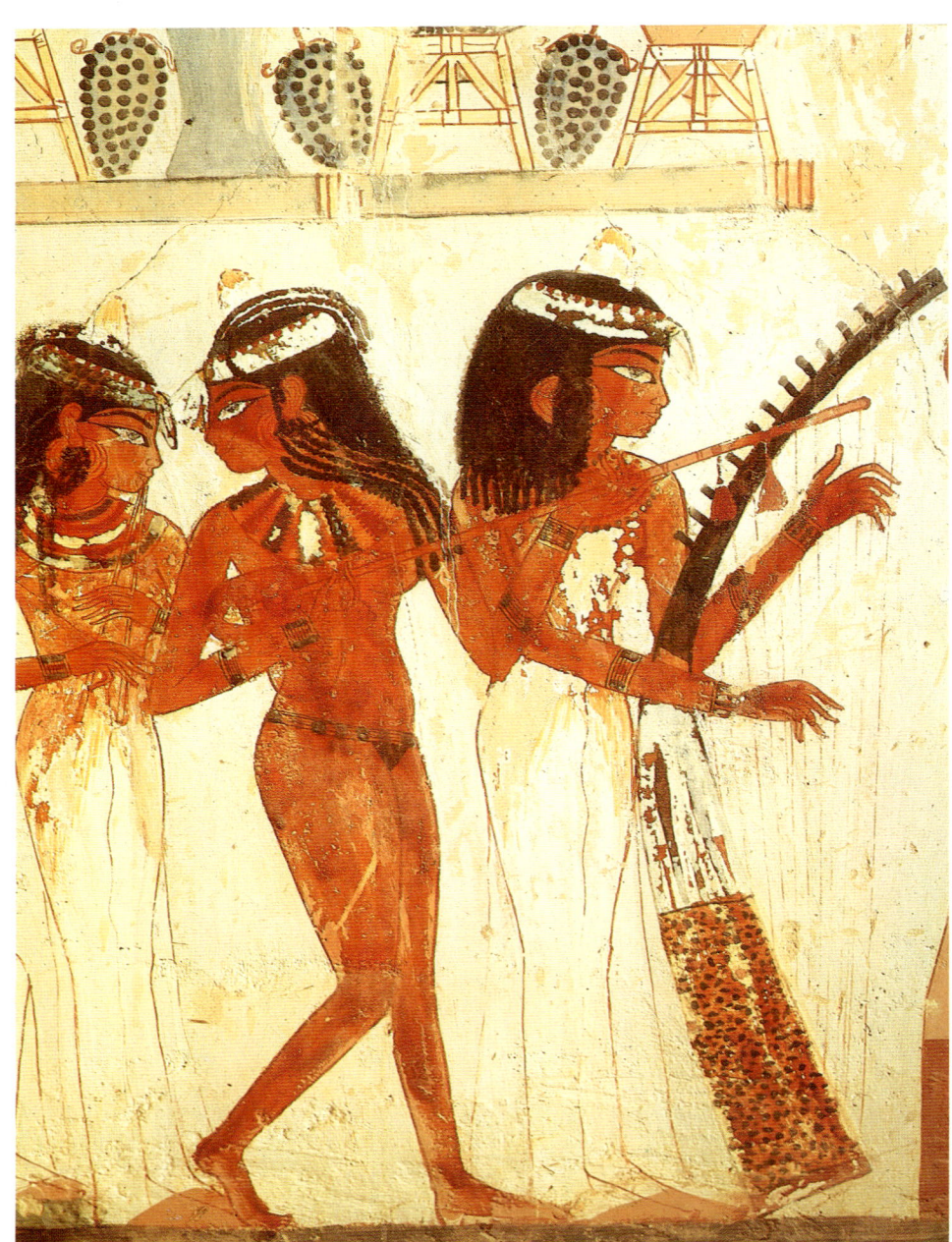

DANCERS AND MUSICIANS

She counseled her husband in all things, participated in the country's foreign affairs. And, very often, she spoke directly to foreign princes: "such was her influence on the pharaoh, so much did she seem the supreme authority in the empire."

When the king died, Tiye's son Amenhotep III, better known as Akhenaton, which means in the tongue of the ancient Egyptians servant of the sun god Aton, came into power.

It is the decisive role she played alongside her son that made Queen Tiye one of the most important figures in human history.

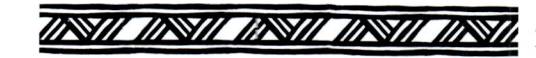

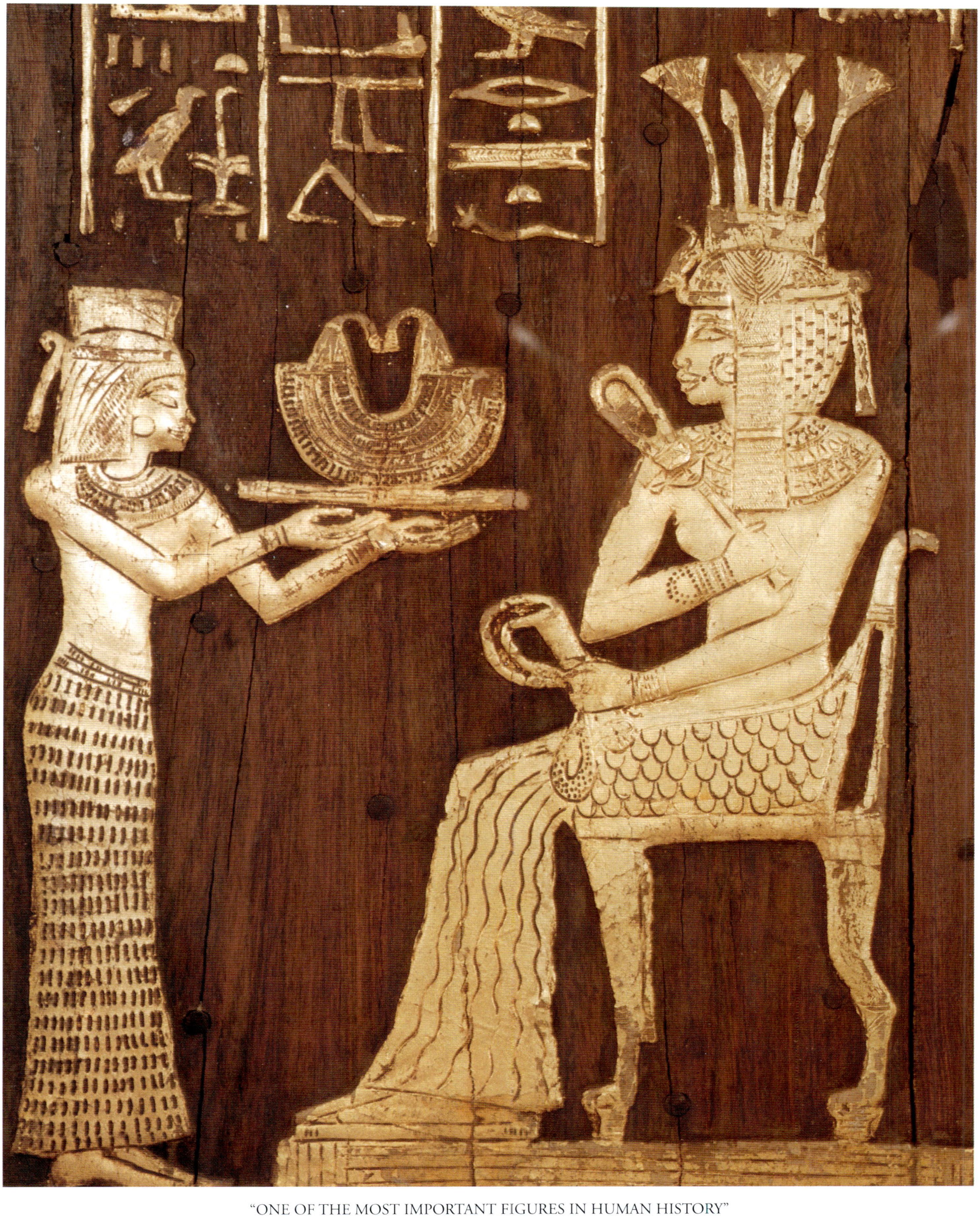

"ONE OF THE MOST IMPORTANT FIGURES IN HUMAN HISTORY"

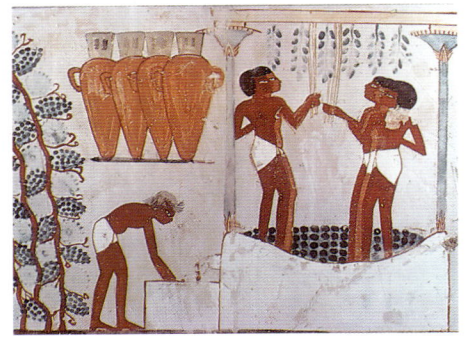

The Grape Harvest

*Come, oh master, see your trellises,
And rejoice in them.
The pickers mash the grapes
with their feet before you.
So many grapes have rolled out onto the ground.
They have more juice than last year.
Drink and get drunk,
Don't stop doing what you love.
They have grown for you, to be at your service
for your heart's desire...
The evening comes.*

*The grapes are heavy with dew,
Let's be quick and press them
And bring them to the house of our master.*

*Offer up some to this good spirit of the vineyard
So that he may love us with wine,
Next year.*

Hymn to the Sun

*You are the one who buries the child
in the women's wombs,
Who has planted the seeds in the men,
Who breathes life into the son
deep in his mother's belly,
Who quiets him so he does not cry.
You, wet nurse in the mother's womb,
Who awakens life to quicken your creation;
You open the son's mouth on the day of his birth,
so that he may speak
when he comes out of his mother's body.
You have given him everything he needs.
How numerous are your works!
They remain hidden to us,
Oh one and only God whose power is absolute!
You have created the earth according to your wish,
When you were alone,
People and beasts, great and small,
All that is on earth,
All that walks on feet,
All that flies through the air with wings.
The lands of Syria and Nubia,
And the land of Egypt.
You put each person in his place,
And you give each what each needs.
Everyone has goods
and days that are numbered.
Their tongues speak many languages,
They come in different colors and shapes,
Because you have sought to make them different.*

Proverb

"Don't hold on to what is in your hand."

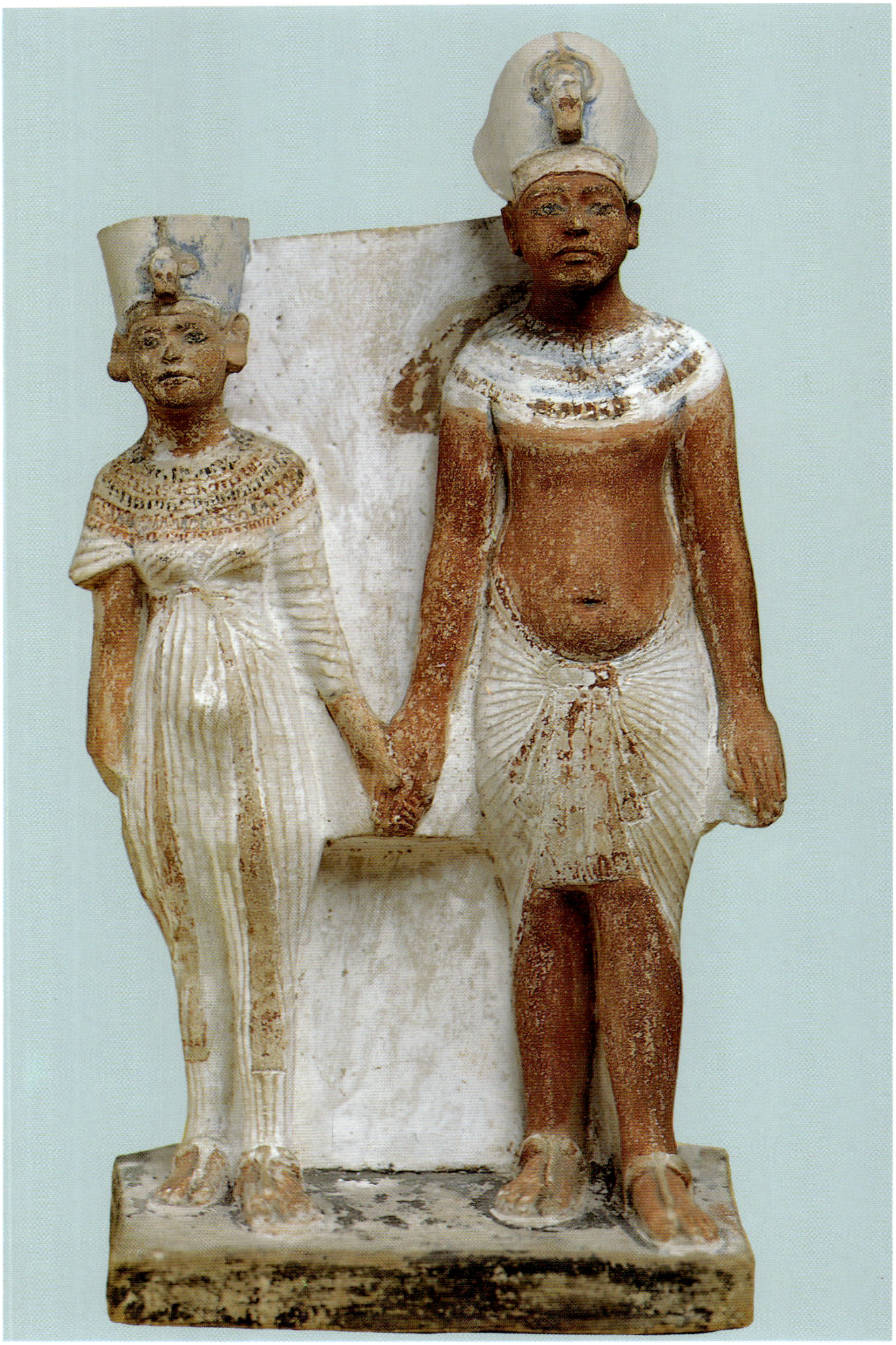

Up until then, the Egyptians, like other peoples, were polytheists. They saw the world around them as governed by several gods whom they adored in various temples.

But suddenly, under the influence of his mother, Queen Tiye, the new pharaoh proclaimed for the first time in human history a single god, Aton, the sun, whom he imposed upon the empire.

NEFERTITI, WIFE OF AKHENATON

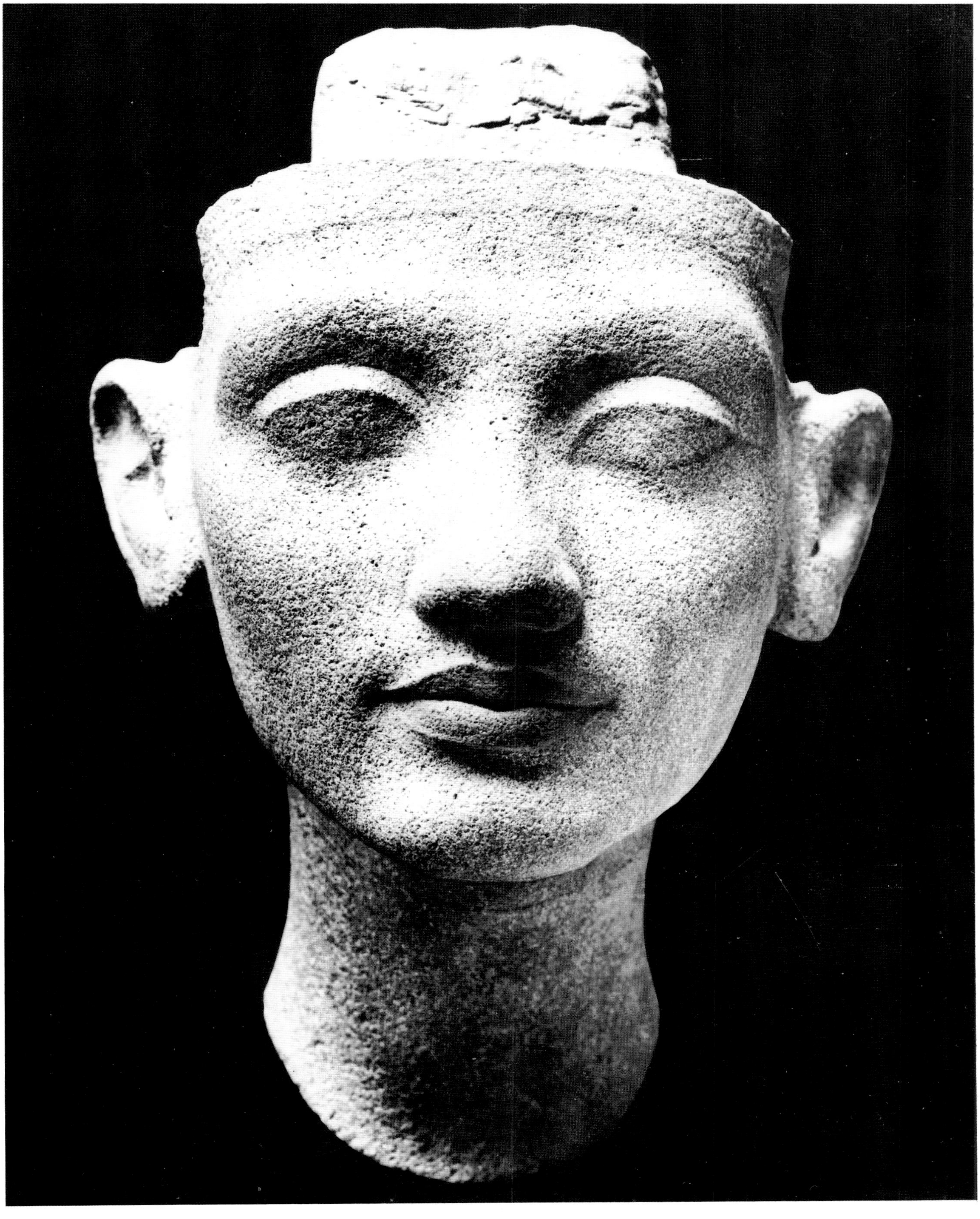

TIYE

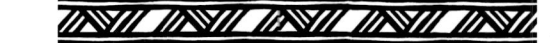

NEFERTITI

This reform may have inspired Moses to definitively establish the monotheism that has since spread all over the globe.

Thus, even nowadays, when people pray to God in a church, a mosque, or a synagogue, they may in some way be under Queen Tiye's invisible influence as it reaches across the millennia.

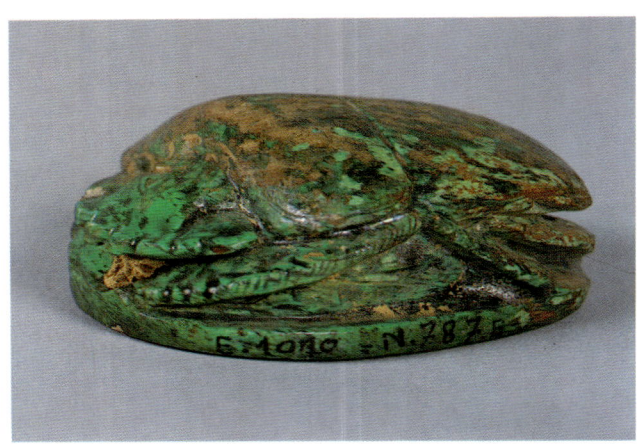

SCARAB OF THE MARRIAGE OF AMENHOTEP III AND TIYE

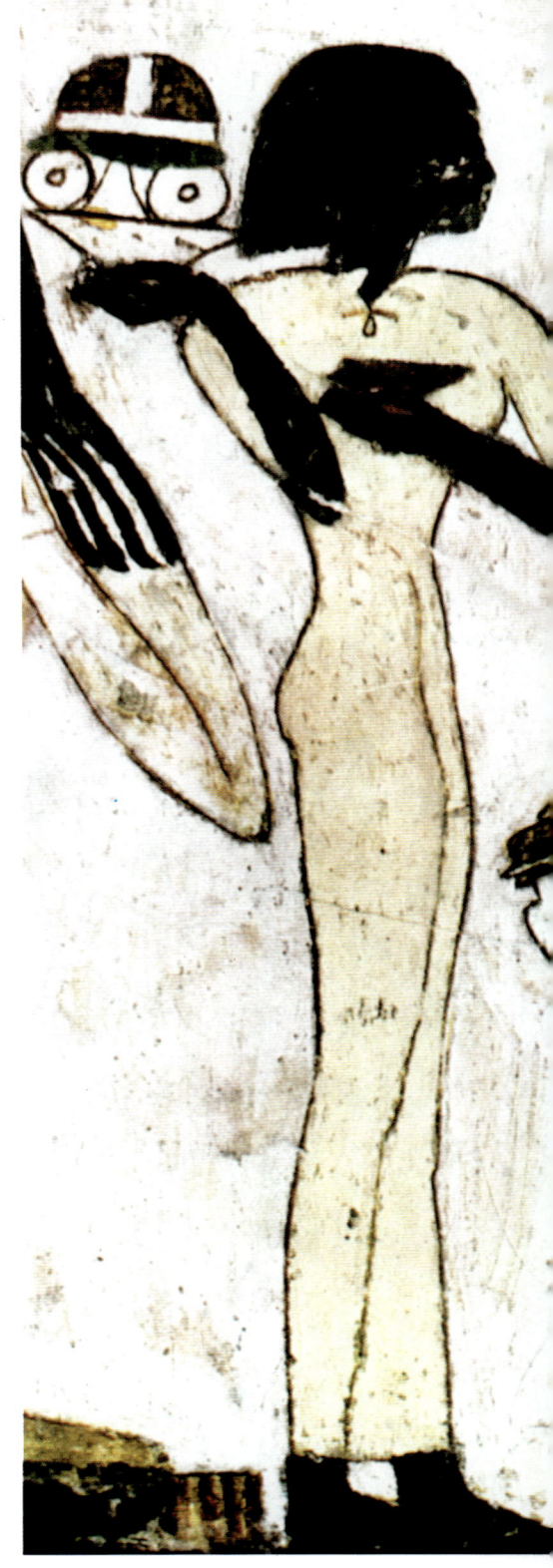

"THE INVISIBLE

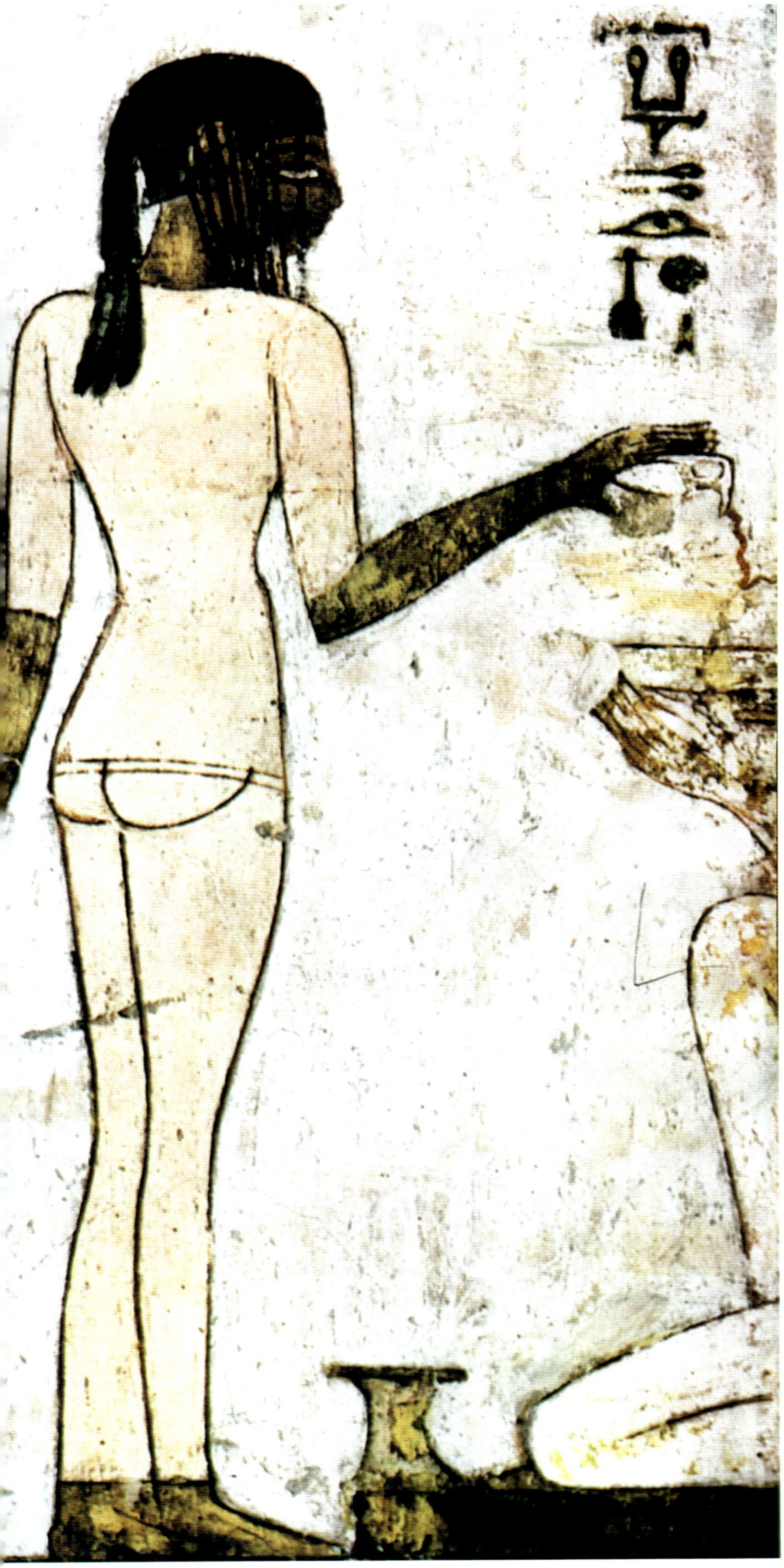

"INFLUENCE OF QUEEN TIYE"

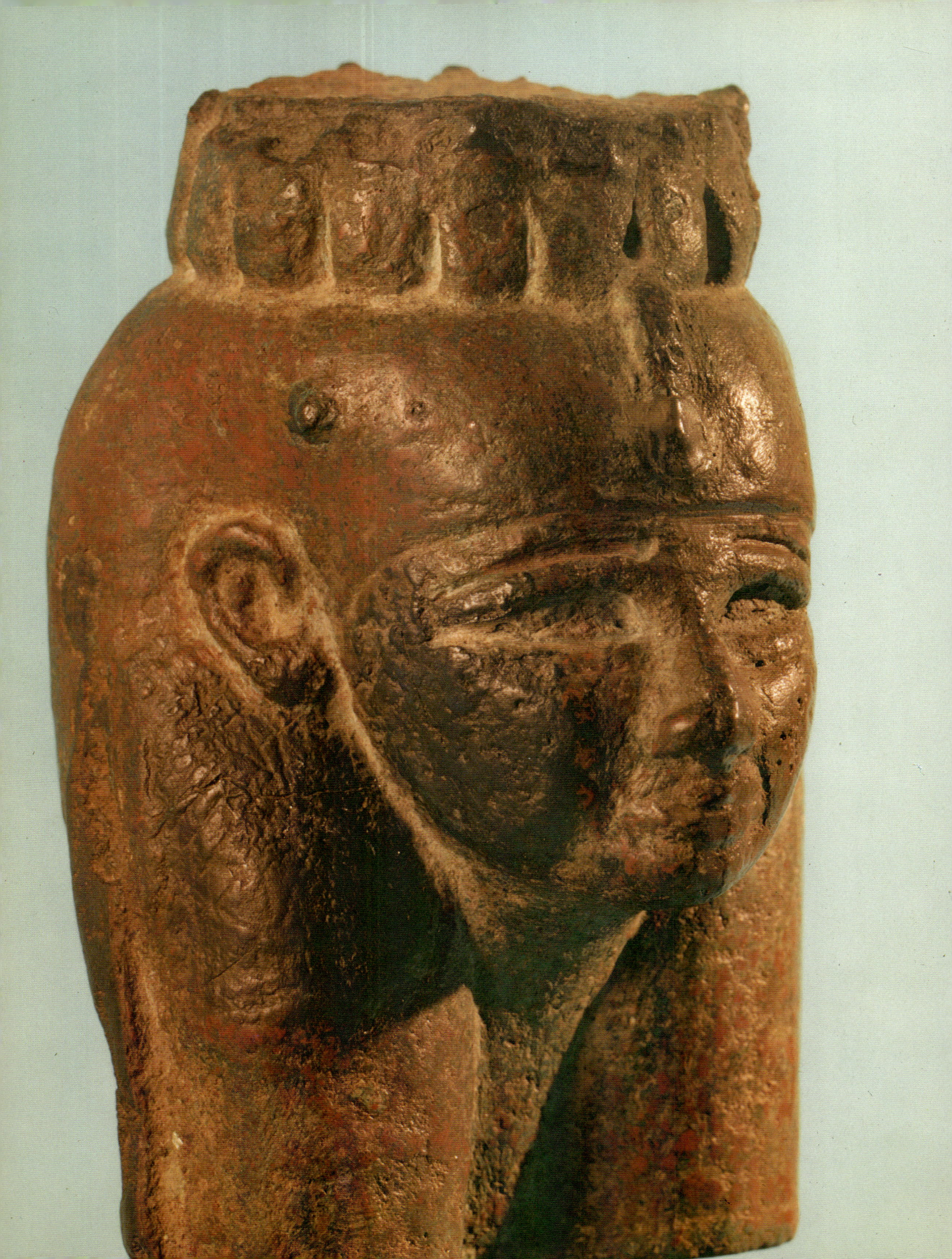

THE CANDACES

RULERS OF THE KINGDOM OF KUSH

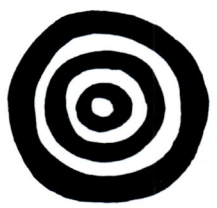

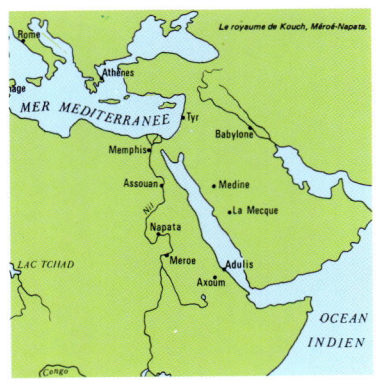

The kingdom of Kush was renowned in antiquity, and its reputation stretched beyond the seas: its queens were called the Candaces...

THE BLACK KINGDOM OF KUSH WAS BORN SOME THREE THOUSAND YEARS AGO. IT WAS TO LAST A MILLENNIUM, UNTIL 350 C.E., WHEN IT DISAPPEARED, AS HAD MANY OTHERS, LEAVING BEHIND ONLY RUINS OF STONE SCATTERED LIKE BONES ACROSS the sand of contemporary Nubia.

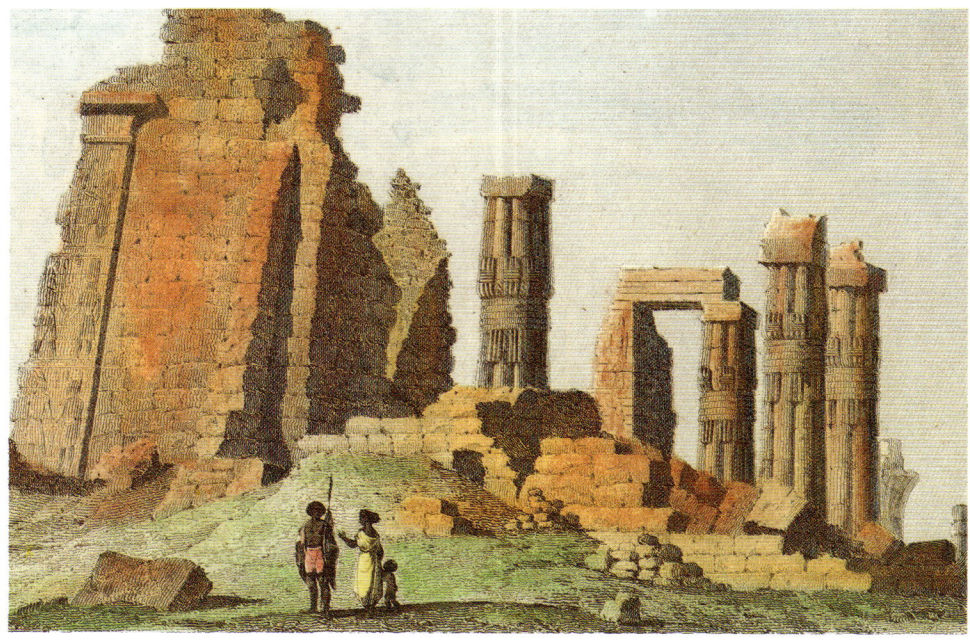

It was very well known in antiquity, and its reputation spread far beyond the seas, thanks to the tales of Greek travelers.

In the year 750 B.C.E., the kingdom expanded north along the Nile and conquered Egypt, founding the twenty-fifth dynasty, the illustrious dynasty of the black pharaohs.

Then, in the year 666 B.C.E., the Assyrians invaded Egypt. Their weapons were made of iron, while those of the Kushites (like those of the Egyptians) were made of stone and bronze. Iron conquered, and the twenty-fifth dynasty collapsed. Its fall shook the entire ancient world, which had been struck by its splendor.

The final battle took place in Thebes, which the Assyrians pillaged and burned, before razing it to a pile of ruins.

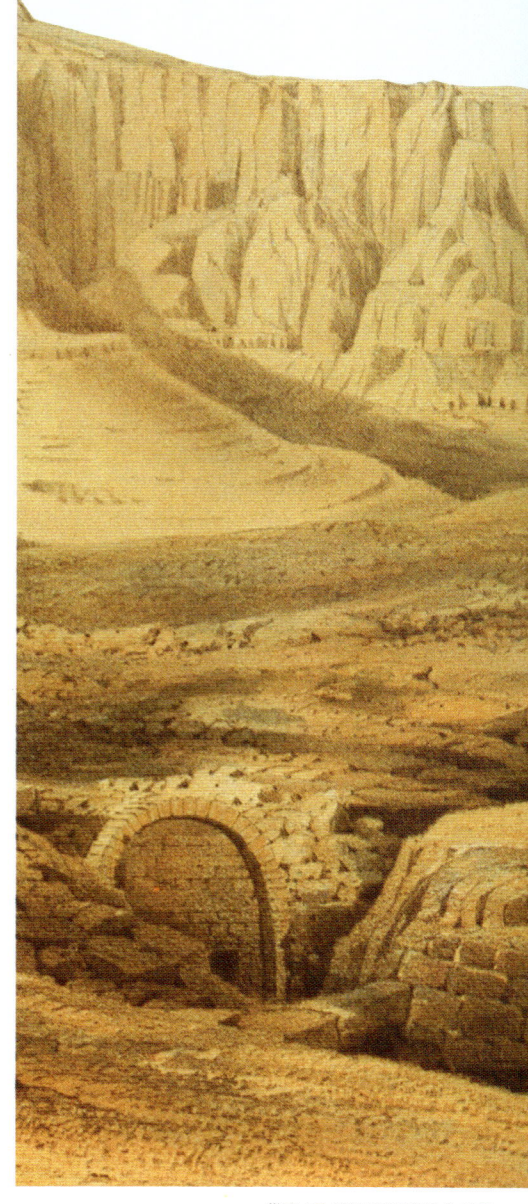

"THE KINGDOM OF

THE CANDACES

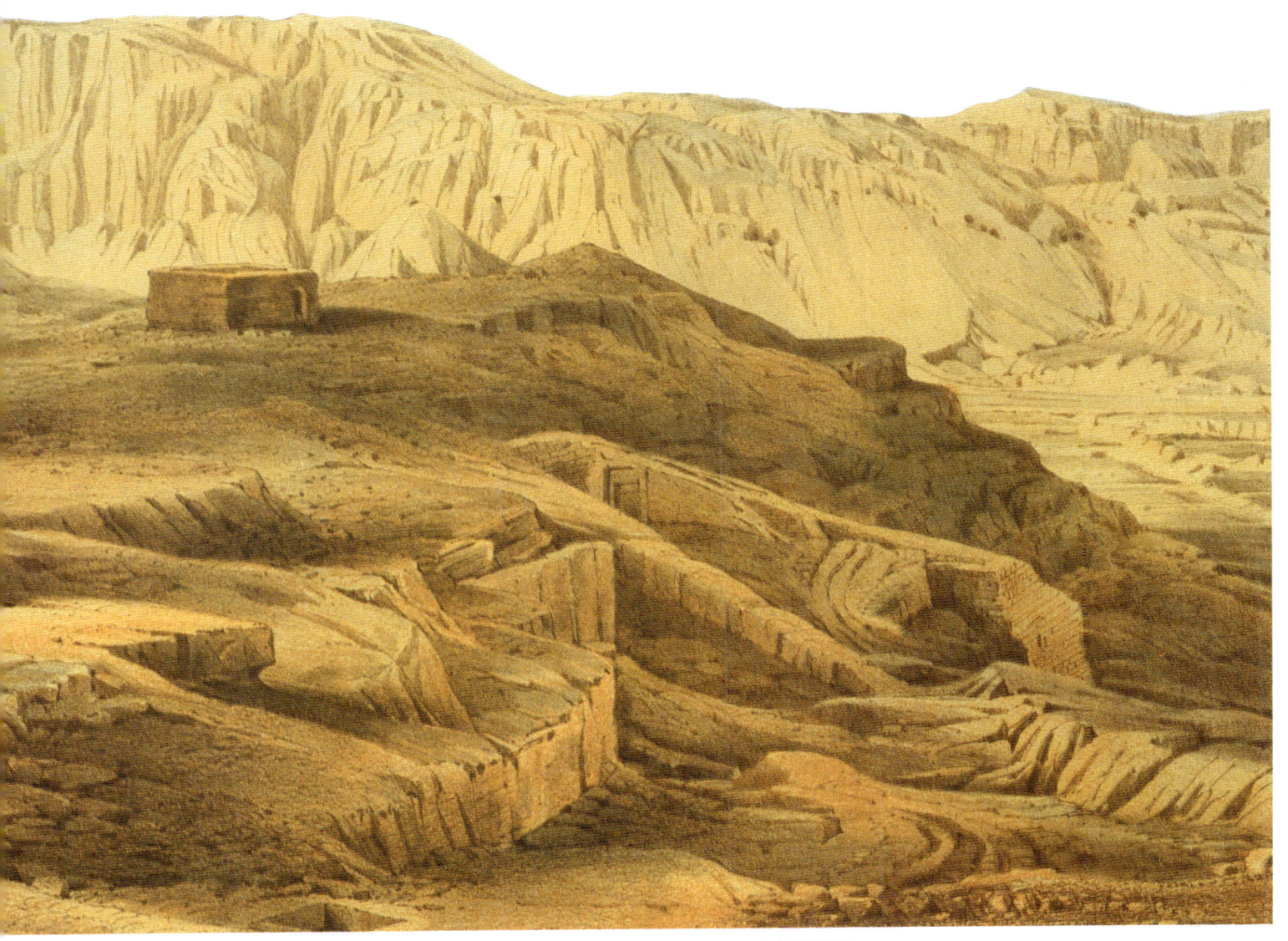

"KUSH DISAPPEARED, AS HAD MANY OTHERS, LEAVING BEHIND ONLY RUINS OF STONE"

> **The Nubian People's Contribution to World History**
>
> "The Ethiopians [Nubians] are the first men ever to exist; here is the usual evidence given to support such a fact:
>
> First, since it is almost unanimously recognized that they have not come from elsewhere, but grew on this very land, one cannot refuse them the adjective of autochthonous without committing an injustice. Furthermore, it is equally clear to all that those who suckled at the bosom of the meridian lands were the first to live; because after having dried up the wetlands, the sun's heat rendered the earth fertile and proper to give existence to the animals, and so it is likely that the places closest to the sun must have first produced living beings.
>
> Ethiopians were also the first to teach that one should render service to the gods, offer sacrifices, and perform ceremonies and sacred rites—in other words to accomplish all of the religious acts by which men honor divinity; thus they are famous all over the world for their piety, and the sacrifices Ethiopians offer are said to be most pleasant to the immortal ones.
>
> People also say that the gods have graciously rewarded the Ethiopians' piety, by keeping them from falling under the yoke of foreigners. Indeed, these people have always remained free and have been able to live together in such harmony that no king who has ever waged war upon their land has ever managed to sow conflict among them.
>
> Most of the customs adopted by the Egyptians have Ethiopian origins, colonies being in the habit of keeping the mores of the motherland: kings honored like gods, the meticulous funerals, and many other such rites are Ethiopian institutions.
>
> Finally, the meanings associated with sculpted figures and the typography of Egyptian letters are likewise borrowed from the Ethiopians. The colleges of priests in both nations are basically the same. Those who devote themselves to the cult are submitted to the same purifications; they both shave the body, wear robes of the same shape, and carry scepters topped with the figure of a plow.
>
> Kings use that same scepter, but they also wear a tall crown that has at the top a sort of knot encircled by spirals shaped like the serpents known as asps. This ornament reminds everyone that whoever dares to conspire against the life of the king will expose himself to lethal bites. Ethiopians have recorded many other particulars, both about their race and about their colony that settled in Egypt."
>
> Diodorus of Sicily, first century B.C.E.

Yes, such a fall, preceded by such splendor, confounded everyone at the time; and so, the prophet Nahum called out to Ninevah:

"Do you think yourselves greater than Thebes, which sits between canals, with the flow of the Nile as wall and as rampart? The infinite lands of Ethiopia and Egypt strengthened it and yet it fell under siege and was dragged into captivity!" (Nahum 3:8)

Tanutamon is the name of the last black pharaoh to rule Egypt; after the fall of Thebes, he succeeded in reaching Napata (Marawi), which was then the capital of the kingdom of Kush, his native land.

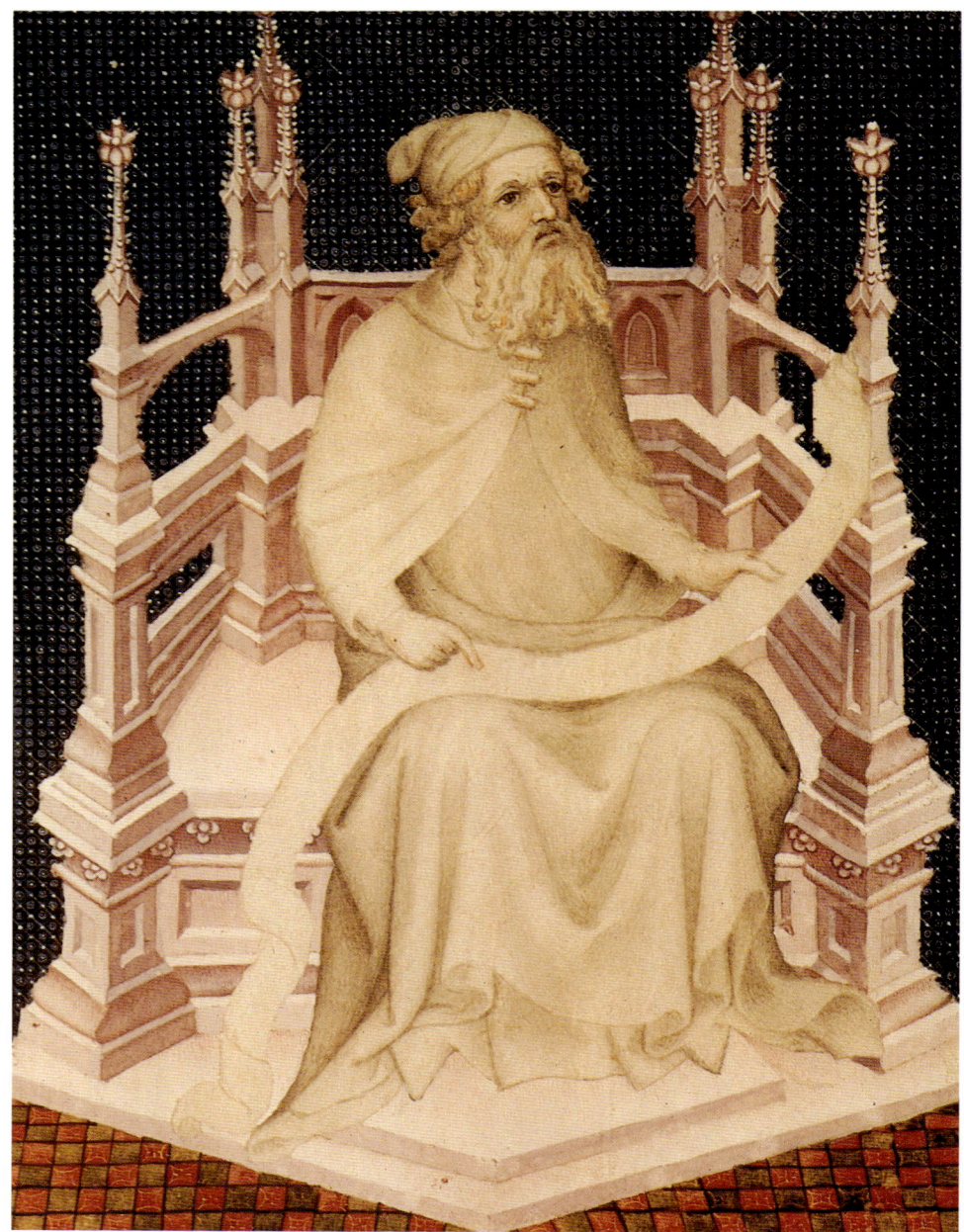

"THE PROPHET CALLED OUT TO THE CITY..."

THE CANDACES

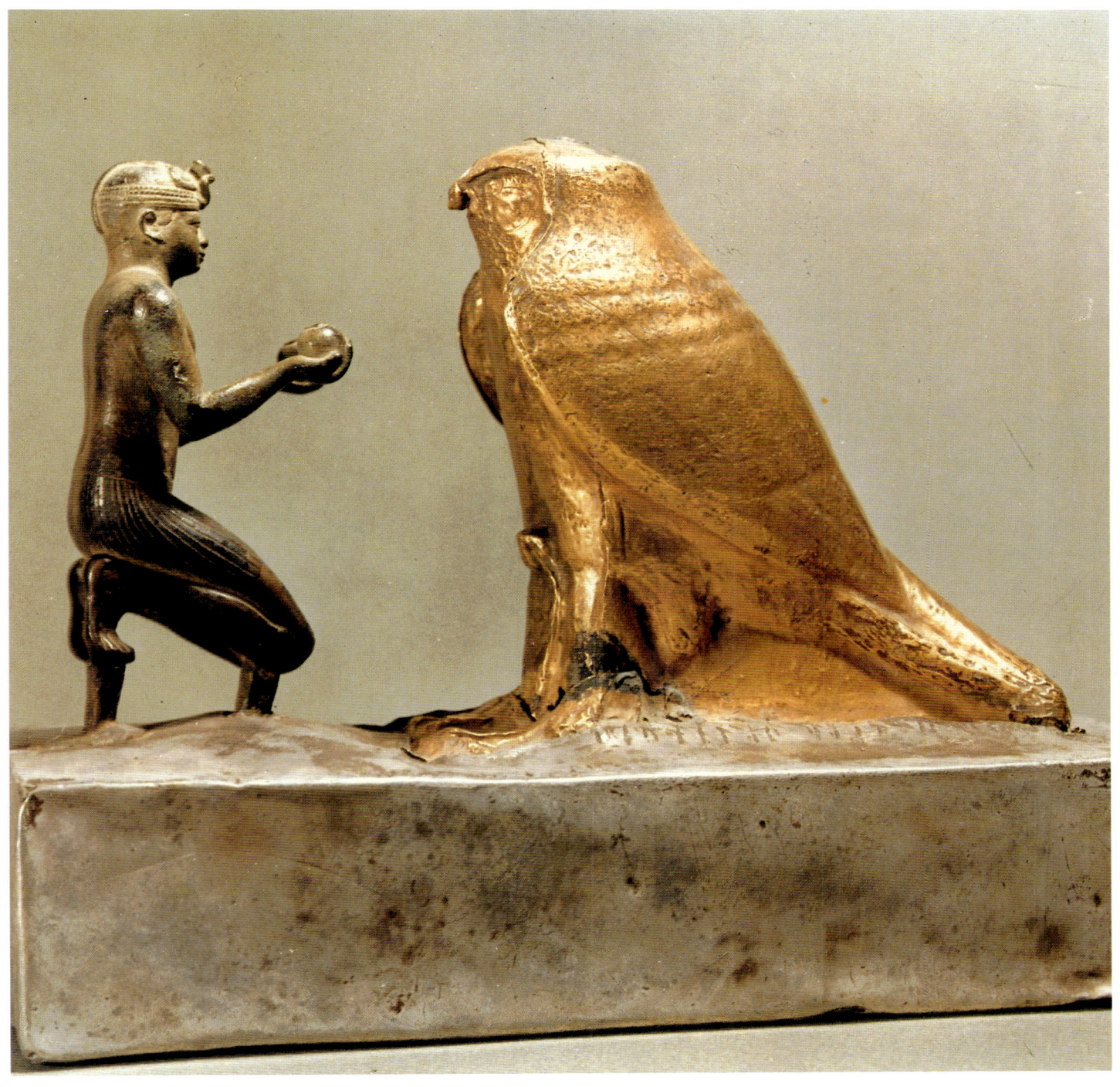

More Research on Nubia

"On March 1st, 1979, Boyce Rensberger drew the attention of *New York Times* readers to the work of Bruce Williams, a scholar at the Oriental Institute of Chicago: "The Oldest Monarchy: The Nubian Monarchy."
Bruce Williams is preparing the complete publication of his work on the Nubian pharaohs. It took an exhaustive analysis of the items found during the excavation campaign, begun as early as 1962 by Keith C. Seele, in order (fifteen years later) to reach the conclusion that the most ancient pharaonic rule was not in Upper Egypt—from which Scorpion and then Narmer once came in order to unify Egypt—but in Lower Nubia, in Qustul.
The items from the royal tombs in Qustul (Nubia) reveal three essential facts:
1. The existence of pharaonic rule in Nubia prior to Upper Egypt.
2. The existence of a cultural and political continuum from Sudan to the Delta. 'It seems,' Bruce Williams points out, 'that at the dawn of history the Nile Valley was occupied not by two but by three related kingdoms: Lower Egypt, Upper Egypt, Lower Nubia,' and that the pharaonic structure that developed in the Egyptian state originated in Nubia.
3. The existence of inter-regional currents of exchange in the fourth millennium B.C.E. between Africa and the Mediterranean Near East: in addition to Nubian pottery, the Qustul tombs also hold Egyptian pottery from the time of Nagada III (Gerzeen) and even a few 'examples from the Syrio-Palestinian tradition.' Narmer, who once conquered Palestine, probably did little else than follow in the footsteps of others from the fourth millennium."

Présence Africaine, Paris, 1985

The queens of Kush were called Candaces; however, two names in particular have come to us across the tides of history.

The first is Amanirenas. She was queen of Kush when the Romans followed the Nile south after Cleopatra's defeat.

Strabo, a historian at the time, tells us that she was "a very masculine woman who had lost an eye in battle." Masculine probably meant courageous.

Remembering her pharaoh ancestors, she went down the Nile to meet the Romans and beat them at Aswan, where her soldiers broke all of the statues of Emperor Augustus. General Gaius Petronius was put in charge of the counteroffensive. He had gathered a strong army and stormed the kingdom of Kush up to Napata, which was sacked. But he was not able to subdue the queen and his endeavor failed; eventually, he had to bring his troops back to Egypt.

The historian Strabo describes him as tired and disappointed, wondering about the outcome of this impossible war, where the heat and Queen Amanirenas joined forces to harass his troops to no end.

Finally, giving up the conquest of Kush, the Roman general suggested that Candace ask for peace, which, to end things, Emperor Augustus granted.

Nineteen hundred years later, archaeologists were digging up the floor of a palace at Philae. And one day they exhumed the bronze head of Augustus, which Amanirenas's troops had brought back from Aswan; from one abduction to another, across the centuries. One can see it at the British Museum.

The Bible evokes yet another Candace, in Acts 8.

One day, it tells us, the apostle Philip heard a voice telling him to go to Jerusalem from Gaza. No sooner was Phillip on the road than he met a eunuch, a minister of Candace, "Queen of Ethiopia" (Kush was called Ethiopia by this time). The Bible simply says that the man "who came to Jerusalem to worship left in his chariot, reading the prophet Isaiah."

Perhaps he had recently converted to Judaism, but the text does not give any details.

So Philip climbed into the chariot and, along the way, announced to the man "Jesus' good news."

The text goes on: "As they continued up the road, they saw water and the eunuch said: 'Here is water, what stops me from being baptized?'

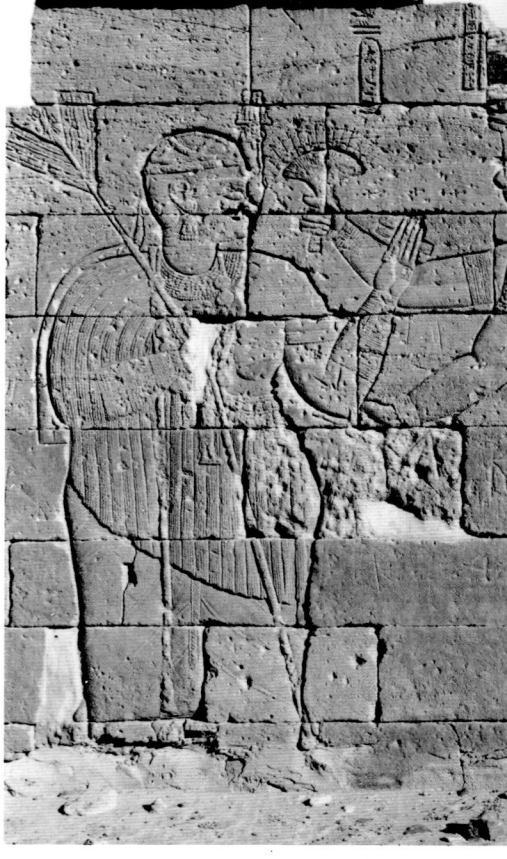

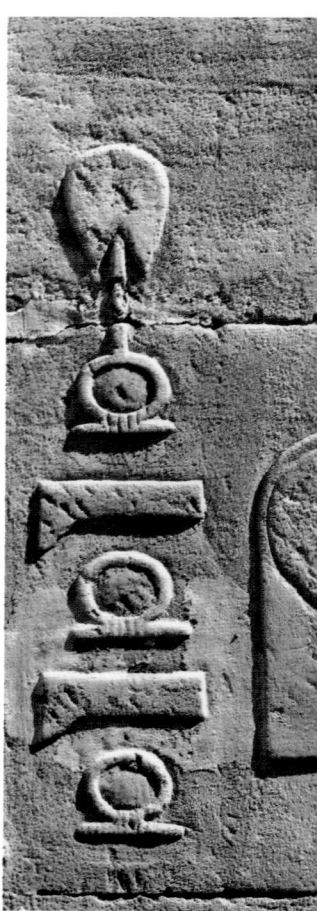

THE CANDACES

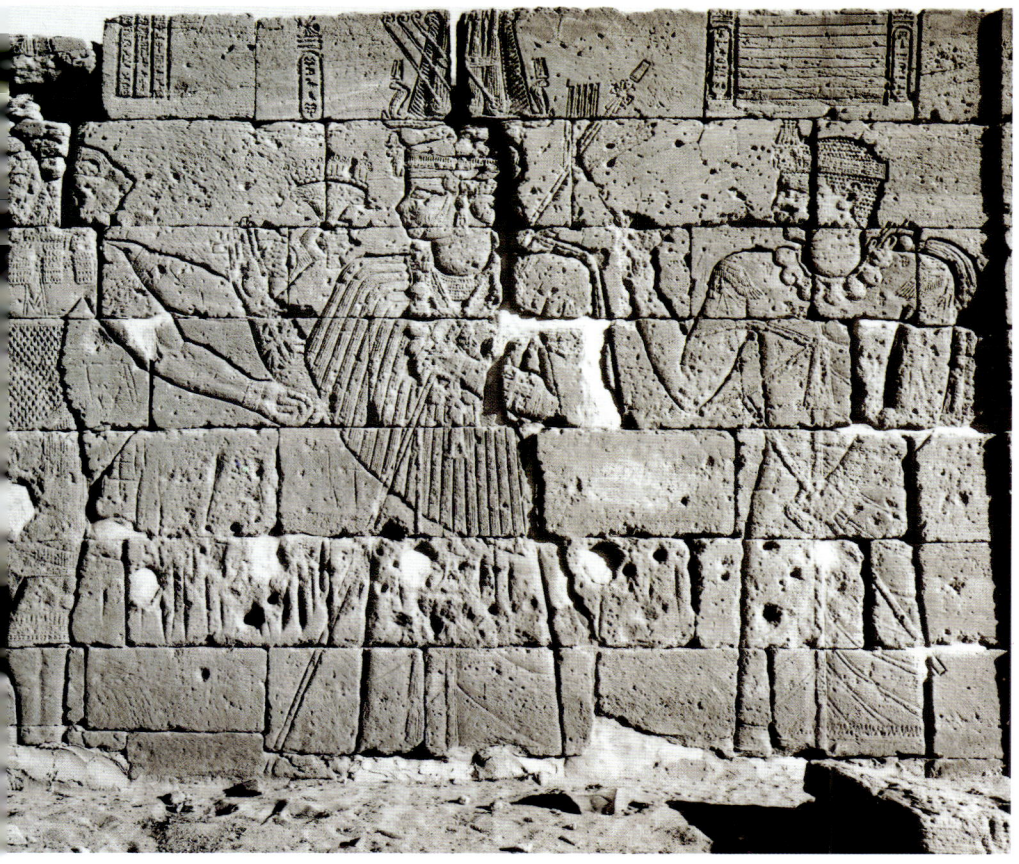

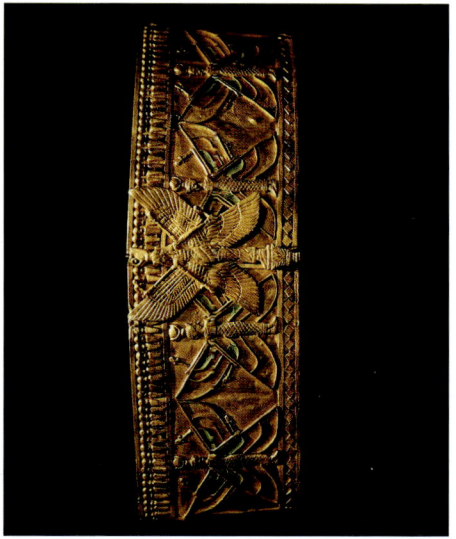

The Queens of Kush

Queens enjoyed an exceptionally important status. They are very visible figures on royal inscriptions and bas-reliefs, and it is evident that they have often fulfilled the roles of counselor and sometimes regent for their sons. Taharqa, the pharaoh of the twenty-fifth dynasty, reports on one of his inscriptions that he had brought back his mother from Napata so that she could may attend his crowning in Egypt. The wealth and splendor of the queens' tombs, which can be seen in the royal cemeteries likewise attest to their high status. The Romans thought that Kush was governed by a dynasty of women all called Candace because of the prestige and power, discreet but important, possessed by the Nubian queens. "Candace" seems in fact to be the deformation of a Meroitic title (kdke) that all of the royal wives and mothers in Kush bore; it does not designate a ruling queen. There were, indeed, at least five queens on the throne toward the end of the Kushite dynasty. It is not certain that they bore the title of kdke. The circumstances that brought them to rule instead of other possible candidates are unknown.

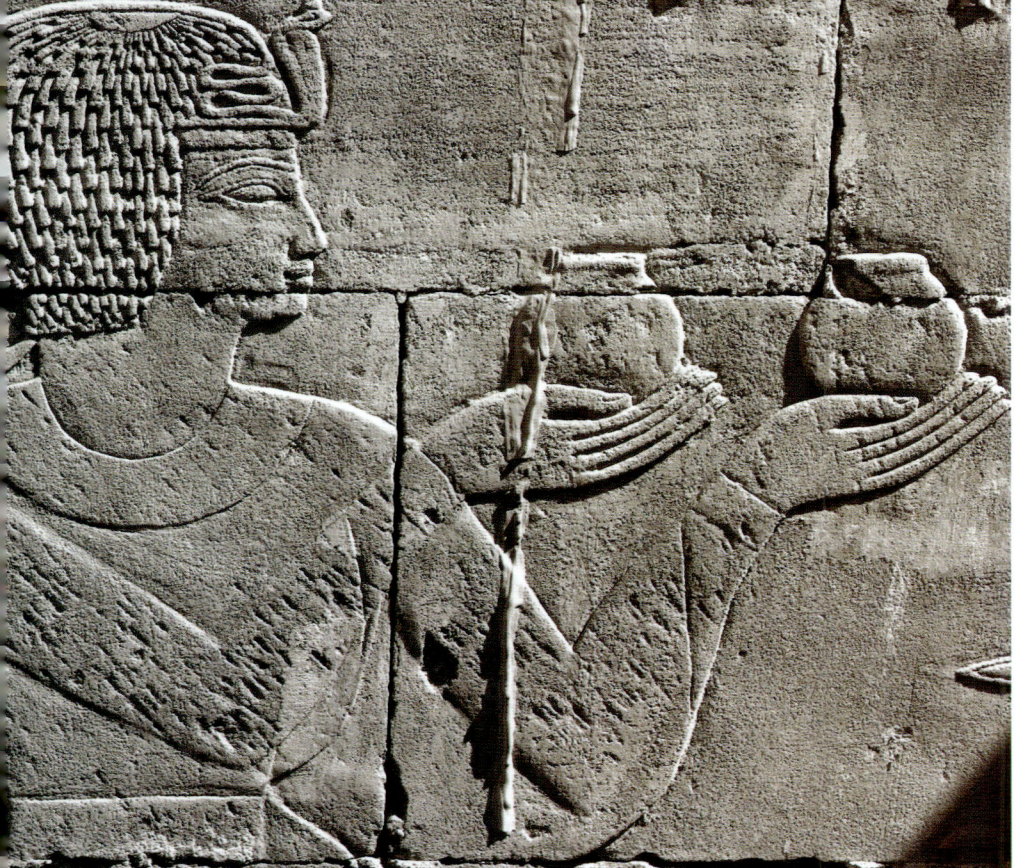

PRESENTATION OF GOBLETS OF WINE TO AMON

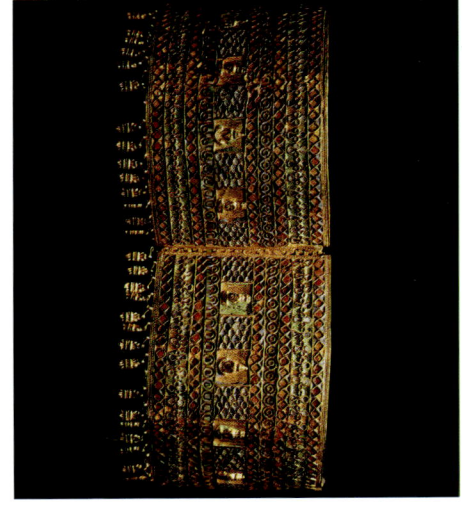

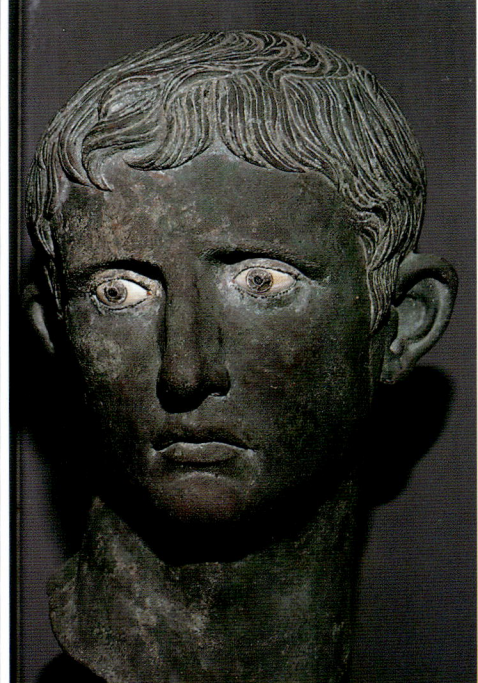

THE BRONZE HEAD OF AUGUSTUS

Daily Life in Meroe

The tone and substance of daily life can hardly be suggested by a handful of objects—most of them from royal tombs, since no other sites have been systematically examined. In fact, this tone and substance did develop, evolve, and become more complex over a thousand years of continuous settlement and technological advance. What was the social nature of this "divine royalty"? How did men and women from Meroe and its sister-cities welcome the emergence of iron, of metal-working, of commerce with half the world? What did these citizens know of China, whose bronzework they copied and whose silk they bought? Of India, whose cotton fabrics they wore? Of Arabia, whose goods they bought? Who were the travelers leaving for and coming from the south and the west? And what became of them?

The Ancient Tombs of Kush

The great necropolis located in Kurru was a burial site from 860 B.C.E., more than a hundred years before the end of the conquest of the north.

Archaeological discoveries have revealed that sixteen of the predecessors of Piankhi, the conqueror of Egypt, have been buried at Kurru. The evolution of the funerary structures attests to historical changes.

The first tombs are made of pits covered with circular mounds. The corpse lies slightly leaning on his right side, head turned toward the north. Later on, the mound is covered with stones. Then we find a rectangular superstructure made of cut stone which ultimately becomes the typical Kushite pyramid.

Philip said: 'If you believe with all your heart, it is possible.' The eunuch answered: 'I believe that Jesus Christ is the son of God.' He stopped the chariot; Philip and the eunuch both went into the water, and Philip baptized the eunuch" (Acts 8:26).

The queen's minister went back to Kush, filled with an ardent desire to proselytize.

Candace, it seems, was the first to embrace the faith preached by her minister. And according to a legend, the example of the queen influenced many other great ones at the court and some of the people as well: thus, Christianity, going up the Nile, then following the course of the Abdarat, finally reached the area we now call Ethiopia.

For many decades, archaeologists have prodded the soil in quest of buried civilizations.

Each stone from the pharaohs' Egypt has been numbered, inventoried, located in time and space; but no one knows why archaeologists have taken so little interest in Kush, whose ground has barely been scratched.

Another mystery hovers over the Kush civilization: Kushite writing, Meroitic, which has not been deciphered.

The Kushite inscriptions are silent; this whole universe of meaning, signs, symbols, essential information about Africa remains concealed in these stones.

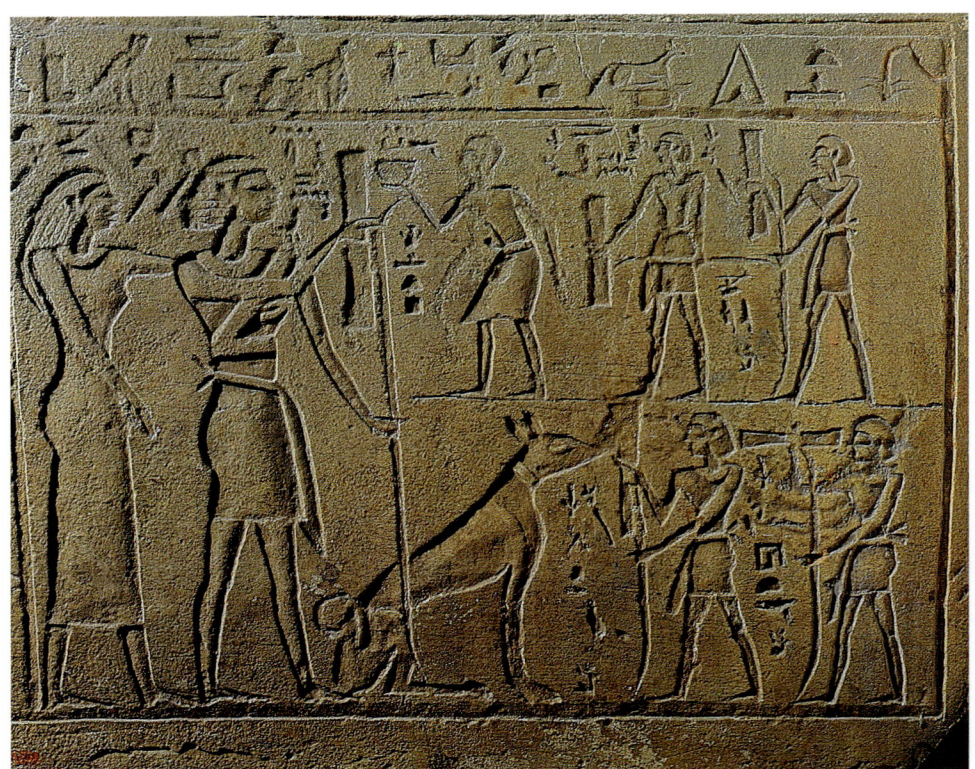

"A UNIVERSE OF MEANING, SIGNS, AND SYMBOLS"

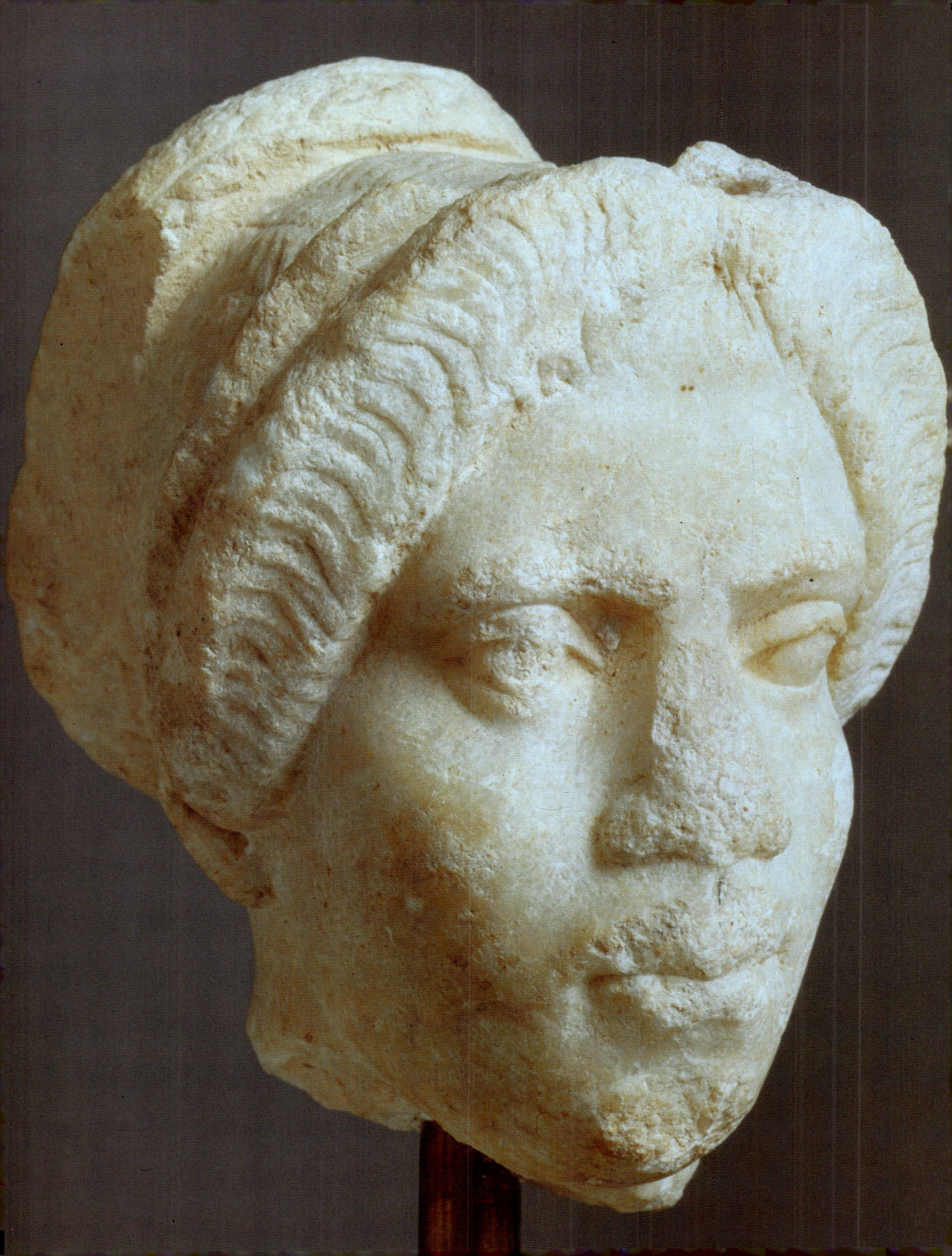

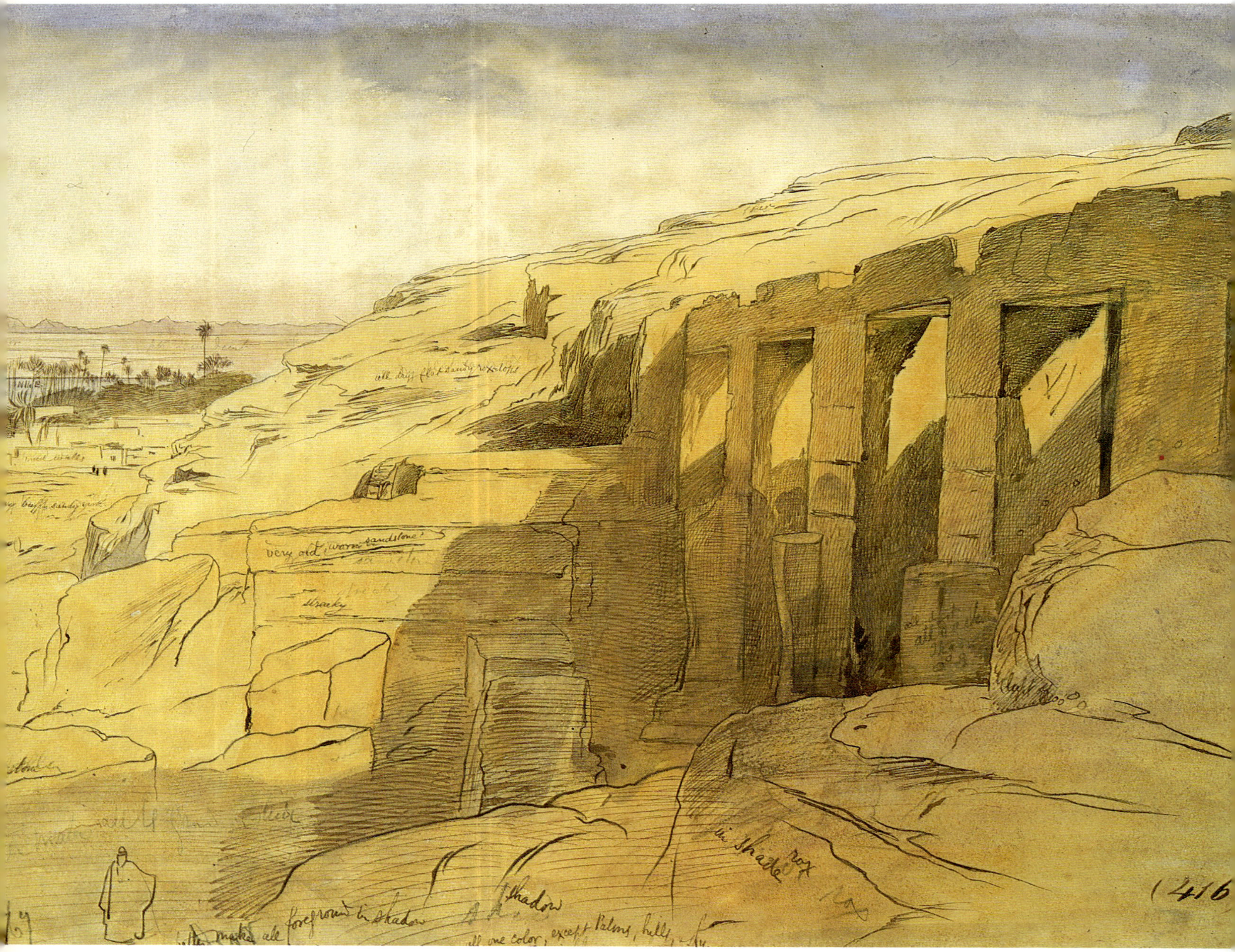

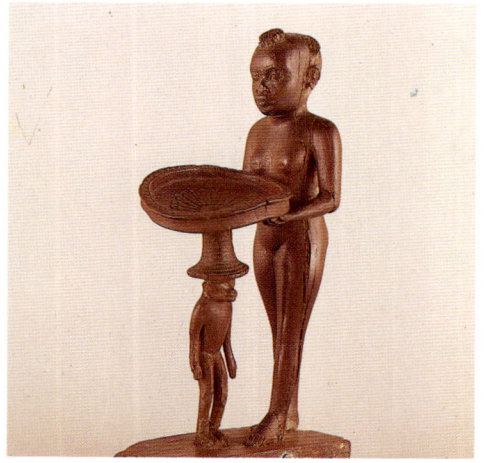

A YOUNG WOMAN

Tomorrow, perhaps, the treasures of Kush will be brought back into broad daylight; and tomorrow, perhaps, it will be possible to decipher these signs, these calls of Kush across time. Then, dozens of queens will come out of the shadows to speak of themselves and their times.

And the biblical Candace will tell us the lost stories about the eunuch who met Philip on the way to Jerusalem.

And finally, Amanirenas, the brave lady with the missing eye, will tell us herself what happened in her struggle against the Romans, and tell us more about what one must call, despite everything, her victory.

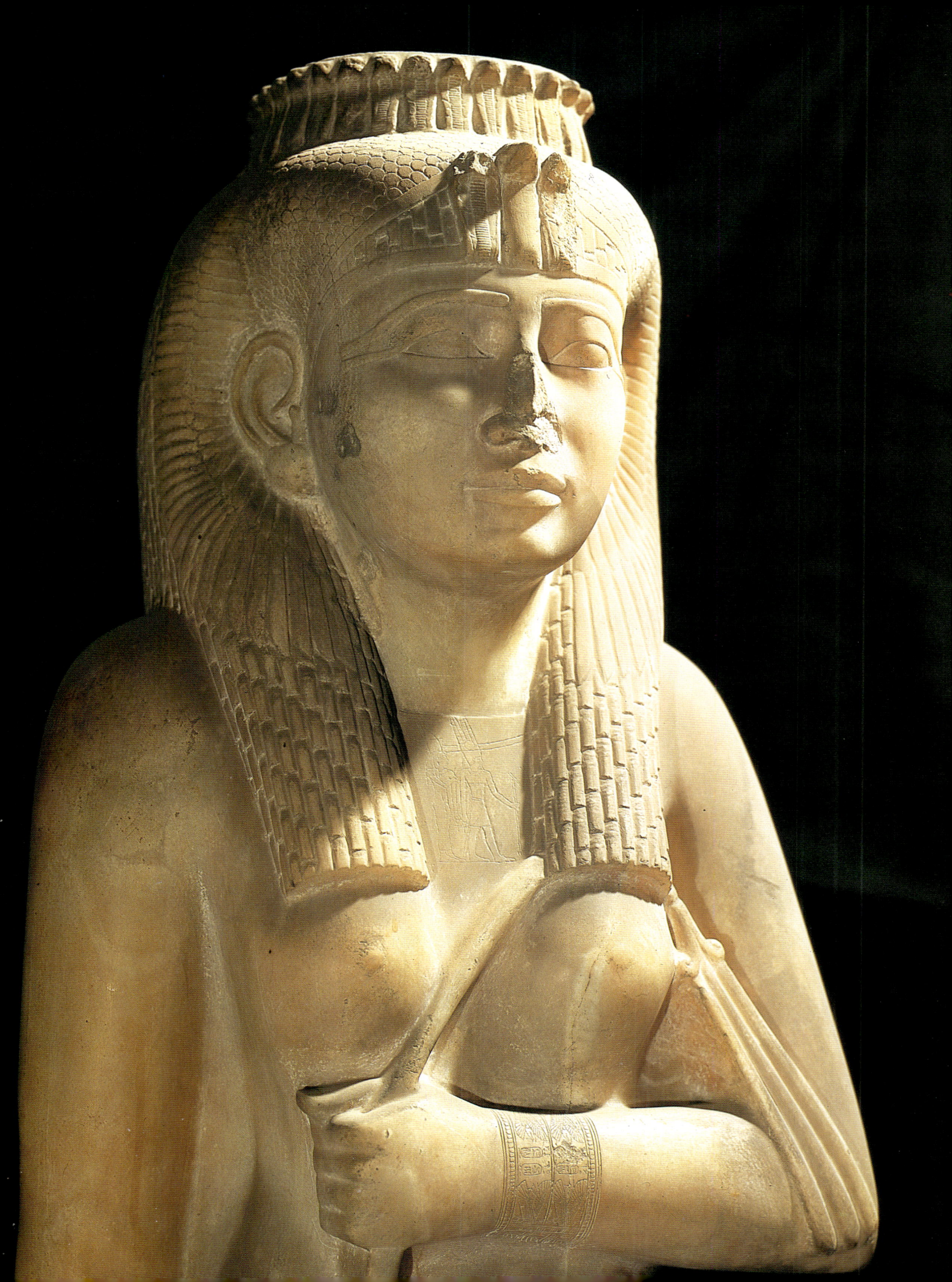

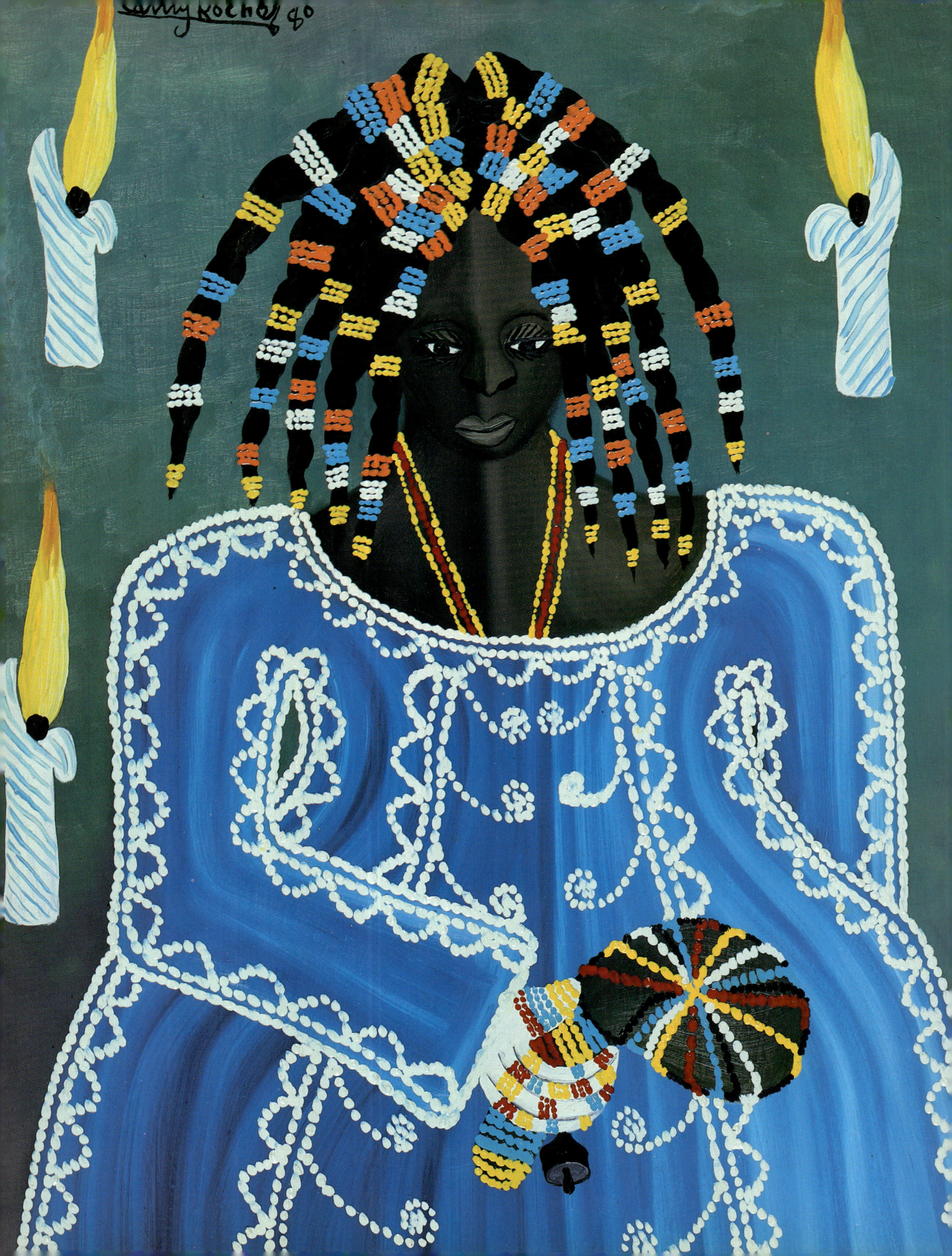

MAKEDA

QUEEN OF SHEBA

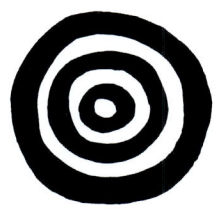

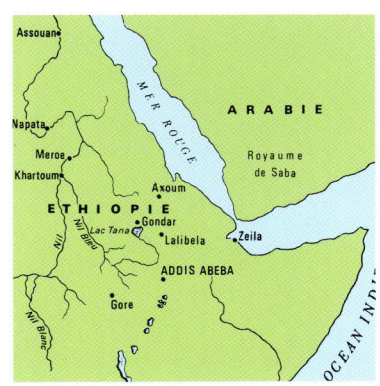

A queen of Ethiopia from the days of the Bible, whose last descendant was the Negus Haile Selassie...

THE STORY OF THE QUEEN OF SHEBA IS RECORDED IN THE BIBLE IN THE SECOND BOOK OF CHRONICLES AND IN THE FIRST BOOK OF KINGS: SHE HAD LEARNED OF THE WISDOM OF KING SOLOMON AND CAME TO JERUSALEM TO TEST IT WITH RIDDLES.

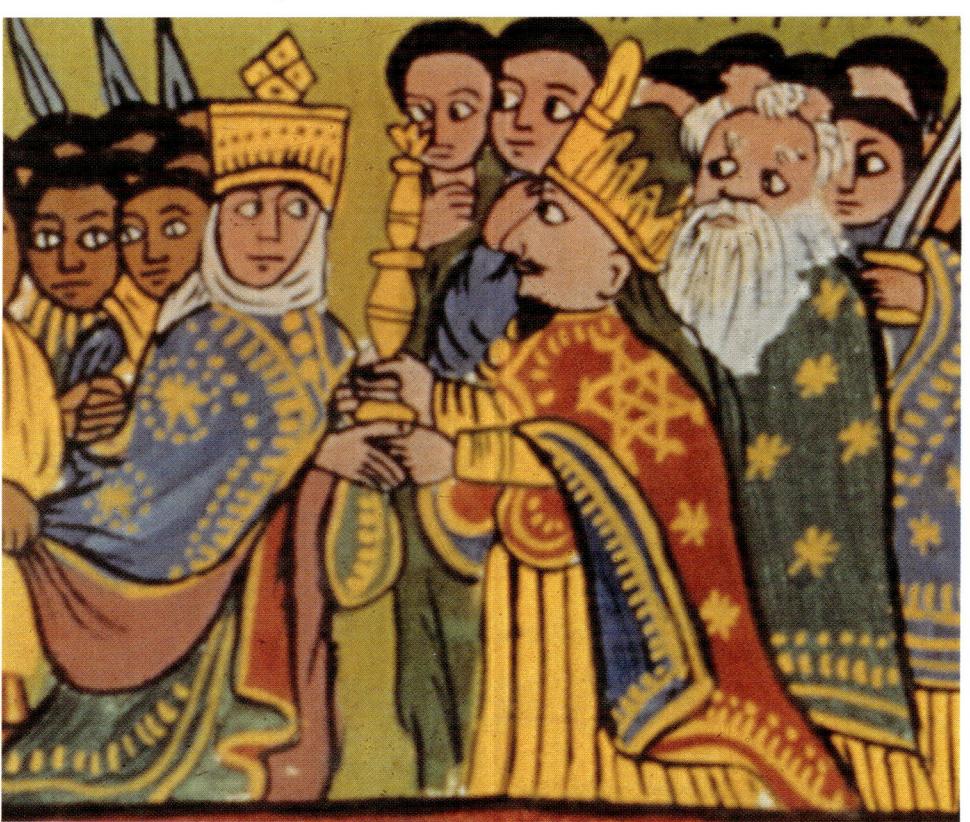

"HE WAS STRUCK BY MAKEDA'S BEAUTY AT FIRST GLANCE..."

According to the *Kebra Negast* ("Glory of the Kings"), a fourteenth-century book of legends written in Ethiopic, the visit of the Queen of Sheba lasted more than six months.

The king of Israel and the Queen of Sheba had exchanged many gifts and spent their time at banquets and in conversations that went on till dawn.

The Songs of Songs

The Shulamite:

*Dark am I, and lovely,
O daughters of Jerusalem,
dark like the tents of Kedar,
like Solomon's pavillions.*

Solomon:

*I liken you, my darling, to a mare
harnessed to one of Pharaoh's chariots.
Your cheeks are graced by earrings,
your neck with strings of jewels.
We will make you earrings of gold,
studded with silver.*

The Shulamite:

*While the king was at his table,
my perfume spread its fragrance.
My lover is to me a sachet of myrrh
resting between my breasts.
My lover is to me a cluster of henna blossoms
from the vineyards of En Gedi.*

Solomon:

*How beautiful you are, my darling! Oh, how beautiful!
Your eyes behind your veil are doves.
Your hair is like a flock of goats
descending from Mount Gilead.
Your teeth are like a flock of sheep just shorn,
coming up from the washing.
Each has its twin; not one of them is alone.
Your lips are like a scarlet ribbon; your mouth is lovely.
Your temples behind your veil
are like the halves of a pomegranate.
Your neck is like the tower of David, built with elegance;
on it hang a thousand shields, all of them shields of warriors.
Your two breasts are like two fawns,
like twin gazelle fawns browsing among the lilies.
Until the day breaks and the shadows flee,
I will go to the mountain of myrrh and to the hill of incense.
All beautiful you are, my darling;
there is no flaw in you.*

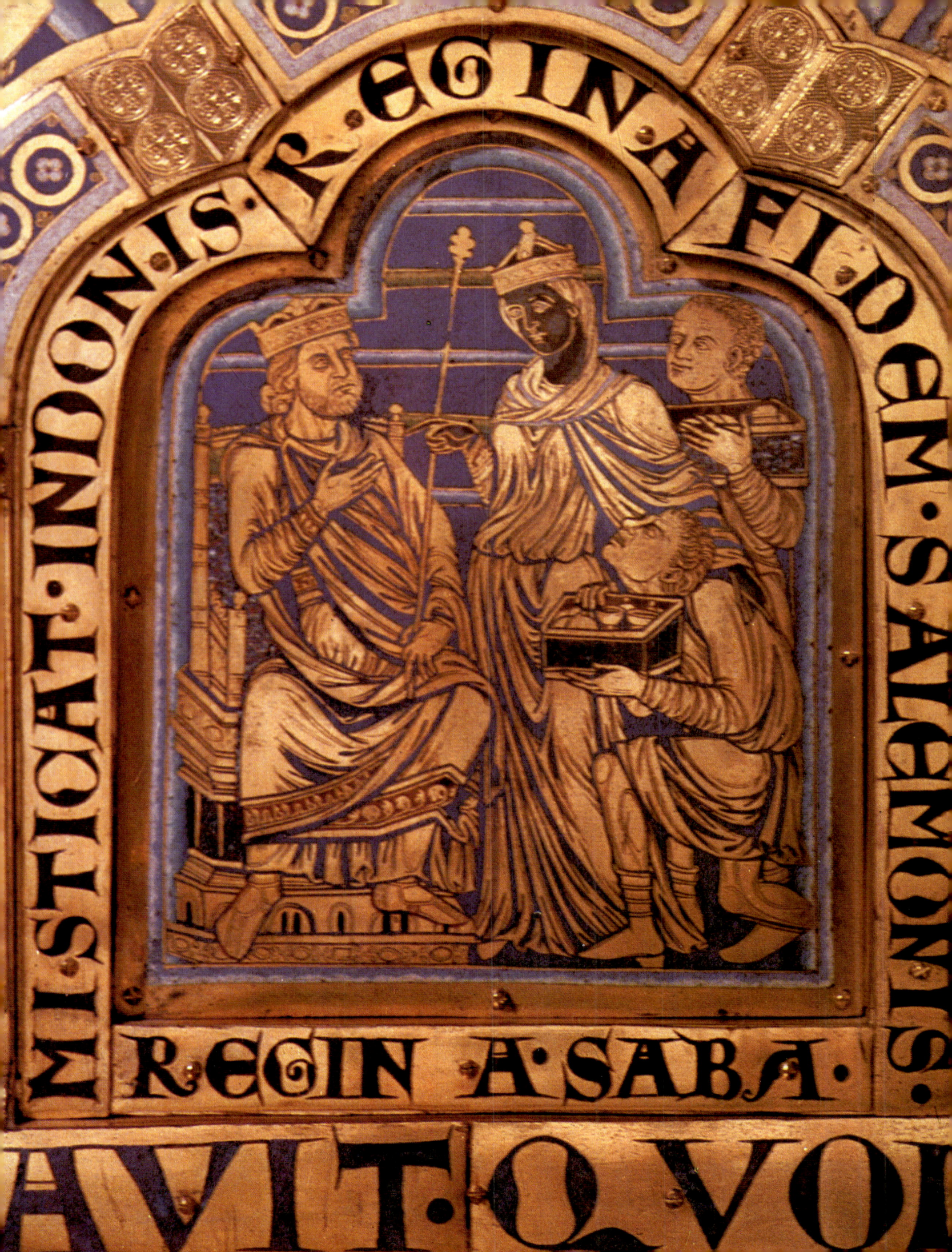

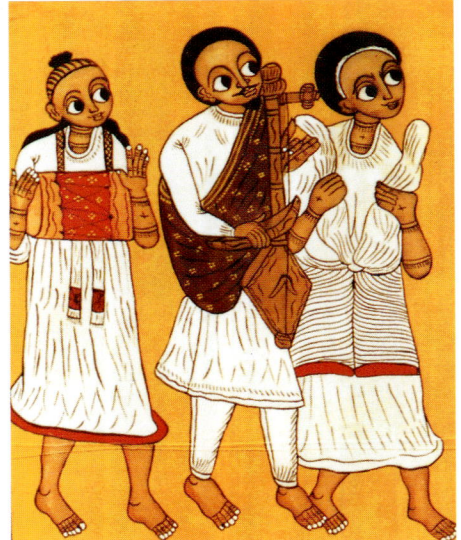

Musicians, Singers, and Jesters

The best known are the azmari, or the ouata, minstrels accompanying themselves on the spike fiddle (masenqo) and by a singer playing the lyre (kerar). Their function is to ennoble or enliven popular ceremonies, depending on the occasion. They know how to express the most profane as well as the most noble feelings. Shuffling nonstop back and forth, they dance and make others dance to love songs or lampoons. They make fun of regular people and condemn the powerful, even the emperor, while begging for gifts. Mischievous or flattering, their verses are reckless: at the end of the sixteenth century, the chronicler Bahrey already deplored their abuse of the freedom of expression that was traditionally granted them. Only Ras Mikael dared take his revenge upon them! They live one day at a time from donations, meals, and drinks which their songs and tunes bring them. Many are famous for their musical virtuosity or verve. Before the crowd, they use between themselves an incomprehensible jargon.

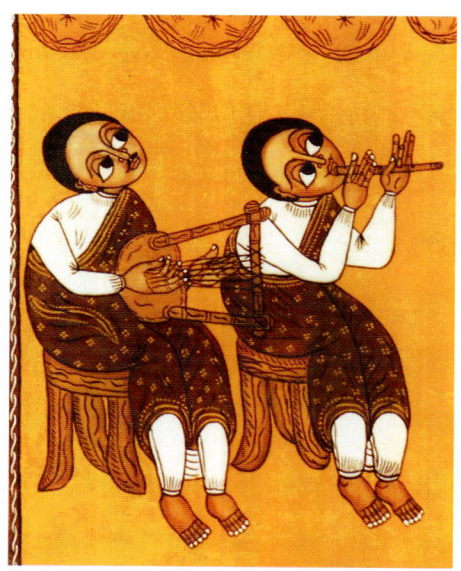

At first glance, struck by Makeda's miraculous beauty, King Solomon said unto his heart: "May God bless me with offspring through her."

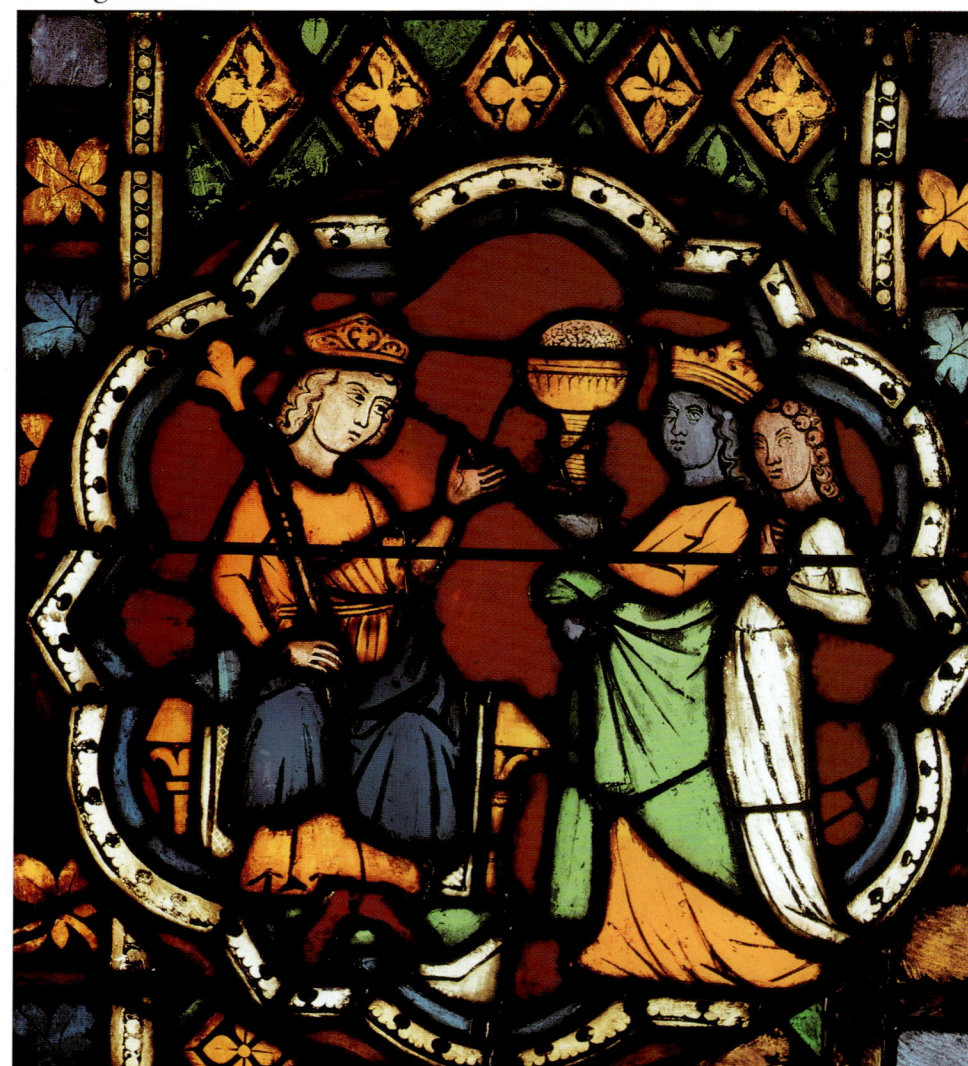

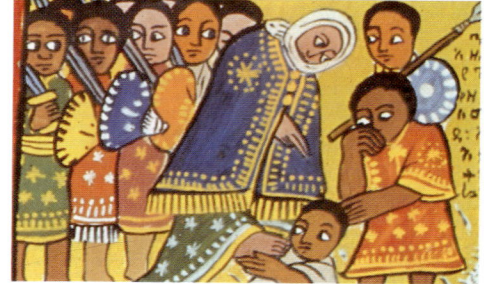

The day of Makeda's departure, Solomon had gifts loaded on six thousand chariots for her, along with, to top it off, a vessel that was to travel in the air.

Then he begged her that if a child should be born of their union that she send him to Jerusalem and give him a ring so that the child would be recognized.

And Makeda went back to her country where she gave birth to a child named Ibn el Hakim: the Son of Wisdom.

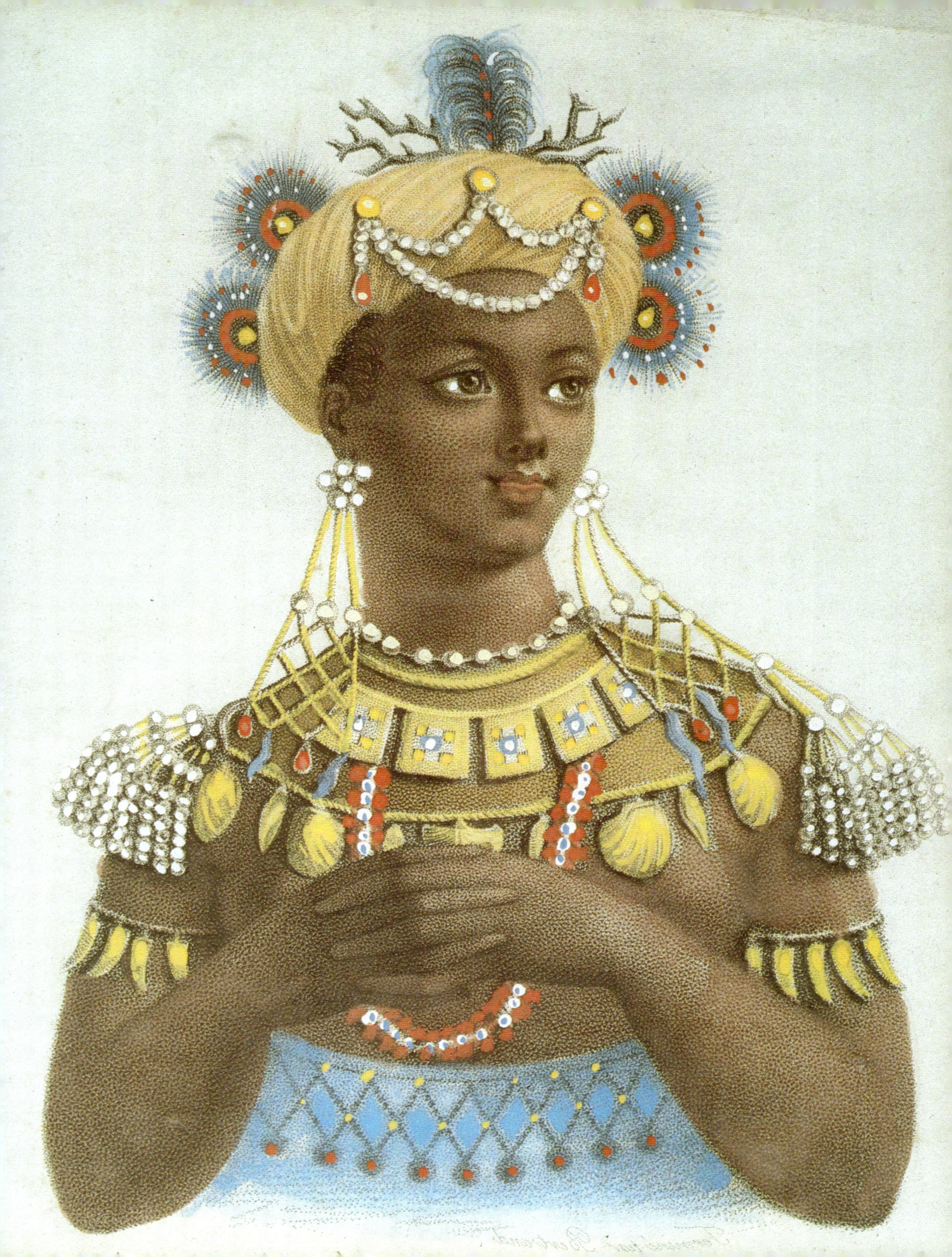

How Solomon Seduced Makeda with a Glass of Water

On the eve of the day set for the departure, Solomon gave a splendid feast of farewell. He had sent for wines from the most illustrious corners of his empire, and on his order cooks had prepared strongly spiced dishes.

The young queen, under the spell of his words and fascinated by his gaze, was not able to resist his invitation; she ate everything he offered her.

After the meal, the queen wanted to go back to her palace, but seeing that the hour was late, and probably under the influence of the good wines, the king invited her to share his tent.

"Have no fear," he said to her, "because I have sworn not to touch your body. You have come here a virgin and you will leave a virgin. But in exchange, and so I may be true to my word, give me your word that you will touch nothing of value that is mine in this palace."

"Agreed. At your request, I swear to take no valuable of yours in this palace"

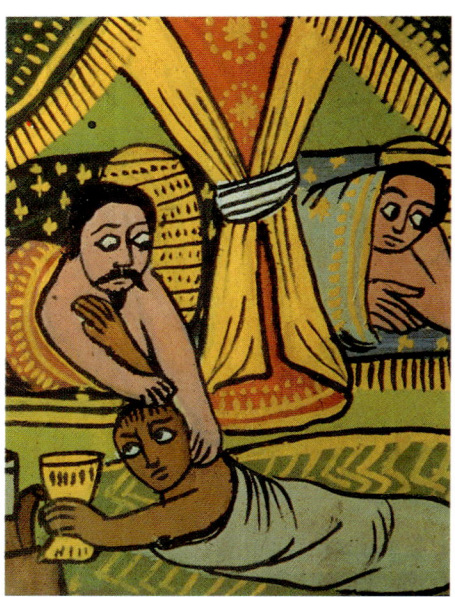

King Solomon's bed was separated from Makeda's by a cloth divider. The king ordered one of his guards to fill a carafe of fresh water and to put it within reach of the Queen of Sheba.

The queen was unable to sleep, consumed by an intense thirst provoked by all the spicy dishes she had eaten. She struggled for a long time to make sure that Solomon was sleeping, and finally, unable to resist, she stole toward the carafe and touched her lips to the fresh water with relish. The king then grabbed the arm that held the tempting vase: "Why do you violate your word? You see, we are a desert people, and no jewels here are more valuable than fresh water." The queen admitted her guilt and accepted, perhaps without much distress, a defeat which her senses had secretly yearned for the instant she had set eyes on Solomon.

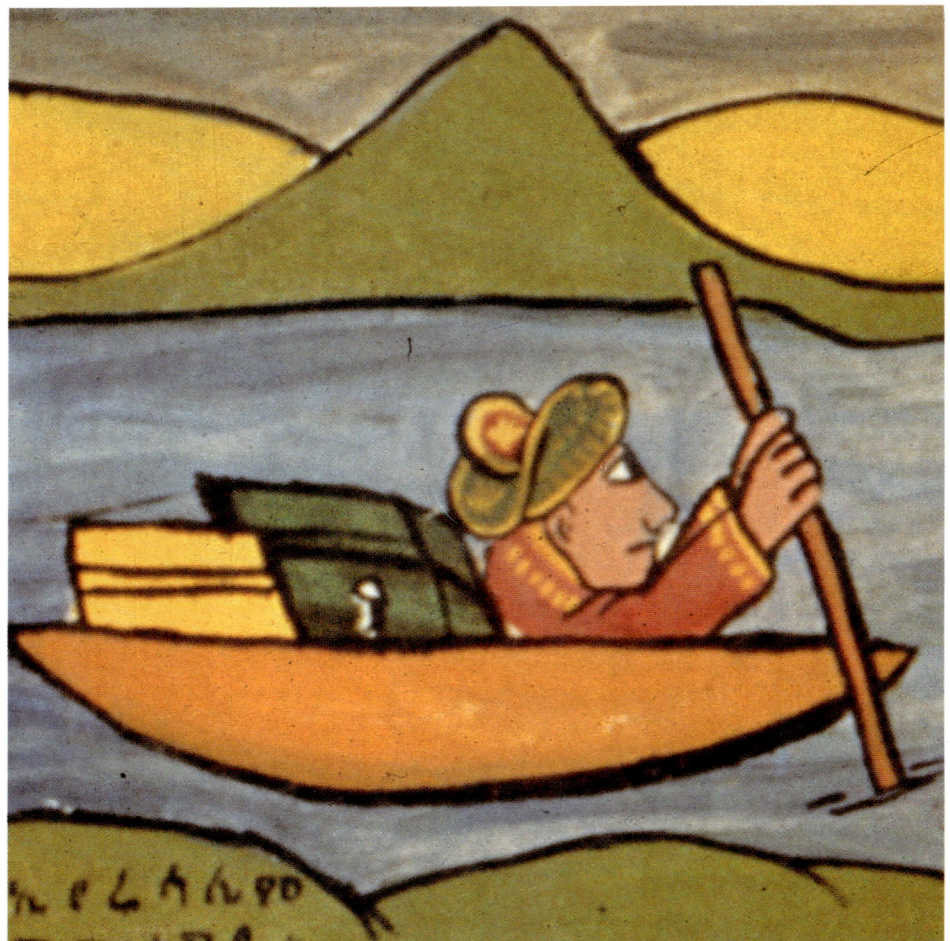

When the child grew up, the Queen of Sheba gave him the ring and sent him to visit his father. The young prince was then twenty-two years old.

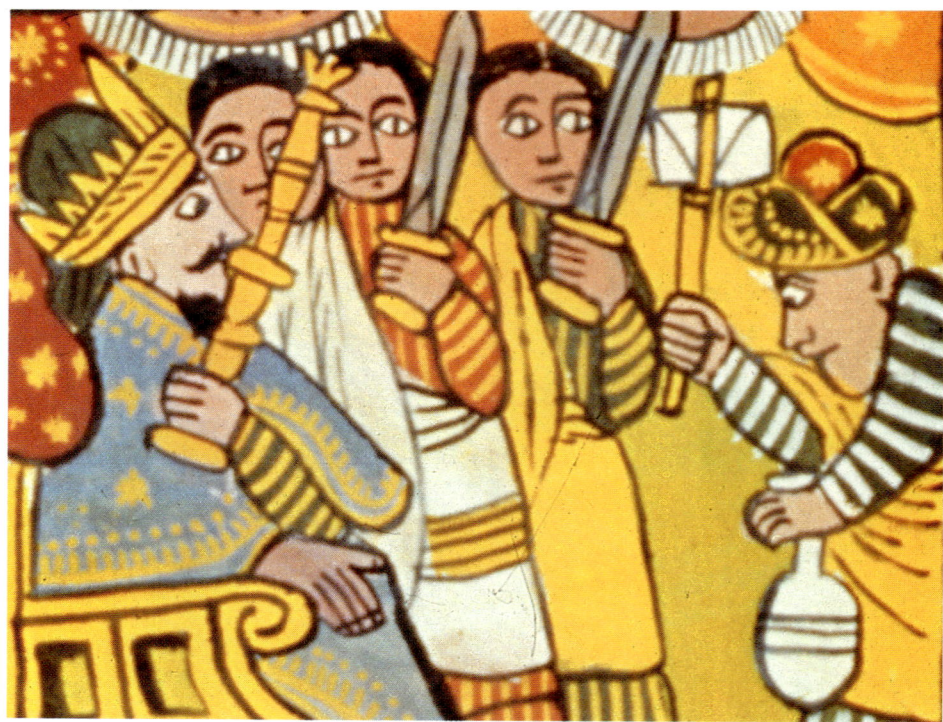

MAKEDA

In Jerusalem, the crowd gathered in the streets was astonished to see two figures who looked like Solomon, so much did the son resemble his father.

But people thought he looked even more like David, his grandfather, and were in awe.

Before he went to Ethiopia, his mother's country, the young man was anointed and consecrated a king in the Temple at Jerusalem.

This is how he became Menilek I, the first king of the famous dynasty of the Lions of Judah, the last of whom was this century's Negus Haile Selassie.

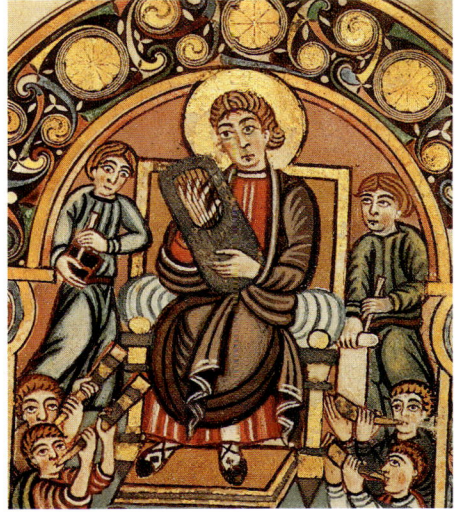
DAVID

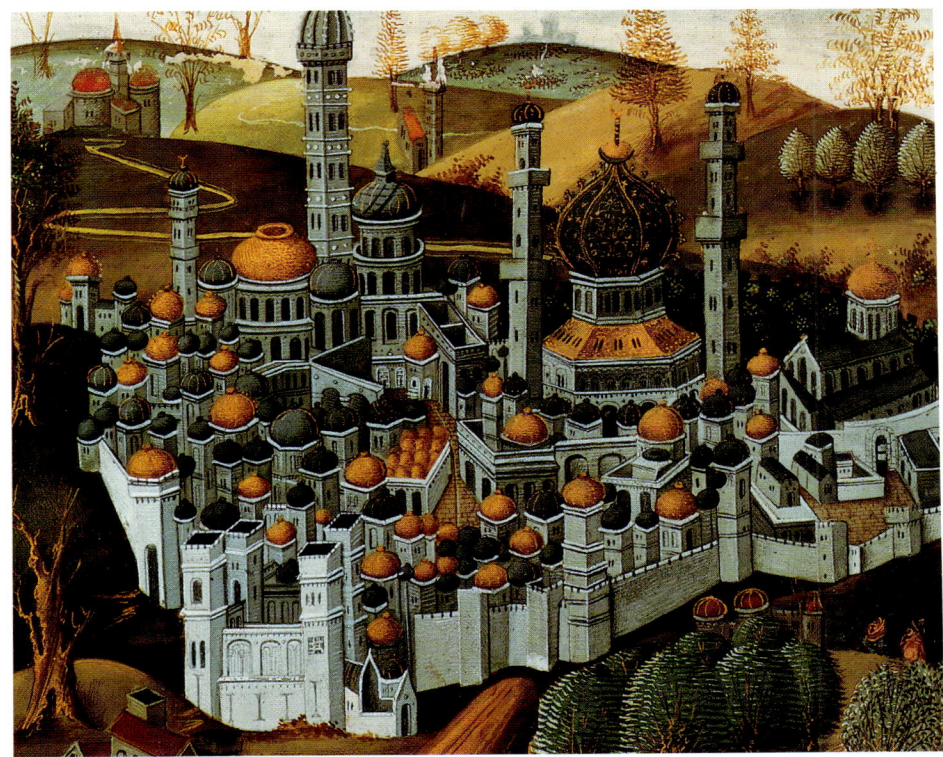
JERUSALEM IN BIBLICAL TIMES

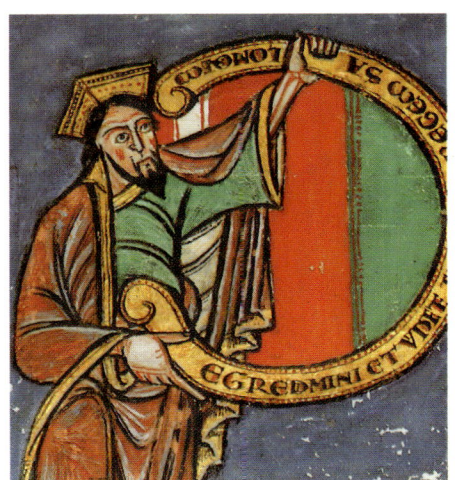
SOLOMON

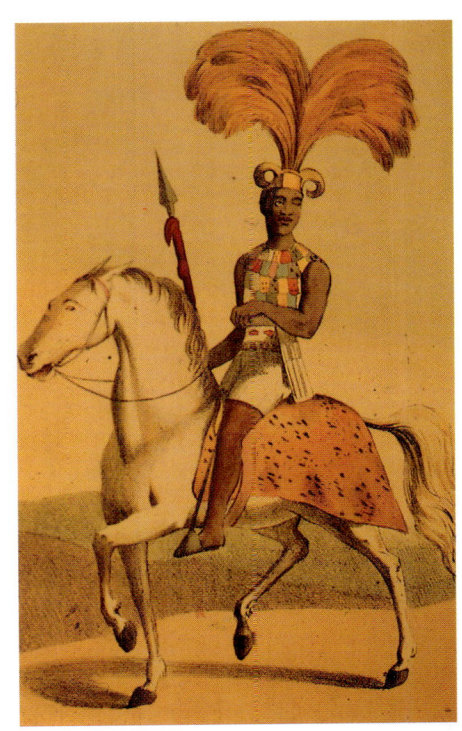
MENILEK I

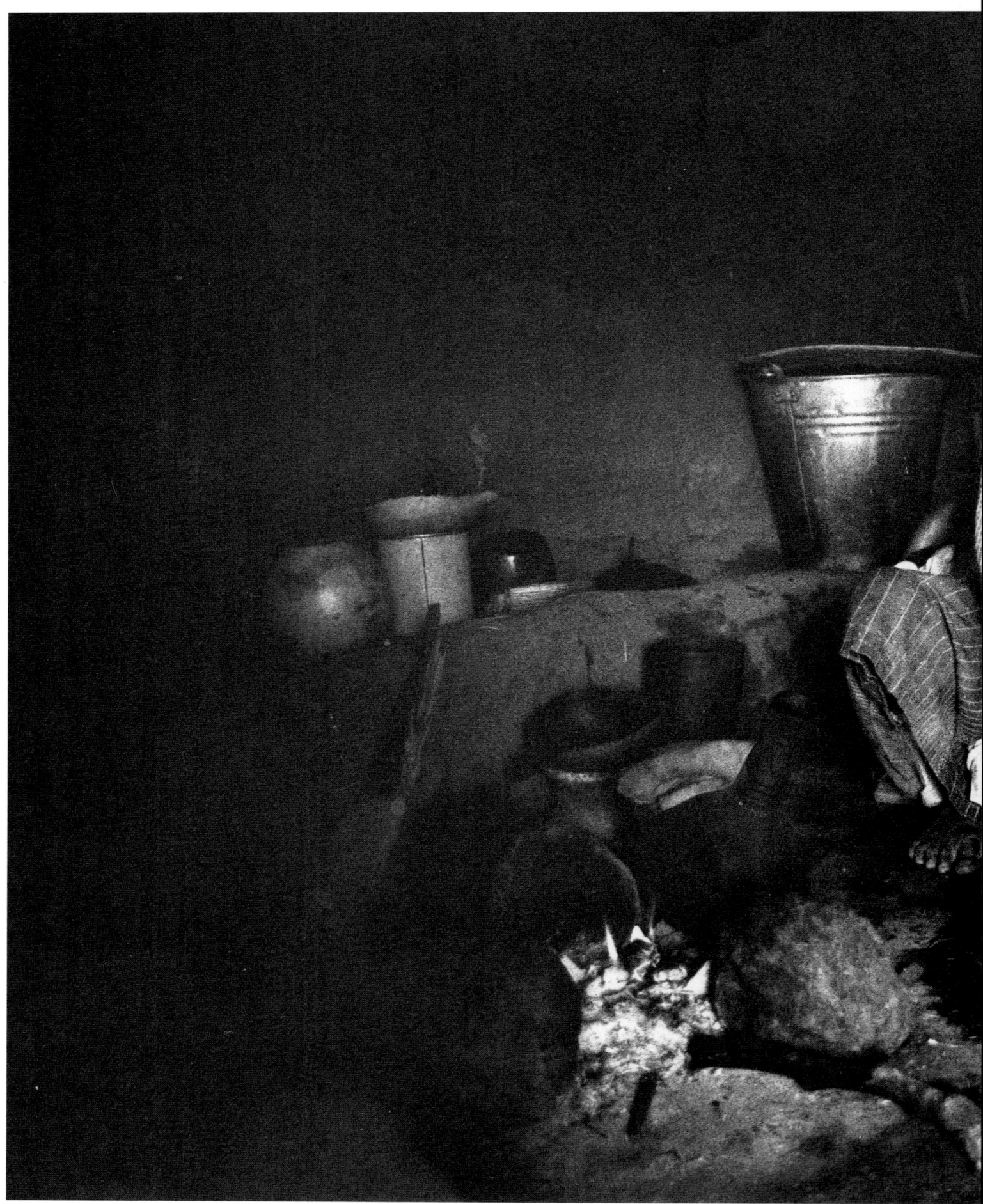

A DESCENDANT OF THE QUEEN OF SHEBA?: A JEWISH

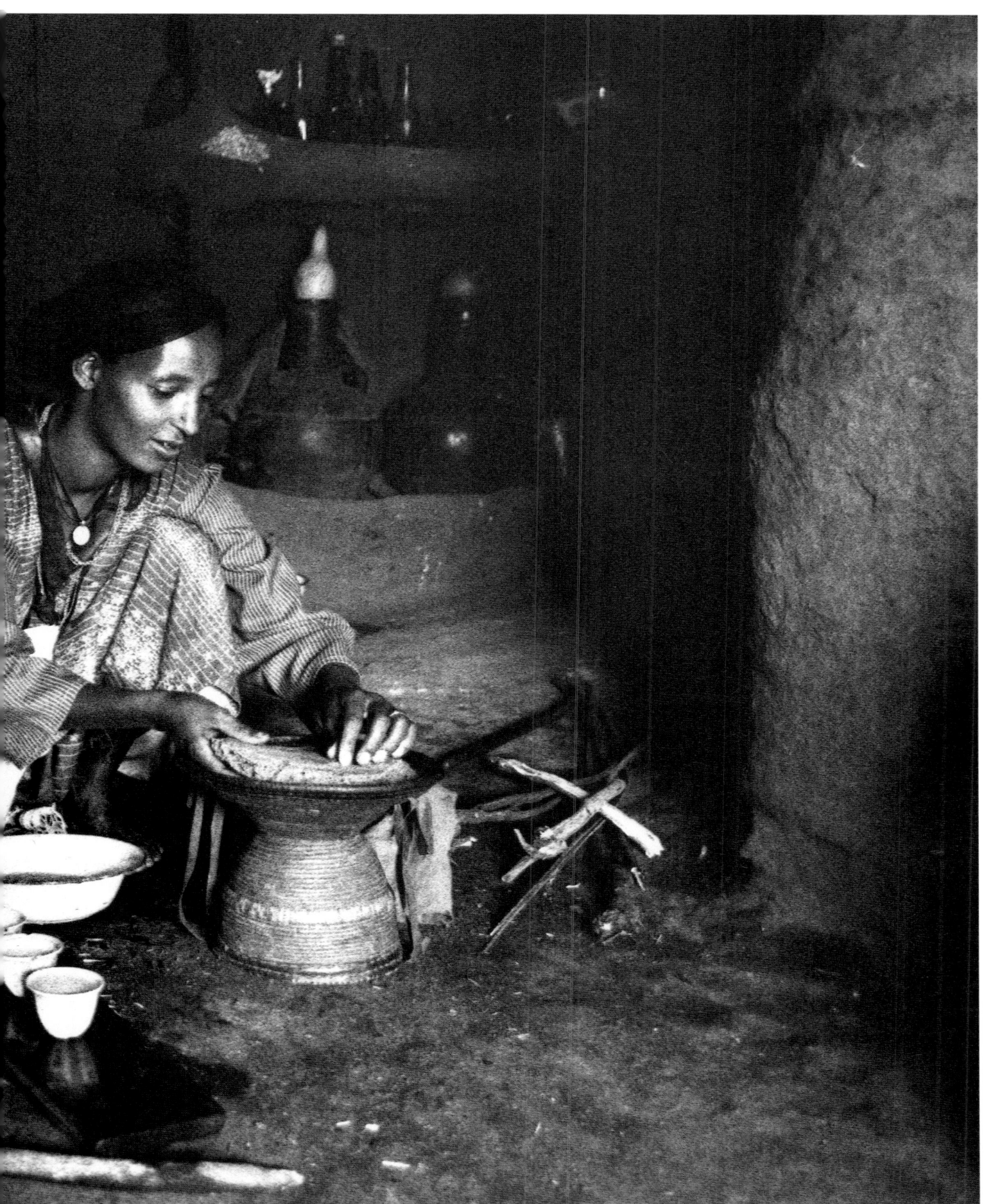

ETHIOPIAN WOMAN, A FALASHA, FROM A VILLAGE OF SIMIENS

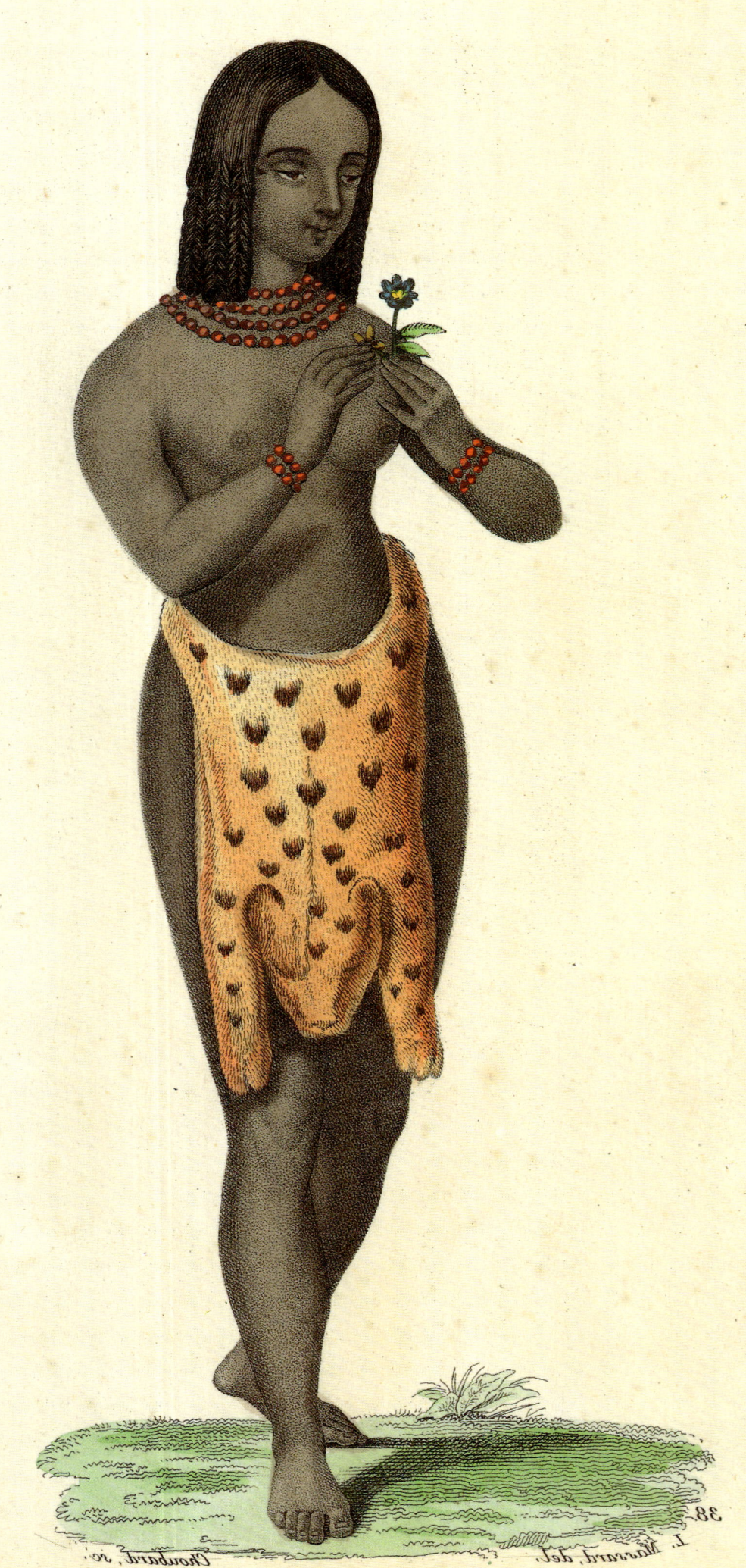

DAURAMA

MOTHER OF THE SEVEN HAUSA KINGDOMS

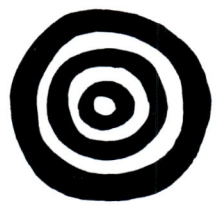

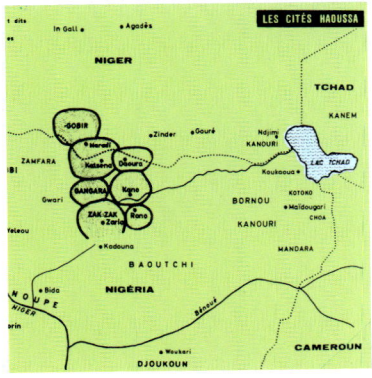

The horseman announced his intention to kill the monster, and the queen warned him, because she had noticed his beauty. Finally she sighed and told him: "If you cut off the monster's head, you'll take the title of king and I will have to go far away from here…"

ONCE UPON A TIME, BE-
TWEEN THE NIGER RIVER AND
LAKE CHAD, THERE WAS A CITY CALLED
DAURA BY THOSE WHO LIVED THERE. IN TRUTH,
SOME PRAISE SINGERS SAY IT WAS RATHER LIKE A VIL-
LAGE—A SIMPLE HAMLET LOST IN THE MIDDLE OF THE
countryside, with a thorn-bush instead of a fortress and a herd of
goats instead of horsemen.

But it's difficult to bring to light events that have taken place over
a thousand years ago.

What is certain is that, whatever the exact dimensions of this
town, it was ruled by a queen, a young woman by the name of
Daurama.

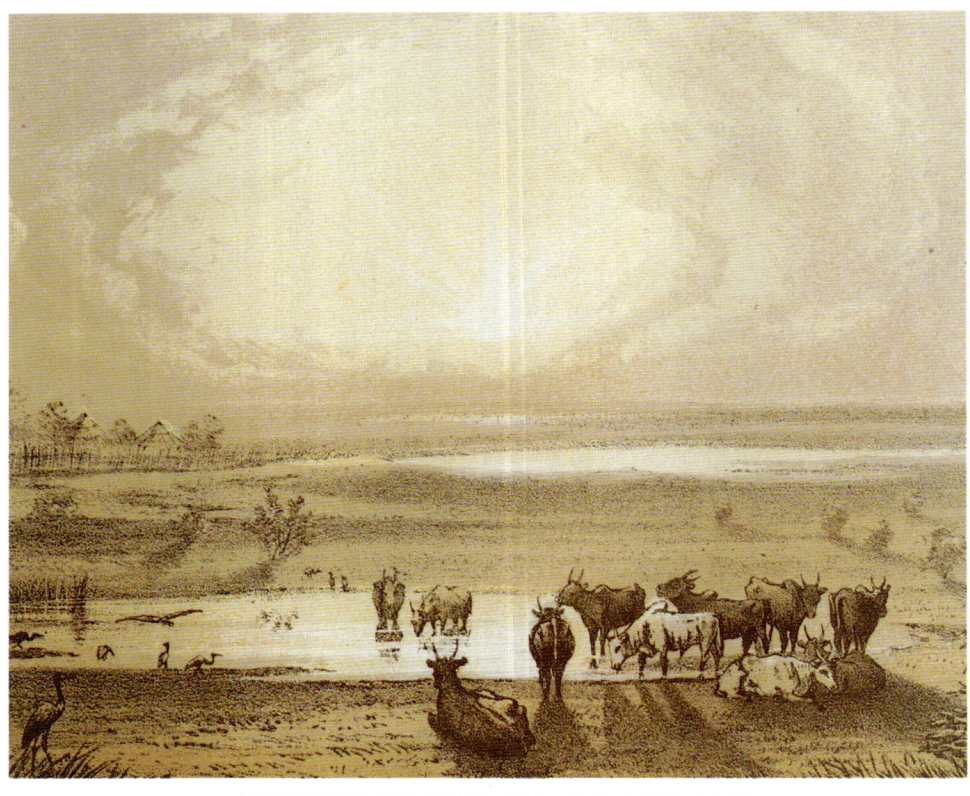

BETWEEN THE RIVER NIGER AND LAKE CHAD

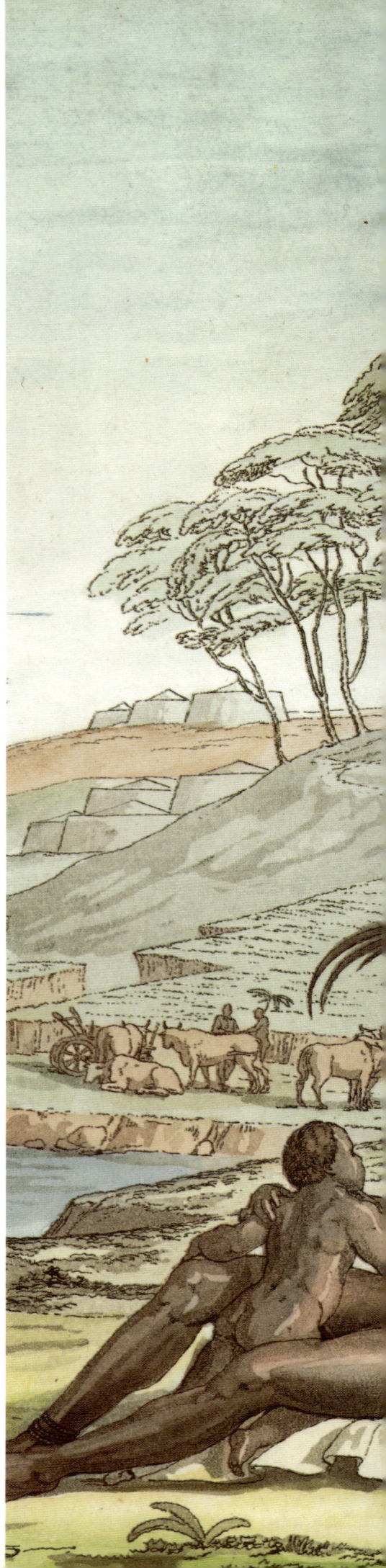

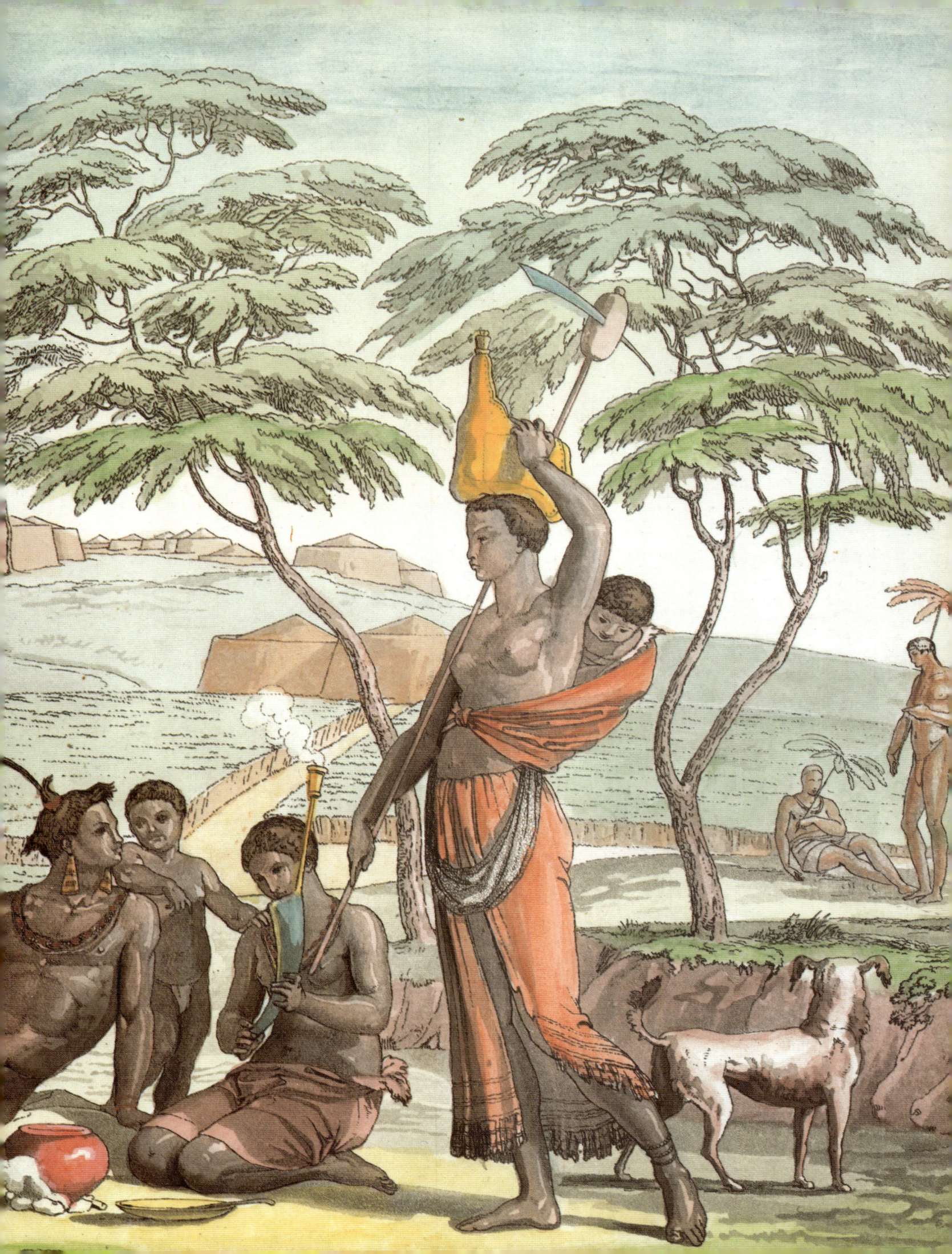

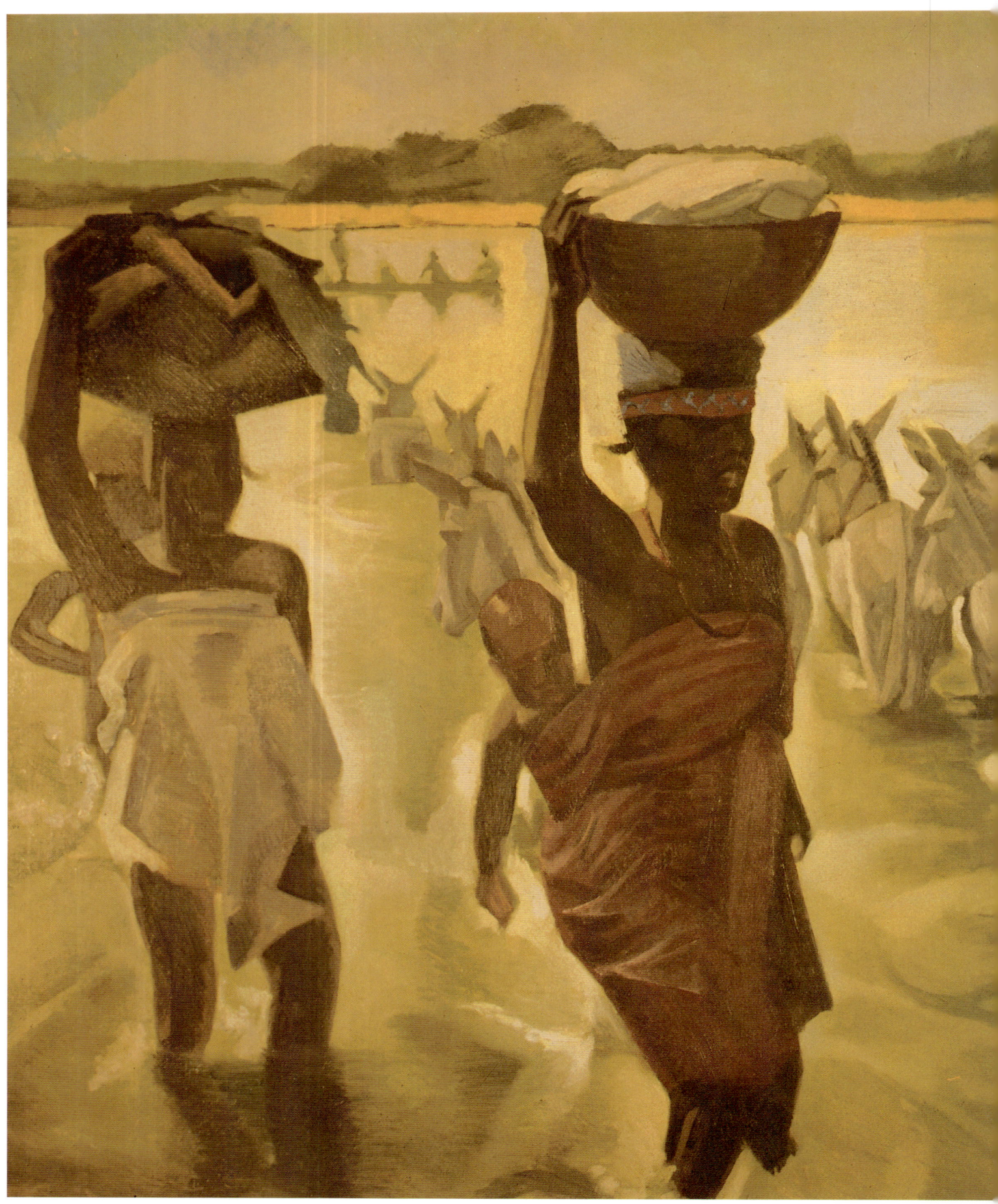

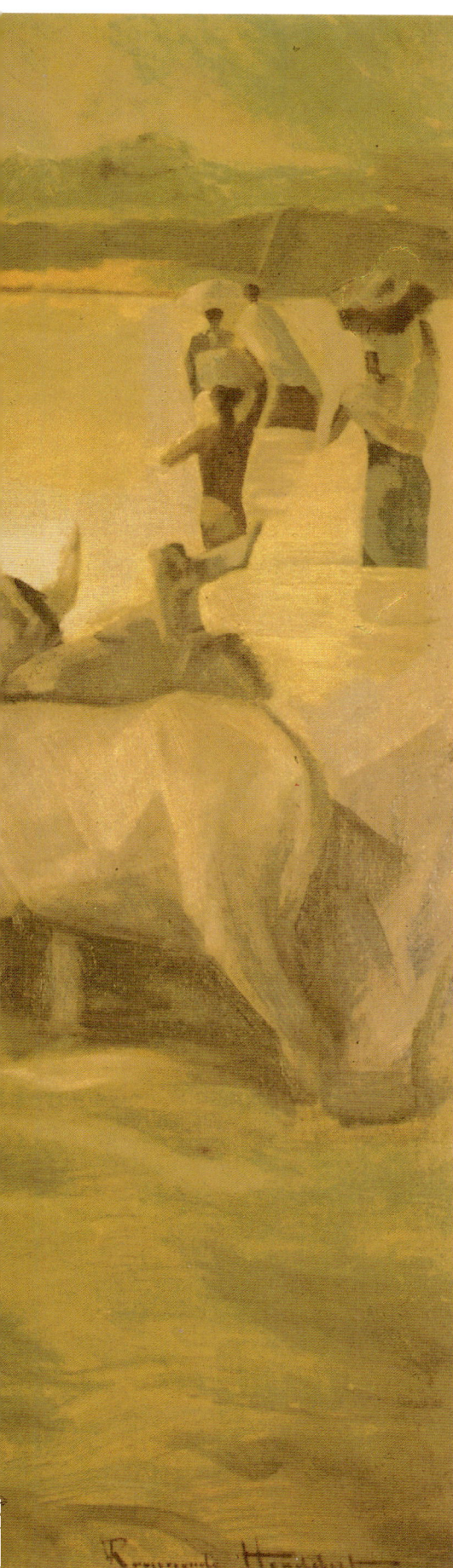

The inhabitants essentially lived on the river, out of which their ancestors had come at the beginning of time.

The waters of the river were teaming with an infinite variety of fish, from the most common species that go their usual way beneath the shimmering surface to those that leave their natural habitat to tread on land and even climb into the trees.

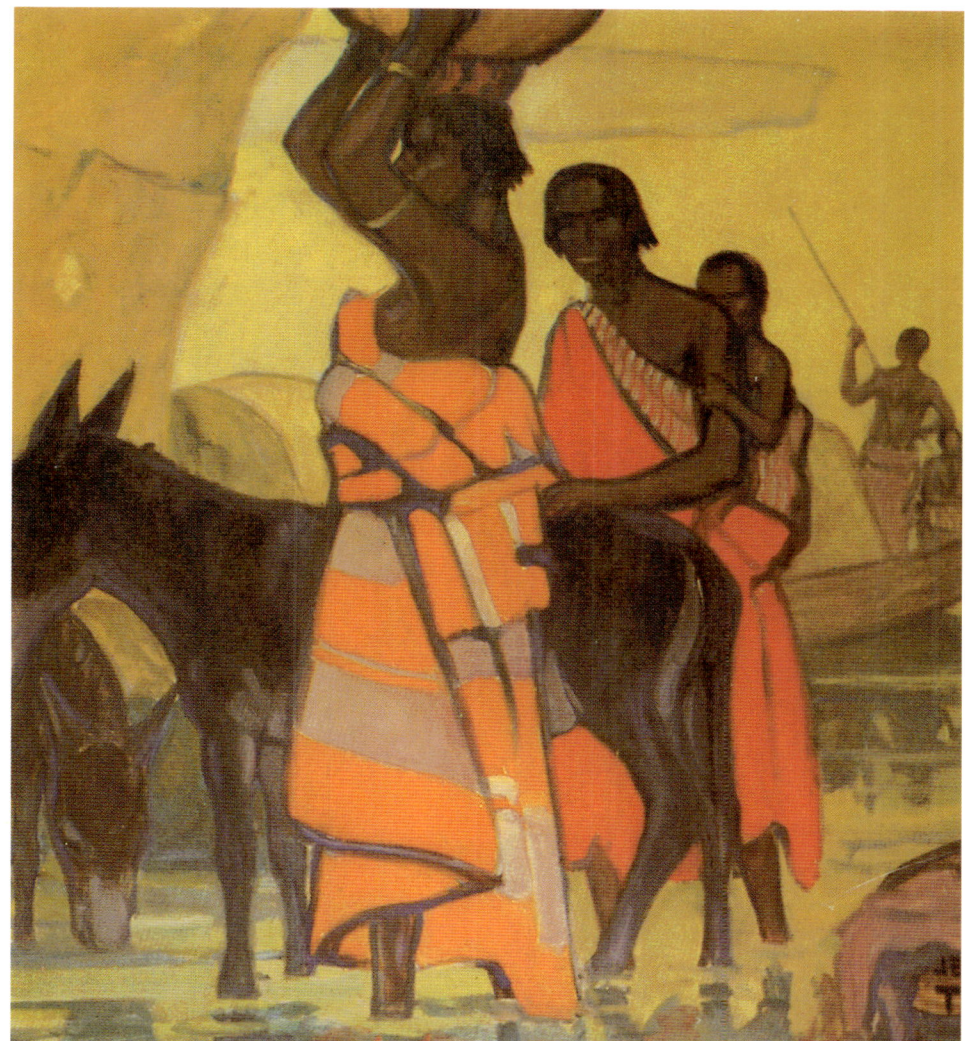

"THE INHABITANTS LIVED ON THE RIVER"

And the banks were furrowed with small creeks where animals would come to drink, putting themselves within reach of lances and arrows.

The inhabitants also drew their water from it with jugs made of baked earth, because the dry savannah began just a few yards from the river and no one had ever heard of anyone finding a well there.

The queen was friendly with the river from which her ancestors had come; covered with scales, they had fallen upon the land, turning into the enormous blocks of rocks that dotted the banks.

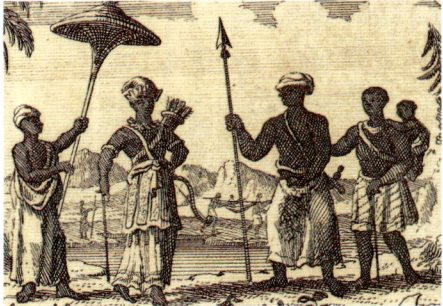

A Hausa Wedding

When the bride has been rubbed with a little henna, all her friends throw themselves on her, covering her, and crying.

After that, the "mothers" of the bride come to tell them to calm down: "Peace, peace, go get a tom-tom player." He comes to the door of the family home (the door of the master if it is a slave wedding). The *kawa* (the bridesmaid) brings a loincloth and wraps it like a turban around the bride's head; then everyone comes out for games and to hear the tom-tom.

The *kawayes* spend a night in the bride's house; they make porridge and eat until they're full.

At night, henna is put on the bride's arms and legs for the second time. In the morning, the bride's grandmother, her mother's mother, washes her with hot water from head to toe. When the bride is taken behind the hut of her grandmother, her kawa comes and puts a loincloth on her head; she takes her hand and guides her. They both go to the "mother" who has been chosen to wash her—one of her mother's younger sisters.

> The kawa sings:
> *From now on you will not go dancing*
> *From now on you will not attend dances*
> *From now on you will not go dancing*
> *You will only dance*
> *on your way to the river.*

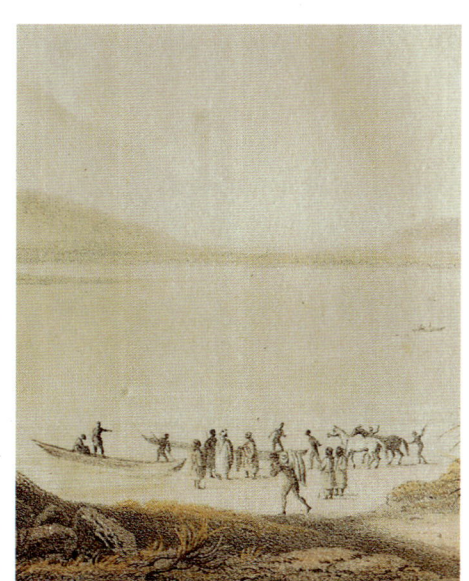

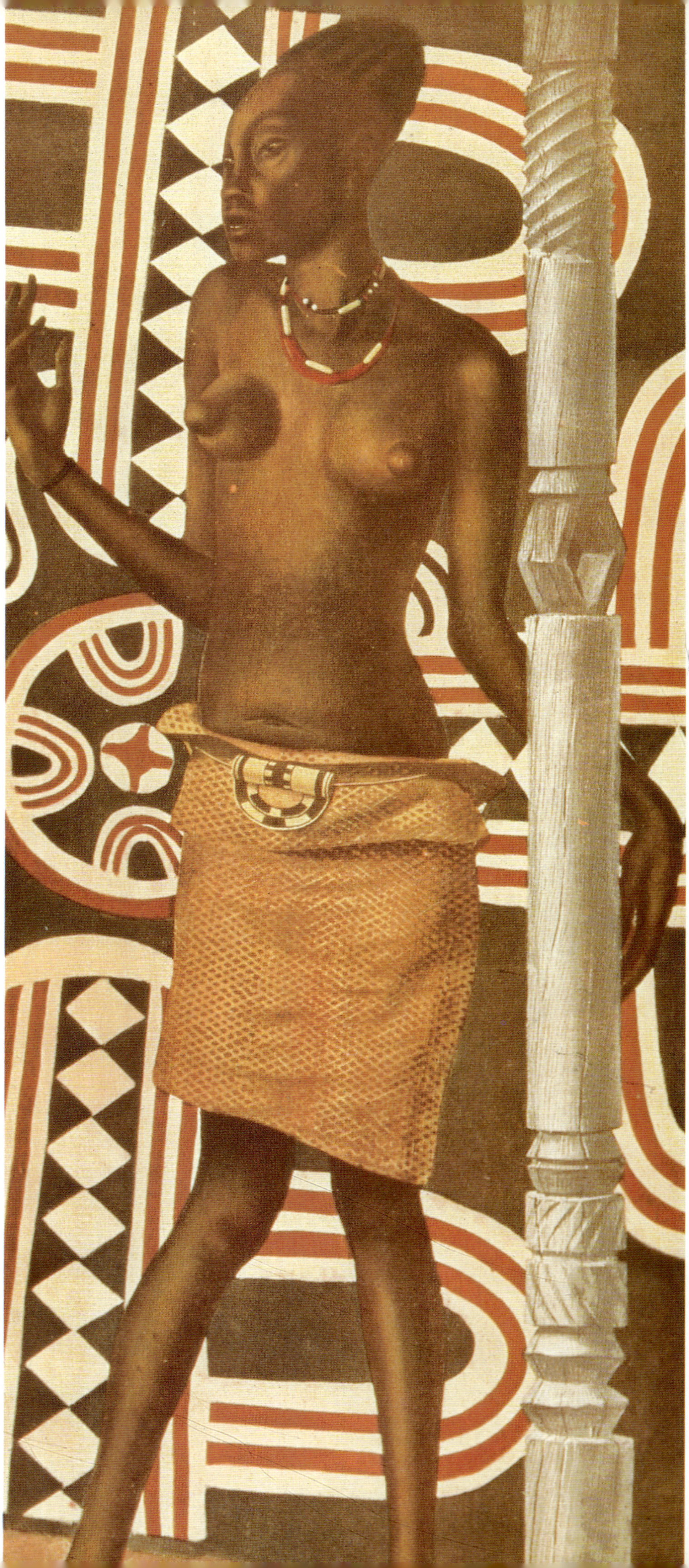

DAURAMA

Once a year, she went to plunge into the river's waters and swim for a long time beneath the surface; then she would reach the bank and shake her arms as if they were fins, as her ancestors had done, all so that the river might never stop in its course.

It was a day of great ceremony.

Helped by two warriors, the queen walked slowly onto the dry grass.

And her toes barely touched the ground while the drums accompanied the injunction: "Slowly, the queen must walk slowly."

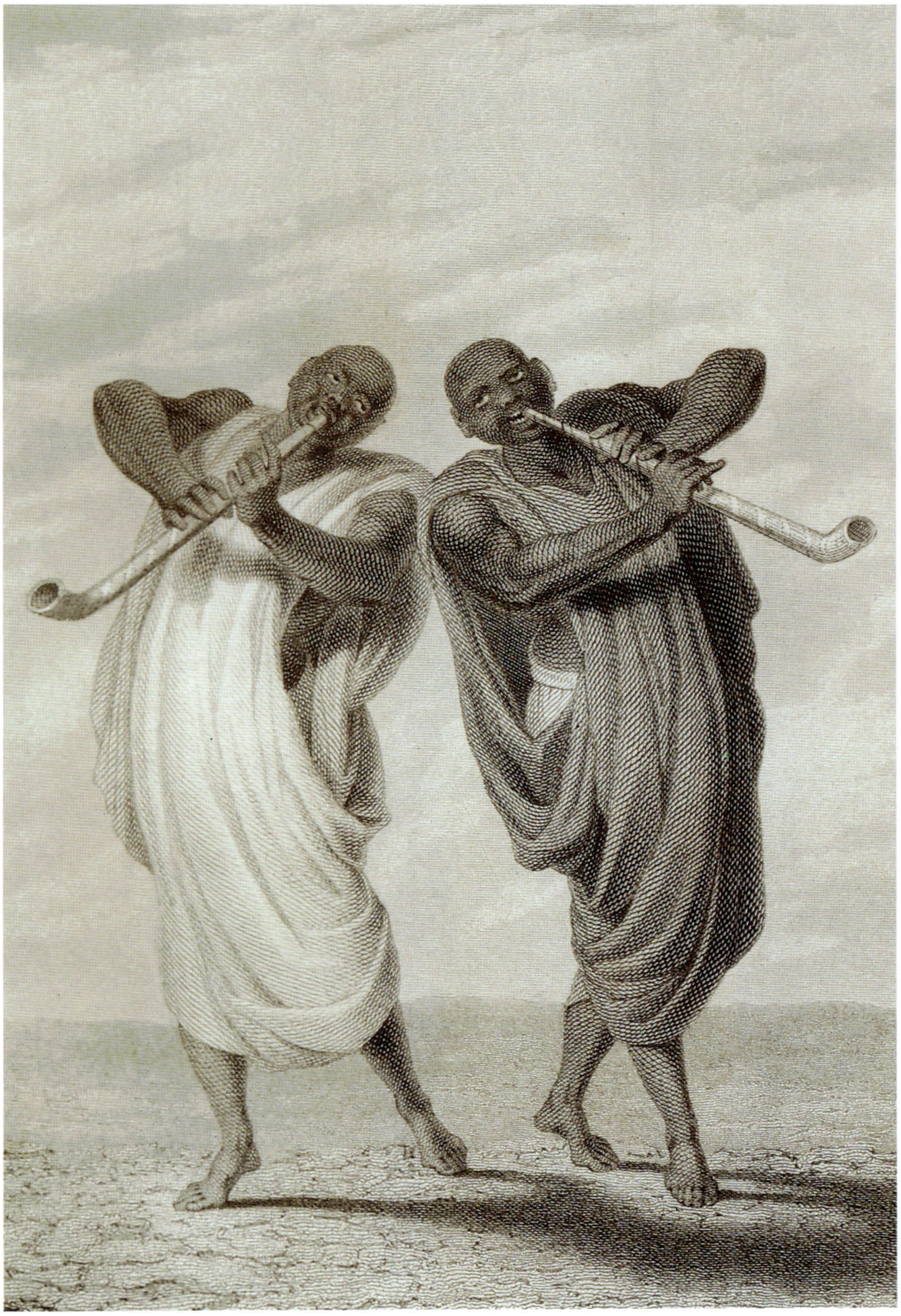

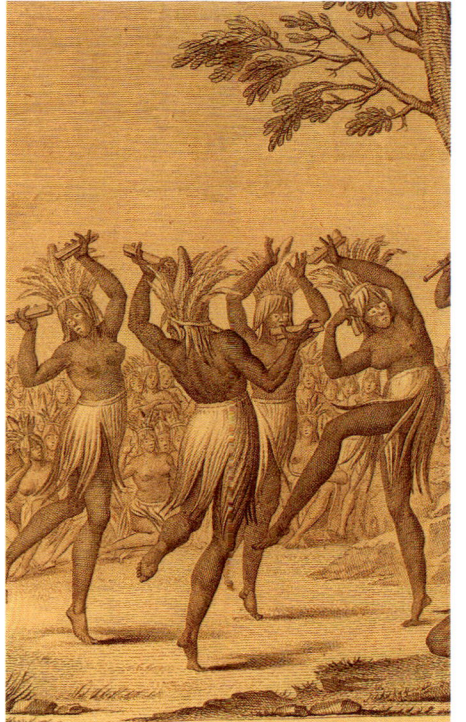

"IT WAS A DAY OF GREAT CEREMONY"

Praise unto Fatou Seydi

What a pleasure it is for me, what pleasure to behold your face, Fatou Seydi!
What a pleasure for me is your nobility, sister Fatou!

Eyes circled in white antimony, gums blue,
Lips like the fine embroideries
of the artisans from Jongaci,
It is sister Fatou!

Face like dawn
piercing a hole into the horizon
Young woman with breasts standing up,
walking proud,
It is sister Fatou!

Lovely young woman
who brings joy to my morning gaze
Beautiful from behind as from the front,
This is sister Fatou!

Fatou Seydi cooked full pots of rice,
covered in butter!

Fatou Seydi offered me some in her house,
so I quickly I washed my hands...

Young woman from Keyin,
even if you cook nothing,
Your beauty is mine,
the gift that fills me.
Young woman from Keyin, smile, laugh for me!

Proverb

"The river is not so full as to hide the fish from the eye."

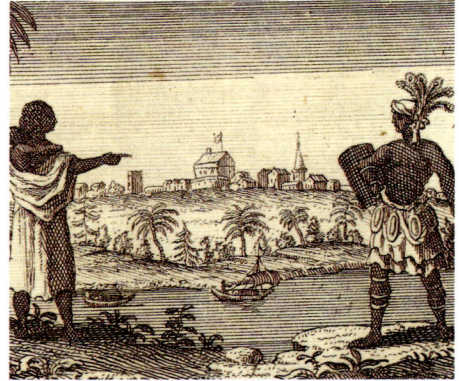

Daura

In the days of Ghana's great prosperity, there used to be, at the other end of West Africa toward Lake Chad, a beautiful land of peaceful people. These people were called the Hausa.

But instead of forming a great kingdom, they preferred to stay quietly gathered around their cities, without any of these cities ever seeking to dominate the others. The most famous of these cities was called Daura. People say that this city "had no history" because it had never attacked anyone and no one had ever attacked it during the more than one thousand years of its existence. But isn't such peacefulness the most beautiful of histories?

Proverb

"Only the body wet with sweat pulls up the well water."

One year, a great serpent called Sarki blocked the way to the river for the inhabitants of the small kingdom.

Such monsters were not rare at the time, and generally the most humble kingdoms were vulnerable to their demands. Humans would leave a herd of oxen on the banks of the river for the monster in exchange for two or three years of peace. But this serpent wanted neither the usual ox nor even a young woman for a sacrifice. Because, in reality, this serpent was a man that the queen had rebuffed; this man happened to be a sorcerer of great power, and his sole desire was to kill all of the inhabitants of the kingdom, to make them die of thirst, young and old, including those still in the bellies of their mothers.

Sarki uncoiled his coils longer than the great tree roots along the banks; and the most thirsty of the inhabitants would stop in front of his giant jaws, then turn back as quickly as humanly possible.

Every morning, the people licked the drops of dew that had settled on the stones at night, and every evening people would turn to the queen and ask her: "Daurama, don't you hear the voice of your ancestors?" The young woman would then turn her ear toward the river, but after a while she would always answer, "I hear only the rolling of the waters and the hissing of the serpent, that is all."

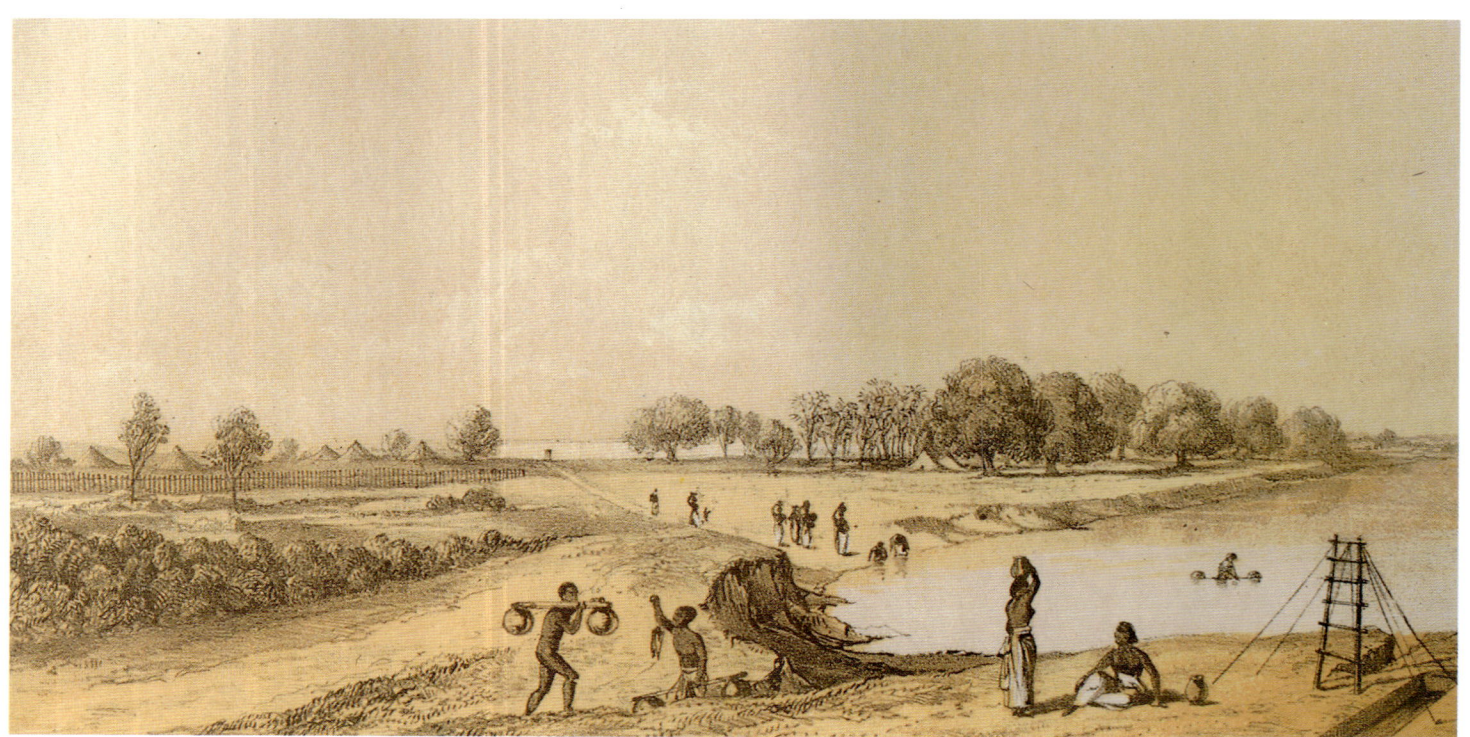

"ONE YEAR, A GREAT SERPENT BLOCKED THE WAY TO THE RIVER"

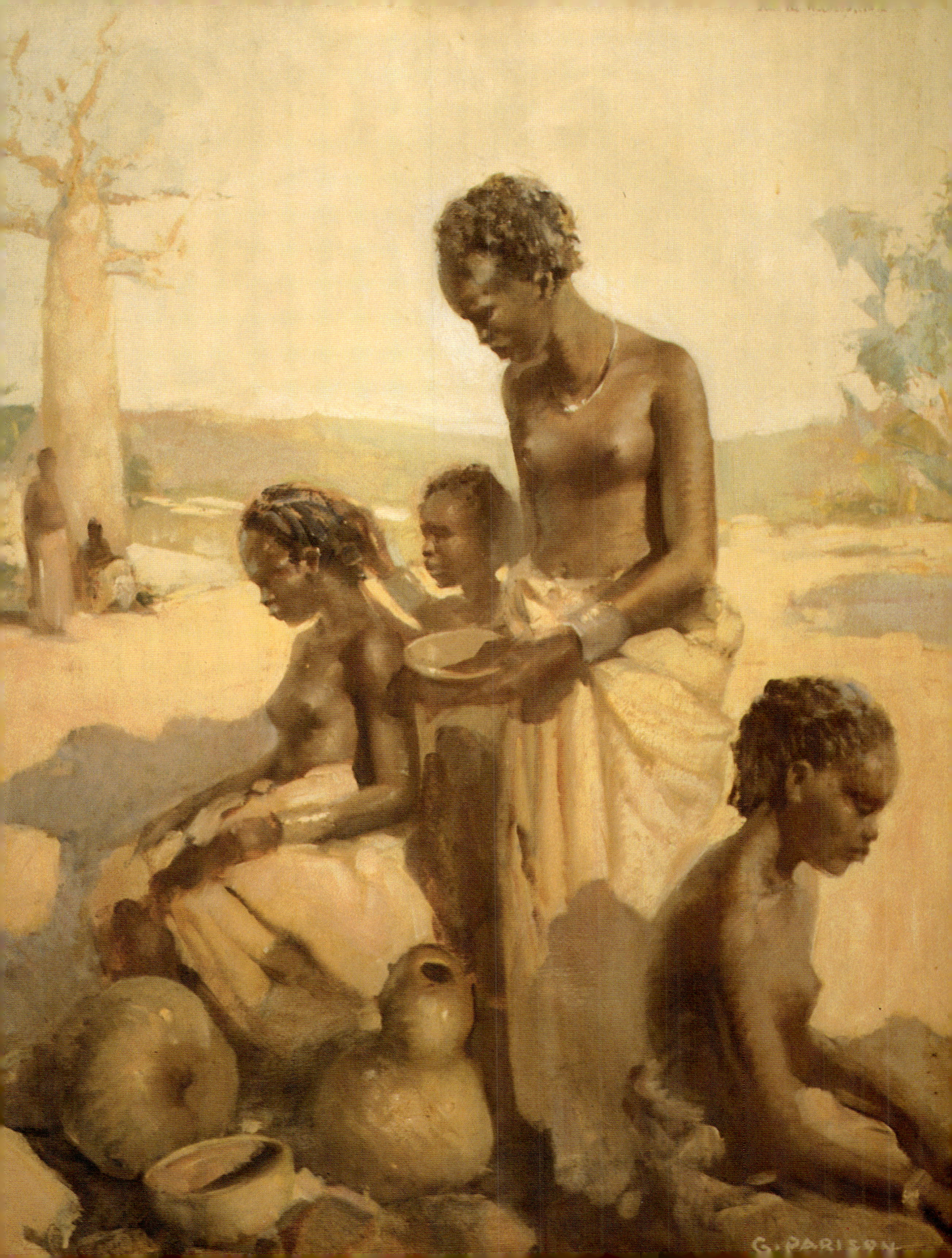

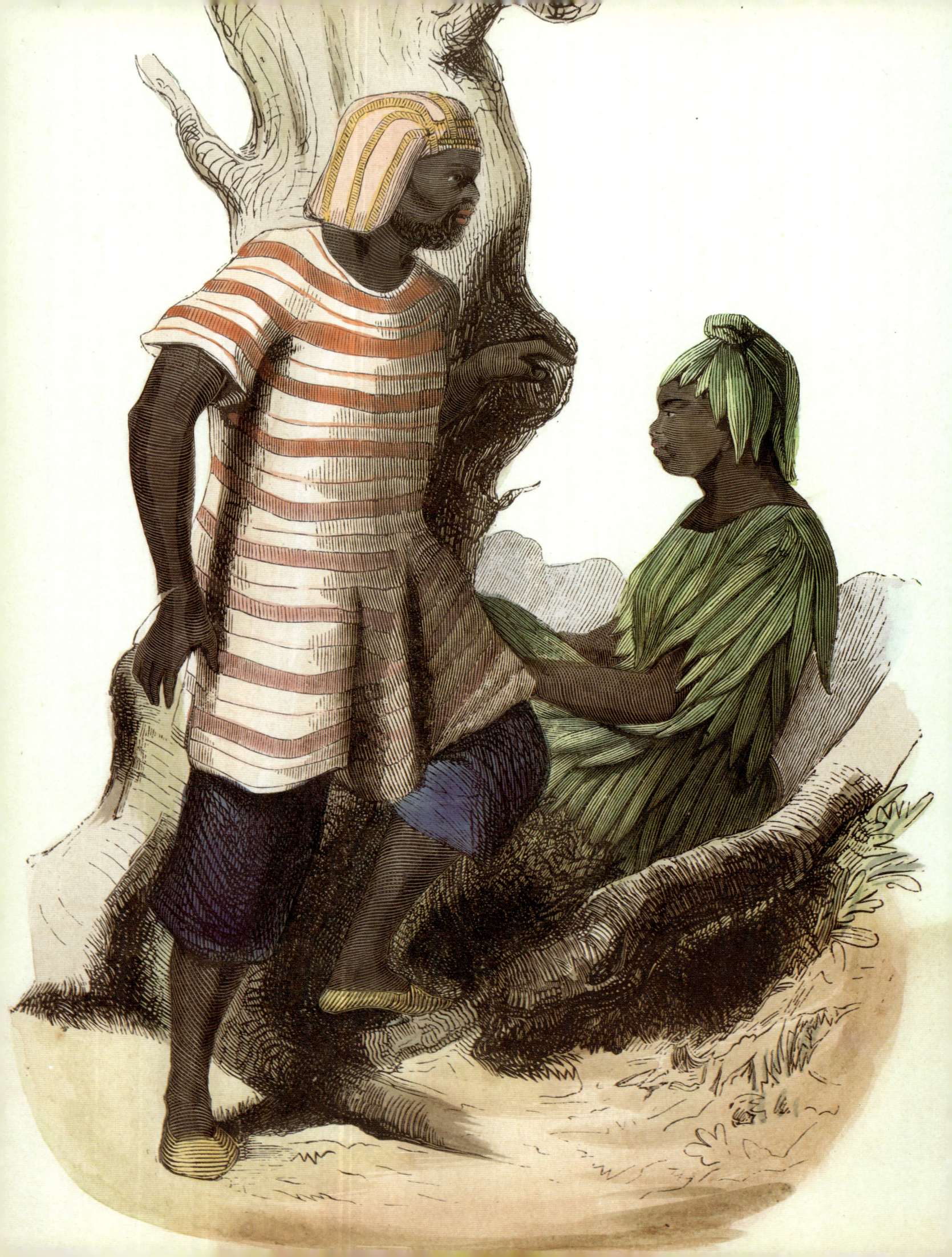

DAURAMA

One day, there appeared a horseman on a three-year-old bay-colored horse. He advanced without paying heed to the parched wretches dragging themselves along the ground; then he noticed the young queen, also lying down, but still radiant despite her emaciated features.

The horseman was a handsome young man wearing a hood and a chainmail tunic, the kind you can still see today: a Hausa warrior from the Niger Valley.

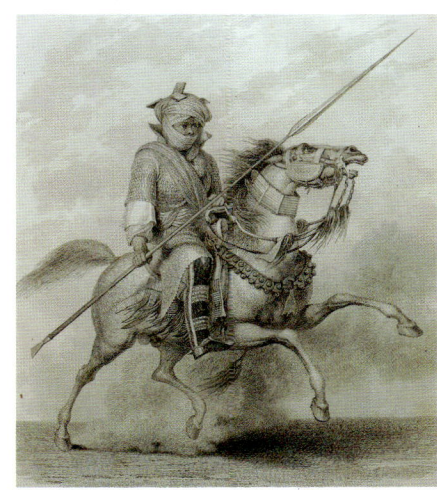

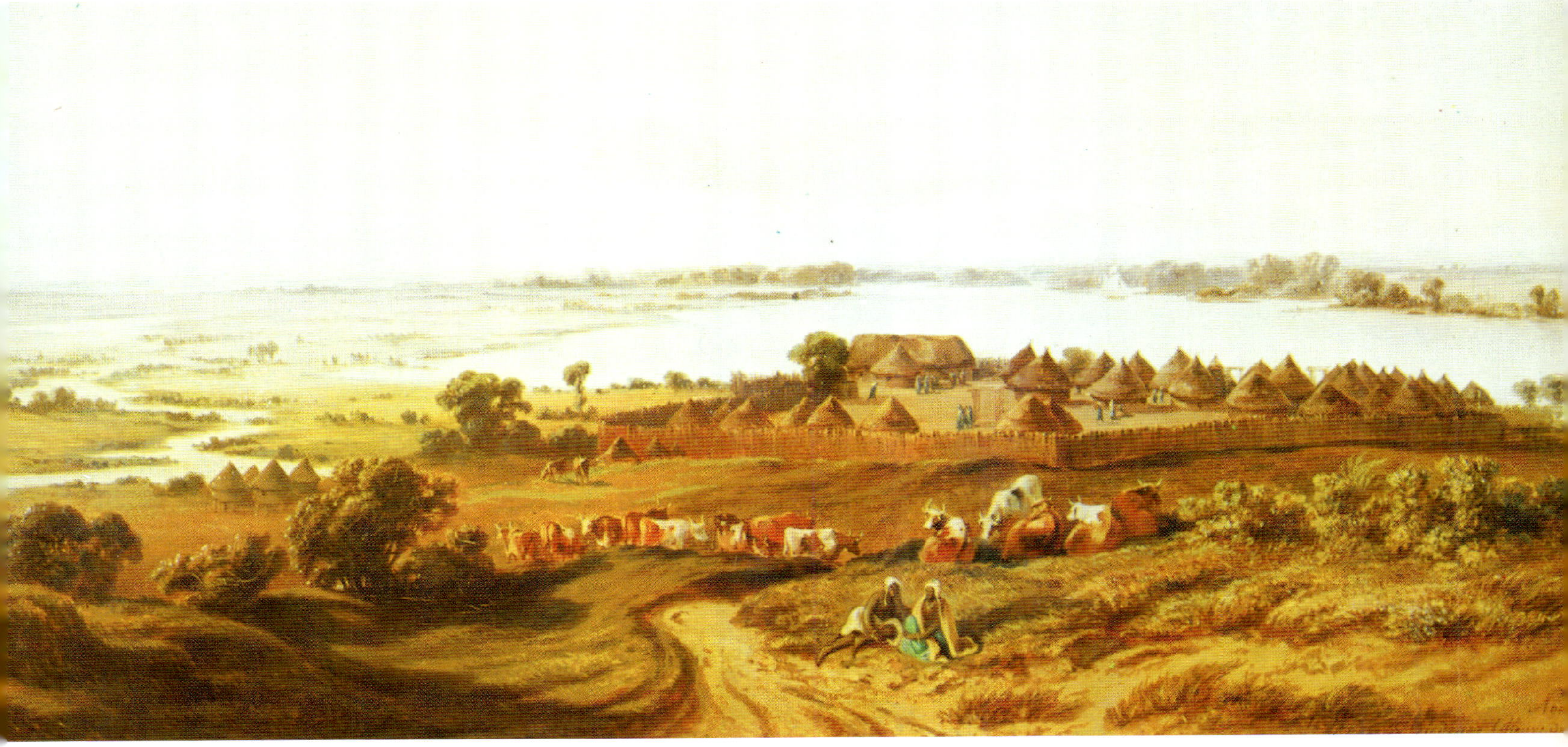

He announced his intention to kill the monster, and the queen warned him because she had noticed his beauty.

Finally, the queen sighed and said to him:

"If you cut off the monster's head, you'll take the title of king and I will have to go far away from here."

The horseman answered.

"You won't go anywhere," said Bayajida. (That was his name.)

When he came back an hour later, a cloud of smoke rose above the river; it was the beast's entrails burning in the sun. The horseman saluted the queen before he went on his way. But just then she said to him:

"You're not leaving."

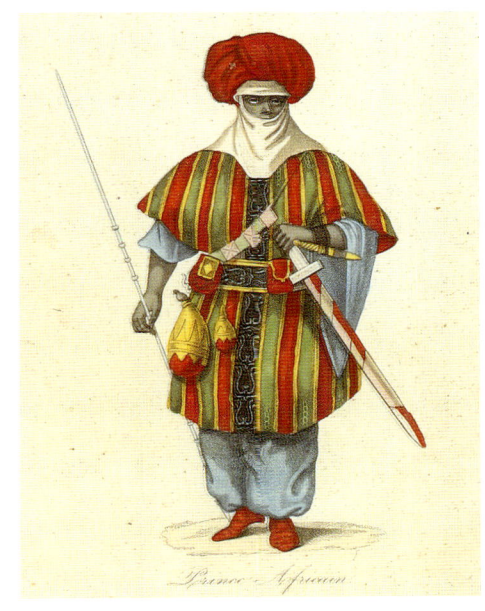

They begat seven sons who founded the first seven Hausa kingdoms, the Hausa Bakwai: Daura, Rano, Zaria, Gobir, Katsina, Biram, and Kano.

Then the sons of their sons spread into the lands of Kebbi, Nupe, Zamfara, Yauri, Gwari, Kororofa, and Yoruba, where they formed seven states that are now called Banza Bakwai, "the seven bastards," or the seven "ne'er do wells," because they never reached the splendor of the first seven Hausa kingdoms.

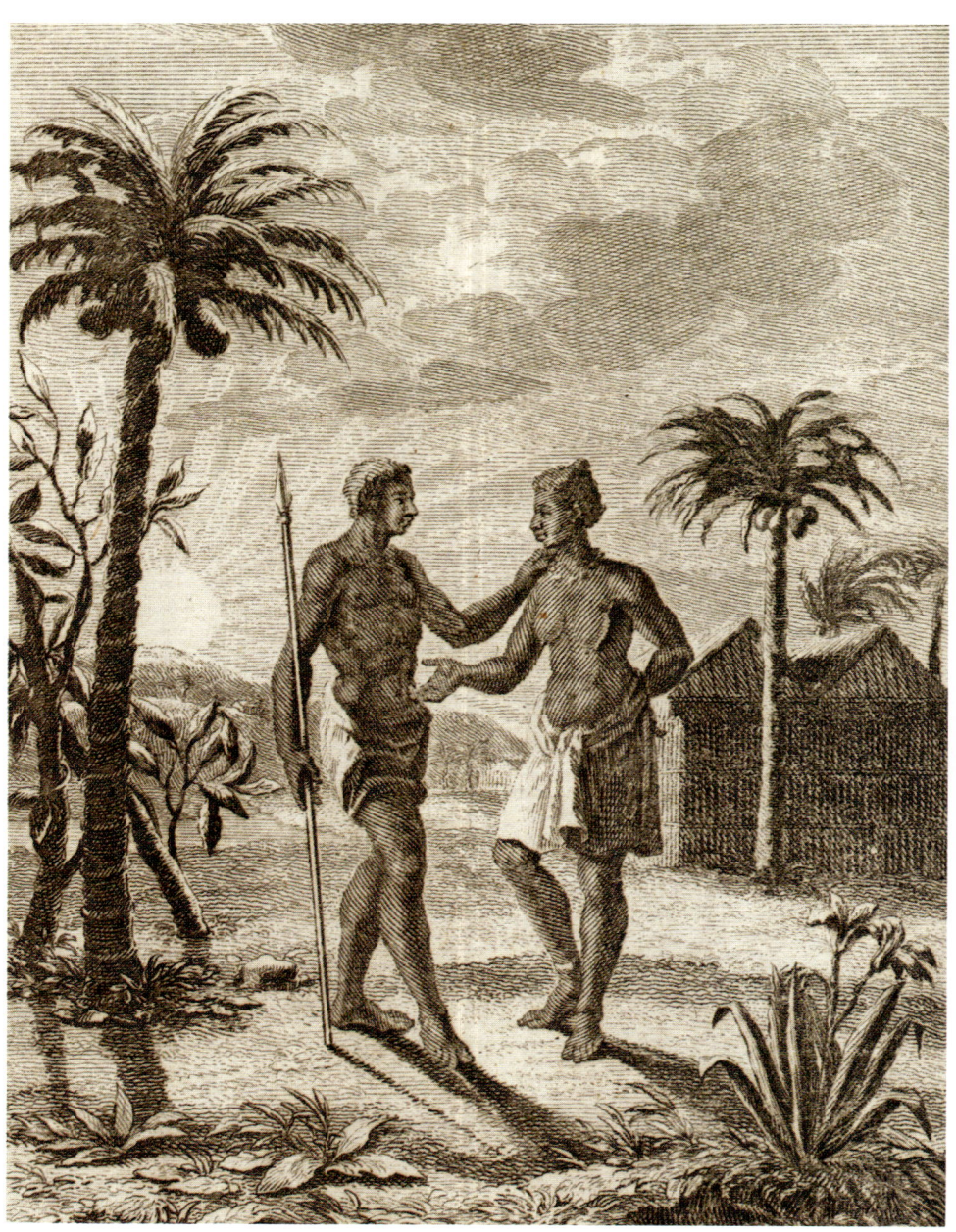

"YOU'RE NOT LEAVING"

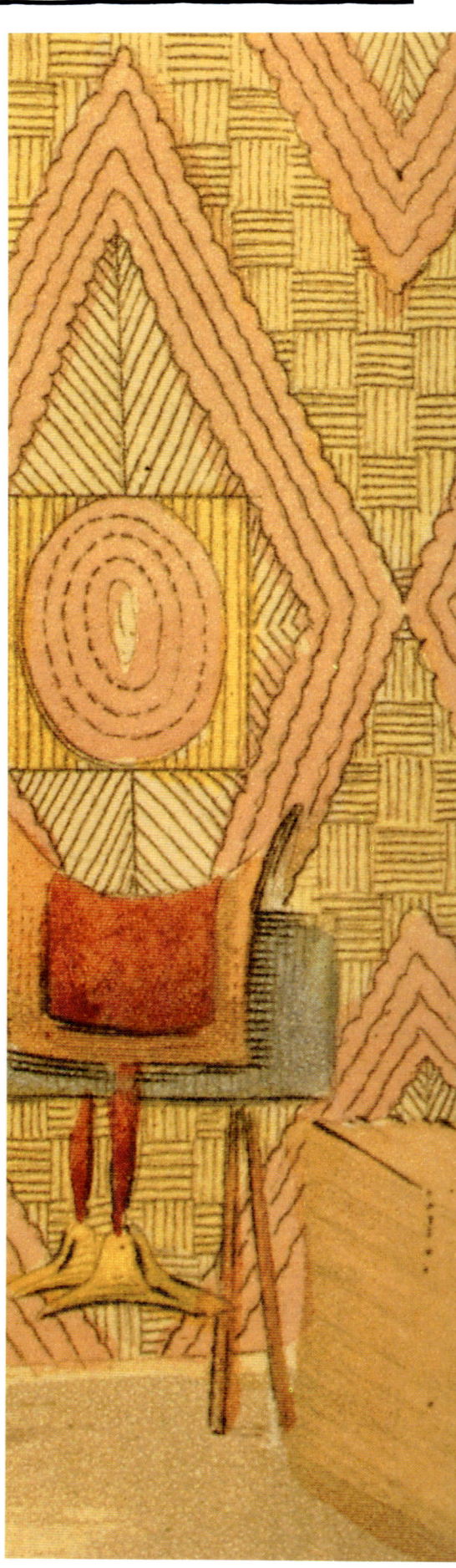

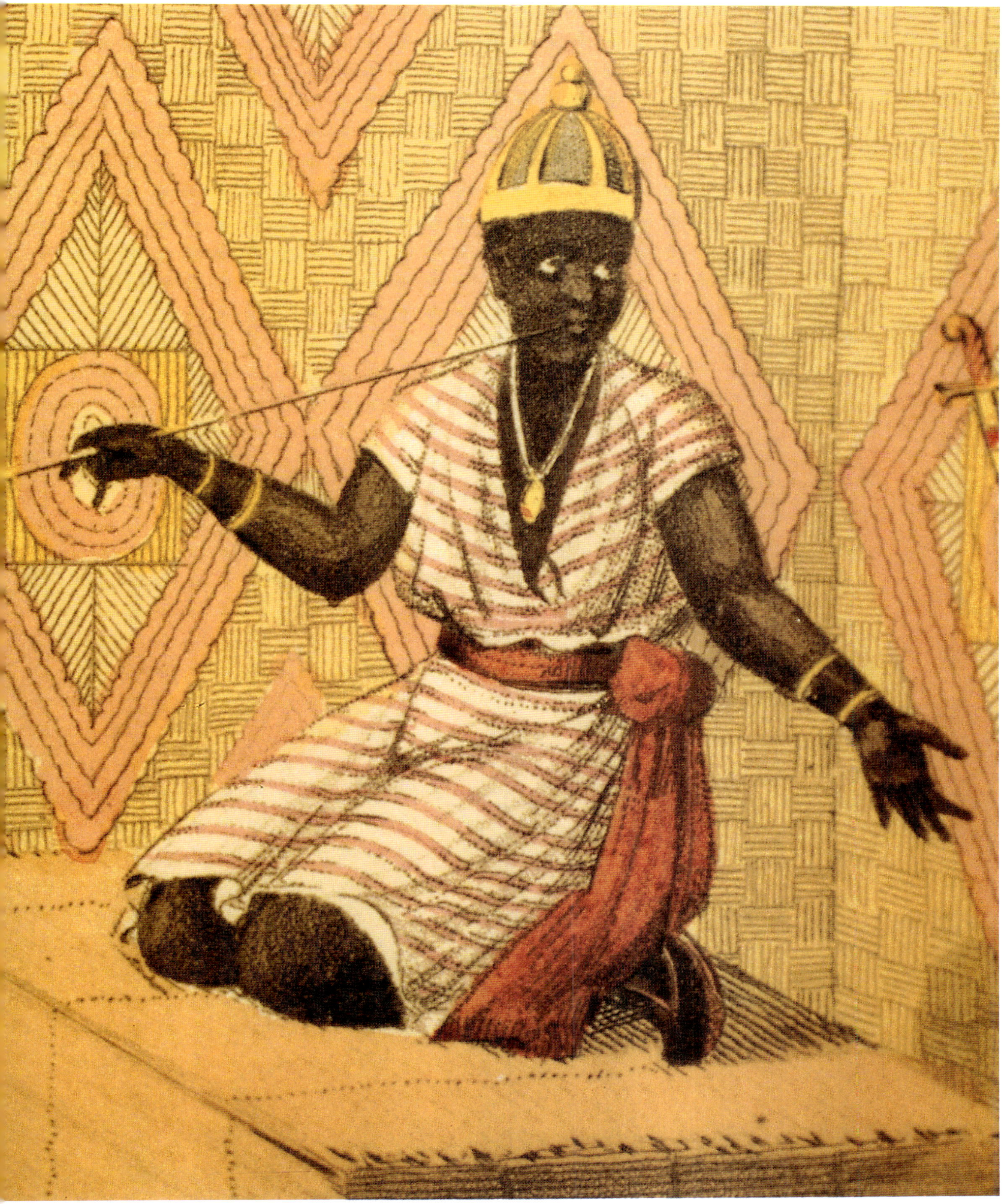

DAURAMA

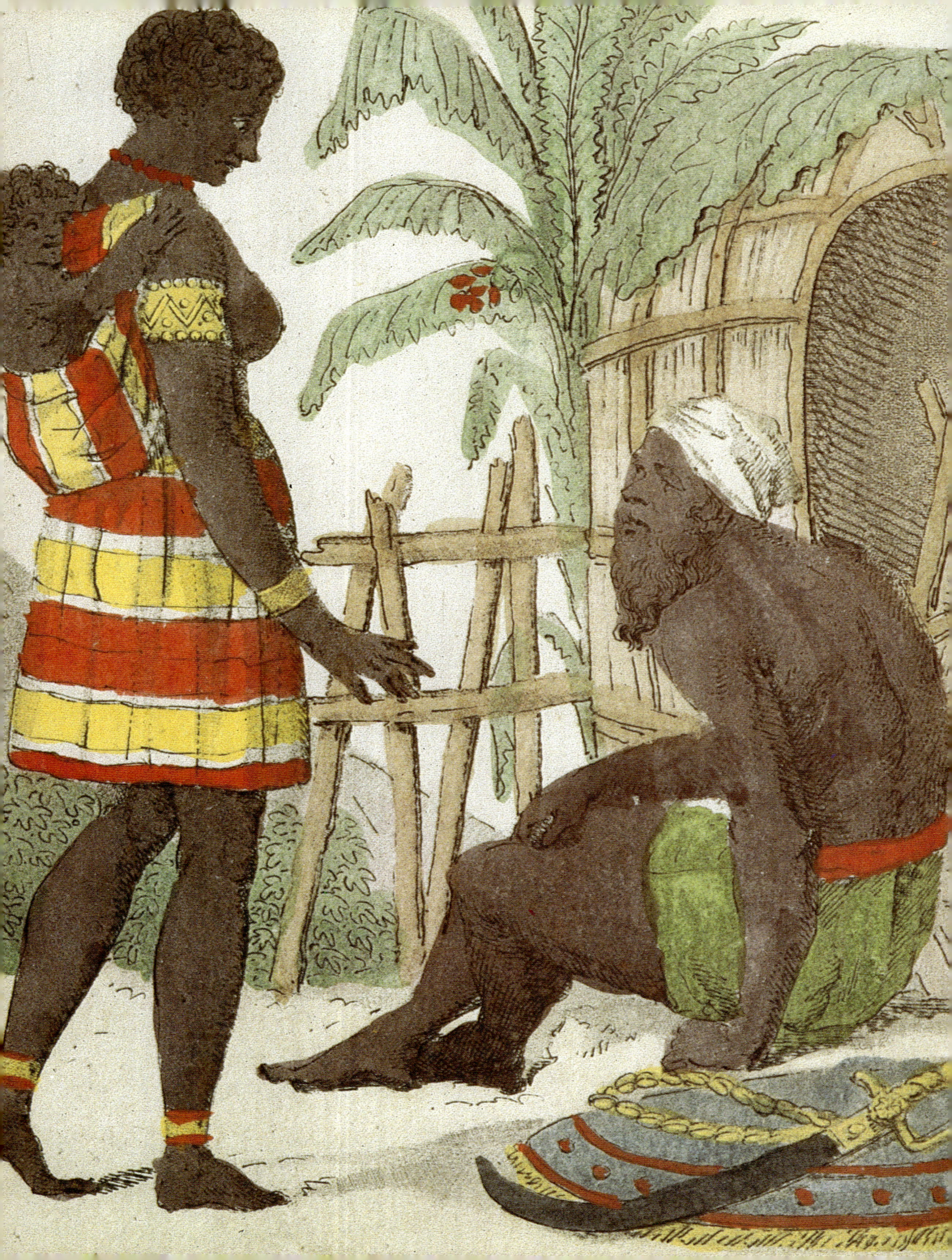

WORDS
OF AN ORDINARY WOMAN

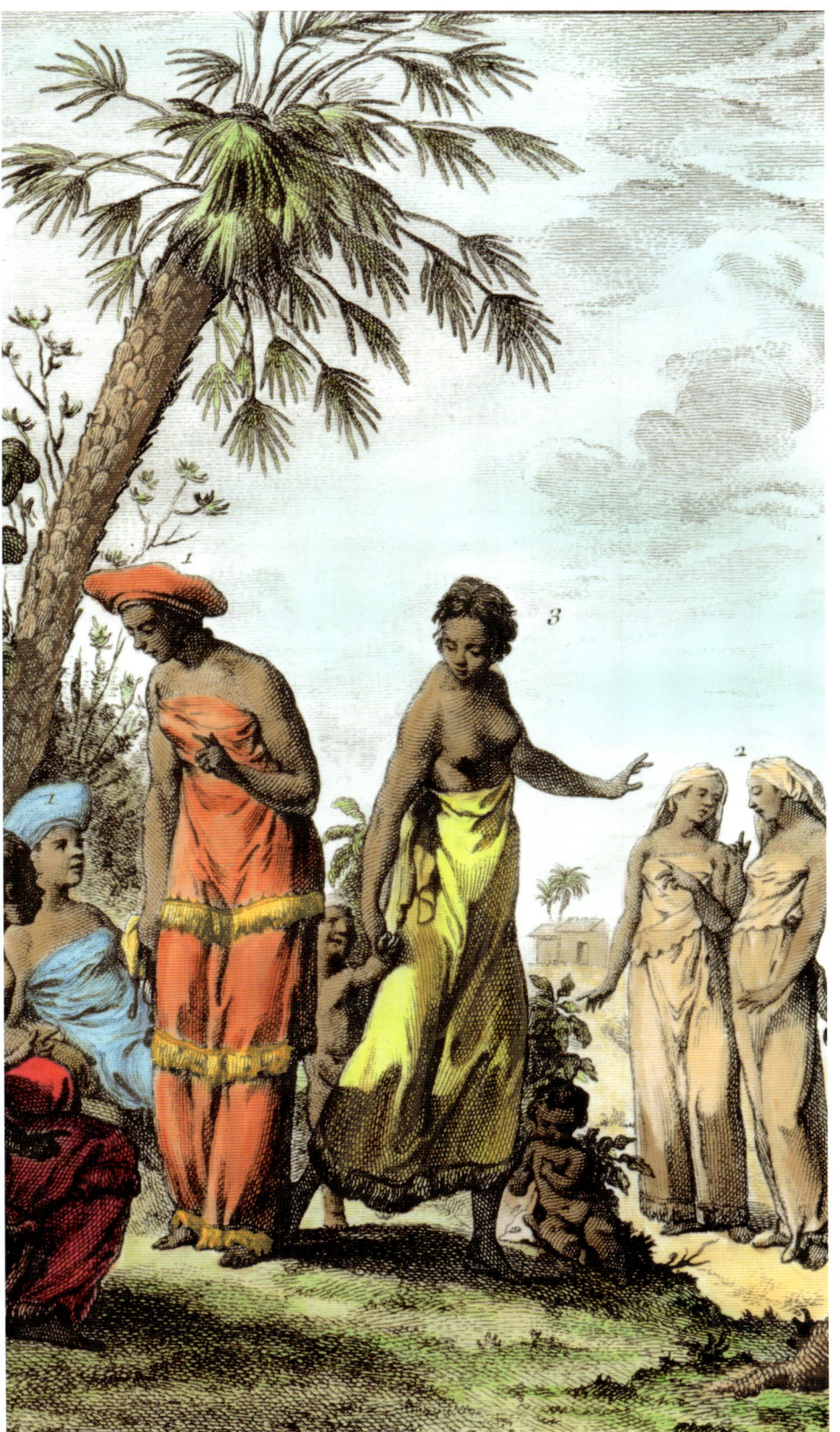

"BEAUTY WITHOUT TOGU IS USELESS"

To the heart also belongs the *togu*.

If people love you, value you, seek you, we say that this is due to your togu.

There are people everyone wants to be with, not because of their wealth but for their company. We say that this is due to the blood in them, the bones in them, the water that fills their whole body.

The togu is like a force. The lack of this force is a weakness.

The togu is linked neither to wealth nor to beauty. It's something else.

Beauty without togu is useless. What good is wealth without togu?

An encampment without togu is a settlement no one comes to, a settlement without hosts. The master of the settlement is there, in the midst of his herds, the food has been cooked, the gourds overflow with milk, but no one has come, no one has stopped by.

Togu is in the heart, in the blood. If someone has togu, we say, he has good blood with people, warm blood.

Togu is in the way one speaks. Whoever has togu has hungry words, and savory words.

Togu is worth more than beauty.

For us women, a man full of togu is worth more than a handsome man. And for men it's the same thing: they look for a charismatic, an attractive woman. They prefer her to a beautiful woman without togu.

Togu is happiness, because it grants love and the admiration of others. Togu always brings fruitfulness.

But togu, like all happiness, does not last. It doesn't stick around. It vanishes without leaving a trace. And its disappearance is final. In saying this we affirm that togu has no previous hosts. It disappears so completely that no one can tell where it lived before.

The happiness of a person is in her charm, in her togu.

Happy is the person who is admired and sought after.

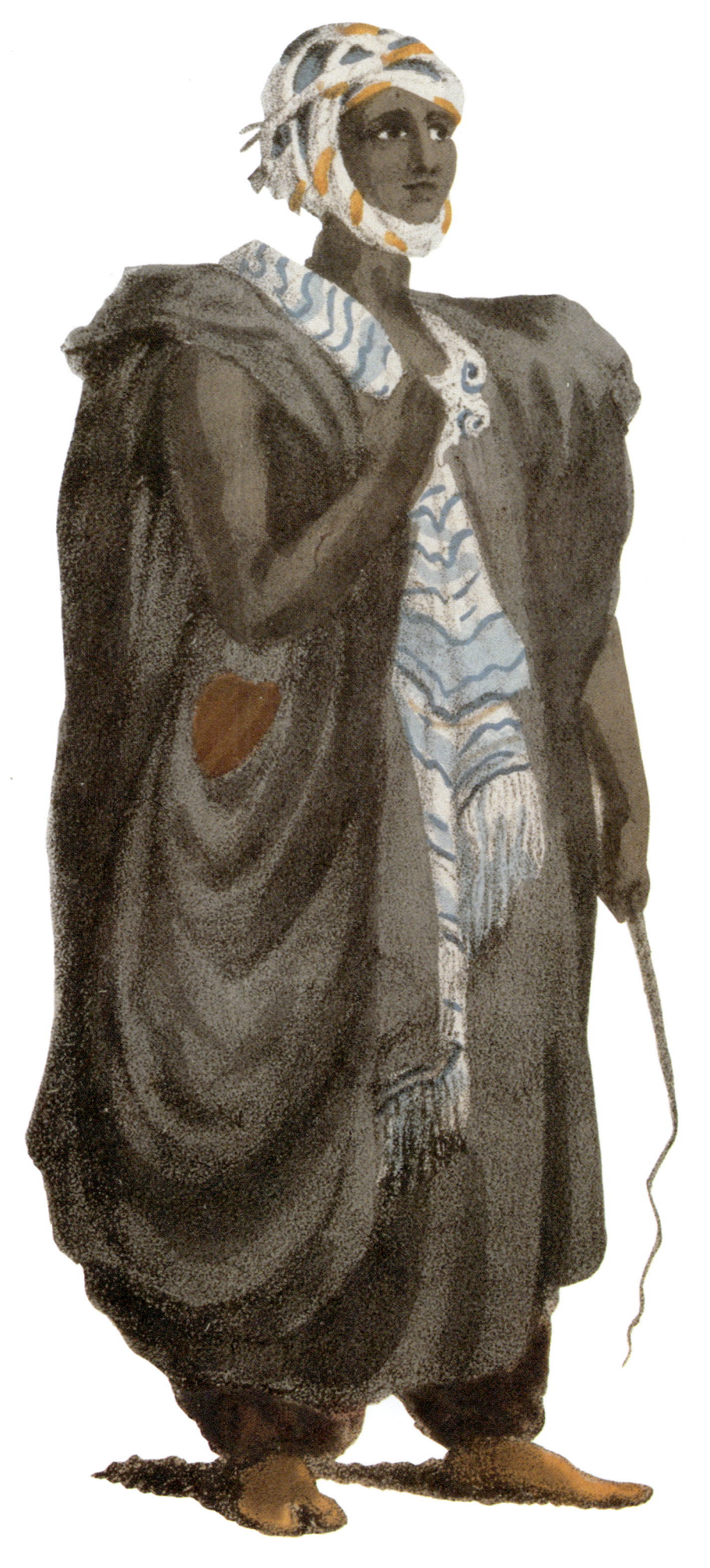

YENNENGA

MOTHER OF THE MOSSI PEOPLE

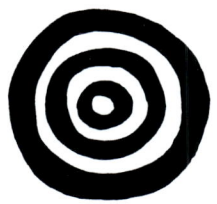

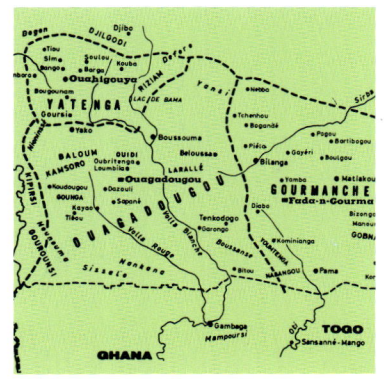

One night, Yennenga dressed up as a man and rode off on horseback from the paternal domain, accompanied by a large entourage of servants...

THE MOSSI KINGDOM IS ONE OF THE MOST ANCIENT IN AFRICA.

IT TRACES A GLORIOUS ARC IN TIME, FROM THE ELEVENTH CENTURY TO OUR OWN, IN WHICH THE MOSSI PEOPLE DISTINGUISHED THEMSELVES IN THE STRUGGLE AGAINST COLONIALISM. THE Mossi kingdom has known but a single dynasty, one ruling family: a hereditary chain in which no single link has ever been missing. Thus, thirty successive monarchs rose in the skies of Mossi, in perfect chronological order, from its foundation until today. The first of them was named Ouedraogo and he ruled until the year 1132: he was the son of the famous amazon, Yennenga the Svelte, who was truly the mother of the Mossi people, the prolific womb that started it all.

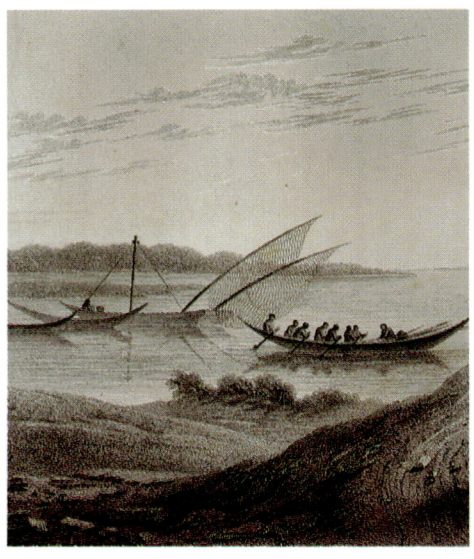

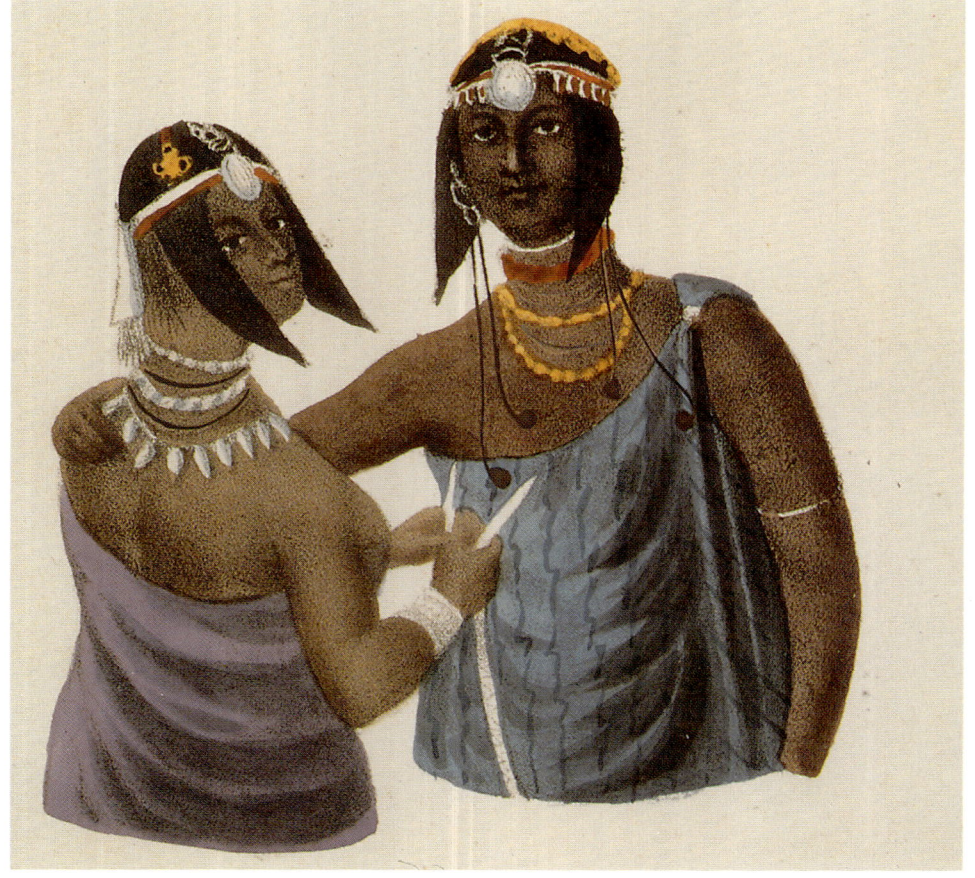

YOUNG WOMEN

IN THE MOSSI KINGDOM

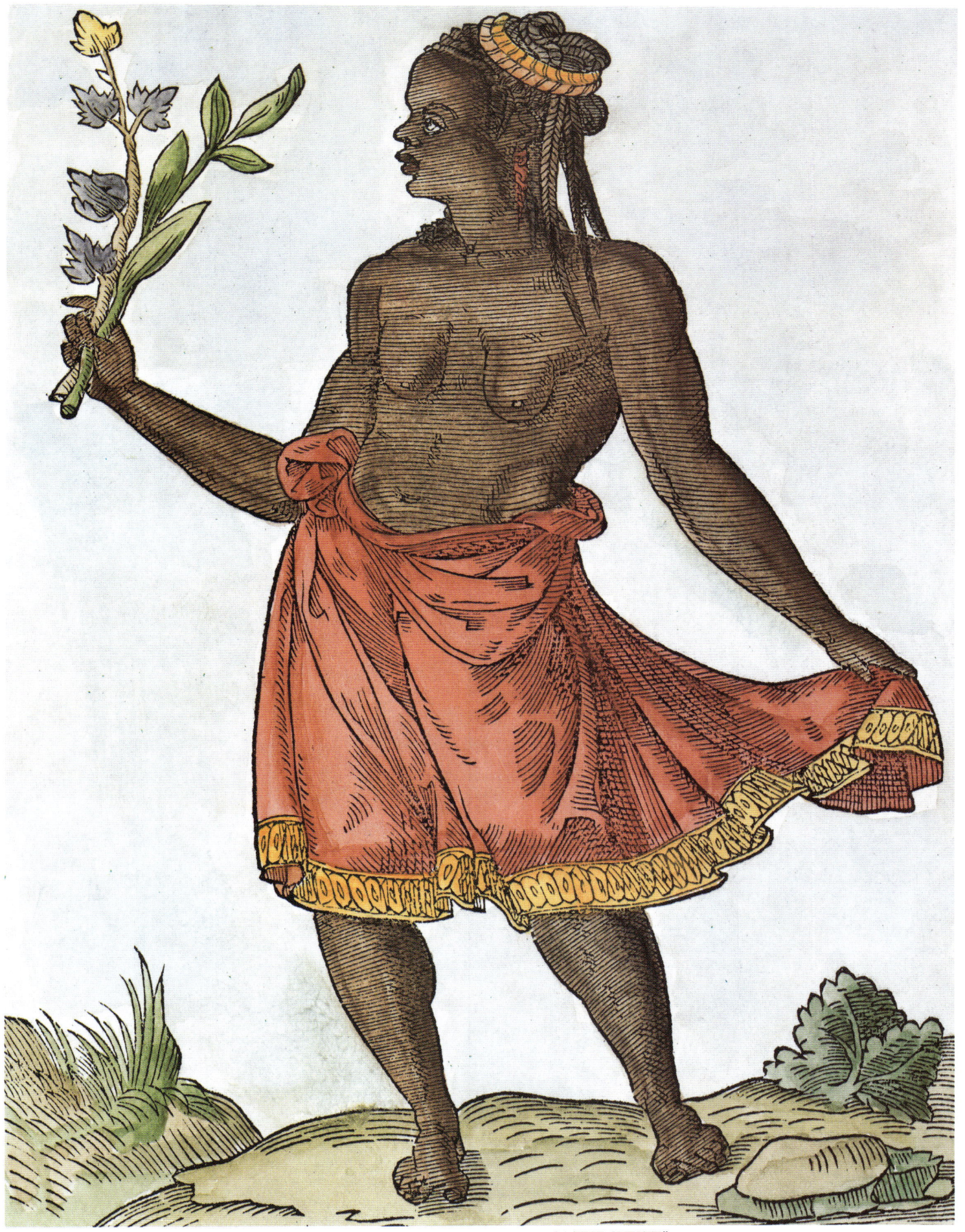

"THE FAMOUS AMAZON, YENNENGA THE SVELTE"

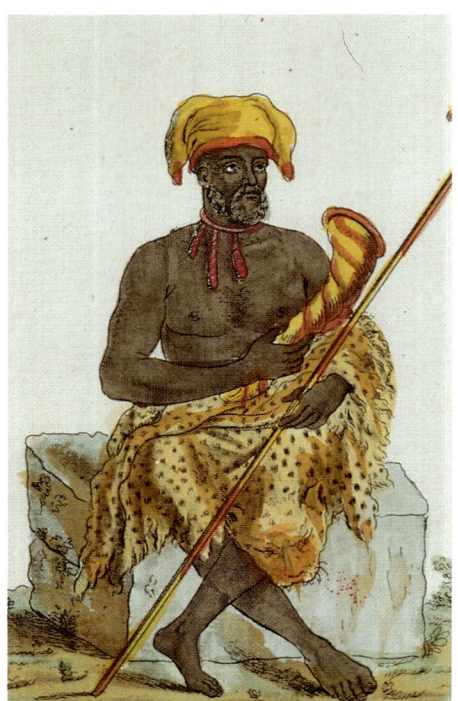

A KING NAMED MADEGA

Once upon a time, around the year 1100, to the north of present-day Ghana, there was a king by the name of Madega who was unusually attached to his daughter. His daughter was the only thing on his mind.

Yennenga was her name. And she was so beautiful that the praise singers compared her to an "open parasol," and a "gingerbread palm," trunk reaching toward the sky.

And she was so fearless in battle that they often described her as a lioness "with stubborn chin and flowing mane".

In the memory and honor of Yennenga and her bravery, the sons of the Mossi people never attack that particular beast.

The elephant, the buffalo, the panther, those are the traditional targets of Mossi hunters: they never go after the lion unless provoked.

As early as the age of fourteen, riding horseback, "her hair floating before the armies," Yennenga participates in the kingdom's war expeditions.

She has her own battalion and is put in charge of the royal guard; the king's granaries, his secret stores and reserves, overflow with the loot brought back by his daughter.

The Might of the Morho Naba

The power of the Morho Naba, of the "great lord," is absolute, total, unlimited. He alone possesses the power to wage war. At his beck and call, the vassals must come running with the full force of their infantry and cavalry; horsemen are the backbone of the Mossi. He alone anoints the chiefs of the provinces and grants fiefdoms to whomever he likes.

The Morho Naba collects an annual tax on the many kinds of agricultural products grown by his subjects. Moreover, the confiscated wealth of those condemned to death is legally his. As for big game, he reserves the right to collect elephant tusks and a quarter portion from each buffalo or koba killed near the capital. The Hausa merchants give him presents in exchange for the protection he grants their caravans.

Finally, the Morho Naba is the appeals judge for all cases brought before the lords. He alone can pronounce a death sentence, either against common criminals or nobles of royal blood. In the case of condemned lords or dignitaries, the Morho Naba supplies a white robe and a poisoned arrow with which the guilty person carries out justice himself, by pricking his own arm or leg.

The Morho Naba and His Ministers

At the height of the Mossi state, one chieftain, symbolizing the sun on earth, the Morho Naba, holds central power. Elected by an assembly of high dignitaries at the court and chosen from among the sons and brothers of the late Morho Naba, he is assisted by four powerful ministers, great feudal lords who partition the country among themselves.

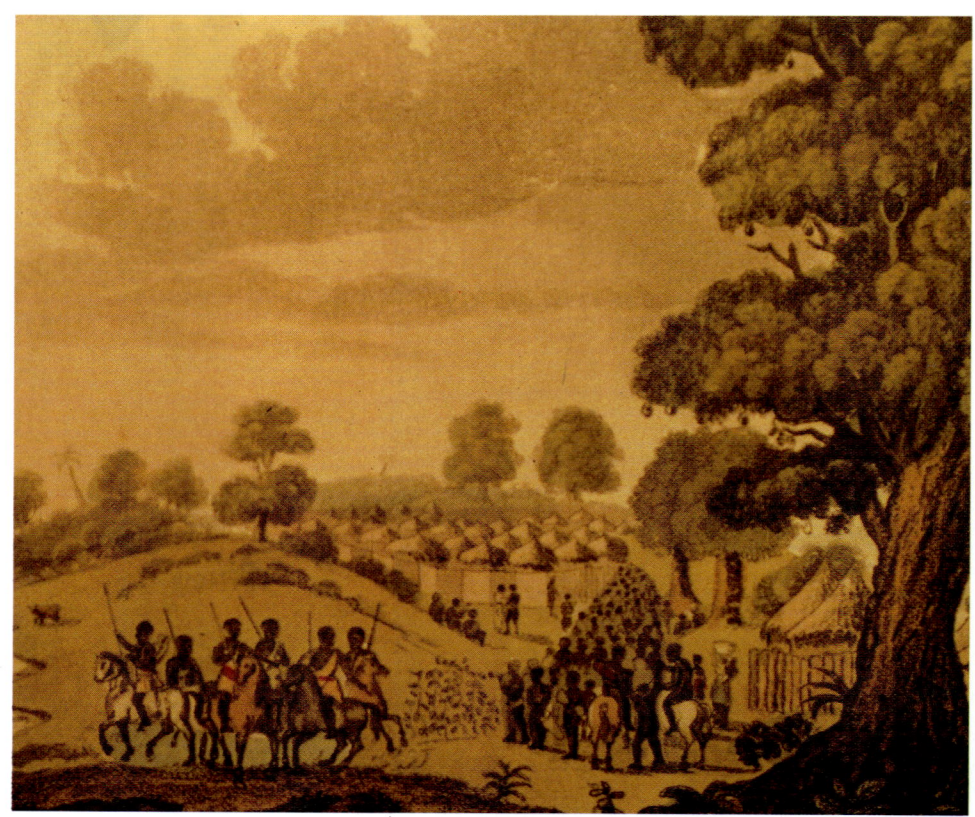

"YENNENGA TAKES PART IN WAR EXPEDITIONS"

YENNENGA

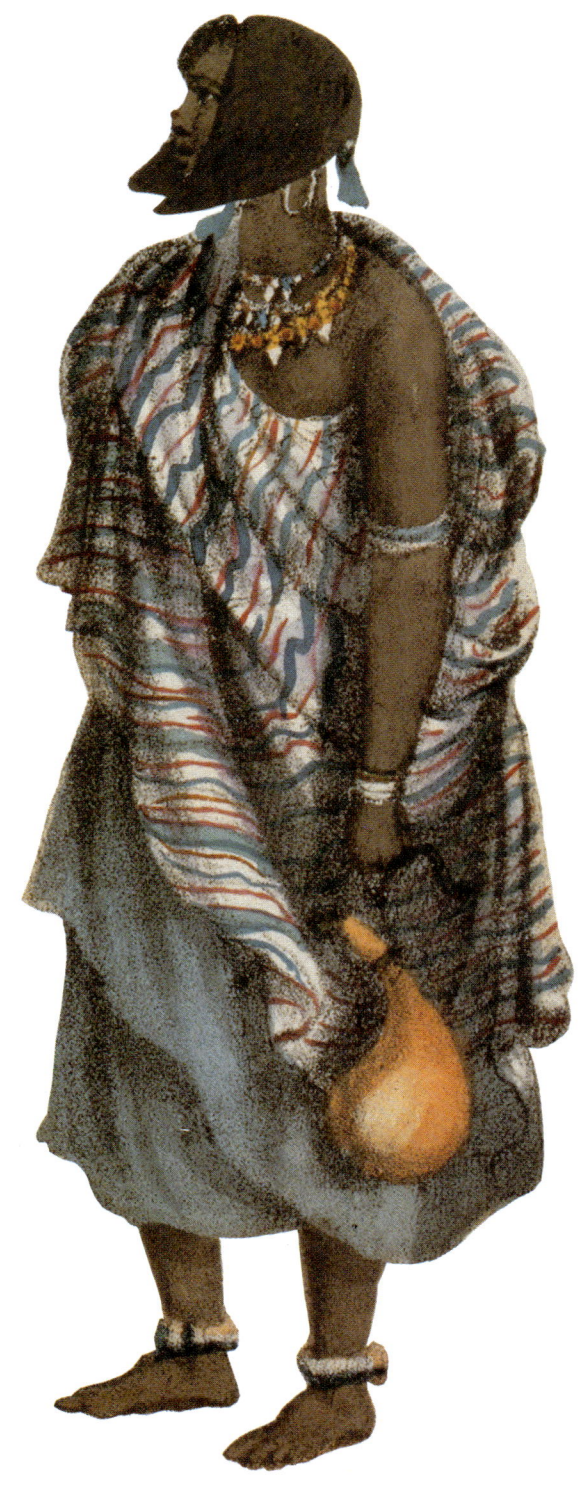

"SHE HAS HER OWN BATTALION AND IS PUT IN CHARGE OF THE ROYAL GUARD"

The Good Fortune and Stability of the Mossi Empires

Although these empires never acquired the renown of those such as Ghana, Gao, and Mali, they were in reality stronger, more homogeneous, and more lasting. Surrounded by kingdoms whose ephemeral peaks were always soon followed by progressive dismemberment or a quick end, the Mossi empires lasted nine centuries without any significant change in either their borders or their internal organization. While the history of the Sudanese people is full of palace revolutions, the present-day rulers of Wagadugu, of Yatenga, trace their genealogy to Ouedraogo and thereby provide the rare example of power having been preserved within the same family for about nine hundred years.

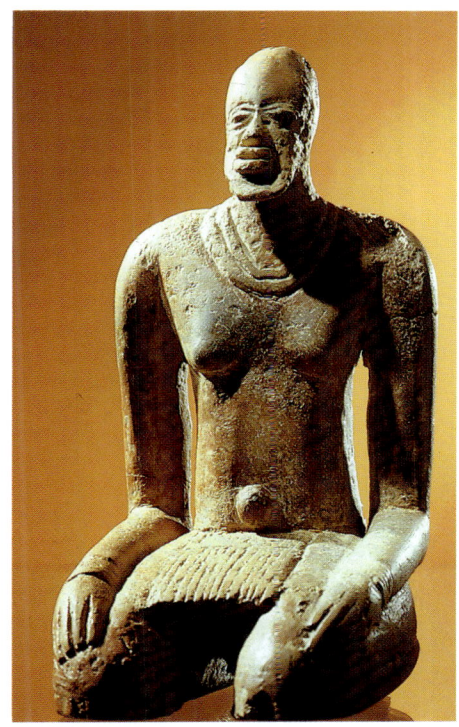

None of these empires have made names for themselves through great extra-territorial conquests. Nor has any one of them ever been a foreign vassal; the integrity of the Mossi states has never been seriously compromised. They've never suffered a true defeat, while they routed such foes as the emperors of Mali, Gao, and Ségou, and the Moroccan pashas of Timbuktu.

Such fortune has had several consequences: first of all, the high population density of the Mossi empires. Second, it must be said that, although the Mossi and Gurma states contained a diverse populace, each formed an ethnically homogeneous whole. Finally, a highly organized national religion, based for the most part on the cult of ancestors, ruled the most minute details of private and public life.

106

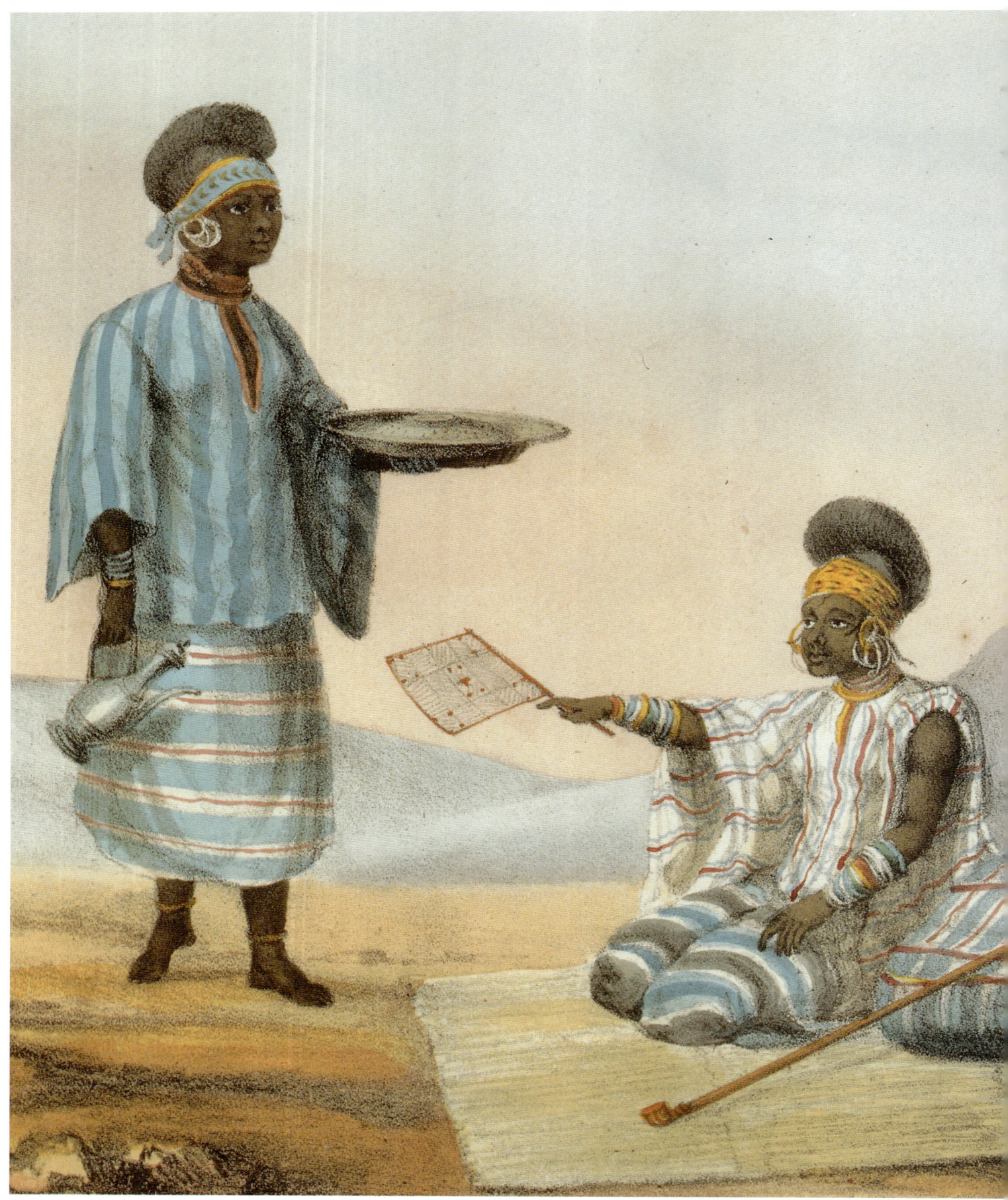

"BUT LITTLE BY LITTLE, A WOMAN AWAKENS UNDERNEATH THE

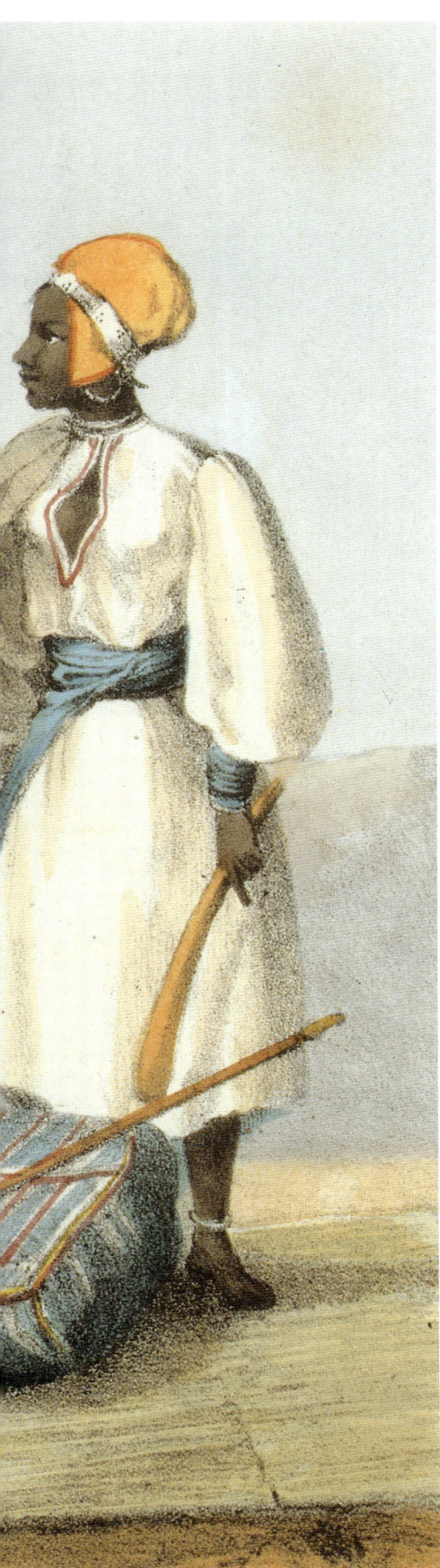

AMAZON'S BREASTPLATE

But little by little, a woman awakens underneath the amazon's breastplate. Yennenga braids her hair around her head and lets her father know that her time for marriage has come: "I want to hear a child laugh," she says simply, using the traditional phrase.

King Madega regularly turned away Yennenga's many suitors, never finding any of them worthy of his daughter. They were either too small, too big, too thin, too fat, even too wise or too crazy. People started to wonder why they were always "too" something and why every suitor seemed repulsive to the king.

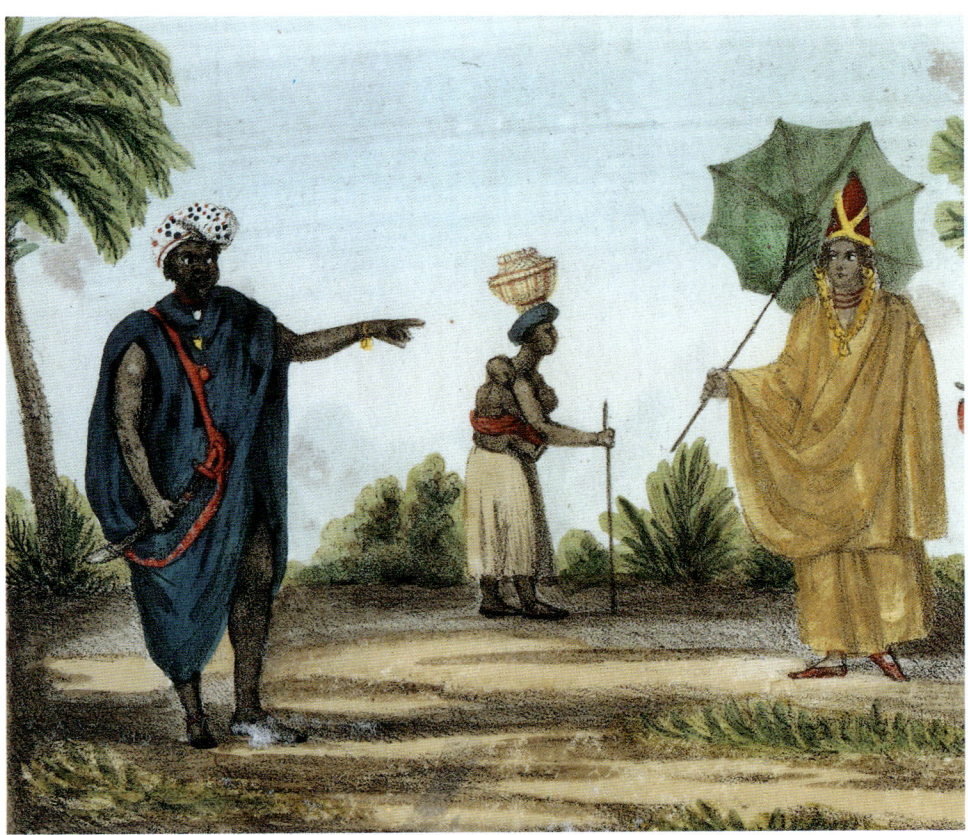

"MANY WERE YENNENGA'S SUITORS"

In the end, Yennenga decided to teach her father a lesson. She had a large field around her quarters planted with okra and let the pods wither on the plants, carefully instructing her servants not to pick a single one. The king suspected a ruse, so he tried not to say anything. But in the end, he wasn't able to keep quiet and asked:

"Why do you let your okra grow old like that?"

"Oh really," replied Yennenga, "so you think I'm letting my okra grow old! And what do you say of a grown daughter like me without husband?"

The Origins of Prince Riale, Yennenga's Husband

When the Malinké Riale left Mali, he had already had a son by the name of Lombo from his first marriage. When his father was alive, Riale was a rugged and intrepid warrior whose reputation made others respect the borders of his father's states.

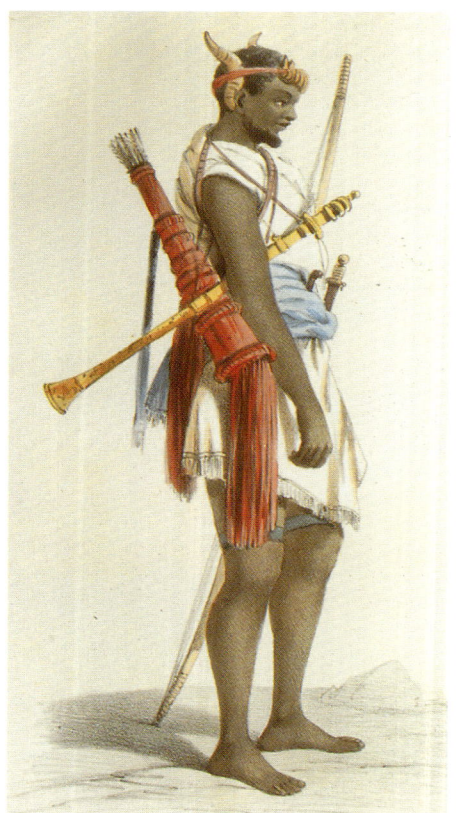

Such a man made many others jealous and envious. The father died, leaving Riale and his older brother to succeed him. The custom forbade Riale, the younger son, to claim the throne, despite his popularity. Another version of the story includes a seer who predicted that Riale would destroy his brother were the two ever to live together. So Riale had to choose exile or fratricide. Faced with such a bitter fate, Riale, out of spite, chose to live alone in the forest far away from Mali, to hunt elephants. Not wanting to expose his son Lombo, still too young, to the worst of the dangers he was about to face, he entrusted him to his brother, thus leaving his boy behind on paternal soil.

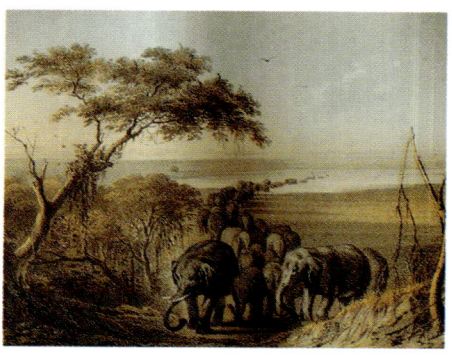

One night, Yennenga dressed up as a man and rode off on horseback from the paternal domain, accompanied by a large entourage of servants. The journey lasted three weeks. Anger kept Yennenga awake, and fear of the king's armies gave wings to her servants. One day, they arrived in an unknown region peopled by the Bousancé and protected by a huge forest. In the middle of a clearing there appeared a hunter's hut, and Yennenga suddenly felt tired. A man stood at the entrance of the hut, holding in his hand a bow, which he lowered as a sign of welcome. Taking her for a man, a high lord accompanied by an entourage, the stranger begged her to honor him by accepting the hospitality of his humble abode.

The name of this strange young man was Riale, and he lived far away from the world as a solitary elephant hunter. He was running away not from a living father, as was Yennenga, but from the ghost of a dead father, king of the Mandé, dethroned and murdered by his own people. He invited the handsome lord into his house, offered him food and a bed, and spoke to him as hunter to hunter, as if both of them had always chased elephants.

As for Yennenga, she did not uncover herself at all, keeping even her hair tucked inside her helmet. But on the third day, as she made a sudden movement, the helmet slipped, a cascade of hair fell on her face, and the game was up.

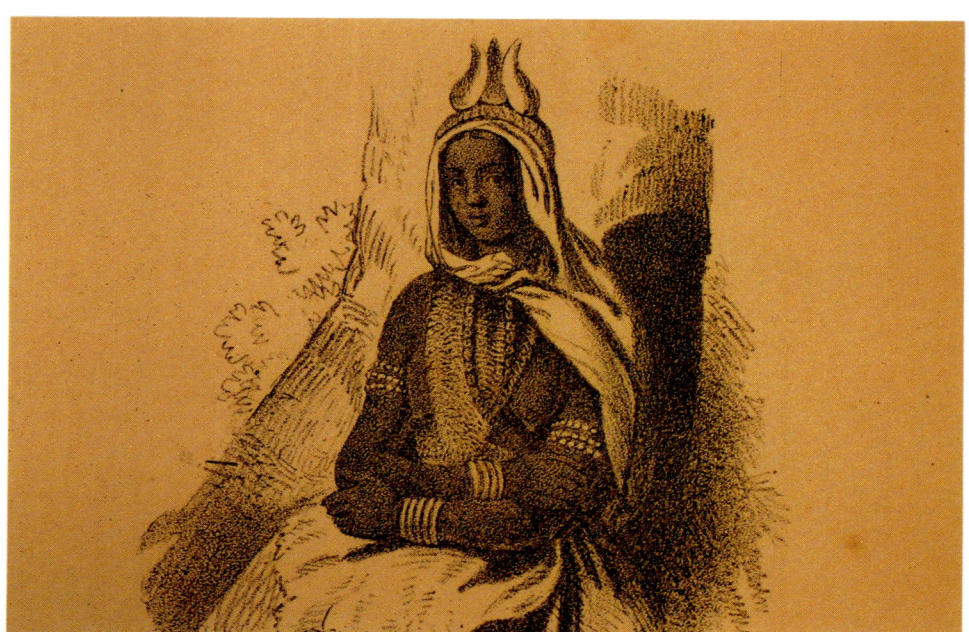

Yennenga had been dreaming of a child's laughter for a while: a boy was soon born of their union. They named him Ouedraogo, Stallion, in memory of the wild horse ride that had carried the young woman to her fate.

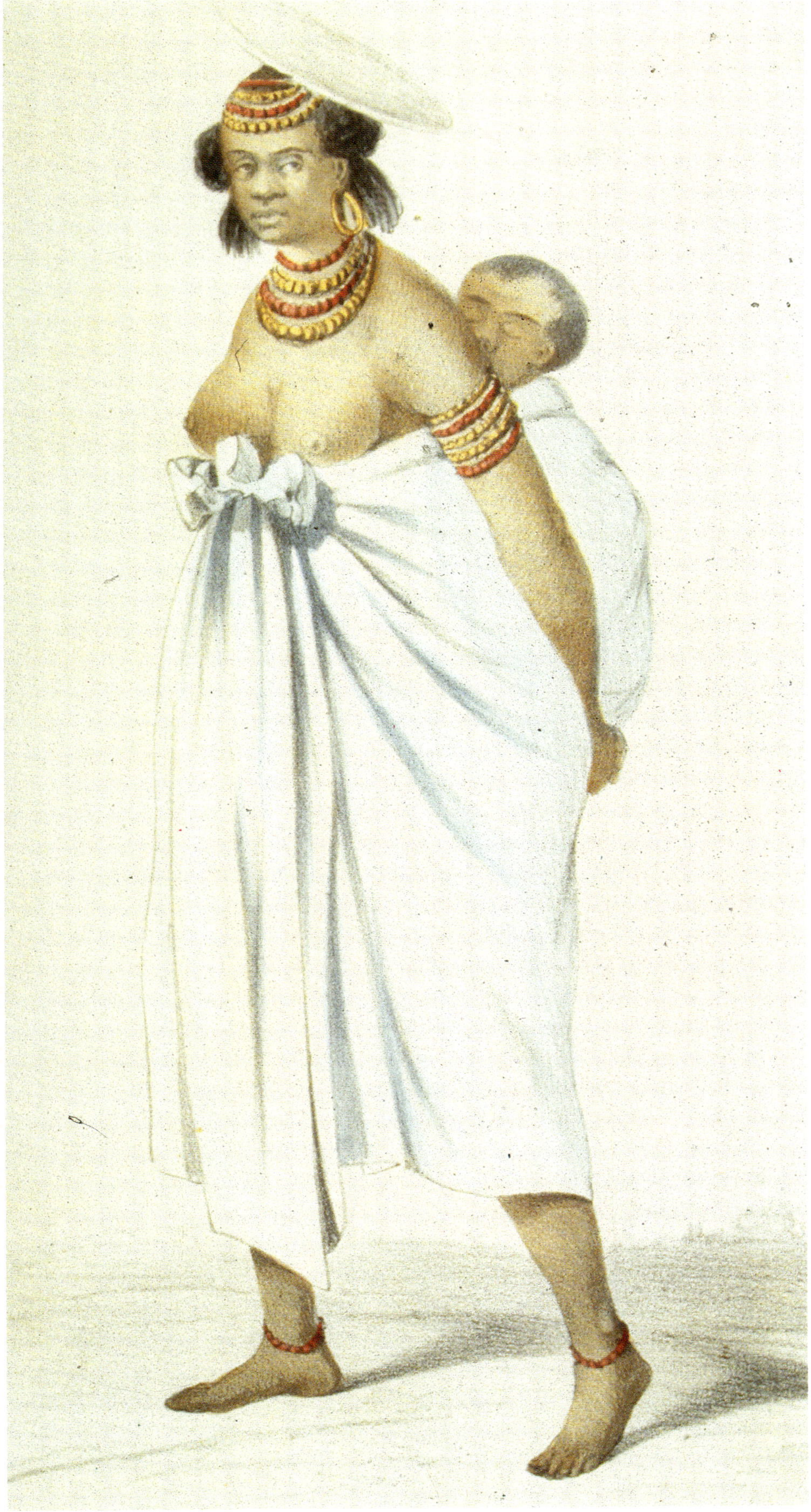

"A BOY WAS BORN OF THEIR UNION"

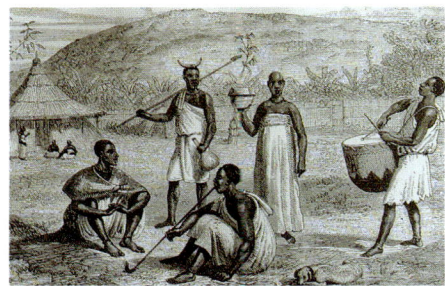

Tinsé

The custom of Tinsé goes back to the time of the Naba Oubri. His mother, Pougtoega, had an extraordinary reputation, because, so the legend goes, she wore a beard like a man. She was a wise counselor for a son over whom she had great influence. She paid special attention to children. She left behind the memory of being a great benefactress whose good deeds outlived her death. She was considered the mother of all. When she died, she was given a most lavish funeral.

This took place toward the beginning of the rainy season, probably in the month of May. There was a great downpour the day of the funeral. The rains delayed the planting, but the millet harvest would be abundant that year. The following year, there was no memorial ceremony, the rain did not fall, and the millet harvest was bad. The peasants were able to survive thanks to the reserves accumulated in the preceding year. After that, the situation got worse, and the idea of re-enacting the funeral of the mother of Naba Oubri came to everyone's mind. And so it was done. The rain fell abundantly and the millet harvest was excellent. Thus it became a tradition and there was famine no more.

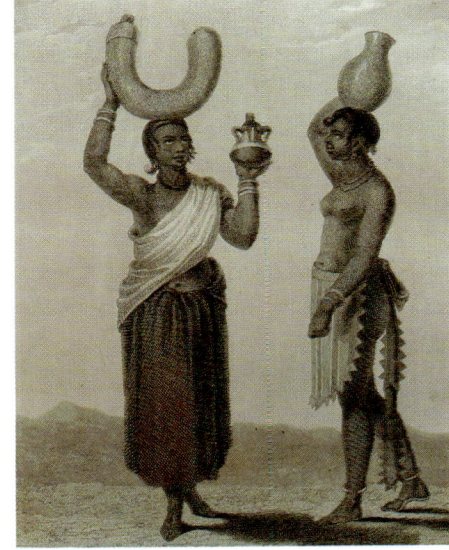

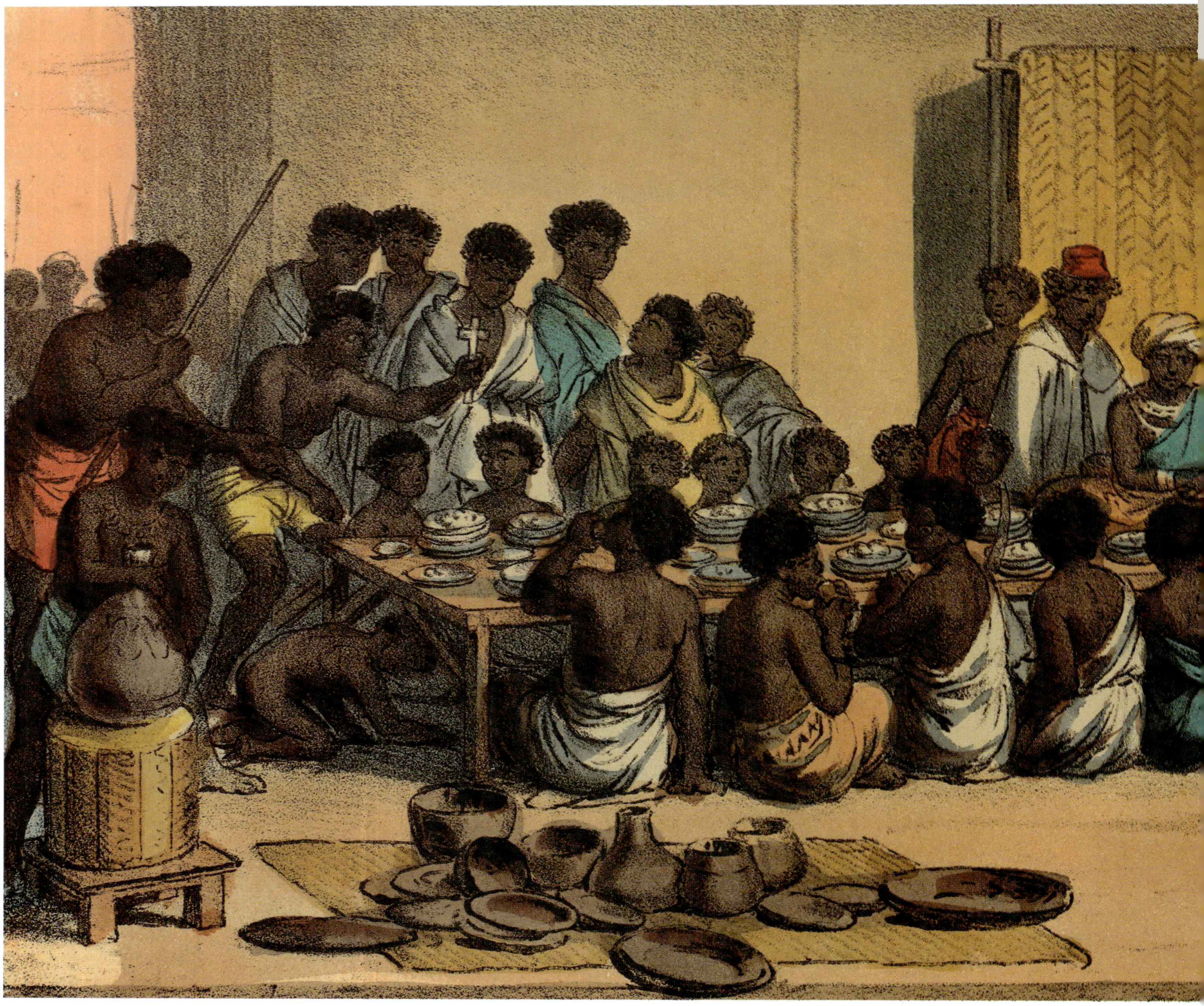

"YENNENGA TOOK HER SON TO VISIT HER FATHER"

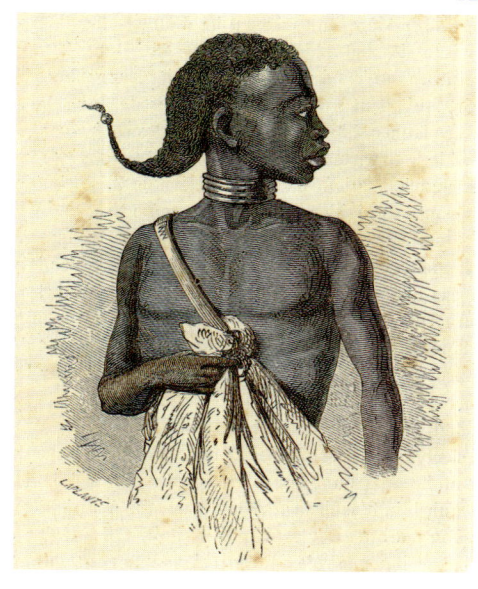

"WHEN HE WAS SEVENTEEN"

When her son reached the age of seventeen, old enough to give life, to mete out and receive death, Yennenga took him to visit King Madega so that no one could say that the young man was without ancestors.

Despite the years that had gone by, Yennenga still feared her father's wrath and wondered if that trip would not be her last. But the king had reflected on much since the night of her departure: he received Yennenga as a father receives his visiting daughter and when the moment came, he did nothing to stop her from returning home.

The king had never smiled since Yennenga's flight twenty years earlier: during Yennenga's stay at court, her servants heard her sing three times during her morning bath, and the news spread throughout the whole kingdom.

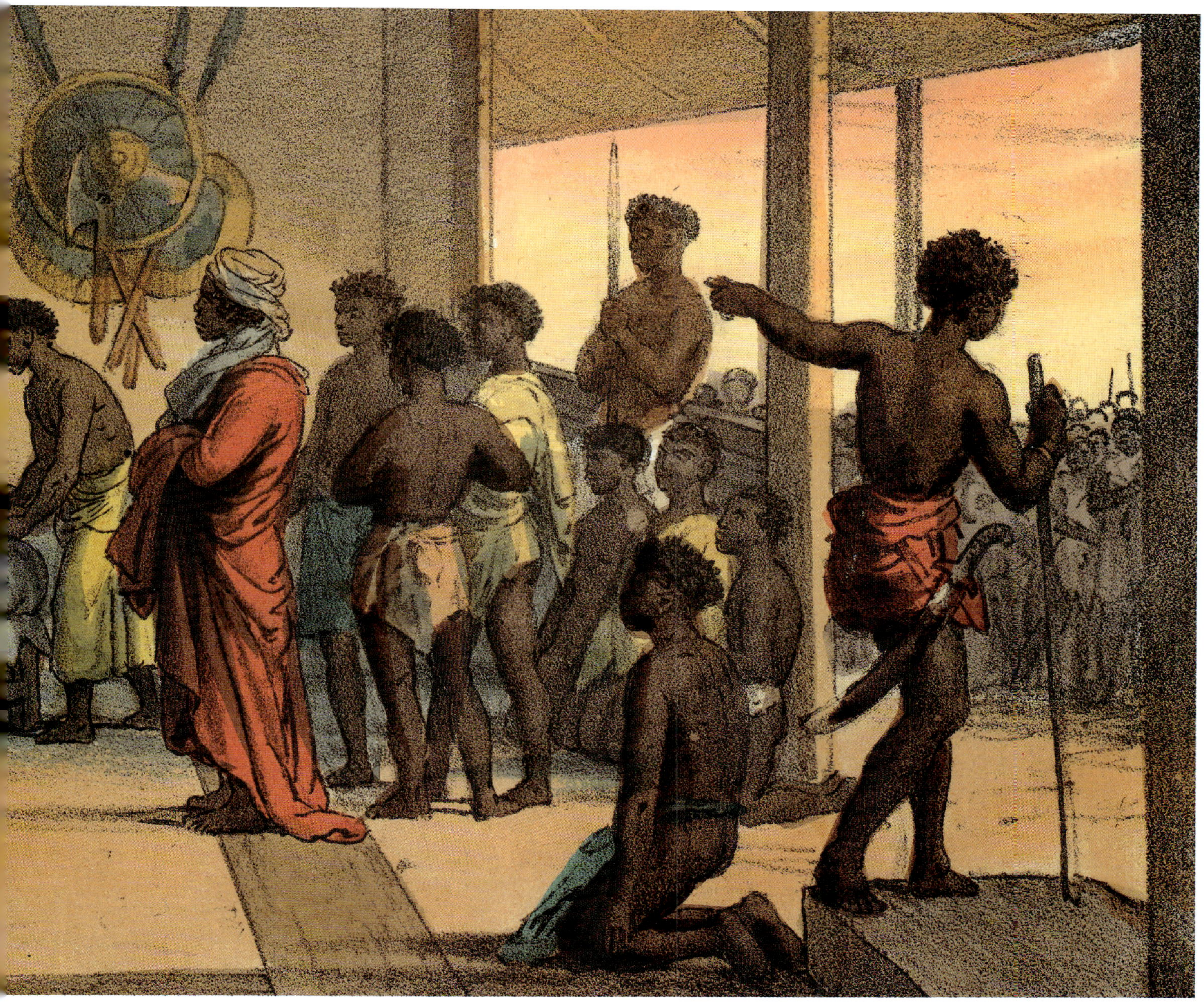

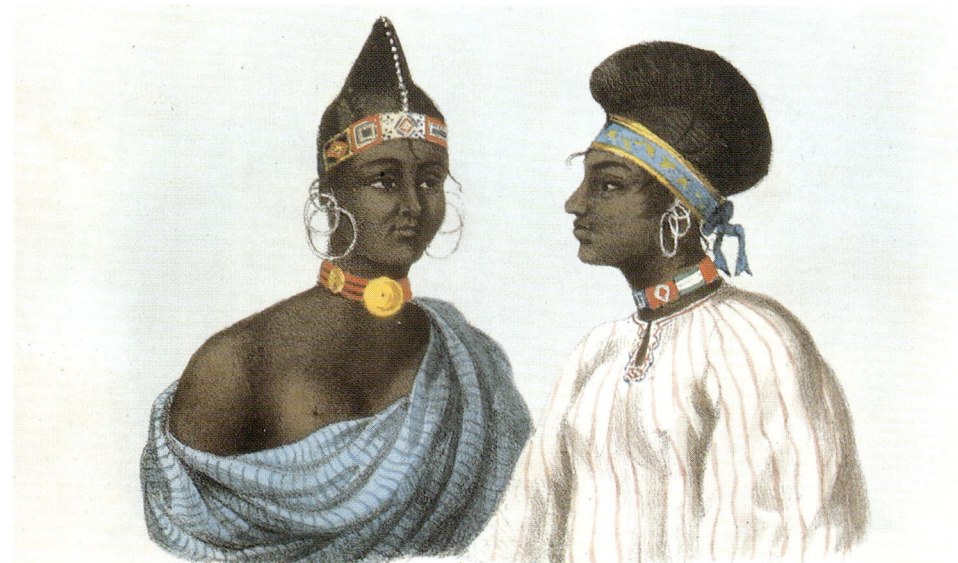

The Family and Entourage of the Morho Naba

The ruler has at his command a great number of women who are not locked up in a harem but whose faithfulness is controlled yearly by the Pouy Naba.

The pages, or "sorhoné", are constantly standing by to fulfill his least desire: they are young handsome males 8 to 16 years old. They bring the ruler his drink and carry his pillow, mat, parasol and sword. They arrange his stirrups when he rides horses, they announce the guests. They wear the same hairstyle and jewelry as the women: large copper bracelets on their ankles and wrists. The stable boys take care of the Morho Naba's horses, and his guards are in charge of palace security. Finally, musicians, drummers and violin players, singers, and minstrels are part of the royal entourage, as in most courts in traditional Africa.

THE ENTOURAGE OF THE MORHO NABA

Dori, the Capital of Liptako

The old traditions say that the north of Upper Volta was once occupied by the Deforobe, cousins of the Dogon people.

In the glorious days of Gao, these people were dominated by the Askia dynasty, who placed Songhai governors over them. When Gao fell beneath the blows of the Moroccans, the Deforobe got their independence back, as did most of the peoples of that immense empire. But at the same time, the Fulanis arrived in great numbers, with all their herds. These Fulanis felt so strong that they called themselves "Liptako," which means "the unconquerable," people that can't be pinned to the ground! So the Deforobe were obliged to leave them alone. Perhaps they even let them handle their herds. A century later, around 1700, the Gurma came from the south and attacked the country. The Deforobe were forced to retreat northwest, toward Aribinda. The Fulanis, on the other hand, didn't budge. But for about a hundred years, both peoples fell under the power of the Gurma.

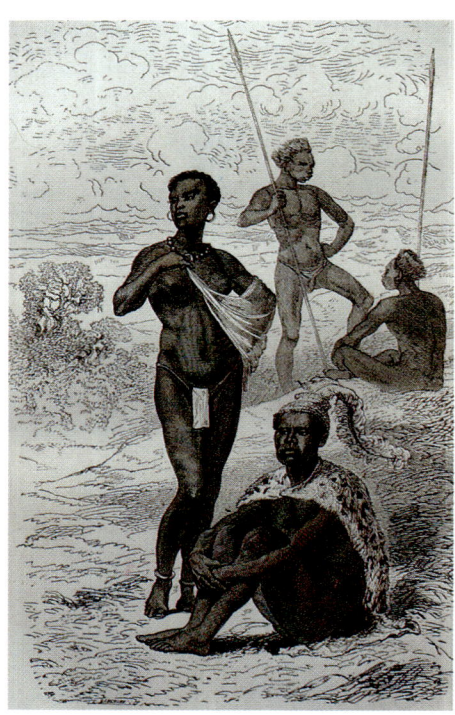

Proverb

"If a little tree is growing on top of a baobab it will die a little tree."

Fable

A merchant came to show his fabrics to a woman. She admired his wares but refused to buy any.

The merchant insisted and the woman said: *"The hawk may want the goat but does not have the strength to catch it."*

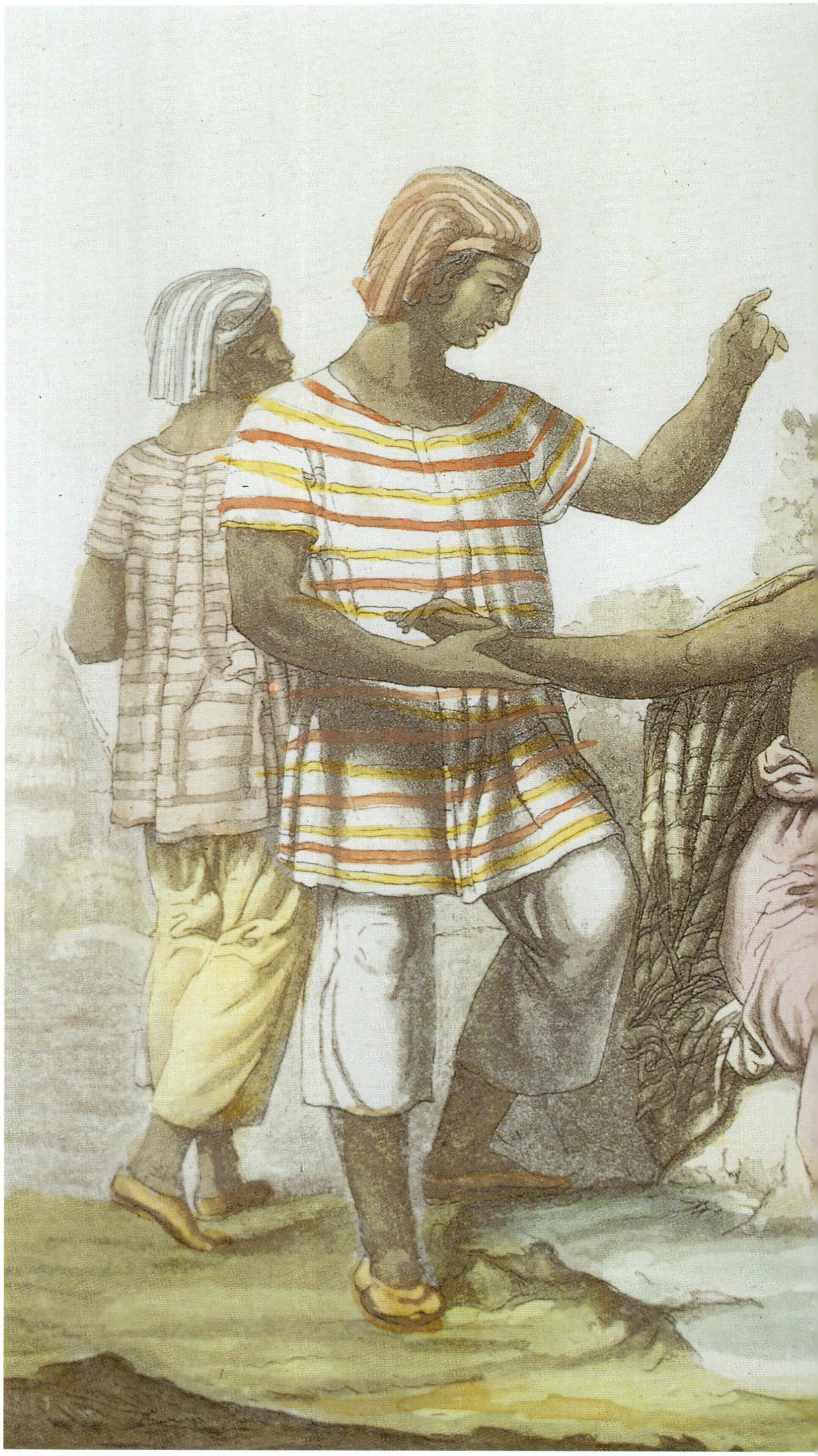

YENNENGA

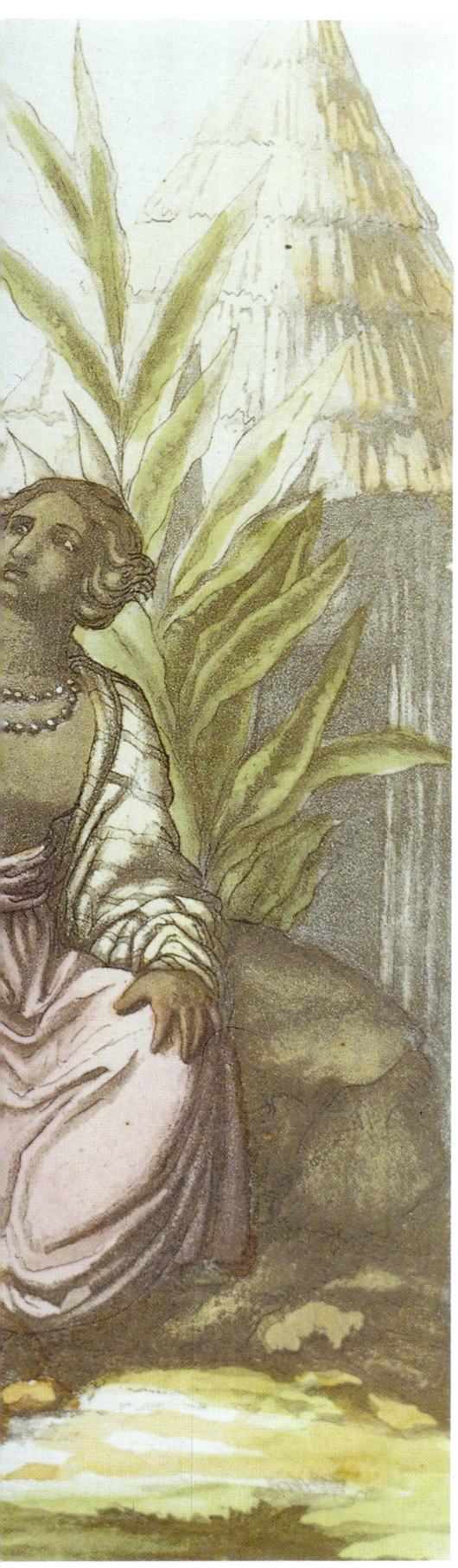

Ouedraogo remained at court after the departure of his mother, and there he deepened his knowledge of the world.

King Madega taught him a thousand and three things. The thousand things are known by all kings on earth. The three other things are: to see beauty in the world and say that it is ugly; to get up in the morning and do what you cannot do; and finally to give free rein to your dreams, because whoever dreams too much becomes a victim of his dreams.

When he came of age and the dough of his being had been sufficiently kneaded, rolled right and left, and baked like a sorghum biscuit, Ouedraogo asked for permission to leave.

Madega, in reply, granted him the succession to the crown. But the young man declared that he wanted to carve out his own kingdom, and the king smiled: "No one can stop the stallion in his course."

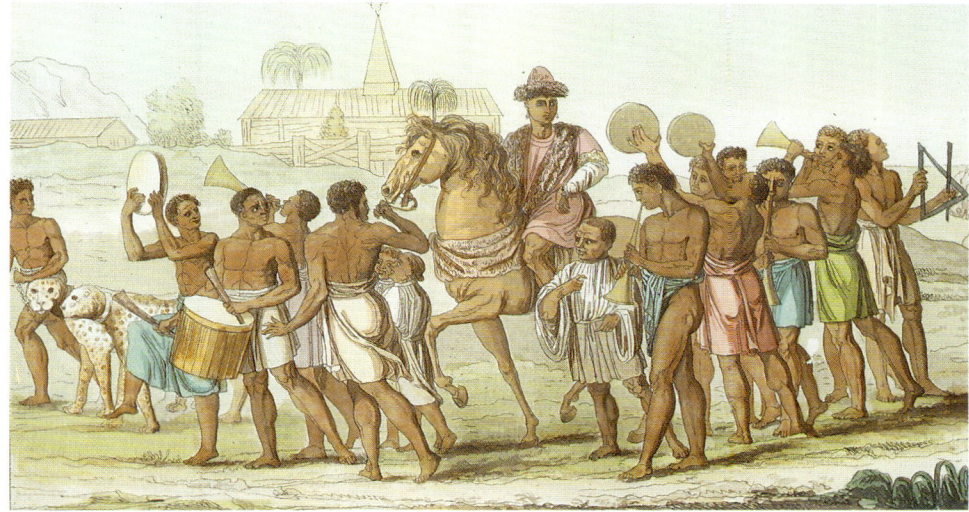

Finally, the king gave Ouedraogo two hundred men-at-arms and the young man left for the country of the Bousancé, in order to pay his respects, one last time, to his mother, his father, and the trees of the great forest. Then, he rode off at the head of his army and galloped north, where he founded the first Mossi kingdom, the father-kingdom, as the tradition goes, in the place now called Tenkodogo.

The children of Tenkodogo are: the kingdom of Zandoma, founded by Rawa, the eldest son of Ouedraogo, which later became the kingdom of Yatenga; the kingdom of Oubritenga, Oubri's land, which later became Wagadugu, as we still know it today; and finally the kingdom of Fada-n-Gurma, Diala-Lompo's land, which won its independence very early on but still recognizes itself as son to the father-kingdom of Tenkodogo, the trunk, the stock, the immortal tree born of the amazon Yennenga.

Here is the list of the Mossi kings, the Morho Naba, such as it was inscribed in the book of the praise singers, engraved as in marble:

Morho Naba Ouedraogo, founder of the Mossi kingdom

Morho Naba Zoungrana, who ruled from 1132 to 1182

Morho Naba Oubri, who ruled from 1182 to 1244

Morho Naba Naskiemde, who ruled from 1244 to 1286

Morho Naba Nasbire, who ruled from 1286 to 1307

Morho Naba Soarba, who ruled from 1307 to 1323

Morho Naba Gnignemdo, who ruled from 1323 to 1337

Morho Naba Koumdoumie, who ruled from 1337 to 1358

Morho Naba Kouda, who ruled from 1358 to 1401

Morho Naba Dawingna, who ruled from 1401 to 1409

Morho Naba Zoetre Bousma, who ruled from 1409 to 1441

Morho Naba Niandfo, who ruled from 1441 to 1511

Morho Naba Nakim, who ruled from 1511 to 1541

Morho Naba Namegue, who ruled from 1541 to 1542

Morho Naba Kiba, who ruled from 1542 to 1561

Morho Naba Kimba, who ruled from 1561 to 1582

Morho Naba Goabga, who ruled from 1582 to 1599

Morho Naba Guirga, who ruled from 1599 to 1605

Morho Naba Zana, who ruled from 1605 to 1633

Morho Naba Oubi, who ruled from 1633 to 1659

Morho Naba Motiba, who ruled from 1659 to 1666

Morho Naba Warga, who ruled from 1666 to 1681

Morho Naba Zombre, who ruled from 1681 to 1744

Morho Naba Saga I, who ruled from 1744 to 1762

Morho Naba Kom I, who ruled from 1762 to 1783

Morho Naba Doulougou, who ruled from 1783 to 1802

Morho Naba Sawadogo, who ruled from 1802 to 1834

Morho Naba Karfo, who ruled from 1834 to 1842

Morho Naba Baongo, who ruled from 1842 to 1850

Morho Naba Koutou, who ruled from 1850 to 1871

Morho Naba Sanem, who ruled from 1871 to 1889

Morho Naba Koukari Koutou, who ruled from 1889 to 1897

Morho Naba Siguiri, who ruled from 1897 to 1905

Morho Naba Kom II, who ruled from 1905 to 1942

Morho Naba Saga II, who ruled from 1942 to 1957

Morho Naba Kougri, thirty-sixth of the dynasty, crowned in 1957

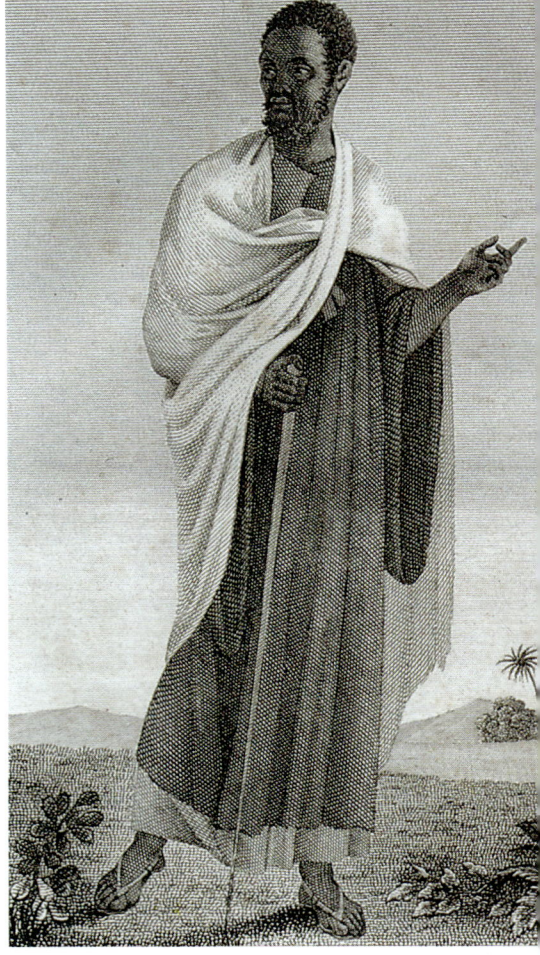

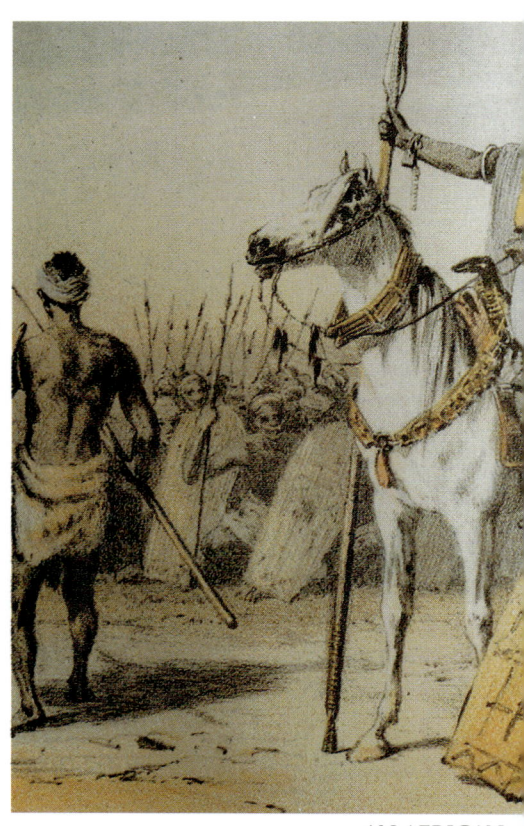

AN AFRICAN

YENNENGA

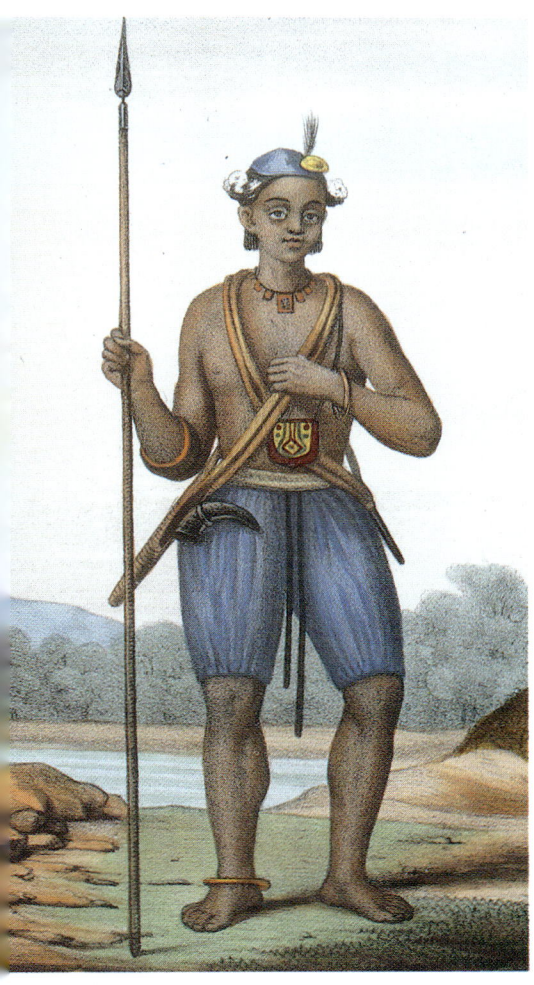

DYNASTY

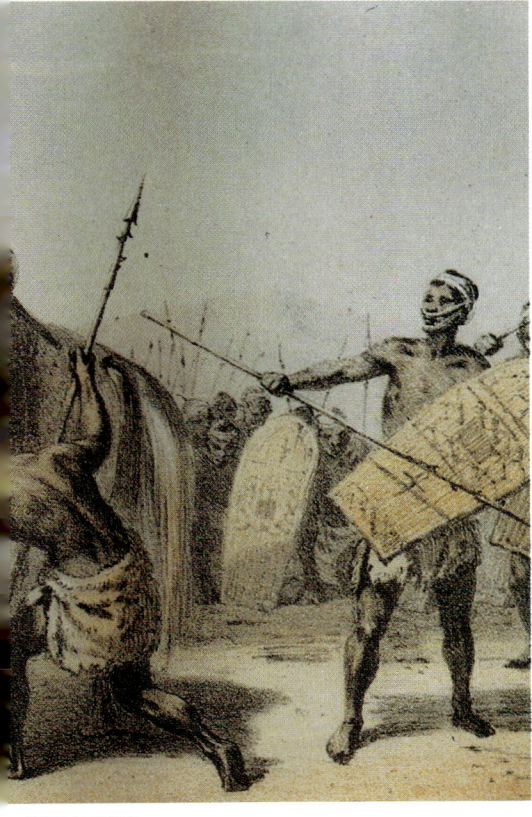

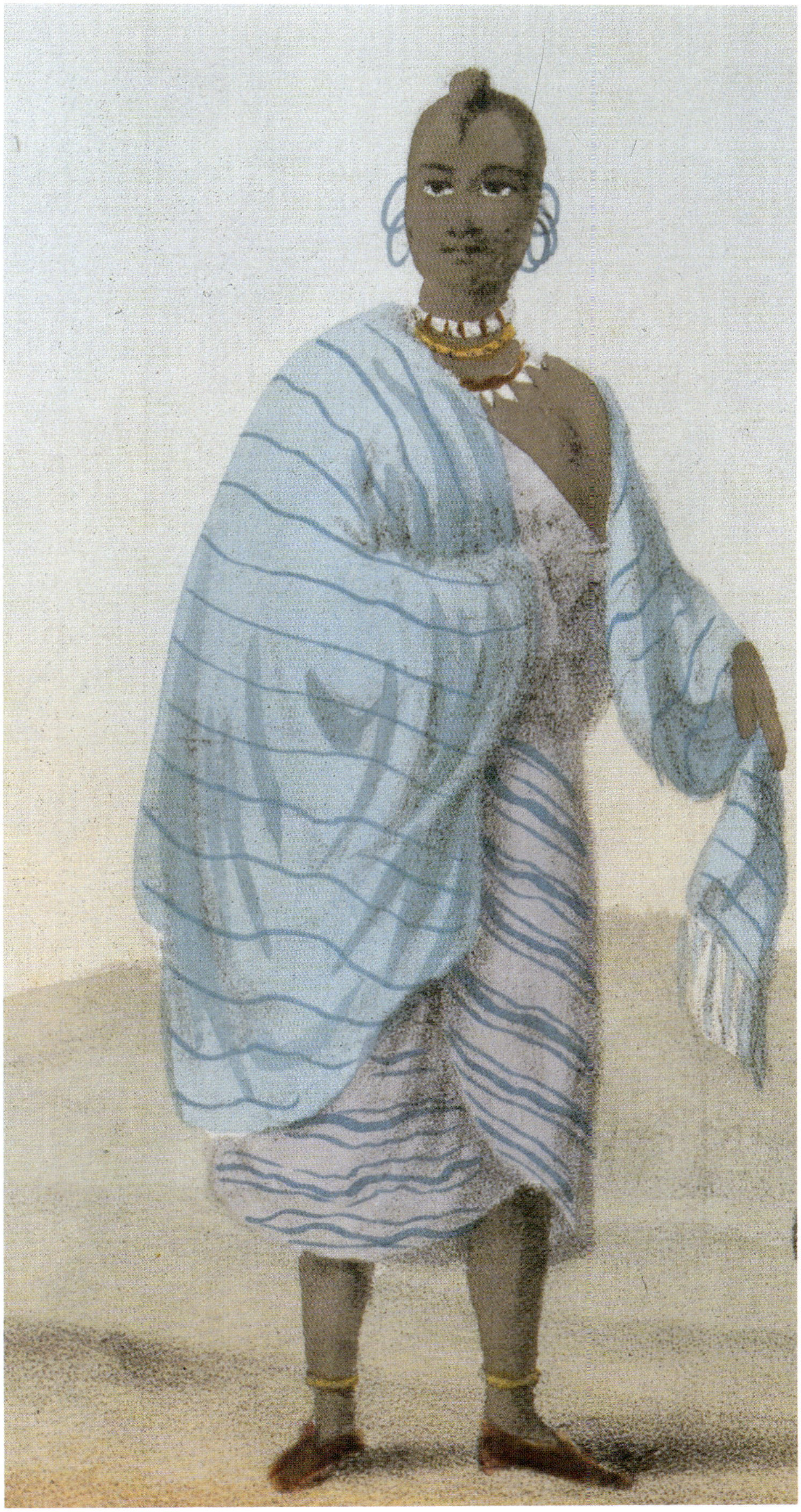

"THE IMMORTAL TREE BORN OF THE AMAZON YENNENGA"

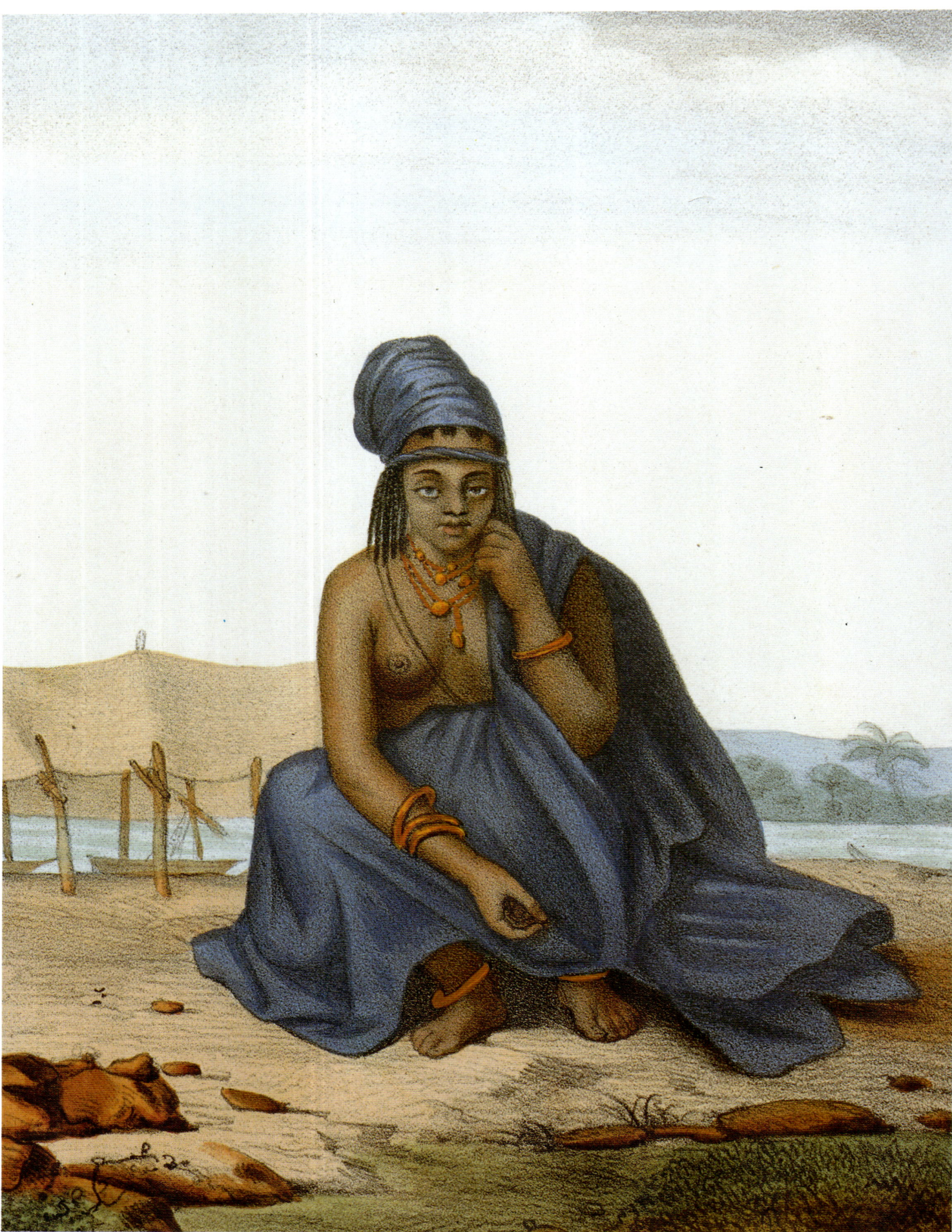

WORDS OF AN ORDINARY WOMAN

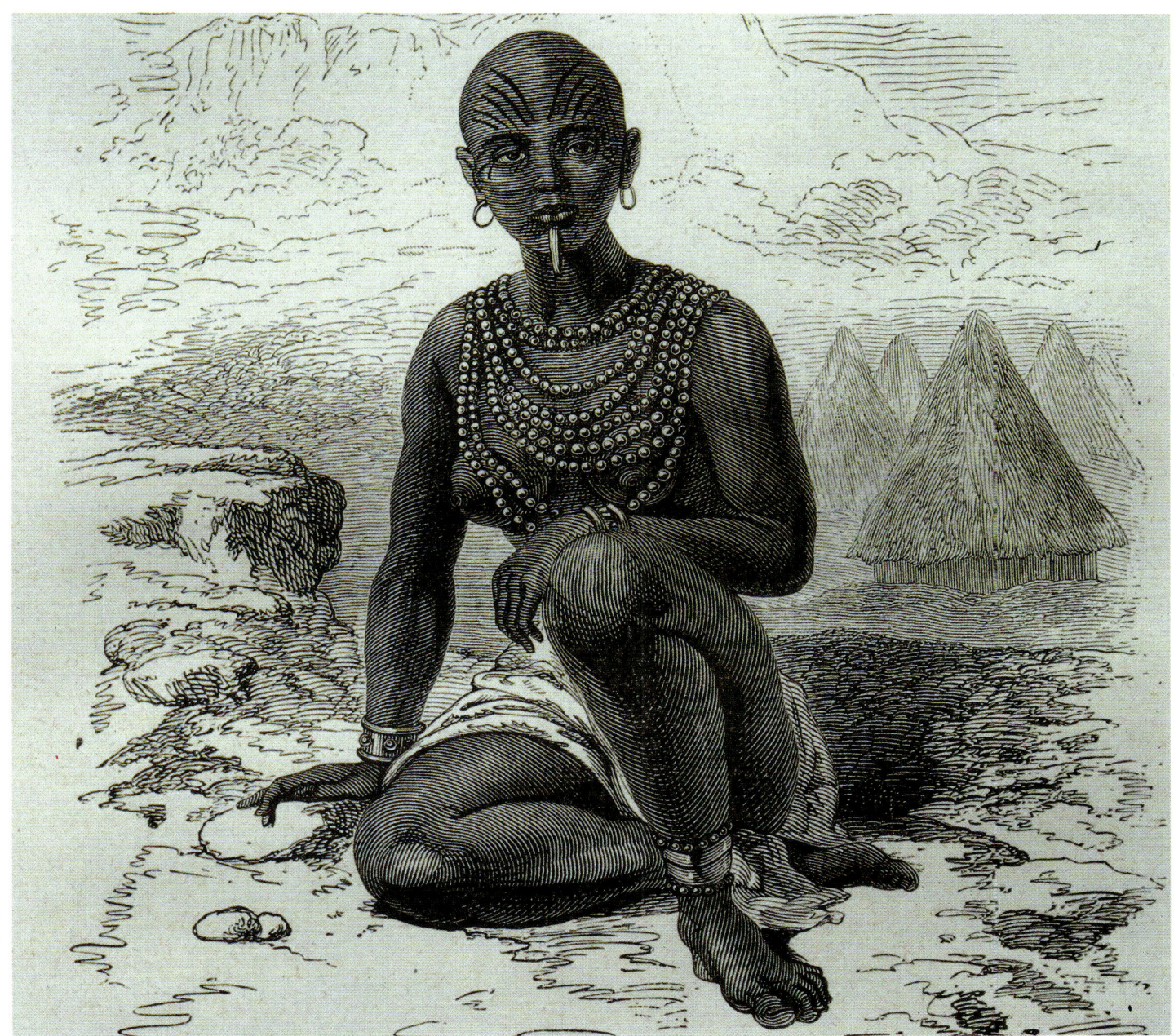

Intelligence is with the heart. It belongs to the heart.

A good word is a word that comes from the heart. A harsh word does not come from the heart.

But intelligence is fleeting: it comes and goes. It takes nothing to make it take flight.

Intelligence is an important thing. To underscore its importance we like to say that it is better to have no cattle than to have no intelligence. If you have no cattle but have intelligence, you will gather a herd one day. But if you have cattle and no intelligence, you'll end up losing the cattle you have.

True poverty is lack of intelligence. And we despise such poverty. Such poverty is a shame and the one who is poor that way will be the object of ridicule.

Intelligence is like personality: everyone has his or her own. We say that it looks like the groove in a stone. A stone will always keep its groove. The groove will never disappear.

Can a dying tree find the sap of life by staying in water? We have a proverb which says that "A dried-up tree trunk in a pond will never turn into a cayman!"

Intelligence is with the heart.

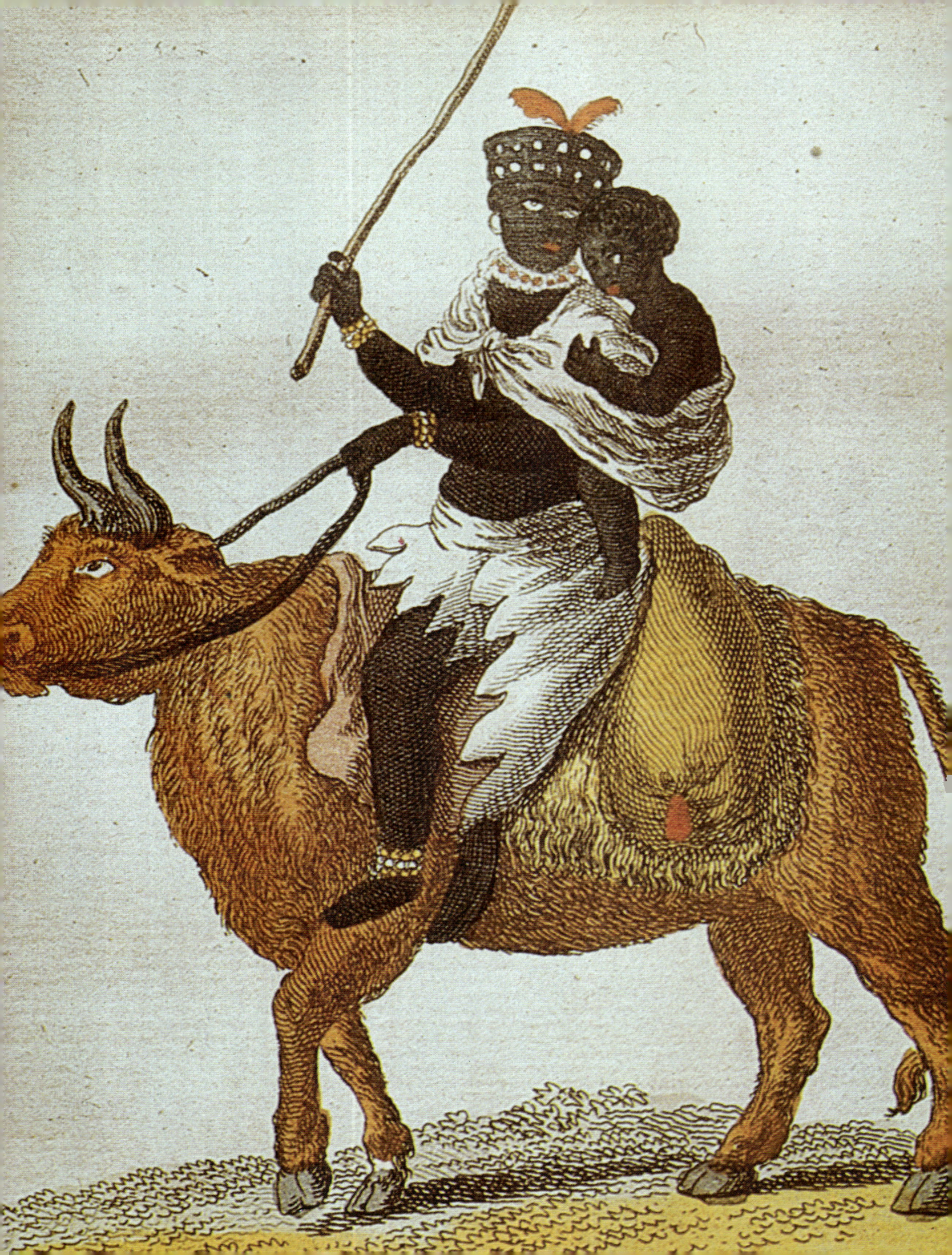

SOGOLON KONTÉ

A WOMAN ENDOWED WITH MAGIC POWERS

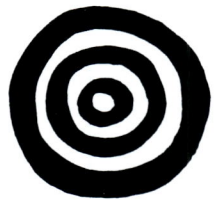

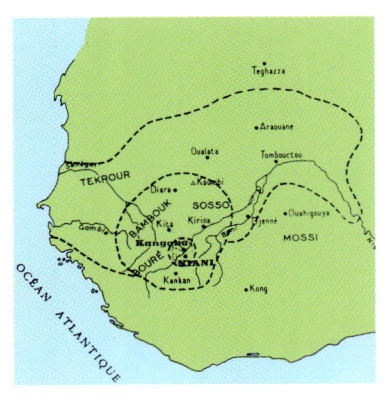

A long time ago in the kingdom of the Malis, on the Upper Niger, a buffalo woman thrice gave birth to a child who would become the hero Sundiata...

A LONG TIME AGO, THE KINGDOM OF MALI STRADDLED THE UPPER NIGER RIVER, UP ALONG THE BAMAKO RIVER AND TO THE EDGE OF GUINEA. THE EXISTENCE OF THIS KINGDOM DATES BACK TO THE TENTH CENTURY, BUT ITS ACTUAL BIRTH GOES back much further.

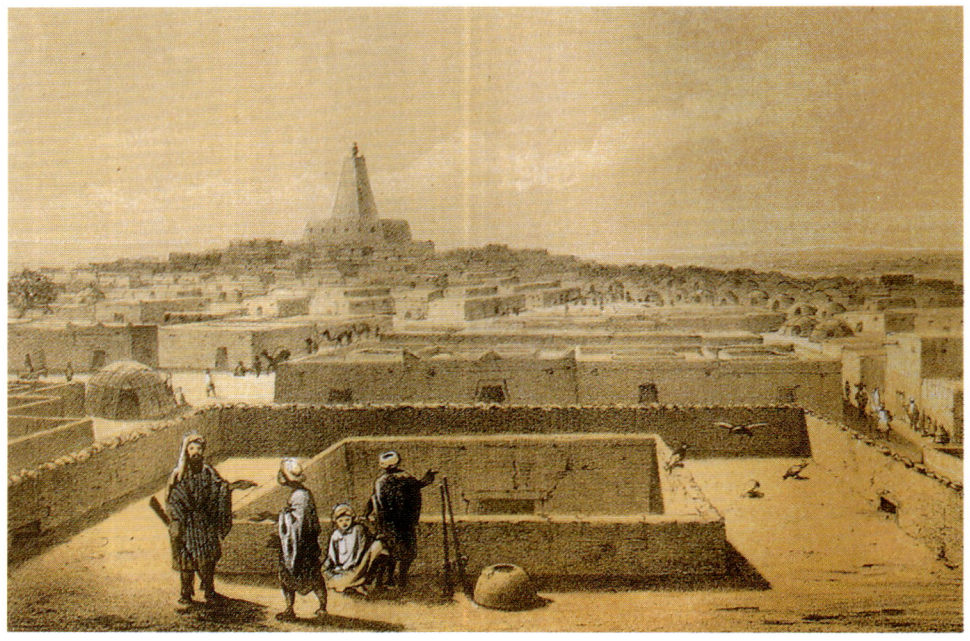

TIMBUKTU

Three centuries later, Sumanguru, the king of the Susu, suddenly conquered the Malian state of Kangaba and had the eleven sons of the defeated king murdered. He spared only the life of the second son, a frail and stiff-jointed child who dragged himself on all fours until the age of ten. This crippled child was to become Sundiata, hero of many names, the one people call Sogolondiata, Nare-Nlagha-Diata, Sogo Sogo Simbo Salaba, and finally Maridiata, which in the Manlinké language means "Lion of Mali." Praise singers still sing of his exploits today, because Sundiata was great amongst kings and incomparable among men.

FEMALE PRAISE SINGER ▷

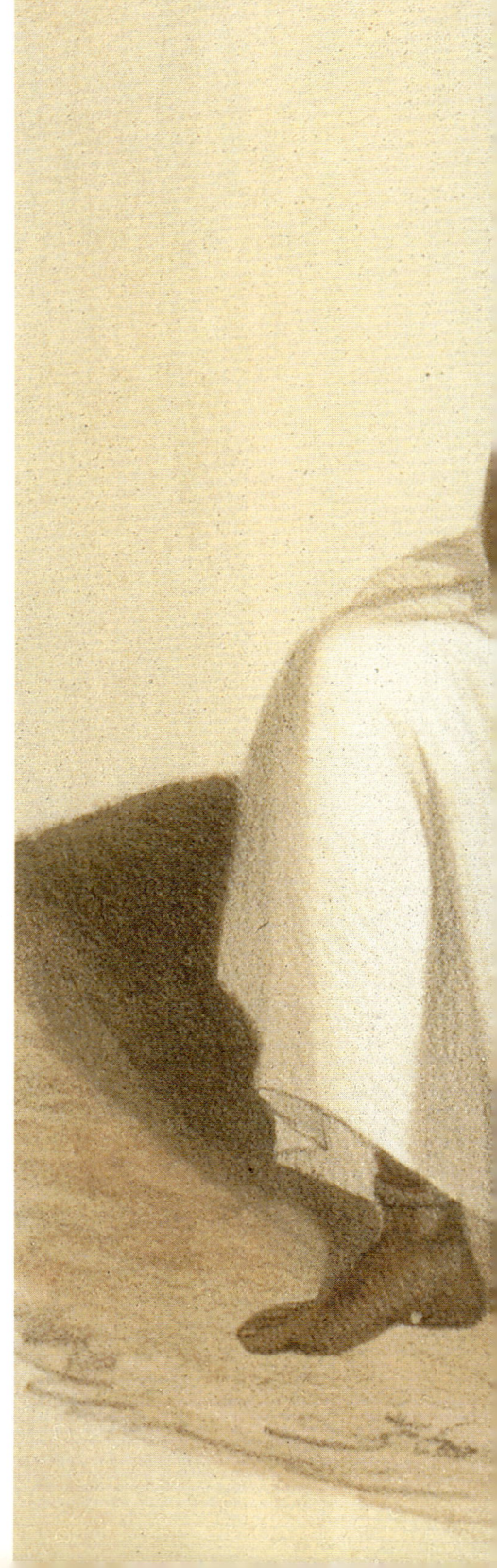

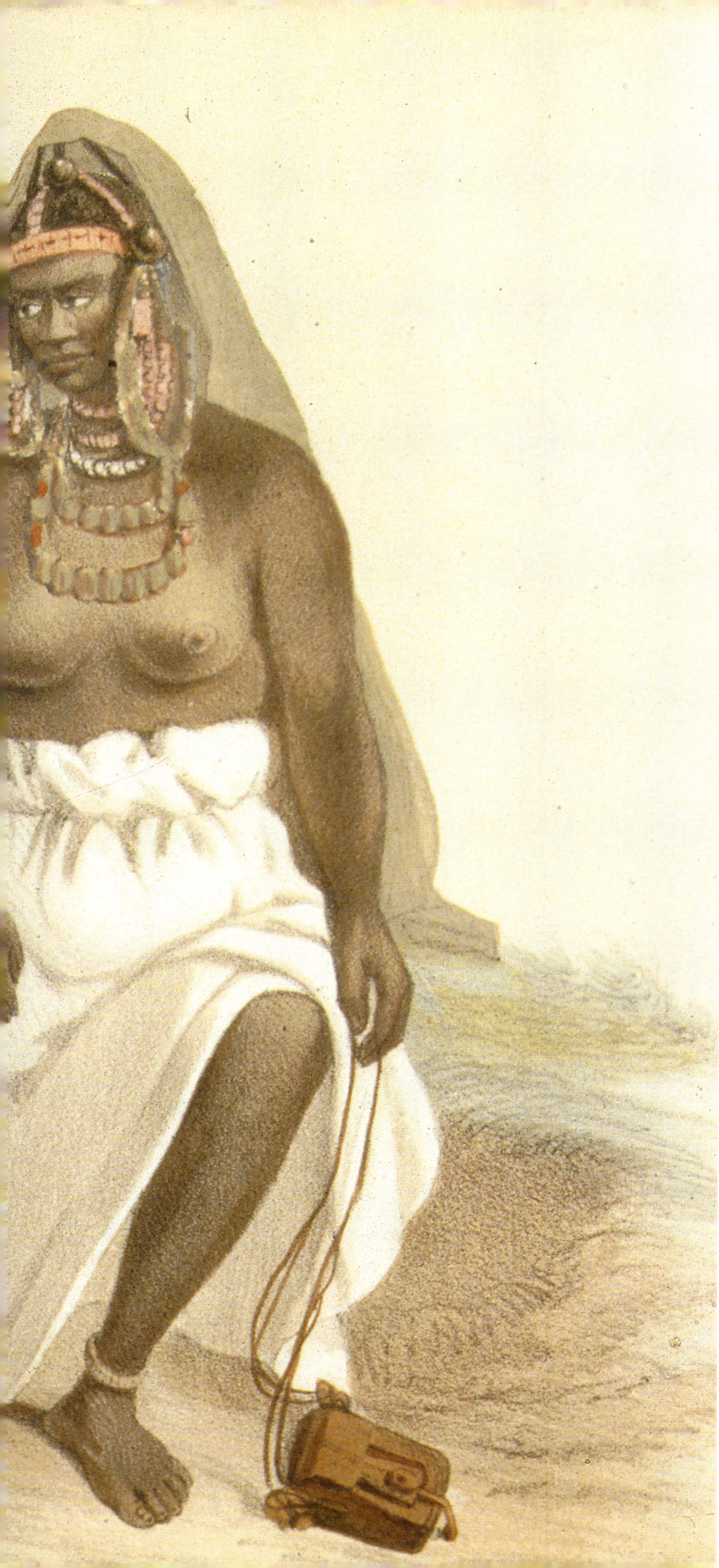

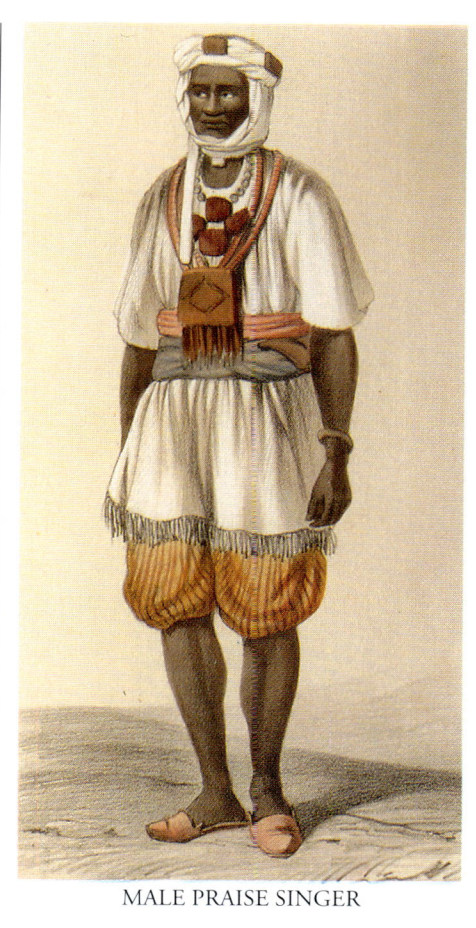

MALE PRAISE SINGER

Anaavoukoutou

In the beginning, at the dawn of life, a few rock pigeons came upon a house. They found a woman sitting outside. She was a married woman, and she had no children. She said: "They have come to make fun of me. They see I am without child, so they add salt to my wound."
There were six pigeons that came. One said: "Voukoutou." Another asked: "Why do you say Voukoutou?" The first repeated: "Voukoutou." A second asked: "Why do you say Voukoutou?"
And so time passed, as the woman looked on.
Then the first bird said to the woman: "Take a thorn and scratch yourself. Take a bead of blood, put it in a pot. Close the pot, turn it upside down, and on the eighth month, uncover it."
When the woman uncovered it she found a child. In that very pot, the bead of blood had a child beside it.
And then the child grew instantly.
Her husband came home in the evening. Astonished, he asked: "Where did you get this child? Who is this child?"
She answered: "This is my child. This is the child from my bead of blood, the child of the pigeons who have taught me wisdom."
And so the husband was happy, thanked her and told her: "I'm happy and glad today. You have now had a child. Very good."

The Mother

The child who did not respect his mother was considered cursed by society. The supreme place of the mother is revealed in the exclamation the Malinkés use when in danger: "be yi babore." The etymology of this expression refers to the notion that each and every one is in the hands of his or her mother.

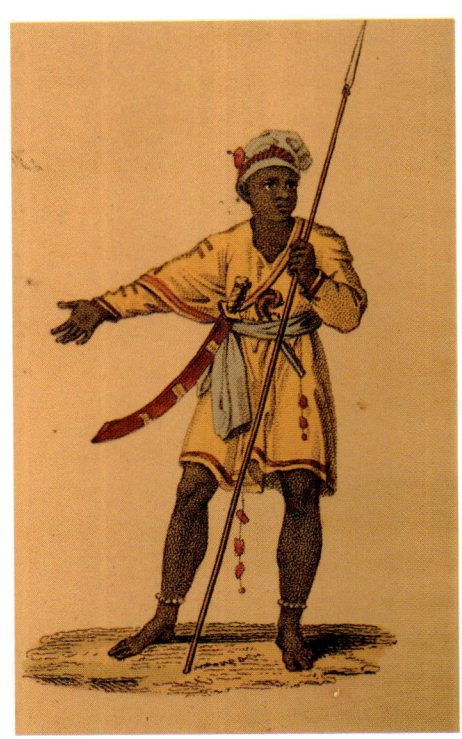

Song for the Mother

A mother comes home after a long day. Sensing that her mother is tired and thirsty, her daughter runs out to her with a gourd full of water, singing:

*There will always be someone
to bring you water,
unless the gods will it otherwise.
There will always be someone
to solve all the problems you may face,
unless the gods will it otherwise.
Because you have renounced
everything for your children.
Gold, money, rings,
bracelets, clothes.
You've sacrificed everything for your children.
If there was no one
to give you water,
I would be there,
even if it made the whole world laugh.
So take this water, wonderful mother.
For accepting so difficult a life,
you surely deserve your fill of water.*

Proverbs

"Whoever refuses to understand what his mother has to say will understand misfortune's words all too well."

"Truth walks through fire without getting burned."

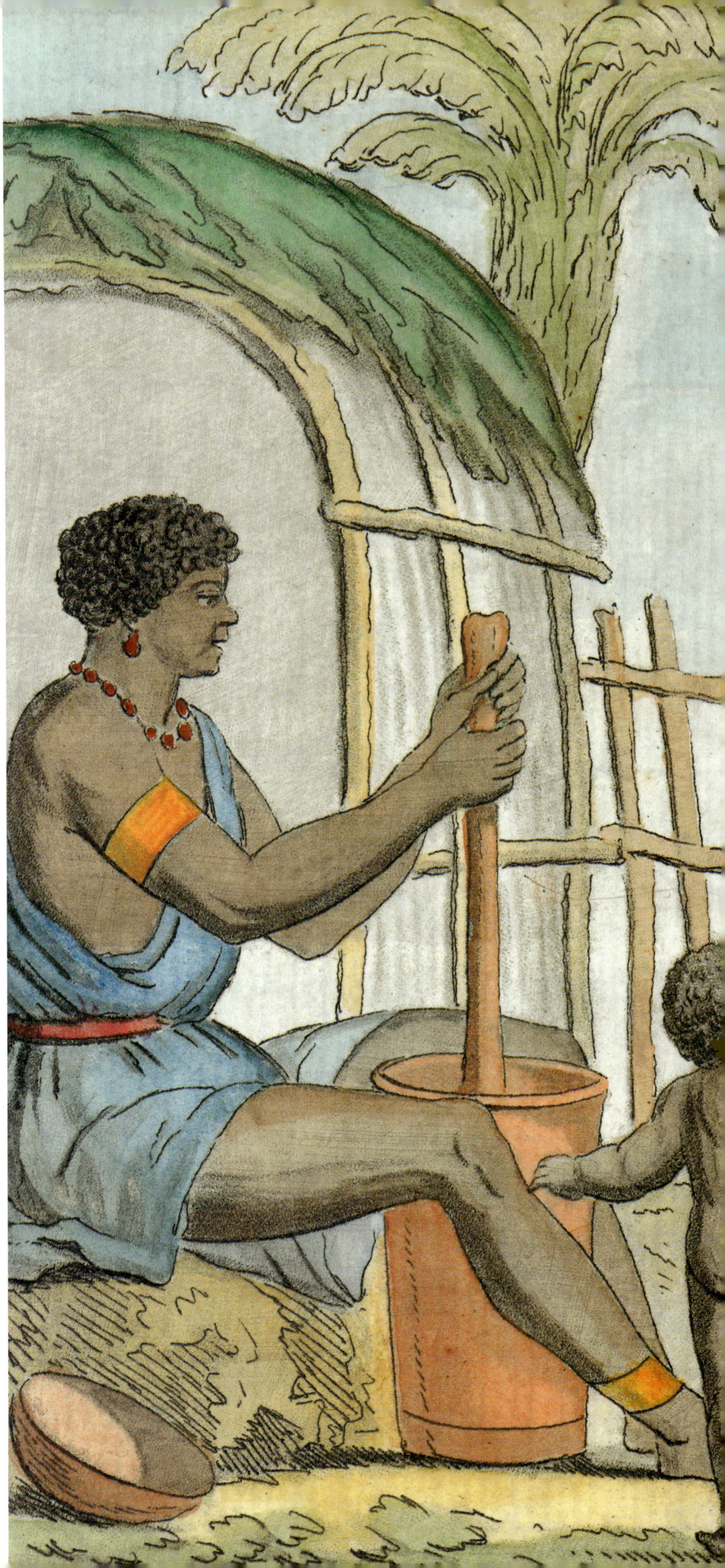

SOGOLON KONTÉ

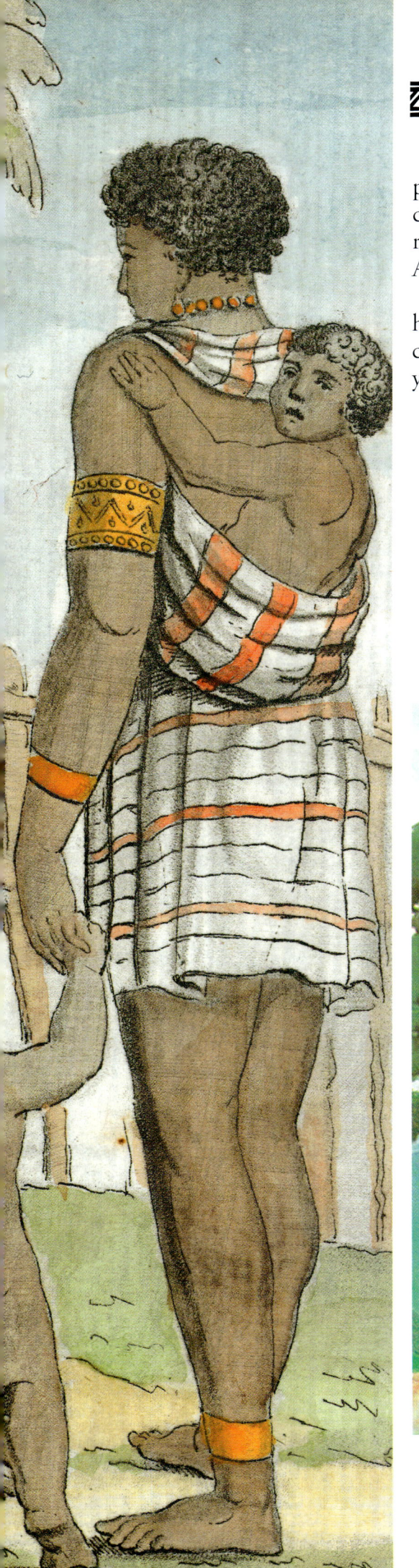

He owed this extraordinary fate to his mother, Sogolon Konté, a powerful woman, who was armed with magic powers, because she carried the spirit of the buffalo within her. She had courageously raised the crippled child, despite the mockery of the other women. And she accepted exile in order to save the life of her child.

Sundiata dragged himself on the ground, and it pained him to see his mother scorned. One day, he said to Sogolon Konté: "The other children may bring a baobab leaf to their mothers, but I will bring you the entire tree."

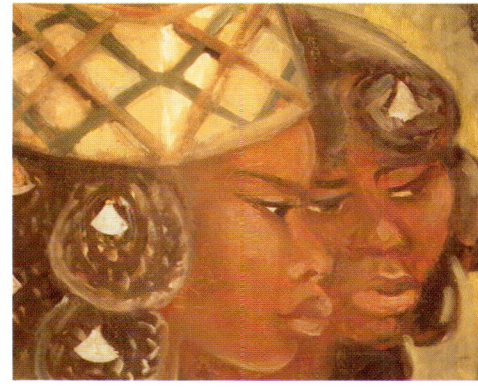

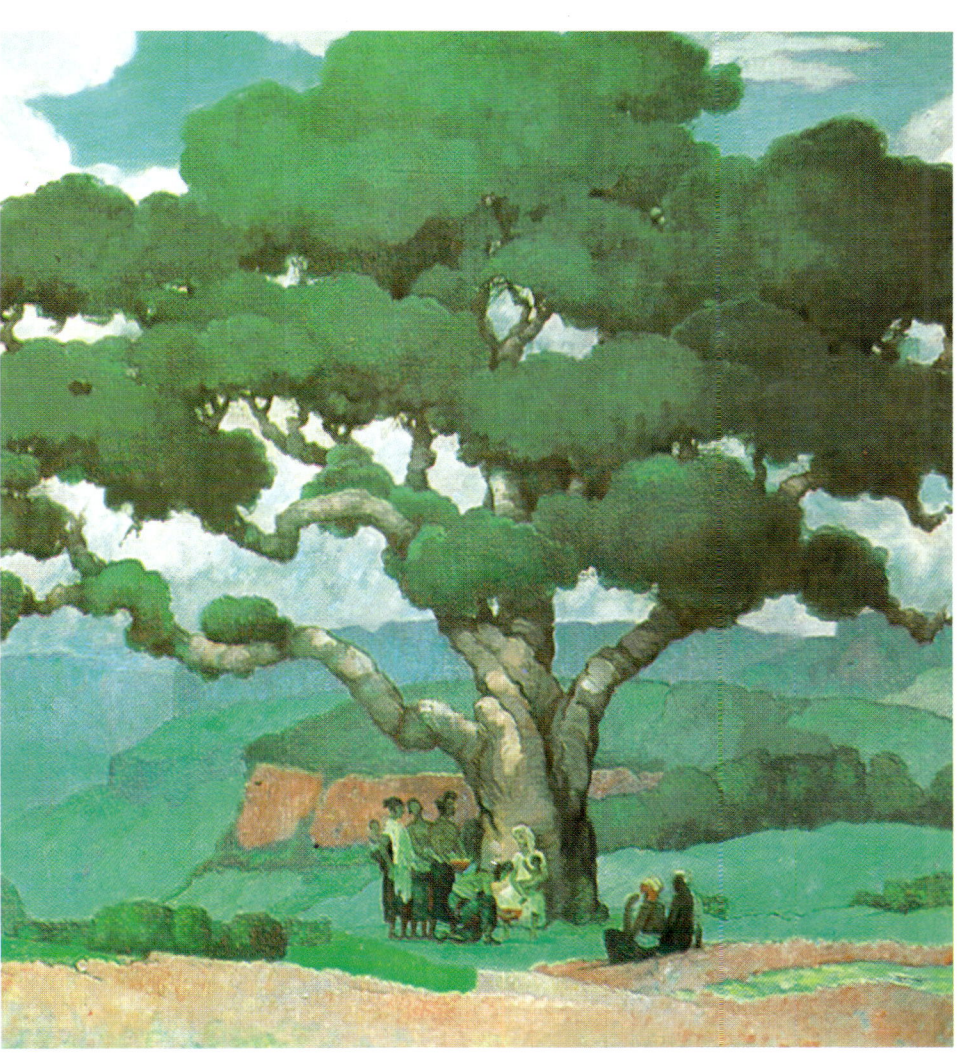

"I WILL BRING YOU THE ENTIRE TREE"

Then the cripple asked for an iron bar to help him to stand on his feet. But the bar bent in two beneath his weight. A second and then an even thicker third bar suffered the same fate. Then an old man suggested: "Why don't you give him his father's scepter, so that he may straighten his back by leaning on his grandeur." And so, leaning on the royal scepter, Sundiata finally managed to stand up for the first time, at the age of ten. Right away, the witnesses of the event made up the "Song of the Bow," whose lyrics and melody have been transmitted through the generations and still echo today in Mali:

> *Lion, take the quiver!*
> *Lion, take the bow of the Mandingo!*
> *My son Sundiata can walk!*
> *Praise!*
> *Better death than shame!*
> *Oh honor!*

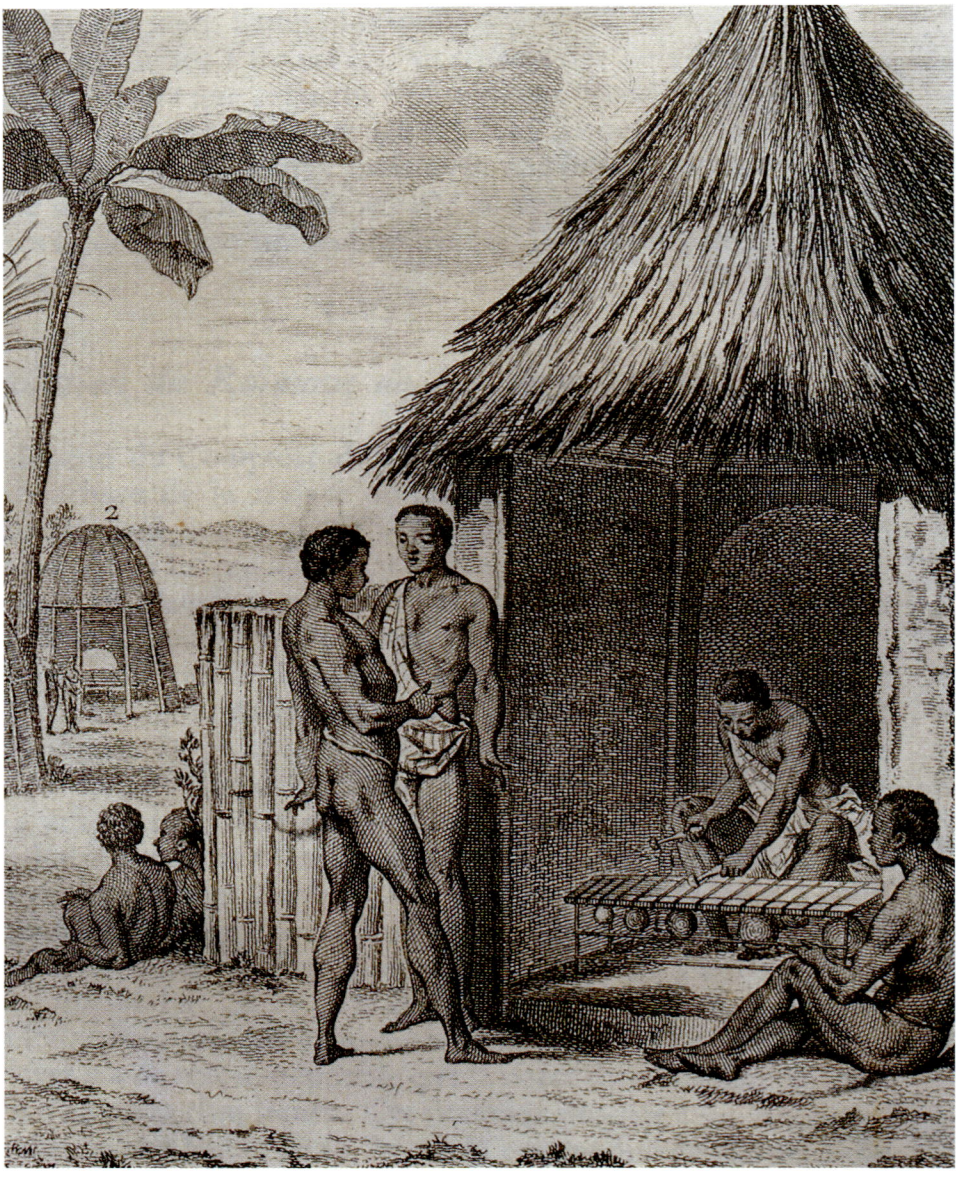

A GROUP OF MUSICIANS

Birth of Biton Kulibali, Founder of the Bambara People

According to the early sources, Biton's father was Tiguiton Kulibali. He was born in Niamina toward the end of the sixteenth century, and his wife, Princess Soulou Souko, apparently gave birth to a son when she was fifty years old. This explains the father's cry of amazement: "Bi to ye na!" ("in my lifetime!"). And the name of the boy would be Biton. He became a great hunter who came to settle on the banks of the Niger near a great shea tree, which eventually became Ségou. The legend says that Biton once captured the son of a river spirit and, because he spared the boy's life, he was dragged all the way to the bottom of the river to meet the boy's mother. Grateful, she promised Biton a great empire.

Proverb

"No well-wished words are finer than 'May God protect your mystery.'"

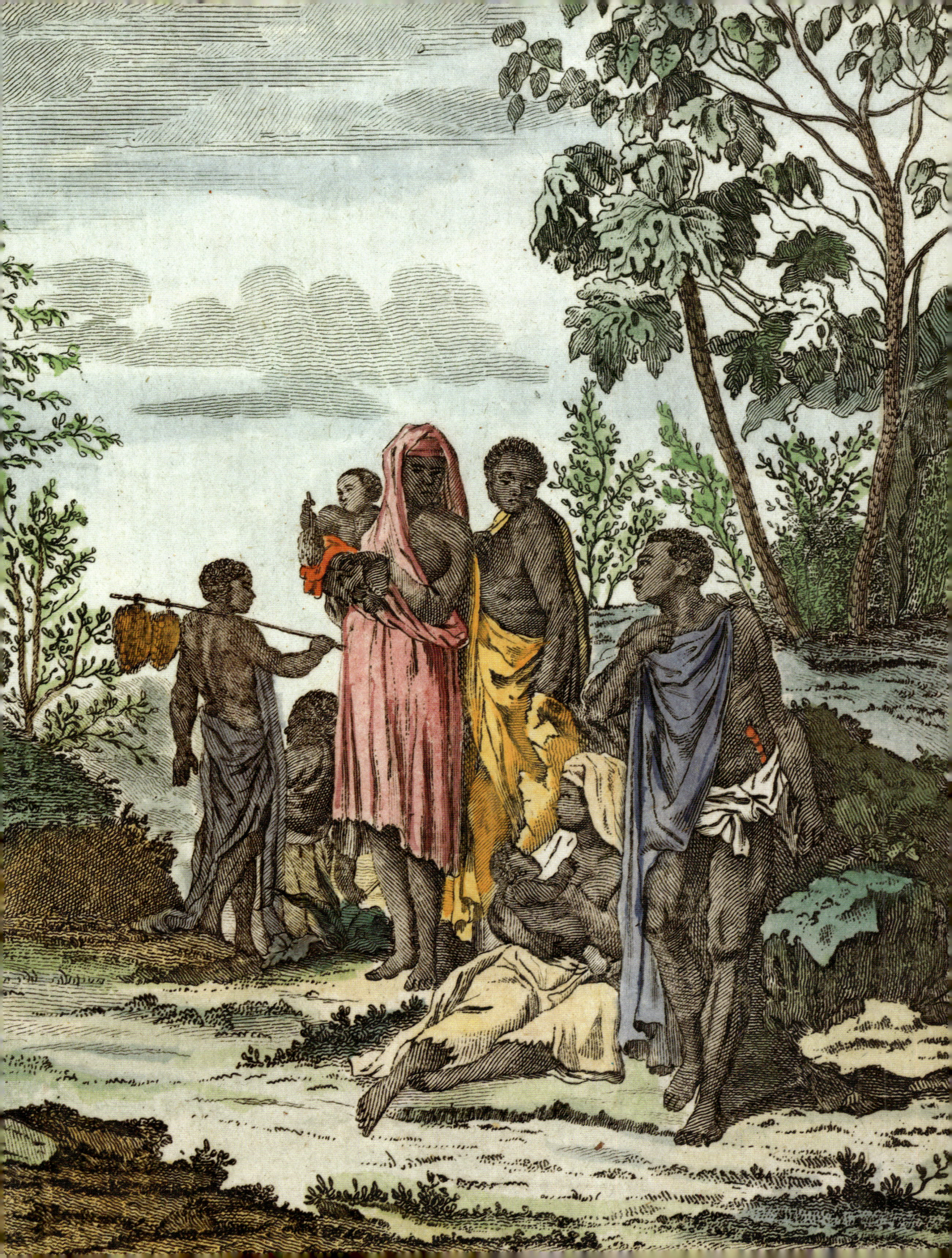

The Words of the Praise Singer Mamadou Kouyaté

I am a praise singer. I am Djeli Mama dou Kouyaté, son of Binou Kouyaté and of Djeli Kedian Kouyaté, master in the art of words. From time out of mind, the Kouyatés have been in the service of Princess Keita of Manding: we are bags of words, we are the bags holding secrets a few centuries old.

The art of words is no mystery to us: without us, the kings would fall into oblivion. We are the memory of men; through the word, we give life to the acts and gestures of kings for the younger generations.

I am heir to the science of my father Djeli Kedia who inherited it from his father; history keeps no mysteries from us.

I have taught kings the history of their ancestors so that the life of the Ancient Ones may be an example for them, because the world is old, and the future comes out of the past.

My word is pure and bare. I tell no lies. I carry my father's words and the words of my father's father.

I will give my father's words the way he gave them to me: the king's praise singer knows nothing of lies.

Thus, it is to honor his mother, who had suffered so much for him, that Sundiata engaged in the struggle that would lead to the reconquest of Mali. His mother advised him in all matters, but she died without seeing her son's triumph. But on her death bed, she gave him one last piece of advice: "Come closer, so I can give you three spells. When I will not be here any more, you will say these words, standing before the shae tree that sticks out its dead branches in the yard. The first spell will make the tree turn green again; the second will make it bloom and give fruit; and when you say the third, three ripe fruits will fall from its tall branches. You will take these three fruits and you will eat of them; and thus, God will grant you power over all the lands where the shae tree grows: from the sands of Timbuktu to the green forests of Fouta-Djallon."

On her death bed, Sogolon Konté also asked her son to abolish slavery among the Malinké people and to overcome all forms of injustice. And that was how Sundiata won the hearts of all the Mandingo; and thus did he conquer the lands that stretch from Timbuktu to Fouta-Djallon.

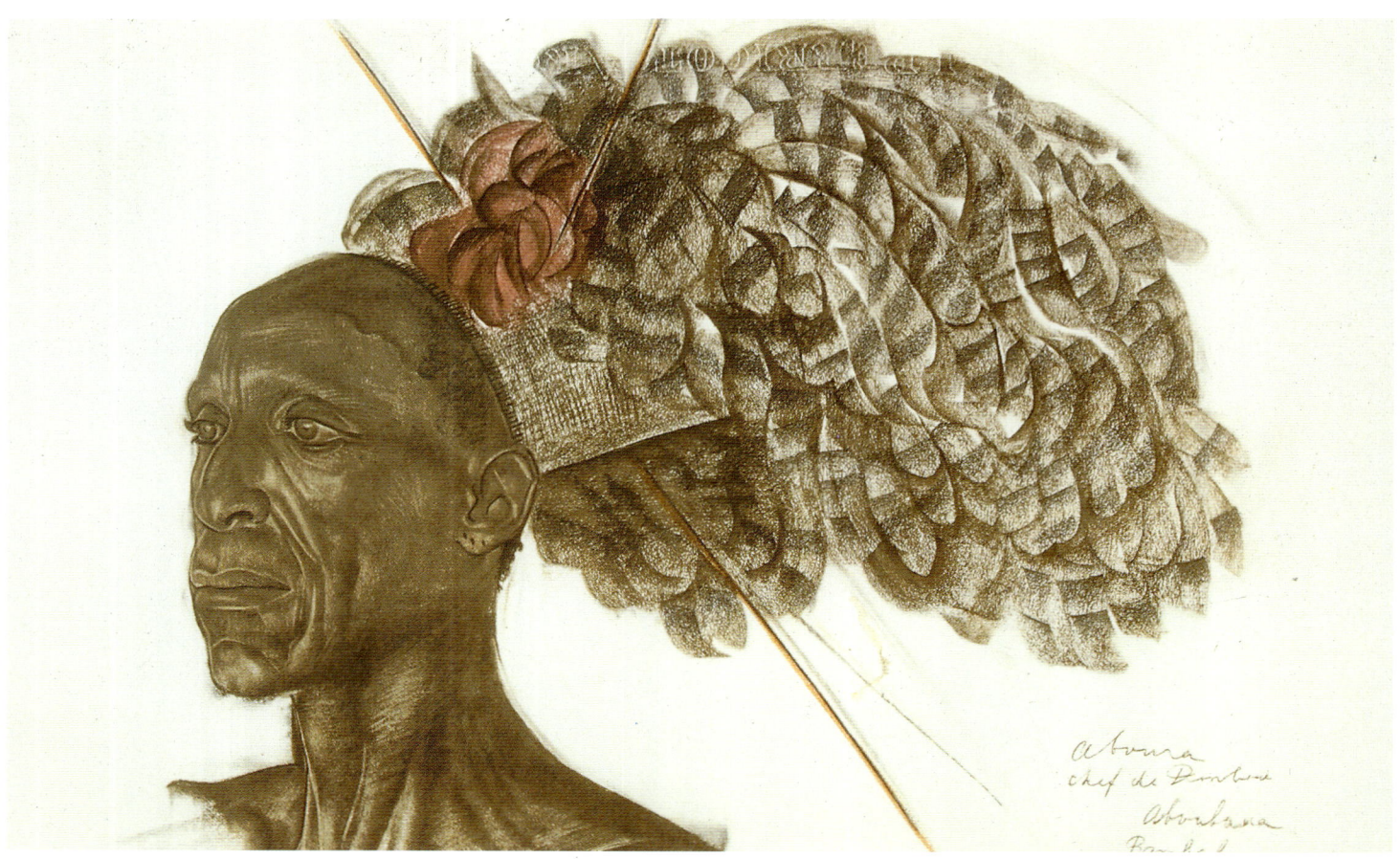

THE PRAISE SINGER

WOMAN FROM THE MANDINGO ▷

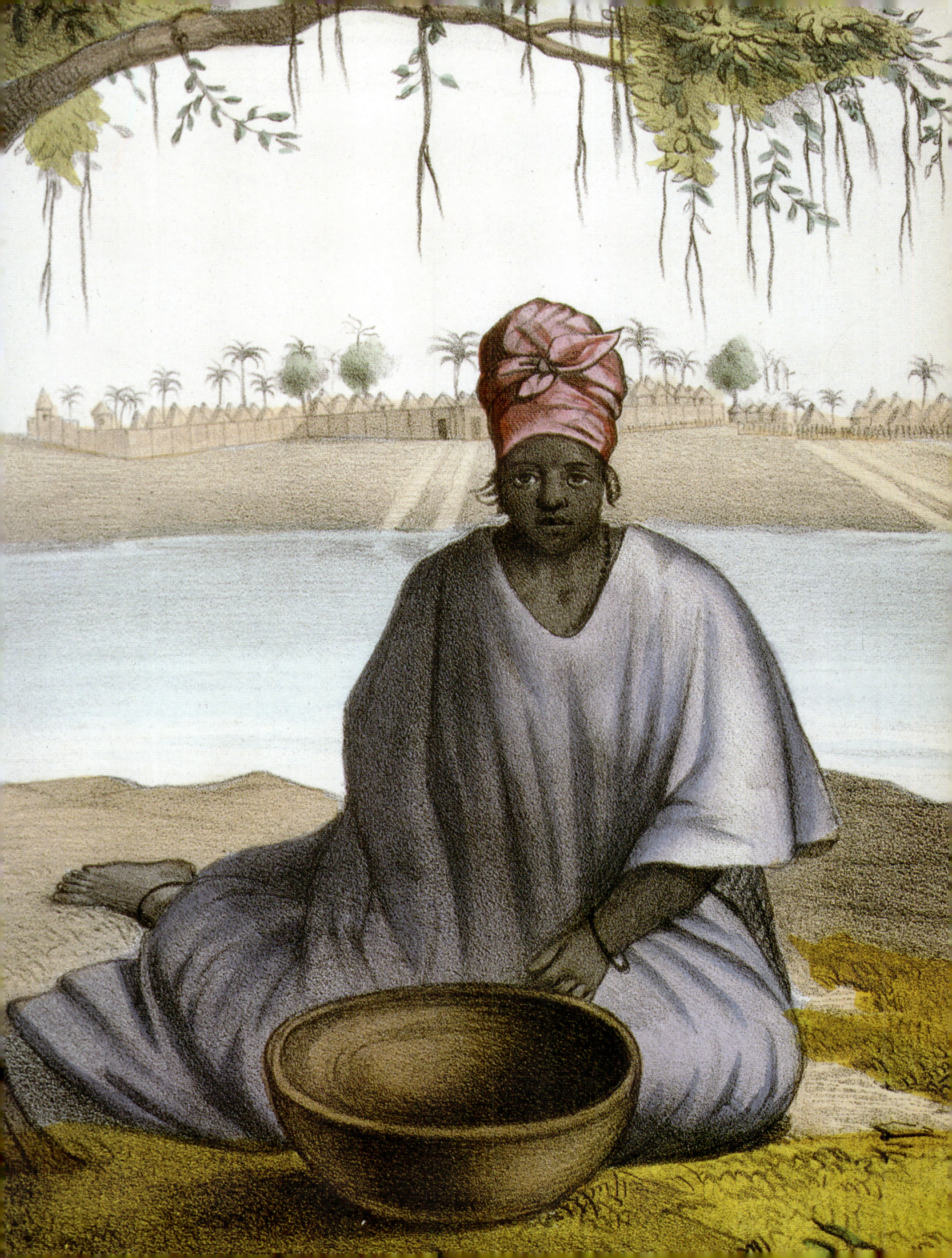

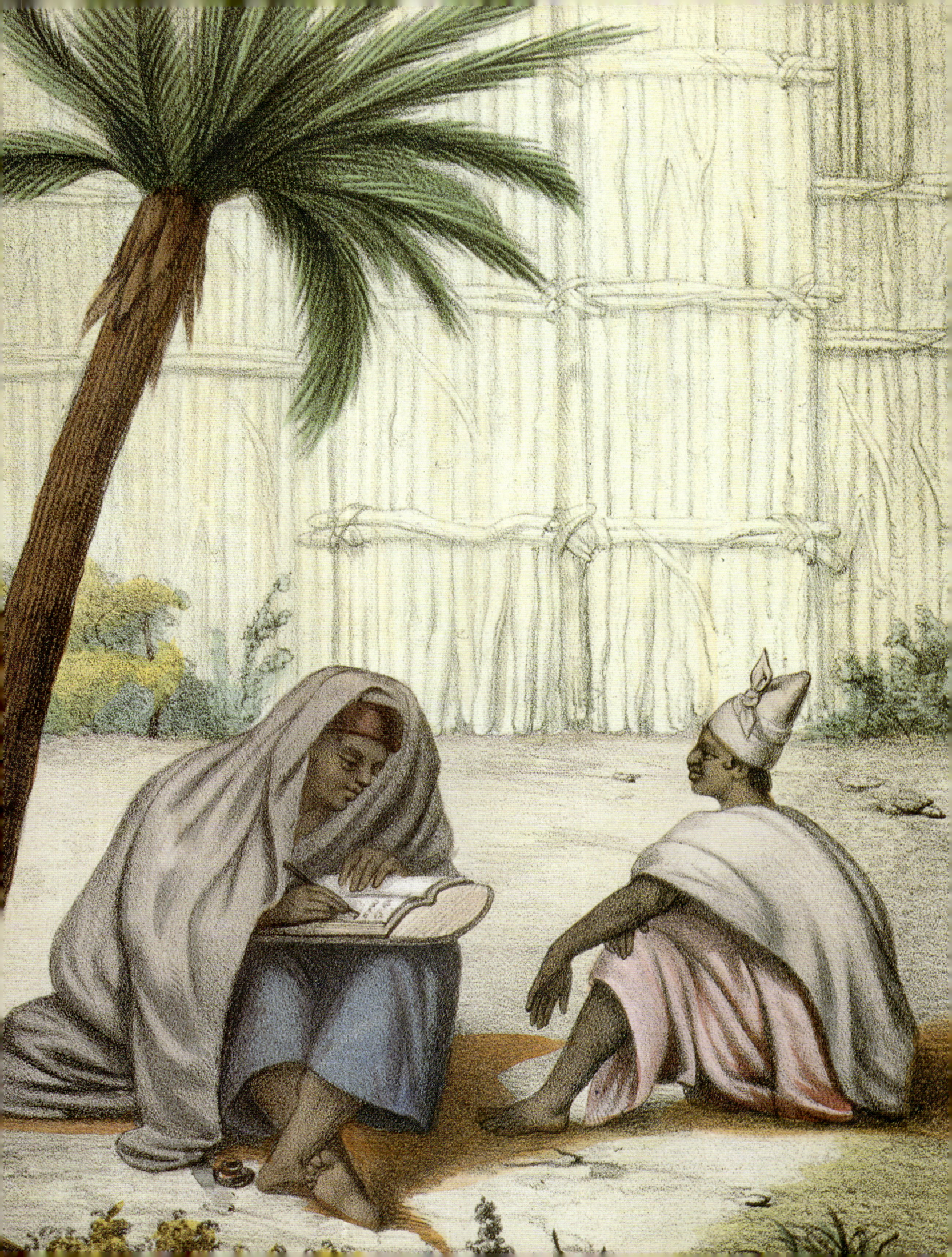

IN PRAISE OF BLACK WOMEN

WORDS
OF AN ORDINARY WOMAN

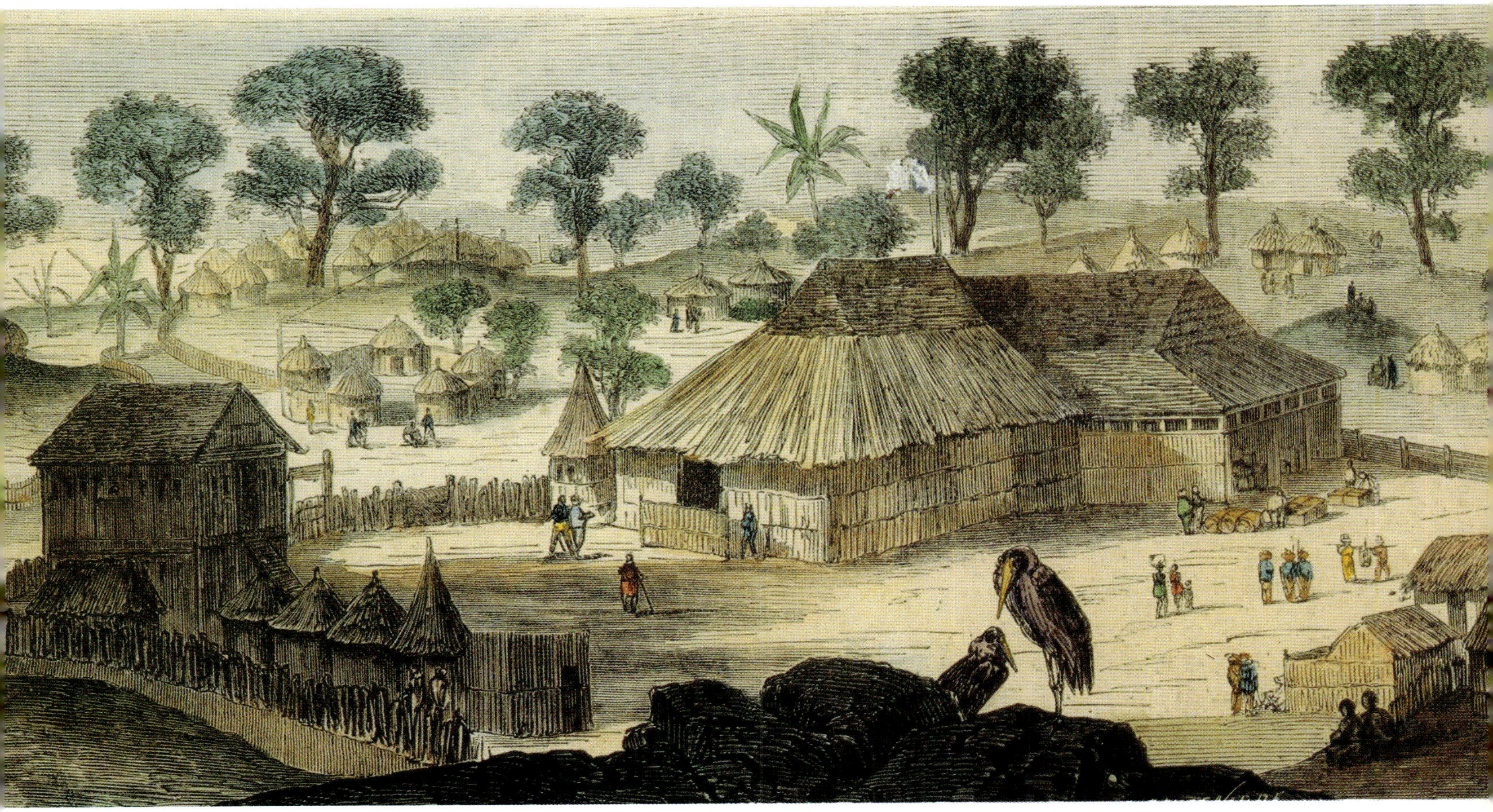

Everyone seeks growth. Everyone wants more. No one can stop desiring. Only the dead want nothing at all, because they've lost everything forever.

But anyone with any breath left wants more. The spirit of everyone points its head in the direction where it thinks it can expand.

The proverb goes: "The bird always has the threshing floor on its mind." That's where the bird finds food and happiness. Wherever the bird is full, it is happy.

For everyone, life is the desire for growth. Because to desire is to live, The dead do not want anything.

The desire for growth is, for everyone, the desire for life. It's not just a part of you, not just your heart, that desires more, but also your blood, and your bones. Desire grabs you. It holds your heart, your bones, your joints, your back.

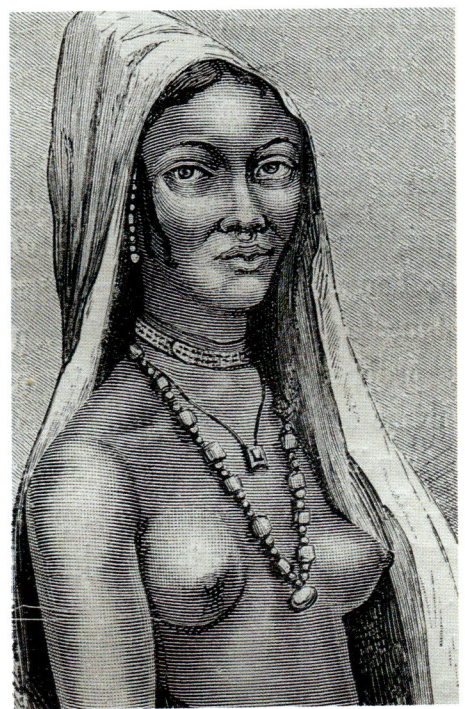

FULANI WOMAN

When you fervently desire something, you find no peace until you have obtained it, until you hold it in your hands. When you desire, you go mad. You don't want food or sleep. All is pain and thirst.

If you strongly desire something, you'll end up getting it. God will grant you the objects of your desire. And there will be plenitude. "It will be for you like it was for the bucket left in the well. The bucket stayed in the well a long time, and one day it came back up full and flowing with water!"

Patience grants every wish: what you haven't gotten today, you can get tomorrow. When the first rains come, the brush is still thirsty. But the rain will not fall everywhere at once. The spot that has not been moistened with rain will have to wait and be patient. The thirst of the brush will eventually be appeased.

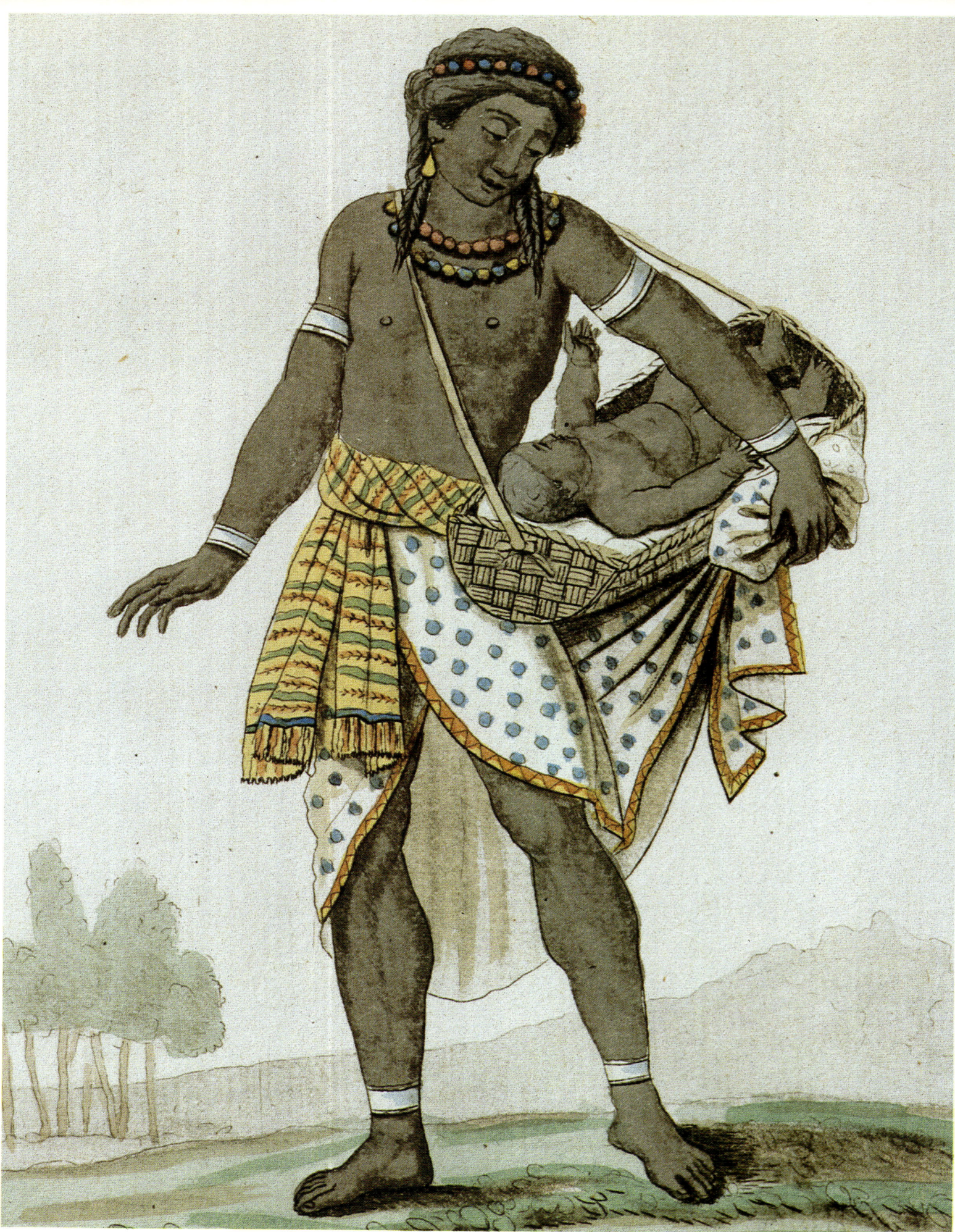

AMINA KULIBALI

FOUNDER OF THE PRINCELY DYNASTY OF GABU

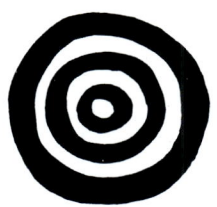

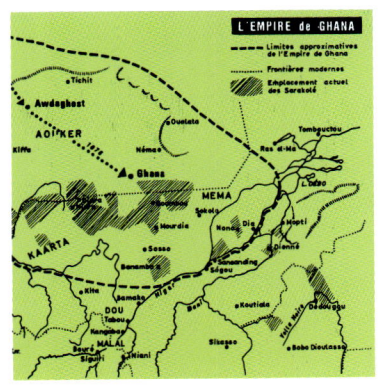

Amina gave birth to a daughter who sneezed thrice, and the king solemnly declared that the children of this girl would become the kings of Gabu...

ONCE UPON A TIME, IN THE REGION OF KAHARTA, IN SOUTH-EAST SENEGAL, THERE WAS A GREAT KING

BY THE NAME OF IKSY GUIEN KIED. HE WAS BUILT LIKE HERCULES, AND PEOPLE SAY HE WAS AS STRONG AS THE LIGHTNING THAT STRIKES THE LIVING AND THE dead without warning. One day an arrow hit him, and his people, the Massaleke, felt like orphans.

Custom dictated the election of a new king. And after having spoken with the ancestors, the elders decided that the people needed a king of less dazzling strength, a king more like the proverbial reed that bends but doesn't break.

So they chose Wade Amedou, a man of lofty intellect, who needn't walk ahead of his troops to lead them well.

However, the elders explained, the new choice should not reflect negatively on the deceased king. The qualities of one were not to throw a shadow on the qualities of the other. And that's why it was decided that the oldest son of the late king would marry the daughter of the new king, the beautiful Amina Kulibali.

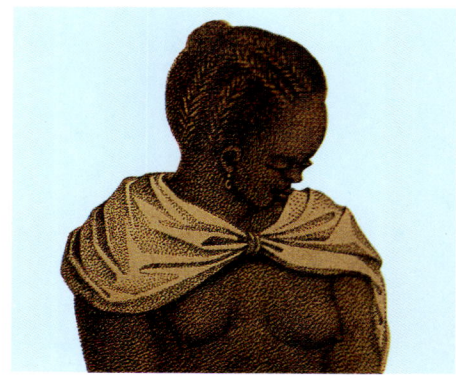

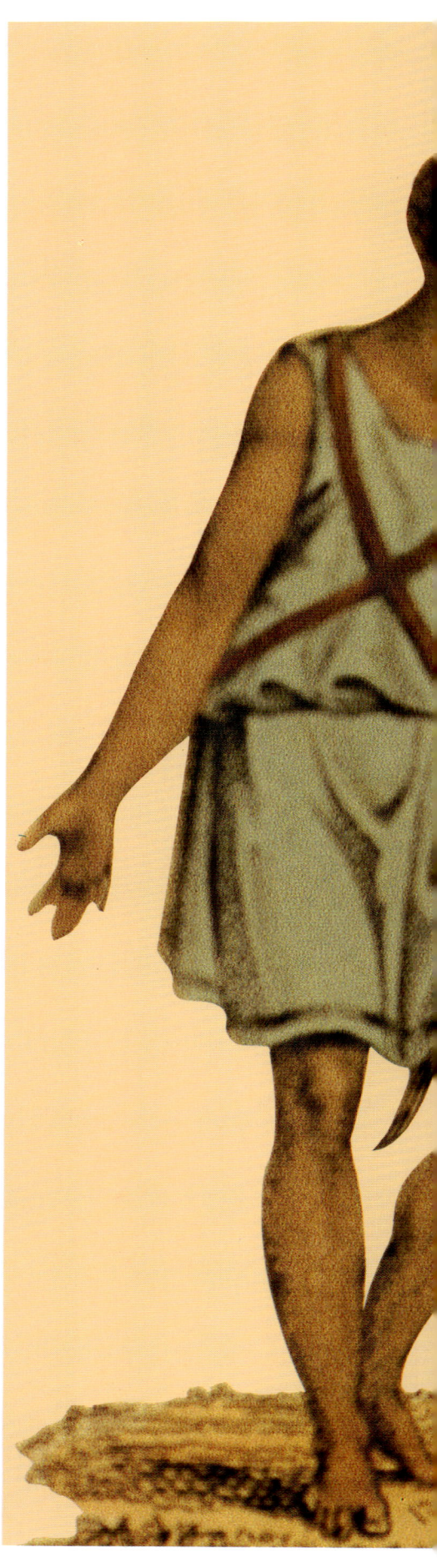

Diakha, Amina's fiancé, had been in love with her since she was but a child. The wedding was to take place a year from the engagement day. But after only a month, Diakha was so impatient he could neither sleep nor eat nor even drink a drop of palm wine. One night, disguised as a praise singer, he sneaked into his fiancé's room and found her asleep. It seemed to him that, out of the depths of her slumber, the beautiful Amina silently invited him onto her mat: so he went unto her and took her.

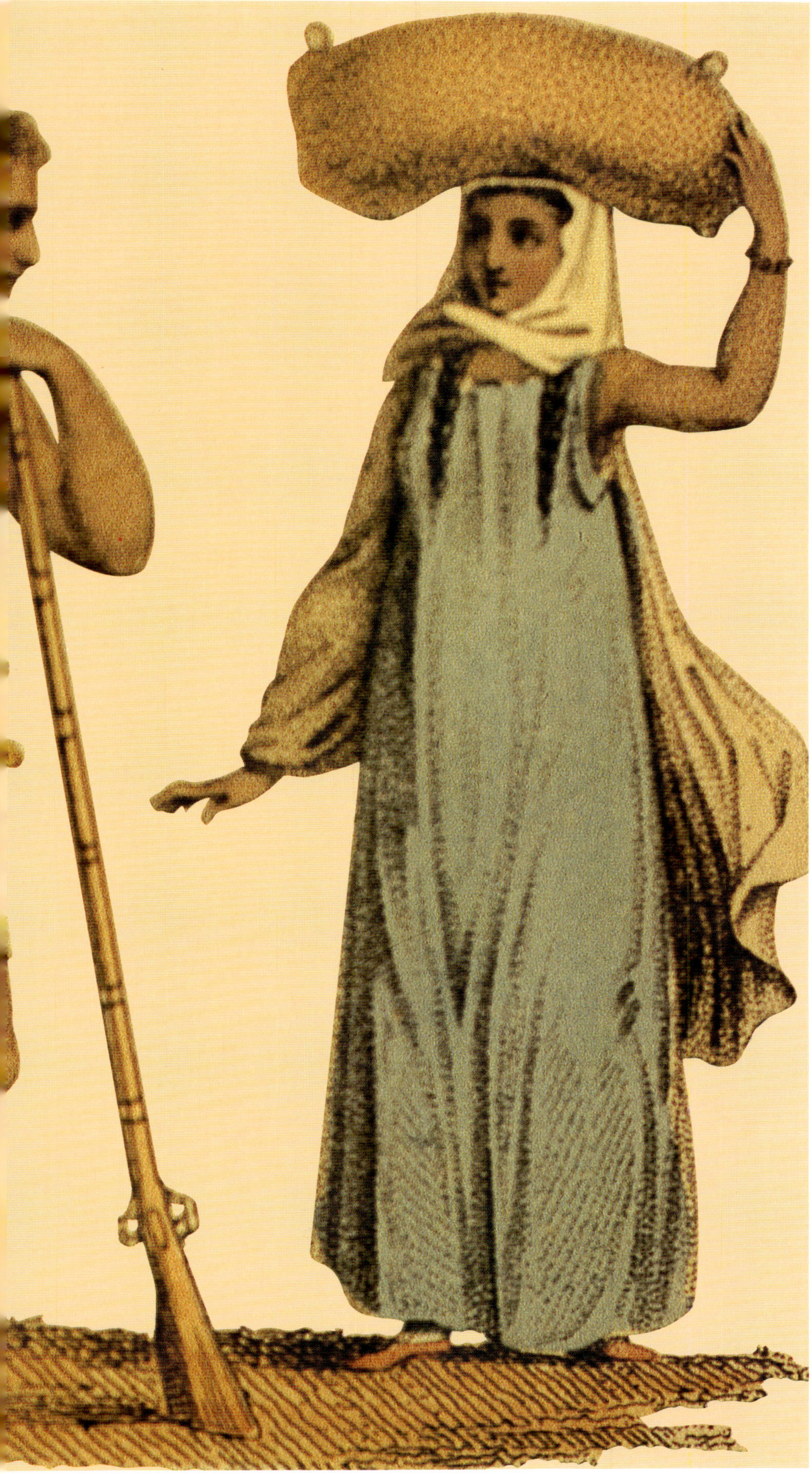

AMINA KULIBALI

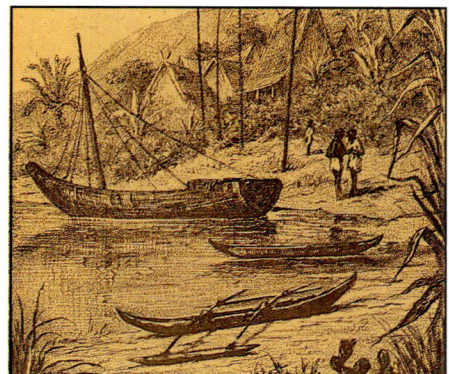

The Name of Senegal

Senegal was probably named by the Berber tribes, the Sanjadja (called the Azanaga by the Portuguese), who lived in Mauritania and went on frequent excursions throughout the river region. The Wolofs have a most poetic etymology: in their language, *suñugal* means "our canoe," a symbol for the future. Some say that the name comes from the naiveté of a cartographer who had asked some fishermen what the name of the river flowing behind them was. They turned around and seeing their boat on the bank replied: "But that's our canoe" (*li siñui gal lë*).

Love Song

*Now that our friendship is but sighs,
I'm sorry I ever met you.
If I had known! If I had known!
A good heart should not seek love,
A good heart is like a virgin bride
It does not last long.
Oh Fulani woman whose name is Roky
The praise singer bids you farewell,
Fulani woman, born of a golden flask,
The praise singer bids you farewell,
Woman with lovely hands, noble pearl,
Most beautiful of all women,
The praise singer bids you farewell,
The praise singer leaves for Bayote;
Bayote's children run away in the night,
On a dark night the journey back is hard,
But only for those who have no
Lovely memory in their hearts.
But I carry within me
The image of my noble Fulani woman,
White teeth, dark lips,
High chest,
And three shining pythons around her neck.
The Hippo of the Great River,
the sacred Hippopotamus
of our fathers has fallen.
My Coumba, born of a golden flask,
Is no more.*

Proverb

"*Before you shake a tree, check to see where the fruits will fall.*"

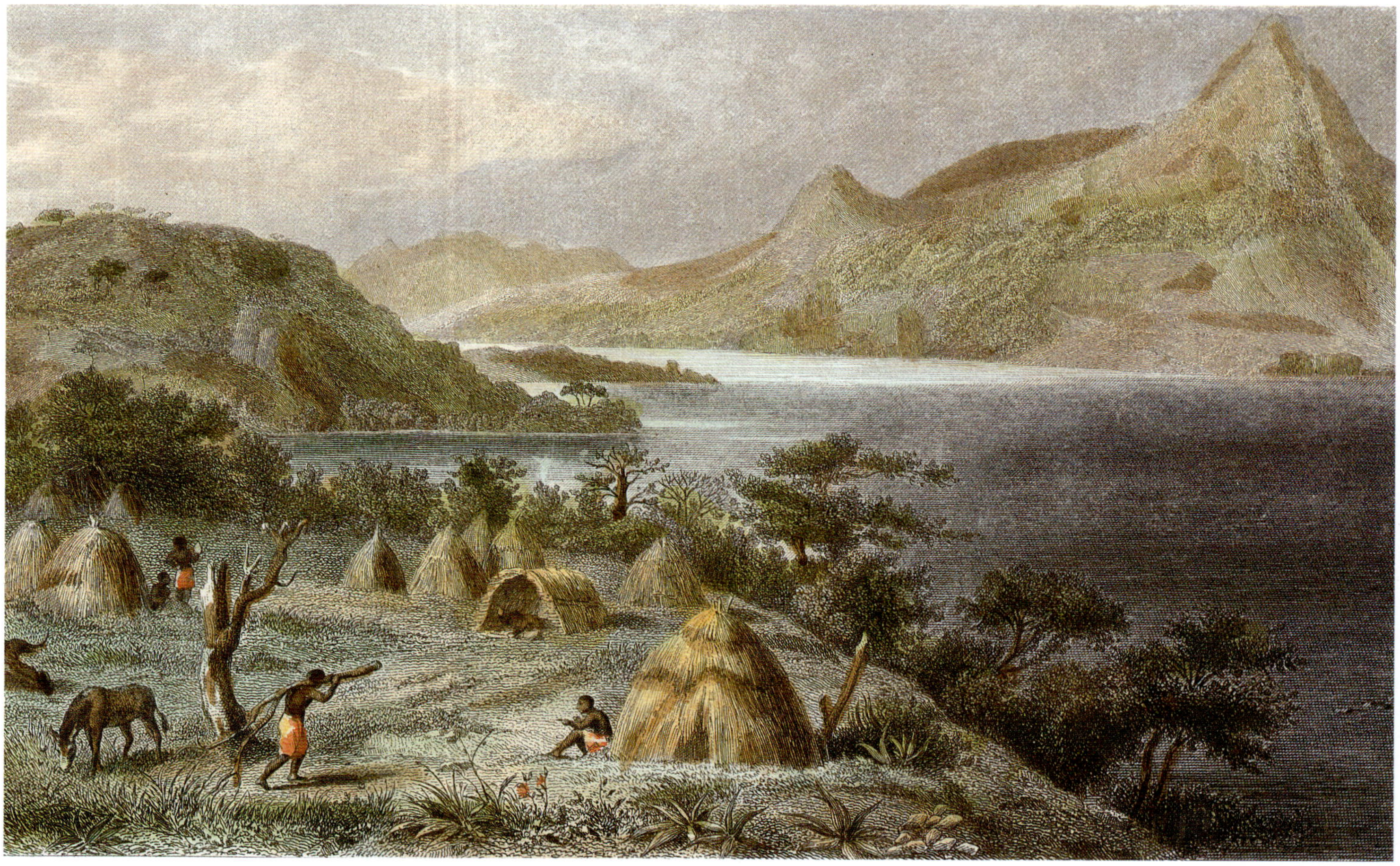

"THEY WENT DEEP INTO THE KINGDOM OF GABU"

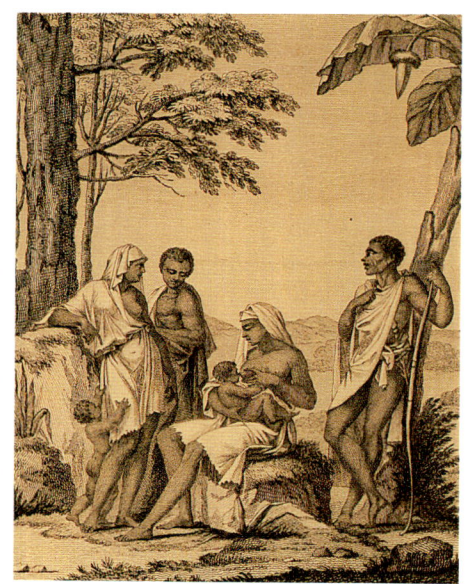

Proverb

In a year of poor harvests, the head of a family told his wives to prepare only one meal a day. One evening, one of the children started crying out for food. And his father said:

"You must learn to carry a burden on your bare head, because sometimes you won't find a rag to cushion it."

Amina was not one of those people who fold at the first wind, like banana plants. When the young man left, it seemed to her that she was going to die of shame upon her sullied bed. And when she realized that she was pregnant, she could not bear the humiliation this was going to bring upon her father the king.

Amina decided to go to a place so far away that everyone would think her dead.

One night, she left her village, followed by a slave who carried her jewelry, as well as twelve boys and twelve girls who escorted them. Bearing her personal belongings, including her twelve bags full of gold, they crossed rivers and climbed over mountains. They reached Gambia and went deep into the kingdom of Gabu. By now, more than six months had passed, and they lacked food and were exhausted; it seemed they would die of hunger, their hands full of gold.

The boys couldn't tighten their bows any more, and the girls had forgotten how to dig up roots. They lived in fear of men and animals. The least noise terrified them.

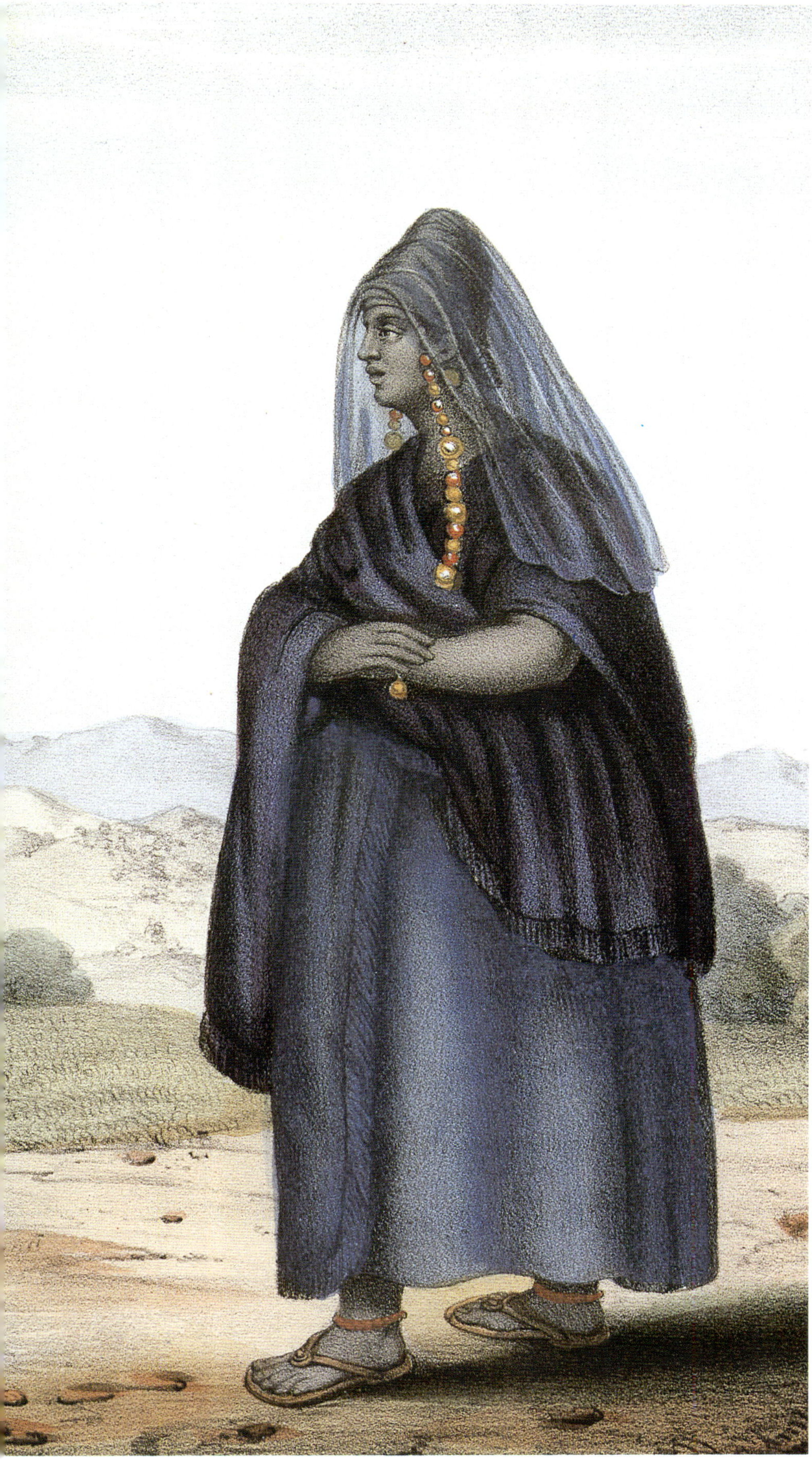

AMINA KULIBALI

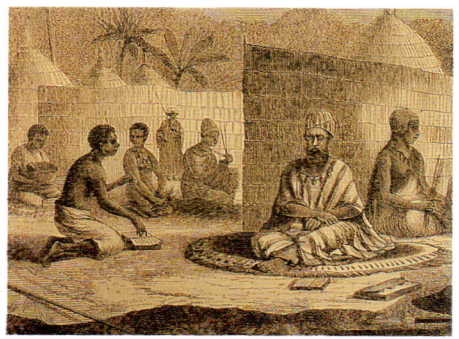

Story of the Sine-Saloum

There were once two kingdoms on the banks of the River Saloum. On the shores of the ocean stood the kingdom of Sine, which was populated by the Serer. East of Sine stretched the kingdom of Saloum, peopled by Serers, Wolofs, and Tukulors. These two kingdoms were well organized. Their rulers were called *burbas*. Powerful and respected, these great kings surrounded themselves with counselors and ministers. They ruled, meted out justice, collected taxes, waged wars.

The Serers were the earliest inhabitants of that country. One day the Malinkés arrived. They crossed the River Saloum, invaded the Sine, and took over the capital of the Serers. The latter, being peaceful farmers, preferred submission and did not leave the country. There were many unions between the victorious chieftains and the Serer women. The two races became one.

A Serer princess married to a Malinké chief gave birth to a boy who was named Ouagana. This Ouagana became a great warrior, dethroned the Serer burba, and moved the capital of the Sine. The ancient burbas never tried to get back the throne. Then, a brother of Ouagana managed to take over Saloum and to dethrone the Tukulor burba who ruled there. Thus the two kingdoms fell into the hands of one family, the family of the Gelowars.

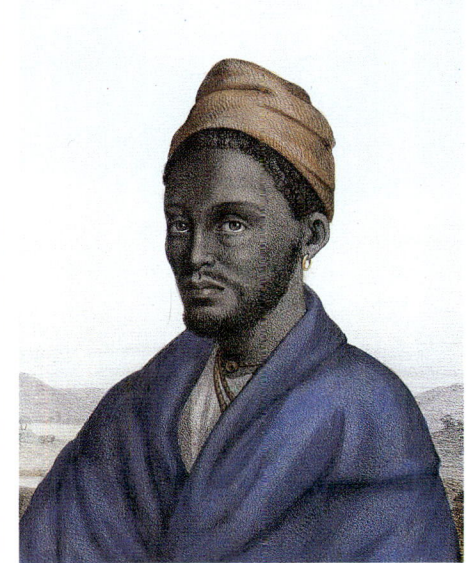

A SERER WOMAN

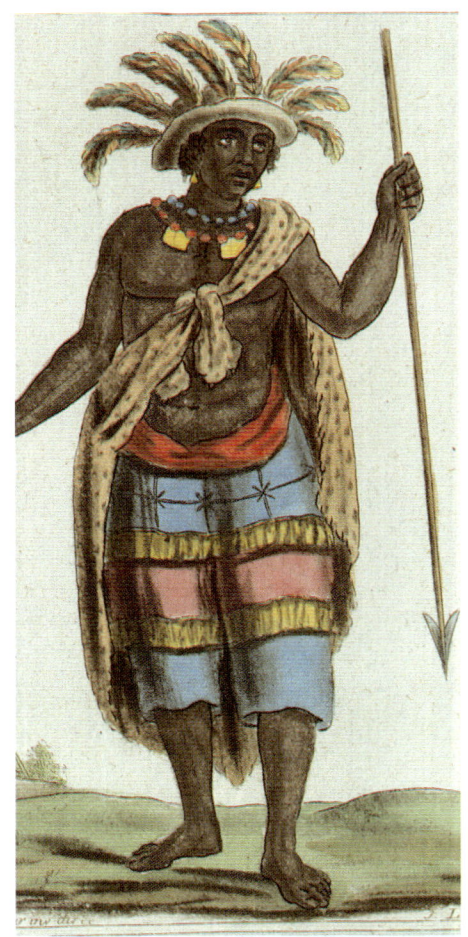

One day they reached a deep ravine whose name they did not know. And there, they took refuge in an immense cave by the sea.

Amina was tired, her heavy belly was dragging her down into the sand, and her heart, which was even heavier, pulled her to the ground that murmured with her ancestors. She let herself just lie there and dismissed her servants, saying that she wished to be buried in the golden sand.

The youngsters with her began to look for a village by the sea; but the girls refused to leave their mistress, whom they tried to soothe with a song:

Go away, dove! Go away, dove!
Today, they call me Amina,
Go away, dove! Go away, dove!
Before, I was Amina, sister of Tiada Kulibali,
Go away, dove! Go away, dove!
Now, I eat from a dirty bowl.
Go away, dove!
Fly away, take me to my father and my mother!

The Oral Tradition

It is time to decolonize history, and to listen to the great voice of oral tradition—to the message that has been passed on from mouth to ear and from one generation to another. Europe has always fetishized writing, reassuring itself with the Latin adage: *Verba volent, scripta maent* (words fly away, writing remains). Long gone are the days of bards and troubadours, of *chansons de gestes* and folk tales. Still, the word is closer to life than writing. Oral tradition shows things in the flesh, full of color. It explains the world, situates history in a sociocultural context, and "waters the dry bones of the past with fresh blood."
In Senegal, in 1941, a well-read man from Dagana, Amadou Wade, wrote, in Wolof (using Arabic characters), a chronicle of the kingdom of Walo spanning six hundred and sixty-nine years, including a list of fifty-two *brak* (kings) going back to the formation of the Wolof ethnic group at the beginning of the twelfth century. It is possible to reconstitute, thanks to the praise singers, or *griots*, the epics of the Damel of Cayor, of the burbas and the Gelowars of Sine, of the Teens of Baol, of the Satifi of Fouta.

Proverb

"Wish good fortune upon others for the love of your own."

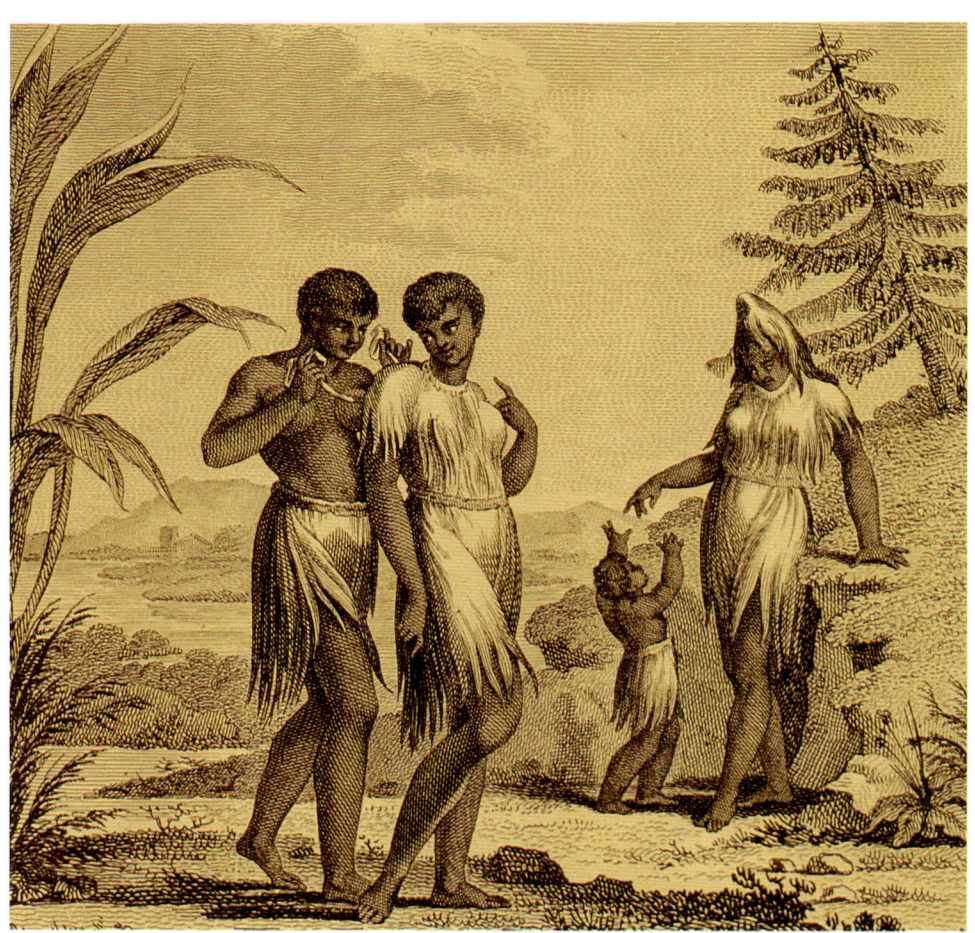

"TAKE ME TO MY FATHER AND MY MOTHER..."

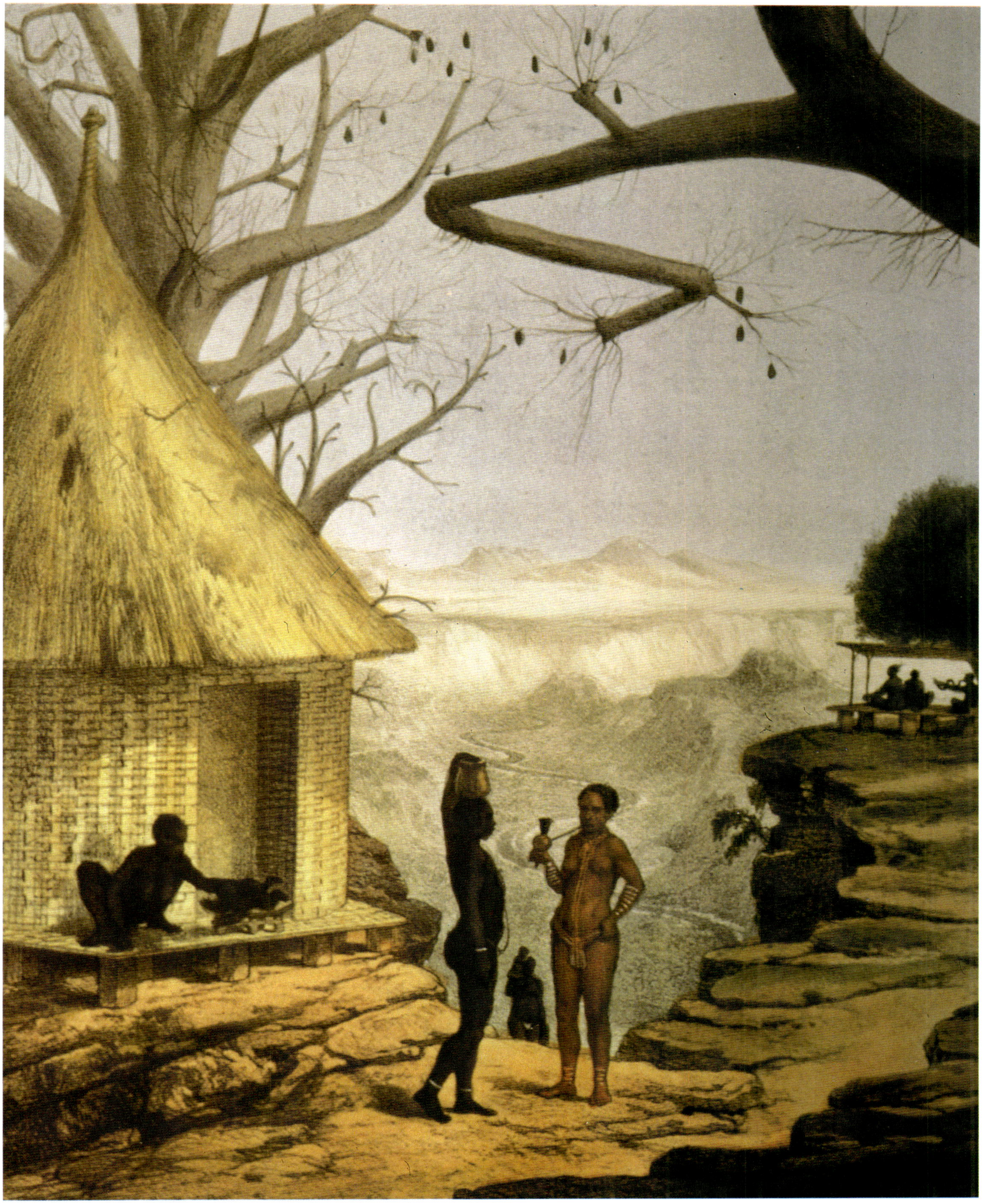

AMINA KULIBALI

"THEY BEGAN LOOKING FOR A VILLAGE BY THE SEA"

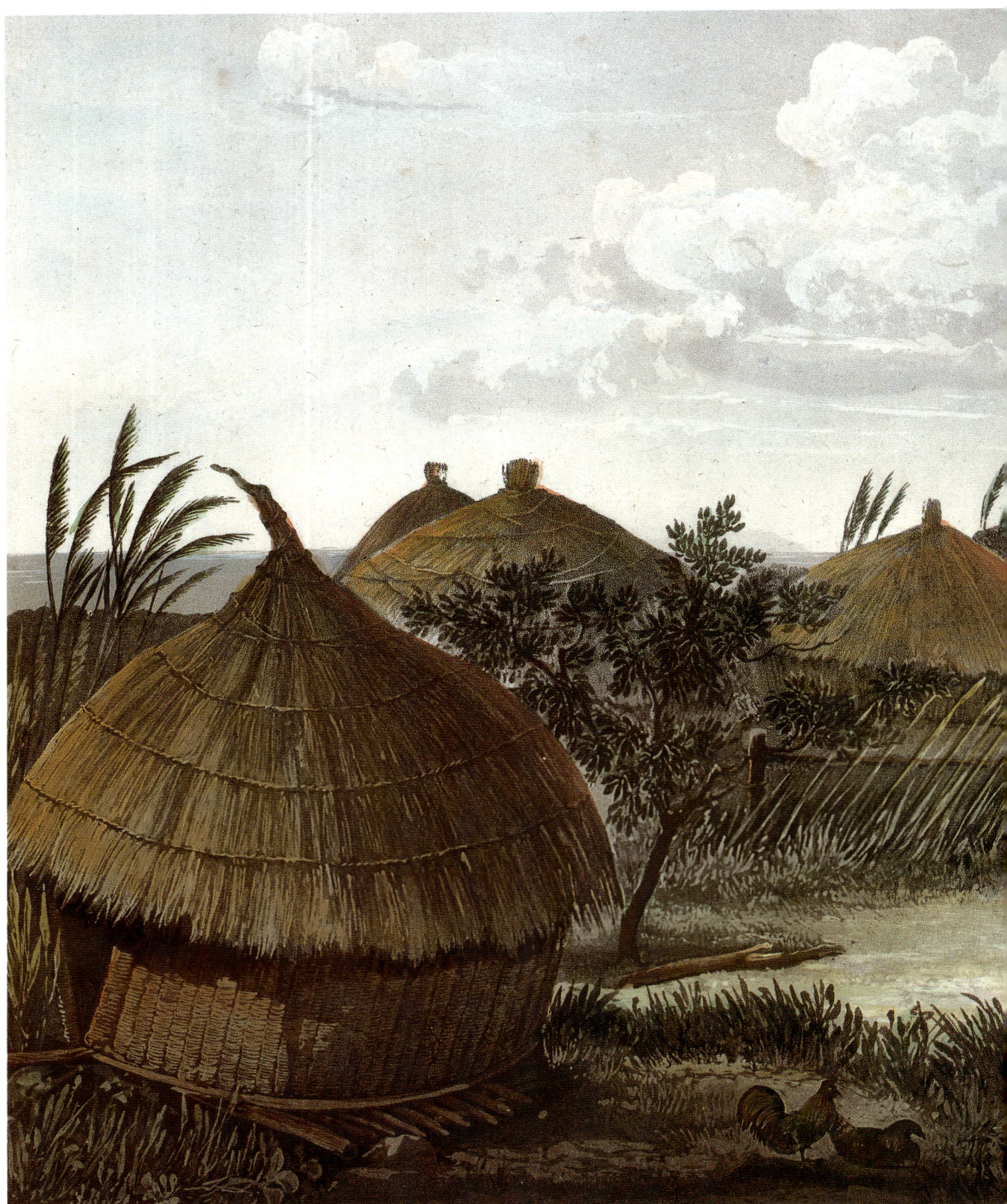

"THEY FOUND A FISHING

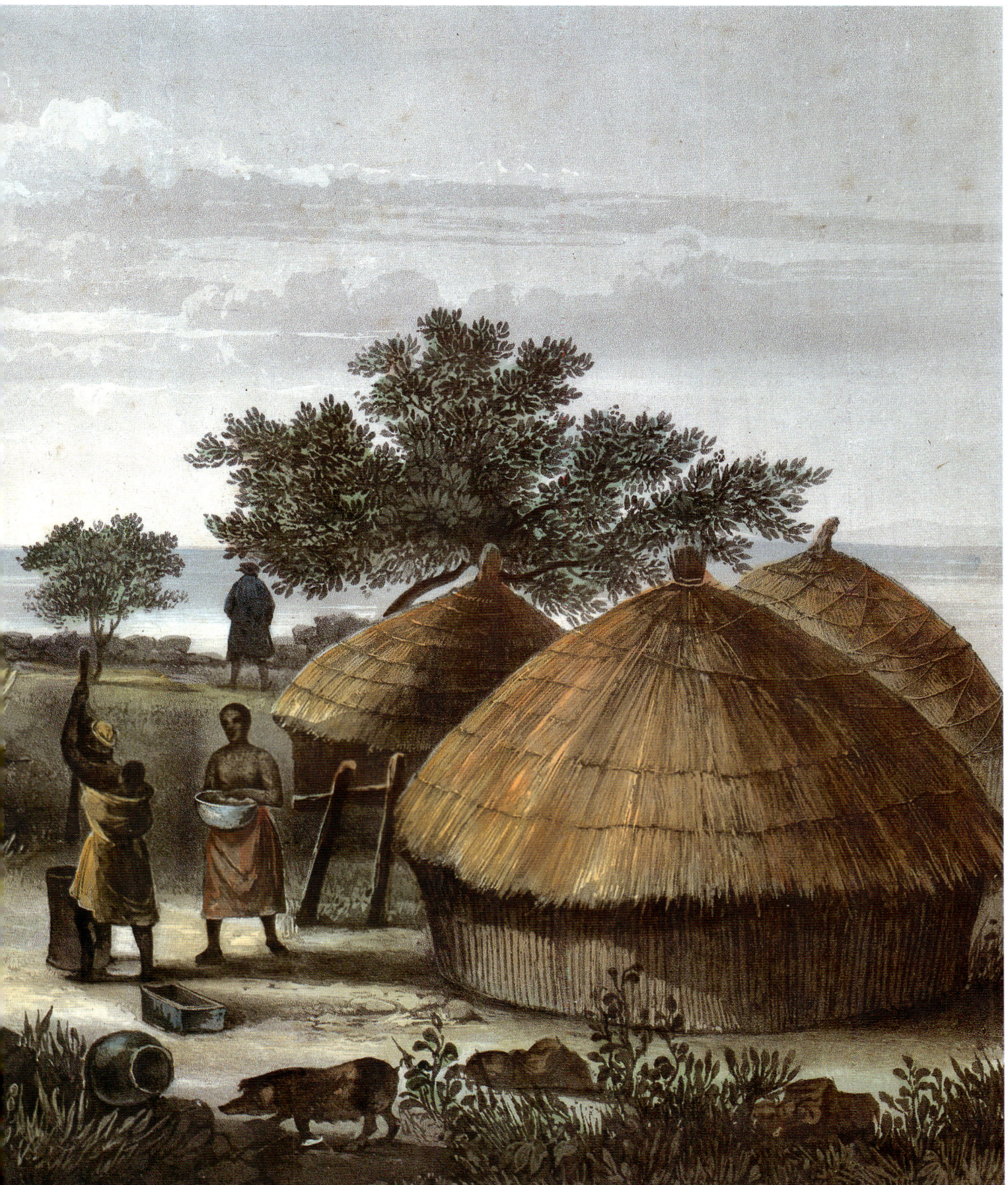

Meanwhile, the boys had found a fishing village, where they were offered a meal of fish and rice as soon as they got there because they looked so thin. They refused to eat before their mistress did and went back to the cave, arms full of food.

A boy by the name of Kaya Manabal had followed them from afar and hid nearby.

The next day, at sunrise, he saw Amina, who was being combed by one of the young women. When Amina saw she was being watched, she put her hands around her belly and ran away deep into the cave.

The child said to his father that he had seen the most beautiful woman on earth in the ravine of Tirindi. The father gave the news to the chief of the village who passed it on to the king of Gabu who raced to the cave wishing to see the most beautiful woman on earth.

Powerful warriors respectfully ran beside the king. Behind them, the king's old chamberlain pulled himself along, out of breath.

Twelve boys and twelve girls stood as a wall before Amina. But the king had noticed Amina's face and he stopped as if struck by an arrow.

The old chamberlain went into the cave, trying to convince the beautiful stranger to give herself up. But Amina stubbornly refused, and the twelve boys and girls tightened around her body like a vine. Getting his arm through the boys and girls, the king tried to bring Amina to him. She examined him closely and said: "If I follow you, the child who is within me will be king in the country where he will be born."

The king answered: "Fine, you will be mistress of my house and your child will succeed me."

Once at the palace, she distributed bags of gold earrings to the important people there. The people were dazzled and threw themselves at her feet because they had never seen such treasures come out of such ordinary sacks. Even those who had waged wars as far as the land of Galam had never seen anything like it.

Many moons went by in endless celebration, and many simple folk said the joy would never end.

Choice cuts of meat were given to the nobles as well as to the village chiefs, to the canoe owners and their servants, to the heads of families and their wives and children. Once the provisions were exhausted, the guests returned to their lands and the king swore before all that never would Amina eat meat that was more than two days old; and finally without any hesitation, he declared that Amina's heart would never be consumed by jealousy because he would have no other wife but her. And as soon as that was said, he chased away all the other wives who lived in his house.

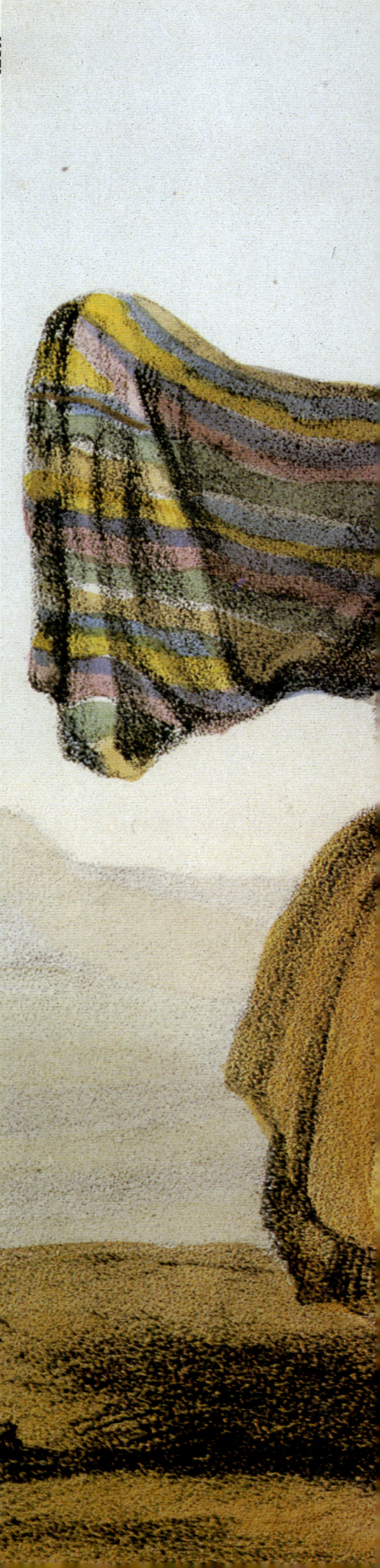

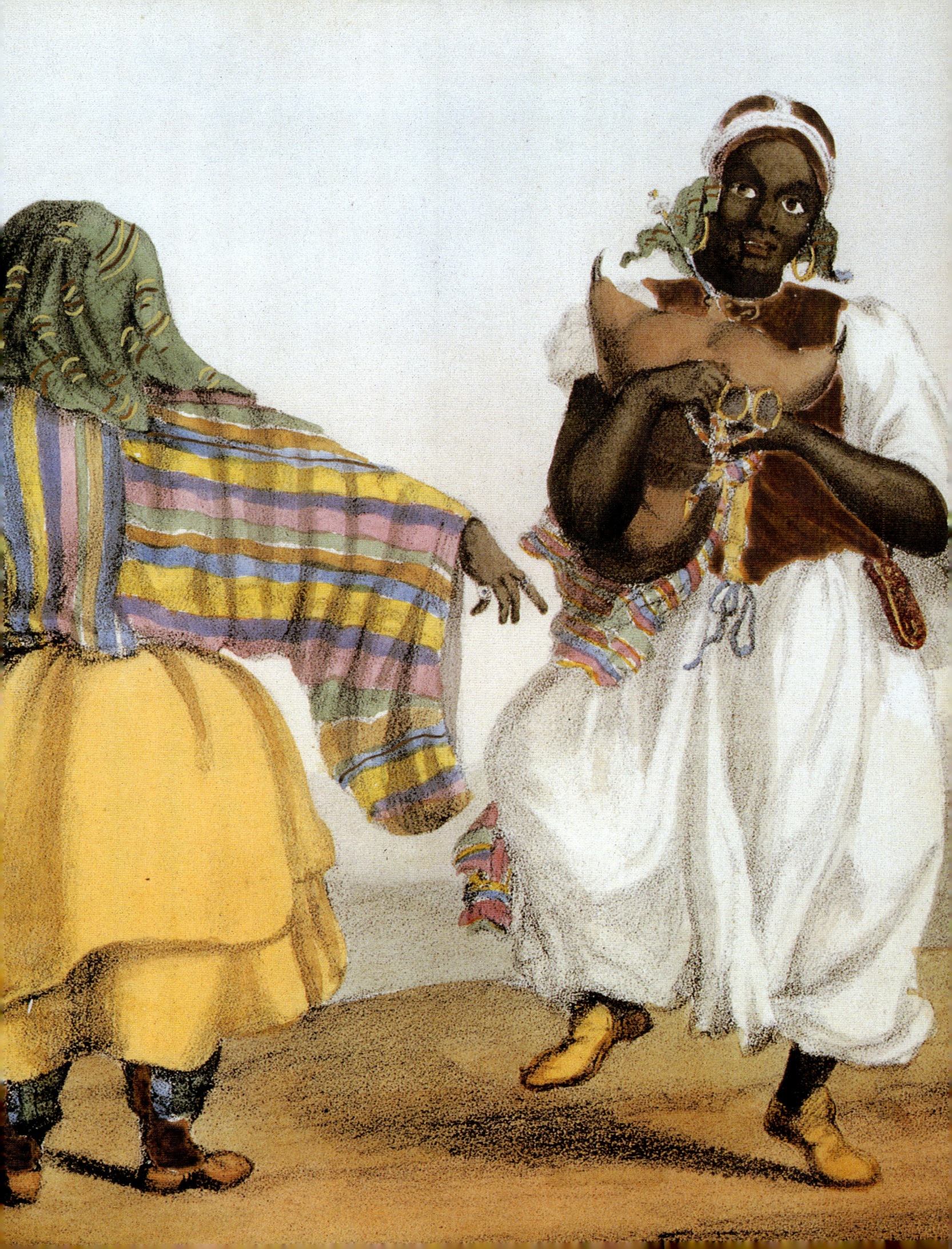

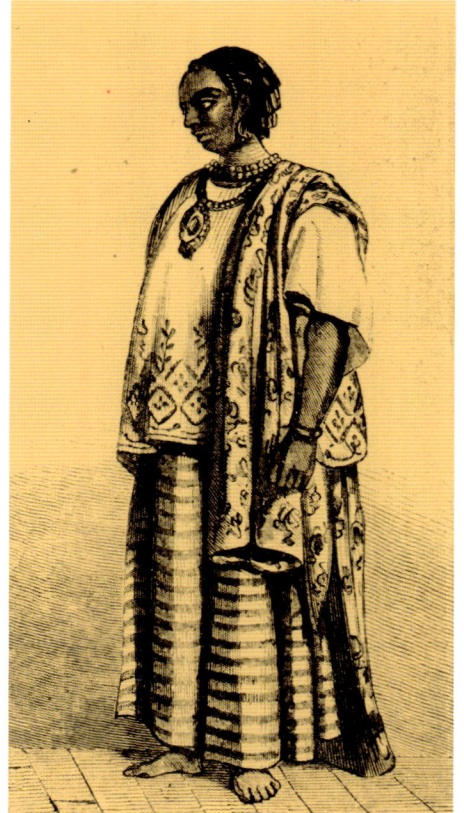

The Lingers

At the end of the sixteenth century, the *linger*, the king's mother or full blood sister, used all her influence at the court—women like Koumba Ngonindiaye, mother of two successive kings, or Yacine Boubou, a true Senegalese Iphigeneia, ready to sacrifice herself so that her husband could be king of Cayor. Some linger did not hesitate to go to war, like the daughter of Lat Soukaabê (1697–1719) who, dressed as a man, went after the Trarza Moors on horseback and beat them at Ngram-Gram.

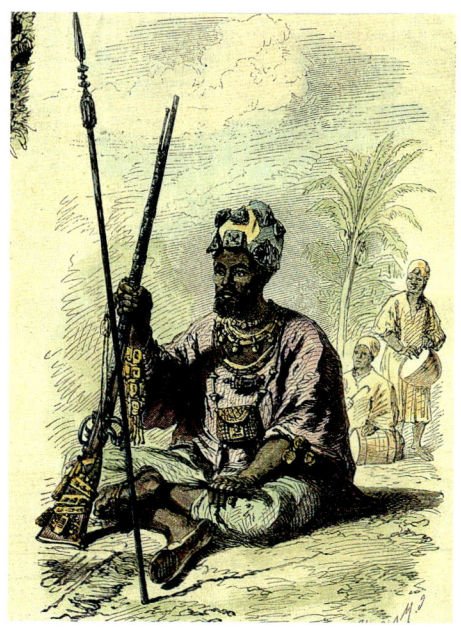

THE KING OF SINE

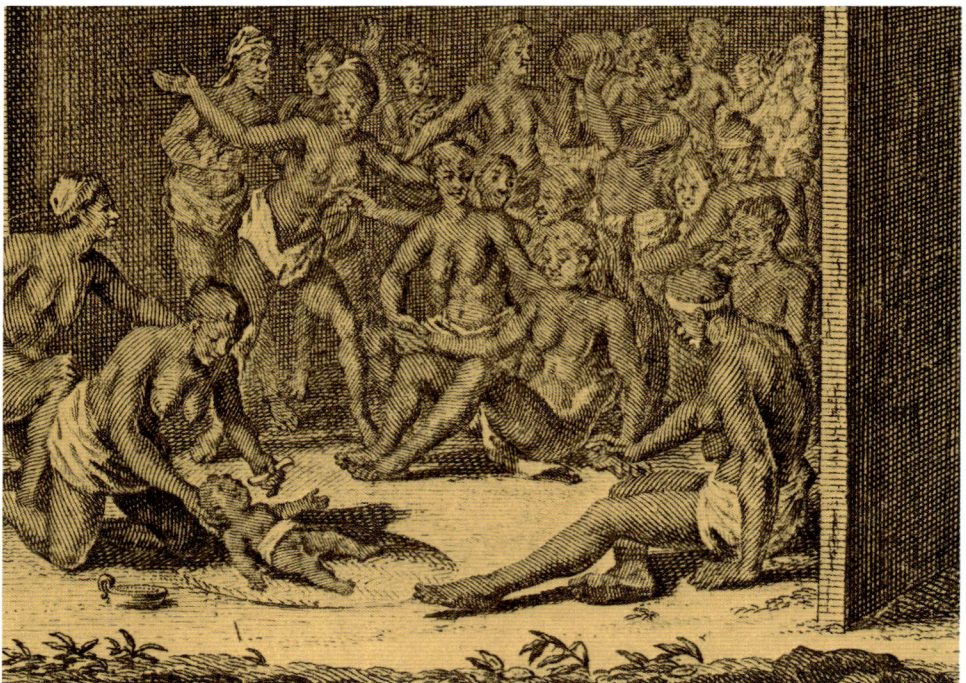

THE BIRTH

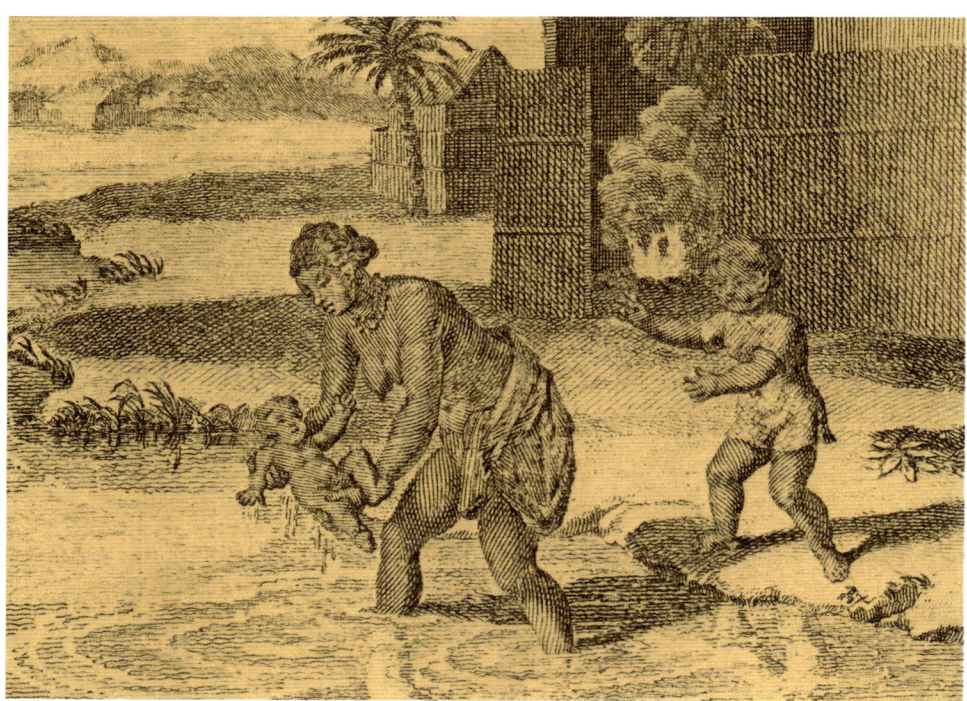

The next day, Amina gave birth to a daughter who sneezed thrice, as if to greet the assembled crowd, then fell asleep. And the king declared that the children of this girl would be the kings of the land of Gabu, as if they were his own, born of the womb of his heart.

So ends the story of Amina Kulibali.

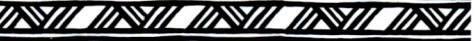

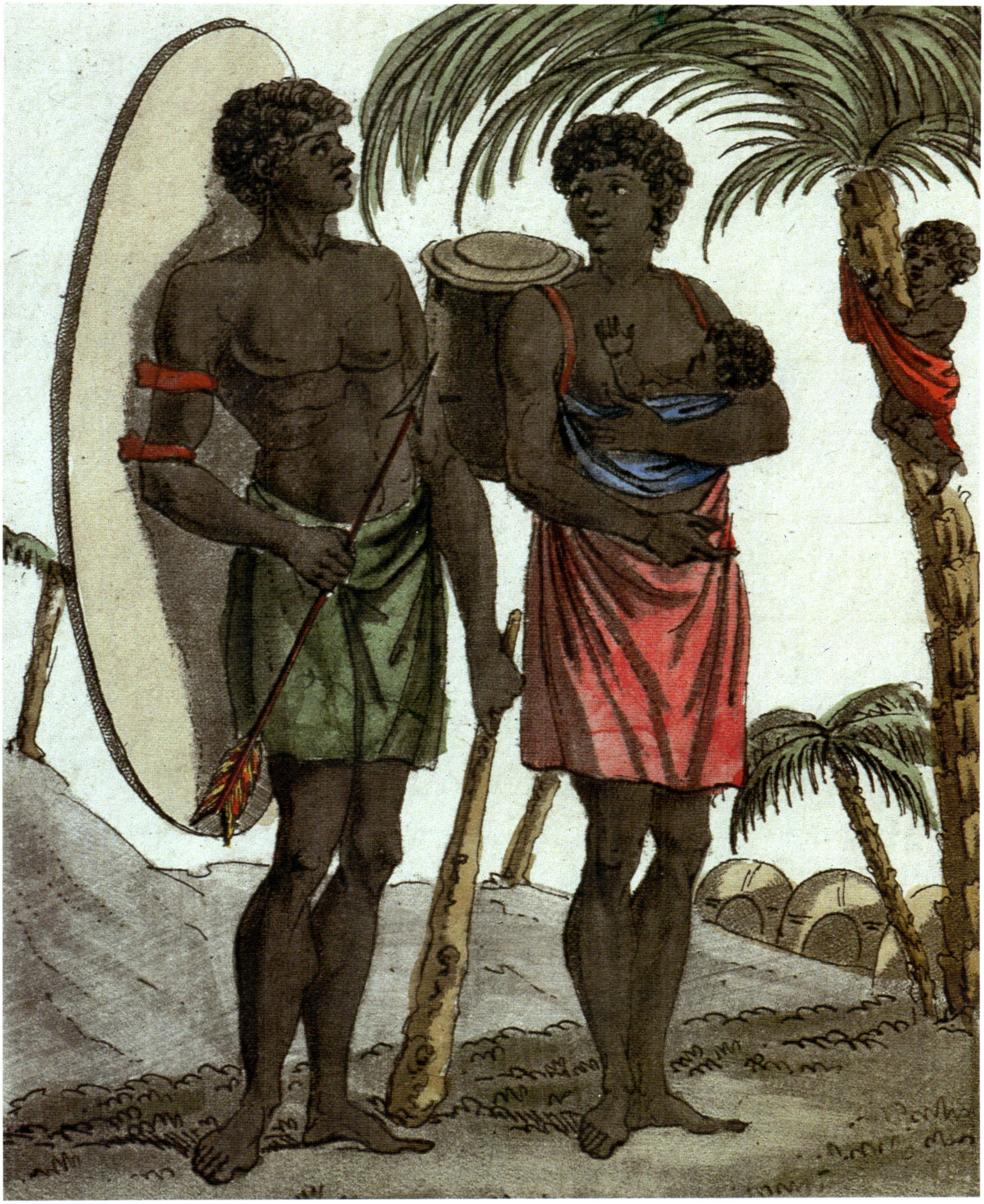

"THE CHILDREN OF THIS GIRL WILL BECOME KINGS OF GABU"

And that's how the celebrated lineage came to be: the golden dynasty of the princes of Gabu, among them Goria and his three sisters, who went to settle in the Koular and in the archipelago of Gaudoul, between Gsangomar and Gambia, where they would remain.

This means that the Gelowars of the Koular have the same mother and father as those from the Sine and the Saloum. From the latter descended Nuick, and from the former came the great Wagane Faye who was so prominent in Serer antiquity.

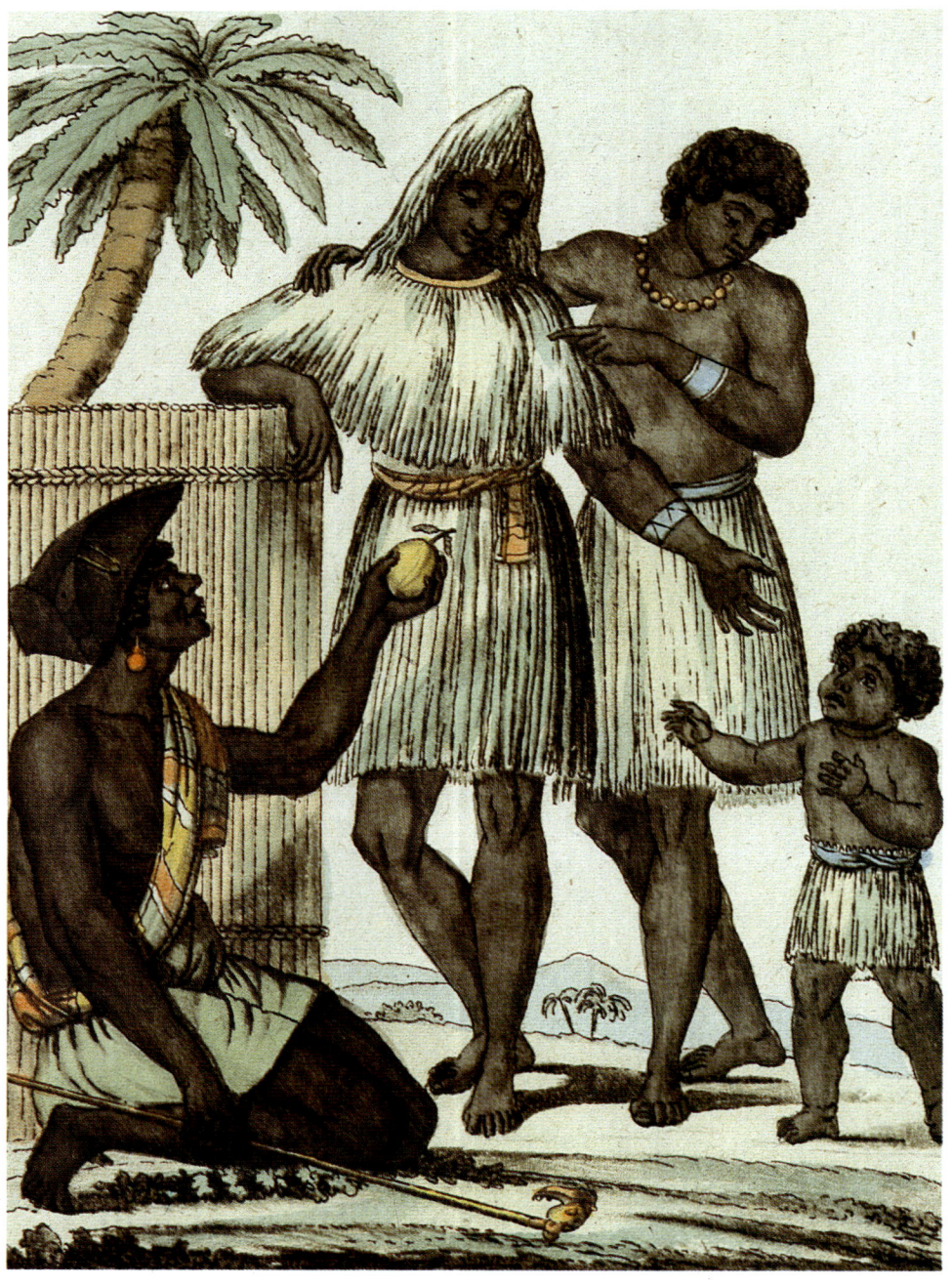

"AND THAT'S HOW THE CELEBRATED LINEAGE CAME TO BE"

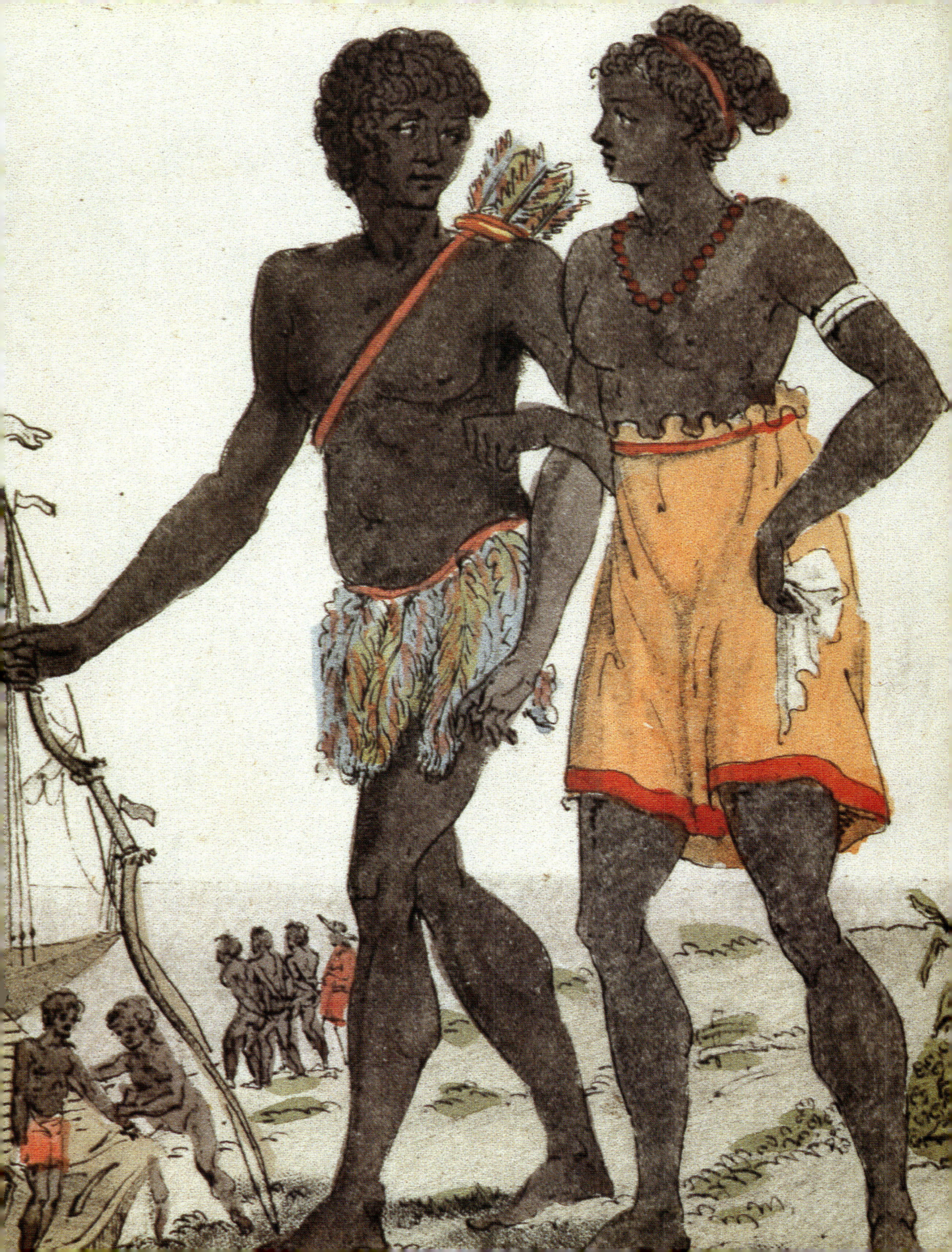

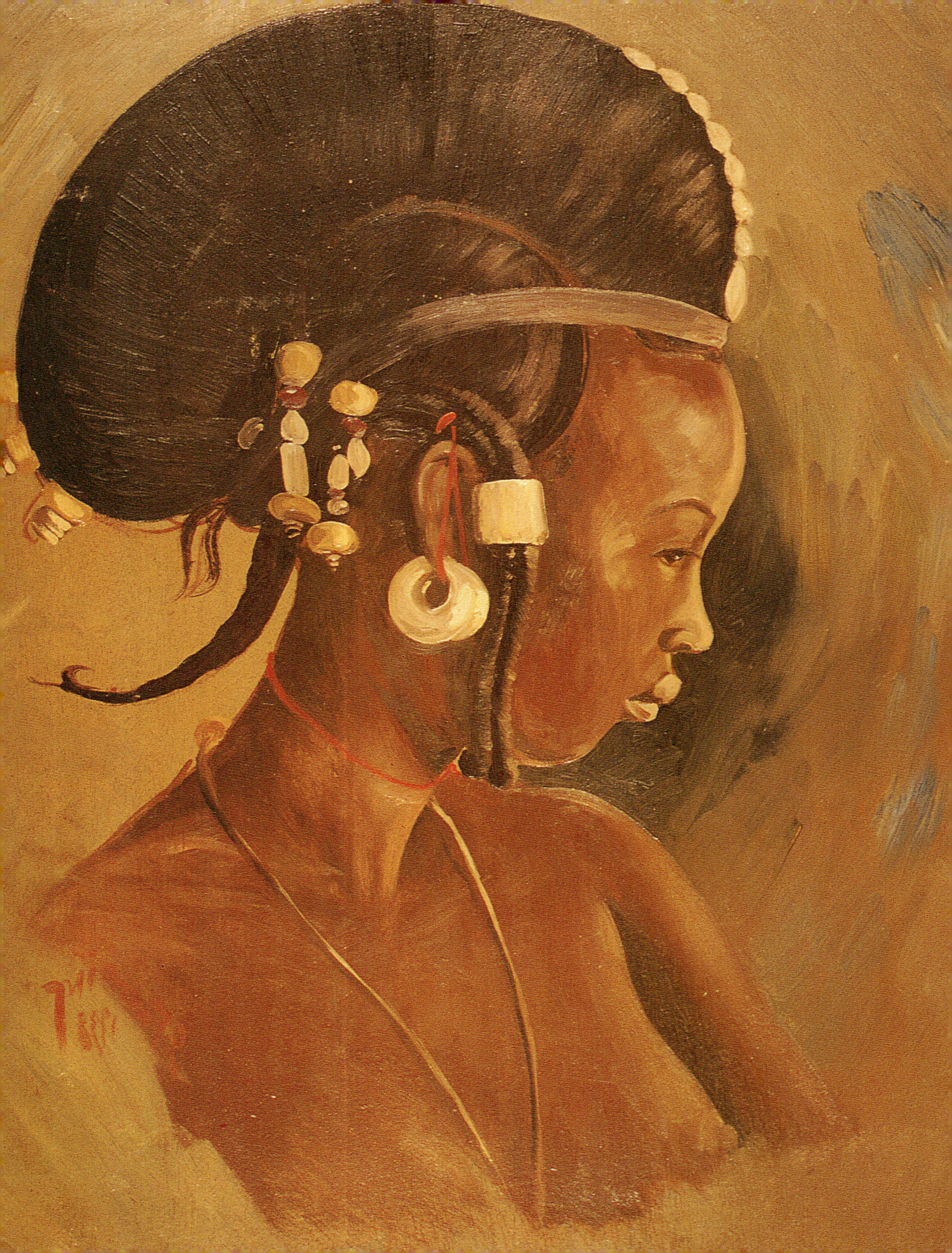

WORDS
OF AN ORDINARY WOMAN

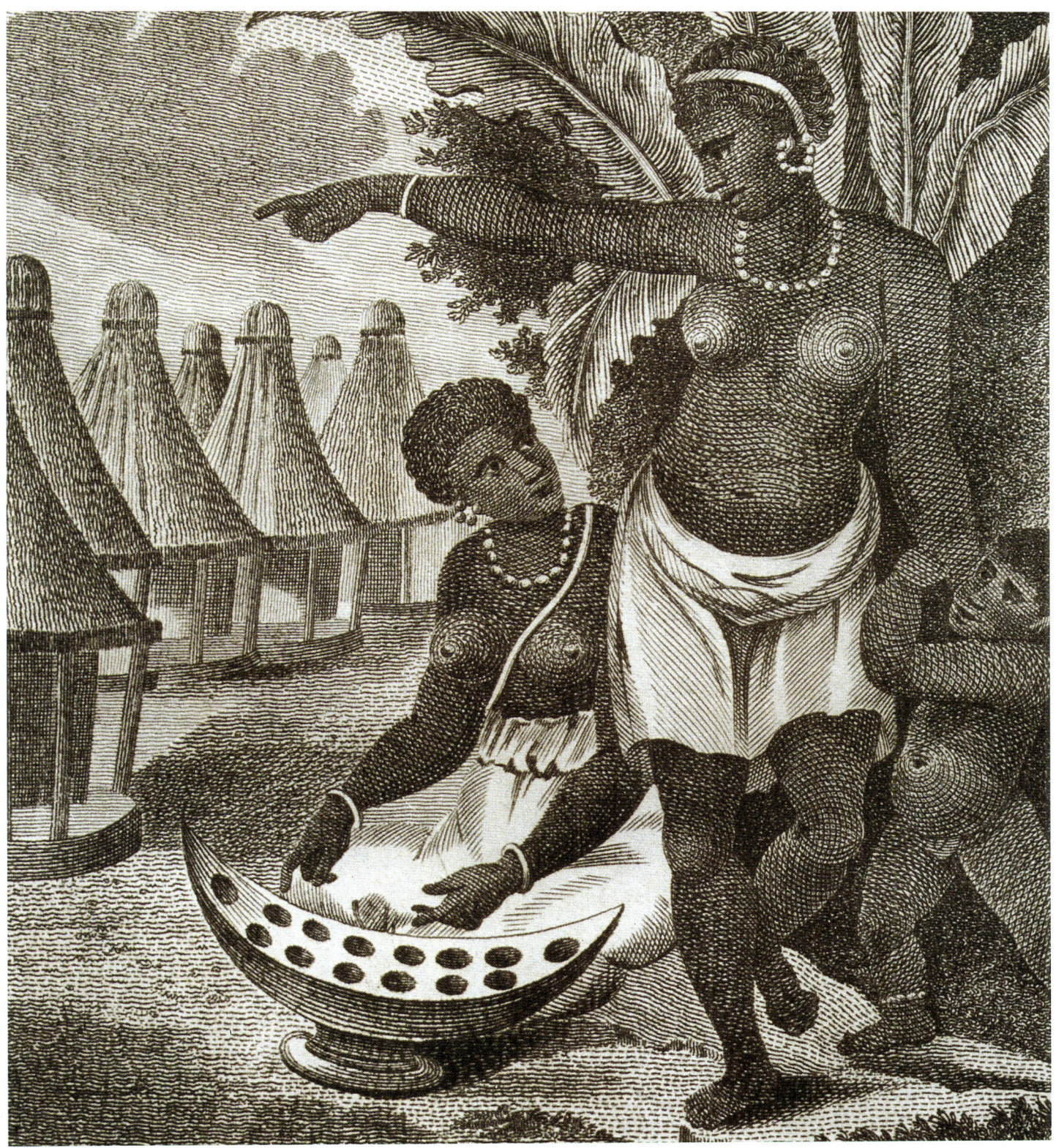

Anything that approaches happiness becomes happiness. When you look for millet stems, you don't seek them for themselves but for the grain of their ears. Do you know the parable of the river? "The more water there is in the river, the more water the river desires." The human heart is like the river. The fuller the heart is, the fuller it wishes to be.

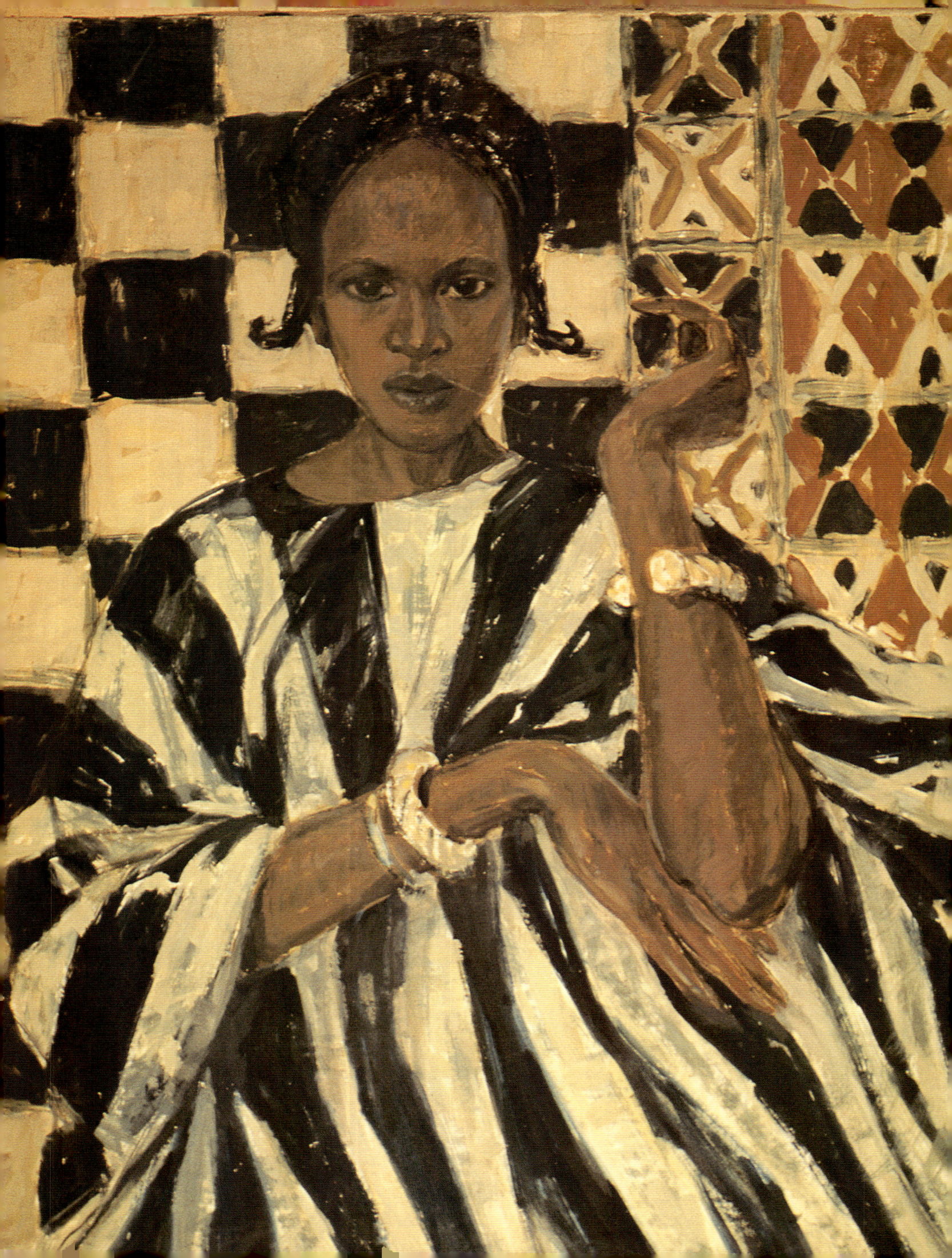

AMINA OF ZARIA

THE PINK-HEELED YOUNG GIRL WHO DEFENDED THE HAUSA PEOPLE

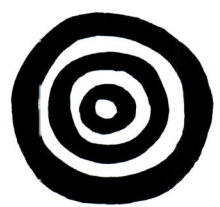

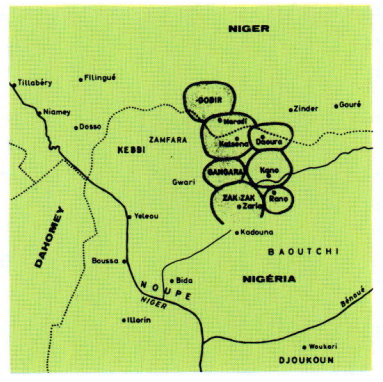

She was the best rider and the finest archer in Hausaland, and she would charge the advancing enemy troops...

BETWEEN THE NIGER RIVER AND LAKE CHAD STRETCHES A FERTILE REGION: HAUSA COUNTRY.

THOUSANDS OF YEARS AGO, WHEN THE SAHARA WAS NOT YET A DESERT BUT A VAST OASIS POPULATED MOSTLY BY BLACKS, THE HAUSA LIVED IN A mountainous zone that is now called the Aïr.

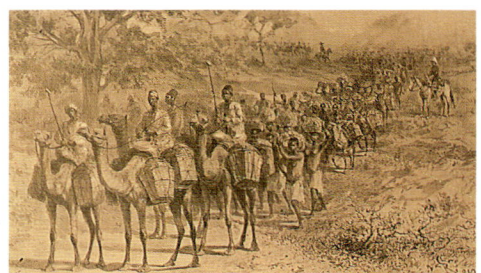

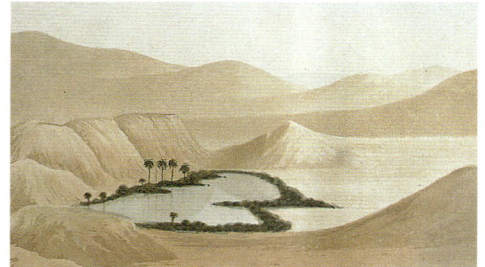

The desertification pushed them toward the loop of the Niger River, while their neighbors went toward the banks of the Nile where they founded a new civilization: many specialists today acknowledge that the Hausa language and that of ancient Egypt are related.

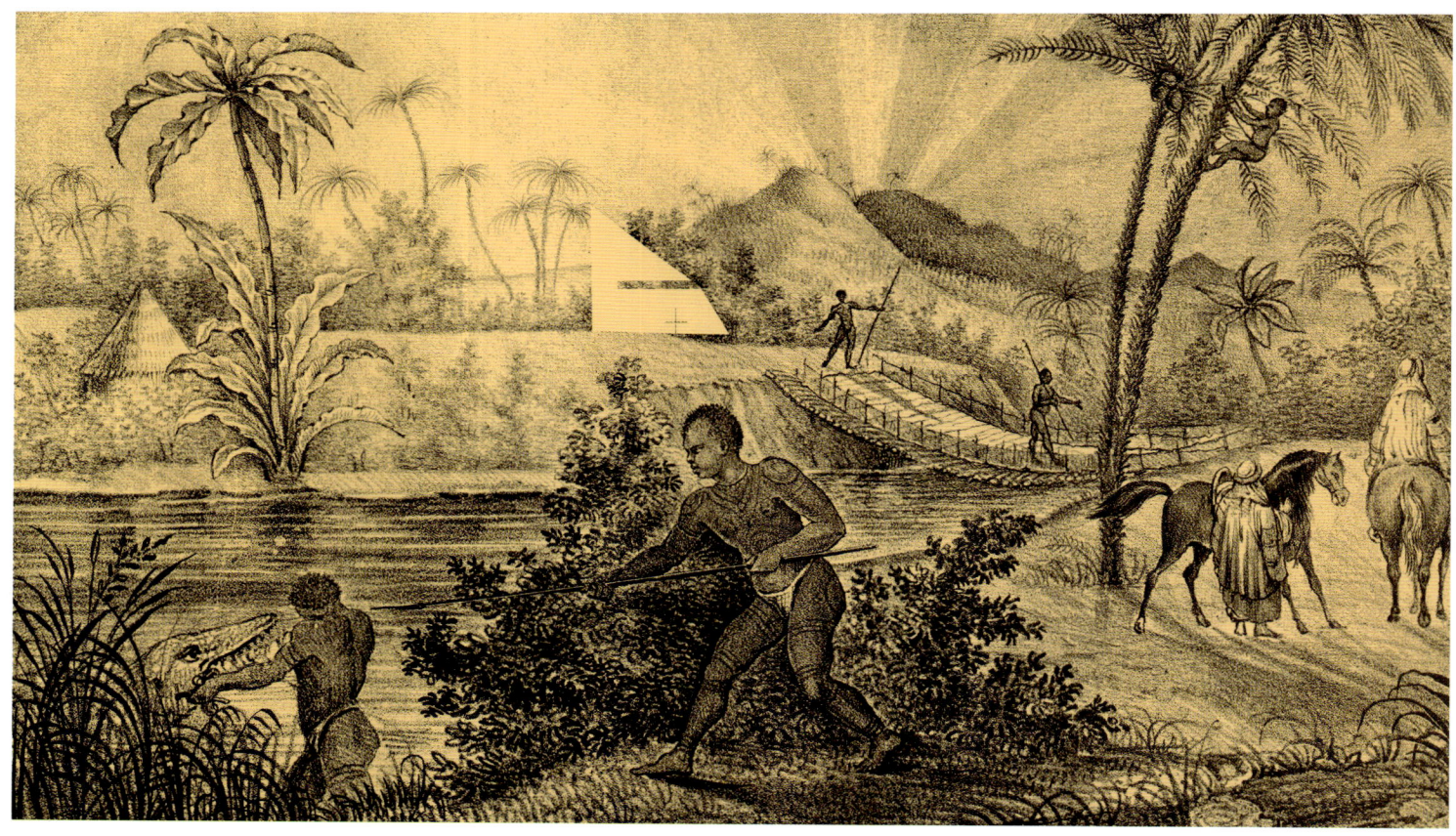

"WHEN THE SAHARA WAS NOT YET A DESERT"

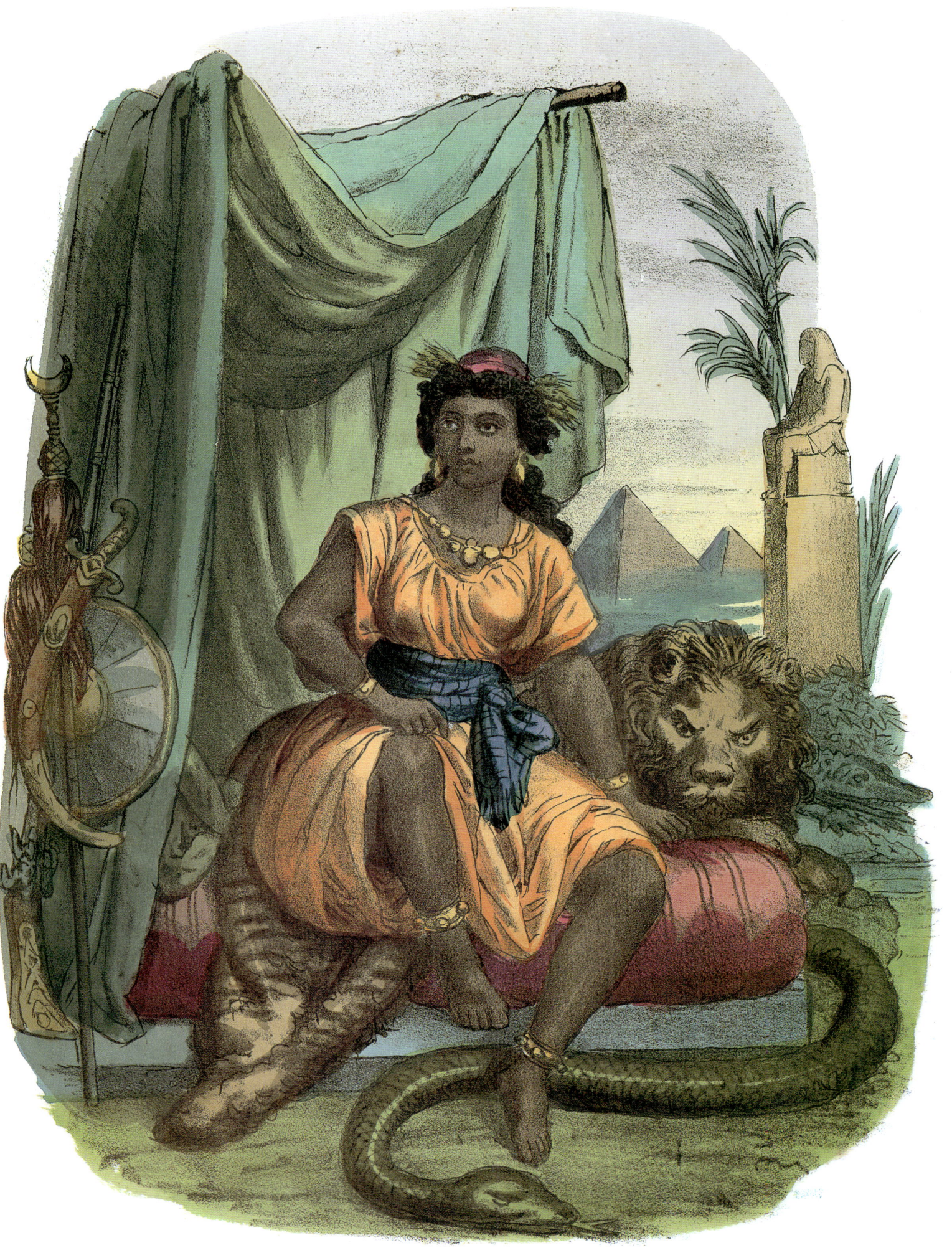

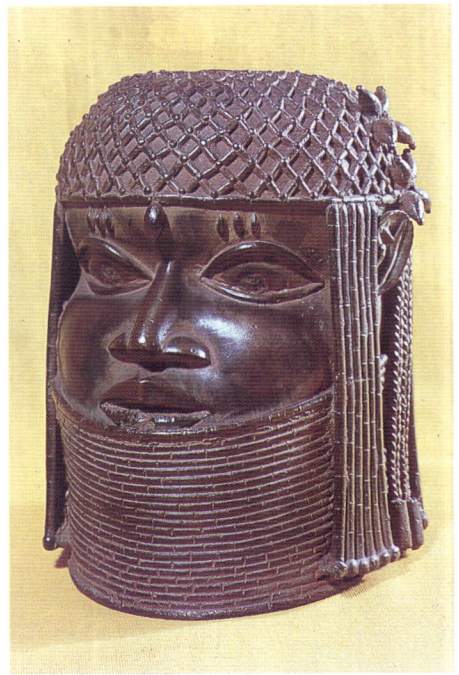

Usman dan Fodio

Usman dan Fodio, founder of the Fulani empire of Sokoto, is the most significant figure in the history of Niger in the nineteenth century. A Fulani born in the Hausa state of Gobir in what is now northwestern Nigeria, he was the thirteenth chief of an old family that had come from the Senegalese Fouta three hundred years earlier. He had received a strict Muslim education and had been sent to study in Agadez. When he came back he began preaching the religion of his forefathers. Because of his education, he was called upon to teach and instruct the king's children. But Usman's reputation became so great that it worried the king. Furthermore, this Hausa king didn't want Usman preaching the word of Mohammed. And so one day, the king sent him back to his village.

There, followers gathered around him. Usman became more and more powerful. The king was beginning to get seriously concerned. One legend claims that he tried to get rid of this new prophet. A member of the Fulani prophet's inner circle, accused of disturbing the peace, was arrested by order of the king. So Usman attacked the royal garrison and freed his follower. This enraged the king and Usman fled to Gudu.

This incident and Usman's flight incited all the Fulanis in the land to rebel. They proclaimed Usman dan Fodio an imam, "Emir of the Faithful," and managed to defeat the royal cavalry at Kwato Pound (1804). They were emboldened by this success, and in 1808 a large part of what is today called Niger fell into the hands of the Fulanis.

Proverbs

"Whoever has a master is not the master of the load he carries on his back."

"Even if a piece of wood soaked in water for ten years, it would never turn into a cayman."

In the fifteenth century, Africans who were recent Muslim converts invaded the land of the Hausa.

They were peculiar horsemen, wearing helmets and chainmail, astride horses covered in metal caparisons.

Nothing stood in their way. One after another, the cities fell under their yoke, and everyone thought that the land of the Hausa was about to fall into foreign hands.

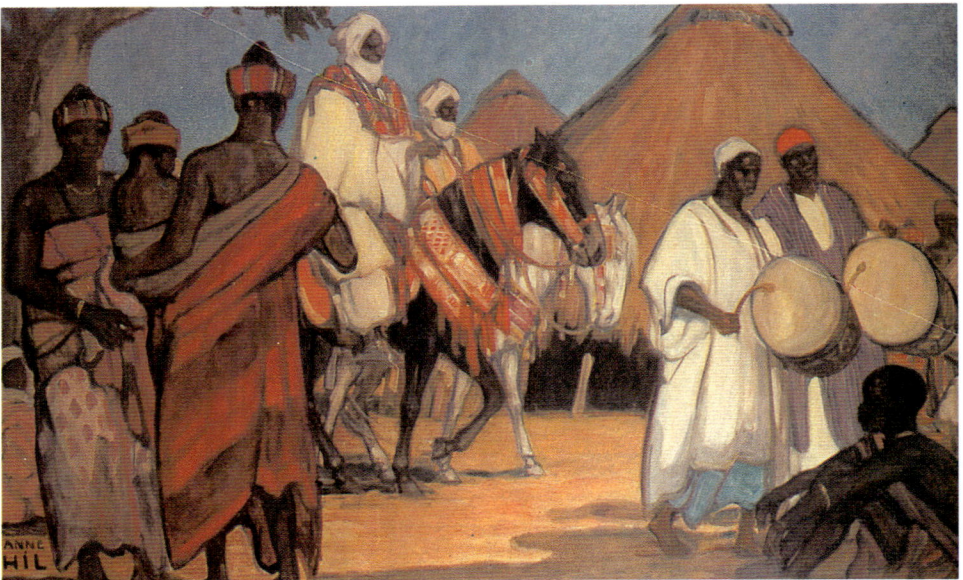

"That's when," the praise singers of Hausaland say, "that's when a pink-heeled young woman, Princess Amina of Zaria, showed her true colors to the world, the ancestors, and the gods."

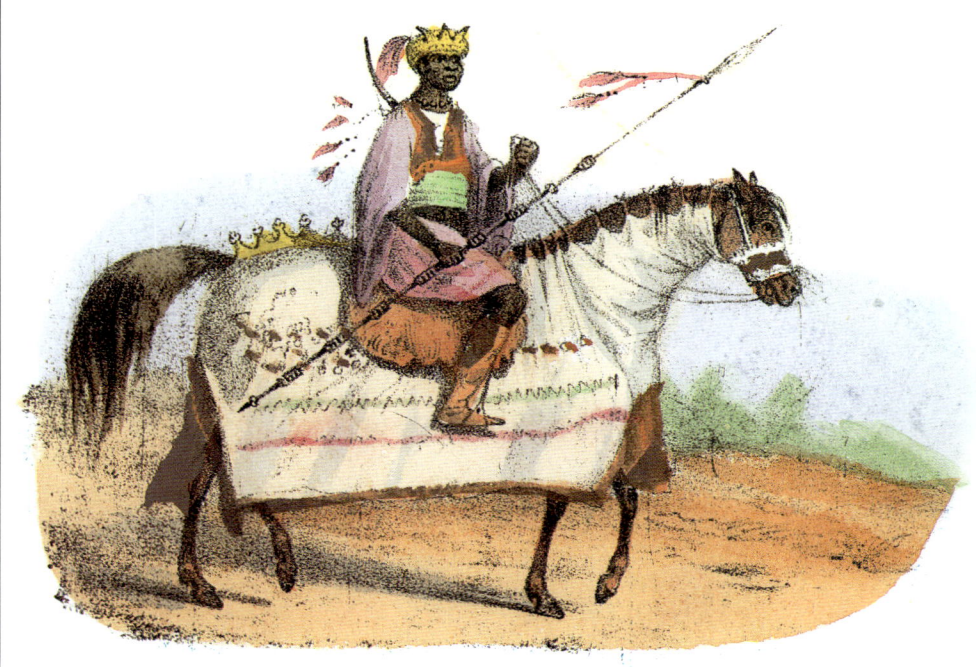

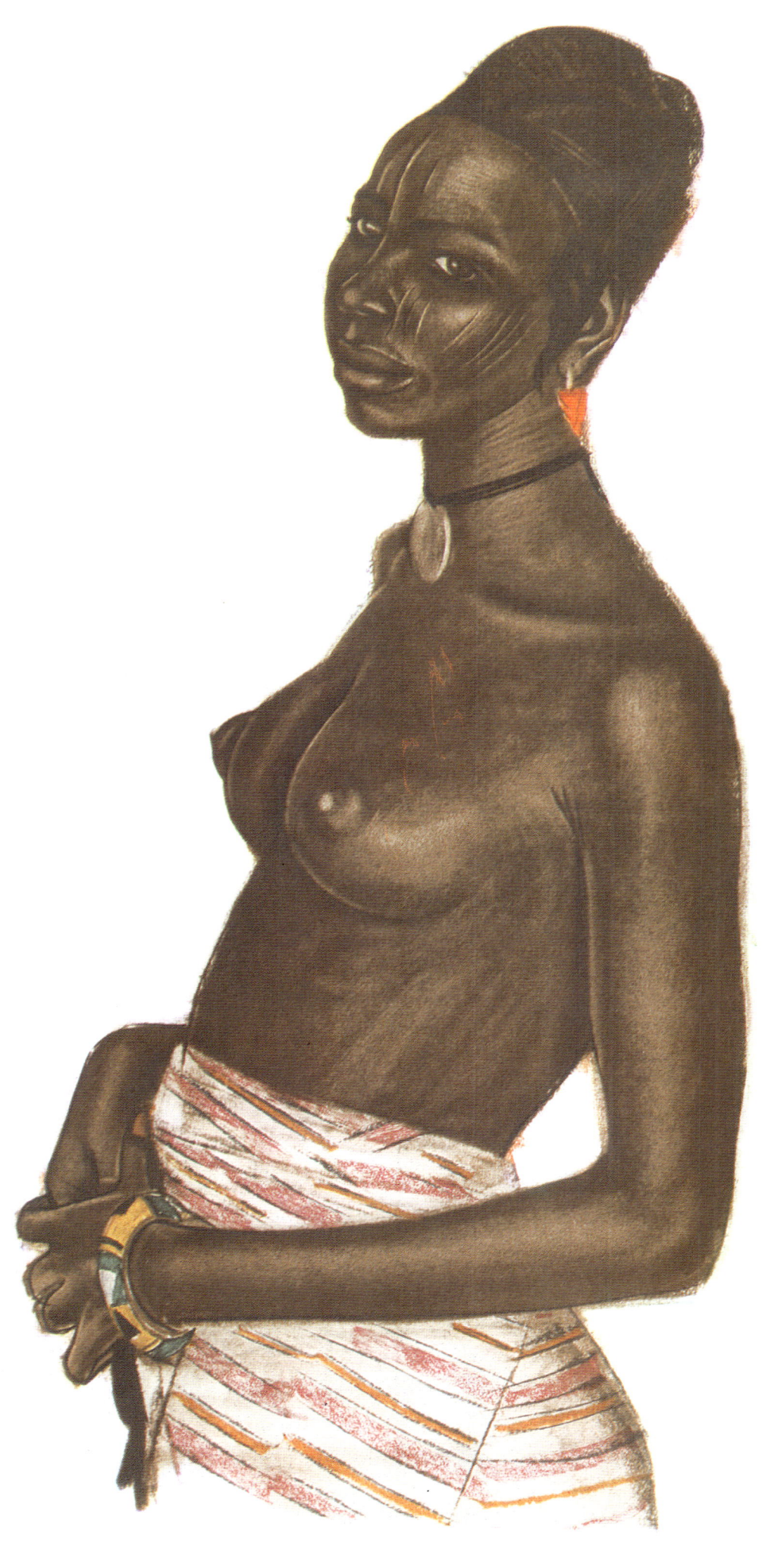

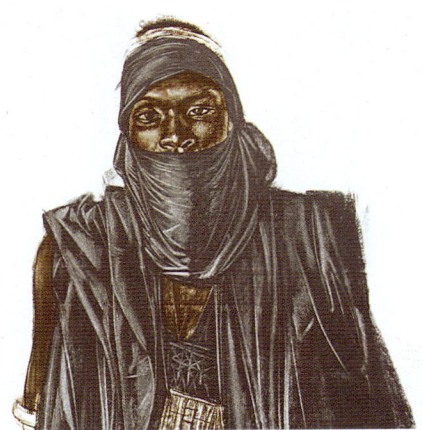

Zaria

In the days when the great Kanta of Kebbi led the invincible armies of his master, when Kano was still the heart of an indomitable state that successfully fought off waves of invasions by the powerful Bornu, Zaria was a bright comet in the skies of Hausaland.
Zaria! Ancient Lazzau, Lazzau of Queen Amina, the intrepid queen, warrior, relentless leader of victorious armies that defeated neighboring lands.

In no time, everyone realized that she was the best rider and the finest archer in Hausaland.

Her arrows reached the most distant targets off in the hills. And flames shot out of the nostrils of her horse Demon, so aptly named, as she charged the advancing enemy troops.

A year after that first assault, to the day, she had reconquered all of the lost territory, where many fortified towns still carry her name.

Kano, Daura, Gobis, Katsina, Zaria, Biram, and Ramo were returned to the hands of the Hausa.

Then the horses of the fearsome amazon charged beyond the borders of her land; and her domain stretched toward the sources of the Niger and the banks of Benue, town after town, kingdom after kingdom, during the thirty-four years of her reign.

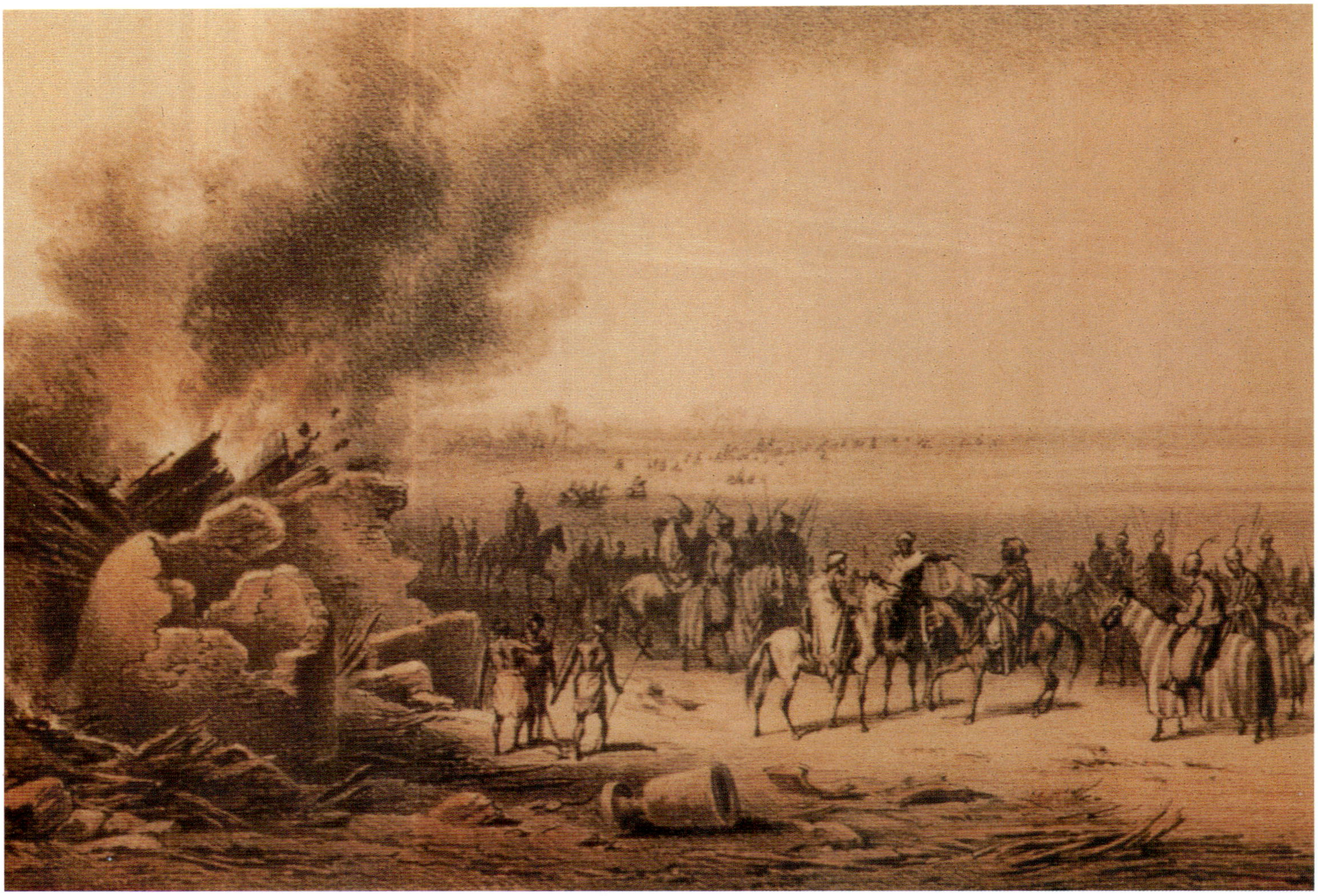

"AS SHE CHARGED THE ADVANCING ENEMY TROOPS..."

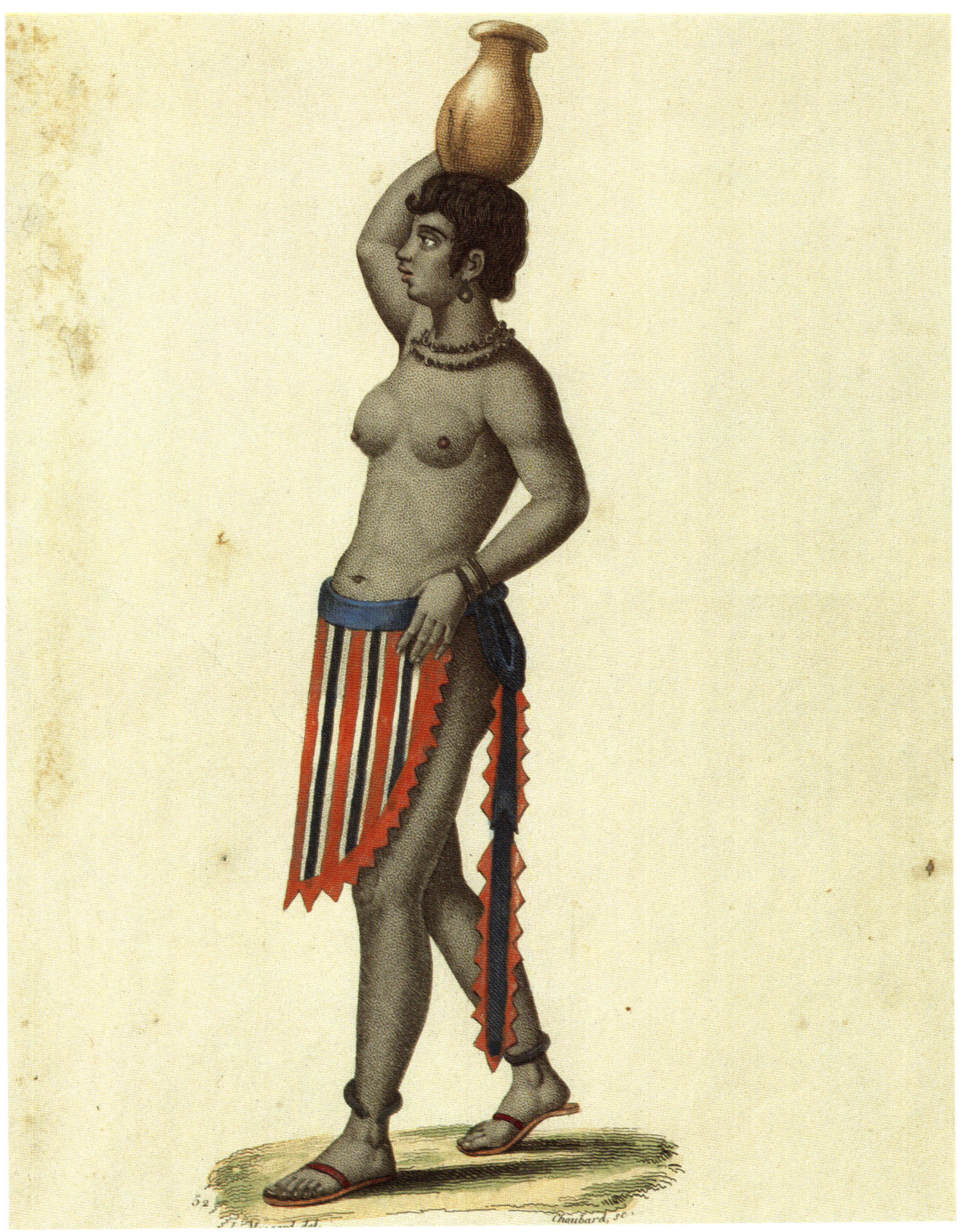
WOMAN FROM KANO

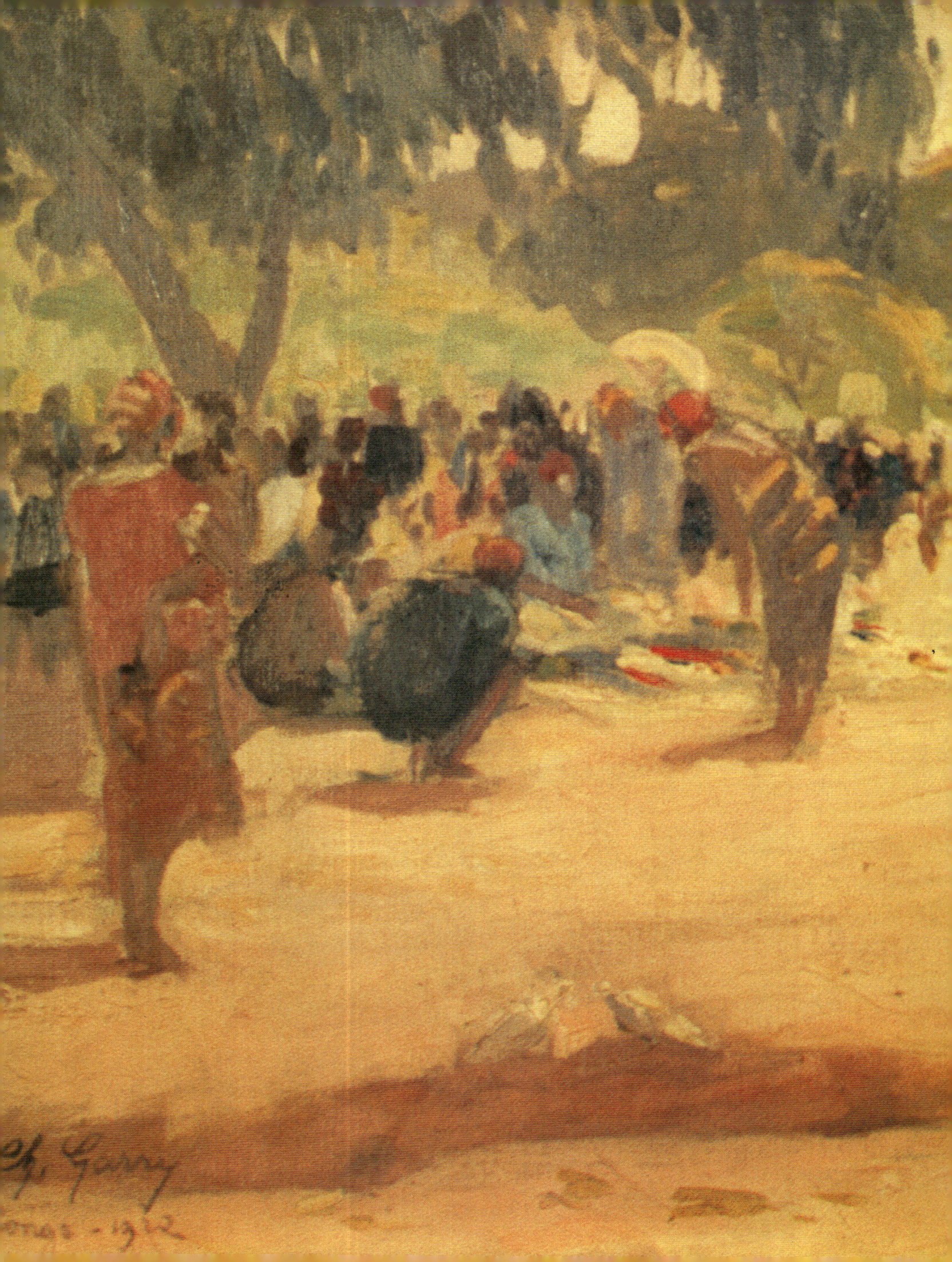

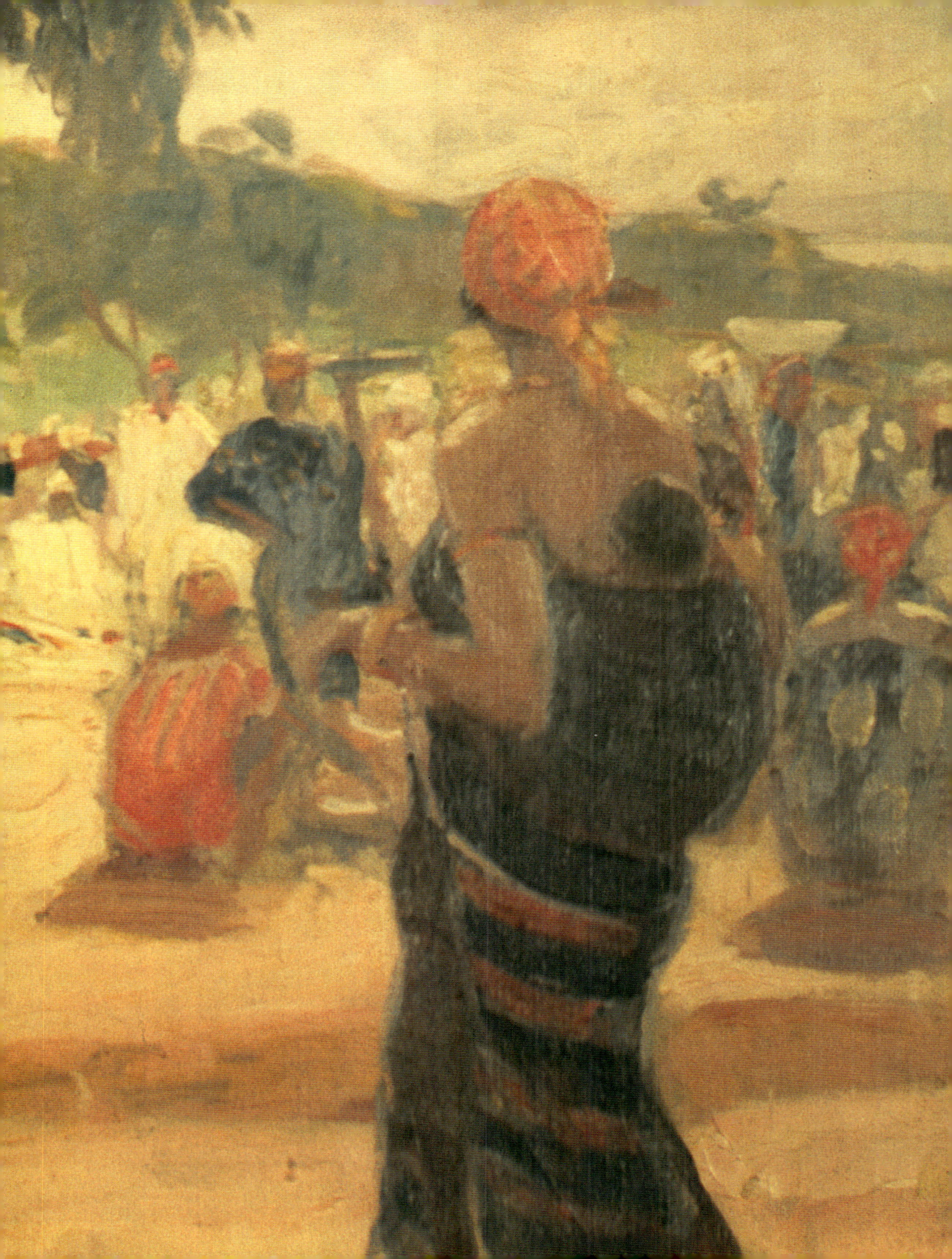

A legend tells us that she took a lover in each city and then abandoned him when she thought it was time to conquer the next town.

"Every city was a lover and every lover a city: such was Queen Amina of Zaria," legend says.

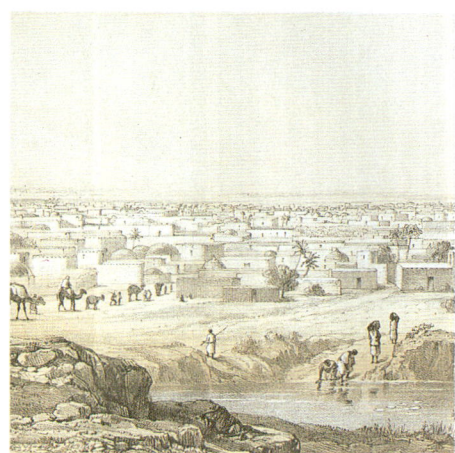

Kano, in the Last Century

Across from shops full of busy merchants and buyers there were stalls full of starving half-naked slaves for sale. And passing in front of boutiques full of the most varied and savory delicacies might be a poor person casting an envious eye, or an opulent chieftain, dressed in bright colored silk clothes, on a richly ornamented horse and followed by a pack of happy slaves. You can picture a blind beggar trying to find his way with his hands in such a city where yards full of fresh mats and straw surrounded pretty and clean huts of polished clay with rounded doors made of meticulously braided reeds. In this city, you can also find the place reserved for the daily chores, in the shade of a few long-branched allelouba, beautiful gondas, or slender date palms. The housewife with hair stylishly braided, dressed in a very clean black cotton tunic tied across her chest, takes care of her absent husband's meal, watches the female slaves who grind the wheat for the *foura,* and is surrounded by happy naked children or by earthenware and wooden bowls. This peaceful scene differs from that of the courtesan in colorful clothing, an infinite number of pearl rows in her hair arranged in a wild manner and capped by a tiara, a multicolor dress arranged loosely beneath her breast and dragging behind in the sand. In this city, you can also find unfortunate cripples, afflicted with a hump or suffering from elephantiasis.

At the docks, men are busy mixing indigo, hanging up clothes that have just been dyed, and beating dried blue clothes to give them a nice finish. Blacksmiths are making astonishingly sharp daggers, hunting spears with fearsome barbs, and farm tools. Men and women are always busy around here.

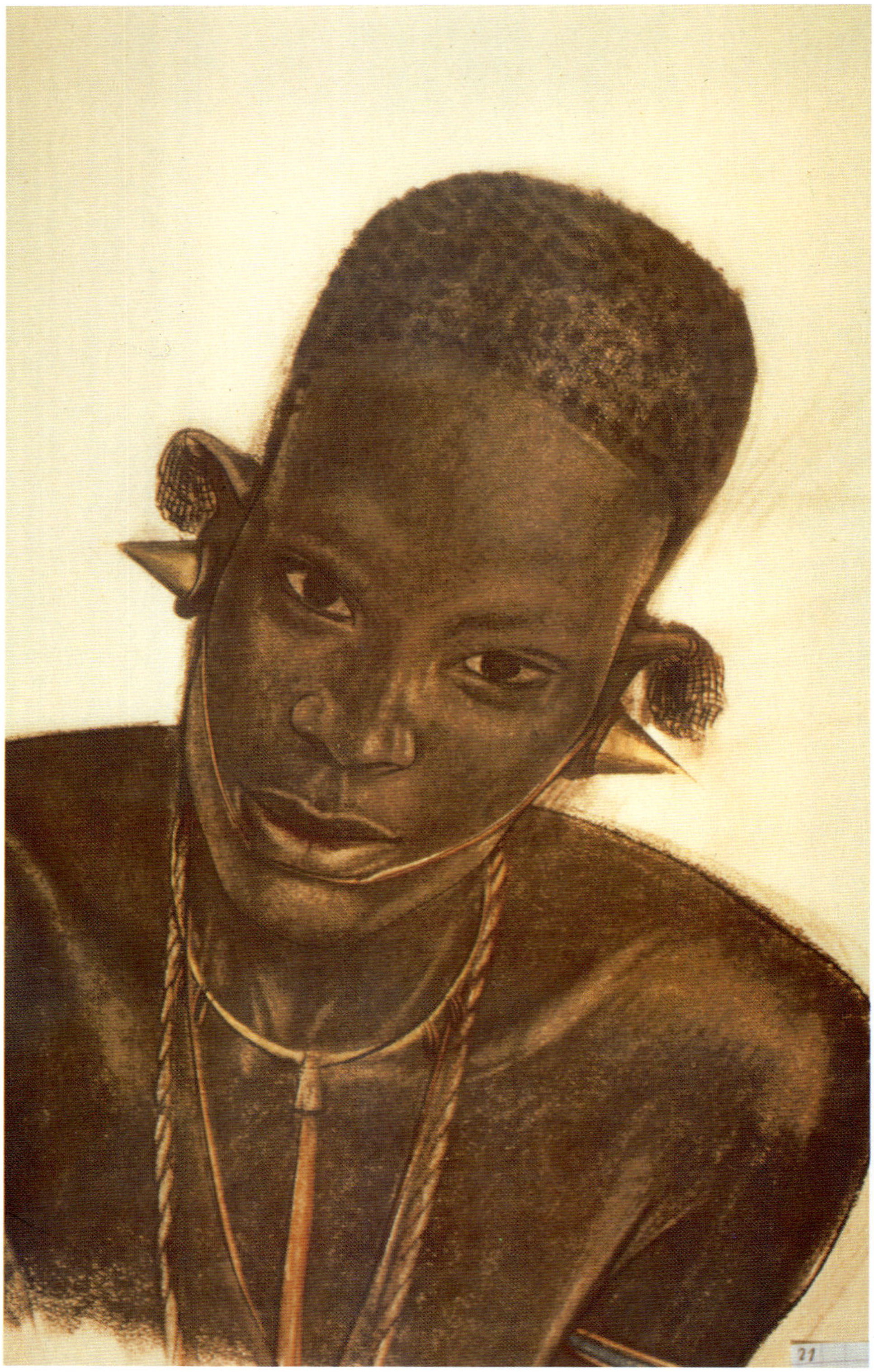

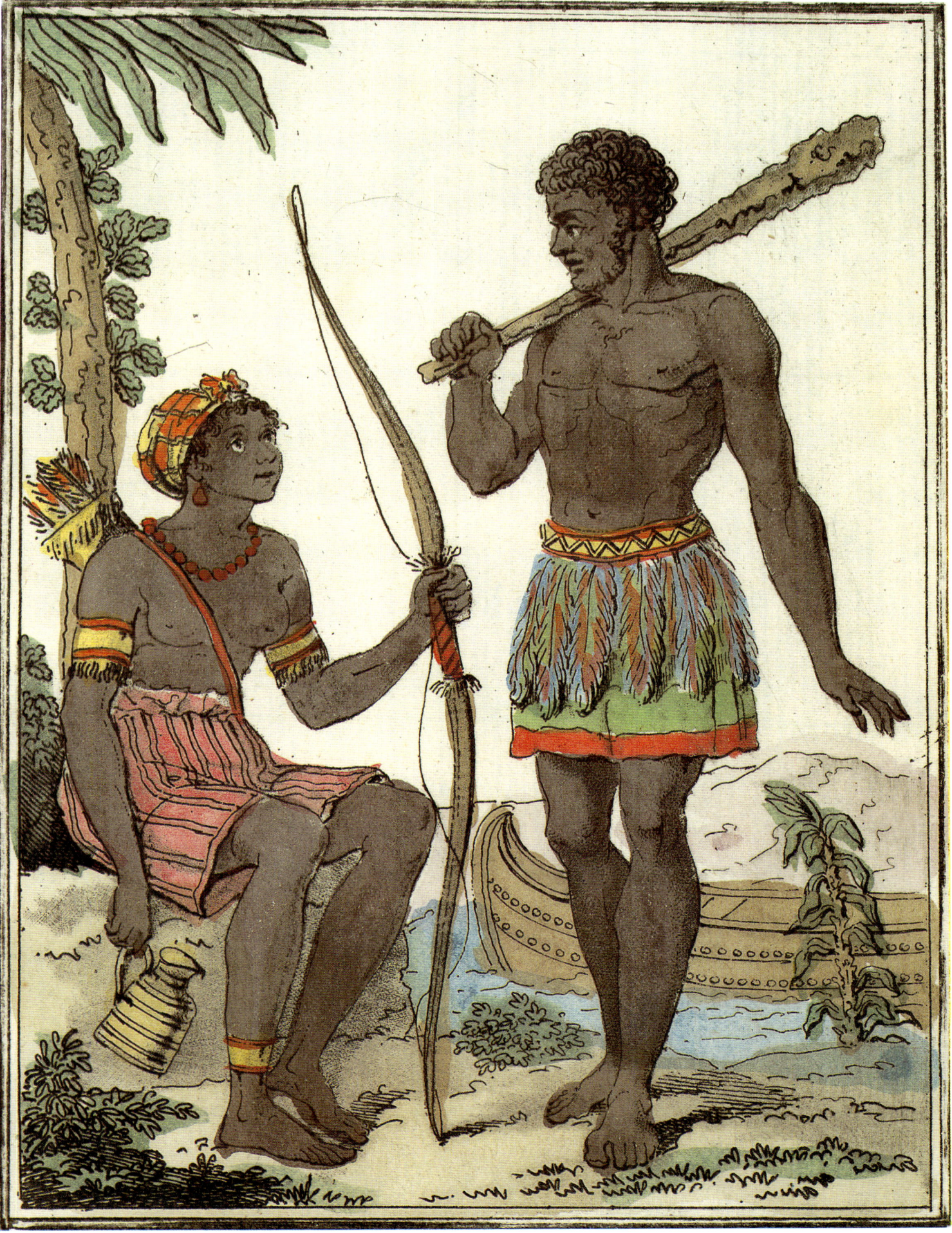

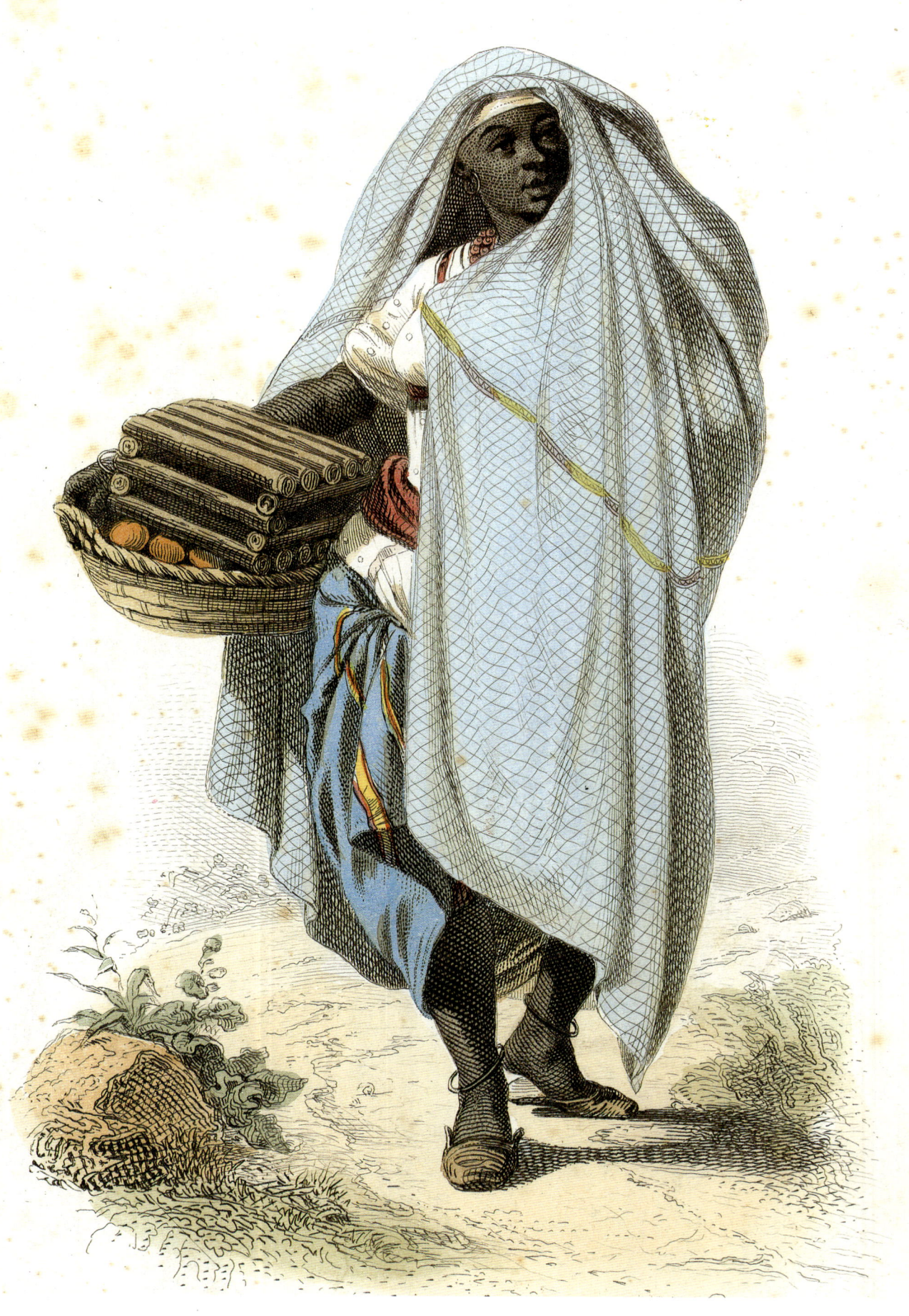

WORDS
OF AN ORDINARY WOMAN

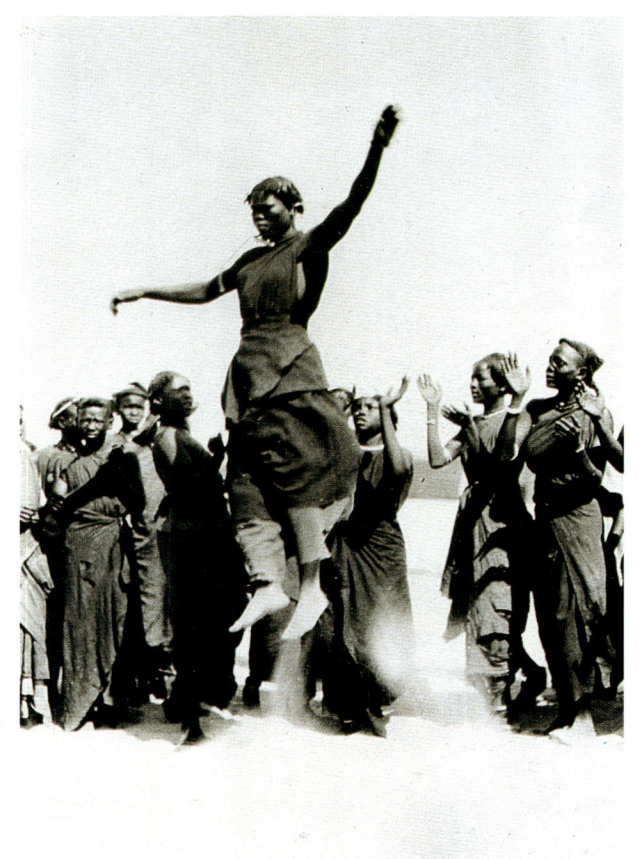
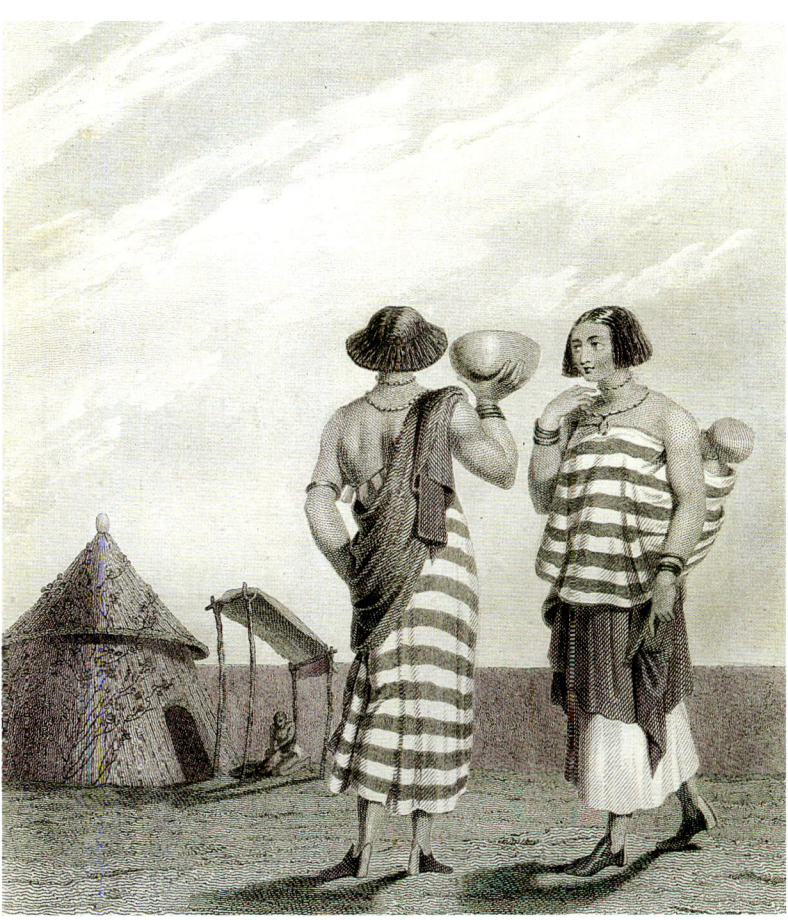

"GREAT IS HAPPINESS..."

Great is happiness; but health is the greatest happiness.

Whoever is in good health can desire anything, can seek out anything.

Health is life. Health is love of life. Without health, life ebbs away. Nothing is left.

Life comes and goes: she comes the same way she came. No one can run away from her. No one can cheat life.

We say that life comes from the hands and hence returns to the hands. So goes the proverb. A newborn is welcomed by hands. He is caught by hands. Hands cut the umbilical cord. Hands wash the infant. Hands give him life.

On your dying day, you go back to the hands. Hands will do the undressing. Hands will wash the body. Hands will wrap it in a white shroud. Hands will lower you down into your grave.

Every proud man must remember this: he is not in charge of his life, because from the beginning to the end, his life is in the hands of others.

After death, there's no more happiness, because there's nothing left.

Only death is true unhappiness, because after death there's nothing left to do. There is no cure for death.

The death of others is also your death. Here, when someone dies, the relatives and the friends go to his house to mourn. They go talk to the family.

We have another proverb: "The blood from the head trickles into the neck." If the head is wounded, covered with blood, won't the neck also be covered with blood? The blood will run from the head down onto the neck. Thus, when another has experienced great suffering, that suffering also becomes your suffering. The death of your brother or your friend is also your death. We have another proverb: "When your neighbor's beard is on fire, wet yours." The fire that caught your friend will probably catch you too, since you are close to him.

The suffering and death of others is your own.

But then, after having suffered and died, you begin to live again. You keep going until the next time.

When you witness the suffering, illness, and death of others, your heart breaks, it grows dark. Your heart also drinks its fill of suffering. But your eye just stands there, looking.

Suffering is in the heart. The eye does nothing, feels nothing. We say: "Suffering doesn't move the eye!" If you feel a great sadness, you can do nothing. You stand there, just looking, as if nothing were the matter. Suffering is only in the heart.

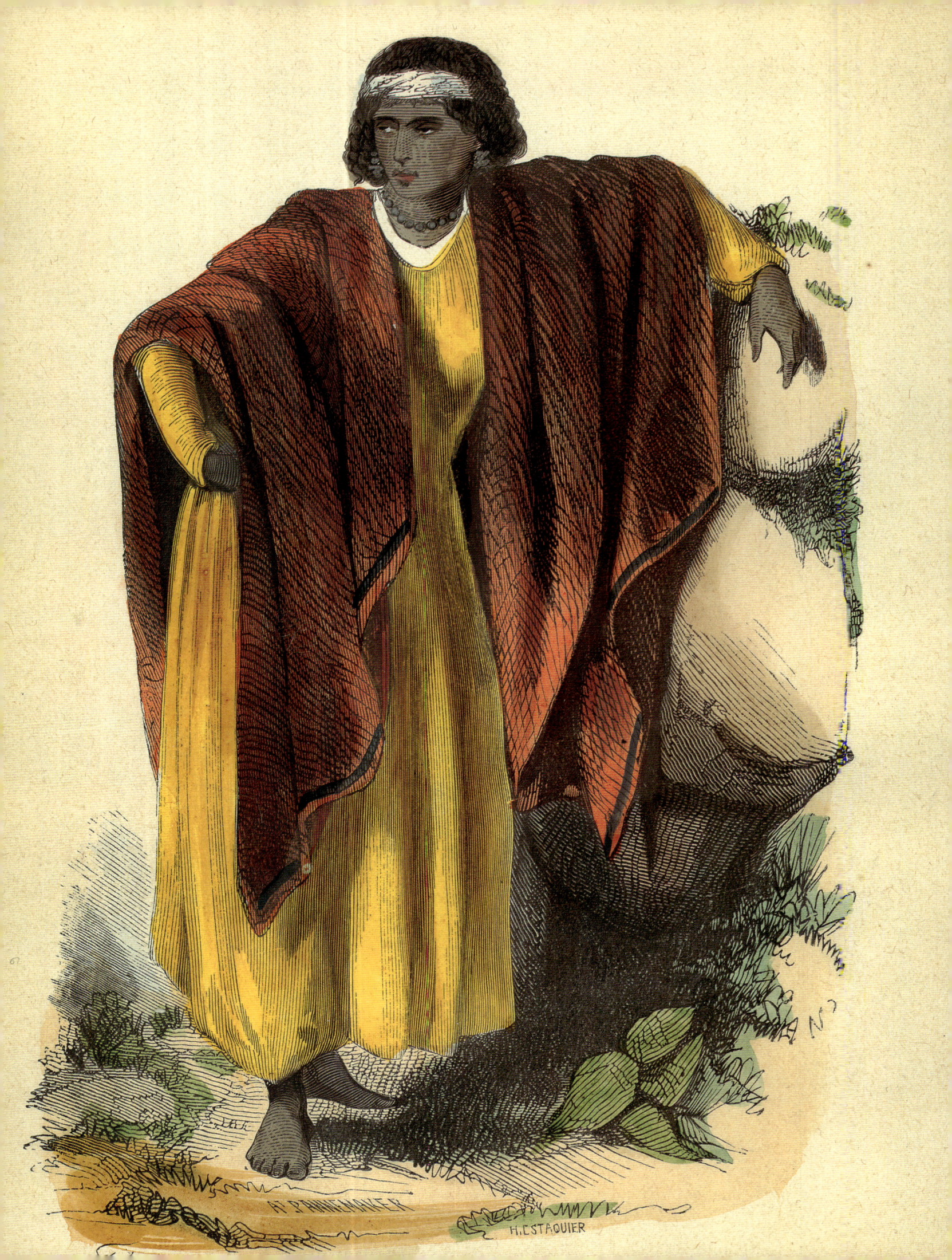

HELENI

QUEEN OF ETHIOPIA

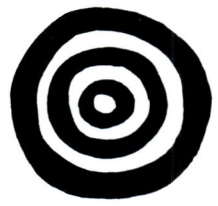

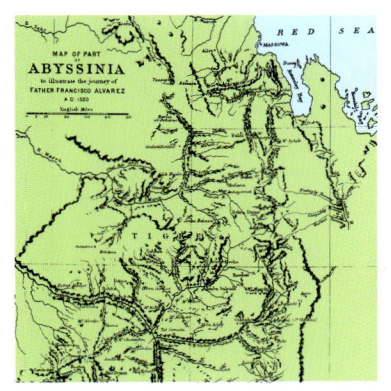

An enigmatic woman, who managed to pull Ethiopia out of its traditional isolation at the very moment when this old Christian kingdom of Africa was in distress...

IN 1441, THE NAVIGATOR NUNO TRISTAO ROUNDS CAPE BLANC; IN 1443, HE VISITS ARGUIN BAY AND BUYS FROM THE MOORS A FEW SLAVES WHO WILL BE SOLD AGAIN AS LABORERS BACK IN PORTUGAL: THESE ARE THE FIRST STEPS OF THE WEST IN AFRICA

and mark the beginnings of the slave trade.

From now on, year after year, new caravels will cruise all along Africa's coasts.

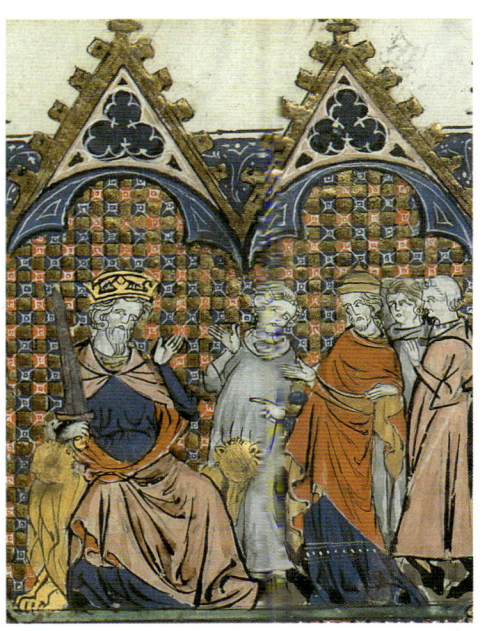

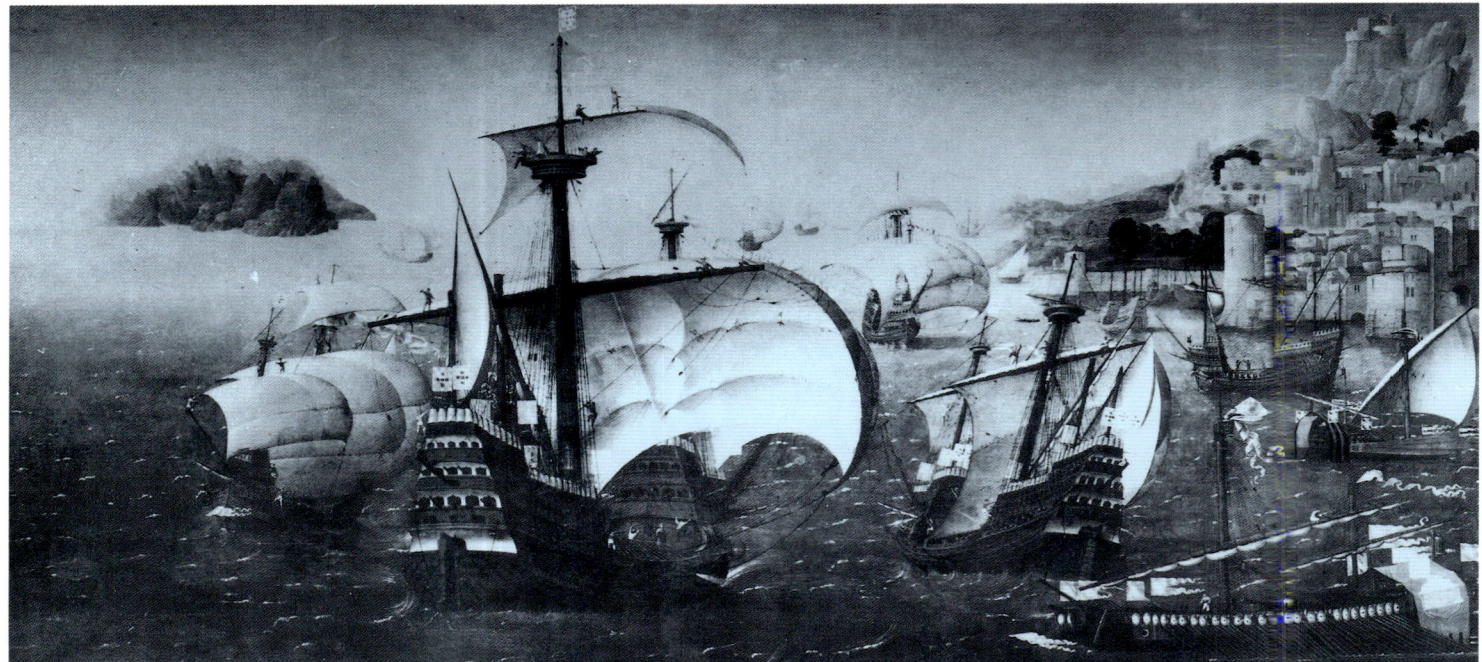

The continent has been ceded to the Portuguese by a papal decree. From time to time, like peasants marking the boundaries of their fields, they disembark and erect high stone columns with a cross on top; one of them, erected at Cape Trosse, 22 degrees latitude, will stand for four centuries before being toppled by the wind.

But these tough navigators, men of cape and sword, who will bloody all of the Indian Ocean, are also, in their own way, poets.

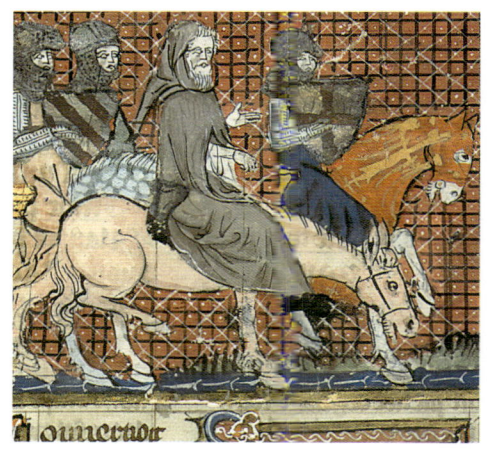

THE PORTUGUESE PRESENCE

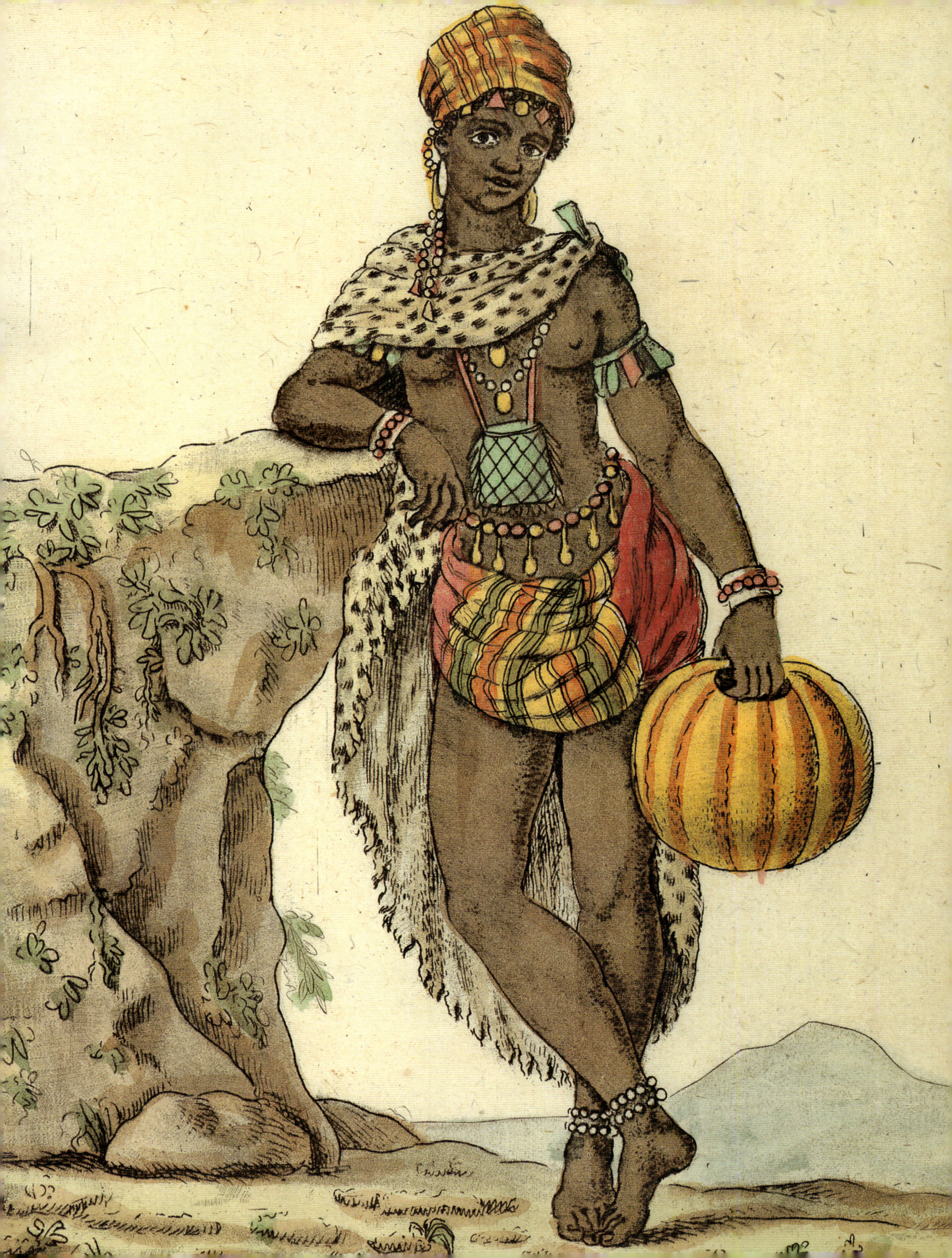

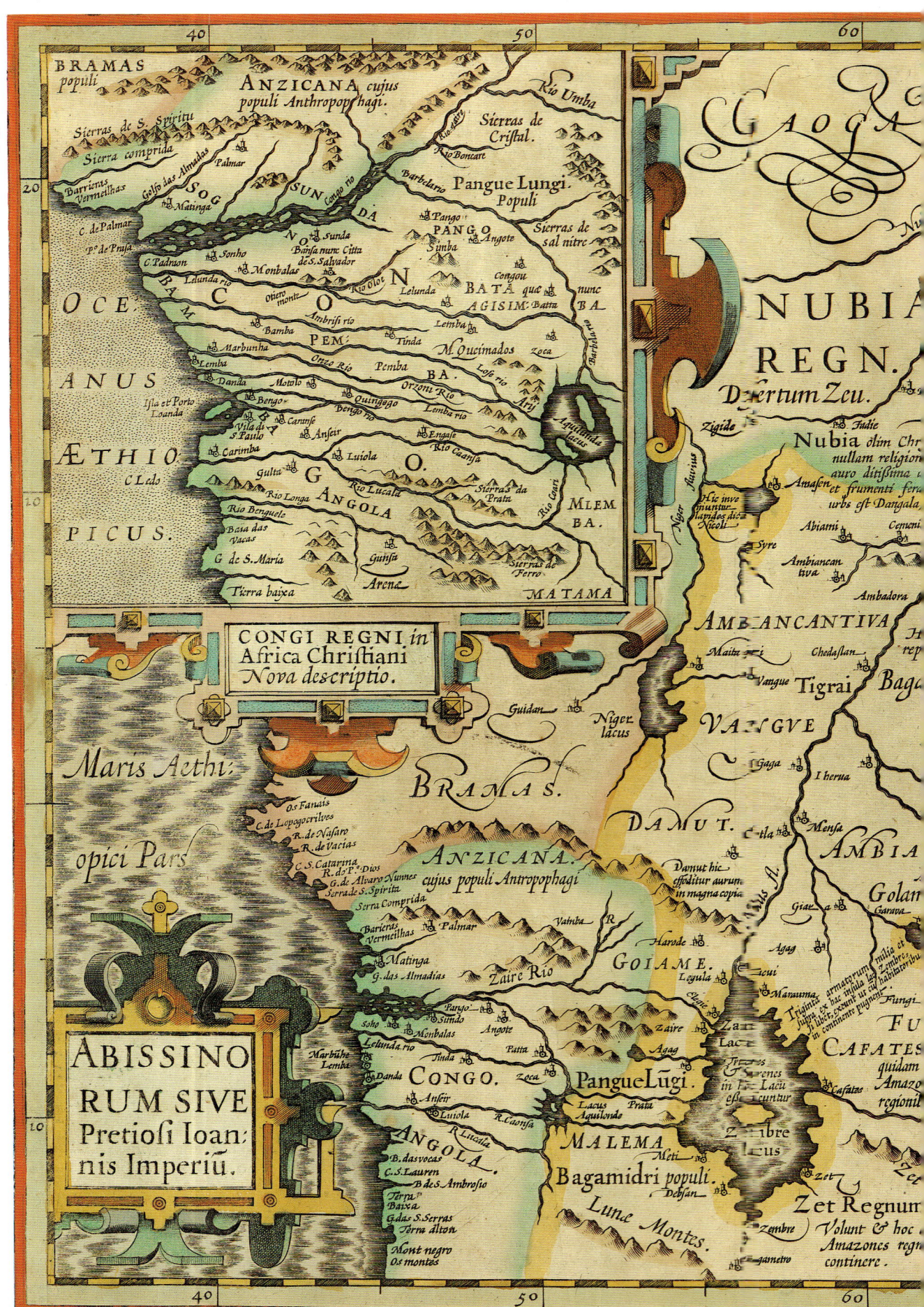

PRESTER JOHN'S KINGDOM AS IMAGINED BY

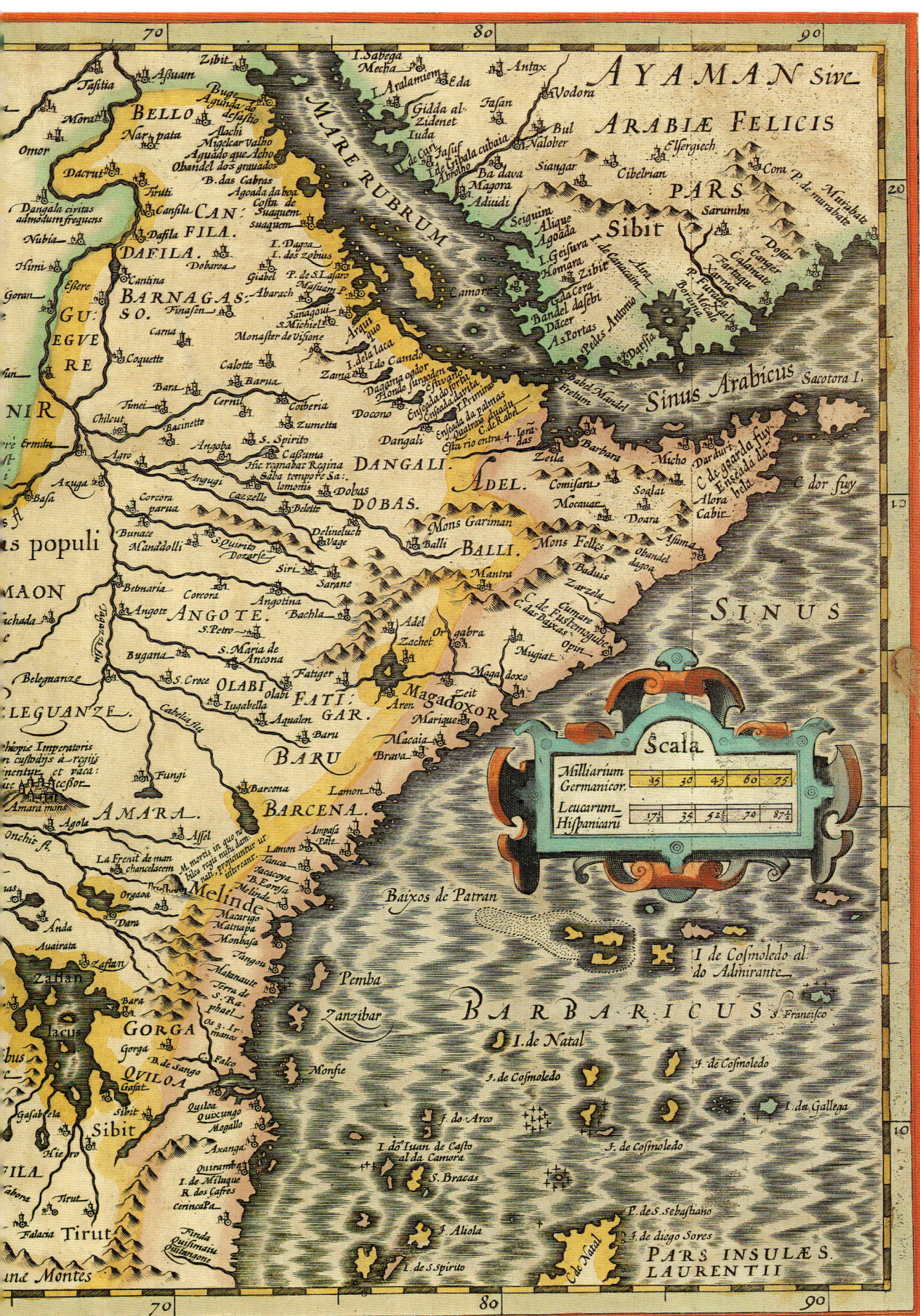

WESTERN CARTOGRAPHERS IN 1600

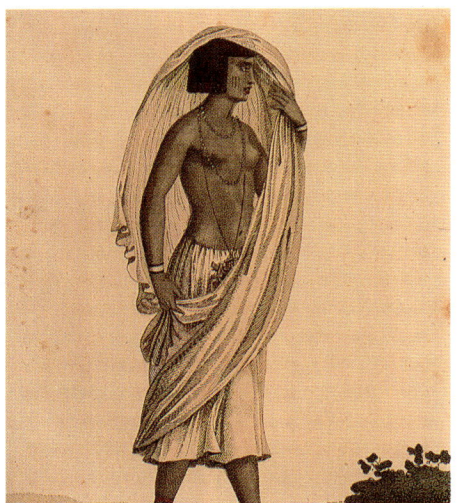

How Women Use the Toga

Women ride mules astride, and thus wear tight ankle-length pants under their robes; the bottoms of the pants are often embroidered with silk of different colors. When pregnant women appear in public, they cover themselves with a fold of the toga so as to reveal only their eyes. Sometimes they wrap a scarf around their heads instead of a fold of the toga. They cover their faces and let the scarf hang in the back.

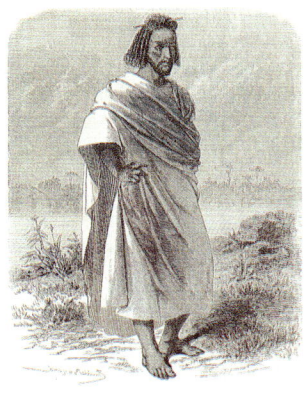

Ways to Wrap the Toga

There are different ways of wrapping the toga, depending on whether one is going to church, to court, to a memorial, to seek the company of a superior or an equal, or to speak before such or such an assembly. They uncover their chests to respond to a greeting, and by wrapping themselves this way or that, may show disdain, vigor, self-neglect, and all the primary feelings that fill the human heart.

Identical accessories often inspire the same things in different people. Thus, without having ever heard of Caesar, more than one Ethiopian has covered his face with a corner of his toga, when dying by the assassin's steel.

They thirst for gold, ivory, and slaves, and meanwhile dream of an imaginary country, the Christian kingdom of Prester John, in which ten thousand knights carry ten thousand crosses, and of the king's immense mirror through which he sees everything that happens in his kingdom. The legend of Prester John is the subject of Europe's dreams for two centuries. It is at the origin of the first explorations of Africa; it also haunts Christopher Columbus's companions a century later. Thus, each time they erect a stone column, a padrao, the Portuguese navigators also leave behind a black slave whom they charge with contacting the legendary Prester John.

It is the king of Portugal, a deeply pious man, who thinks of sending these ambassadors. Magnificently dressed and supplied with gold, silver, and spices, they are charged with giving the compliments of His Very Catholic Majesty to Prester John. One by one, these poor souls are left in unknown lands among people whose language they do not understand. None will ever be heard from again.

A few years later, two Portuguese, João Gomez and João Sanchez, take their first steps in the "legendary kingdom" of Prester John.

This kingdom is simply Ethiopia, and the man they take for the mythical ruler is Emperor Vayda Maryam. But the real authority in this kingdom is in the delicate hands of a woman, the wife of the man they mistake for Prester John: she is Empress Heleni.

Since its conversion to Christianity twelve hundred years before, Ethiopia has survived almost miraculously in a sea of enemies.

By the time the Portuguese arrive, this small courageous country seems doomed: the Muslims from the coast are about to do away with it, and the end of the kingdom seems near and ineluctable.

Empress Heleni welcomes the envoys from Portugal with much fanfare. She is a pious woman. She has written two books of theology: *The Organs of Praise* and *The Light's Ascension.* But most of all, she is a great politician and she immediately realizes the value of an alliance with this faraway kingdom whose Christianity is not exactly hers. The treaty is signed without delay, and soon thereafter, Portugal sends troops to support "Prester John's Kingdom" in its fight against the Muslim invaders.

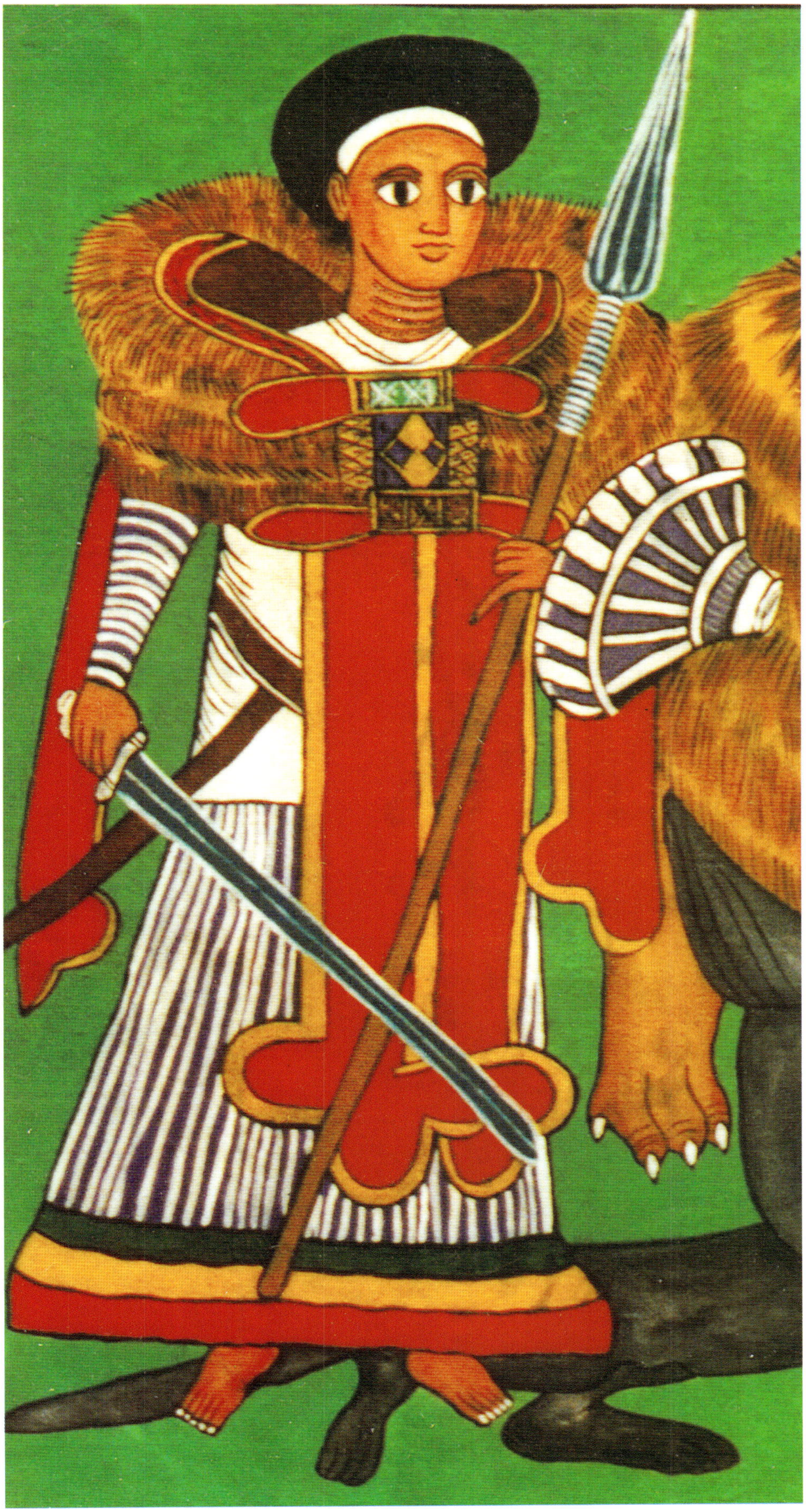

HELENI

THE EMPEROR VAYDA-MARYAM (FOLK PAINTING)

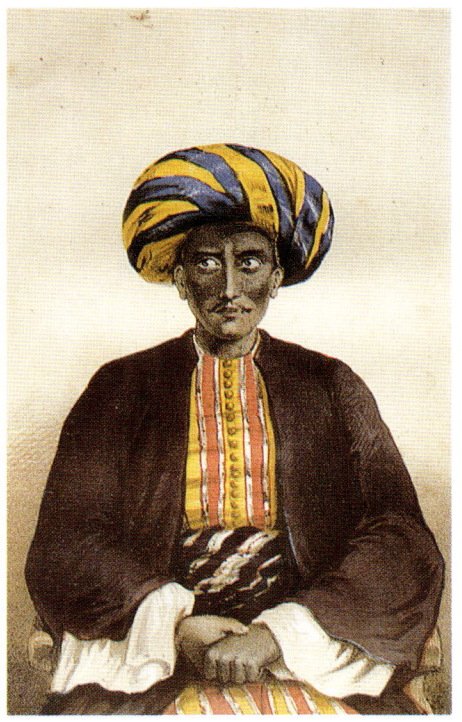

The Struggle against Islam

The Muslims are soon ahead in the war, and many of their leaders wage a relentless and merciless campaign against Abyssinia.

The Somali chief Ahmed Gran swears to exterminate the Abyssinians or convert them to Islam. In 1527, he passes through Ethiopia, wreaking havoc; villages and churches are set ablaze. Anyone who refuses to reject their faith faces the sword. Emperor David does not give up; he slowly retreats before this terrible onslaught, until five hundred Portuguese men led by Christopher da Gama arrive and turn the tide. Christopher da Gama is killed right at the start of the fighting. His unhoped-for reinforcements, however, deliver victory to the hands of the Abyssinians, and Ahmed Gran, struck down by a Portuguese bullet, dies on the field. David dies soon after this and is succeeded by Claudius. This new Negus continues the war, defeating the Muslims on many occasions, and falls in battle as did Christopher da Gama and Ahmed Gran before him. After this, victorious Abyssinia has been able to breathe freely.

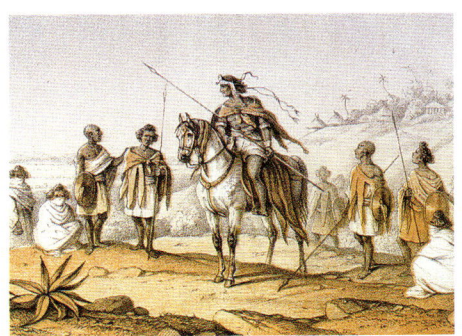

Disguised Politeness and Insults

In order to express themselves freely even in the presence of the powerful, Ethiopians have become masters in the art of double meanings, of the ambiguities concealed in a gesture. An insult, if it is dressed in a polite formula or a joke, can only be avenged by an insult of the same kind. The greats know how to answer each other unpleasantly while being polite to each other: by sending gifts with double meanings, for example. Offering gold bracelets to someone, no matter how sumptuous, is a way of reminding him that he is the vassal of the person who can afford such gifts. Offering feminine clothes to a man is even more outrageous.

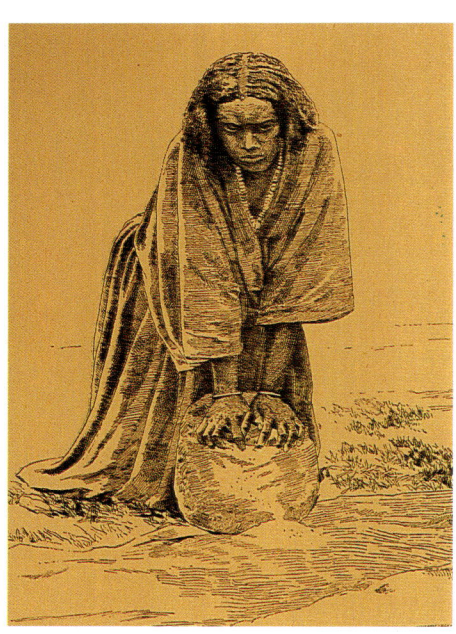

Bread Making

Bread is made with *tief* flour, sorghum, or *durra,* grain (a very common grain in Abyssinia), barley, or wheat. Women are in charge of making bread. First, they place the grain in the empty trunk of a tree, using it as a kind of mortar where they hull the grain using a wooden pestle. After that step, the grain is carefully stone-ground. Then they add water to the flour, turning it into a liquid paste to be fermented. The cooking is done on a shallow disk made of baked clay that is slightly greased and placed over a small fire; a cone-shaped lid seals the heat in for a few minutes, and the bread is ready.

Proverb

"Even if you know you're right, don't argue with the judge if he says you're wrong."

The expedition is led by Don Christobal, fourth son of the famous navigator Vasco da Gama.

This distinguished nobleman comes dressed in rose satin and brocade, with a gold-specked, black French cape. But his soldiers wear breast plates and carry harquebusiers, rifles that rule the battle field; and since the harquebusiers always carry the day, "Prester John's kingdom was saved from the infidels."

Throughout her lifetime, Heleni endeavors to preserve her alliances between land and sea, between Ethiopia and the maritime power of Portugal. First as queen, then regent, she rules for fifty years, deciding Ethiopia's fate.

Ethiopia was not within her present boundaries. This little mountainous country had to guard itself from all sides: northern kingdoms, sultanates along the Red Sea, as well as smaller sultanates to the south, all threatened Heleni's rule. The personality of this empress was many-sided: she was a pious believer, perhaps even a mystic; she was a smart politician, a fearsome warrior and a good-hearted being who could forgive her worst enemies; she was the leading figure in the kingdom; and she was an exquisite woman whose charm dazzled anyone who came near her.

Heleni: an enigmatic woman who managed to pull Ethiopia out of its traditional isolation at the very moment when this old Christian kingdom of Africa was in distress.

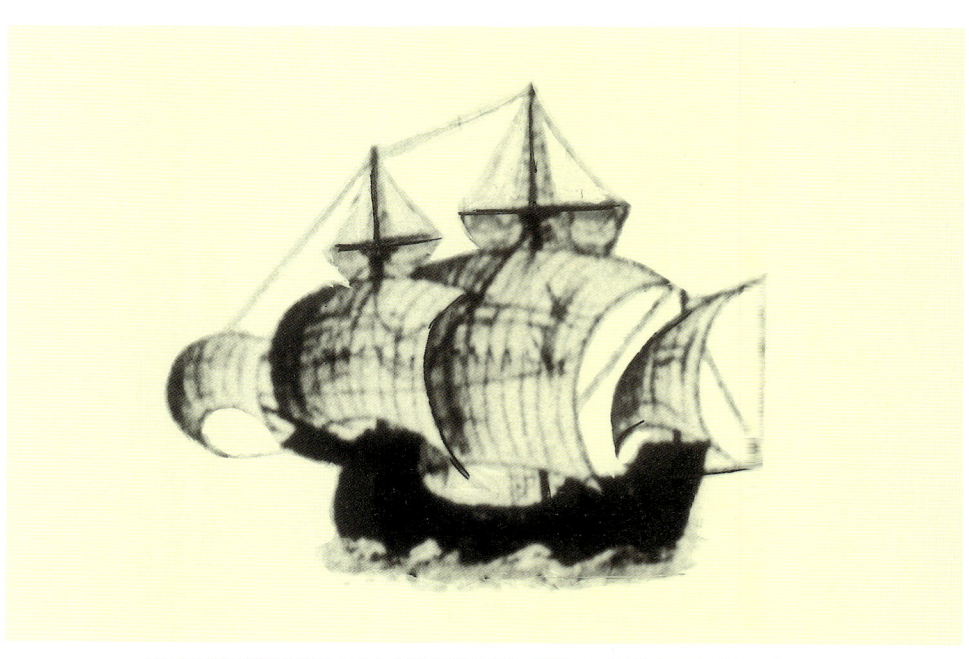

PORTUGUESE TROOPS ENTER TO HELP PROTECT ETHIOPIA

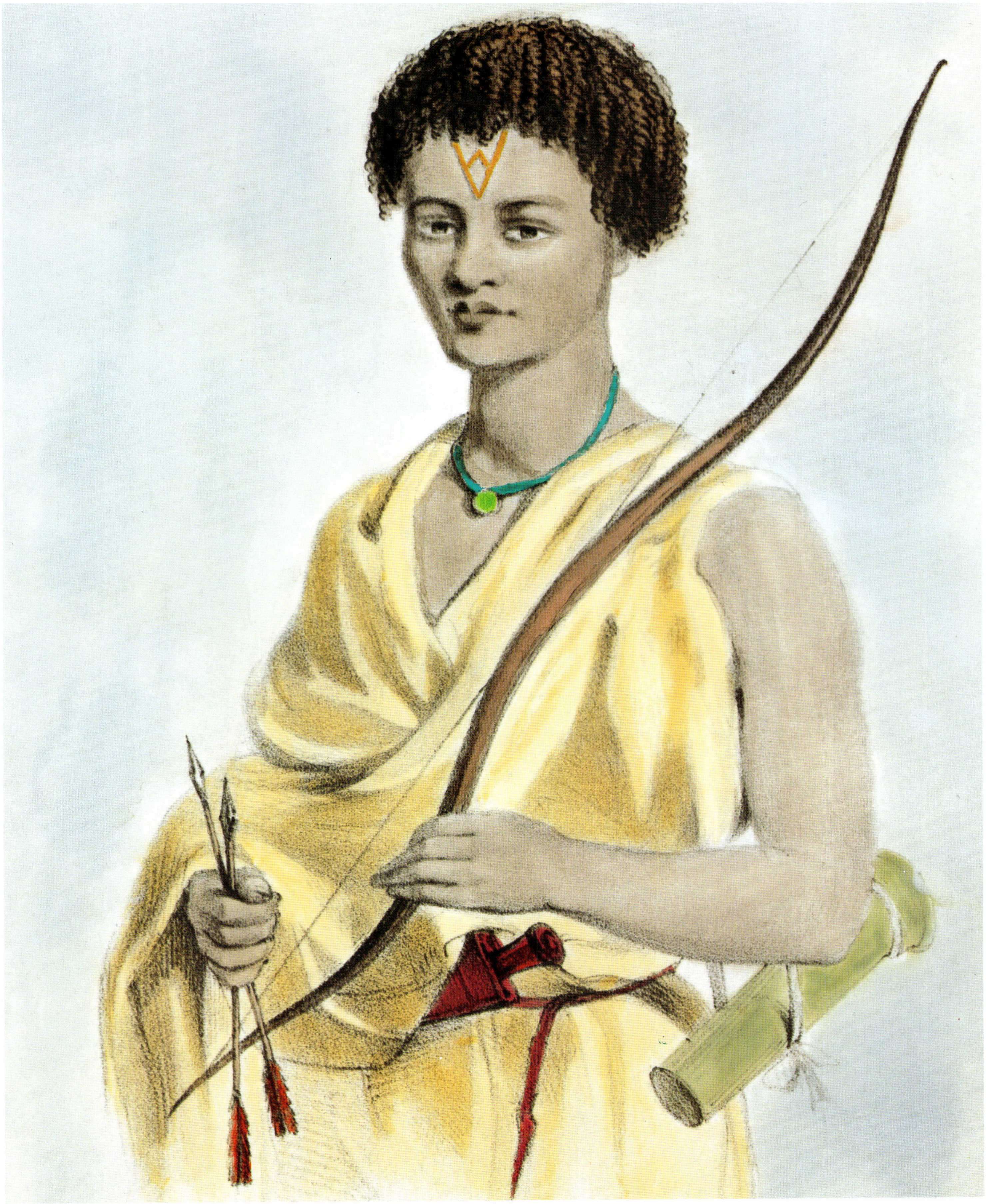

HELENI

ETHIOPIAN ARCHER

"She was the mother and father of us all," the Ethiopians said to the chronicler Alvarez, to whom we owe this story. Some also said that she was most beautiful when she was young: they would call her Romani Ouarq, Golden Pomegranate.

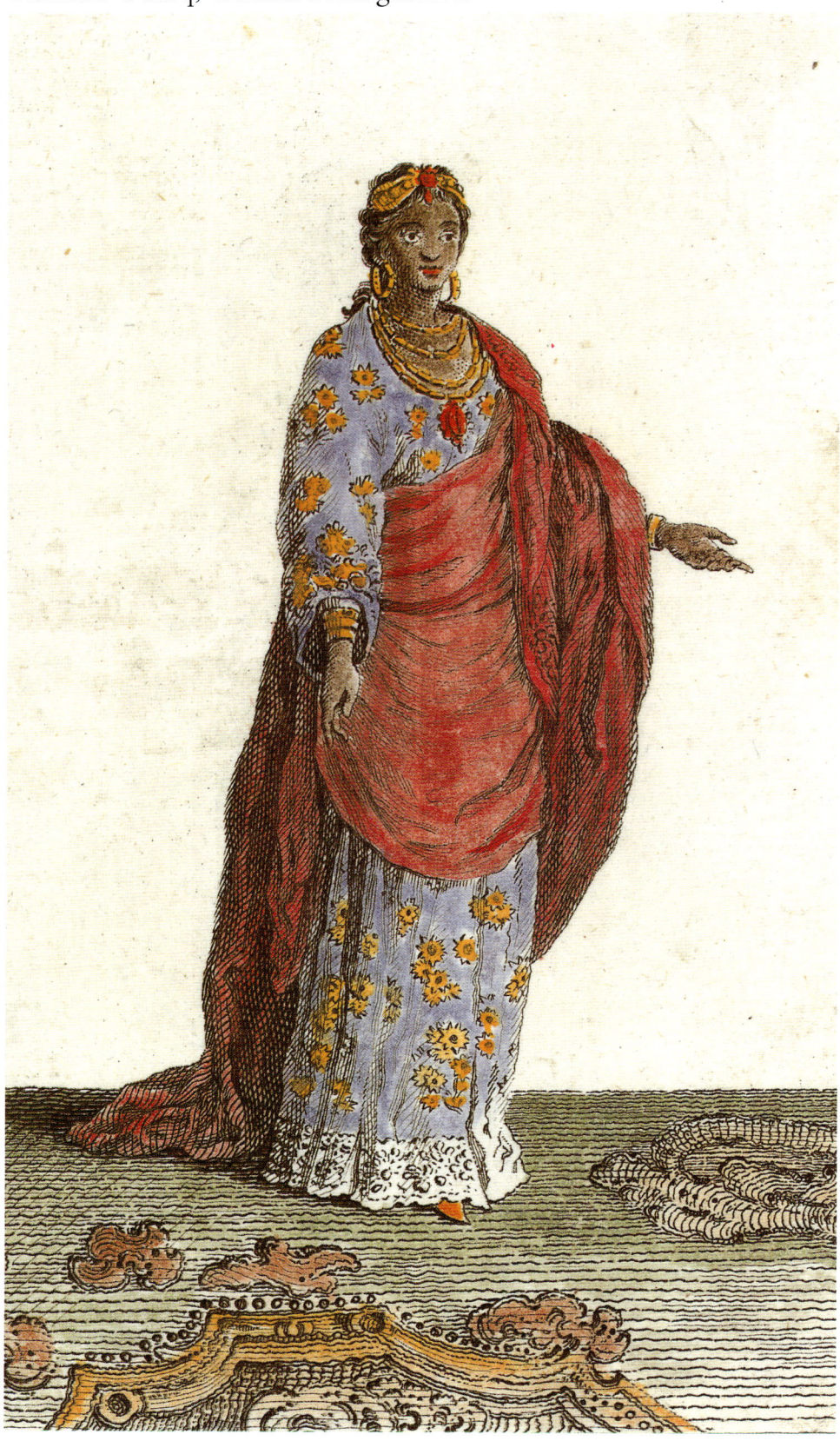

"THEY WOULD CALL HER GOLDEN POMEGRANATE"

HELENI

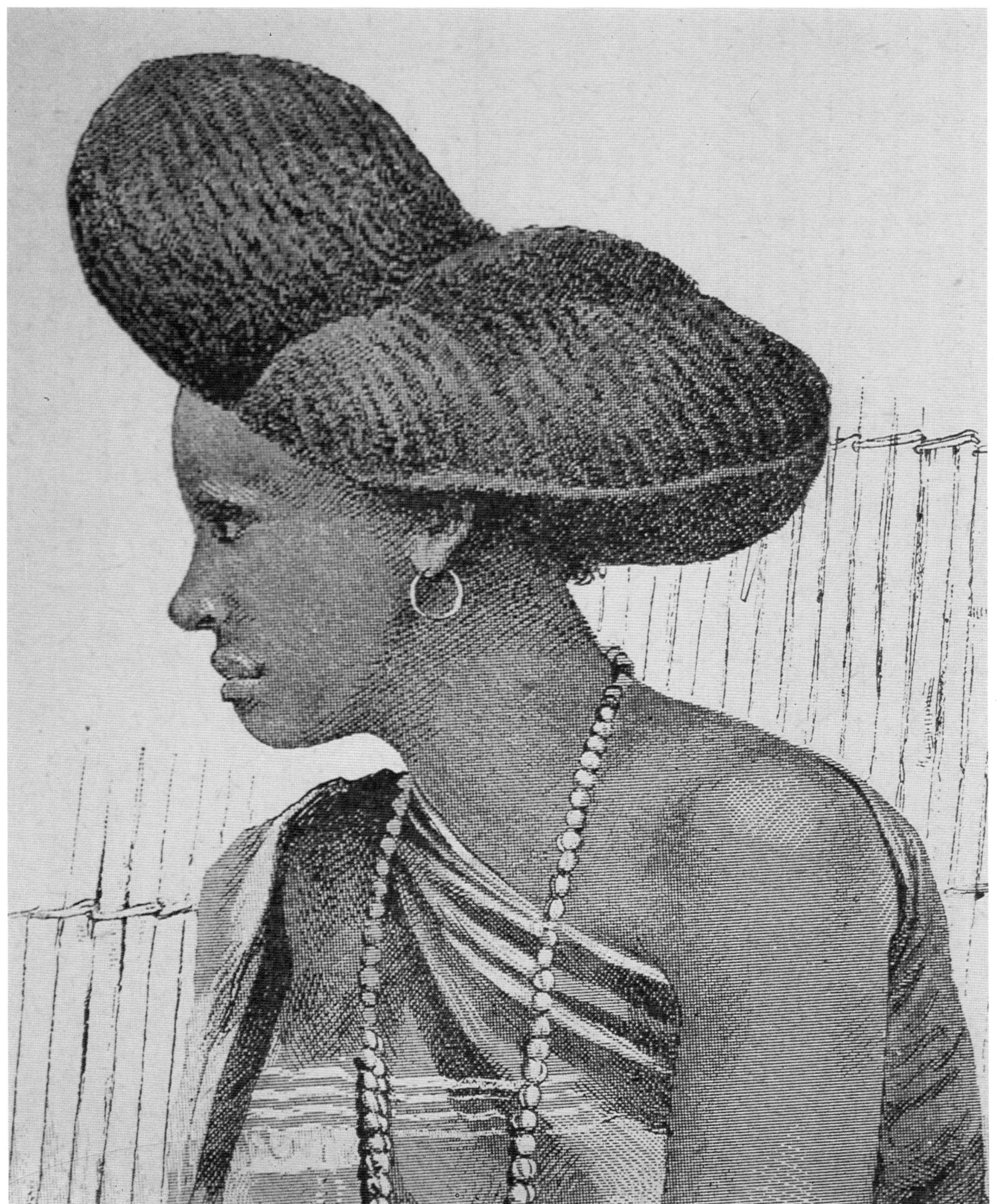

AN ETHIOPIAN HAIRSTYLE

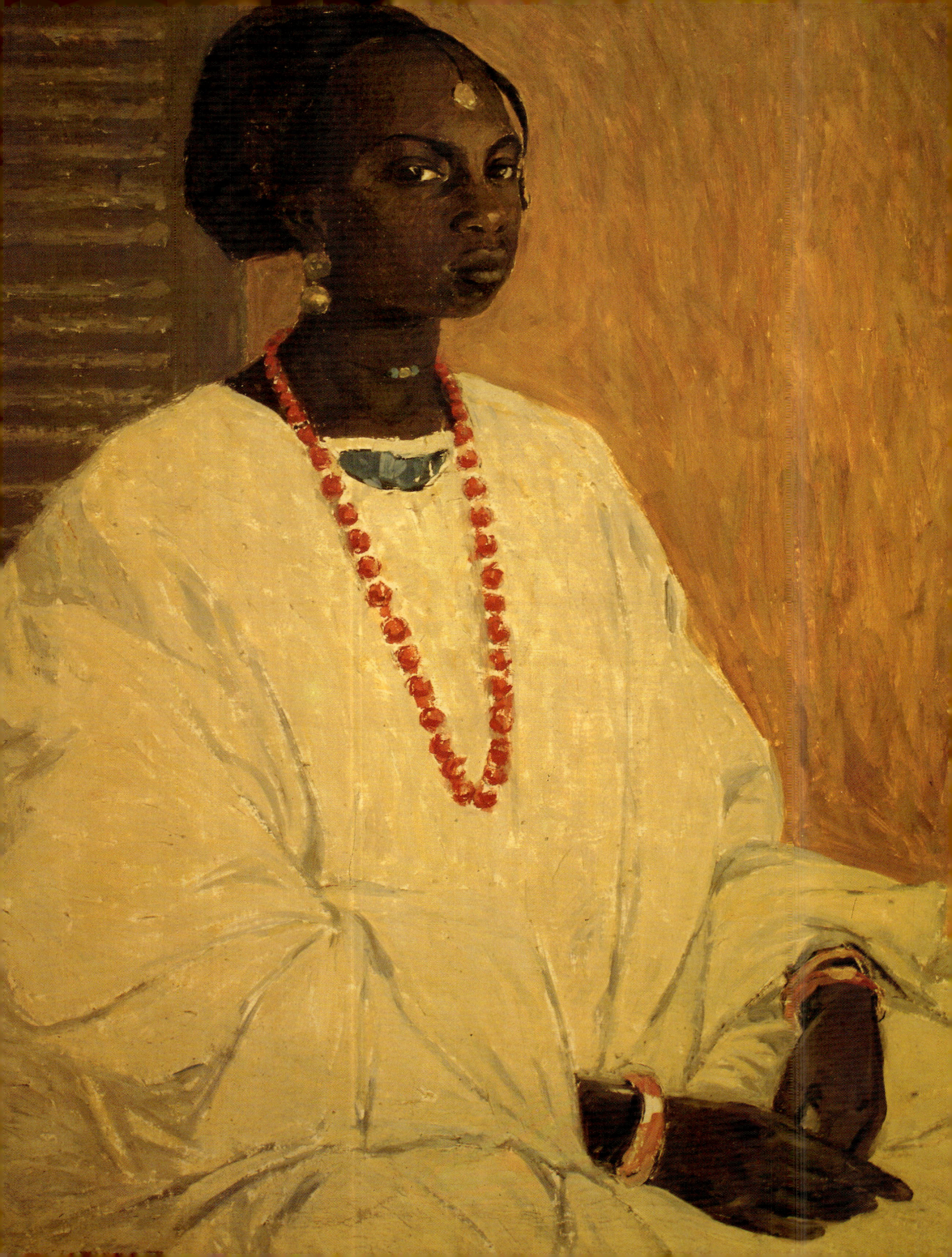

ANA DE SOUSA NZINGA

THE QUEEN WHO RESISTED THE PORTUGUESE CONQUEST

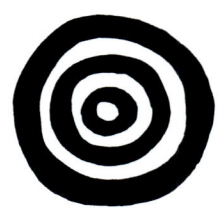

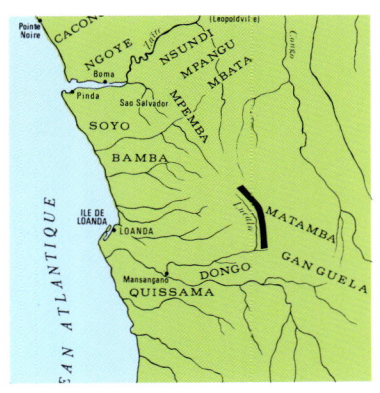

In Angola, every living, breathing thing, down to the least blade of grass in your path, still remembers our great queen, Ana de Sousa Nzinga...

IN 1860, AFTER HAVING CROSSED AFRICA FROM ONE CORNER TO THE OTHER, FROM ONE OCEAN TO THE OTHER, THE SCOTTISH MISSIONARY-EXPLORER DAVID LIVINGSTONE REACHED THE OLD PORTUGUESE STRONGHOLD OF LUANDA. BARE STAIRS, cells, shackles bolted to stone testified to much of the recent history of Africa here. Then, as he reached a courtyard, he saw the imprint of a woman's foot engraved in stone. He was astonished.

He asked the Portuguese, but they couldn't seem to answer. So an Angolan man stepped forward and declared that it was the imprint of the great Ngola Nzinga who had set foot in this courtyard three hundred years ago.

The man who had spoken was a simple convoy bearer. Suddenly tears of emotion filled his eyes and he added: "These stones are not the only ones to have remained faithful to her. In Angola, every living, breathing thing, down to the least blade of grass in your path, still remembers our great queen, Ana de Sousa Nzinga."

Ana de Sousa Nzinga was born in 1581 in Kabasa, the capital of the kingdom of Ndongo, a land ruled by leaders called *ngolas*.

At this time, the Portuguese have already converted the whole kingdom of Kongo and are advancing south toward the silver mountains of Kambandé.

But the greatest treasure, in their minds, is the very people of Angola (the kingdom of the ngola), which they consider to be an inexhaustible source of manpower—of "black ivory," as slaves were called then.

But Ngola Karensi, Ana de Sousa Nzinga's father, has given much thought to the European domination of neighboring Kongo. He decides to bar missionaries from his country, and soon the language of cannons replaces the entreaties of pious discourse: this is war, a war that will last more than forty years, until his very last breath.

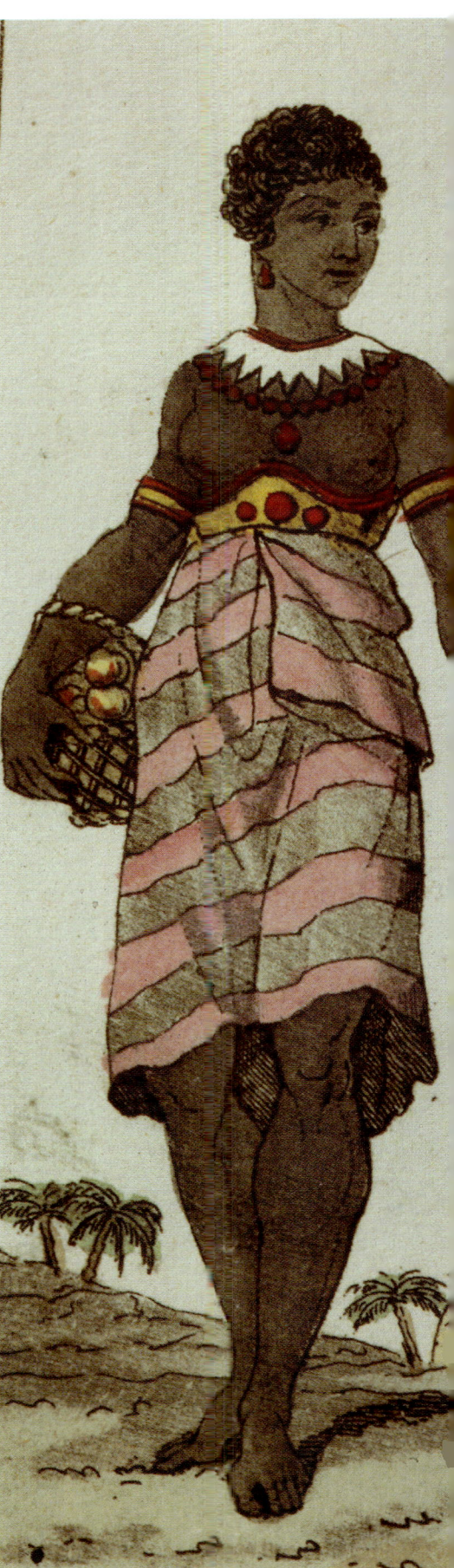

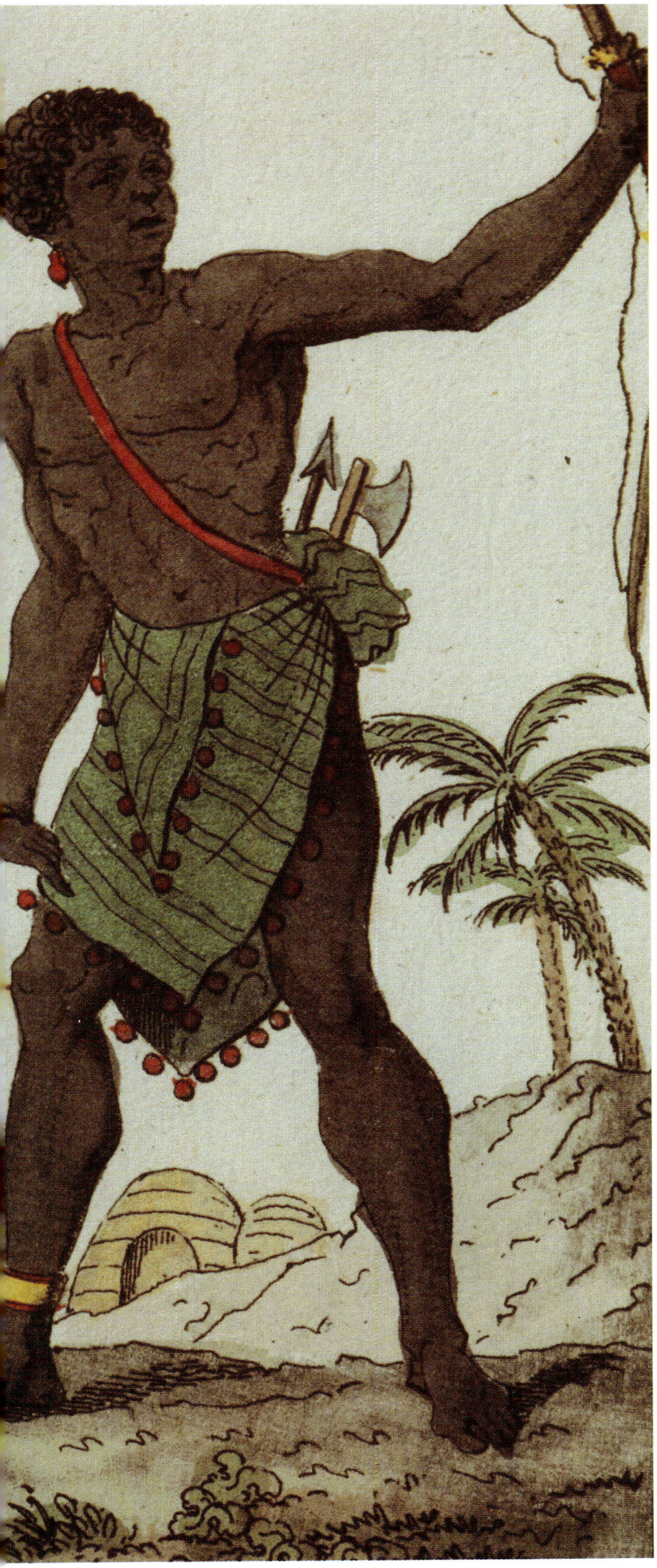

ANA DE SOUSA NZINGA

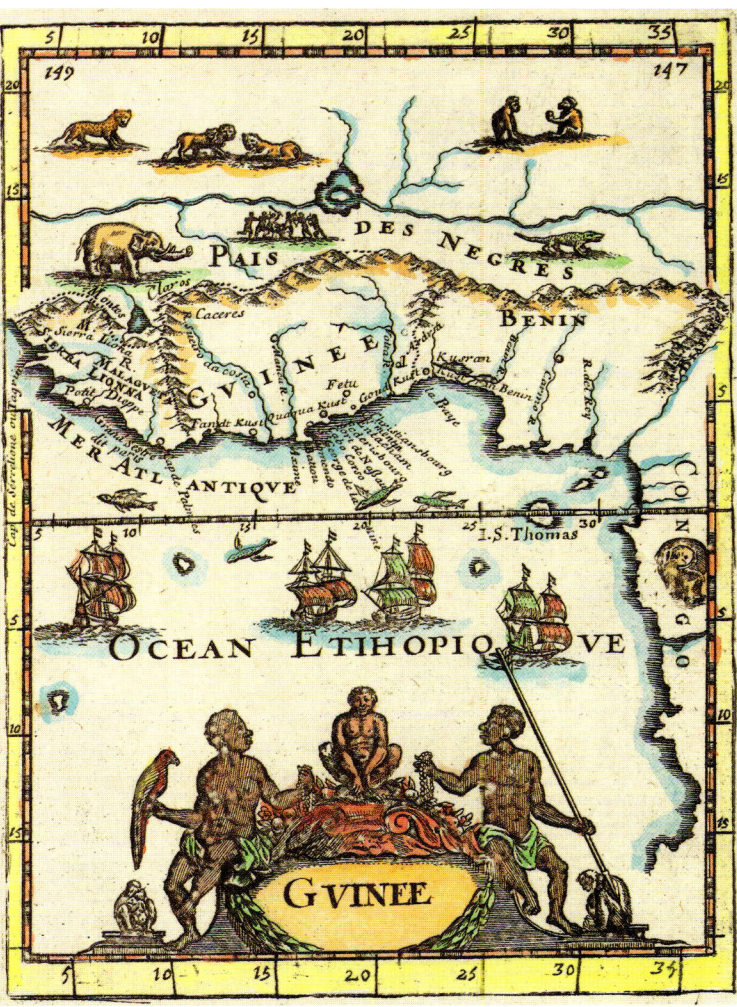
WEST AFRICA WAS THEN CALLED GUINEA

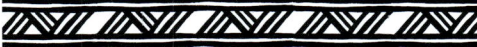
COUPLE FROM ANGOLA

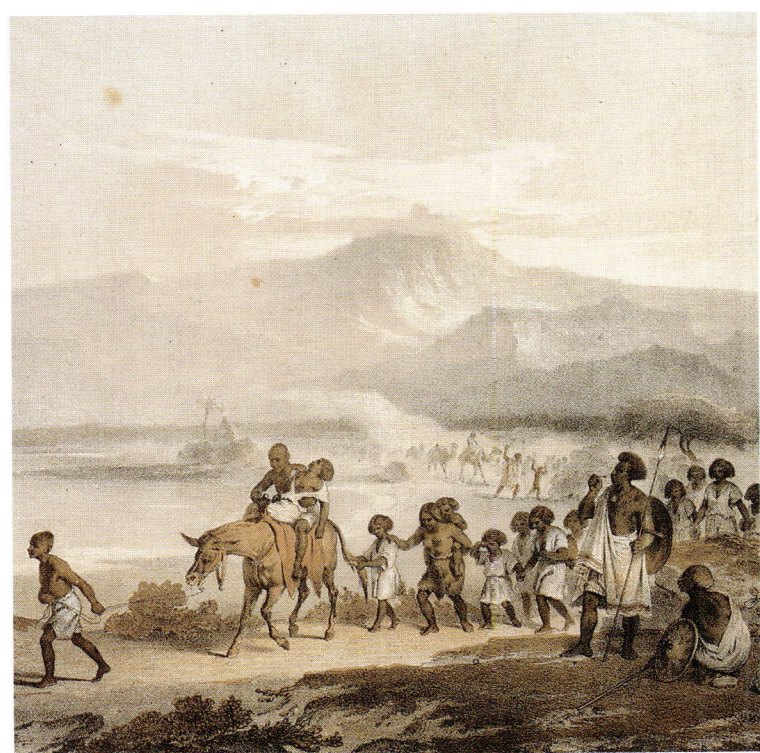
SLAVES ON THEIR WAY TO THE COAST

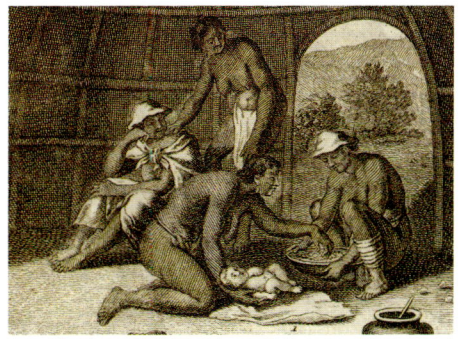

The Birth of Ana de Sousa Nzinga

Among the folk songs that honor Ngola Nzinga, one tells the story of how when the prophet-soothsayers, the *xinguilas*, bent over her cradle, they looked at each other mischievously, grumbling, "Ayayai, Mama! Ayayai! The stars say that the little princess will not have an easy-going nature."

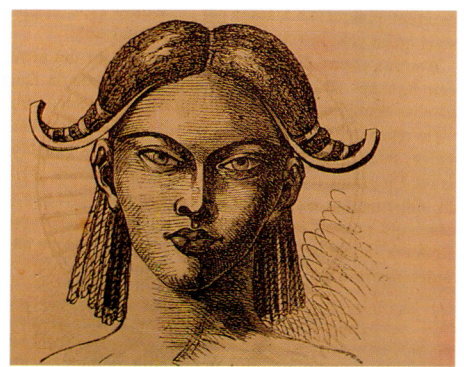

Kimbundu Young Women

The way women arrange their hair is remarkable. Some add cowries to make it resemble a hat. Others tease, curl, or roll up their hair so as to make it look like a Roman helmet.
The use of cowries to decorate the head is widespread among the women. White or red glass trinkets are also used, though less so, amongst the people who live west of the Kwanza River. These extraordinary styles are set with a red balm made from resin powder and castor oil. This balm is especially common among people who produce a great quantity of castor oil. First they pick the seeds and dry them out, before grinding them into a powder. This powder gives off oil once it has been boiled in water for several hours. After the water cools, the oil is extracted and preserved in small gourds.

Proverb

"No matter how *full* the river, it wants to grow more."

Upon the king's death, power falls into the hands of his oldest son, Ngola Mani a Ngola.

He has raised an army of thirty thousand men and intends to engage the Portuguese in pitched battle: traditional lances against mortars and guns.

Ana de Sousa Nzinga, amazon and warrior, beautiful though dressed like a man, is already considered the greatest political mind of her time.

In the middle of a council meeting, she says to the king: "My dear brother, your warriors are many, but their chests are bare: if you go this course, your defeat will be that of the whole nation."

Furious, the king has the throat of Nzinga's only son cut and hands the princess over to the matrons, who sterilize her using a red hot poker, say some praise singers, or scalding water, other versions claim.

A few months later, having suffered one defeat after another, the king begs Ana de Sousa Nzinga to negotiate a peace agreement with the governor of Luanda: she speaks Portuguese and has studied their customs, ways of thinking, and military strategy. She is, as a member of the council clumsily put it, "the man of the hour."

Nzinga cannot forget her dead son, and her ruined womb; but then she hears the lamentations of her people and agrees to go to Luanda.

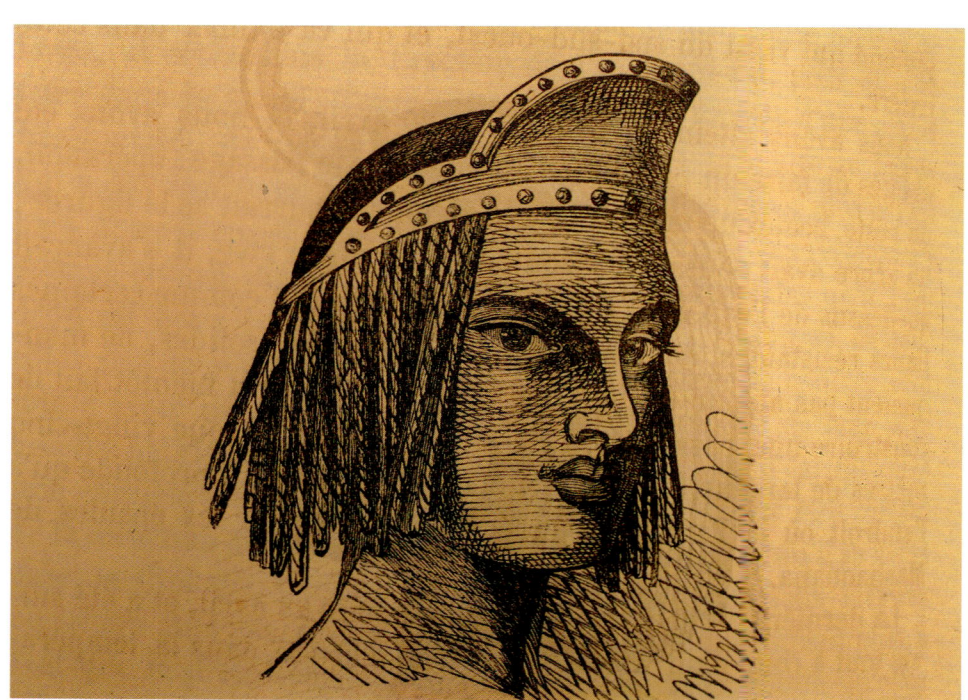

"FURIOUS, THE KING HAD THE THROAT OF NZINGA'S ONLY SON CUT" ▷

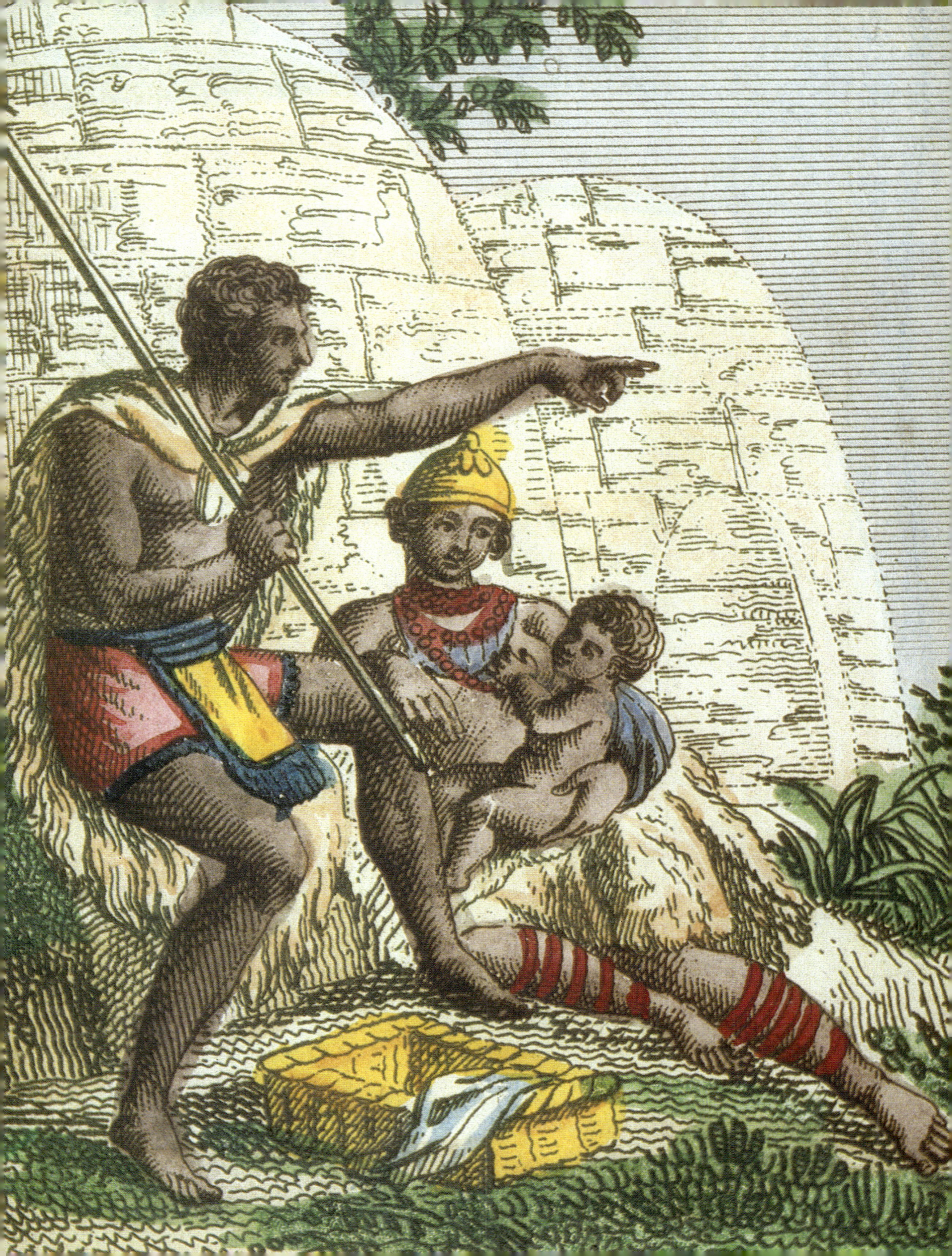

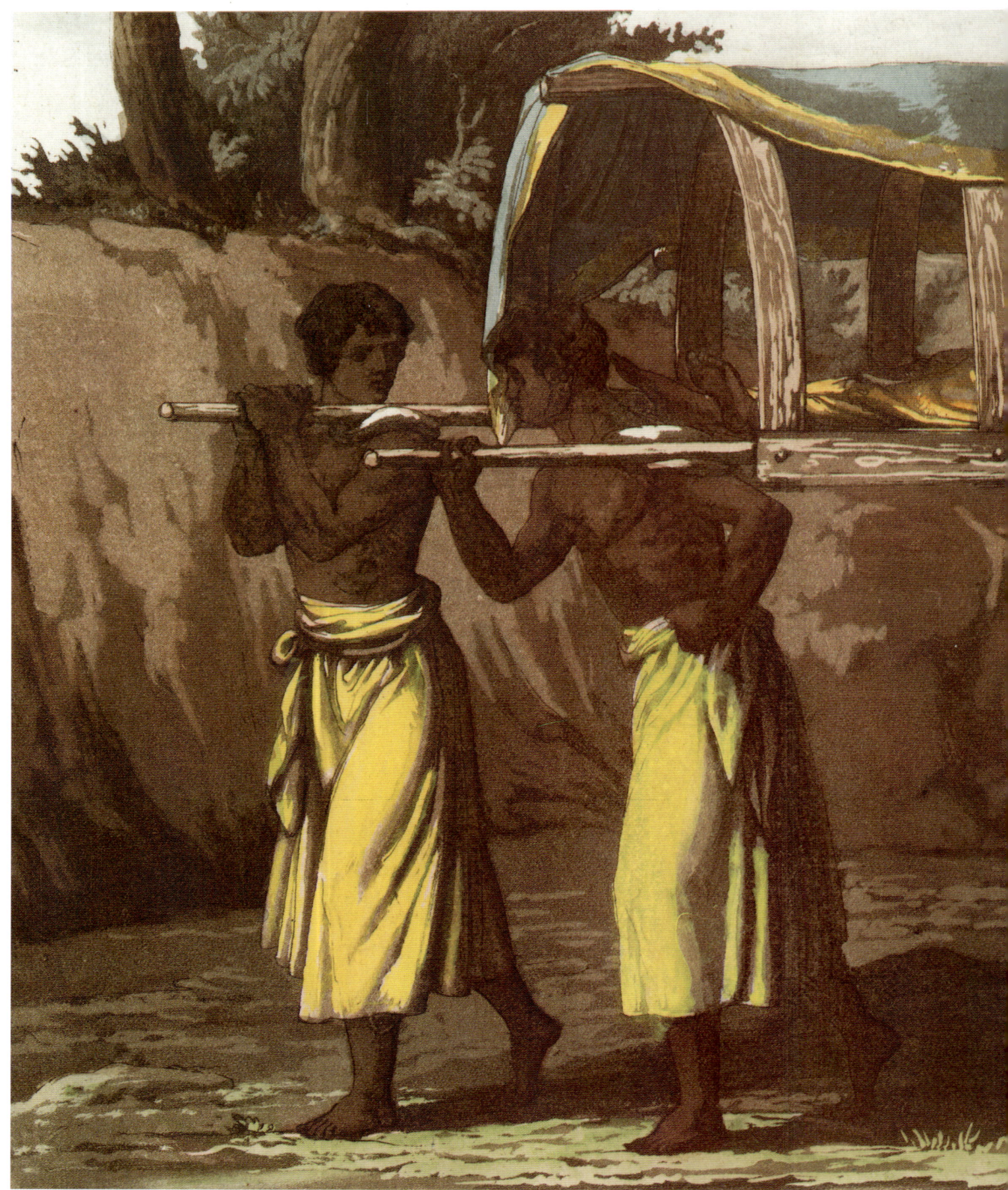

"A HUGE CROWD ESCORTS HER AND THROWS

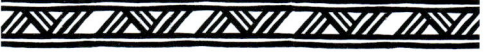

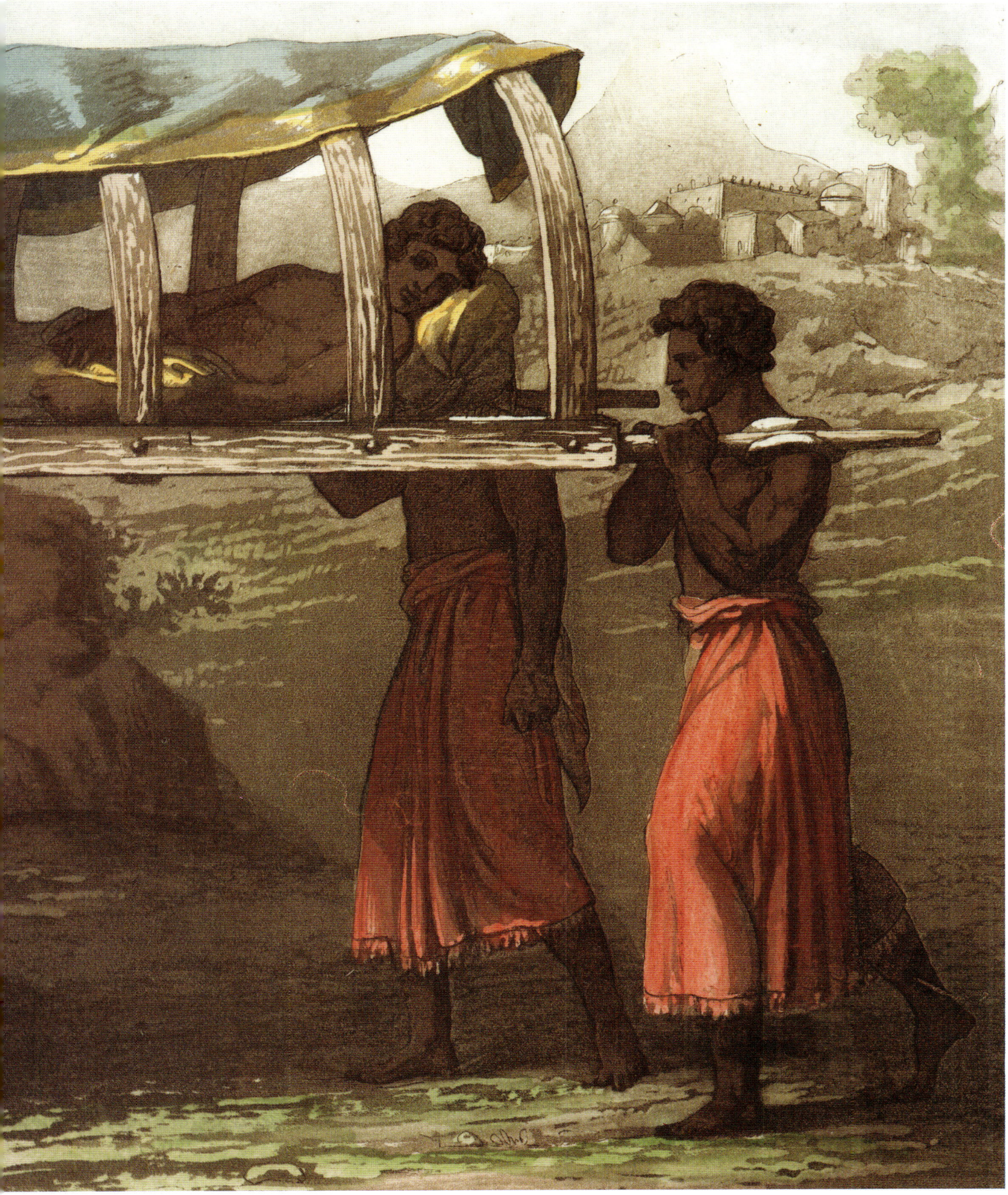

"FLOWERS ALONG HER PATH OF EXILE"

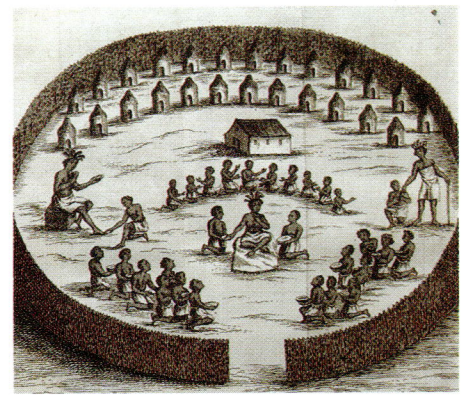

Ngola Nzinga's Regular Meals

The queen was served by three hundred women. They were at her service ten at a time for ten-day shifts, and during that time they never left her presence. Unless she was taken ill, the queen always ate in a public place. The table was set under the arch where she received people.

She simply helped herself with her hands, breaking the meat into pieces and eating it.

During her meals, she spoke to the ladies and officers around her and gave them pieces of meat that they respectfully accepted and ate with her. When she drank, all those in attendance clapped hands and used their fingers as castanets, and one of her highest ranking officers would touch the big toe of her left foot with his index finger to let her know that her subjects wished her good digestion, that the food should spread throughout her body from head to toe.

Once she had eaten, she distributed the leftovers among her women, and there were always many people to feed. When she received strangers, she ate in the European fashion. She would sit on her throne, richly dressed in Portuguese clothes, and her ladies and officers served her as one serves a ruler in Europe; but this happened rarely because she disliked customs that made her uncomfortable.

Ana de Sousa Nzinga's Trip

There were about a hundred people in Nzinga's entourage, not counting the military escort. From Kabasa to Luanda, a distance of two hundred and fifty miles, the princess was carried in a litter, as custom dictates in a country where the few horses and mules belonged to the Portuguese. The litter was large and comfortable enough so that Nzinga was able to travel reclined on brightly colored pillows. The four corners of the litter were sturdily pegged together by two pieces of supple wood that the porters placed on their shoulders. These bearers switched places with each other every few miles. They could walk for about twenty-five miles without tiring.

A huge crowd escorts her, throwing flowers on her path of exile.

But once she gets to Luanda, she enters the fortress, the bastion of the whites, without an escort, accompanied only by a few of her women.

At that moment, wishing to test rather than honor her, the governor fires a twenty-one gun salute.

But the princess has already heard this music in the course of many battles; and her eyelids don't even blink as she enters the fortress, crosses the courtyard, where her step leaves an imprint in the stone, and makes her entrance in the main reception room, the floor of which has been covered with velvet, the walls of which are covered with hangings, and the ceiling of which is like a sky covered with stars.

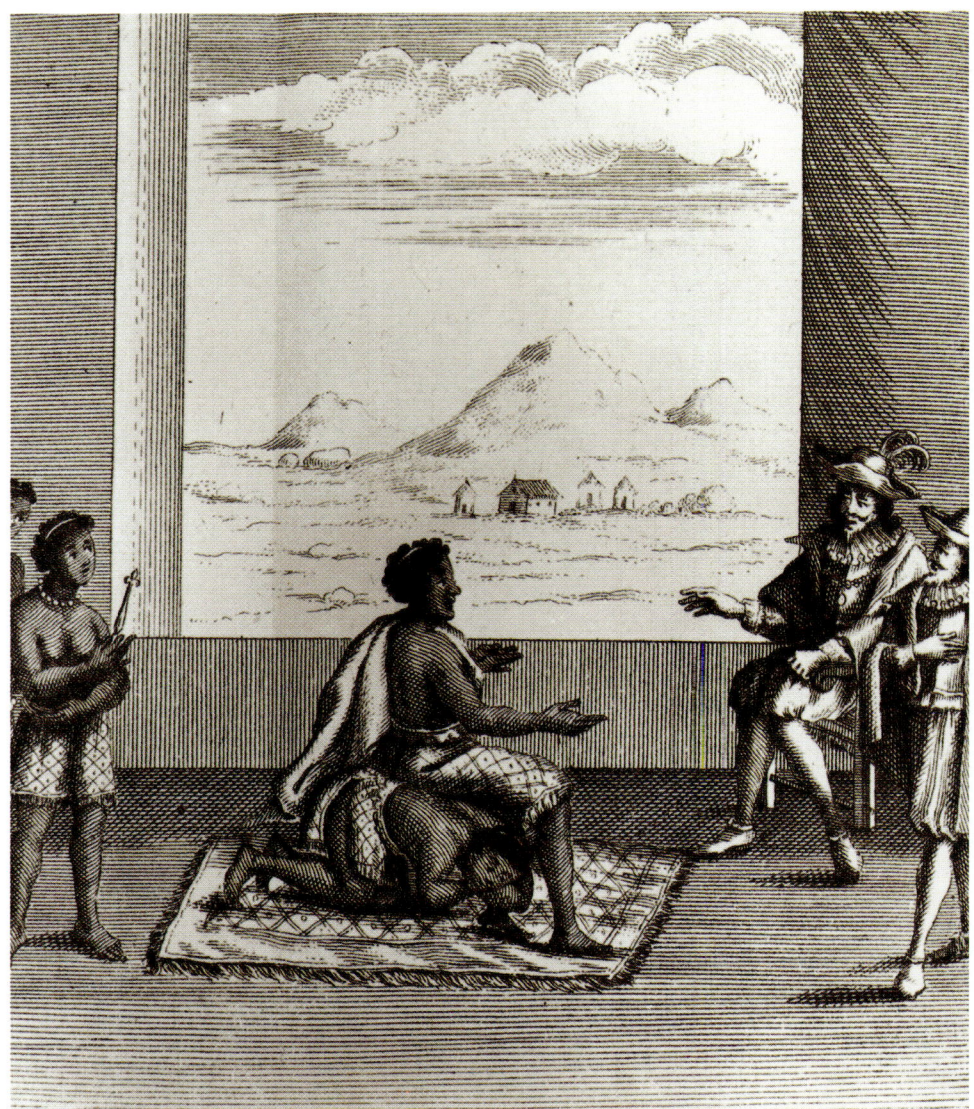

"IN RESPONSE TO A SIMPLE GESTURE, A SERVANT KNEELS"

The stone room is full of men-at-arms.

All the way in the back, from atop a resplendent throne, the governor gestures for her to step forward.

But still wishing to challenge, if not humiliate, her, he has not prepared a seat for the ambassador.

In response to a simple gesture, one of her women kneels and Ana de Sousa Nzinga gingerly sits down upon this human throne.

The governor, in a haughty tone, asks her what the conditions of her capitulation are. But Nzinga's eyelids don't budge at those words. She calmly replies: "I represent a sovereign people, and I am ready to continue this conversation only on that basis."

A few months later, in 1623, a peace treaty is duly signed between the kingdoms of Angola and Portugal. Ana de Sousa Nzinga has taken the diplomatic route so far as to convert to Catholicism. But the princess has not been duped: she knows this alliance is stillborn and the Europeans' promises will not be kept; she saw their words break at their own feet as if they were dead leaves.

A Conversation Booth in Huambo

In each village there is a kind of conversation booth. Most of the inhabitants come around eventually to sit on stumps and chat, especially if it rains. People go there to tell each other moving tales of love or hunting or war. They speak of themselves, instead of others as they tend to do in Europe.

Spinning and Weaving Techniques

The spinning and weaving techniques used in the kingdom of Angola, as well as other parts of southern Africa, are similar to those used in ancient Egypt, as depicted in these engravings from Sir Gardner Wilkinson's interesting work. In the lower part of the illustration, women are spinning thread in the true African manner, while the women at the upper left set their threads in Angolan fashion.

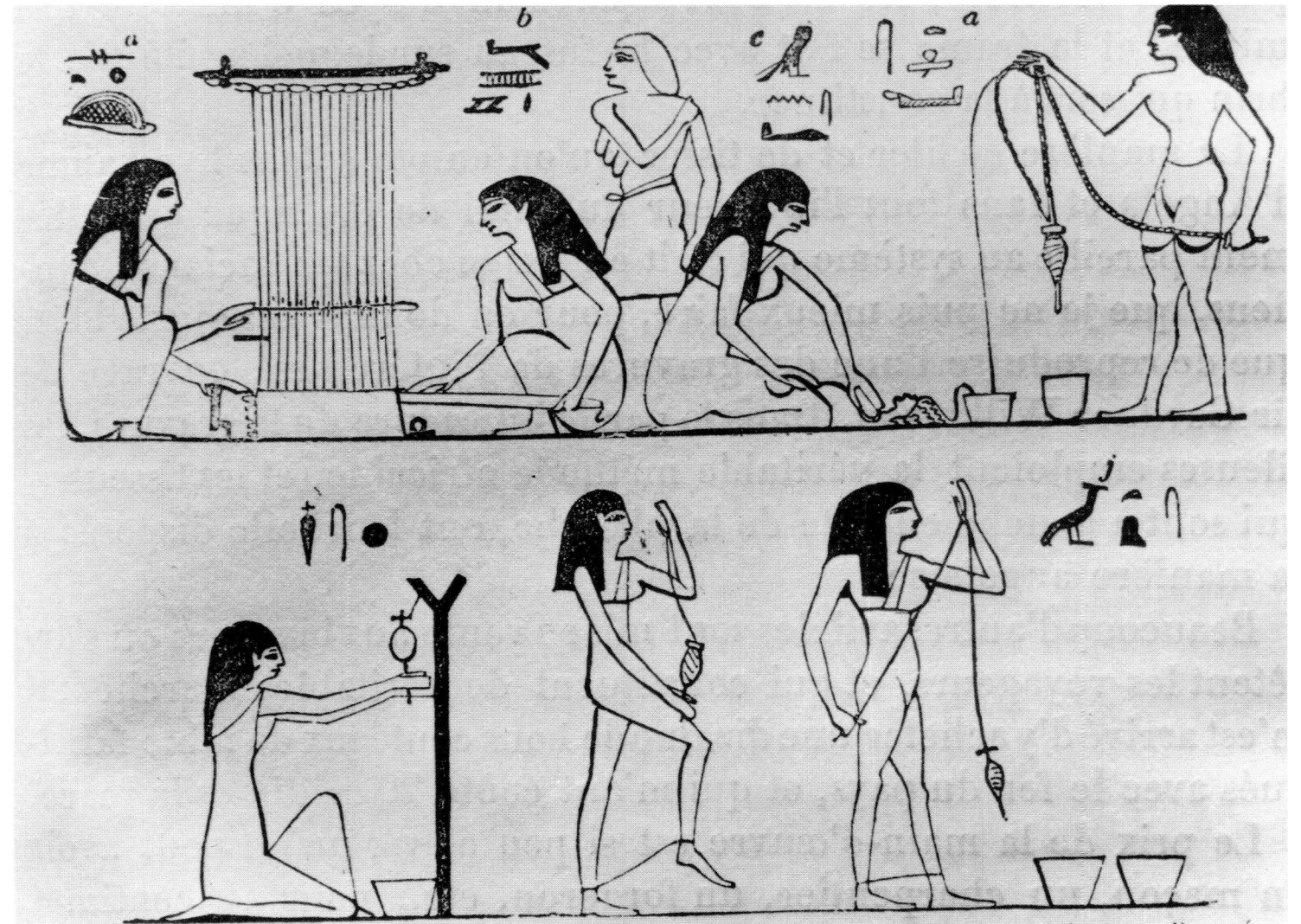

THE TECHNIQUES OF SPINNING AND WEAVING ARE THE SAME AS THOSE IN ANCIENT EGYPT

For her part, from the moment she leaves the gates of the fortress, she has decided to continue the fight in order to protect her people from the slavers: the cruel and desperate war that Ngola Karensi and after him his daughter Ana de Sousa Nzinga will carry on for more than seventy years.

She has seen the lion in his den. She knows the length of his claws. A feeling of urgency fills her now. As soon as she gets back, she jails Ngola Mani, and while her father is still fresh in his grave and the first rolls of the funerary drums resound, she proclaims herself ngola and issues her first orders.

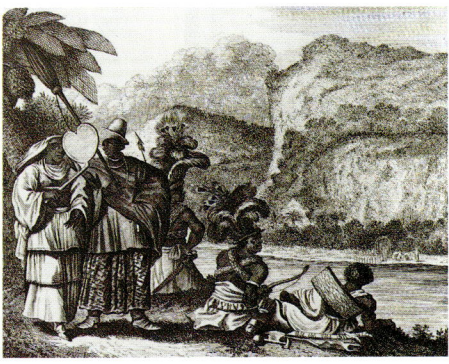

Kabasa Notables Conspire Against the Queen

From the beginning of Nzinga's reign, in 1623, a number of notables from Kabasa begin to ferment plots against the queen. Forewarned that a conjurer is to poison her, Nzinga decides to make an example. She lets the suspect go on with his treason. The man never misses an opportunity to flatter the queen. He is always the first to applaud any of her decisions. One day when Nzinga has been particularly merciful to a prisoner who had attempted to run away, the plotter steps forward and gives a long speech:

"Nzinga, you are a great ngola. You know that your generosity, and not ill-treatment, will win the love of your subjects. Only an egregious offense would justify shedding blood here. You are right, you rule over us better by winning over our hearts than you would…"

"Sir," the queen interrupted him, "your words are just. Only an egregious offense justifies shedding blood here. That's what you said, isn't it?"

"Indeed," says he, all flushed and glad to be conversing with the queen in front the people.

"So," Nzinga asks, "tell us why you've been carrying poison hidden in your loincloth since the new moon!"

Before the man knows what is happening, the queen's men take him away. A few minutes later, he is publicly executed along with all of his accomplices.

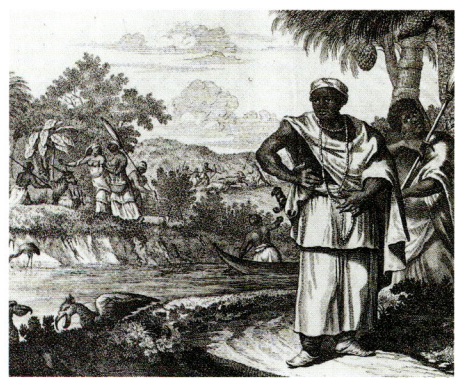

Proverb

"Human blood is heavy: it will prevent the one who sheds it from running off too quickly."

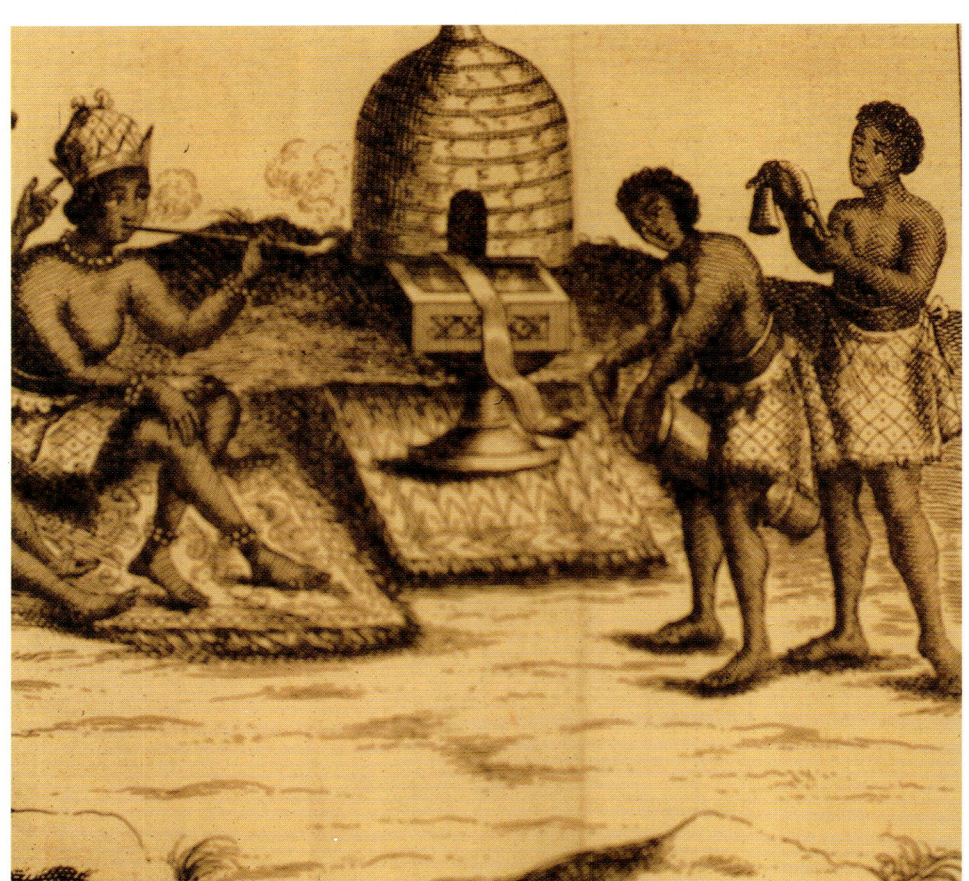

VENERATION OF THE QUEEN

She wasn't wrong: the peace treaty lasts only the space of a dream. The Portuguese are already moving deeper into the kingdom, buying off her friends, establishing alliances with her enemies. Ana de Sousa Nzinga has to retreat. And from one setback to another, always vanquished but never defeated, she goes into the mountains of Matamba where she will hang on until the very end.

GROUP OF REBELS ▷

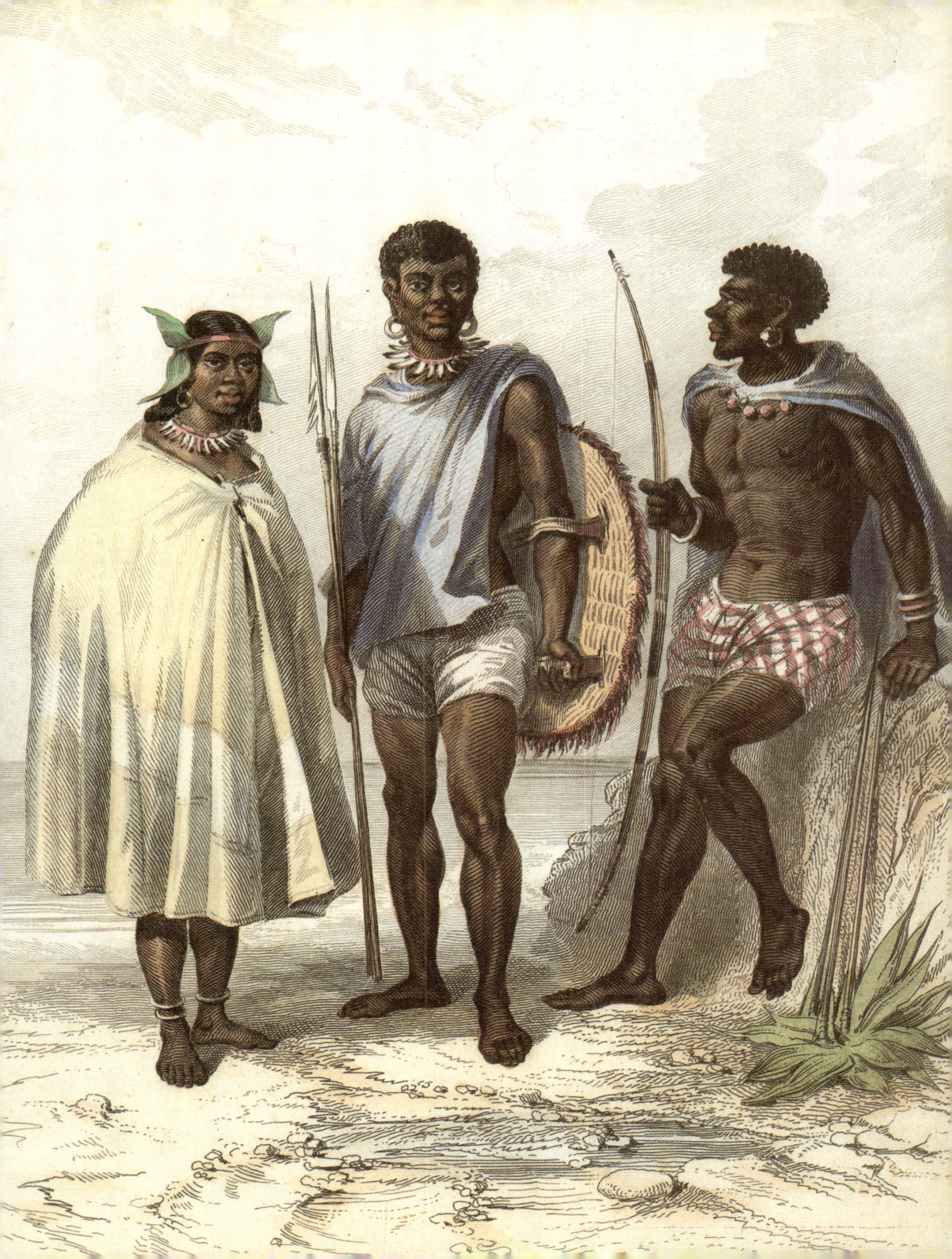

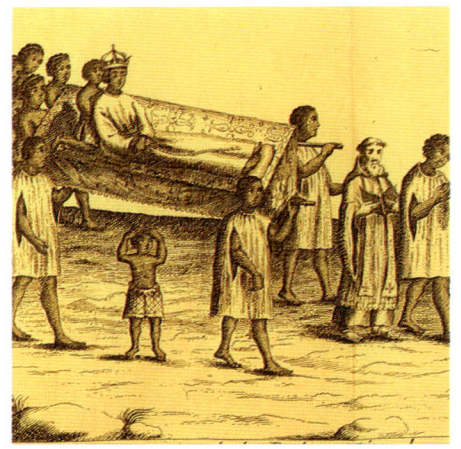

Ana de Sousa Nzinga's Death

On December 14th, 1665, Nzinga called for a council meeting one last time. She begged her first minister, the Tandola (a title she had just created before she had taken ill) to make sure that her sister Cambo would succeed her.

The morning of the 17th, Nzinga was dead. The news of her death was kept secret until the morning of the 19th. The members of the royal council gathered the people.

In her hut, sitting upright, Nzinga was dressed in her royal clothes. Held up on her chest by a pin, a sheer gold-embroidered textile fell from her shoulders and spread over the pillows. She wore a helmet crowned with feathers and a golden wreath in her hair. Rare shells and large pearls hung from her neck, pearls and gold earrings adorned her ears. Her arms were covered in bracelets, made alternately of gold and elephant tail hair, worn up to the elbow, her legs had anklets down to the heels, and her feet were encased in velvet slippers fastened by two glass buttons. The rest of her body was covered in rich gold brocades.

She looked like a statue covered with necklaces, bracelets, and flowers.

On the afternoon of the 19th, Nzinga was carried, in this attire, into the courtyard of her compound. The crowd marched before its queen.

One hundred warriors who were usually combat soldiers played musical instruments. Other regiments lined up to imitate a battle, the way Angolans usually do on the days of feasts.

People were so used to seeing Nzinga dressed beautifully that for a moment they thought she had been resurrected.

A cry of joy rushed out of everyone's lungs, but the reality of her death imposed itself in the end and no one could hide their pain.

Proverb

"If your bedfellow kicks you, kick him back, otherwise he'll think your legs are too short."

For thirty years, she will fight to win back her homeland.

She will exact blood for blood and answer terror with terror, slaughter with slaughter: all so that her people may not know slavery.

She will die at the age of eighty-four, without having been able to rebuild her homeland. Nevertheless, says Fernando Monteiro de Castro Soromenho, a twentieth-century writer and a man of his people, "She lost many battles, but she never lost the war: because Ana de Sousa Nzinga lived a queen and died a queen."

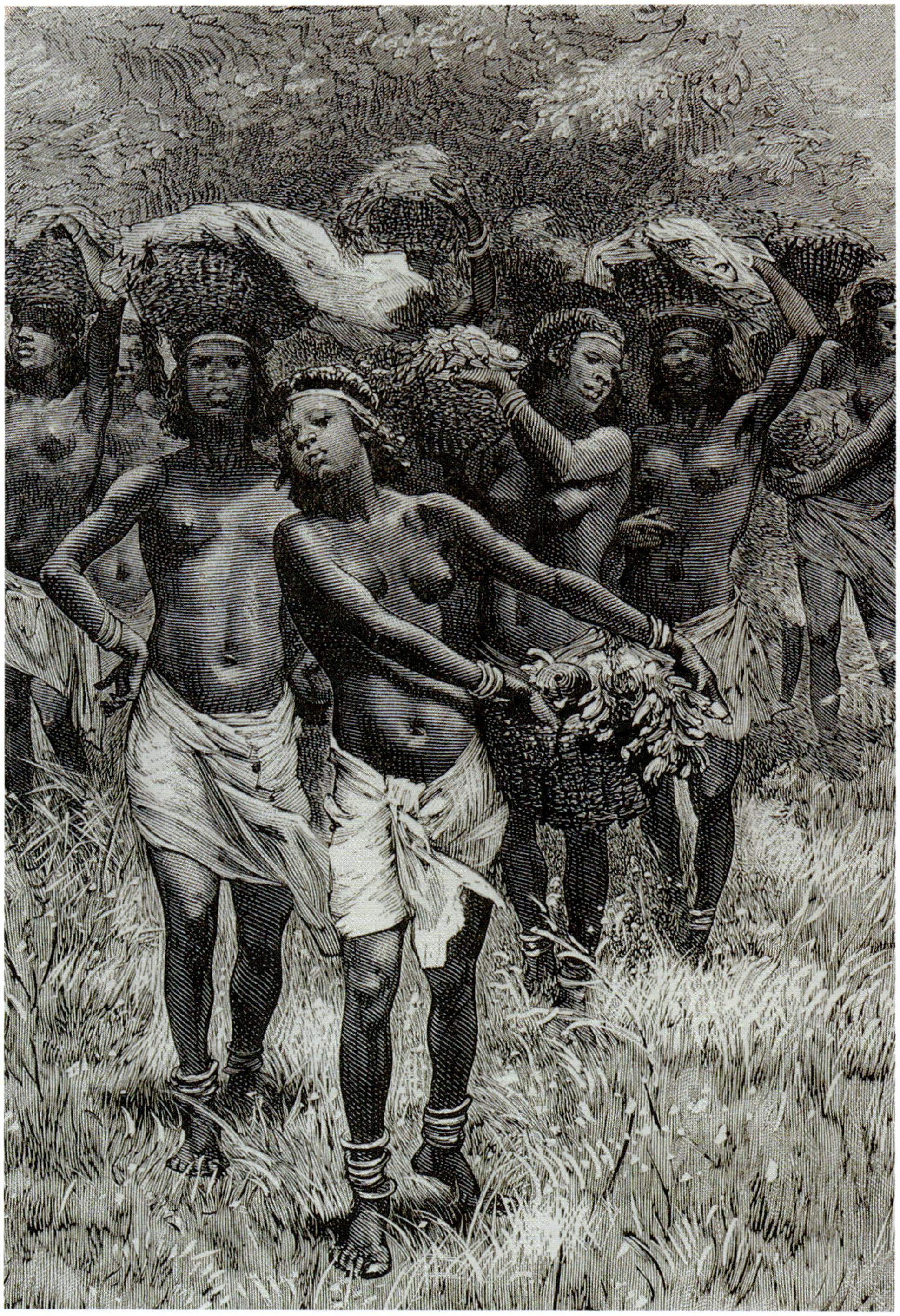

YOUNG WOMEN FROM HUAMBO BEARING FLOWERS

WORDS
OF AN ORDINARY WOMAN

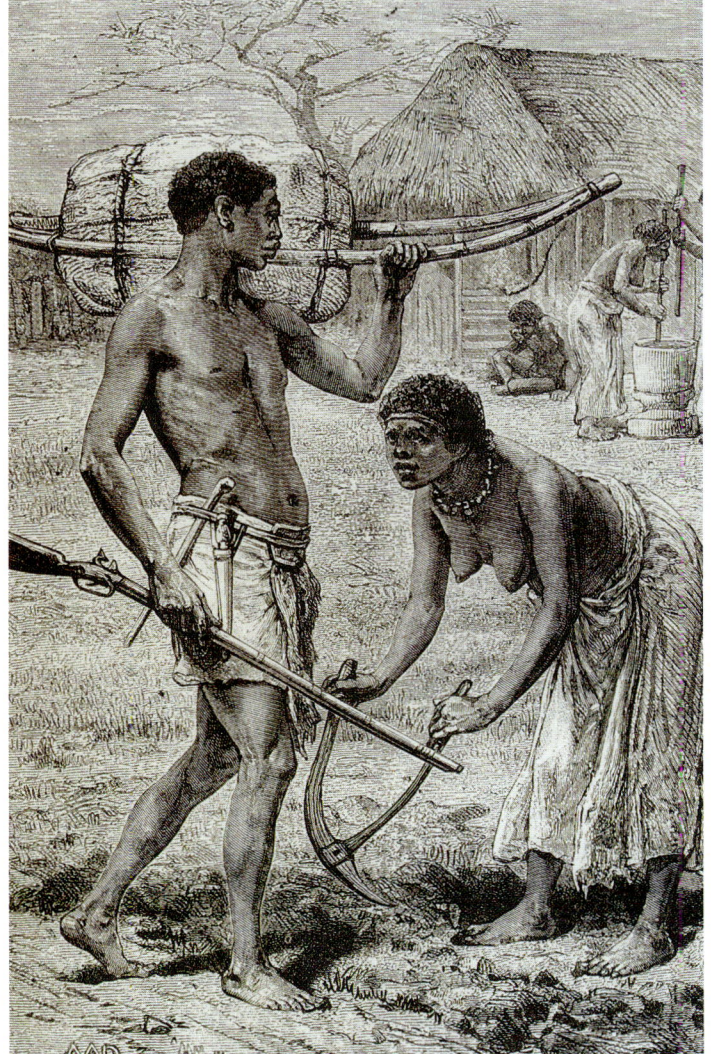
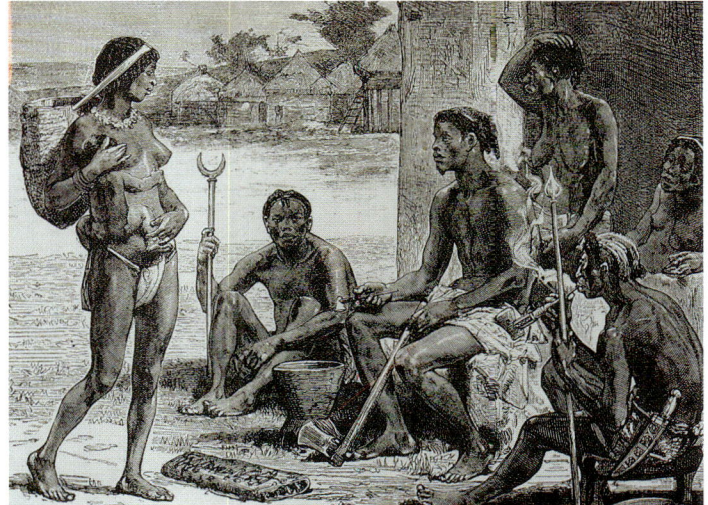
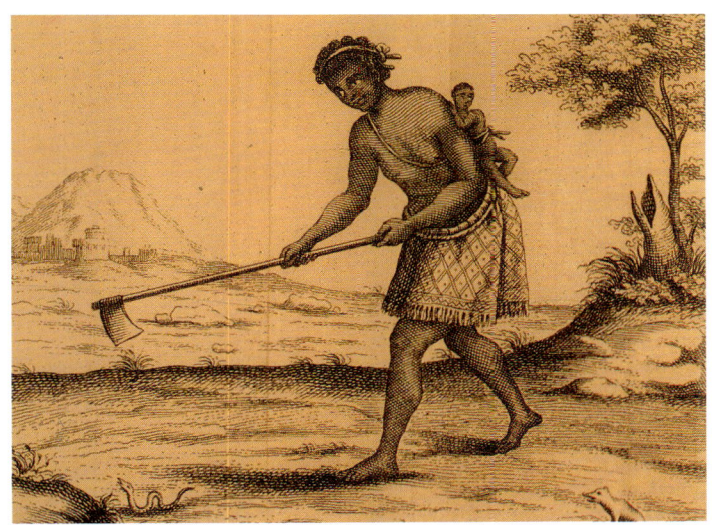

"PATIENCE IS NECESSARY IN ALL THINGS"

Patience is necessary in all things: before death as before life.

If you show no patience, you won't be able to live with anyone. To live with someone means to be patient with that person. Love doesn't last more than three days if a couple has no patience. Love is about patience!

At the end of the rainy season, the pond water is polluted. It's dirty and it stinks. But if you are thirsty, you have to drink it because there is no other. You even have to spare it as if it were precious. From the few puddles left you must draw water with care, by making it run into holes that you have dug, at least until you are able to get good well water. When you have clear water then you'll be able to pass up dirty water. But not before. That's why we have this proverb: "Keep the dirty one until you have the clean one." One has to know how to be patient and wait.

When you light a fire, at first there's a lot of smoke. But if you can't put up with it, you'll never know the joy of a flame. The pleasure of sitting by the fire and warming yourself up comes after being patient with the smoke.

Patience is necessary in all things. Be patient with others. Be patient with thirst. Be patient with weariness. Be patient with children.

Things change. Years bring change. After suffering comes happiness. After happiness comes suffering. After the dry season comes the wet season. And after the rains, the dry season returns again.

Human life is made of suffering and happiness. Do you know what we compare happiness to? To the drops of milk the cow gives. And do you know what suffering is like? It's like the sparks that burn you when you sit by the fire. The suffering of fire and the happiness of milk are not like each other. In the life of every single person, there is fire and there is milk!

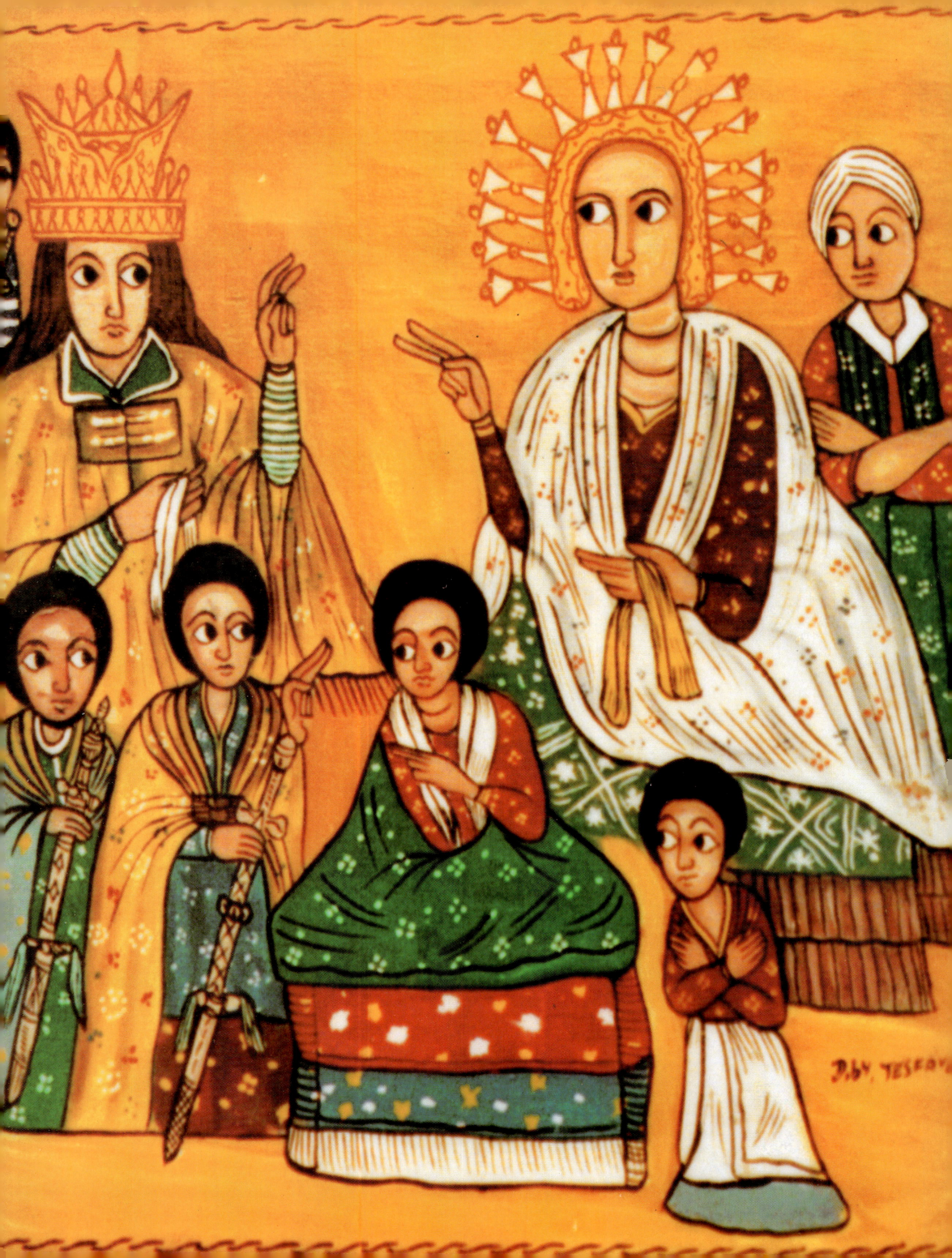

MENTOWAB

EMPRESS OF ETHIOPIA

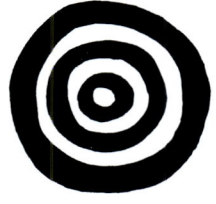

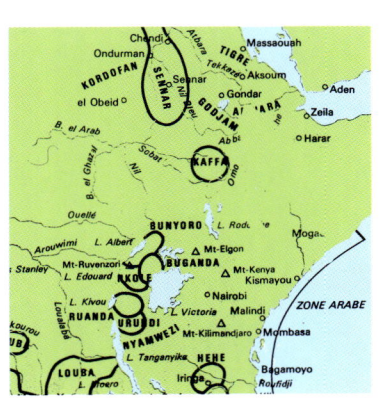 *Her name means: "Oh how beautiful you are!" She is one who will not give up, who will bend only to stand taller...*

A CHRONICLER BY THE NAME OF ALVAREZ WAS AMONG THE FIRST PORTUGUESE AMBASSADORS TO ETHIOPIA DURING THE TIME OF QUEEN HELENI. HIS DESCRIPTION OF PRESTER JOHN'S KINGDOM STUNNED ALL OF EUROPE. THE BOOK WAS PROMPTLY translated into all the known languages.

In those days, black skin was not talked of pejoratively when considering the African civilizations. The whole world discovered along with Alvarez a society rooted in traditions millennia old, where the poor and the powerful were ruled by one law, where the power of the great did not trump the basic rights of the most humble subject in the kingdom.

In the old city of Aksum stands a granite obelisk, taller than Egypt's pyramids, which seems to symbolize the kingdom of Ethiopia: both rooted in the ground and reaching into the sky.

Full of enthusiasm, the renowned writer Johnson included an Ethiopian scene in a novel popular throughout Europe.

Three centuries later, things have changed greatly. Domestic pressures have struck chords of disunity in the kingdom, which enters a period of sound and fury, darkness and trouble.

Then a great Solomonic king, Bekaffa, appears and takes power in 1721. Bekaffa is soon revered by the people and hated by the great lords, who nickname him "The Stubborn." One of his habits, among others, will give birth to a thousand legends: Bekaffa, king of kings, the descendant of Solomon walks disguised among the common people in order to see if justice is carried out, to make sure the widow and the orphan are not harmed.

And so, on one of these long solitary walks, the king hears a troubling prophecy: a man of God, a priest from Gondar says to him that "after the current king's death, a woman will rule the kingdom for many years, a woman by the name of Walatta-Giyorgis."

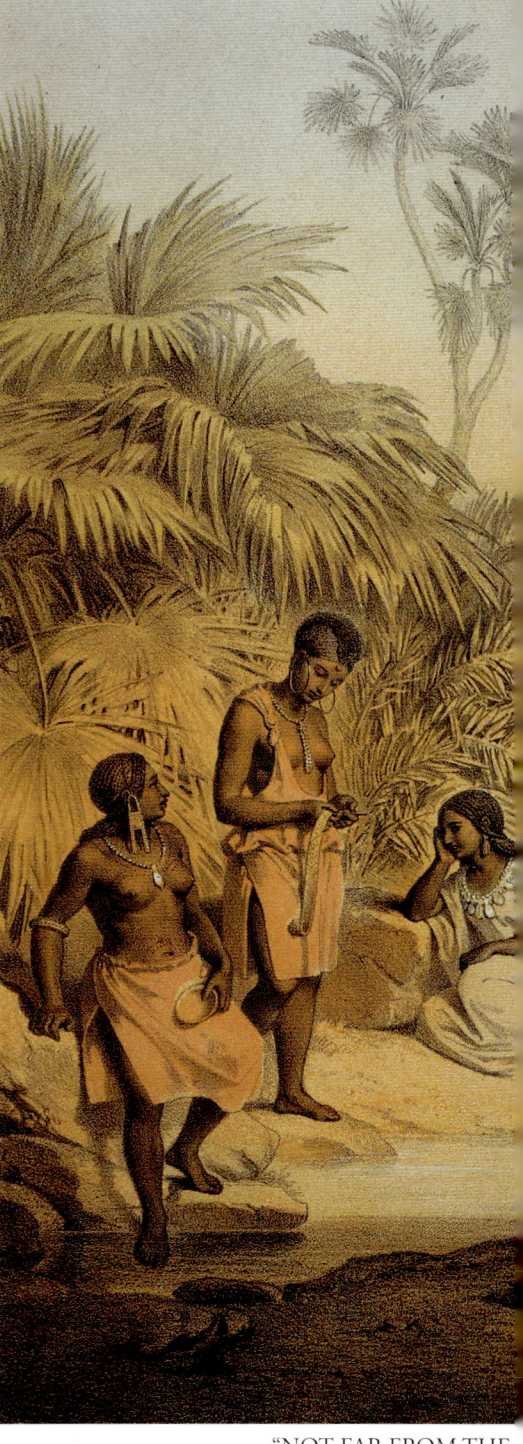

"NOT FAR FROM THE

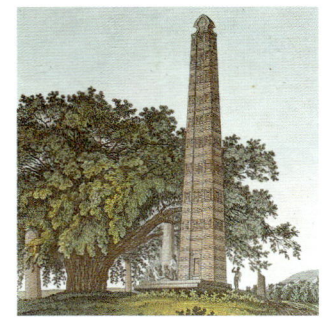

THE OBELISK OF AKSUM

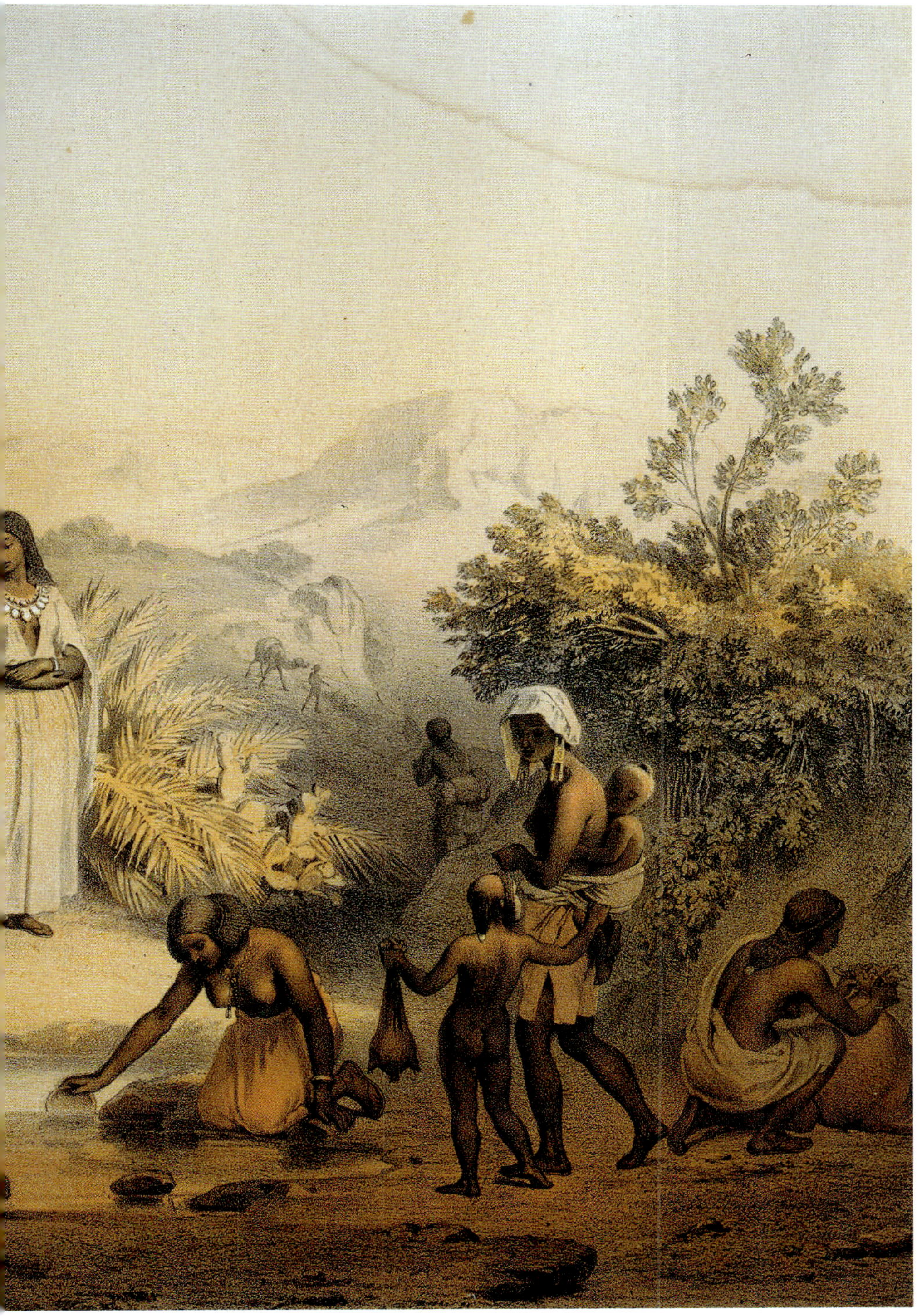

"SOURCE OF THE BLUE NILE"

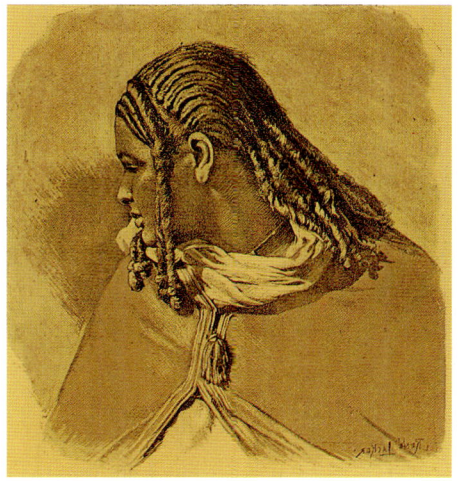

Women's Stylishness

Like men, women may arrange their hair however they please and are not subject to class restrictions in this respect. Peasant women, artisans' or priests' wives, even slaves have their hair braided just as rich ladies do. Like men, they like to put a long, carved pin made of buffalo horn or wood in their hair. Rich people's pins have silver or vermilion tips, and sometimes gold leaf. Women wear many thin silver rings on their fingers, shown off between rings of buffalo horn. In their hair, they wear silver dangles, small oval-shaped silver grains or glass beads. They also wear bracelets on their wrists and on the fleshy parts of their arms. They comb both butter and raw Arabian essences into their hair, and also place essence in their amulets.

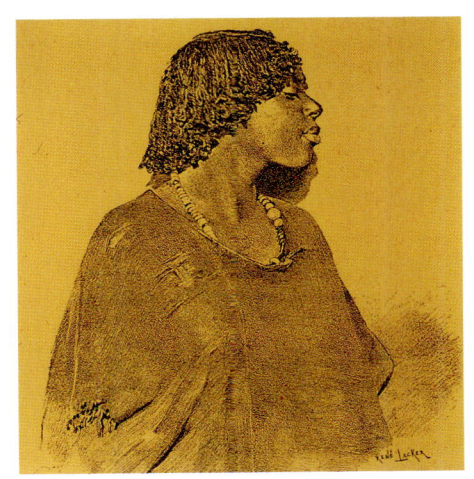

In the course of another trip, he becomes sick in the mountainous region of Quara, east of his kingdom, not far from the source of the Blue Nile. Although unknown to all and poorly dressed, he is welcomed by a local lord and is cared for by the lord's own daughter, a child named Barhan-Mugasa, which in Amharic means "Splendor of the Light." But the young woman's secret name is Walatta-Giorgis, the very name that had been prophesied, and Bekaffa will ultimately humbly bow before the will of God.

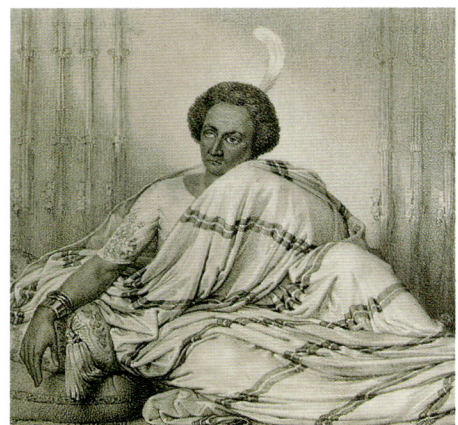

The Ethiopians' Beauty

What always first strikes one in Ethiopia is the nobility of people's faces, the seemliness of their behavior, the artful clothing that evokes antiquity. Arnaud d'Abbadie, who lived in Ethiopia when Gondar was still the capital, noted that the ancient classical statues "are astonishingly accurately depictions of young Ethiopian women from good homes." The explorer James Bruce, who made many true friends in Gondar, believed that Mentowab, who was past sixty years old by then, was the most graceful woman of her time.

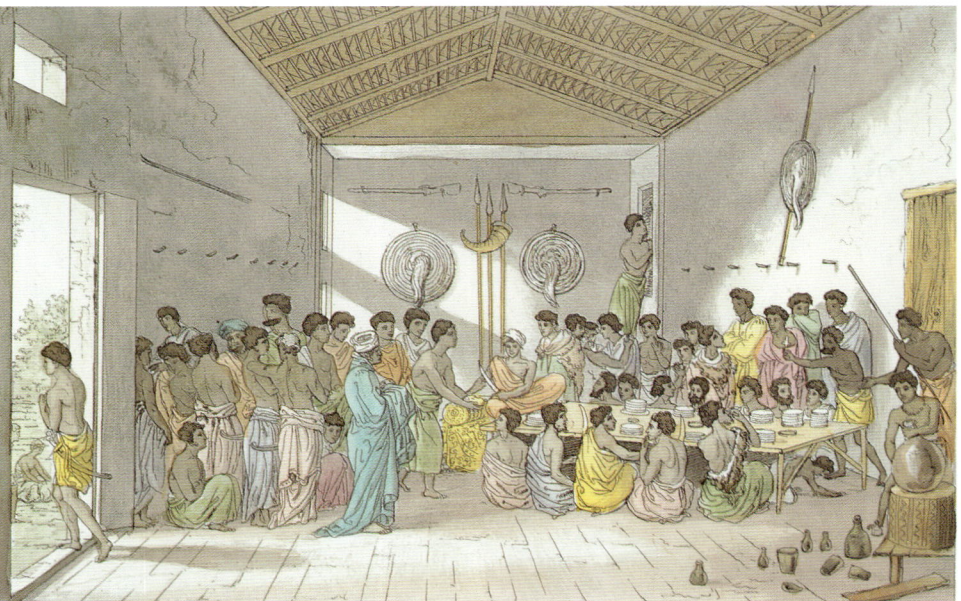

"THE KING BRINGS THE YOUNG WOMAN BACK TO HIS PALACE IN GONDAR"

Once cured, the king reveals his identity and brings the young woman back to his palace in Gondar where she gives him a son who will be his successor, Jesus II. She herself will become the famous empress known as Mentowab, which in Amharic means "Oh how beautiful you are."

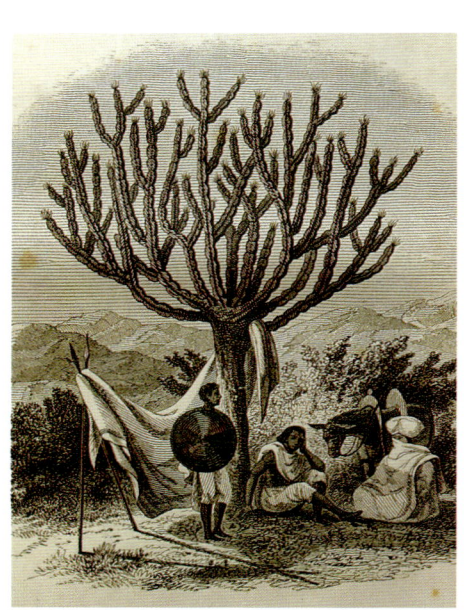

Attachment to the Soil

Ethiopians value their soil most highly. Many anecdotes report their suspicions concerning the foreigner, the *farendj*, the "French" who had come to steal part of their heritage. A king, according to tradition, made Europeans leave their shoes with him when they left Ethiopia lest they take any soil with them under their soles, a bit of Ethiopia and therefore a bit of her wealth.

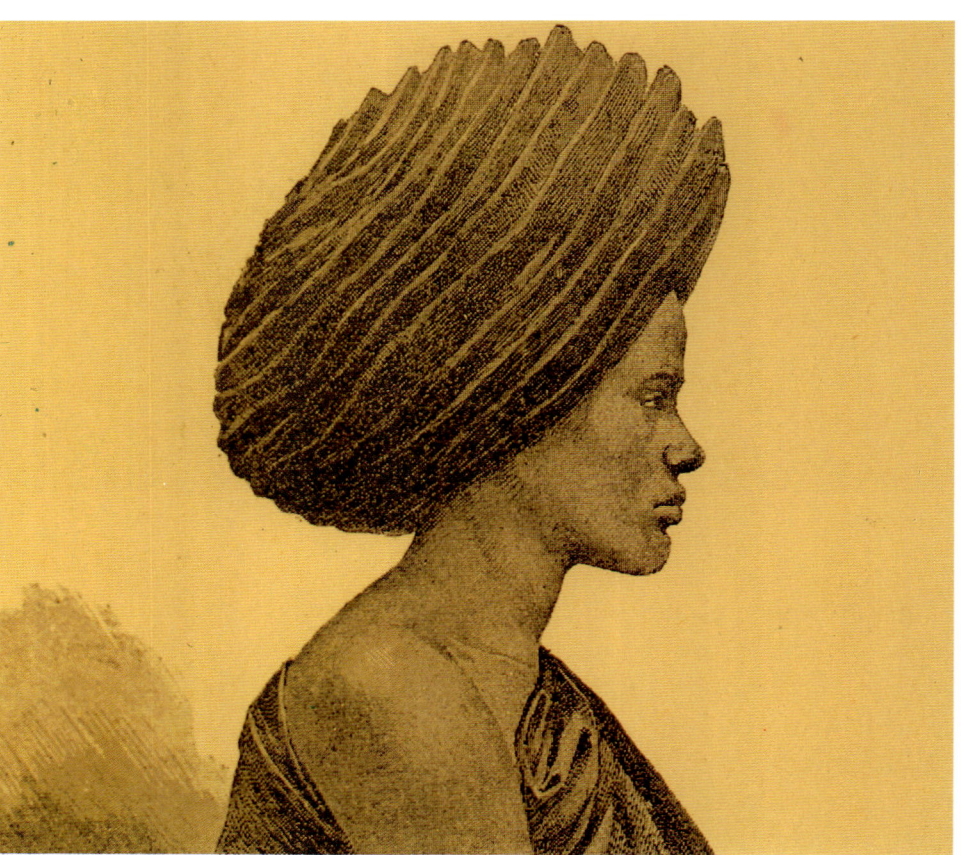

YOUNG WOMAN FROM HARAR

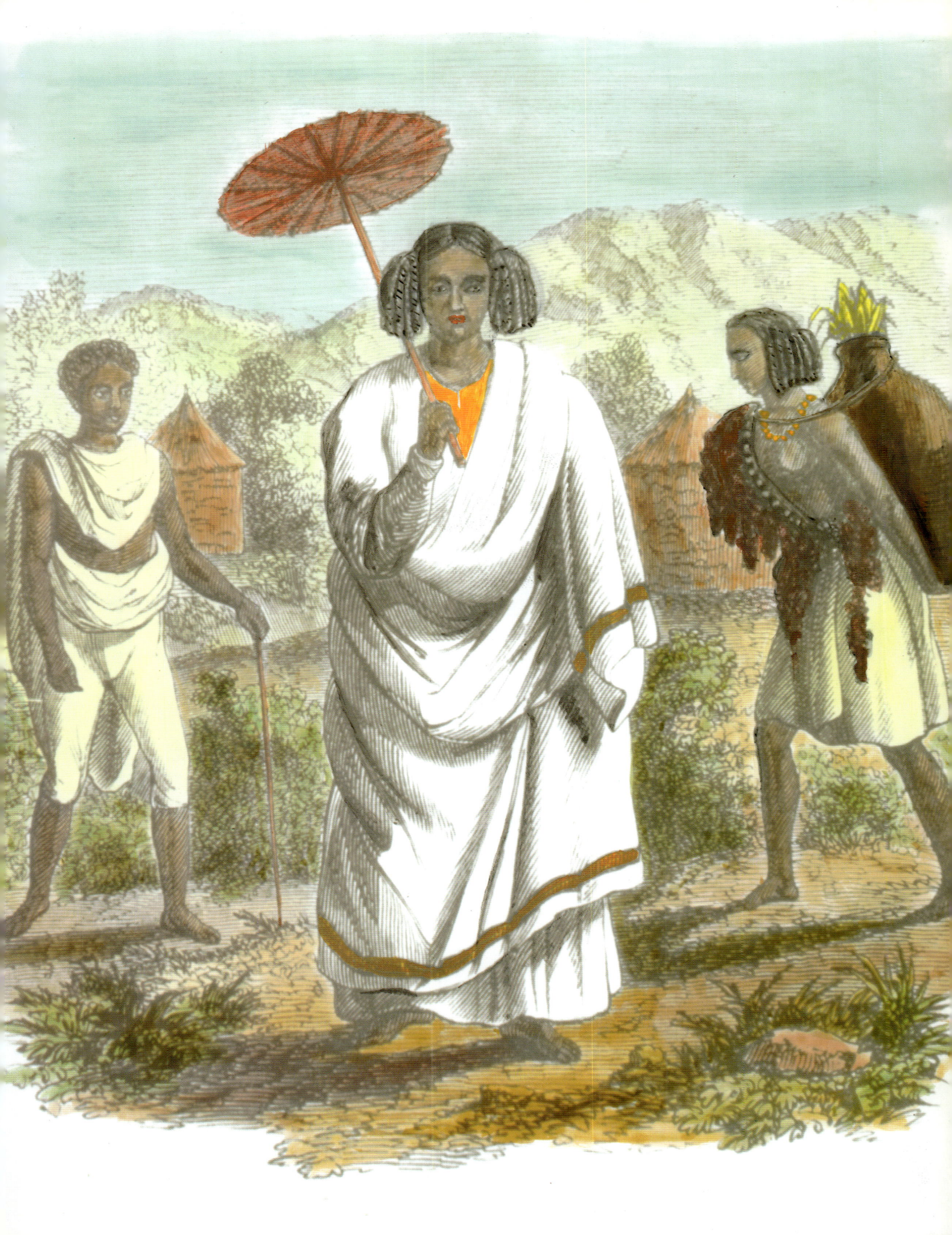

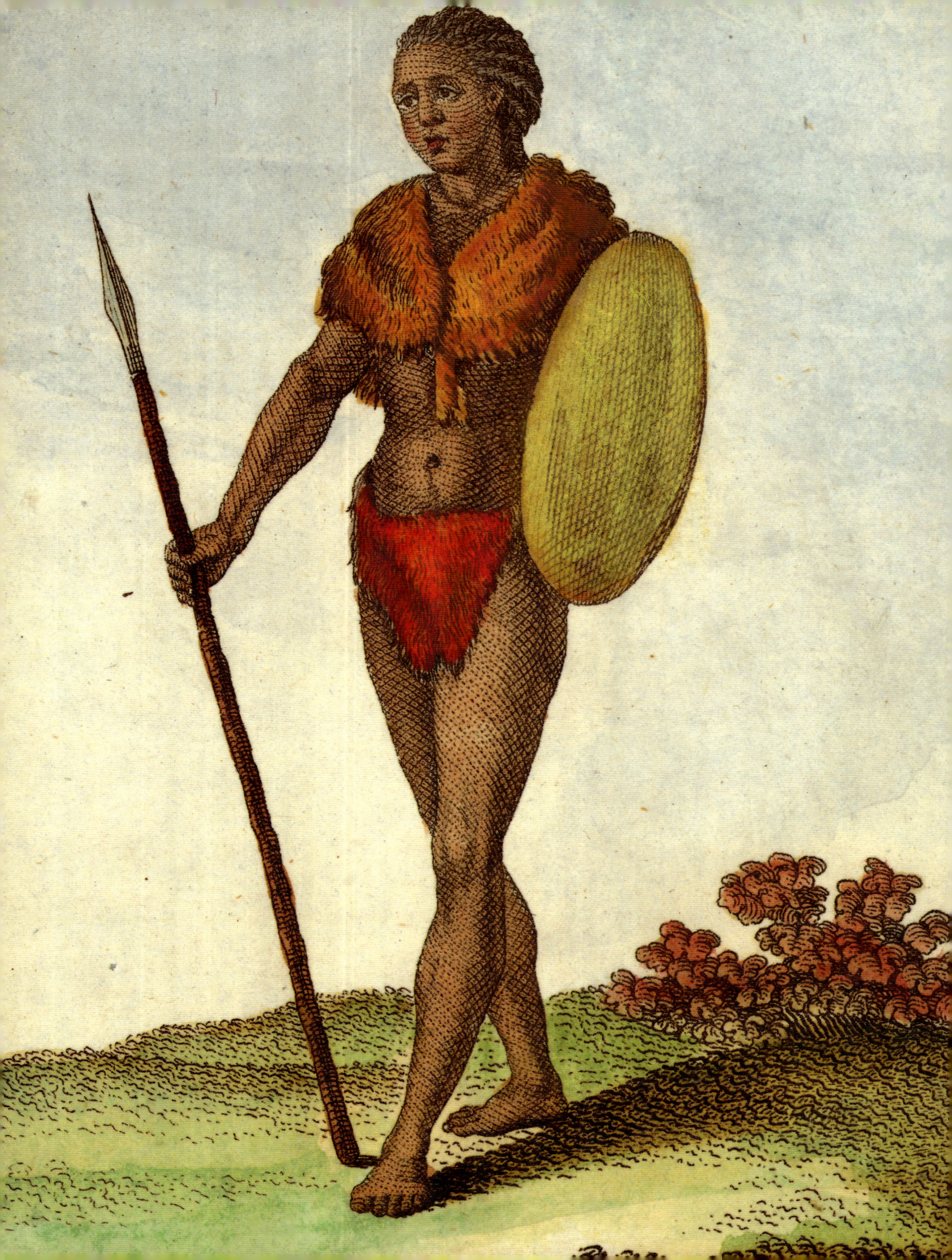

Mentowab is twenty-four years old upon the death of King Bekaffa the Stubborn, whose life she once saved.

She does not spread the news of the king's death right away, but instead reflects and considers an effort to make some alliances.

The future seems gloomy: Islam is beating at the doors of the kingdom. It awaits an opportunity to knock down the last stronghold of Christianity in Africa. And civil war threatens from within: civil war, this canker, this diabolical emanation that bleeds Ethiopia for more than two centuries. Throughout his life, Bekaffa had held the kingdom together with all his might. He banned Lord Ras Giorgis. He cut short the ambitions of Balata Rufaed; he crushed the Damot rebellion and pacified Rasta, whose Lord Lubala became a great friend of his. He had set his powerful hand on the Tigré region and upon Lord Taklé, who personally came to pay him tribute at Gondar, the capital of the kingdom. Will Mentowab be able to continue her husband's work? The young woman knows her husband died peacefully, sure of the future, because he had discovered that his wife's birth name was the very one predicted by the prophecy.

Mentowab is a young woman without experience, suddenly prey to palace intrigues, regional rivalries, and the quarrels of various lords. For two months, she keeps the death of the king a secret; then, having brought all the threads together like an embroiderer who has carefully prepared her canvas, she officially has herself proclaimed empress and orders a period of mourning for the whole kingdom.

Two months in the throes of lonely deliberation in the darkened palace have transformed her: she has come into her own, she is now wholly Mentowab, the one who will not give up, who will bend only to stand taller, who will follow the path once traced by the wandering Bekaffa the Stubborn, who had been welcomed into her father's house. The ends shall justify the means. She will submit all men to the hard yoke of the empress, and, at times, a delicate yoke, suffused with the scent of a woman.

Several conspiracies await her, and even a large-scale revolt in December 1732, when she will be surrounded in her Gondar castle in a desperate last stand, until a friendly officer rescues her from the final assault.

She uses a few men to insure her power, to clear a path through Ethiopia's stormy skies. Then, she marries Jesus Garazmach and has three daughters with him: Princesses Esther, Aletash, and Walatta-Israel.

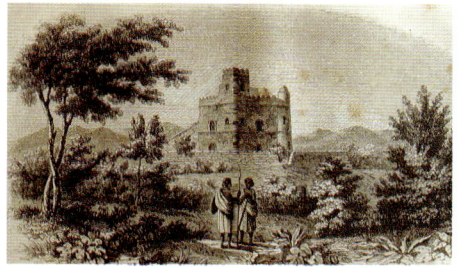

Gondar

Oh Gondar, with your lovely buildings,
Gondar, the dream of the wretched
and of the great,
One and only Gondar, to whom nothing compares,
Mother Gondar who satisfies all desires
Gondar, beyond delirium,
Gondar with your the delightful name,
Gondar, more beautiful than David's City,
than the land of Salem,
You who should have kept your splendor until the end of time.
Why were you destroyed like Sodom,
You who could never have deserved it?

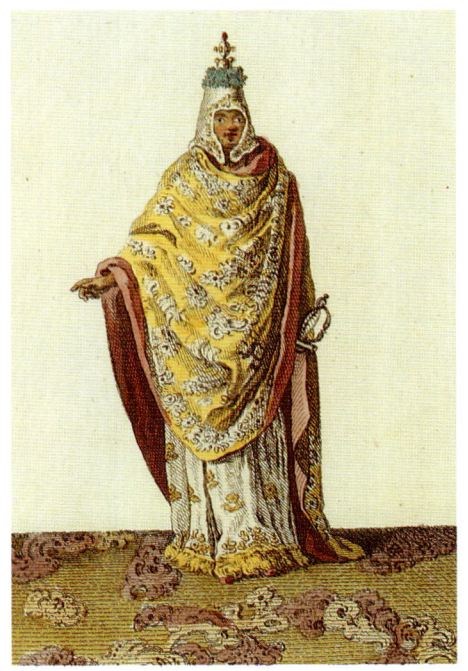

The Royal Hunt

Upon his ascension to the throne, the ruler takes possession of the palace and its hierarchy. Eventually, he decrees a reduction of all earlier taxes and frees the prisoners. But most of all, he hunts wild animals to demonstrate his courage and skill.

This institution, whose origins date back to antiquity, though not as respected in Gondar as in centuries past, is still alive and well.

The king must be an example of valor. But once the ruler has had the chance to face the lions and tigers, he lets his companions enjoy the bloody ritual of fighting these big cats.

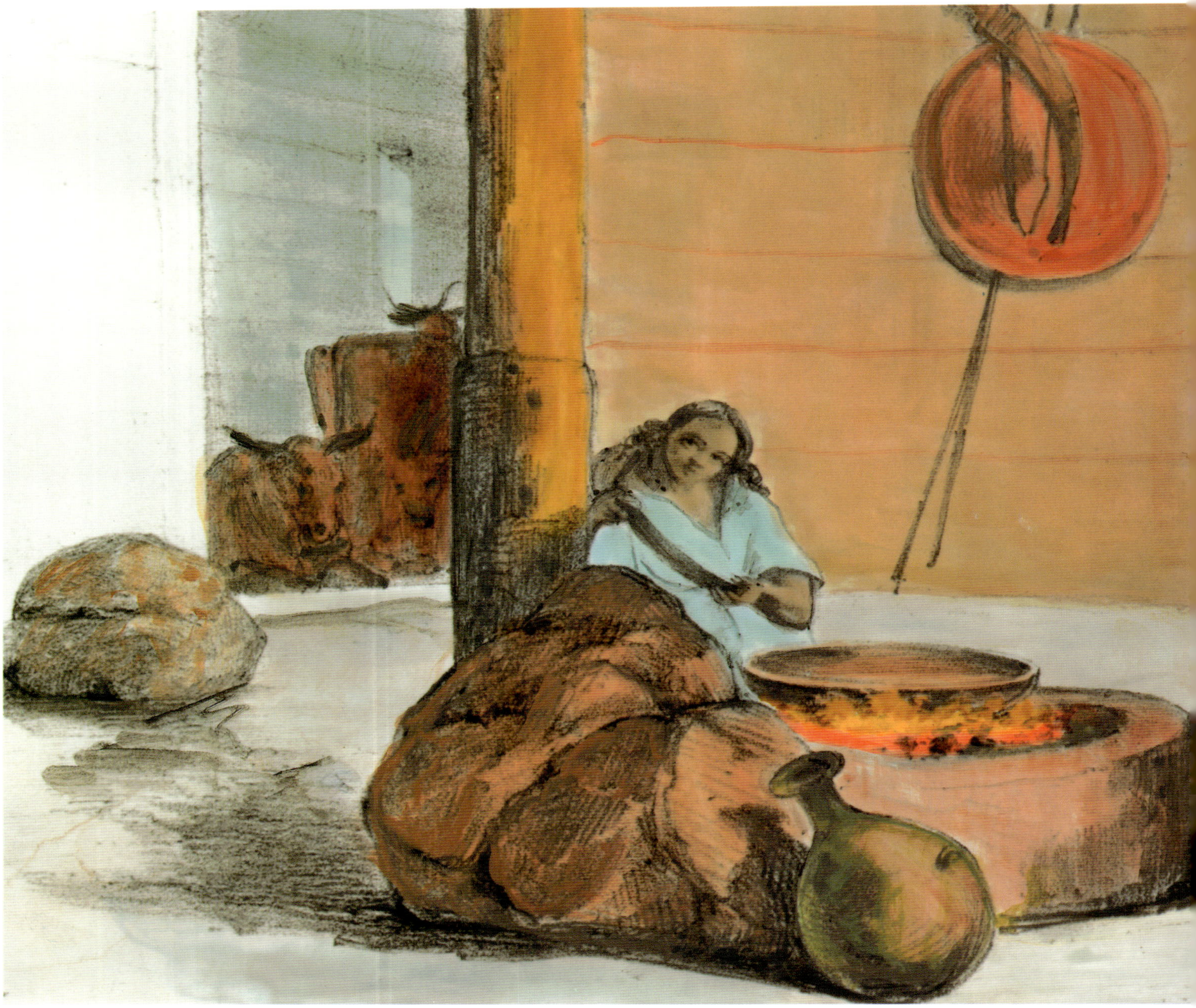

INSIDE AN ETHIOPIAN HOUSE

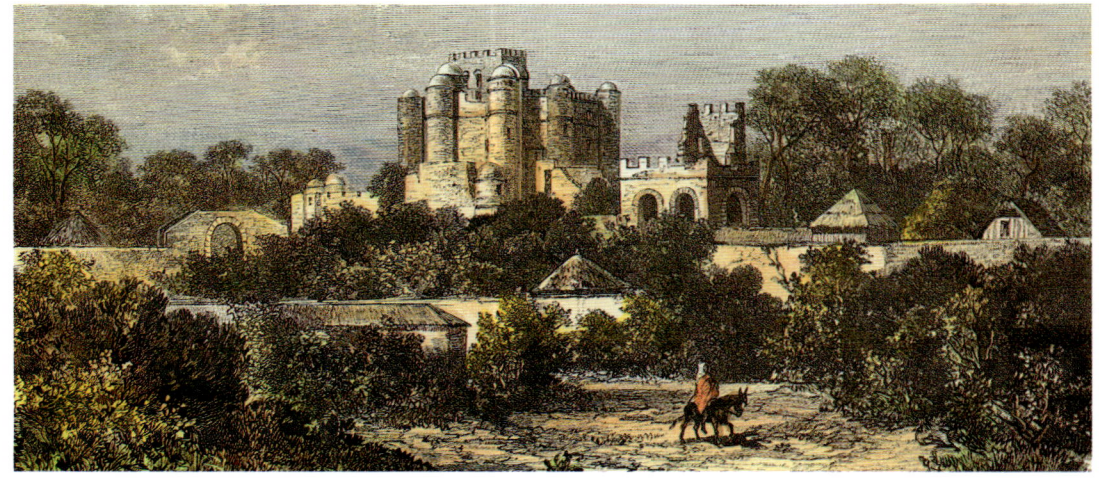

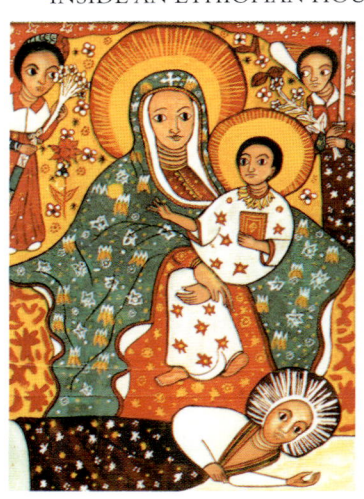

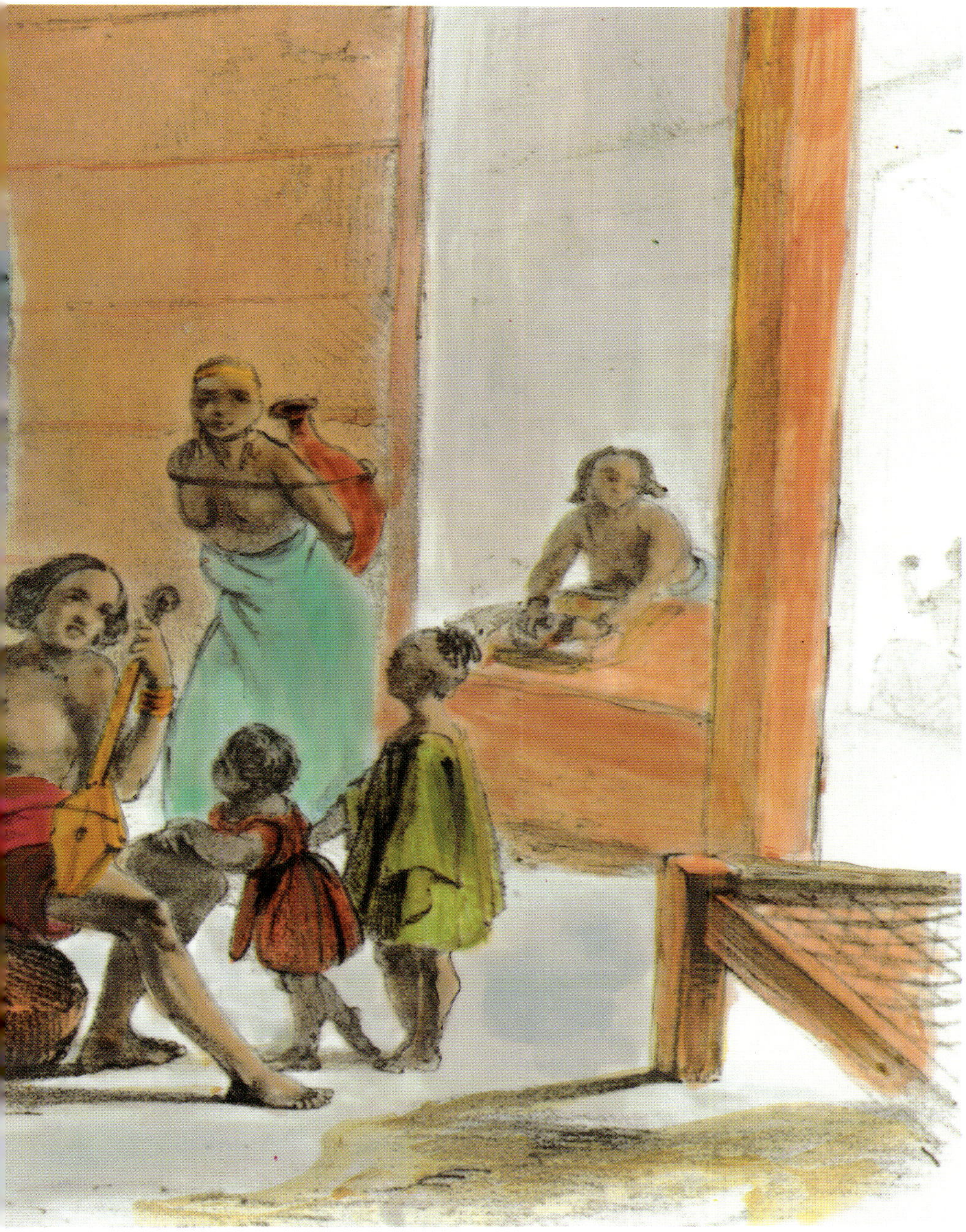

MENTOWAB

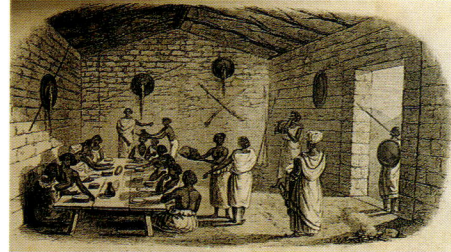

Daily Life

It is customary for a couple to live with their unmarried children all in one house. Servants and slaves are housed separately in huts. Among the domestic animals, the cat is the favorite; every house has pets. Cats are considered especially distinguished. If they wander into a church, no one chases them out, not even out of the Holy of Holies, the area where usually only priests and deacons are permitted. The body of a cat is not cast in the dump but carefully buried in the garden or in the cemetery next to the Christians. The breeding cock, the uncastrated cock, is entitled to almost the same treatment. It is neither killed nor eaten. And if it dies, it is carefully buried. Pigeons, because they resemble the dove that symbolizes the Holy Spirit, are likewise spared.

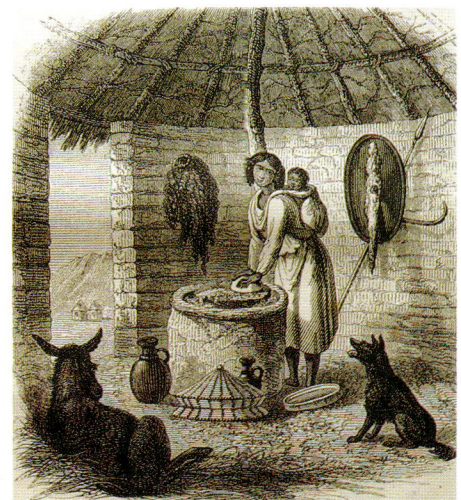

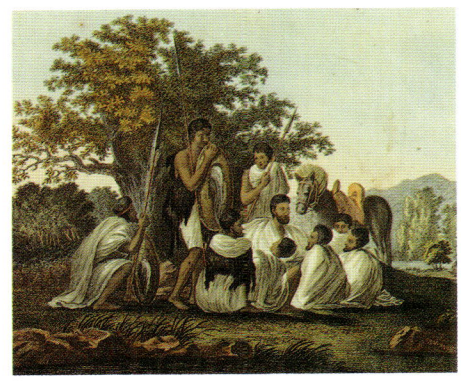

TRADITIONAL DRESS

A relatively tranquil period of stability sets in. Mentowab uses this time to insure peace within the church of Ethiopia, which had been torn by fierce infighting between the two main monastic orders. She builds churches, erects many monuments, encourages the production of illuminations and paintings. Her son, Jesus II, personally takes part in the decoration of the palace: he dreams only of painting and architecture, and it is Empress Mentowab who will take over upon the death of this heir, who would later be known as Little Jesus because of his humble ambitions. At that point she becomes regent of the kingdom in the name of her grandson Iyoas.

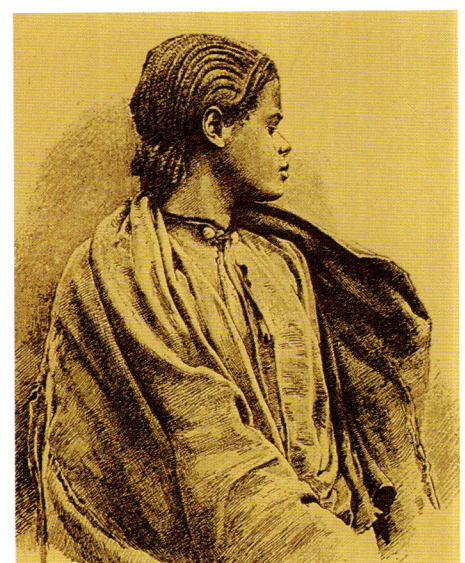

Esther, Daughter of Mentowab

Ouanzaro Esther was, like her mother the empress, one of the most beautiful women of her time, which did not stop her from also having the courage of a Roman legionnaire and to follow in the footsteps of other warriors. She attended the bloody parades in celebration of victories. On the back of her swimming horse, she crossed the raging Abbai (that is how the Blue Nile is known in Ethiopia). Whether Esther was at home or in the Abbey of Cousqam, beside Mentowab, she spent her time talking, joking, and taking part in celebrations. She could be capricious, pretending to be afflicted by various conditions she claimed were going to be the end of her. It was only a way to get more attention: to be cared for and flattered. She was so good and sweet and her conversation and ways were so pleasant that her doctor wished she would always need his attention. Ouanzaro Esther was in her third marriage, which was actually a modest number: the explorer Bruce remembered having met another lady whom fortune had blessed with a succession of seven husbands.

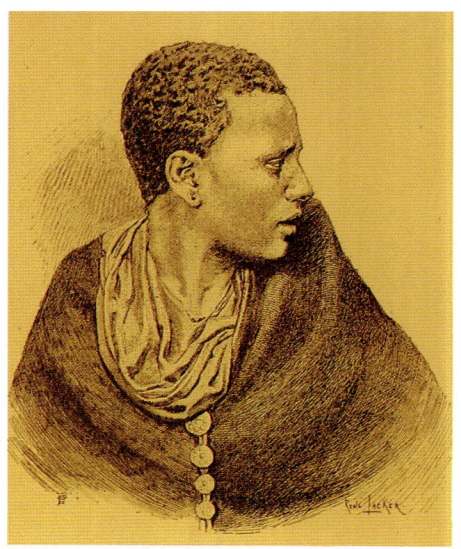

The greatest threat during Mentowab's reign will come from Ras Mikael Sehul, a man who has killed two emperors. He is an old gray-haired general, but his body is as strong as iron and his mind is among the keenest in the land. He is a leader on the field, as well as in the civil life of the kingdom, where his penetrating thought, scathing rhetoric, and talent for ruse help him to triumph over his opponents.

He wants power, but he is not of Solomonic lineage. That is why he needs to seat what he cynically calls a puppet on the throne.

Mentowab uses all the weapons a woman can marshall against him. She marries one of her daughters to the favorite son of her eminent enemy. Then she gives her second daughter to the old man himself, who will find the strength to father a last child.

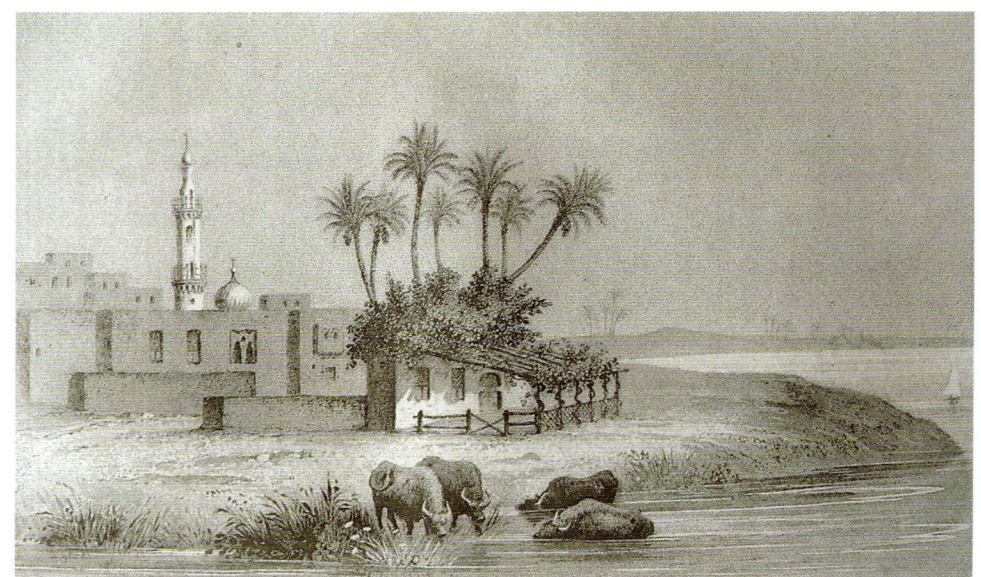

Meanwhile, after intrigue upon intrigue, Ras Mikael has all of the empress's opponents assassinated and now stands alone: the kingdom's greatest friend, its strongest pillar, and Mentowab's most dangerous enemy.

Then, in 1769, when Iyoas, the grandson of the empress and the legitimate heir, attempts to have Mikael assassinated, the Ras tries and hangs the emperor and sets up a puppet on the throne who is at his beck and call. He has become the de facto ruler of Ethiopia. But he cannot rule without the presence of the old Empress, who is still revered throughout the country, at his side. Mentowab, who had fled north, is brought back to the Gondar Palace for the sake of appearances.

Here, she will soon end her days, treated as a queen but having no real power. This catastrophe ushers in a bleak 150 years of feudal anarchy, the period of the *Zamana Masafent*, the Age of Princes, in Ethiopia.

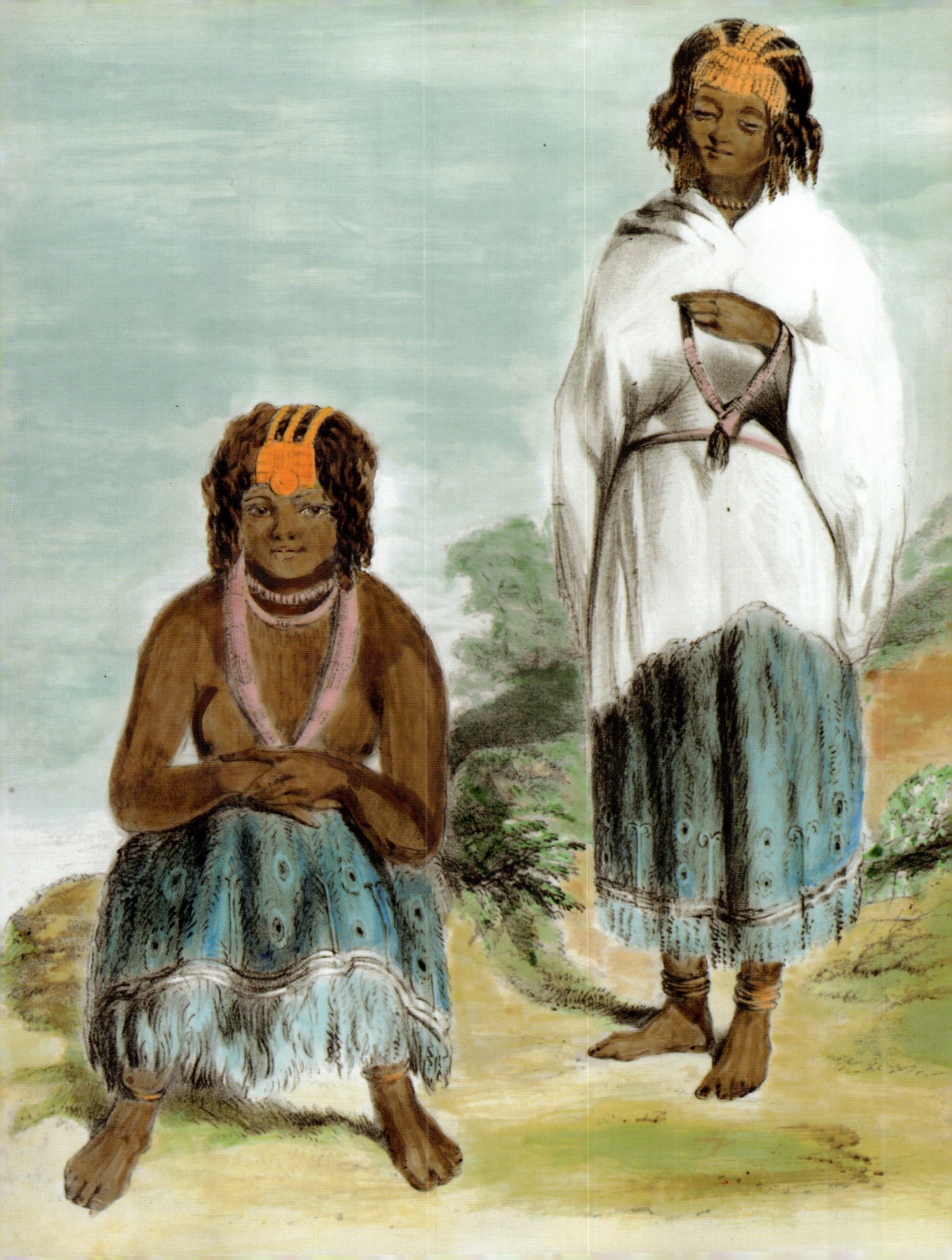

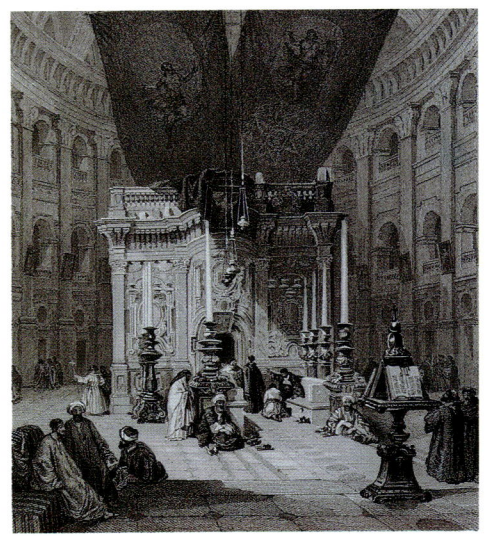

In 1770, the famous explorer James Bruce is traversing the kingdom searching for the source of the Nile. He meets an old woman in the palace at Gondar who has done away with all earthly ties. She tells him: "See what strange things God does with our puny fates. You come from Jerusalem where you have lived under Turkish rule; you have also gotten used to our uncomfortable hot climate: all of this so you can see a simple river and the swamp that is its source. And I, an old woman who has been sitting on a throne more than thirty years, I only wish I could enter Jerusalem as a simple beggar and sit in front of the Church of the Holy Sepulchre to beg for my bread until my dying day."

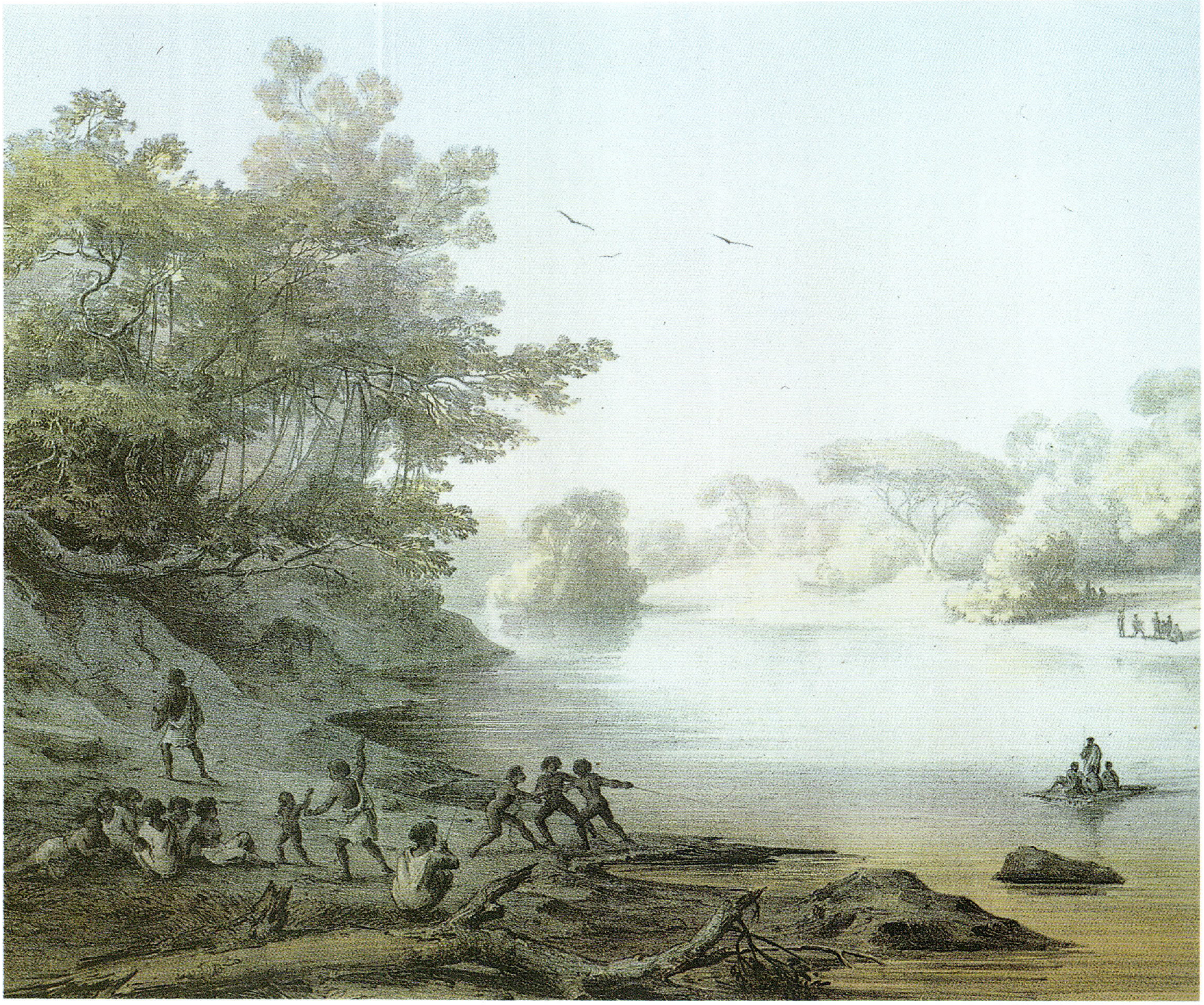

THE SOURCES OF THE NILE

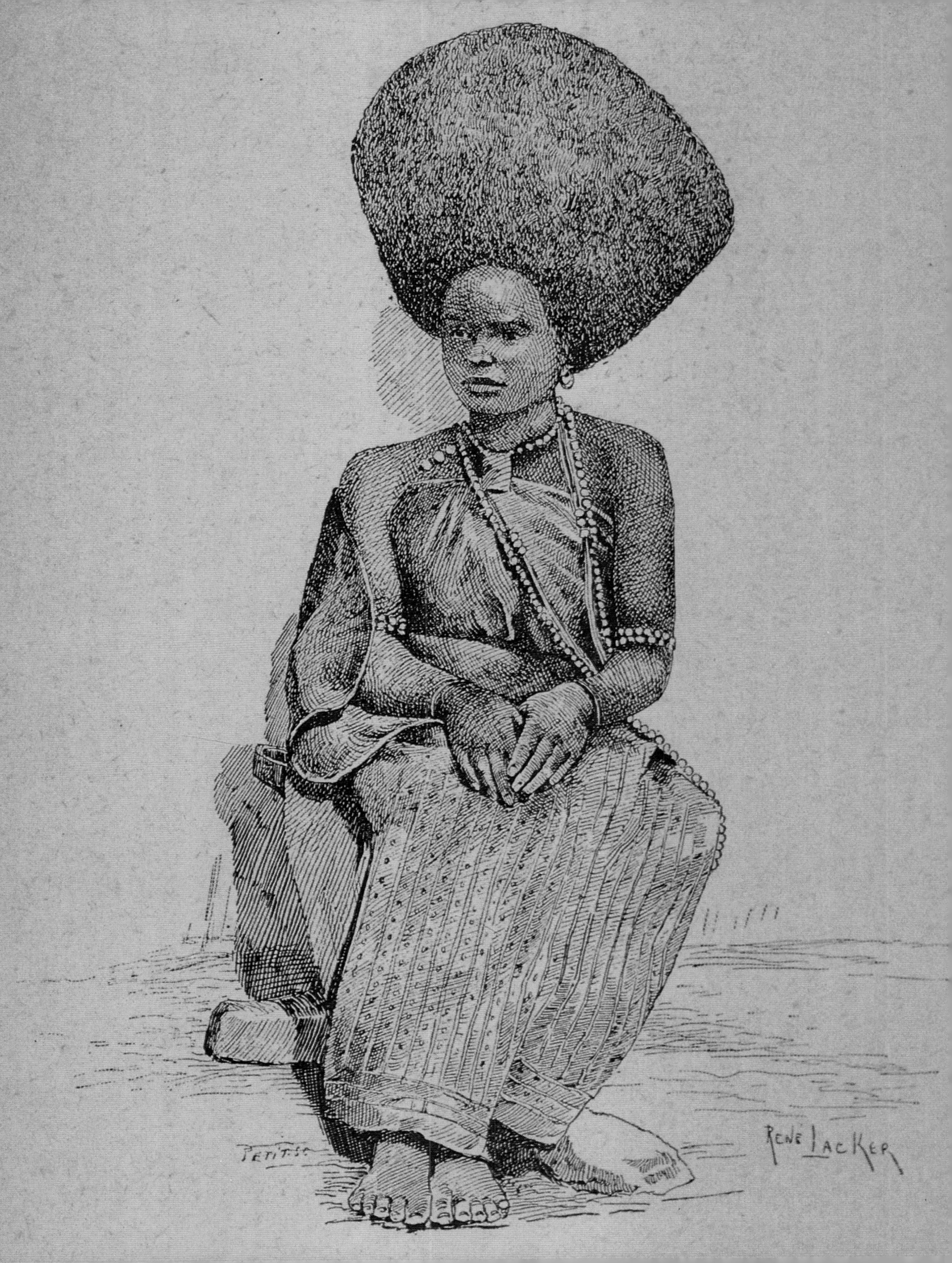

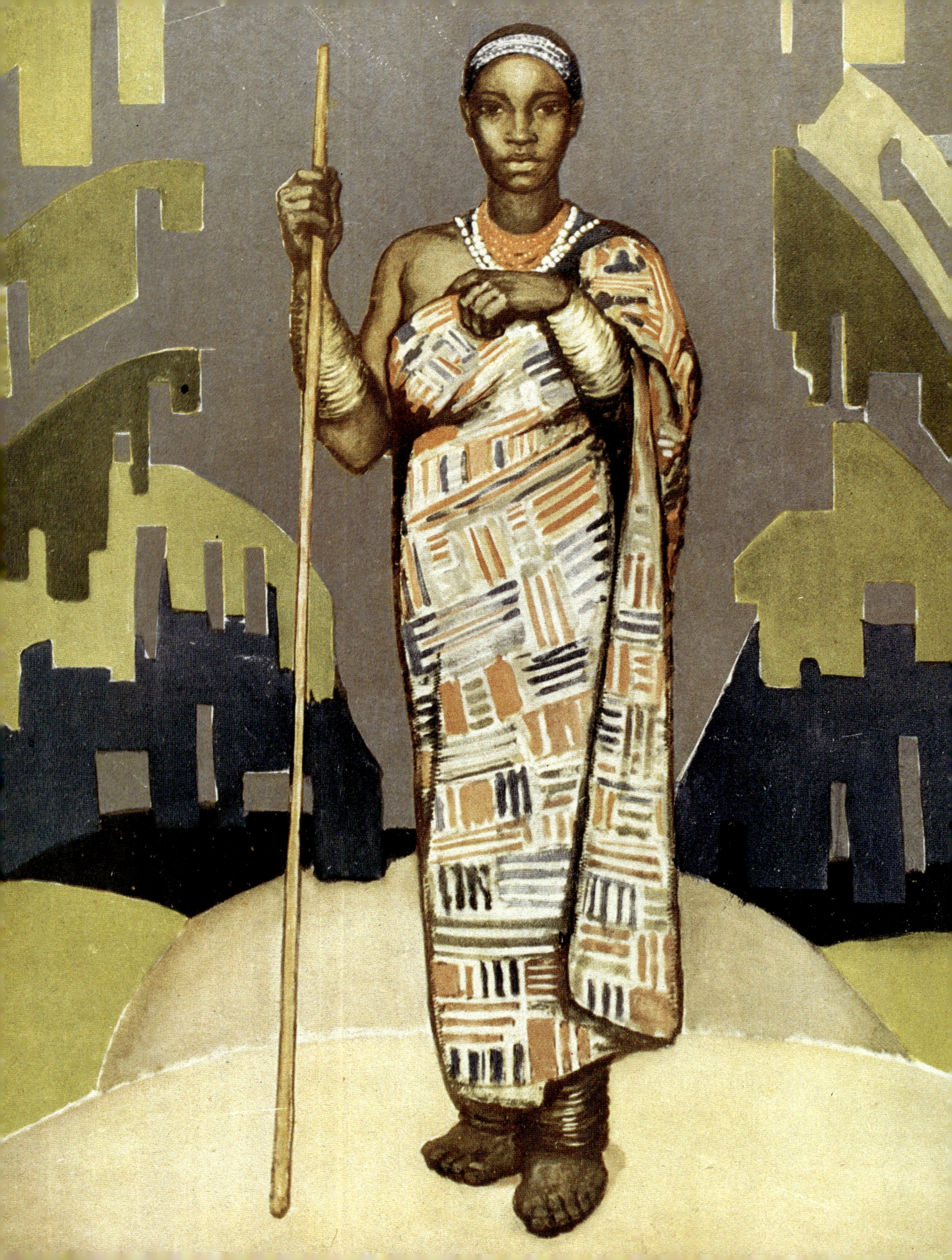

BEATRICE KIMPA VITA

THE JOAN OF ARC OF KONGO BURNED ALIVE IN THE YEAR 1706

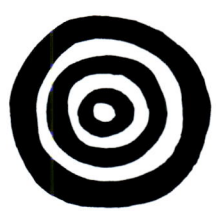

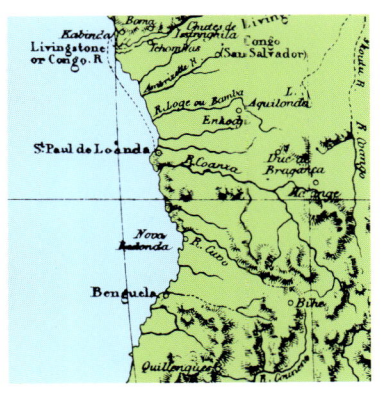

Disciples known as "angels" are sent to the four corners of the earth, all wearing crowns of musenda, the emblem of Beatrice Kimpa Vita.

IN 1483, WHEN THE PORTU-
GUESE SAILED INTO THE MOUTH
OF THE CONGO RIVER, THEY THOUGHT
THEY WERE ENTERING THE KINGDOM OF
PRESTER JOHN, LEGENDARY CHRISTIAN RULER OF
THE EAST. AS FOR THE KONGO PEOPLE WHO WITNESSED
these white men emerging from the sea, they thought they were dealing with spirits of the ancestors, come from the beyond and condemned to return there after a brief stay among the living.

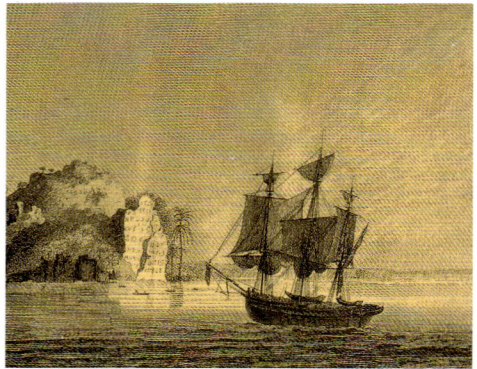
AT THE MOUTH OF THE CONGO

Little by little, the visitors from the beyond seemed more and more like living men—but powerful, dangerous men, whose weapons and writing, methods of navigation and metalworking, appeared to be the work of a most powerful magic, beyond the grasp of the riverbank dwellers.

The king of Kongo was convinced that the secrets of this magic resided in the strange ritual practiced by the white men; he converted to Christianity and quickly endeavored to acquire this knowledge, so new and disconcerting, so laden with promise for his people.

He wished to buy a boat in order to conduct trade with Portugal. And in a famous letter addressed to King Manuel I, he asked that carpenters, blacksmiths, coppersmiths, weavers, and other masters of white knowledge come as well; he was ready to give all the gold in his kingdom to have them.

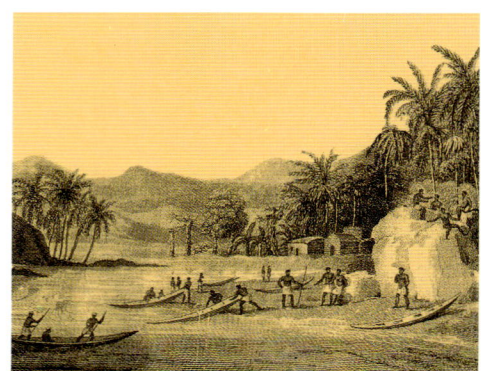
THE VILLAGE ON THE BANK OF THE RIVER

Unfortunately, the only thing the king of Portugal would be generous with was missionaries, who would teach the Kongo king the writing of the whites, or rather, their Holy Scriptures, with which he would have to make do. The poor king of Kongo could study the Bible, that formidable object, all he wanted, but he would do so in vain, for the text would never reveal to him the secrets of European sorcery. Two centuries later, the kingdom of Kongo was but a shadow of its former self. The state was divided, traditional power had weakened. Mbanza Kongo, the capital, the holy city, was deserted by the sovereign, whose authority now came from his anointment by the missionaries and who impatiently awaited the Pope's blessing. The slave trade was at its height, trailing in its wake war, famine, and great turmoil for the Kongo people. And at that moment, out of this very confusion and despair, a young woman by the name of Beatrice Kimpa Vita appeared, a native of the M'Bligha Valley, deep in the heart of Kongo.

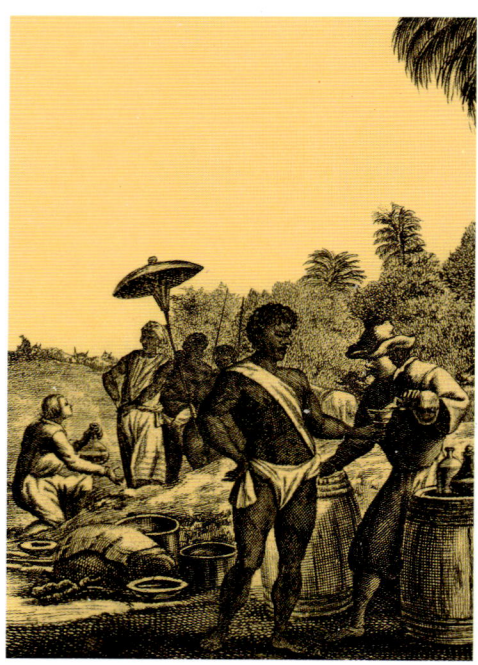
"THE PORTUGUESE WOULD GIVE NOTHING..."

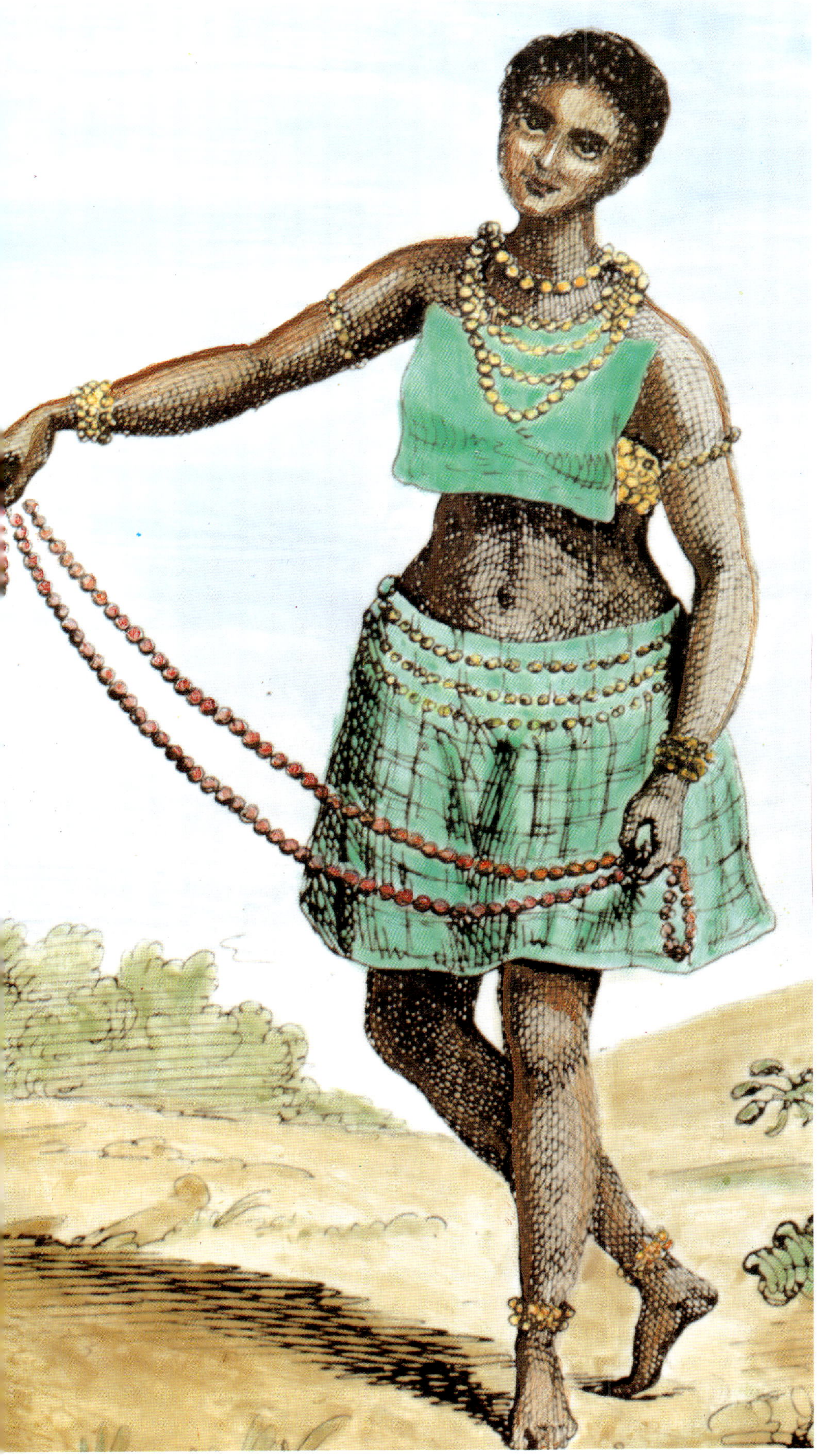

BEATRICE KIMPA VITA

Feminine Attire

Women cover the lower part of the body with three lengths of cloth; one long one goes down to the feet, the next one is shorter, and the next one shorter still; each is draped all the way around and opens in the front. They cover their chests with blouses that come down to the waist. These clothes are made of palm cloth. Slaves and lower-ranking women cover only the bottom half of the body, and the upper half remains naked.

Menswear

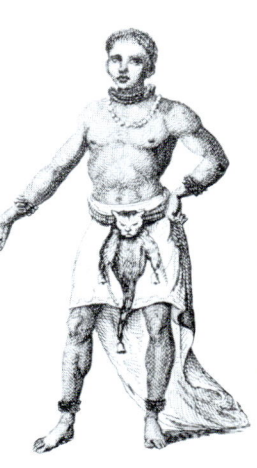

Men dress in similar fabric. They cover the bottom half of the body, holding up the cloth with a finely worked belt woven of the same material; in front, around their waists, they wear beautiful decorative skins: the pelts and heads of small tigers, civet cats, sables, martens, and other such animals.

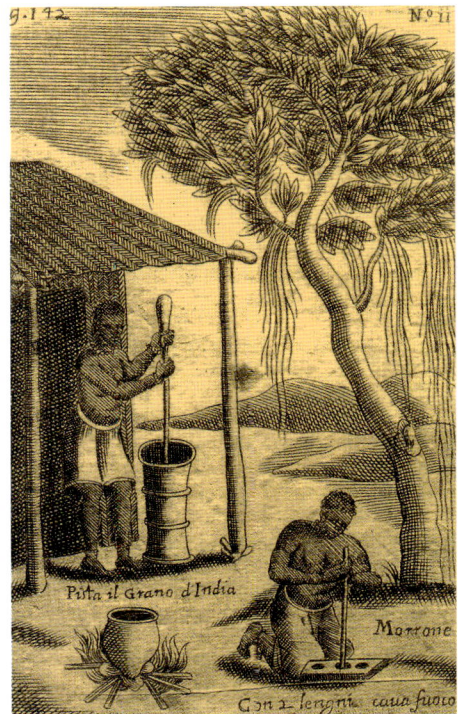

The Sun

Daily life, calm and uneventful, goes on during daylight hours. A proverb serves as a reminder: *Tudianga ye ntengu, ka tudianga ye ngonda,* "We live and eat with the sun, we eat not with the moon."

YOUNG WOMAN OF KONGO

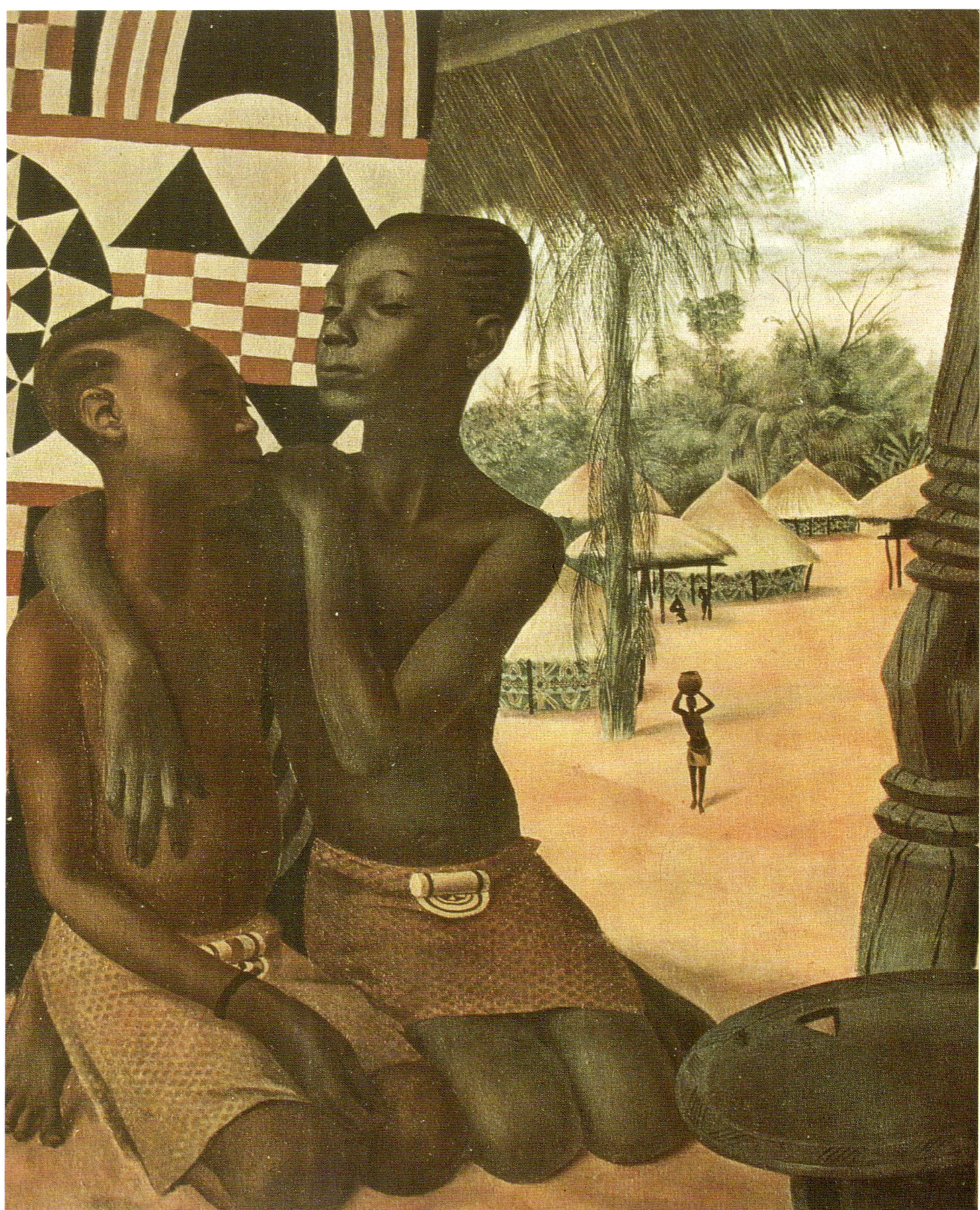

BEATRICE KIMPA VITA

Beatrice Kimpa Vita is a young woman of the most ancient Congolese nobility, and her village is ruled by a woman, as most villages are at the time. She rapidly becomes a priestess of the Marinda cult, after being initiated at the youngest possible age. As a young girl, she has a vision of white figures who speak to her and touch her: as everyone in the village knows, these are the spirits of the ancestors, whitened by death. From that time on, she wears a crown of the musenda plant as a sign of her special link to the spirit world. She is no longer simply a priestess: she is a *bango,* Initiate of Initiates.

The child is stricken with grief by her people's troubles. The king, the world's foundation, lives high on the Kibangu Mountain, under the thumb of the missionaries who control his power. He and all the members of his court, who belong to the most noble families of the country, dress in the Portuguese style: the men wear capes and cloaks from another world, and the women wear their hair bedecked with jewels and veils.

Beatrice Kimpa Vita is twenty when she first hears of Matuffa, an old woman traveling around the country prophesying: a black Virgin Mary had appeared to Matuffa, outraged at the king's ways, and promised the imminent destruction of Mount Kibangu if the sovereign did not descend immediately. Matuffa saw the Virgin surrounded by black saints, each wearing a crown of musenda. The one closest to the Virgin was Saint Anthony, patron of the humble and the poor, who had the special ability to be in several places at once, just like the traditional spirits of the ancestors.

When Beatrice Kimpa Vita hears of this, she starts to wonder about this black Virgin and these black saints, watching over the well-being of the ancient kingdom of Kongo, now draped in the frightening robes of the missionaries. And then suddenly she has a revelation: she is visited by Saint Anthony himself, who enters the young woman's body and speaks through her mouth, urging her to go straightaway to the king, to the faraway heights of Mount Kibangu.

Beatrice Kimpa Vita sets out followed by a throng of men and women who march forth singing and dancing around the saint, stopping only to call out, in unison, the cry that will be heard all over Kongo during the short life of the prophet: *"N'yari! n'yari! n'yari! Mercy! mercy! mercy!"*

◁ CHILDHOODS, A. IACOVLEFF

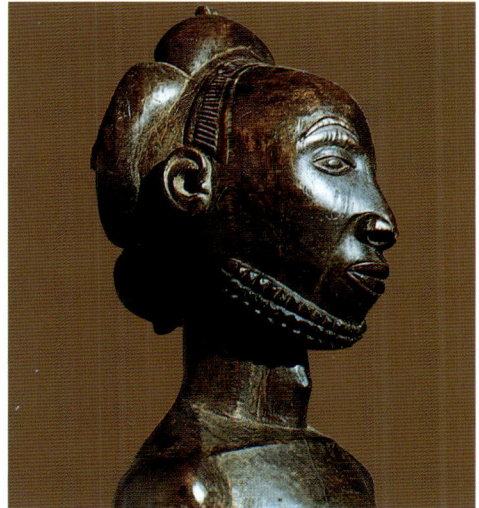

ANCESTRAL FIGURE

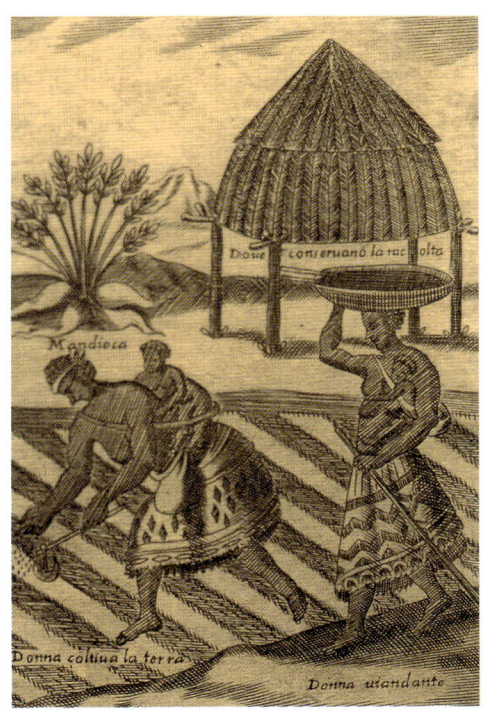

IN THE VILLAGE

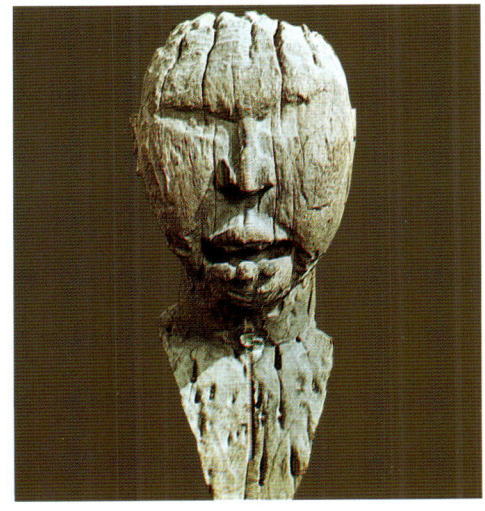

"...THE SPIRITS OF THE ANCESTORS..."

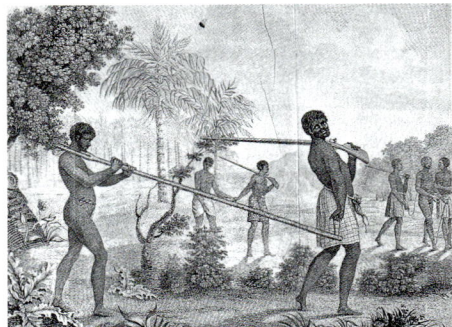

Black Ivory

Slaves were called "black ivory." The best slave, was referred to in Spanish jargon as a "coin of the Indies."

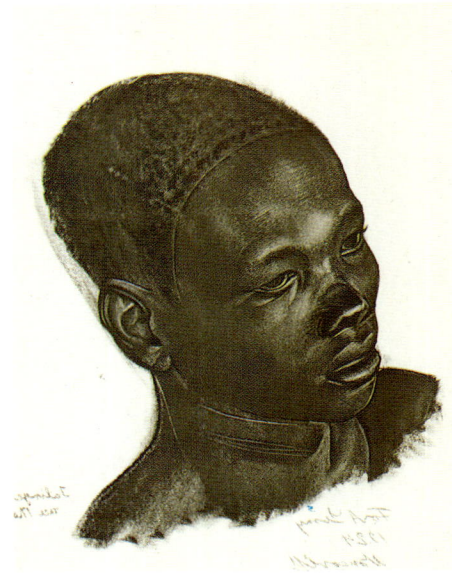

The Coin of the Indies

The base unit in the slave trade, the "coin of the Indies," was a black adult male, age fifteen to thirty-five,. 5 ft. 4 in. tall, without any physical defects, baldness, missing teeth or fingers, in excellent health, and with good eyes. To verify this last quality, a trader only had to cover one of the Negro's eyes at a time, while violently thrusting one finger at the uncovered eye as if he were going to poke it. The subject's reaction attested to his good vision! And so there was a baseline for establishing value according to the health, age, and sex of the merchandise. Three children aged eight to fifteen might be worth two "coins of the Indies," two children, three to seven years old, one "coin." Until the age of three, the child was considered part of the mother.

Proverbs

"If you see nothing above you, you will not see what you are above."

"At the end of patience, there is heaven."

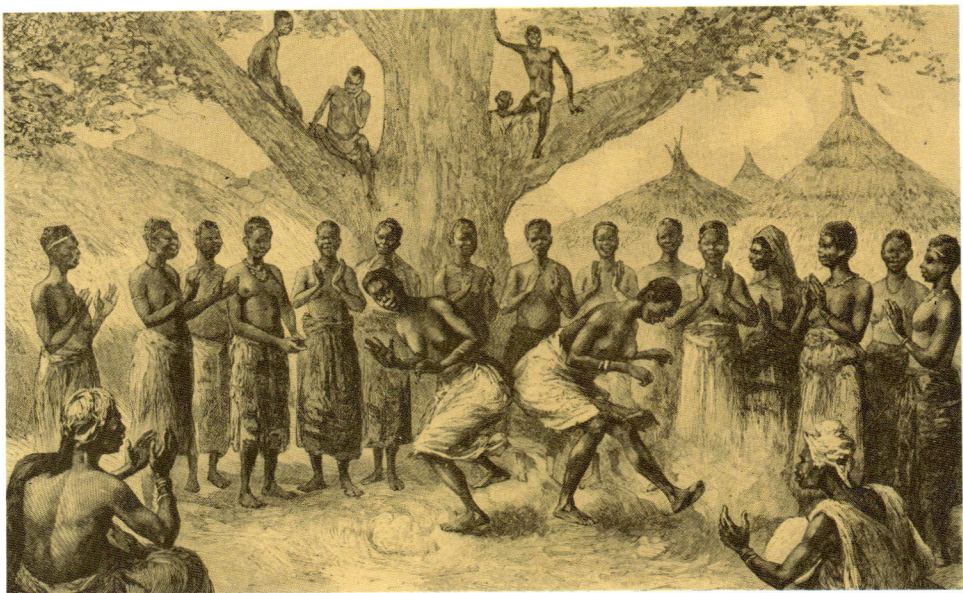

"A WAVE OF JOY SPREADS OVER KONGO..."

Beatrice Kimpa Vita is twenty-two when she undertakes her final journey. In his report to Rome on December 17, 1710, Father Bernardo do Gallo describes her in these terms: "She had a rather slender waist and delicate features; she spoke with gravity, seeming to weigh each word, and she walked on tiptoe, almost without touching the ground."

Around this slender figure, advancing with the gracious, airy step of an antelope, a wave of joy slowly spreads over Kongo.

A new church is born, bearing new hope.

Disciples known as "angels" are sent to the four corners of the earth; they all wear a crown of musenda, the emblem of Beatrice Kimpa Vita. They call for the destruction of all crosses in their path and spread the new gospel: Jesus Christ was born in Mbanza Kongo and baptized in Nsundi; Saint Francis was born in Vunda, and Our Lady Madonna traced her origins to a slave from Nzimba-Npanghi. The missionaries have made God white for their own profit, Beatrice Kimpa Vita's emissaries explain: that is why they blessed the slave ships; that is why they upheld all the conquerors' undertakings for more than two centuries; that is why they supported their armies all the way to the great Battle of Mbinta, in 1665, a battle that witnessed the destruction of the capital and the death of the king, whose head would long be on display at the church of Luanda. And last but not least, they were the ones turning the new king away from his people, forbidding him to rebuild the sacred capital, the rock of ages, without which there is no kingdom of Kongo.

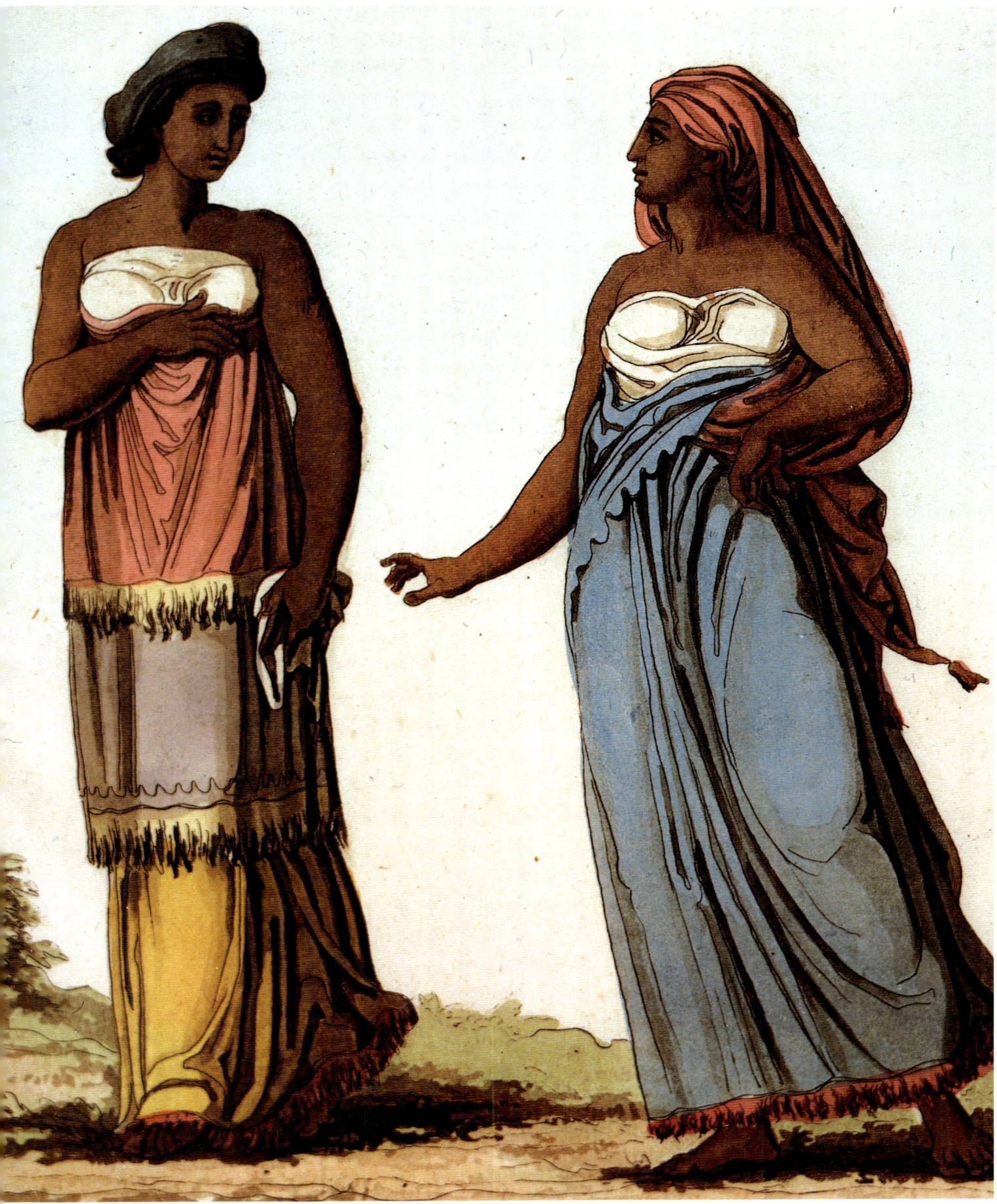

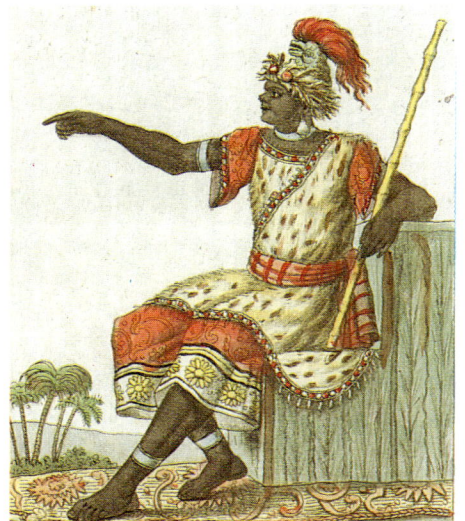

The King of Kongo Grants an Audience

The king gives two public audiences each week, but the liberty of speaking to him is granted only to nobles. In 1642, when the Dutch ambassadors from Luanda were received, right after Holland had taken that city from the Portuguese, they were brought into the palace during the night. First they were made to pass between two rows of torch-bearers through a gallery two hundred strides long. The king was seated in a small alcove, whose walls were covered with mats, and in the middle of which hung a chandelier weighed down with candles. He was dressed in a jerkin of gold cloth, with high breeches of the same material. Around his neck, he had for a cravat three massive gold chains. One could see glittering on the thumb of his right hand a garnet of extraordinary size, and two large emeralds on his left hand. He wore a white hat on his head, and boots on his feet.

WARRIOR OF KONGO

An immense crowd climbs the slopes of Mount Kibangu with the young woman; high above, one can just make out the outline of the palace towers.

Beatrice Kimpa Vita wears a crown of musenda, now adorned with gold leaf.

Marimba players make their instruments sing with the help of flat wooden sticks.

The people kiss the hem of Beatrice Kimpa Vita's tunic. They beg for her blessing. And Beatrice Kimpa Vita addresses the crowd with the same words she will repeat later before the king and his petrified missionaries (as reported by Father Bernardo do Gallo): "You say 'God Save the Queen' and you do not know why. You might just as well say 'God Save the Bloodshed' and you would do no worse. Well, God cares only about our good intentions, and he takes only these into account. Marriage is useless; God counts our intention. Baptism is useless; God judges our intentions. And all the prayers in the world are useless, for God wants only our good intentions."

And the crowd takes up the refrain: "God wants our intentions, our good intentions," a clamor now being drowned out by the cry that marked the rhythm of Beatrice Kimpa Vita's whole journey:

"N'yari! n'yari! n'yari! Mercy on the world: mercy! mercy!"

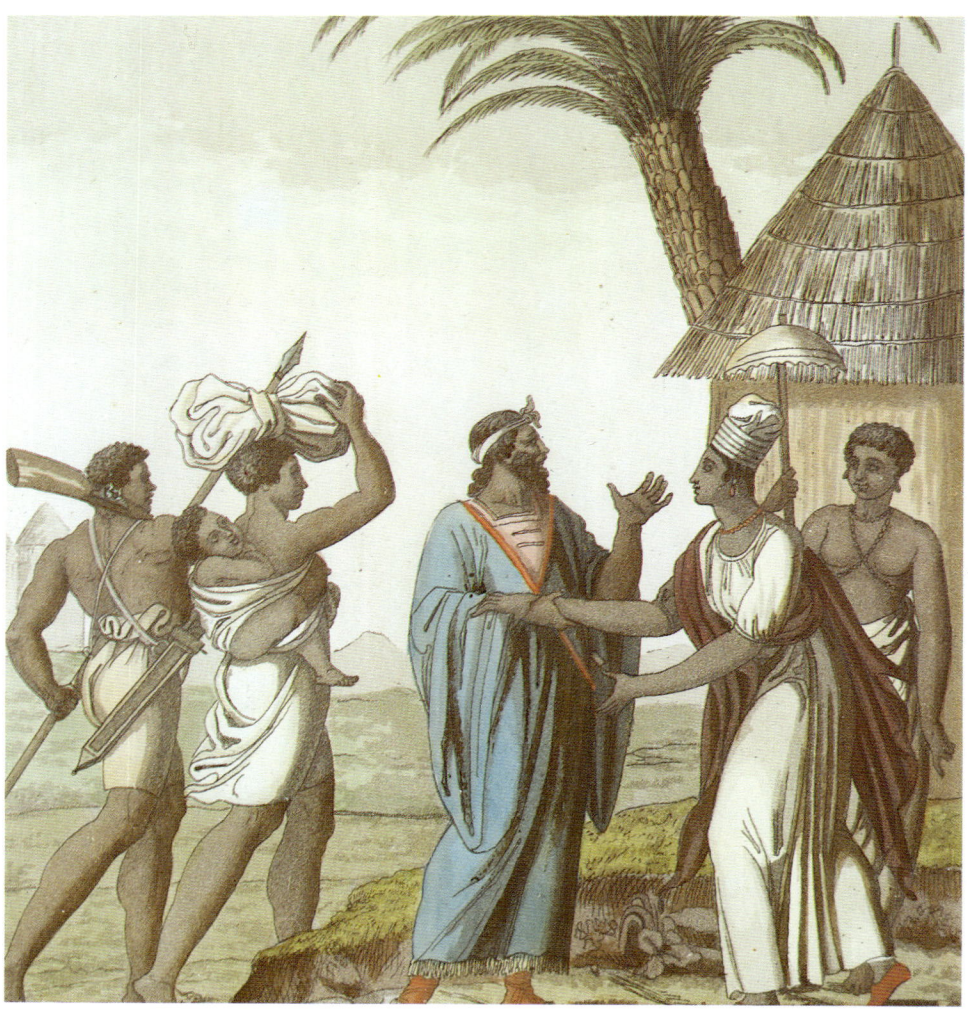

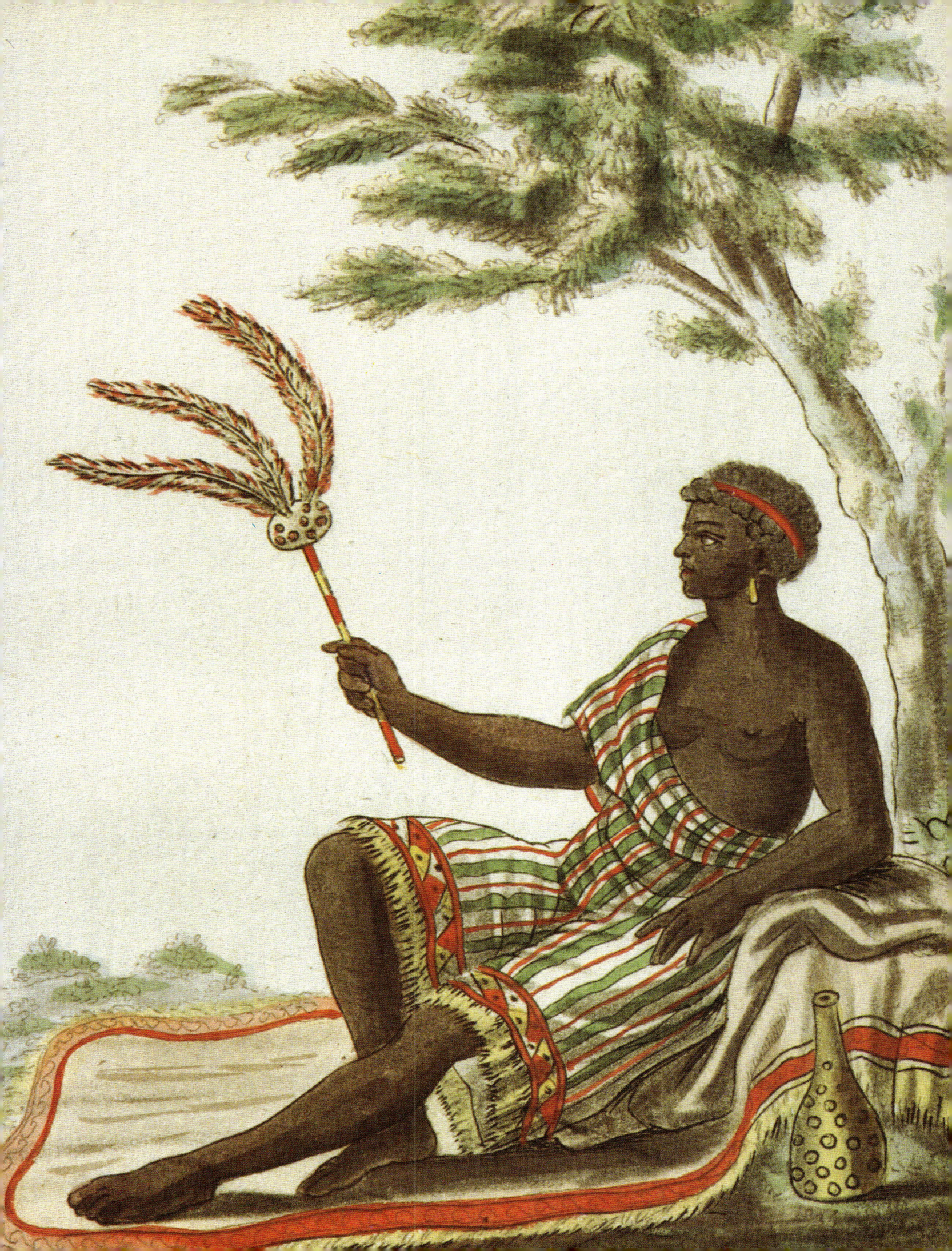

According to an oral tradition recounted by Father Bernardo do Gallo, "twisted and fallen trees stand straight" as Saint Beatrice Kimpa Vita passes by, on her way up Mount Kibangu; and the gates of the Lumba, the stockade around the king's palace, open on their own, pushed back by invisible hands.

Immediately, she presents to the king the old prophet Matuffa, who had been persecuted by the missionaries, who wished to "tame her by iron," according to Bernardo do Gallo. Then, in a fit of indignation:

"We have saints in Kongo as well," she proclaims before the assembly of so-called counts, dukes, and princes, looking as ridiculous as if they were at a costume party, who even in their wildest dreams never could have imagined a saint in black skin.

The crowd around the stockade dances and sings, carried away by holy fervor. The courtiers take fright. Offended by the tribute rendered to the "old fetishist," the missionaries retreat to the church; later, they refuse to say mass as long as Beatrice Kimpa Vita remains in the king's palace.

Nonetheless, captivated by Beatrice Kimpa Vita's speech, and giving in to her pleas, the whole court leaves the mountain of Kibangu and solemnly proceeds to the village of Evelulu, a day's march from Mbanza Kongo, the old ruined capital, which the zealous crowd undertakes to clear of the plants that have overgrown it.

Beatrice Kimpa Vita lives in a hut adjoining the only cathedral wall still standing. She is given the traditional insignia of the kings of Kongo. The paths leading to her hut are swept by women of the aristocracy; and when she sits on the ground to eat, great lords spread their capes of gold brocade at her feet for a tablecloth. People pounce on the smallest crumbs that fall from her hand; and lick with devotion the drops of water that fall from her small, simple gourd. They know that with a mere touch of her hand, the young woman can make barren wombs flower. And entire compounds rise around her on the chalky earth of Mbanza Kongo: sacred ground, traditional sustenance of the spirits, and now fruitful once more by the grace of the prophet. The unity of Kongo seems imminent. One king, one kingdom: this good news spreads in the provinces torn by war over the slave trade.

Little by little, Beatrice Kimpa Vita's message takes on a new tone: it is no longer simply a matter of restoring the kingdom to its ancient splendor. Through the voice of St. Anthony, the prophet now calls on the people to build a more humane society with neither splendor

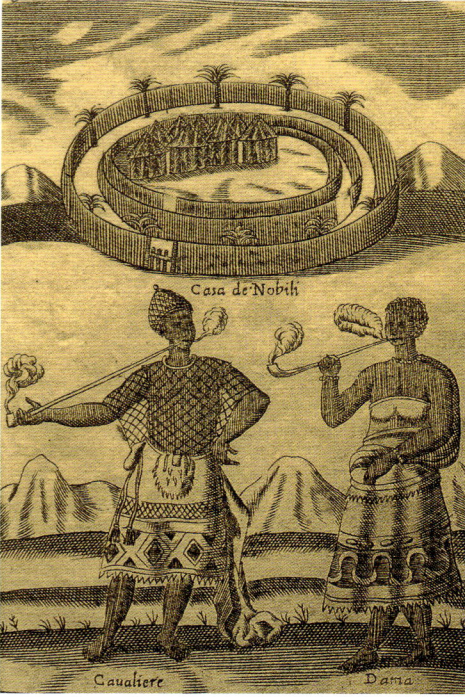

STORY OF A VOYAGE TO KONGO

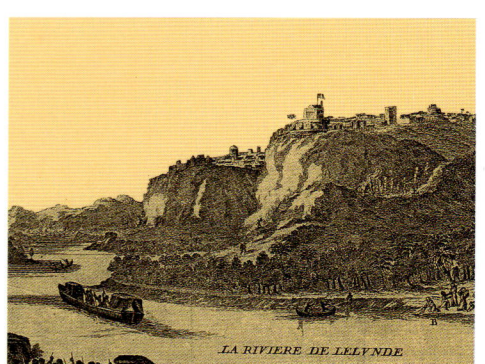

THE CAPITAL OF KONGO

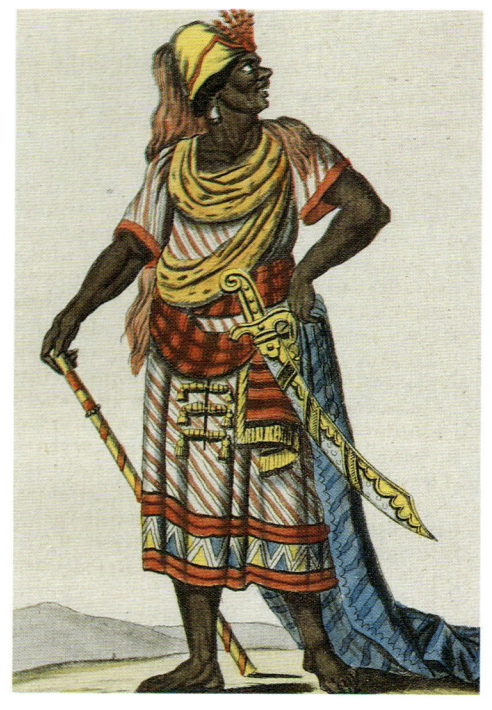

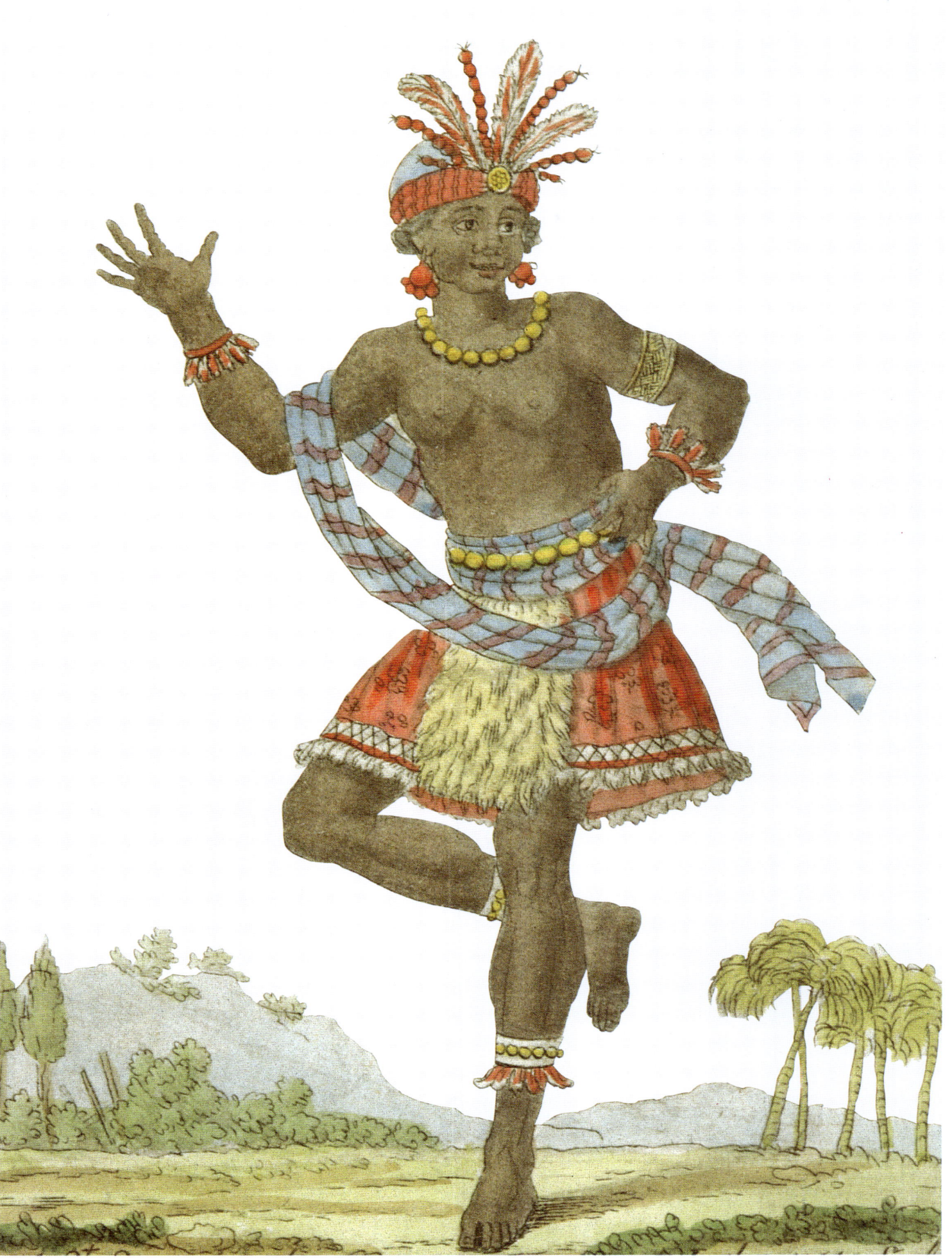

"THE CROWD DANCES AND SINGS, CARRIED AWAY BY HOLY FERVOR"

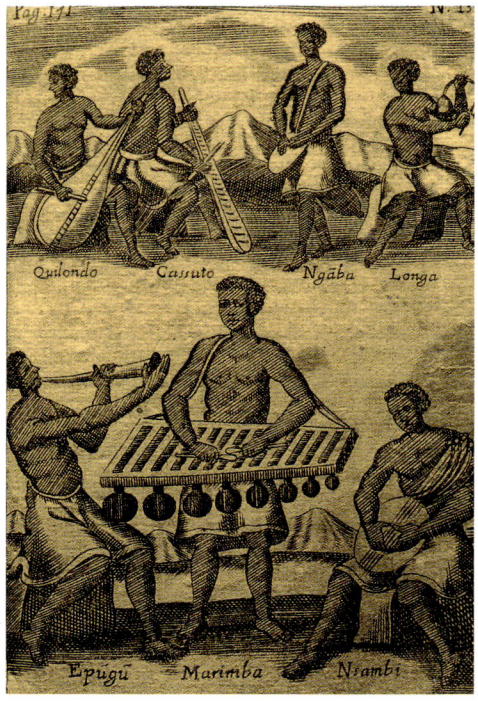
MUSICIANS

nor misery, neither masters nor slaves, like the one the ancestors have built in the underworld.

The crowd's enthusiasm rises to heights never before seen. There are no more weddings or baptisms, no more prayers or holy sacraments. Not even sin: for God, ever present, keeps a loving eye on every one of his creatures.

One song rises night and day over the ruins of Mbanza Kongo. There is no more sin; people's hearts are open. There is no more marriage: bodies draw near and unite in a sort of holy purity.

Beatrice Kimpa Vita herself is overcome with tenderness for a young man who has been faithfully keeping watch over her from the beginning. He is the "Borro," in whom the faithful saw a reincarnation of St. John. The prophet gives birth to a little boy: this is the moment her enemies have been waiting for since the day she entered the palace on Mount Kibangu.

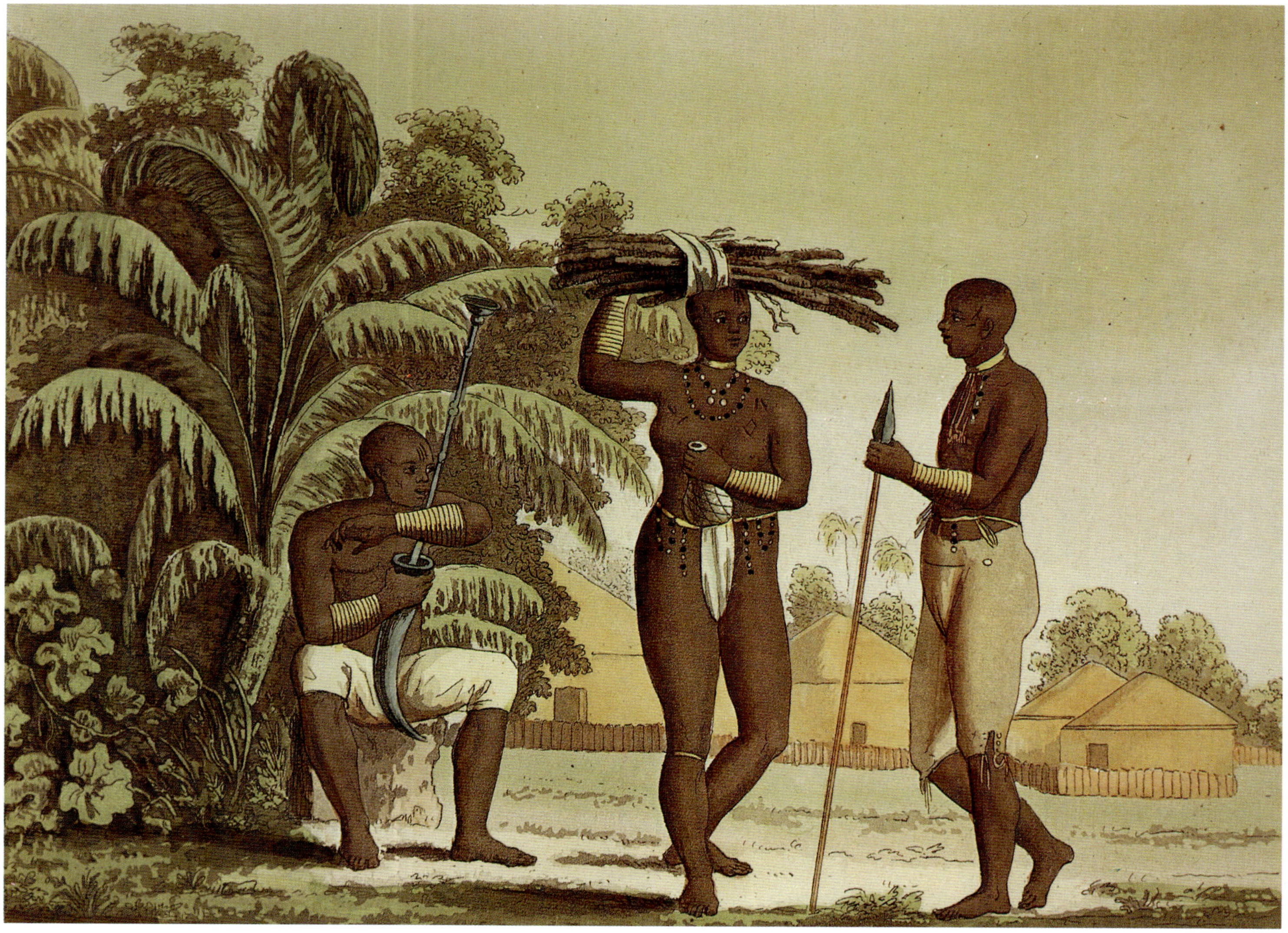

"THERE IS NO MORE SIN; PEOPLE'S HEARTS ARE OPEN..."

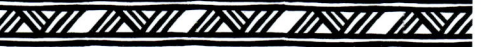

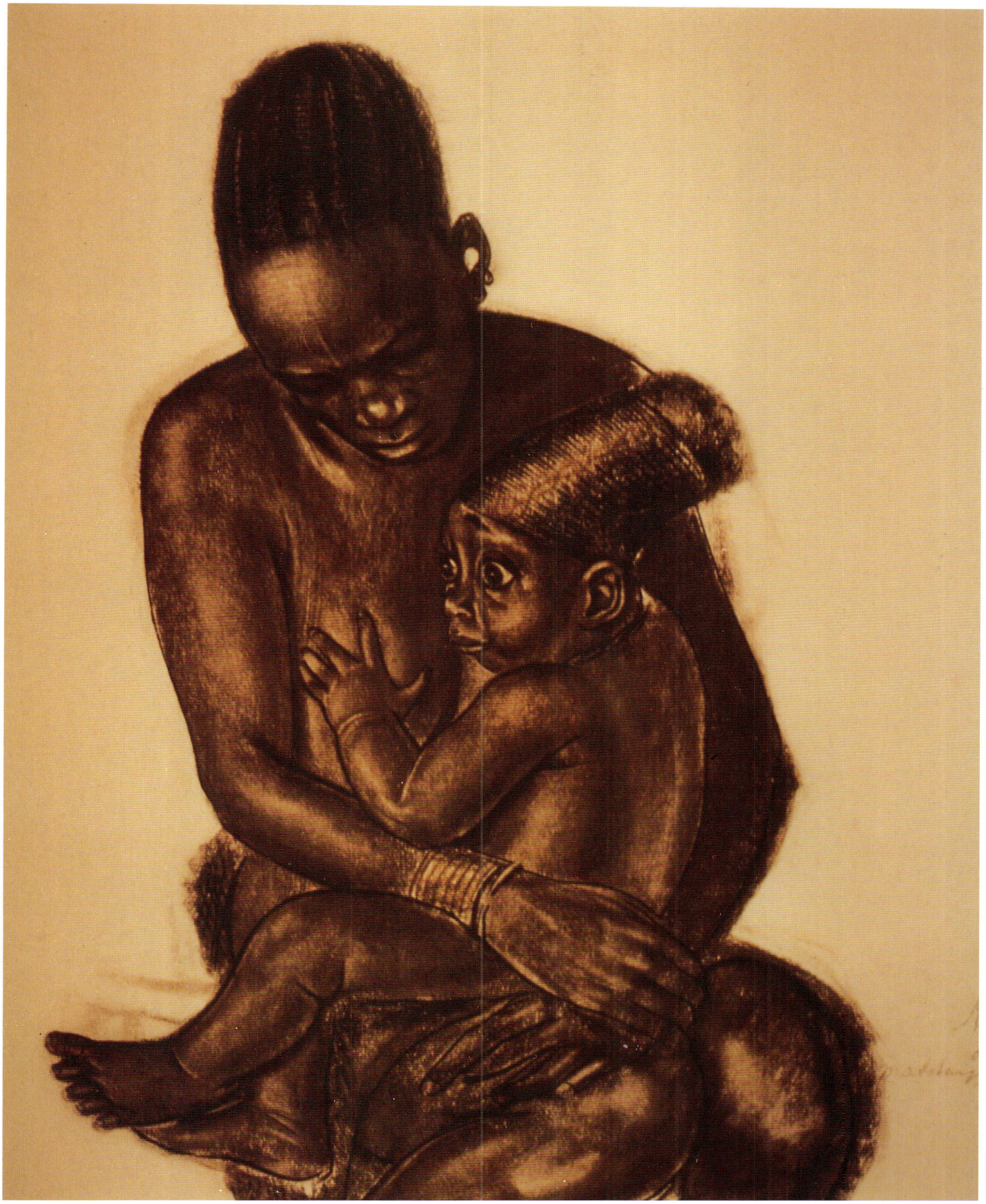

"BEATRICE KIMPA VITA GIVES BIRTH TO A LITTLE BOY..."

From this time forward, things happen very quickly. In early July 1706, Prince Chibangé's soldiers seize the prophet and turn her over to the feeble King Pedro IV, who works directly for Italian missionaries, having been enthroned by Father Francesco di Pavia. A travesty of justice is rendered at the palace. But behind the scenes are the Capuchin monks Laurenzo da Lucca and Bernardo do Gallo, notorious brutes and village-burners. They send ahead a troop of Portuguese harquebusier gunners, the better to lead the people to baptism; and so, in his report to Rome, Father Bernardo will lay claim to eighty thousand conversions.

The young woman is weighed down with chains and crowned, out of who knows what sort of mockery, with a musenda wreath of sparkling gold.

Father Bernardo asks her to introduce herself; she says that she is simply a young woman of Kongo, whose only merit is to have welcomed the voice of St. Anthony when it came down one day from heaven.

Then Father Bernardo jeers: "Well, what news do you have for us from up there? Tell me, are there Negroes from Kongo in heaven, and are they black up there?" She replies, "In heaven there are blacks from Kongo and those who have observed God's law; but they have neither the color of Negroes nor whites, for in heaven people are of no color." (As reported by Father Bernardo.)

The prophet is dragged in chains to the foot of a hastily erected stake. Her child in her arms, the young woman weeps; then the child is taken from her, and she becomes perfectly calm, looking out at the world serenely.

And now her chains are removed and rope is coiled around her. Father Laurenzo da Lucca interrogates her one last time. "What does it matter to me if I die," she replies, "It is a step I must take but once. My body is nothing more than the dust of the earth. I do not set great store by it; sooner or later, it will return to ashes." The old proselytizer is moved. He later admits: "Those words and others which she spoke brought tears to my eyes." (Report of Father Laurenzo da Lucca, translated from by Father Jean Cornélius.)

When the first flames erupt over the silent body, the crowd can no longer contain itself and the two missionaries are beaten and shoved, barely escaping death.

"And the next morning, men came to burn the few bones that were left and reduced everything to very fine ashes." (Father Laurenzo.)

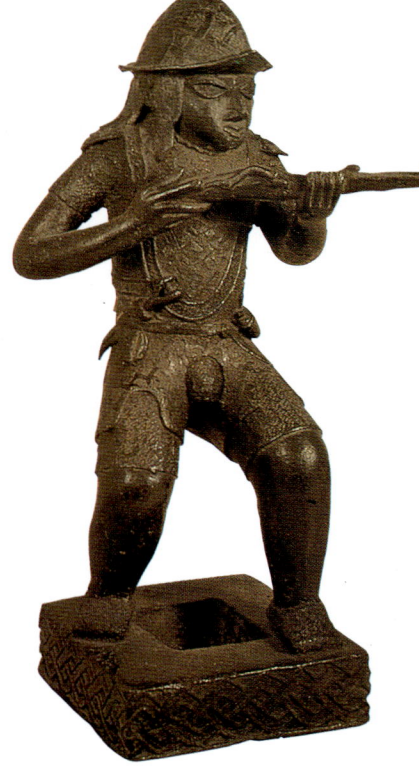

PORTUGUESE HARQUEBUSIER

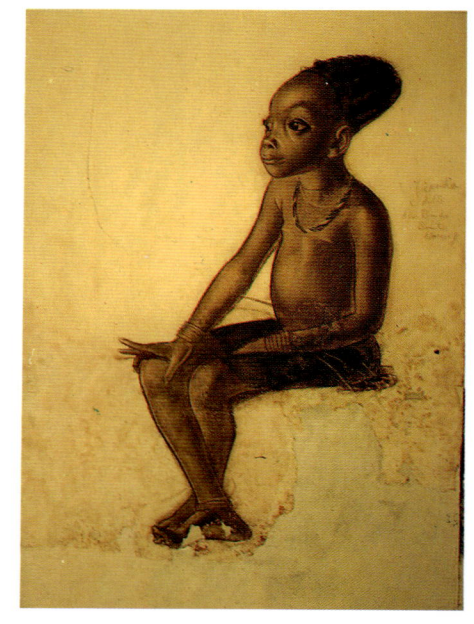

"THE CHILD IS TAKEN FROM HER..."

"N'yari! n'yari! n'yari!" The ancient kingdom of Kongo has certainly known its ups and downs since that astounding cry rang out over Mount Kibangu and the tall grasses of the plains, and over the madness of the tall trees and the unchanging course of the river which bore Beatrice Kimpa Vita's ashes to the sea.

N'yari! n'yari! n'yari! Ashes crushed so fine they should have left nothing but oblivion behind.

Nonetheless, the memory of Beatrice Kimpa Vita has not faded away, and her words have given birth to many religions, century after century, some of which still breathe life into the soul of the old Congo.

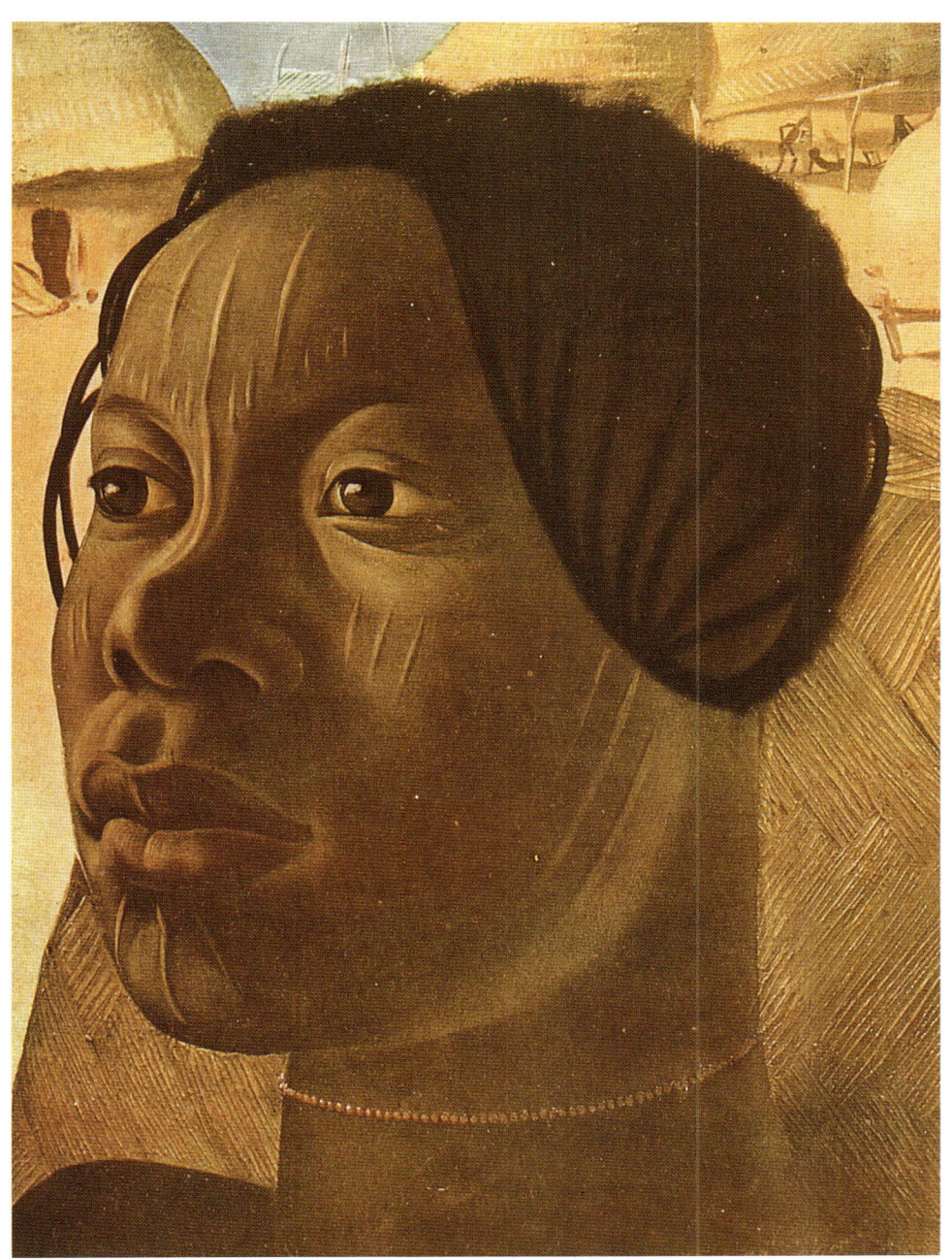

FACE OF A WOMAN, A. IACOVLEFF

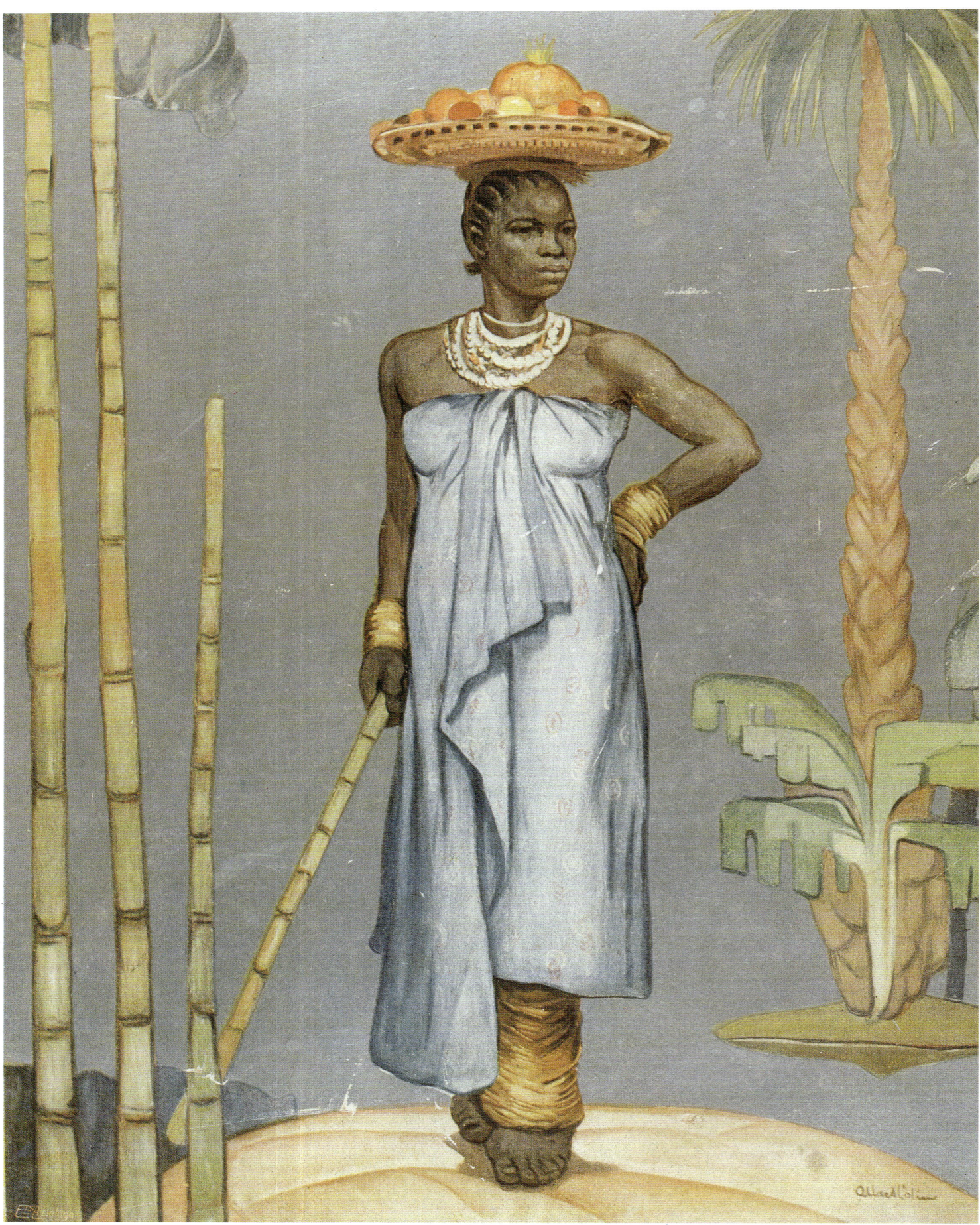

IN PRAISE OF BLACK WOMEN

WORDS
OF AN ORDINARY WOMAN

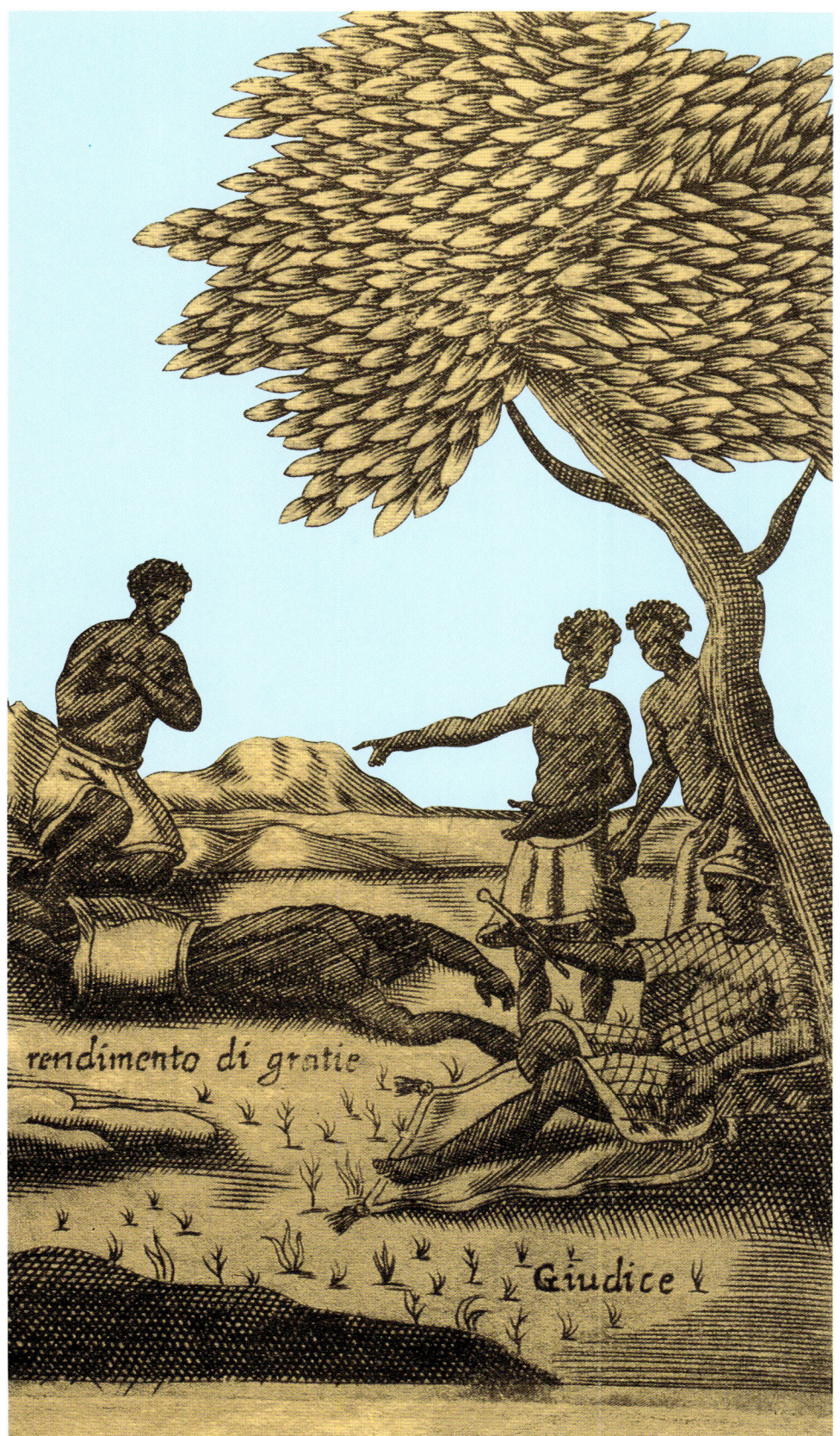

"PULAAKU IS RESTRAINT..."

Fear can mean a lot of different things. We always use the same word, *kulol*, but there can be different fears, various anxieties.

The fear of an enemy who wants to harm you or kill you is not comparable to the fear of your in-laws. The fear of the spirits of the bush is not the same thing as the fear of old people. And the fear of spiteful gossip is not the same thing as the fear of God. We use the same word, but it is a figure of speech, a way of expressing yourself.

Yes, fear is many things. It can be fear of what you know, as well as what you don't know.

The fear of people is the fear of their names. Yes, we are afraid of certain names. We cannot say the names of certain people. We could never speak the name of our oldest son or daughter, nor the name of our spouse. I could never speak the name of my husband, or the names of his father and mother.

We call this type of fear *pulaaku*: it is this mutual fear that binds the Wodaabe together.

Someone who has no pulaaku does not fear others, does not respect them. He has no propriety. Not to show pulaaku is very shameful for us.

The other day, my little brother Bammi came here. I asked him about his oldest daughter's health—she has been quite sick lately. I begged him to tell me, not to use pulaaku with me, since there was no one else around. But he did not answer me. He did not even look at me. He became a deaf-mute. This way of acting, we call pulaaku.

Pulaaku is many things. It is like fear. Moreover, it depends on fear: it is the fear of showing everyone what is in your heart, what your heart desires. Pulaaku is restraint, to hide the love you feel for someone.

For us, pulaaku is something very important. It is a way of acting that is part of who we are. It is part of our traditions, our heritage.

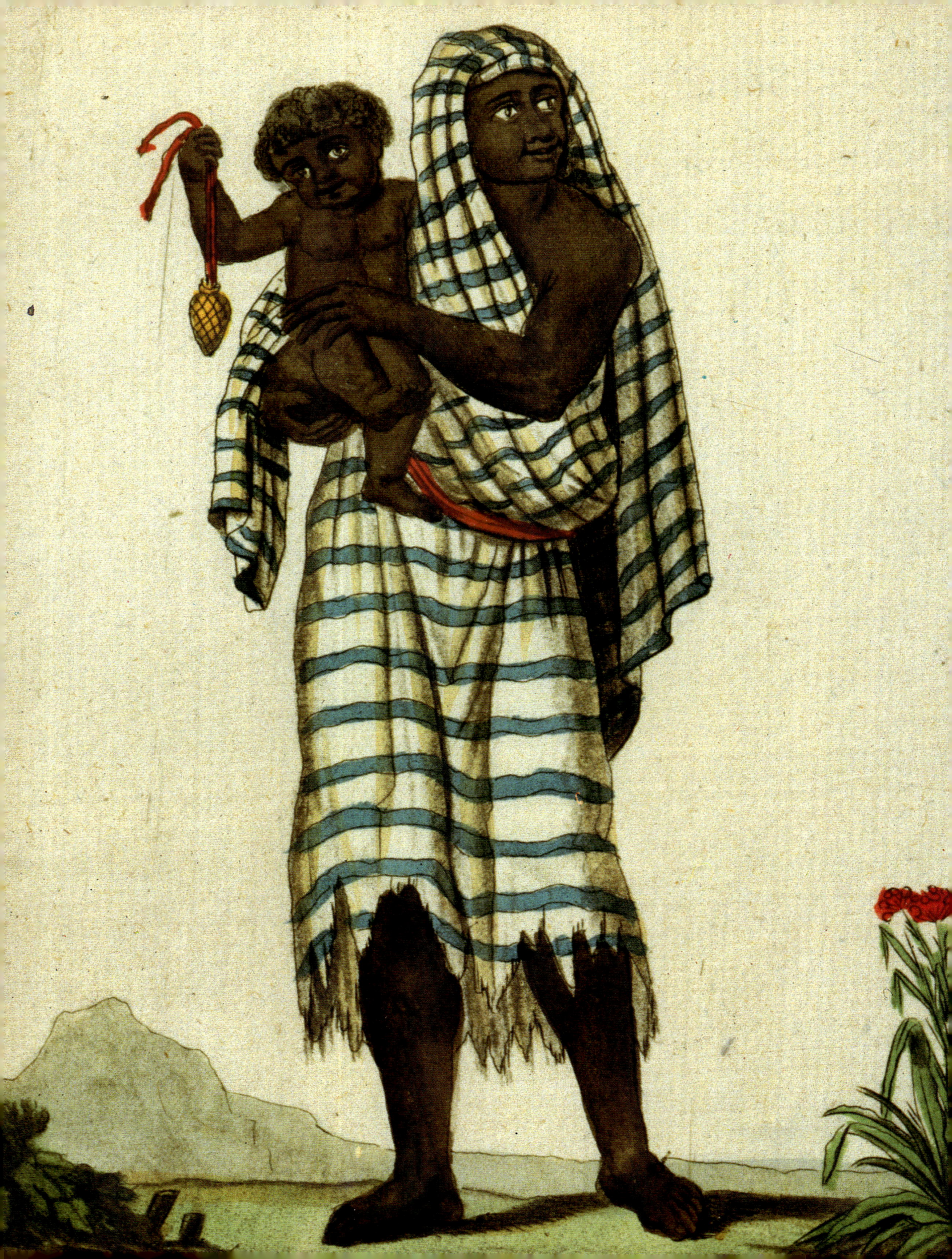

QUEEN POKU

FOUNDER OF THE BAULÉ PEOPLE

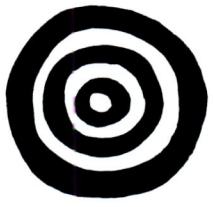

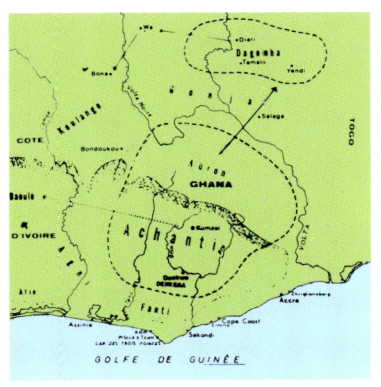

Childless until the age of forty, Queen Poku at last gave birth to a son, only to sacrifice him for the sake of her people...

AWURA POKU, NIECE OF THE GREAT OSEI TUTU, RULER OF THE ASHANTI KINGDOM, WAS THE MOST BEAUTIFUL GIRL IN THE LAND. IN THE VILLAGE OF SIKASSO, WHERE HER DESCENDANTS CAN STILL BE FOUND, PEOPLE STILL RECALL HER LONG FACE, shaped like a little water flower, and her eyes like two shimmering lakes.

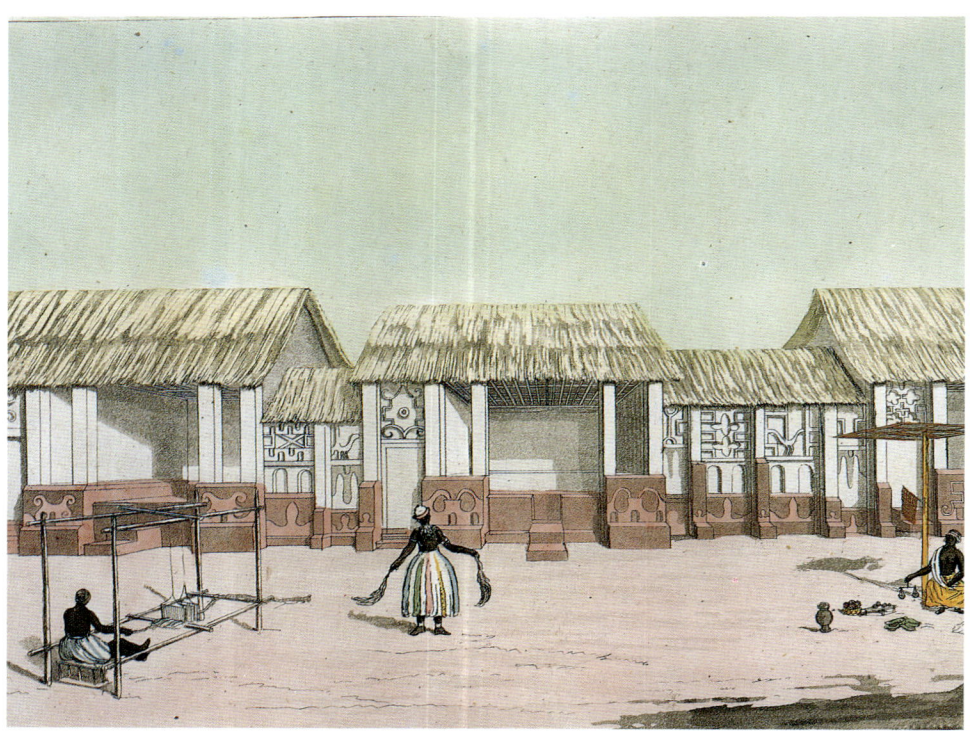

VILLAGE STREET

Among the Akans of West Africa, only the king's sister or niece can bear royal heirs, since the crown is passed down through the mother's line. Unfortunately, it turned out that the beautiful Poku could not bear children. In vain did she invite men to her chamber; her womb remained barren. The others snickered. They murmured that she was guilty in the eyes of the gods; and soon the pregnant women avoided her gaze, so that she would not wither the fruit growing in their bellies.

IN THE VILLAGE OF SIKASSO ▷

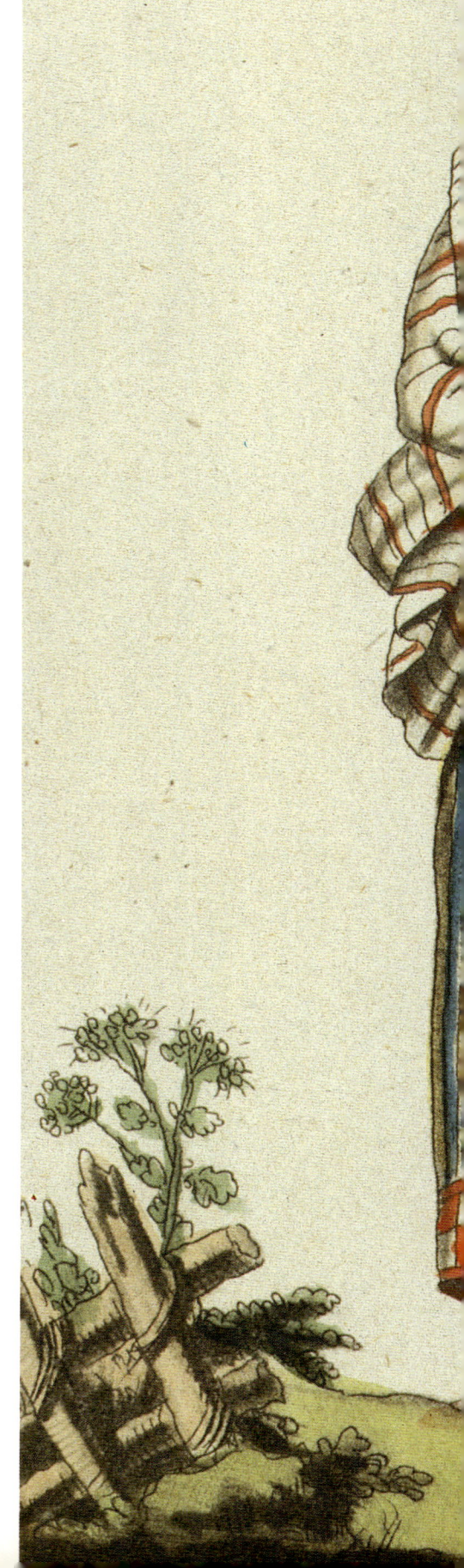

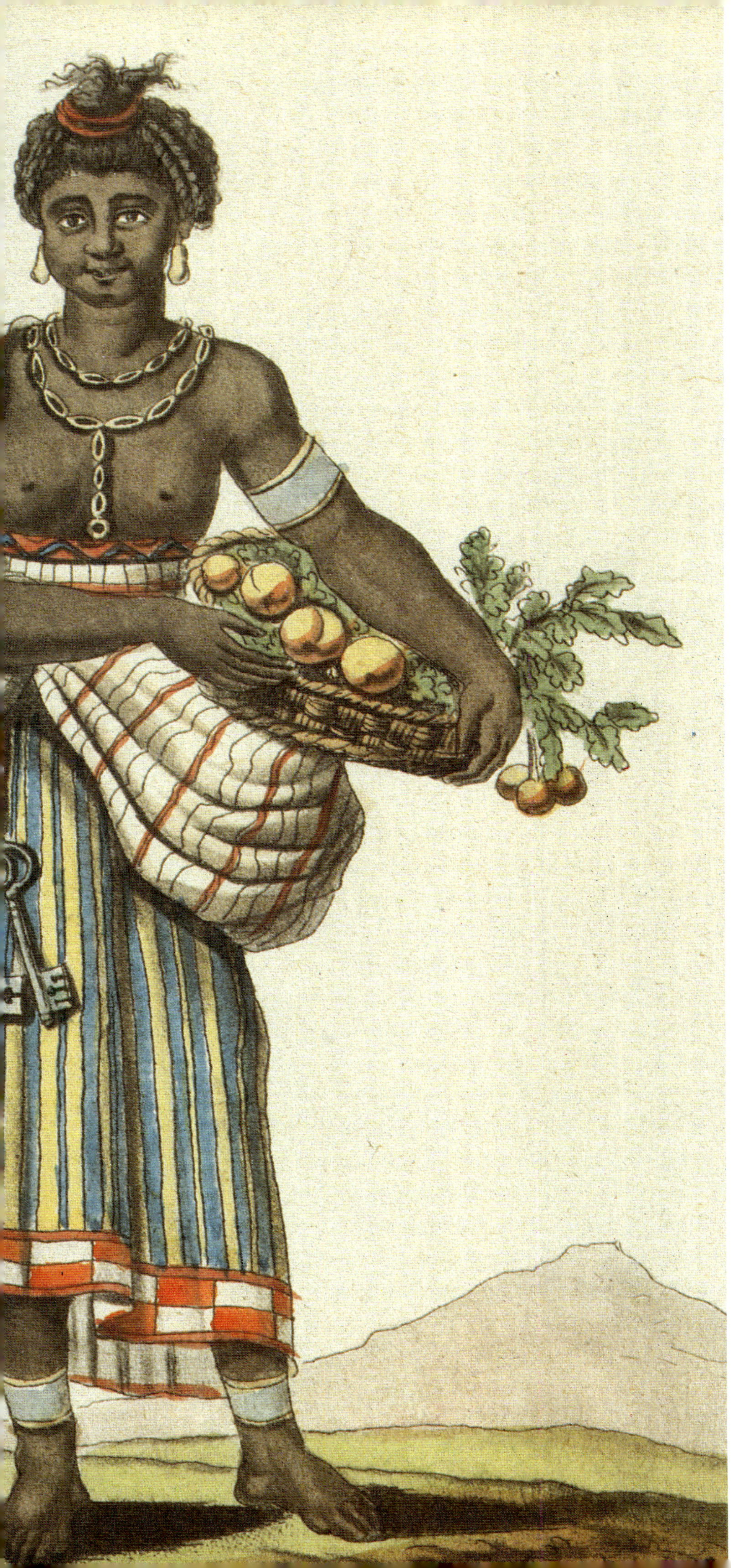

Woman Without Child

If I had only known!
If I had only known, I would have died the day
I was born!
Who will tell any comer?
Who will tell the other young women?

If I had only known!
Let them tell my brother...
Let them tell my mother...
That though it was time for me to be a mother,
I lacked the strength
That when it was time for me to be a mother
I was a piece of dry wood.

If I had only known!
You, mother of an only child,
Mock not my barrenness!
Don't you see I've nothing
To keep the worries away?

If I had only known!
What good is it to envy
What I will never have!
My hands washed, I missed the taro season.
The field I worked was fit for yams
But I had no mother-yams.
The yams rotted.
My basket is empty.
Maybe I look happy;
I am miserable at heart.

If I had only known!

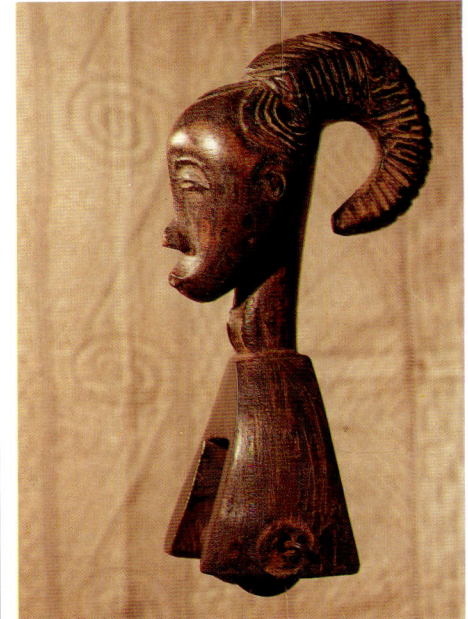

Heddle Pulley Carving

The meticulous decorativeness of the pulley is remarkable given the rustic simplicity of the loom, which is made of branches. This is because heddle pulleys, like the shuttlecocks and combs likewise embellished with carvings, are the personal objects that accompany the weaver when he goes from village to village, exchanging his services for food and small gifts, working with thread that the women have spun at home.

I Have Just Given Birth

Lefelele, for the first time,
I have just given birth
Given birth for the first time.
Lefelele, she who has no child
Lends an ear
Lefelele, she who has no child
Sits up straight
Lefelele, she who has none
Makes herself small.
Lefelele, for the first time,
I have just given birth
Given birth for the first time.

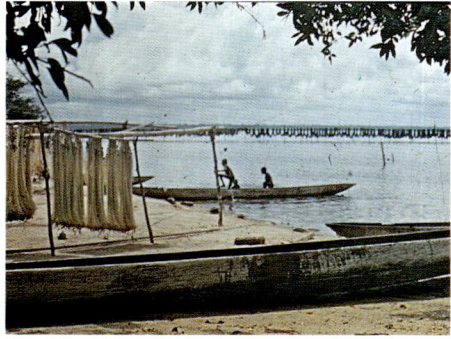

Origins of the Anyi Kingdoms

On the banks of the Efe River, in Ghana, lived the tribe of the Brafé, belonging to the Anyi-Ashanti group. The chief of this tribe had a dispute with his king, and it was decided that it should be settled by combat. Now, before the battle, lightning struck down a tree between the two armies and, according to the legend, an exquisite sword descended from heaven. The two adversaries rushed forward to seize it. In the ensuing struggle, the blade ended up in the hand of one and the hilt in the hand of the other. Instead of stopping at that, the Brafé people mocked the enemy king. So the latter was determined to have it over with then and there. The assault was terrible and the Brafé were vanquished. Too proud to submit, they fled southwest under the leadership of Aka, nicknamed "Esoin," the elephant hunter. Aka Esoin arrived with his people at the mouth of the Bia River on the shores of the Aby Lagoon. He immediately sent word to the local chief of his intention to settle in the country and to rule there as its master. The chief, furious, cut off the hand of Aka Esoin's messenger: this meant war. The Brafé triumphed, burnt the village to the ground, and slit the people's throats. Then they subjugated the whole region and settled at Krinjabo (which means "at the foot of the tree"). Aka Esoin called his new kingdom Sanwi, which meant: "The Ashanti are like porcupines: kill a thousand, and a thousand will take their place." Later, a group of Brafé-Ashanti from Sanwi went beyond the Komoé and settled in Molonou, near the Baulé, their kin, who had also left Ghana to settle in Ivory Coast.

Baulé Proverb

"Even a blind doe can still recognize the trail of a panther."

In 1742, when she was forty, Awura Poku knew that she would be buried with nothing but a chunk of coal for adornment: coal, burnt wood, is all a childless woman deserves. People called her *Apae,* the one through whom misfortune strikes. And yet, it was at the age of forty that she brought into the world a son named Kwaku. That's when Poku the Barren, Poku the Unfortunate, the *Apae,* became Poku the Mad, the one whose eyes never left her child.

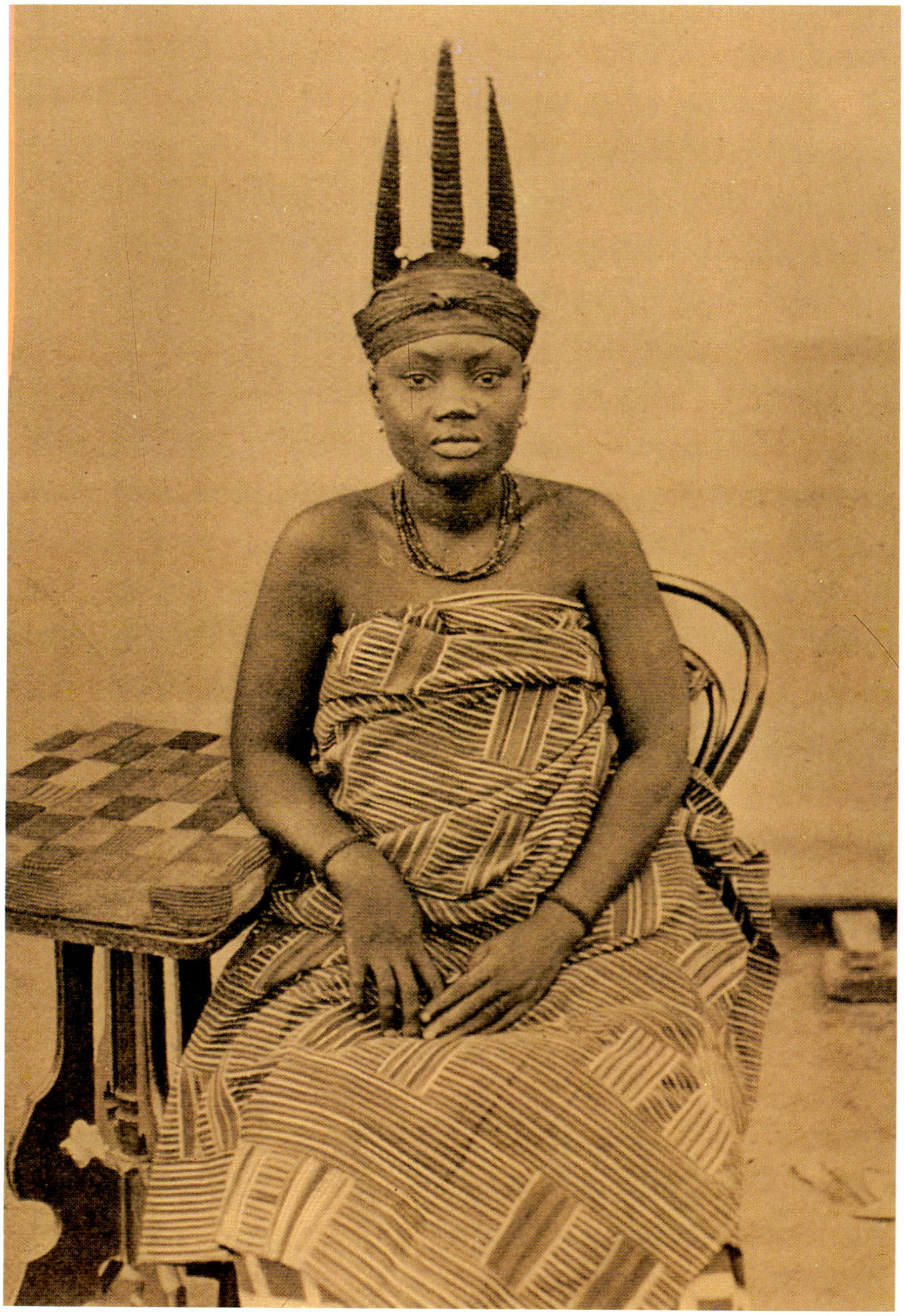

ASHANTI WOMAN

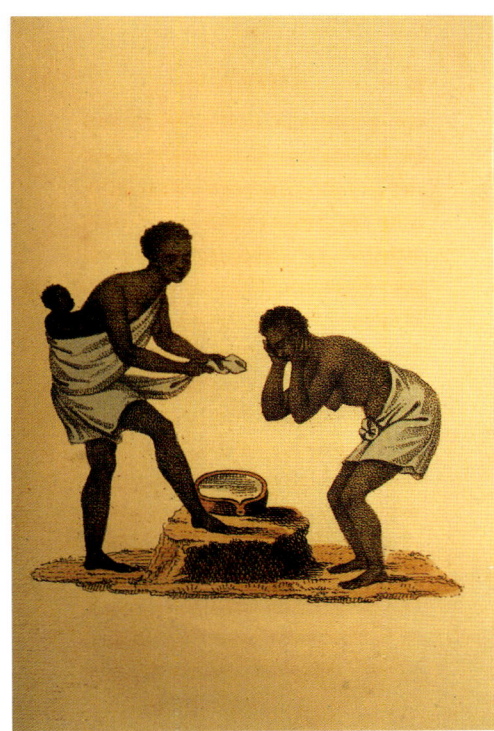

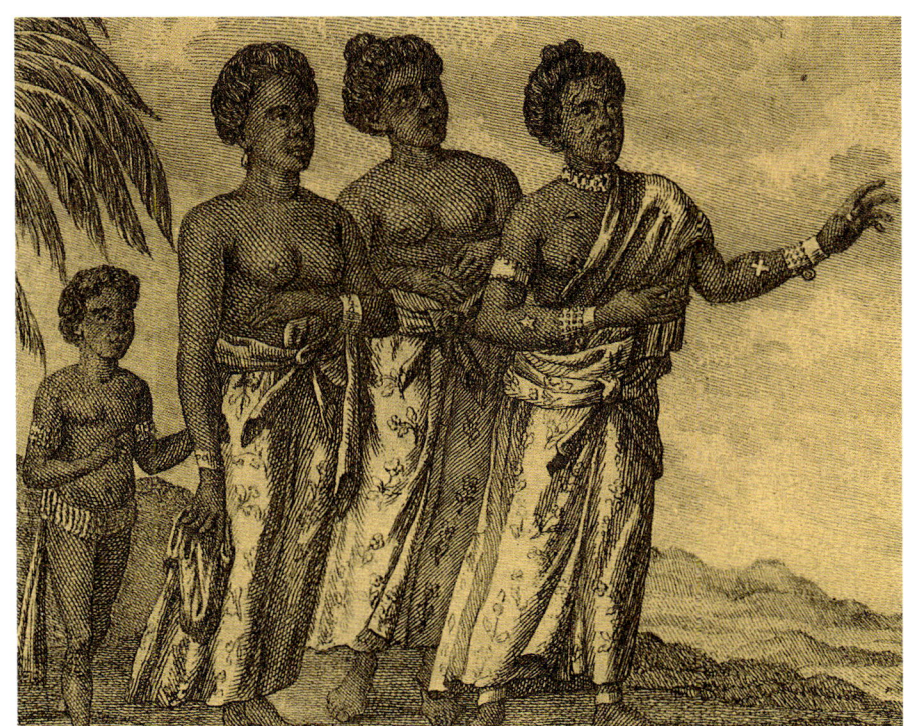

AKREAN WOMEN

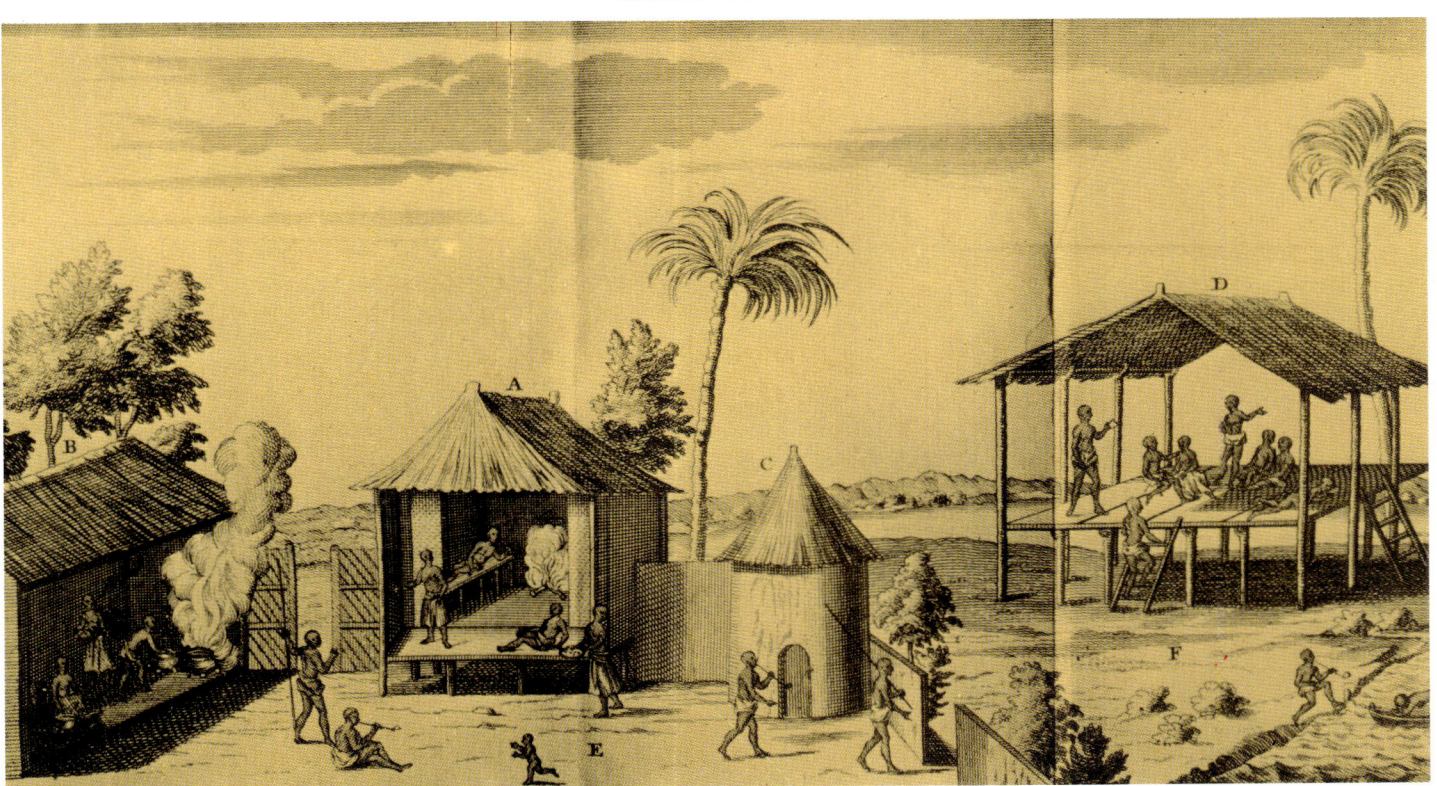

The Houses of Cape Mezurado

The kitchens are on ground level, surrounded by walls on three sides, with the open side facing away from the wind; the stilts that support the ridgepole are planted in the ground. They are connected to each other by means of wickerwork covered over with mud clay, which binds quite well and lasts a long time, even though it is not mixed with lime. Their bedrooms are raised three feet above ground level.

The front is completely open, and the floor juts out five or six feet across. The three sides of the bedroom are enclosed by wickerwork walls, covered with thick, neatly packed red earth about one foot thick. The tent-shaped roof is covered with reed or palm leaves, woven or neatly braided, so tight and thick that the rain and the heat of the sun cannot penetrate within.

In the middle of each village there is a large room similar to a meeting hall, raised six feet off the ground. It is called the "Caldé," that is, the place of conversation. These houses are accessible by ladder.

Funeral Song

Oh Bat, I have no village
I have become like the bat
I have no village
If I have a village,
I have no house...
The green tree doesn't fall without reason,
my son
A man made it fall
I am the bird
That weeps all day
The bird that weeps all night
And finds no one to console it.

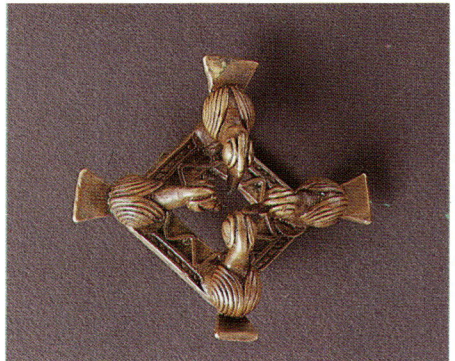

Weights for Measuring Gold

It is possible to group the weights for measuring gold into two large categories:
• Geometrical weights decorated with various motifs including a swastika-shaped cross (symbol of the astral rotation), diamonds, spirals, Greek crosses, trapezoids, squares, stepped pyramids, crescent moons, etc.
• Proverbial weights, in the shape of men, animals, plants, and objects.
These include the forms of almost all the objects common to craftsmen: knives, hatchets, dippers, gourds, stools, baskets, chairs, musical instruments, adzes, etc. One can almost re-create all of Baulé life in miniature thanks to the diversity of these weights. Each weight corresponds to a common saying; each depicted scene possesses a specific meaning. One may find many representations of family life, such as a woman caring for a child or a baby on a chair, or of religious life: dance scenes, ivory horns, and talking drum players.

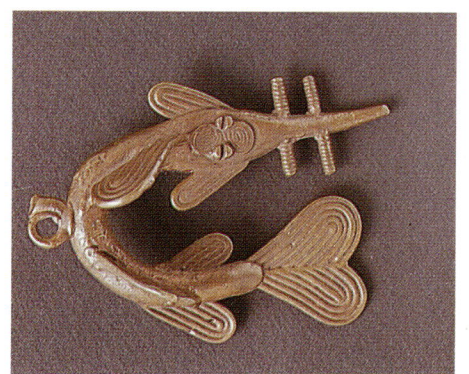

Kwaku was about ten years old when the throne was usurped by Kusi Obodum, a tyrannical old man, who would have anyone who had the misfortune of displeasing him strangled in the night.

Poku, who feared for her son, led all those faithful to the late and rightful king in a desperate flight across savanna and forest.

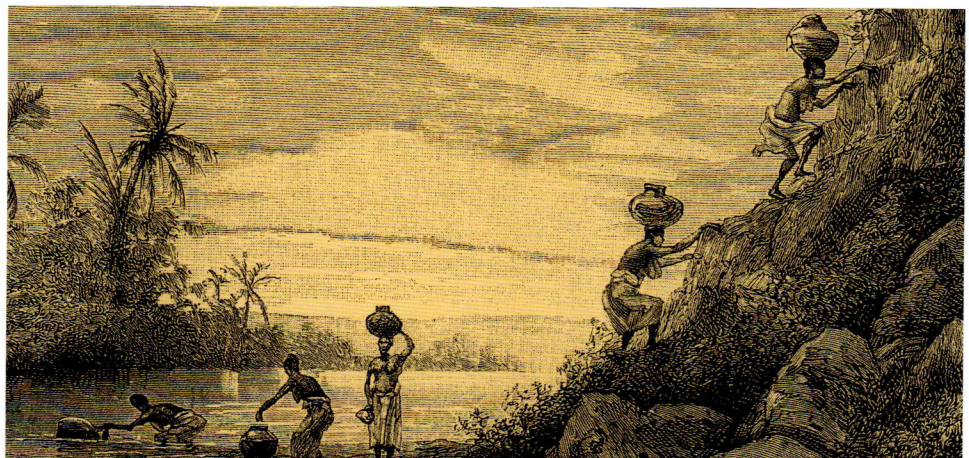

THE KOMOÉ

One day, pursued by the armies of the usurper, the refugees arrived on the banks of an overflowing river, the Komoé, not far from the present-day border between Ghana and Ivory Coast. The armies were on their heels and there seemed no way to escape certain slaughter. The high priest interrogated the River Spirit, which told him:

"I will let your people pass, on the condition that they sacrifice unto me their purest and best."

"Let us give him our jewels and our gold," said Princess Awura Poku.

But the high priest shook his head:

"Do you really think the gods are fond of metal?"

"Let us give him the best goats of our flock," said Princess Awura Poku.

Once more, the great priest rebuked her:

"Woman, do you regard the gods as if they were but common hyenas?"

"Let's give him the flesh of a warrior," said Princess Awura Poku.

The high priest smiled:

"Men are not pure, and even youths smell of sludge: the River Spirit craves the life of a child, the purest, the best of our children."

Poku turned toward the fathers who had many sons, toward uncles who had many nephews, and even toward those whose children were sick and on the threshold of death: but no one wanted to give the flesh of his flesh to the river. So Poku grabbed her only son and held him out before the crowd, proclaiming in a dead voice:

"This one will save our people."

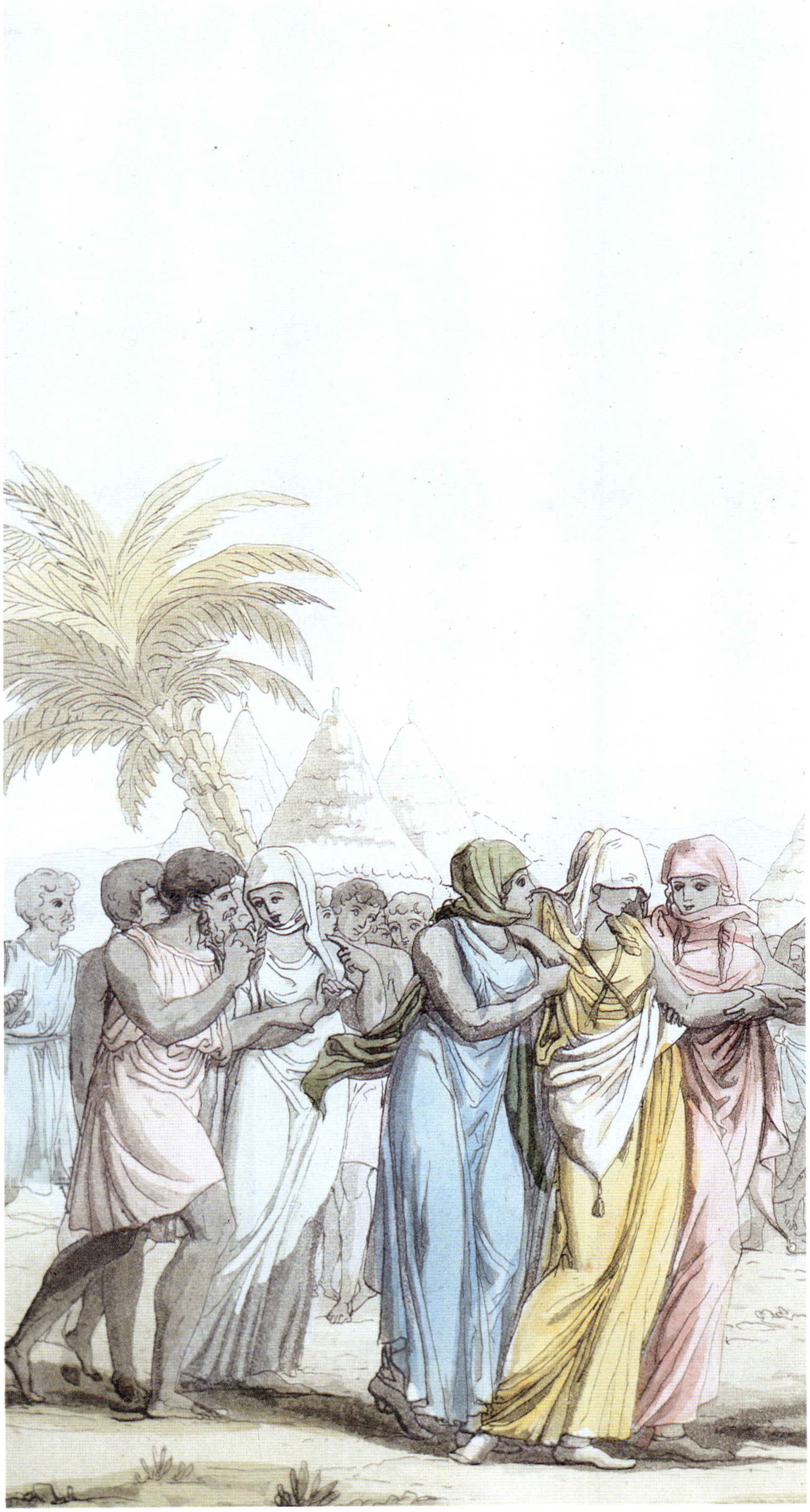

QUEEN POKU

"BUT NO ONE WANTED TO GIVE THE FLESH OF HIS FLESH…"

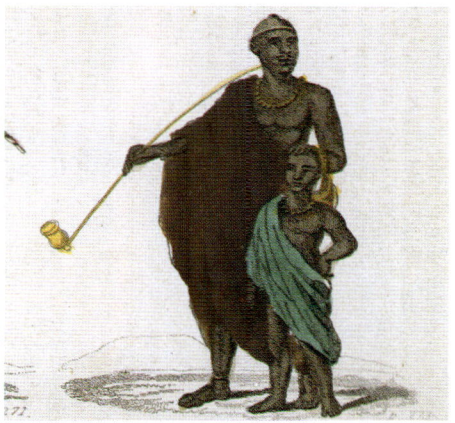

Nangui Founds Korhogo

Sekou Ouattara, first king of Kong, possessed a captive named Nangui. He was a brave warrior, and monks predicted to Sekou that Nangui would one day become king. Sekou, fearing that Nangui would seize power from his sons, freed Nangui and told him to settle wherever he wished, as long as he left the kingdom.

Nangui left Kong and went west until he crossed the Bandama River. There, he stopped under a tall tree, unsure which direction to take. Then he headed east. On his way, he met monks coming from Timbuktu who told him: "The place of your kingdom is in the north and your city will be called Korhogo."

Nangui therefore retraced his steps and set out resolutely in the direction indicated by the monks. He finally stopped on the west bank of a creek. There he found a praise singer and made him this proposition: "I am going to settle here, and we can become allies." The praise singer answered: "I will pray for the prosperity of our descendants." This is how Nangui and his followers settled in Korhogo.

Nangui's descendants reigned throughout Sénoufo country.

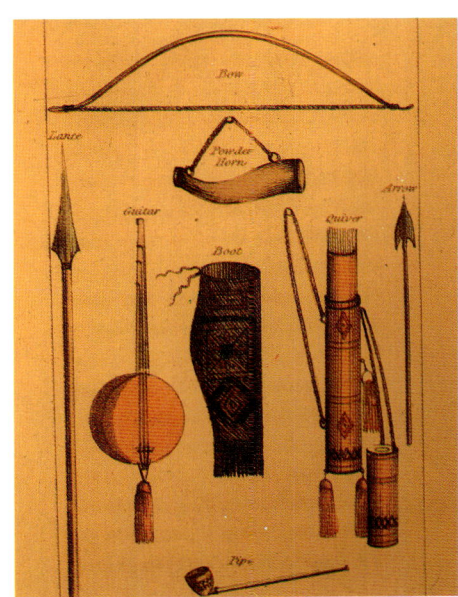

WEAPONS AND OBJECTS

Then, like a zombie, she led the child to a cliff above the river, picked him up in her embrace, and then let go. The crowd let out a howl, but Princess Poku kept silent.

All at once, the great trees along the river banks laid themselves down atop the water, forming a huge bridge over the Komoé.

When night fell, the high priest noticed that all the refugees had crossed the river except for the princess, who remained on the cliff, standing there like a statue. He came near the old woman and said:

"Look, you have to cross now, you're the last one."

The princess obeyed, crossing the river in her turn on that strange bridge of trees. When she reached the other side, she knelt in the mud and gently dipped her hand into the black water. And only the great priest heard her utter these words:

"*Ba-Uli*... The child is dead."

At that instant, the trees stood up again, swaying over the tumultuous flow, and the first shadowy outlines of the pursuing army appeared on the opposite bank. And then a woman cried out:

"Poku, think of the thousands of children who are yours and think no more of the one who is dead."

And the high priest added:

"Poku, Poku, this little child has become our father. We were Ashanti, but the Ashanti have cast us out. Your child has carried us into new lands, and so I propose that we change our very name. *Ba-Uli* was the first word you uttered on this side of the river. This word, I ask that we preserve it. The Ashanti have remained on the other side: long live the Ba-Uli people!"

And so it was that Princess Awura Poku became queen of the Baulé, who still live on that side of the river, in present-day Ivory Coast. Her descendants were rulers in Baulé country for well over a century. The last great king, Anublé, died in 1958 in the village of Sikasso, the same village where Queen Poku spent her last days.

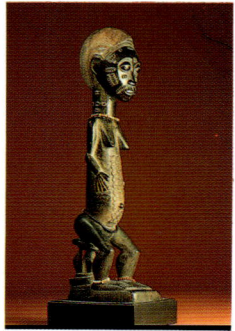

WORDS
OF AN ORDINARY WOMAN

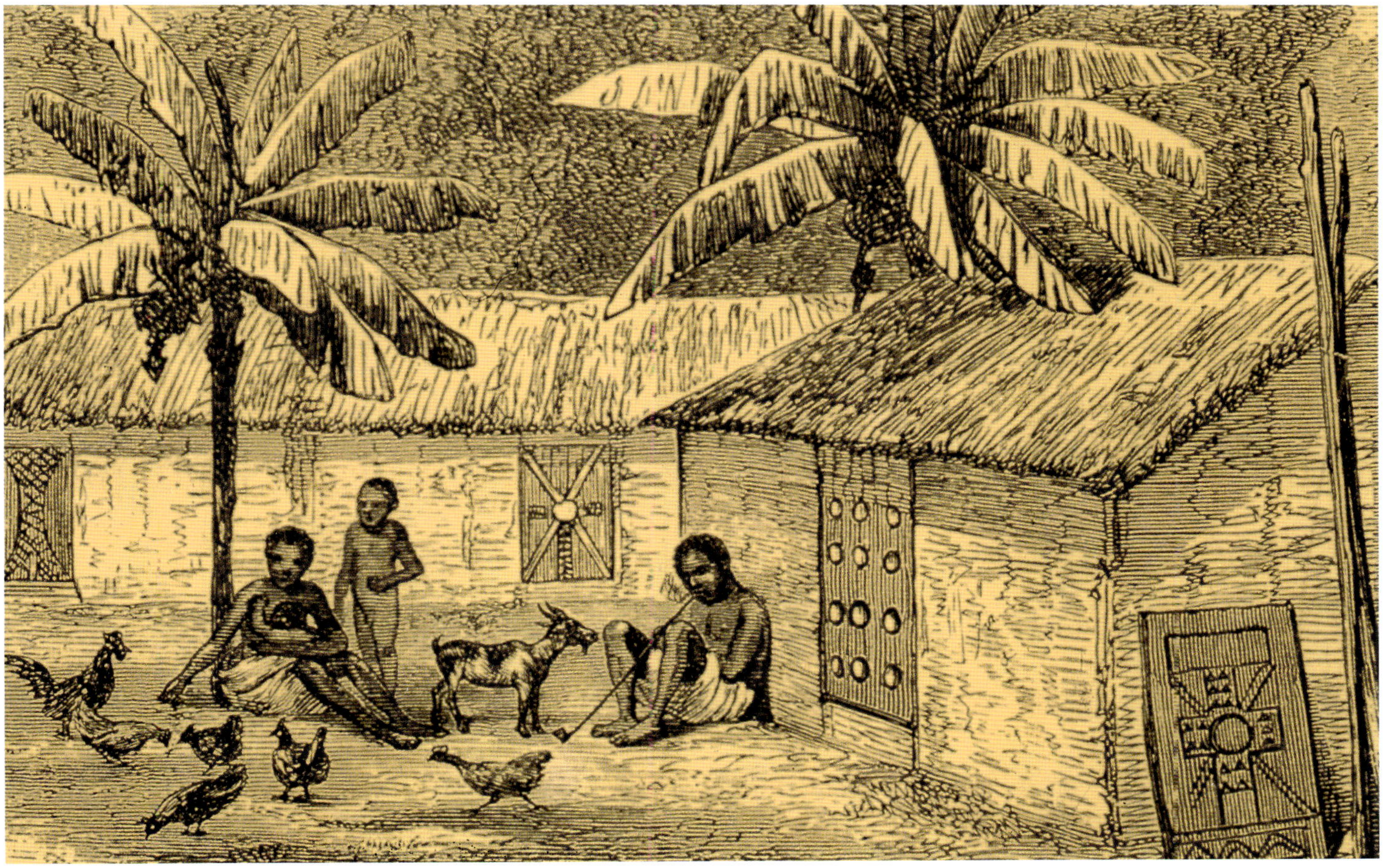

IN THE VILLAGE

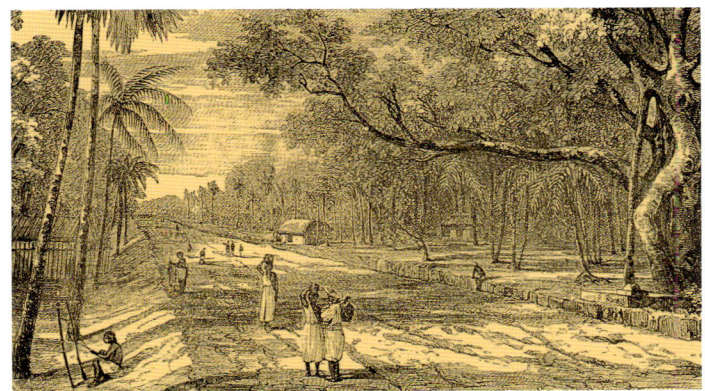
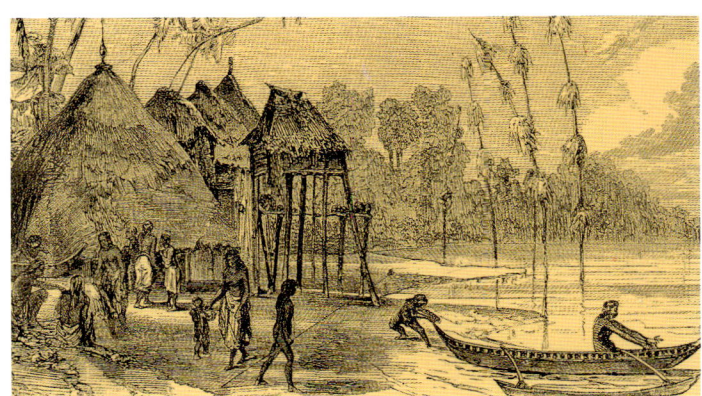

Children are happiness. Yes, having descendants brings happiness to everyone, to all men and all women.

Children are life.

If you live and you have no children, you are already dead. You are not truly living.

If you die without leaving any children behind, you die twice. Who will speak my name after my death?

Who will remain among men after my death? If someone has no children, he is already dead before dying. But if he has many children when he dies, he is not really dead: he remains. Because people will keep saying: look, it's Dubu's son, those are Mbiinam's sons! And in this way the name will last. It will not be forgotten, shall not vanish. The person will not die, because his name will live.

For men as for women, children are their life, their happiness. They are the remedy for death.

Last year, our uncle Jaho died, leaving only one child. And that child died a few days ago. You know what people said? They said now Jaho is truly dead. They said he died a second time. Now there is nothing left of him, his name will be forgotten.

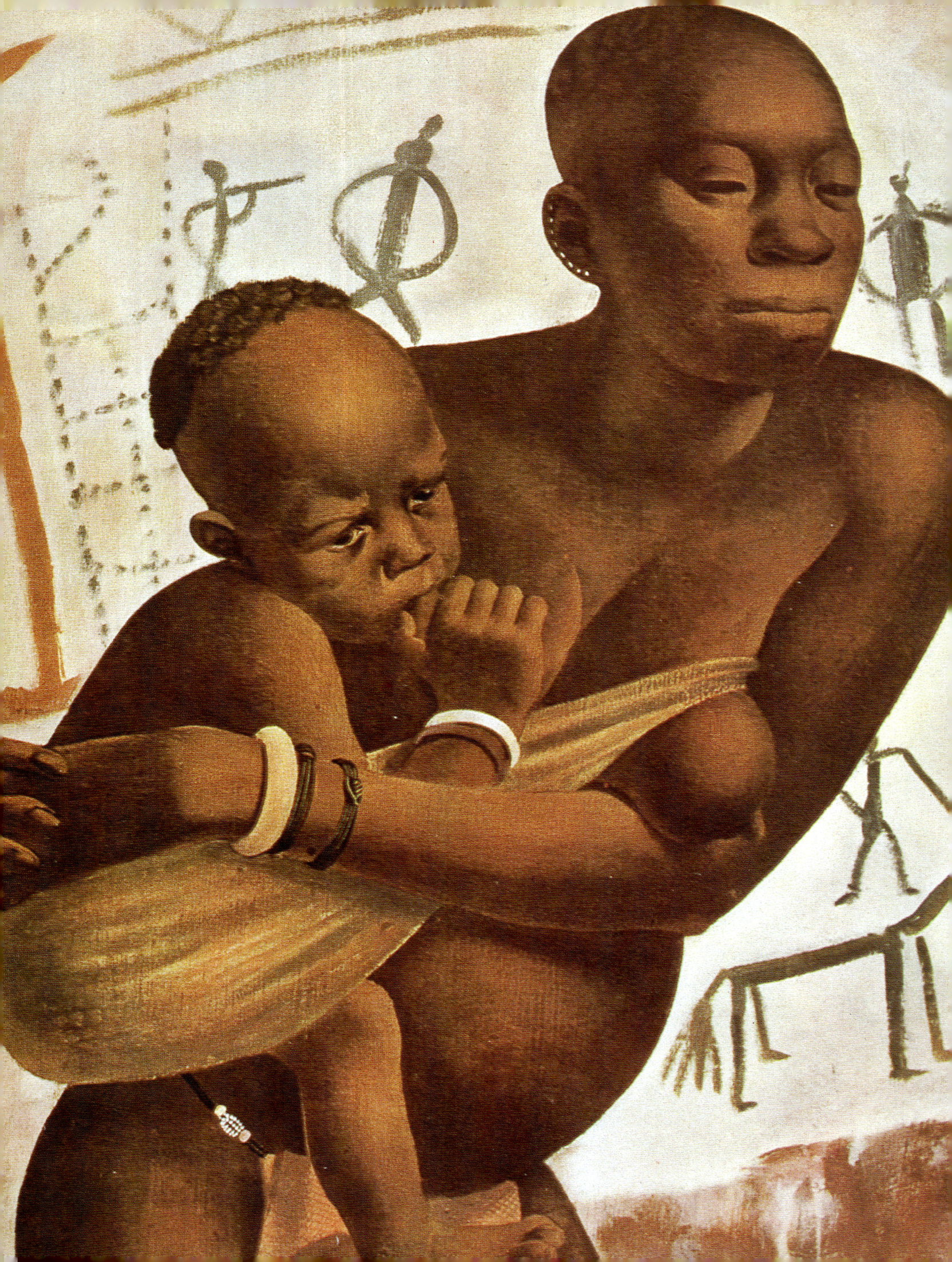

SOGANÉ TOURÉ

SHE WHO WOULD NOT ACCEPT THE WAY OF THE WORLD

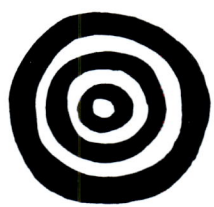

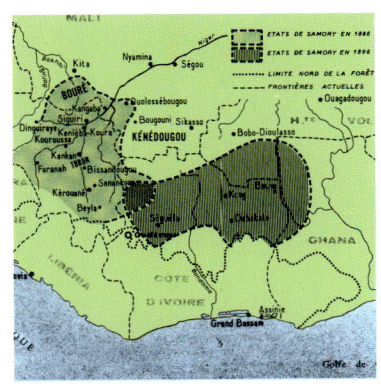

And then she spoke these last words, known to all the children of Mandé: "My son, you have been a slave for me for seven years; may the world now be your slave…"

TWO CENTURIES AFTER THE DEATH OF SOGOLON KONTÉ, MOTHER OF THE GREAT SUNDIATA, THE MANDINGO PEOPLE WITNESSED THE BIRTH OF A COMPLETELY ORDINARY WOMAN; A WOMAN WHO WAS NEITHER A LIONESS NOR EVEN AN ANTELOPE WITH a graceful figure, but a simple creature made to serve, the kind who seems to murmur, barely moving her lips: "I am a goat, I cry when my throat is slit." This plain woman was named Sogané Touré: we do not even know the meaning of her name.

Like all girls in the country of Mandé, Sogané Touré had been raised to be obedient. If the gods had given her attentive parents, she could have learned all the ways of the world from them; had the gods put a drop of noble blood in her body, this drop might have infused her with an awareness of her dignity; and if the gods had given her an aura of beauty, she might have conducted herself with more confidence along life's journeys.

But the gods were looking elsewhere the day she was born; and for a long time she was like an invisible breath of air in the village of Magnanbalandugu, where her parents had given her as a child to the old Laviaafiya Touré. Sogané became the weaver's sixth wife.

Since her mouth did not know how to grumble, and since her stomach remained perfectly flat, she became the servant of the other wives and all their children. This went on until she became pregnant; then, it was as though a wind had lifted her up from the kingdom of the dead and suddenly set her down among the living.

To her great surprise, she gave birth to a male child, a child just like all the others, with everything in place right down to his toenails.

And as his little mouth nuzzled at her breast, gulping down her milk, which was just like the milk of all the other women all over the world, Sogané Touré felt a great anger rising up from deep down inside her, a rage like the wind when it rips the roofs off houses and throws down great trees; she was tempted to open her mouth but remained mute, as before, her lips sealing up her secret: she had given the child the traditional name of Samory.

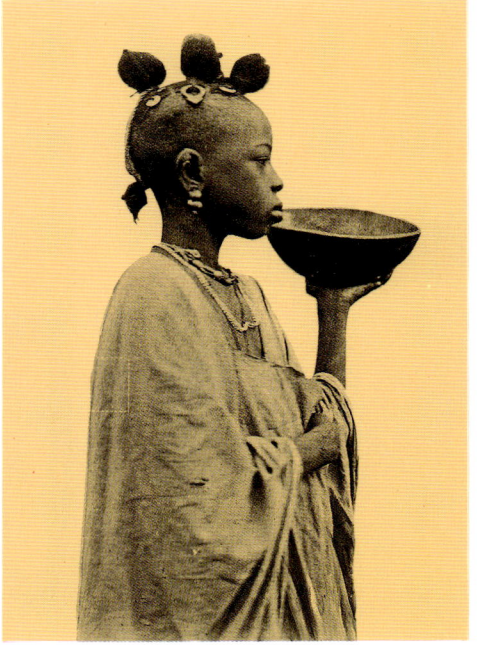

YOUNG GIRL OF TIMBUKTU

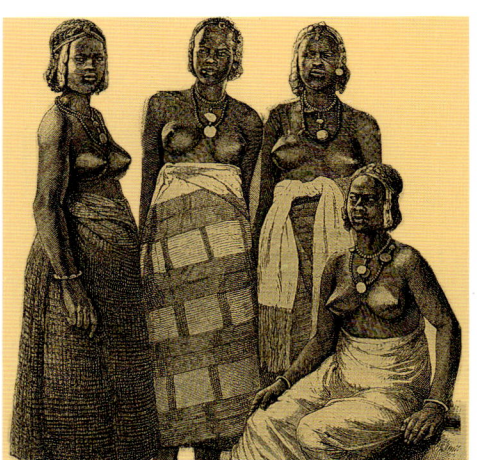

MALINKÉ WOMEN

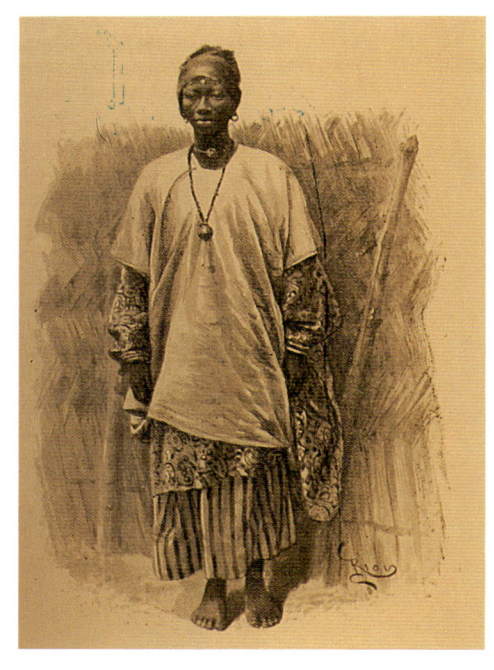

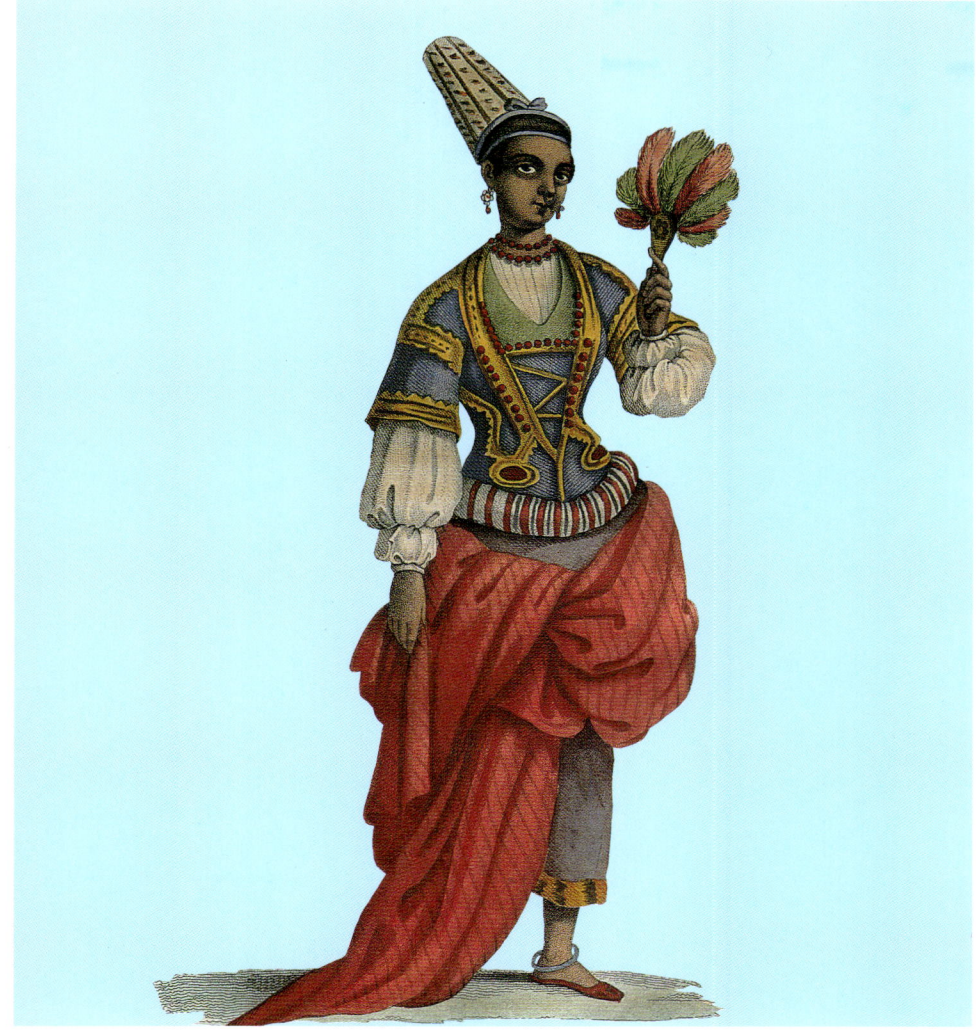
WOMAN OF TIMBUKTU

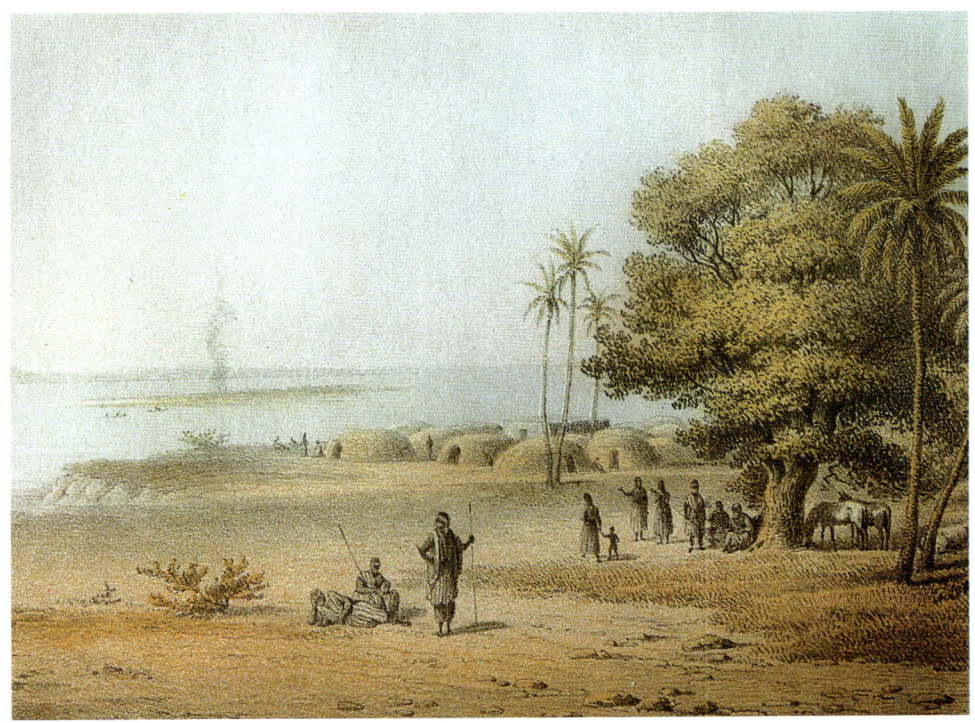
BAMBA

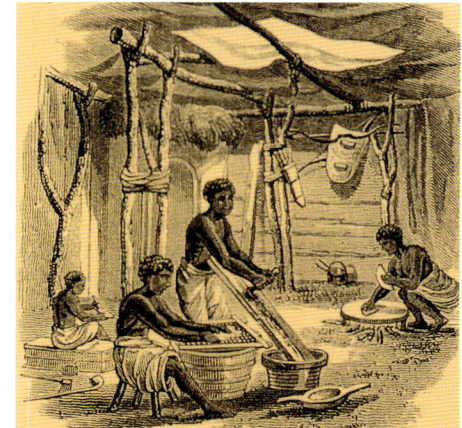
A Woman's Day

In pre-colonial Mandé, women played a large part in the work of the fields. A small cloth tied around their waists, they would crouch for hours at a time, tending the crops. Five days a week, they tended the family fields; they spent the rest of their time in their individual fields, or *logodiougoniforo*. This prompted one of our sources to comment: "In that era, a woman was very busy; one might agree with the poet Senghor in saying that woman was at the beginning and the end of everything in Mandé."

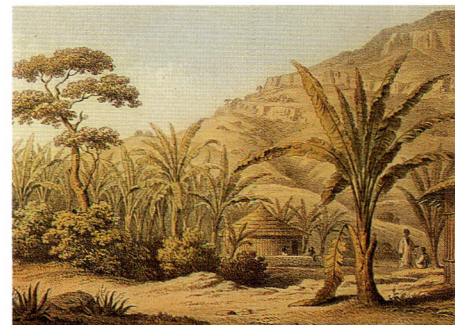

In the morning, she got up, cleaned her home, drew water, and prepared the noon meal, which she would finish around nine or ten o'clock; the other wives who were not cooking would already be in the fields. She fed the old men and women and the small children, and then she joined the others in the fields where her husband's other wives and daughters were already working. She would come back in the evening carrying the wood she used for cooking; she heated water for her husband and prepared the evening meal, which was sometimes not ready until ten o'clock. That is when she would wash, and after eating, begin her evening activities: that is, evenings spent in the company of the other women of the house and the adolescent boys and girls. This is when the mothers told the little ones stories and legends that they themselves had learned from their parents, tales that played an important role in the children's moral education.

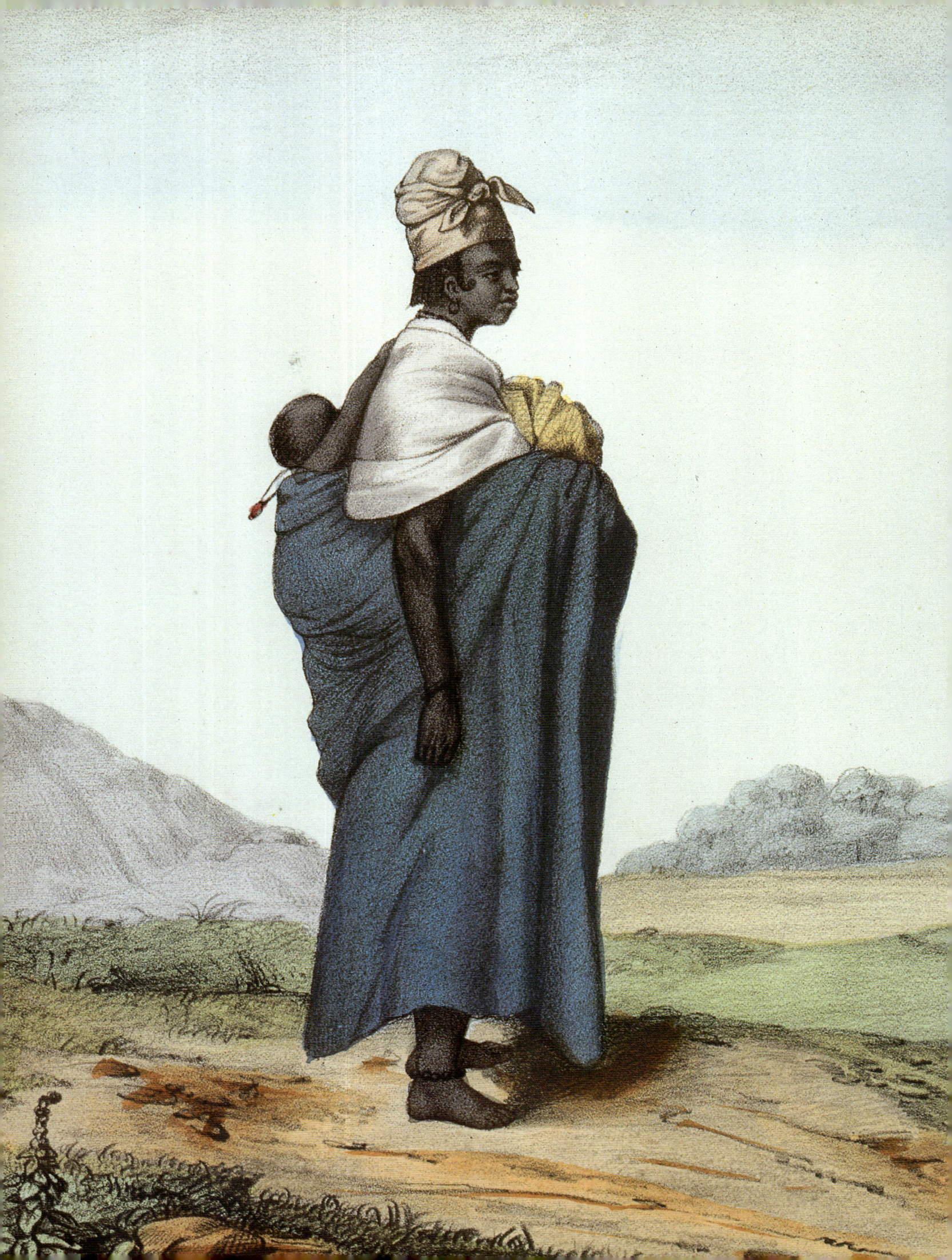

Whenever she had a moment to rest, whenever the people around her let her catch her breath, she would lift up the child secured on her back, the better to see his face, and call him nicknames unknown in Mandé country: "My little fire," she would say to him, "my little fury, my anger that does me good."

One night, she had a dream: she saw herself in labor in the birthing hut, her feet raised up toward the thatch roof. Then an old woman pushed on her belly, which opened suddenly on a serpent that shot straight up into the sky, its mouth open on all of Mandé country. Sogané Touré would not mention this vision until later, and later the praise singers would cite it repeatedly.

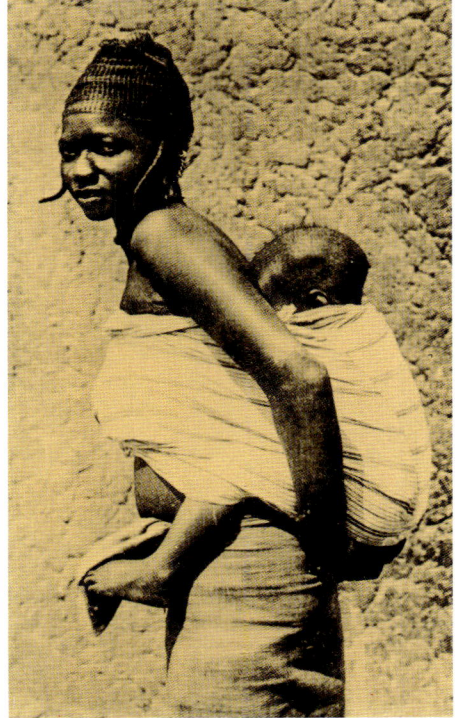

Black Woman, African Woman

Black woman, African woman
Oh you, my mother, I think of you...

Oh Dâman, oh my mother, you who carried me
on your back
You who nursed me, who watched over my first
steps
You who first opened my eyes to the wonders of
the world
I think of you...

Woman of the fields, woman of the rivers
Of the great river, oh you my mother

Oh you Dâman, oh my mother
You who wiped my tears away, you the delight
of my heart
Whose patience cradled my mischief
How I would love to be near you still,
to be a child by your side!

Simple woman, resigned to fate
Oh you my mother, I am thinking of you!

Black woman, African woman
Oh you my mother, thank you
Thank you for all you did for me,
Your son, so far so close to you!

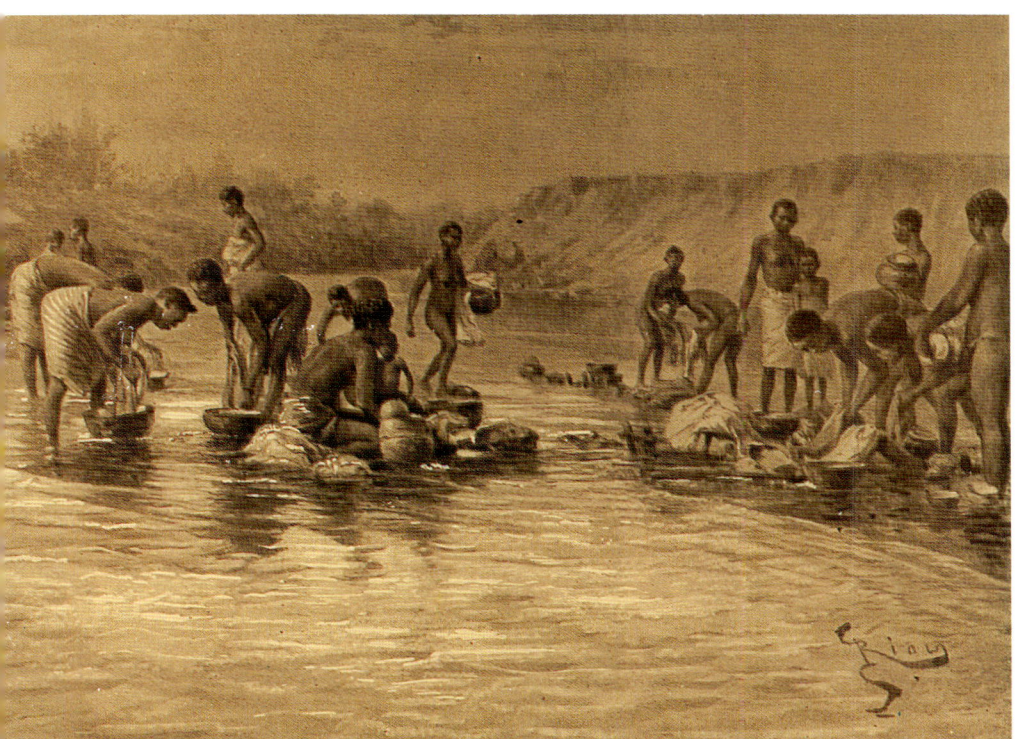

Her belly had given birth to a great devourer of men: and this news appeased her heart. For him, she toiled more than ever before, collecting shae tree nuts in secret and spinning cotton into the darkest hours of the night. She would blow on the sleeping child to cool him. She nourished his body with the choicest morsels, and fed his mind little phrases to stoke his fire.

◁ "THE CHILD SECURED ON HER BACK..."

Oh Mother, My Mother

Oh mother, oh my mother
Best friend among mothers
When my mother starts cooking
Her cooking is better than anyone's
When my mother goes to the fields
She grows more crops than all the others
When my mother goes to wash
her children's clothes
She washes them better than any other mother
Oh mother, oh my mother
Best of mothers
Mother whose tenderness will always shine
Like the Djoliba.

El-Hadj Omar

El-Hadj Omar was born in Senegal to a Muslim Tukulor. He undertook a pilgrimage to Mecca, as well as a long journey that lasted eighteen years. He returned with not only the title of grand marabou, but great wealth besides. He settled in Fouta-Djalon, in Guinea, quickly won over many people to his views, and purchased ammunition, for his goal was to conquer the Sudan and to oust the whites. Even as a child, Omar displayed surprising intelligence and irresistible charm. He was remarkably handsome. He never looked older than thirty. He could go indefinitely without eating or drinking. He never seemed to tire, whether it be from walking, riding, or lying still on a mat.

He had a sweet voice and was able to make himself heard as well afar as up close. He never laughed or cried, nor got angry. His face was always calm and smiling. He never used a weapon, even in war.

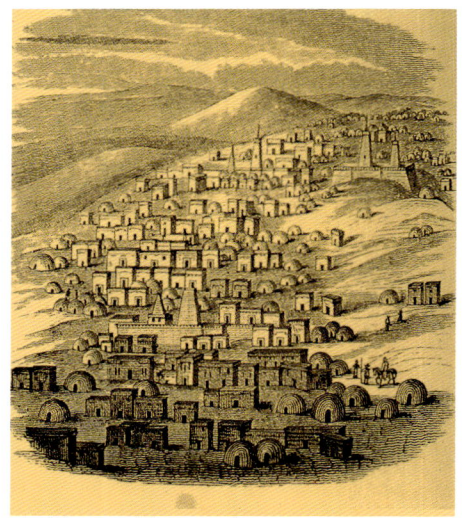

TIMBUKTU

When his soldiers retreated in combat, he would move to the front line and say: "You're giving up on paradise today?" Everyone would march, shouting "Allah is great!"

It is not hard to imagine that, with such qualities, he was able to achieve much of his ambitious dream in just a few years.

First he attacked the pagan Bambaras of Kaata. He conquered them, entered their capital and had their king's head cut off. The Bambaras of Ségou and the Peuls of Massina took fright and united their forces. El-Hadj Omar vanquished them, entered Ségou as its master, then Hamdallahi, and there too he executed the royal families.

In a short time, fifteen years or so, the empire of El-Hadj Omar stretched from Middle Senegal to Timbuktu. But the marabou's fall would happen quite suddenly. In 1863, Omar was conquered by the Peuls of Massina.

His son Ahmadou and his nephew Tidiani reigned after him in Ségou and Massina, until the arrival of the French colonialists.

Samory was taller than the other boys, with large, very black hands covered with rosy patches, which made him look a little like a leper. He had his teeth filed down to points, like all the other boys of the village; but when he burst into laughter, his upper lip rose into a sneer, a sort of pouting, sullen grimace, which made him look like a lion.

After Samory turned fourteen, Sogané urged him to leave, to flee the petty tyranny of their neighbors; but despite his considerable strength and the lion's laugh that he sometimes displayed, Samory was a desperately peaceful boy, who seemed to wish to live in his mother's shadow.

A few months later, prodded by Sogané's pleas, he latched on to a Diula kola nut peddler and took the road to Konanka and Sankaran. Two or three times, Muslim bandits fell upon him, and he would instantly transform into a mighty warrior, flailing his arms and legs, which seemed to multiply every which way. Then he would tie up the ends of his bundle and walk away with great tranquil strides, which would take him back to the village of Magnanbalandugu once a month.

One day the boy returned home to find his mother's hut deserted: the knights of Sérébouréma, king of Wasulunka, had sacked the village and taken his mother into slavery. She was in Madina, capital of Sérébouréma. Now, a peddler's trade is not terribly lucrative. So Samory asked his father for a few cattle to buy his mother back from King Sérébouréma. His father refused; he preferred his cattle to that frail toothless creature, who was never of great use to him as a wife, and who exhausted herself in her servant's duties.

Samory went to the capital of the Wasulunka Kingdom and offerred himself as a captive in exchange for his mother's freedom. (She belonged to a chief by the name of Kouyaté.) But the master kept both mother and son. Every day, Sogané begged him to flee and every day, Samory once again chose slavery: seven years went by like this.

According to legend, Sogané, out of desperation, became a Yégou Niéoumanmusso: a woman who could wring out a potent fluid from solid iron. Every day she washed her son's face with this water. Or so the legend goes.

ON THE ROAD TO TIMBUKTU... ▷

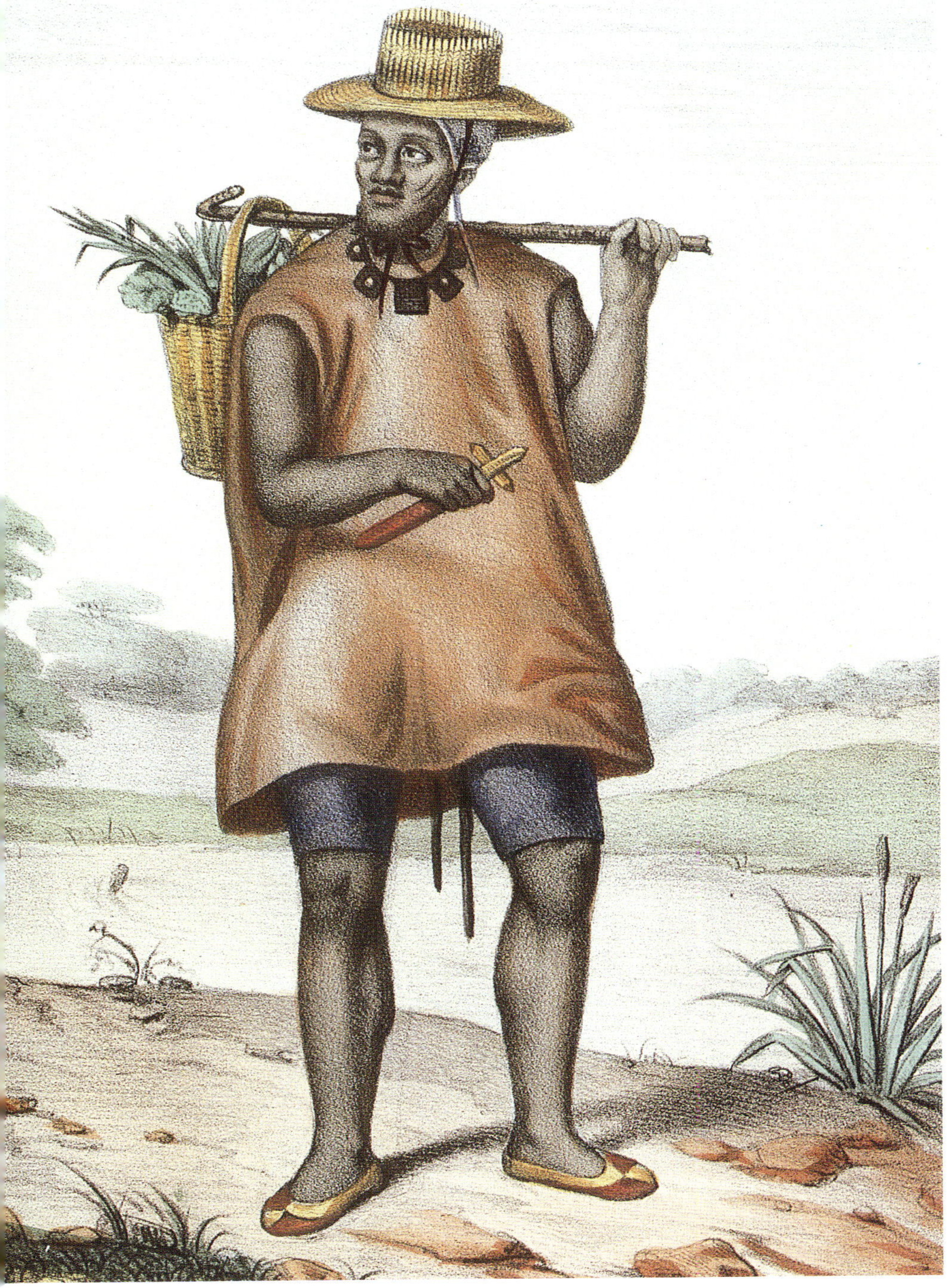

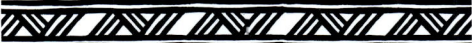

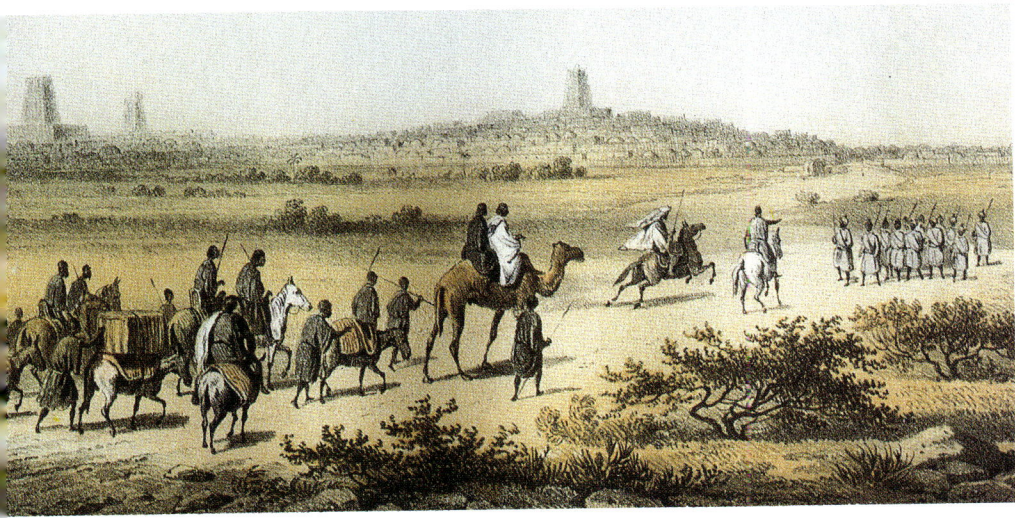

TIMBUKTU

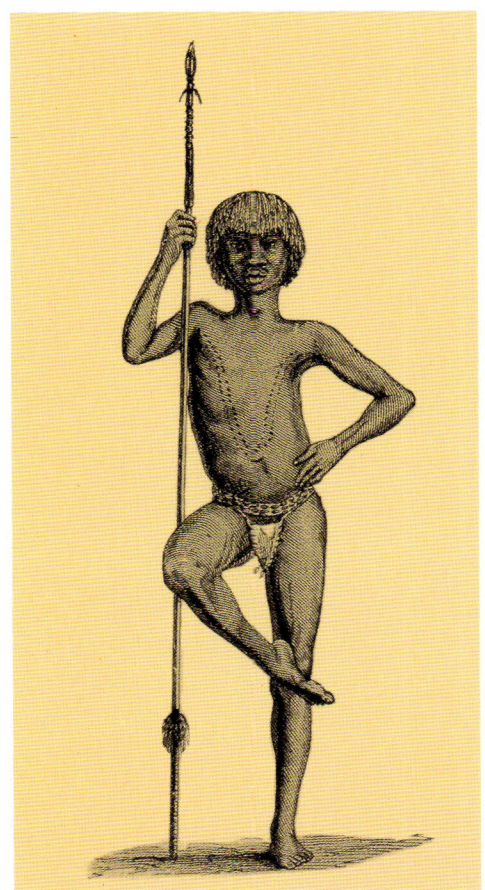

"HE WAS TALLER THAN THE OTHER BOYS..."

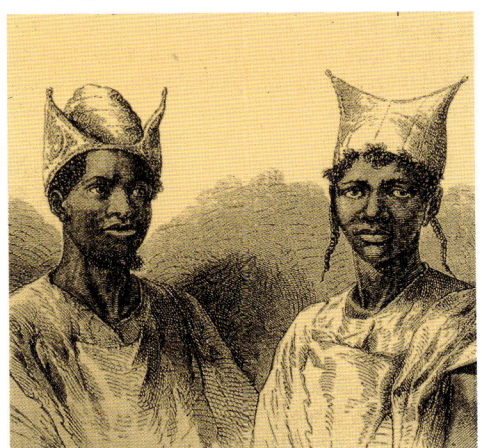

A BAMBARA COUPLE

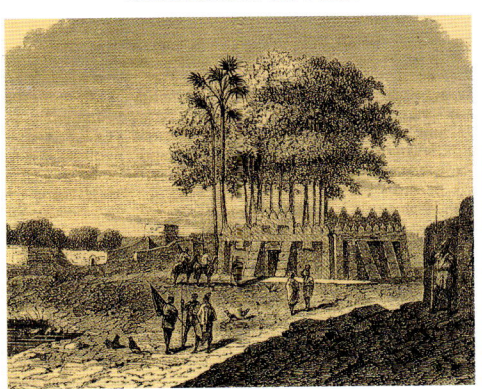

SÉGOU

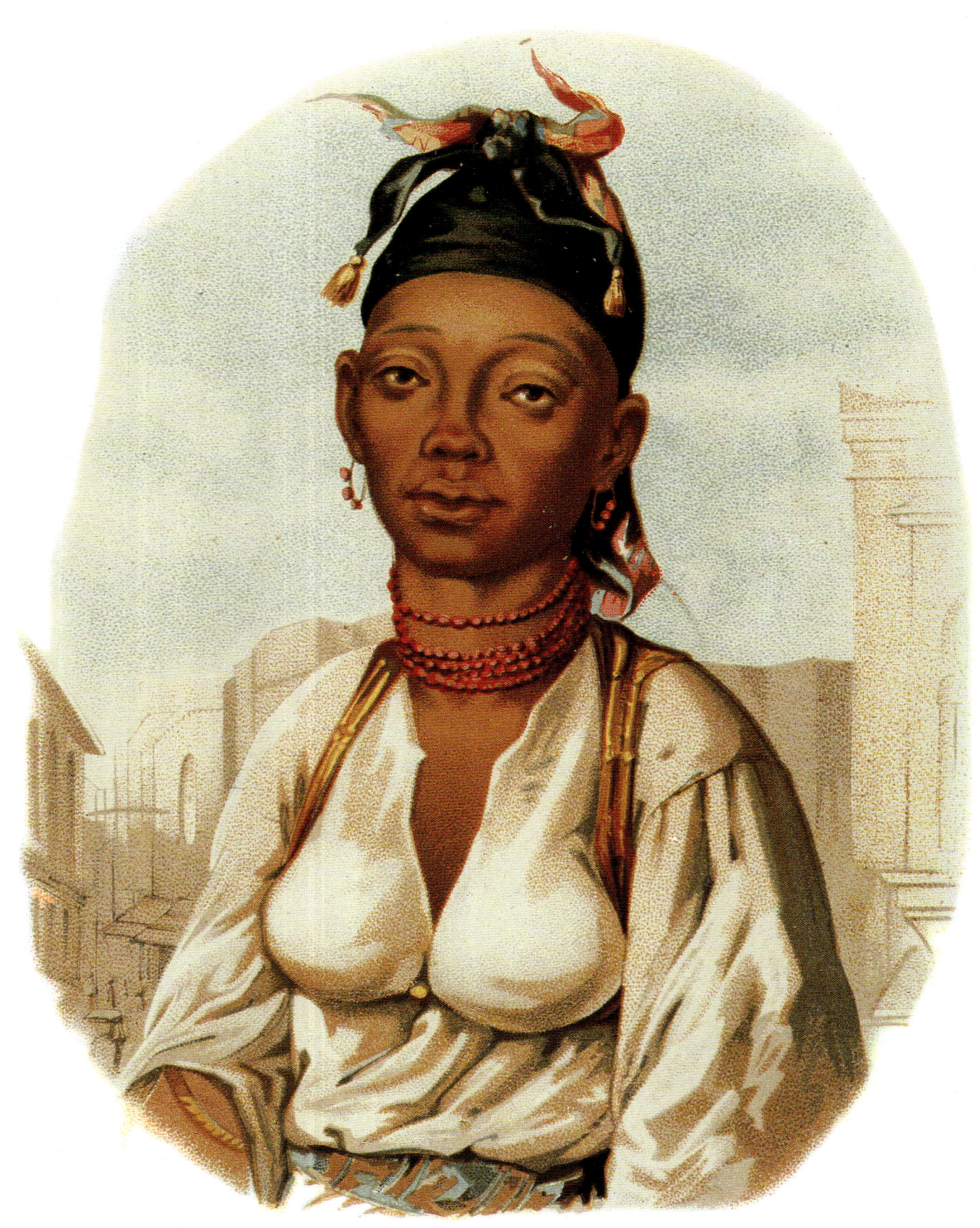

WOMAN OF TIMBUKTU

The seventh year, Samory, still a slave, is drafted into the army to serve with the king's troops; in this way, he captures a slave, then a second slave, and a third; each time he gives these slaves to his mother's master in exchange for her liberty.

But the master will hear nothing of it and Samory now throws himself into the heart of battle, in the hope that his merit as a warrior will release his mother from bondage.

One day during a battle, the king of Wasulunka notices his prowess and asks who this man is, this lion whose teeth gleam in the midst of combat. He asks to see him immediately, but the slave is gone: having only one scratch, he has gone to wash it in the creek and is waiting in the bushes for his clothes to dry. Finally, Samory appears before the throne of the king, who asks him how he came to be in the king's army.

Samory has been a merchant, and a slave, and a warrior: he now knows about all the dark sides of human nature.

He tells the story of his kidnapped mother, his voluntary servitude, the three slaves he brought in vain to trade for her: he would be proud to serve in the army of the king of Sérébouréma all his life, if his majesty would release old Sogané from bondage. He would be more than proud: he burns with the desire to serve the great monarch, who has been so good as to give him the honor of his attention.

Sérébouréma is moved by his words: "I do not want you as a slave. I have seen you in combat; you are a lion with shining teeth and I want you under my flag as a free warrior. Go, faithful man, take old Sogané back to her village and return quickly to me, for a chieftaincy awaits you, as well as a rifle and a horse."

Samory has read the king's mind well: as soon as he and old Sogané are outside the capital, Samory advises his mother to take a narrow hunting trail, for Sérébouréma will surely change his mind; and, sure enough, a little later, men on horseback burst from the city gates to go prepare an ambush for the mother and son near a creek on the path they are expected to take.

With orders to bring the two back to the capital, the riders wait a long time; but mother and son calmly follow their path until nightfall. They arrive at a clearing. Samory cuts some wood, cooks a piece of meat until it is tender enough for his mother's gums, and lies down next to the fire to protect old Sogané from wayward sparks.

Women of Timbuktu

In Timbuktu, the women do not wear veils; they go out when they wish and are free to see anyone. The inhabitants are kind and friendly to strangers; they are industrious and clever in trade, which is their only resource. Women's dress consists of a *coubasse* like the men's, except that it does not have large sleeves; they also wear Moroccan

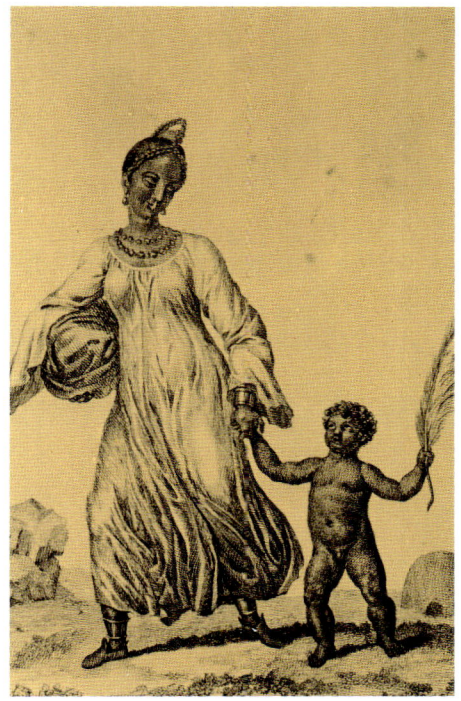

leather shoes. There is some variation in hairstyle, which consists mainly of a *fatara* of pretty muslin or other European cotton fabric. Their hair is artfully braided: the main braid or plait starts on the back of the head, then comes around to the front, and ends in a round carnelian bead; they place a small cushion under this braid to hold it up, and attach many other trinkets such as imitation amber and coral, and pieces of carnelian carved to resemble coral. They are also accustomed to rubbing butter on their heads and bodies. Rich women wear much glass-beaded jewelry on their necks and ears; as in Jenné, they wear rings in their noses. Those who are not rich enough wear a piece of red silk instead of a ring. They wear bracelets of silver and bands of silvered iron on their ankles. The anklets are manufactured domestically; instead of being rounded like the arm bands, they are flat and about four inches wide; women engrave pretty designs on them.

Proverb

"Patience is a tree: its roots are bitter, but its fruit is sweet."

During the night, Samory's blanket catches fire and one of his legs is seriously burned.

He bandages it with leaves and they set back out, the mother helping the son and the son helping the mother, drawing on each other's strength. Struggling along in this way, they arrive in the village of Magnanbalandugu, where Sogané lies down to die.

Her death was as silent as her life had been. Sitting in the doorway of her hut, the villagers, cousins, friends, and relatives heard only her light breathing, which came and went, sometimes rose with a start, then fell, but never turned into moaning; and from time to time, they would hear a deep sigh well up from a man's throat.

At dawn she began to sing and then fell back into silence: she sang the song of young girls going to fetch water, to everyone's surprise, for no one had ever heard her hum that melody.

The next evening, before the sun disappeared behind the hills to go light up the world of the dead, Sogané's voice rose one last time inside the hut and she said these final words, known to all the children of Mandé: "My son, you have been a slave for me for seven years: may the world now be your slave; my son, your blanket burned because of me: may the whole world be your blanket."

These words were pronounced in a surprisingly firm tone. Then she stopped breathing, and her son spent the whole night next to the death bed, forbidding anyone to enter the hut.

He did not come out until dawn of the third day. Those who were present at this event, so well known to the praise singers, said that the man who came out of the hut was not the same man they had seen go in. He was now like a beast of prey, an impassive beast of prey, with that cruel curl at the corner of his mouth that never again would leave the lips of Samory Touré, conqueror of the Mandingo country and one of the greatest statesmen that Africa has ever known: he who would not bow down to the white man.

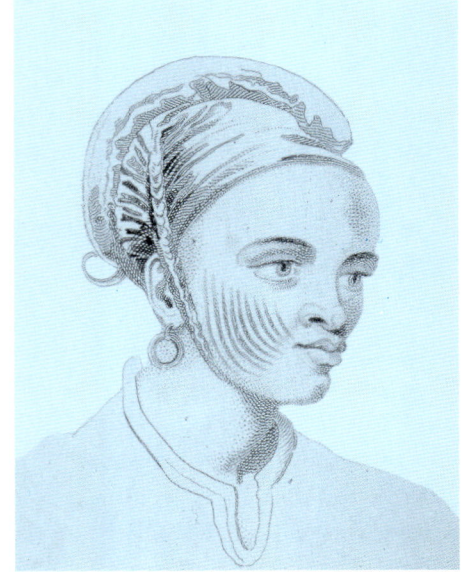

Sacrifice of a Young Girl

The Soninké-Nono, on the advice of the Bozo, moved to the Kanaja Plateau, overcame the marshes they found there, and built a village which they called Jenné. The local spirits demanded that they offer up a young virgin as a sacrifice in order to insure the future prosperity of the new village. So the Bozo of Dioboro brought a little girl to the patriarch of the Mana (who was the chief of the Soninké-Nono), who had her walled in alive within the stockade that was being built near what is now called Kanafa's Gate. Before the young girl drew her last breath, she could be heard through the still-soft clay with which she had been covered, counseling the Soninké always to remember that it was to the Bozo that they owed the prosperity of their city.

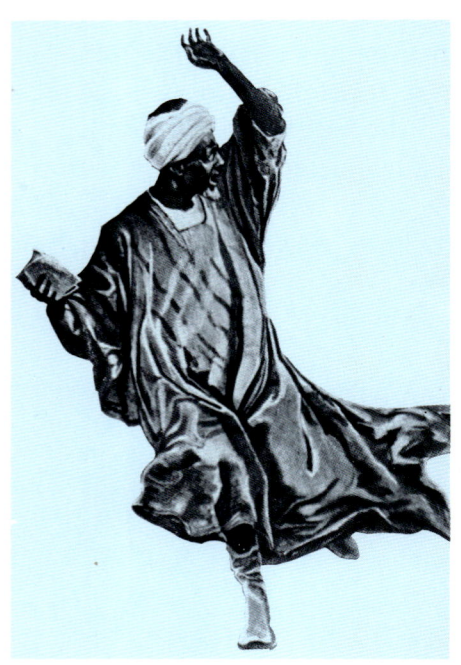

LAST DEPICTION OF SAMORY TOURÉ

WORDS OF AN ORDINARY WOMAN

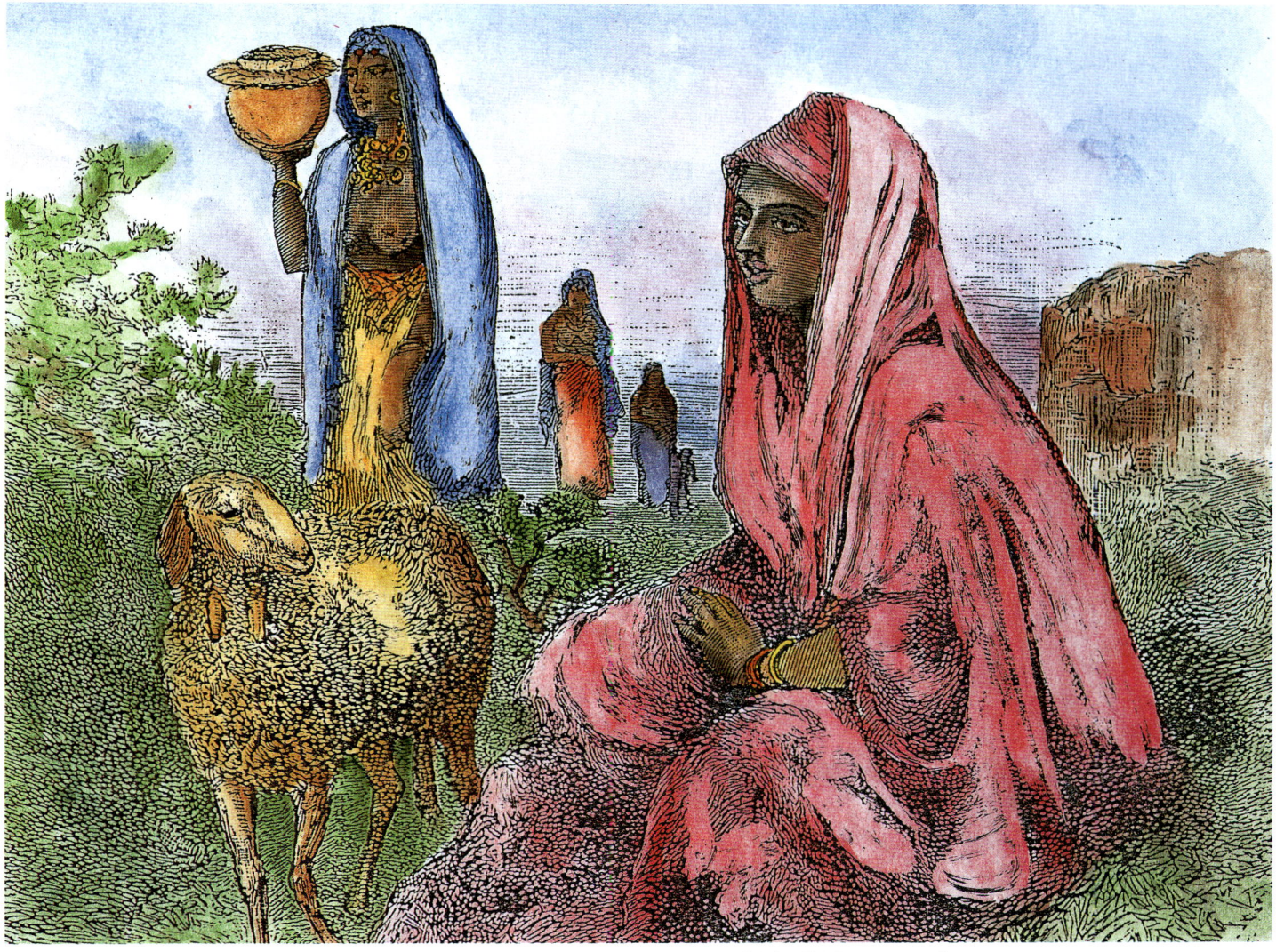

"A TREE ISN'T UPROOTED WITH THE FIRST GUST OF WIND..."

It's not with the first gust of wind that a tree is uprooted. Everything takes time, everything takes endurance.

Being able to endure brings happiness all by itself to all beings blessed with the breath of life. A long life is a gift from God.

A long life brings happiness, because living long means increase, growth.

An old man is a fulfilled man, a happy man. Endurance has shown him everything. He is familiar with everything. He knows everything.

We say that an old man sees everything, even if he has gone blind. He sits, and in his eyes there is only fog. And yet he sees everything, he examines everything. Whereas a young man stands, his eyes focused on the distance, and yet he sees nothing.

The happiness of a long life is the happiness of knowing things. "He who preceded you in sleeping also preceded you in waking." So goes the proverb. The waking in the proverb is knowledge of things. He who was born before you knows more than you. He can always show you something that you don't know.

For all the things that you can know, an old man can tell you where they came from. He knows the past of everything you know about, because he has gone before you, because he saw when you were born, because he ate the meat of the bull killed on your naming day.

An old man, to whom God has granted the sight of his sons and the sons of his sons, is a man overcome with happiness. We say that he has grown northward, like a creeping vine.

In any encampment, an old man will be found in the southern portion. The south is the place for old men. His sons, with their families and flocks, will settle in the north.

An old man who has had a long life and who has fathered many children takes up space and stretches northward. He fills the bush. He grows and stretches everywhere like the calabash vine, full of life.

We say that someone who dies at the peak of his strength has gained nothing. But a man who dies in his old age, surrounded by his children and his flocks, has earned everything. His eye has not seen shame, his enemy has not defeated him.

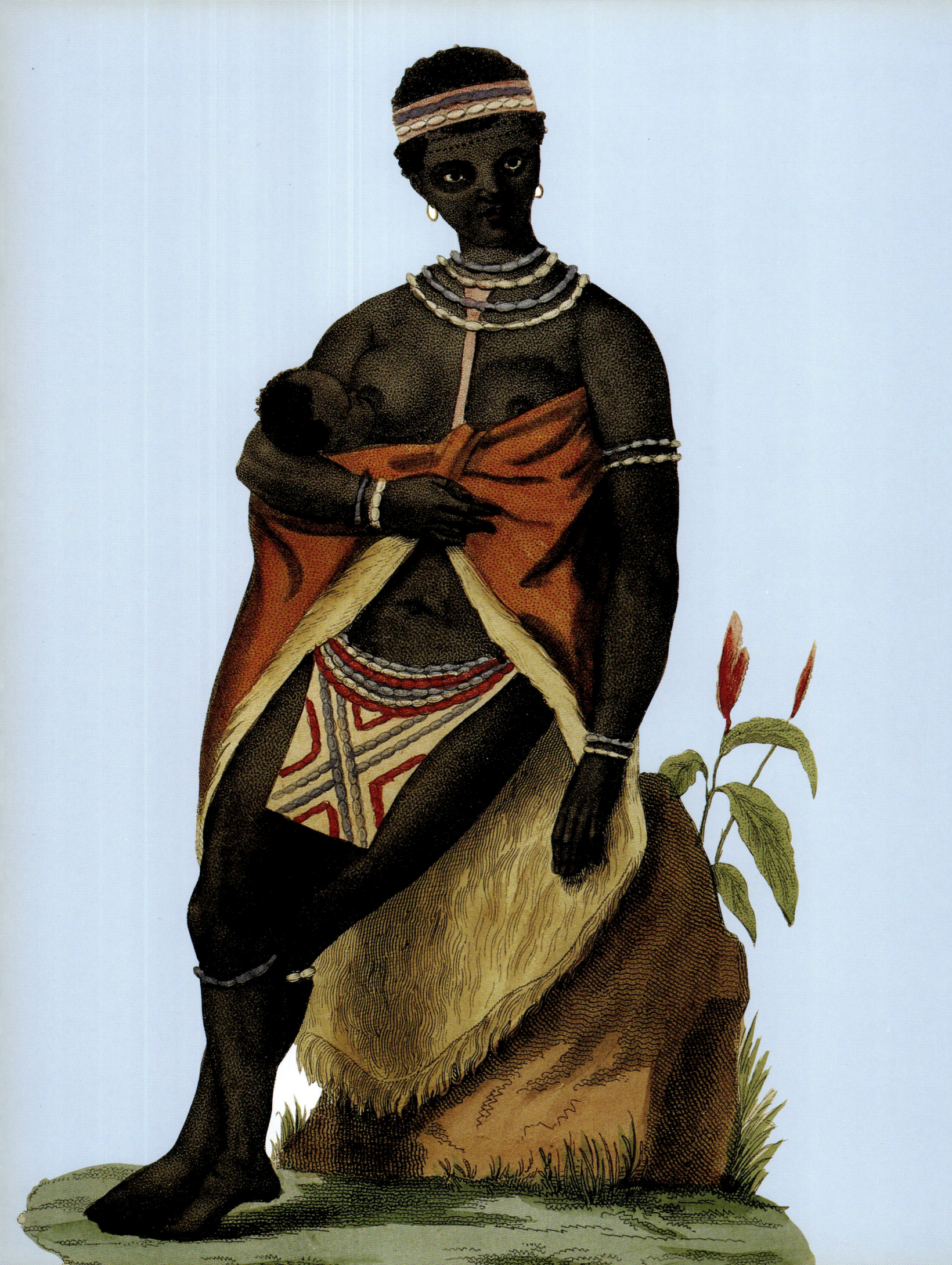

THE STORY OF NANDI

MOTHER OF THE FEARSOME SHAKA

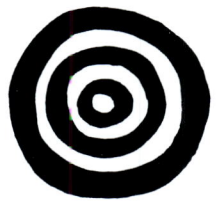

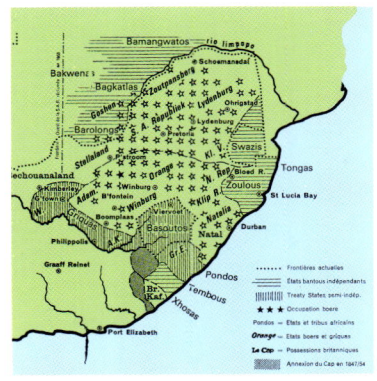

King Senzangakona noticed a young woman who danced better than all the rest: when she leapt in the air with her feet together, it seemed to him that the nape of her neck touched the clouds...

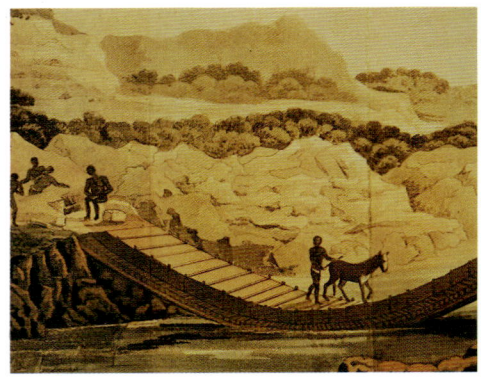

"BORN TO A MODEST CLAN...

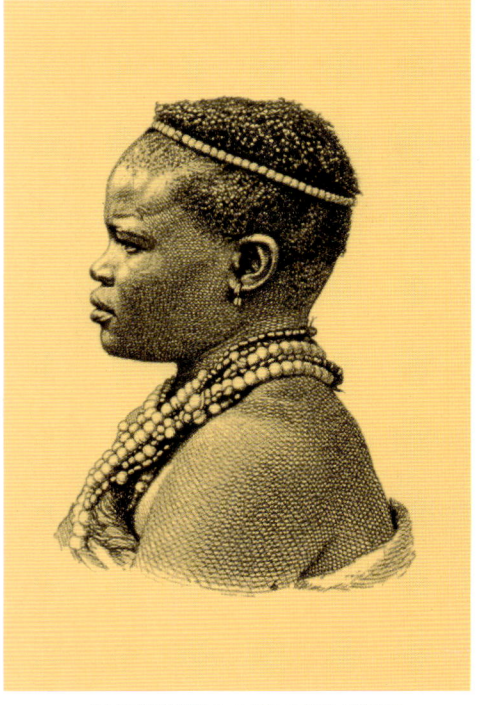

NANDI WAS A SIMPLE GIRL WHO WISHED FOR LOVE: ONE DAY, ON HER WAY TO GO DANCING, SHE MET WITH THE HIGHEST HONOR AND THE GREATEST INDIGNITY. SHE WAS A SIMPLE WOMAN WHO WISHED FOR A SON: SHE GAVE BIRTH TO A LION OF A MAN, WHO gave her the greatest joy a mother can know, and also the greatest pain—Shaka, Shaka Zulu, who shaped an empire and a people with his own hands and who still casts a somber shadow over Africa more than a hundred years after his death.

Nandi was born into the Nguni nation, which then occupied the east coast of the Cape of Good Hope.

At that time, the Europeans were knocking at the gates and famine was already showing its hyena snout in the heart of the kingdom. The population had been in decline for the past several years, and the country was not expanding.

The clan into which Nandi was born was one of the weakest of the weak. It was not a proud clan of warriors or hunters, but a modest clan of artisans who produced wooden vessels and utensils; she was the orphaned daughter of Makedaba, a dignitary of the modest Langeni clan.

...NANDI WAS A SIMPLE GIRL"

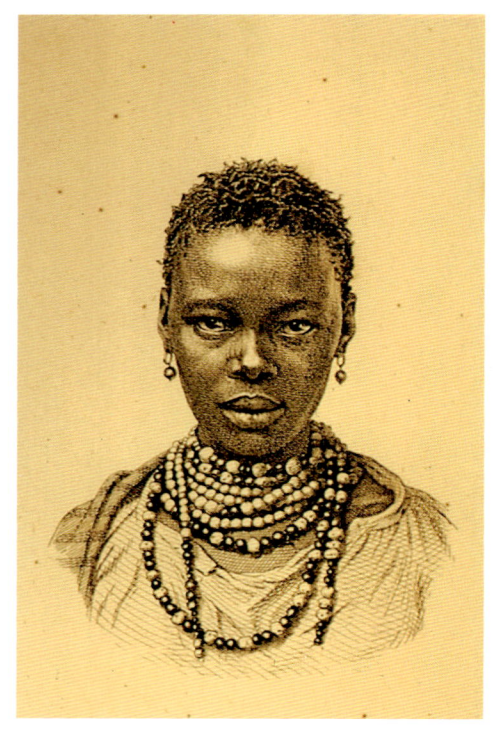

The highest chieftain of the clan was named Senzangakona. He was a father who dreamt every night of a male child, while his three wives gave him only daughters. And he was a young man who dreamt of making "kana" with every beautiful woman on earth, which was forbidden in the Zulu nation under penalty of death.

One day, Senzangakona resolved to find a fourth wife, who might perhaps give him a male child. To this end, he organized a great celebration, complete with dancing. During the dance, he noticed a young girl from the Kubé village who danced the Muchocho better than all the others. She was pudgy, but when she leapt in the air with her feet together, it seemed that the nape of her neck touched the clouds. The prince had forgotten about finding a wife; all he saw was a plump young girl whose head floated in the stars.

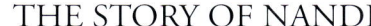

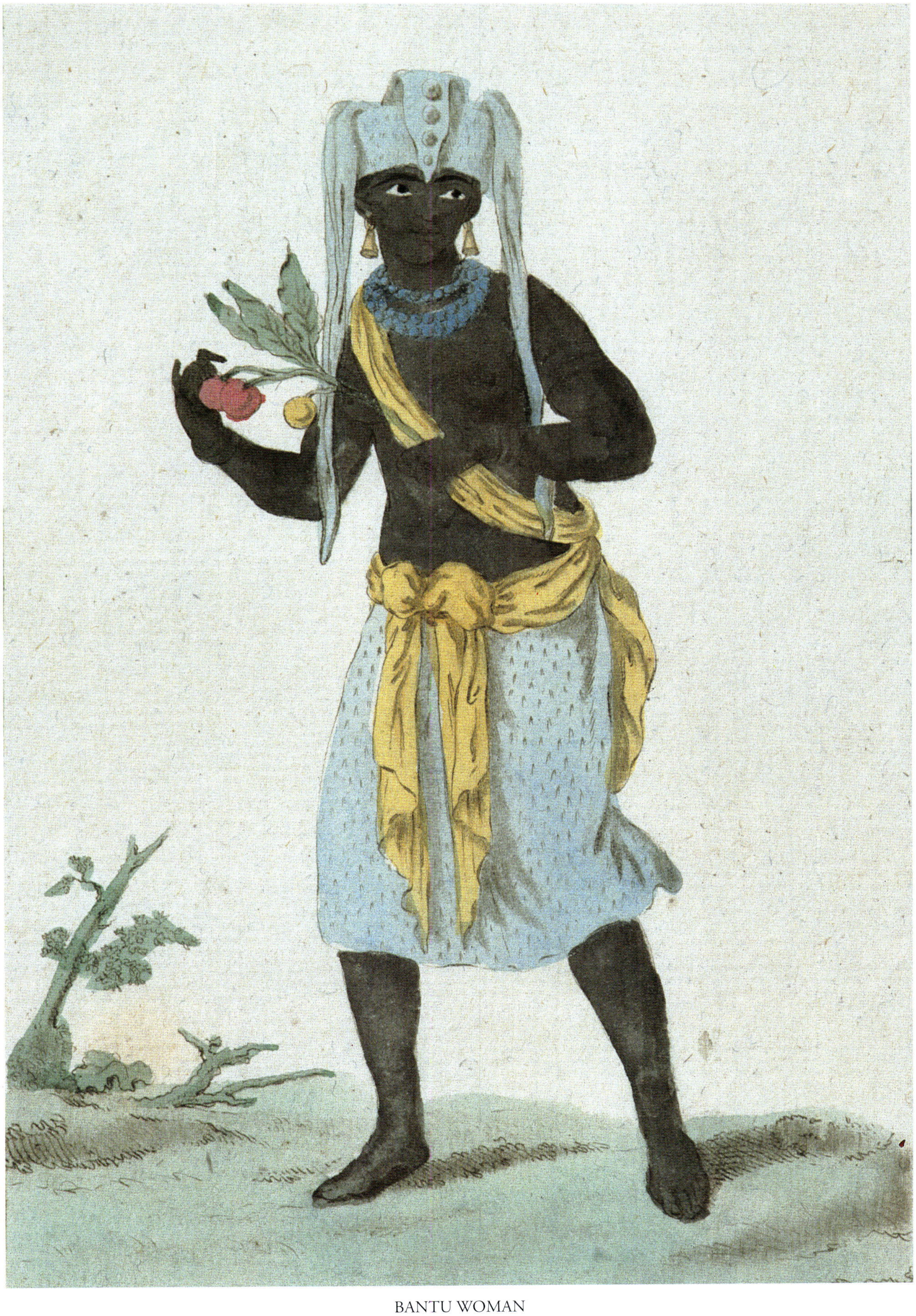

BANTU WOMAN

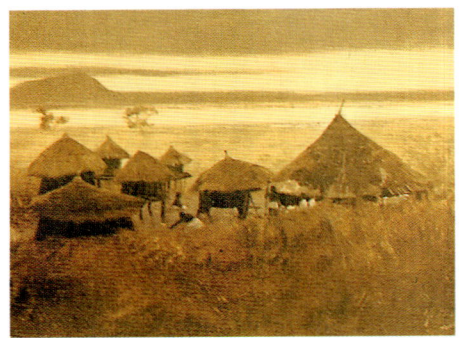

Daily Life in the Village

Near the huts occupied by the patriarchs, the married women, headbands on their foreheads, weeded the fields, brewed the beer, prepared the meals, nursed the babies, fashioned ornaments, molded and fired clay utensils, winnowed and crushed the grain. Near the livestock pastures, the men passed their leisure time talking and drinking; but they also built and repaired the huts, crafted decorations and wooden utensils, and constructed lookout towers to keep an eye on the ripening harvest.

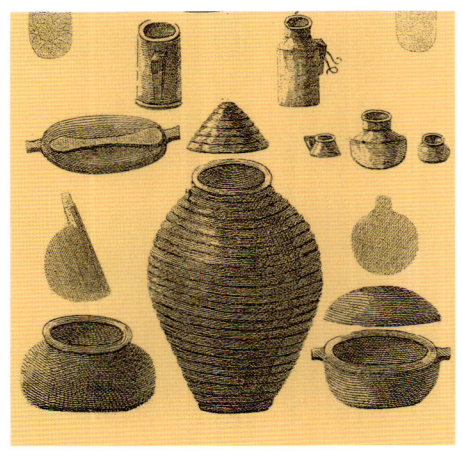

They also watched over the farm animals and the milking of the cows; they attended religious ceremonies and celebrations in the capital and at tribunal gatherings.

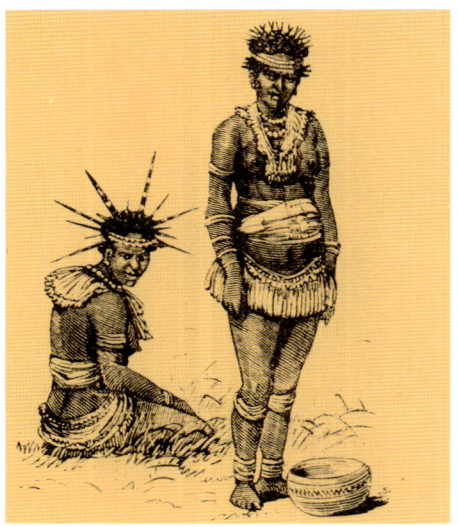

He learned that her name was Nandi. Nandi was aptly named, for this name means "the delicious one" in Zulu.

Senzangakona showered her with compliments and waited for her the next day in the middle of a field, in a deep valley near the village of Kubé. There, he lay with the young woman in the shadow of a tree and, having accomplished the irreparable, went on his merry way.

In the Zulu nation, dishonor exacted death upon the man as well as the girl he seduced, not to mention all her female companions in the common hut; thus, the women who saw Nandi come back that day fell silent in fear.

Soon Nandi realized that her month had passed, and she told Senzangakona, who married her in all haste, so that no one would notice her state. Some time later, a messenger came to Senzangakona and spoke to him in these terms: "A son has been born to you, a bull destined for the vultures." This last phrase meant, in the ancient tongue of the Zulus, a warrior who would perish in combat and become prey for the vultures.

When the child reached his second month, Nandi took him to his father, who gave him the name Shaka. But she returned home the same day, her child in her arms, for fear that Senzangakona's wives would kill the baby; she ran so fast, holding the child to her breast, that the wind undressed her without her knowing, and suddenly she was naked.

But the tyranny of the ladies of the court hounded Nandi all the way to her village; little by little, since they eventually came to have sons of their own, they asked the king to disinherit the eldest, whose mother's blood was not noble enough. They added: "If you refuse to understand, we will publicize your relations with Nandi, and we will take the affair to the Great Council of all the Zulus." So Senzangakona declared: "Shaka will have no share in my succession and the heir will be Mfo Nkazana; as for Nandi, she may never set foot here again."

News is not bread, and no one wants to keep it for himself: already the rumor that had started in the court filled all the huts of the village, arousing great animosity toward Nandi and her son.

Then, in response to some of the more insidious rumors started by the king's wives, people began to whisper that it would be a good and righteous deed to kill Shaka, the child of sin: and that is when the time of persecution began for him.

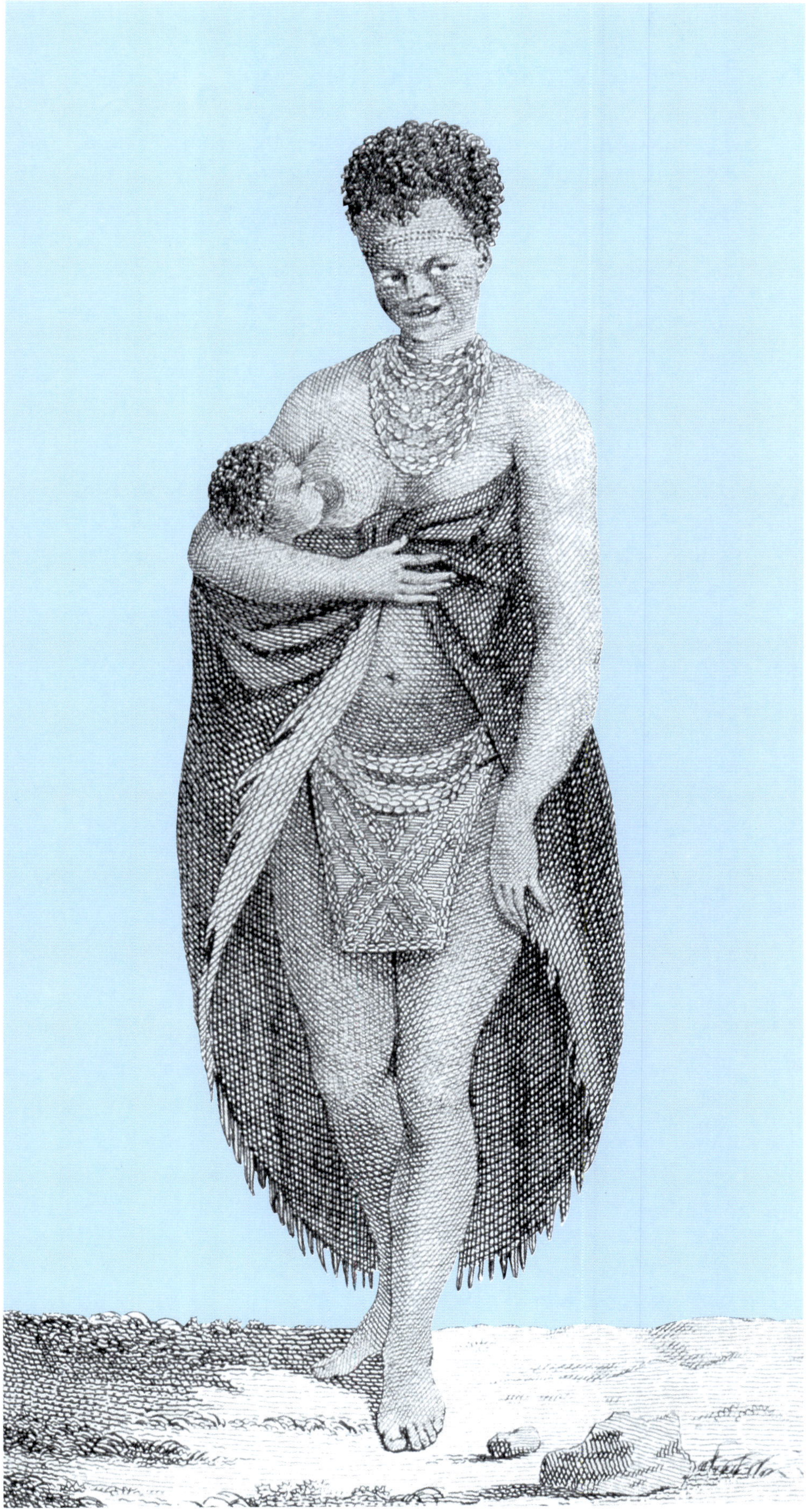

THE STORY OF NANDI

BANTU WOMAN

The Amazulus

The Zulus are a beautiful black race, taller than the Tswanas in height. Their shape is muscular and elegant.

A Mosotho told me: "Seeing those men so strong and well made, completely naked, with their fierce and cruel eyes, armed with a short, wide assegai, the *mokondo*, and a shield of buffalo or cattle skin twice as large as ours, we were all overcome with fear and called them Matébélés (those who disappear behind their great shields), whereas they call themselves Amazulus, the heavenly ones."

The Tswanas also call them Lifakani, which means those who chop or carve the enemy into pieces with a *chaké,* their formidable war hatchet.

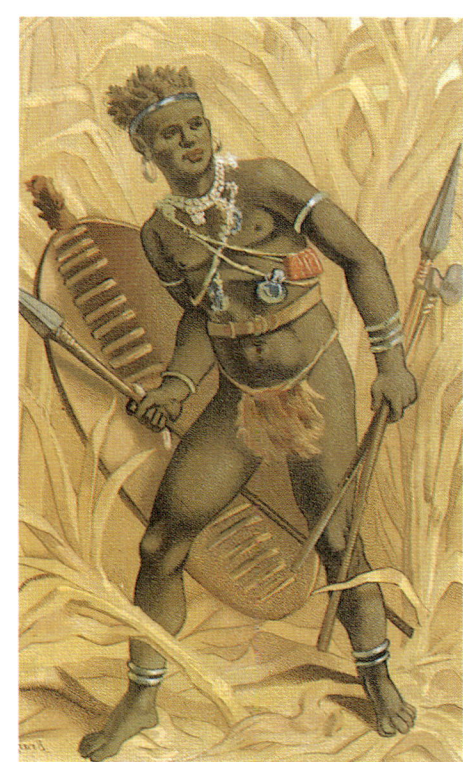

Song of Celebration

Princess "Poorly Loved."
See the feast of dance,
Bright as a wreath.
In the morning sun, pretty as
The chieftain's speckled horse.
Take it easy:
Dance is not about haste.
The dancing must last till dawn.
Great and beautiful from the back,
The chief of the women stands proud.
The celebration is in full swing.

Proverbs

"Death is not a room where you can go in and out."
"A burning heart makes no smoke."

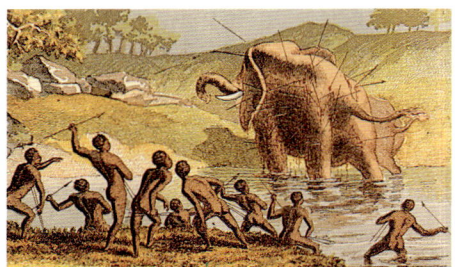

The Elephant Hunt

A female was standing and fanning herself with her great ears, while her calf rolled in the mud. The hunters arrived in a long line.
The excellent beast did not suspect the enemy's approach and nursed her little one, who might have been two years old. Suddenly her enemy's whistles sounded; some whistled through tubes, others through both hands pressed together, and all cried out to get the animal's attention:

> O chief! we have come
> to kill you;
> Oh chief! and not only you,
> many of your kind will die;
> The gods have decreed it.

The elephants pricked up their ears and came out of the ditch at the same instant as their assailants rushed toward them.
The mother placed herself between the threat and her offspring, caressing his back over and over again with her trunk to reassure him. Moving away, she watched her enemies all the while, as if she were torn between the need to protect her son and the urge to reprimand her tormentors. They were about a hundred strides behind her until the point at which she was forced to cross a stream. The time she took crossing it and climbing back up the other side allowed the hunters to gain ground; they threw their javelins at her. Red with blood flowing from her wounds, the mother fled. The elephant calf moved as fast as he could; nonetheless, elephants, young or old, cannot gallop: a very rapid walk is their fastest gait. He sought refuge in the water, where the hunters finished him off. The mother's pace gradually slowed down; then, turning around, trumpeting with rage, she rushed at the hunters, who scattered left and right. Four times, she repeated this furious charge; then finally, turning in a circle, she stumbled, fell to her knees, and died.

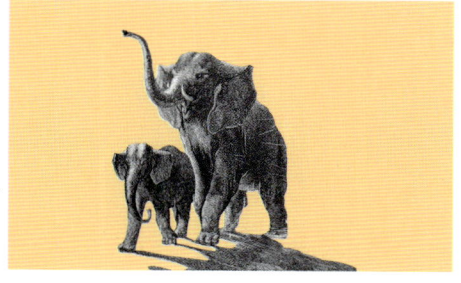

As soon as he was old enough to tend the calves in some far-off pasture, the other boys waited for him along the path and beat him senseless. After that Nandi gave him chores closer to the village, begging him to call her if the boys tried to beat him up again. He watched over the fields, shooing away the birds that pilfered grain. But he would not make the slightest cry when the boys beat him until he bled and lost consciousness.

Two or three times, Shaka asked them why they wanted him dead; they just sneered and laughed. He asked his mother the same question, but she remained silent.

Nandi had cried every day and every night since her return to the village. But one fine morning, as she awoke, her cheeks covered with tears, she dried them with the corner of her dress and said: "Today, I will not weep." Then she went to Shaka and held out to him a stick covered with knots, saying in a strange voice:

"My son, hit whoever hits you, hit anyone who so much as looks at you."

The child gazed at her a long time in silence and took the stick from her hands.

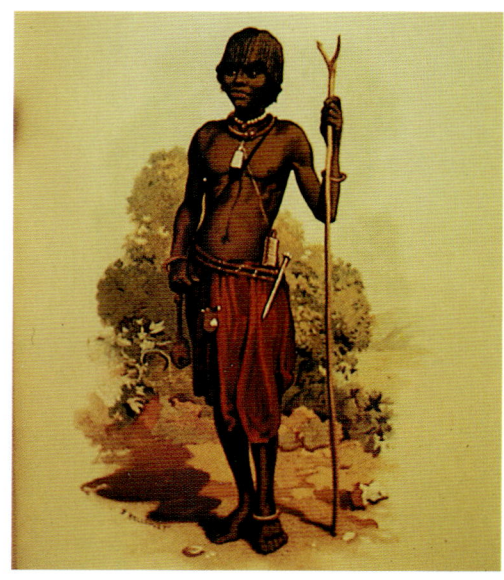

From that moment on, he was as if possessed, plagued by a constant itch. He had never picked fights with anyone: now it seemed he wanted to wage war against the whole world. Wielding the club was his joy, and his greatest delight was to hear the plaintive cries of his enemies. It seemed the blows were weighted with a secret virtue, which multiplied their force, while the blows of his rivals seemed weakened by the time they reached his flesh, "as if they had really been dealt with a corn husk."

Soon, the shepherds let him come and go as he pleased and gave him the right of way at the watering hole; he had become their leader, the Manpoli.

Every morning before leaving, Nandi held out the club to Shaka and gazed at him; and every evening when he came back, she read the child's day on his face and lowered her eyes in approval.

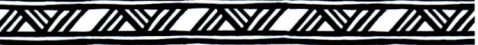

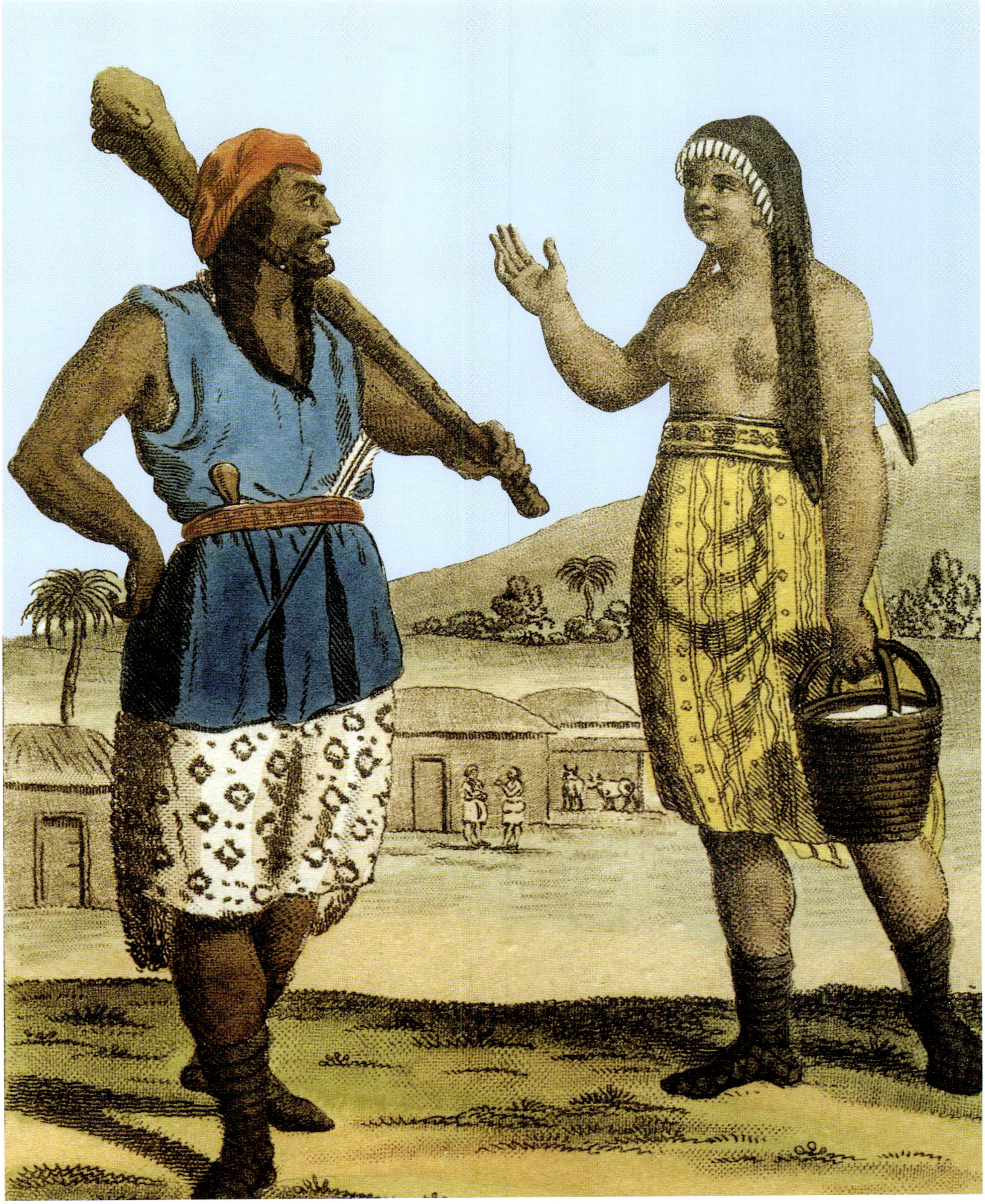

INHABITANTS OF BAHAHARA

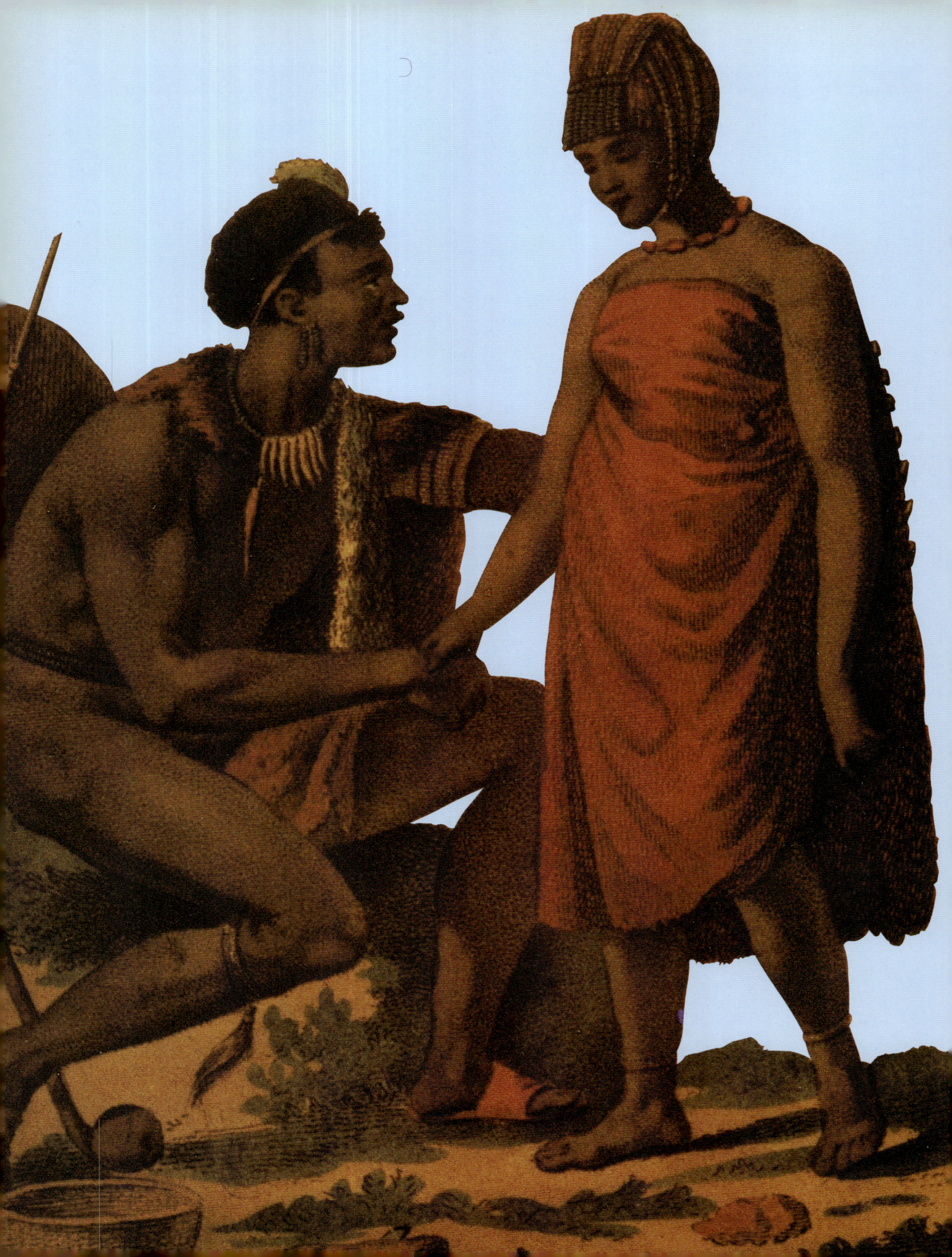

THE STORY OF NANDI

The things that happened to Shaka during his youth have been told many times by the praise singers.

Yes: the famous lance throw with which the skinny adolescent boy felled a lion; and the way he got the better of the giant hyena that had been terrorizing the whole Kubé region—all that has been reported many times by praise singers old and new, by Thomas Mofolo and Ibrahima Baba Kaké.

But just as the watchfulness of the ancestors coaxes the harvest, in the same way the great deeds of the young man were contained in the gaze his mother directed on him every morning as she handed him his shepherd's crook.

It was Nandi's gaze that gave Shaka's arm its power.

That is what infused him with the taste for glory.

And that is also what gave him the courage to return when his father Senzangakona died, to win back his inheritance by force; thus the unloved, illegitimate child now commanded his whole clan. His vengeance was complete.

And Nandi's gaze pushed him higher, ever higher, as if to distance him even further from his former humiliation; each triumph fed into new triumphs. The chief of the clan had become the king of all the Nguni, and as an indication of his power, he decided that with him commenced a new people, for whom he would be like a god; and he called these people the Amazulu, which means in the ancient tongue "those who live in the sky."

But Nandi's gaze had not followed him that far. She had been satisfied calling him king: it was Shaka who wanted to make himself a god.

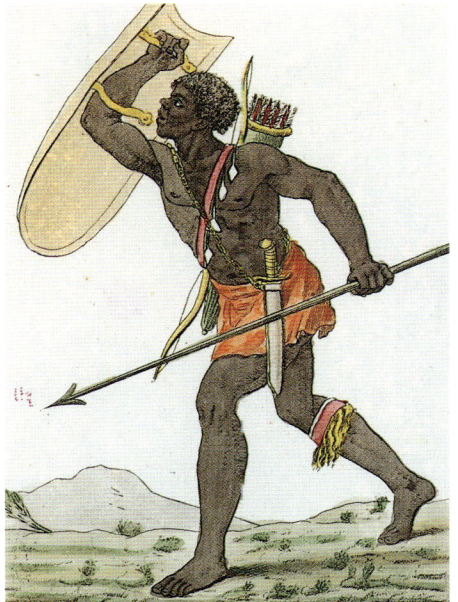

Shaka's Kraal

Workers had planted a circle of flexible poles in the ground and curved them in toward the center, making the skeleton of a dome. These frameworks were placed at regular intervals in a great circle, and agile hands had woven supple stems solidly attached to the poles. Successive layers of lime covered everything. The huts of the royal *kraal*, or Bantu village, in the hollow of the valley, were like the beads of a great necklace, with a winding barrier in the center sheltering the home of the new chief.

The Names of the Regiments

The regimental names all have various, more or less striking, meanings. For example, Omobapankué means "panther trapper." About twenty years earlier, a panther had devoured one of the king's young shepherds, and a detachment was sent out against it. The regiment that had made the capture was called "panther trapper." Its soldiers mimic the roar and utter ferocity of the animal whose name their regiment has the honor to bear. Its leaders wear nothing but mantles of panther or leopard skin.

The Precariousness of Life

It is a fact that the Zulu emperors do not value men. The subject shouts respectfully to his master, "Zii, our father!" and the latter responds coldly "I saw you."
There is no tomorrow for the Zulu! This is the proverb he quotes in response to anyone who promises him something: "Give me today, for tomorrow I may be killed."

Proverb

"There is no roof without smoke, no man without sadness."

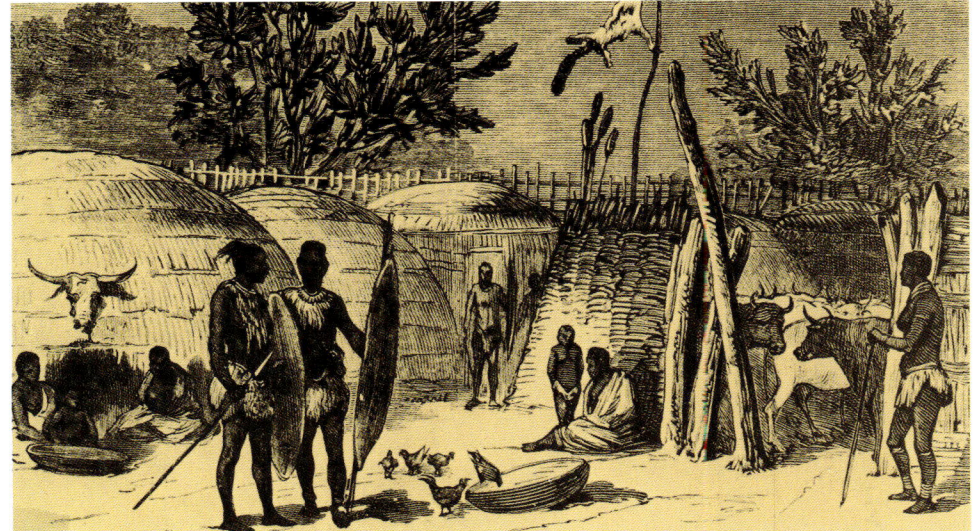

SHAKA'S KRAAL

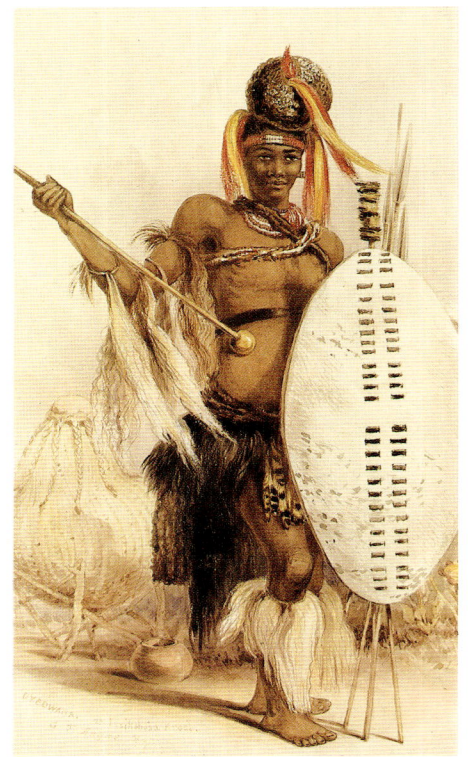

Shaka's Warriors

One morning, three regiments of young men arrived to pass review. There were nearly six thousand of them, all with black shields. The respective regiments were distinguishable by the style and ornamentation of their hair. One regiment's style resembled a Malay coiffure with a six-inch point and a bouquet of feathers on top. Another wore an otter turban, with a crane feather or two on either side; the third wore little bunches of feathers all over the head, tightly attached.

They went through the gate, ran through the kraal, stopped in front of the palace, and saluted the king. A boy stepped out of rank and made a long speech. When the orator had concluded, all his comrades, after an acclamation, began a race, each striving to outdo the other in prowess and agility, paying no attention to order, rhythm, or discipline. After this demonstration, which lasted three hours, a regiment of men arrived with white shields marked in the center with one or two black spots. The men saluted Shaka, went to set down their shields, and assembled as one group to dance. They formed a semicircle, the men in the center and the youths at both ends. The king took his place in the center and about fifteen hundred young girls stood opposite the three male formations in a perfectly straight line. His majesty then began to dance and the warriors followed, while the young women kept time by singing, clapping their hands, and rising up on their tiptoes.

From that moment on, Nandi was a stranger to her son's destiny: she followed him from one end to the other of the new empire, without praising or criticizing him, having hardly any more influence on him than a bird flying off into the sky. Shaka carved people up the way a woodcutter squares planks. There were no more Sothos or Ngunis, Basothos or Tswanas; all the conquered peoples had to give up their names and their native tongues to become Amazulus: Sky dwellers.

They all wore the same uniform: a headband of feathers, monkey or wildcat skins around the waist, bracelets on the arms and legs, and long-bladed, short-hafted stabbing lances for hand-to-hand combat, for slaughter.

The first time he introduced these lances, the Buffalo and Hatchet regiments used them like assegais, throwing them at the enemy from afar. Shaka made an announcement in front of the whole army that it was as if these two regiments had retreated from the enemy: his words caused a sudden silence, for in Shaka's armies any soldier who retreated so much as an inch was executed. Then Nandi came to throw herself at her son's feet:

"Master, deign to hear me out! Oh Zulu, pull in your claws and moderate your anger; these men have understood the seriousness of their mistake and will not do it again. Let them live!"

Nandi was still on the ground, eating the dust at her son's feet. Then Shaka declared in a loud voice, for all the regiments to hear, from one end of the plain to the other:

"For the love of my mother, and only because she is my mother, I will allow the Buffalo and Hatchet regiments to live; but from now on, the lance must never leave the hand of the Zulu warrior."

Then, turning to his mother:

"As for you, get away from here and go home, now that you have gotten what you asked for; and never interfere in my affairs again."

From that day on, Nandi no longer dared bend Shaka's course as it was traced in the sky: except in one case, and one case only.

The discipline in Shaka's armies was inflexible: his soldiers were not allowed to marry and were not even allowed to have sexual relations, upon pain of death. All their energy was to be directed toward combat, and all their earthly attachments to the king.

Only Shaka had the right to visit the young women of his people; but all the children they gave him were killed the day they were born, for he wanted nothing to soften his soldier's heart.

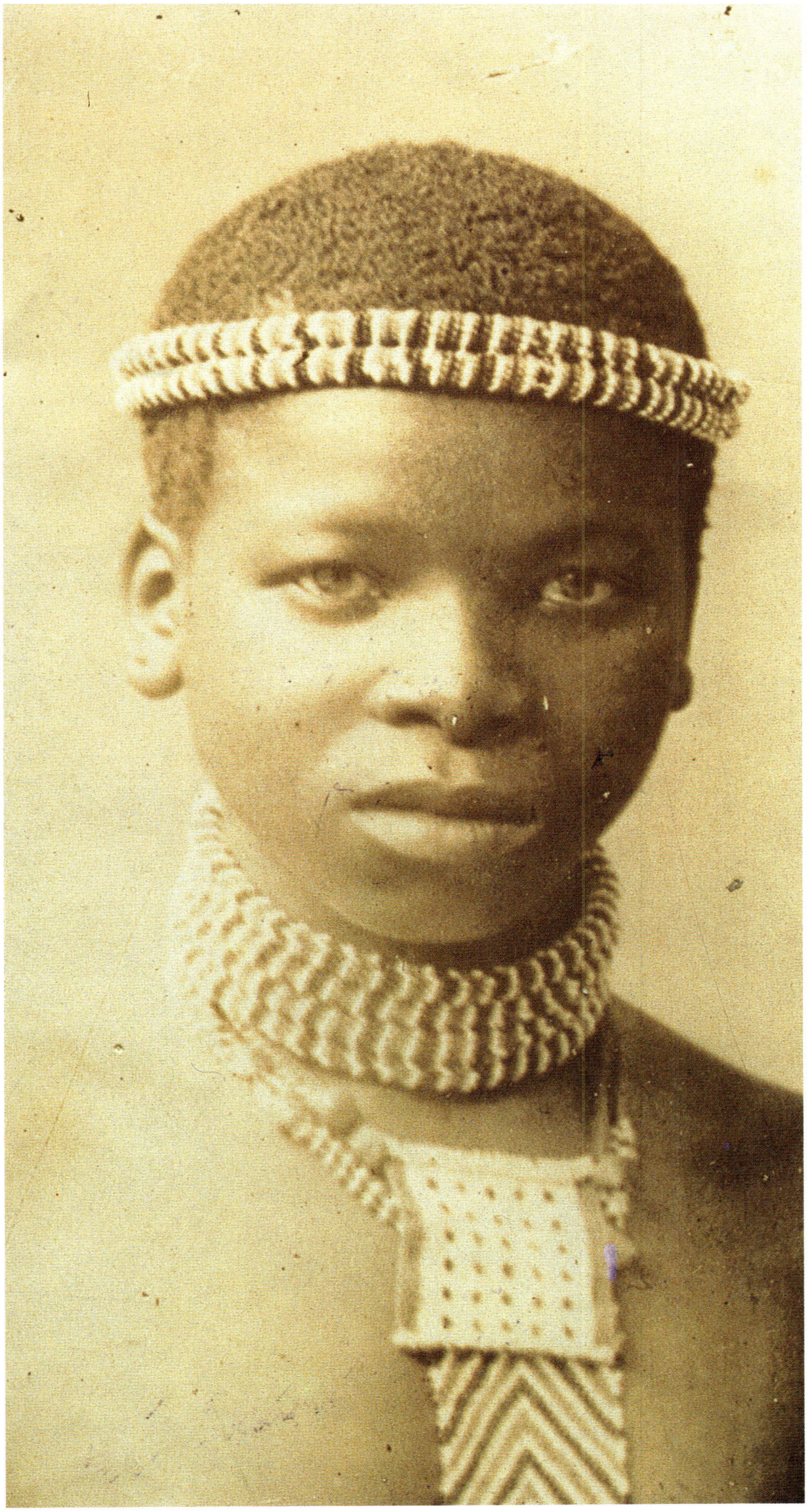

THE STORY OF NANDI

"ONLY SHAKA HAD THE RIGHT TO VISIT THE YOUNG WOMEN OF HIS PEOPLE"

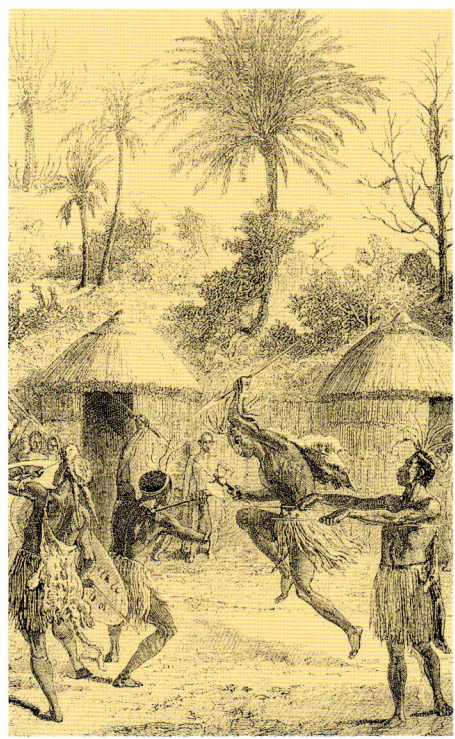

Shaka, the Military Genius

The Mfecane, the Crushing, the time of the great migrations, brought war and destruction, famine, sickness, and death. As eyewitnesses recalled years afterward, "the assegai killed people, but hunger killed the earth."

Nonetheless, the Mfecane was not merely a horrible time of murder, pillaging, and destruction, for this maelstrom also gave birth to new peoples and nations. The demography of southern, central, and eastern Africa, as well as its political and social configuration, were profoundly altered. The invaders challenged anyone they failed to crush, offering them the example of a new form of military and social organization.

Besides being a military genius, Shaka was actually a social revolutionary who made a multi-tribal nation out of the disparate chiefdoms of Nguniland, a nation that outlasted the military power on which its greatness had been founded and which has preserved its identity up to the present day.

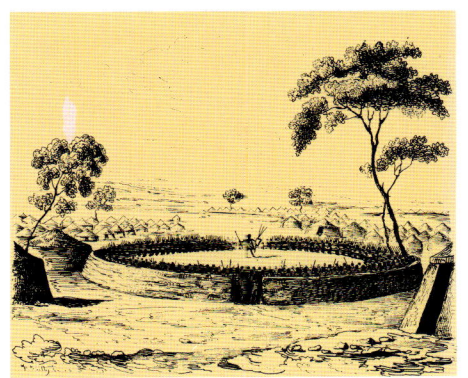

Nandi suffered in silence as she watched her grandchildren perish. She had repeatedly encouraged her son to take a wife, so that he would leave behind heirs to his name. But seeing him always with his tyrant's head in the clouds, she took under her wing one of the women he had gotten pregnant and placed her far from her son's eyes, until the child was born. For a long time, she kept this child out of Shaka's sight; but she could not hold out any longer and sent for him, so that she might behold her own son.

One day, Shaka burst into her home while she was quietly playing with the child. He said to his mother: "Put that child in the middle of the courtyard." Then, once the child was placed there, Shaka drew near and bent over the little being, so that his shadow fell over him; and when the king's shadow covered the child, the little one died.

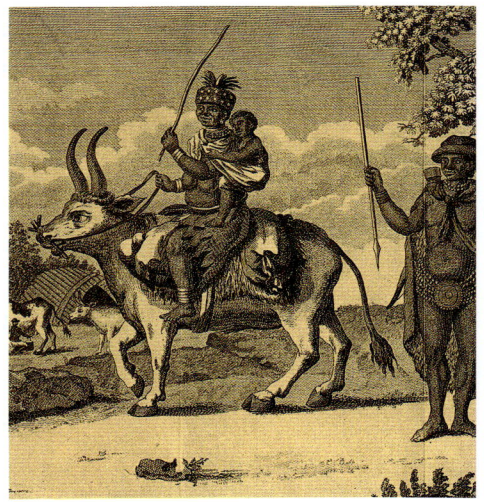

Nandi silently went back inside; her heart was swelling in her chest like a broken bird trying to open its wings. She could see Shaka as a child, beaten senseless by the other boys; then she relived the moment when she had handed him the stick and said: "Hit those who hit you and even those who so much as look at you." Suddenly the light of day hurt, and she lay down, pulling the blanket over her eyes; the bird in her chest opened its wings, a drop of blood formed at the corner of her mouth: she was dead.

Shaka stood at the foot of the death bed and remained silent for a full hour.

He wanted to justify himself to his mother, tell her the secret reasons of his vast enterprise: the growing presence of white men on the Cape, and the need to meet them with a powerful state that would stop their momentum.

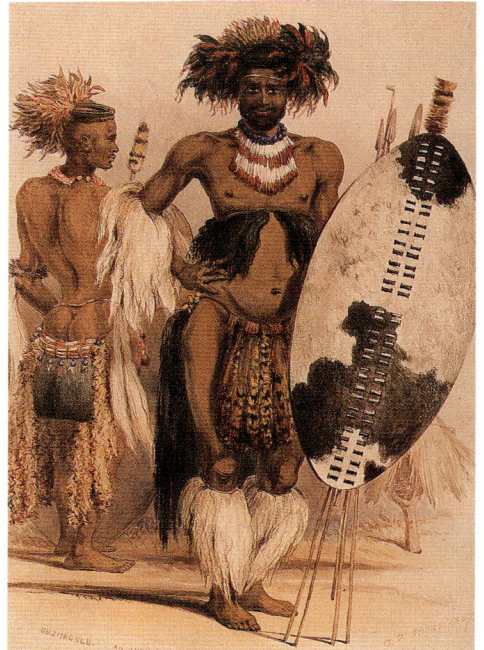

Shaka thought too of his enemies, those in his own camp who strove to bring him down and would one day succeed. And in his mind he said to them: "You will not take my place, for Umulungu, the white man, is on the move; he is the one who will dominate you, and you will become his subjects." After an hour of contemplation, great tears came to Shaka's eyes and he let out a shout.

And those around him, and then those who were outside the tent, and then those who heard them in the camp, all let out the same shout; the cry of mourning went from person to person throughout all of Zulu country. Men and women threw down their ornaments and gathered around Shaka, who was soon surrounded by a circle of sixty thousand people, all wailing the same desolate cry.

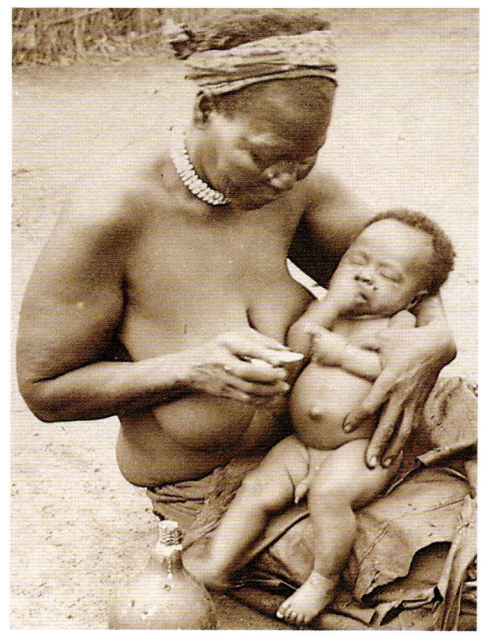

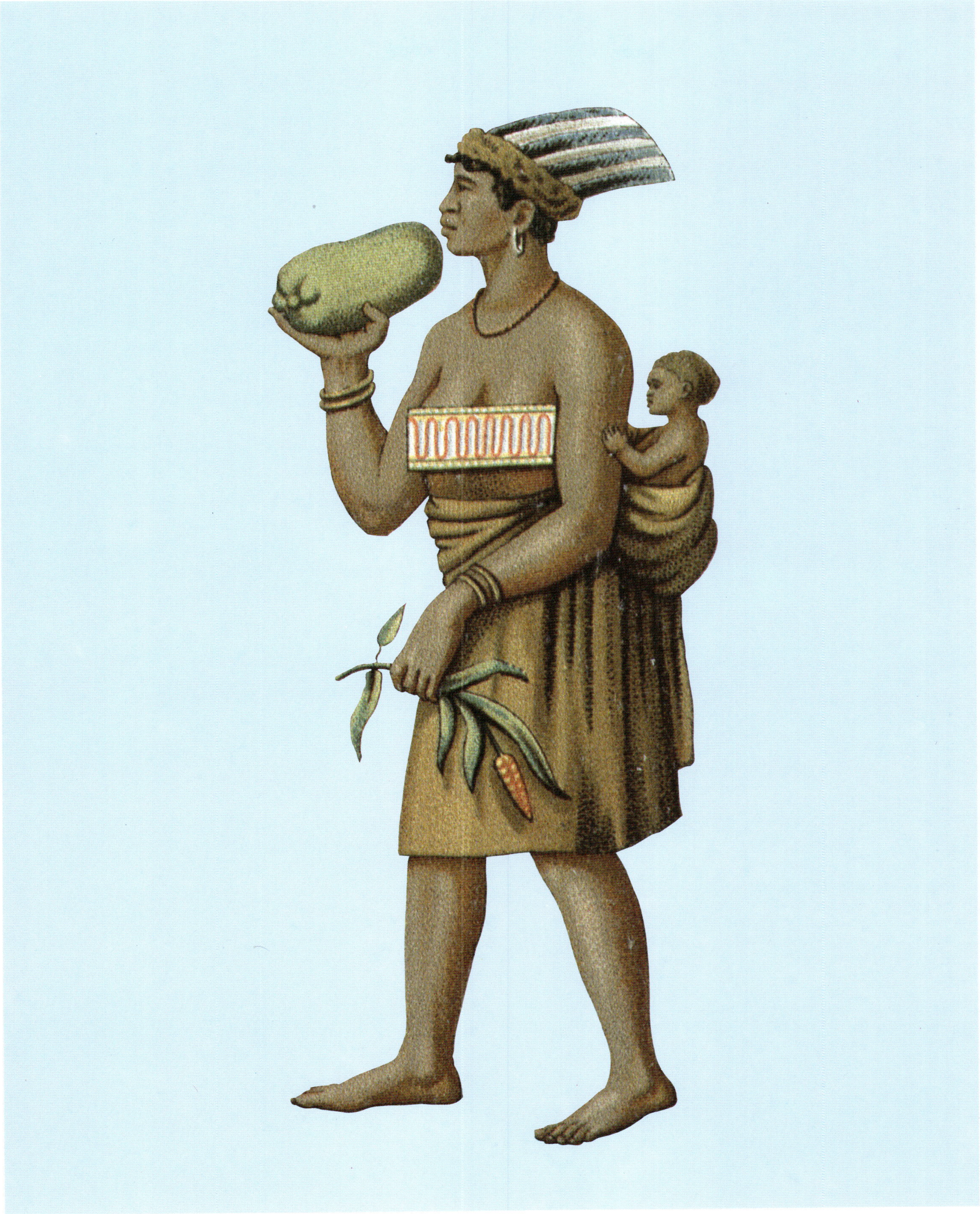

THE STORY OF NANDI

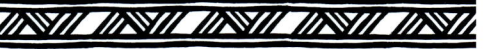

"SHAKA WANTED NOTHING TO SOFTEN HIS SOLDIER'S HEART"

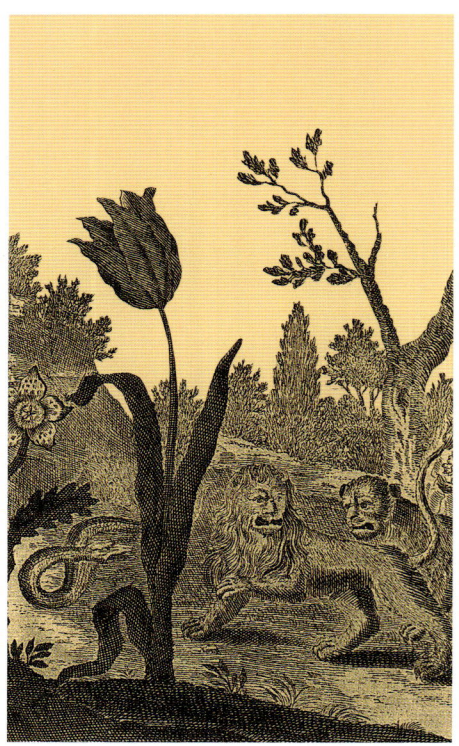

Shaka's Assassination

Shaka had a dream that he was dead and that Mbopa served another king. When he woke, he told his dream to one of his sisters, who within the hour reported it to Mbopa. Knowing that this did not leave him many hours to live, he urged conspirators to seize the first opportunity to assassinate the king; and the opportunity presented itself very quickly.

Some Bantus had arrived from far-off lands, bringing crane feathers that the king had sent them to fetch; Shaka displayed his unhappiness at their lengthy absence. Shaka asked them in a harsh tone of voice what could have taken so long in getting the feathers. Mbopa threw himself on one of them with a stick in his hand, demanding that they explain why they had taken so long to carry out royal orders, and struck them. Aware that their lives were in danger, and supposing that Mbopa had received a secret signal, as usually happened when an execution was ordered, they all fled.

Mhlangana and Dingane had hidden behind a small barrier, very close to Shaka, each hiding an assegai under his cloak. Seeing the people flee and the king alone, the first stabbed him in the back at his left shoulder. Dingane came up and struck him as well. Shaka had only time to ask, "What is the matter, children of my father?" But the three men struck him with so many quick blows that he expired after running a few yards past the kraal gate. The few people in the kraal and its surroundings fled into the brush, thinking that "the sky was going to meet the earth."

The next day, Shaka ordered the nation to mourn for a full year. No crops were planted, nor could milk—the staple of the Zulu diet—be used.

During this time, it was forbidden for women to lie with their husbands. Any woman who became pregnant was killed for having neglected the mourning period, as were thousands of milk cows, so that even the calves might know what it was to lose a mother.

Shaka did not know how to adequately express his pain: he proclaimed law after law and enacted ever more extravagant measures. For example, he posted men along the roads to watch over the people passing by and to kill all those who walked with a carefree step, or simply those who were not weeping.

The sun's gaiety offended him.

It was whispered that he wanted to paint the sky and the earth the colors of his mourning.

Shaka did so much and did it so well that he did too much, even for a demigod.

In the spring of 1828, he was stabbed to death by Senzangakona's sons, with the complicity of the commander of his armies, Mbopa.

And so Shaka died at the height of his power, because of the death of his mother Nandi; so passed the man who had been taken for a demigod, a Baïété who reigns between heaven and earth; so vanished the illegitimate son, the keeper of calves, the young lion-killer, the general to whom his troops addressed this greeting every day:

Baïété, oh father! Lord of Lords!
Oh great lion, oh elephant to whom no one can answer.
Baïété, Lord of Heaven!
The shadowy one, born to govern with clemency,
You who possess the power of an elephant,
You who devour men,
You with lion claws,
You whose grandeur reaches to the sky,
To the sky over our heads,
Oh Zulu, oh heavenly one, lead us with clemency,
Baïété, lord! Baïété, Baïété, oh father!
Baïété, heavenly one!

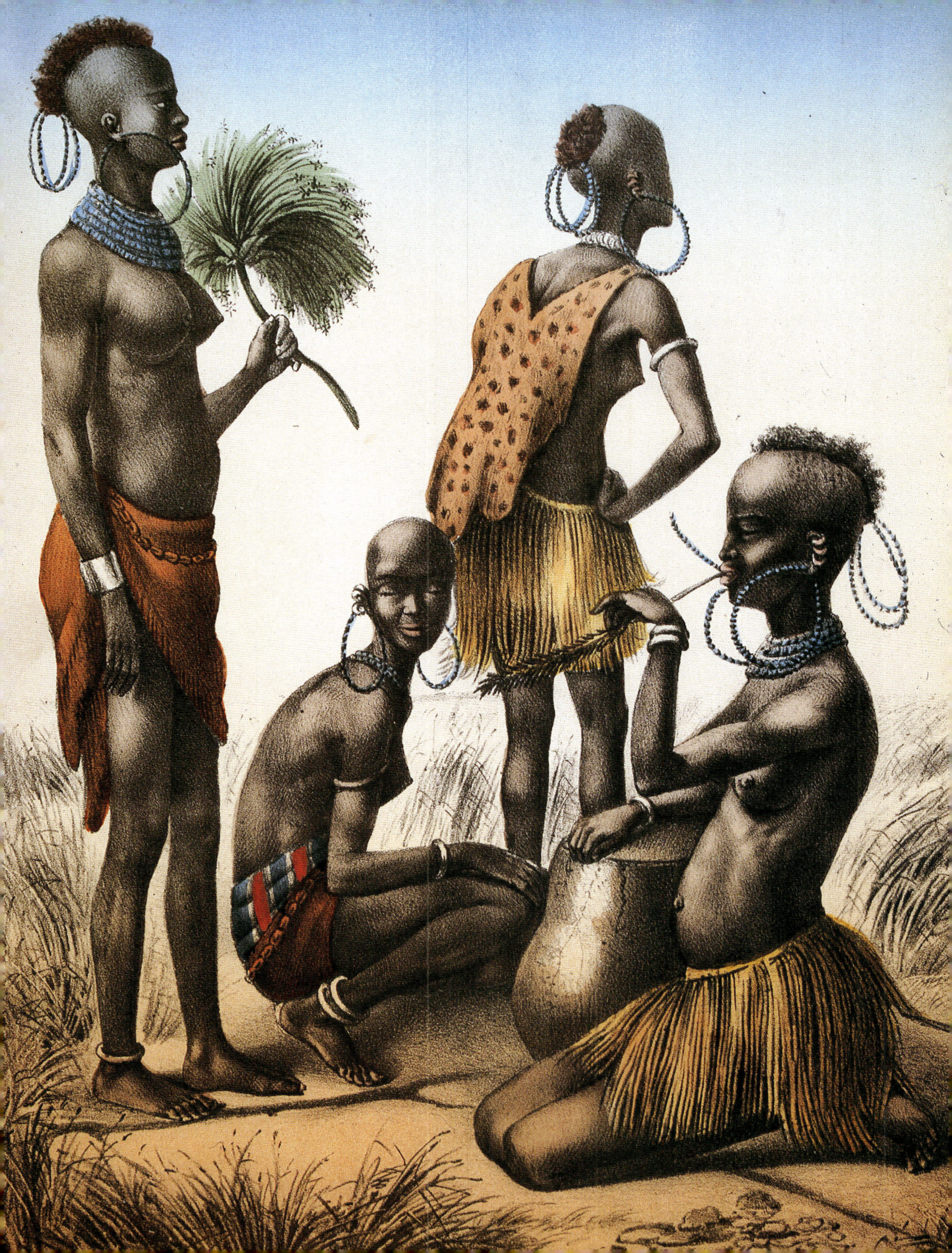

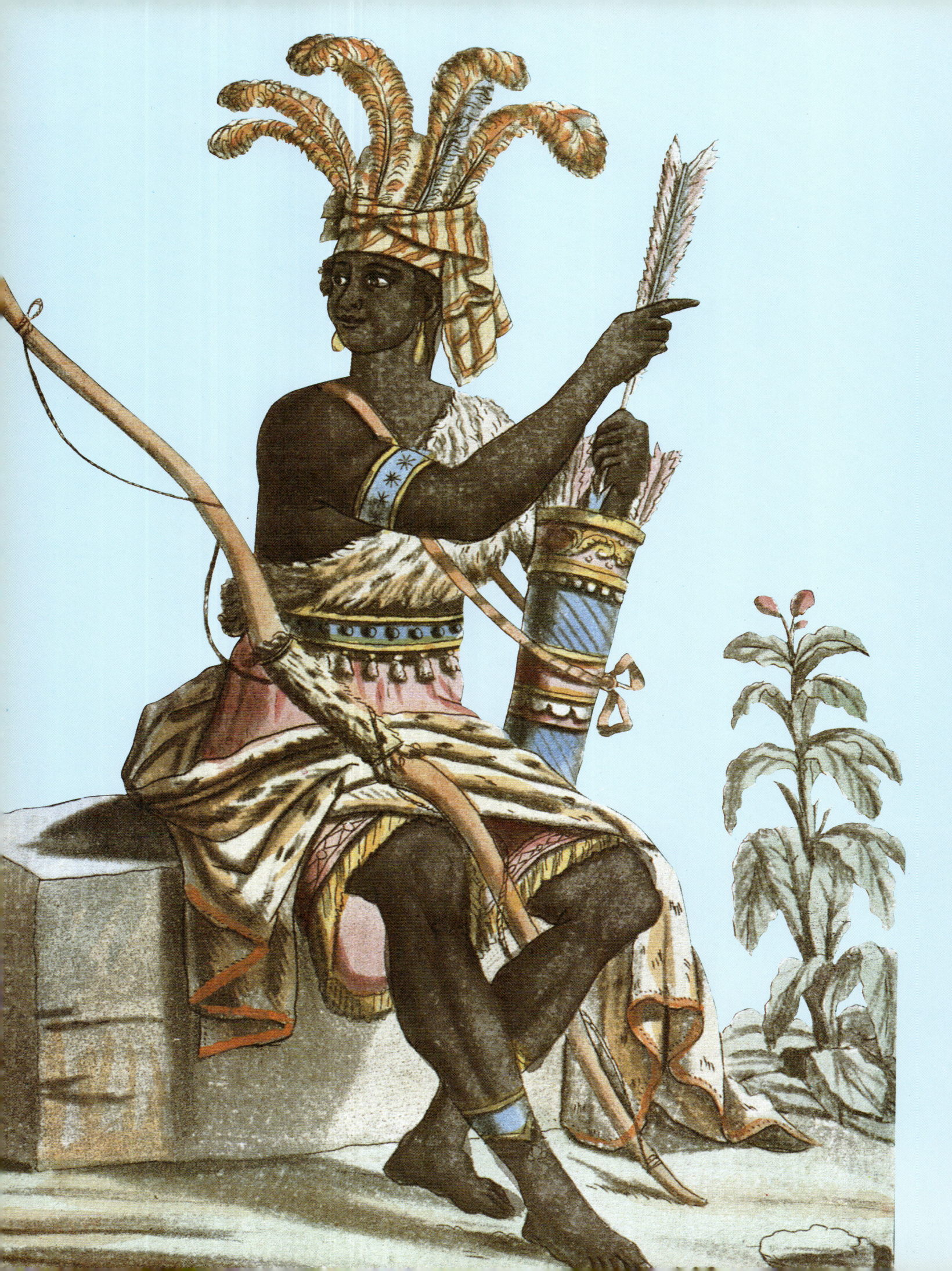

TATA AJACHÉ

THE SLAVE WHO BECAME QUEEN

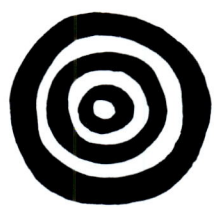

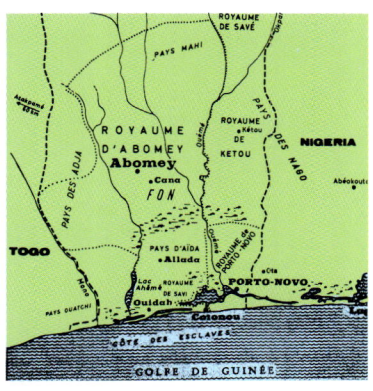

Lionesses are more fearsome than lions because they have their little ones to defend, and we amazons have our king to defend...

SEVERAL AFRICAN NATIONS HAVE GIVEN RISE TO AMAZONS; BUT IT WAS IN DAHOMEY THAT THIS INSTITUTION HAD ITS BRIGHTEST PERIOD, FROM THE BEGINNING OF THE NINETEENTH CENTURY UNTIL THE FALL OF KING BÉHANZIN ON JANUARY 25, 1894.

Everything began with the white settlement at Ouidah. There, all along the African coast, the slave traders' presence set in motion a strange mechanism, like a never-ending spiral. The neighboring kingdoms coveted the weapons of the Ouidah slave traders. In exchange, they provided them with heaps of slaves, obtained during wars ever more cruel and devastating, which in turn required ever more numerous and improved weapons: the slave trade fed the war, and the war fed the slave trade, which spread like a sore along Africa's flanks.

Thus grew the Dahomey kingdom: a warrior kingdom par excellence, a great purveyor of slaves, transformed by the tide of events into a sort of intermediary between the human granaries of western Africa and the far-off plantations of the New World.

The amazons were organized into several army corps. The Gulonento, the "riflewomen," were equipped with long trade rifles loaded with bullets manufactured locally. The Gohento, the "archers," wore on their left arms ivory bracelets along which the arrow slid, and their quiver held arrows with barbed arrowheads, which stuck in the skin like fishhooks. The Nyekplonento, the "reapers," were armed with great two-handed razor-shaped cutlasses that could slice a man in half with one blow, according to one missionary. Finally, the Gbeto, the "hunters," were distinguished by the two antelope horns on their foreheads, attached to an iron circle worn like a crown. Some were volunteers, some were drawn from the king's wives, others were chosen from among the delinquents of the kingdom, others still were foreign captives: this was the case for Tata Ajaché, the little war trophy who would become an amazon before destiny made her a queen.

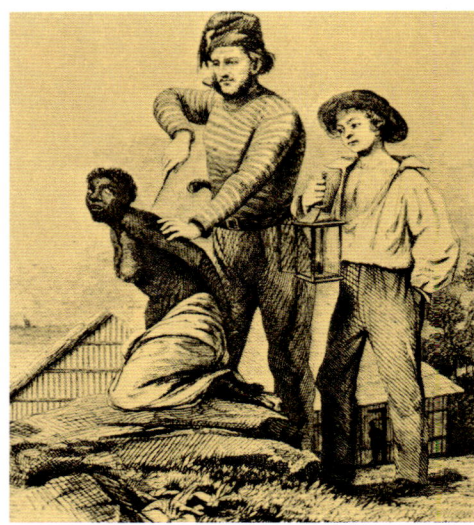

"THE WAR FED THE SLAVE TRADE..."

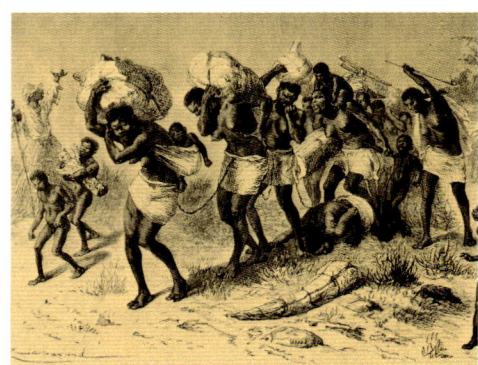

"...THE SLAVE TRADE FED THE WAR"

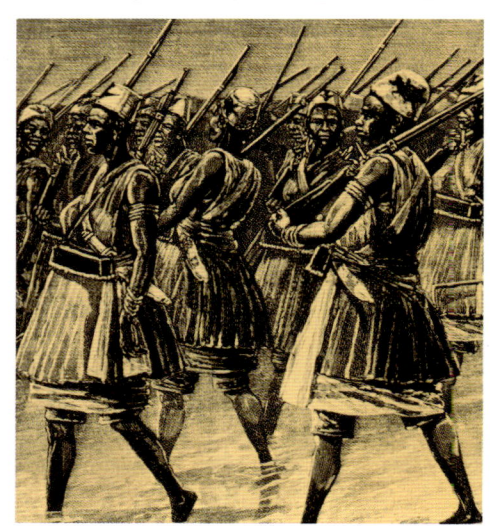

THE KING'S AMAZONS

TATA AJACHÉ

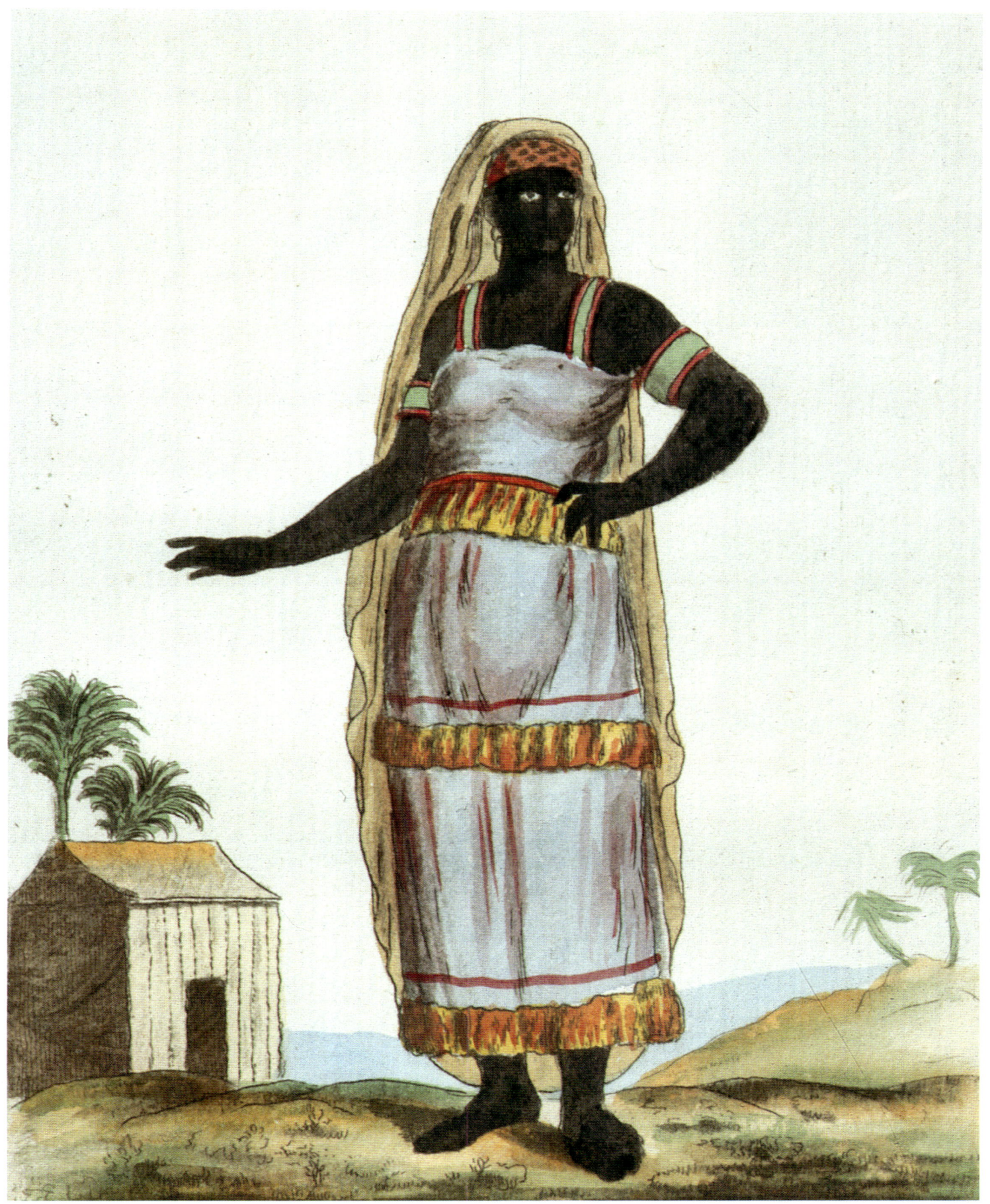

DAHOMEY WOMAN

Tata Ajaché was born among the Holli people, who had been prey to the rulers of Dahomey for two centuries; cunning prey but prey nonetheless.

There was no longer any slave trade, since slavery had been abolished, but war had been inscribed into the very being of the kingdom—the nation lived and breathed war. In 1858, after a raid on the Holli, King Gezo was being carried on his litter through a region that had just been subjugated. A poisoned dart hit him, from who knows what corner: immediately the inhabitants of Ekbo were pillaged and massacred.

In the doorway of one hut, a little ten-year-old girl stood among the bodies. Her mouth was shut and she held out her little hands in front of her. The shadow of a lance fell on the child for an instant. Then a woman's voice spoke:

"Look, she is silent, and she's showing us her claws: she'd make a good amazon."

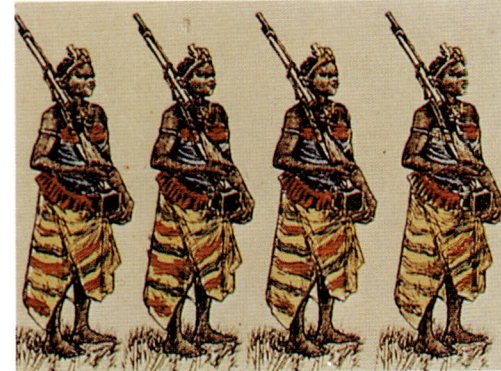

The little girl is led away with the baggage train of the enemy army.

The years pass. Immersed in another world, submitted to discipline at every moment, the memories of her former life shrivel: a green leaf that falls from a tree and dries up will soon dissolve completely into the earth.

For a long time, she is the slave of a huntress; and then the child's calm in the middle of the elephant hunt meets with approval. She is given a blue shirt and white striped leggings: she has become a Gulonento. She practices archery, wrestling, fencing, she is made to overcome all sorts of obstacles, she must even run barefoot over a carpet of bramble, to learn to control her pain. She is abandoned in the forest to risk hunger, thirst, and the great beasts of the night. Before each battle she takes an elixir and becomes like the god Bloukon whose blood begins to boil in the heavens when he drinks palmetto oil. Finally, in the company of other women in training, she is stripped and led into the necropolis of the kings of Dahomey. Her arm is cut open and she is made to drink her own blood in a skull, mixed with the blood of the other young women.

The little leaf in the depths of her memory has completely disappeared: the child of Ekbo village has become Tata Ajaché, an amazon of the guard of King Glélé, successor to Gezo.

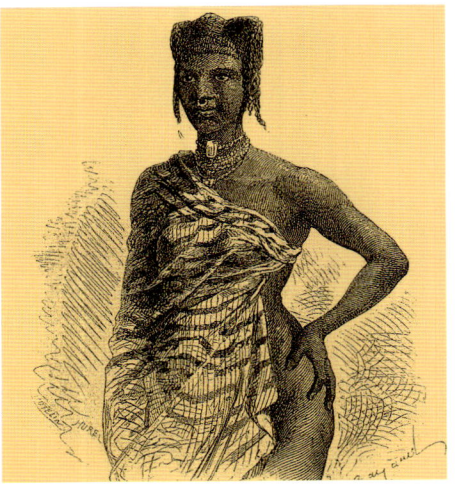

The Legendary Origins of the Dahomey

One day when Adowi, one of the king of Tado's wives, was going to the forest for wood, she found herself in the presence of a male panther, who pounced on her. From this meeting was born Agassou, the son of the panther, the ancestor of the Dahomey lineage. At the same time as she brought this half-human, half-beast into the world, the mother also gave birth to a little panther that immediately escaped into the bush; another boy normal in every way, named Goun; and a pair of white doves.

Raised in his mother's family, Agassou lived in the Tado court, where he was distinguished by his physical appearance and strength. He was tall, with lots of red hair, and wore his fingernails very long, like a panther's claws. Since no girl wanted to marry the half-human, half-animal, his mother gave him in marriage to one of his aunts. They produced numerous offspring who aspired in vain to the throne of Tado.

One of them killed the prince and heir Adja and broke the symbolic calabash from which the kings of Tado drank, so that no other sovereign would ever quench his thirst from it again, something that would signify the end of the kingdom.

The murderer left Tado with his family and allies, taking the skull of his ancestor Agassou, his lance, his ceremonial chair (*kataklé*), as well as an ancient musical instrument, an adjoguin, made up of sticks on which rings slid. After crossing the Mono, he moved eastward, starting villages in every place where he spent some time; then he arrived in a region where he settled for good, founding the kingdom of Allada. From then on that is where the rest of the Agassou would flourish.

His state rapidly grew in importance. Nonetheless, quarrels arose among his successors, either his sons or grandsons, according to different versions of the story. They decided to separate. The third brother, Do-Aklin, taking the kataklé with him, went north with his two children, Gangyé-Hessou and Dako-Donou, who brought his body back to Allada when he died a few years later. The kings of Dahomey would descend from him.

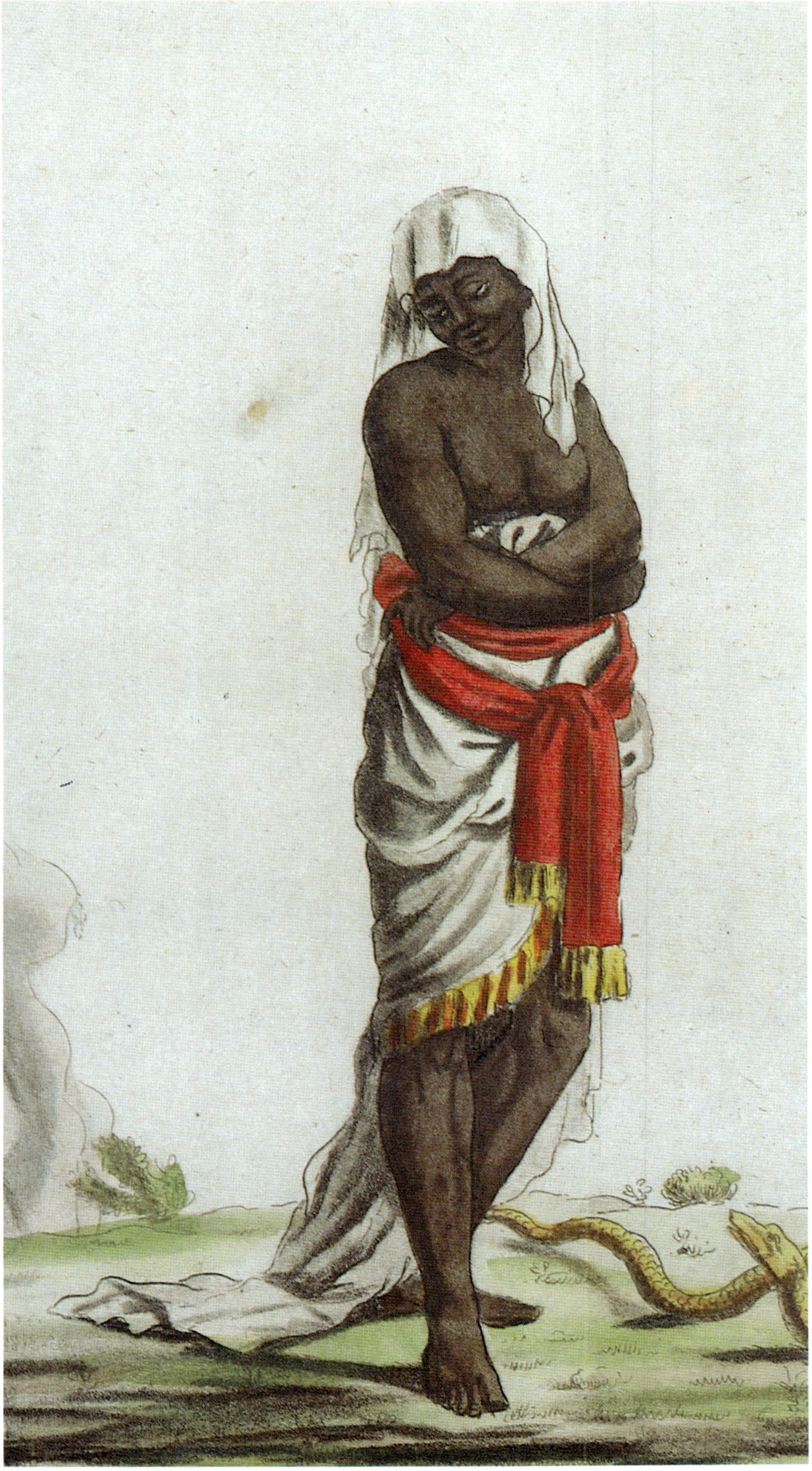

TATA AJACHÉ

YOUNG PRIESTESS OF DAHOMEY

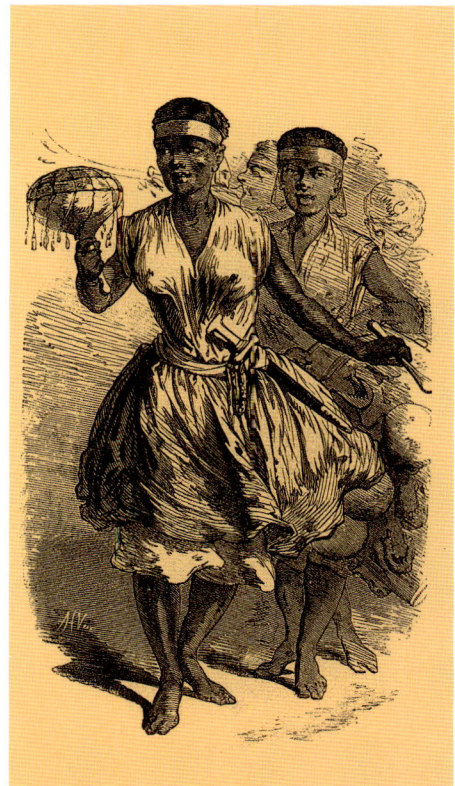

Dahomey Women

Dahomey women are smaller than the men; with well-formed, gracious bodies, they are ravishing when they go to the fair gracefully draped in their bright-colored cloths, carrying white calabashes on their heads.

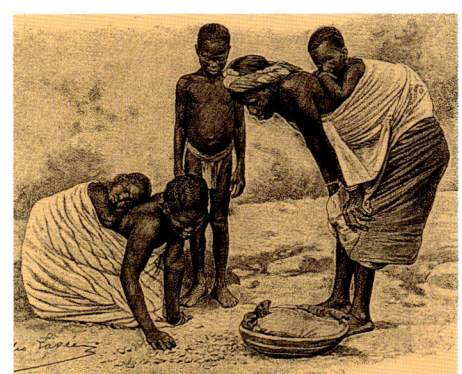

Cowry Counters

The merchants have their own cowry counters, women who use their fingers with astonishing agility and push the shells by fives, from right to left.

Proverb

A group of old men settle down to discuss business, in a place usually occupied by children. A child approaches the old men. One of them says to him:
"If a lie follows a path, truth looks in the grass."

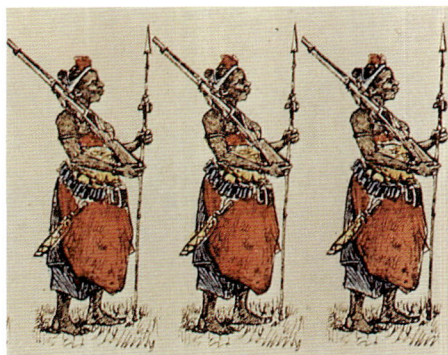

Amazon Organization

The central group, formed by the Fanti company, makes up the king's guard. At its head, a "general-in-chief" is recognizable by the horsetails attached to her belt. This group is divided into two parts, which cover the king during expeditions. Each is placed under the direction of a captain or a commander.

The three wings are made up of several units—Burton calls them battalions, the French historian Dunglas calls them regiments—directed by women officers.

The name of each group commemorates some great deed or specialty of its members. The Aligossi, for example, evoke the sacrifice of the amazons massacred in Aligo (part of the palace of Abomey) because of their fidelity to their king.

The Djedokpo, whose name means "kneeling," form an élite corps whose members are "strictly confined to the palace, and on whose passage common people must prostrate themselves." These marks of respect are perhaps due to the rank of the women who make up this unit, for, according to the Benin historian Amélie Degbelo, they are amazon queens whose duty is to protect their spouses when they go out into the country.

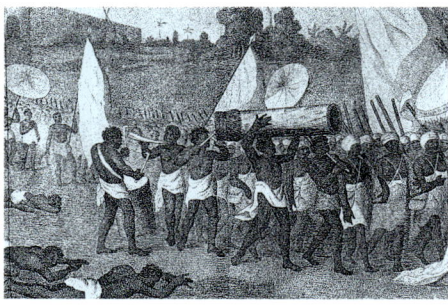

The Amazons' First War

The year in which the women's armies were created cannot be pinpointed with precision. However, the latest research has pushed back the time of their appearance. It is in the oral histories of the Ouéménou that the earliest mention of their participation in combat is made, during the war the Dahomey waged against the Ouéménou in 1708.

Tata Ajaché is first made a member of the regiment led by Dan-Jihunto, "the rainbow rules the sky"; then, no one knows why, she comes to be under the command of Captain Jibihowé-ton, "the whole sky belongs to the sun."

The amazons' discipline is most strict, and their devotion to the king is boundless. In 1818, the guards of King Adandozan confront a plot to overthrow their king; every last one of them dies fighting. More than the male warriors, they are the kingdom's true backbone, its most solid foundation. This is expressed in one of their songs, where devotion to the king takes on a maternal tone:

> *Lionesses are more fearsome than lions*
> *because they have their little ones to defend.*
> *And we amazons have to defend*
> *our good king and our god Kini.*

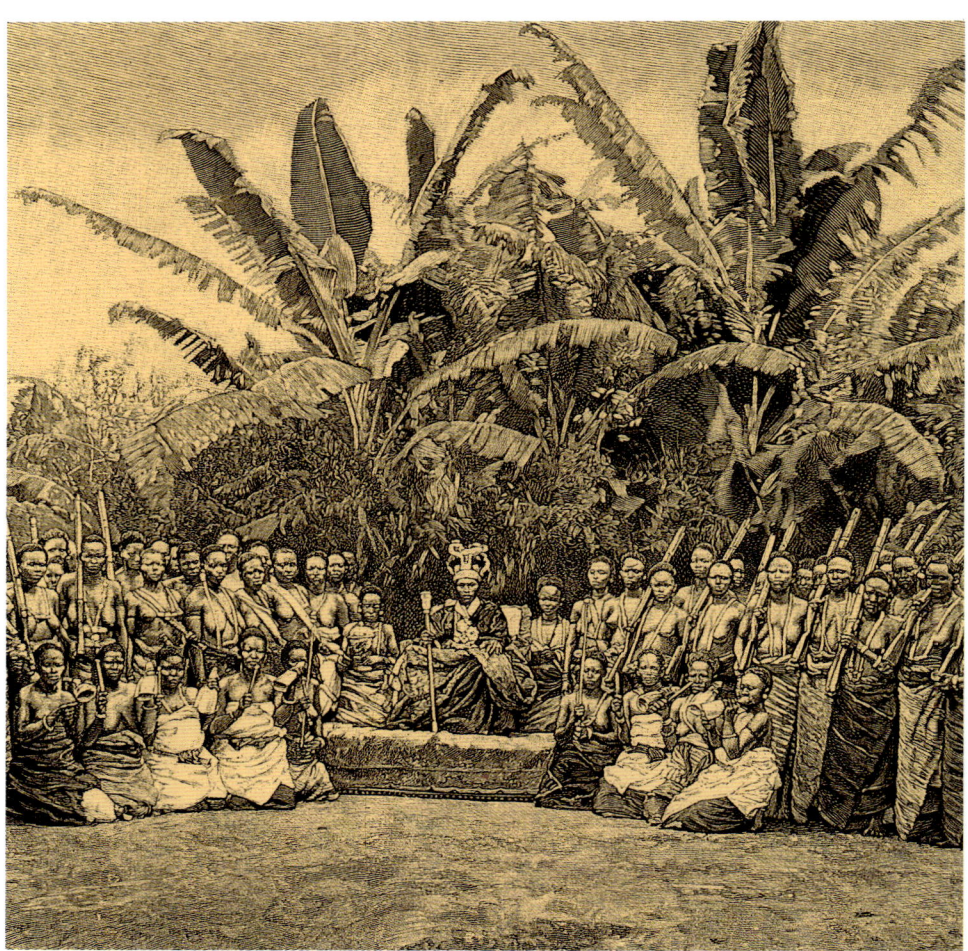

"WE AMAZONS HAVE TO DEFEND OUR KING"

The amazons are required to remain chaste: neither wives nor mothers, their life is reduced to defending the king's will. Any violation of this rule of rules is punishable by death. And this is the fate that awaits Tata Ajaché the day she is denounced: she allegedly goes to see a man one night, and is supposed to have "dropped her tunic" before him.

She denies it, claiming there is a conspiracy: they torture her to tear out the truth.

King Glélé attends one of these interrogations: tied to the central post of the necropolis, Tata Ajaché does not shed a single tear, does not even raise her voice to refute the accusations. She replies to the inquisitor's questions with a calm voice and then falls silent; she answers and falls silent, her mouth shut on a secret stronger than the instruments of torture, a secret that was already hers, long ago, a little girl silent in the face of death. The king is moved to see her so proud and asks:

"How long will you deny it?"

"Until my innocence is recognized."

"And yet you were seen with a man: admit it."

She laughs disdainfully:

"What use would I have for a man, my lord?"

And under the eyes of the mute spectators, she sings an old amazon song, through which she expresses the woman she has become:

We tear, and turn, and tear our hearts out.
Let the men take care of the cassava harvest!
We tear, and rip, and turn over our hearts.
Let the men take care of the cassava harvest!

Take Aim!

Take aim! Take aim! Shoot!
Spread out so you can shoot well!
Let the one who fires follow the rifle's smoke!
We eat to serve you,
King of Pearls!
So that one day, if we find ourselves in the presence
Of an audacious army
We will fear nothing;
We will be invincible;
We will be like the buffalo
Who is not lost
Among the sheep!

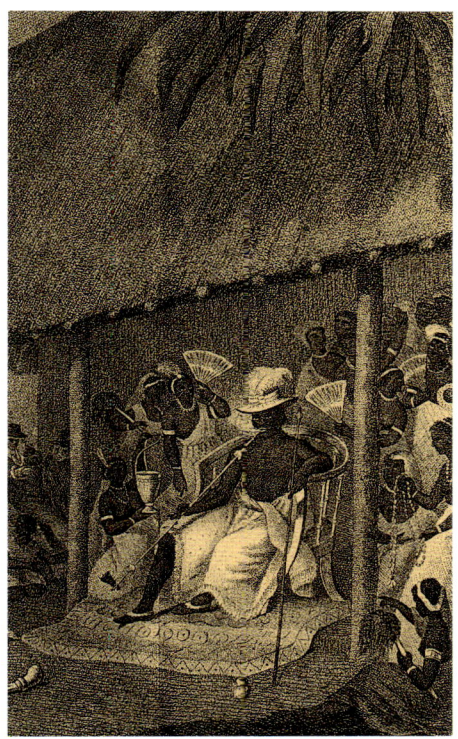

The General's Challenge

Around 1880, the Chacha of Ouidah led several amazons to Agoué. Their general issued this challenge to the warriors of the city: "You say men are stronger than women. Well, we shall see! Let the cleverest among you come to me, and I will give him my saber or my neighbor's, the choice will be his. Then the two of us will go at it and within two minutes, his head will be stuck on the tip of my saber!" No Agoué soldier dared accept the challenge.

We Die No Matter Where

When the fire burns, we can put it out.
And when there are many people,
An army of multitudes,
The Dahomey can put it out.
All the fire, all the anger,
We will leave to go put them out.
We have proclaimed it.
But when the day arrives,
We die no matter where.
You die or another dies,
That is war.

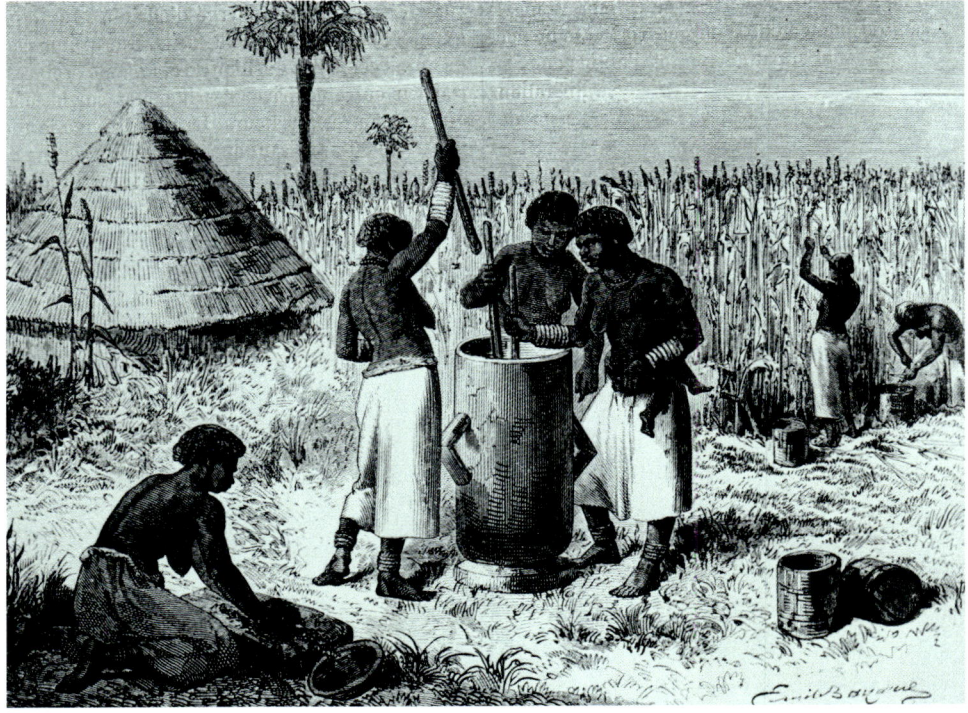

ORDINARY WOMEN IN THE FIELDS

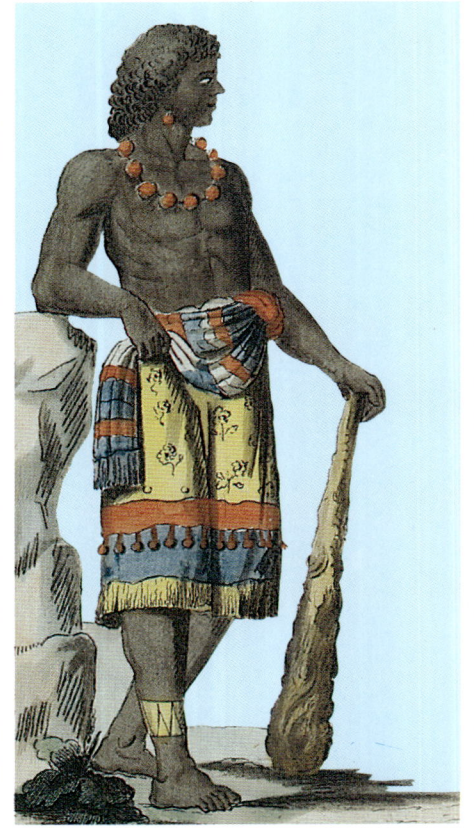

Proverb

"If you want honey, you have to put up with the sting of the bee."

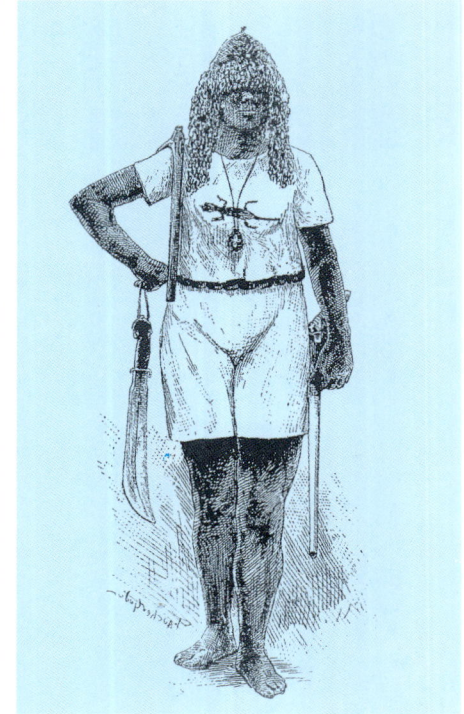

Proverb

"The word that stays in your stomach is your mother's child, the word that comes out of your mouth is your father's child."

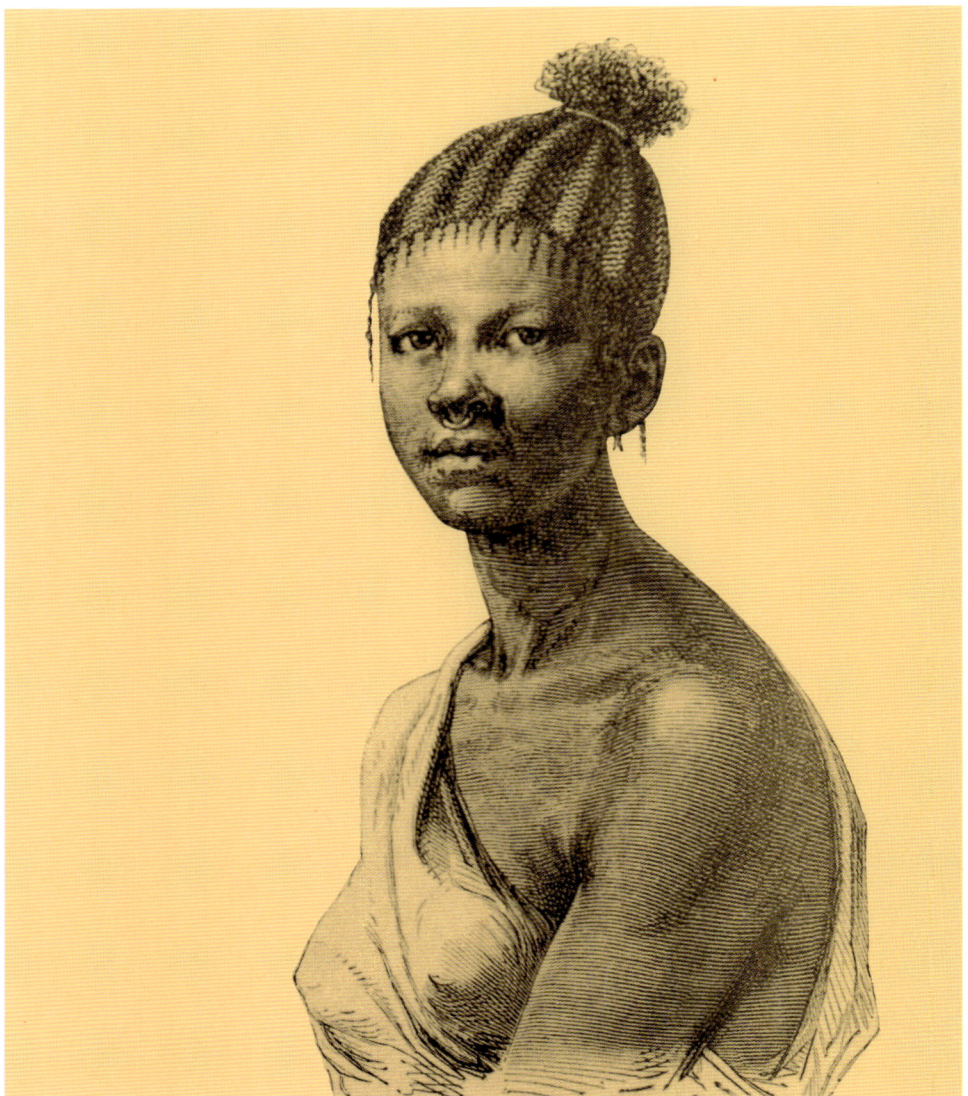

The king's mouth falls open, like a young man who has discovered beauty. Then he goes to the amazon and removes her bonds, wipes her face covered with blood, wipes her arms and shoulders, and has her taken to his palace where she is tended to for nine weeks. When her body has recovered, she is dressed in her blue amazon tunic, her white leggings with blue stripes, her cap decorated with a little blue crocodile; the straight little saber is slung over her shoulder from a strap decorated with cowries. Then she is brought before the king, who contemplates her for a while and says:

"Tata Ajaché, my uncle King Gezo married Avognondé because of her bravery at the battle of Agbomé. And my grandfather Agaja married the amazon Ahinajé because of her bravery at the siege of Tchetti. I have never seen you wield a weapon in combat, but I have seen you engaged in a combat without arms, a battle from which few men emerge victorious."

He finishes with an ironic smile:

"Tata Ajaché, I know that in your eyes I am nothing but a cassava harvester; nonetheless, would you be my Djedokpo, she before whom all the others must kneel?"

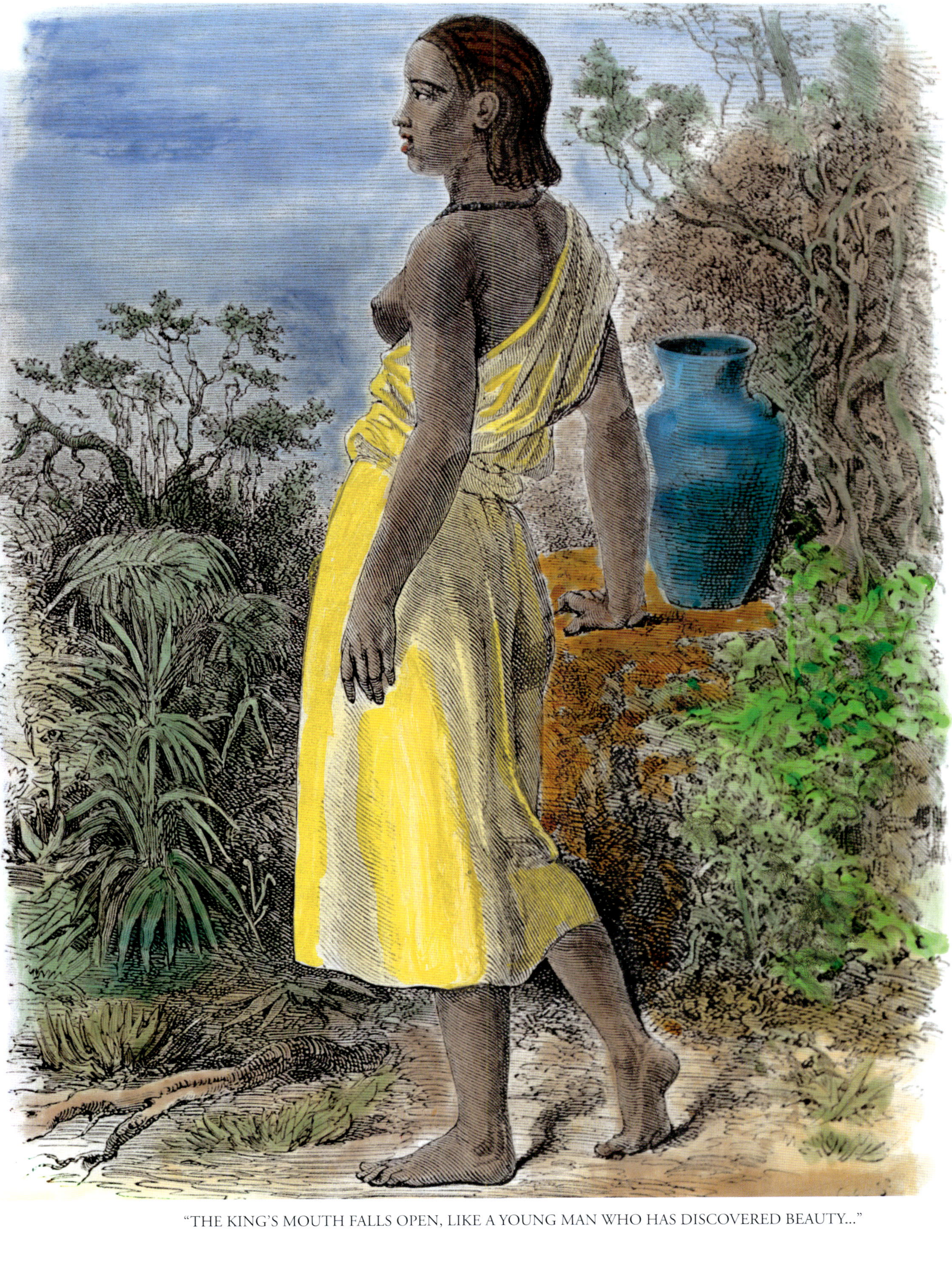

TATA AJACHÉ

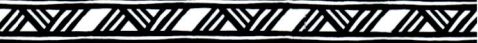

"THE KING'S MOUTH FALLS OPEN, LIKE A YOUNG MAN WHO HAS DISCOVERED BEAUTY..."

For the Dahomey peoples, the name of Tata Ajaché has continued to be associated with that of the king who recognized her, and the memory of the little slave queen will not fade.

In spite of her crown, she participated in all the kingdom's wars, advancing as just another blue amazon; then, upon Glélé's death in 1889, she retired like a royal widow, and no one ever saw her again.

According to legend, when she was very old, she went one day to the village of Ekbo where she stopped for what seemed like an eternity in front of a little hut: but no one knows what she was thinking, for the old woman's worn mouth remained closed.

Thus ends the story of Tata Ajaché, the silent little slave who was transformed into an amazon, before fate made her the greatest queen of Dahomey.

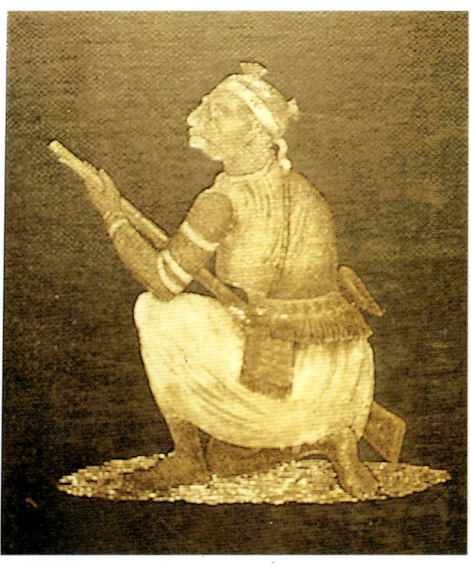

OLD AGE

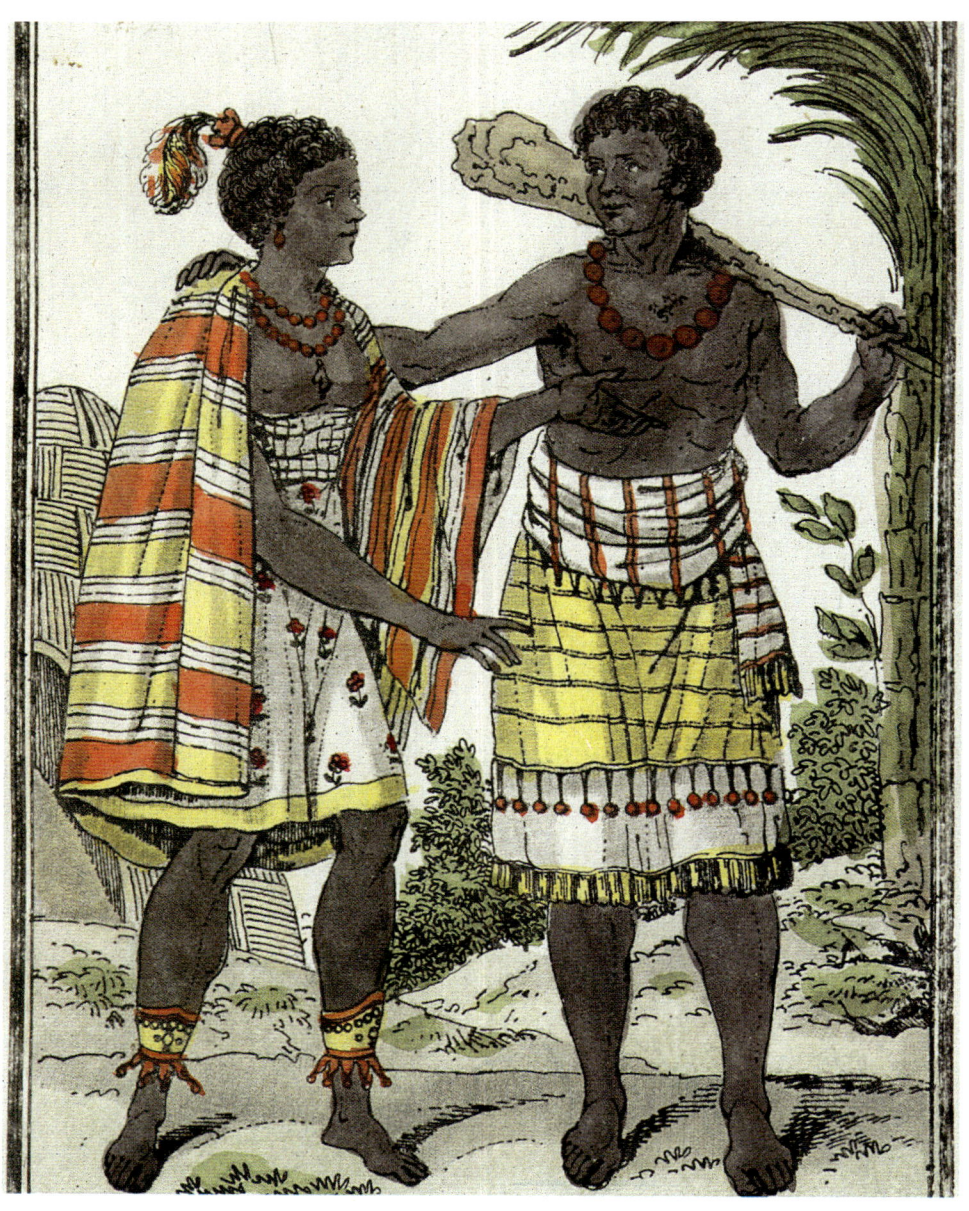

WORDS
OF AN ORDINARY WOMAN

A woman cannot explain many things to you. A woman knows nothing.

We women make no decisions, we cannot do anything. We follow, that is all.

If you want to learn many things about the life of the Wodaabe, you must go see the old men. You must go see the men and listen to them. They are the ones who know everything, who decide everything, who can do everything.

A woman is worth nothing. She is always behind the men. She can never make important decisions for the life of the camp. Yes, a woman only follows.

It is the man who takes care of the flocks, and for us the flock is everything: prestige, the breath of life. It is our only strength.

We do not know the bush very well. We women risk getting lost, because we do not recognize places well.

But men, they know everything. They know the bush, as if it were the family compound: each tree, each hill, each valley.

But on the other hand, we women can do certain things that the men cannot. We know things that men do not know.

You saw what happened during the year of the drought. It meant destruction for the flocks and death for people. It was terrible. And we will never be able to forget what we suffered.

Well, the men, after losing their flocks, also lost all their power. They didn't know what to do anymore, they no longer knew how to make decisions.

We abandoned the bush to come take refuge in the villages like the sedentary folk. Now what can a Wodaabe man do in a village?

How could he feed his family? With trade or masonry? No, he doesn't know a thing about all that. The only work he knows is the flock.

That was when we women showed what we knew how to do. A Wodaabe woman in a village can always get along:

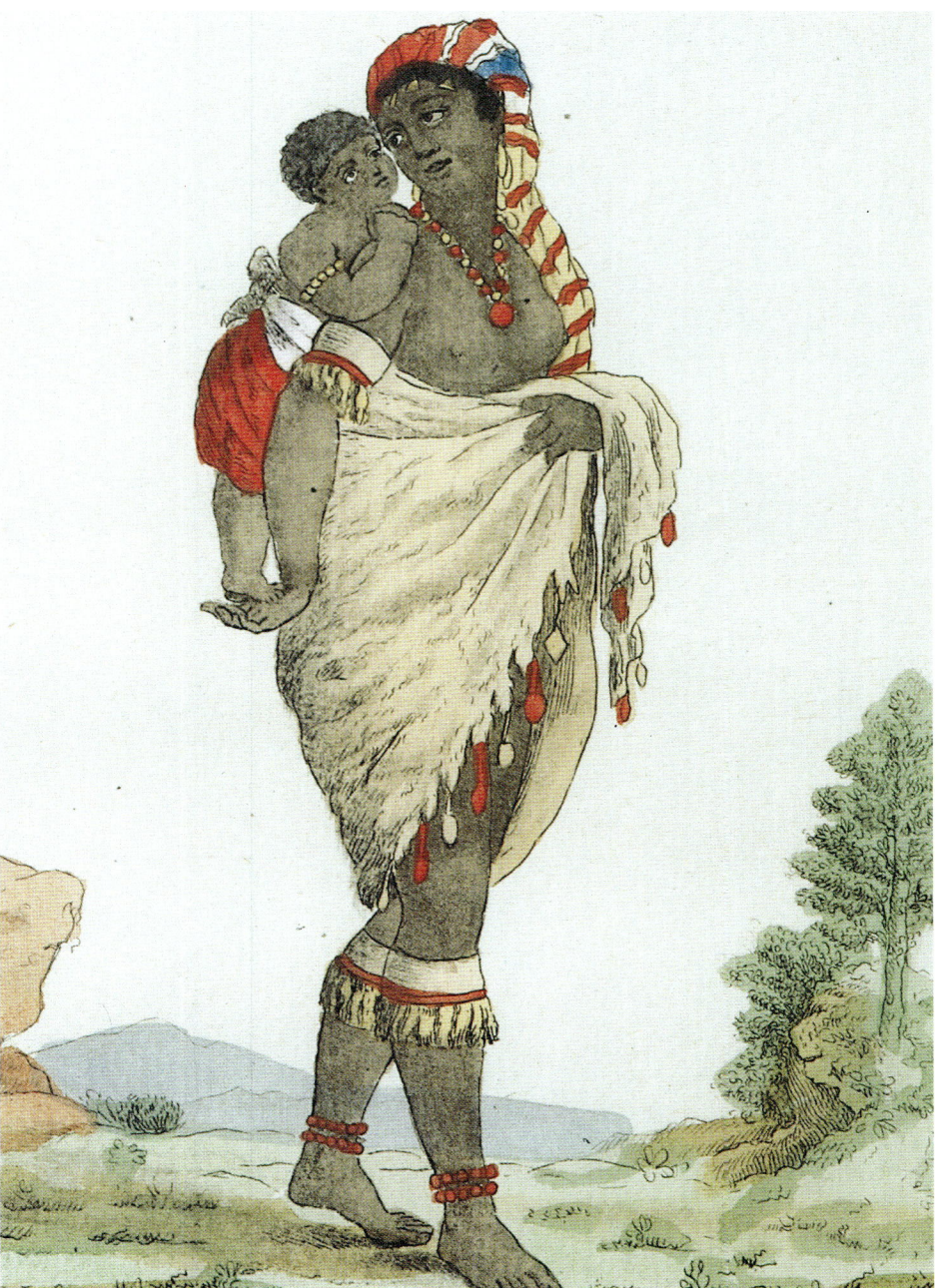

WOMAN AND CHILD FROM OUIDAH

she can do the women's hair, she can fix gourds or grind grain in the compounds. She will always find a way to get food. No, a Wodaabe woman never loses her courage.

It's true. A woman knows nothing. She's not as valuable as a man. But during the year of the drought, it was the women who saved the men.

Yes, in a camp, a man is everything. We say he is the *jom wuro,* the master of the camp. But the woman is the *fom suudu,* the mistress of the house.

All that you see in the family compound belongs to the woman: the gourds, the mats, the pot, the bed. Everything. The man doesn't even own the little gourd for milking his cows.

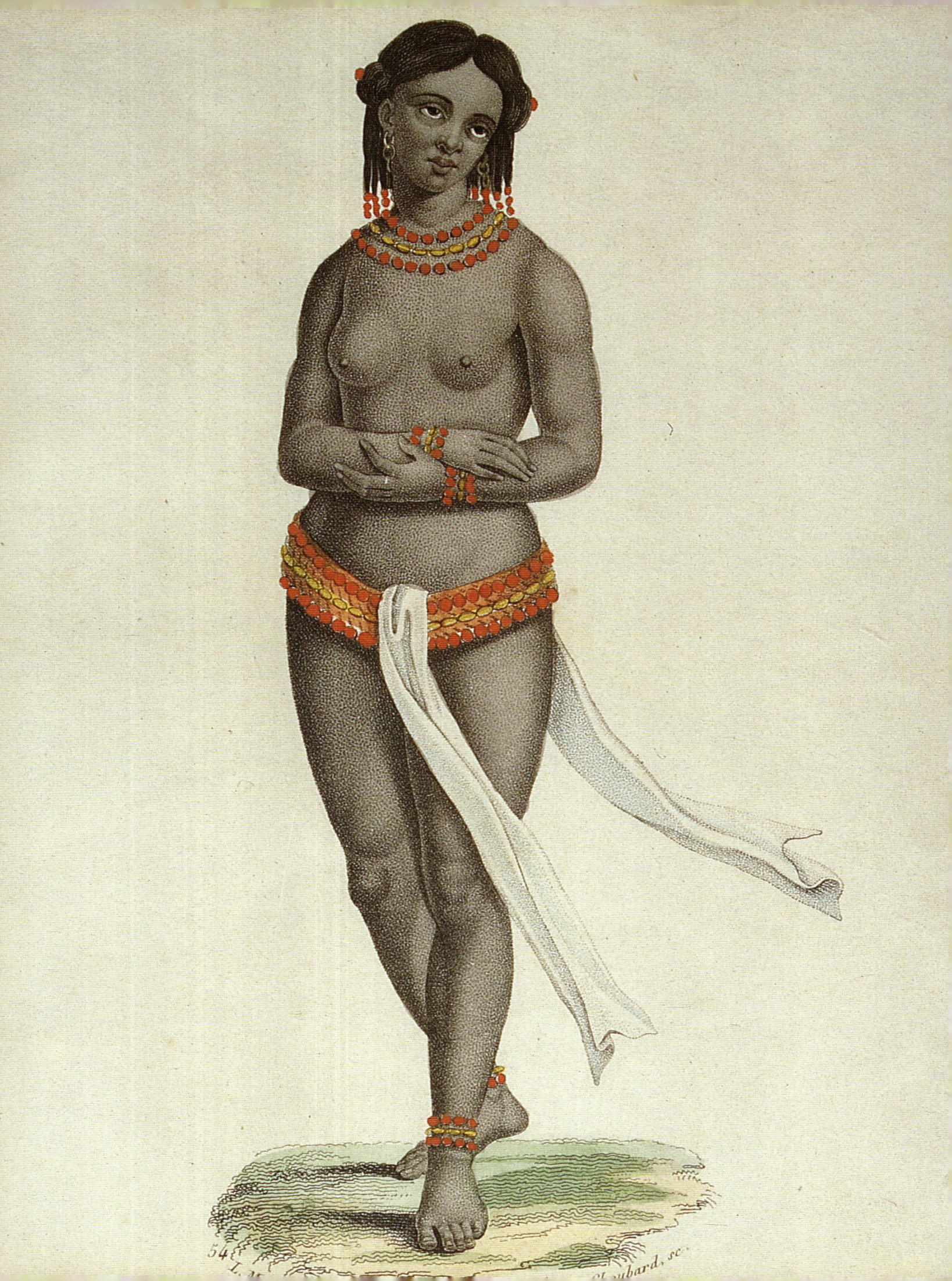

MODJADJI I

RAIN QUEEN
OF THE LOVEDU

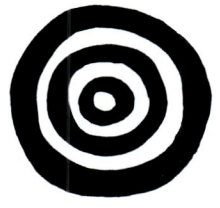

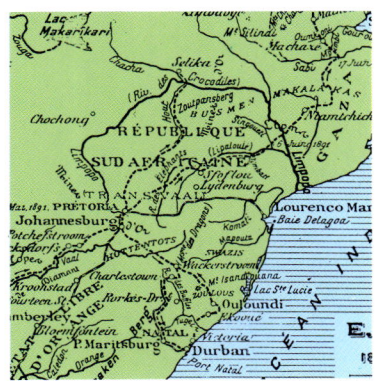

This young girl had no name, did not call herself anything; people used to shout at her like a beast of burden. But after she made the rain fall, they began to take notice...

ONCE UPON A TIME, BETWEEN THE ZAMBEZI RIVER AND THE VAST STRETCHES OF THE HIGH PLATEAUS, THERE CAME TO BE A NEW PEOPLE UNDER THE SUN, A TRIBE WITHOUT A NAME. THIS TRIBE HAD BEEN BORN FROM THE COMING TOGETHER OF VARious people fleeing from different directions who said to each other: "We are fleeing the North,...we are fleeing the South,...and we are fleeing the East and West: let us make one people and put a stop to our flight."

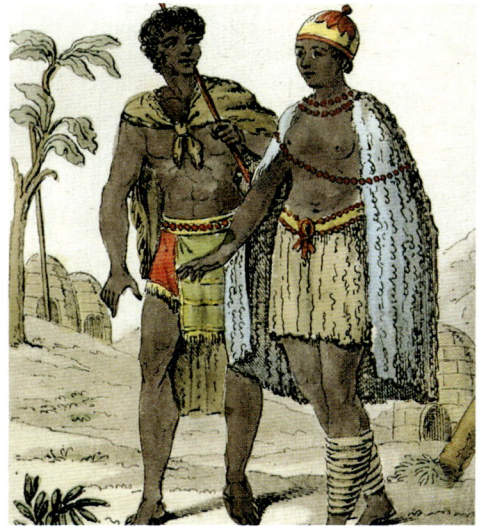

Unfortunately, other tribes in the area did not see things the same way; and in vain did the nameless ones seek their own place, a mark on the ground, a corner of earth around which they could put up borders and watchtowers manned by archers.

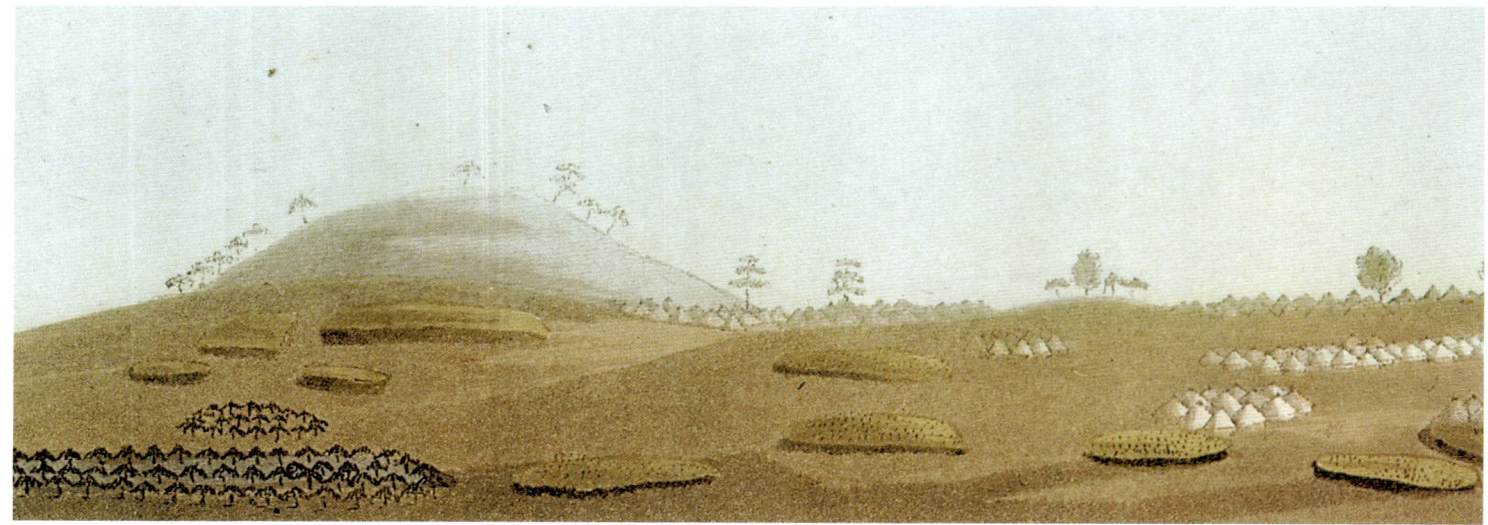

"BETWEEN THE ZAMBEZI AND THE VAST STRETCHES OF THE HIGH PLATEAUS..."

One day, they arrived at the foot of a mountainous massif, which rose up straight as a sword. No man had ever set foot on this mountain, nor on its plateau, which they could barely make out in the cloud-covered heights: the Oliphant River embraced it on the left, and on the right, the Limpopo Valley, shrouded in a fog of tsetse flies.

After much searching, they found a secret trail up the mountain and reached a large flat plateau, which was, alas, a land without water, where the rains never fell: misfortune, such misfortune.

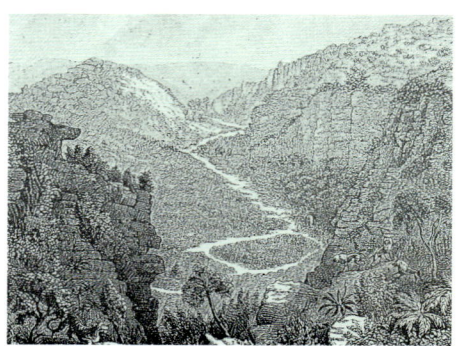

"...A SECRET TRAIL..."

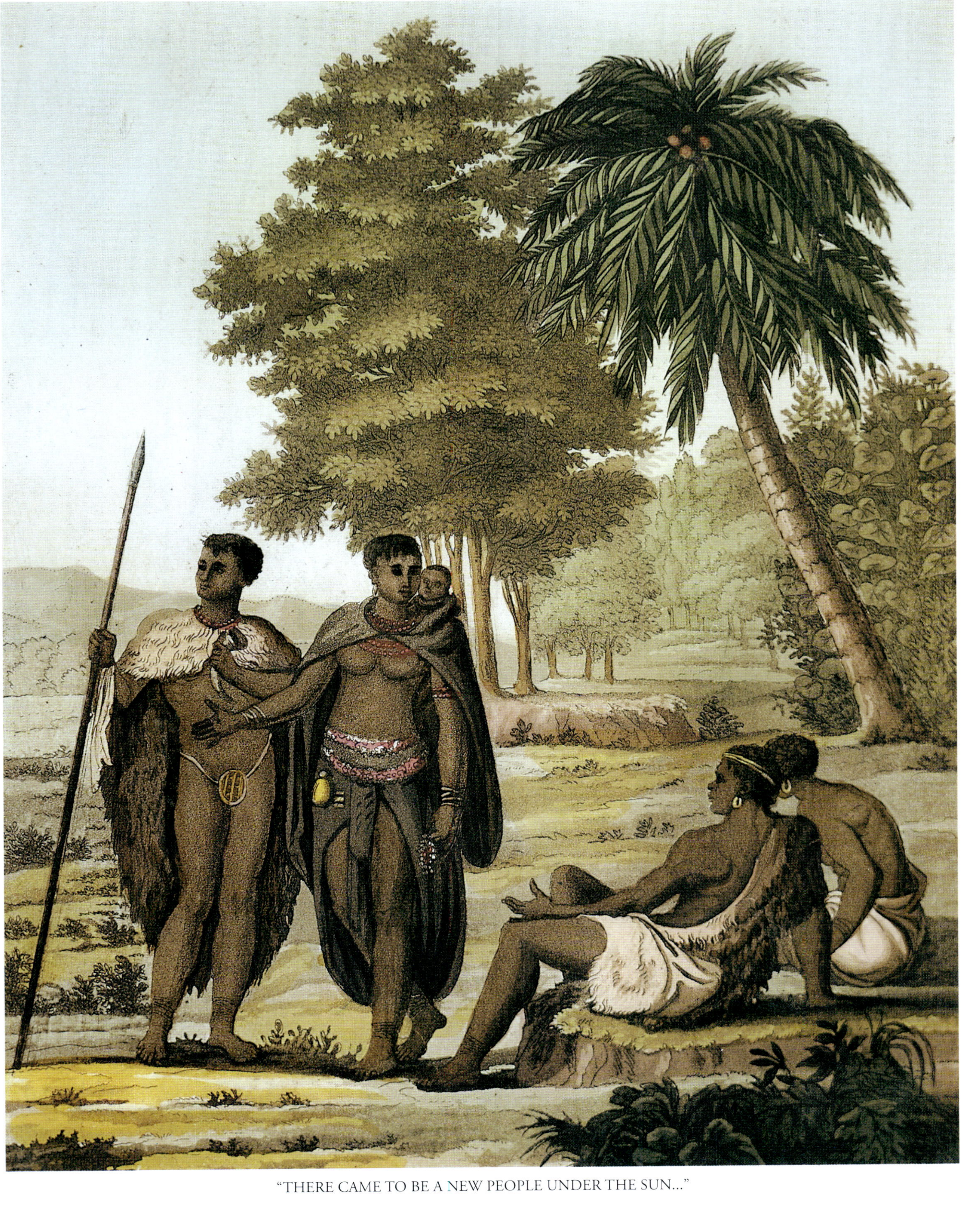

MODJADJI I

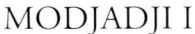

"THERE CAME TO BE A NEW PEOPLE UNDER THE SUN..."

Rainmakers

Rainmakers were in great demand in central South Africa. In the village where they had been invited to put an end to the drought, these sorcerers began by choosing the ingredients necessary for their potions; then, they taught the villagers the rituals for summoning the rain and the prayers to the spirits of the dead ancestors. When they could not manage to draw storm clouds, they would sacrifice an animal and, at dawn, followed by the villagers and some livestock, they would go into the countryside and display their unhappiness by destroying bushes, killing any game that crossed their path, and defiantly throwing rocks into the dried-up ponds. Toward noon, the tribe would return to the village, and the women, pushing the animals along, would moan and pray, begging the ancestors to send rain.

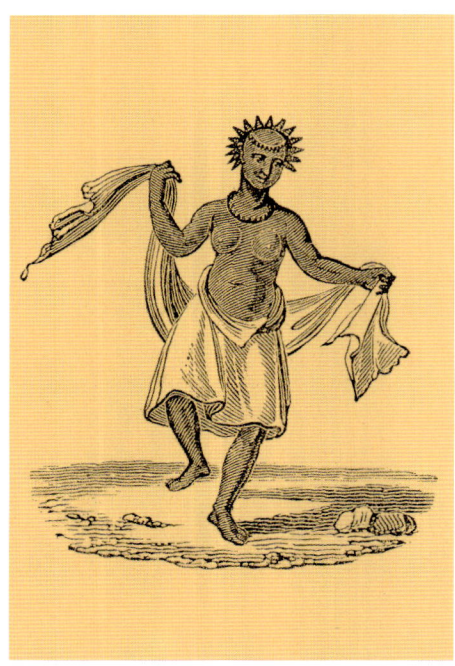

If the drought persisted, they prayed even more, and during these new ceremonies even a humble spoonful of porridge could serve as a magic wand. A black bull would be sacrificed over the tomb of a renowned ancestor, Chief Mathibé. The beast's innards would be buried in the tomb and the members of the tribe, after taking part in the ceremony, would consume its flesh. Then the Bamangwato people, standing in the holy necropolis, would once again begin their prayers and lamentations.
"We have come to beg for rain in exchange for this bull," they would sing in unison, their voices wavering. "Here he is, oh chief, our father! Pula! Pula! Pula! Chief, we are dead, we who are your people."
And under the burning sun of Bechuanaland, the Bamangwato would call for the rain and dance before the tomb.

After a month, an old man heard a voice saying that perhaps the sky would spill its gourd if only it would see a woman dance.

At first the people laughed, but since the sun kept beating down harder and harder, and since the old man still heard the voice, one by one the women entered the circle and began to dance; and one by one they left the circle, and the sky remained dry.

Finally, when they had all danced, they noticed a young slave girl with thick hands and few charming features, with as much expression as the bottom of a bowl or the sole of a foot, and who alone had remained seated on her rock.

She was ordered to enter the circle; she took a few awkward steps, like an animal that was only used to work: she twisted her neck, one arm went left, one leg went right, that was all she knew how to do.

But little by little, no one knew how, her movements became smooth as if someone put grease on her joints. She acquired a grace no one had known her to possess.

It was as if wings had sprouted on her shoulders, on her heels, and on her cheekbones stretching gravely toward the sky: and suddenly, there was a rolling crash and the rain began to fall.

This young girl had no name, did not call herself anything; people used to shout at her like a beast of burden. But after she made the rain fall, they began to take notice, and they gave her the name Dzugudini, which means Face of Light; and the refugee people gave themselves the name Lovedu, which they have kept to this very day.

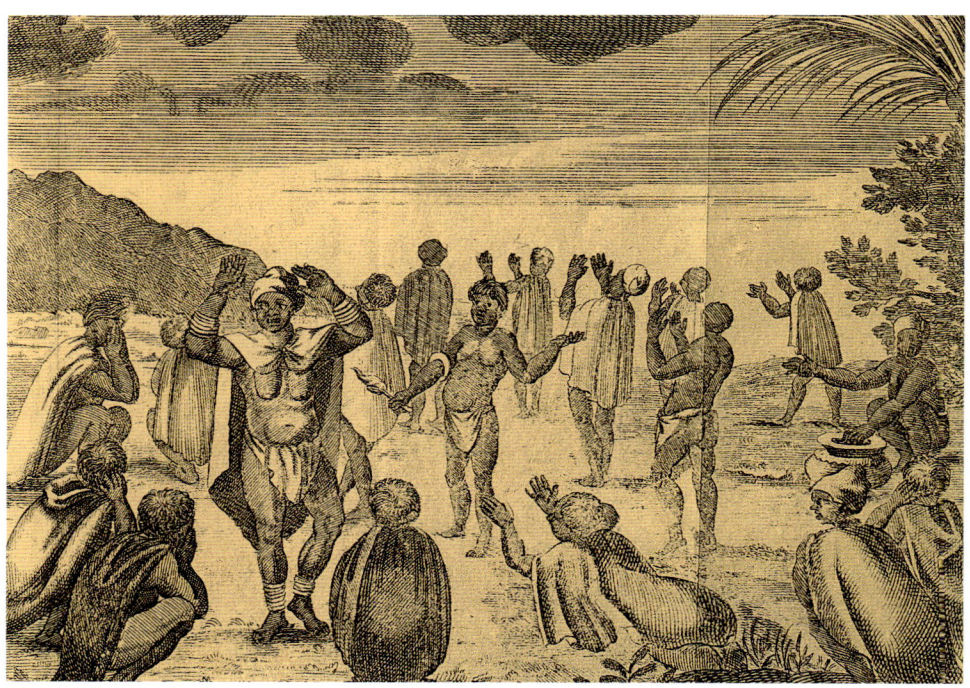

"...SHE TOOK A FEW AWKWARD STEPS..."

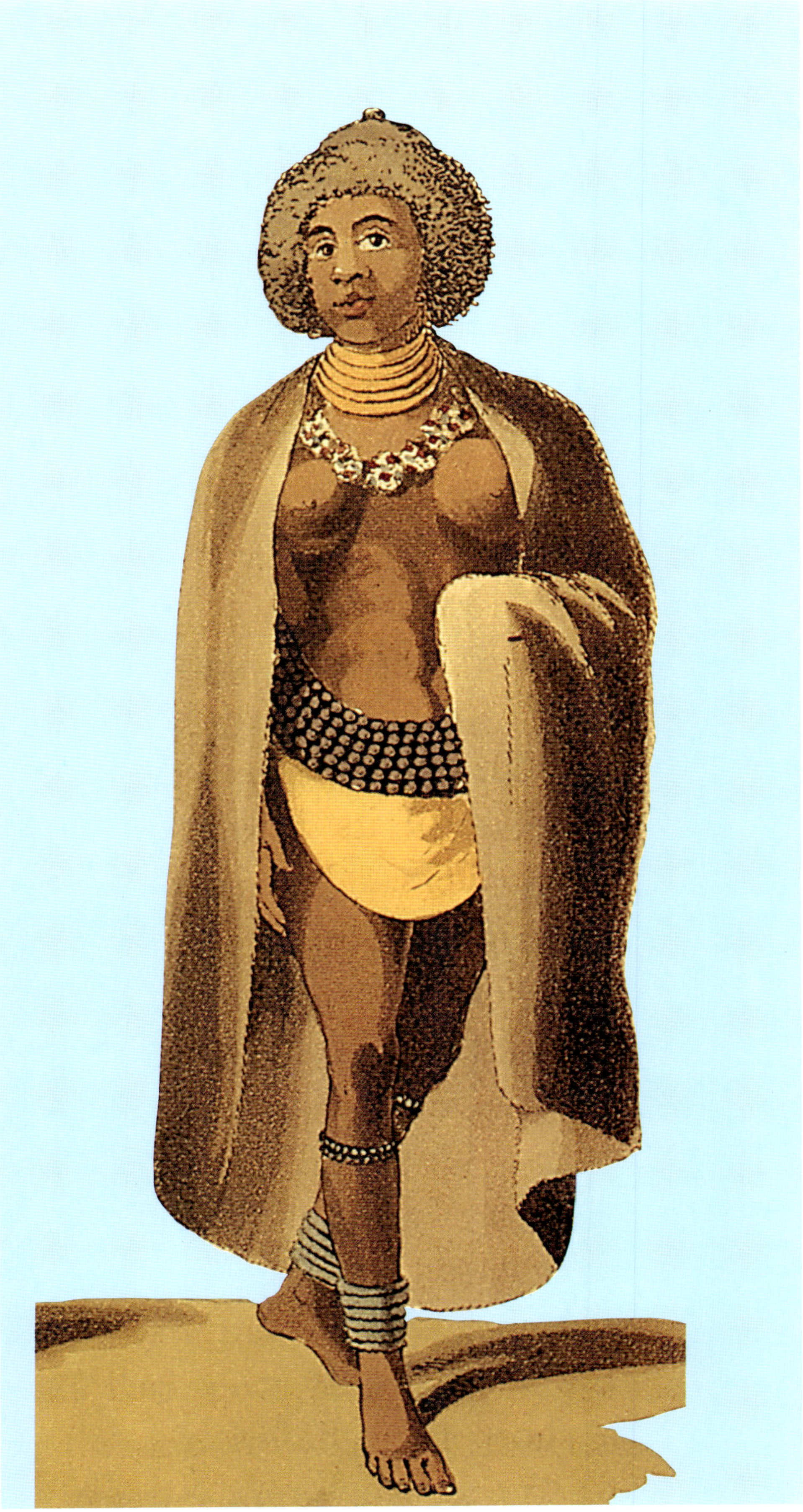

MODJADJI I

THE RAINMAKER

The Tale of Tsélané

A Mochuana had a daughter named Tsélané whom he loved dearly. One day he decided, following the example of the other Mochuana, to emigrate with his family and flocks to new pastures. He said to his wife: "We shall leave tomorrow." His wife said to Tsélané: "Follow us, my child." But Tsélané replied: "No, mother, I will not follow you. Our house is decorated with red and white glass beads, it is too pretty for me to leave behind." Her mother answered, "My child, since you are so stubborn, you can stay here all alone, but shut the door tight, Tsélané, so you don't get eaten by the spirits." And she left.

A few days later, she came back to see her daughter and bring her some food. But Tsélané would let nothing change her mind, neither her mother's prayers, nor the glowing descriptions of her parents' new home, nor the fear of spirits.
But then one day, a spirit imitating her mother's voice managed to fool Tsélané. She opened the door for him and he grabbed her, put her in a leather sack, and carried her off.

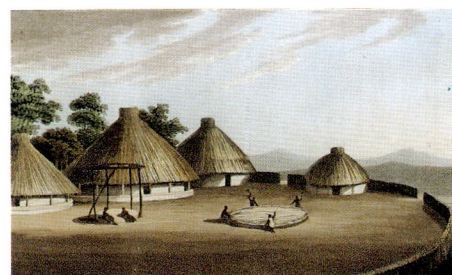

On his way, the spirit became thirsty; so he entrusted his burden to a group of young girls for safekeeping, and went to ask for beer in a nearby village, where Tsélané's aunt lived and where Tsélané's mother happened to be visiting. While he was gone, the young girls looked through a little hole in the sack and saw a finger. "Whose finger is this?" they asked. "Mine," answered a muffled voice. "I'm Tsélané."
They immediately ran to Tsélané's mother, who pulled her daughter out of the sack and put in her place a dog, a couple of scorpions, vipers, poisonous insects, rocks, and shards of broken pots.
The spirit, tipsy from the beer, came back to get his sack and took it to his house. But when he opened it and reached in, the dog and the vipers bit him, the scorpions stung him, the shards cut him, and the rocks bruised him. He jumped up and ran like a madman through the village, fell in the mud, and was turned into a tree, in whose trunk the bees came to make honey.
And the young girls of the region would go there in the spring to gather *makapetla a linotsi,* honeycombs.

Proverb

"The earth holds out its hand to whatever rains down from heaven."

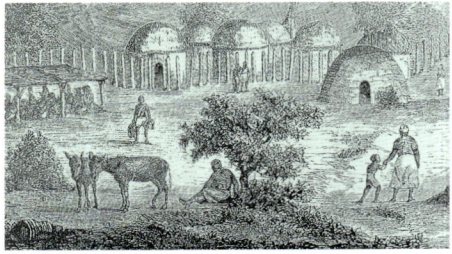

Daily Life in a Sotho Village

The Sotho tribes cultivated their fields, tended their flocks, participated in rituals, and hunted to put food in their cooking pots; they also took part in a host of other activities. The men softened and tanned animal skins to make clothing and sandals; they sculpted milk tubs, bowls, basins, spoons, and other utensils; they extracted metals from minerals to make adzes, war hatchets, hunting lances, knives and assegais. With clay, the women made cooking utensils and pots of different sizes and shapes for storing milk, water, beer, and grain. Out of woven reeds, they made sleeping mats, baskets, and enormous spherical grain sacks.

Each year, in the proper season, the villagers led their livestock to well-watered pastures. These pastures, at considerable distances from the principal settlements, were visited from time to time by livestock thieves from neighboring clans. These organized raids were a popular pastime, particularly during the winter months, once the harvest was brought in.

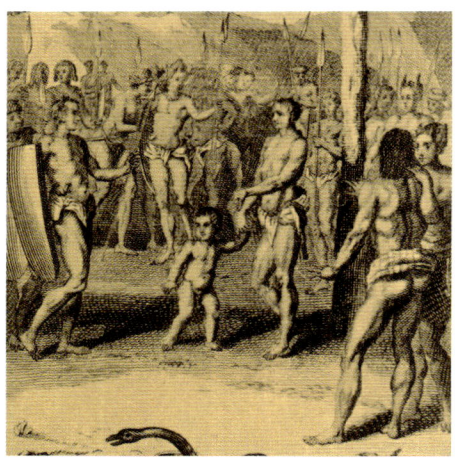

The Empire of the Mwene Matapa

This empire is vast, peopled by noble and polytheistic blacks, of average height, but quick and most valiant in war.

Their weapons are bows and light arrows and darts: the emperor has many armies parceled out among his provinces, divided into legions in the Roman manner; as a great lord, he is obliged to wage war constantly in order to defend his territory.

---------- 2 ----------

Many centuries passed for the Lovedu, suspended between heaven and earth, like little birds who seek shelter high up in a tree. They had not learned the art of war, since they had always been protected by the hidden mountain trail; and, in good years and bad, the sky opened fairly regularly on the high plateau, which yielded cassava roots as heavy and deep as the roots of trees.

The most celebrated descendant of Dzugudini was Modjadji I, who reigned over the Lovedu people from 1800 to 1850.

She was born without grace, her movements uncertain; yet she became a rainmaker such as had never been seen before and as will never be seen again as long as the world shall last.

Modjadji I did not simply dance, as her ancestor Dzugudini had; she also knew many words as effective as dancing, and sometimes even more effective.

She was a somewhat plump woman, with calm eyes beneath a rounded forehead, one of those women who, the others say, have eaten a bit too much millet porridge.

But when she danced, it seemed that mountains and valleys moved, even though she was content to limit herself to the most traditional of steps.

But best of all was to see her when she was not dancing, when she stood up straight in the center of the circle on certain days, imploring a sky reluctant to open up and part with its water. Her body stretched slowly, became gaunt, her bones held up her skin like tent posts, and the folds of fat along her neck gave way to empty, wrinkled skin, as her mouth hurled curses at the sky.

Nonetheless, as soon as the first drops fell on her, her whole body came back to life and gradually swelled up again under the rain; and once more she looked like a slightly plump woman, one of those, with all due respect, who have enjoyed a bit too much millet porridge.

It rained regularly during the fifty years of her reign. Yet this was a difficult period for the people of Africa, a time when men and the elements seemed to be conspiring to make life hell. The empty sky brought drought upon drought, but there was an even greater drought in the human heart, for they were living through the terrible wars of Lifaqané, the wars that followed Shaka's arrival in the world.

Yet the Lovedu plateau lived in peace and prosperity; the rains fell regularly, swelling the millet kernels and fattening the cassava roots.

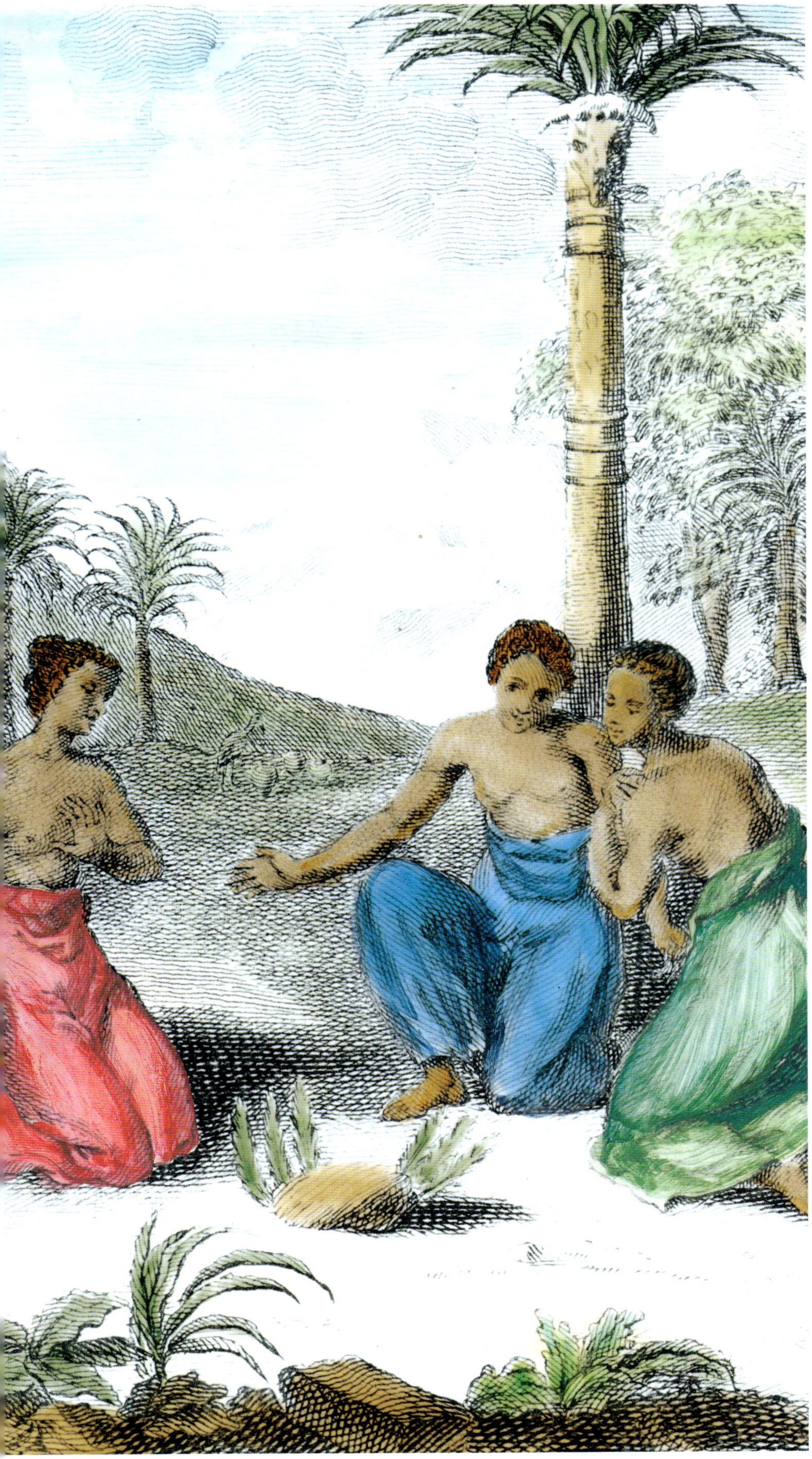

MODJADJI I

RAINMAKING CEREMONY

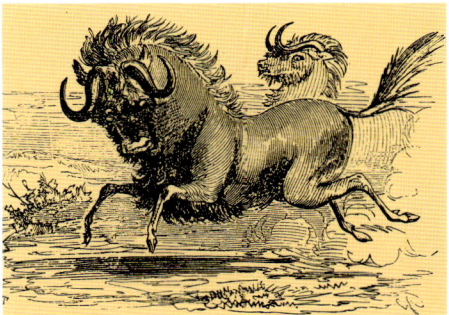

The Gnu

Of all the animals of southern Africa, the gnu, or wildebeest, is the one whose shape is the most extraordinary. It has the eyes, coloring, and nostrils of a buffalo, the feet of an antelope, the mane and the tail of a donkey, the neck and bearing of a horse; its horns come down perpendicularly to the level of its eyes, then extend forward at a right angle in the most fearsome way.

Its movements have a threatening air; it shakes its tail violently like a lion. As soon as it is surprised or frightened, it pirouettes, turns in a circle, stops, takes a few steps toward the object that is the source of its anxiety, flees bucking, and stops again. One may often see herds of gnus form a circle and play, chasing each other without leaving the circle; they seem to take pleasure in the whirlwinds of dust that their exercise raises around them.

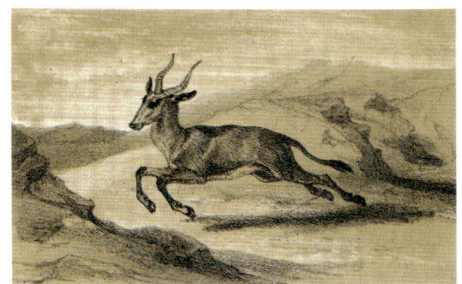

The Bubal Antelope

The Basutos attribute to the herds of bubal antelopes, or hartebeests, a mysterious shepherd whom they call Unkonagnana, "little nose." He lives in the Maloutis and hides from human eyes. They also claim that the bubal has, between its horns and hidden in its fur, a very dangerous yellow viper called a kuane. And so when a bubal is slain, they hit the top of its head with a stick several times before piercing its heart.

Song of the Bubal

Fawn-colored trotter, she can't gallop,
she goes the way her flanks go.
She's a cow who hides her calf
in the streams' secret fords;
She's Unkonagnana's cow.
And now, she's not trotting anymore
She has stopped to cry out.

The Moon and the Newborn

Nearly two months go by after the birth before the mother comes outside with her newborn. A small ceremony decides when their seclusion must come to an end.

On a clear evening, the baby is carried out into the courtyard. They point at the moon, and if the child's eyes focus on the heavenly body, it is concluded that the child may safely make its appearance in the human world.

And the conquerors would stop at the foot of the mountain, without crossing the invisible boundary that separated them from the kingdom of the famous rainmaker Modjadji, she who was then called the Immortal.

She always confined herself to her palace, and only appeared on the days of great drought, when a powerful remedy was required.

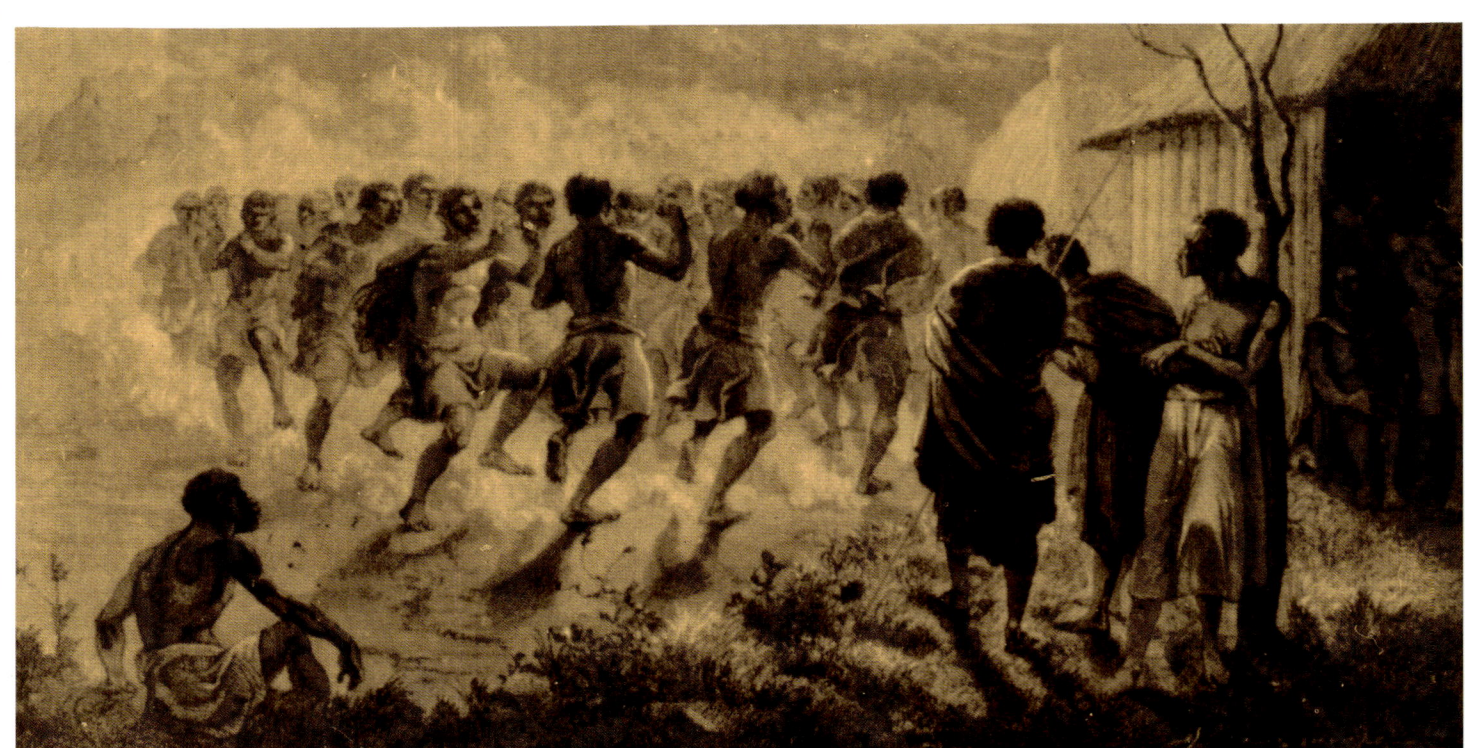

PRESENTATION OF THE BABY TO THE MOON.

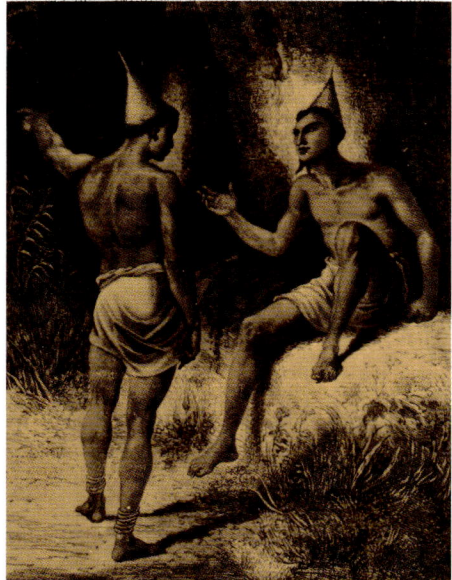

RIVER-DWELLERS OF THE ZAMBEZI

Then she would appear with her hair braided in the shape of antelope horns; and she would dance on the edge of the cliff, accompanied by the crystalline music of the digoma drums, the famous sacred drums of the Lovedu, the only ones capable of moving the spirits of the ancestors.

Little by little, clouds would form on the horizon, would come and go, draw near, then stop precisely above the plateau; and suddenly rain would fall on the territory of the Lovedu, without ever going so much as an inch onto neighboring lands.

It was this extraordinary precision that dazzled all her contemporaries: the clouds arrived at the chosen time at the chosen spot, and then disappeared on her command, when she judged that the earth had drunk its fill and was no longer the least bit thirsty.

Ambassadors presented themselves at her court, laden with sumptuous gifts. They would describe their countries in great detail; and, if she so decided, Modjadji would make rain fall on the land they had described, no matter how far it was from the high plateaus of the Lovedu.

MODJADJI I

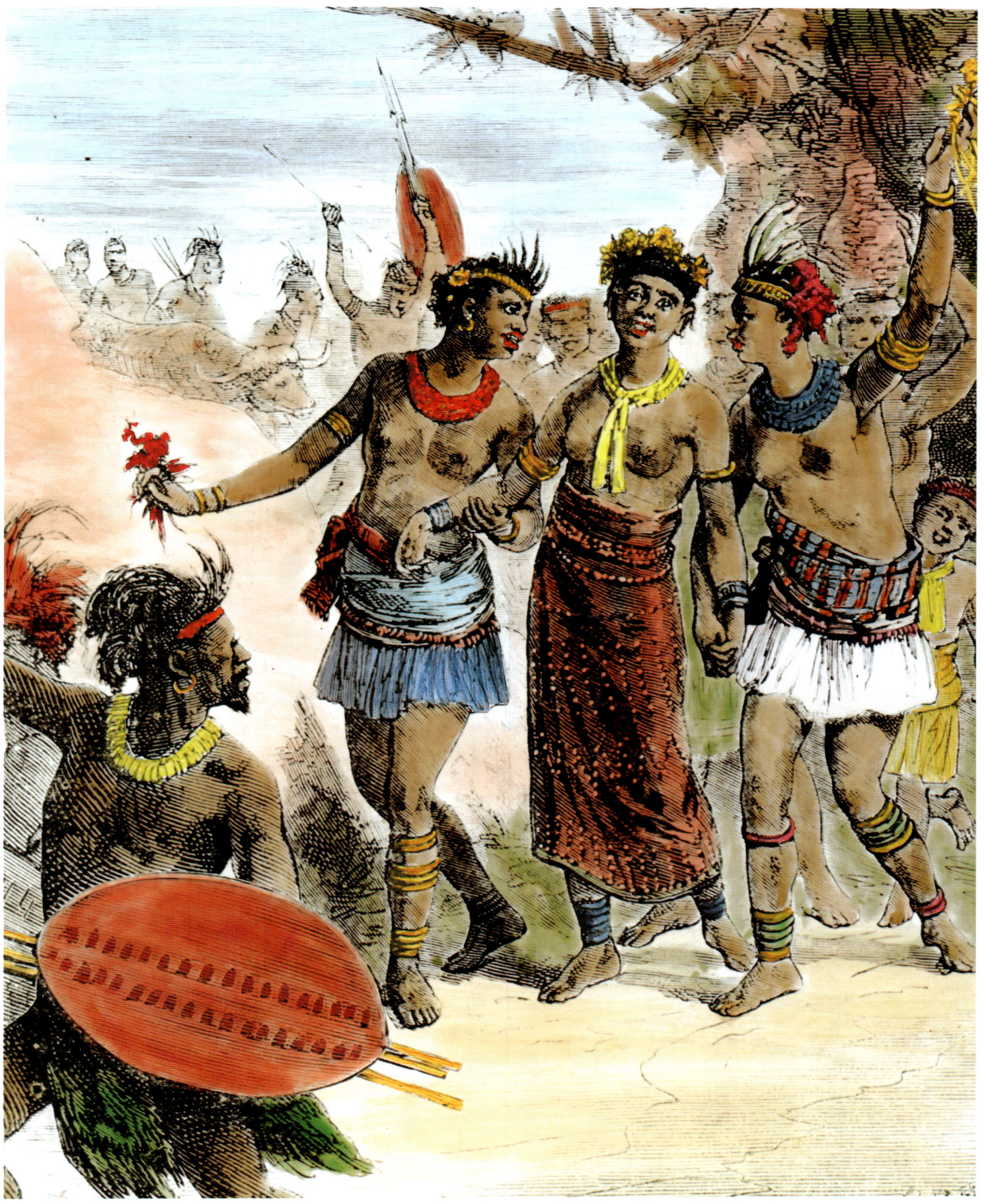

"...AND SHE WOULD DANCE TO THE SOUND OF THE DIGOMA DRUMS..."

Song of the Rainy Season

First one hears the cries of joy that welcome the rains and continue all through the winter, that privileged time during which the young people gather and celebrate:

Hello, end of winter!
It is raining: let's go back to Bumsa!
Great gazelles, put on your makeup,
Let Walo be beautiful!
Let's go to the esplanade
Let your bells ring out,
Rake the ground for those who have come.
Let us lunge and draw back!
Watch and admire!
Let us work hard, and admire!

Politeness

These tribes have rules of etiquette that must be observed. If you should interrupt someone, it is advisable to say: "Permit me to strike you on the mouth." If you approve of what another says: "I rise for you." A chief speaking to his subjects calls them his "lords and masters." You address an older person as "my father, my mother"; an equal as "my brother"; inferiors as "my children." You kiss a superior on the knee; if you do not fear him too greatly, you kiss him on the hand; a little more familiarity allows you to kiss him on the shoulder; finally, only equals kiss each other the way we do, on the cheeks. Courtesy requires that before you serve your guests you taste in their presence the dishes you are going to serve them. He who kills a cow would never dream of not sending the head and brisket to his father, a shank to his older brother, a shoulder to his little brothers, the backbone to his sisters. The head is symbolic of the dignity of the father as head of the family.

The Rain Song

Sung by a men's and a women's chorus, who answer each other.

Both:
Get up, get up...
The rain is coming.
The men:
Get up, get up...
The rain will come.
The women:
Get up, get up...
Where is the rain?
The men:
Drizzle...
The women:
Drizzle rain!
The men:
Drizzle...
Meanwhile, the women:
The striped one (the quagga) is braying with thirst
The men:
Drizzle...
The women:
We are calling for the rain!

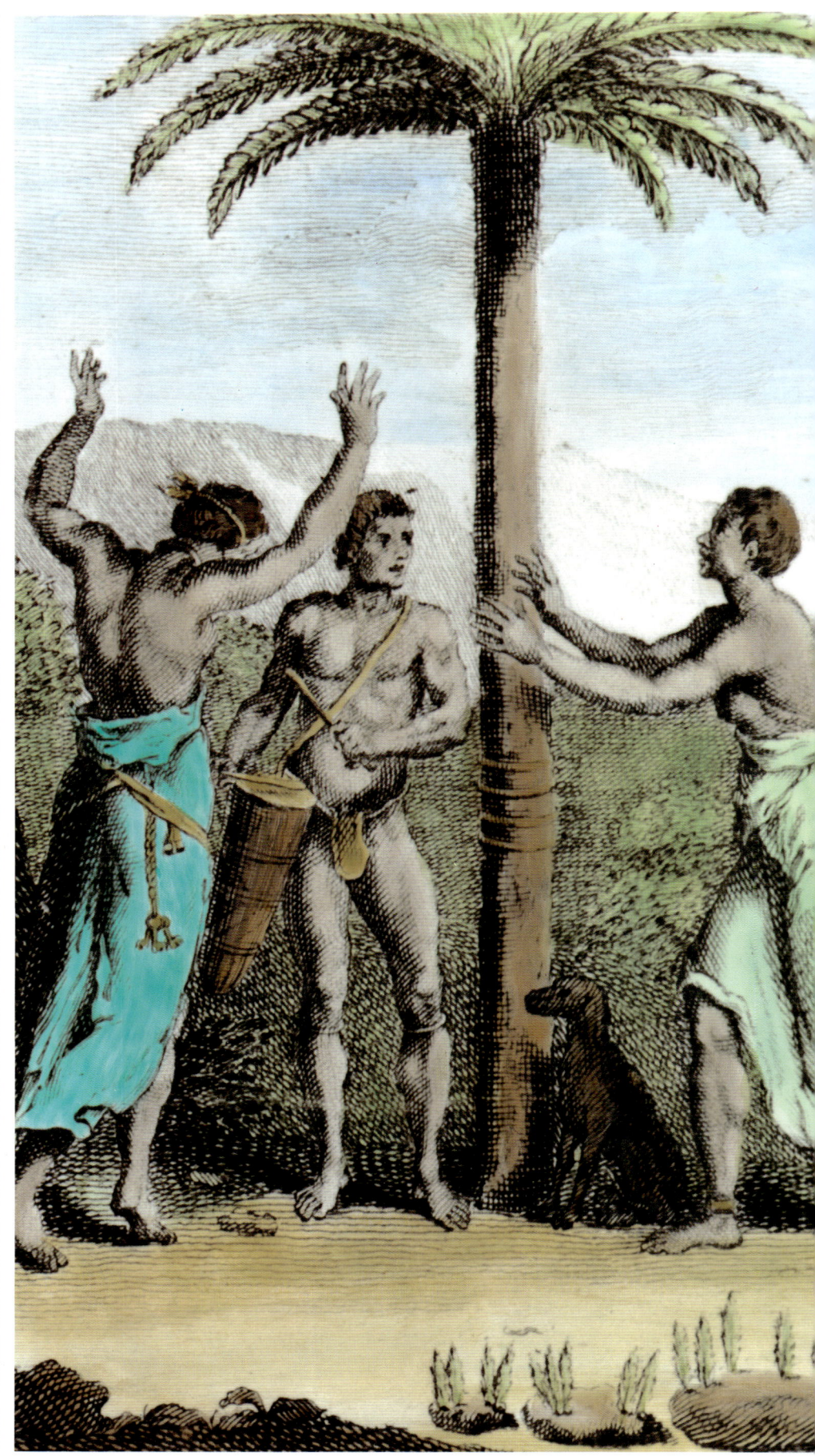

SUMMONING THE RAIN

MODJADJI I

First came the messengers of King Manukuza, their hands full of the gold of Mwene Matapa. Then came the envoys from Ventaland, giants whose knees shook, who did not dare lay eyes on the queen and always addressed her in the third person as "she who gives us water to wash our faces." There came, too, envoys from Phalacora, from Chopiland, from Wurwa and from Tswana, from Khatta and from Magépia, from Letswalo; some wanted to avoid natural disasters, and others supernatural calamities, for the rainmaker also had a reputation as a miracle worker.

Shaka himself was in the habit of sending flocks as an offering to the queen, whenever the rain would not obey his all-powerful sorcerers. And it is said that at the peak of his glory, he and his troops came within two days' march of the little kingdom of the Lovedu and then just stood there, suddenly frozen with terror at the thought of what had happened to Zwidé, the great Zwidé, who had been struck dead on the banks of the Oliphant River.

During this same period, while Modjadji danced up rainstorms on the edge of her cliff, all the peoples of the central plateau were throwing themselves at each other, in the cycle of wars of the Lifaqané.

But this fury, as if by a miracle, always stopped at the banks of the Oliphant River; and as empires were built up and smashed down, the minuscule kingdom of the Lovedu quietly followed its path in the sun, the wind, and the rain, wisely apportioned by Queen Modjadji.

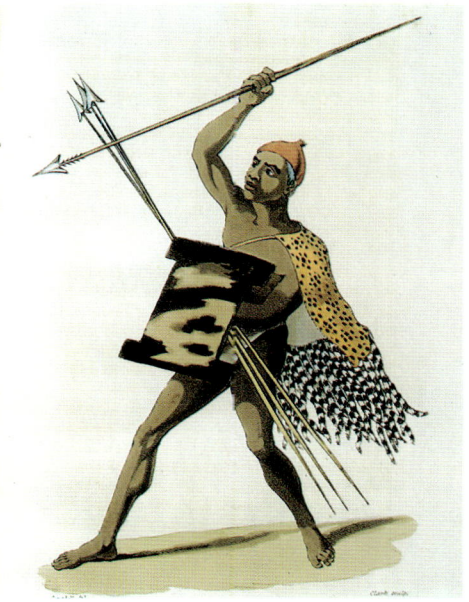

"THERE CAME...

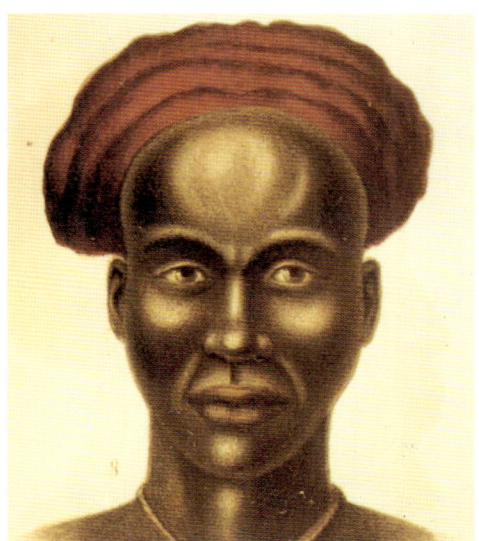

...THE KING'S MESSENGERS...

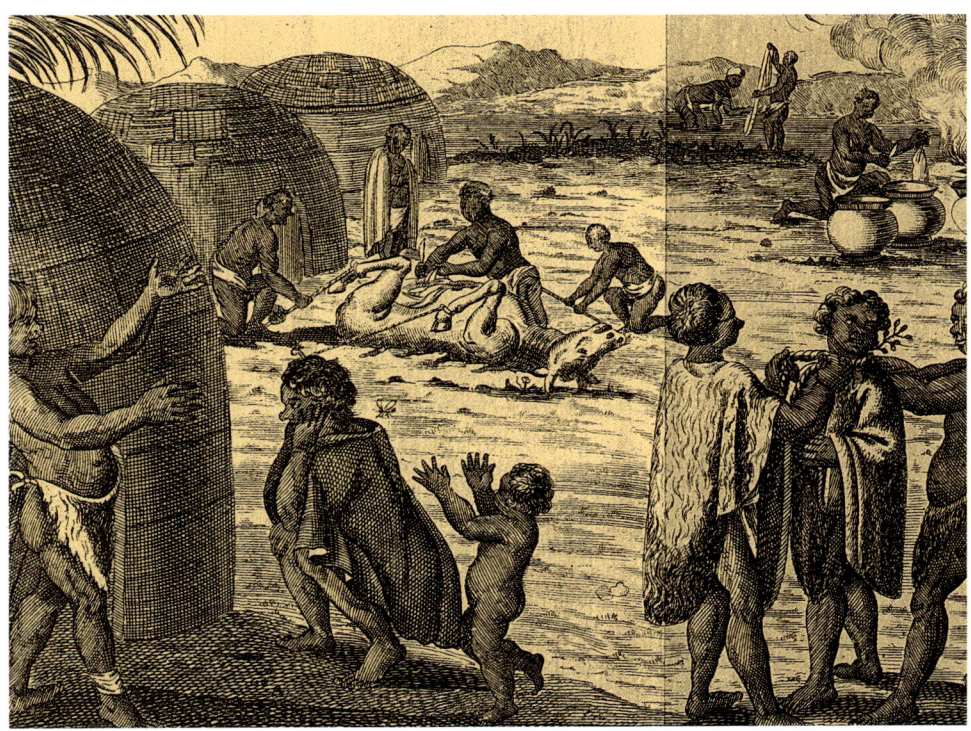

"...THE TINY KINGDOM OF THE LOVEDU..."

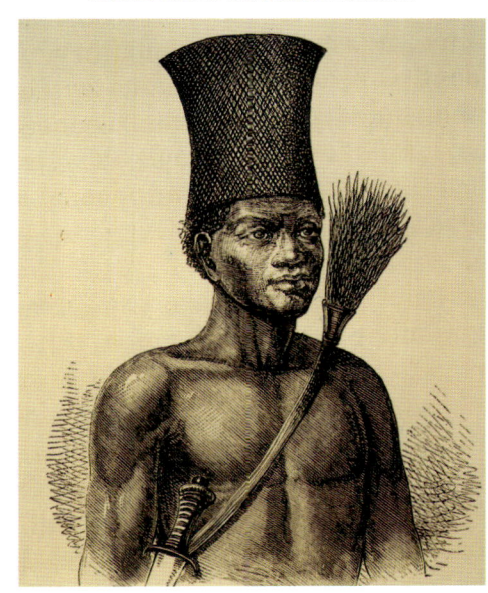

...THEIR HANDS FULL OF GOLD."

The little fairy-tale kingdom seemed invincible.

When Modjadji I died in 1850, the succession was arranged according to the usual rules.

One by one, the young girls of the palace were led into the room of the late queen, where each raised an arm toward a little door half-hidden by a bark wall hanging; this was called the "night door," for it opened onto the beyond.

Suddenly, the little false door was opened by the hands of the ancestors, and one of the young girls came out into the light of day, becoming Modjadji II.

Some years later, the whites crossed the Oliphant River and the new queen attempted to turn them against each other, the missionaries against the men from the Boer government.

But the two forces walked hand in hand, and little by little the gods turned away from the modest kingdom of the Lovedu.

Despite the queen's prayers and dances, soon the rain fell no more often than in the neighboring countries; and the clouds of locusts returned.

In 1894, it seemed that the drought and the locusts were even more abundant than anywhere else: then Modjadji II withdrew into the farthest corner of her palace and drank a cup of poison, as was advised for those who had failed.

It is true, the force of the ancient queens is no more, but the faith of the Lovedu people has remained intact.

They know—they know that one day, tomorrow perhaps, a little queen, humble and unassuming, will draw near the cliff and begin to dance, her plump neck stretching its folds out toward the sun; and a cloud will form far away on the plain and come to rest over the plateau, precisely above it, as in the days of old.

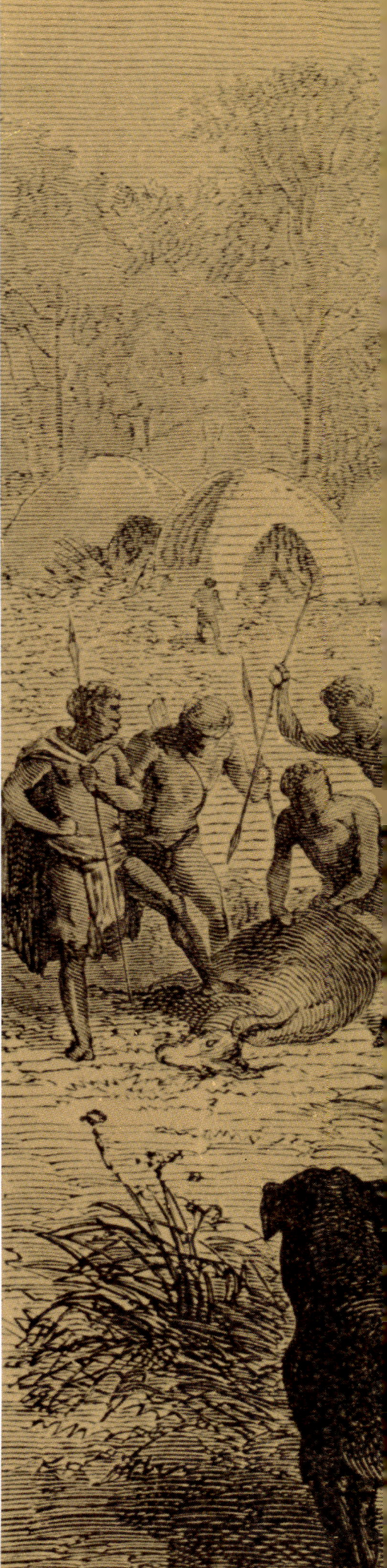

WOMEN COLLECTING WATER IN OSTRICH EGGS ▷

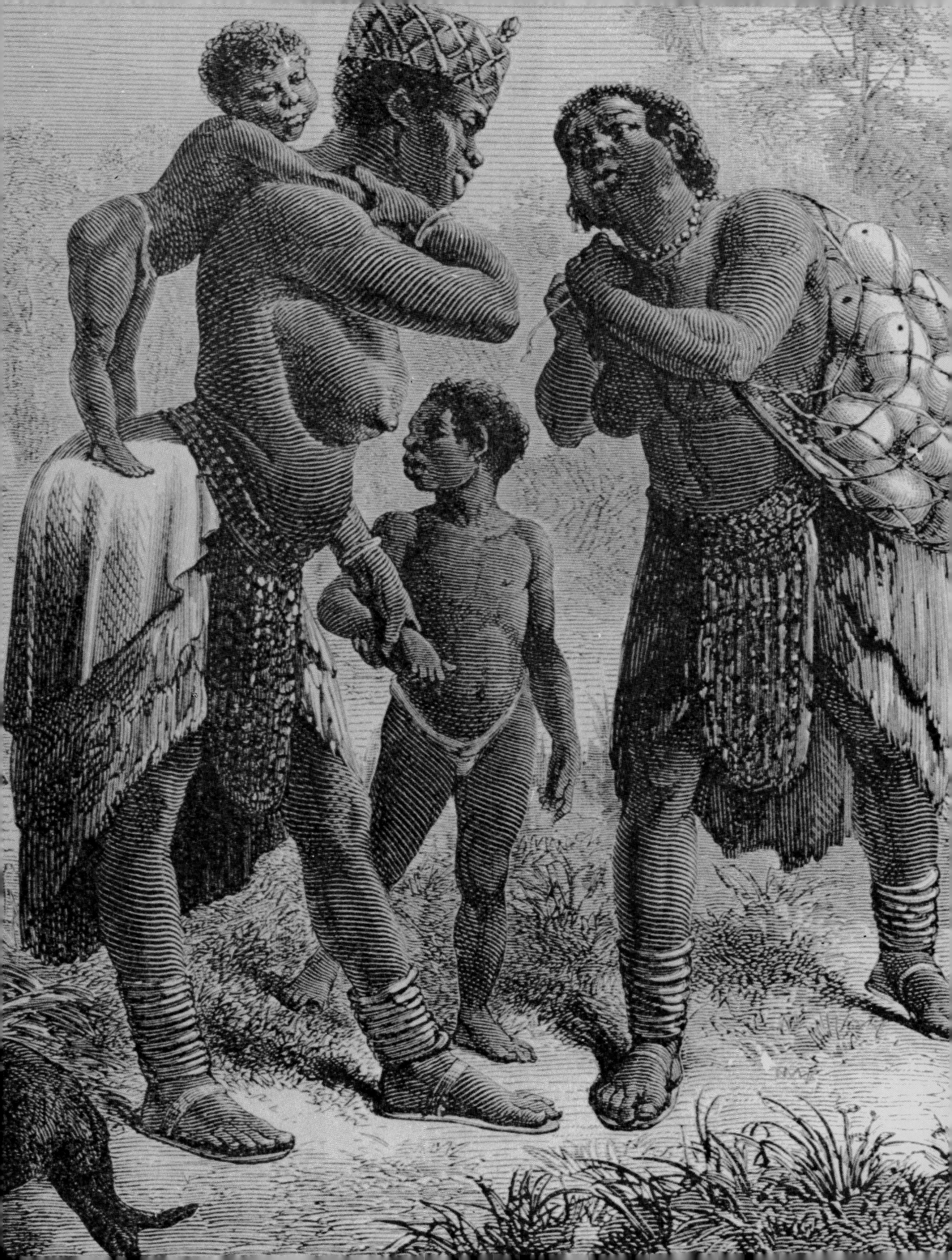

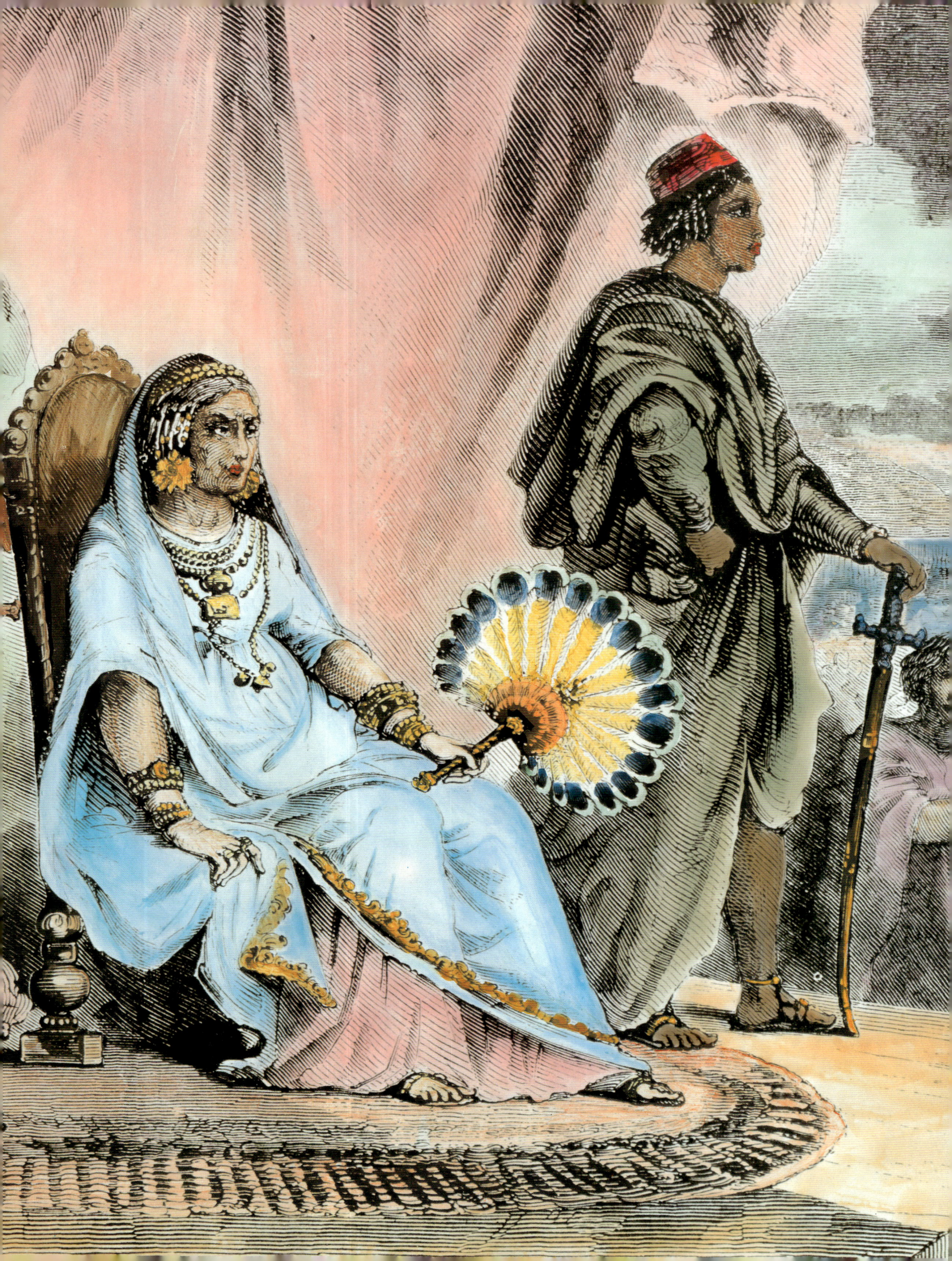

RANAVALONA I

MOTHER AND FATHER OF THE MALAGASY PEOPLE

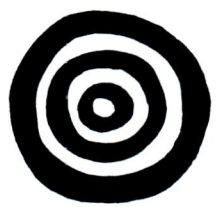

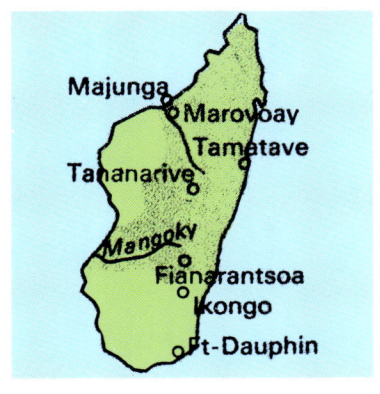

"Oh my people, I am here to tell you that I will not pray to the ancestors of the Europeans, but only to my gods and my ancestors!" Ranavalona I declared on the day of her coronation...

MADAGASCAR IN THE EIGHTEENTH CENTURY WAS STILL AN ENIGMA, A KIND OF SLEEPING CONTINENT WHOSE PEOPLE WERE JUST BARELY STARTING TO OPEN THEIR EYES TO THE REST OF THE WORLD. THEN A LITTLE KINGDOM APPEARED AROUND Tananarive (the present-day city of Antananarivo), on the central plateau; an audacious man had himself crowned there under the name of Andrianampoinimerina, "the lord at the heart of Merina."

He wished to unite all the tribes of the island and adopted the following motto: "The sea is the border of my rice field."

The monarchy brought with it a mystical grandeur: the living king was the visible god, "the father and mother of the people"; and the dead king was the invisible god, more powerful still, more fearsome in the bottom of his grave than the living king with his flesh and bones.

In 1810, on his deathbed, Andrianampoinimerina had his two older sons killed in order to better assure the succession of the youngest, Radama I, whom he considered the most worthy.

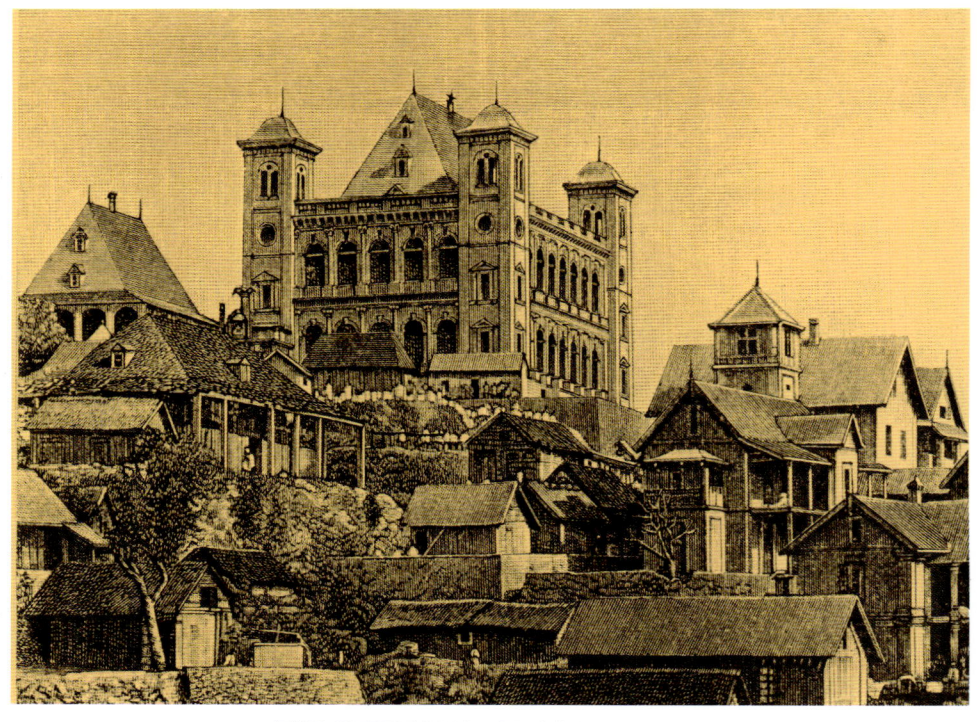

THE QUEEN'S PALACE AT TANANARIVE

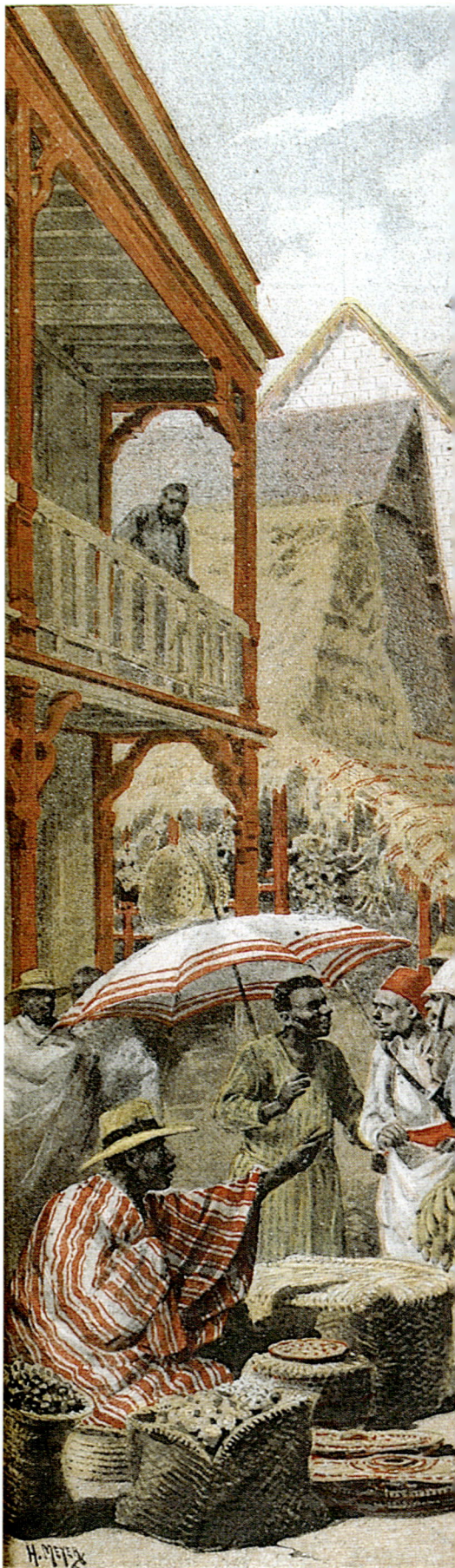

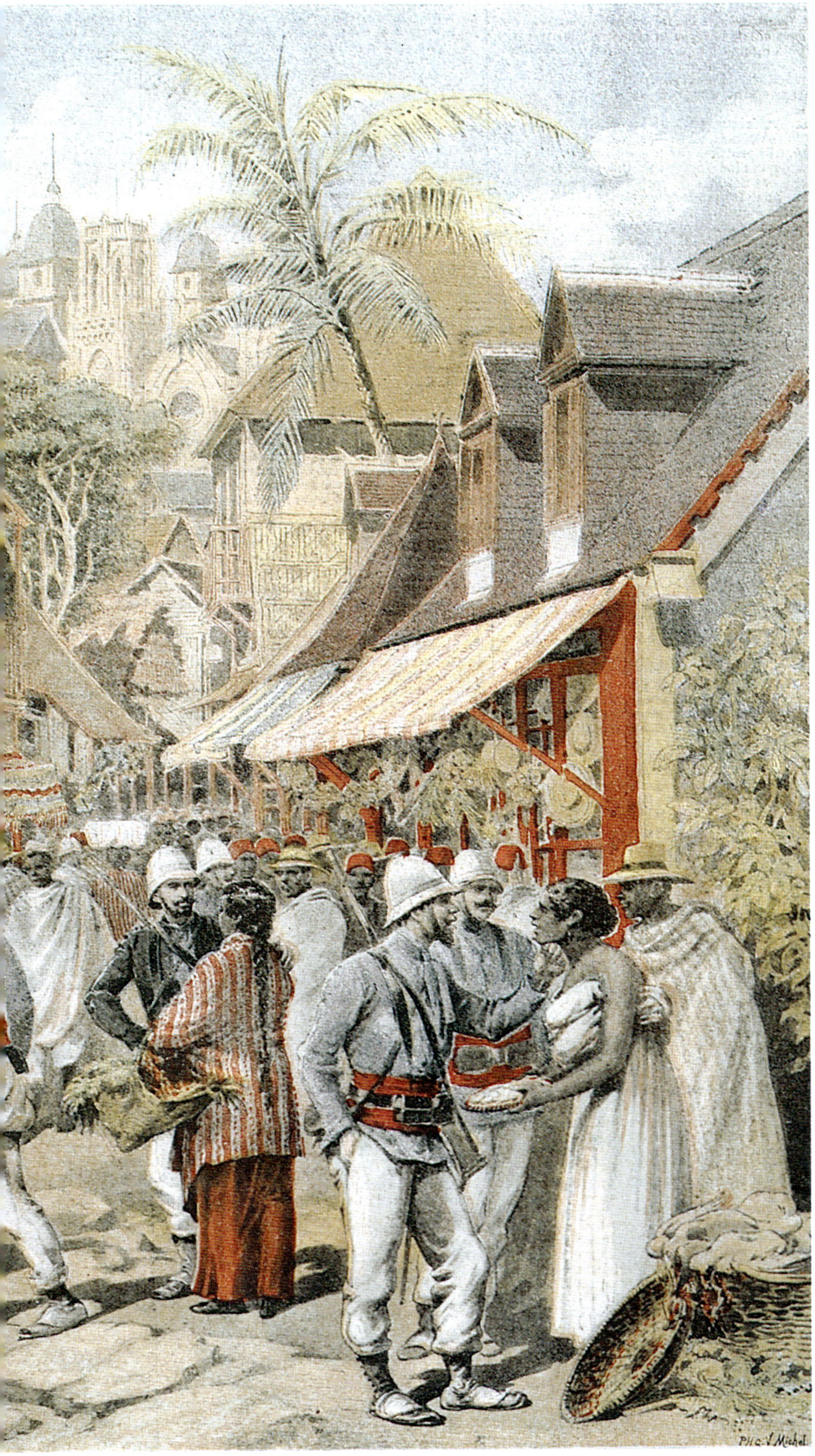

RANAVALONA I

TANANARIVE UNDER FRENCH OCCUPATION, 1895

Ravahiny

Ravahiny was a great ruler of Boina, the Sakalava kingdom of the west, who governed from 1780 to 1808. She was at once feared and worshipped as a goddess, and her subjects maintained a veritable cult in her honor. Her long reign left an undying impression on her subjects. She changed men according to her pleasure, as easily as kings change wives, and no one had anything to say about it. Invited by the king of Merina, Andrianampoinimerina, she went in great style and told him: "I have brought you, oh Andrianampoinimerina, three cannons as big as my thigh, as well as seven barrels of powder and twenty rifles."

Jumping up and down for joy, the king Andrianampoinimerina had the cannons fired three times, then declared: "This is very pleasant and I like it very much; this is overwhelming and I can't get over it."

Ravahiny stayed for more than a month in Merina and concluded a treaty of friendship that allowed Andrianampoinimerina to supply himself with weapons more easily through Majunga, which was under the queen's control.

This northwestern port knew prosperity under Ravahiny, thanks to the maritime privilege that was in the hands of the Antalaotra. Their sailboats linked Majunga with neighboring Africa and traded along the western coast. For all practical purposes, they held a monopoly on port traffic, in return for the taxes they paid to the queen.

Ravahiny died in 1808, during the era of the great Lahidama; she was laid to rest in Trongay, west of Majunga.

As is written in the *Tantaran ny Andriana*, or the Book of Kings of Madagascar: "Even when the Sakalava were at war, they did not dare point their rifles at Majunga, for that is where Ravahiny was."

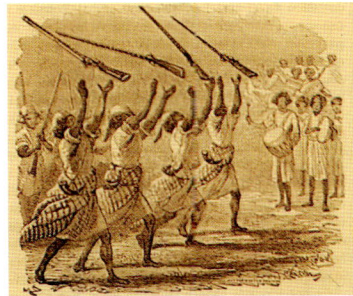

War Dance of the Sakalava

The Sakalava have a particular dance in which groups of men reproduce the various movements of an army at war. They act out attacks, scrimmages, pursuit, triumph after victory. They repeatedly throw their long rifles into the air, rifles decorated with copper-headed nails, and catch them with one hand, while the other throws a kerchief so that it floats in the air. The spectacle remains serious and restrained throughout.

Indeed, Radama I was a young sovereign graced with talent, who ended up getting his hands on three-fifths of the great island.

He yearned to be an absolute monarch, master of the body and soul of all his subjects. But in truth, he did not consider himself a messenger from heaven, an incarnation of the gods: a skeptical thinker, clad in an elegant cynicism, he was the high priest of a religion in which he had ceased to believe, though he still cashed in on its benefits. Fascinated by Western civilization, he saw in it a powerful means for extending his power: he modernized his army, suppressed certain elements of the ancient religion, proclaimed his sovereignty over the whole island, and, after gaining recognition from England, sent young nobles to study in London with his Western "brothers."

His ambition was clear: to transform Madagascar into a modern power, along the model of the white nations which had been knocking at the gates of the Great Land for three centuries.

In 1818, Radama I of Merina opened the island to the pastors of the London Missionary Society. The latter played their usual role with finesse: they introduced Western ways, romanized the Malagasy writing system, and in general, portrayed themselves as being much more than priests—they played assistants to the less developed world. They also helped spread Merina culture and power across the whole island, which until then had been divided into several kingdoms.

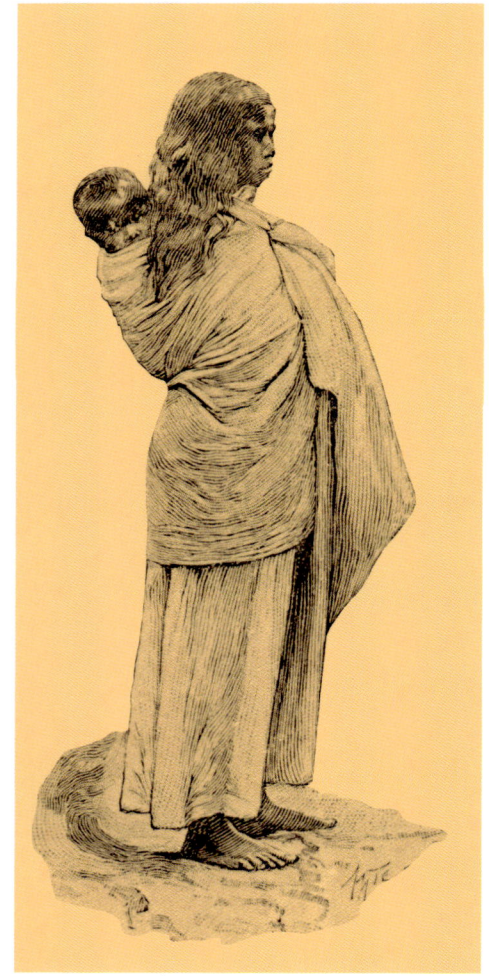

MALAGASY WOMAN

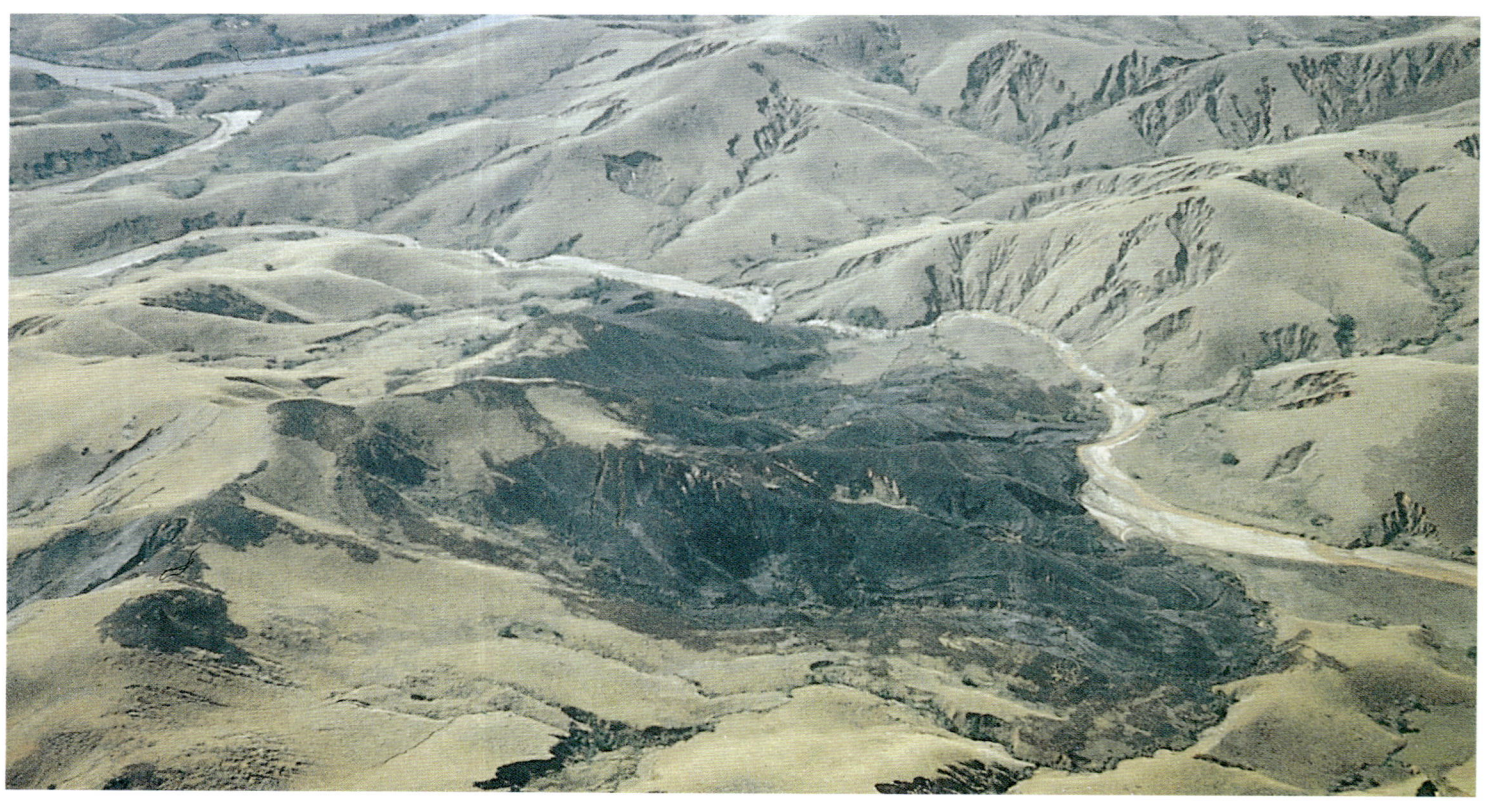

MERINA

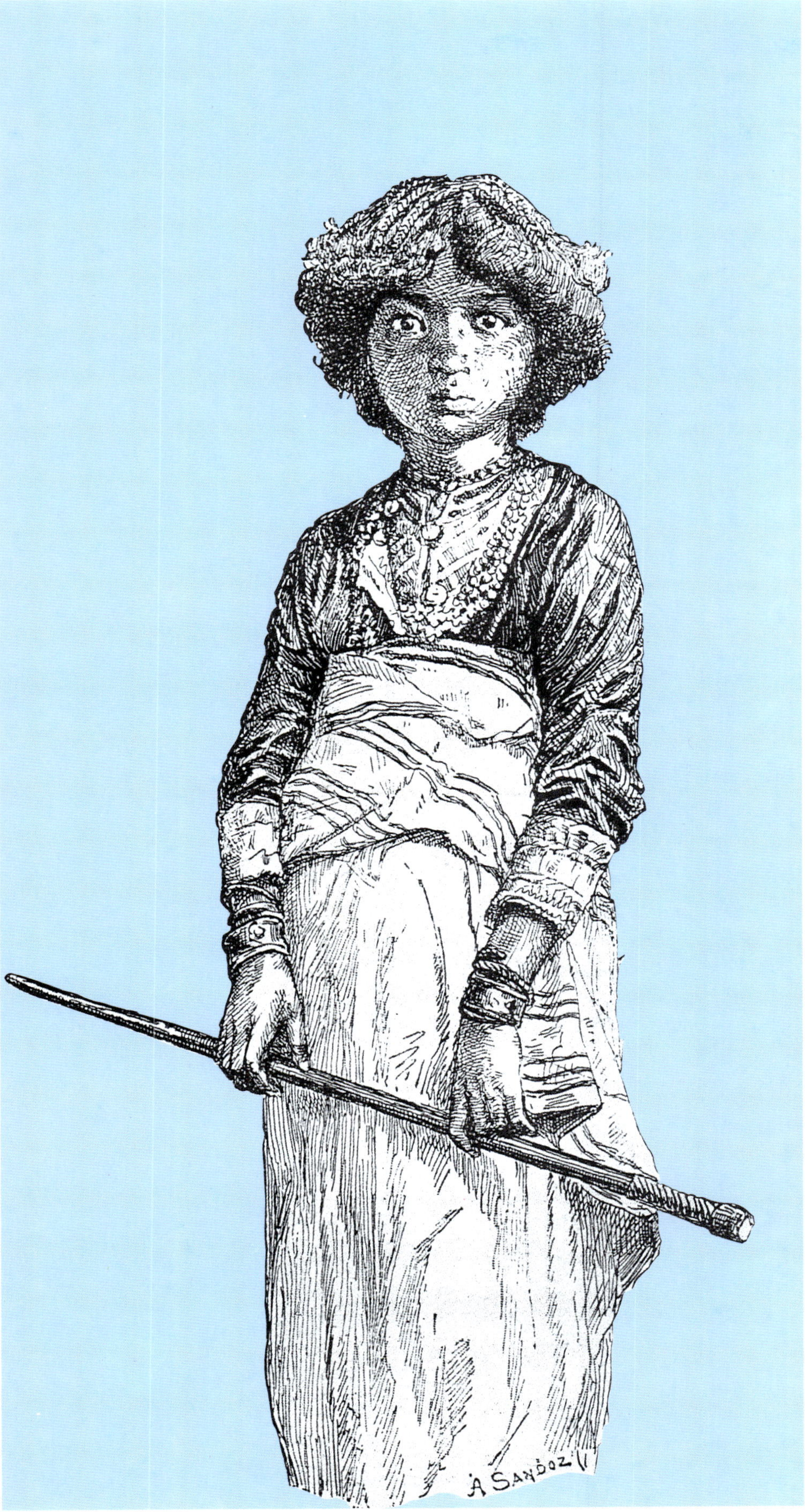

RANAVALONA I

BINAO, QUEEN OF THE SAKALAVA

Tananarive

Tananarive, now called Antananarivo, the capital of the country, is situated almost in the center of the plateau, on one of the most beautiful hills. The outlying areas, which surround the city proper on all sides, were originally separate cities that came together as they grew. Most of the houses there are built of earth or clay.

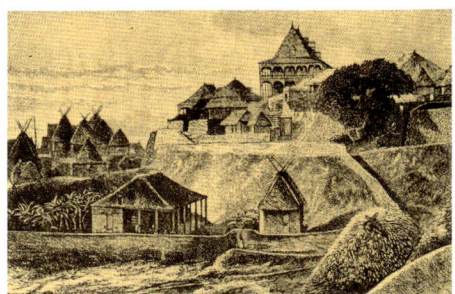

Tananarive, the Palace Quarter

The royal palaces are grouped together in a vast enclosure. One of these buildings is much taller than the other structures not only in the capital, but on the whole island; this is the main palace, "Manjaka-Miadana."
A wide three-story veranda encircles the palace and rests on enormous wooden columns linked by arcades. Everything, the walls, the roof, the veranda, is painted white, except for the balustrade.

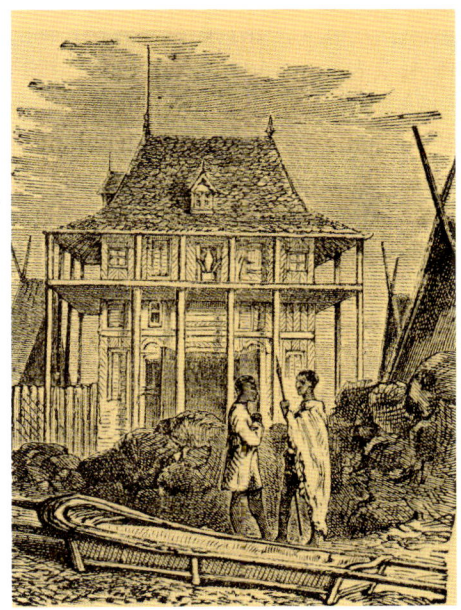

The Chief's House in Ambatomanga

A wide veranda encircled it, supported by wooden pillars and topped off by a gallery on the third floor; the moldings were shaped with care and the walls solidly constructed. Shutters and paneled doors gave it a truly civilized flavor.
The ground floor was divided into three rooms, with the largest in the center.

That was how it began. Then, little by little, preceded by its carpenters and masons, its gunsmiths and schoolteachers armed with their primers, Christianity opened a breach in the traditional soul of the Malagasy people. The people began to show reluctance, which they expressed in court. Radama suddenly died, most likely poisoned by a few notables, by "men of the past," as Radama liked to call them, on July 27, 1828.

That is when a strange feminine figure arose, seemingly from another era: Ranavalona I, Radama I's own wife, a fabulous creature, a sphinx, an archaeopteryx stepping suddenly out of the shadows of the past, and whose whole ambition would be to annihilate her husband's work in order to return to the olden days, to the golden years of the great Andrianampoinimerina.

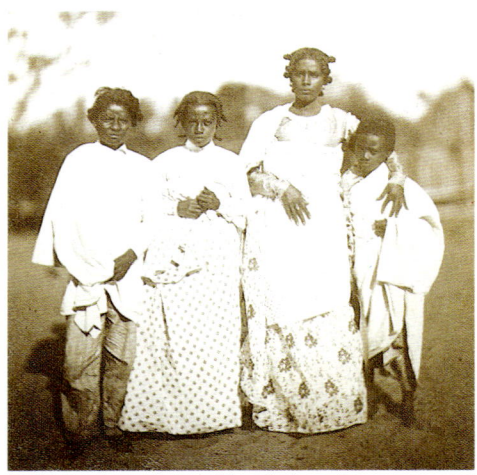

Ranavalona was forty when she assumed power. All the advisors to the late king were executed during the night of mourning; and the organizer of the plot, Rahiniahay, the queen's agent and secret lover, soon joined them in the other world. Ranavalona knew no debts, neither of the heart nor of the body. She had cleared the playing field: from now on she could govern as she wished; she could play her role as an instrument of the gods.

On the day she was crowned, she declared:

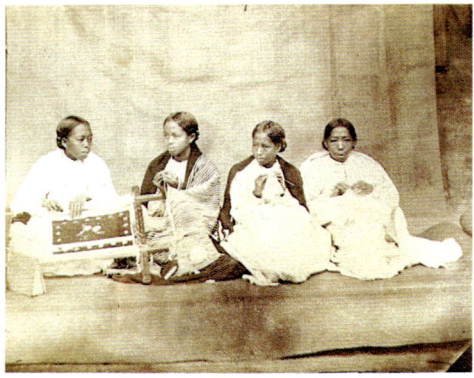

"Oh, children of Merina, learn now and remember that I will change nothing that our ancestors did; and learn now and remember that I am no longer a woman in her toga, but that from this moment forth I am your *Rayaman dreny,* your father and mother under heaven."

"I am no longer a woman in her toga": the creature who expressed herself this way had hard features, a wide jaw, and thick eyebrows, and one might naturally assume that she had risen above her sex. But perhaps one must place these words in the context of their time: in the past, young unmarried girls went barefoot, while married women were supposed to wear shoes so that young people would know that the "woman had a master," as the accepted expression went. And this is most likely what the words decreed on the day of her coronation meant: Ranavalona would have no "master"; she would choose among men as one chooses fruit at the market, simply to satisfy the hunger in one's belly.

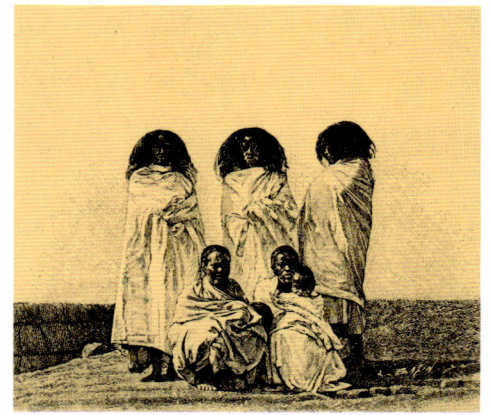

In fact, all throughout her reign, the men whom she came to love to excess, who would make her feel a little too much like a woman and forget that she was a queen, would one day be led to the great flat stone at the far end of the royal terrace. From there, they would be thrown into the void of the Mahamasima Valley, which even today, more than a century later, still bears the indelible nickname of Red Valley.

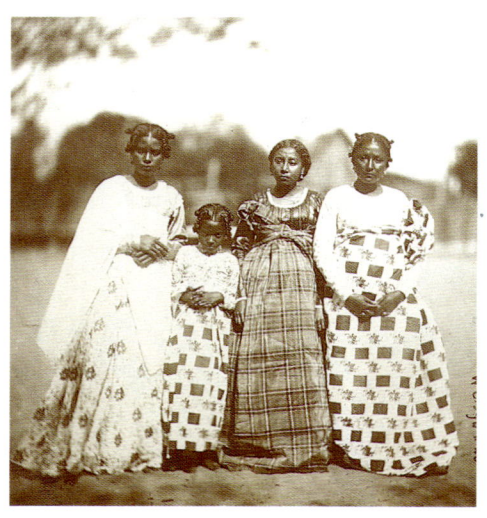

MALAGASY WOMEN

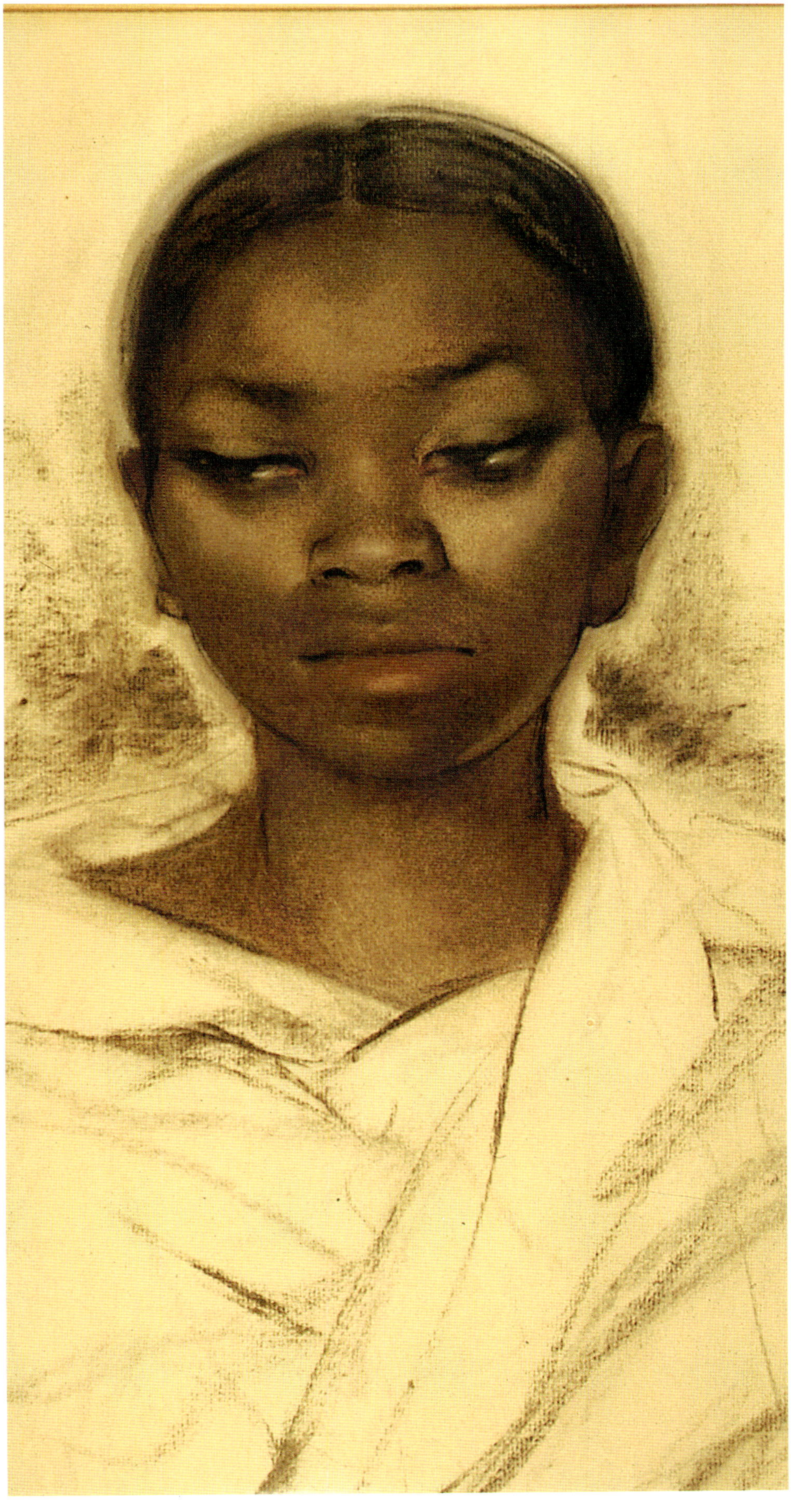

The Fiséhoana of Ranavalona I

At the *fiséhoana,* or coronation, of Ranavalona I in June 1829, there was an imposing deployment of military force. The goal of the government was to loudly affirm the queen's attachment to ancient customs and her resolution to maintain them at any price, by force if necessary.

The Kabary

Nothing was neglected that might inspire submission and respect for the royal authority. On the city's heights, the cannons fired a prolonged salvo early in the morning; troops numbering fifty thousand men were led to the place of assembly, in order to show everyone the force at the queen's disposal.

The queen's message was this: "I declare to you, people of Madagascar, that I am not a deceitful queen. What man here wishes to change the customs of our ancestors and of the twelve rulers of this country? If someone here would like to change the customs of our ancestors and of the twelve rulers, know that I detest it.

"Now, if anyone is thinking of dishonoring the idols, of calling divination childish, or of desecrating the tombs of the Vazimbas, know that I detest it, and anyone in my country who would destroy them is guilty in my eyes.

"As for baptism, congregations, places of worship separate from schools, and observing the Sabbath, how many masters are there in this kingdom? Am I not the sole ruler? Those things must no longer take place."

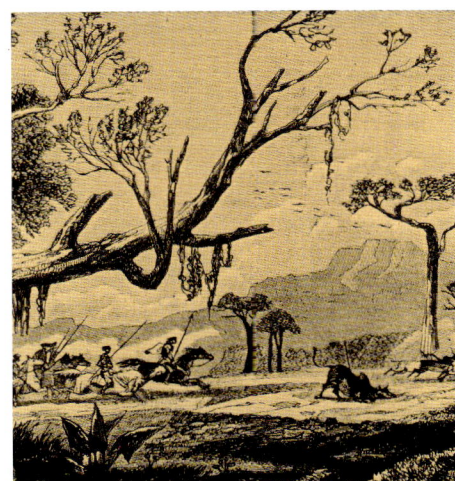

Hunting Wild Cattle

In ancient times, the chiefs' favorite pastime was hunting the wild cattle and boars that populated the uninhabited regions of the island; during these expeditions, carried out on an enormous scale, thousands of animals would be brought down.

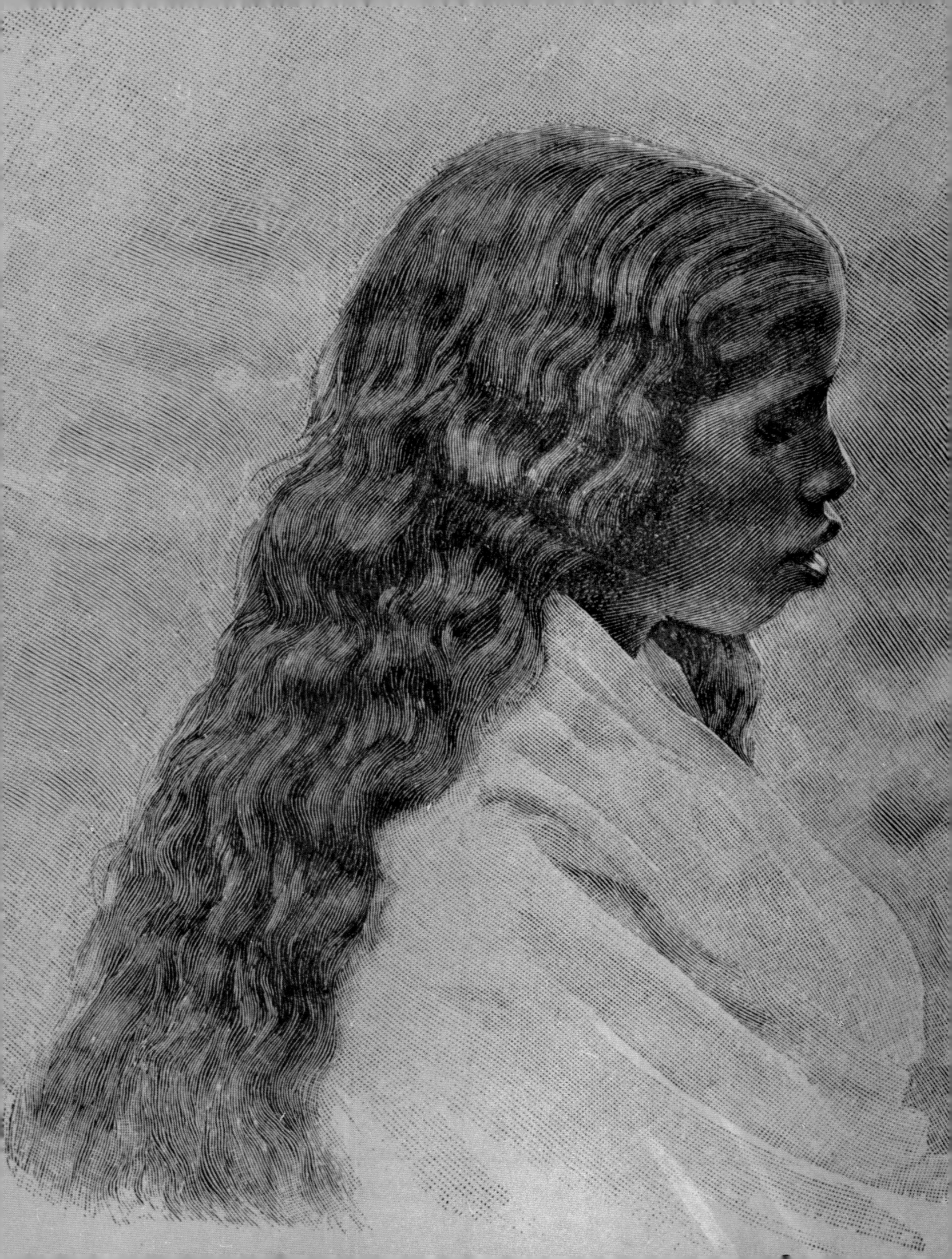

RANAVALONA I

On March 1, 1835, the queen made the following proclamation:
"Oh my people, I am here to tell you that I will not pray to the ancestors of the Europeans, but only to my gods and my ancestors! It was thanks to custom that the twelve kings reigned and it is thanks to custom that I myself reign. Your own ancestors respected the customs, and custom itself respects custom. I will put to death anyone who shall practice a foreign religion, oh my people, for that person is a renegade, a traitor, and a liar to his own blood. Oh my people, let it be so, for I am heir to the Twelve Kings!"

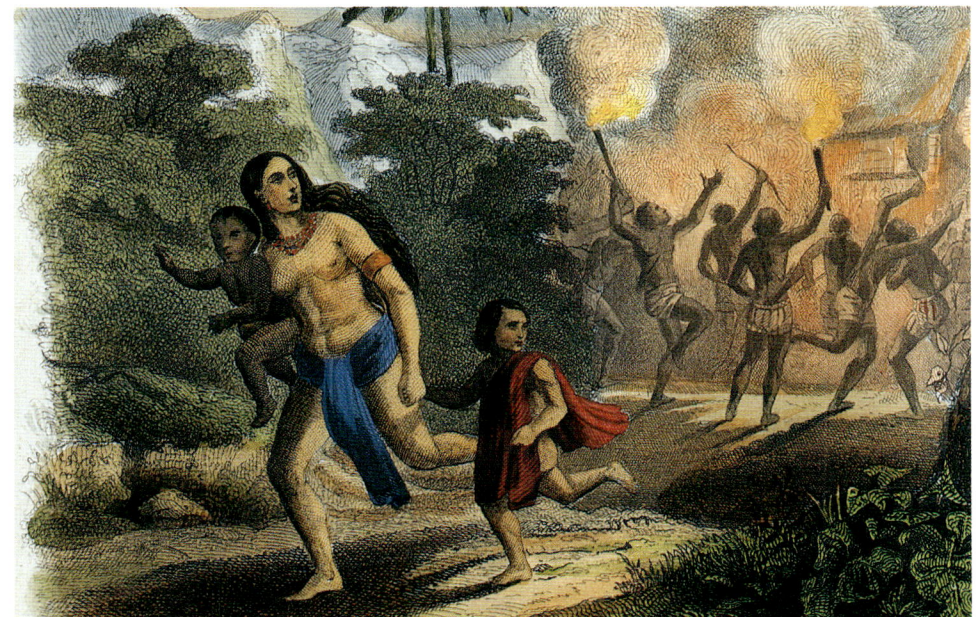

From then on it was open season, and a wave of denunciations inundated the plateau of Merina. The memory of that time has preserved the name of the first Malagasy martyr for Christianity, a woman called Rasalama. But the others rapidly sank into anonymity: they were burned and stoned, torn apart, and submitted to the treacherous trial by poison called the Tangéna; and they were thrown from the rocks into Mahamasima Valley.

A process had been set in motion that led inevitably to the ultimate step: Ranavalona I decided to banish all whites from the kingdom.

For a century, and especially since the reign of Radama I, France and England had been fishing in the waters of the Great Island, which seemed to them a highly desirable prey.

The queen's attitude gave the two great colonial powers something in common, creating for an instant an unexpected and most unlikely alliance: on July 20, 1845, a joint Franco-British fleet bombarded the port of Tamatave but was ultimately repulsed.

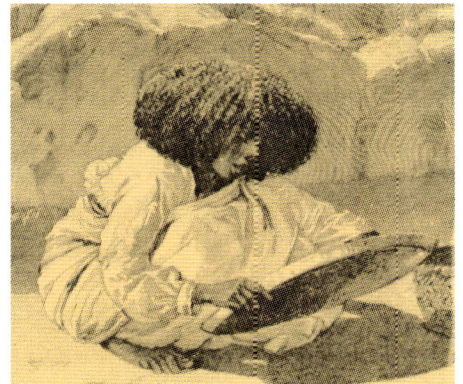

The Royal Infant and the Boar

Randapavola gave birth six times, but not one of her children survived; when she became pregnant a seventh time, she consulted the *sikidy* (divination) with the help of Andrianmanalina, the chief of the sorcerers. The sikidy was favorable.
So Randapavola left and crossed the water at Mahitsiandriana. When she arrived at Ambohiboaladina, above and to the east of Betafo, the slaves who accompanied her built some huts that looked like little boats and Randapavola gave birth.
Then a boar came from the east and climbed into the hut where the newborn lay. They chased it and caught it.
This earned that place the name Ankadindambo. And the royal infant was called Ralambo, because of the boar that had climbed into the hut when he was born in Ambohiboaladina.

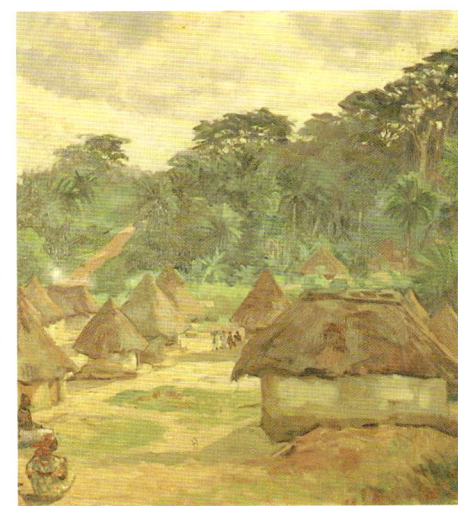

A Malagasy Village

Several coconut trees wave their green plumes and their clusters of fruit high above the rooftops. In front of the doors, women stand, each wearing a simbou necklace at the base of her throat, pounding their rice in wooden mortars with a vigorous and graceful motion. They are clothed in the two squares of red-patterned white fabric that make up the essentials of their garb; some chat with neighbors; others string coral beads.

Then things began to happen very quickly: cunningly coached by outside forces, the Christians of the kingdom organized themselves, forming a secret network, and finally hatching a plot to bring the life of Ranavalona I to an end, and her reign with it. The queen's only son, her "sweet rice," her "blue-rooted plant," was at the head of the conspiracy. The plot was thwarted, and hundreds of implicated Christians were publicly executed. But her son, Rakotond Radama, the serpent she had sheltered in her breast, was curiously spared: this would be the only weakness the queen ever showed during the entire imposing course of her existence.

Even better: before she suddenly passed away, in August 1861, she chose this same Rakotond Radama, her cruelest enemy, the very child who had tried to assassinate her, as her successor.

Ranavalona I was seventy-three years old when she died.

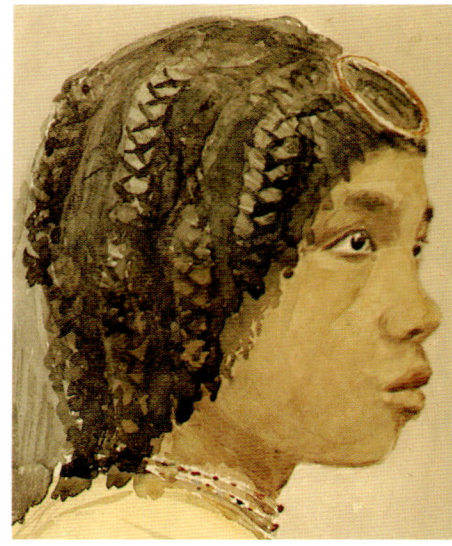

The night before, a few hours before the end, an orange glow appeared around Tananarive, floating above the hills and reflected in the lakes, the water hollows, and the silvery stretches of the rice fields.

The queen wondered about this strange phenomenon, and learned from a dignitary that similar fires had been observed rising from Amanyché, west of Ambonimanga, the night before the great Andrianampoinimerina died; and the old man added: "Queen, these are not fires lit by the hand of man; they come straight from the mouth of the gods."

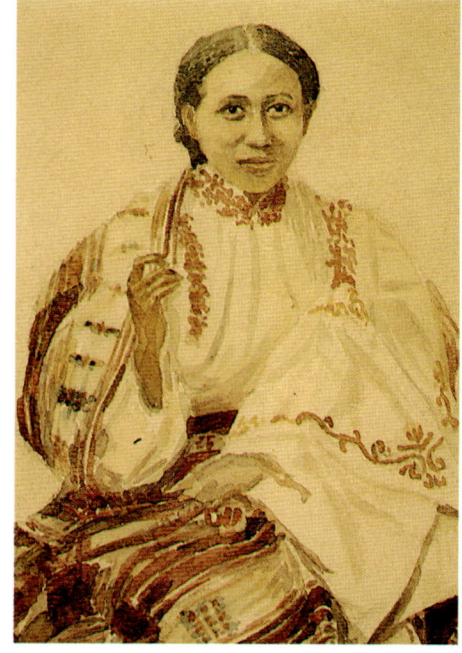

The next morning, Ranavalona was found dead in her bed. They wrapped her in her "robe of power," now a shroud, in the same dress she had worn for her coronation and which must, according to Merina custom, accompany her to the grave.

Ranavalona I had hardly been beloved while she was alive. Yet, upon the news of her death, no inhabitant of the kingdom went to bed for a week; partisans and adversaries alike, they did not wash their feet or hands during that week of mourning; no one, whether victim or agent of her politics, cut their nails or hair.

She had come, she had gone. She had been like a great flame over the world; and all felt in some way that a piece of Malagasy grandeur had plunged into the void on that day, in August 1861.

Thus ends the story of Ranavalona I.

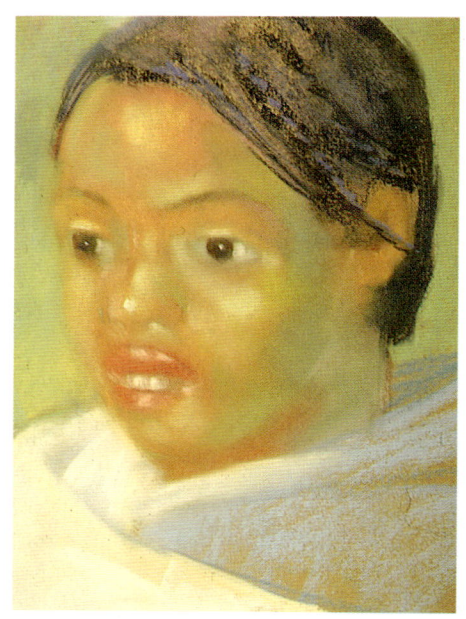

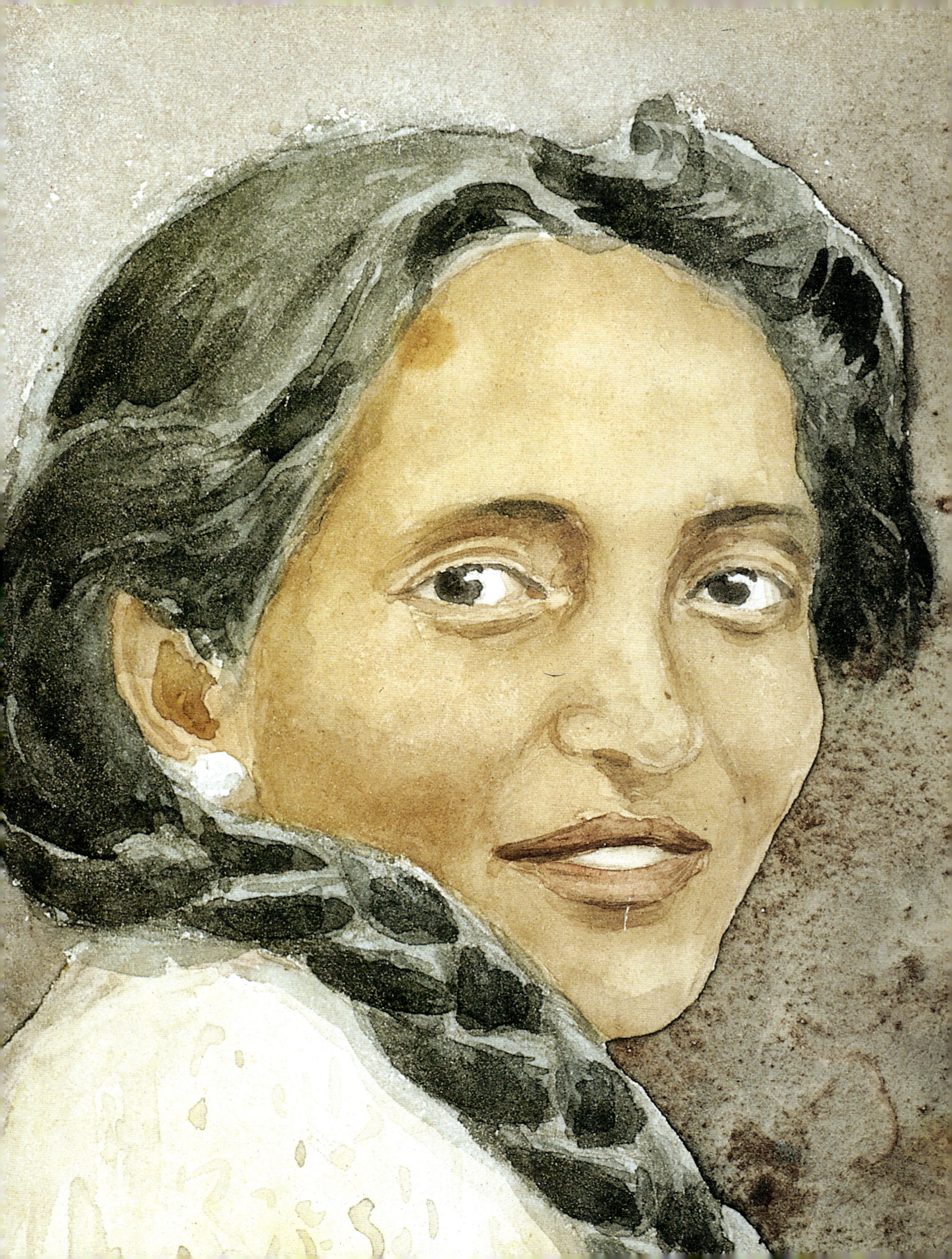

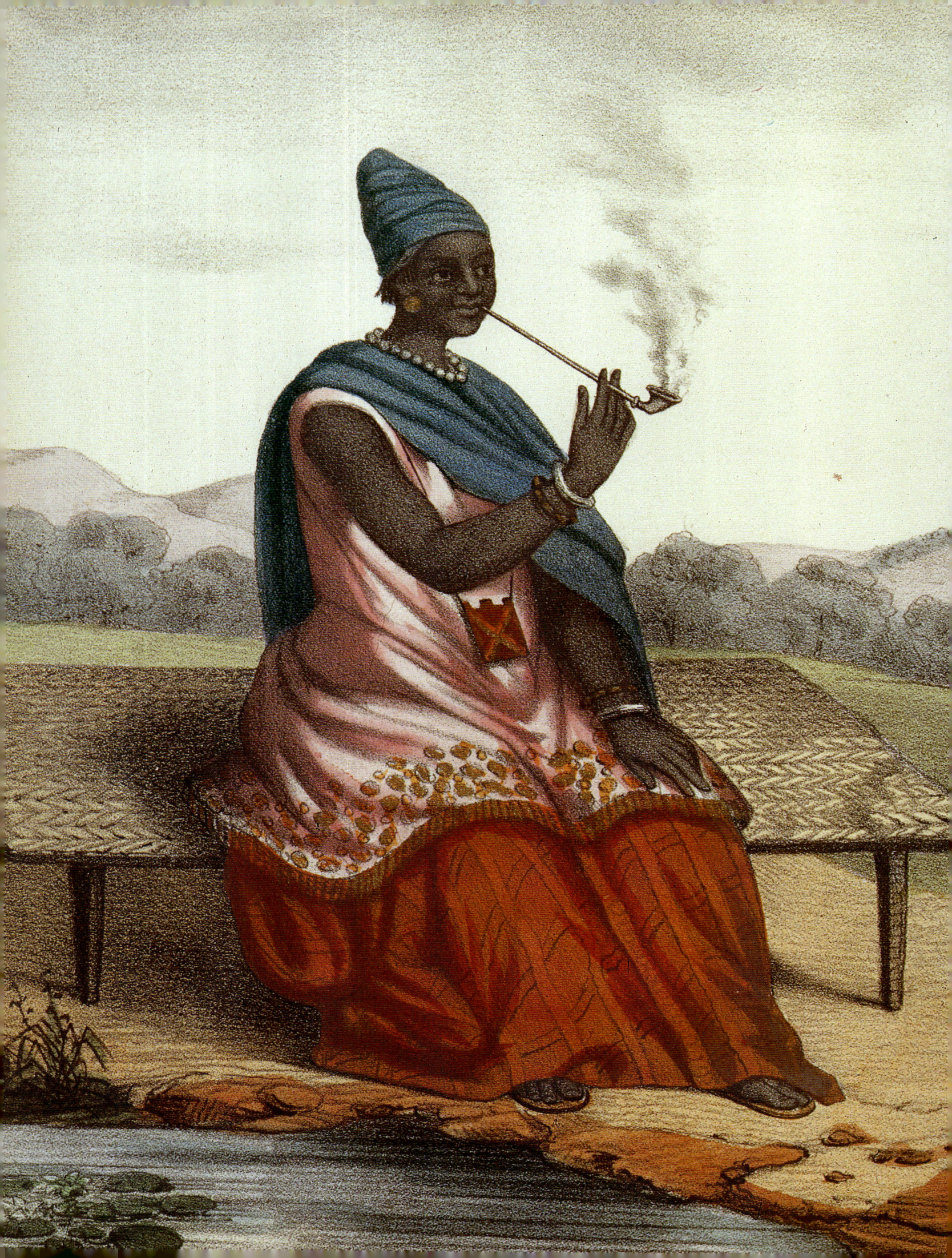

N'DATÉ YALLA

LAST RULER OF THE WALO

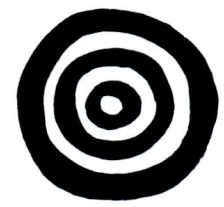

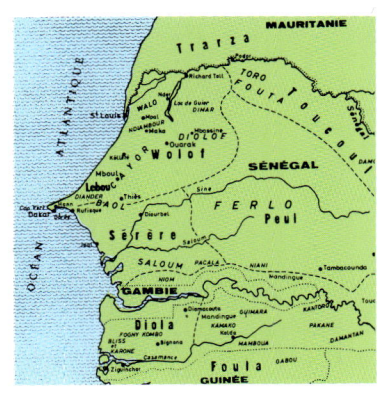

Century after century, more than fifty monarchs reigned over the Walo; the last ruler of this prestigious line was a woman...

CENTURY AFTER CENTURY, MORE THAN FIFTY MONARCHS REIGNED OVER THE WALO; THE LAST RULER OF THIS PRESTIGIOUS LINE WAS A WOMAN, N'DATÉ YALLA, WHO WATCHED OVER THE LIFE OF HER PEOPLE UNTIL 1885, THE YEAR WHEN THE FRENCH

annexed this little kingdom to their colony.

As a child, Princess N'daté Yalla lived in her father's household in the capital, N'der, on the western bank of Lake Guiers.

But more than anything else she loved to walk along the edge of the river, which marked the northern border of the kingdom. Barges of all kinds sailed up and down: some, manned by whites, conveyed to the river's mouth ivory and rubber destined for Europe and captives destined for the Americas; others, piloted by Tzarza Moors, carried only slaves, who were unloaded on the right bank of the river, where caravans guided them toward the countries of North Africa across the deadly stretches of sand.

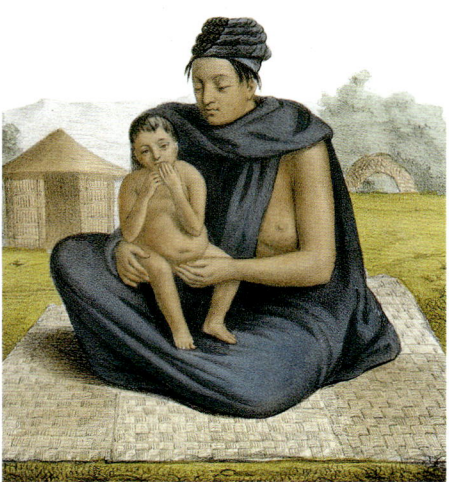

MOORISH WOMAN

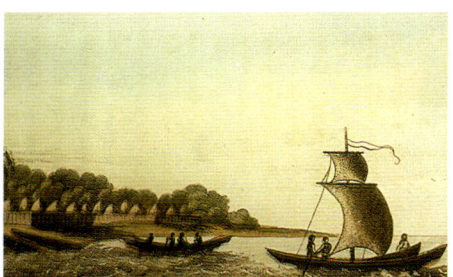

TO THE AMERICAS

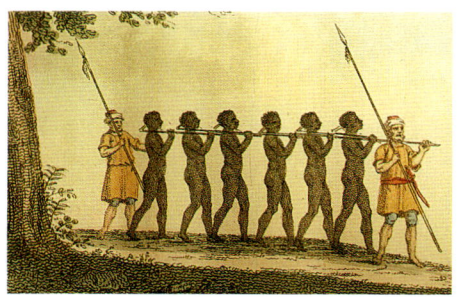

CONVOY OF SLAVES

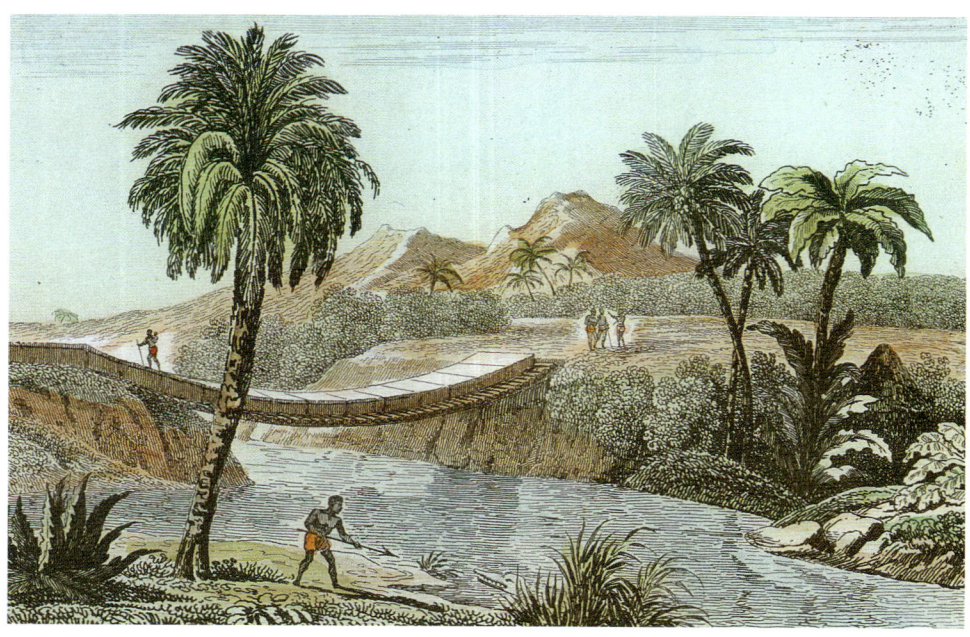

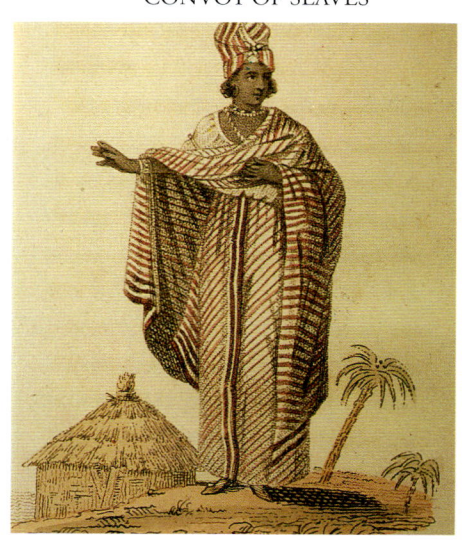

SIGNARE LADIES OF SAINT-LOUIS

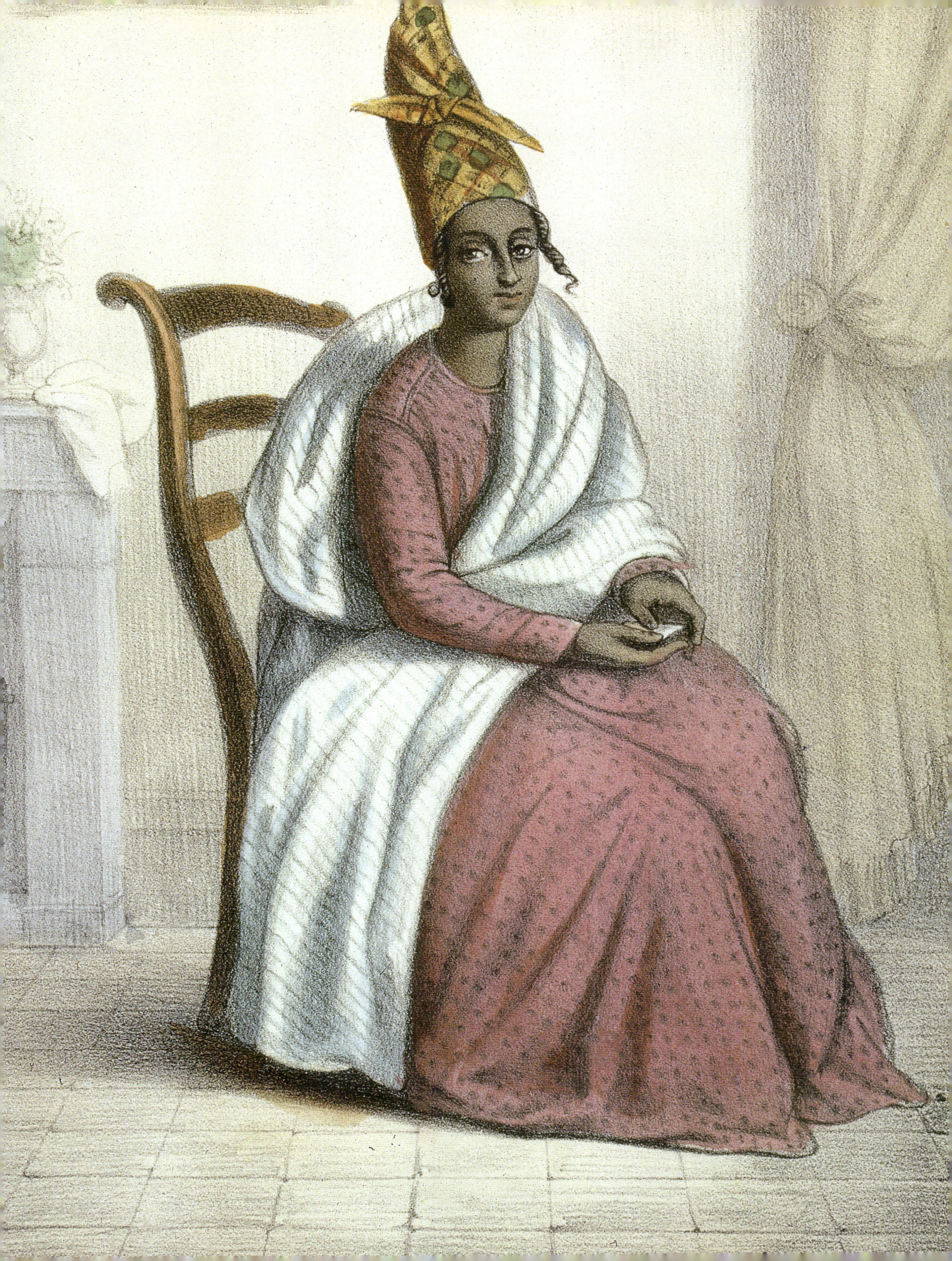

Lat Jor

In Senegal, a principal adversary of French encroachment was Lat Jor, born around 1842, who became king of Cayor in 1862. Cayor was the most important kingdom in Senegal, situated between Dakar and Saint-Louis. The "lingers," the king's mother, aunts, and sisters by his mother, played an important political role. Some did not hesitate to march into combat, such as the young woman Lat-Saoukaabé, who, dressed as a man, set out on horseback against the Trarza Moors and beat them at Gramgram.

Lat Jor was born an animist. Supported by Demba-Waar, he confronted and beat King Ma Dyodyo, a French favorite. Lat Jor was crowned in his place. Later, however, after the tables had turned and he was beaten by Dyodyo, Lat Jor was forced to flee. He tried in vain to interest the chiefs of Sine and Saloum in his cause, and finally entrusted himself to the great Sufi marabou Ma Bâ, who converted him to Islam. But in 1867, the Almamy Ma Bâ was killed in a battle against the Serers, and Lat Jor was obliged to surrender.

The hostilities with the French flared up again, until February 1871, when a treaty recognized him as king of Cayor under French protection. But in 1879, the French decided to build a railroad from Dakar to Saint-Louis, a railroad that was to be a commercially vital piece of infrastructure but above all the axis of their political influence. Lat Jor understood that this railroad would be the death knell for traditional society. And so he rebelled once more and was obliged to seek refuge in Baol. Untiring, refusing to accept what had come to pass, Lat Jor persevered in his guerrilla war until the day he fell, October 26, 1886, near the well of Dyaglé, at the age of forty-four, surrounded by his last Tyeddo. He was a valiant man who loved to say, "I wish to live free and generously."

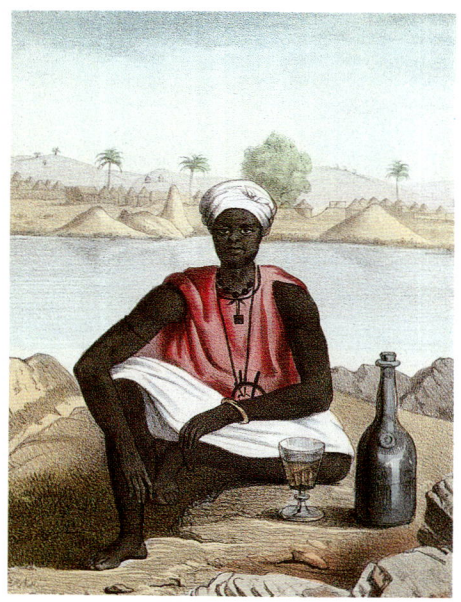

TYEDDO WARRIOR

Proverb

"A single heartache cannot break your heart in a single day."

One day when N'daté Yalla was about ten years old, the Moors crossed the river to attack the capital of Walo.

The army was away and the Badolo men were working in the fields, so the women found themselves defending the houses by themselves. After a long struggle, they shut themselves in the king's main residence and set themselves on fire so that they would not fall into the claws of the slave merchants.

That day, standing before the burnt ruins of the palace, the little girl swore she would live free or die, like all those noble black women who had refused to wear shackles.

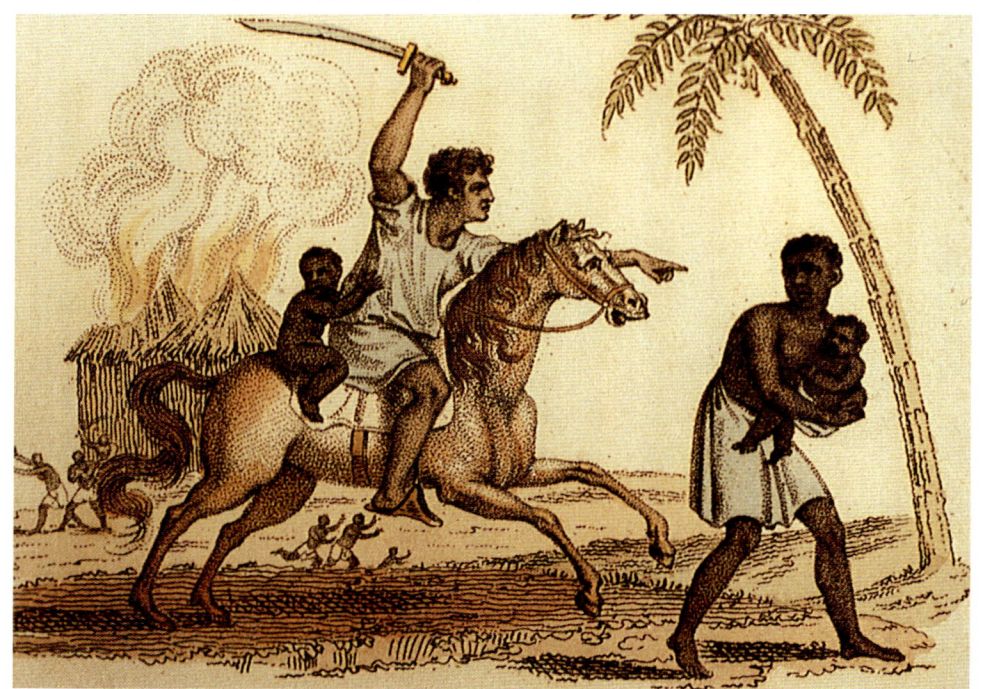

THE MOORS RAID ALONG THE RIVER

Upon the death of her sister N'dyëmböt, N'daté Yalla takes the fate of the kingdom into her own hands.

Immediately, she feels caught between a rock and a hard place: the Moors along the right bank and the French in Saint-Louis, who have challenged her trading rights on the river. In a letter to the governor, she expresses herself in these terms: "We are doing no harm to anyone, but the country belongs to us and we must govern it; we guarantee passage for the flocks, and it is for this reason that we take one-tenth of them, and we will never accept anything less. Saint-Louis belongs to the governor, Cayor belongs to the *damel* (king), and Walo belongs to the queen; each of these chiefs governs the lands as he or she sees fit."

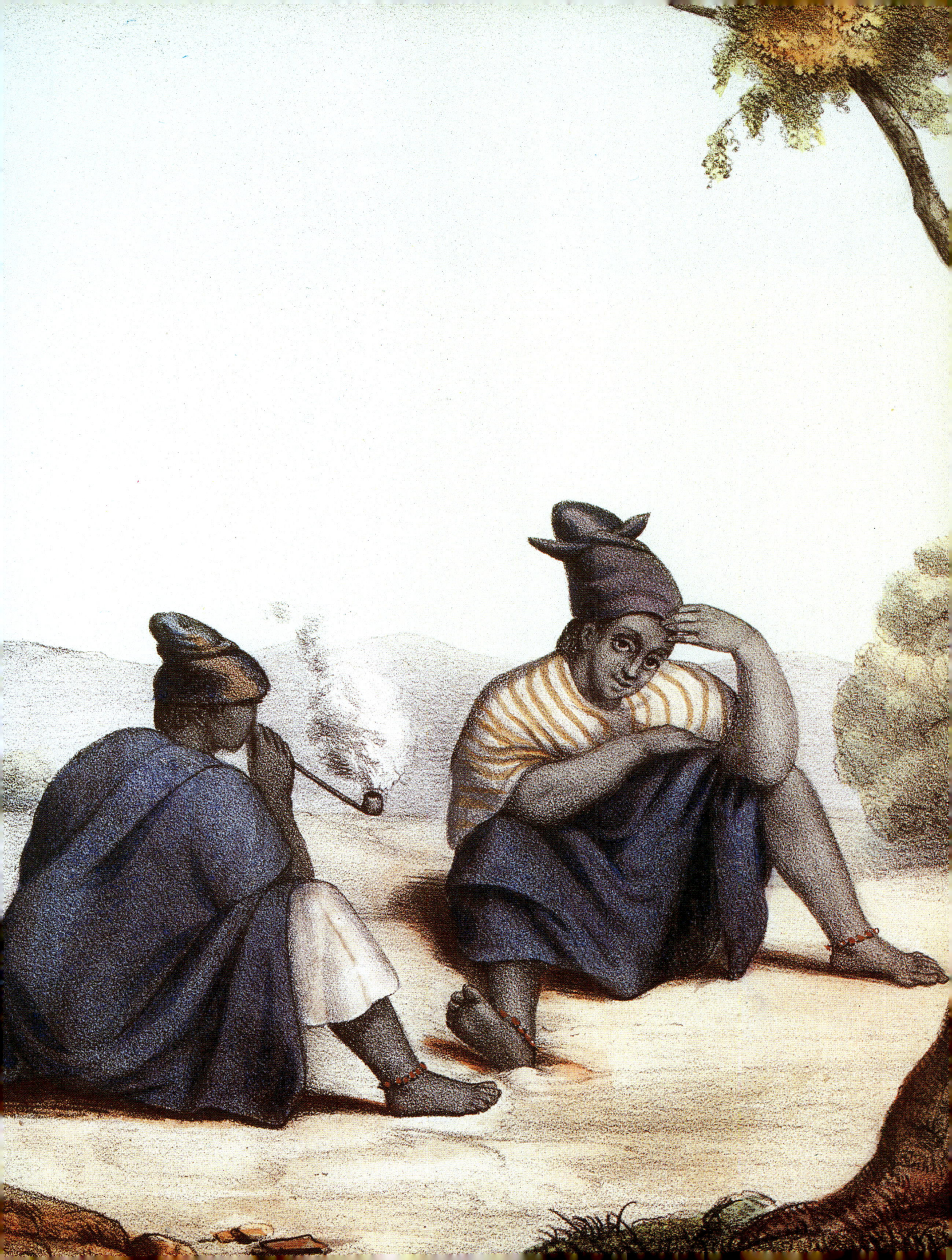

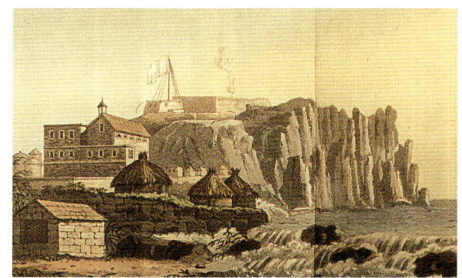

Gorée, Isle of Horror...

At the end of the seventeenth century and throughout all of the eighteenth, Gorée was generally the most important location in Senegal for the slave trade.

At the end of the seventeenth century, the mayor reported: "we buy the best captives for ten francs apiece and we resell them for more than a hundred gold florins." The demand kept growing, so the price per head rose to as much as forty pounds or thirty bars of iron in 1697. The slaves were penned in dark low enclosures, underneath the rooms reserved for the dealers.

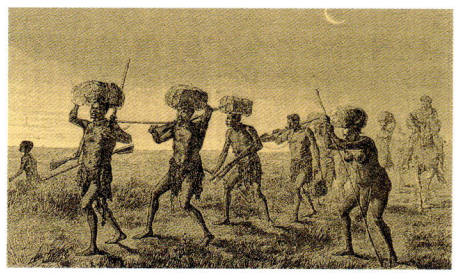

On the eve of the French Revolution, the traffic had reached its peak; never had the ships transported so many victims to those wealthy islands that demanded an ever-increasing supply of labor.

The main "producers" of "black wood"—as the captives were called—were Galam and Cayor in western Africa, and farther south, the Slave Coast (from Cape Saint-Paul to the mouth of the Niger). The Gold Coast and Kongo were also plundered by the English traders.

The great French trading posts for warehousing and expeditions were Gorée and Saint-Louis.

The blacks were captured in their villages, or by bush-beaters, or by neighboring petty kings trying to get rich quick, or sometimes by their own greedy princes. The "living ebony" was stacked, naked, in narrow passages, not much more than hallways, grim back alleys with little air and even less light. Resisters were shut up in long, narrow cells, where the sun could barely pass through the solid bars securing narrow slits of windows. Often the slaves who had any strength left to complain after such an ordeal were shackled to heavy chains sealed into the walls of the darkest and dankest rooms of that sinister island.

She also opposes the Moors, who seed division in her kingdom, stirring up a dynastic feud in order to better ensure their domination. Certain great families abdicate under pressure from the nomads; and, not strong enough to prevent the Moors from pillaging their subjects, they join the pillagers to get their share of the loot. In response, N'daté Yalla supports a sort of national party directed by her own son, Sidia, who reunites all the country's sentiments in one figure: and soon one phrase is in everyone's mouths, ordinary people and warriors, dignitaries, lords of the royal house alike: "Sidi Walo Reck"—Only Sidia for Walo.

But pressure from the French increases. Captain Louis-Léon-César Faidherbe, appointed governor of Saint-Louis, has decided upon the military conquest of the whole river kingdom; and soon N'daté Yalla orders a general Walo uprising.

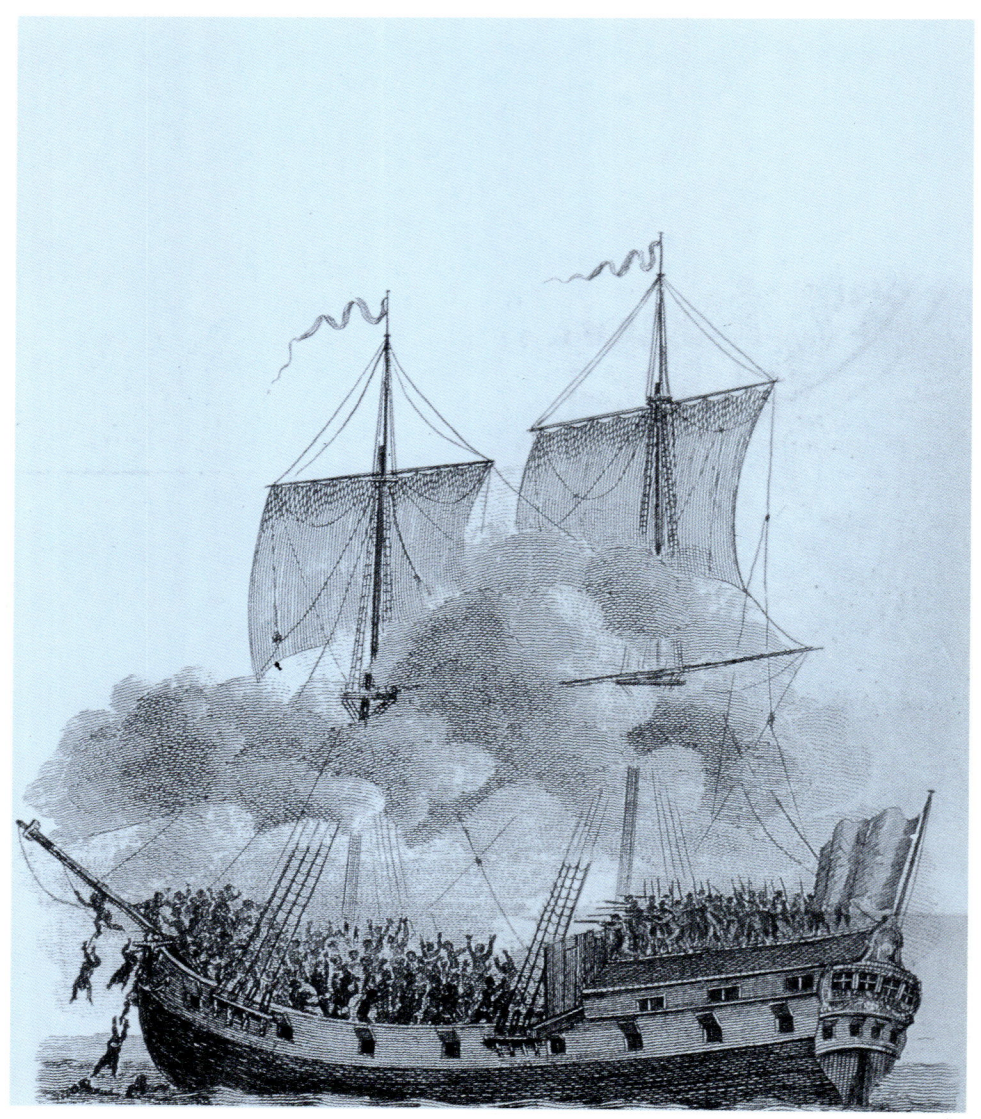

SLAVE SHIP

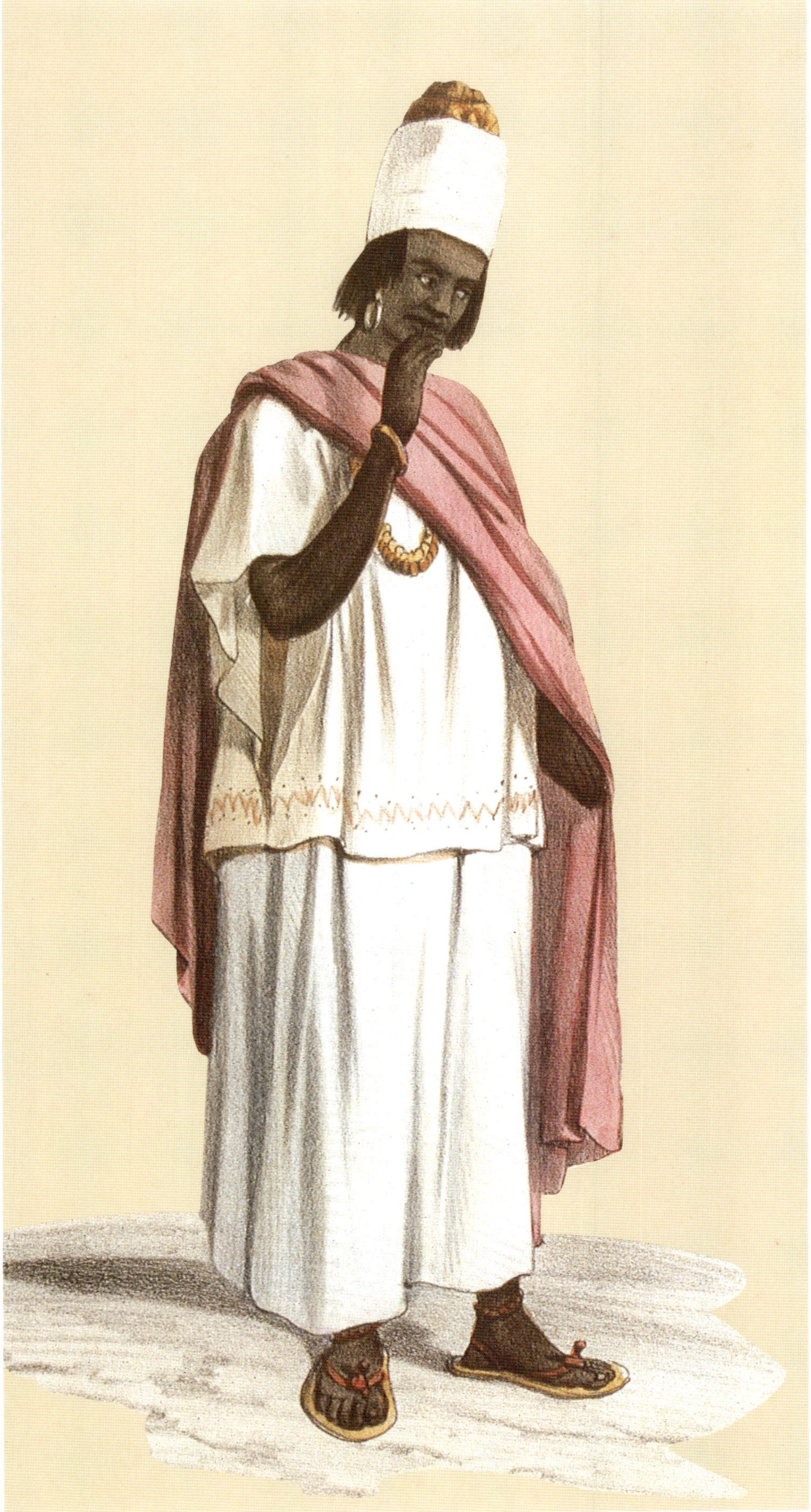

N'DATÉ YALLA

WOMAN OF THE SAINT-LOUIS AREA

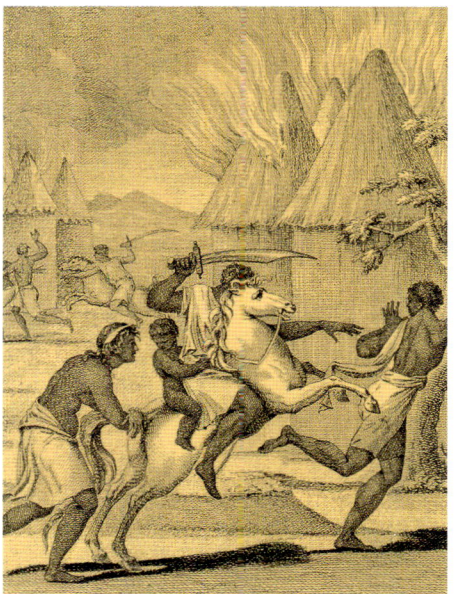

The Saharan Slave Trade

The oldest written accounts of slaving in the Sahel concern the Fezzan region in Libya and date from the seventh century. But as early as the ninth century, the effects of this traffic are noted in West Africa. Kawar, fifteen days by foot from Zawila, has a Muslim population of various origins, primarily Berber, engaged in trade with the Sudanese. In the tenth century, this trade, already apparently well organized, is centered in Zawila on the edge of North Africa. A medium-sized city with a large surrounding district extending into the Sudan, it is the source of slaves sold in Muslim countries. "They are a race of a very pure black color." Also from the Sudan, situated between the ocean to the west and the desert to the north, come the majority of eunuchs. "The merchants from Egypt traveling to this region... steal children.... They castrate them and import them into Egypt where they sell them. Among the Sudanese themselves there are people who steal children from each other to sell to the merchants when they come." Edrisi, around 1154, mentions on several occasions that the people of the desert and the Sudanese states (Barisa, Silla, Tekrur, Ghana, Ghiyaro) reduce the local inhabitants to captivity, "transporting them to their own country and selling them to visiting merchants, who then pass them along elsewhere. A great number leave that country currently, heading for western North Africa."

These slave exports are mentioned at different moments in North African history: El Biruni in around 1050, El Zuhri, around 1154-1161, El Sharishi around 1223, Ibn Khaldun, around 1375. And again in 1416, El Makrisi noted that "a caravan was arriving from Tekrur for the pilgrimage [to Mecca] with 1,700 slaves, men and women, and a large amount of gold, which they intend to sell there."

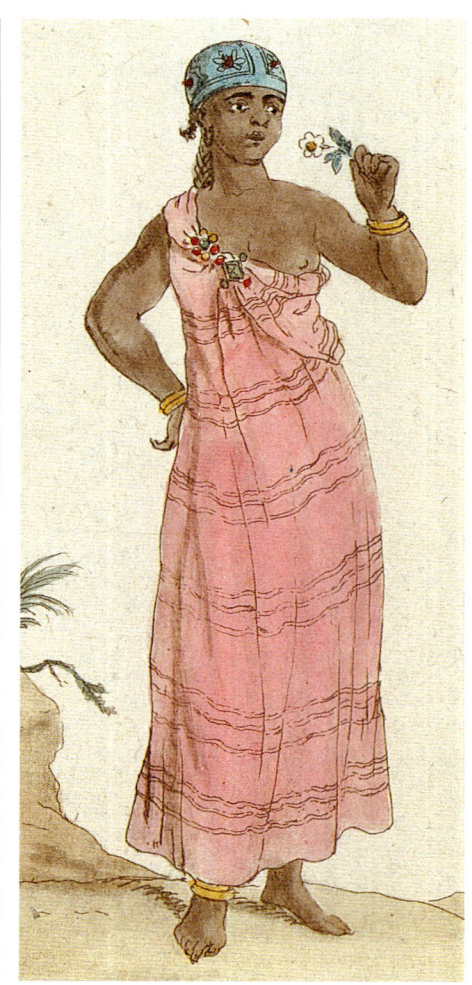

On January 25, 1885, a battalion dispatched from Saint-Louis pillages and destroys all in its path. The villages of Darhaliga, Naeri, and Temy are reduced to ashes. N'daté Yalla succeeds in convincing the Moors to unite with her before the common threat. But it is too late; the French are already at the gates of N'der, the capital, and the language of cannons manages to drown out the courage of men. On January 31, 1885, N'daté Yalla watches her capital fall, defended by the Moorish and Walo armies.

As the flames rise up into the sky, the queen remembers the heroic women of days gone by and wishes only to die like them; but already, the warriors of her entourage are pulling her away, and the poor woman seeks refuge in the Kadjoore, where she will finish her days in exile: conquered to the very bone, but still a rebel.

How can I deny my love for Ablah,
when my tears bear witness to the sorrow
her absence causes me...
I weep so much that even the birds
will know my sorrow
and will cry with me.
Oh beautiful Ablah! my spirit and my heart
are far away while your flocks
are safe under my watch.
Have pity on my sad state,
I will be faithful to you forever...

Prince Antar

It is said that Antar, who thus sang of his love for his cousin, gave her three pieces of cloth scattered with jewels and placed a golden diadem on her head. This story took place in the Near East in the sixth century. Antar was the son of a slave. But this child of black Africa, having rapidly demonstrated his military worth, found himself a young man at the head of his master's warriors. His poems made him famous. One of them was even engraved at the entry of a temple in Mecca. But above all he is remembered for being the first to sing of the beauty of his race:

I am the son of a woman with a black forehead,
with the legs of an ostrich, with hair
like grains of pepper...
In black hues, there is virtue,
there is beauty.

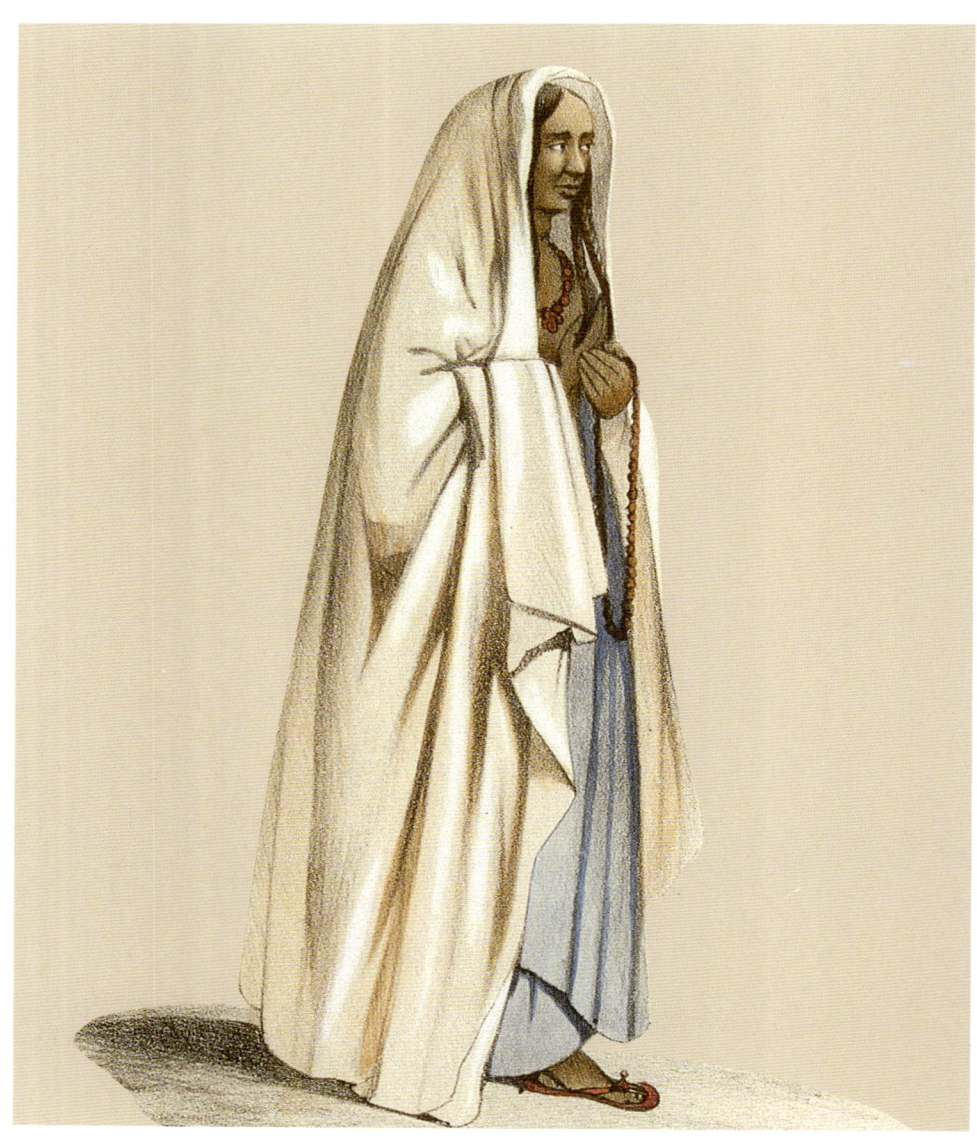

WOMAN OF THE BANKS OF THE SENEGAL

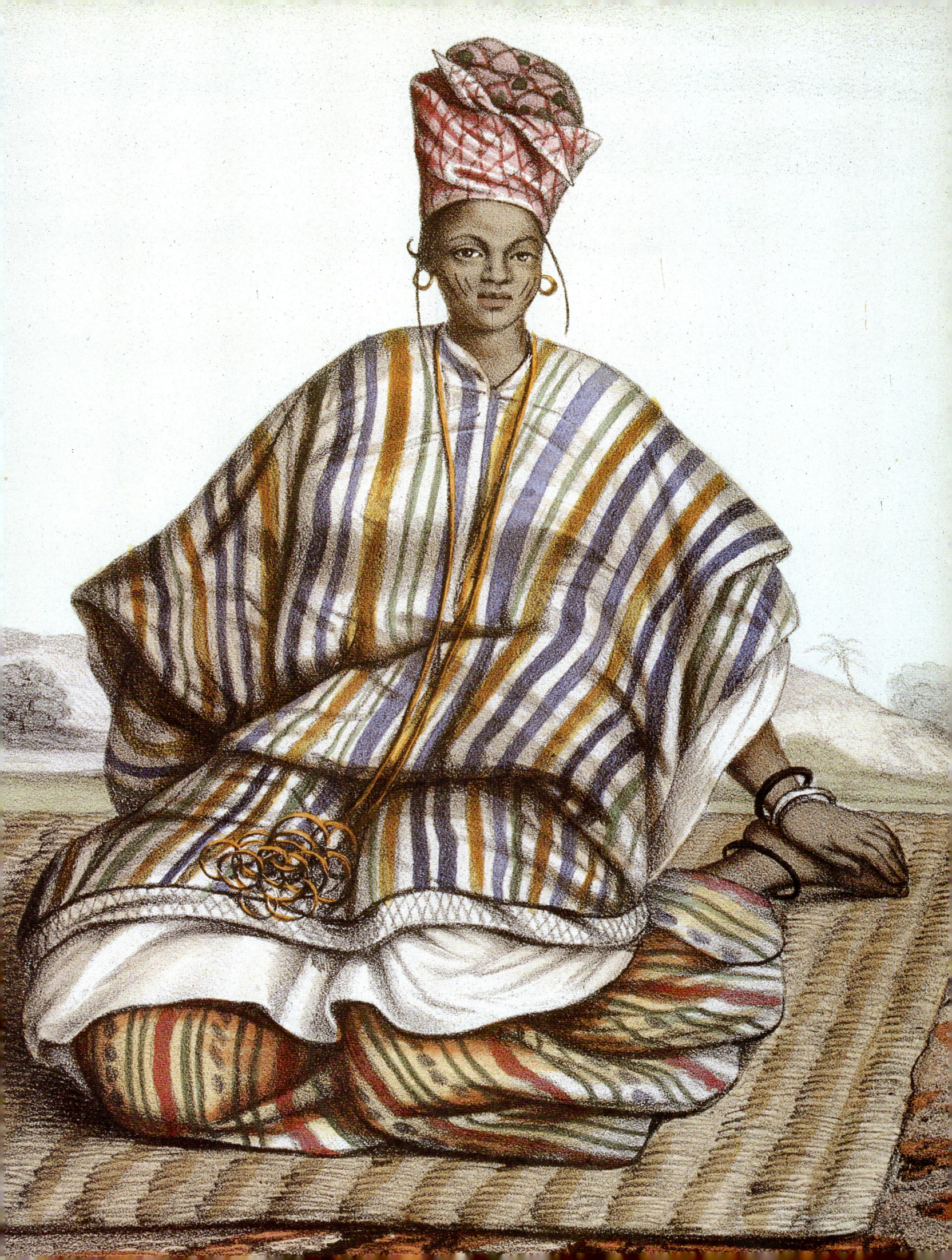

A few years later, a young man from Senegal finishes his studies in France with flying colors. His future holds the promise of high positions in the colonial empire, like all the sons of dignitaries who have attended the William Ponty School, the school for future leaders in Dakar. But in fact, this particular young man will not become a bureaucrat or an administrator or a military man like his schoolmate Alfred-Amédée Dodds, who would one day participate in the conquest of Dahomey.

As soon as he returns to his homeland, having completed his studies, his diplomas signed and sealed, the young man in exile becomes the very soul of resistance against colonialism: for his name is Sidi—you remember Sidi, the very one that the crowds of river people used to salute with the cry "Sidi Walo Reck!"

Sidi: heir to N'daté Yalla, the last queen of the ancient kingdom of Walo.

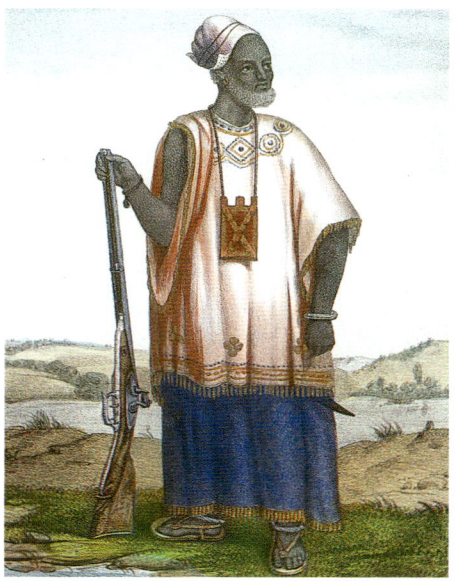

THE QUEEN'S HUSBAND

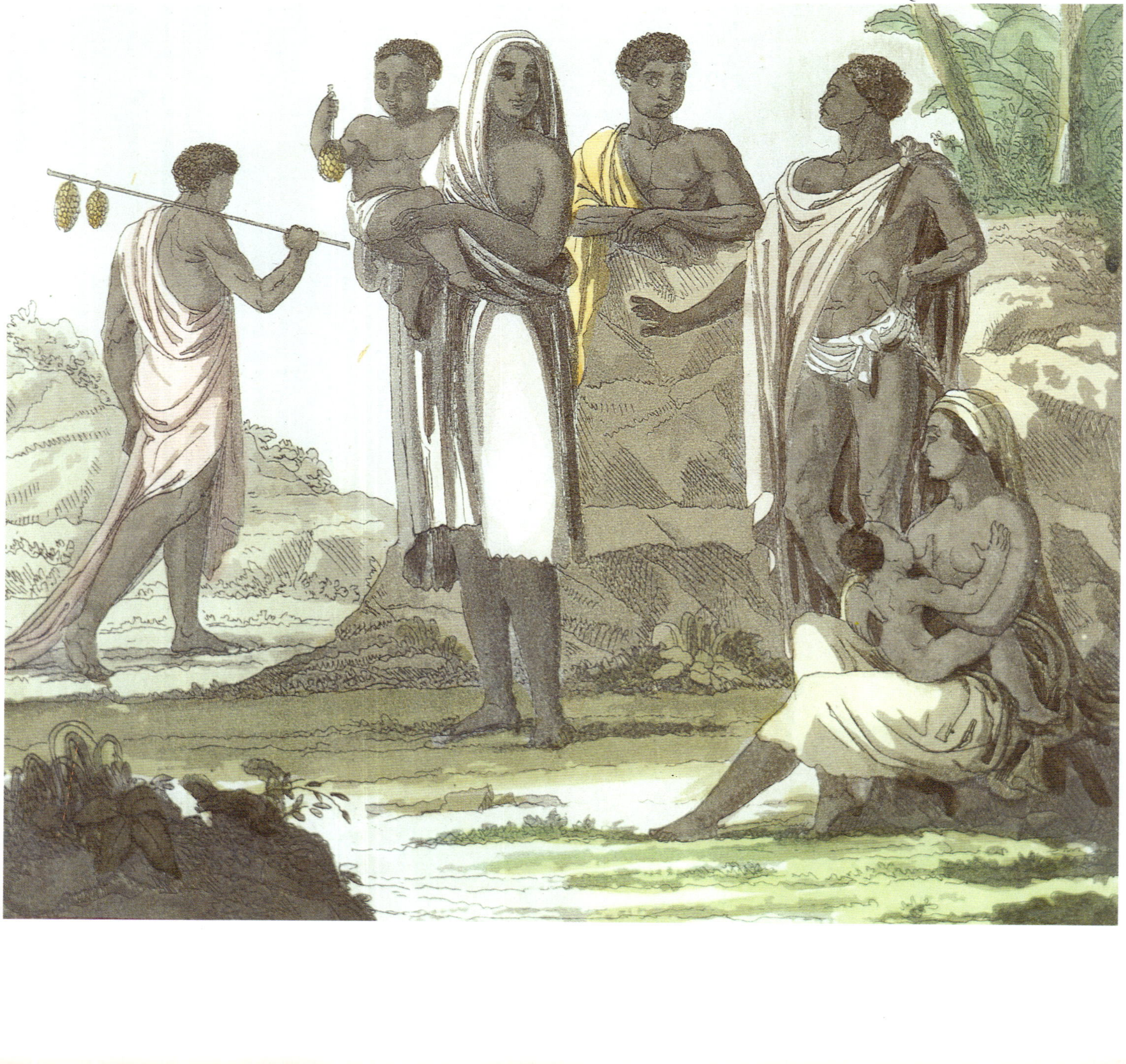

WORDS
OF AN ORDINARY WOMAN

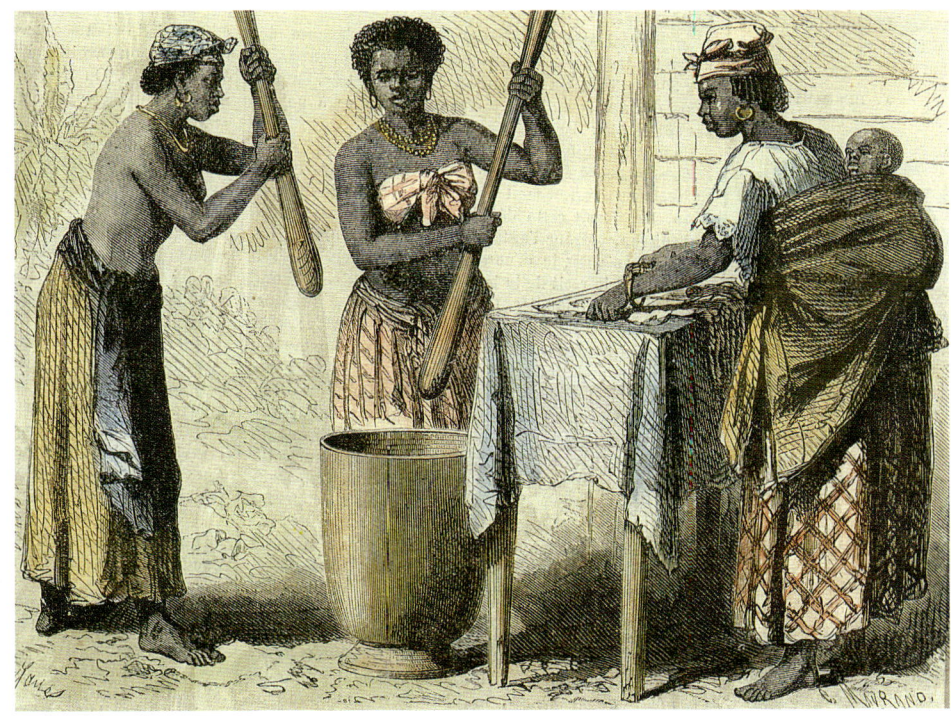

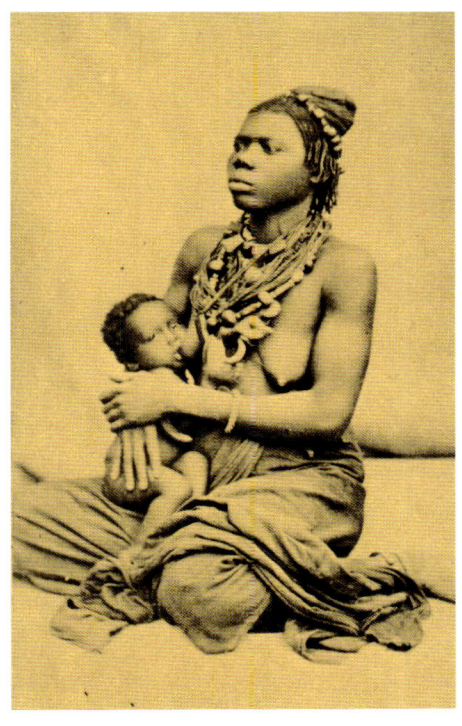

Three of my children are dead. Two were lost when they were still babes. The third one, a boy, was already three or four years old.

Each of their deaths was like my own death. It was even worse than death. Because the one who dies, once he's dead, feels nothing any more, sees nothing else. But the one who stays behind, she is the one who bears the burden of death.

I had the feeling that I was just there because I had to be there. But inside, in my heart, there was nothing left. It was as if my life's breath had gone. And yet, there I was.

The boy died in the heart of the drought year, the one we called the "great, horrible year."

There was a measles epidemic. We all got sick. The children, their father, and I.

We did not know how to stop our children from crying: they kept asking for milk.

Even today, sometimes, I can hear my children crying. I truly feel like I can hear them. Then at night, I can't sleep. Some days it even keeps me from eating. Every day, death is right before our eyes. And we don't know what to say. We don't know what to think.

Life, charm, and happiness: three things that do not last. Their days are numbered.

A proverb says: "Happy things do not camp close together." When you leave one happiness behind, you know that you will have to walk for a long time before you reach another happy place. Happy things do not camp close together.

If you know happiness today, you will need much patience before you find it again. A long road, a lot of pain. Sometimes, you come across an old camp abandoned by happiness. But it's just an old camp, happiness doesn't live there any more!

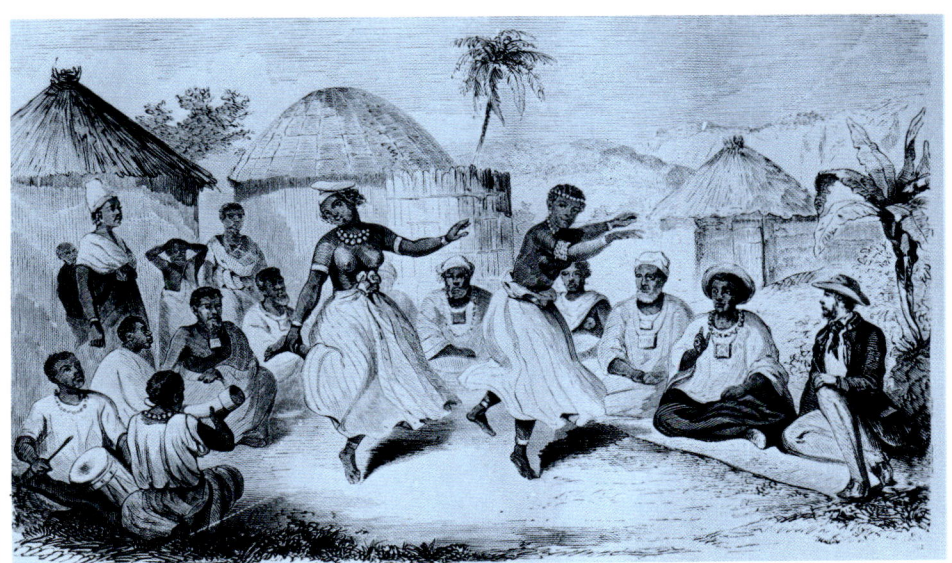

A HAPPY ENCAMPMENT

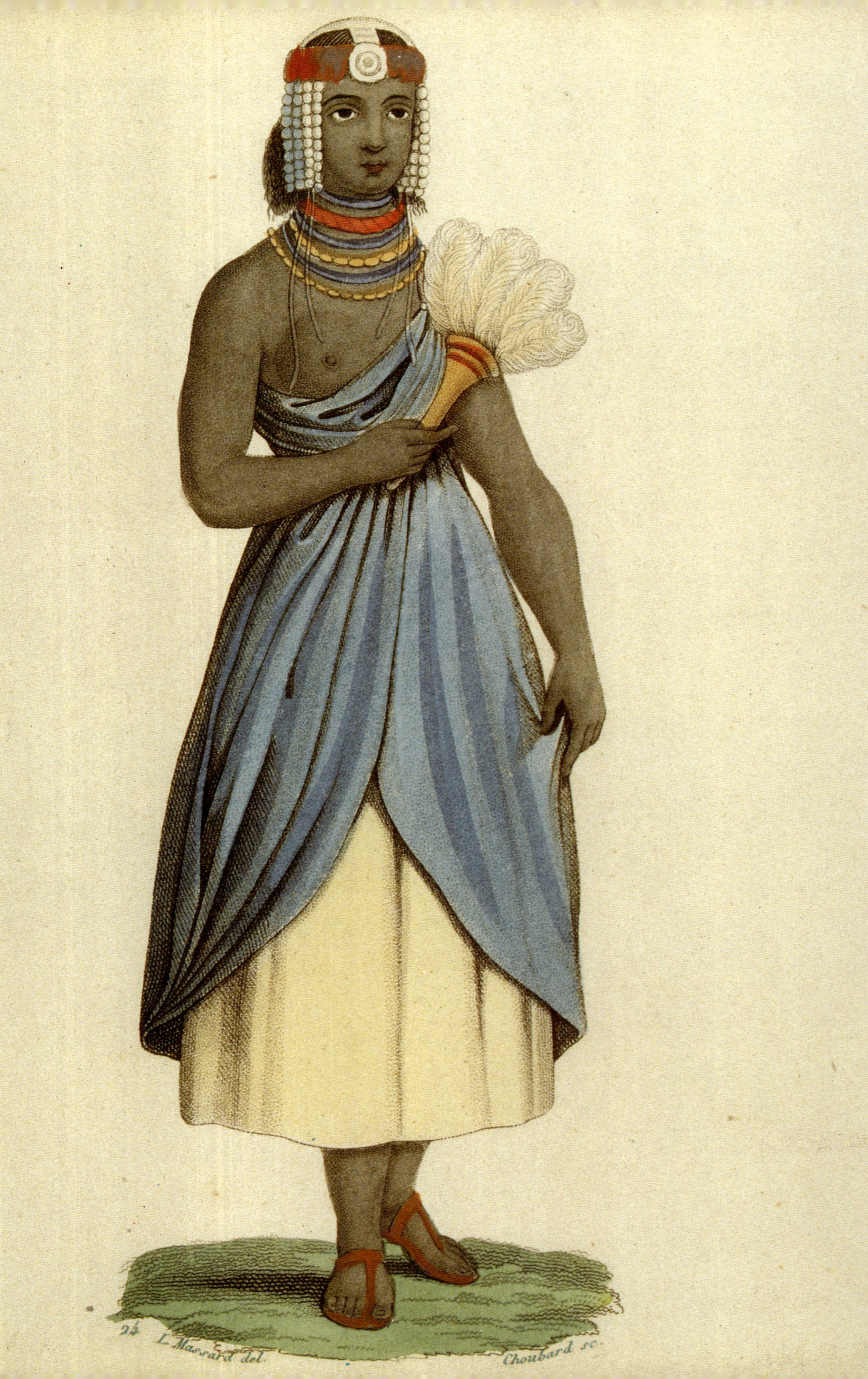

NONGQAWUSE

THE YOUNG WOMAN WHO HEARD THE VOICE OF A GOD

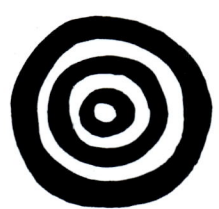

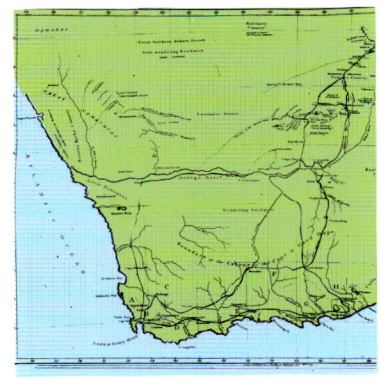

The grass you burn makes more grass grow, but a place ruined by God is difficult to make green again...

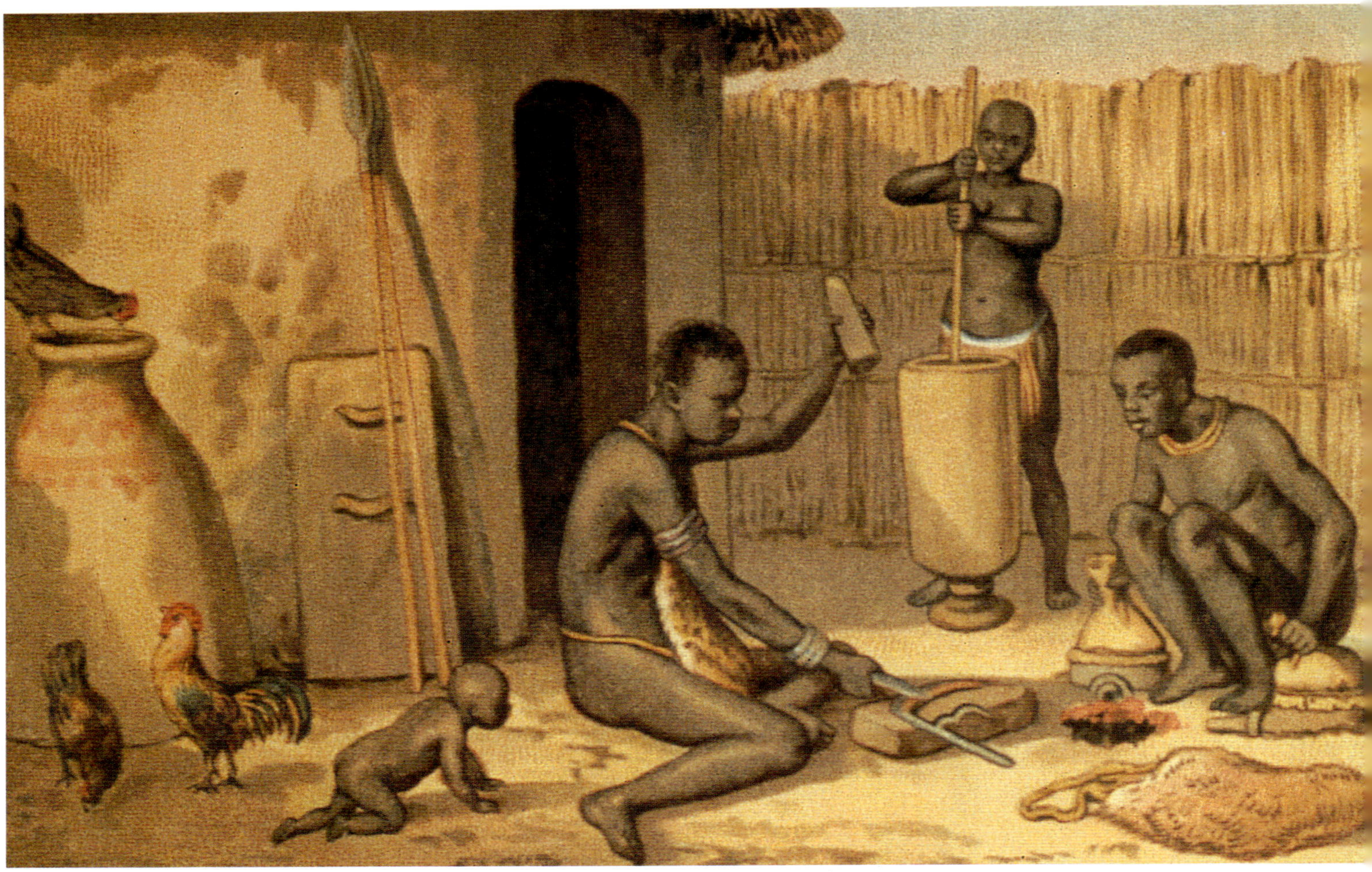

"THE XHOSA LIVED AS SHEPHERDS...

STARTING IN THE NINETEENTH CENTURY, THE TERRIBLE BOER EXPANSION TOWARD THE NORTH UPSET THE CHESS BOARD MADE UP OF THE NATIONS OF SOUTHERN AFRICA. ALL THE TRADITIONAL FRAMES OF REFERENCE WERE BROKEN: A SORT OF frenzy shook the immense zone from Transkei to Tanzania, and from Basutoland to the coast of the Indian Ocean.

The name Shaka sums up this period of atrocious wars that were called the Lifaqané.

Shaka was at the eye of this storm, but he had not provoked it: it all started with the white pressure moving up from the Cape, which would ruin so many tribes and nations that South Africa is still reeling and gasping for breath a century later.

The first to submit to this pressure were the Xhosa, a herding people, who lived to the east of the Cape Colony, between the Great Fish River and the southern border of the Natal.

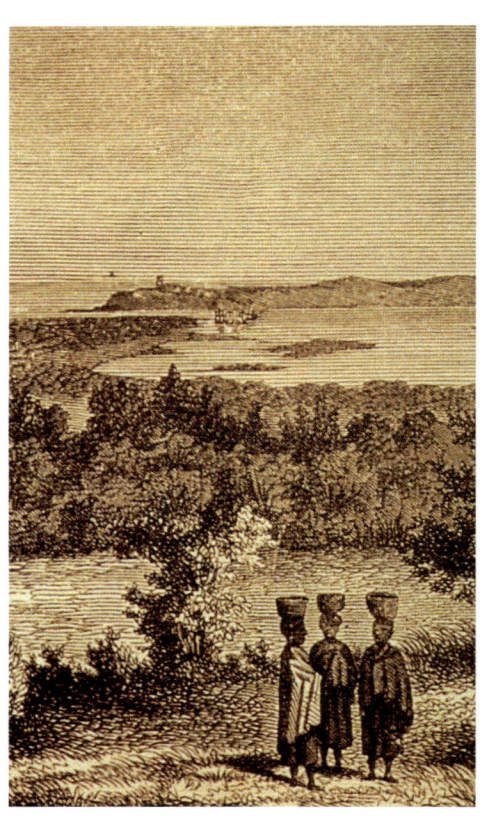

EAST OF THE CAPE COLONY

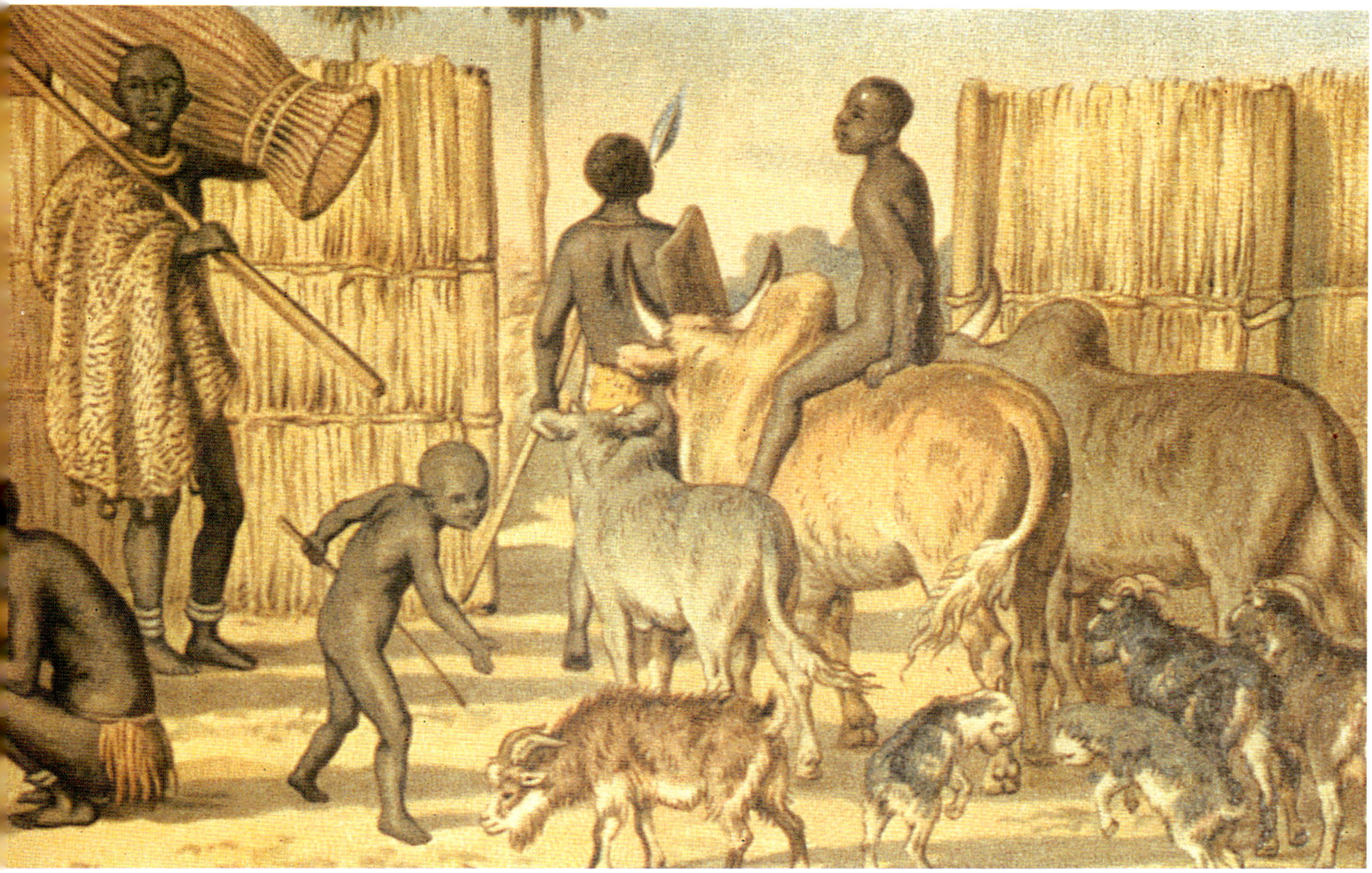

"...AND WANDERING HERDSMEN"

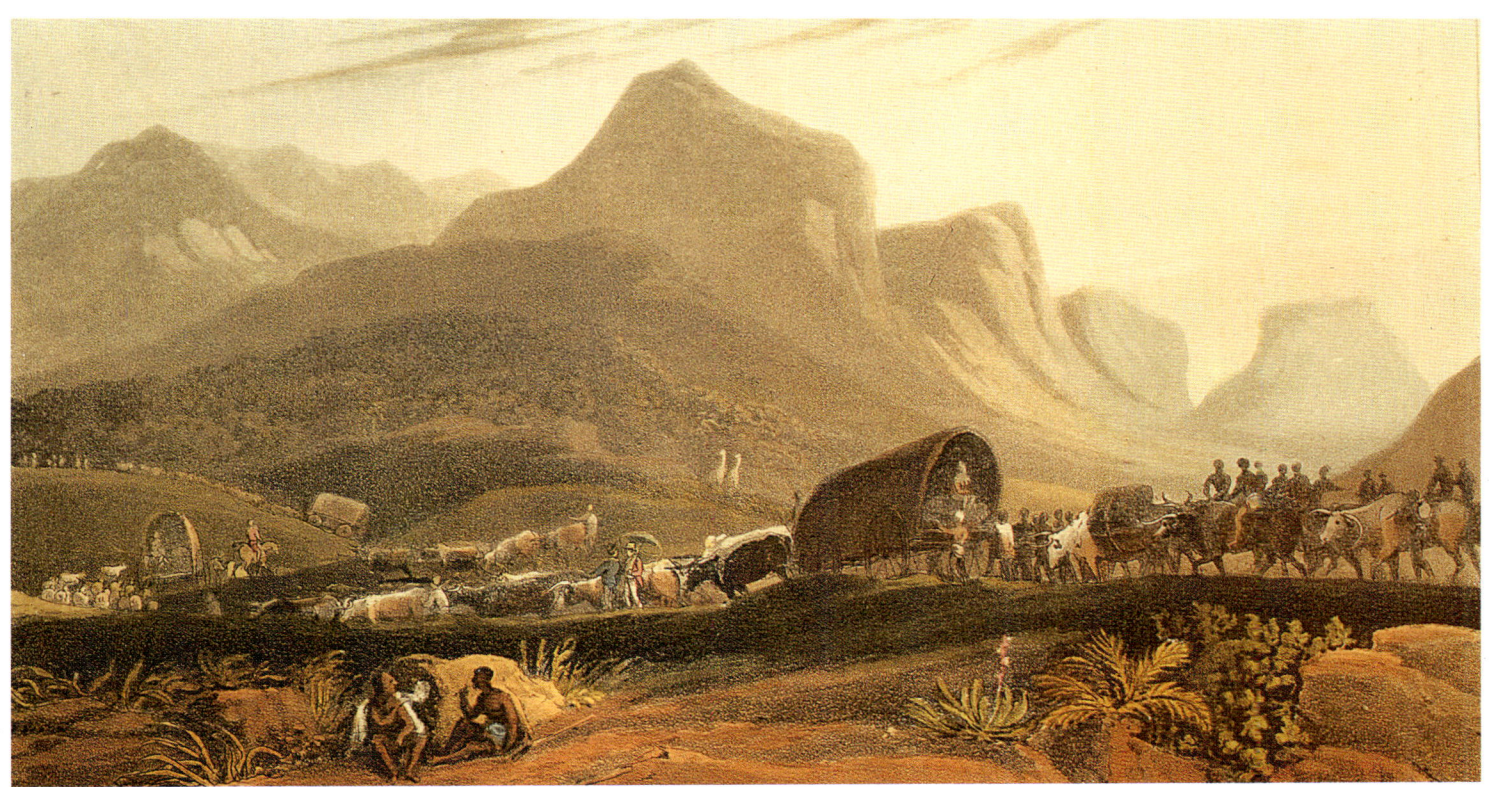

"IT ALL STARTED WITH THE WHITE PRESSURE COMING FROM THE CAPE"

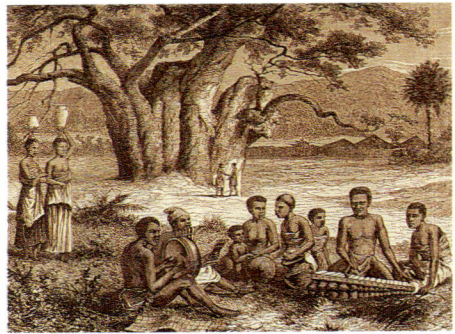

Praised Be the Women

Praised be the women!
Praised be the night!
Praised be the feast!
Praised be the hawk!
Praised be the fair sex!
Praised be the bells!
Praised be the beautiful women!

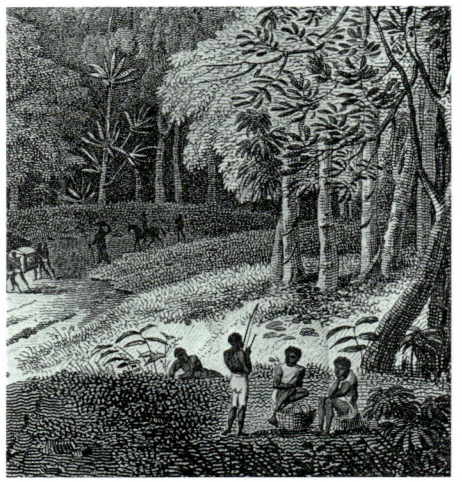

The Ford of the Orange River

The willows, mimosas, and olive trees that shade the banks of this river, the clear and delightful coolness of its waters, the masses of shining rocks that frame its course, the waterfalls and the green isles sprinkled on its surface, are in most agreeable contrast to the dry harshness of the surrounding uncultivated countryside, deserted, sandy, and spiked with yellowish, rocky hills.

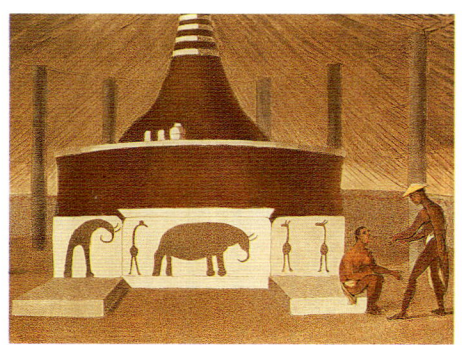

INSIDE A ROYAL HUT

In 1770, they found themselves face to face with the Boers, who were inexorably pushing back their flocks: ten wars followed, until the final defeat of the Xhosa over eighty years later in 1853.

Shrunk like a raisin in the sun, the Xhosa's territory no longer allowed them to live as shepherds, wandering herdsmen, as they had done since the beginning of time; they whose beautiful flocks were their reason for living, on earth as in heaven, suddenly found themselves reduced to despair.

And up from the depths of this despair rose a young woman, Nongqawuse.

The grass you burn makes more grass grow, but a place ruined by God is difficult to make green again. Nongqawuse was a girl like all others, but she was not made for unhappiness.

She was about ten years old when the last war against the whites broke out, the one that ended with defeat deep as an abyss. She was, as they say, "a smiling little girl, wet behind the ears," whose calling as a cook was surprisingly precocious. She had a special talent for the traditional stew made with pumpkin, sorghum, corn, roots, and certain leaves that she picked in the bush.

Her mother was named N'Sudu, and her father, Sandilé, was a priest of the traditional Xhosa religion.

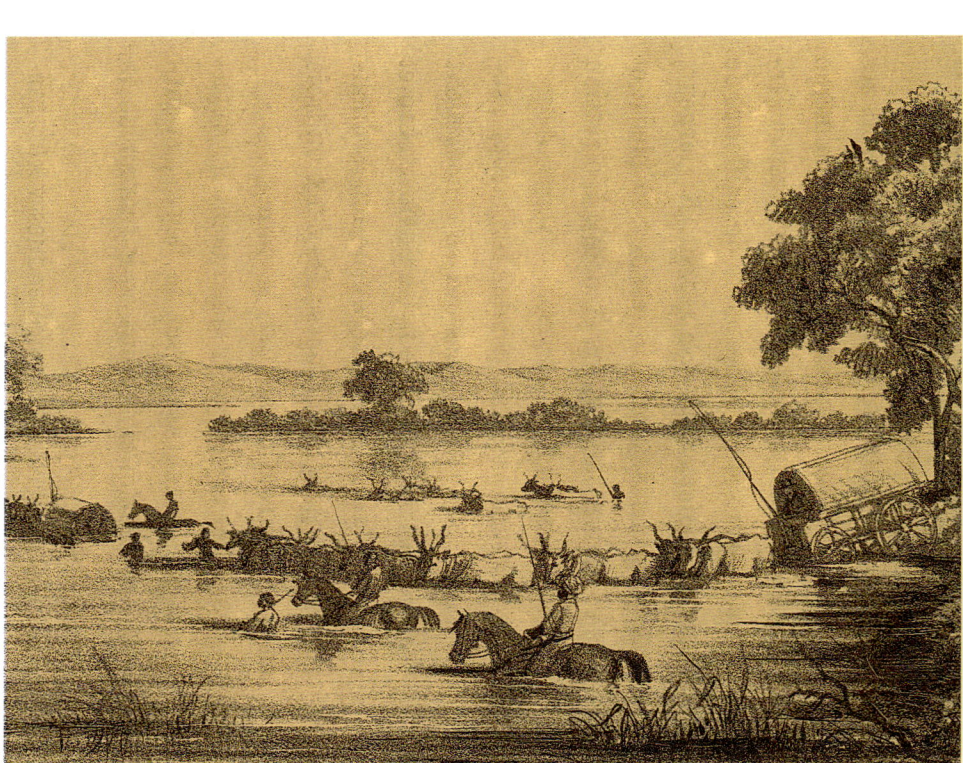

THE ORANGE RIVER

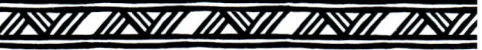

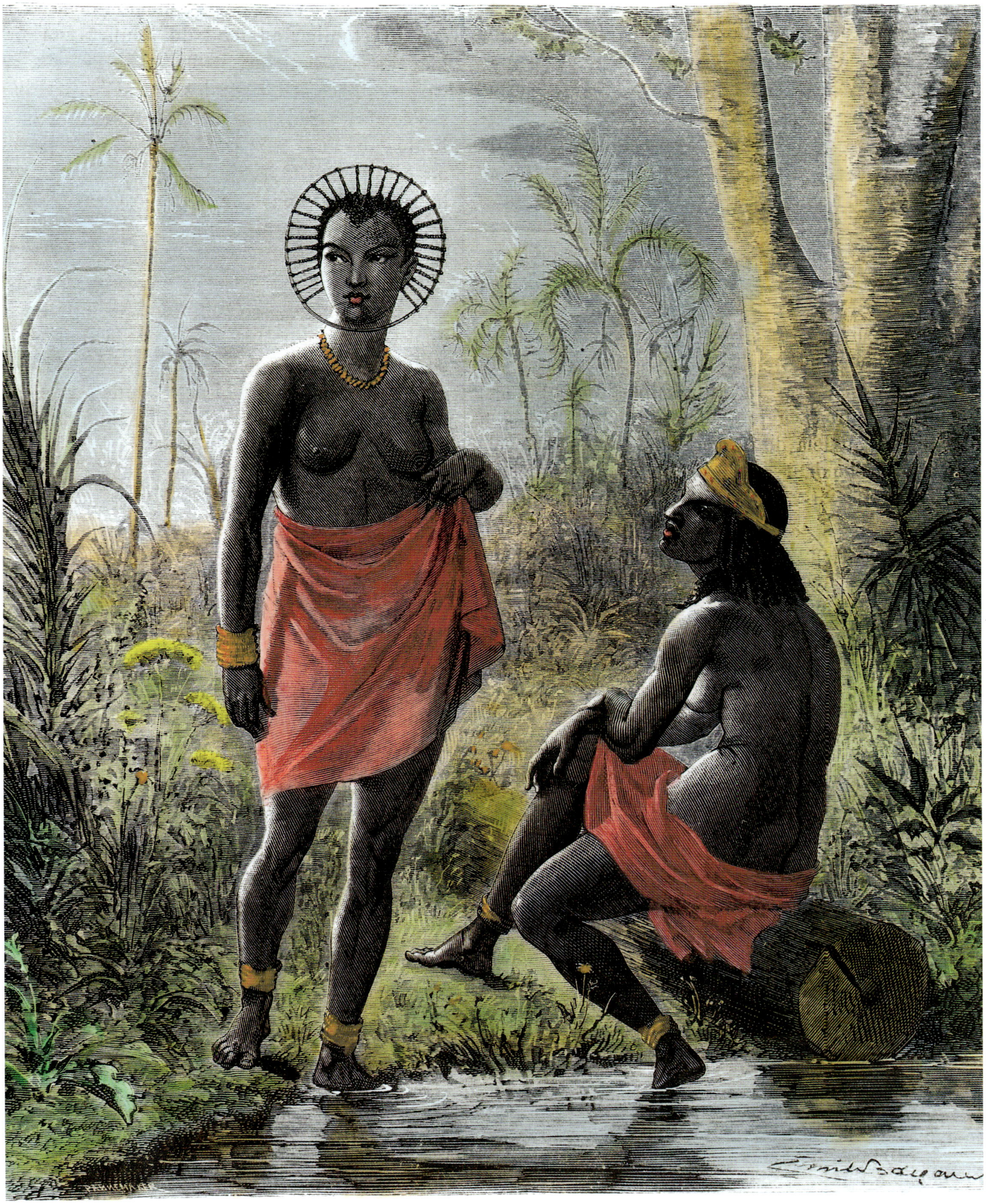

"AND UP FROM THE DEPTHS OF THIS DESPAIR ROSE A YOUNG WOMAN..."

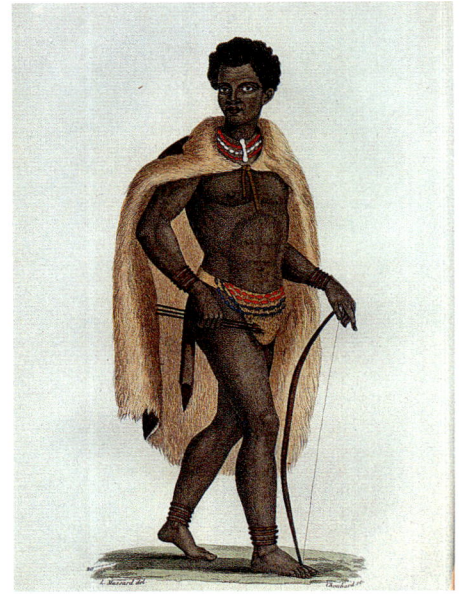

Attachment to the Land

The stubborn resistance of the Amakosas, the Temboukis, and the Basutos to the colonizers' tramplings are sufficient evidence of the extent to which these peoples are attached to the lands that they inhabit. They designate them with expressions meant to touch the heart or arouse fervor: "Our home, our land, the country of our fathers." A chief who learned that certain people to whom he had extended his hospitality claimed to own the districts they now occupied, observed coldly: "The land of my ancestors knows who her children are! She will reject the newcomers!" This was more than a figure of speech. "You are asking me to *cut up* the land!?" exclaimed the ruler of the Basutos to the whites who had settled in his country.

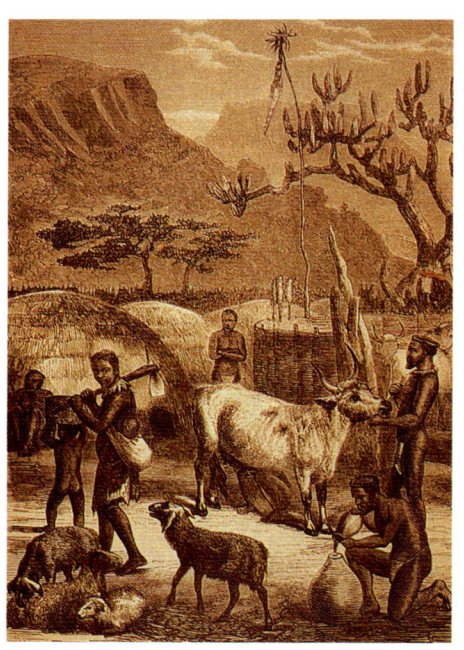

Old Sandilé had told her at length about the prophet Makana, who would lead the Xhosa in their fifth war against the whites in 1818 and 1819. The prophet Makana had said that the Xhosa were under the direct protection of Dalidipu, the supreme god, who reigns over all worlds visible and invisible, whereas the whites obeyed a subordinate god by the name of Tixo. The priest added that the supreme god had sent Makana to chase the whites back across the seas and to bring back the Xhosa's stolen livestock: that is how the fifth war against the whites began. Fifteen years later, another war would follow, the war in which N'Sudu and Sandilé, Nongqawuse's mother and father, were killed.

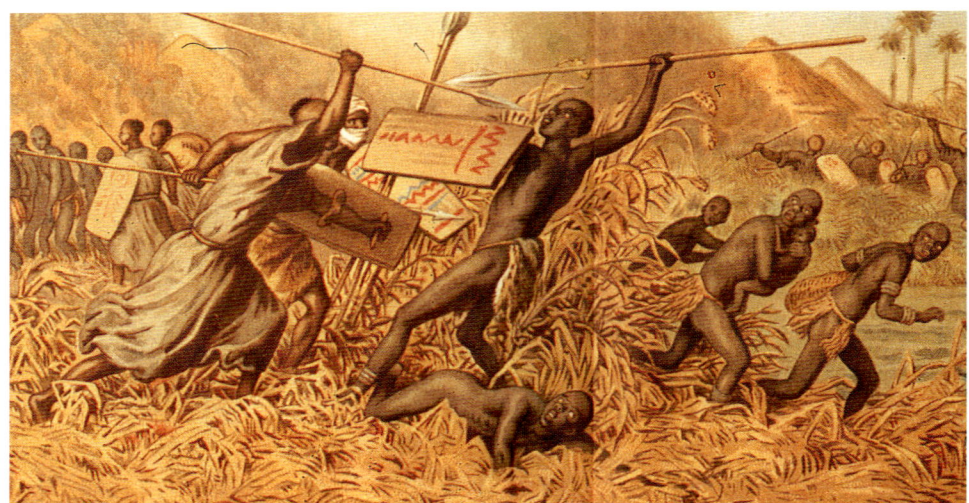

"...THAT IS HOW THE FIFTH WAR AGAINST THE WHITES BEGAN..."

Little by little, life started up again in the sheep and cattle pastures and in the pens that sheltered the cows with their calves. The "little girl wet behind the ears" had lost her smile and her taste for cooking. The sorrow is far too great, she said to herself, prostrated on the floor of a hut day and night. She could still see her mother N'Sudu and her father Sandilé, and once again she heard all the stories the old priest had told her about the prophet Makana who had foretold that the whites would leave and that the plundered animals would return.

One night, she dreamt of a flock that came out of the Xara River and set out into the plains streaming with water that sparkled in the sun.

Since she was a priest's daughter, she took note of her dream and confided it to her uncle Mlankazana, with whom she had been living since her family had been killed. Mlankazana gazed at her for a long time in silence. Then, the next day, when she went to get water from the Xara River, that same flock came out of the blue water and went off calmly toward the plains, where it suddenly disappeared.

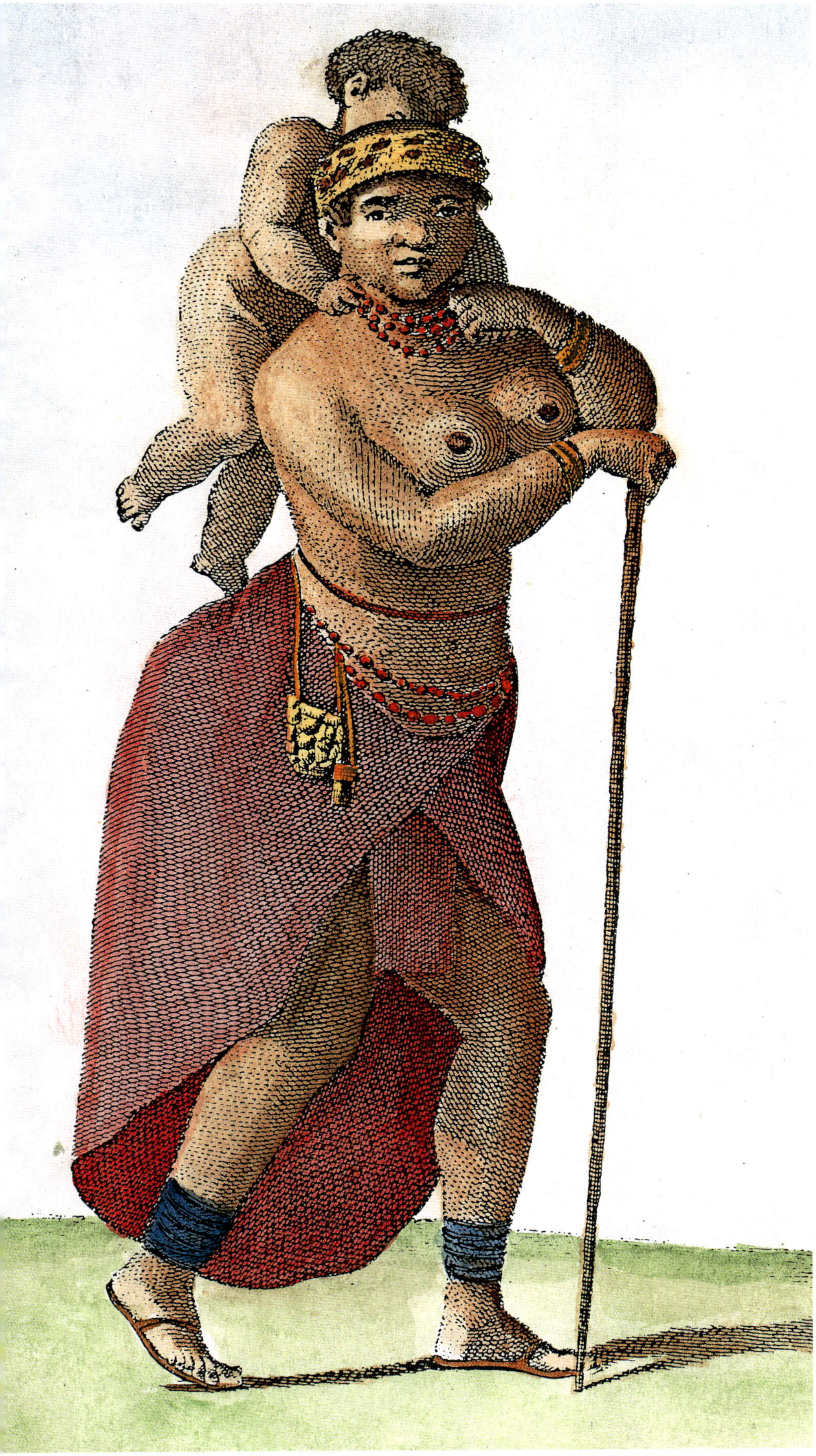

NONGQAWUSE

"SHE COULD STILL SEE HER MOTHER N'SUDU..."

The Arrival of the Portuguese

Twenty years had not yet passed since Bartolomeu Dias had discovered the Cape of Good Hope when Francisco de Almeida, viceroy of India, dropped anchor in Table Bay to take water. The Khoikhoi rebuffed these strangers with their suspect intentions, killing Almeida.

Shortly thereafter, other Portuguese appeared on the coast. Knowing the indigenous people's passion for copper, they brought a well-polished cannon and pretended to present it to them as a gift. As the Khoikhoi crowded around the instrument of death and started dragging it, unsuspecting, toward their homes, the Portuguese, who had loaded the weapon earlier, set it off and thus brought about horrifying carnage.

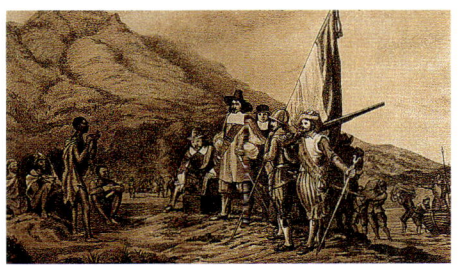

The Cape Frontier Wars (1779–1879)

In the southern part of Zulu country, between the Kei and Gamtoos Rivers, the history of the Xhosa (or Kafirs, as the whites called them, from the Arab word for "infidel") becomes intertwined with that of the Cape Colony and the expansion of the "frontier," at the price of an interaction both hostile and peaceful. Early on, the expansion assumed economic terms. Its fundamental instrument was the livestock trade that supplied the ocean-going vessels with meat; thanks to this trade, the Xhosa obtained metal, beads, alcohol, cloth, and especially the rifles and horses they coveted.

The missionaries followed close on the traders' heels: the first regular outpost of the Church Missionary Society in Xhosa territory was founded in 1816 on the Kat River. Seven Methodist stations followed; the missionaries studied the language, printed the Gospels, and created village schools. In 1834, the teachers' seminary destined to become the famous coeducational Lovedale School was founded.

But the Xhosa also struggled fiercely to hold on to their lands. Despite British efforts to avoid an irreversible confrontation between colonists and Africans, the frontier moved rapidly east. There were between six and nine wars, finally resolved after a century of incessant conflict by the annexation of Kaffraria in 1848.

The definitive decline of the Xhosa was confirmed by the desperate, violent revolt of 1857; this doomsday movement left the country starving and bled dry; from then on it was in no state to oppose incorporation into white society.

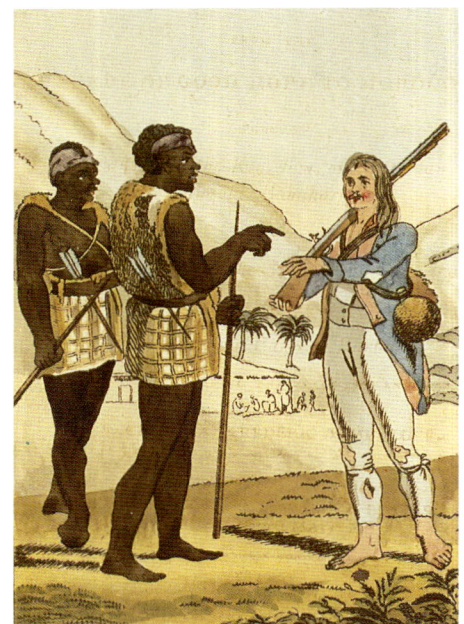

The White People's Weapons

The whites, according to the Xhosa, do not seize their enemy by the body as we do; but strike him down with thunder from afar. Their artillery fire is for men what the fires of August are for ripe pastures. How far can you run from the flame of their muskets? Where can you hide from the thunder vomited by their cannons?

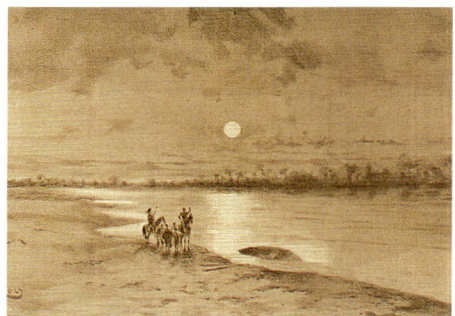

"THEN THE SKY WOULD OPEN..."

The Importance of Livestock

The chief's position and his people's prosperity depended on the number of animals they possessed. Livestock were slaughtered only for ritual purposes; beef constituted a delicacy consumed only on occasion, as when a beast died in the field and was brought back to the kraal and cut into pieces. Livestock provided the village with milk, buttermilk, skins for clothing, and the dung they used to cover the floor of the huts and to line and seal the grain storage pits. The health and safety of the animals were therefore constantly on the minds of the people who raised them.

Proverb

"Even the white man who lives in a palace will still be buried in the ground."

After this event, she decided to keep her ear to the ground, and that is how she heard the voice of the god Dalidipu for the first time: he prophesied the return of the dead, who would put everything back in place for the Xhosa, down to the least snuffbox of the last prisoner. She went home with her gourd of water and told her uncle what had happened. He fetched one of his friends, Kréli—one of the greatest Xhosa chiefs—to tell him in detail the story about the dream and about the god's voice.

And the two men looked at her in silence: this was in May of 1856.

During the days that followed, the flock would come out of the water again, always more numerous and more brilliant in its splendor.

And the voice of the god became more precise, giving new details each time, details that made Uncle Mlankazana and his old friend the great chief Kréli shudder: the dead were coming back to drive out the white men and to live eternally with the living; they would bring so much livestock with them that no one would be able to count it. From then on, death would lose its sting, it would be definitively banished from the land of the Xhosa; they would live in plenty until the end of time, like gods.

They simply had to listen to the voice of the dead and follow their instructions: kill the livestock and destroy the harvests in homage to the ancestors, who demanded this proof of trust and submission. Then the sky would open up like a fruit and two stars would appear: a yellow sun that would follow its usual course from east to west, and a red sun that would rise in the west and set in the east. Millions of animals would come out of the earth; and all who had died in years past would mingle with the living, so beautiful in their flesh and bones that no one would be able to tell them apart. And a sweet, calm wind would carry the white men to sea, with no hope of resistance, whence they would disappear forever.

The child who uttered these words of hope was no longer a little girl: Nongqawuse was now a Xhosa woman of austere bearing, dressed in an animal skin apron that fell to her knees; and her staccato gestures, her now commanding voice, her steady gaze, her eyes darker than the eyes of the dead, served as witnesses for every word that left her mouth.

The resurrection was to take place on August 15, 1856.

Little by little, each example serving to convince new converts, the Xhosa began to destroy their livestock and to devastate their harvest in the fields, to burn or flood their stores of grain.

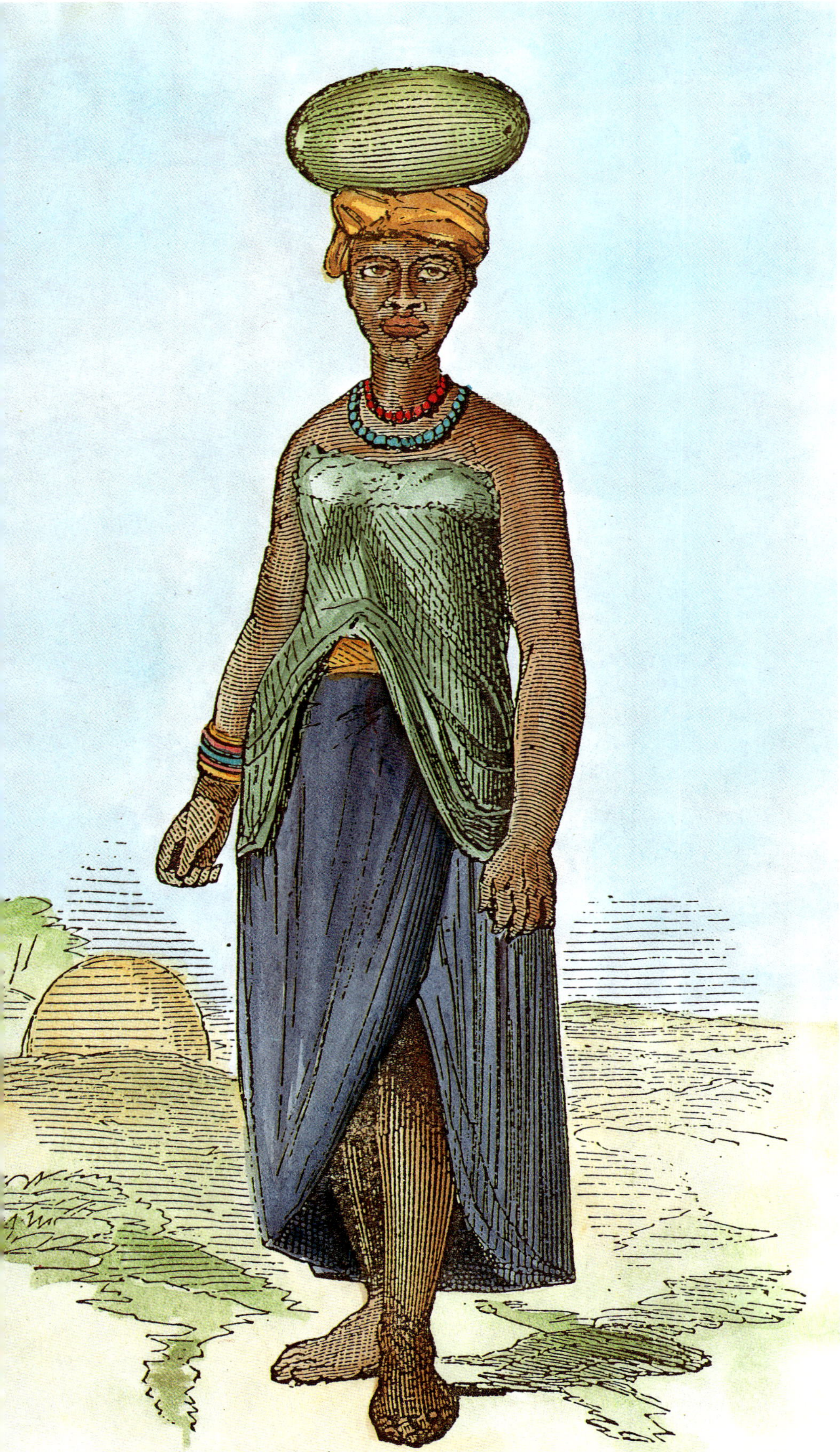

NONGQAWUSE

"SHE WAS NOW A WOMAN OF AUSTERE BEARING"

The Tragic Story of Siwitani, King of Mangoli

After the death of his father, King Siwitani gathered his subjects together and told them that they could not remain much longer in the vicinity of the Matébélés. He had personally resolved to seek a new, less exposed homeland in the northeast.

They traveled for one long month through the deserts, followed by their wives and children, and herding the rest of their flocks before them. They took shelter under overhanging cliffs, and when they went to sleep, all the warriors stuck their lances in the ground near their heads. Finally they arrived at the Indian Ocean. Surprised, they gave it the name *great river*. There, white men came down from two houses floating in the middle of the great water. They spoke amicably to the king. They seemed to feel great sympathy for his unhappy people and offered to transport them beyond the great river, into a peaceful country where they could plant their gardens.

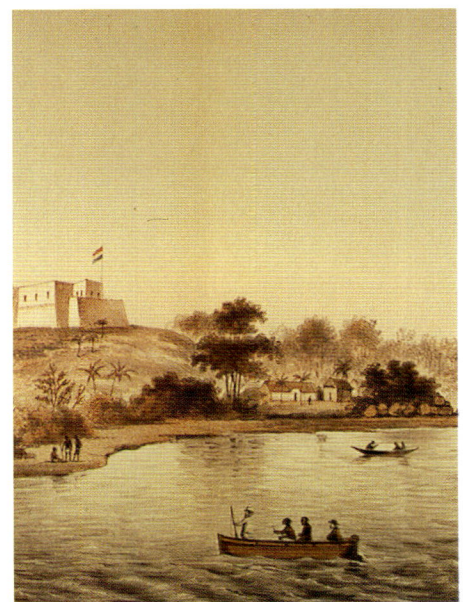

The king and his people accepted the offer. Immediately, launches were brought to shore and the people got on board with their animals, their wives, their children, their provisions, and all their possessions. At the end of the day, there remained on the bank only a hundred or so Mangolés who called out proudly:

"No! We will not follow the king to go with strangers that we do not know any more than we know their country or their language; we would rather go back to the desert, and when our beef and millet run out, we'll live on tigers and jackals—together with our brothers! *Ré tla ya linkué lé lipokouyaié kua ha éssou*!"

It was these few survivors of the Mangolés who returned to their country and told this story. They did not know what happened to their comrades, for they knew nothing of the slave trade.

They pleaded with those who did not believe, threw themselves at their feet and kissed their knees. On Friday August 15, 1856, an ordinary sun rose and followed its usual course from east to west.

But the destruction continued and the last holdouts were put to death, since the faithful were convinced that these unbelievers were the reason for the persistence of the white man's domination, of death and misery. And suddenly there was starvation, and the dead numbered in the tens of thousands.

A cloud of carrion birds hovered over the mingled carcasses of men and beasts; the survivors begged along the roads of the Cape Colony.

The whites had won without weapons in this last war, the worst one of all, which had been played out between the ever-renewed hope of the Xhosa people and their despair; because that Friday in August, hope wore a death mask.

There exist different versions, sometimes unpleasant, of the story of the young woman Nongqawuse, and especially of her disappearance in the final disaster.

Certain versions are brought back to life with pain, others by the will to make a mockery of the suffering of the Xhosa people.

For our part here, we simply recall a legend—a legend born of history, or history transformed into legend: we can see the young prophet lying in the dark of the hut and refusing to eat, in spite of the pleas of those around her; waiting and waiting and refusing to take nourishment, refusing to lose hope until her last breath.

So ends the story of Nongqawuse, the young woman who had heard the voice of a god.

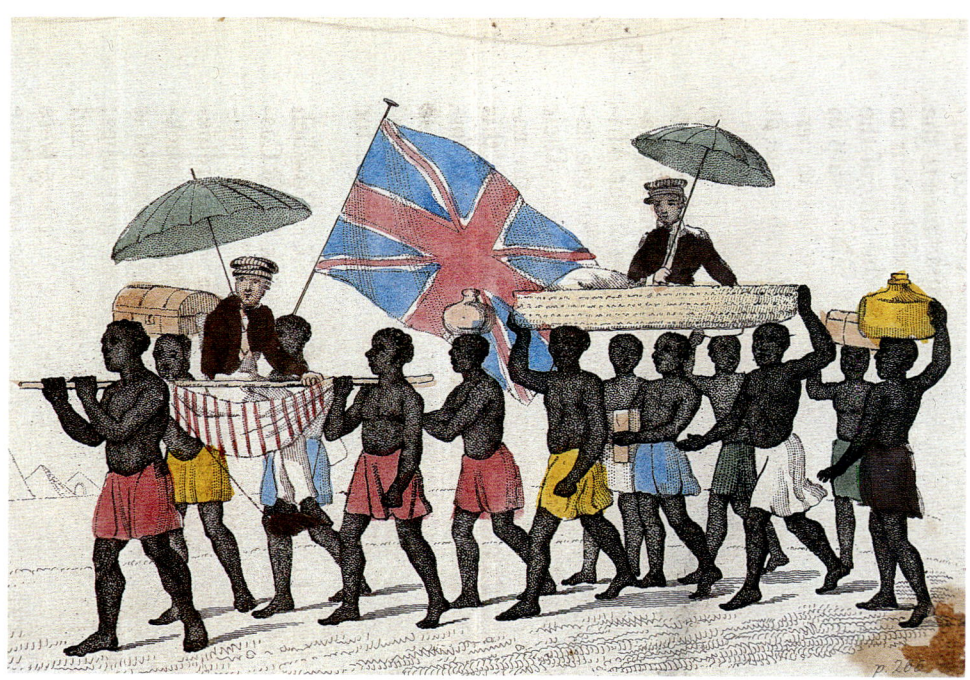

AFTER THE DEFEAT

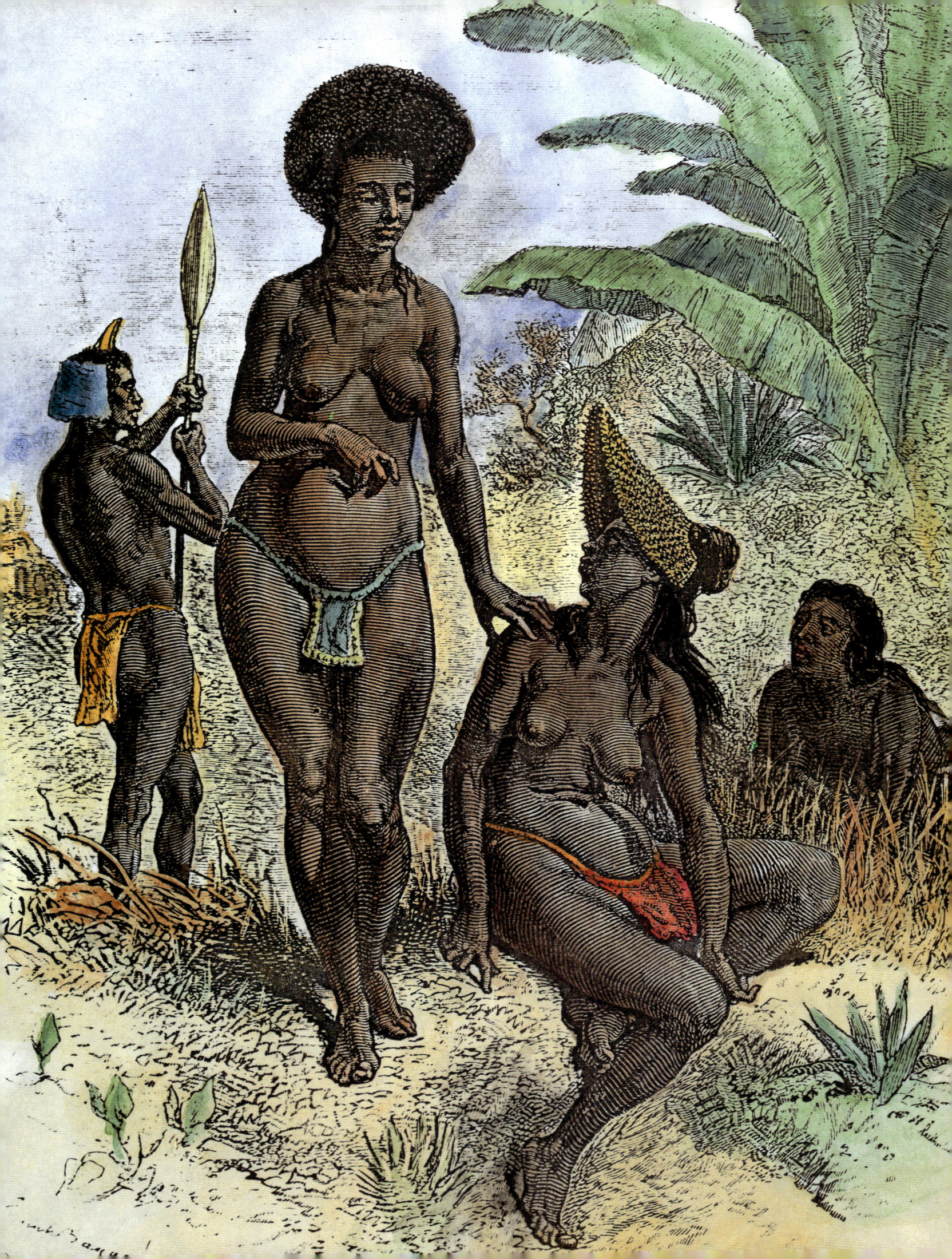

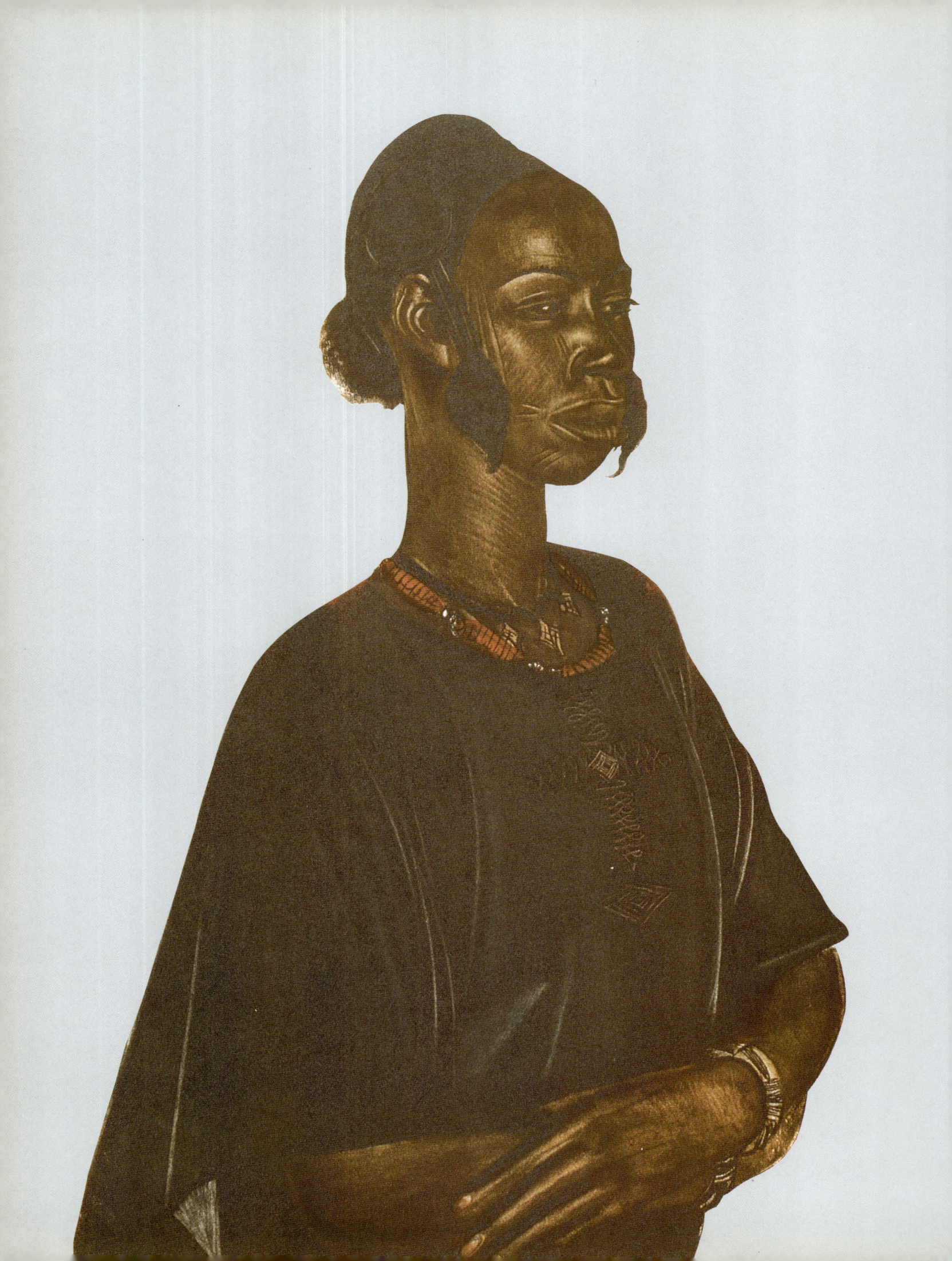

SARRAOUNIA

THE PANTHER QUEEN

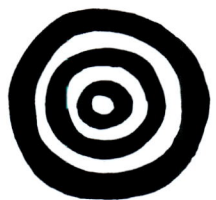

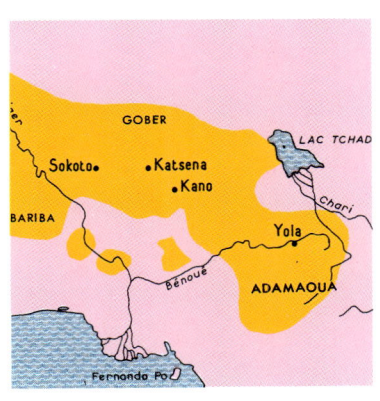

The story of the woman who opposed bayonettes with the strength of her soul, and the white man's tricks with the traditional magic of Africa...

IN 1880, JULES VERNE PLANNED A NOVEL ABOUT A BAND OF WHITE PIRATES WHO CARVED OUT AN EMPIRE ALONG THE BEND OF THE NIGER; SEVERAL YEARS LATER, IN THE 1890S, A FRENCH COLONIAL OPERATION SADLY FULFILLED THIS PROPHECY. THIS WAS THE Voulet-Chanoine mission, which would trace a horrible arc between Ségou and Chad, before succumbing to its own fantasies.

In the beginning, Lieutenant Voulet and Captain Chanoine were colonial officers. Their mission was to quickly overtake France's competitors: the English coming from Nigeria and the Germans from Cameroon, each striving to be the first to plant its flag at Lake Chad.

On May 2, 1899, in Ségou, they numbered about a dozen white men followed by a company of native soldiers, called "tirailleurs," with three cannons, one hundred and sixty rapid-firing rifles, and the same number of short automatic rifles.

War feeds war; such was the motto of all the colonial conquests.

Like all those that had preceded it, the Voulet-Chanoine regiment advanced by feeding off the indigenous peoples; it conscripted hundreds of porters by force, punished villages that resisted, burned cities, and practiced a policy of terror that facilitated the signing of treaties.

But so far, all of this was nothing new: it had been like this in western Africa for twenty years. "Friendly" villages were ransomed. The others were simply "broken," to use the horrid language of the colonialists, that is, reduced to ashes.

This was not Voulet's and Chanoine's first expedition. In February 1896 and in 1898, they had splendidly ravaged Gurunsi country. But after all was said and done, they had no exceptional feathers in their caps; and it was only in 1899 that they would go all out, during their third and final, fatal, expedition to Chad.

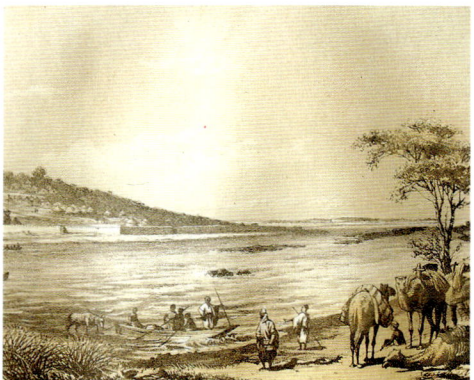
"A FRENCH COLONIAL MISSION...

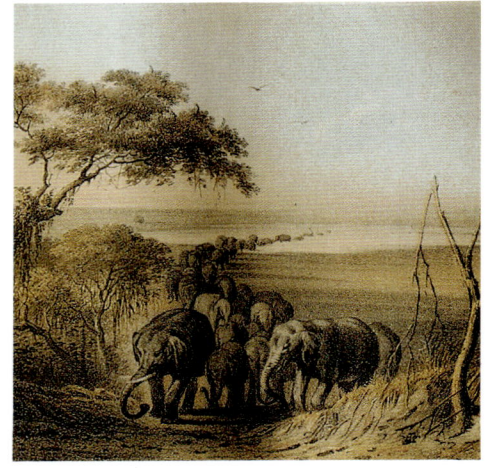
...TRACED AN ARC OF HORROR...

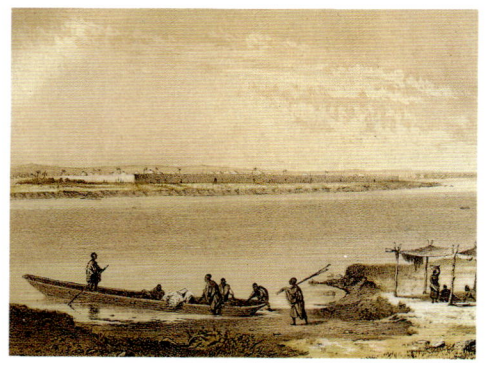
...TO BE THE FIRST TO PLANT A FLAG AT LAKE CHAD"

SARRAOUNIA

Something astonishing happened then: Voulet and Chanoine suddenly took themselves for gods.

Up until then they had acted as officers, conscious of French rights upon these "savage" lands, on which they were planting the flag of civilization.

And then slowly, as they advanced among the Mossi, the Sperma, the Gurma, in the midst of these terrorized populations, everything began to get confused in their minds. They forgot that their strength was not in themselves, but in the nation that had delegated them to a purpose: it was the power of the West that had forged their weapons and cast their cannons. They forgot that. It was the power of the West that had given them mastery over its people. They forgot that.

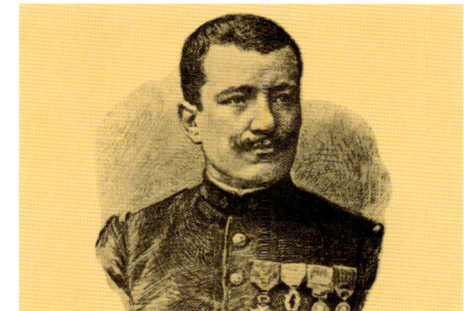

CAPTAIN VOULET

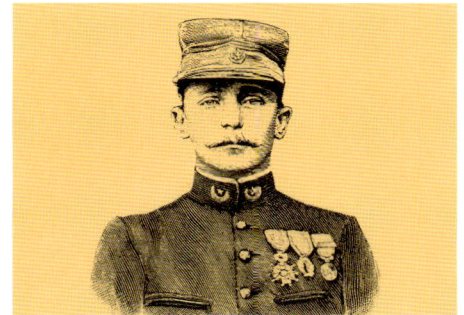

LIEUTENANT CHANOINE

The Voulet-Chanoine Expeditions in Western Africa

The ministry sent the following telegram from Dakar to Lieutenant-Colonel Klobb, in Timbuktu, on April 19, 1899:
"I have learned that atrocities have allegedly been committed by the Voulet mission in the Say and Sananné Hausa regions, peaceful villages attacked with bayonets for the purpose of conscripting porters against the will of the inhabitants; and two tirailleurs have allegedly been killed; Voulet is said to have massacred fifteen women and children near his camp; a tirailleur who defended himself, against orders, with bullets instead of his bayonet was said to have been summarily executed by Voulet. Then, during the march from Sananné Hausa to Liboré, many porters too tired to march were allegedly decapitated; then, new massacres to acquire porters; tirailleurs were obliged to show the captain(s) [the plural has been added] the severed hands of those executed [?, illegible] as proof that orders had been carried out. Chanoine himself is said to have impaled on stakes the heads of natives caught unawares, and all villages within a twelve kilometer radius are alleged to have been burned."

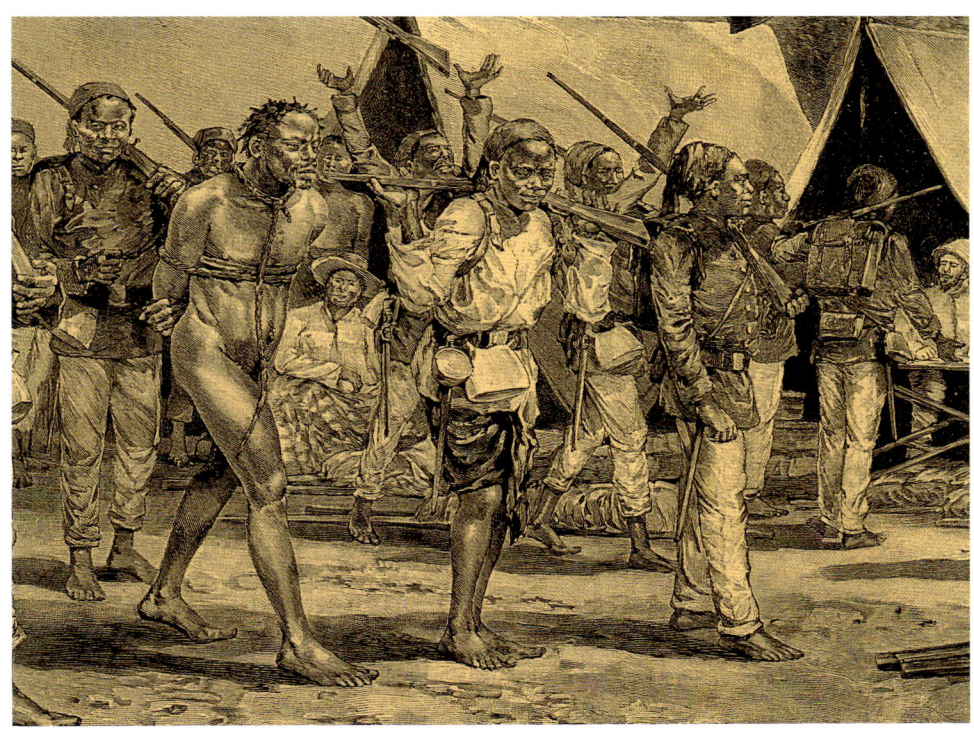

"A TRAIN OF CAPTIVES DESTINED FOR SALE..."

Before them, all they saw were submissive villages, crowds on whom to exercise their fantasy.

And they dreamt of carving out a kingdom of their very own, between Lake Chad and the first foothills of the Darfur region.

A strange logic took shape in their minds: they were gods because they spread death, they spread death because they were gods.

A train of captives now swelled the ranks of the caravan: men, women, and children fated to be sold at the markets in Sudan. The laggards were executed on the spot and their bodies left to the vultures.

Song of the Mercenaries

Gone to war
Gone to follow the whites
Gone for women
Gone far, far, far
Warrior
You'll never see your house again
Gone far, far, far
You'll never see the river again
Gone to war
Gone to follow the whites

Proverb

"A man falls with his shadow."

Two or three women had to give birth during the march. All resistance was mercilessly penalized by pillage, fire, and slaughter.

The column kept growing, and each passing day it advanced more slowly; eventually, it entered Hausa country, the territory of a little kingdom inhabited by the Aznas.

And suddenly the unforeseeable came to pass, astonishing everyone at the time: the gods Voulet and Chanoine were stopped by a simple woman, Sarraounia, the queen who opposed the bayonets with the strength of her soul, and the white man's tricks with the traditional magic of Africa.

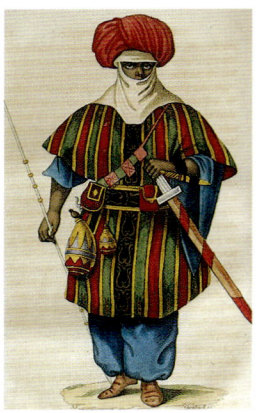

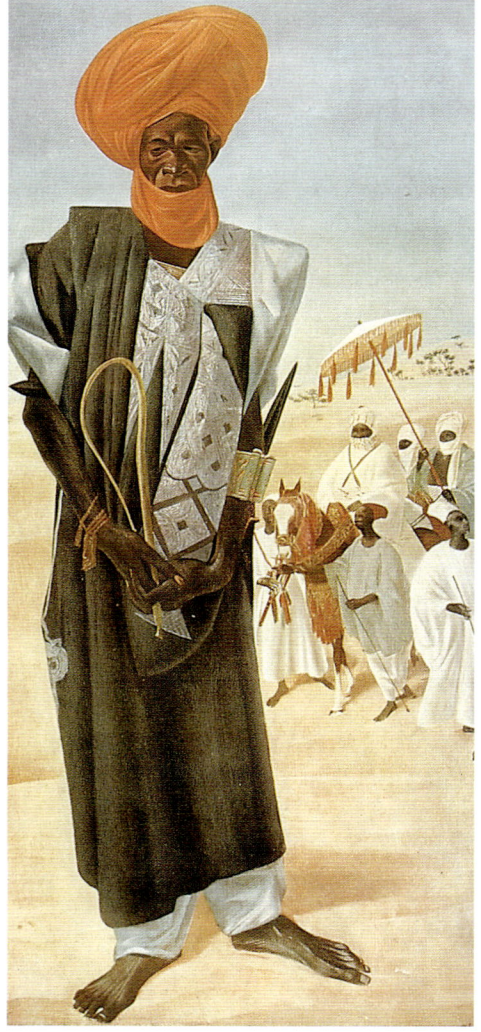

"HE WAS A WARRIOR WHO NEVER SHRANK FROM FEAR"

Sarraounia's father was a warrior who never shrank from fear, whose deeds for the Azna people had earned him the status of a king.

He had particularly distinguished himself in his defiance of the Tuaregs, who were always hungry for black men to sell to the caravans from the north and for beautiful Azna women to take back to their goatskin tents. He had also had to struggle against the powerful Muslim marabous of Sokoto, who yearned to convert all the "fetishists," as they called them, to their strange religion from another world.

And so, by prying apart these two jaws that gripped his people, Sarraounia's father had become the serkin, king of the tiny territory of the Aznas.

Sarraounia's mother had died giving birth, and everyone had thought that her child would soon follow her to the grave, for her pinched mouth and her clenched little fists did not seem to want to open to this world. But just then, the little creature had raised her delicate bluish eyelids and revealed shining yellow eyes with a vaguely metallic sheen; and the people recognized the sign of the panther.

The Aznas always knew that they had been born of a panther; and it was this animal, sculpted on the fronts of their houses and embroidered on the long striped cotton garb of their chief, that was their symbol among the other tribes.

A panther does not die without a fight, and so the Aznas were not surprised to see Sarraounia survive her difficult birth and grow into a strong, beautiful young woman.

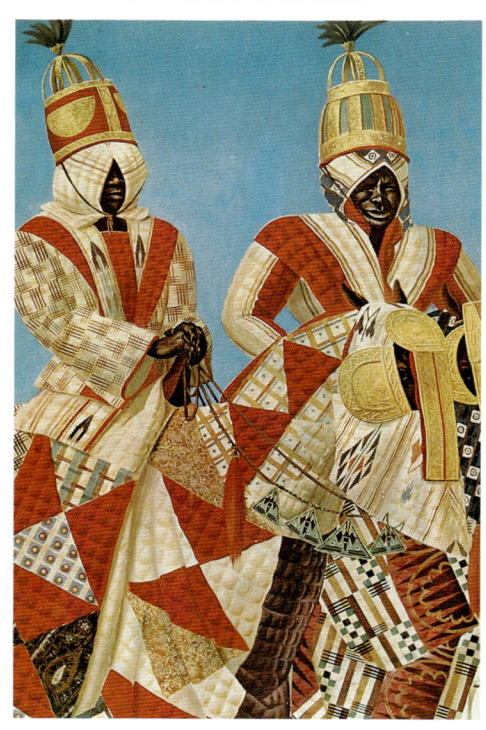

"...KING OF THE AZNA TERRITORY"

SARRAOUNIA

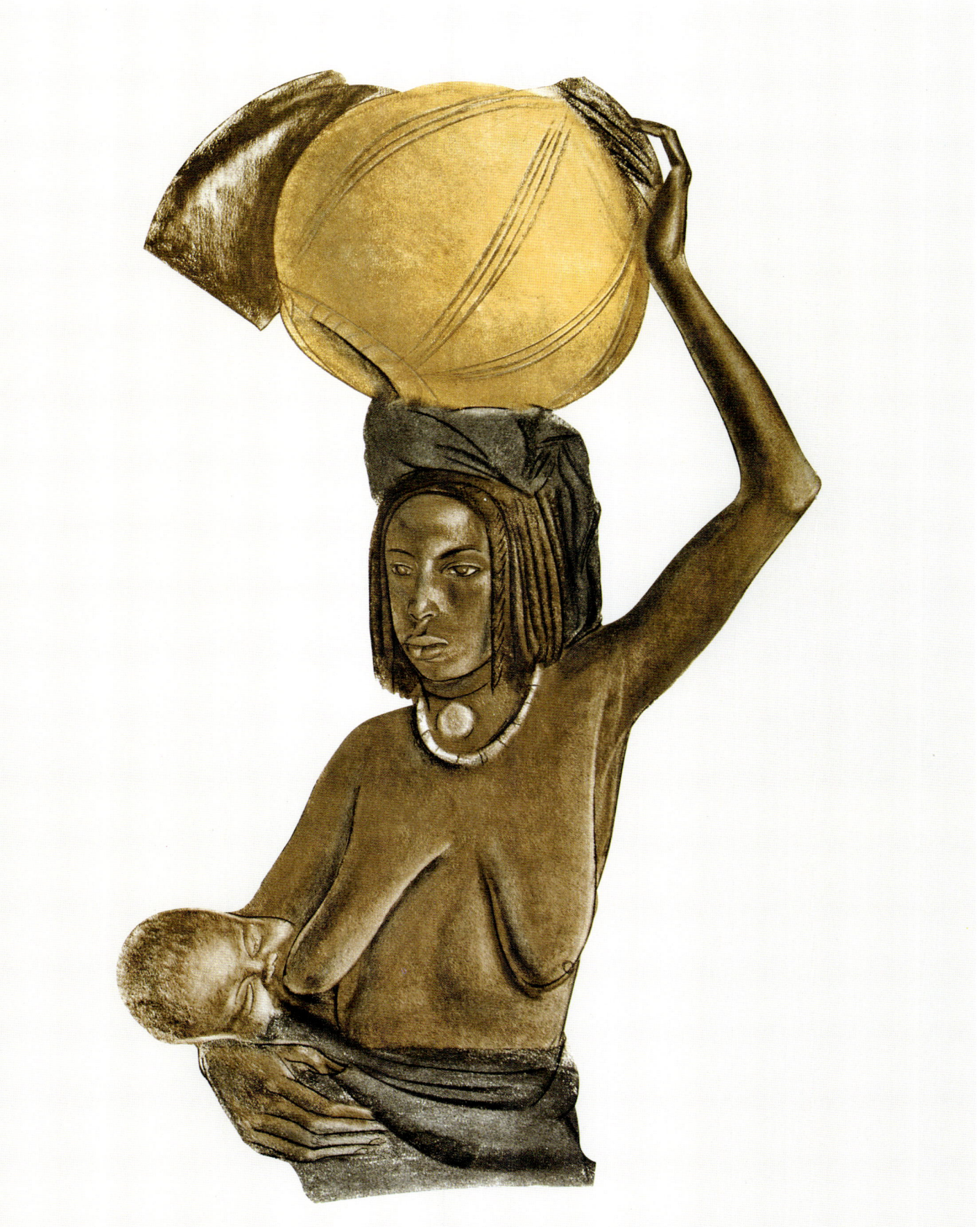

"A PERSON WHO HAS NO MOTHER MUST KEEP EVERYTHING IN HIS HEART" (PROVERB)

Sarraounia's Childhood

At the age of ten, Sarraounia was already a pretty girl with the beginnings of voluptuous curves. Her wide eyes had softened, and her two little well-set breasts adorned her proud chest. Not a single tribal scar marred her full little cheeks, smooth as an overripe mango.

The Advice of the Wiseman

Do not stifle your two little fruits in a cloth. Let them grow and fill out freely. Let your body breathe. The wind, rain, and sun will ripen and soak the body. Your body will be firm and supple as the wood of the tamarind tree. For your body will not know the torments of childbirth. Never forget, my daughter, that you were not nourished with a mother's milk. No woman gave you her breast. You were not raised by women. Do not let yourself be distracted by the childish pleasures of the senses. When the time comes, you will know man as your servant and not your master. The male will be an instrument of relaxation and fleeting pleasure for you, not an arrogant and egotistical lord.

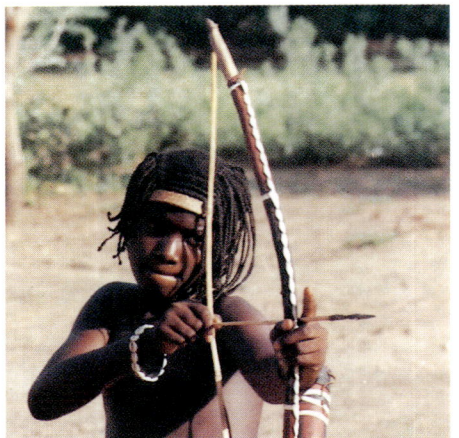

Sarraounia's Initiation

As trials of initiation, Sarraounia dove into the muddy water of the streams, fishing for the fearsome and slippery electric eel with her bare hands or with a harpoon. She knew the fear and anguish of the tumultuous evenings when the wild beasts roam in search of food. More than once she used the bow and arrow to defend or feed herself. She learned to handle all the weapons of hunting and war. She learned the secret of the blowgun, of the curved saber, and of the sling as terrifying as thunder from the sky.

Certain illustrations for this story are taken from the remarkable film by **Melmed Hondo,** *"Sarraounia,"* **produced by Soleil Ô.** *The author was kind enough to place them at our disposition, and we thank him.*

Panthers are made for the bush, as everyone knows: the gods did not put them on earth to haunt the courtyards and fill their ears with the hammering of the pestles.

The panther child soon learned to use a bow and arrow. She climbed trees, leapt among the rocks, and dove into the brown water of the ponds to catch the pink-mouthed fish with her bare hands. Then she learned the secret of "hyena's ear," that poison that lends arrowheads a merciless power over everything that breathes under the sun. Now, armed with a lance and a saber shaped like the crescent moon, she haunted the tall grass of her hunting grounds, aloof and solitary as her animal ancestor whose reflection she bore among the Azna.

She was the king's daughter; she went with men as she pleased, but never wanted a child clinging to her breast.

Sometimes she would disappear for weeks at a time; and they said that she would talk to the spirits of the Shadow, who taught her all the secrets of good and evil, of the plants that kill and those that bring back to life, the elixirs of power and wisdom.

This is how she became Sarraounia, daughter of the king, sorceress, great dame of the Shadow.

She was twenty when her father died, and naturally she was brought to the throne, where a long wooden panther offered her its spine as an armrest.

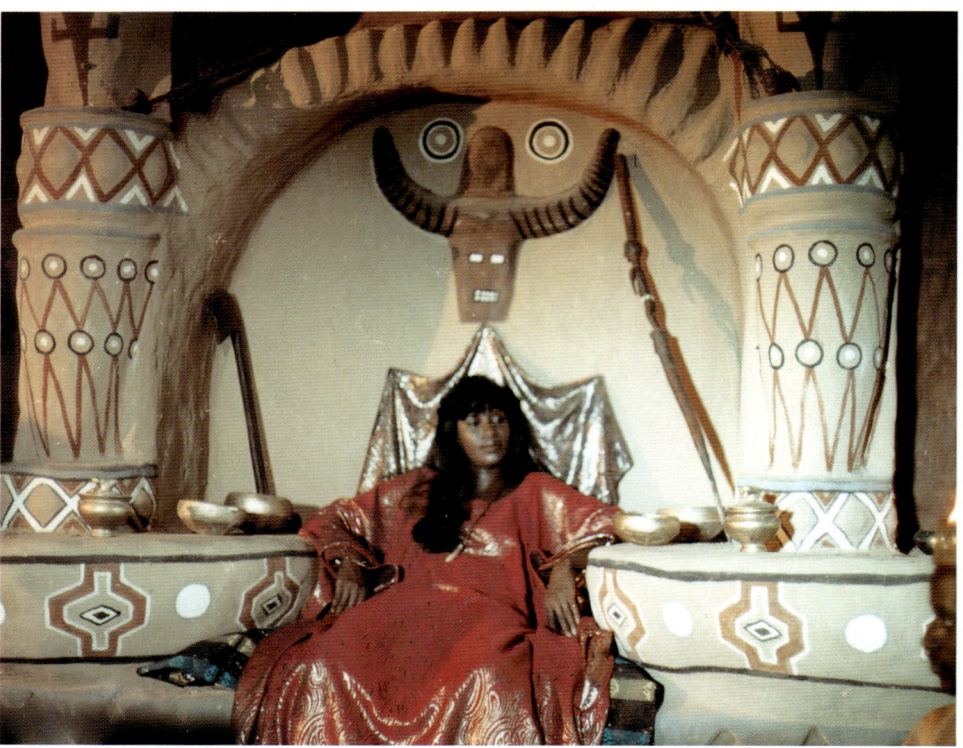

"SHE WAS BROUGHT TO THE THRONE..."

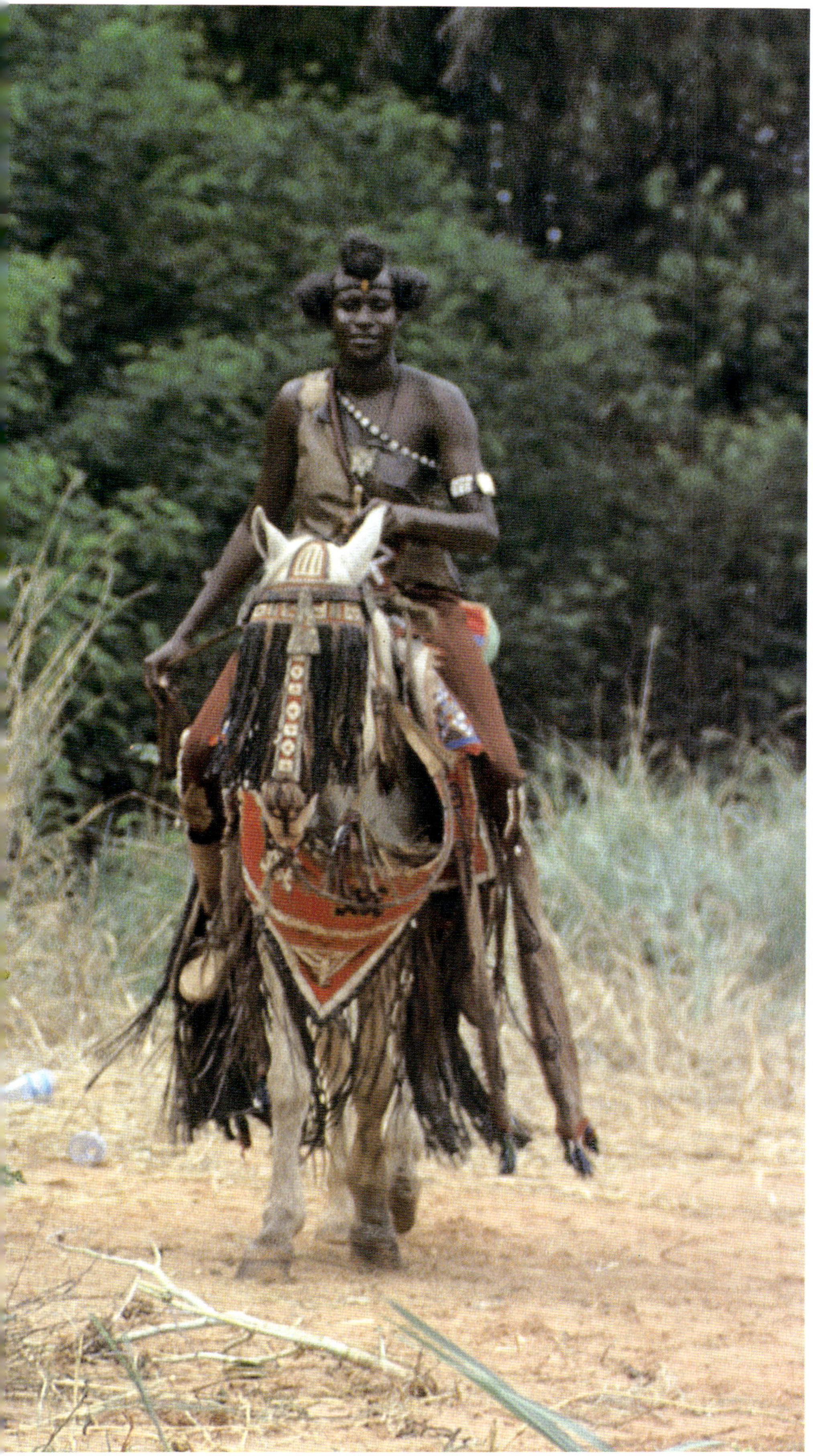

SARRAOUNIA

"AT THE SLIGHTEST DANGER, SHE WOULD BE AT THE HEAD OF HER TROOPS..."

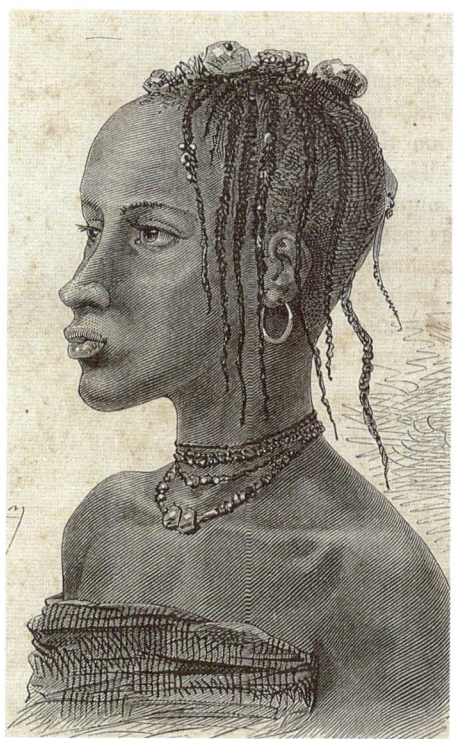

Song of the Praise Singer Gogué, the Queen's Lover

*"I love you because you are my night lover
I fear you because you are the great sorceress
I respect you because you are my queen
I adore you because you are my lord
I sing your glory because you are the strongest
You are the eye and the honor of the Aznas
Sweet Sarraounia with iron claws
You break your enemies as surely as
The panther breaks the bones of its prey..."*

The Great War against the Whites is Announced

"What do the cowries say, serkin Boka?"
"Nothing. Or rather, they are talking, but they're not saying anything. And saying nothing is not good. I don't like it when the cowries don't speak. Yes, Sarraounia, the cowries' silence scares me. Something serious is going to happen in Azna country. The last time the cowries were quiet, do you remember, Sarraounia? That was the year of the cram-cram grass, just before the harvest. That year, a cloud of locusts covered our fields and chewed them down to the roots. Today, the cowries are silent, as they were on the eve of that great plague. Something serious is about to happen, Sarraounia."
"Yes, something serious. You said it, serkin Boka! Those who are preparing to invade our country are indeed locusts armed to the teeth. White men from god knows where are traveling to Lougou, destroying everything in their path."

Proverb

"It is not for no reason that we run into thorns: if you aren't chasing the snake, then the snake is chasing you."

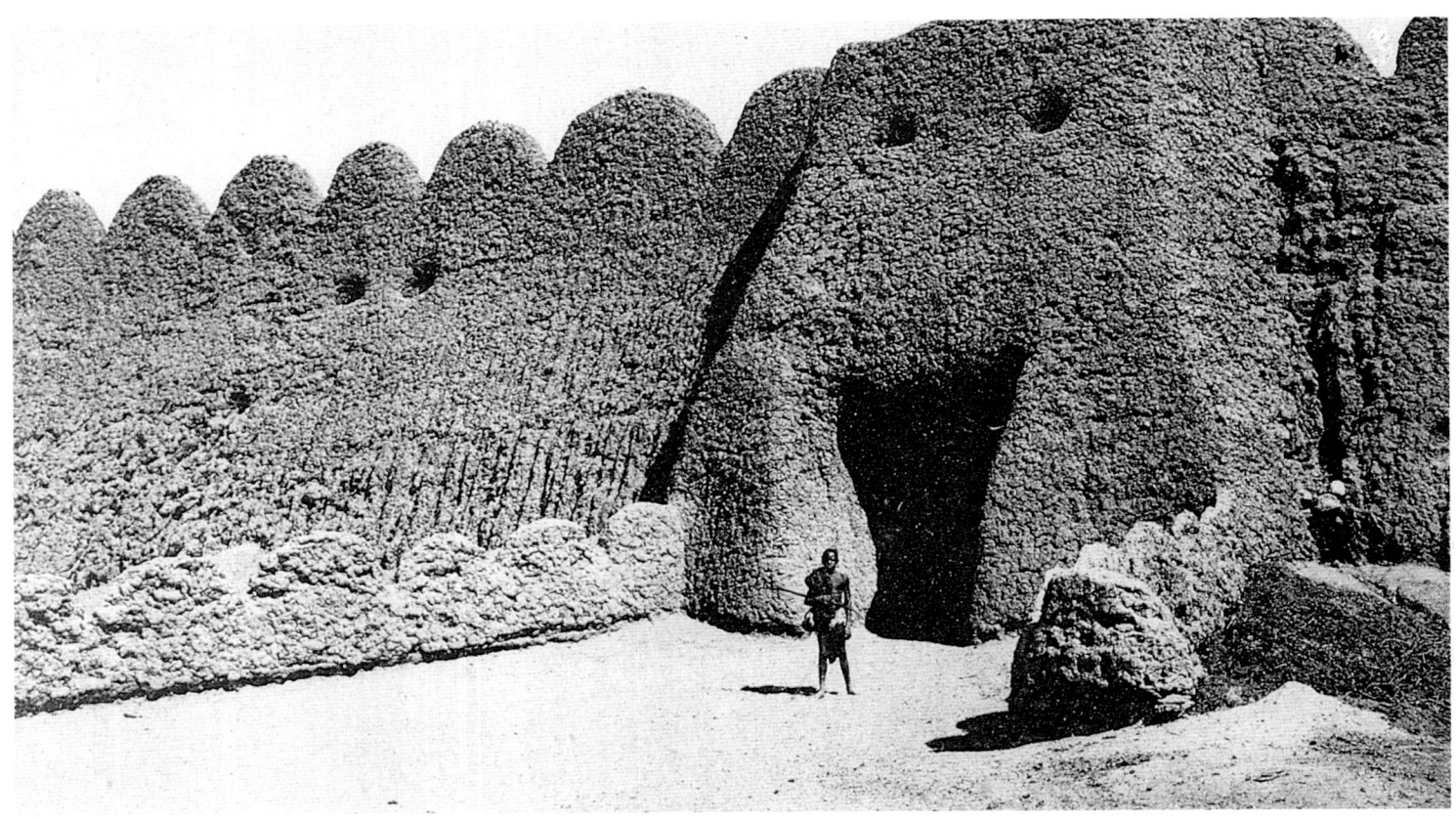

"SARRAOUNIA HAD A FORTRESS WALL BUILT"

Organizing the Defense

The best archers, those able to shoot their saw-edged arrows black with poison over five hundred feet, form the front line on the vast towers. At all costs they must deflect the attackers on the plain. Then come the riflemen, armed with their sturdy muskets, accompanied by young amazons.

The blows must fall one after the other with no time to think. Exhausting work for the bare-chested amazons, crouching next to the riflemen and armed with long iron rods; and all this in a suffocating atmosphere of smoke and powder stinging their eyes and nostrils like hot pepper. Inside are the lancers, protected behind their enormous rawhide shields reinforced with plant fibers. The old *griots* (praise singers) too weak to bear arms have brought out their musical arsenal: hollowed-out antelope horns, thirteen-tone copper bells, single-scale reed flutes, the one-stringed fiddle, and the enormous war drum, three feet high, with a deep muffled sound like thunder, all to maintain the courage and energy of the warriors. Even the children have been mobilized in the tremendous commotion of this combat for the sake of honor and dignity.

The Queen Sarraounia

Through her constant interest in state affairs and in the education of the youth, she developed the consciousness of the Aznas. She transformed them into a powerful community of animists. Nevertheless, the Aznas remained threatened by the intolerance of the Muslim tribes to the north and south.

The people rejoiced to see her in her palace in Lougou, the capital of the Azna kingdom. From then on the men of the north and the Muslims of the south would keep to themselves.

At the slightest danger, she would be at the head of her troops, hair flying like a madwoman's, chest bare, her pale eyes shooting lightning; her silhouette became legendary throughout the steppes that separated the dunes of the north from the great equatorial forest.

Then a rumor gradually made its way through all the tribes of the region: a column of white men was marching east, devastating everything in its path. Villages had been razed, venerable cities reduced to ashes. The whole river valley had become a tomb. Djoundjou, Sananné, Hausa, Tessa, and Baban and the Zerma country, Nalankani, Koma, and Berni N'Konni were rotting in the sun.

Sarraounia immediately dispatched messengers north and south, proposing to the Tuaregs and the Sokoto peoples that they unite to face the common threat. She did not plead for forgiveness of old hatreds; she simply said, "If your neighbor's beard is burning, hurry up and put water on your own." But the Tuaregs did not even bother to reply: you don't make alliances with the seeds of slaves.

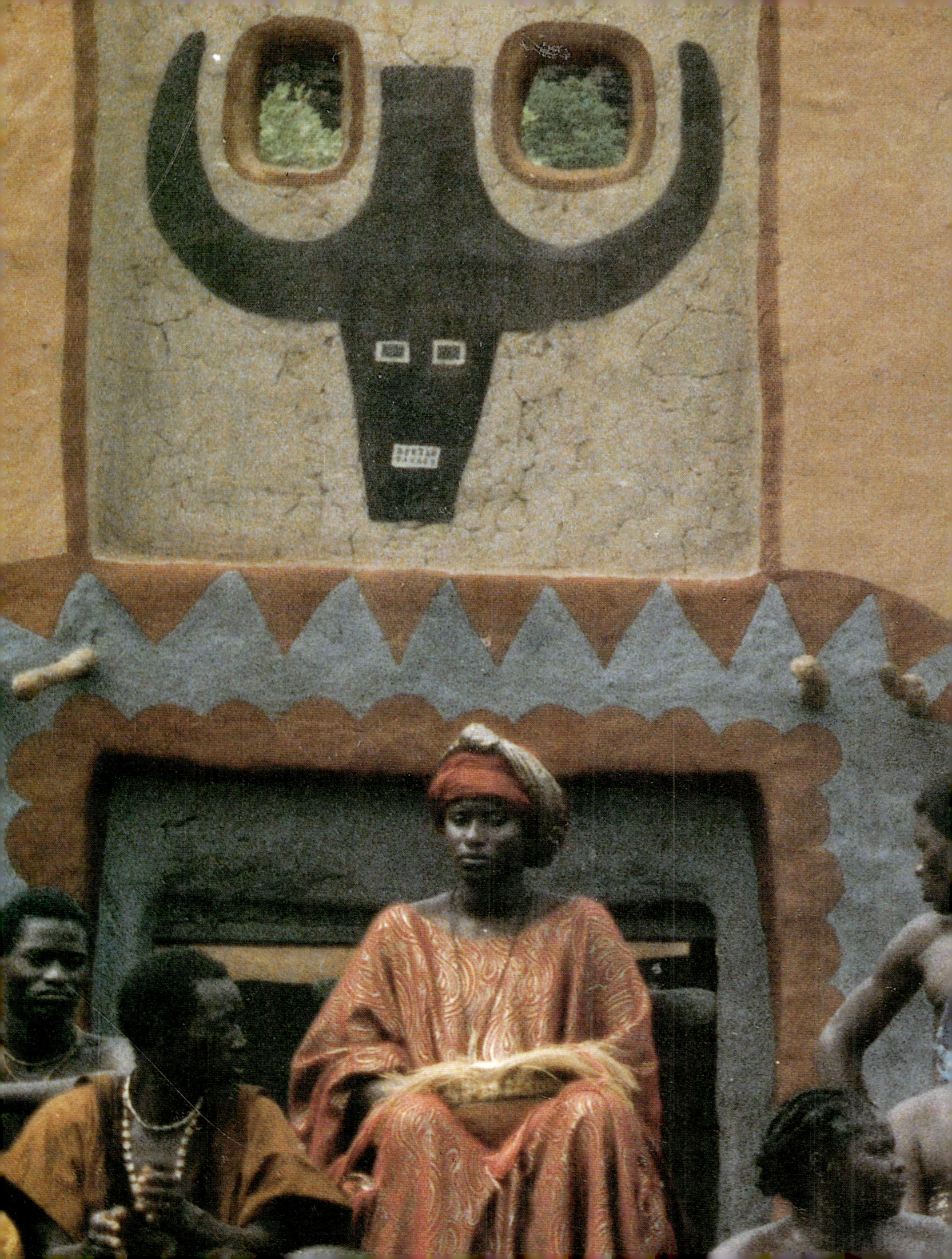

And entrenched behind their fortress with its triple ramparts, the Fulanis of Sokoto responded to her by sending back the decapitated head of her emissary: let her accursed superstitions help her now, let them protect her from the white creatures who pissed standing up and did not prostrate themselves to Mecca!

So Sarraounia had a fortress wall built around Lougou, her capital. She smashed open the granaries and sent the women, children, and old men to a safe place in the bush. Then the warriors waited, armed with spears and old piston rifles, while the queen applied an ointment that was supposed to stop bullets. Anxiously, the men stretched out their foreheads to receive this magical protection.

On the plain, the first wisp of smoke was already rising.

Sarraounia gave her final orders, finished the last preparations: the food was rationed, her personal effects distributed, the royal emblems put in deep pits for safe-keeping.

Then, having hand-picked a group of archers, silent warriors, she slipped into the tall grass to seek out the enemy: and in this way, when night fell, a cloud of arrows from nowhere threw the Voulet-Chanoine expedition into a state of chaos for the first time.

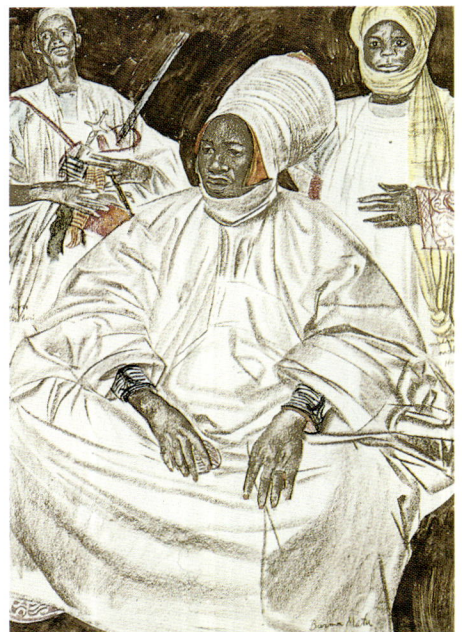

So That the Name of the Aznas May Live On

"I will cover my throne with their monkey hides. Let them come, we will receive them as bandits of their sort should be received. Close all the gates to the city, order the nimblest archers to the towers, gather tons of powder and rounds for your rifles. The struggle will be hard, but we will fight to the last, for no one will ever say the Aznas surrendered without a fight. Do not forget that as we struggle to defend our homes and our freedom, we are also fighting for the honor of all the Aznas, for the Azna NAME! When our bones have turned white in the sand, our griots, our griots' sons, and our griots' grandsons will sing the courage and the honor of the Aznas. I have not given the Aznas a son, but I will leave them more than a son, more than life, more than all the world's riches, I will leave them a NAME. I have given the Azna people the pride of BEING. Shame on him who has no name left! Yes, all who will come after us will hear about the Aznas, thanks to our deeds of bravery against those who wish to control and humiliate us. We must die to leave a name behind. For he who dies without a NAME is dead forever."

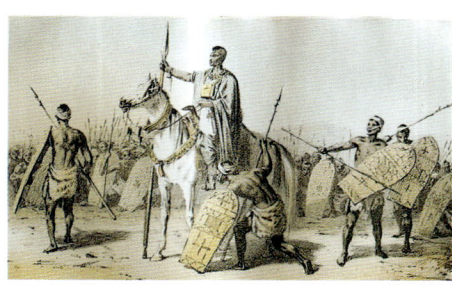

Proverb

"In the house of the brave man there are tears; in the coward's house no one cries."

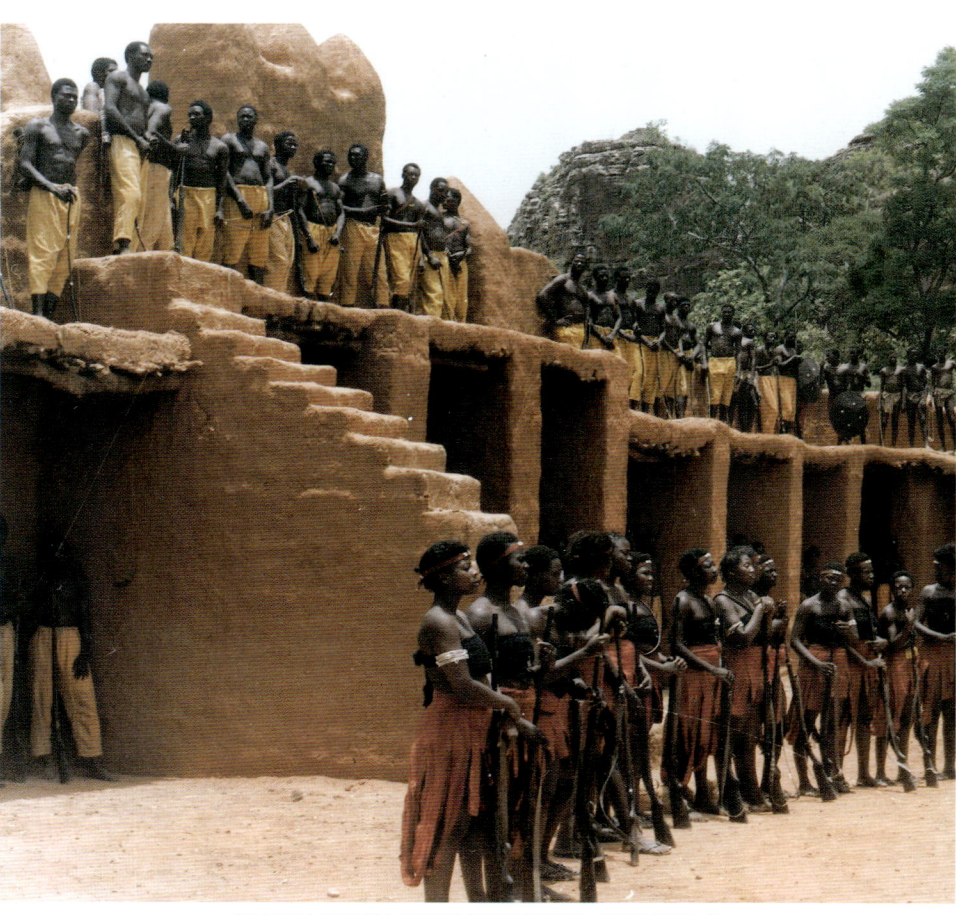

"SARRAOUNIA GAVE HER FINAL ORDERS..."

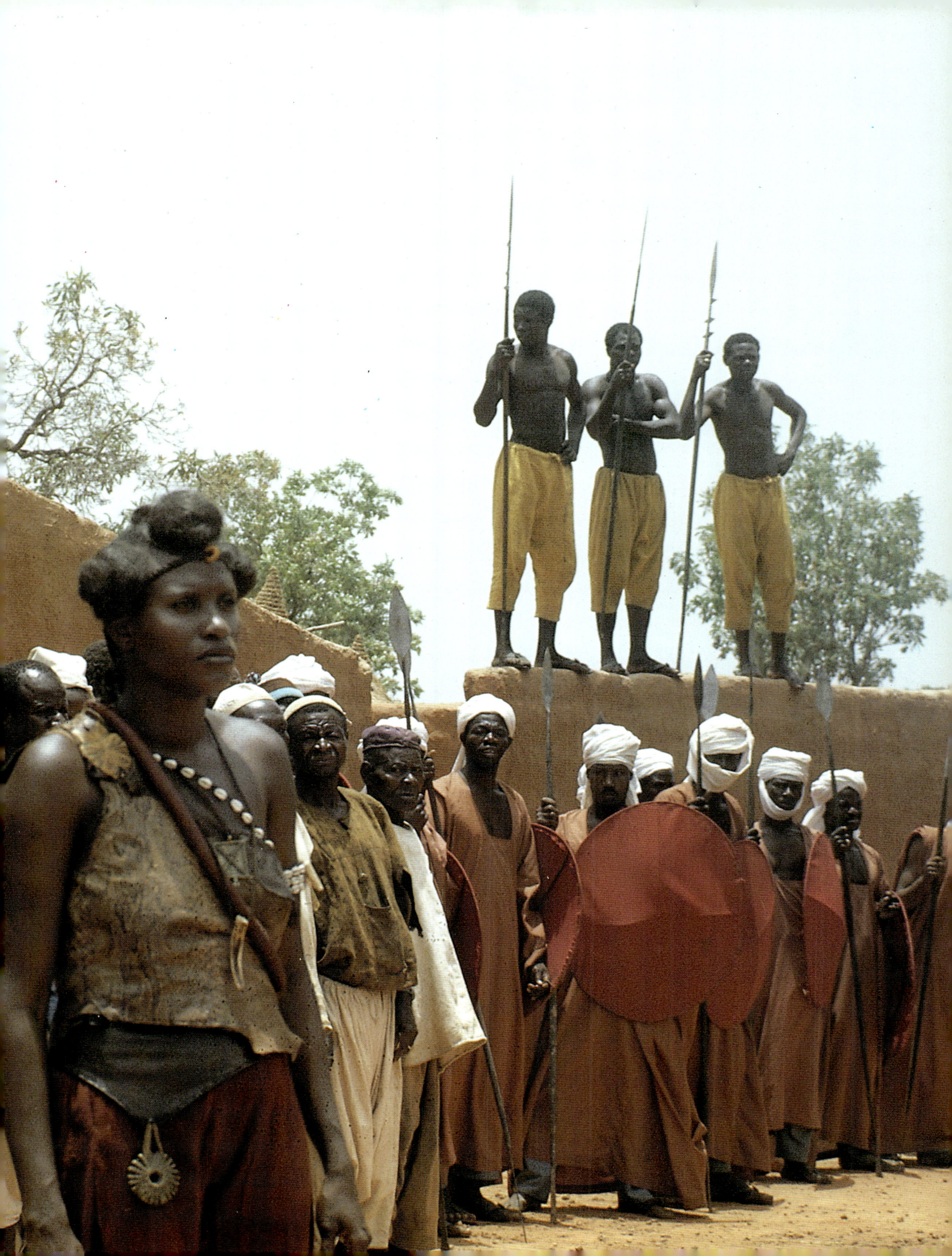

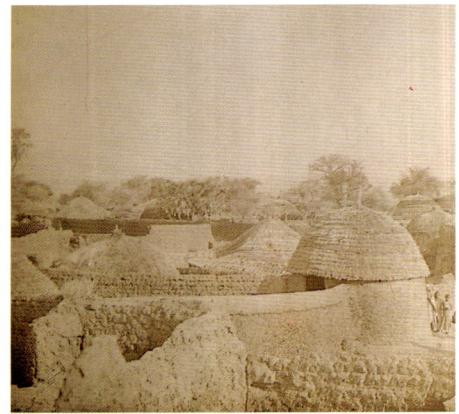

The Queen's Speech to the Brothers and Sisters of the Other Nations of Africa

"Brothers and sisters coming from afar, you are welcome in Azna country. We do not speak the same tongue, we do not have the same beliefs, but we share the same will, the will to live free. And you appreciate even more than we do the price of liberty for having once lost it. Your decision to slip away from your masters honors you and honors all the people of the black lands. Brothers and sisters from afar, you are welcome in Azna country. Here, no one will disdain you or your customs, and the use that you make of your goods and your bodies won't upset anyone. No one will trouble your prayers and meditations, for you alone are responsible for your souls. Our community is a community of tolerance where all live according to their strength, their habits, and their principles. We have our fetishes and our totems. Respect them, we shall respect yours. The Azna land is rich. You will have plots for your crops, you will build your houses next to ours, you will drink from our wells, and hunt in our forests. Our rivers are full of fish. You will fish in our streams and you will grow corn, yams, and cassava in the fertile peat of our basins. Brothers and sisters, black of skin like us, you are welcome. You will live in Azna country in love and dignity."

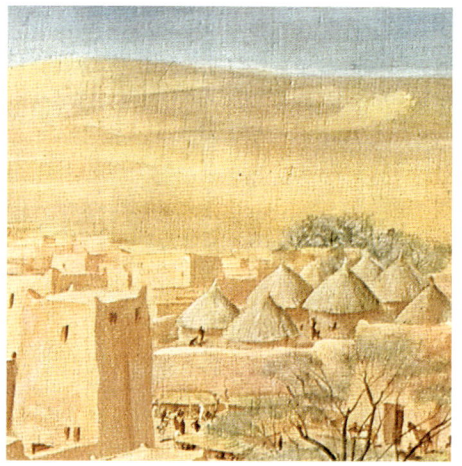

"THE TROOPS ENTERED A DESERTED CITY"

For several days, Doctor Casenave and Lieutenant Pallier had been advising that they avoid Lougou, the Azna capital; the tirailleurs were petrified, they said, at the idea of confronting the dreaded sorceress, of whom they would only speak in hushed tones, as if afraid to wake her. But Voulet and Chanoine would hear nothing of it; they were enraged at the idea that a simple black woman could block their path, make them change their course, their road to glory, for even just a day.

And witnesses would later recount the effect of the silent rain that fell on the horde assembled around the campfires: white officers and black mercenaries, captives with yokes on their necks, and the whole string of women and children who had survived the march.

The next morning, one hundred and fifty porters were missing at roll call, and a dozen native infantrymen had deserted, preferring to wander in a strange land rather than confront Sarraounia.

But that very day, Voulet and Chanoine launched an attack against Lougou, whose earthen walls crumbled beneath the hail of cannonballs.

The troops entered a deserted city: empty huts, empty animal pens, empty granaries.

Another arrow flew out in silence and shouts rang out, a woman's laughter was heard: that was the beginning of the end for the French force.

Day after day, night after night, Sarraounia harassed the divided, crippled column, all the way to Maffi Guirgui, where a black mercenary brought down the god Chanoine with a rifle shot, while the god Voulet was slain farther along, near Nakouta. That was the end of their adventure.

The capital of the kingdom was rebuilt, but new columns of soldiers followed the first, and traditional cunning could not sustain the unity of the Azna people. Little by little, the mysterious strength of the invaders carried the day; a French flag was eventually raised in the middle of the great court of Lougou, and the queen shut herself up in the shadows of her palace. One day, at the end of a fiery hot afternoon, a yellow-eyed panther burst out of the throne room and flew in one bound over the ramparts, disappearing into the bush: Sarraounia was never seen again.

All the griots of the Azna people had died in combat, and no voice rose to salute the queen's memory, her rise and her final fall, the leap with which she lost herself in the night.

But happily, the people had retained every detail of her life and soul, and taught these to their children at night around the fire.

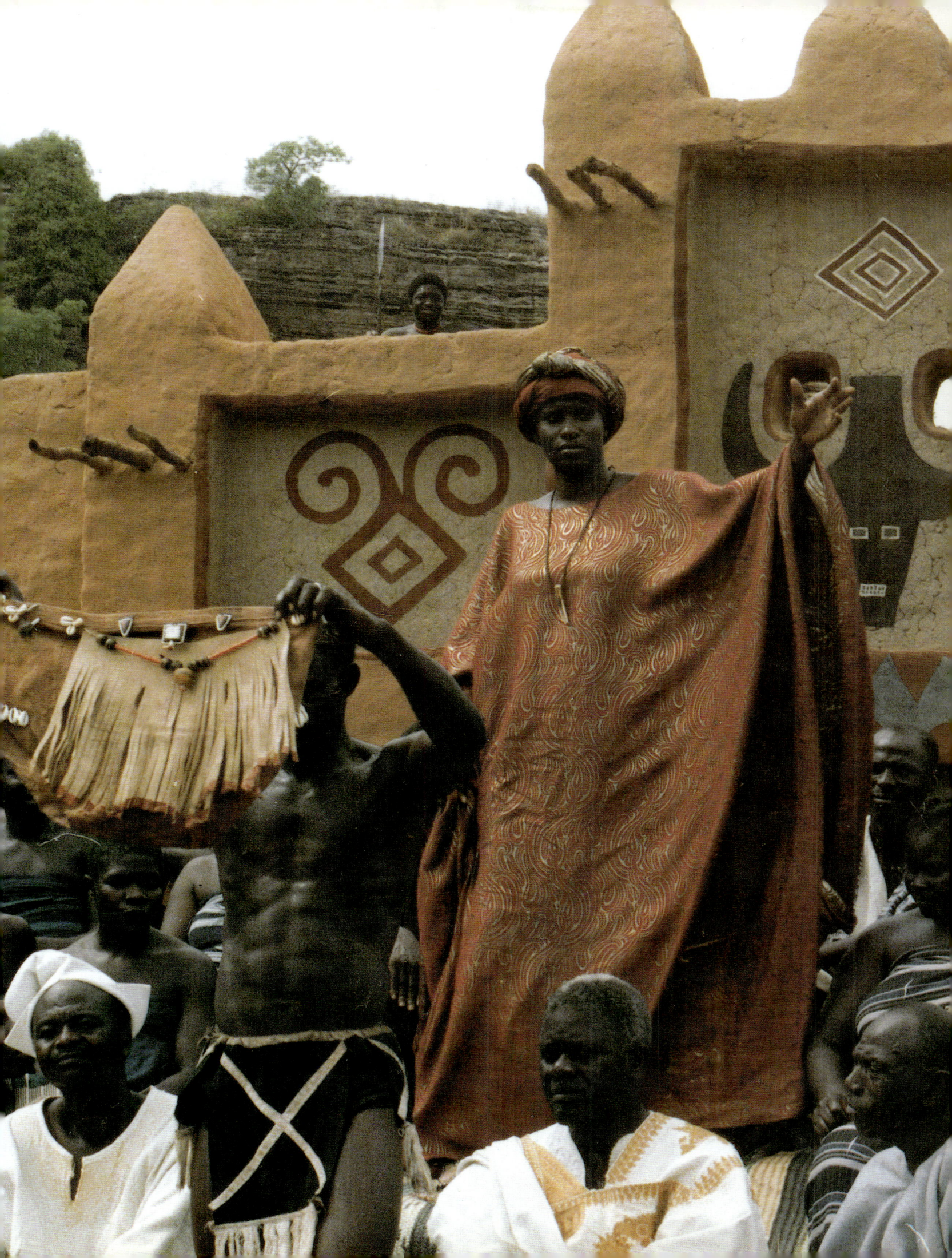

And that is how, half a century later, there was a griot by the name of Abdoulaye Mamani who evoked the memory of the sorceress in a noble song, too little known today. May Mamani be thanked here, for, as he himself says, "What would remain of the feats and the high deeds, if there were no griot with a memory deep enough to sing of them and keep them alive throughout time? Yes, what will remain of men's actions when their authors have vanished and their bodies are reduced to dust?"

So ends the story of Sarraounia.

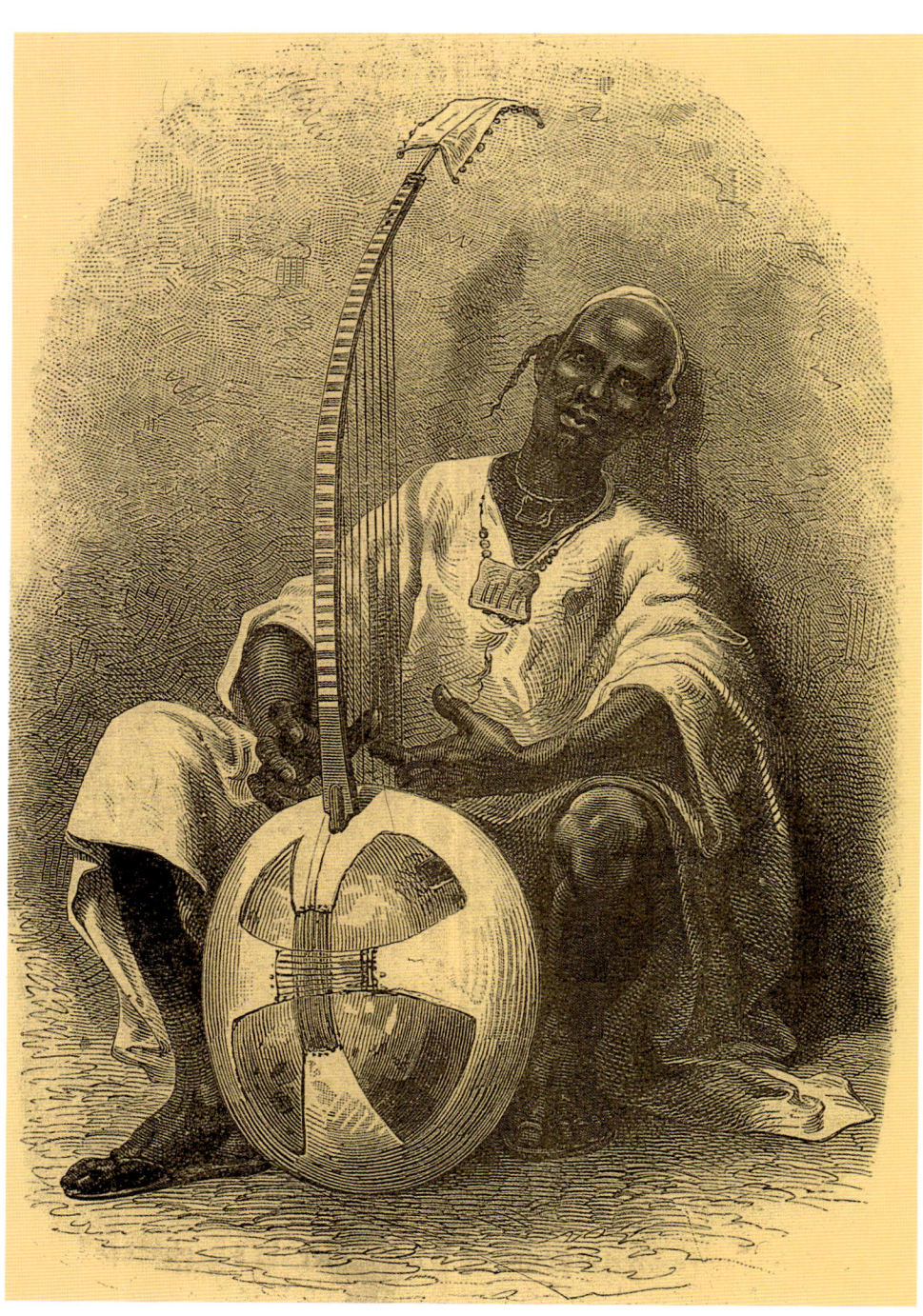

THE GRIOT

WORDS
OF AN ORDINARY WOMAN

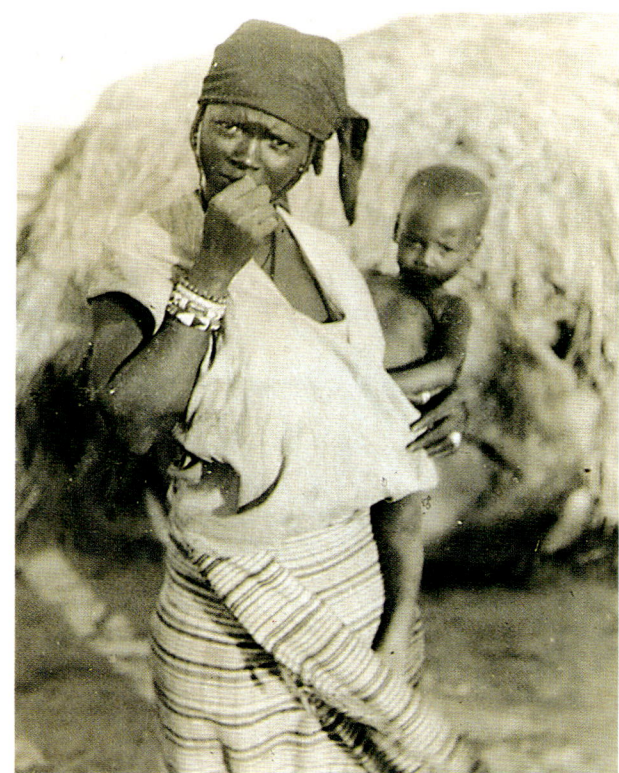

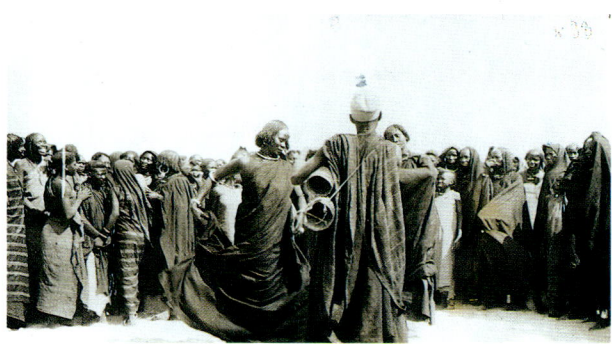

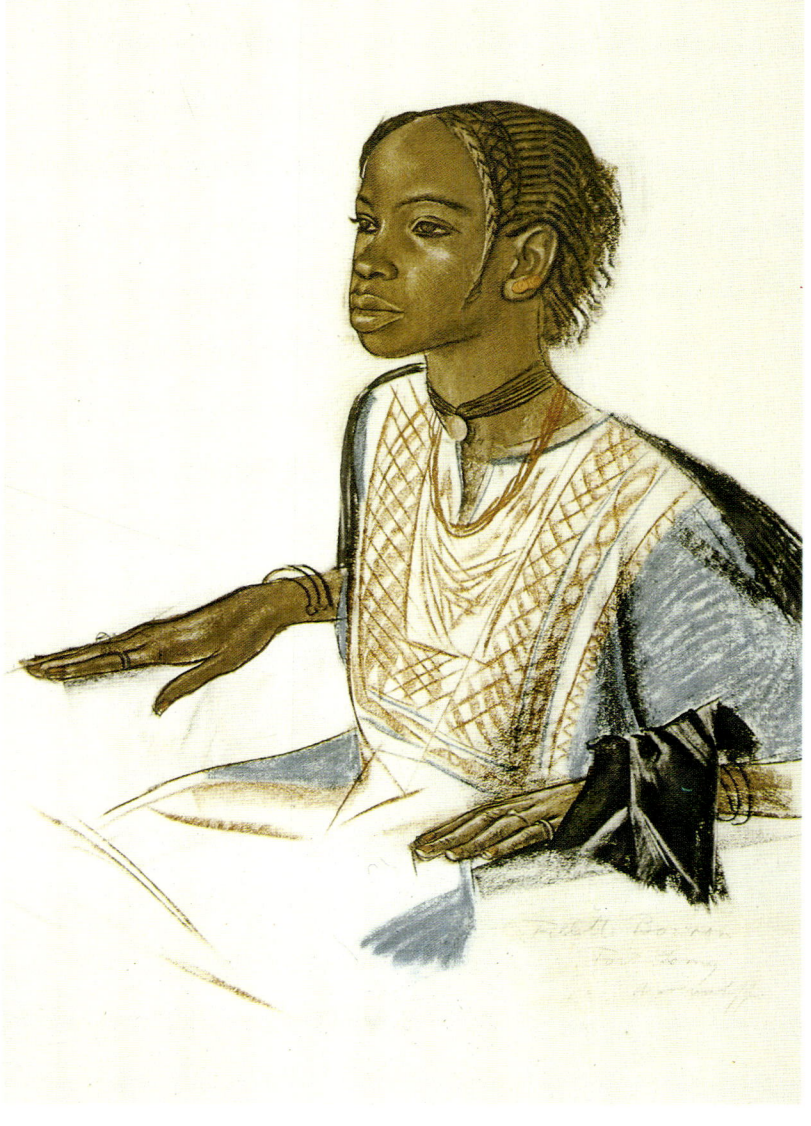

A man who is not feared and respected by others is not a happy man. A man without the esteem of others cannot know happiness.

Their esteem makes you great and important. It gives you happiness and glory. It gives you weight.

Others' fear is a joy for any man.

You can be old, rich, surrounded by your children and your flocks, but if no one respects you, if no one is afraid of picking a fight with you, then where is your happiness?

If they forget you when there is a council or goods are being divided, then where is your happiness?

If my husband leaves me, if my husband's clan takes no interest in me, then where is happiness?

If you are feared, if you are respected, you become great, important. You have prestige.

Mutual fear is the community of life. If, among people who live together, there is no fear, they will not last together. That is what the proverb says: "Living together means foundering together."

Old people do not mix with young people, and young people do not go where the old people are. They respect each other. They fear each other.

An old man will not eat with a young one, unless he is his grandson. He will not agree to eat in the presence of young people. We say he is afraid of their eyes, of their faces.

The same thing goes for children. They never go rubbing up against the old men. If a young person or a child doesn't fear adults and is always among them, we say he "bites goats in the eye"! Yes, he has no fear, no respect. We don't like that kind of child.

Someone who does not fear others covers himself with shame in front of everyone. Lack of fear leads to shame.

He who is not feared is not really loved. Not to fear someone means to forget him.

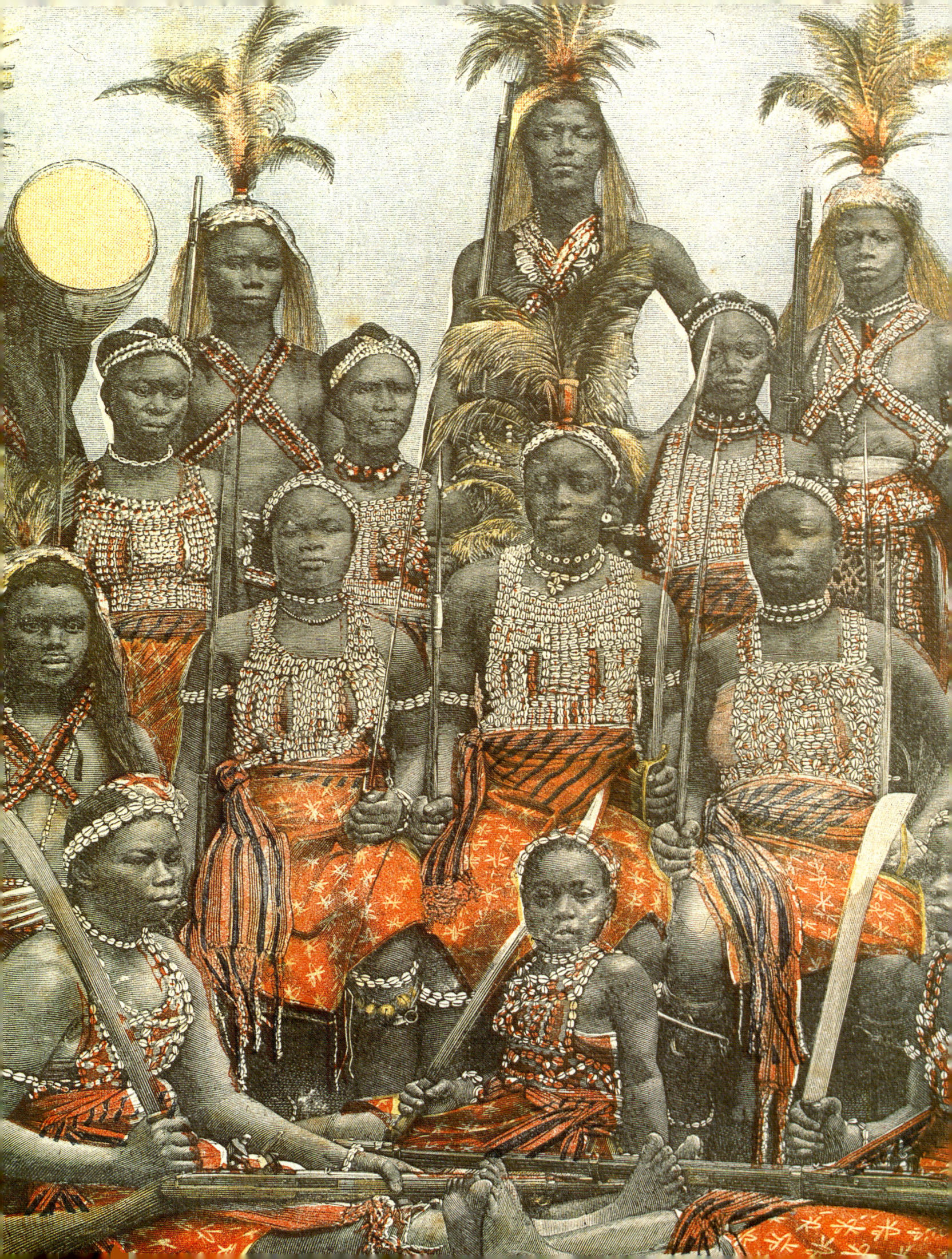

THE STORY OF NAGA

THE SIMPLE BLUE AMAZON

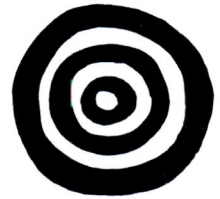

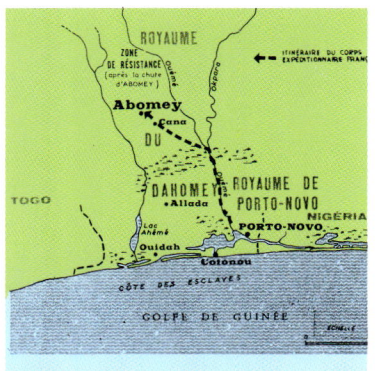

Her name means "tall one," and it was her exceptional height that caught the attention of the recruiters who had come sniffing around the swamp region, where the people rivalled the water birds in grace...

IN 1885, THE GREAT POWERS MEET IN BERLIN AND DIVIDE UP THE BLACK CONTINENT. IMMEDIATELY AFTERWARD, THE RUSH FOR THE INTERIOR BEGINS, AND WITH IT COMES THE ERA OF GUNBOAT DIPLOMACY, OF AMBITIONS BURSTING LIKE CANNONballs in the skies of Africa.

For two centuries, the French have been ensconced in their fort in Ouidah on the Slave Coast, where they ship "living ebony" off to the Americas. More recently, they have achieved sovereignty over the city of Cotonou, which they use as a base for their push toward the interior: they want to gobble up all of Dahomey.

The war will last four years. Dahomey's King Béhanzin deploys all his forces only to be forced to give in at the last moment, reduced to the shadow of a king.

Conscious of what is at stake, the amazons are the most relentless of all.

Wave after wave, archers and hunters, reapers, riflewomen and king's guards, brandishing cutlasses and carbines, they rise up to charge the French troops; wave after wave, over waves of corpses.

But the cutlasses cannot overpower the bayonets; the wheezy seventeenth-century cannons cannot overpower modern artillery, whose land and sea batteries cripple every attack one after the other.

And the blunderbusses, the ancient firearms called espingnoles, and other weapons gained in trade, cannot overcome the bolt action Lebels of 1888, the stuff of crazed nightmares with their rapid firepower, whose explosive bullets slaughter rows of troops and burrow holes clean through the thickest trees. These guns are so powerful you could sometimes find, behind the leafy giants of the forest, piles of astonished corpses gaping open-mouthed at such supernatural destruction.

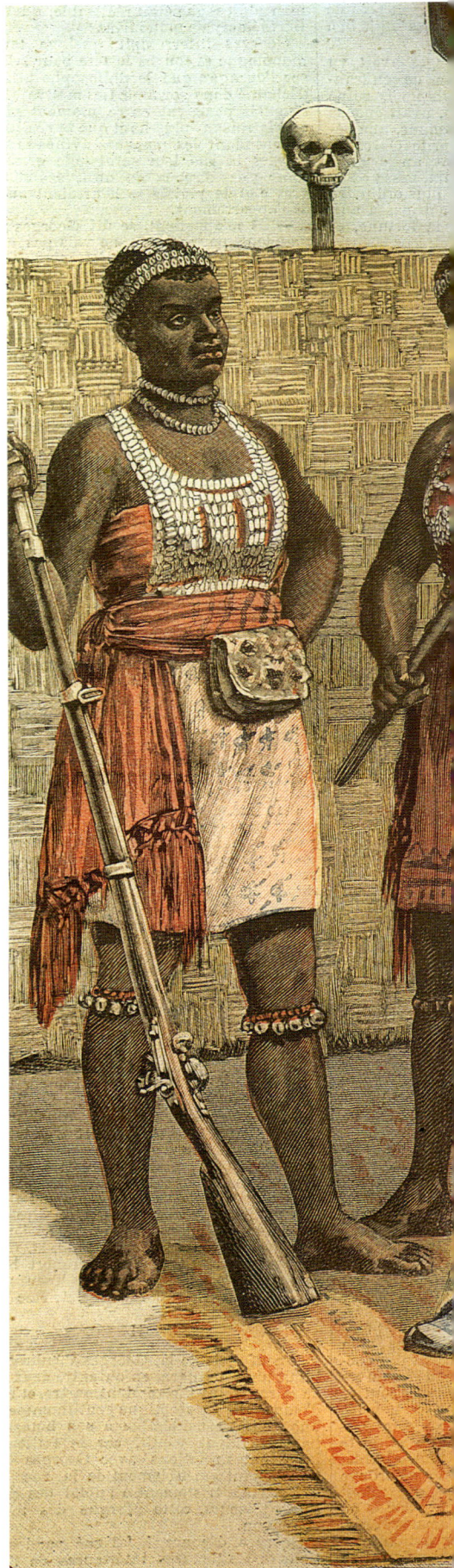

BÉHANZIN, KING OF THE DAHOMEY, SURROUNDED BY HIS AMAZONS ▷

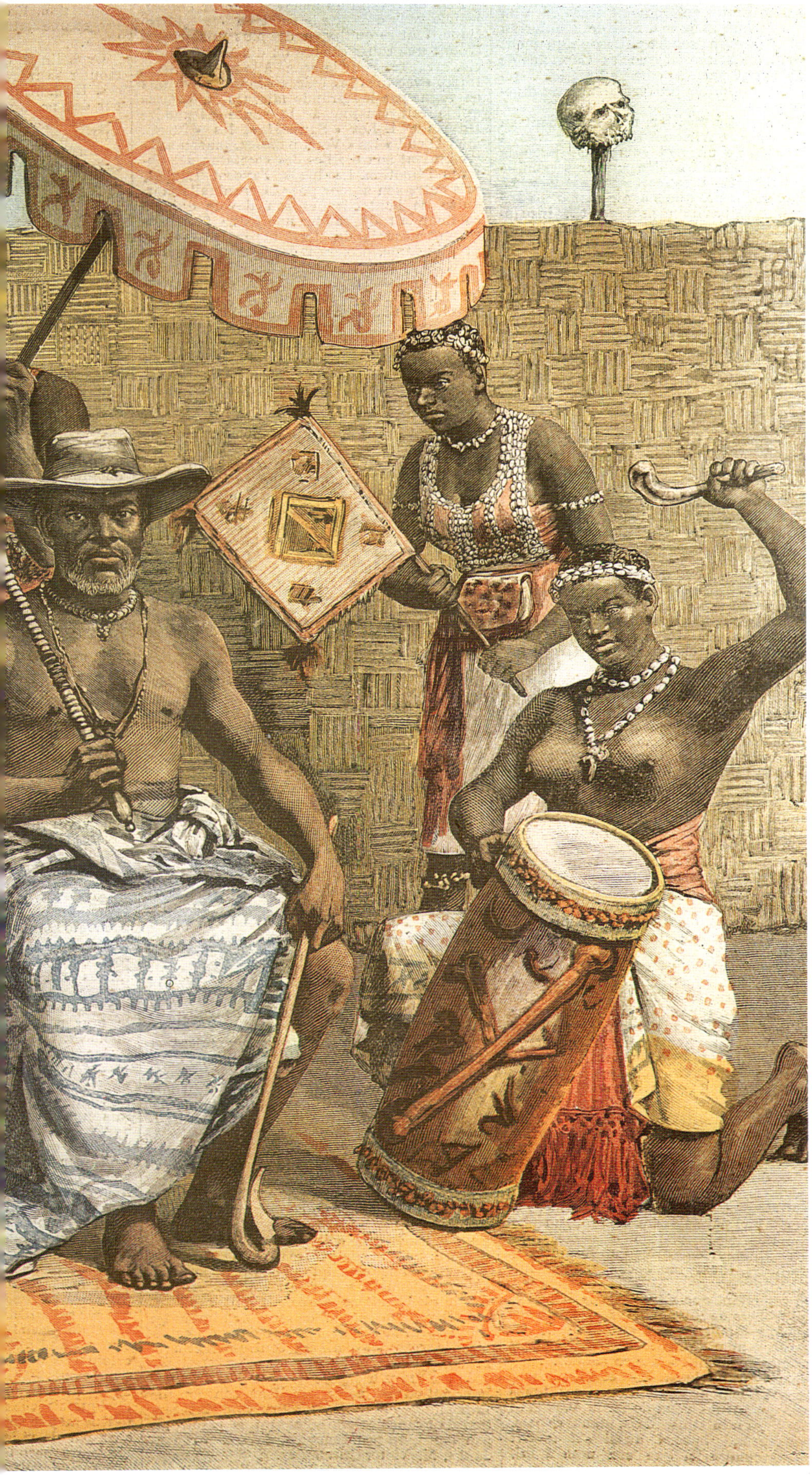

THE STORY OF NAGA

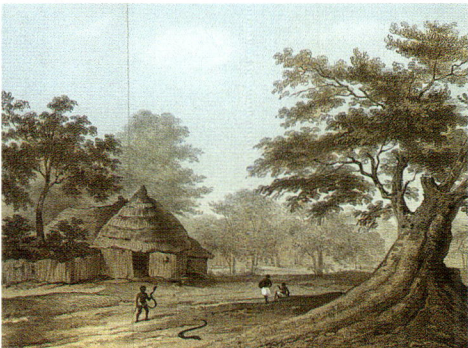
OUIDAH

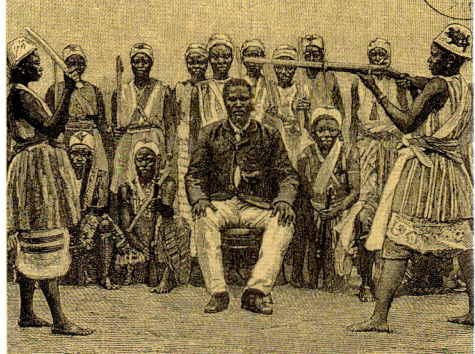
AMAZON TRAINING

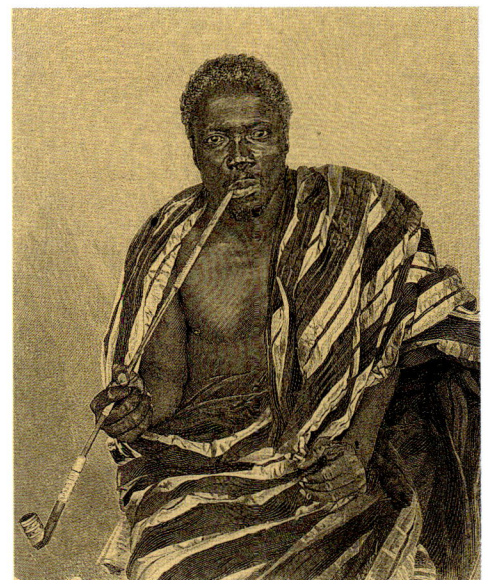
BÉHANZIN

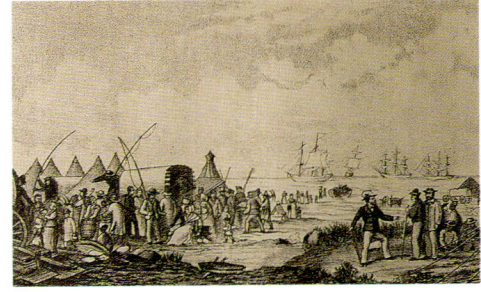
Proverb

"Only one thing is stronger than the elephant: the wilderness."

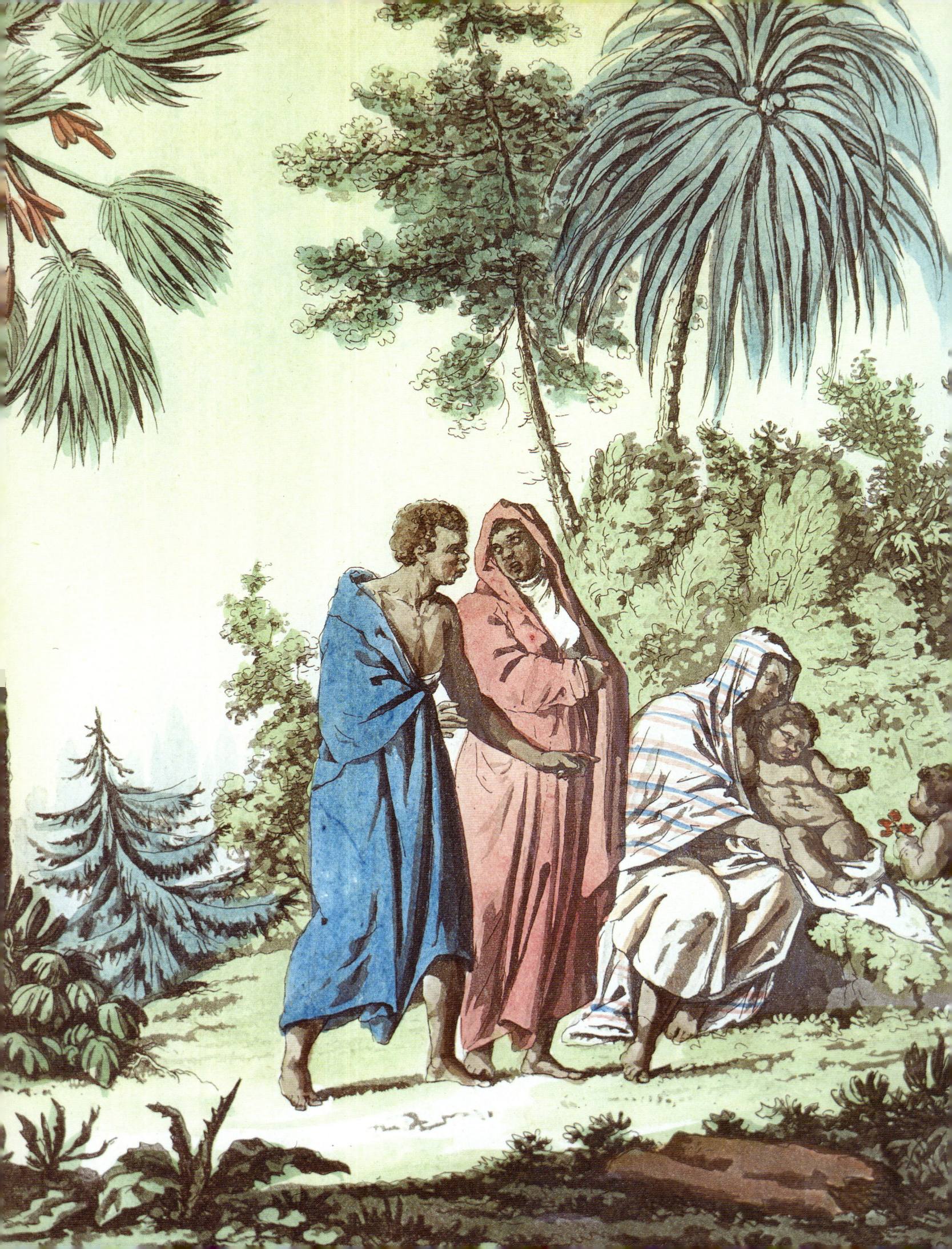

THE STORY OF NAGA

Naga was born in the village of Abassi, not far from the western marshes where she spent quiet days at her mother's side. Zimbadji was the third wife of a peasant about whom we know nothing except that he had the longest legs in the province.

Naga's name means "tall one," and it is her exceptional height that catches the attention of the recruiters who have come sniffing around the swamp region, where the people rival the water birds in leanness and grace. In this same long-legged village, they also recruit a young girl by the name of Nausika, Naga's neighbor and playmate.

As they leave, first the village vanishes, then the high marsh grass, then the long-necked, clumsy birds, who disappear in the sky.

Despite her agility and her giraffe-like height, Naga will remain a simple blue-uniformed amazon all her life. She will bend without complaint under the amazon discipline, but without joy. She does not have the spark that makes top-ranking amazons.

But fate gives her a rank: she will learn her trade as a killer, just as she might have learned to be a housewife with the same studiousness of a woman who knows her place. They will put a long jointed razor in her hands and she will reap; then, seeing how tall and strong she is, they will give her a heavy blunderbuss with a muzzle like gaping jaws, as deafening as a cannon. Before each war, she will receive from the king the cloth that, if necessary, would become her shroud. And she will confront the enemy toe to toe, always head on, like all the other amazons, for she knows that all whose backs are wounded will be severely punished.

But she will never forget the village of Abassi, and her heart will always quicken at the sight of a woman carrying a baby; nor will she ever lose hope of returning to the soil, to have another chance at living out a life as an ordinary woman, between a field and a river, in a house with a peaked roof like all the other houses of Abassi.

Sometimes, when she visits the palace, she meets her childhood friend Nausika.

Nausika had given up the short tunic of the blue amazons some time ago. She wears the white cap, scarlet pants, and flowered vest of the king's guards, who live inside the palace.

◁ PEACEFUL DAYS IN THE VILLAGE

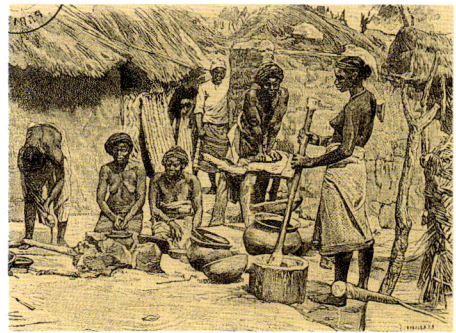

Woman's Work

When she is young, a Dahomey woman contributes to her parents' well-being by doing her share of work until the day she is married. As a wife, she enters the domain of her lord and master. The hardest household tasks fall to the woman. Her baby tied behind her back, she grinds the corn, makes cassava flour, cracks the almonds, and goes to fetch water, often very far away. Her only distraction is in the evening, when the moon lights up the beautiful African skies, and she gathers with the other women. Then they dance, sing songs, or tell each other stories.

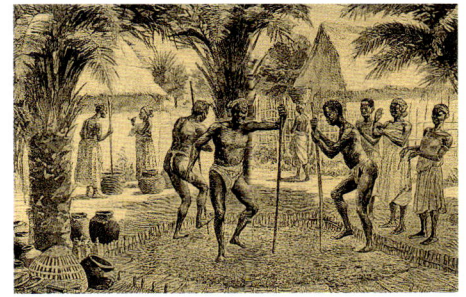

Manufacturing Palm Oil

The fruit of the palm oil tree is picked as soon as the clusters of nuts are red; first they are thrown on the ground into a heap that the fowl come to peck at and left there to ferment for a few days; then they are shelled. The fruit is piled into red earthen pots that are filled with water and left over a fire to boil for six or seven hours. The nuts are then dried. As soon as the water has evaporated, they are ground in mortars carved from tree trunks or in old dugouts; the women use their feet as pestles. This work lasts three or four days. They stomp and stomp, singing work songs in time to their rhythm: repeated again and again is the word Dahomey, Dahomey. As they get tired, the women rest and accompany the melodies on primitive instruments: broken bottles or cracked bells. When it is judged that the nuts have been sufficiently crushed, water is poured into the containers and everything is stirred up by hand: a sort of orange foam with an aroma of iris and violet begins to rise to the top.

Her white cap is decorated with a red moon, the royal emblem of Dahomey. She advances with a slow and ceremonious gait, as princesses do, paying careful attention not to make the slightest false step. One can see that her mind is constantly repeating to her body, as the chief attendant has commanded: "Let us walk straight, let us walk slowly, majestically, let us not deign to look at our feet." Not a gleam shows beneath her eyelids, not a particle of red powder strays from her cheeks. But as soon as she returns to the countryside, she will turn into a lioness with her hair standing on end in rage.

Nausika wants the king to notice her; she wants to shine with the special brilliance that attracts a royal crown to your head. She is very beautiful, with the longest neck in the kingdom, and her courage in battle knows no limits: but King Béhanzin never says the words she is waiting for. So when she meets her old friend Naga, companion from a distant childhood, she sometimes confides to her in a strange, fierce voice: "Tomorrow, I will be dead or queen."

The war against the French will soon give her the opportunity to shine one last time.

As for Naga, she has no such lofty ambitions. And her thoughts fly no higher than usual that year, 1890, by the end of which the future of all Dahomey children is laid out: the sparkling children of princes, the delicate city children, and the thick-skinned country children, playing in the sand of some obscure, forgotten village like Abassi.

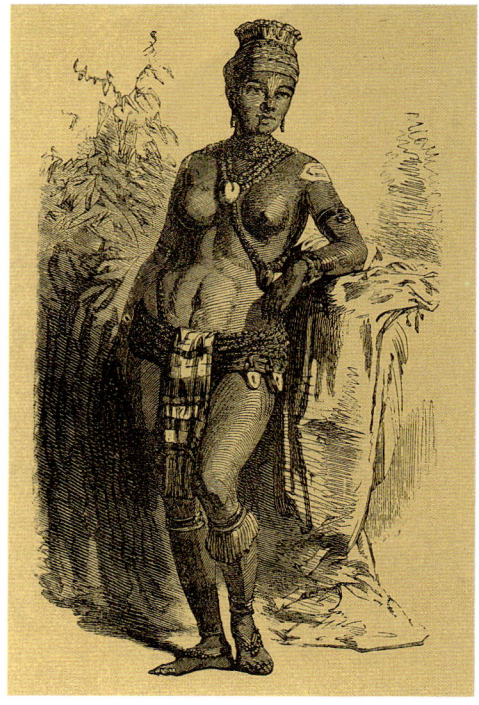

DAHOMEY WOMAN

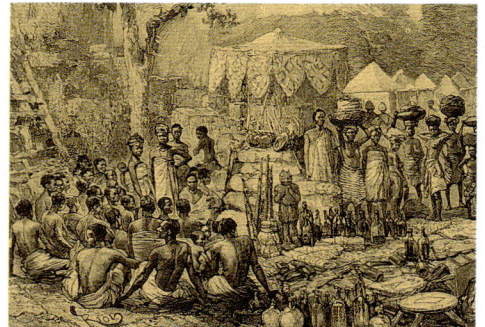

ON THE ABOMEY SQUARE

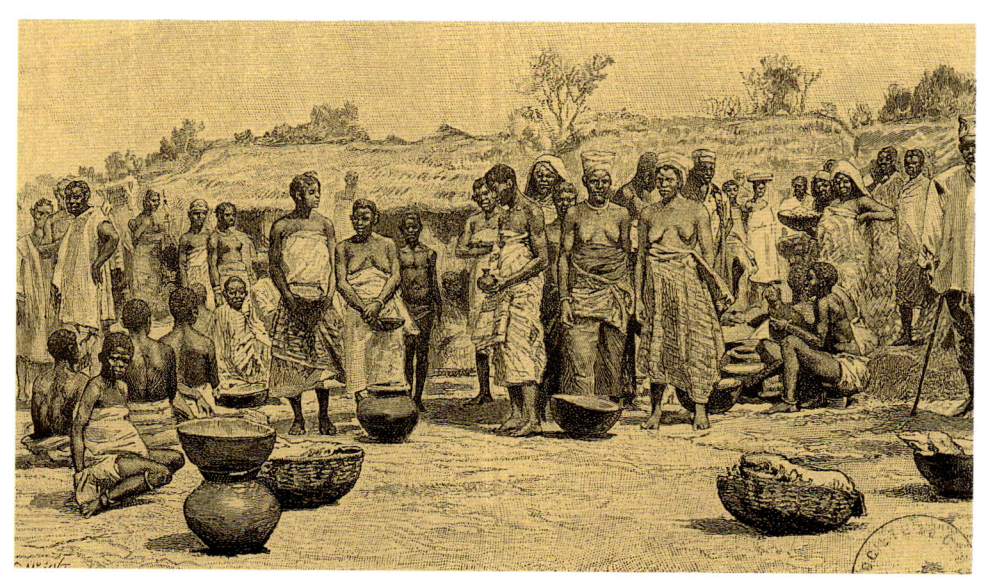

MARKET SCENE

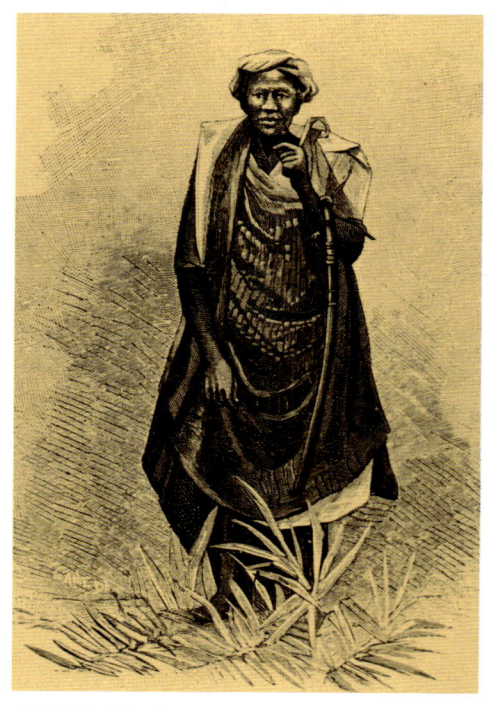

MITHA, RENOWNED AMAZON OF MOLEKI

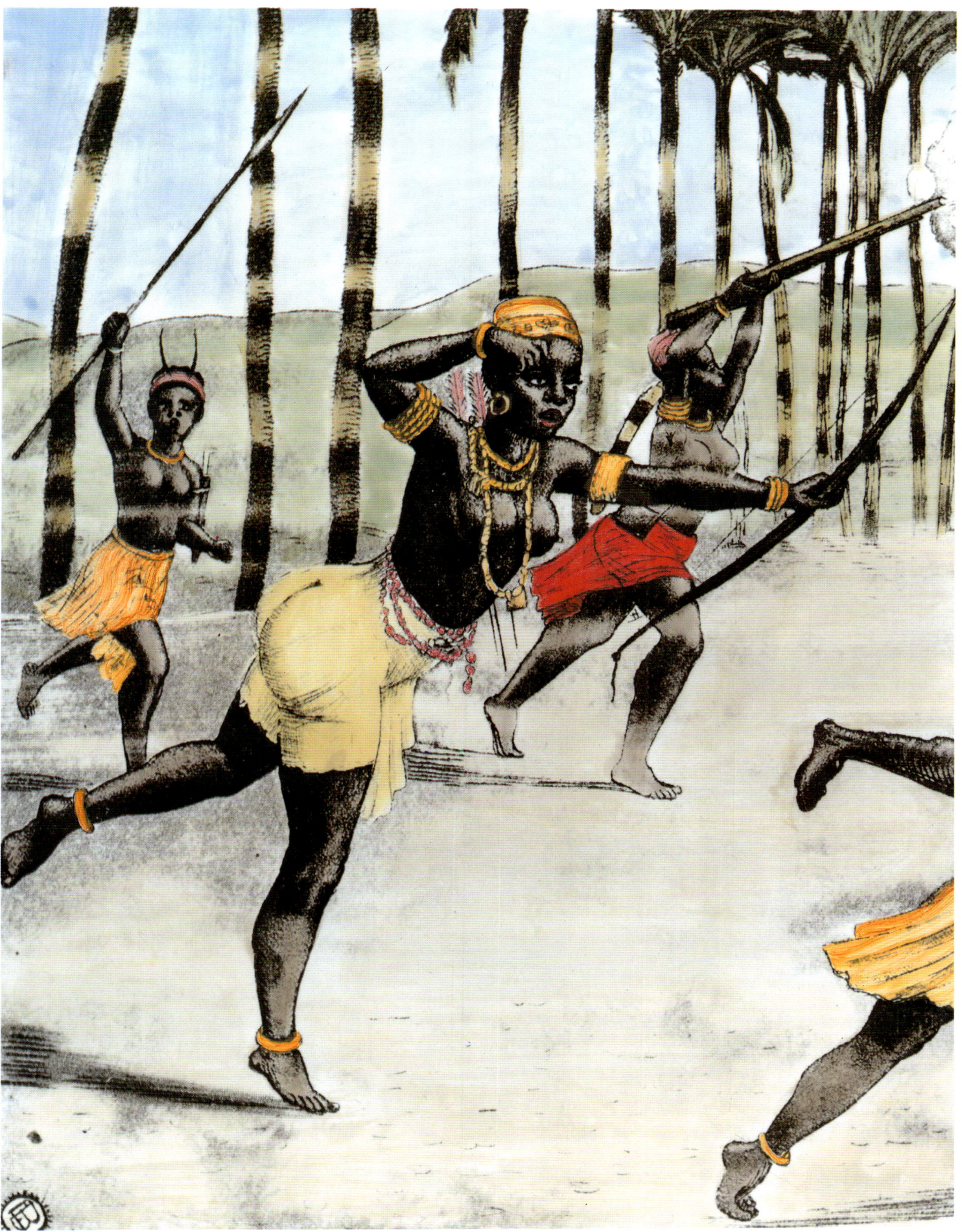

AMAZONS

Women's Courage

According to certain sources, women played an important role in the Dahomey ruler's decision to resist France and answer war with war. The men are said to have been more defeatist. The amazons seem to have defended the hawkish perspective more fiercely than anyone else. With the support of a few responsible female decision makers, a group of novice amazons, greedy for shining moments of glory, had adroitly pressured the other amazons to hold a meeting at night in order to convince the king to fight the colonizers to the end.

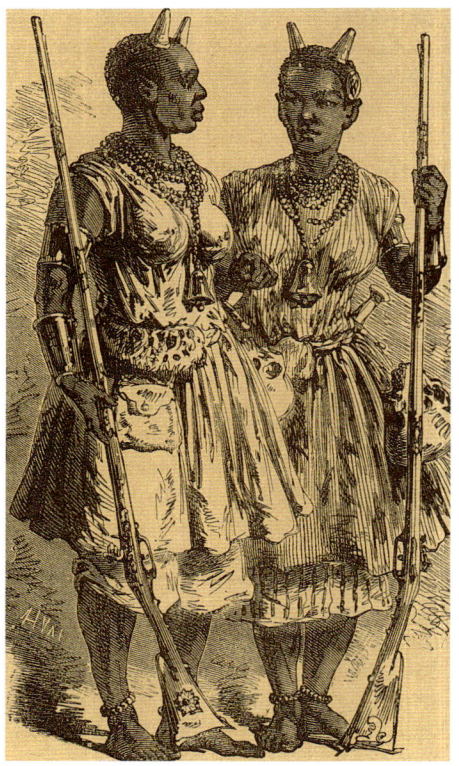

A Letter from Béhanzin

"Now, I have this to say to you: if you remain peaceful, I will do the same, and we will continue in peace. But if you do something rash, I will ruin everything, our trade as well, and I will conduct trade with other nations. I have so many men, they are like worms coming out of holes in the ground. I am the king of the black people and it is none of the whites' business what I do. The villages you speak of are indeed mine. I would like to know how many independent French villages I, the king of the Dahomey, have broken? Let us remain peaceful; carry on your business in Porto-Novo, and we will remain in peace as before. If you want war, I am ready. Yet I will not be the one to see it end, for it would last a hundred years and kill twenty thousand of my men."

Proverb

"War is a cow you milk in the thorns."

The war does not surprise her. At the sound of the first drumbeats, Naga runs to her little amazon hut behind the palace ramparts, and carefully bathes in a wash of violet grasses, the same ones they used in the village of Abassi. She braids her hair. She rubs oil on all of her joints. She checks her whetstone, her flint and tinder, with the same meticulous care in which her mother had swathed the gestures of everyday life. She roasts her corn. She cooks a few spicy bean patties, flat, oval cakes like they made in the village. She puts everything in her bag, padded with grass, and adds a dozen smoked fish. Finally, with her water gourd hanging from her belt, her heavy blunderbuss hoisted like a hoe over her shoulder, she joins the regiment with her long careful stride not exactly like the stride of an amazon; a stride you would be more likely to see in the country, in a housewife methodically hurrying along, a woman whose road is laid out before her, one day after the next.

The attack on Cotonou takes place on February 23, 1890; the night before, the native quarter has been burned down, the inhabitants scattering into the surrounding countryside.

At the head of the army come the amazons, their general in the very front, her horns brandished above her graying skull. The priests and royal guards follow, shaking their horse tails; then come the regular troops, and finally, the volunteers hastily recruited from all the villages in the kingdom.

The bells ring and throats are already spouting battle cries. Nausika marches at the general's side, hackles raised in fury and holding a heavy, two-handed axe for breaking down doors. The assault on the fort of Cotonou is lightning quick. The cannon doesn't even have time to fire before the amazon Nausika has crossed the barricade and decapitated the post leader; behind her, other amazons seize the cannon loaders by the legs, throw them to the ground, and finish them off.

A few minutes later, the bulk of the French troops appear. Rounds of fire tear into the assailants, hurling bullets that explode through the victims' backs, opening up holes the size of fists. Then the warships anchored in the harbor fire off long volleys of shells that slice rows of death among the amazons and soldiers.

Seeing this, the archer Kata Goa, followed by a dozen of her companions, throws herself into the sea to try to sink the ships: but none of them can reach the great boats, and now they are all at the bottom of the ocean.

THE TAKING OF KANA ▷

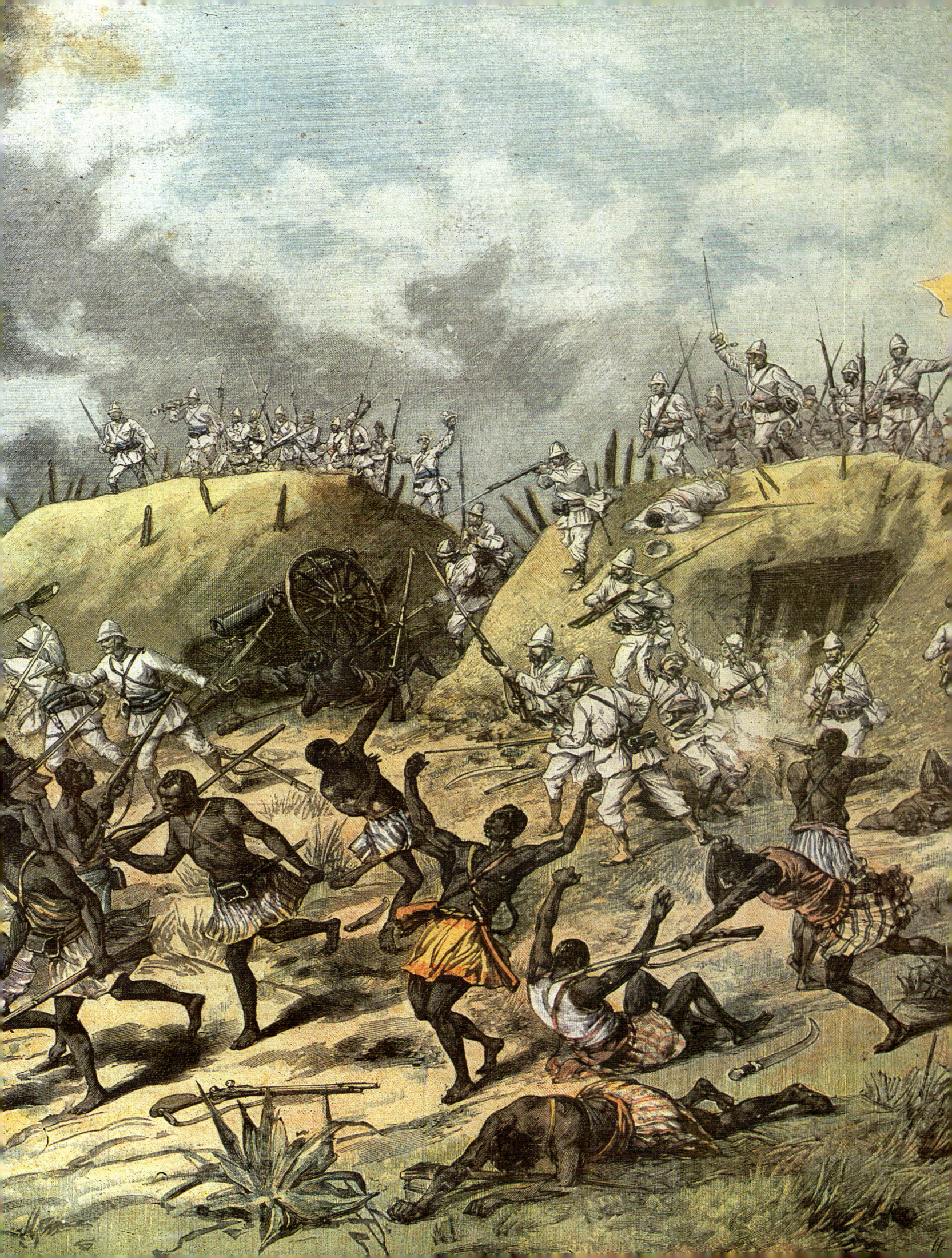

Naga is infuriated by these great holes being blown through the women's backs, while the invaders remain safely sheltered from the gunfire.

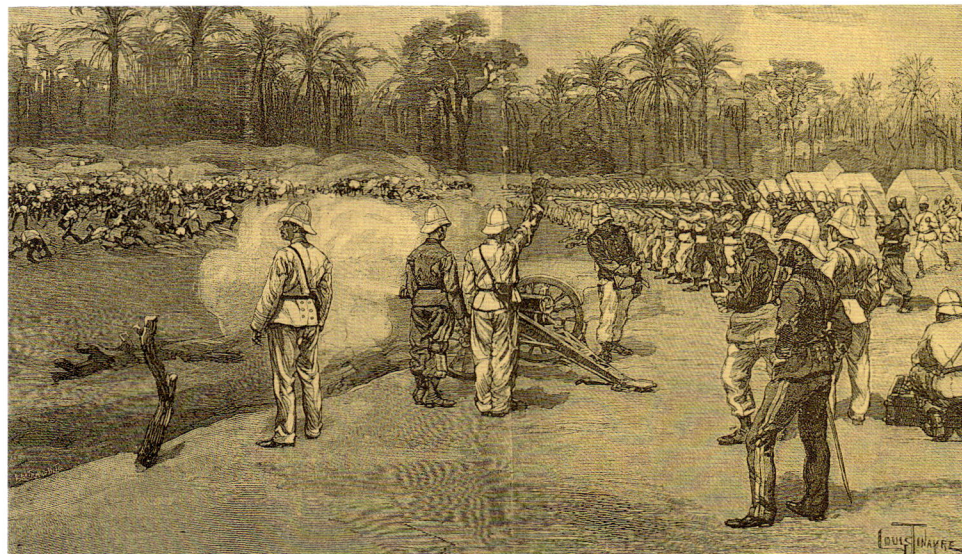

THE BATTLE OF DOGBA

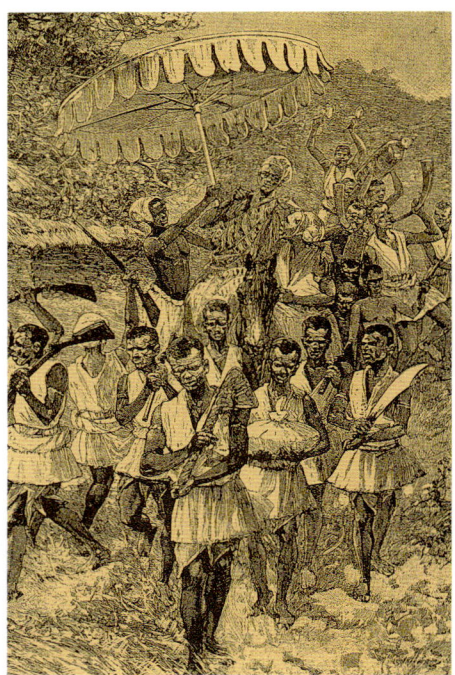

AMAZONS

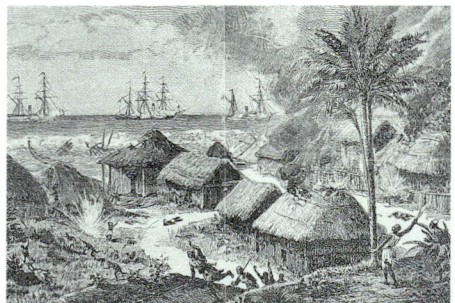

BOMBARDING THE COAST

These people, she thinks to herself, these people have no business on Dahomey land, with their eyes that don't recognize the plants, their feet that don't know the trails, their skin that flinches at a mosquito bite. For a split second, she sees them as intruders who go into a hut and make themselves at home; and this domestic metaphor sticks with her. She feels like the mistress of the house who pushes out the undesirables and slams the door in their faces. Suddenly, moved by this thought, Naga leaps forward over a fresh wave of corpses, among whom she has caught sight of her friend Nausika stretched on her back, her face intact, a sort of smile floating on her curled lips.

A bullet tears her blunderbuss from her hands; she falls on the ground, pulls herself forward in the grass; then, coming out of a fog, she sets off again toward the intruders who suddenly grow huge in front of her eyes, close enough to touch.

She throws her arms out in front of her. And suddenly realizing that she has no weapon, no gun or blade of any kind, not even her little jet cutlass, she opens her mouth and bares her teeth at the throat of the squadron leader, Sergeant Major Duparc; and she grips him tight, determined not to let go. She holds on even after death, despite the bayonets plunging into her from all sides, according to a report found in the colonial archives.

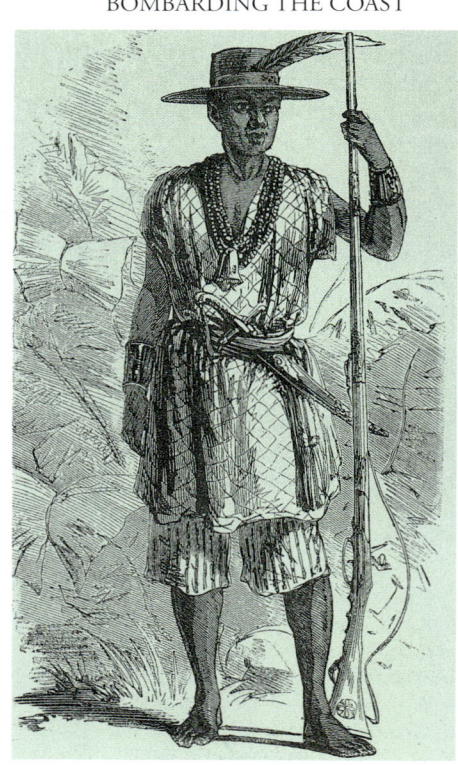

CHIEF ESCORT

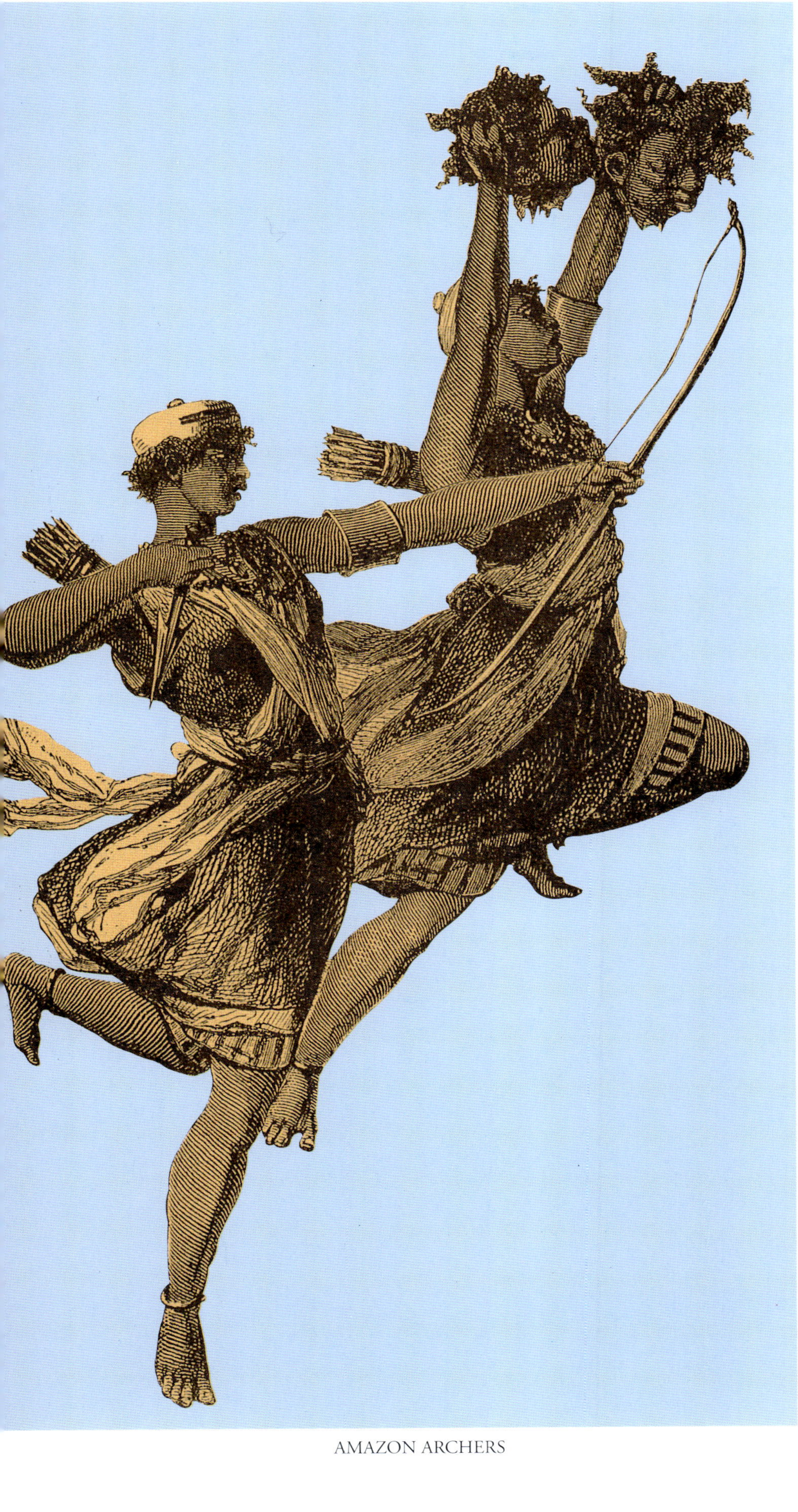

THE STORY OF NAGA

The Survivor

Who knows the name of this woman, whom one of our friends met in Cotonou when he was a child in the early thirties?

"I was maybe five or six years old," says our friend. "I often played in the street with a group of friends. Sometimes, a very old woman would stop to watch us. Doubled over with age, she walked with a stick and grumbled nonsense.

"One day, one of us threw a stone that hit another stone. It made a noise and sent a spark flying. Suddenly we saw the old lady stand up straight. Her face was transfigured. She started walking proudly, with a rhythmic step. Arriving at a wall, she got down on her belly and crawled along on her elbows to get around it. She thought she was holding a rifle, for suddenly, she lifted it and fired, reloaded her imaginary weapon and fired again, making the sound of gunfire. Then she leapt up, tackled an imaginary enemy, rolled on the ground in a furious wrestling match, and pinned her adversary. With one hand, she seemed to be holding him to the ground, while with the other she stabbed him over and over. She was shouting from exertion. She made a gesture of slicing flesh and stood up brandishing a fictitious trophy. Later I was told that she probably thought she was cutting off the genitals of the vanquished. She danced and sang a victory song:

> *The blood flows,*
> *You are all dead.*
> *The blood flows,*
> *We have won.*
> *The blood flows, it flows, it flows,*
> *The blood flows,*
> *There is no more enemy.*

But suddenly she stopped, in a daze. Her body drooped, hunched over. How old she looked, even older than before! She went away with hesitant steps.

"'She's an old warrior,' a grownup explained to us. 'In the time of our former kings, there were soldier-women. Their battles have been over for a long time, but she is still at war in her head.'"

Royal Courage

The case of Dimèdji, as reported by Amélie Degbélo, is exemplary. This warrior had broken her cutlass in combat, so she jumped against the end of a rifle, took a bullet to her left breast, and despite her wound, quickly brought down the rifleman whose weapon she had seized. Béhanzin had her treated by his best healers, gave her cowries, cloth, and a horse—an animal most precious to the Dahomey—then, in supreme compensation, he married her.

Proverb

"When someone bites you, he reminds you that you too have teeth."

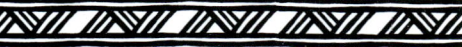

AMAZON ARCHERS

During the night, two archers slip behind the French lines to bring Naga back among her own, where she is buried according to the old tradition of the amazons, who never leave their dead to the enemy. And it is during her funeral that Naga's famous song is born; it can still be heard floating around today over the plains of Cotonou, between the new city far away and the depths of the bush:

Dahomey, Dahomey,
We were created to defend you
We will drive the wart hogs from their holes.

Dahomey, Dahomey,
There are shouts, tears, people who have fallen
And it's over, it's over.

So ends the story of Naga, the young woman from the village of Abassi.

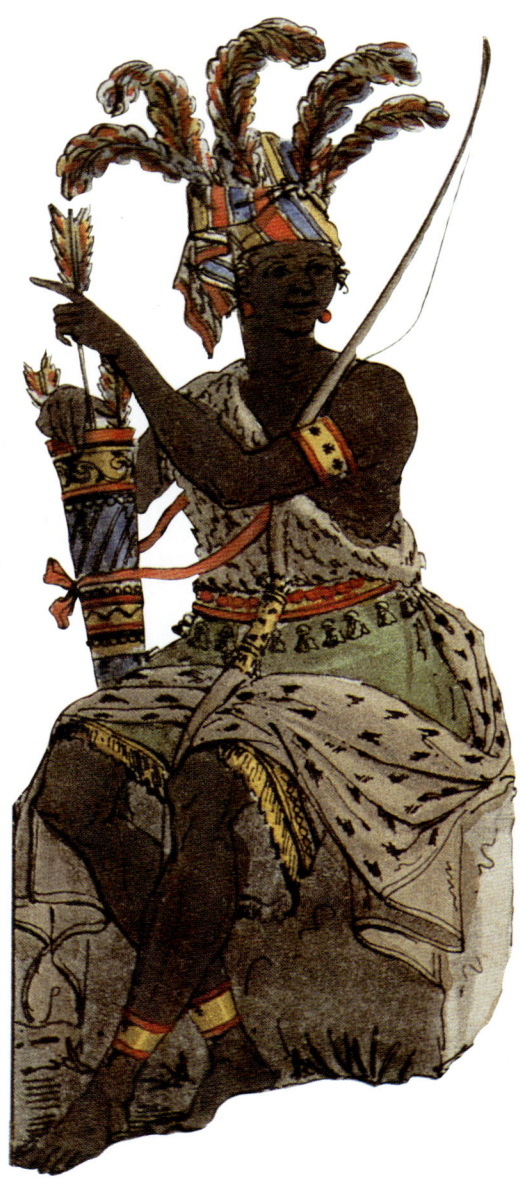

WORDS OF AN ORDINARY WOMAN

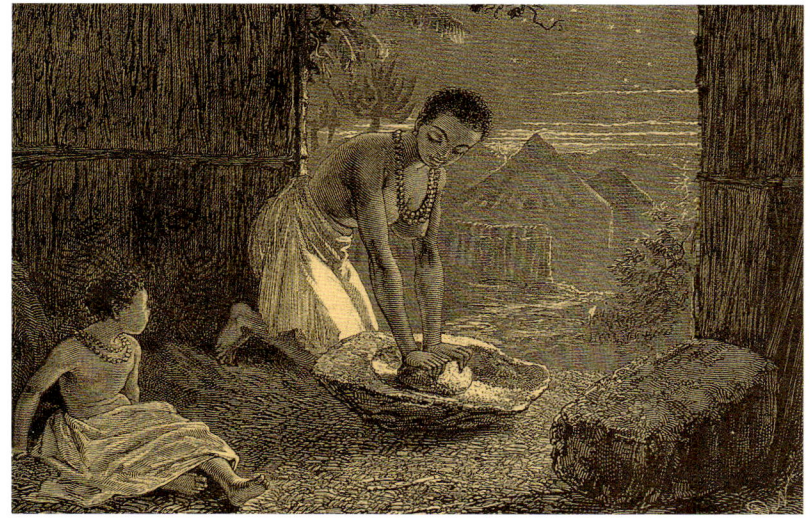

WOMAN GRINDING GRAIN

DAHOMEY WOMEN

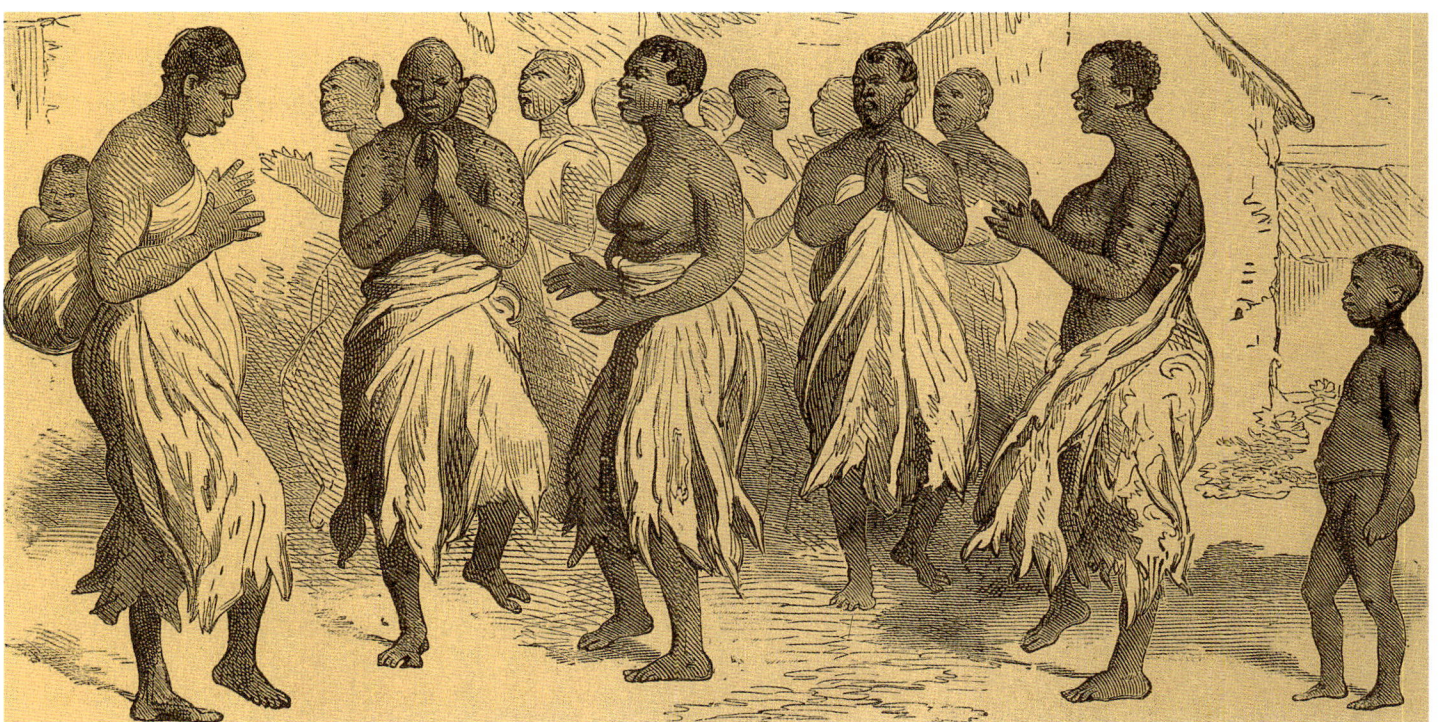

"A WOMAN'S STRENGTH IS THE CHILDREN SHE BRINGS INTO THE WORLD"

There are certain people who say that a woman who has had no children is worth nothing. They say even a dog is worth more. Who will defend a woman who has no children? Who will work for her? Who will grind her grain or fetch her wood and water?

A woman's only strength is the children she brings into the world.

Charm and beauty are fated to pass: they are like the dew, which disappears as the sun rises above the horizon.

Beauty and charm fade, children remain. Children alone are certainty and security for a woman. Anything else is only a lie.

People are very hard on a barren woman. As if it were her fault, as if she were the one who had refused to have children.

But who else could give what God has not given? Who could grant what God has refused?

A woman who has had no children is filled with shame, with sorrow. She will always be alone, until she dies.

The suffering of a barren woman is solitude. Everywhere, even in the middle of the clan, she will be alone: and her solitude will only increase.

All the happiness of marriage is in the children. A marriage without children is worthless. It is like a tree without fruit.

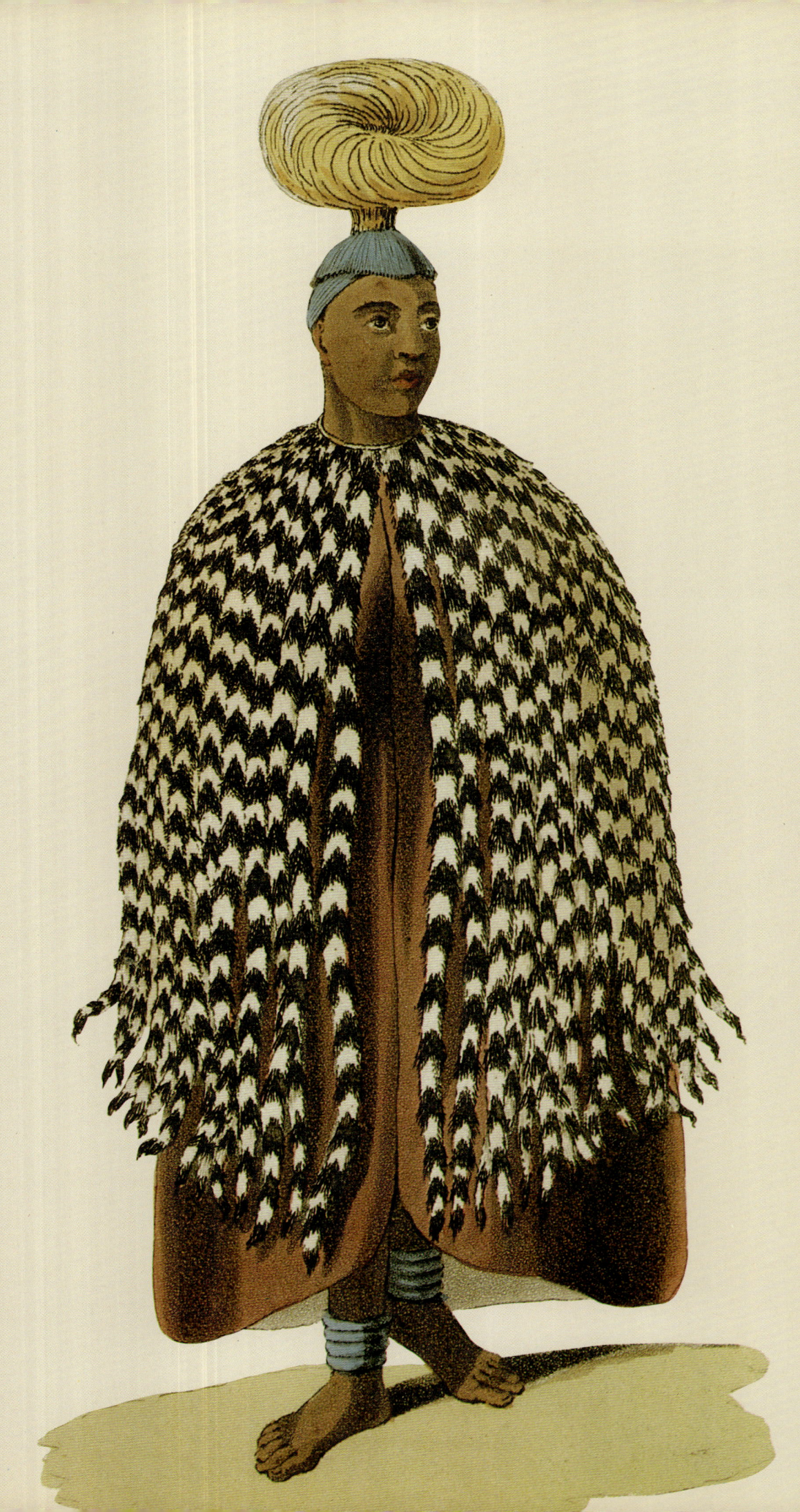

MANTA TISI

THE QUEEN
OF THE WILD CATS

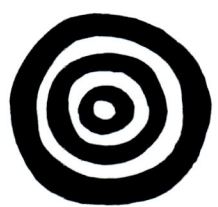

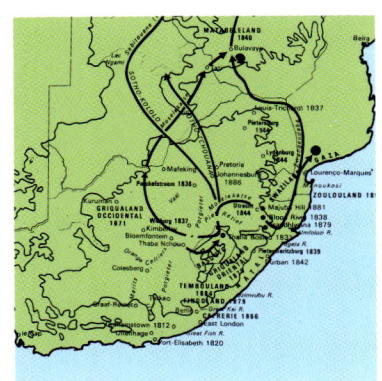

As the years passed, the whole tribe would rally around her, and the first to adore her were the very ones who had once plotted her death...

SHAKA ZULU WAS ONE OF THE GREATEST CONQUERORS OF ALL TIME. THE WARS HE INSTIGATED BLOODIED ALL OF SOUTHERN AFRICA DURING THE FIRST HALF OF THE NINETEENTH CENTURY. THE DEFEATED TRIBES FLED BEFORE HIM. AND IN THEIR FLIGHT, they encountered other tribes, who defended their territory against the refugees; and so, little by little, the war spread like an enormous brushfire.

One of these tribes, the Batlokwa, or Wild Cats, was led by a woman, Queen Manta Tisi.

When her husband, the king of the Batlokwa, died, Manta Tisi found herself alone with her son, Sekonyela, still a child. The parents of the late king wanted to kill her, and thus prevent her son from succeeding to the throne. But Manta Tisi triumphed over all her enemies and became regent of the kingdom. As the years passed, the whole tribe would rally around her, and the first to adore her were the very ones who had once plotted her death.

The Batlokwa, the Wild Cats, belonged to the great Sotho nation. When the Zulus undertook their terrible campaign, the clans of the Sotho nation retreated toward the central plateau, overrunning each other and fighting for survival, for there was not enough food for everyone. This bloody struggle was called Mfecane: twenty-eight Sotho clans disappeared in it without a trace.

Manta Tisi had attacked and destroyed the Bakofengs—the People of the Mist. Then she fled their land, propelled by the approaching troops of King M'panga Zita, who was himself fleeing Emperor Matiwane, who was himself marching day and night trying to keep ahead of Shaka's invasion. The brushfire had been started, and its flames would soon cover all of the central plateau.

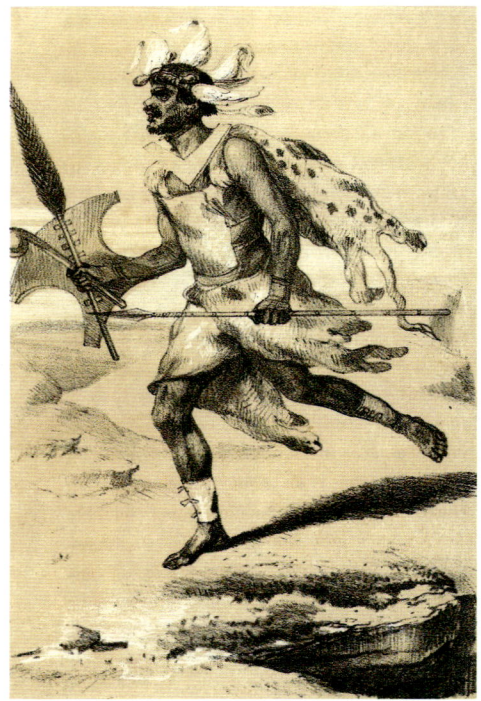
MARIMO

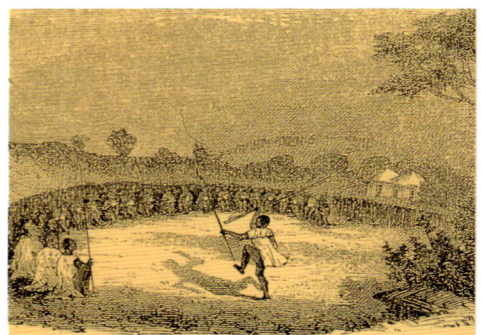
WARRIOR ASSEMBLY

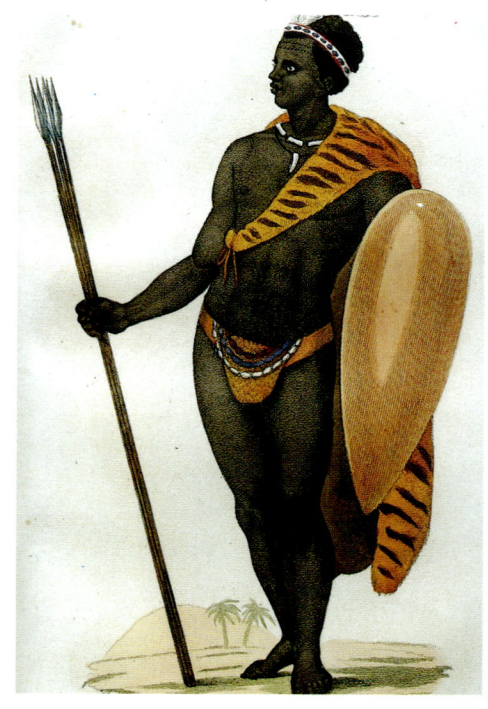
BANTU WARRIOR

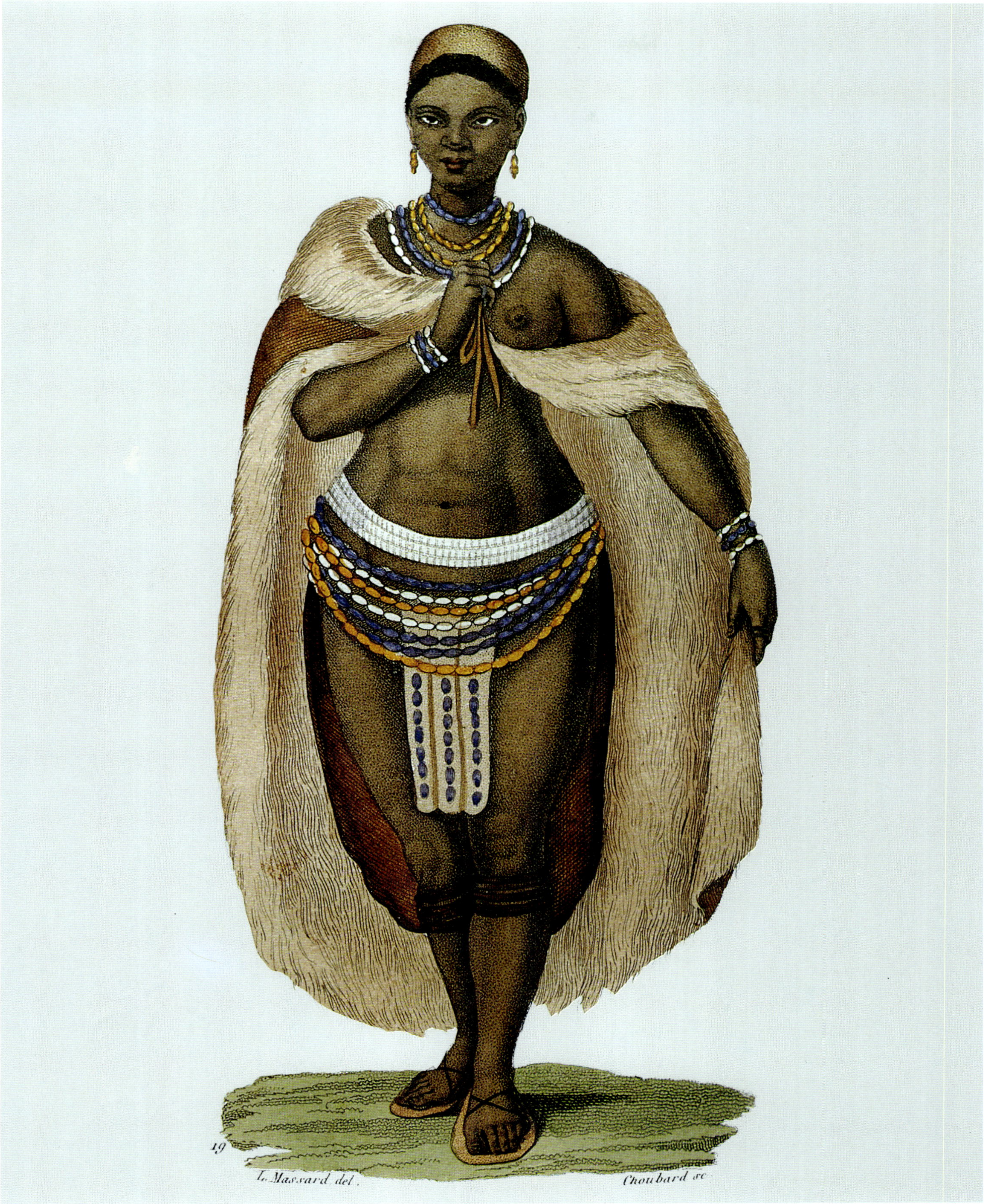

MANTA TISI

KHOISAN WOMAN

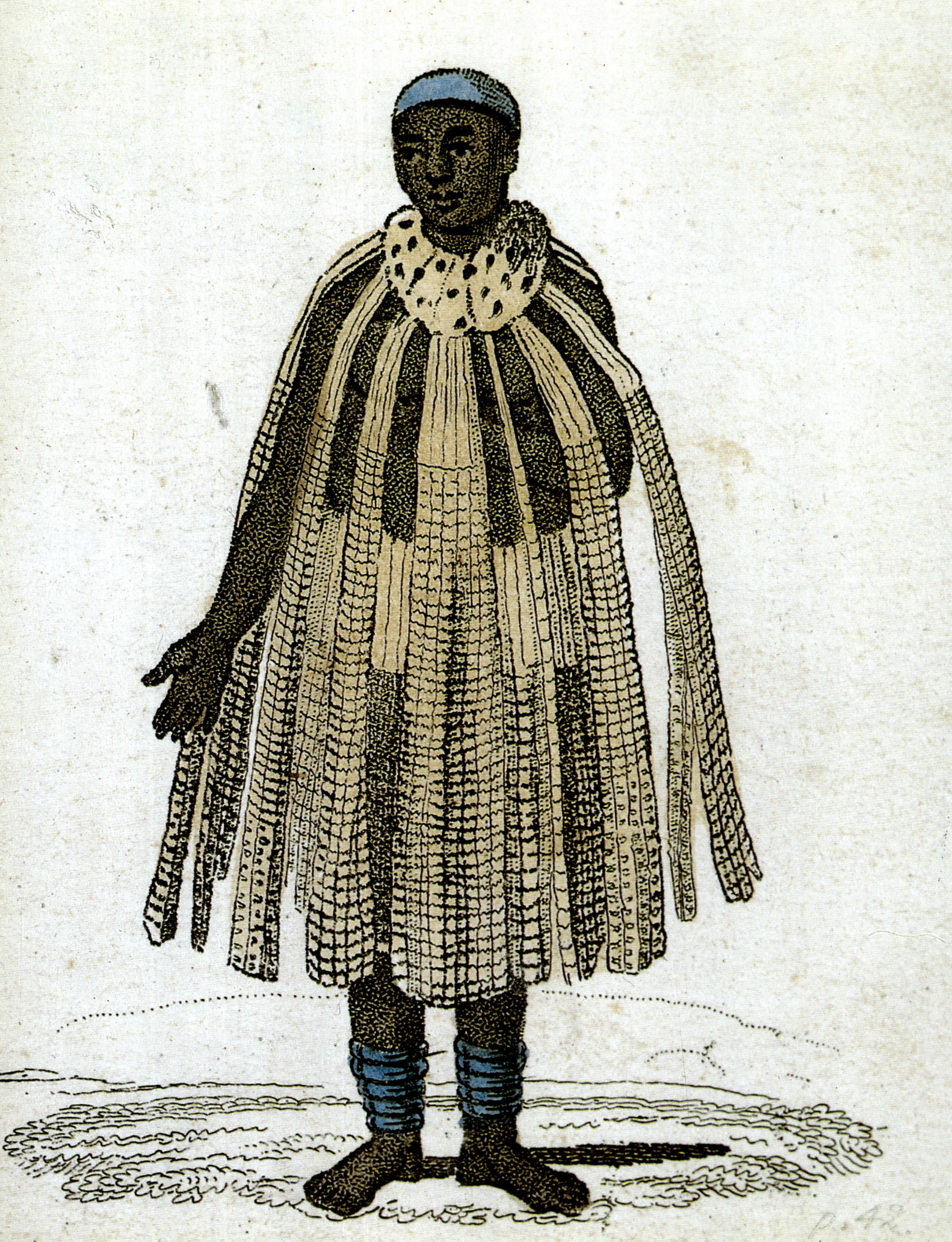

MANTA TISI

Accompanied by her son, who was by then eighteen years old, Manta Tisi led her people into the valley of the Caledon, a river with waters clearer than the sky.

She had changed greatly since the beginning of the upheaval. Still straight, tall, and slender, she had lost her "gentle and agreeable face," as certain English missionaries had once described it. Her eyes were cold, always wide open; she almost looked as though she had no eyelids. And her cheeks were as flat as two metal plates, with a deep crease of bitterness around her mouth. People said that she was impervious to human suffering.

To this she always replied: "War is the cauldron of the seven sorrows, and no one will come out unscathed."

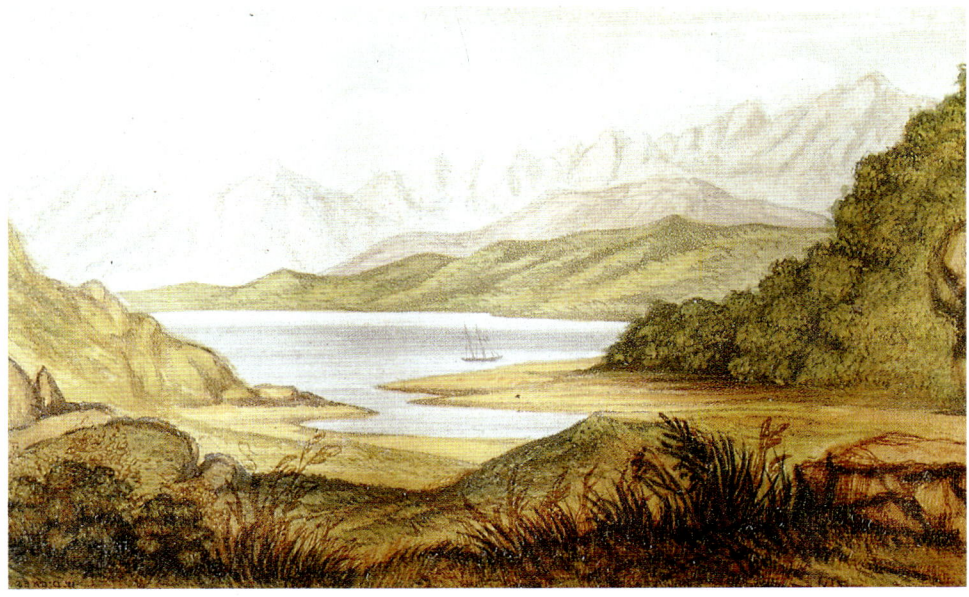

Her goal was quite simple: she wanted her son to survive the wars of the Mfecane, even if the whole world should disappear in the meantime.

Nothing would stop her.

She advanced along the Caledon River, killing, seizing the livestock in her path, and leaving nothing but desolation in her wake.

Her legend spread throughout the central plateau. According to the legend, a powerful woman named Manta Tisi was at the head of an army of spirits, innumerable as a cloud of locusts, and was overrunning the regions of the interior, sowing ruin in her path. She fed her army on her own milk, sent swarms of wasps as the advance guard, and could throw eight spears at a time, each aimed at a different enemy.

◁ LATTAKOO WOMAN

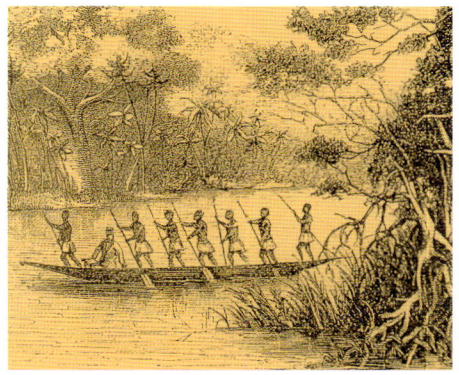

The Lizard and the Chameleon

Long ago, the Lord sent the gray lizard to deliver this message to the world: "Men die...and they will come back to life." But a chameleon ran ahead, arrived panting and blurted out: "Men die...and it is forever." Then along came the gray lizard shouting, "The Lord has spoken, he says: Men die, and they will come back to life." But the people replied: "Only the first message counts, what is said afterward means nothing."
And so, the unbelieving mortals of this country hate the chameleon, nimble and clever, whereas they love the slow, innocent gray lizard.

The Caledon

The Caledon is a European name. The natives call it Mogakare, "through the middle," because it flows through the middle of Mantatee and Basuto country.
The Caledon starts out only a few feet deep near its source, widens considerably as it approaches the minor valleys, and becomes dangerous when it rains and the snow melts. When it reaches Mérabing, it is joined by the Tlotse, which, like the Caledon, comes from the western slopes of the Blue Mountains. Sixty feet wide, the Tlotse polishes a blue shore sparkling with mica, like the Caledon. Both banks are lined with willows.

Manta Tisi's Response to the Missionary

On August 1, 1834, the Mantatee witnessed the arrival of Mr. Allison, a missionary from the Wesleyan Society. They welcomed him warmly. But once their initial curiosity was satisfied, they proved indifferent and inaccessible to the white man's efforts. One day, the queen asked him:
"Why, if what you preach is true, did the Lord not reveal it to my people sooner? How can it be that our ancestors died entirely ignorant of all these things? And why am I only hearing of them in my decline, when the taste for the new has already left me?"

Proverb

"You can bend a knee, but not a heart."

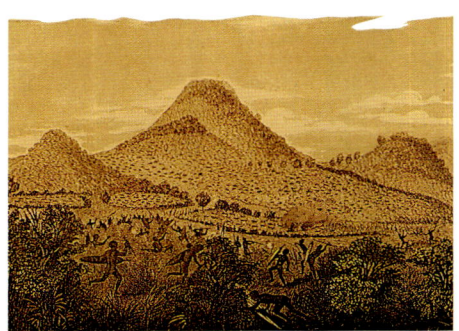

The Siege of Thaba Bosiu

The Mantatee, the refugees, had camped at the bottom of the mountain. Every morning, when the Basutos came down, before them a troop of soldiers, behind them flocks led by their shepherds, a skirmish would take place between the two sides.
It goes without saying that from time to time the enemy would capture a few of the inhabitants' livestock; many of them also wasted away. Toward the end of the siege, the starvation on top of Mount Thaba Bosiu was so great that the people ate dogs, sandals, and old leather coats. Nevertheless, they sang war songs, and down below the enemy responded to their bravado with dances.

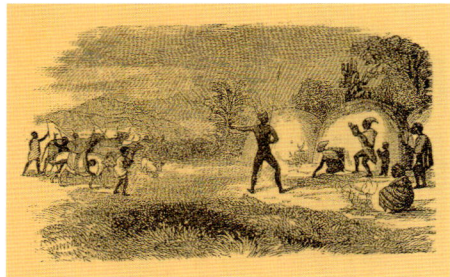

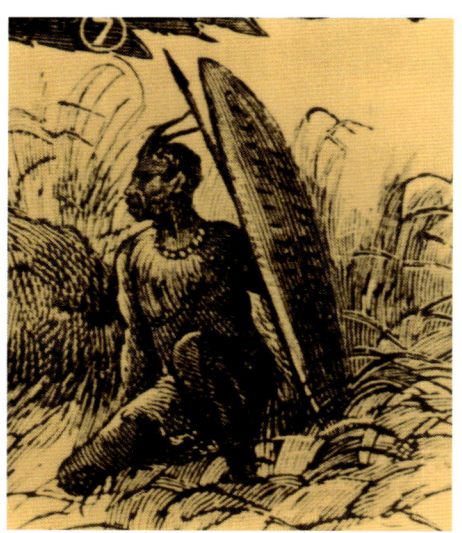

Proverb

"An honest man should buy a good horse so he can get away when he tells the truth."

In 1823, Manta Tisi's army was made up of forty thousand men, women, and children.

She left the devastated banks of the Caledon and headed for the mountain of Thaba Bosiu, the Place of Sweet Repose, whose peak was occupied by a young chief named Mshweshwe. Her army plundered the plain, destroying huts. And it was preparing to attack Mshweshwe's pitiful little band when a messenger came down from the mountain and presented himself at Manta Tisi's tent with a simple red hen.

The gift of a little red hen means: I have heard of your beauty.

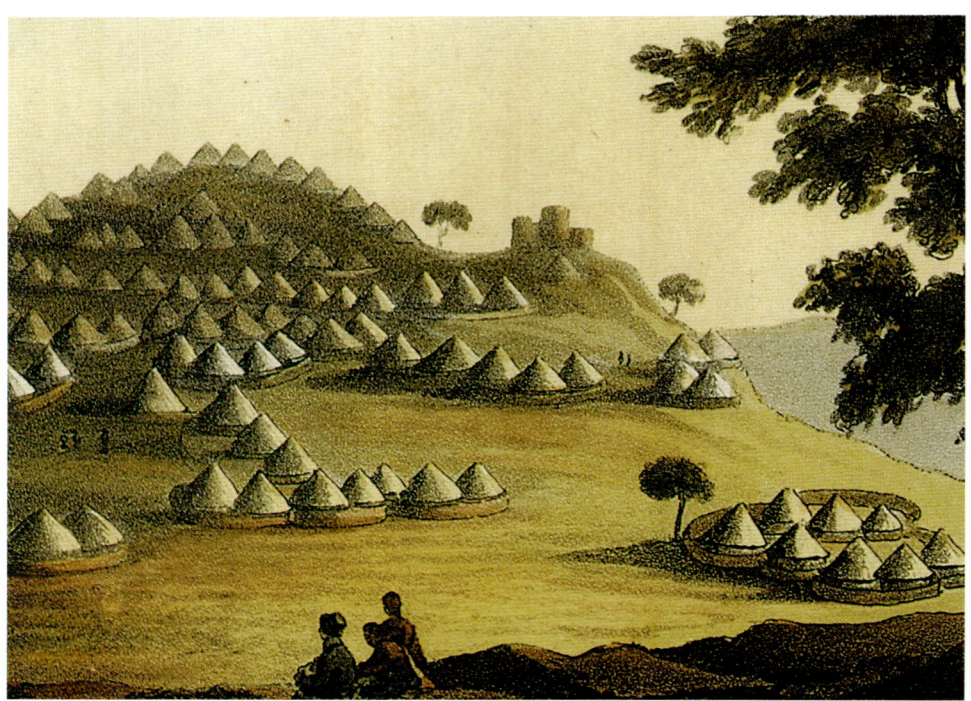

In the royal tent, the messenger was complimented for his master's gesture. He knew that Manta Tisi was going to order a bloodbath, and yet he sent her a little red hen: this was good.

At that moment, Manta Tisi smiled sweetly and sent the messenger back to his master, bearing the following reply: "A red hen sang in the cemetery, and this morning the dead rejoiced."

Then she gave orders for their departure and, having shown mercy to Mshweshwe, the Wild Cats set off in the direction of Bechuanaland, where the grain still swayed on the plains and where many flocks still thrived.

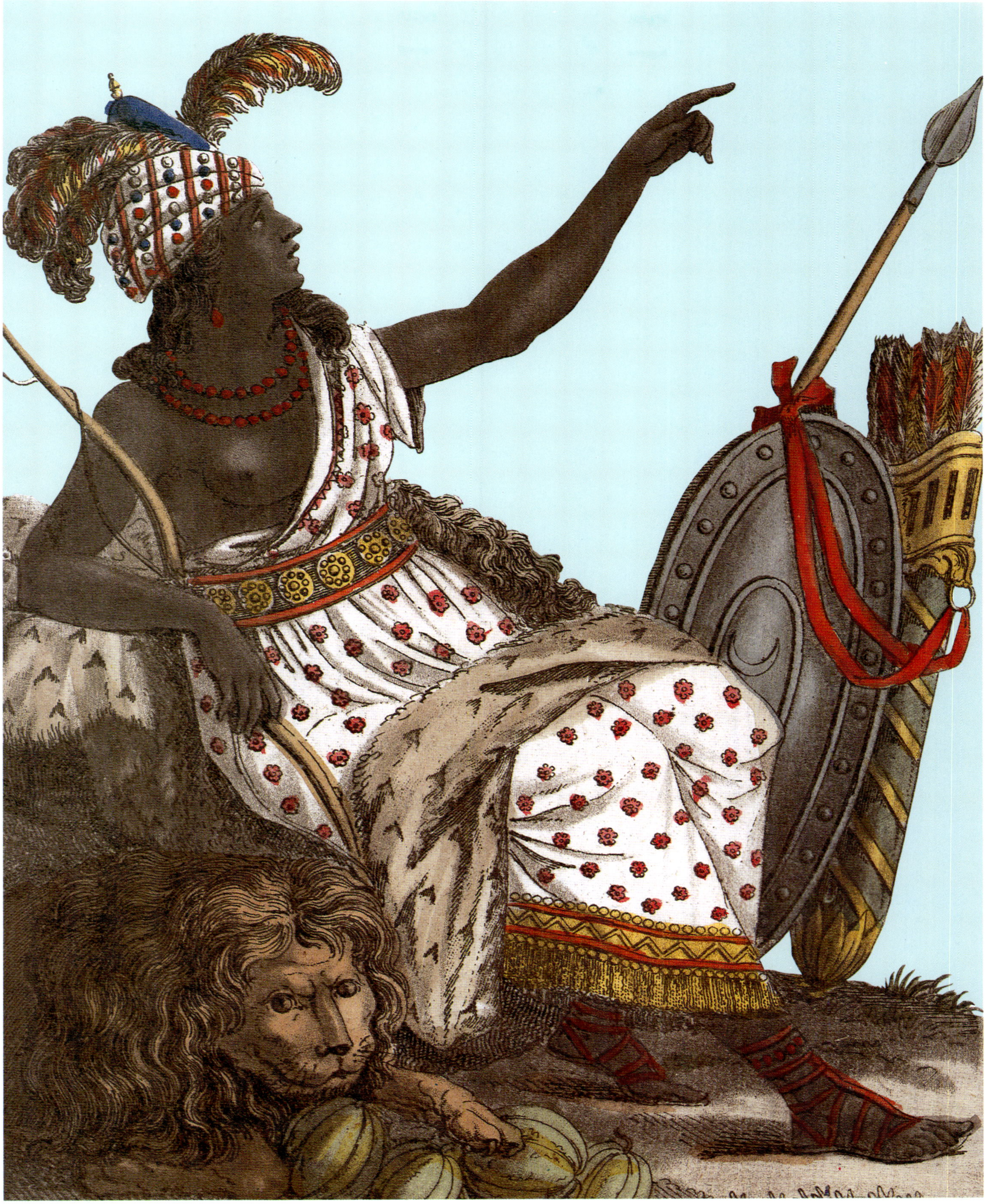

MANTA TISI

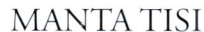

"MANTA TISI GAVE ORDERS FOR THEIR DEPARTURE..."

Anticipating the invasion, the king of Bechuanaland had prepared traps, trenches where enemy troops of the vanguard would fall like animals and would be instantly buried under a hail of javelins.

This was the Wild Cats' first defeat; they retreated, starving, toward Bathutsi territory.

Death and ashes as usual: thousands of refugees plunging into the Kalahari desert.

However, on the other side of the desert, the threatened tribes raised troops to confront the Wild Cats; they were mostly Griquas, a mixed-blood people of Dutch colonial heritage, Bushmen, and black slaves.

Armed with rifles, a troop of Griqua horsemen met Manta Tisi's army. The Batlokwa warriors had never seen a horse, never heard the explosion of gunpowder. They hurled themselves at the horsemen, who promptly backed off, all the while shooting at the front lines of their adversaries.

The mechanism was in place, and would not stop until the final defeat: the Batlokwa warriors advanced, the Griqua cavalry retreated, pelting the enemy from a distance, in such a way that they always remained beyond the range of the arrows and spears.

Riddled with bullets, the Wild Cats did not manage to unhorse a single Griqua; they lost ground and scattered under the blows of the horsemen sent to pursue them.

The rest of the army was dispersed by the Zulu troops of King Matiwane.

And the remainder of this remnant would disappear in the great storm of the Mfecane, burned up, no one knows where, by the great brushfire Shaka had lit.

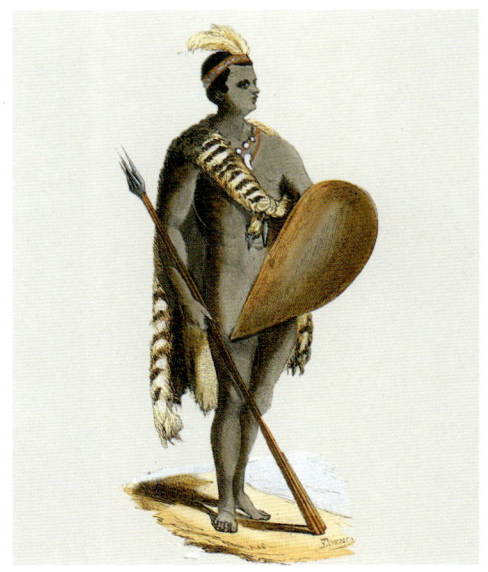

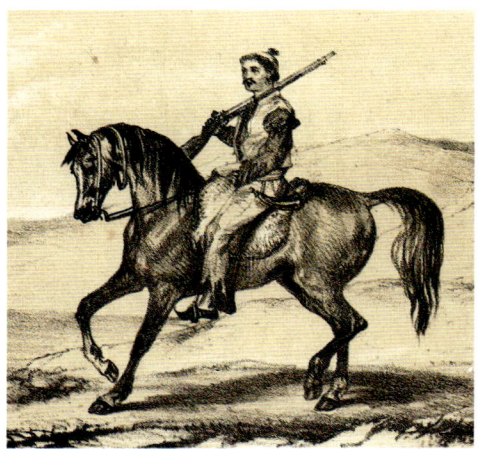

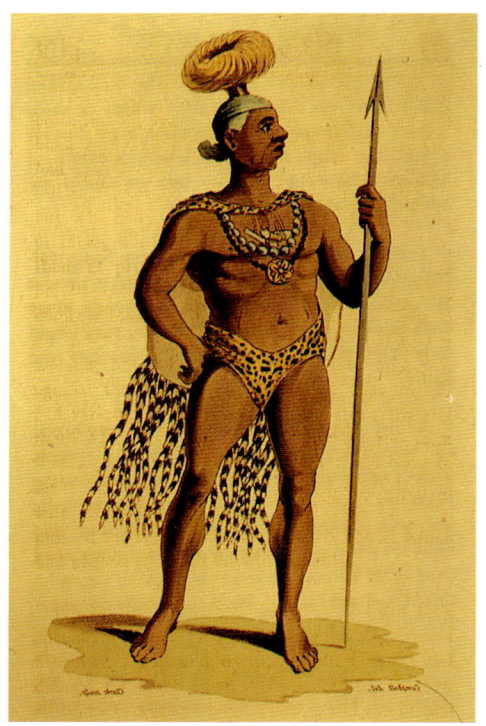

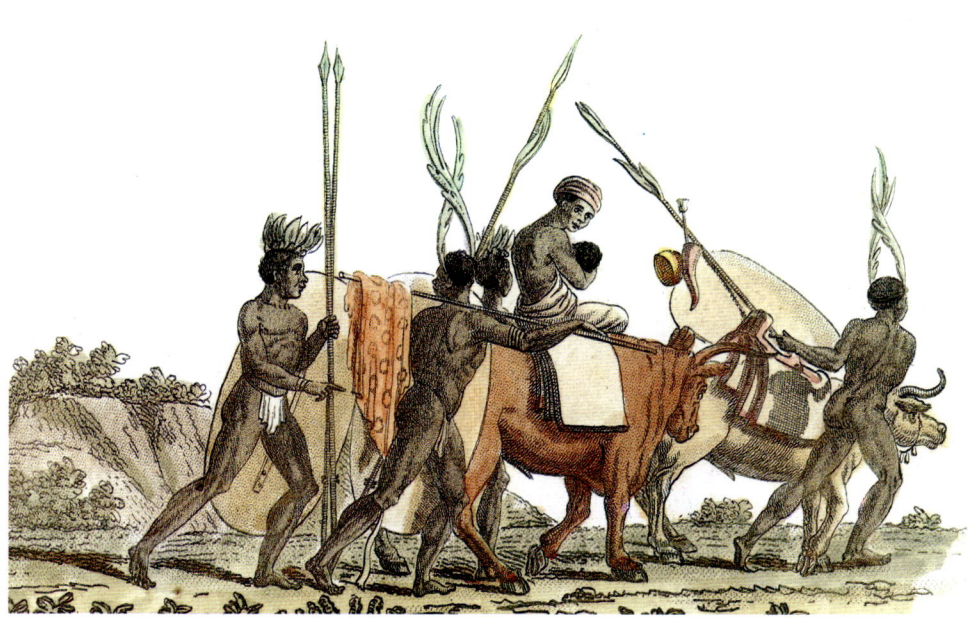

"AND THE REST DISAPPEARED INTO THE STORM..."

WARRIORS

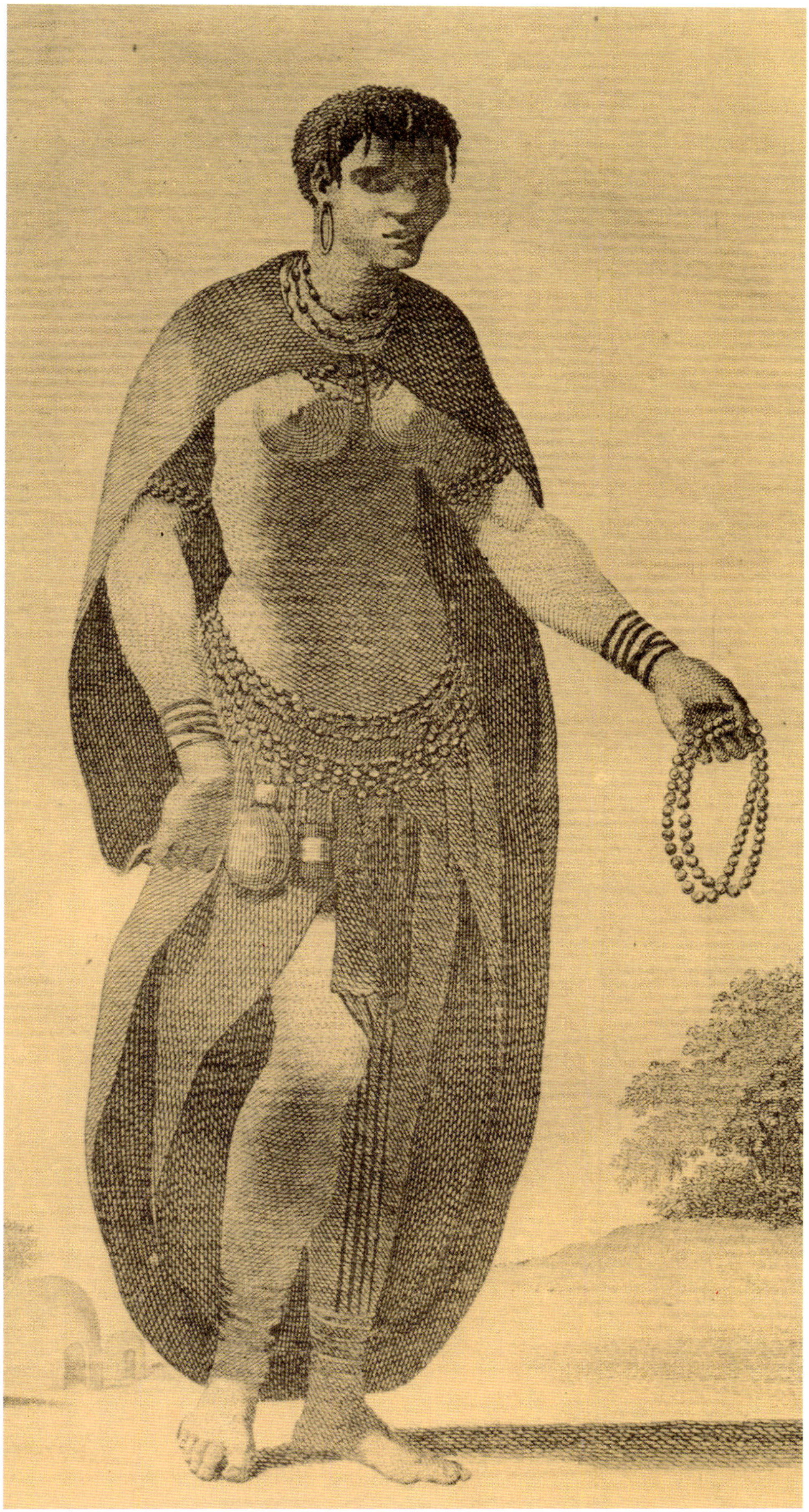

NAMAQUOIS WOMAN

Invitation to Dance

Shake for Diija!
Shake for Perfume!
Shake for what is yours!
Shake for Dawn!
Shake for the Lively One!
A brunette courtesan.
A bolt of lightning in the night.
Shake for the Widow!
Red, white-speckled cow!
Diija the tattooed woman.
Shake for the palms!

Court

The interested parties always plead their own case and do it with truly remarkable skill. Cases are always debated in public, and it is praiseworthy for all those who attend to take part.

One day, the chief and a few hundred of his subjects were seated in a somber circle, their heads bare, in deep silence, as a woman, carrying a young child in her arms, walked slowly around the circle, examining them in turn with the greatest care. She had been the victim of indecent exposure, but she knew neither the name nor the residence of the guilty man's family. After having tried in vain to identify him by the description she had given, the chief proposed that all the men of the area be summoned to appear before her, so that the woman could identify him herself. She was now in the middle of this task, and one could see all the importance she attached to getting it right. Suddenly she stopped, cried out, and thrust the child she had been carrying onto the knees of a young man: "Here," she said, "this is the man who insulted the mother of this little baby." The stunned man confessed his guilt and was obliged to go into exile after paying a heavy fine.

Song for the Departure of the Herds

The Do'Aawol is sung on the last morning of the festival in the corral, after the cattle leave. All the boys and girls hold a branch of "barkehi," a plant that brings good luck, which they throw on the ground as they leave, to invoke prosperity for the herds of their hosts.

May the herd turn its head and come home.
   Children of the Ancestor,
   Children of Vooja,
   Oh sons of Mudaana,
   Like a flight of herons
   Take flight too.

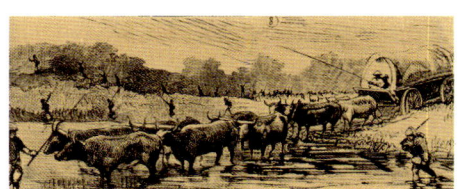

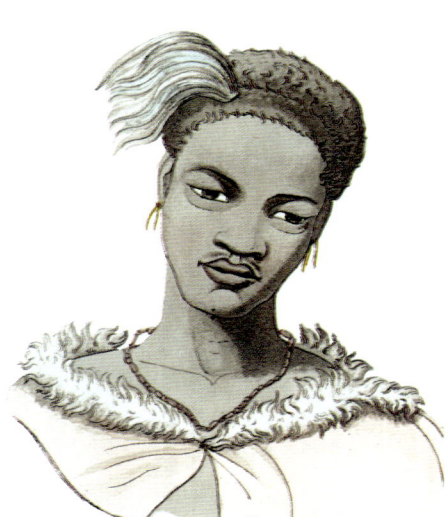

A few years later, Manta Tisi sought refuge in the land of Mshweshwe, the famous young man with the red hen, who housed her in his fortress on Thaba Bosiu, the Place of Sweet Repose.

She had lost her son, she had lost her kingdom and her people; and yet it is said that she remained serene until her last days, content simply not to speak, retreating into an eternal silence.

And until her final day, her very last breath, Mshweshwe watched over her as if they were blood kin.

This is the same Mshweshwe who one day became a hero for gathering the wanderers, the refugees of the plain, in order to shape them into a new nation, the Basutos, who now live in Basutoland.

So ends the story of Manta Tisi, the queen who lost her son, her kingdom, and her people.

Creole Expressions for the "Heart"

They say that the seat of life, emotion, thought, and will is the heart, and this is perhaps their only word for the rational being, generally speaking. They say of a person who is thinking, "the heart is listening to itself," "the heart is weighing," "the heart is seeking." An intelligent person has a "large heart," a patient person "a long heart," an irritable person "a short heart." A brave man has "a strong heart," a happy man "a white heart," an unhappy man "a black heart"; he is "heartsick." They ascribe the more abrupt or violent emotions to the lungs: "his lungs are keeping him from speaking," "her lungs jumped." The uneasiness that results from a bad deed is ascribed to the spleen: "my spleen is accusing me," "my spleen is gnawing at me." Persistence and standing one's ground in danger or suffering are credited to the liver: "He has a hard liver" means he has endurance.

The Marriage Proposal

Nowhere is childhood shorter than in these countries. A child is barely fourteen years old when people start talking about his or her marriage. This transaction takes much deliberation on the part of the parents. Usually, several months pass between the preliminaries and the definitive conclusion of the contract. The choice of the first wife generally falls to the father of the groom. He is the one who goes to ask for her. If his proposal is welcomed, they kill a bull and feast upon it together. Soon afterward, the young man's kin will present the livestock required for the acquisition of the bride. The groom's sister opens the procession. She holds in her hand a long white baton, symbol of peace and harmony, which she throws in the doorway of her future sister-in-law's hut without saying a word.

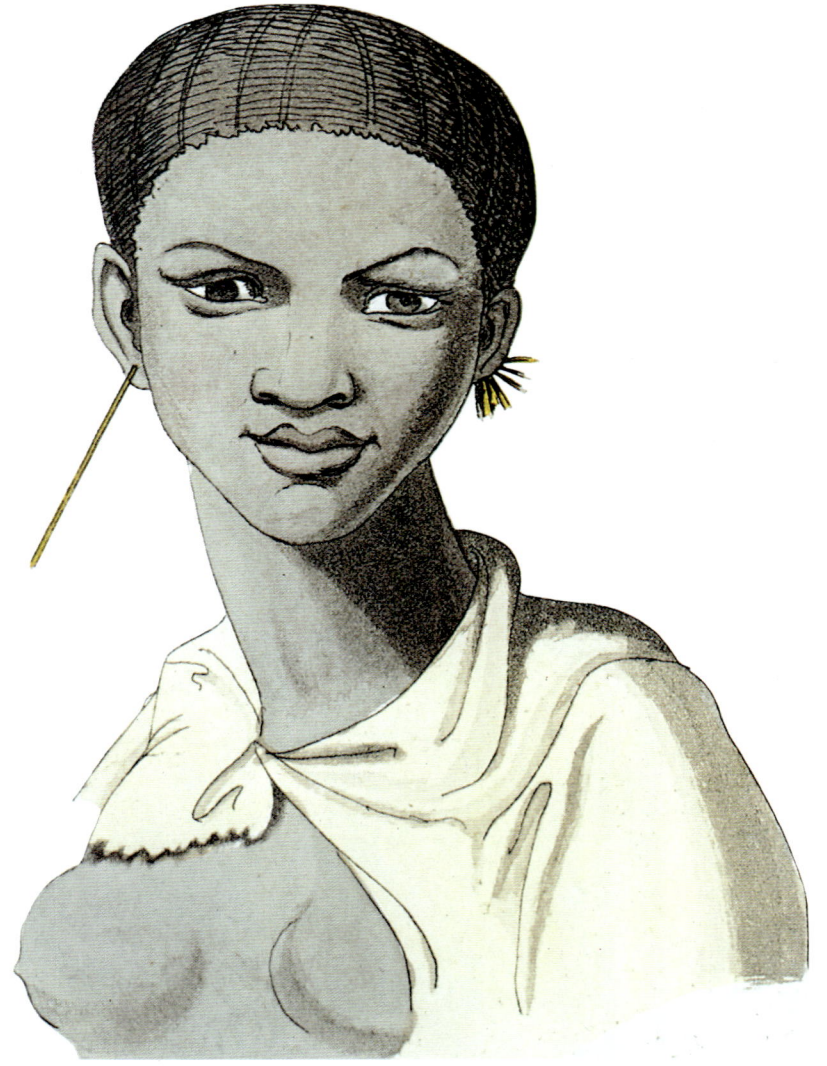

FACE OF A BANTU WOMAN

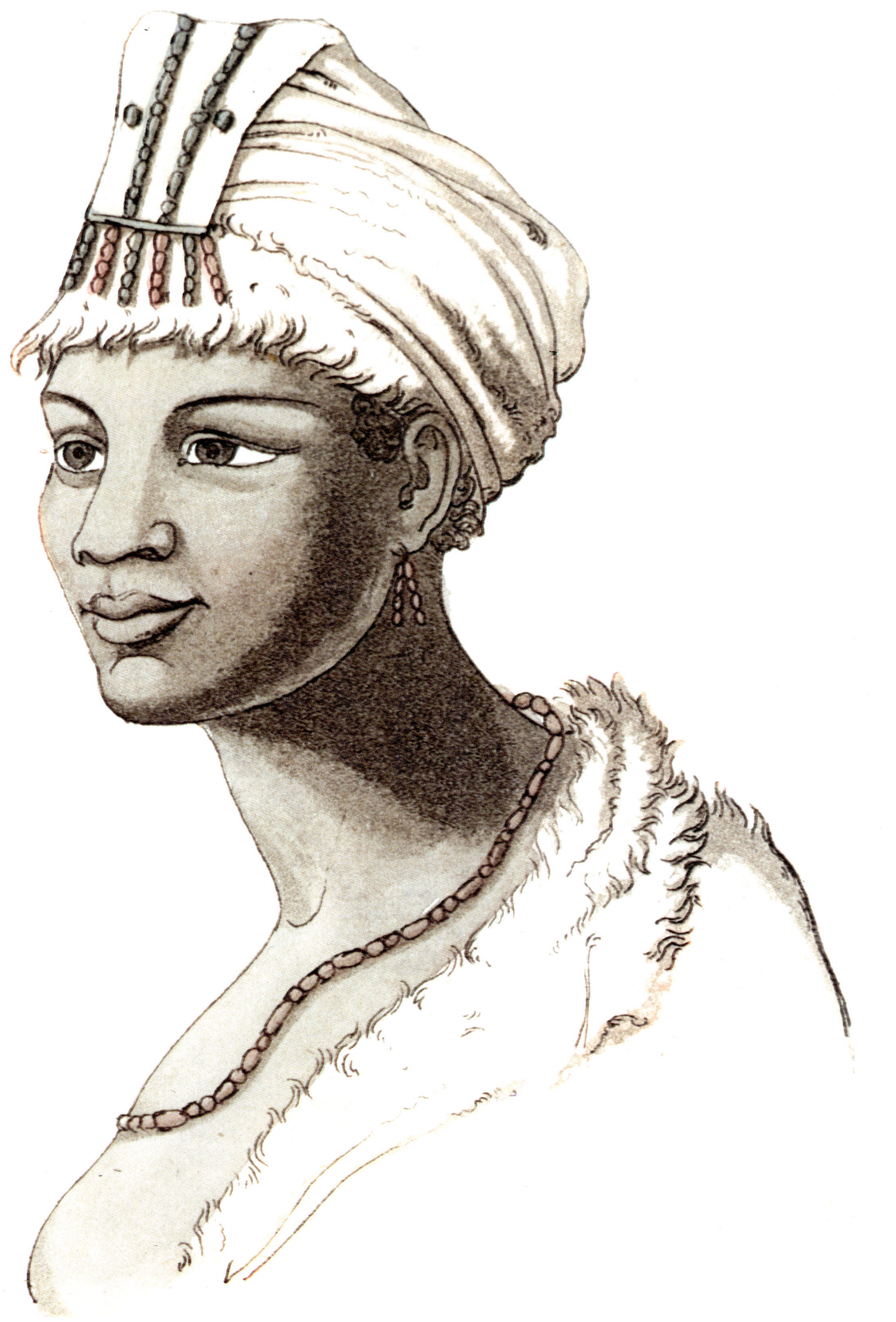

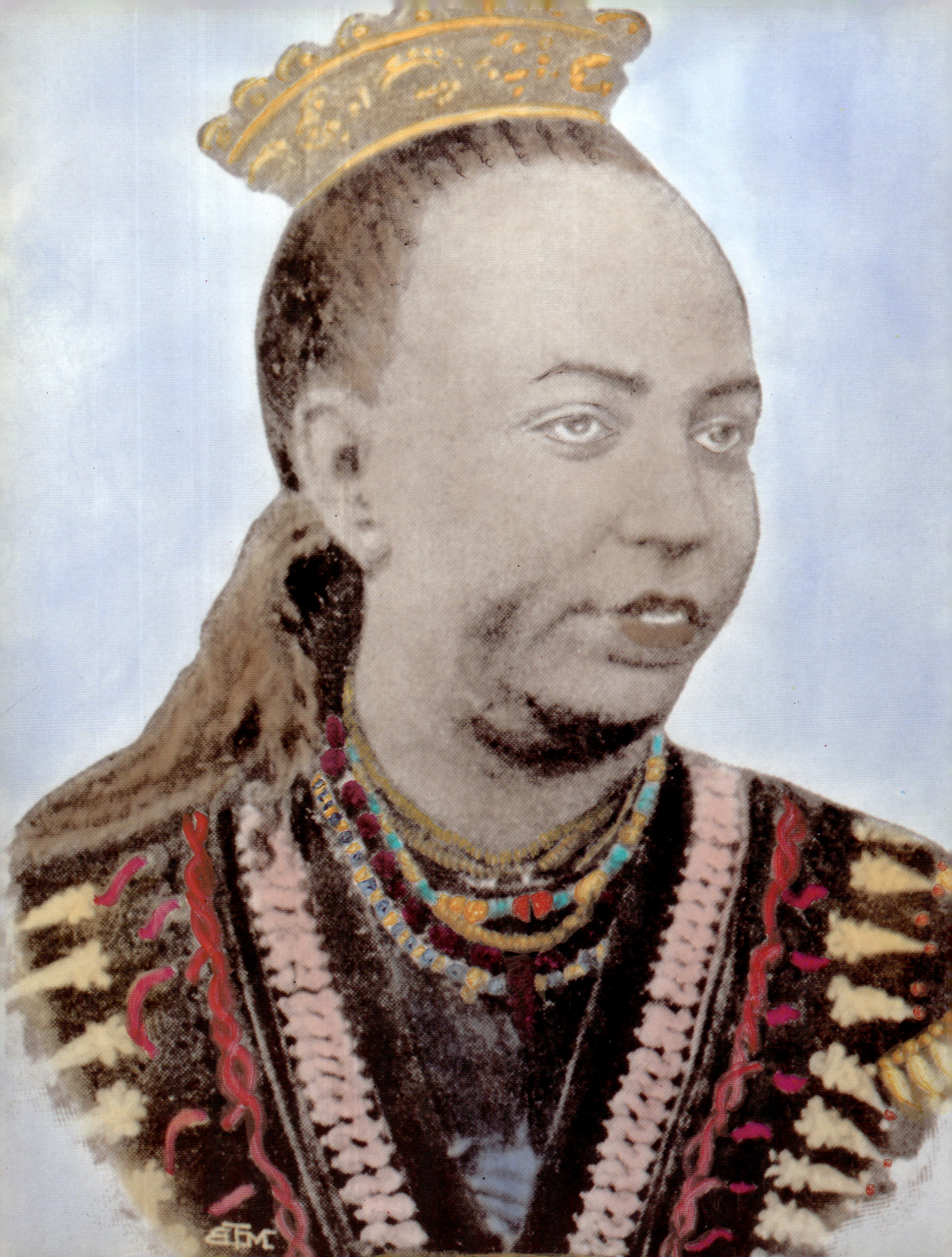

TAITU BETHEL

EMPRESS OF ETHIOPIA

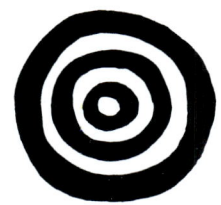

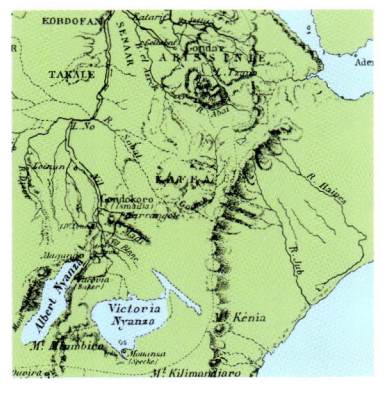

The work of Menilek II, as imposing as it may have been, depended wholly upon the delicate breath of a woman, the most ordinary and the most extraordinary woman of her time...

AS WE SAW IN THE STORY OF MENTOWAB, THE BETRAYAL OF RAS MIKAEL INAUGURATED A SOMBER TIME WHICH THE ETHIOPIANS CALL *ZAMANA MASAFENT,* OR THE AGE OF PRINCES, ALLUDING TO THE VERSE OF THE BIBLE THAT SAYS: "IN THOSE DAYS THERE was no king in Israel: every man did that which was right in his own eyes" (Judges 21:25).

Then came Emperor Johannes IV, who undertook the pacification of the kingdom. And succeeding him, the great Menilek II, the Lion of Judah, who would bear the title king of kings, for he was the culmination of the entire Solomonic line beginning with the coronation of the son of the Queen of Sheba, Menilek I, the founder of the dynasty.

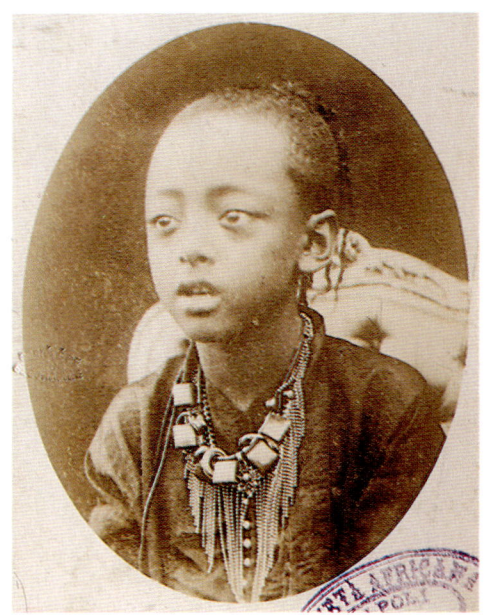

SON OF TAITU BETHEL AND MENILEK II

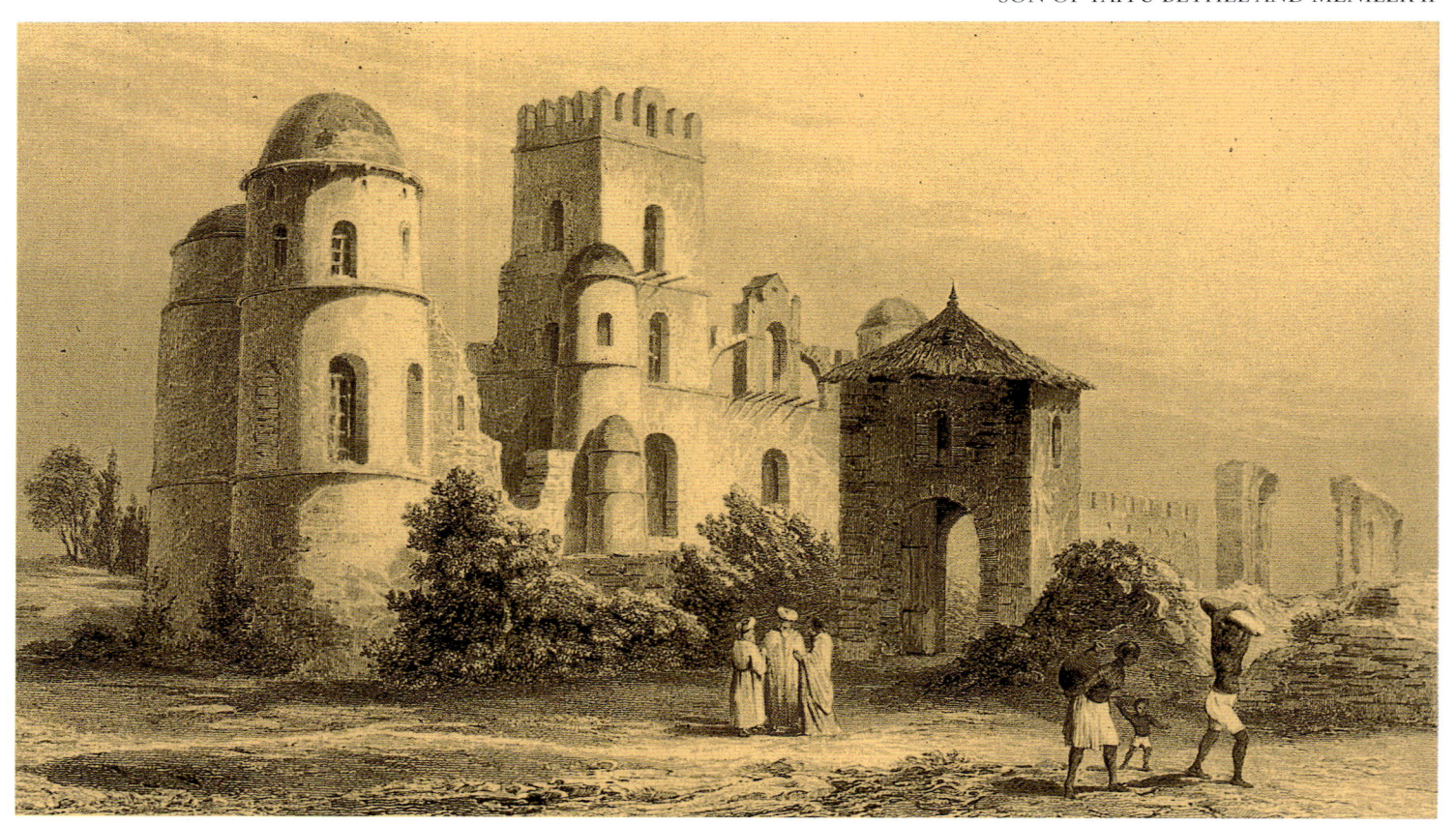

THE EMPEROR'S RESIDENCE IN GONDAR

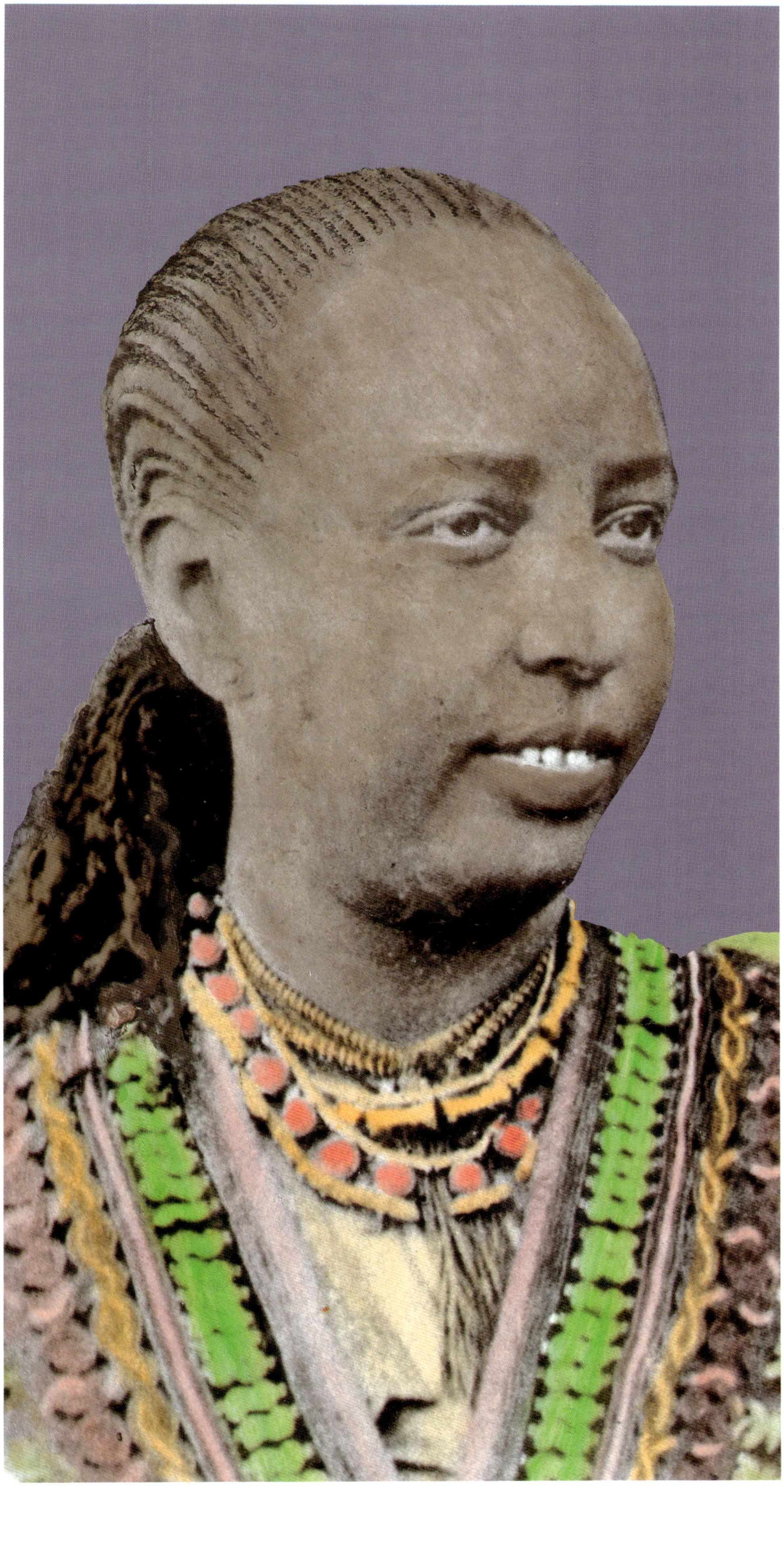

TAITU BETHEL

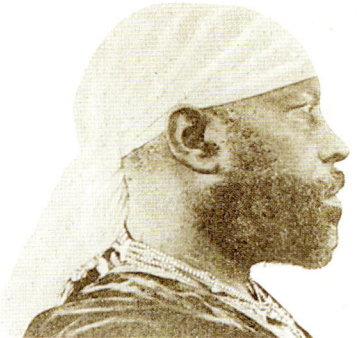

Menilek II

Menilek was six feet tall and powerfully built. His skin was very black and his teeth a brilliant white. He had a small, slightly turned-up nose, a fine moustache, and a thick goatee hiding the smallpox scars that marked his skin. His eyes sparkled with intelligence.

The emperor gave audience in the manner of an oriental satrap, sitting Indian style on a couch covered with rugs and cushions. He dressed in the old-fashioned style, in white cotton and muslin, a black cape with golden ornaments thrown over his shoulders. A silk handkerchief knotted at the back of his neck hid his premature baldness, and he protected himself from the bright sun with a wide-brimmed Quaker-style hat.

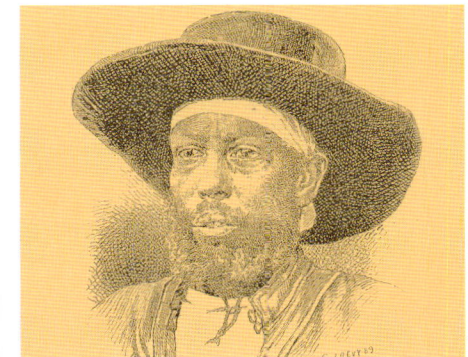

Menilek's Grandfather

Menilek's grandfather, Sahalé Selassie, used all of his treasure to give each impoverished peasant a cow and a plow, telling them to "work and dig." Every year, he gathered together all the poor and paid off their debts himself.

In the twenty-third year of his reign, when his eldest son was already a young man, he wanted to abdicate in his son's favor and withdraw from the world to a monastery. But the monks talked him out of it, knowing what they would suffer in losing this good king, being uncertain of what his son would bring. According to custom, they cited religious considerations and invoked a prophecy. Sahalé's mystical nature was shaken by such a prophecy, and he consented to keep his crown even though the loss of his left eye affected him like a curse.

But the work of Menilek II, as imposing as it was, majestic and engraved in the marble of history, depended wholly upon the delicate breath of a woman, at once the most ordinary and the most extraordinary woman of her time: Taitu Bethel.

The destiny of little Taitu does not seem to be written in the stratosphere of queens. Born in 1853, she begins her conscious life with violation, by a procedure called "the antelope's horn"; that is, a method of deflowering young girls in such a way that they often become barren for life. Thus "opened," she will pass successively through the arms of four husbands, who always leave her without much ado, since her belly remains flat.

But, with her perfectly oval face, her eyes bright as torches, she is nonetheless one of the most beautiful women of the kingdom. Above and beyond her beauty, she is gifted with talents unique in her time. She reads and writes Amharic and even knows Ge'ez, the holy, liturgical language, the privilege of priests. She composes poems, is a first-rate chess player, and divinely plays the bégawa, a court instrument similar to the lyre. But all these qualities are in vain: a woman is judged by her womb. And a creature with a barren womb will sooner or later find herself confronted with the traditional choice: to become a nun or a prostitute. Taitu will choose a third, unexpected path: she will become an empress.

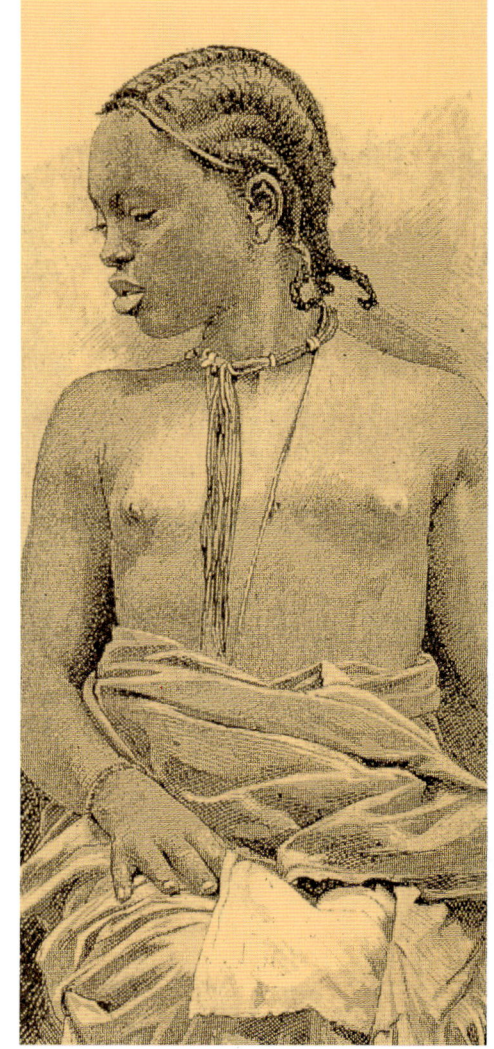

YOUNG ETHIOPIAN GIRL

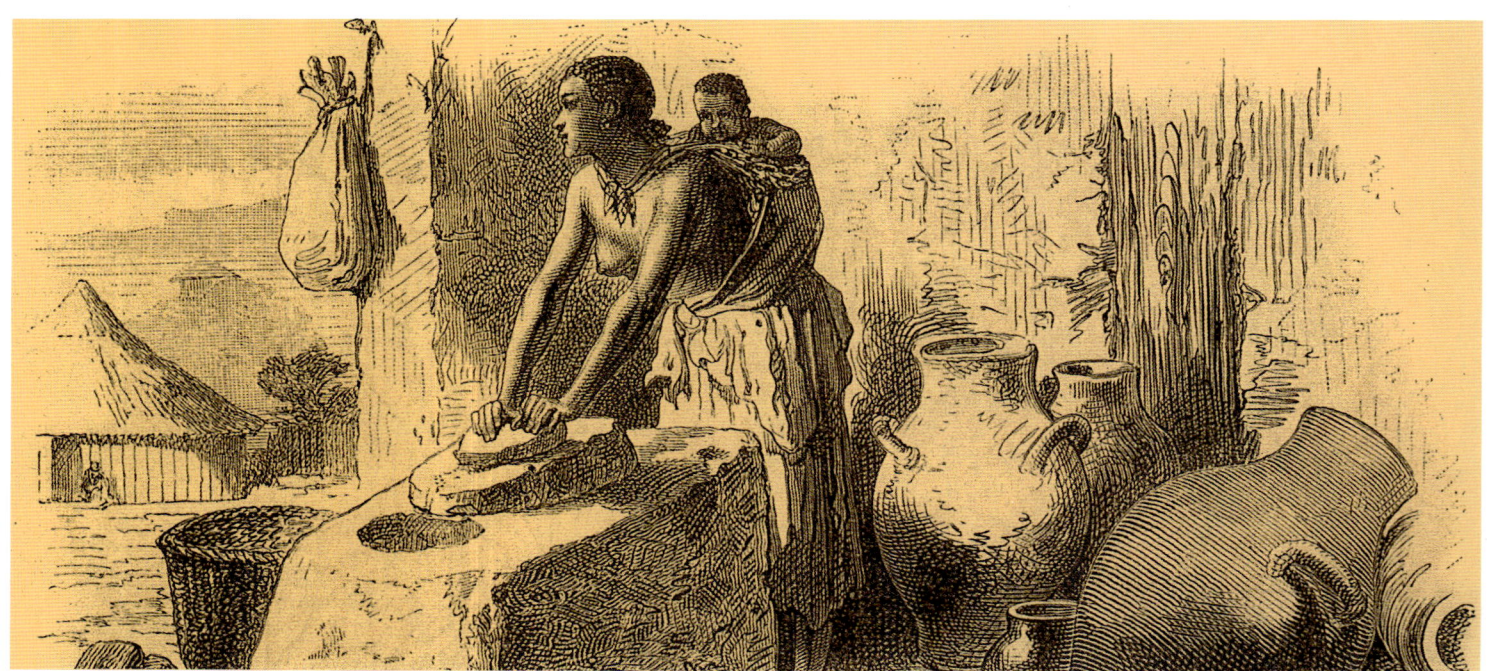

MOTHERHOOD

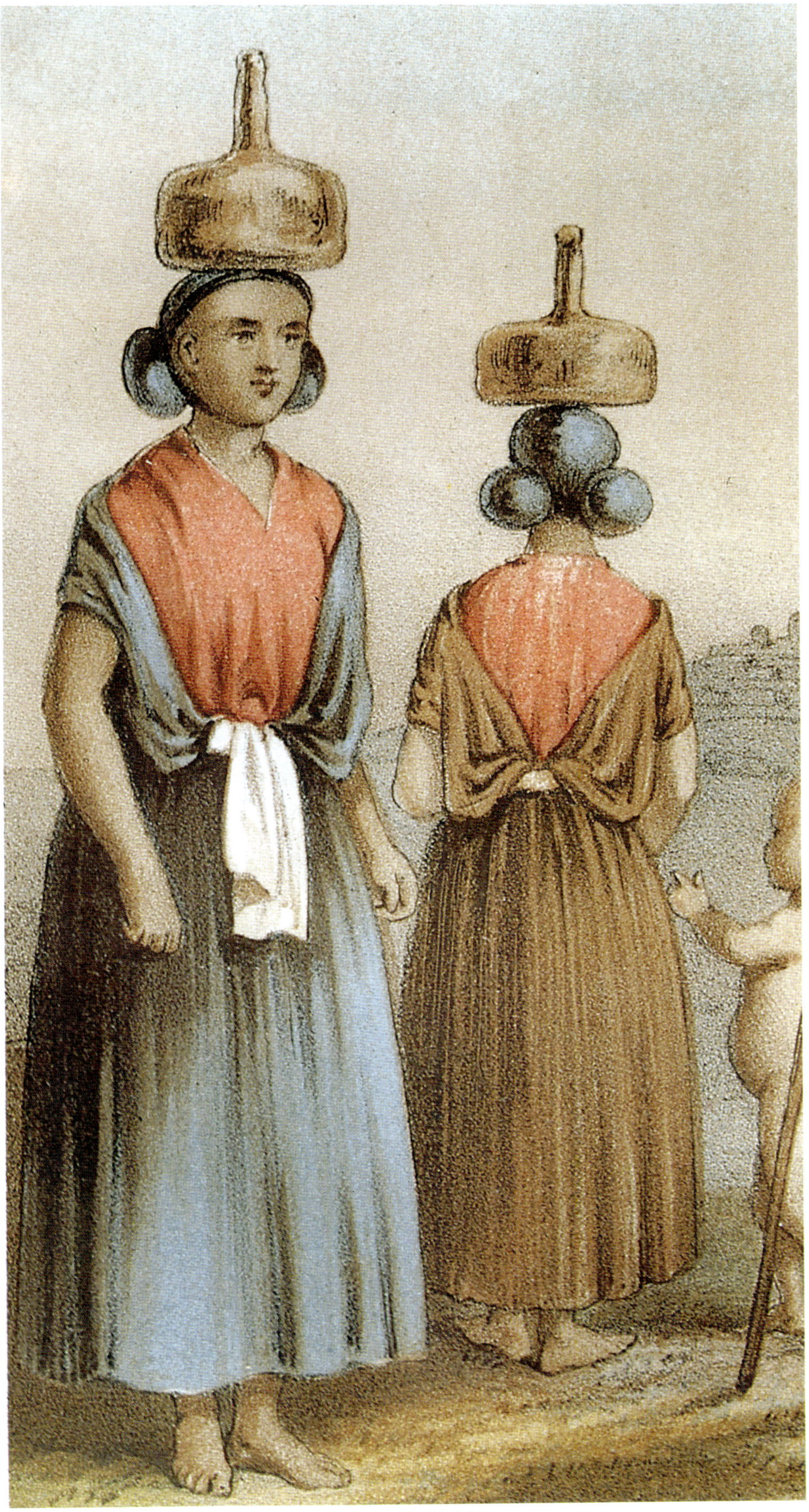

HARAR WOMEN

Women's Hairstyles

The thick hair of young women is arranged in many different ways: they may braid it into tiny plaits and decorate it with finely worked metal pins, as the ladies of quality do; they may arrange it in several heavy shells; they may pile it high, sometimes with a framework of reeds underneath—it all depends on the region. When these coiffures are periodically undone, large, hard wooden combs must be used to untangle the locks.

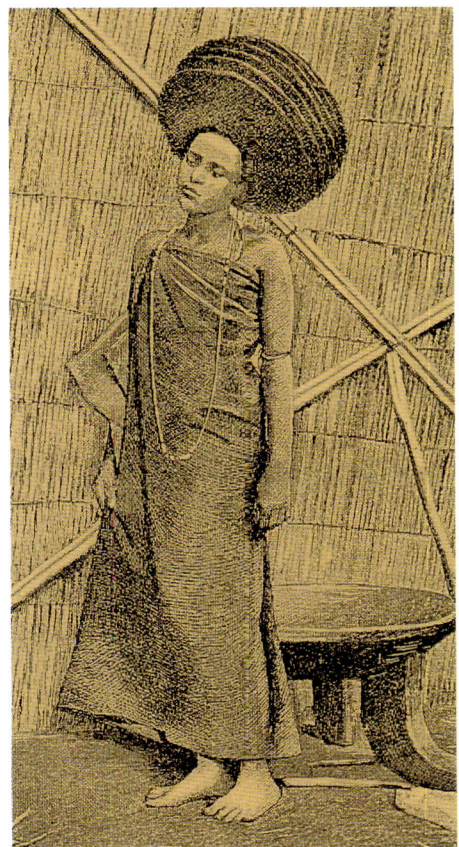

Agriculture

Agriculture, complemented by the raising of livestock, is Ethiopia's greatest resource; in this regard, Ethiopia is one of the few rich countries of the African continent. A prehistoric drawing that may be seen in the province of Eritrea, in Amba-Focada, depicts a peasant working with an instrument drawn by oxen. Furthermore, the Ancients credited Ethiopia with being the country that originated wheat and the olive tree.

Certain pieces of land, wide, flat stretches, quickly lent themselves to farming. Farmers had to patiently work the other plots into terraces and remove stones from them. They knew about irrigation. They practiced crop rotation and allowed land to remain fallow for a year or two. On this fallow land, they grazed their livestock so that the soil would benefit from the manure; or they burned grass and then worked the ashes into the ground to improve the land.

Proverb

"Wisdom that is kept prisoner in the heart is like light in a jar."

Taitu is forty on her wedding day, and she has worn out a certain number of mounts in her race through life: four marriages and belly that has never swollen and never will.

As for Menilek II, he enters the church with his head full of visions of another, the beautiful Bafana, whom he has just repudiated with a heavy heart for a sin that the kings would not pardon.

Thus, it is a sad and extravagant marriage of convenience that unites Taitu Bethel, daughter of a great family of Sémen, and the sovereign drunk on glory, who for the first time in the history of Ethiopia has himself called Negusa Nagast, which means king of kings in Amharic.

The world that awaits them is a difficult one. In 1885, the Conference of Berlin has fated Africa to be butchered and divvied up like an animal. And the construction of the Suez Canal gives the Ethiopian coast global strategic interest. Around the Red Sea, a stiff ballet takes place between France and England, Italy, and Czarist Russia. These noble partners have only one point in common: they have mutually agreed not to furnish arms to Ethiopia, who is to remain the prey.

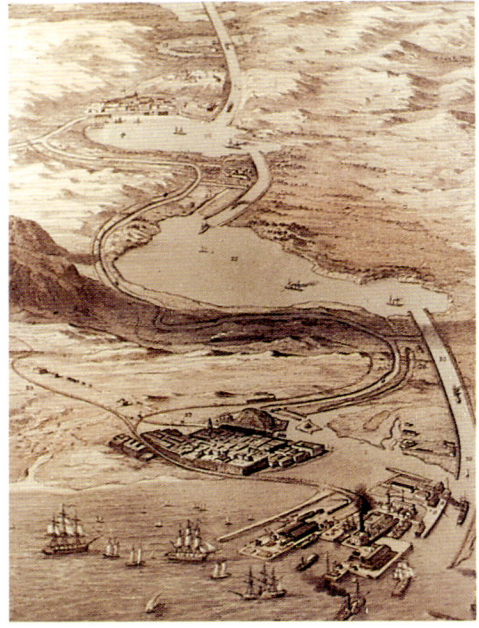

THE CONSTRUCTION OF THE SUEZ CANAL

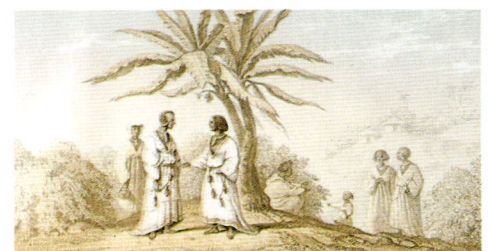

TRADITIONAL COSTUMES

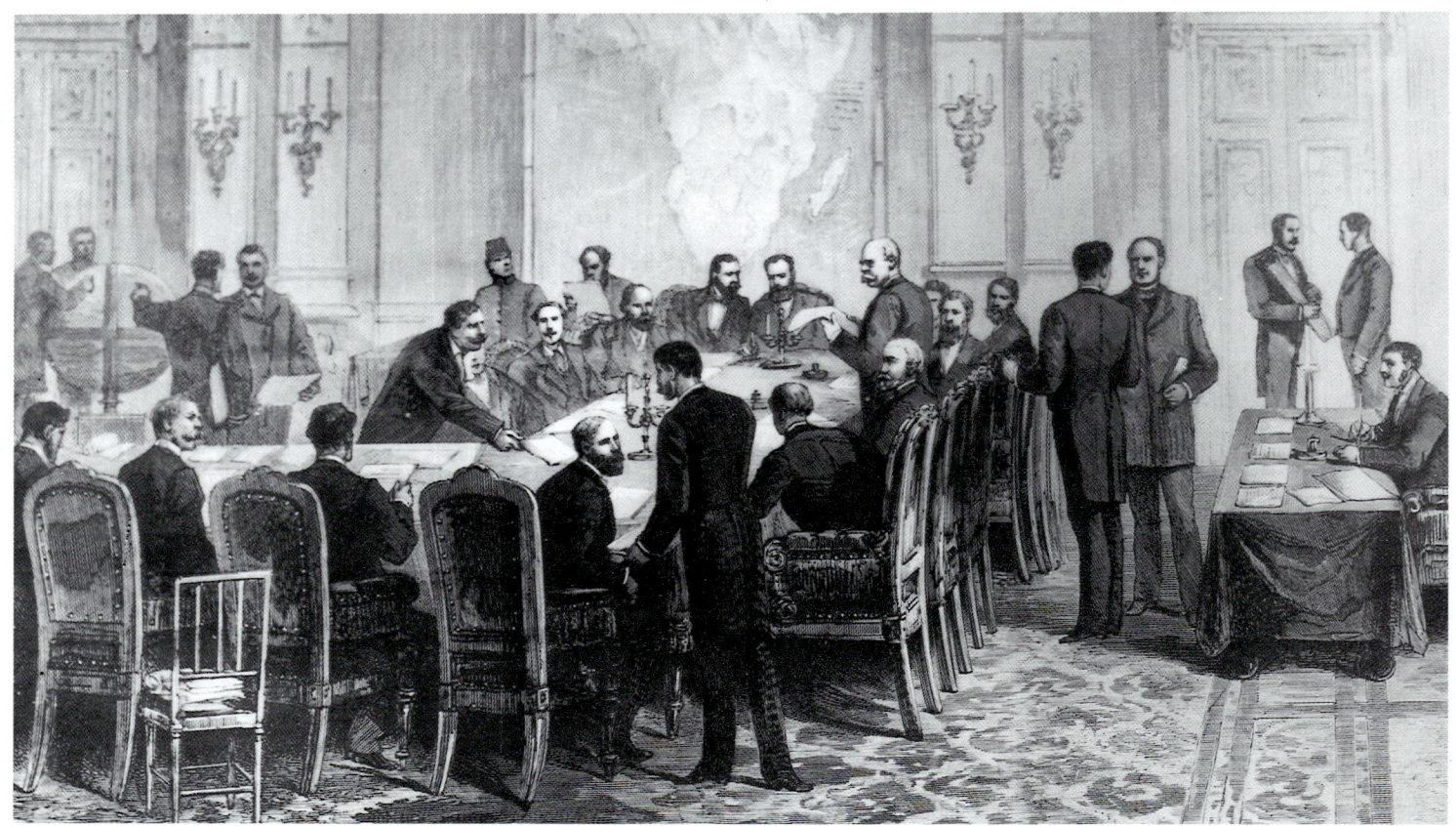

THE BERLIN CONFERENCE

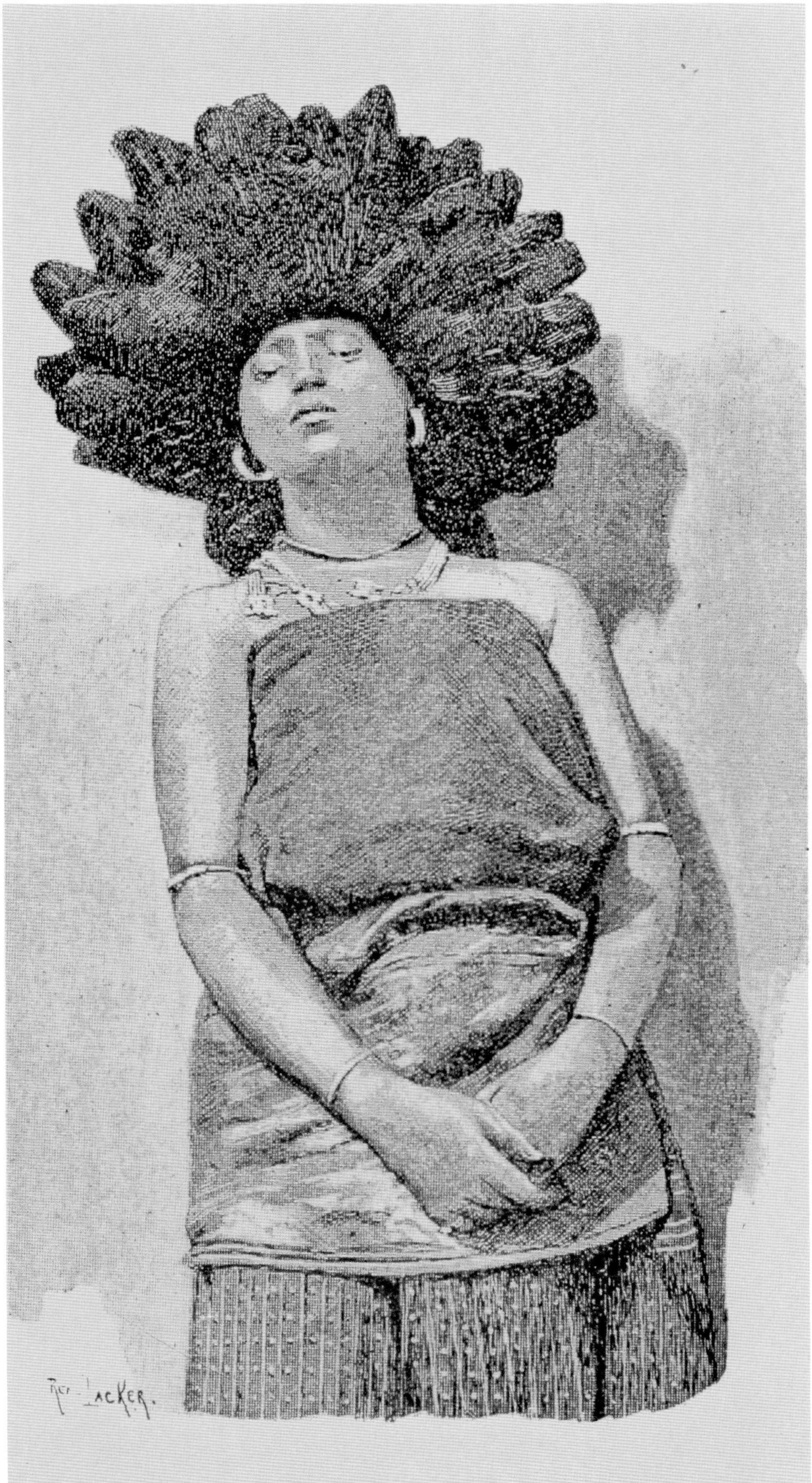

Queen Warquit

The queen of Gallas Wallos, known as Queen Warquit, was most beautiful. She rode horseback and handled a lance and slingshot like the most able warrior. Barechested, leopard skin flying over her shoulders, her dark mane of hair carefully braided, she would gallop ahead of her cavalry and lead them into furious attacks where they would charge through the bullets and arrows, indifferent to danger.

It is said that a charm protected her, but more simply, a sort of superstitious fear checked the arms of her adversaries, as if they were faced with an awesome divinity. What's more, her courage was matched by her cruelty, if we can believe the number of male trophies that she cut off with her dagger from those she conquered.

This fierce amazon, who spurred those around her to carnage with her battle cry and defied death with her white-toothed laughter, this African Valkyrie was an ardent romantic for whom many lovers, princes or paupers, lost their reason and often their lives.

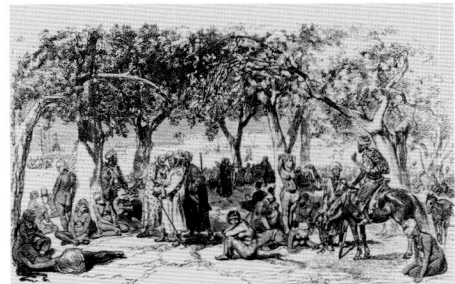

The Slave Trade

Sudan and Abyssinia have furnished the Arab kingdom with so many slaves for so many years that their children suffice to fulfill most needs in this regard. Owners scheme to multiply these offspring. There is even a special group of matchmakers who guide the masters in the steps they should take to obtain good products and who earn a commission when a baby is born.

The king of Nedjed and Hedjaz (who is recognized as a genius by all those who have been in his presence) has shown an unmistakable hostility to the slave trade ever since he defeated the Hashemite dynasty. Just six years ago, King Hussein officially recognized the slave trade, since his customs office charged a ten percent tax on each imported slave.

Ibn Séoud repealed this barbarous tax, forbade the unloading of slaves in Djeddah, asked the representatives of powerful nations to furnish the many pilgrims with passports, and granted legations and consulates the right to provide asylum for escaped slaves. But his acts had to be tempered by political considerations, and were therefore relatively modest. He was brought to the power he now exercises by the fanaticism of his warriors, and he now must take that into account.

A WOMAN OF OLDEN TIMES

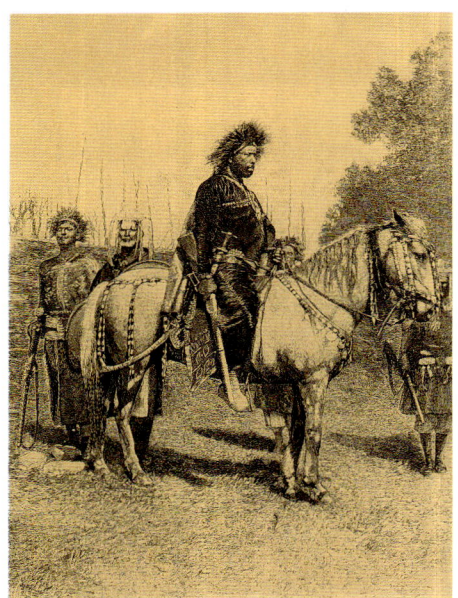

Menilek's Will

"Now, my children, my friends, do not be jealous of one another. Do not say 'I will take the land of another.' I beg you to live in the unity and charity that I have assured until this day. If you are one of heart and if you do not destroy each other with envy, you will never hand our country over to foreigners and it will suffer no harm. To keep the wind out, keep the door shut, and, each at his post, defend your country valiantly. Call each other 'my brother.'

If I have written this advice to you, it is because, by the Lord's grace, I have governed for many long years; but since I am a man, I must wonder, 'How long do I have left to live?'"

As a chess player, Taitu knows she must attempt an opening move.

On her advice, a treaty of perpetual friendship (the Treaty of Wichale) is signed with Italy on May 2, 1889. Her people stock Italian arms. They eagerly import Italian technicians, engineers, teachers, and printers, who will bring ancient Ethiopia into the dawn of the twentieth century.

This lasts six months, a year. Then the Italian government publishes a map on which Ethiopia is identified as an Italian protectorate: this brings about a crisis.

By 1893, Menilek II renounces the treaty, and an Italian diplomat comes to threaten the emperor: war is knocking at the gates.

This historical episode has witnesses. Menilek begins by holding his tongue, calculating the consequences of a conflict with Italy: white men are at this time masters of the world, so he needs to consider carefully. But then, interfering in the debate, Taitu brusquely asks the diplomat to leave. "You cannot threaten Ethiopia," she says, "please take your leave." Commander Antonnelli lends no weight to a woman's words, but he immediately uses Taitu's tirade as a pretext for raising the stakes: the entire Italian nation, as embodied by him, has just been insulted; this is serious and demands immediate redress.

Menilek hesitates and the great council holds its breath. Then, feeling the wind change direction, Taitu considers the Italian diplomat and says: "*Amigi*, little *frengi*, I advise you to take your leave at once, if you do not want me to have you thrown out like a bum."

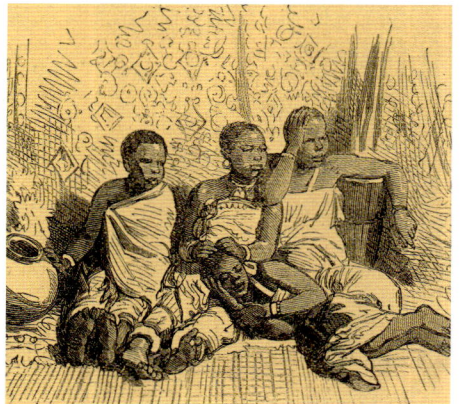

CHILD SLAVES IN KHARTOUM

Proverbs

"*Do not grab the leopard's tail, but if you do have it, don't let go.*"

"*The wee hours and the great truths come to light in time.*"

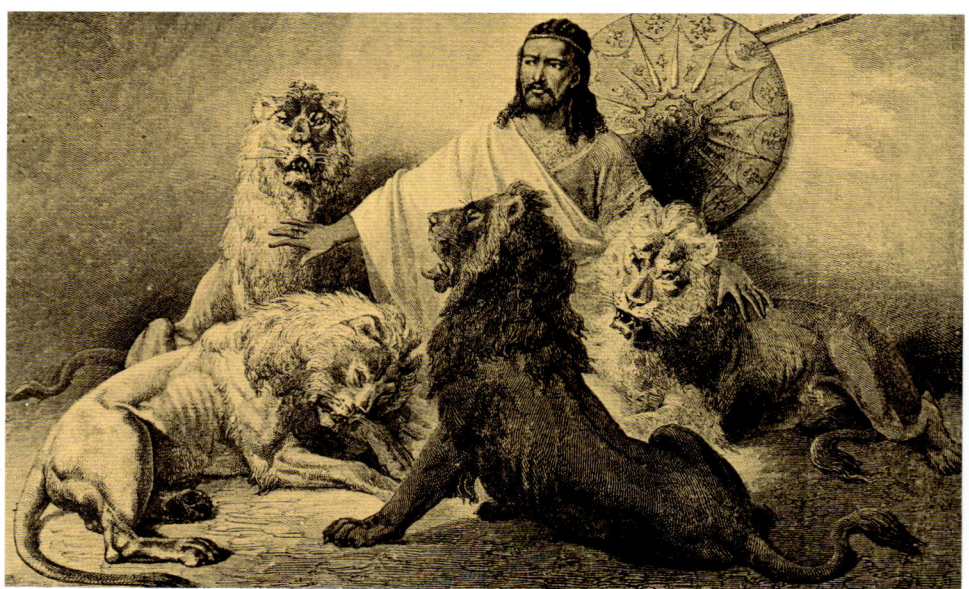

THE SPLENDOR OF THE KING OF KINGS

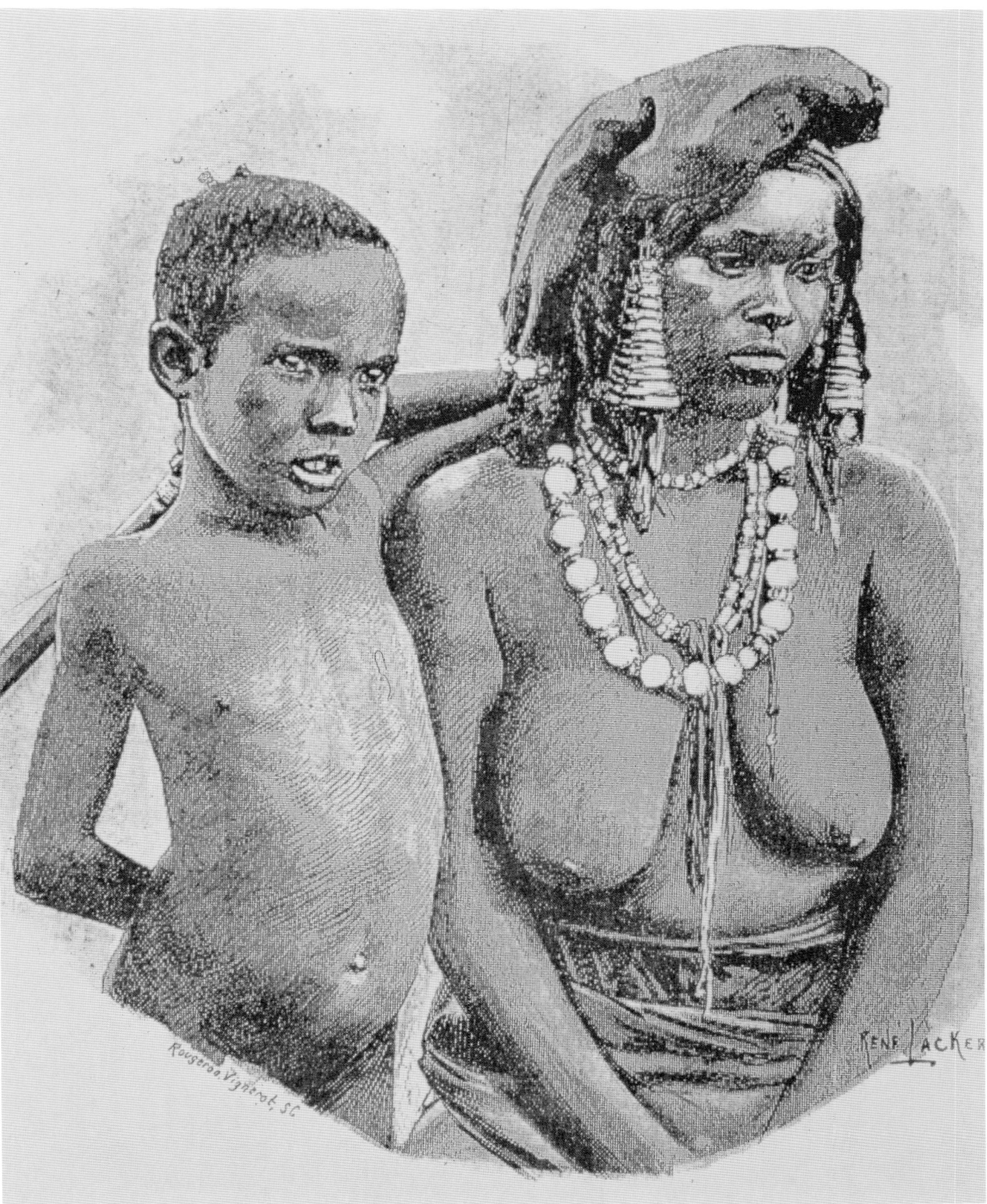

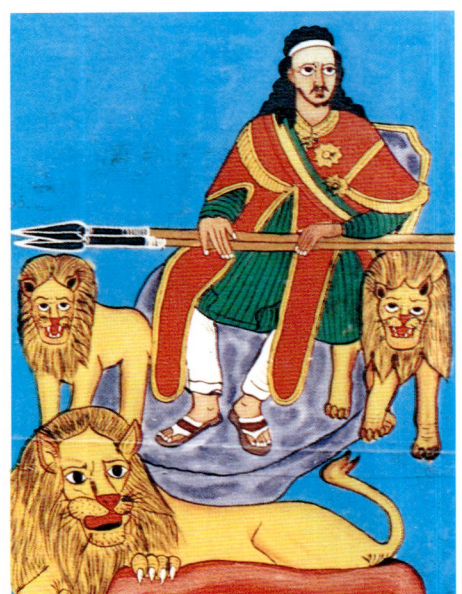

MENILEK II (FOLK PAINTING)

The Battle of Adowa, March 1, 1896

Taitu came out of her tent at the moment when the soldiers, seeing so many comrades falling around them, were hesitating to offer their chests to the bullets. She reprimanded them and revived their courage. How could a man flee when a woman was setting such an example of scorn for death?

She had the four cannons at her disposition placed near her and had them aimed at the center of a small Italian platoon, which soon surrendered. That is when the general ordered the troops to fall back, but as the battery that was supposed to protect the retreating men had fallen into enemy hands, their flight soon degenerated into chaos. Of eighty-one Italian officers, forty-eight were killed and the others wounded, among them Albertoni, who was made prisoner. Two thousand corpses remained on the field, for the wounded did not survive their hideous mutilations, which had been carried out against Menilek's orders.

It was ten o'clock in the morning. Only then did the second Italian detachment arrive, the Arismondi brigade of two thousand men and a good part of the Helena reserve of four thousand five hundred men, who had been able to join them. The combat was even more bloody than that of the night before, since daylight allowed for better aim, and, what's more, the wind dispersed the smoke from the Gras rifles.

Taitu, seeing her men falling like wheat under a scythe, urged them on anew, sending back into combat those who had carried in the wounded. Together with the other women, she administered first aid and gave them water, while the priests performed last rites for the dying.

An Incredible Victory

Henri d'Orléans wrote: "March 1, 1896 witnessed the impossible in colonial history: an army of whites was beaten, crushed, toppled, in organized combat, without ambush, by blacks."

Commander Antonnelli leaves without a word and the great council meets immediately. After a brief deliberation, they agree to issue an apology to the Italian nation. If need be, they will even concede some piece of territory on the edge of the Red Sea: anything to avoid war.

And that is when Taitu, the *yégésit*, the light of Ethiopia, utters the famous words that will guide the king's decision and lead their kingdom away from the grim angels of slavery and death:

"Oh Menilek," she says, her voice quavering, "Oh Negusa Nagast, I am the last of your servants, but I beg you to give the white men nothing. I beg you, along with all of Ethiopia, oh Menilek. For what you give them today will be a ladder to scale the walls of your fortress, and tomorrow they will come into your house: if you must lose, let it be with a weapon in your hand."

Taitu has known war since her childhood, its disasters and its sudden triumphs. Like other officers' wives, she has followed her four husbands in their faraway campaigns and has cared for them: she has lived through hunger, thirst, long marches, the horror of blades and the atrocity of firearms. And so in 1898, on the back of a mule, she sets out to meet the Italian troops along with her army of five thousand. This is the first time she has accompanied Emperor Menilek II to war; and it is also the first time she finds herself face to face with soldiers of white skin, conquerors of people of color all over the earth.

At the battle of Morelle, she opposes a frontal attack from the Italian lines; and, following her precise orders, the imperial army captures the enemy's water reserves. The Italians are soon obliged to surrender.

Then comes the great, the immense victory at Adowa, which will ring a death knell for the Italian presence in Ethiopia. Taitu is in the front line. At one point, the imperial troops hesitate. So the empress removes her veil, gets down from her mule, and walks toward the European troops protected by nothing more than a black silk parasol. Inspired, the Ethiopian troops leap into action: the Italian army will be utterly defeated.

At the end of the day, Taitu goes to the imperial tent and bows before the throne, before taking her seat next to the Negus. Despite the cries of the wounded around the tent, the moans of the dying, the queen's clothing is impeccable, and her behavior perfectly proper.

TAITU BETHEL AT THE BATTLE OF ADOWA (FOLK PAINTING) ▷

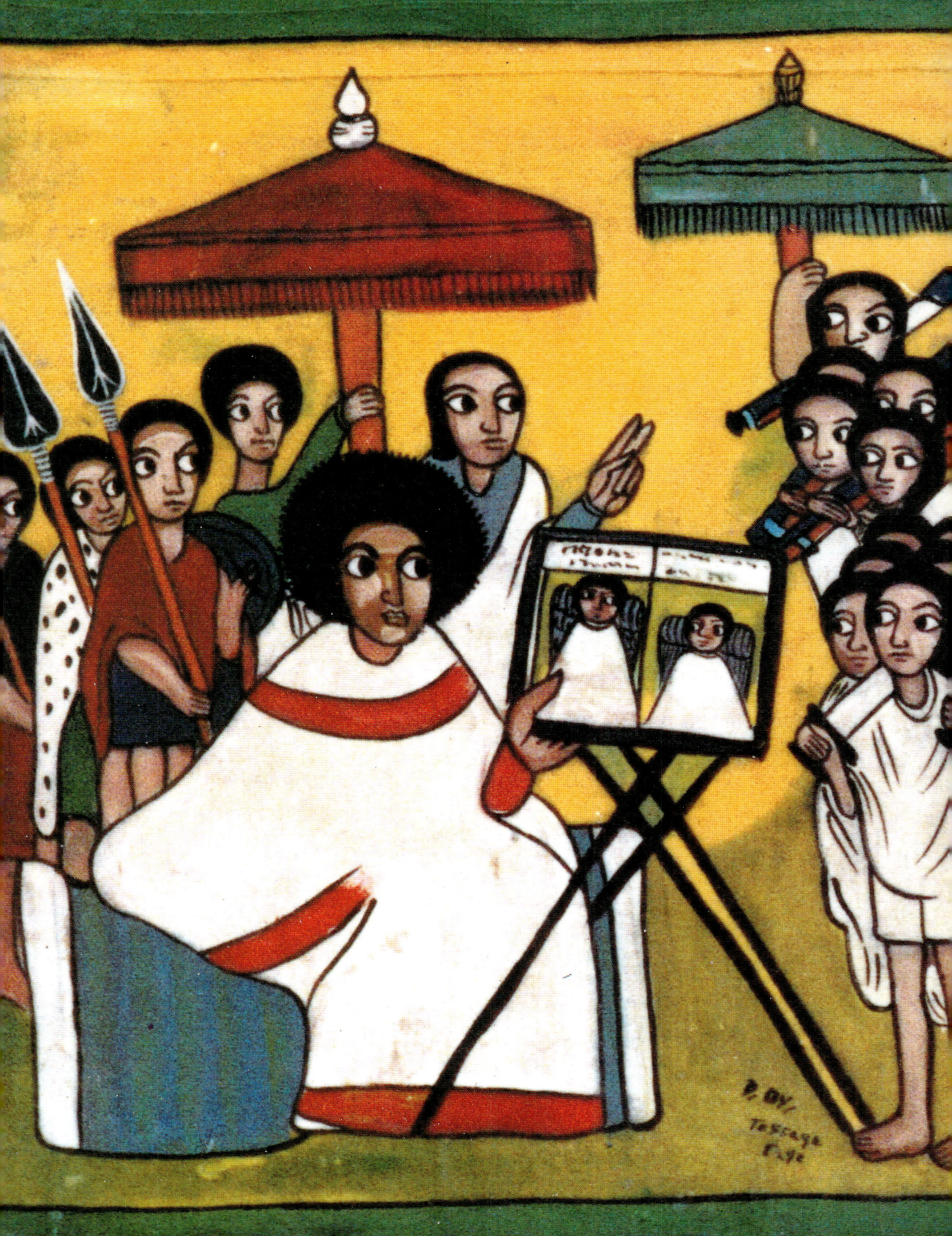

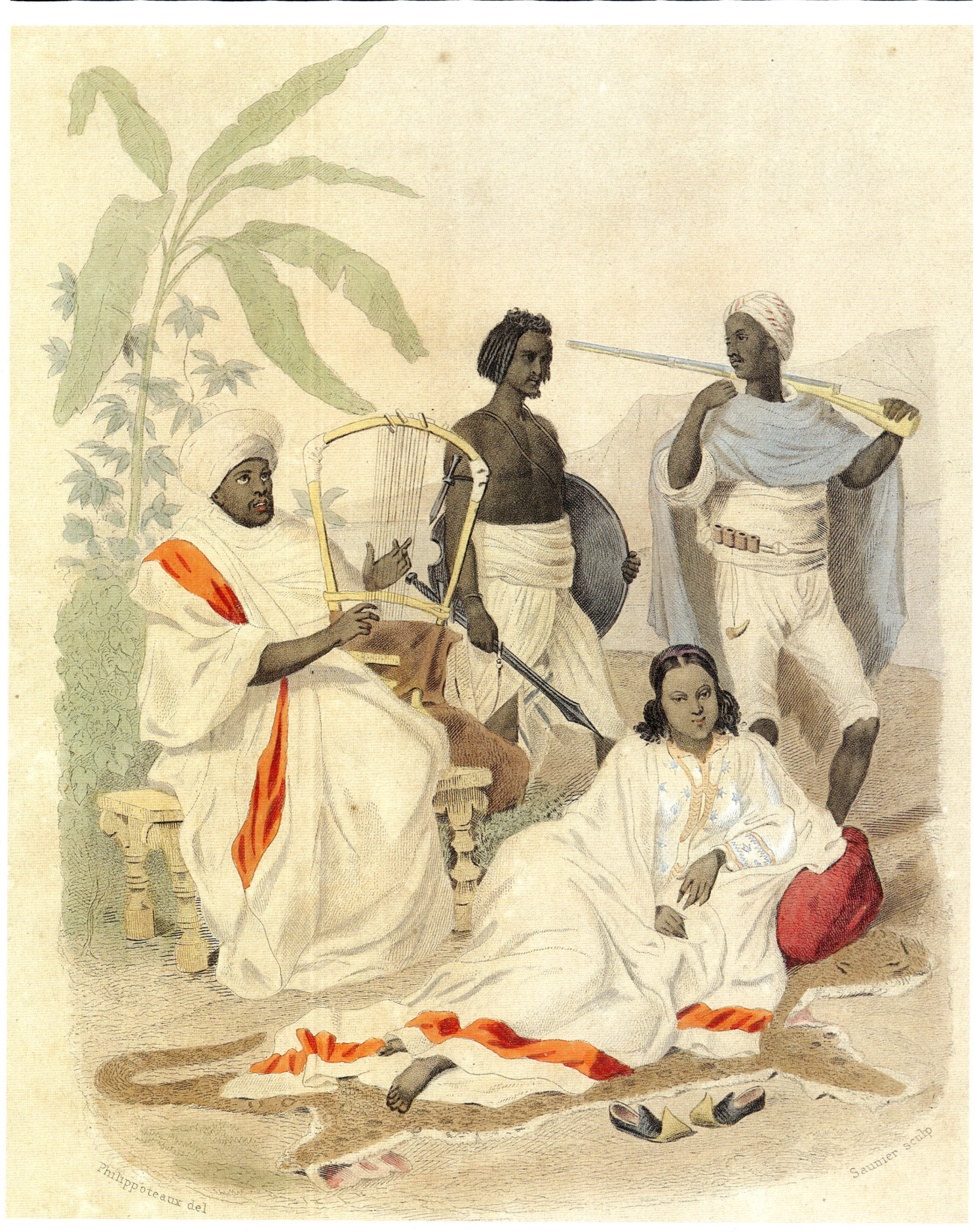

However, according to witnesses, her beautiful face is bathed in silent tears that flow without stopping throughout the audience given by the king the evening of the battle of Adowa.

Adowa gave Menilek international prestige. In the following months, the French and English governments signed treaties of friendship with him. The nations of Europe and the Middle East opened permanent diplomatic posts. It was the first time since Carthage, the first time in 2,500 years, that an African nation had beaten a Western country. This had a considerable effect throughout the black world. Numerous African American intellectuals came from the United States and even from Haiti to visit the region in the first years of the twentieth century. The first churches of Ethiopia were born, which would completely transform the relationship of black people with Christianity; Marcus Garvey and negritude were not far behind.

During the heyday of colonialism, the battle of Adowa reminded the world that the whites were not gods, that they too were subject to human limitations: it was the first note of hope in the midst of the chorus of lamentations of the conquered.

As soon as the war ended, the empress recovered her taste for poetry and chess, for theological debates, and for the little dishes she cooked, of which she seemed prouder than of all the rest. Many of her character traits have been noted, a thousand anecdotes have been told about her role in the country's domestic affairs, in which she appears, according to her friends, like an angel of light, and according to her enemies, like the "Great Spider" of the kingdom.

But above all, her memory is tied to the birth of Addis Ababa, the present capital of Ethiopia.

Ethiopia has known many imperial cities since the founding of Aksum at the beginning of the Christian era. Over the centuries, the role of capital city has been played by Nush, Arka, Tegulet, Sokota, Barra, Gondar, Dabra-Tabor, Adowa, Antawlou, and Entoto.

It was there, in Entoto, that Menilek II had established himself, at the summit of a mountain over 9,000 feet above sea level: it was very cold there, the slopes were bare, and there was hardly any wood to burn for heat.

One day, Taitu came down to bathe at the foot of the mountain and felt that the air was mild. She said to Menilek: "I would like to build a house here, on the bank of this river." And she had a house built there, then a second, a third, a fourth: and all these houses became the new capital of the kingdom. Taitu baptized it Addis Ababa, which means "new flower" in Amharic.

◁ "THE EMPRESS RECOVERED HER TASTE FOR POETRY..."

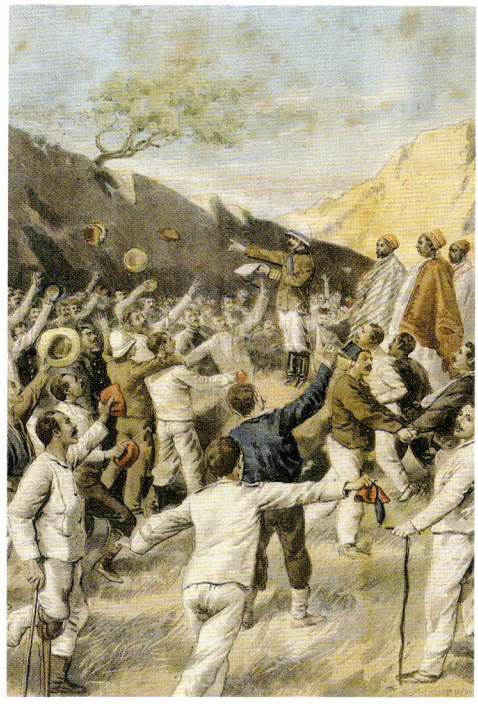

LIBERATION OF THE ITALIAN PRISONERS

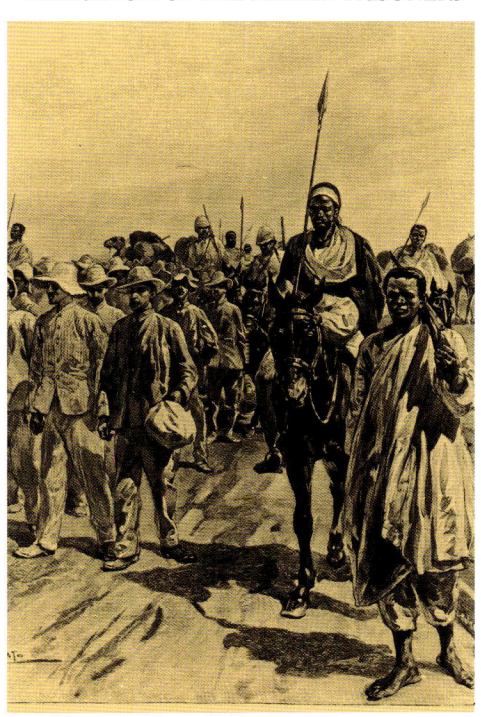

ITALIAN PRISONERS

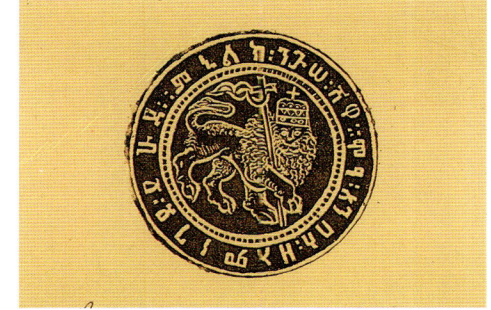

MENILEK'S SEAL

But Taitu wanted all the glory of the founding of the city to belong to the king; and when he installed a water purification system, she wrote the following poem for the occasion:

We have had news from Addis Ababa
They say that the waters adore Emperor Menilek
Oh Menilek, what wisdom will you bring us next?
Already you made the water climb mountains
And now the water becomes pure
Now the impure becomes bright as a baby's eye
And the thirsty may drink
Oh Menilek!

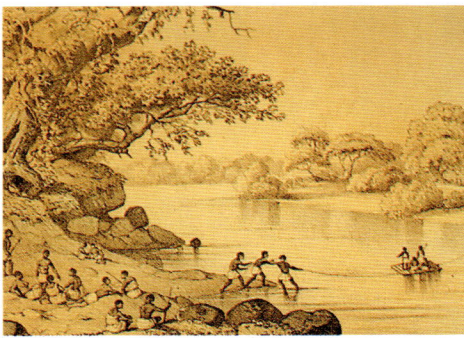

THE HAWASH RIVER

Menilek fell ill in 1906, and Taitu Bethel stayed by his side until his death in 1913, governing the kingdom from a back room. Then she withdrew into a convent, soon to die there out of grief over the passing of the man she thought she had married without love.

So ends the story of Taitu Bethel.

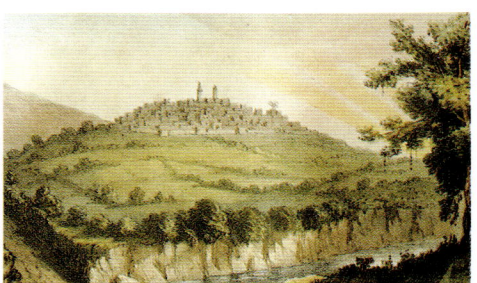

HARAR VILLAGE

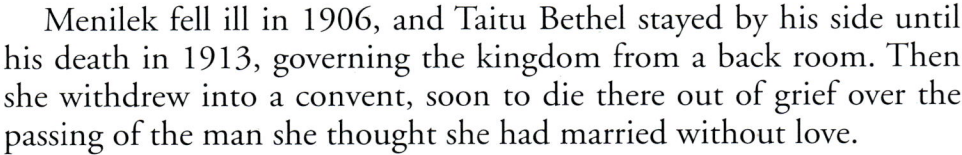

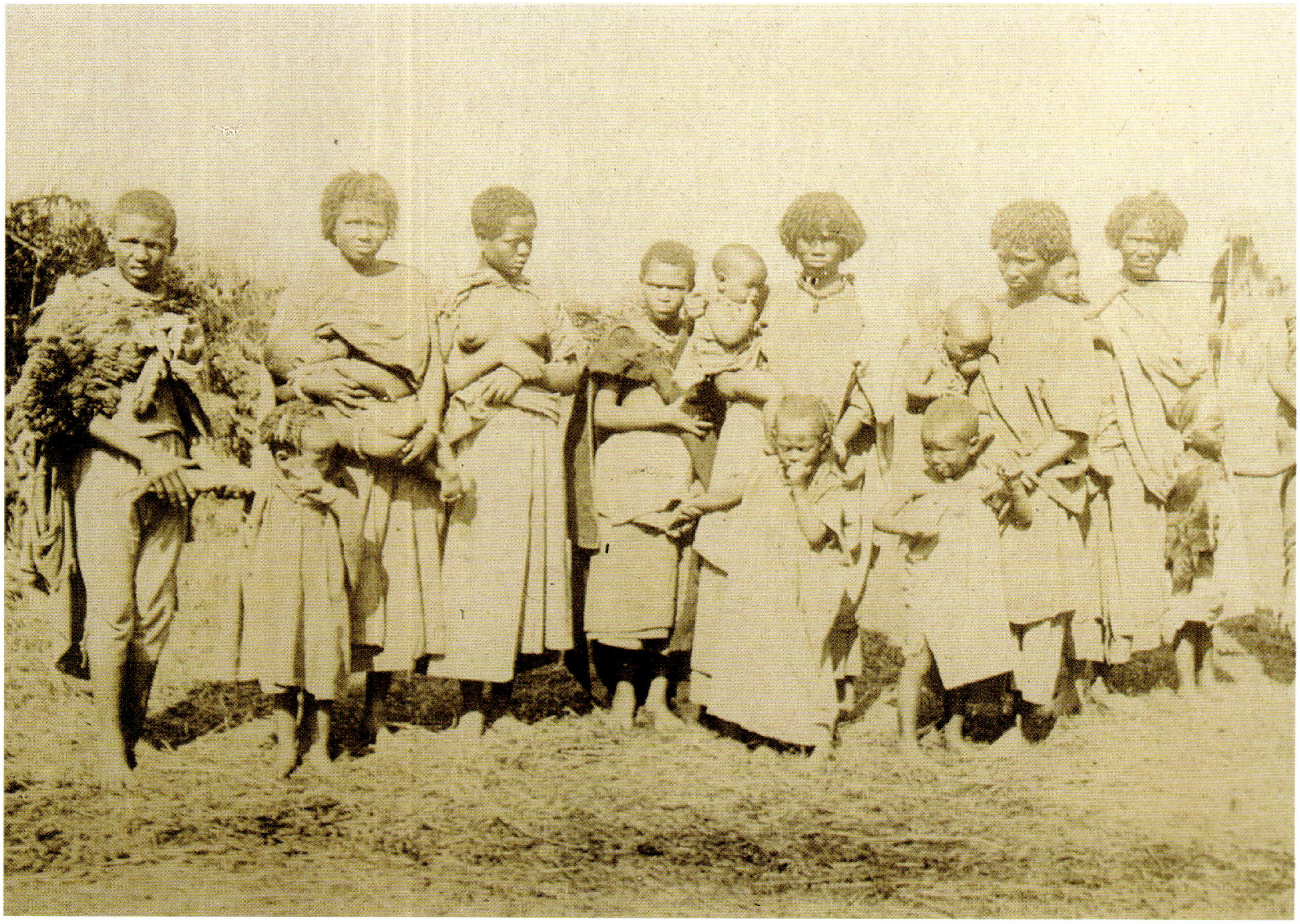

WOMEN OF HARAR

KOULLO WOMAN ▷

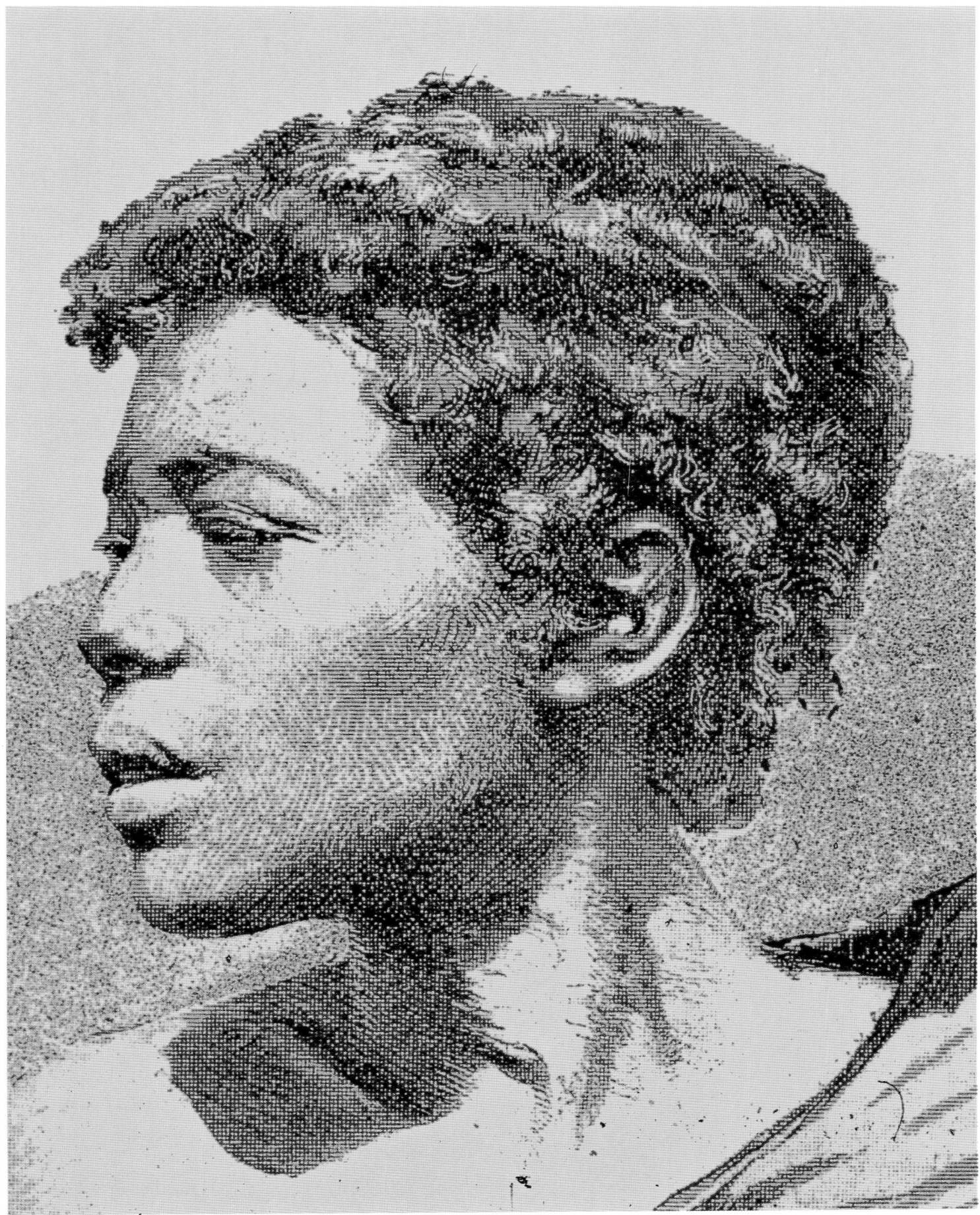

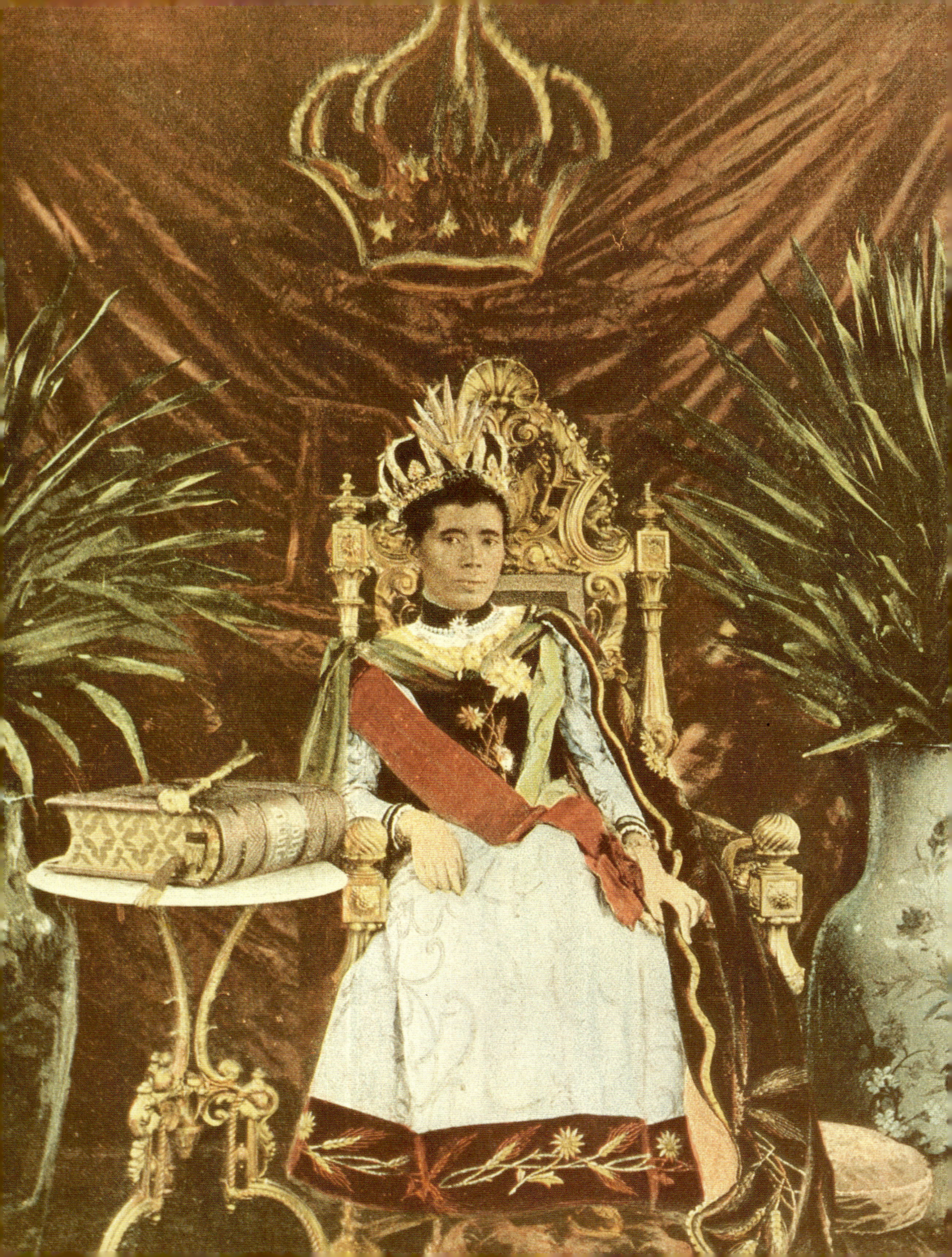

RANAVALONA III

LAST MONARCH OF MADAGASCAR

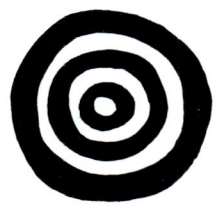

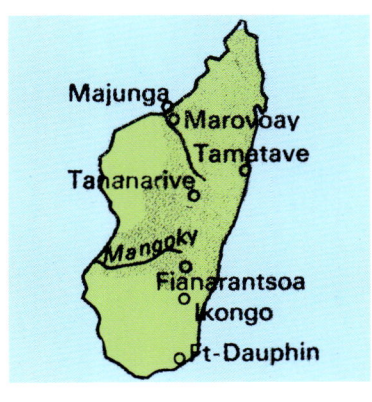

Short, slight, with a tiny child's face, she was twenty-two the day of her coronation; and she was perhaps the young woman least likely to wear the crown in the whole kingdom...

ALL HER LIFE, THE GREAT RANAVALONA I BITTERLY OPPOSED WESTERN PENETRATION. SHE WANTED ORDER, INDEPENDENCE, AND THE CONTINUATION OF THE TRADITIONAL IDENTITY OF THE MALAGASY PEOPLE.

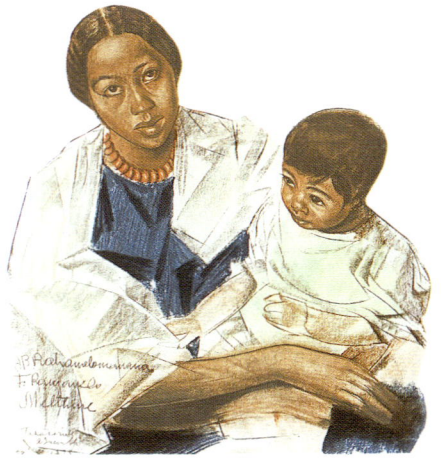
MALAGASY MOTHER AND CHILD, A. IACOVLEFF

Her death marked the end of her policies: the scales again tipped in favor of the whites and the emulation of Europe.

In the years to come, the royal palace would be deluged by clocks, porcelain vases, and Bibles.

Each of the rulers who succeeded her added his or her own touch to the tableau: Rakotond Radama II (1861–1863), Ranavalona I's son, a whimsical modernist who loved mechanical toys and three-piece suits and died strangled by a silk toga; then Queen Rasohérina (1863–1868), expert in frills and flounces and fragile knickknacks; and finally Queen Ranavalona II (1868–1883), a great pusher of prayer books, who introduced the Protestant religion to the court and made it the be all and end all of high fashion.

During this time, colonial ideas were making headway in the West: by 1885, the Conference of Berlin had carefully carved up black Africa like a Christmas goose and Admiral Pierre had attacked the port of Majunga.

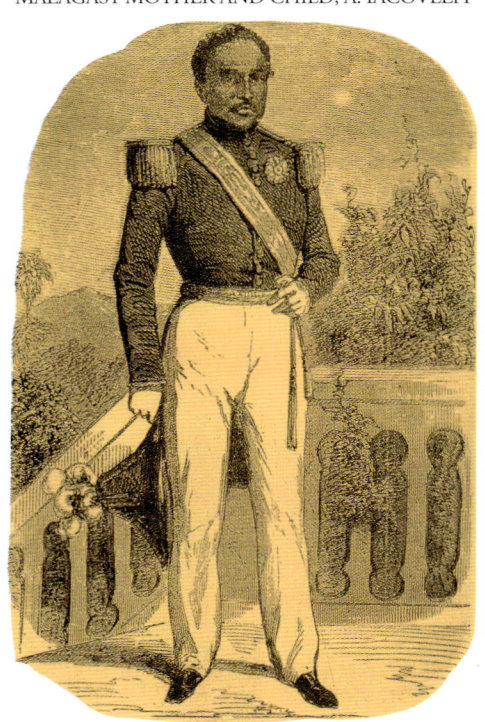
KING RADAMA II, A WHIMSICAL MODERNIST

On hearing this last news, the delicate Ranavalona II spoke up for the first time in her life, and rejected France's ultimatum. But all the emotion was too much for her heart: a month later, she expired in her palace, exhausted with rage, still trembling with indignation.

The power then fell into still weaker, more languid hands, so to speak: the tiny, frail, barely formed, childish hands of Ranavalona III, the last sovereign of Madagascar.

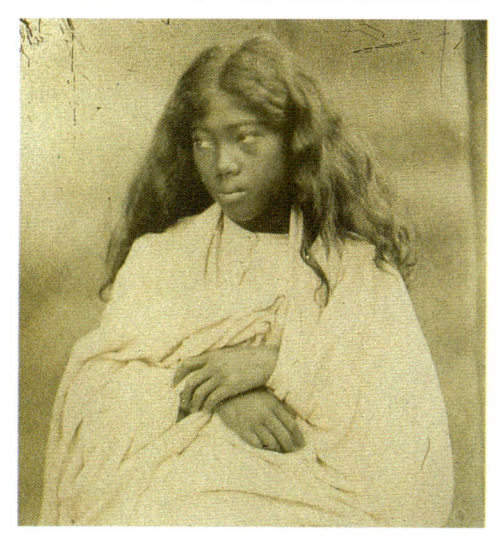
YOUNG HOVA GIRL

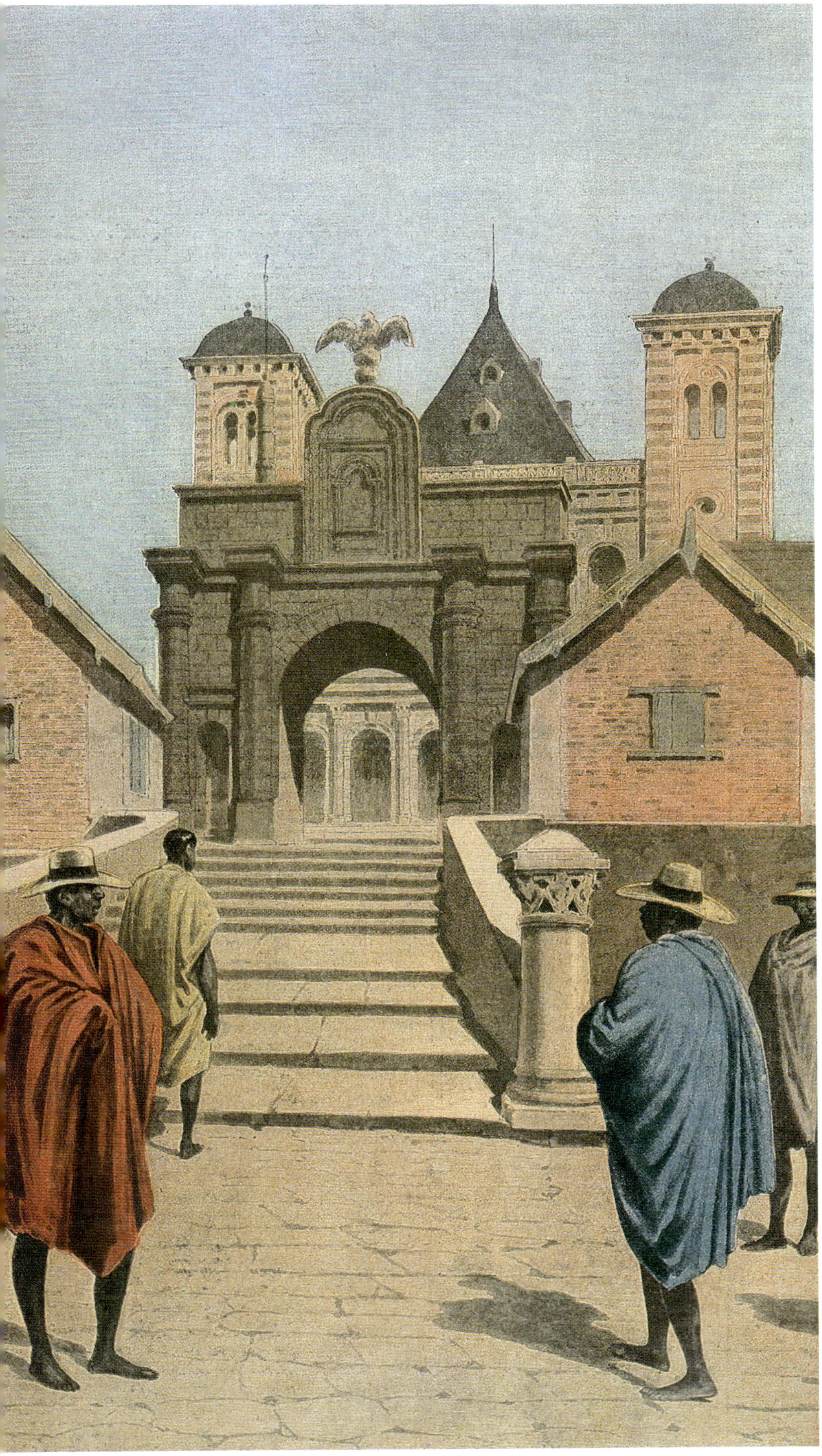

RANAVALONA III

THE QUEEN'S PALACE AT TANANARIVE

The Giant Darafély

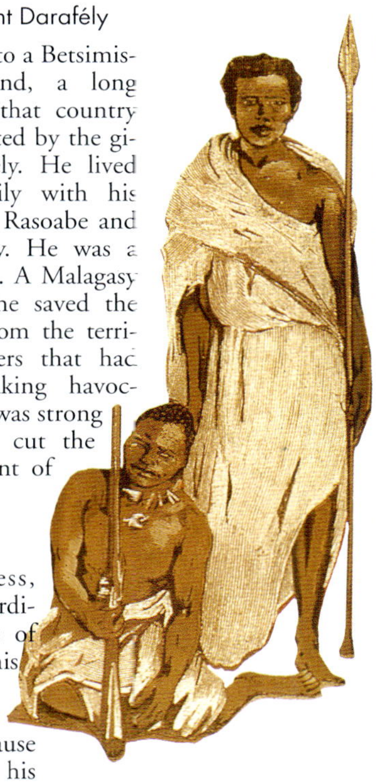

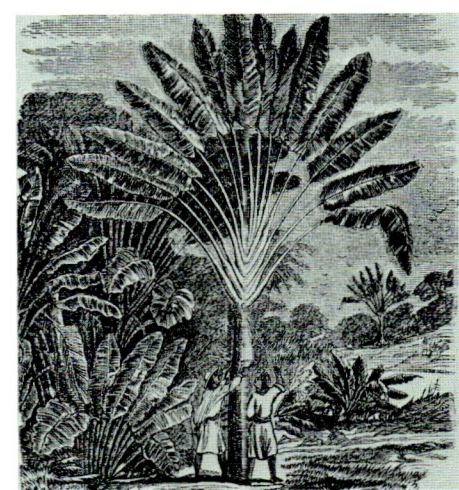

According to a Betsimisaraka legend, a long time ago, that country was inhabited by the giant Darafély. He lived very happily with his two wives, Rasoabe and Rasoamasay. He was a good genie. A Malagasy Hercules, he saved the province from the terrible monsters that had been wreaking havoc there, and was strong enough to cut the huge serpent of Tanifotsy into tiny pieces. Nonetheless, the extraordinary deeds of one of his neighbors troubled him because they hurt his pride. Darafély declared war on his neighbor, and in an epic struggle, managed to throw him into the waves, but not without losing his right hand, which the vanquished man tore off in his last effort. Some time afterward, Darafély died from his wound. The powerful right hand of the giant forms Fonga Island, and the site of the battle was called Maitanana. Rasoabe and Rasoamasay, Darafély's inconsolable widows, cried torrents of tears in the deserted forests, turning them into immense lakes.

The Traveler's Tree

The traveler's tree owes its name to the following quality: it always furnishes a certain amount of fresh water that is safe to drink when you pierce a petiole, that is, a leafstem, with a spear or other pointed instrument.

The Woman Child

The woman-child walks forward with rhythm,
dressed in blue—a second morning!
She has a rose lamba, dragging along,
and a wild rose in her hair.

Is it a sheaf of high grass,
is it a reed
that trembles at the edge of the wood?
Is it a swallow on a calm day,
or a blue dragonfly along the river?

The woman-child walks forward with rhythm,
suddenly silent with happiness,
She is listening to three valihas, a wooden drum,
fiddles and flutes.

But now her lips are trembling,
dreams are pouring out
so irresistible they become moans
and later even songs!

And the old woman is touched too
and comes to take part in the dance:
a piece of her cloth is in the dust,
like her declining days.

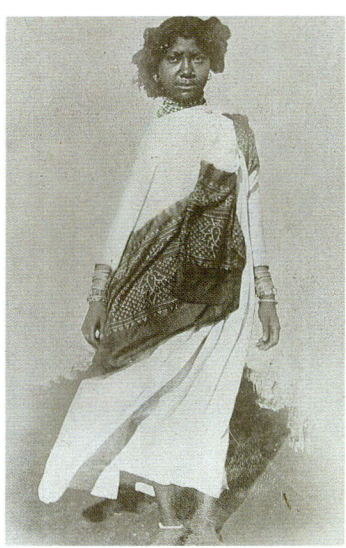

SAKALAVA WOMAN

Neither moans nor songs
flutter on her face:
only tears suffuse it
with the memory of all the dead...

Remembering... Like a full moon
Close to tipping over and disappearing,
here is springtime losing its leaves
becoming nothing more than a tomb of dead
leaves...

And their fingers meet:
the frail fingers of the woman-child
and the lifeless fingers of the old woman,
fingers alike in their translucence,
meet and form
a sort of bridge
that links the dusk
on the hills, already closing
the day the cock had crowed!

J.-J. Rabéarivelo
Presque Songes
(Almost Dreams)

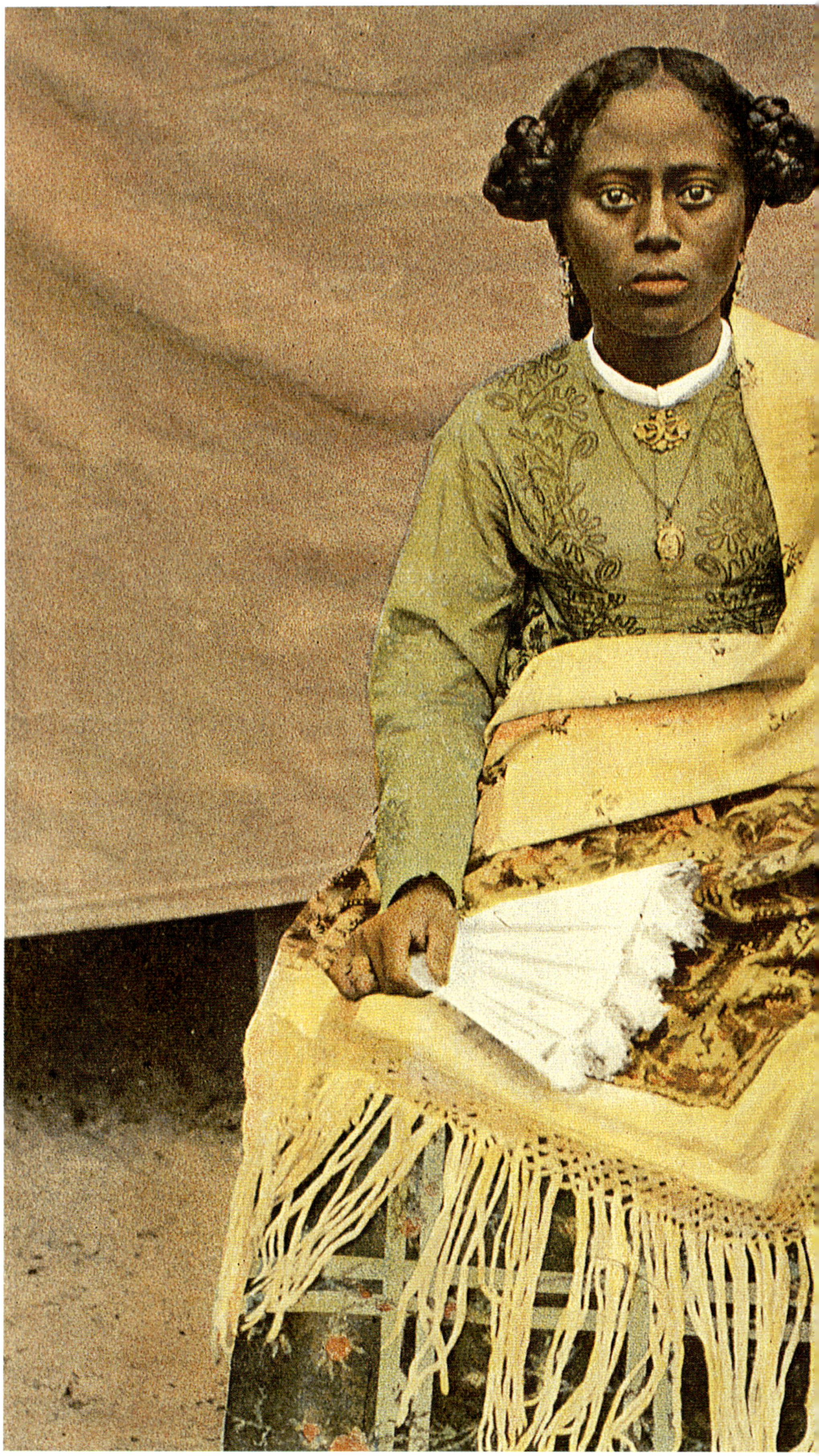

BENINKA WOMAN

RANAVALONA III

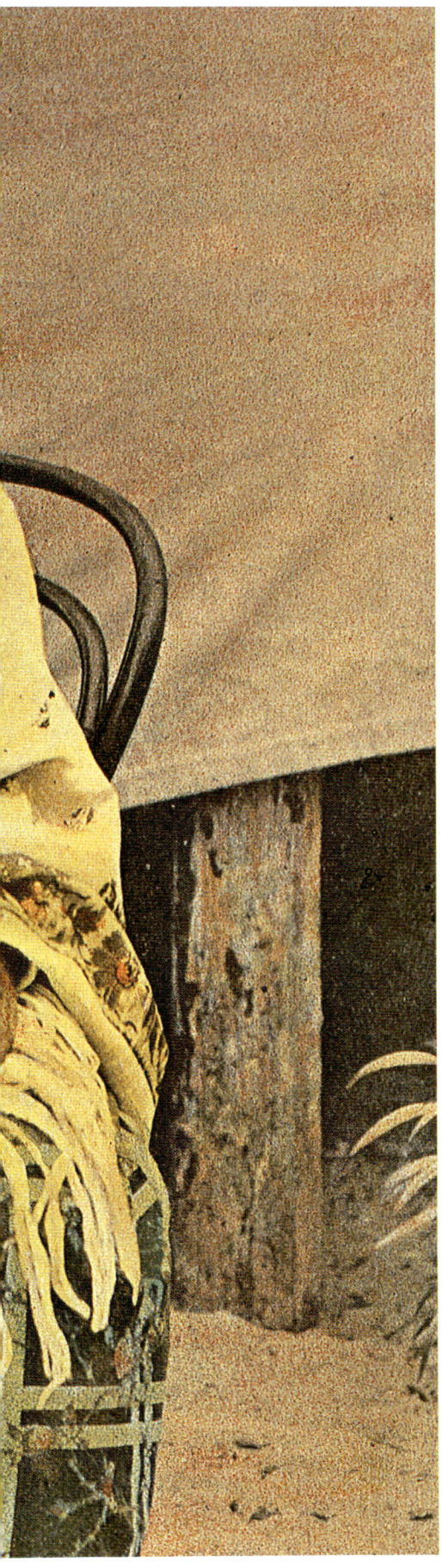

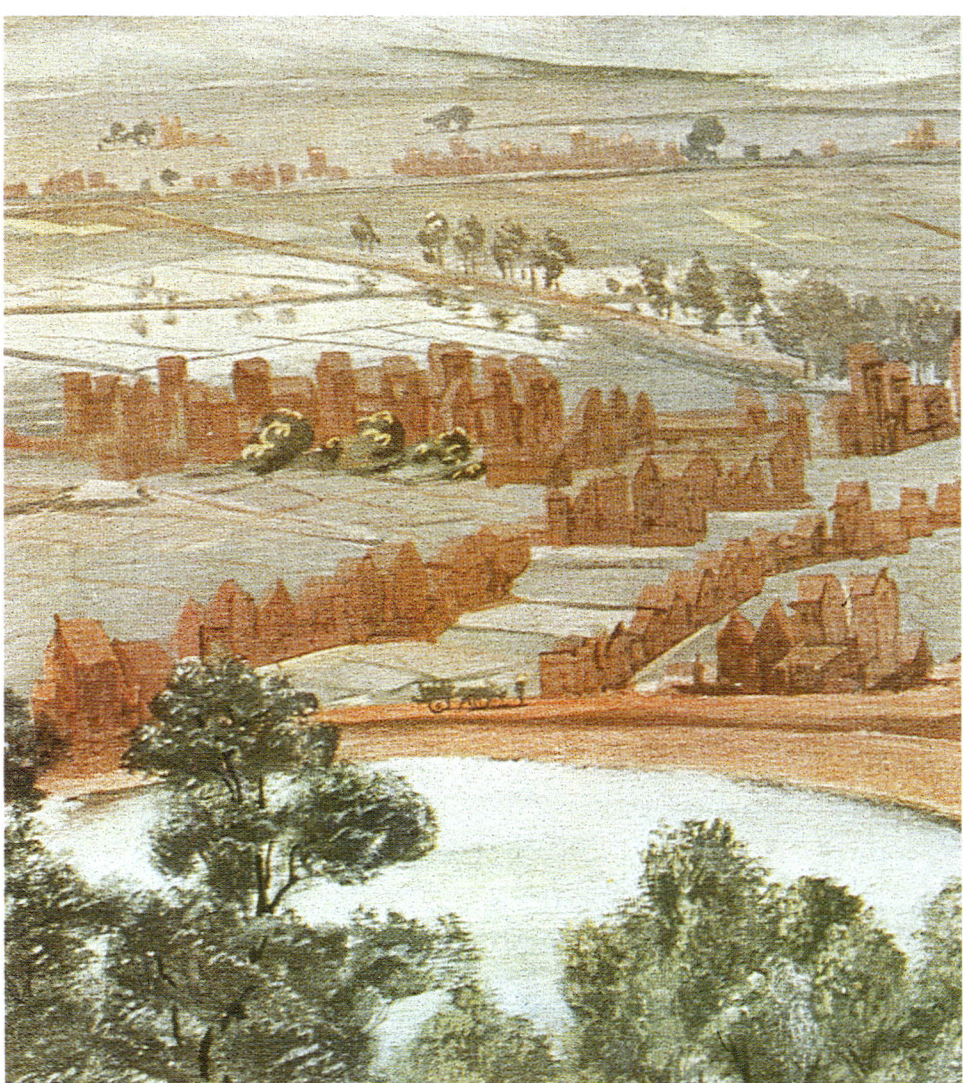

TANANARIVE, A. IACOVLEFF

According to Malagasy wisdom, "Being a girl without a mother is being on a mountain without a path; and being a girl without a father is being on a mountain without water." Ranavalona III was on a mountain with neither path nor water. She was a simple young country girl taken in by her aunt, Ranavalona II, who had taught her, as well as could be expected, her profession as a queen, which she hardly knew herself.

Short, slight, with a tiny child's face, she was twenty-two the day of her coronation; and she was perhaps the young woman least likely to wear the crown in the whole kingdom. Her aunt had often repeated to her: "Be a monster if you must, but be a queen." But Ranavalona III was, and would be until the end, a monster of sweetness, insignificance, and true humility.

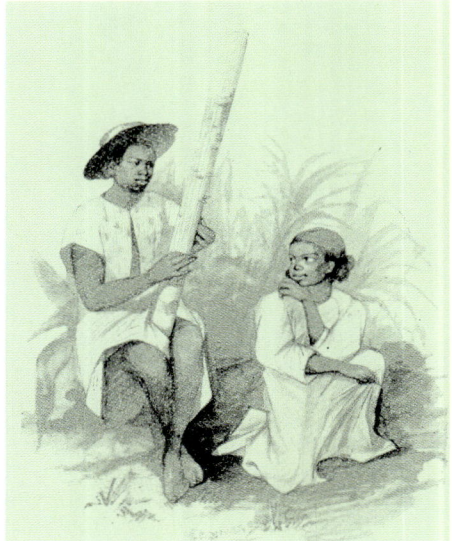

The Legend of Tritriva

Down in the west, at the foot of a mountain, there were two villages next to each other: in one lived a young man renowned for his strength and agility; in the other lived a young woman of remarkable beauty. The two young people were engaged; they had sworn eternal love. However, they could not marry. Their families, divided by violent hatred, would never consent to the union they desired. Neither prayers, nor tears, nor entreaties could move the inflexible parents of these poor children. Desperate and tired of life, the young couple climbed the mountain of Tritriva. They tied themselves together with their silk lambas (togas) and threw themselves into the bottomless lake.

From that day on, each time a young woman died in the village of the unhappy girl, half the water of Lake Tritriva would be tinted red. And each time that a young man passed away in the village of the desperate boy, all the water of the lake would turn red.

Andrianampoinimerina, who reigned in Tananarive at that time, understood the will of fate. In a solemn decree, he ordered all his subjects no longer to resist their children's desires but to let them follow their tastes and inclinations.

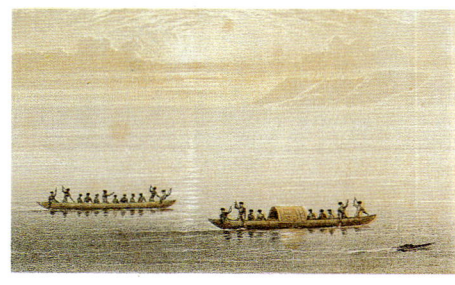

Proverb

"Fate is like a chameleon on top of a tree. All it takes is for a child to blow on it for it to change color."

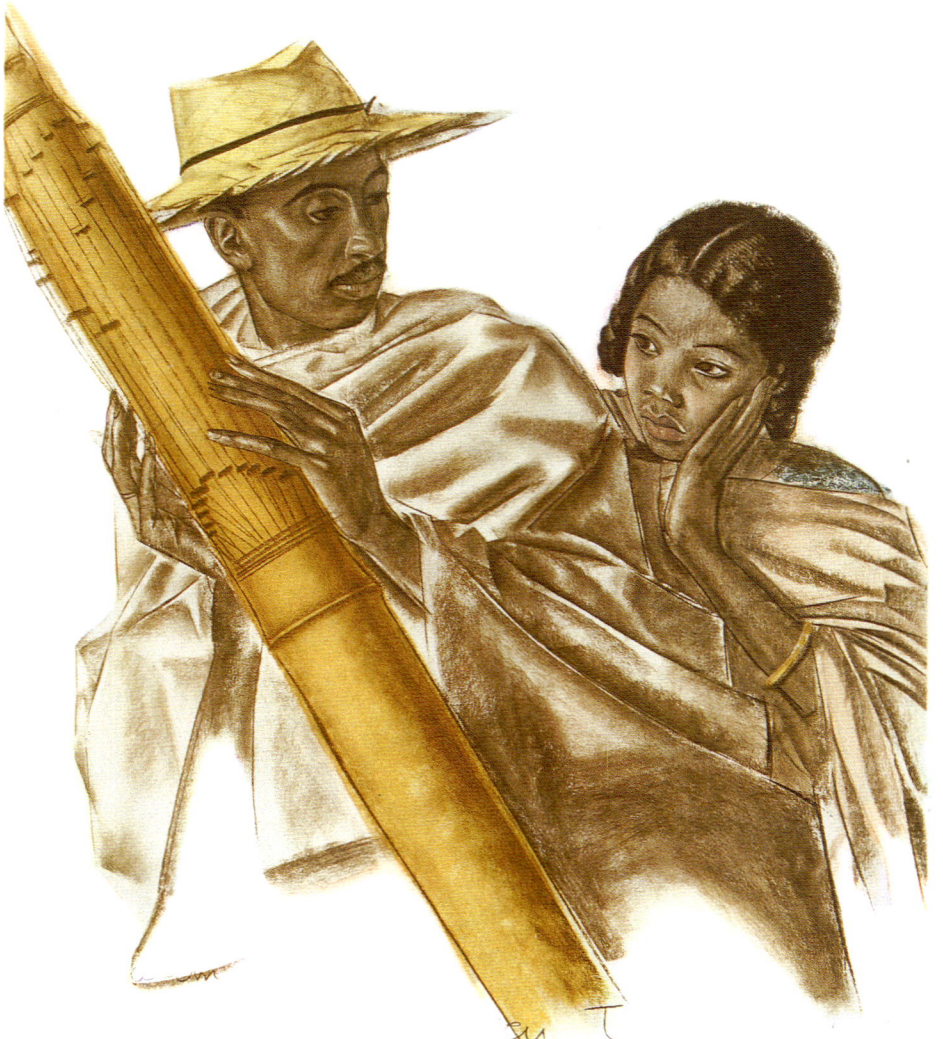

MUSICIANS, A. IACOVLEFF

Ah! If the gods had asked her, she would probably have chosen to live in one of those houses of reddish clay, red brick over ocher earth; one of those poor huts that melt under the strong rains and that must be rebuilt by hand as time passes, just as every day we rebuild our lives. Yes, if the gods had asked her, as a little girl, she would have preferred corncob dolls to silken ones; and later, she would have gone to plant the rice in the plains of Tananarive, sinking down to her ankles in the soft, creamy earth trampled like malanga puree by the zebus. Then, after the harvest, she would have gone to the festival of the first sheaf of rice, the Santa-bary, where she would have danced among the oxen, their horns adorned with balls of gold, and among the young men in red waistcoats, who would have romped around her whispering provocative songs:

May I come in, precious Rasoa?
Come in, Randriamatoa, I will spread a clean mat for you.
I do not want a clean mat, I want a corner of your lamba.

RANAVALONA III

On November 22, her birthday and the day of her coronation, she went dressed in white to Ambohimanga, the city of the founding princes, to acquire the "holiness of the ancestors" there; then, wearing a long dress with an endless train like the tail of a Chinese dragon, she went to the stone of Mahamasina to obtain the "power of the ancestors."

A crowd of five hundred thousand people surrounded the hill of Andrahalo. Ranavalona climbed up on the holy rock and stood in the wind.

Spread out in the distance were the little clay huts, so much like her, an ordinary young woman, the most ordinary of all, a simple blade of grass in Madagascar.

She knew that she would never know the sweetness of these huts, and, after a sigh of regret, she turned her gaze toward the Blue Mountain that sheltered the "Rova," the palace of King Andrianampoinimerina. Finally, she stood as straight and tall as she could on the sacred rock and proclaimed in a shrill voice that flew out and then slowly descended over the silent crowd:

"Here is what I have to say to you, oh my People! God gave me this country, God gave me this kingdom, and I thank him. The great Andrianampoinimerina, and Radama I, Ranavalona I, Rasohérina, Ranavalona II, have bequeathed this kingdom unto me as my heritage. Consequently, if anyone should wish to take a piece of this land, so much as a hair of it, I will go forth as if I were a man to defend our country. Is this not true, oh my People?"

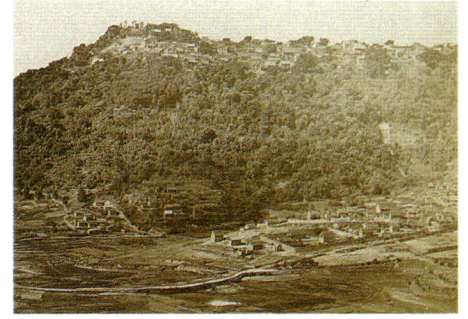

If You Went to Ambohimanga

If you went to Ambohimanga,
I would ask you for a little favor.
Please bring me three mangoes,
So I may leave you for three years.
But today I am yours alone,
Tomorrow, I am my mother's and father's.
Love is a seed of rice:
It grows in its new place...

The Charms of the Malagasy Language

The frequent usage of figurative expressions is one of the great charms of the Malagasy language. Many of these expressions are compound words or sentences. Here are a few examples: *mitsamboki-mokympi*, literally, "jump with closed eyes," means "venture forth boldly." *Mitsipi-dòhà-àkà-mitana* is an expression formed from the contraction of several words which means "kick the bow of a passing canoe," that is, "misconstrue a demonstration of kindness." There is a corresponding proverb in English: "Don't bite the hand that feeds you." *Rùmomàso-tsy-miàrak'àman-pàty:* "not to accompany the dying with water from the eyes," in other words, "not to cry at (a friend's) death," means to do something at the wrong time, or not to take advantage of an opportunity or, even, to repent too late.

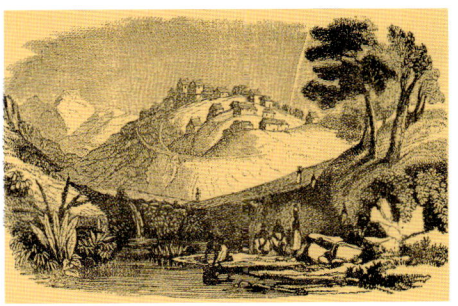

Tell the Clouds to Wait

Tell the clouds to wait
The wind is dying down
Tell the lake to forget
The birds are not coming to sleep.
It is bad to forget everything at once
It is good to forget little by little.

Proverb

"Soft wood is not split by lightning."

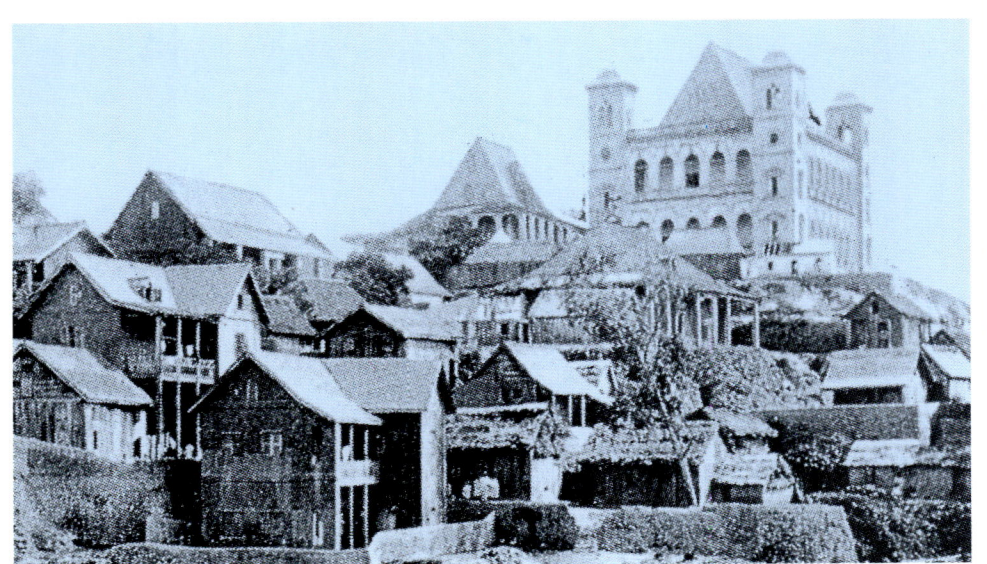

ROYAL PALACE AND COURT OF JUSTICE

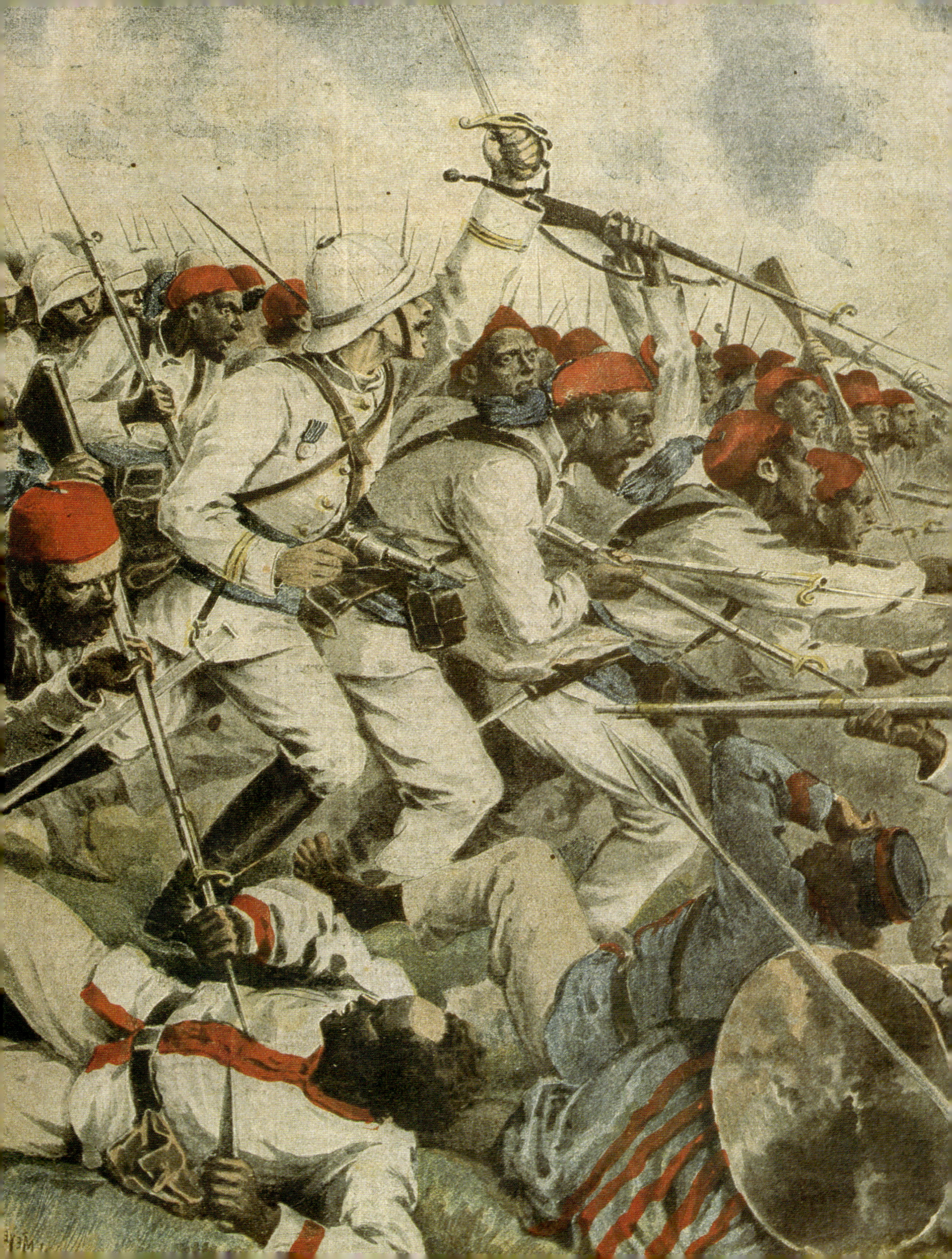

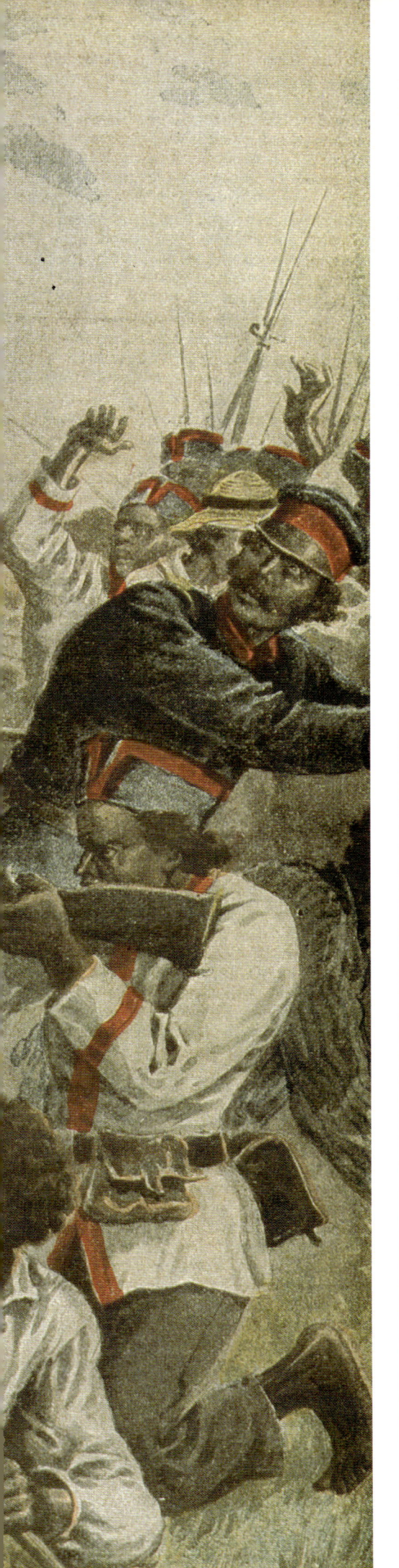

RANAVALONA III

On August 16, 1890, the two pearls of the Indian Ocean entered the sphere of influence of the great colonial powers: England claimed Zanzibar, and the French Republic cast its beneficent shadow over the island of Madagascar.

Fifteen thousand French soldiers were ready to get to work. After the usual barrage of the artillery, the ports of Tamatave and Majunga were taken by force in January 1895. To the ears of the Malagasy peasants, the cannons thundered like gods. By September, six thousand men had arrived at the outskirts of Tananarive. The little queen was prepared to continue the resistance in the south, but a rain of cannonballs crashed through the palace roof; with such an eloquent demonstration, the great council decided in favor of surrender. An act of protectorate was signed, and the royal army turned its weapons over to France.

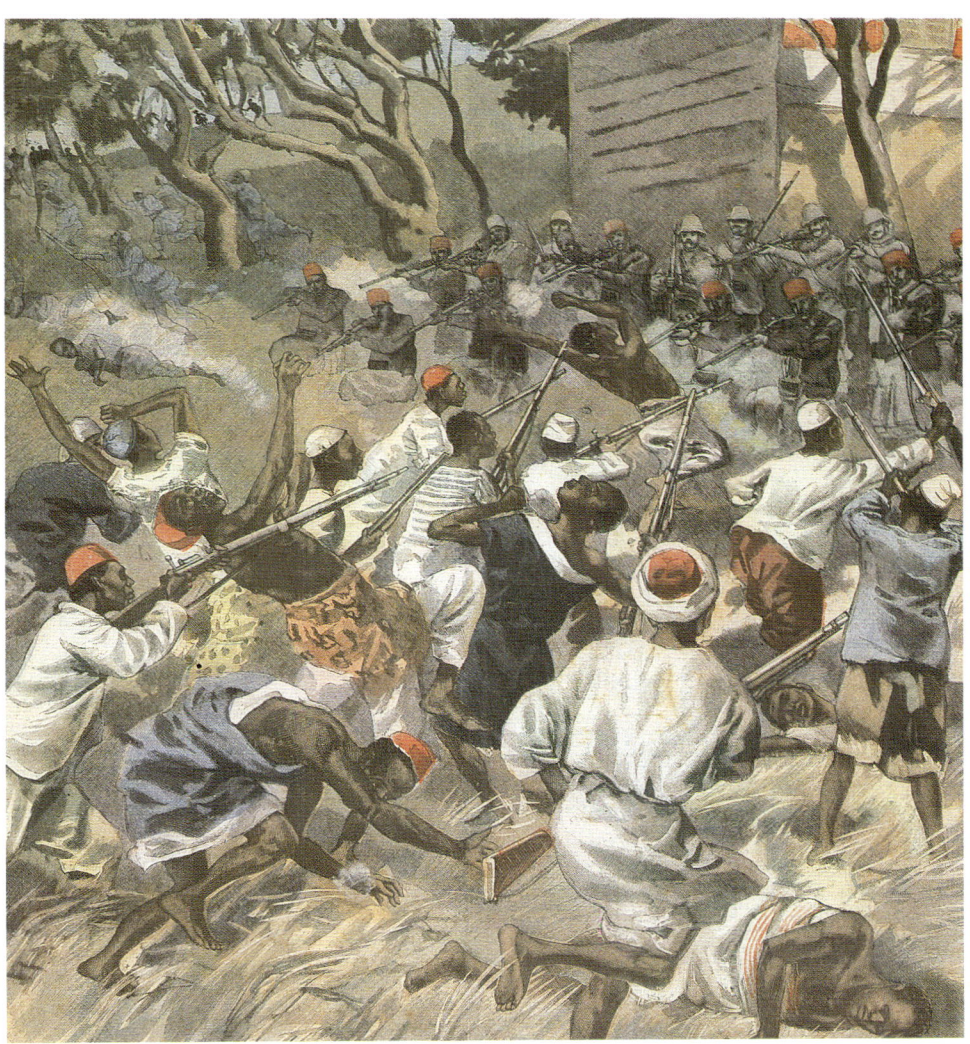

"THE CANNONS THUNDERED..."

Zebu

The cattle of Madagascar are humped oxen related to the zebus of India and eastern Africa. With long legs and horns, they are gentle and docile. Their meat is good. The hump on its shoulders can grow very large when the beasts are fattened up; it is considered to be a delicacy.

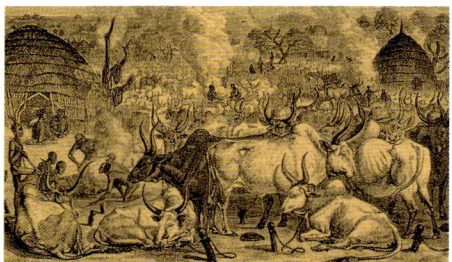

Blue Root Onion

Blue root onion
Blue leaf sugarcane
Even the shadow of her lamba smells good
The lamba she wears, even better.

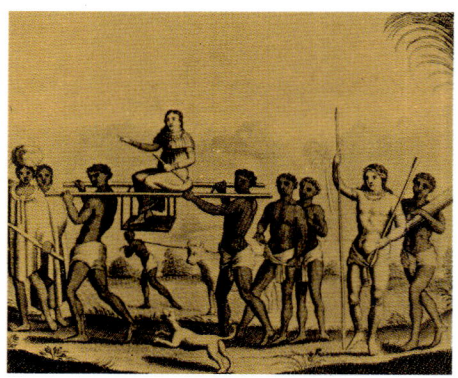

The Filanzana

The royal litter, or *filanzana,* is made up of a large armchair, attached to two wooden bars, and carried by four strong men, *maromitas,* as they are called in the region. They travel at a run and yet their movement is not jolting, since the porters have trained to run in step with one another. Every five minutes they shift the bar to the other shoulder, passing it over their heads without slowing their pace.

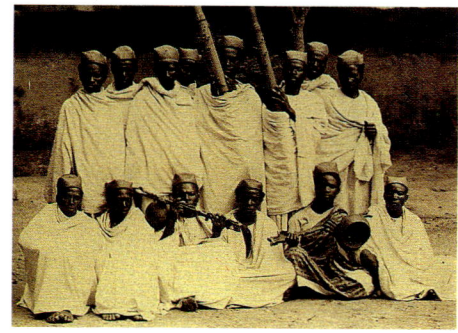

FILANZANA PORTERS

Yet a murmur rose from the depths of Madagascar, and the conflict that had scarcely been ended gave way to a popular revolt. The whole country could think of nothing but freeing the little queen, held prisoner, it was said, by the cruel French. The rebels wore a sun shell, the *falana,* on their foreheads, and their shoulders were draped with the *menalamba* (red togas) of the holy wars. France, taking the plunge, decided on annexation, pure and simple, on August 5, 1896.

General Joseph-Simon Gallieni was the great theoretician of French colonization. His doctrine, more clever than it might seem, rested on the systematic occupation, down to the last hamlet, of the conquered territory. His troops tracked down the "men with shells" and massacred a few rebel groups who did not understand the benefits of civilization. Half of the queen's entourage was exiled, the rest executed.

Commerce followed in the footsteps of combat: in Paris, the Madagascar Committee was created, an important financial group seduced by the economic prospects of the Great Island. Forced labor was introduced; then, and this was the fruit of Gallieni's subtle genius, laziness was criminalized, and thus the Department of Bridge and Road Works was furnished with "convict" laborers.

But the rebellion did not die out; it was said to be supported by the queen in her palace in Tananarive, by means of rays of light sent as signals from the windows of her room.

Finally, in 1897, General Gallieni eliminated the Malagasy monarchy with a stroke of his pen and decided that the last sovereign was to be exiled; and so she had to pack her bags.

She left at about two o'clock in the morning, February 27, 1897. The weather was stormy, and the tropical rain blew through the canopy of the filanzana, drenching the young woman. This was followed by a blazing sun; and the litter and its porters trundled along through the inclement weather for days and nights. Finally, the little queen, who had never left the region of Tananarive, was so astonished at the extent of her territory that she asked:

"Will we be in France soon?"

The queen, throned and dethroned, but still an ordinary young woman, was first deported to the island of Réunion, where the colonizers came to examine her with interest, with that curiosity tinged with sympathy that people have for extinct species. Then she boarded a great ship that took her even further from the royal palace, from Tananarive, Madagascar, and the Indian Ocean, to end the eternal captivity that was her life in 1917 in a villa in Algiers.

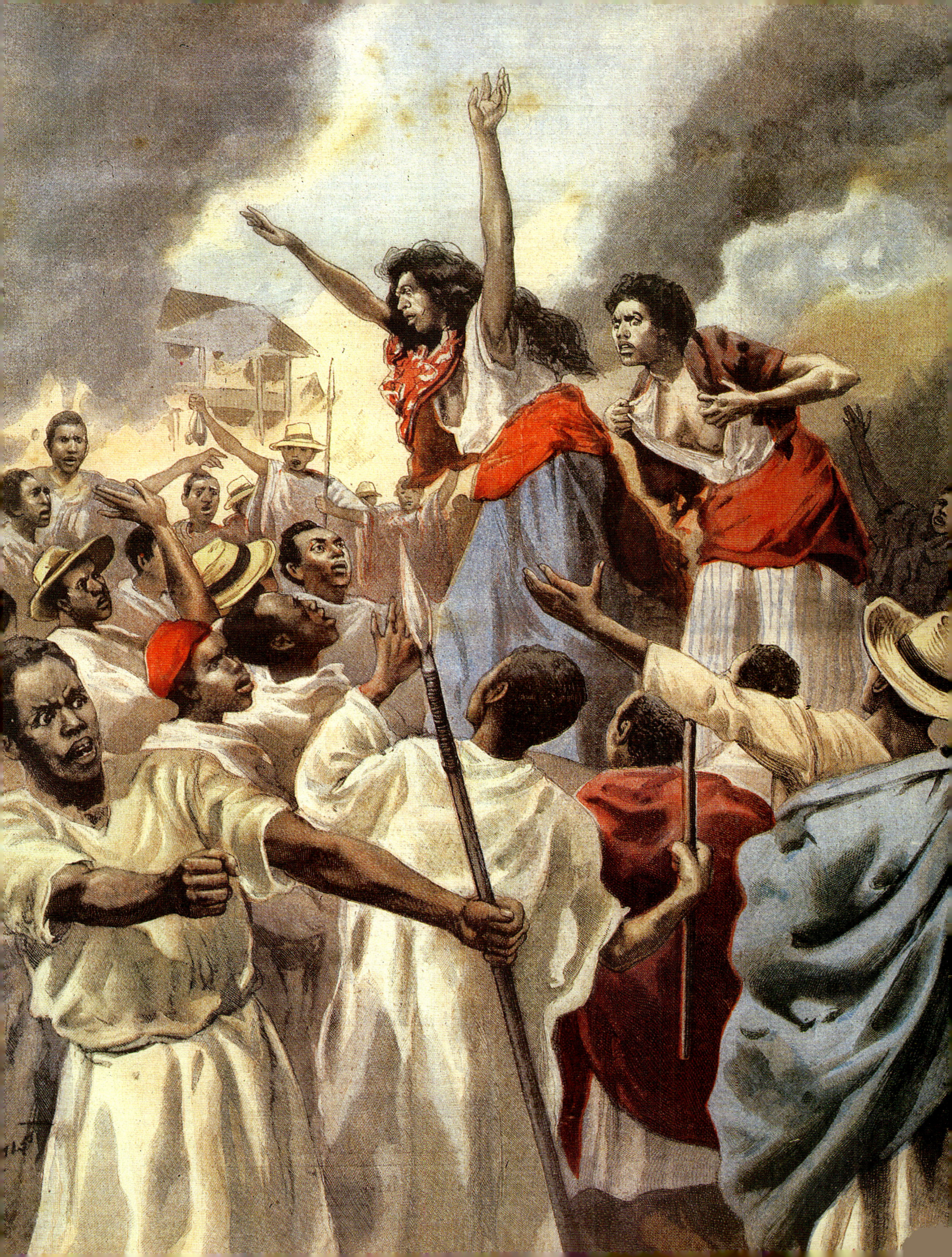

There, on the city's heights, she met old Béhanzin, the hero of Dahomey's struggle for independence, who had just been extricated from Fort Tartenson in Martinique. For a few months, a strange friendship developed between the old man and the little girl, both sharing a common nostalgia for their lost homelands, and, of course, a common sense of their dignity, intact with respect to and in spite of History.

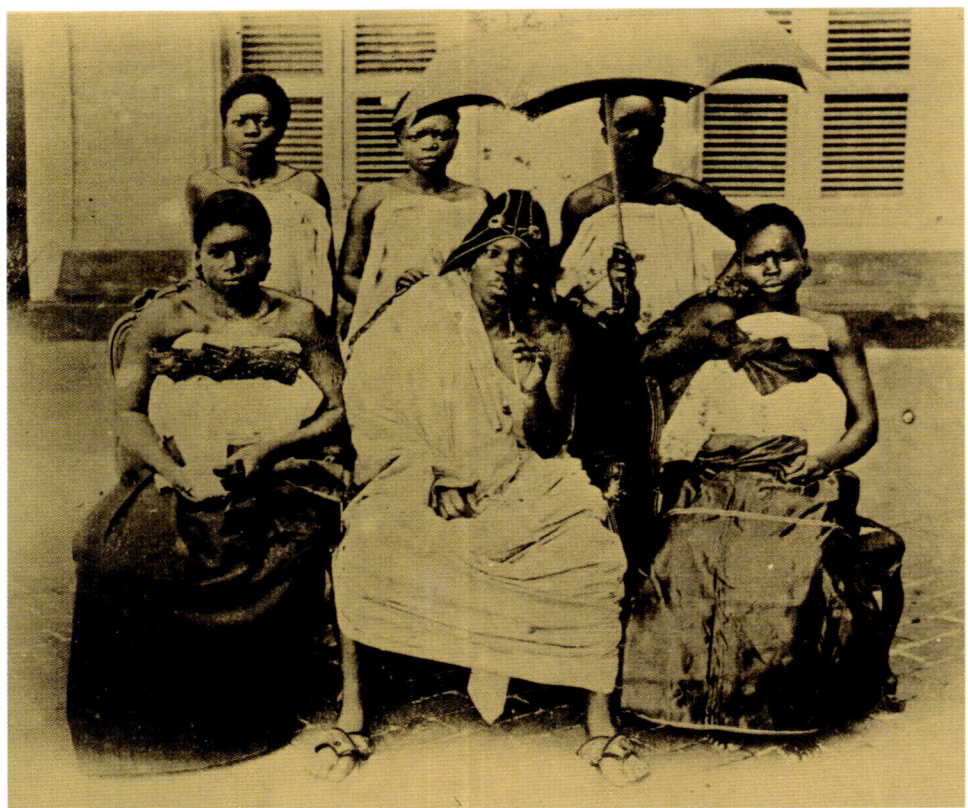

BÉHANZIN AND HIS FAMILY IN FORT DE FRANCE

The Madness of Desire

*I would like to be very sick without dying
Rather than to be this mad with desire
Even the hairs on my head wear themselves out
Desiring you...*

I Am the Rice, You Are the Water

*I am the rice, you are the water
In the fields they never leave each other
In the village they stay together
And every time they meet
They fall in love again.*

Proverb

"Friends are like those who have a father, and lovers are like those who have a mother."

Tree Ferns

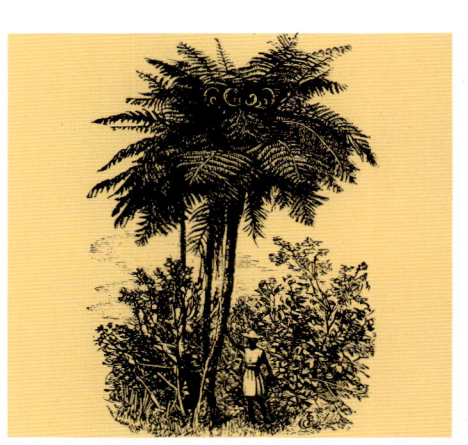

RANAVALONA III IN ALGIERS ▷

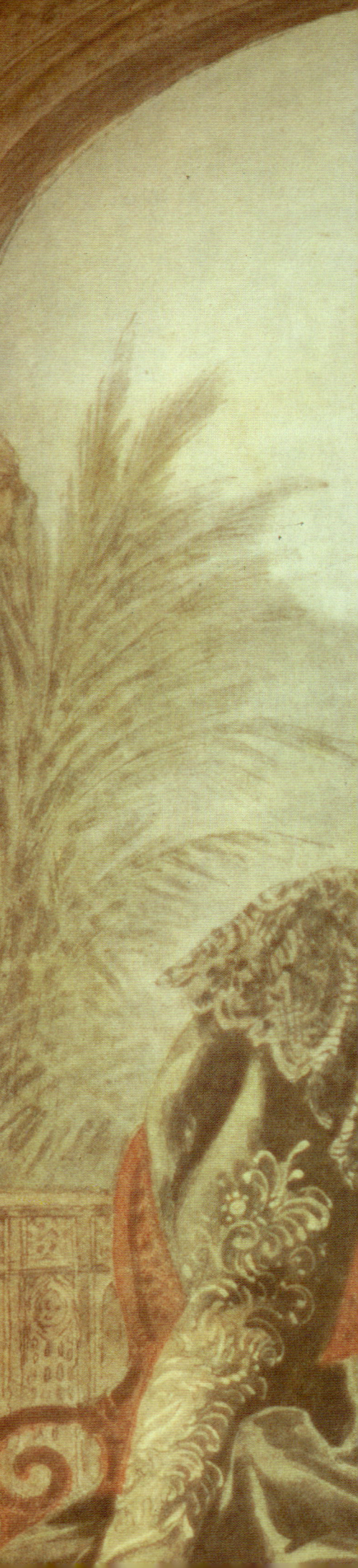

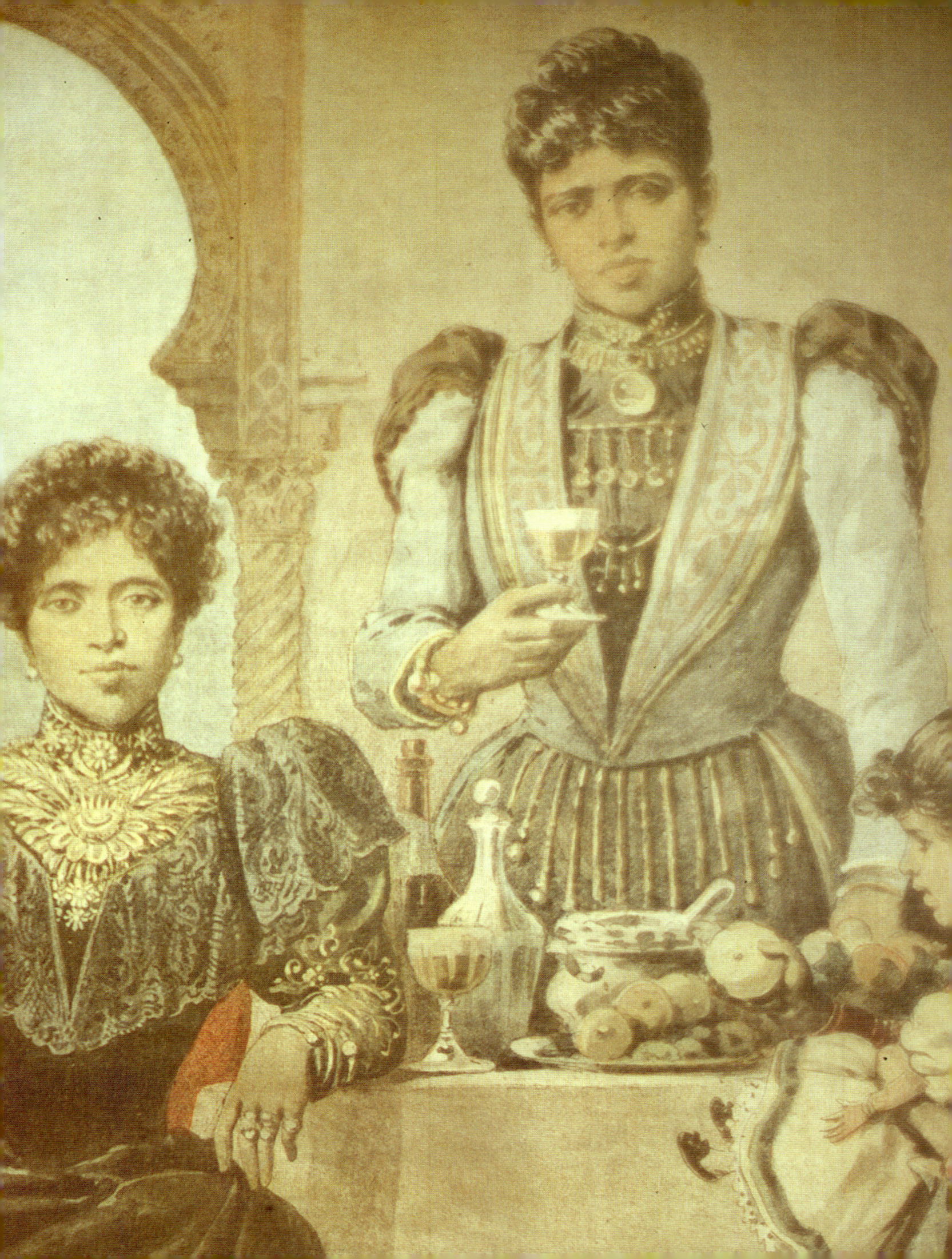

In 1938, Georges Mandel, the French minister of colonies, decreed that France must restore the body of the little queen to the land of her ancestors: so ended the captivity of Ranavalona III.

On October 29, 1939, a ship brought the body to Tamatave. The queen would complete by train the journey she had made forty years earlier in her traditional chair, the filanzana. The very next day, the ceremony of the *faluadihama* took place, the procession to the "holy house" that stored the ashes of Andrianampoinimerina, Ranavalona I, Rasohérina, and Ranavalona II. All the Malagasy people gathered around the queen, as they had on the day of her coronation. Their endless tears and silence seemed to build a bridge across time and space.

As the ceremony took place, the old dignitaries in the first row remained alert, watchful.

They knew that the soul of royalty was immortal and they kept their eyes peeled for any omen near the tomb, the tiniest of signs: a spider, even a fly taking flight.

Suddenly, a very common butterfly, most ordinary, flew off a tuft of grass at their feet and stretched out its little white wings, like a young woman shaking her lamba; then, with a few shy, hurried wingbeats, it disappeared into the blue air of Merina.

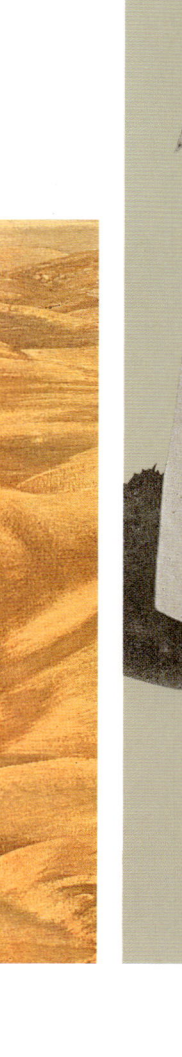

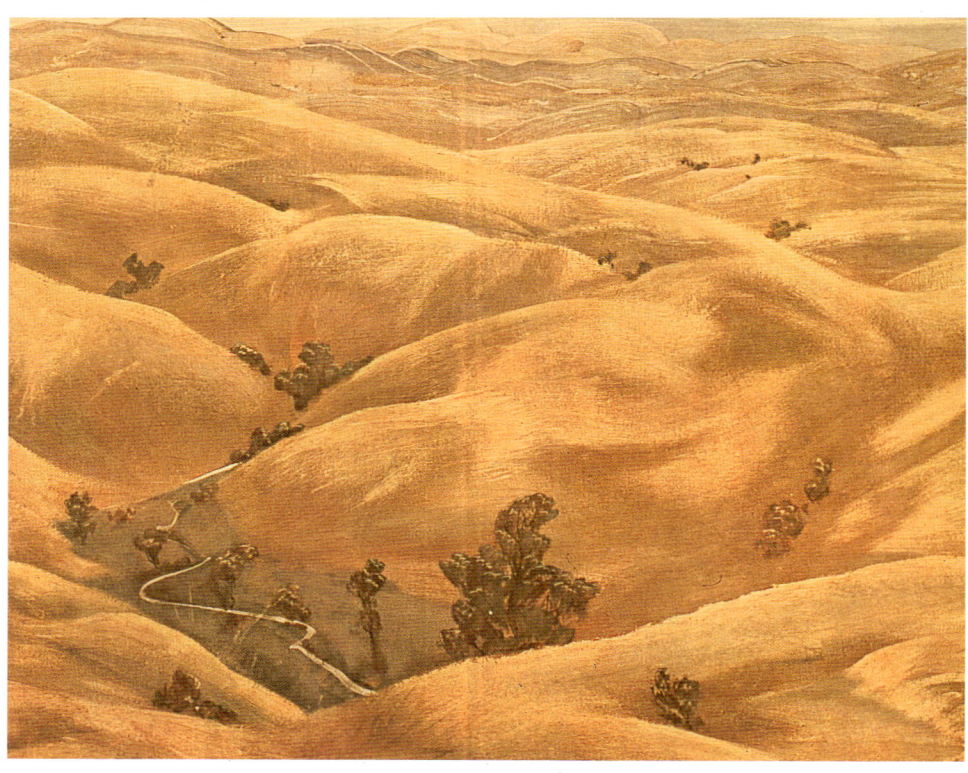

HIGH PLAINS OF MADAGASCAR, A. IACOVLEFF

WORDS
OF AN ORDINARY WOMAN

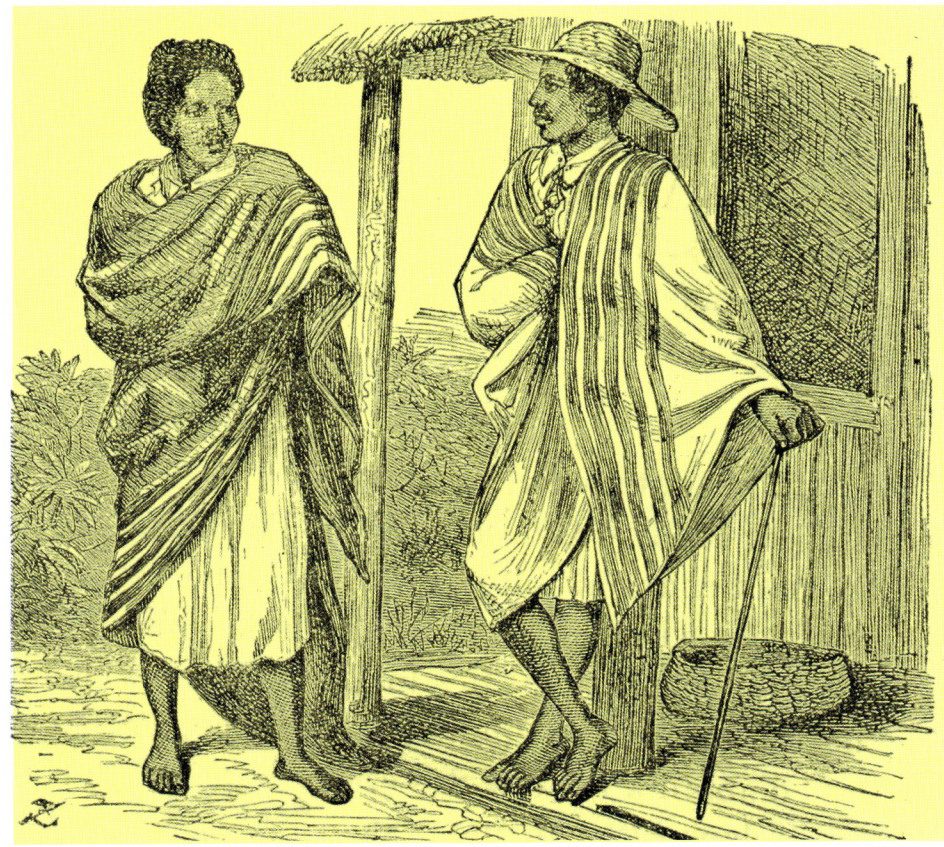

HOVA COUPLE

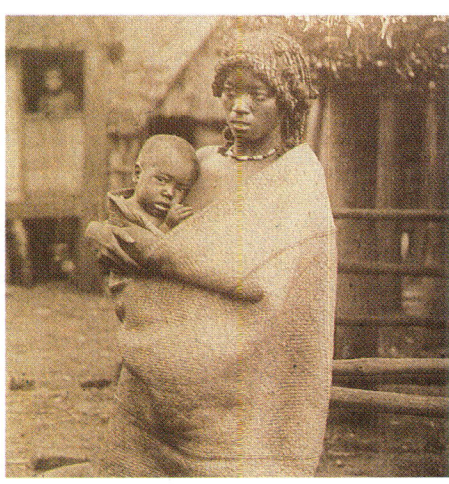

WOMAN OF THE SOUTHEAST COAST

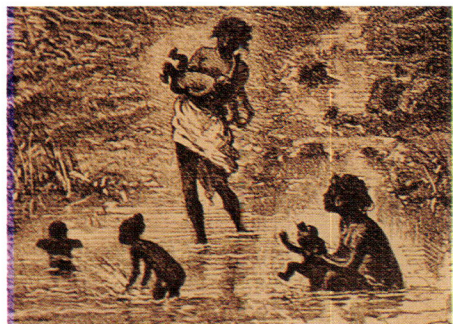

BATHING

People have a breath of life, and so do animals. People have hearts and so do animals. And when the breath leaves with death, people and animals are no more.

But people are worth more than animals. Because you can talk to people, and people can talk.

People are beings you can talk to. That is the difference between people and animals. That is what makes people higher than animals.

An animal, even if it has intelligence, a mouth, and a heart, has no words, cannot speak.

But people are speech.

People can do everything with words.

People can say savory words that give others joy. Salty words that have flavor. Words that grab you, that seize your chest, your heart, your back. Words that jab you in the stomach, that reveal hidden thoughts. Words that can make your whole body shiver from head to toe.

You can tell foolish people by the way they speak. They say everything that comes to their lips. Any words that come into their mouths, they just spit them out. Whereas prudent people, discreet people, know how to be quiet, to speak at the right moment.

It is words that make people worth more than animals. Do you know what we say to show the superiority of people over animals? We say that anything you can buy at the market is worthless next to what you can't buy. An animal can have all the good qualities possible. A cow can give lots of good milk and have many calves. If she dies, it is a misfortune. But that misfortune has its limits, because you can always get another cow like her. You can always buy another one at the market.

But a human being can't be bought. There is no money that can buy back someone who has died. So what you can't buy is worth more than what you can.

People's words come from their hearts. Words ripen in the heart, they simmer there. They grow in the heart. People's words belong to their hearts, not their mouths.

We have a proverb: we say that "the mouth keeps blood and spits saliva. If someone's mouth is hurt, it bleeds. But if he spits, he is only spitting saliva." The meaning of the proverb is this: you shouldn't say mean things, but only good things. You don't say every word that comes to your lips. Words belong to the heart. If words didn't belong to the heart anymore, that would be crazy. Only crazy people say any word that comes to their lips.

What is insanity if not the fact that words no longer follow the heart, that speech no longer belongs to the heart?

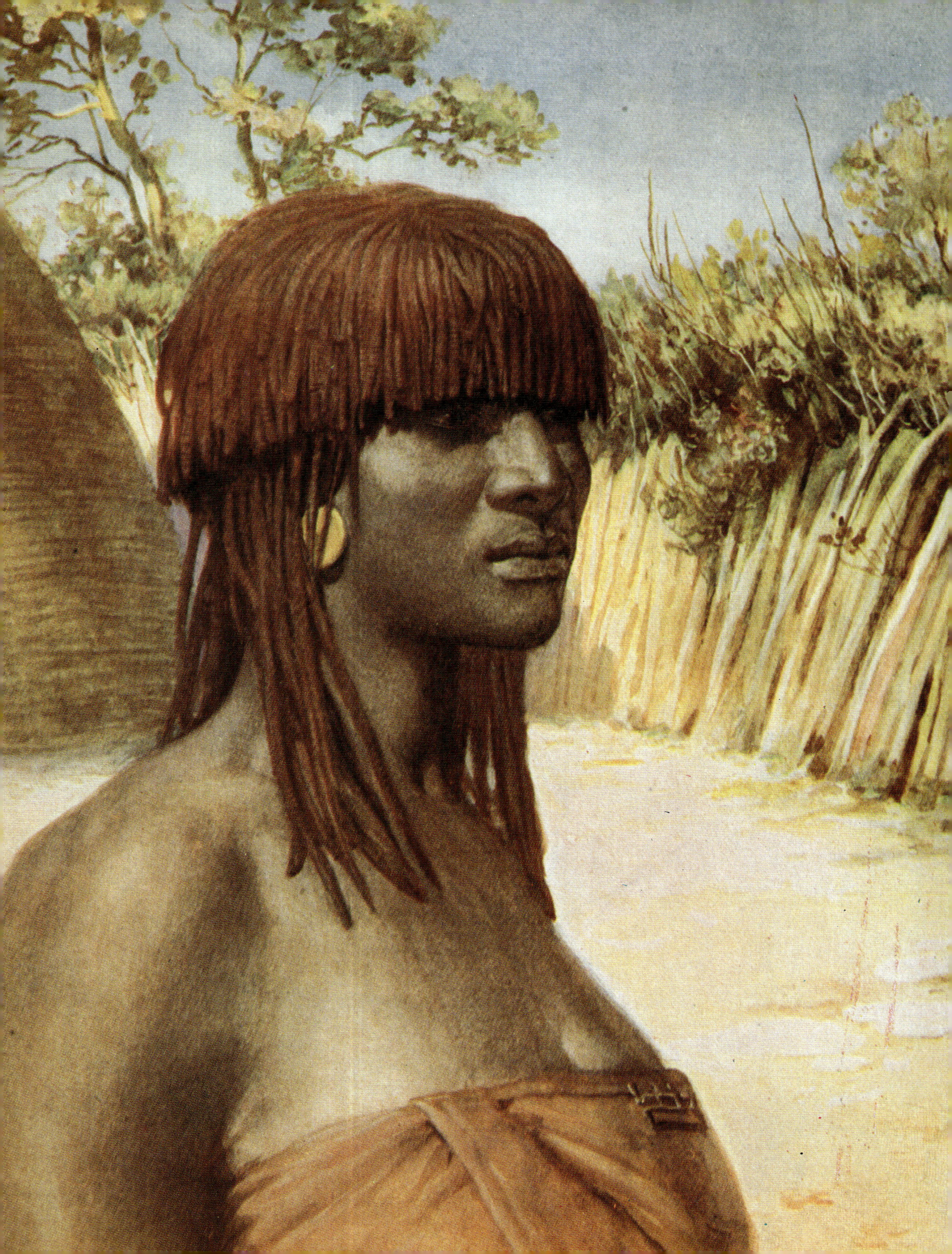

MAMOCHISANE

THE BANNER OF THE KOLOLO PEOPLE

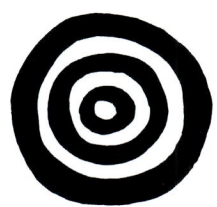

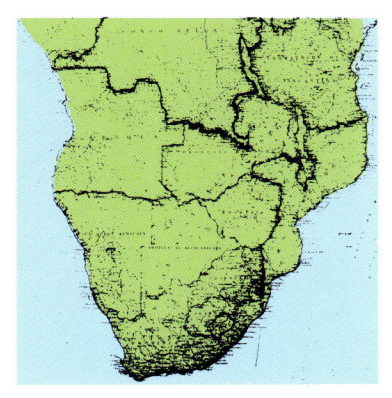

She was a frail and graceful child with narrow shoulders, whose eyelids seemed always to be fluttering; but her slender neck would not bow to anyone, not even to the king. . .

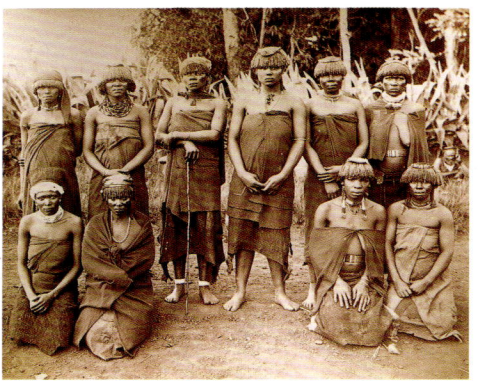

WOMEN OF NATAL

AT THE BEGINNING OF THE NINETEENTH CENTURY, SOUTH AFRICA KNEW SEVERAL GREAT CONQUERORS, HEROES OF HORROR, STARS OF SLAUGHTER, GREAT KILLERS OF MEN, WOMEN, AND CHILDREN. THERE WAS SHAKA, THERE WAS MZILIKAZI, there was Zwidé, there was Dingane, there was Soshangane, there was Manta Tisi, whose legend still floats along on the Caledon River. They all started out as refugees, except for Shaka, the first, the root of all the others' flight.

Sebetwane (1842-1916) was once nicknamed the African Caesar: ruler of the Kololo people as they fled from the Lesotho, he mounted an attack on Zambia.

Mamochisane was King Sebetwane's only child.

She was a frail and graceful child, with narrow shoulders, whose eyelids seemed always to be fluttering; but her slender neck would not bow to anyone, not even to the king. When she was a little girl, the king already called her the crutch of his old age and indeed, he used her as such during important ceremonies, his hand covering the child's head like the knob of a walking stick. She participated in camp life, attended the debates of the great council, slept next to his "wives of a single night," and voiced her opinion on everything with a seriousness and aplomb that made the king laugh. He had never had any child other than her, and it was said that his seed had dried up.

One day, one of these one-night women brought him a little boy and said: "Sebetwane, you who reign over life and dust, you who come and go like the wind, look, here is a little seed that you spilled in my body."

The king did not recognize the woman and wanted to have her removed from his sight.

But Mamochisane told him when and where this stranger, this woman of a single night, had shared the king's bed, and so they summoned the old women, who examined the baby's skull. Indeed, they said after a while, this baby was the reincarnation of Sebetwane's maternal grandfather, no doubt about it.

This is how Sebetwane received a male heir; a spear into the future, as the Kololo used to say.

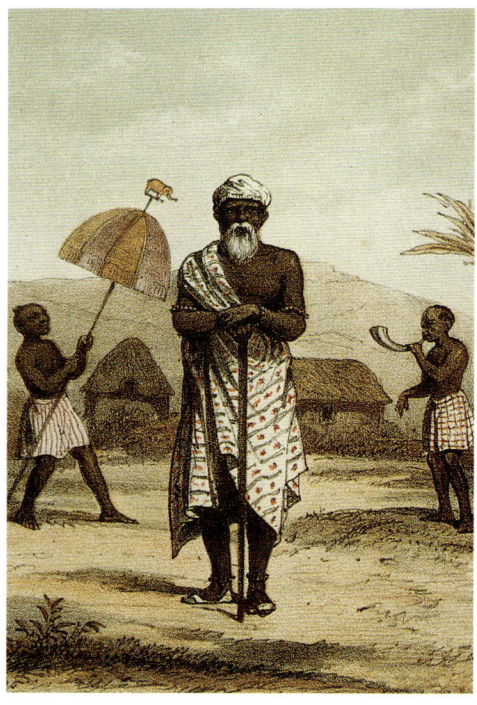

"THE AFRICAN CAESAR"

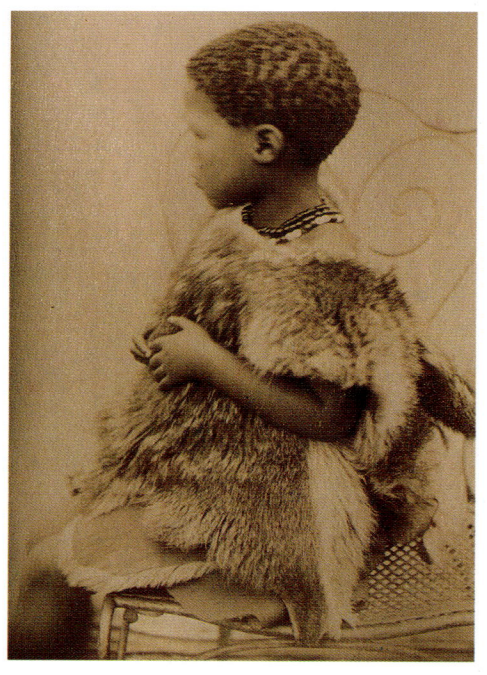

LITTLE KHOISAN GIRL

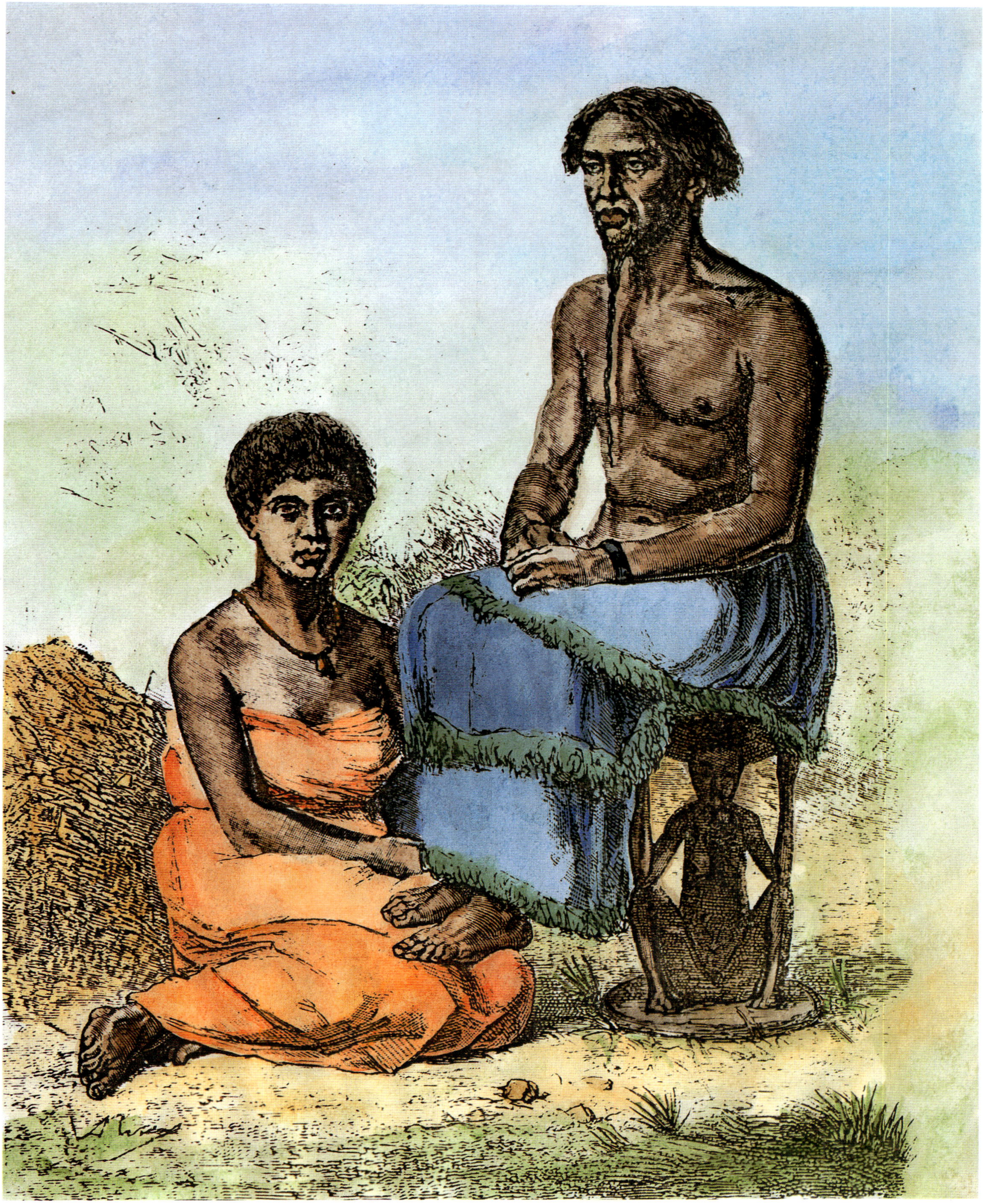

"AS A LITTLE GIRL, MAMOCHISANE WAS THE KING'S CRUTCH IN HIS OLD AGE"

Funeral Song of the Basutos

We have stayed outside,
We have stayed for the sorrow,
We have stayed for the tears.
Oh! If only there was a place for me in heaven!

Why don't I have wings to fly away!
If a strong rope came down from the sky,
I would tie myself to it, I would climb up high,
I would go live there.

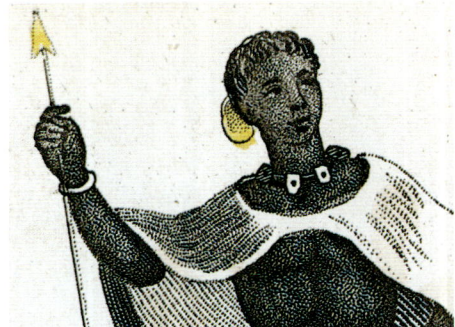

The Hunt

The warriors took part in the hunt by the thousands. Directed by their captains, they would go to areas with lots of game, then position themselves to form a circle several miles in circumference. When the order was given, they would march forward singing, whistling, and stomping, herding the animals toward the center of the circle. Soon, all the animals—large and small, timid and fierce—would begin to struggle, trying to escape the hunters' menacing circle. Finally, the lions, rhinoceroses, and buffaloes would be terrorized to such a point that they would charge blindly through the openings that the warriors had made for them.

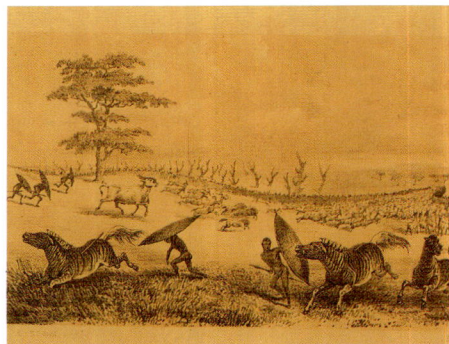

The soldiers brought the kills back to their king's kraal. The regiments divided up the meat and the festivities would last several days. The tribe got its supply of game primarily thanks to traps.
The most efficient trap was the *umhopo*. This was a great ditch dug near a river and carefully camouflaged. On each side of this ditch, hedges formed a sort of funnel. When the animals approached or left the river, they would walk between the two hedges and then be obliged to go toward the ditch.

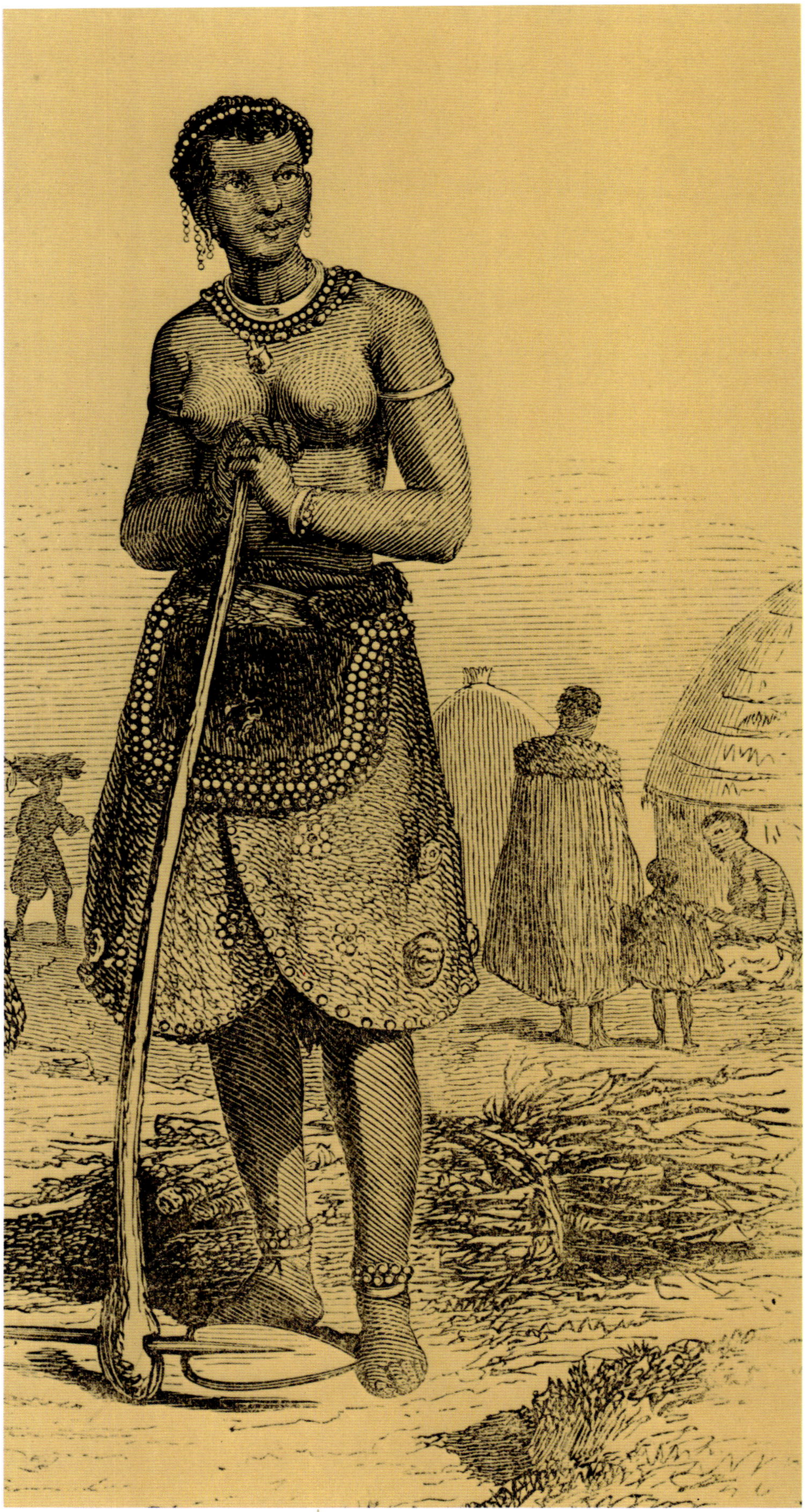

BANTU WOMAN IN THE FIELDS

MAMOCHISANE

Mamochisane was about fifteen years old when the Kololo invaded Lozi country, to the west of what is now Zambia.

She had imbibed the art of war like milk since she was very small, and now she would attend the meetings of the great council and pronounce her opinions like an old warrior. She was at the king's side during combat and carried his lances, warned him of danger, gave him a gourd of water in the middle of battle. She now had breasts like mangoes and the king laughed to see her in the middle of combat: "The most beautiful woman of the Kololo and the bravest warrior," he liked to say. But she herself never threw a spear at enemy chests. And ever since she had developed a woman's breasts, she had been formally opposed to the killing of prisoners: they were bargaining chips, and she took care of them accordingly, making sure that they were not harmed in any way.

The Kololo had never had a queen; but their enemies the Lozi believed in the power of women. And soon enough, they came to act on their belief.

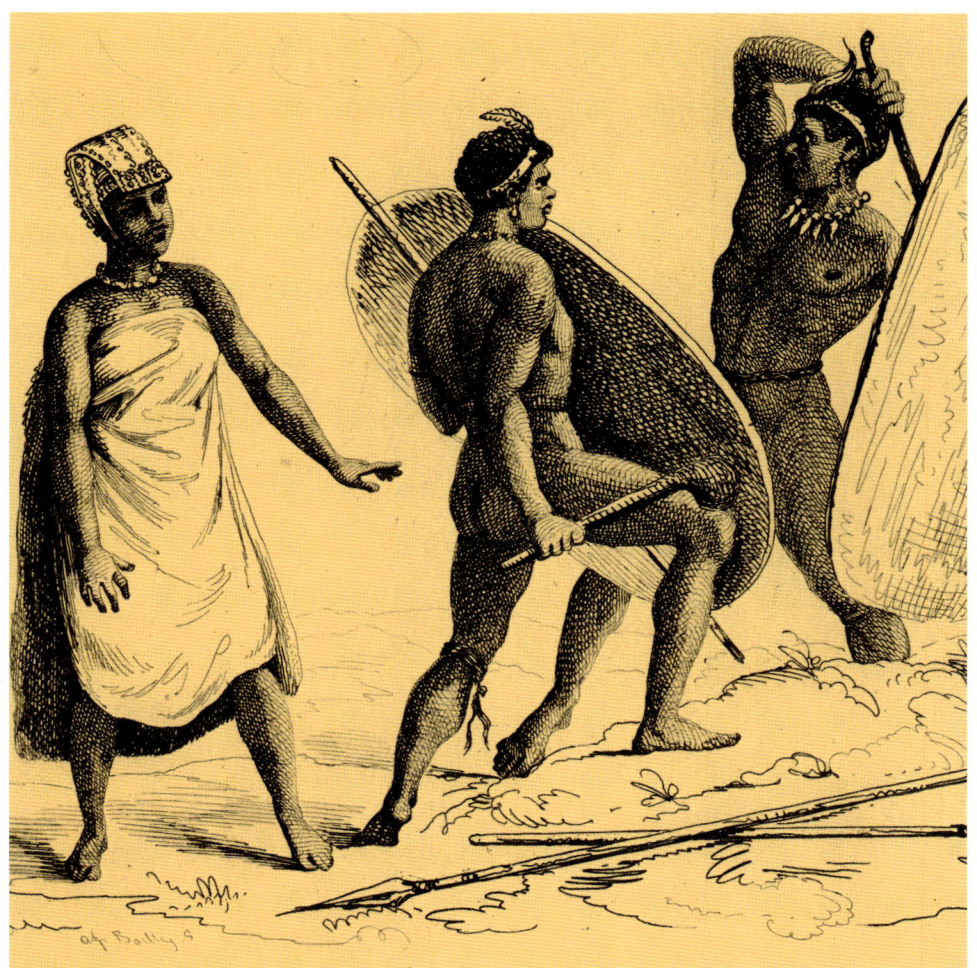

"THE KING LAUGHED TO SEE HER IN THE MIDDLE OF COMBAT"

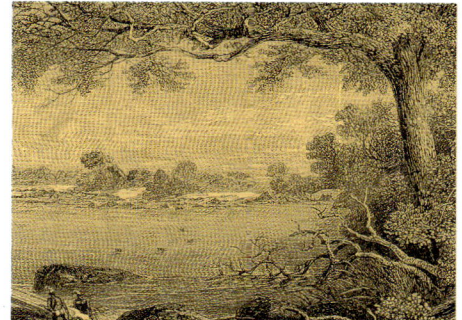

The Legend of Lake Dilolo

One evening, a woman named Moéné Monenga, who was a village chief, went to the house of a certain Mosogo, her neighbor. She was hungry and asked for food; Mosogo's wife gave her enough to eat her fill. Monenga continued on her way and arrived in another village, where the lake is today. She requested the same thing from the villagers that she had requested from Mosogo's wife, but they would not give her anything to satisfy her hunger. When she sternly reproached them for their greed, they asked in mocking voices: "What can you do to punish us?" Without answering, she began singing slowly, and as she drew out the last syllable of her name, the whole village, down to the last fowl and dog, sank down and disappeared into the earth, where the water came to take its place. Casimacaté, the village chief, was away; when he returned to his family and found nothing there, not even the ruins of his hut, he threw himself in the lake, where he must still be to this day; and it is from the word *ilolo,* which means despair, that this lake where that unhappy man sought his death takes its name.

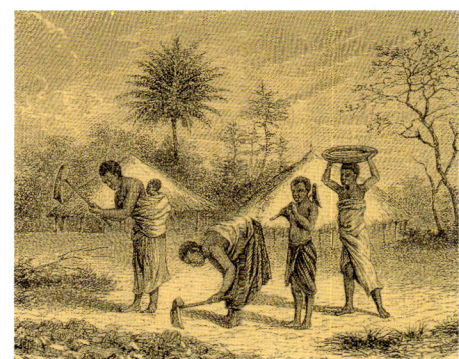

Work in the Fields

The Sothos would begin farming two moons after the harvest. Every morning, the young boys milked their fathers' cows and led them to the community pastures; then the women left for the fields, carrying simple hoes, and there, singing all the while, they labored halfway through the afternoon.

Monsoon Song

Sing, sing the "ndeerooda"!
Let's have fun: it's the monsoon!
Go wake up the sleepers!
Go raise the women!
Play for the sleepyheads!
Make your bells ring!
Let us go to the promenade!
Full of hope, though we may be conquered.
Full of hope, though we may be kicked out.
Let's have fun: it's the monsoon!
Pass the days, pass the nights!

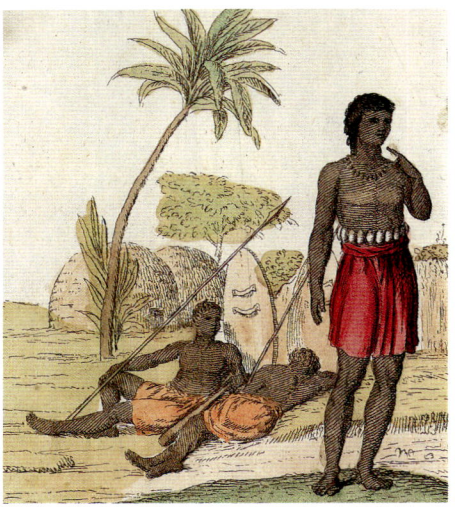

Proverb

"The great floods make the little fish proud."

The Falls of the Zambezi (Victoria Falls)

At Gonyé, the falls are not the result of the outpouring of a mass of water that can no longer be contained in its banks, like the Niagara Falls. Instead, these falls are caused by a kind of strangulation of the river, held tightly for several miles in a gorge barely one hundred yards wide and fifteen to eighteen yards deep at flood stage.
Upriver from the falls, the islands are covered with marvelous vegetation, and the landscape from the rocks that overlook the falls is one of the most beautiful that I have ever contemplated.
David Livingstone (1859)

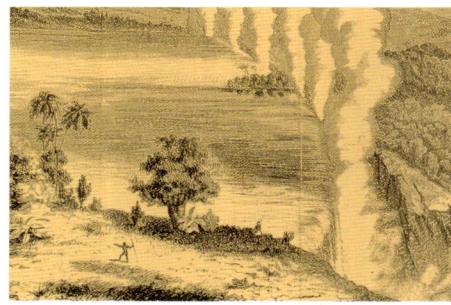

Proverb

"Life is a dance that you only dance once."

For a long time, there had been a rumor that a young woman served as the banner of the Kololo people; when this rumor reached the Lozi camp, King Waga Lozi hatched a plan to seize the young woman in the midst of a battle.

The prisoner was led before him. She was covered with dust and her face was as white as those who live in the Kingdom of the Dead. She was trembling. The king said: "Calm down, Mamochisane, you will be treated as you treated Lozi prisoners."

He settled her in a hut reserved for privileged guests and treated her with the greatest respect. Two years passed. The Lozi rejoiced, and the Kololo seemed lost without their banner. In a desperate attack, Sebetwane reached the heart of the enemy camp and found the way his daughter had been treated. So he said: "I have been fighting a kindly people, with whom from this day on I shall form one nation."

Around 1840, he had the king of the Lozi killed, took the king's wives for his own, and adapted the Lozi customs to the those of the Kololo, and the Kololos' customs to the those of the Lozi. They formed one people, one nation, as Sebetwane said.

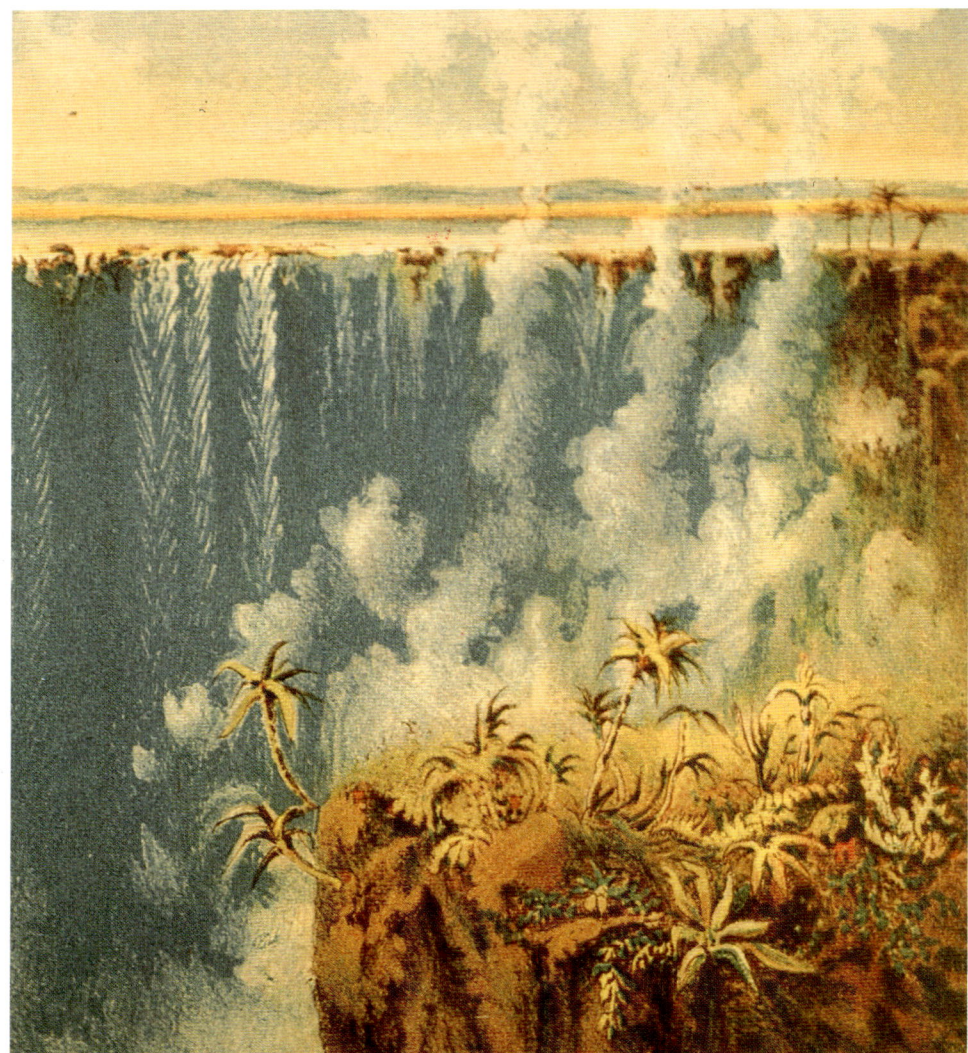

FALLS OF THE ZAMBEZI

LATTAKOO WOMAN ▷

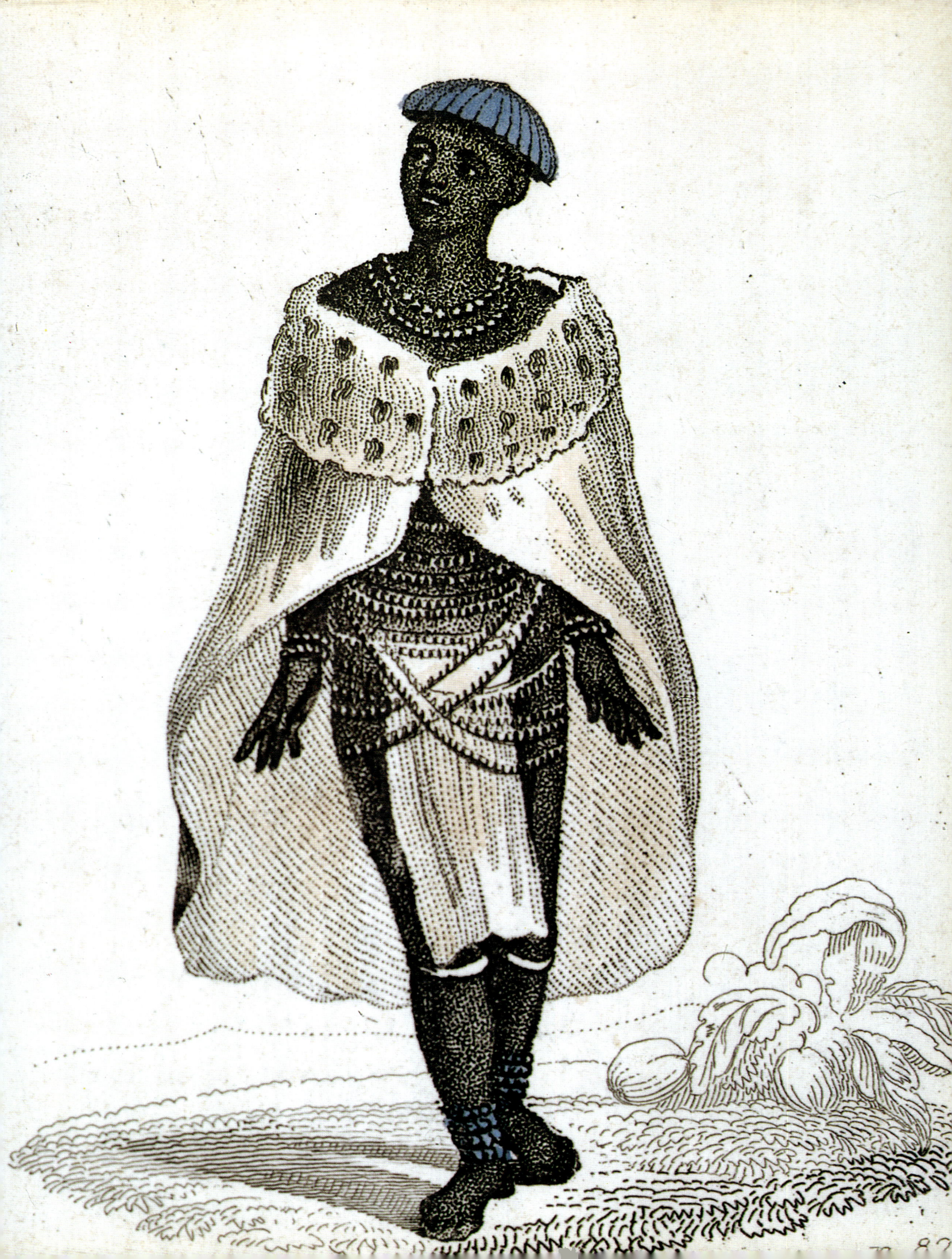

When the old king died, Mamochisane succeeded him and reigned for three days. On the first day, her new dignity thrilled her and she made important decisions. On the second day, she suddenly seemed indifferent to everything. And on the third day, her head sagged under the weight of the crown and the royal scepter dangled sadly from her hand.

At the end of the third day she declared: "I am a woman, I did not come into the world to decide matters of life and death: see, King Sebetwane's crown is not the right size for my head; let me take it off and put it on the ground." And the people cried: "Queen, we will make you a crown that will fit your head perfectly." And then she said again, now backed against a wall: "You see, I am a woman, I was not born to decide matters of life and death; this crown weighs on me; let me put it on the ground."

And they let her remove the crown. She passed it on to her little brother, the son that Sebetwane had had with the woman of a single night.

So ends the story of Mamochisane, she who was her father's crutch in his old age, the banner of his armies; and who had no desire to inherit his crown.

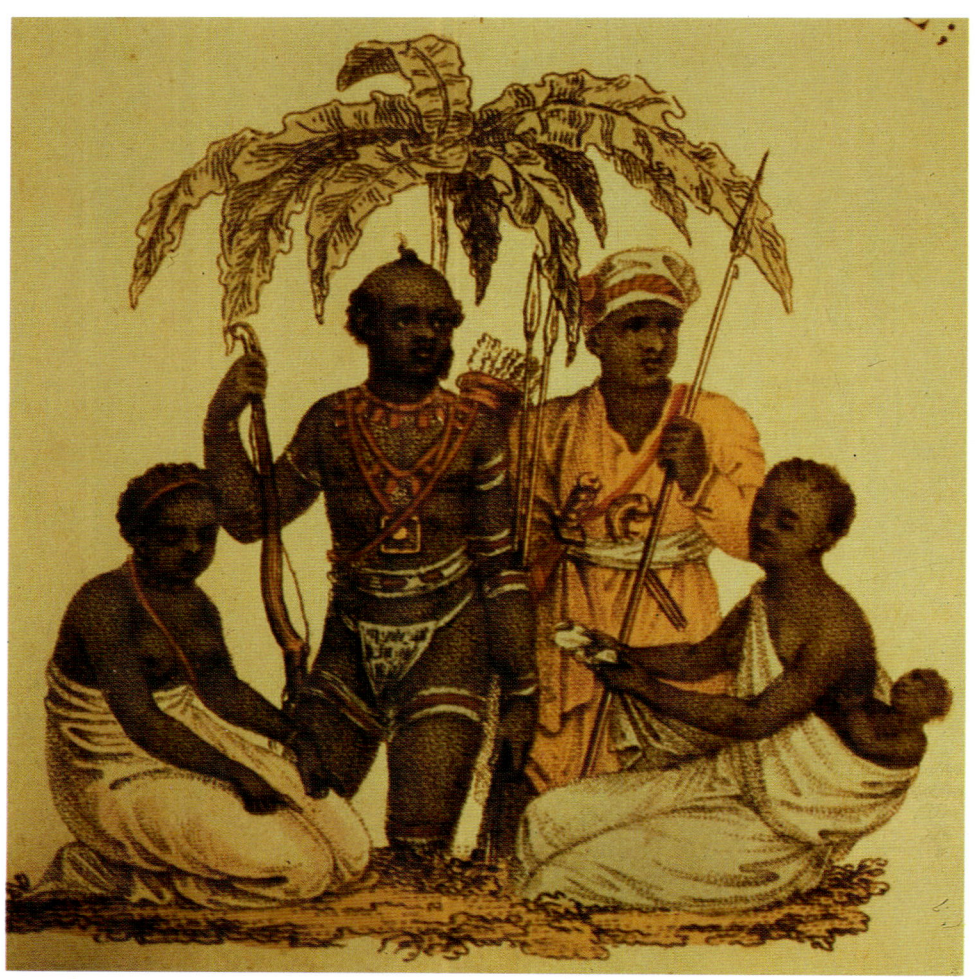

"SHE WHO DID NOT WANT TO INHERIT ROYALTY"

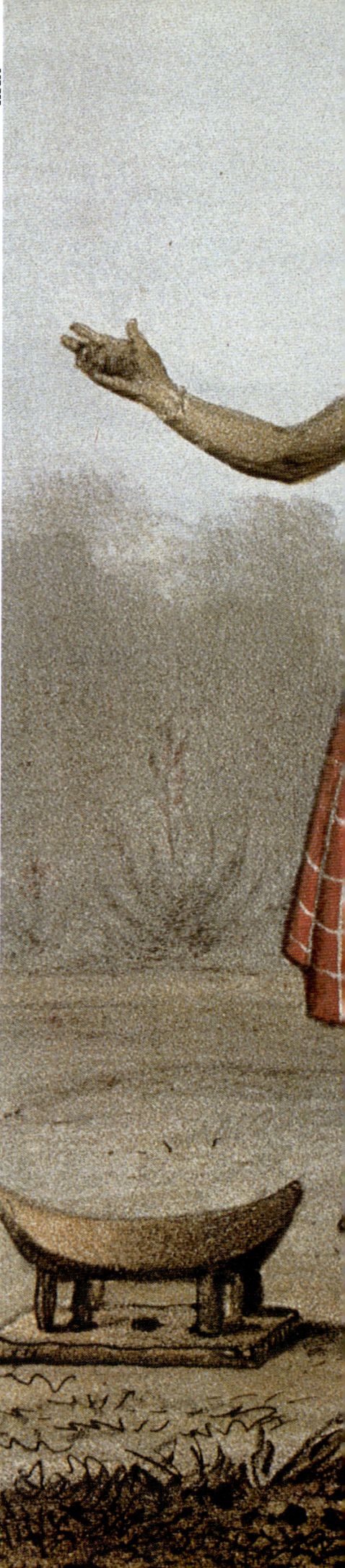

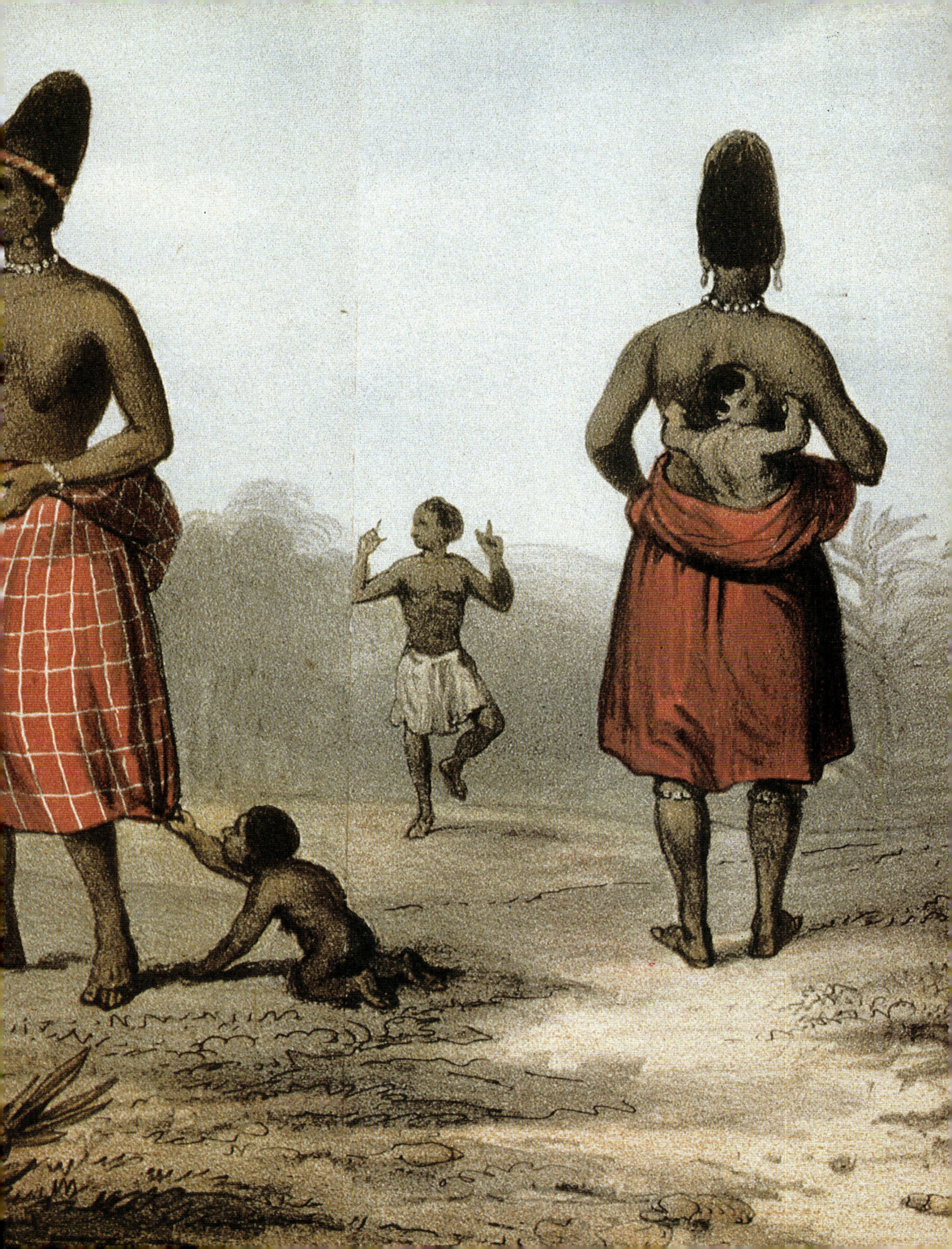

PRINCIPAL WORKS CONSULTED: pp. 1-201

Arnault d'ABBADIE
Douze ans de séjour dans la Haute-Éthiopie (Abyssinie)
Citta Del Vaticano.

William Y. ADAMS
Nubia corridor to Africa.
Princeton University Press.

Cyril ALFRED
Akhénaton le pharaon mystique
Jardin des Arts/Tallandier.

Cyril ALFRED
Les Égyptiens. L'empire des pharaons
Armand Colin.

Ola BALOGUN
Nigéria, du réel à l'imaginaire
« Grands Livres ». Jeune Afrique.

Boubacar BARRY
Le royaume du Waalo. Le Sénégal avant la conquête
François Maspéro.

Henri BARTH
Voyages et découvertes dans l'Afrique septentrionale et centrale pendant les années 1849 à 1855
1860. A. Bohne Librairie. Paris.

Abbé David BOILAT
Esquisses sénégalaises
Karthala.

Nazi BONI
Histoire synthétique de l'Afrique résistante
Présence Africaine.

Françoise BRETOUT
Mogho Naba Wobgho
Nouvelles Éditions Africaines/ABC.

Jacques BUREAU
Éthiopie. Un drame impérial et rouge,
Ramsay.

Aimé CÉSAIRE
Cahier d'un retour au pays natal
Désormeaux.

Lionel CASSON
Les pharaons
Éditions du Fanal.

Blaise CENDRARS
Anthologie Nègre
Buchet-Chastel.

Jacques CHEVRIER
L'arbre à palabres. Essai sur les contes et récits d'Afrique noire
Hatier.

Catherine COQUERY-VIDROVITCH
et Henri MONIOT
L'Afrique noire de 1800 à nos jours
P. U. F.

Robert CORNEVIN
Histoire de l'Afrique
Payot.

Histoire des peuples d'Afrique noire
Berger-Levrault.

Les mémoires de l'Afrique
Robert Laffont.

Luc CROEGAERT
Premières Afriques
Didier-Hatier.

Basil Davidson
L'Afrique ancienne
François Maspero.

Mère Afrique
P. U. F.

Le réveil de l'Afrique
Présence Africaine.

André Davy
Éthiopie d'hier et d'aujourd'hui
Le Livre Africain.

Maurice Delafosse
Haut-Sénégal-Niger
Maisonneuve et Larose.

Paulette et Maurice Deribere
L'Éthiopie, berceau de l'humanité
Société Continentale
d'Éditions Modernes Illustrées.

Christiane Desroches-Noblecourt
La femme au temps des pharaons
Stock/Laurence Pernoud.

Djibril Dione et Sékéné Mody Cissoko
Histoire de l'Afrique
Présence Africaine.

Cheikh Anta Diop
L'Antiquité africaine par l'image
Dakar.

Nations nègres et culture
Présence Africaine.

Jean Doresse
La vie quotidienne des Éthiopiens chrétiens aux XVIIe et XVIIIe siècles
Hachette.

Walter B. Emery
Egypt in Nubia
Hutchinson of London.

Elian J. Finbert
Le livre de la sagesse nègre
Robert Laffont.

Pierre Grimal
*Histoire mondiale de la femme
Préhistoire et Antiquité*
Nouvelle Librairie de France.

Marcel Guilhem, Boubou Hama
Niger, récits historiques
Ligel.

Marcel Guilhem, H. N'Diaye
Sénégal, récits historiques
Ligel.

Marcel Guilhem
Précis d'histoire de la Haulte Volta
Ligel.

E. Guernier
*L'apport de l'Afrique
à la pensée humaine*
Payot.

La guerre de Sassa-Dengel contre les Falachas
Texte éthiopien
Manuscrit de la Bibliothèque Nationale, n° 143.

Journal of Ethiopian Studies. Vol. X, n°1.
Addis-Abebba.

Charles-André Julien
Les Africains
Jeune Afrique.

Ibrahima Baba Kaké
Anna Zingha, reine d'Angola, première résistante à l'invasion portugaise
« Grandes Figures Africaines »
ABC/NEA.

Combats pour l'histoire africaine
Présence Africaine.

Mémoire de l'Afrique. La diaspora noire
ABC/NEA.

Ibrahima Baba Kaké et Elikia M'Bokolo
*Histoire Générale de l'Afrique
La dispersion des Bantous*
ABC/NEA.

*Histoire Générale de l'Afrique
Les grands résistants*
ABC/NEA.

Ibrahima Baba Kaké et François Poli
« Grandes Figures Africaines. »
ABC/NEA.

Joseph Ki-Zerbo
*Histoire de l'Afrique noire.
D'hier à demain*
Hatier.

K.A. Kitchen
*Ramsès II le pharaon triomphant
Sa vie et son époque*
Éditions du Rocher.

Claire Lalouette
L'empire des Ramsès
Fayard.

Textes sacrés et textes profanes de l'ancienne Égypte
Gallimard.

Wolf Leslau
Coutumes et croyances des Falachas
Institut d'Ethnologie
Musée de l'homme. Paris.

Henry Lhote
A la découverte des fresques du Tassili
Arthaud.

David Livingstone
Explorations dans l'intérieur de l'Afrique australe et voyages à travers le continent de St Paul de Loanda à l'embouchure du Zambèze (de 1840 à 1856)
Hachette. Paris. 1859.

Angelo B. Maliki
Bonheur et souffrance chez les Peuls nomades
Edicef/CILF.

Gaston Maspero
*Histoire ancienne des peuples de l'Orient classique.
Les premières mêlées des peuples.*
Johnson Reprint Corporation.
New York. Londres.

Jacques Mauduit
La vie quotidienne à l'époque des premiers chasseurs
Hachette.

Pierre Montet
La vie quotidienne au temps des Ramsès
Hachette.

Henry de Monfreid
Ménélik tel qu'il fut
Bernard Grasset.

Djibril Tamsir Niane
Soundiata ou l'épopée mandingue
Présence Africaine.

Théophile Obenga
Afrique centrale précoloniale
Présence Africaine.

Achola O'Pala et Madina Ly
La femme africaine dans la société précoloniale
Unesco.

Major Serpa Pinto
Comment j'ai traversé l'Afrique depuis l'Atlantique jusqu'à l'océan Indien
Hachette. Paris. 1881.

Georges Posener
Dictionnaire de la civilisation égyptienne
Fernand Hazan.

Christian Roche
Histoire de la Casamance.
Conquête et résistance : 1850-1920
Karthala.

J.A. Rogers
World's Great Men of Color
New York, The Macmil.

Robert I. Rotber
Protest and Power in Black Africa
New York. Oxford University Press.

Christian Saglio
Sénégal
« Petite Planète ». Seuil.

Serge Sauneron
Villes et légendes d'Égypte
Institut français d'archéologie orientale du Caire.

Gabriel Simon
L'Éthiopie, ses mœurs, ses traditions, le Négouss Iohannès, les églises monolithes de Lalibéla
Challamel Ainé. Paris. 1885.

Mary F. Smith
Baba de Karo
« Terre humaine ». Plon.

Castro Soromenho
Portrait de la reine Zingha
Revue *Présence Africaine* n° 42.

Alfâ Ibrahim Sow
La femme, la vache, la foi
Petters.

Taddesse Tamrat
A short Note on the Traditions of Pagan Resistance to the Ethiopian Church (XIV)
Journal of Ethiopian Studies,
Addis-Abebba.

André Terrisse
Contes et légendes du Sénégal
P. Nathan.

Philipps Vandenberg
Nefertiti
Belfond.

Jan Vansina
Kingdoms of the Savanna
The University of Wisconsin Press.

Arthur Weigall
Le pharaon Akh-En-Aton et son époque
Payot.

PRINCIPAL WORKS CONSULTED: pp. 202-404

Arnault d'ABBADIE
Douze ans de séjour dans la Haute-Éthiopie (Abyssinie)
Citta Del Vaticano.

William Y. ADAMS
Nubia corridor to Africa.
Princeton University Press.

Cyril ALFRED
Akhénaton le pharaon mystique
Jardin des Arts/Tallandier.

Cyril ALFRED
Les Égyptiens. L'empire des pharaons
Armand Colin.

Ola BALOGUN
Nigéria du réel à l'imaginaire
« Grands Livres ». Jeune Afrique.

Boubacar BARRY
Le royaume du Waalo. Le Sénégal avant la conquête
François Maspéro.

Henri BARTH
Voyages et découvertes dans l'Afrique septentrionale et centrale pendant les années 1849 à 1855
A. Bohne Librairie. Paris. 1860.

Abbé David BOILAT
Esquisses sénégalaises
Karthala.

Nazi BONI
Histoire synthétique de l'Afrique résistante
Présence Africaine.

Françoise BRETOUT
Mogho Naba Wobgho
Nouvelles Éditions Africaines/ABC.

Jacques BUREAU
Éthiopie. Un drame impérial et rouge,
Ramsay.

Aimé CÉSAIRE
Cahier d'un retour au pays natal
Désormeaux.

Lionel CASSON
Les pharaons
Éditions du Fanal.

Blaise CENDRARS
Anthologie Nègre
Buchet-Chastel.

Jacques CHEVRIER
L'arbre à palabres. Essai sur les contes et récits d'Afrique noire
Hatier.

Catherine COQUERY-VIDROVITCH
et Henri MONIOT
L'Afrique noire de 1800 à nos jours
Presses Universitaires de France.

Robert CORNEVIN
Histoire de l'Afrique, Payot Paris.

Robert CORNEVIN
Histoire des peuples d'Afrique noire
Berger-Levrault.

Robert CORNEVIN
Les mémoires de l'Afrique
R. Laffont.

Luc CROEGAERT
Premières Afriques
Didier-Hatier.

Basil DAVIDSON
L'Afrique ancienne
François Maspero.

Basil DAVIDSON
Mère Afrique
Presses Universitaires de France.

Basil DAVIDSON
Le réveil de l'Afrique
Présence Africaine.

André DAVY
Éthiopie d'hier et d'aujourd'hui
Le Livre Africain.

Maurice DELAFOSSE
Haut-Sénégal-Niger
Maisonneuve et Larose.

Paulette et Maurice DERIBERE
L'Éthiopie, berceau de l'humanité
Société Continentale
d'Éditions Modernes Illustrése.

Christiane DESROCHES-NOBLECOURT
La femme au temps des pharaons
Stock/Laurence Pernoud.

Djibril DIONE et Sékéné Mody CISSOKO
Histoire de l'Afrique
Présence Africaine.

Cheikh Anta DIOP
L'Antiquité africaine par l'image
Dakar.

Cheikh Anta DIOP
Nations nègres et culture
Présence Africaine.

Jean DORESSE
*La vie quotidienne des Éthiopiens
chrétiens aux XVIIe et XVIIIe siècles*
Hachette.

Walter B. EMERY
Egypt in Nubia
Hutchinson of London.

Elian J. FINBERT
Le livre de la sagesse nègre
Laffont.

Pierre GRIMAL
*Histoire mondiale de la femme
Préhistoire et Antiquité*
Nouvelle Librairie de France.

Marcel GUILHEM, Boubou HAMA
Niger, récits historiques
Ligel.

Marcel GUILHEM, H. N'DIAYE
Sénégal, récits historiques
Ligel.

Marcel GUILHEM
Précis d'histoire de la Haulte Volta
Ligel.

E. GUERNIER
*L'apport de l'Afrique
à la pensée humaine*
Payot.

*La guerre de Sassa-Dengel contre les
Falachas*, Texte éthiopien, Manuscrit de
la Bibliothèque Nationale, n° 143.

Journal of Ethiopian Studies. Vol. X, n°1.
Addis-Abebba.

Charles-André JULIEN
Les Africains
Jeune Afrique.

Ibrahima Baba KAKÉ
*Anna Zingha, reine d'Angola
première résistante à l'invasion
portugaise*
« Grandes Figures Africaines »
ABC/NEA.

Ibrahima Baba KAKÉ
Combats pour l'histoire africaine
Présence Africaine.

Ibrahima Baba KAKÉ
Mémoire de l'Afrique. La diaspora noire
ABC/NEA.

Ibrahima Baba KAKÉ et Elikia M'BOKOLO
*Histoire Générale de l'Afrique
La dispersion des Bantous*
ABC/NEA.

Ibrahima Baba KAKÉ et Elikia M'BOKOLO
*Histoire Générale de l'Afrique
Les grands résistants.* ABC/NEA.

Ibrahima Baba KAKÉ et François POLI
« Grandes Figures Africaines. »
ABC/NEA.

Joseph KI-ZERBO
*Histoire de l'Afrique noire.
D'hier à demain*
Librairie A. Hatier.

K.A. KITCHEN
*Ramsès II le pharaon triomphant
Sa vie et son époque*
Éditions du Rocher.

Claire LALOUETTE
L'empire des Ramsès
Fayard.

Claire LALOUETTE
*Textes sacrés et textes profanes
de l'ancienne Égypte*
Gallimard.

Wolf LESLAU
Coutumes et croyances des Falachas

Institut d'Ethnologie
Musée de l'homme. Paris.

Henry LHOTE
A la découverte des fresques du Tassili
Arthaud.

David LIVINGSTONE
*Explorations dans l'intérieur de l'Afrique
australe et voyages à travers le continent de St Paul de Loanda à l'embouchure du Zambèze (de 1840 à 1856)*
Hachette. Paris. 1859.

Angelo B. MALIKI
*Bonheur et souffrance chez les Peuls
nomades*
Edicef/CILF.

Gaston MASPERO
*Histoire ancienne des peuples de
l'Orient classique.
Les premières mêlées des peuples.*
Johnson Reprint Corporation.
New York. Londres.

Jacques MAUDUIT
*La vie quotidienne à l'époque des
premiers chasseurs*
Hachette.

Pierre MONTET
La vie quotidienne au temps des Ramsès
Hachette.

Henry de MONFREID
Ménélik tel qu'il fut
Bernard Grasset.

Djibril Tamsir NIANE
Soundiata ou l'épopée mandingue
Présence Africaine.

Théophile OBENGA
Afrique centrale précoloniale
Présence Africaine.

Achola O'PALA et MADINA LY
*La femme africaine dans la société
précoloniale*
Unesco.

Major Serpa PINTO
*Comment j'ai traversé l'Afrique depuis
l'Atlantique jusqu'à l'océan Indien*
Hachette. Paris. 1881.

Georges POSENER
Dictionnaire de la civilisation égyptienne
Fernand Hazan.

Christian ROCHE
*Histoire de la Casamance.
Conquête et résistance : 1850-1920*
Karthala.

J.A. Rogers
World's Great Men of Color
The Macmillan Company. New York.

Robert I. Rotber
Protest and Power in Black Africa
New York. Oxford University Press.

Christian Saglio
Sénégal,
« Petite Planète ». Seuil.

Serge Sauneron
Villes et légendes d'Égypte
Institut français d'archéologie orientale du Caire.

Gabriel Simon
L'Éthiopie, ses mœurs, ses traditions, le Négouss Iohannès, les églises monolithes de Lalibéla
Challamel Ainé. Paris. 1885.

Mary F. Smith
Baba de Karo
« Terre humaine ». Plon.

Castro Soromenho
Portrait de la reine Zingha
Revue *Présence Africaine* n° 42.

Sow
La femme, la vache, la foi
Classiques africains.

Taddesse Tamrat
A short Note on the Traditions of Pagan Resistance to the Ethiopian Church (XIV)
Journal of Ethiopian Studies, Addis-Abebba.

André Terrisse
Contes et légendes du Sénégal
Nathan.

Philipps Vandenberg
Nefertiti
Belfond.

Jan Vansina
Kingdoms of the Savanna
The University of Wisconsin Press.

Arthur Weigall
Le pharaon Akh-En-Aton et son époque
Payot.

Arnault d'Abbadie
Douze ans de séjour dans la Haute-Éthiopie
Citta Del Vaticano.

Agendafrique
Librairie Larousse. RFI.

Alexandre L.-D. Albeca
La France au Dahomey
Hachette. Paris. 1895.

Hélène d'Almeida-Topor
Les Amazones
Rochevignes.

Jacques Anquetil
Côte d'Ivoire, l'artisanat créateur
A.C.C.T.

Arbousset et Daumas
Relation d'un voyage d'exploration au cap de Bonne-Espérance
Arthus Bertrand. Paris. 1842.

Georges Balandier
La vie quotidienne au royaume de Kongo du XVIe au XVIIIe siècle
Hachette.

Jean-Claude Barbier
Femmes du Cameroun
Karthala.

Boubacar Barry
Le Royaume du Waalo
Maspéro.

Peter Becker
L'Attila Noir
Librairie Plon.

Abbé David Boilat
Esquisses Sénégalaises
Karthala.

Nazi Boni
Histoire synthétique de l'Afrique résistante
Présence Africaine.

Jean Boulegue
Le grand jolof
Karthala.

Françoise Bretout
La résistance du royaume Mossi de Ouagadougou
Nouvelles Éditions Africaines/ABC.

Jacques Bureau
Éthiopie, un drame impérial et rouge
Ramsay.

René Caillie
Journal d'un voyage à Tombouctou et à Jenné, dans l'Afrique centrale
Imprimerie Royale. Paris. 1830.

R.P. Callet
Histoire des rois Tantaran Ny Andriana
Ed. de la Librairie Malgache
Tananarive.

Vera Cardot
Belles pages de l'histoire africaine
Présence Africaine.

E. Casalis
Les Bassoutos
Lib. de Ch. Meyrueis et Cie. Paris. 1859.

Blaise Cendrars
Anthologie Nègre
Buchet/Chastel.

E. Chaudoin
Trois mois de captivité au Dahomey
Hachette. Paris. 1891.

Jacques Chevrier
L'arbre à palabres.
Essai sur les contes et récits traditionnels de l'Afrique noire
Hatier.

Catherine Coquery-Vidrovitch et Henri Moniot
L'Afrique noire de 1800 à nos jours
P.U.F.

Robert Cornevin
Histoire de l'Afrique
Payot.

Robert Cornevin
Histoire des peuples d'Afrique noire
Berger-Levrault.

Robert Cornevin
Histoire du Dahomey
Berger-Levrault.

Robert Cornevin
Les mémoires de l'Afrique
Robert Laffont.

Basil Davidson
Le réveil de l'Afrique
Présence Africaine.

André Davy
Éthiopie d'hier et d'aujourd'hui
Le Livre Africain.

Maurice Delafosse
Haut-Sénégal-Niger
Maisonneuve/Larose.

Dominique Desanti
Côte d'Ivoire
Rencontre.

Djibril Dione et Sékéné Mody Cissoko
Histoire de l'Afrique
Présence Africaine.

Cheikh Anta Diop
Nations nègres et culture
Présence Africaine.

Jean Doresse
La vie quotidienne des Éthiopiens chrétiens aux XVIIe et XVIIIe siècles
Hachette.

Elian J. Finbert
Le livre de la sagesse nègre
Robert Laffont.

Robert Gaffiofa
Gorée. Capitale déchue
L. Fournier.

Célestin Goma Foutou
Histoire des civilisations du Congo
Anthropos.

Henry Gravrand
La civilisation Sereer
Nouvelles Éditions Africaines.

Marcel Guilhem et A. Traore
Mali, récits historiques
Ligel.

Djibril Dione et Sékéné Mody Cissoko
Histoire de l'Afrique
Marcel Guilhem et Michel Yapi
Côte d'Ivoire, récits historiques
Ligel.

Histoire générale de l'Afrique
UNESCO/Nouvelles Éditions Africaines.

J. Janvier
Autour des missions Voulet-Chanoine en Afrique occidentale
Revue *Présence Africaine* n° 22.

Charles-André Julien
Les Africains
Jeune Afrique.

Ibrahima Baba Kaké
Chaka
ABC/NEA.

Ibrahima Baba Kaké
Mémoire de l'Afrique. La diaspora noire.
ABC/NEA

Ibrahima Baba Kaké
Dona Béatrice
« Grandes figures africaines ». ABC.

Ibrahima Baba Kaké
Combats pour l'histoire africaine
Présence Africaine.

Ibrahima Baba Kaké et Elikia M'Bokolo
*Histoire Générale de l'Afrique.
La dispersion des Bantous*
Nouvelles Éditions Africaines.

Joseph Kessel
Marché d'esclaves
Union Générale d'Éditions.

Joseph Ki-Zerbo
Histoire de l'Afrique noire
Hatier.

R.P. Labat
Le voyage du Chevalier des Marchais en Guinée, Isles voisines et à Cayenne (1725, 1726, 1727). Amsterdam.

Roger Labatut
Chants de vie et de beauté chez les Peuls nomades du Nord-Cameroun
Publications Orientalistes de France.

Recueil de littérature mandingue
ACCT.

David Livingstone
Explorations dans l'Afrique australe.
Librairie Hachette. Paris. 1868.
Karthala. 1981.

Jean-Noël Loucou et Françoise Ligier
La reine Pokou
Nouvelles Éditions Africaines/ABC.

René Luneau
Chants de femmes au Mali
Luneau-Ascot Éditeurs.

Angelo B. Maliki
Bonheur et souffrance chez les Peuls nomades
Edicef/CILF.

Abdoulaye Mamani
Sarraounia
« Encres Noires »
L'Harmattan.

Claude Meillassoux
Anthropologie de l'esclavage
P.U.F.

Elikia M'Bokolo
L'ère des calamités. L'Afrique australe au XIXe et au XXe siècle
Nouvelles Éditions Africaines/ABC.

Henry de Monfreid
Ménélik tel qu'il fut
Bernard Grasset.

Djibril Tamsir Niane
Soundiata ou l'épopée mandingue
Présence Africaine.

Pius Ngandu Nkashama
et Bernard Magnier
L'Afrique noire en poésie
Gallimard.

Théophile Obenga
Afrique centrale précoloniale
Présence Africaine.

Achola O. Pala et Madina Ly
*La femme africaine
dans la société précoloniale*
UNESCO.

Jean Paulhan
Les Hain-Tenys
Gallimard.

Yves Person et Françoise Ligier
Samori
Nouvelles Éditions Africaines/ABC.

Protest and power in Black Africa
Oxford University Press.

Proverbes et contes Mossi
Edicef/CILF.

Christian Roche
Histoire de la Casamance, Conquête et résistance : 1850-1920
Karthala.

La Sagesse des nations
Les Libraires Associés
Club des Libraires de France.

Christian Saglio
Sénégal
Seuil.

Léopold Sedar-Senghor
Anthologie de la nouvelle poésie nègre et malgache
P.U.F.

James Sibree
Madagascar et ses habitants
Société des livres religieux de Toulouse
1873.

Gabriel Simon
L'Éthiopie, ses mœurs, ses traditions, le Négouss Iohannes, les églises monolithes de Lalibella
Challamel Aîné. Paris. 1885.

Alfa Ibrahîm Sow
La femme, la vache, la foi
Julliard.

Solange Thierry
Madagascar
« Petite Planète ». Seuil.

Victor Tissot
L'Afrique pittoresque
Librairie Delagrave.

Jeanne Vilardebo
Connaissance des Arts
numéro d'Octobre 1968.

Bruce Williams
A lost Kingdom in Nubia at the Dawn of History
Notes and News
The Oriental Institute. Chicago. 1977.

SOURCES OF TEXTS CITED: pp. 1-201

Black Eve

───── PAGE 8 ─────

La mère du genre humain
Anthologie nègre
Blaise CENDRARS, Buchet-Chastel

La légende de la création
Blaise CENDRARS, *opus cité.*

Pourquoi le monde fut peuplé
Blaise CENDRARS, *op. cit.*

───── PAGE 10 ─────

Ève noire origine de l'homme
et unité de la race humaine
Phéhistory and the humanities
C. Van RIET LOWE
South African Journal of Science.

Ève noire, une preuve supplémentaire par
la génétique
L'Express (janv. 87).

───── PAGE 15 ─────

Parole d'une femme ordinaire
Bonheur et souffrance chez les Peuls nomades
Angelo B. MALIKI, Edicef, CILF.

Black Women 10,000 Years Ago

───── PAGE 18 ─────

Homme à califourchon
A la découverte des fresques du Tassili
Henry LHOTE, Arthaud.

L'art
La vie quotidienne aux temps des premiers chasseurs,
Jacques MAUDUIT, Hachette.

La découverte
Henry LHOTE, *opus cit.*

───── PAGE 22 ─────

Les trois styles rupestres
Premières Afriques
Luc CROEGAERT, Didier-Hatier.

───── PAGE 24 ─────

Le désert
L'Afrique ancienne
Basil DAVIDSON, François Maspéro.

───── PAGE 25 ─────

Histoire du peuplement de l'Afrique
Histoire de l'Afrique
Djibril DJONE, Sékéné Mody CISSOKO,
Présence Africaine.

Ahmose Nofretari

───── PAGE 32 ─────

Scène d'amour
La femme au temps des pharaons
Christiane DESROCHES-NOBLECOURT
Stock/Laurence Pernoud

───── PAGE 34 ─────

Ahotep
Christiane DESROCHES-NOBLECOURT, *opus cité.*

───── PAGE 35 ─────

La toilette d'une dame
La vie quotidienne en Égypte au temps des Ramsès
Pierre MONTET, Hachette.

Chant d'amour
L'empire des Ramsès
Claire LALOUETTE, Fayard.

───── PAGE 36 ─────

La belle heure
Les chants d'amour de l'Égypte ancienne
Siegfried SCHOTT
L'Orient Ancien Illustré.

Ivresse
Christiane Desroches-Noblecourt, *op. cit.*

La vérité
Siegfried Schott, *opus cité*.

Chant d'amour
Claire Lalouette, *opus cité*.

──────── PAGE 39 ────────

La musique
Pierre Montet, *op. cit.*

Musiciens et danseuses
Christiane Desroches-Noblecourt, *op. cit.*

Hatshepsut

──────── PAGE 48 ────────

L'inondation et les larmes d'Isis
Pierre Montet, *op. cit.*

──────── PAGE 49 ────────

Elle est un champ fertile
Siegfried Schott, *op. cit.*

Lettre d'un fils à sa mère
Siegfried Schott, *op. cit.*

──────── PAGE 50 ────────

Sénemout
La femme au temps des pharaons
Christiane Desroches-Noblecourt, *op. cit.*

Tiye

──────── PAGE 55 ────────

Chants d'amour
Siegfried Schott, *op. cit.*

Les fêtes
L'Éthiopie, berceau de l'humanité
Paulette et Maurice Deribere
Société Continentale d'Éditions Modernes Illustrées.

──────── PAGE 56 ────────

Les divines adoratrices
Paulette et Maurice Deribere, *opus cité*.

──────── PAGE 60 ────────

Les vendanges
Siegfried Schott, *op. cit.*

Hymne au soleil
Nefertiti
Philipp Vandenberg, Belfond.

Proverbe
Siegfried Schott, *op. cit.*

The Candaces

──────── PAGE 66 ────────

Contribution du peuple nubier à l'histoire universelle
Diodore de Sicile, Bibliothèque Historique.
Présence Africaine, nos 133-134, 1985.

──────── PAGE 67 ────────

L'état actuel des recherches sur la Nubie
Alain Anselin
Présence Africaine, nos 133-134, 1985.

──────── PAGE 69 ────────

Les reines de Kouch
Nubia corridor to Africa
William Y. Adams
Princeton University Press.

──────── PAGE 70 ────────

La vie quotidienne à Méroé
Basil Davidson, *op. cit.*

Les premières tombes de Kouch
Egypt in Nubia
Walter B. Emery
Hutchinson of London.

Makeda

──────── PAGE 76 ────────

Le Cantique des Cantiques.
Bible

──────── PAGE 78 ────────

Musiciens, chanteurs et bouffons
La vie quotidienne des Éthiopiens chrétiens au XVIIe et XVIIIe siècles,
Jean Doresse, Hachette.

──────── PAGE 80 ────────

Comment Salomon séduisit Makéda avec un verre d'eau
Ménélik tel qu'il fut
Henry de Monfreid, Bernard Grasset.

Daurama

──────── PAGE 90 ────────

Un mariage Haoussa
Baba de Karo
Mary F. Smith, « Terre humaine », Plon.

──────── PAGE 91 ────────

Louange à Fatou Seydi
La femme, la vache, la foi,
Alfâ Ibrahim Soro Sow
« Classique africains », Petters.

Proverbe
Blaise Cendrars, *op. cit.*

──────── PAGE 92 ────────

Daoura
Niger, récits historiques
Marcel Guilhem, Boubou Hama, Ligel.

Proverbe
Le livre de la sagesse nègre,
Elian J. Finbert, Robert Laffont.

──────── PAGE 99 ────────

Paroles d'une femme ordinaire
Angelo B. Maliki, *op. cit*

Yennenga

──────── PAGE 104 ────────

La puissance du Mogho Naba
Précis d'histoire de la Haute Volta
Marcel Guilhem, Ligel.

Le Magho Naba et ses ministres
Marcel Guilhem, *op. cit.*

──────── PAGE 105 ────────

Fortune et stabilité des empires mossi
Précis d'histoire de l'Ouest africain
Marcel Guilhem, Ligel.

──────── PAGE 108 ────────

Les origines du prince Riâlé, époux de Yennenga
Tidugu, « Journal catholique de Fada N'Gourma »,
Raphaël Lompo.

──────── PAGE 109 ────────

Le Tinsé
Histoires et coutumes royales des Mossi du Ouagadougou,
Yemba Tiendrébéogo.

──────── PAGE 111 ────────

La famille et l'entourage du Mogho Naba
Marcel Guilhem, *op. cit.*

──────── PAGE 112 ────────

Dori, capitale du Liptako
Marcel Guilhem, *op. cit.*

Proverbe
Elian J. Finbert, *op. cit.*

Fable
Proverbes et contes Mossi
« Fleuve et Flamme », Edicef, CILF

──────── PAGE 113 ────────

Paroles d'une femme ordinaire
Angelo B. Maliki, *op. cit.*

Sogolon Konté

──────── PAGE 121 ────────

Amavoukoutou
Blaise Cendrars, *op. cit*

──────── PAGE 122 ────────

La mère
La femme africaine dans la société précoloniale, Achola O'Pala, Madina Ly
Unesco.

Chant à la mère
Achola O'Pala, Madina Ly, *op. cit.*

Proverbe
Elian J. Finbert, *op. cit.*

──────── PAGE 124 ────────

Naissance de Biton Coulibaly
Histoire de l'Afrique Noire,
Joseph Ki-Zerbo, Hatier.

Proverbe
Elian J. Finbert, *op. cit.*

---PAGE 125---

Paroles d'une femme ordinaire
Angelo B. Maliki, *op. cit.*

Amina Kulibali

---PAGE 133---

Le nom du Sénégal
Sénégal,
Christian Saglio, « Petite Planète », Seuil.

Complainte d'amour
Contes et légendes du Sénégal,
André Terrisse, F. Nathan.

Proverbe
Proverbes et contes Mossi, op. cit.

---PAGE 134---

Proverbe
Elian J. Finbert, *op. cit.*

---PAGE 135---

Histoire du Siné Saloum
Sénégal, récits historiques,
M. Guilhem, H.N'Diaye, Ligel.

---PAGE 136---

La tradition orale
Christian Saglio
Sénégal
« Petite Planète », Seuil.

Proverbe
Elian J. Finbert, *op. cit.*

---PAGE 142---

Les lingers
Christian Saglio, *op. cit.*

---PAGE 144---

Paroles d'une femme ordinaire
Angelo B. Maliki, *op. cit.*

Amina of Zaria

---PAGE 152---

Ousmane dan Fodio
Boubou Hama, Marcel Guilhem
Niger, récits historiques.

Proverbes
Elian J. Finbert, *op. cit.*

---PAGE 154---

Zaria
Nigéria du réel à l'imaginaire
Ola Balogun, « Grands livres »
Jeune Afrique.

---PAGE 158---

Kano
Voyages et découvertes dans l'Afrique septentrionale et centrale pendant les années 1849 à 1855
Henri Barth, A. Bohne Librairie, 1850.

---PAGE 161---

Paroles d'une femme ordinaire
Angelo B. Maliki, *op. cit.*

Heleni

---PAGE 168---

Comment les femmes utilisent la toge
Douze ans de séjour dans la Haute-Éthiopie (Abyssinie),
Arnauld d'Abbadie
Biblioteca Apostolica Vaticana, Citta del Vaticano.

Différentes façons de draper la toge
Arnauld d'Abbadie, *opus cité.*

---PAGE 169---

Guerre avec l'Islam
L'Éthiopie, ses mœurs, ses traditions, le Négouss Iohannès, les églises monolithes de Lalibéla,
Gabriel Simon, Challamel Aîné, 1885.

---PAGE 170---

Politesse et insultes déguisées
Jean Doresse, *op. cit.*

Préparation du pain
Gabriel Simon, *op. cit.*

Proverbe
Elian J. Finbert, *op. cit.*

Ana de Sousa Nzinga

---PAGE 178---

Naissance d'Anna Zingha
Anna Zingha, reine d'Angola, première résistante à l'invasion portugaise
Ibrahima Baba Kaké
« Grandes figures africaines », ABC/NEA.

Jeunes filles Quimbandès
Comment j'ai traversé l'Afrique depuis l'Atlantique jusqu'à l'océan Indien
Major Serpa Pinto, Hachette, 1881.

Proverbe
Elian J. Finbert, *op. cit.*

---PAGE 182---

La Reine Zingha
R.P. Labat, Charles Jean-Baptiste Delespine.

---PAGE 183---

La manière de tisser et de filer
Explorations dans l'intérieur de l'Afrique australe et voyages à travers le continent de St Paul de Loanda à l'embouchure du Zambèze (de 1840 à 1856)
Hachette.

---PAGE 184---

Conspiration des notables de Cabasso
Ibrahima Baba Kaké, *op. cit.*

Proverbe
Elian J. Finbert, *op. cit.*

---PAGE 186---

Mort d'Anna Zingha
Ibrahima Baba Kaké, *op. cit.*

---PAGE 187---

Paroles d'une femme ordinaire
Angelo B. Mamiki, *op. cit.*

Mentowah

---PAGE 191---

Coquetterie des femmes
Douze ans de séjour dans la Haute-Éthiopie (Abyssinie),
Arnauld d'Abbadie, *op. cit.*

---PAGE 192---

Beauté des Éthiopiens
Jean Doresse, *op. cit.*

L'attachement à la terre
Éthiopie, un drame impérial et rouge,
Jean Bureau, Ramsay.

---PAGE 194---

Gondar
Jean Doresse, *op. cit.*

Chasse royale
Jean Doresse, *op. cit.*

---PAGE 197---

La vie quotidienne
Jean Doresse, *op. cit.*

---PAGE 198---

Esther, fille de Mentowab
Jean Doresse, *op. cit.*

SOURCES OF TEXT CITED: pp. 202-404

Beatrice Kimpa Vita

PAGE 205

Habillement des femmes
La vie quotidienne au royaume de Kongo du XVIe au XVIIIe siècle
Georges BALANDIER. Hachette.

Habillement des hommes
Georges BALANDIER, *op. cit.*

Le soleil
Georges BALANDIER, *op. cit.*

PAGE 207

L'ivoire noir
Histoire des Civilisations du Congo
Célestin GOMA FOUTOU. Anthropos.

La pièce d'Inde
Célestin GOMA FOUTOU, *op. cit.*

Proverbes
Le livre de la sagesse nègre
Elian J. FINBERT. Robert Laffont.

PAGE 209

Audience publique du roi du Congo
d'après PIGAFETTA
Histoire générale des voyages. Tome V.
Didot.

PAGE 219

Paroles d'une femme ordinaire
*Bonheur et souffrance
chez les Peuls nomades*
Angelo B. MALIKI. Edicef/CILF.

Queen Poku

PAGE 223

La femme sans enfants
Femmes du Cameroun
Jean-Claude BARBIER. Karthala.

Sculpture de poulie
Connaissance des Arts
Jeanne VILARDEBO, numéro d'Octobre 1968.

PAGE 224

J'ai accouché
Chants de femmes au Mali
René LUNEAU. Luneau-Ascot Éditeurs.
Origine des royaumes Agni
Côte d'Ivoire, Récits historiques
Marcel GUILHEM, Michel YAPI. Ligel.

Proverbe Baoulé
Côte d'Ivoire
Dominique DESANTI. Rencontre.

PAGE 225

Maisons du cap Mezurado
Le voyage du Cheval'er des Marchais en Guinée, Isles voisines et à Cayenne (1725, 1726, 1727). Tome I. R.P. LABAT. Amsterdam.

PAGE 226

Chant funèbre
Dominique DESANTI, *op. cit.*

Les poids à peser l'or
Côte d'Ivoire, L'artisanat créateur
Jacques ANQUETIL. A.C.C.T.

PAGE 227

Nanguin fonde Korhogo
Marcel GUILHEM, Michel YAPI, *op. cit.*

PAGE 229

Paroles d'une femme ordinaire
Angelo B. MALIKI, *op. cit.*

Sogané Touré

PAGE 233

Journée d'une femme
*La femme africaine
dans la société précolcniale*
Achola O. PALA et Madina LY. UNESCO.

―――――― PAGE 235 ――――――

Femme noire, femme africaine
L'enfant noir
Camara LAYE. « Liminaires ». Plon.

O mère, ma mère
Achola O. PALA et Madina LY, *op. cit.*

―――――― PAGE 236 ――――――

El-Hadj Omar
Mali, récits historiques
M. GUILHEM et A. TRAORE. Ligel.

―――――― PAGE 238 ――――――

Femme de Tombouctou
Journal d'un voyage à Tombouctou et à Jenné, dans l'Afrique Centrale
René CAILLIE. Imprimerie Royale. Paris. 1830.

Proverbe
Elian J. FINBERT, *op. cit.*

―――――― PAGE 239 ――――――

Sacrifice d'une jeune fille
Haut-Sénégal Niger, tome I
Maurice DELAFOSSE. Maisonneuve/Larose.

―――――― PAGE 240 ――――――

Paroles d'une femme ordinaire
Angelo B. MALIKI, *op. cit.*

The Story of Nandi

―――――― PAGE 246 ――――――

Vie quotidienne au village
L'Attila Noir
Peter BECKER. Librairie Plon.

―――――― PAGE 247 ――――――

Les Amazoulous
Relation d'un voyage d'exploration au nord-est de la colonie du cap de Bonne-Espérance, entrepris dans les mois de mars, avril et mai 1836. T. ARBOUSSET et F. DAUMAS
Arthus Bertrand. Paris. 1842.

Chant de fête
Chants de vie et de beauté chez les Peuls nomades du Nord-Cameroun
Roger LABATUT
Publications Orientalistes de France.

Proverbe
La sagesse des nations
Les Libraires Associés
Club des Libraires de France.

―――――― PAGE 248 ――――――

La chasse à l'éléphant
Explorations dans l'Afrique australe (1840-1864). David LIVINGSTONE
Librairie Hachette. 1868. Karthala. 1981.

―――――― PAGE 251 ――――――

Le kraal de Chaka
Peter BECKER, *op. cit.*

Les noms des régiments
T. ARBOUSSET et F. DAUMAS, *op. cit.*

La précarité de la vie
T. ARBOUSSET et F. DAUMAS, *op. cit.*

Proverbe
Blaise CENDRARS, *op. cit.*

―――――― PAGE 252 ――――――

Les guerriers de Chaka
Travels and Adventures. Tome I. N. ISAACS.

―――――― PAGE 253 ――――――

Chaka, génie militaire
Les Africains, tome II et VIII
Charles-André JULIEN. Jeune Afrique.

―――――― PAGE 256 ――――――

L'assassinat de Chaka
Birds, Annals of Natal. Tome I. H.F. FYNN.

Tata Ajeché

―――――― PAGE 262 ――――――

Les origines légendaires du Dahomey
Les Amazones
Hélène d'ALMEIDA-TOPOR. Rochevignes.

―――――― PAGE 263 ――――――

Dahoméennes
Trois mois de captivité au Dahomey
E. CHAUDOIN. Hachette.

Compteuses de cauris
La France au Dahomey
Alexandre L.D. ALBECA. Hachette.

Proverbe
Proverbes et contes Mossi
Édicef. CILF. Paris. 1982.

―――――― PAGE 264 ――――――

Organisation des Amazones
d'après Hélène d'ALMEIDA-TOPOR, *op. cit.*

La première guerre des Amazones
d'après Hélène d'ALMEIDA-TOPOR, *op. cit.*

―――――― PAGE 265 ――――――

En joue !
cité par Hélène d'ALMEIDA-TOPOR, *op. cit.*

Le défi de la générale
Charles-André JULIEN, *op. cit.*

On meurt n'importe où
cité par Hélène d'ALMEIDA-TOPOR, *op. cit.*

―――――― PAGE 266 ――――――

Proverbes
Elian J. FINBERT, *op. cit.*

―――――― PAGE 269 ――――――

Paroles d'une femme ordinaire
Angelo B. MALIKI, *op. cit.*

Modjadji I

―――――― PAGE 274 ――――――

Les faiseurs de pluie
Peter BECKER, *op. cit.*

―――――― PAGE 275 ――――――

Le conte de Tsélané
T. ARBOUSSET et F. DAUMAS, *op. cit.*

Proverbe
La sagesse des nations, op. cit.

―――――― PAGE 276 ――――――

La vie quotidienne en village sotho
Peter BECKER, *op. cit.*

L'empire du Monomotapa
d'après PIGAFETTA, *op. cit.*

―――――― PAGE 277 ――――――

Le gnou
Les Bassoutos
E. CASALIS. Librairie de Ch. Meyrueis et Cie.
Paris. 1859.

L'antilope bubale
T. ARBOUSSET et F. DAUMAS, *op. cit.*

Chant du bubale
T. ARBOUSSET et F. DAUMAS, *op. cit.*

―――――― PAGE 278 ――――――

La lune et le nouveau-né
E. CASALIS, *op. cit.*

―――――― PAGE 280 ――――――

Chant de l'hivernage
Rober LABATUT, *op. cit..*

La chanson de la pluie
T. ARBOUSSET et F. DAUMAS, *op. cit..*

Ranavalona I

―――――― PAGE 287 ――――――

Rahaviny
d'après R.P. CALLET, *Histoire des rois*
Éditions de la librairie malgache.

Danse guerrière des Sakalaves
d'après James SIBREE
Madagascar et ses habitants
Société des livres religieux de Toulouse
1873.

―――――― PAGE 289 ――――――

Tananarive
L'Afrique pittoresque. Ida PFEIFFER
Lectures choisies par Victor TISSOT
Librairie Delagrave. Paris. 1888.

Tananarive, quartier des palais
d'après James SIBREE, *op. cit.*

La maison du chef à Ambatomanga
d'après James SIBREE, *op. cit.*

―――――― PAGE 291 ――――――

Le fiséhoana de Ranavalona I
d'après James SIBREE, *op. cit.*

Le Kabary de Ranavalona I
d'après James SIBREE, *op. cit.*

Chasse aux bœufs sauvages
d'après James SIBREE, *op. cit.*

―――――― PAGE 293 ――――――

L'enfant royal et le sanglier
R.P. CALLET, *op. cit.*

Village malgache
L'Afrique pittoresque. Charles SEGARD, *op. cit.*

N'Daté Yalla

—— PAGE 300 ——

Lat-Dior
D'après J. Ki Zerbo
Histoire de l'Afrique noire. Hatier.

Proverbe
Elian J. Finbert, *op. cit.*

—— PAGE 302 ——

Gorée, île d'épouvante
Gorée, capitale déchue
Robert Gaffiofa. L. Fournier.

—— PAGE 303 ——

La traite saharienne
Anthologie de l'esclavage
Claude Meillassoux. P.U.F.

—— PAGE 304 ——

Le Prince Antar
Agendafrique. Librairie Larousse. RFI.

—— PAGE 307 ——

Paroles d'une femme ordinaire
Angelo B. Maliki, *op. cit.*

Nongquwuse

—— PAGE 312 ——

Le gué de l'orange
T. Arbousset et F. Daumas, *op. cit.*

—— PAGE 314 ——

L'attachement à la terre
E. Casalis, *op. cit.*

—— PAGE 315 ——

L'arrivée des Portugais
E. Casalis, *op. cit.*

Les guerres cafres
L'Afrique noire de 1800 à nos jours
Catherine Coquery-Vidrovitch
et Henri Moniot. P.U.F.

—— PAGE 316 ——

Les armes des Blancs
T. Arbousset et F. Daumas, *op. cit.*

L'importance du bétail
Peter Becker, *op. cit.*

Proverbe
La sagesse des nations, *op. cit.*

—— PAGE 317 ——

Histoire tragique de Siwitani, roi du Mongoli
T. Arbousset et F. Daumas, *op. cit.*

Sarraounia

—— PAGE 323 ——

Les missions Voulet-Chanoine en Afrique Occidentale (1896-1899)
Autour des missions Voulet-Chanoine
Jacques Janvier
Revue *Présence Africaine*, n° 22.

Chant des mercenaires
Sarraounia, Abdoulaye Mamani.
« Encres Noires ». L'Harmattan.

Proverbe
Anthologie Nègre
Blaise Cendrars. Buchet-Chastel.

—— PAGE 326 ——

L'enfance de la Sarraounia
Abdoulaye Mamani, *op. cit.*

Les recommandations du sage
Abdoulaye Mamani, *op. cit.*

L'initiation de la Sarraounia
Abdoulaye Mamani, *op. cit.*

—— PAGE 327 ——

Chant du Griot Gogué, amant de la reine
Abdoulaye Mamani, *op. cit.*

L'annonce de la grande guerre contre les Blancs
Abdoulaye Mamani, *op. cit.*

Proverbe
Blaise Cendrars, *op. cit.*

—— PAGE 328 ——

Organisation de la défense
Abdoulaye Mamani, *op. cit.*

—— PAGE 330 ——

Pour que vive le nom des Aznas
Abdoulaye Mamani, *op. cit.*

Proverbe
Elian J. Finbert, *op. cit.*

—— PAGE 332 ——

Discours de la reine aux frères et sœurs des autres nations d'Afrique.
Abdoulaye Mamani, *op. cit.*

—— PAGE 335 ——

Paroles d'une femme ordinaire
Angelo B. Maliki, *op. cit.*

The Story of Naga

—— PAGE 339 ——

Proverbe
Elian J. Finbert, *op. cit.*

—— PAGE 341 ——

Le travail des femmes
E. Chaudoin, *op. cit.*

Fabrication de l'huile de palme
Alexandre L.D. Albeca, *op. cit.*

—— PAGE 344 ——

Le courage des femmes
Hélène d'Almeida-Topor, *op. cit.*

Une lettre de Béhanzin
Hélène d'Almeida-Topor, *op. cit.*

Proverbe
Blaise Cendrars, *op. cit.*

—— PAGE 347 ——

La survivante
Hélène d'Almeida-Topor, *op. cit.*

Un courage royal
Hélène d'Almeida-Topor, *op. cit.*

Proverbe
Elian J. Finbert, *op. cit.*

—— PAGE 349 ——

Paroles d'une femme ordinaire
Angelo B. Maliki, *op. cit.*

Manta Tisi

—— PAGE 355 ——

Le lézard et le caméléon
T. Arbousset et F. Daumas, *op. cit.*

Le Calédon
T. Arbousset et F. Daumas, *op. cit.*

Réponse de Manta Tisi au missionnaire
T. Arbousset et F. Daumas, *op. cit.*

Proverbe
La sagesse des nations, *op. cit.*

—— PAGE 356 ——

Le siège de Butha-Buthé
T. Arbousset et F. Daumas, *op. cit.*

Proverbe
Blaise Cendrars, *op. cit.*

—— PAGE 357 ——

Invitation à la danse
Roger Labatut, *op. cit.*

Plaidoirie
E. Casalis, *op. cit.*

Chant pour le départ des troupeaux
Roger Labatut, *op. cit.*

—— PAGE 360 ——

Style créole pour le cœur
E. Casalis, *op. cit.*

La demande en mariage
E. Casalis, *op. cit.*

Taitu Bethel

—— PAGE 365 ——

Ménélik
Ethiopie d'hier et d'aujourd'hui
André Davy. Le livre africain.

Le grand-père de Ménélik
Ménélik tel qu'il fut
Henry de Monfreid. Bernard Grasset.

—— Page 367 ——

Coiffures des femmes
L'Éthiopie, ses mœurs, ses traditions, le Négouss Johannes, les églises monolithes de Lalibéla
Gabriel Simon. Challamel Aîné. Paris. 1885.

L'agriculture
La vie quotidienne des Éthiopiens chrétiens aux XVIIe et XVIIIe siècle
Jean DORESSE. Hachette.

Proverbe
Dictionnaire des proverbes du monde op. cit.

───── PAGE 369 ─────

La reine Warquit
Henry de MONFREID, *op. cit.*

La traite
Marché d'esclaves
Joseph KESSEL. Union Générale d'Éditions.

───── PAGE 370 ─────

Le testament de Ménélik
Henry de MONFREID, *op. cit.*

Proverbes
Dictionnaire des proverbes du monde, op. cit.

───── PAGE 372 ─────

La bataille d'Adoua, le 1er Mars 1896
Henry de MONFREID, *op. cit.*

Une victoire inouïe
Éthiopie un drame impérial et rouge
Jacques BUREAU. Ramsay.

Ranavalona III

───── PAGE 381 ─────

Le géant Darafély
d'après James SIBREE, *op. cit.*

L'arbre du voyageur
d'après James SIBREE, *op. cit.*

───── PAGE 382 ─────

La femme enfant
Presque Songes, J.J. RABEARIVELO.
Anthologie de la nouvelle poésie nègre et malgache. Léopold SEDAR-SENGHOR. P.U.F.

───── PAGE 384 ─────

La légende de Tritriva
d'après James SIBREE, *op. cit.*

Proverbe
Madagascar, Les hains tenys
Solange THIERRY
« Petite Planète ». Seuil.

───── PAGE 385 ─────

Si vous alliez à Ambohimanga
Les Hain-Tenys
Jean PAULHAN, Gallimard.

Les charmes de la langue malgache
d'après James SIBREE, *op. cit.*

Dis aux nuages d'attendre
Jean PAULHAN, *op. cit.*

Proverbe
Dictionnaire des maximes et proverbes op. cit.

───── PAGE 388 ─────

Bos Zebu
d'après James SIBREE, *op. cit.*

Oignon aux racines bleues
Jean PAULHAN, *op. cit.*

Le filanzana
d'après James SIBREE, *op. cit.*

───── PAGE 390 ─────

La folie du désir
Jean PAULHAN, *op. cit.*

Je suis le riz, vous êtes l'eau
Jean PAULHAN, *op. cit.*

Proverbe
Dictionnaire des maximes et proverbes, op. cit.

───── PAGE 393 ─────

Paroles d'une femme ordinaire
Angelo B. MALIKI, *op. cit.*

Mamochisane

───── PAGE 398 ─────

Chant funèbre des Bassoutos
E. CASALIS, *op. cit.*

La chasse
Peter BECKER, *op. cit.*

───── PAGE 399 ─────

La légende du lac Dilolo
David LIVINGSTONE, *op. cit.*

Travail des champs
Peter BECKER, *op. cit.*

───── PAGE 400 ─────

Chant d'hivernage
Roger LABATUT, *op. cit.*

Proverbe
La sagesse des nations, op. cit.

Les chutes du Zambèze
David LIVINGSTONE, *op. cit.*

Proverbe
La sagesse des nations, op. cit.

LIST OF ILLUSTRATIONS: pp. 1-201

Black Eve

_____ PAGE 2 _____

Peinture de Henri ROUSSEAU (1844-1910).
La charmeuse de serpents. H/t. 46 × 55 cm.
Paris, Musée d'Orsay. Snark/Edimédia.

_____ PAGE 4 _____

Gravure anonyme. Création du monde,
Dieu bénit Adam et Eve.
Coll Part. D.R.

Jeune fille africaine.
Paris, Documentation française.

_____ PAGE 5 _____

Jeune fille africaine.
Paris, Documentation française.

_____ PAGE 6/7 _____

Peinture de Henri ROUSSEAU (1844-1910).
La cascade. 1910. H/t. 116 × 150 cm.
Chicago, Art Institute.
Munich, Schirmer Mosel Verlag.

_____ PAGE 8 _____

Sculpture. Femme à la cruche.
Bois. Coll. part. D.R.

_____ PAGE 9 _____

Peinture naïve haïtienne de P. AUGUSTE.
Le jardin d'Eden. 1972
in Jean-Marie DROT. *Journal de voyage chez les peintres de la fête et du vaudou en Haïti.*
Genève, Skira. Photo ORTF.

Canthare. Têtes de femme blanche et de Noir. VIe siècle av. J.C. Terre cuite. H : 19,2 cm.
Boston, Museum of Fine Arts.
Houston, Menil Foundation/Hickey and Robertson.

_____ PAGE 10 _____

Kenya. Réserve d'Amborelli.
Au fond, le Kilimandjaro.
DIAF/Photo Jean GABANOU.

_____ PAGE 11 _____

Femme africaine.
Paris, Documentation française.

_____ PAGE 12/13 _____

Peinture naïve haïtienne d'André NORMIL.
Le paradis terrestre. in J.M. DROT. *op. cit.*
Genève, Skira. Photo ORTF.

_____ PAGE 14 _____

Femme du Kenya.
DIAF. Photo Jean GABANOU.

_____ PAGE 15 _____

Jeunes femmes africaines.
Paris, Documentation française.

Black Women
10,000 Years Ago

_____ PAGE 16 _____

Fresques du Tassili. Femmes.
Photo J.D. LAJOUX.

_____ PAGE 18 _____

Fresques du Tassili. Gardien et son troupeau.
Photo J.D. LAJOUX.

Fresques du Tassili. Homme à califourchon.
Coll. Henri LHOTE.

_____ PAGE 19 _____

Fresques du Tassili.
Photo J.D. LAJOUX.

_____ PAGE 20/21 _____

Fresques du Tassili. Femmes et enfants.
Photo J.D. LAJOUX.

_____ PAGE 22 _____

Fresques du Tassili.
Troupeau de bovidés. Coll. Henri LHOTE.

Fresques du Tassili. Chars au galop.
Coll. Henri LHOTE.

_____ PAGE 22/23 _____

Fresques du Tassili.
Photo J.D. LAJOUX.

_____ PAGE 23 _____

Fresque du Tassili. Site de Sabbaren.
Coursier avec arc.
Photo J.D. LAJOUX.

_____ PAGE 24 _____

Paysage du Tassili en Algérie.
Photo J.D. LAJOUX.

Fresques du Tassili. Campement.
Photo J.D. LAJOUX.

_____ PAGE 25 _____

Fresques du Tassili. Femme et enfant.
Coll. Henri LHOTE.

_____ PAGE 26/27 _____

Femmes du Tassili, dans les oasis.
Photo J.D. LAJOUX.

Ahmose Nofretari

_____ PAGE 28 _____

Statuette représentant Ahmose Nefertari.
Bois polychrome.
MAGNUM/Photo Eric LESSING.

_____ PAGE 30 _____

Aquarelle de G.S. CAUTLEY.
Pyramides vues du Nil, près du Caire.
XIXe siècle.
Londres, Victoria and Albert Museum/
Edimédia.

Peigne africain. Coll. part.

Peigne égyptien. XVIIIe dynastie. Bois.
Photo R.M.N.

Peigne africain. Coll. Part.

_____ PAGE 31 _____

Chasse aux oiseaux avec le bâton à jet.
Relevé de la tombe de Nakht.
in Nina M. DAVIES. Ancien Egyptian Paintings.
University of Chicago Press/Photo Hachette.

_____ PAGE 32 _____

Musicienne jouant du hautbois, danseuses.
in Nina M. DAVIES. op. cit.
Photo Hachette.

Scène de réjouissances. Danseuses.
Bas relief en calcaire. 10×51 cm
CdA/Photo GUILLEMOT/Edimédia.

Miroir.
Photo R.M.N.

_____ PAGE 33 _____

Vase avec tête d'un membre de la famille
royale. 1350 avant J.C.
Le Caire, Musée égyptien.
MAGNUM/Photo Eric LESSING.

_____ PAGE 34 _____

Akmès-Nofertari, mère d'Aménophis 1er.
1550-1530 av. J.C.
Berlin Est, Musée égyptien/Edimédia.

Égypte. Louxor. Deir el Medineh.
Tombe de Sennedpem. XVIIIe dynastie.
Edimédia/Photo TAGHER.

_____ PAGE 35 _____

Égypte. Thèbes. Vallée des Nobles.
Tombe de Nakht.
Toilette des dames. XVIIIe dynastie.
Photo J.D. LAJOUX.

Égypte. Cuillère à fard représentant
une jeune femme.
Bois clair et couvercle en tamaris. H : 31,5 cm.
Paris, Musée du Louvre/Edimédia.

_____ PAGE 36 _____

Fresque représentant la reine Nofertari
conduite par Horus. XIXe dynastie.
Le Caire, Musée égyptien/Snark/Edimédia.

Chapelle du roi Touthmosis. XVIIIe dynastie.
Le Caire, Musée égyptien/Edimédia.

_____ PAGE 37 _____

Neferhotep et sa femme Meryt font une
offrande aux dieux.
in Norman G. DAVIES. The Tomb of Nefer-
Hotep. Thèbes.
New-York, Metropolitan Museum ; s.d.
Photo Hachette.

_____ PAGE 38 _____

Statuette en bois représentant la Dame Toui.
XVIIIe dynastie.
Paris, Musée du Louvre/Lauros-Giraudon.

_____ PAGE 39 _____

Fragment de stèle de Nubien représentant
une femme. Photo J.D. LAJOUX.

Tombes des Nobles. Louxor. Fresque
de la tombe de Nakht. XVIIIe dynastie.
Edimédia/Photo TAGHER.

_____ PAGE 40 _____

Égyptien. Le défunt Queb suivi de sa mère
et de sa sœur joueuse de sistre.
Edimédia.

_____ PAGE 40/41 _____

Égypte. Fragment de fresque en grès
représentant des joueuses et des danseuses.
XVIIIe dynastie.
CdA/Photo J. GUILLOT/Edimédia.

Hatshepsut

_____ PAGE 42 _____

Détail du sphinx de la reine Hatshepsout
provenant du Deir el Bahari. Nouvel Empire.
XVIIIe dynastie.
Le Caire, Musée égyptien/G. Dagli Orti.

_____ PAGE 44 _____

Le peuple de Canaan. Thèbes. Bas relief de
la tombe de Horemheb. XIVe siècle av. J.C.
Leiden, Rijksmuseum.
MAGNUM/Photo Eric LESSING.

Couple seigneurial en vêtements d'apparat.
XVIIIe dynastie.
Paris, Musée du Louvre/Edimédia.

Statue de « la dame Henut Taoui ».
Nouvel Empire. Bois polychrome et or.
Coll. Gulbenkian/Edimédia.

_____ PAGE 45 _____

Tête de princesse amarnienne.
XVIIIe dynastie.
Paris, Musée du Louvre/Giraudon.

_____ PAGE 46 _____

Statuette de jeune Nubienne portant un vase
d'onguent. XVIIIe dynastie. H : 13 cm.
Gulbenkian Museum of Oriental Art and
Archaeology
Houston, Menil Foundation/Hickey and
Robertson.

_____ PAGE 47 _____

Fragment de fresque : délégués asiatiques
apportant des offrandes.
Londres, British Museum/Edimédia.

Photo J.D. LAJOUX.

_____ PAGE 48 _____

Osiris momiforme aux chairs noires des
Domaines des Morts. XIXe dynastie.
Paris, Musée du Louvre/Edimédia.

Fresque. Thèbes. Transport du blé en
Égypte. 1555-153 av. J.C.
Paris, Musée du Louvre/Snark/Edimédia.

Détail de fresque. Don de produits
d'Afrique tropicale. Vers 1400 av. J.C.
Londres, British Museum/Edimédia.

_____ PAGE 49 _____

Femme tenant un enfant. Calcaire.
XVIIIe dynastie.
Paris, Musée du Louvre.
MAGNUM/Photo Eric LESSING.

Pêche au filet. Relevé d'une peinture de
la tombe de Payry. in Nina M. DAVIES. op. cit.
Photo Hachette.

Deir el Medineh à Louxor.
Fresque de la tombe de Sennedjem :
travaux des champs.
Edimédia/photo TAGHER.

Page d'un livre des morts. Papyrus.
Berlin Est, Musée égyptien/Edimédia.

Deir el Medineh à Louxor. Fresque de la
tombe de Inerkha : prêtre officiant.
Edimédia/Photo TAGHER.

_____ PAGE 50 _____

Fresque représentant des ouvriers
construisant des temples. Thèbes.
Tombe de Neckmère.
MAGNUM/Photo René BURRI.

_____ PAGE 51 _____

Détail d'une fresque représentant la femme
de Sennufur apportant de la bière à son
mari. XIXe dynastie.
Photo Ronald SHERIDAN.

Tiye

_____ PAGE 52 _____

Buste de Tiyi. Vers 1370 av. J.C.
XVIIe dynastie.
Berlin, Musée égyptien/Edimédia.

_____ PAGE 54 _____

Égypte. Cuillère à fard représentant une silhouette de petite fille nue.
XVIIIe dynastie. Gournah. Bois. H : 22 cm.
Paris, Musée du Louvre/Photo R.M.N.

C.R. LEPSIUS (1842-1845).
XVIIIe dynastie. Construction des pyramides.
Edimédia.

Égypte. Louxor. La reine Tiyi.
Roger VIOLLET.

_____ PAGE 55 _____

Sarcophage de la dame Madja : la dame et son époux (détail). XVIIIe dynastie.
Paris, Musée du Louvre/Edimédia.

Amenophis III en sphinx. Faïence.
New-York, M.M.A./Edimédia.

Fresque. Détail d'une scène de banquet. En haut : les convives reçoivent des colliers et du vin. En bas : les femmes avec de lourdes perruques ornées de lotus.
Londres, British Museum/Edimédia.

Cuillère à fard représentant une nageuse.
XVIIIe dynastie. Bois et ivoire. L. : 32,5 cm.
Paris, Musée du Louvre/Edimédia.

_____ PAGE 56 _____

Fragment d'une fresque mortuaire : dame aux fleurs de lotus. XVIIIe dynastie.
Berlin, Musée égyptien/Edimédia.

Akhenaton. Statuette.
Berlin Ouest, Musée égyptien/Edimédia.

Égypte. Thèbes : Vallée des Nobles.
Tombe de Nakht. Joueuses d'instruments.
XVIIIe dynastie.
GIRAUDON.

_____ PAGE 57 _____

Fauteuil de Satamon (détail). XVIIIe dynastie.
Le Caire, Musée égyptien/GIRAUDON.

_____ PAGE 58 _____

Peinture murale : foulage du raisin.
(1580-1314 av. J.C.).
Égypte, Musée de Thèbes/Snark/Edimédia.

Akhenaton et Nefertiti. XVIIIe dynastie.
Calcaire peint.
Paris, Musée du Louvre/GIRAUDON.

_____ PAGE 59 _____

Nefertiti.
Berlin, Staatliche Museum/Snark/Edimédia.

_____ PAGE 60 _____

Scarabée du mariage d'Aménophie III et de Tiyi. XVIIIe dynastie.
Paris, Musée du Louvre/LAUROS GIRAUDON.

_____ PAGE 60/61 _____

Servantes. Thèbes. tombe de Rekhmirâ.
in Arpag MEKITARIAN. *La peinture égyptienne.*
1954/1978. Genève, éditions d'art Albert Skira.

The Candaces

_____ PAGE 64 _____

Gravure anonyme. Temple à Soleb, Nubie.
Coll. part. D.R.

_____ PAGE 64/65 _____

Paysage nubien.
Edimédia.

_____ PAGE 66 _____

Psaultier de Jean de Berry. XVe siècle.
Le prophète Isaïe.
Paris, B. N./Snark/Edimédia.

_____ PAGE 67 _____

Le pharaon Taharqa devant le faucon Hemen. XXVe dynastie.
Paris, Musée du Louvre/Edimédia.

_____ PAGE 68 _____

Art Koushite. Règne de Chabataka.
XXVe dynastie. Amenirdis présente les godets de vin à Amon (détail). Paroi de pierre sculptée de la chapelle d'Osiris Heqadjet.
Houston, Menil Foundation/Photo M. CARRIERI.

_____ PAGE 68/69 _____

Art koushite. XXVe dynastie.
Natakamani, Amanitore et le prince s'avance vers Apédémak aux quatre bras. Relief en grès du temple du Lion à Naga.
Houston, Menil Foundation. Photo M. CARRIERI.

_____ PAGE 69 _____

Art Koushite. Bracelets.
G. DAGLI ORTI.

_____ PAGE 70 _____

Stèle de Nubiens. Période intermédiaire.
Turin, Musée égyptien/G. DAGLI ORTI.

Buste d'Auguste.
Photo Ronald SHERIDAN.

_____ PAGE 71 _____

Tête de femme. Athènes. IIe siècle.
Marbre. Hauteur : 11,6 cm.
Athènes, Musée d'Agora.
Houston, Menil Foundation/Photo M. CARRIERI.

_____ PAGE 72 _____

Aquarelle de Edward LEAR.
Derr, Egypte. 1867.
Londres, Victoria and Albert Museum/Searight Coll. Edimédia.

_____ PAGE 73 _____

Statue en albâtre de l'adoratrice Amenardis, dite épouse du dieu (détail). Karnak. 700 av. J.C. Le Caire, Musée égyptien.
Paris, Dagli-Orti.

Makeda

_____ PAGE 74 _____

Peinture haïtienne de Camy ROCHER.
Celle dont je rêvais. 1980.
Paris, Coll. Max Fourny. D.R.

_____ PAGE 76 _____

Peinture d'église.
Légende de la reine de Saba (détail).
Paris, Musée de l'Homme.

Peinture populaire éthiopienne. Harpiste.
Coll. part.

_____ PAGE 78 _____

Vitrail de 1270. Salomon et la reine de Saba.
Strasbourg, Musée de l'Œuvre Notre Dame.
LAURO-GIRAUDON.

Peinture d'église.
Légende de la reine de Saba.
Paris, Musée de l'Homme.

Peintures populaires éthiopiennes. Musiciens.
Coll. part. D.R.

_____ PAGE 79 _____

Gravure anonyme XIXe siècle.
Coll. part. D.R.

_____ PAGE 80 _____

Peintures d'église.
Légende de la reine de Saba (détail).
Paris, Musée de l'Homme.

_____ PAGE 81 _____

Miniature du XVe siècle : vue de Jérusalem.
in *Voyage d'Outre Mer.*
Snark/Edimédia.

David et ses musiciens.
Manuscrit du VIIIe siècle.
Londres, British Museum/Edimédia.

Le roi Salomon. Lettrine de la Bible limousine.
XI-XIIe siècles.
Paris, Bibliothèque Mazarine.
CdA/Photo Guillot/Edimédia.

Gravure anonyme. Cavalier.
Paris, Sté de Géographie.

_____ PAGE 82/83 _____

Femme juive éthiopienne du village du Simiens, au nord du Gondar. 1983.
Photo Frédéric BRENNER. D.R.

Daurama

_____ PAGE 84 _____

Gravure aquatintée de CHOUBARD.
Jeune fille kirrée.
in Richard et John LANDER. *Voyage en Afrique.*
Coll. part. D.R.

_____ PAGE 85 _____

Gravure de HANHART. Berges du Tchad.
25 avril 1851.
in Henri BARTH. *Travels in North and Central Afrika. 1849655.* 1857.
Paris, Sté de Géographie.

_____ PAGE 86/87 _____
Gravure aquatintée de BONATTI.
Costumes en cafrerie. Coll. part.

_____ PAGE 88/89 _____
Peinture de HEUDEBERT.
Africains traversant un oued. H/t.
Paris, Musée des arts africains et océaniens.

_____ PAGE 89 _____
Peinture de Jeanne THIL. Africaine au bord de l'eau.
Paris, Musée des Arts africains et océaniens.

_____ PAGE 90 _____
Gravure. Scène de mariage.
Coll. part. D.R.

Lithographie de EMMINGER. Taepe, point de jonction du Benou et du Faro. 13 juin 1831.
in Henry BARTH. Voyages et découvertes de l'Afrique septentrionale et centrale. 1860.
Paris, Sté de Géographie.

Peinture de A. IACOVLEFF.
Molande, la Mangbetou.
in A. IACOVLEFF. Dessins et peintures d'Afrique exécutés au cours de l'expédition.
Paris, Sté de géographie.

_____ PAGE 91 _____
Gravure de FINDEN. Musiciens Mandara.
in Dixon DENHAM, Uhgh CHAPPERTON. Narratives of Travels and Discoveries in North and Central Africa in Years 1822-23-24. 1826. Paris, Sté de géographie.

_____ PAGE 92 _____
Gravure anonyme. Femme avec enfant et guerrier. Coll. part.

Lithographie de HANHART. Yo et le Komadugu. 17 septembre 1861.
in H. BARTH. op. cit.
Paris, Sté de géographie.

_____ PAGE 93 _____
Peinture de PARISON.
Femmes malgaches à leur toilette. H/t.
Paris, Musée des arts africains et océaniens.

_____ PAGE 94 _____
Gravure aquatintée anonyme.
Mandingue. Femme de Gazgut.
Coll. part. D.R.

_____ PAGE 95 _____
Peinture anonyme. Vue du village de Diodoumé sur le Sénégal en 1845.
Paris, Musée des arts africains et océaniens.

Gravure de FINDEM. Corps de garde. 1820.
in DENHAM, Hugh CHAPPERTON. op. cit.
Paris, Sté de géographie.

Gravure anonyme.
Manière de saluer le matin en Guinée.
Coll. part. D.R.

_____ PAGE 97 _____
Gravure anonyme.
Appartement du roi Salum.
in Frederic SHOBERL. Afrika : Senegal and Gambia. 1821.
Paris, Sté de géographie.

_____ PAGE 99 _____
Gravure de TARDIEU. Royaume de Ouida.
in Histoire générale des voyages. 1746.
Paris, Sté de géographie.

Yennenga

_____ PAGE 100 _____
Gravure de GAVEI. Femme (détail).
in G.P. LYON. A Narrative of Travels in Northern Africa in the Years 1818-1820. 1821.
Paris, Sté de géographie.

_____ PAGE 102 _____
Gravure aquatintée de GAUCI. Femmes Tibboo en costumes d'apparat.
in G.P. LYON. op. cit.
Paris, Sté de géographie.

Gravure de FINDEN.
Le Shary vu de Kussvy. 1826.
in DENHAM, Hugh CHAPPERTON. op. cit.
Paris, Sté de géographie.

Lithographie de HANHART. Le fleuve Niger. 26 juin 1864. in Henry BARTH. op. cit.
Paris, Sté de géographie.

Gravure de HEATH. Le voyage du capitaine Tuckey en Afrique. Village près d'Embomma.
in J.K. TUCKEY. The river Zaïre. 1816. 1818.
Paris, Sté de géographie.

_____ PAGE 103 _____
Gravure aquatintée anonyme. XVIIIe siècle.
Femme. Coll. part.

_____ PAGE 104 _____
Gravure de LAROQUE. Ganga magicien, médecin du Congo.
Coll. part. D.R.

Gravure anonyme. Vue de Criesala ou Soal.
in Frederic SHOBERL. op. cit.
Paris, Sté de géographie.

_____ PAGE 105 _____
Gravure de GAVEI. Femme (détail).
in G.P. LYON. op. cit.
Paris, Sté de géographie.

Personnage agenouillé. Sculpture Djenné.
H : 20,5 cm.
Coll. part. CdA/Photo HINOUS/Edimédia.

_____ PAGE 106/107 _____
Gravure de GAVEI. Négresse du Soudan.
in G.P. LYON. op. cit.
Paris, Sté de géographie.

_____ PAGE 107 _____
Gravure de HULLMANDEL.
Costumes de la Gambie (détail).
in T.E. BOWDICH. Excursions dans les îles de Madère et de Porto-Santo.
Paris, Sté de géographie.

_____ PAGE 108 _____
Gravure aquatintée d'après RAFFENEL.
Mandingue de Wollie en costume de guerre.
in Anne RAFFENEL. Voyage dans l'Afrique occidentale. 1843-1844.
Paris, Sté de géographie.

Gravure aquatintée de WOELFSLE. Horde d'éléphants au Tchad. 25 septembre 1851.
in Henry BARTH. op. cit.
Paris, Sté de géographie.

Gravure anonyme. Jeune femme.
Paris, Sté de géographie.

_____ PAGE 109 _____
Gravure aquatintée d'après RAFFENEL.
Femme Foulah du Cantorouch.
in A. RAFFENEL. op. cit.
Paris, Sté de géographie.

Gravure de GRANT. Baraza et la résidence du roi Mtesa.
in John SPEKE. Journal of the Discovery of the Source of the Nil. 1863.
Paris, Sté de géographie.

Gravure de FINDEN. Femme de Kanemboo, femme célibataire du Soudan.
in Dixon DENHAM, Hugh CHAPPERTON. op. cit.
Paris, Sté de géographie

_____ PAGE 110 _____
Gravure anonyme.
Le prince royal des Obbois. Coll. part.

_____ PAGE 110/111 _____
Gravure anonyme aquatintée.
Festin en Abyssinie. Coll. part.

_____ PAGE 111 _____
Gravure aquatintée de GAVEI. Costumes du Soudan. in G.P. LYON. op. cit.
Paris, Sté de géographie.

_____ PAGE 112 _____
Gravure anonyme.
Le chef de Kytchs et sa fille.
in Samuel WHITE BAKER. Découvertes des sources du Nil. 1868.
Paris, Sté de géographie.

_____ PAGE 112/113 _____
Gravure aquatintée. Mandingues.
in Giulio FERRARIO. op. cit.
New-York, Schomburg Center. Photo BEY.

_____ PAGE 113 _____
Gravure aquatintée de BIASIOLI.
Marche du roi du Bénin. Guinée. Ibid.
New-York, Schomburg Center. Photo BEY.

_____ PAGE 114 _____
Gravure d'Ambroise TARDIEU.
Diai-Boukari en costume de marabout du Foutatoro.
in G. MOLLIEN. Voyage aux sources du Sénégal et de la Gambie. 1820.
Paris, Sté de géographie.

_____ PAGE 114/115 _____
Lithographie de WOELFSLE. Amsäkai.
in Henry BARTH. op. cit.
Paris, Sté de géographie.

_____ PAGE 115 _____
Lithographie de LLANTA. Homme seul.
in D. BOILAT. Esquisses sénégalaises.
Paris, Sté de géographie.

Gravure de GAVEL. Femme (détail).
in G.P. LYON. op. cit.
Paris, Sté de géographie.

_____PAGE 116_____
Lithographie de LLANTA. Femme maure.
in D. BOILAT. op. cit.
Paris, Sté de géographie.

_____PAGE 117_____
Gravure de GAUCHARD. Bokké, femme du chef des Latoukias.
in Samuel WHITE BAKER. Découvertes des sources du Nil. 1868.
Paris, Sté de geographie.

Sogolon Konté

_____PAGE 118_____
Gravure coloriée.
Femme portant un enfant sur le dos.
in General History of Voyages by Land and Sea. 1747.
Gotha, Forschungs Bibliothek/Edimédia.

_____PAGE 120_____
Lithographie de HANHART. Tombouctou.
in Henry BARTH. op. cit.
Paris, Sté de géographie.

_____PAGE 120/121_____
Lithographie d'après RAFFENEL.
Griotte du pays de Bondou.
in Anne RAFFENEL. op. cit.
Paris, Sté de géographie.

_____PAGE 121_____
Ibid.
Paris, Sté de géographie.

_____PAGE 122_____
Gravure anonyme aquatintée. Guerrier.
in Frederic SHOBERL. op. cit.
Paris, Sté de géographie.

_____PAGE 122/123_____
Gravure aquarellée de SAINT SAUVEUR.
Femmes d'Issini pilant du riz.
Coll. part.

_____PAGE 123_____
Peinture de Juliette DELMAS. Têtes de femmes Tanla. H/t. 46×33 cm.
Paris, Musée des arts africains et océaniens.

Peinture de Jules Louis MORÉTEAU.
René Caillié recevant des offrandes à Brouel-Tagé. Fouta-Djalon (détail).
Paris, Musée des arts africains et océaniens.

_____PAGE 124_____
Gravure anonyme. Femme et enfant.
Coll. part. D.R.

Gravure de TARDIEU. Royaume du Kayor.
Nègre jouant du balafo. XVIIIe siècle.
in Histoire générale des voyages.
Paris, Sté de géographie.

_____PAGE 125_____
Scène de vie quotidienne.
in Giulio FERRARIO. op. cit.
New-York, Schomburg Center/Photo D. BEY.

_____PAGE 126_____
Dessin de A. IACOVLEFF.
Aboura, chef Ababova (Bambili).
in A. IACOVLEFF. op. cit.
Paris, Sté de géographie.

_____PAGE 127_____
Lithographie de LLANTA. Femme mandingue.
in D. BOILAT. op. cit.
Paris, Sté de géographie.

_____PAGE 128_____
Lithographie de LLANTA.
in D. BOILAT. op. cit.
Paris, Sté de géographie.

_____PAGE 129_____
Gravure coloriée. Village africain.
Coll. part.

Gravure. Femme peule.
Paris, Sté de géographie.

Amina Kulibali

_____PAGE 130_____
Gravure de LABROUSSE.
Négresse du royaume d'Aardra.
Coll. part. D.R.

_____PAGE 132_____
Gravure anonyme. Jeune fille.
in F. SHOBERL. op. cit.
Paris, Sté de géographie.

_____PAGE 132/133_____
Gravure anonyme Maure et Mauresque.
Ibid. Paris, Sté de géographie.

_____PAGE 134_____
Gravure de DUREAU. Lac et Pic d'Ougombo.
Afrique centrale.
Paris, Sté de géographie.

Gravure de JOURDAN. Habits des Noirs du Sénégal et du Cap Vert.
in J.B.L. DURAND. Atlas pour servir au voyage du Sénégal. 1802.
Paris, Sté de géographie.

_____PAGE 135_____
Lithographie de LLANTA. Femme Sarackoullée.
in D. BOILAT. op. cit.
Paris, Sté de géographie.

Gravure anonyme. Intérieur wolof.
Sénégal. XIXe siècle.
Paris, Sté de géographie.

Lithographie de LLANTA, Homme sérère.
in D. BOILAT. op. cit.
Paris, Sté de géographie.

_____PAGE 136_____
Gravure aquarellée de LAROQUE.
Prêtre sacrificateur du Sénégal.
Coll. part. D.R.

Gravure de HULK.
Habits des femmes de Kazegut.
in J.B.L. DURAND. op. cit.
Paris, Sté de géographie.

_____PAGE 137_____
Lithographie anonyme.
Scène de village à Fa-Doul.
Coll. part. D.R.

_____PAGE 133/139_____
Gravure aquarellée de HIMELY.
Village de Bel-Air sur la côte d'Afrique.
Coll. part. D.R.

_____PAGE 140/141_____
Gravure aquarellée de GAUCI.
Danse de femmes de Tripoli.
in G.P. LYON. op. cit.
Paris, Sté de géographie.

_____PAGE 142_____
Gravure de NOUSVEAUX. Costume iolof.
Sénégal. XIXe siècle.
Coll. part. D.R.

Gravure aquarellée de MAURAND.
Boukakila, roi de Sine.
Coll. part. D.R.

Gravure de PICART.
Cérémonie de l'accouchement. 1726.
Coll. part. D.R.

Gravure de PICART. L'accouchée va laver son enfant à la rivière. 1726.
Coll. part. D.R.

_____PAGE 143_____
Gravure aquarellée de LACHAUSSÉE.
Homme et femme du Loango.
Coll. part. D.R.

_____PAGE 144_____
Gravure de SAINT SAUVEUR.
Nègres et Négresses de Cazegut.
Coll. part. D.R.

_____PAGE 145_____
Gravure aquarellée de LACHAUSSÉE.
Homme et femme du Sénégal.
Coll. part. D.R.

_____PAGE 146_____
Peinture de FONTAINE.
Jeune fille peule.
Paris, Musée des arts africains et océaniens.

_____PAGE 147_____
Gravure. Femmes et enfant.
Paris, Sté de géographie.

Amina of Zaria

_____PAGE 148_____
Peinture de Fernand LANTOINE. (1876-1956).
Duco Sanghari, peuhl. H : 85 × 60,5 cm.
Paris, Musée des arts africains et océaniens.

_____PAGE 150_____
Gravure anonyme allemande.
Noirs du Niger. Coll. part. D.R.

Gravure XIXe siècle. Nigeria.
Caravane Haoussa en marche.
Paris, Sté de géographie.

Gravure de FINDEN. Vue de Bahir Mandia.
in DENHAM et CHAPPERTON. *op. cit.*
Paris, Sté de géographie

_____PAGE 151_____
Gravure anonyme coloriée. Africa.
Coll. part.

_____PAGE 152_____
Bénin. Tête de roi. Bronze.
Vienne, Museum für Volkerbunde.
Edimédia.

Peinture de Jeanne THIL.
Un sultan au Cameroun.
Paris, Musée des arts africains et océaniens.

Gravure anonyme aquarellée.
Nègre de Guinée.
Coll. part. D.R.

_____PAGE 153_____
Peinture de A. IACOVLEFF. Arima Bossonou.
Femme Kanembou (N'Guignin).
in A. IACOVLEFF. *op. cit.*
Paris, Sté de géographie.

_____PAGE 154_____
Peinture de A. IACOVLEFF.
Mahana, race Songhai (Ansonzo).
in A. IACOVLEFF. *op. cit.*
Paris, Sté de géographie.

Lithographie d'EMMINGER.
Das Ingalpam Bei Demmo. 31 décembre
1851. *in* H. BARTH. *op. cit.*
Paris, Sté de géographie.

_____PAGE 155_____
Gravure coloriée de CHOUBARD. Kano.
Coll. part. D.R.

_____PAGE 156/157_____
Peinture d'Achille de GARRY. (1891).
Place du marché à Brazaville.
H : 54 × 65 cm.
Paris, Musée des arts africains et océaniens.

_____PAGE 158_____
Lithographie de HANHART. Kano. Vue de la
montagne Bala. 10 février 1850.
in Henry BARTH. *op. cit.*
Paris, Sté de géographie.

Peinture de A. IACOVLEFF.
Paris, Sté de géographie.

_____PAGE 159_____
Gravure aquarellée de LACHAUSSÉE.
Homme et femme Anzikos.
Coll. part. D.R.

_____PAGE 160_____
Gravure aquarellée de PORTIER.
Négresse à la ville.
Coll. part. D.R.

_____PAGE 161_____
Photographie anonyme. Lac Tchad.
Danse de femmes Kanembou. 1924.
Paris, Sté de géographie.

Gravure de FINDEN.
Femme Shoa, royaume de Bornou.
in D. DENHAM and H. CLAPERTTON. *op. cit.*
Paris, Sté de géographie.

Heleni

_____PAGE 162_____
Gravure de ESTAQUIER. Abyssinienne.
Coll. part. D.R.

_____PAGE 164_____
Miniature du XIVe siècle. Prise de
Jérusalem par les Turcs (détail).
Paris, BN/Edimédia.

Caraques portugais et vue de Naples.
Snark/Edimédia.

Miniature du XIVe siècle. Expédition
entreprise par les Croisés (détail).
Paris, BN/Edimédia.

_____PAGE 165_____
Gravure aquarellée de LAROQUE.
Négresse Namaquas.
Coll. part. D.R.

_____PAGE 166/167_____
Carte anonyme du XVIIe siècle.
Coll. part. D.R.

_____PAGE 168_____
Gravure aquarellée de BLANCHARD.
Costume de Chendy et de Sennar.
Nubie supérieure.
Coll. part. D.R.

Dessin d'Emile BAYARD. Type bogos.
Coll. part. D.R.

_____PAGE 169_____
Peinture populaire éthiopienne.
Coll. part. D.R.

Lithographie de HANHART.
Le « Hammal ». XIXe siècle.
in Richard F. BURTON. *op. cit.*
Paris, Sté de géographie.

Lithographie de Vincent BROOKS.
Hommes du Shoa. *in* Lewis KRAPE. *op. cit.*
Paris, Sté de géographie.

_____PAGE 170_____
Gravure de MICHEL. Femme broyant du grain
pour faire de la farine.
in Jules BORELLI. *Ethiopie médionale.* 1878.
Paris, Sté de géographie.

Atlas de Lazaro Luis. XVIe siècle.
Monastère de Jeronimos.
Snark/Edimédia

_____PAGE 171_____
Gravure anonyme. Archère éthiopienne.
in William C. HARRIS. *Illustrations of
Highlands of Ethiopia.*
Paris, Sté de géographie.

_____PAGE 172_____
Gravure anonyme.
Femme d'Abyssinie.
Colle. part. D.R.

_____PAGE 173_____
Gravure anonyme. Coiffure de femme. Nadda.
in Jules BORELLI. *op. cit.*
Paris, Sté de géographie.

Ana de Sousa Nzinga

_____PAGE 174_____
Toile de Fernand LANTOINE (1876-1956).
Fatpi sénégalaise. H/t. 80×60 cm.
Paris, Musée des arts africains et océaniens.

_____PAGE 176/177_____
Gravure aquatintée de LACHAUSSÉE.
Homme et femme Taggaanl.
Coll. part. D.R.

_____PAGE 177_____
Carte de la Guinée. XVIIe siècle.
Coll. part. D.R.

Lithographie de MUTTENTHALER.
Caravane d'esclaves.
in BERNATZ. *Scènes in Ethiopia.* 1852.
New-York, Schomburg Center/Photo BEY.

_____PAGE 178_____
Gravure anonyme. Naissance d'un enfant.
Coll. part. D.R.

Gravure anonyme. Coiffure de femme de
Londas le long du Loajima. Les cheveux sont
disposés sur des morceaux de cuir de buffle.
in D. LIVINGSTONE. *Exploration dans l'intérieur
de l'Afrique australe et voyage à travers le
continent de St-Paul de Loanda à
l'embouchure du Zambèze de 1840 à 1856.*
1881. Paris, Sté de géographie.

Gravure anonyme. Coiffure de femme du
Londa, avec diadème de perles formé de
cuir et de poils tissés.
Ibid. Paris, Sté de géographie.

_____PAGE 179_____
Gravure aquatintée. Couple et enfant.
Coll. part. D.R.

_____PAGE 180/181_____
Gravure aquatintée de GALLINA. XVIIIe siècle.
Différentes façons de voyager en Afrique
au Congo.
Coll. part. D.R.

_____PAGE 182_____
Gravure anonyme.
Repas ordinaire de la reine Zingha.
in J.B. LABAT. *Relation historique de
l'Ethiopie occidentale.* 1732.
Paris, Sté de géographie.

Gravure aquatintée. Angola.
Coll. part. D.R.

Gravure anonyme. Audience du vice-roi
d'Angola à la reine Anna Zingha.
in J.B. LABAT. *op. cit.*
Paris, Sté de géographie

_____PAGE 183_____
Gravure anonyme. Manière de filer et de
tisser employée autrefois en Egypte.
in D. LIVINGSTONE. *op. cit.*
Paris, Sté de géographie.

_____PAGE 184_____
Gravures anonymes. Congo. XVIIe siècle.
Coll. part. D.R.

Gravure anonyme. Vénération de la reine Anna Zingha pour les ossements de son frère. *in* J.B. LABBAT. *op. cit.*
Paris, Sté de géographie.

──────── PAGE 185 ────────

Gravure aquatintée de ROUARGUE.
Madégasse. Mozambique et Cafre.
Coll. part. D.R.

──────── PAGE 186 ────────

Gravure anonyme.
Enterrement de la reine Zingha.
in J.B. LABAT. *op. cit.*
Paris, Sté de géographie.

Gravure anonyyme.
Jeunes filles du Huambo (Angola).
in Serge PINTO. *Comment j'ai traversé l'Afrique.* 1881.
Paris, Sté de géographie.

──────── PAGE 187 ────────

Gravure anonyme.
Hommes et femmes du Bihi.
in Serge PINTO. *op. cit.*
Paris, Sté de géographie.

Gravure anonyme. Hommes et femmes du Luchazes avec leurs ustensiles.
in Serge PINTO. *op. cit.*
Paris, Sté de géographie.

Gravure anonyme.
Femme labourant. XVIIe siècle.
in J.B. LABAT. *op. cit.*
Paris, Sté de géographie.

Mentowah

──────── PAGE 188 ────────

Peinture populaire éthiopienne.
Mentowab au Conseil.
Coll. part. D.R.

──────── PAGE 190/191 ────────

Gravure anonyme. L'obélisque d'Axoum.
Coll. part. D.R.

Lithographie de CORRENS.
Coutumes des femmes dankali.
in BERNAT. *op. cit.*
New-York, Schombourg Center/Photo BEY.

──────── PAGE 191 ────────

Gravure anonyme. Dame Ambara.
in Jules BORELLI. *op. cit.*
Paris, Sté de géographie.

Gravure anonyme.
Femme Oromo des Oborrah.
in Jules BORELLI. *op. cit.*
Paris, Sté de géographie.

──────── PAGE 192 ────────

Gravure anonyme.
Sahelé Salassé, chef du Choa.
in Théophile LEFEBVRE. *Voyage en Abyssinie de 1839 à 1843.*
Paris, Sté de géographie.

Gravure anonyme de colqual.
in FERRET, GALINIER. *Voyage en Abyssinie.* 1847.
Paris, Sté de géographie.

Gravure anonyme aquatintée.
Festin d'apparat en Abyssinie.
in Giulio FERRARIO. *op. cit.*
New-York, Schomburg Center/Photo BEY.

Gravure anonyme.
Coiffure de femme à Djimma.
in Jules BORELLI. *op. cit.*
Paris, Sté de géographie.

──────── PAGE 193 ────────

Gravure anonyme.
Grande dame de l'Abyssinie.
in FERRET, GALINIER. *op. cit.*
Paris, Sté de géographie.

──────── PAGE 194 ────────

Gravure anonyme. Palais du Ras à Gondor.
in FERRET, GALINIER. *op. cit.*
Paris, Sté de géographie.

Gravure aquatintée anonyme.
Roi d'Abyssinie. Coll. part. D.R.

──────── PAGE 195 ────────

Gravure aquatintée de MARTI.
Soldat Gala d'Abyssinie. Coll. part. D.R.

──────── PAGE 196 ────────

Gravure de MEUNIER. Gondar, le Gimp.
Coll. part. D.R.

Peinture populaire éthiopienne.
Coll. part. D.R.

──────── PAGE 196/197 ────────

Intérieur d'une maison d'Abyssinie.
in William C. HARRIS. *Illustration of Highlands of Ethiopia.*
New-York, Schombourg Center/Photo BEY.

──────── PAGE 197 ────────

Gravure. Scène de festin.
Paris, Sté de géographie.

Gravure anonyme. Intérieur d'une habitation.
in FERRET, GALINIER. *op. cit.*
Paris, Sté de géographie.

Gravure anonyme aquatintée. Groupe d'hommes.
Coll. part. D.R.

──────── PAGE 198 ────────

Gravure anonyme.
Jeune fille Amhara du Koat.
in Jules BORELLI. *op. cit..*
Paris, Sté de géographie.

Gravure anonyme.
Dame Amhara d'Ankobœr en deuil.
Ibid. Paris, Sté de géographie.

Gravure de HIMELY.
Vue des bords du Nil.
in Théophile LEFEBVRE. *op. cit.*
Paris, Sté de géographie.

──────── PAGE 199 ────────

Gravure. Ethiopie. Femmes Galla.
in W.C. HARRIS. *op. cit.*
New-York, Schomburg Center/Photo BEY.

──────── PAGE 200 ────────

Gravure de ROUARGUE.
Tabernacle du Saint Sépulcre.
in l'abbé GD, *Jérusalem et la Terre Sainte.*
Paris, Sté de géographie.

Lithographie de LOFFLEN
Le fleuve Hawash.
in BERNATX. *op. cit..*
New-York, Schombourg Center/Photo BEY.

──────── PAGE 201 ────────

Gravure de LACKER. Femme de Djimma vêtue de peaux tannées.
in Jules BORELLI. *op. cit.*
Paris, Sté de géographie.

LIST OF ILLUSTRATIONS: pp. 202-404

Beatrice Kimpa Vita

———— PAGE 202 ————

Dessin de Allard L'Olivier
Femme Mutusi. Droits réservés. Coll. part.

———— PAGE 204 ————

Vue du Rocher du Fétiche, près du fleuve
in Relation d'une expédition de 1818 pour reconnaître le Zaïre communément appelé Congo. 1818. Sté de Géographie.

Vue du marché du village près d'Embomma
Ibid.

Sénégambie
Commerce avec les Hollandais
in Dapper. Description de l'Afrique. 1686.
Sté de Géographie.

———— PAGE 205 ————

Gravure aquarellée
Congo. Femme de Malembe. Coll. part. D.R.

Homme de Loango
Coll. part. D.R.

Vie quotidienne
in Cardinal Acciaioli. Relatione del Viaggio del Regno di Congo. 1692.
Sté de Géographie.

———— PAGE 206 ————

Peinture de A. Iacovleff
Titi et Naranghé, filles du chef Eki Bondo (Haut Oulellé)
in A. Iacovleff. Dessins et peintures d'Afrique. 1927. Sté de Géographie.

———— PAGE 207 ————

Zaïre, Figure ancestrale. Sculpture.
Hauteur 79,5 cm.
Berlin. Museum für Vökerkunde.

Travaux des champs
in Cardinal Acciaioli. op. cit.
Sté de Géographie.

Bakongo. Fragments de fétiches. Hauteur 30,6 cm. Amsterdam. Koninkiij Institut Voor de Tropen.

———— PAGE 208 ————

Congo. Noirs au bois Mayombe.
in L. Degrampré. Voyage à la côte occidentale de l'Afrique 1786/87.
Sté de Géographie.

Peinture de A. Iacovleff
Ialingedé, race Mandja (Fort Lamy)
in A. Iacovleff, op. cit. Sté de Géographie.

Gravure. La danse.
in Capitaine Binsa. Du Niger au Golfe de Guinée, par le pays de Kong et le pays Mossi. 1892. Sté de Géographie.

———— PAGE 209 ————

Femmes du Congo
Gravure de Basioli
in Giulio Ferrario. Africa il costume antico e moderno. 1827.
New-York, Schomburg Center/Edimédia.

———— PAGE 210 ————

Gravure de Labrousse
Roi de Loango. Coll. part. D.R.

Gravure de Labrousse
Guerrier du Congo Coll. part. D.R.

Gravure aquatintée de Biasoli
in Giulio Ferrario. op. cit.
New-York, Schomburg Center/Edimédia.

———— PAGE 211 ————

Gravure de Laroque
Femme du Congo. Coll. part. D.R.

———— PAGE 212 ————

Gravure de Labrousse
Danseuse de Loango. Coll. part. D.R.

———— PAGE 213 ————

Un voyage au Congo
in Cardinal Acciaioli. op. cit.
Sté de Géographie.

Bansa ou S. Salvador, capitale du Congo
in M. de la Croix. *Relation Universelle de l'Afrique*. 1688. Sté de Géographie.

San Salvador
Coll. part. D.R.

─────── PAGE 214 ───────

in Cardinal ACCIAIOLI, *op. cit.*
Sté de Géographie

Gravure de BIASIOLI
Habitants de la rive méridionale
du Mafirmo. in Giulio FERRARIO. *op. cit.*
New-York, Schomburg Center/Edimédia.

─────── PAGE 215 ───────

Peinture de A. IACOVLEFF
Femme Banda avec son enfant
in A. IACOVLEFF. *op. cit.* Sté de Géographie.

─────── PAGE 216 ───────

Arquebusier Portugais. Sculpture. Bronze.
Courtesy of the Trustees of the British Museum. Londres.

Peinture de A. IACOVLEFF. Enfant
in A. IACOVLEFF. *op. cit.* Sté de Géographie.

─────── PAGE 217 ───────

Peinture de A. IACOVLEFF
Aoua, femme Banda
in A. IACOVLEFF. *op. cit.* Sté de Géographie.

─────── PAGE 218 ───────

Dessin de Allard L'OLIVIER
Femme Kivu. Droits Réservés. Coll. part.

─────── PAGE 219 ───────

Recueillement. in Cardinal ACCIAIOLI. *op. cit.*
Sté de Géographie.

Queen Poku

─────── PAGE 220 ───────

Gravure anonyme aquarellée. XVIIe siècle.
Femme et enfant de Guinée. Coll. part. D.R.

─────── PAGE 222 ───────

Gravure aquatintée de ROSSI
Une rue d'Adum, pays des Ashanti
in Guilio FERRARIO. *op. cit.*
New-York, Schomburg Center/Edimédia.

─────── PAGE 222/223 ───────

Gravure de LABROUSSE
Femme de la Côte d'Ivoire. Coll. part. D.R.

─────── PAGE 223 ───────

Poulie baoulé
Ex. collection Roudillon
C d A/Photo P. Hinous/Edimédia.

─────── PAGE 224 ───────

Côte d'Ivoire
Lagune Aby
Photo J.J. Cavreul/Musée de l'Homme.

A Fantee Belle d'Ashanti. in Bennet BURLEIGH
Two campaigns Madagascar and Ashantee. 1896. Sté de Géographie.

─────── PAGE 225 ───────

Femme et enfant
Sté de Géographie.

Maisons des nègres du Cap Mezmado
in Père LABAT. *Voyage du chevalier des Marchais en Guinée, isles voisines et à Cayenne*. 1731. Sté de Géographie.

Femme Akréennes
in Pauwel ENDHMEN ISERT. *Voyage en Guinée et dans les isles Caraïbes en Amérique*. 1783-85. Sté de Géographie.

─────── PAGE 226 ───────

Femmes puisant de l'eau au Comoë
in BINGER. *Du Niger au golf de Guinée*. 1892. Sté de Géographie.

Côte d'Ivoire
Poids en laiton baoulé
Photo Ponsard/Musée de l'Homme.

─────── PAGE 227 ───────

Gravure aquatintée
Cérémonie de mariage dans l'île St Louis
in Giulio FERRARIO. *op. cit.*
New-York, Schomburg Center/Edimédia.

Cabossier en habit d'Ashanti
in W. ADAMS. *The Modern Voyager and Traveller*. 1839.
New-York, Schomburg Center/Edimédia.

Instruments divers
in Frédéric SHOBERL. *Africa : Senegal and Gambia*. 1821. Sté de Géographie.

─────── PAGE 228 ───────

Côte d'Ivoire. Femme Baoulé. Sculpture.
CdA/Photo J. GUILLOT/Edimédia.

─────── PAGE 229 ───────

Village Igoumbié
in Paul du CHAILLU. *L'Afrique sauvage*. 1868. Sté de Géographie.

Aschango, route de Mayolo
in Paul du CHAILLU. *op. cit.*
Sté de Géographie.

Aschango, Yengué sur l'Ougoulor
Ibid.

Sogané Touré

─────── PAGE 230 ───────

Peinture de A. IACOVLEFF
Femme Banda et son enfant
in A. IACOVLEFF. *op. cit.*
Sté de Géographie.

─────── PAGE 232 ───────

Carte postale
Jeune fille de Tombouctou
Coll. part. D.R.

Type de jeunes femmes malinkés du Gadougou
in Gallieni. *Voyage au Soudan français*. 1879/1881/1885. Sté de Géographie.

Gravure
L'Intendante en chef du Fama Sansanding
Sté de Géographie.

─────── PAGE 233 ───────

Jeune fille de Tombouctou
in August WAHLEN. *Mœurs, usages et costumes de tous les peuples du monde*. 1843. Sté de Géographie.

Lithographie de EMMINGER
Bamba. 25 mai 1854. in Dr Henrich BARTH
Voyage en Afrique du Nord et Centrale 1849/1855. 1857. Sté de Géographie.

Journée d'une femme
Sté de Géographie.

Lithographie de EMMINGER
Paysage. Sté de Géographie.

─────── PAGE 234 ───────

Lithographie de LLANTA
Femme Wolof portant son enfant
In Abbé BOILAT. *Esquisses sénégalaises*. 1853. Sté de Géographie.

─────── PAGE 235 ───────

Groupe de lavandières à Sikasso. XIXe siècle.
Sté de Géographie.

Carte postale
Bamako. Moussô Bambara et son fils
Agence Edimédia.

─────── PAGE 236 ───────

Tombouctou
Coll. part. D.R.

─────── PAGE 237 ───────

Lithographie de LLANTA
Homme Bambara
In Abbé BOILAT. *op. cit.* Sté de Géographie.

Lithographie de EMMINGER
Tombouctou. 7 septembre 1853.
in Dr Henrich BARTHS. *op. cit.*
Sté de Géographie.

Jeune guerrier
Sté de Géographie.

Couple Bambara
Sté de Géographie.

Vue de Ségou
Sté de Géographie.

─────── PAGE 238 ───────

Femme de Tombouctou
Sté de Géographie.

─────── PAGE 239 ───────

Femme de Tombouctou
In René CAILLIÉ. *Journal d'un voyage à Tombouctou*. s.d. Sté de Géographie.

─────── PAGE 240 ───────

Gravure de FINDEN
in Dixon DEAMAM et Hufh CLAPPERTON
Narratives of Travels and Discoveries in Northen and Central Africa in Year 1822/23/24/1826. Sté de Géographie.

Dessin fait d'après les indications
du capitaine Gourand.
La capture de Samory. Coll. René Dazy.

───── PAGE 241 ─────

Femmes peules
in Gallieni. op. cit. Sté de Géographie.

The Story of Nandi

───── PAGE 242 ─────

Gravure de Choubard
Afrique du Sud. Femme cafre.
Voyage de Cowper Rose. 1828.
in Albert Montemont
Bibliothèque universelle des voyages. 1836
Sté de géographie.

───── PAGE 244 ─────

Traversée du fleuve
Sté de Géographie.

Portrait de femme
in Gustave Fritsch. Süd Afrika's. 1872.
Sté de Géographie.

───── PAGE 245 ─────

Gravure anonyme coloriée. XVIIIe siècle.
Femme cafre.
Coll. part. D.R.

───── PAGE 246 ─────

Village du Bari
Sté de géographie.

Ustensiles (détail)
in John Campbell. Travels in South Africa.
1815. Sté de géographie.

Gravure
Femmes africaines. Sté de Géographie.

───── PAGE 247 ─────

Femme cafre
in F. le Vaillant
Voyage dans l'intérieur de l'Afrique.
1783-84-85. Sté de géographie.

Gravure de Brandin
Zoulou. 1865. Coll. part. D.R.

───── PAGE 248 ─────

Dessin de Emile Bayard
Chasse à l'éléphant
in Livingstone. op. cit. Sté de géographie.

Cannibale
Sté de Géographie.

───── PAGE 249 ─────

Habitants de Bahahara
in Christian Frédéric Damberger. Travels in the
Interior Parts of Africa, From The Cape of
Good Hope to Morocco. 1801.
Sté de géographie.

───── PAGE 250 ─────

Lithographie.
Couple. Sté de Géographie.

───── PAGE 251 ─────

Scène villageoise. Dessin de Meyer
Sté de Géographie.

Gravure aquarellée de J. Laroque
Coll. part. D.R.

───── PAGE 252 ─────

Aquarelle. G.F. Angas.
Chef Zoulou en costume de guerre
1847. British Museum/Edimédia.

───── PAGE 253 ─────

Photographie anonyme. vers 1900.
Jeune fille. Sté de Géographie.

Dessin de Emile Bayard d'après Livingstone
Danses des landines ou des Cafres-Zoulous
à Shoupanga. Sté de Geographie.

Gravure
Grand conseil des Matelhapis
Sté de Géographie.

───── PAGE 254 ─────

Gravure de Poisson. Hottentots.
Coll. part. D.R.

Aquarelle. G.F. Angas
Deux guerriers zoulous
British Museum/Edimédia.

Photographie de G.T. Ferneyhough.
vers 1880. Sté de Géographie.

───── PAGE 255 ─────

Femme et enfant
Coll. part. D.R.

───── PAGE 256 ─────

En Cafrerie
in de la Croix. op. cit. Sté de Géographie.

───── PAGE 257 ─────

Lithographie de Meyn-Nuwër
in Robert Hartmann. Die Nigritier. 1876.
Sté de Géographie.

Tata Ajeché

───── PAGE 258 ─────

Gravure aquarellée de Labrousse
Amazone d'Afrique
Coll. de Selva/Tapabor.

───── PAGE 260 ─────

Scène d'esclavage
Sté de Géographie.

Dessin de Emile Bayard
Les esclaves de Coimbra
Sté de Géographie.

Les amazones du roi traversant un torrent
in Le journal des voyages. 1890.
Coll. Jean-Loup Charmet.

───── PAGE 261 ─────

Gravure de Laroque
Femme du Dahomey
Coll. part. D.R.

───── PAGE 262 ─────

Dessin de Emile Bayard
Jeune fille Soninké
Coll. part. D.R.

Image d'épinal
Amazones et guerriers (détail)
Paris, B.N.

───── PAGE 263 ─────

Gravure aquarellée de Laroque
Jeune prêtresse du Dahomey
Coll. part. D.R.

Féticheuses
in E. Chaudoin. Trois mois de captivité au
Dahomey. 1891. Sté de Géographie.

Compteuses de Cauris
in Alexandre L. d'Albeca. La France au Dahomey. 1895. Sté de Géographie.

───── PAGE 264 ─────

Image d'épinal
Amazones et guerriers (détail). op. cit.

Amazones (détail)
in A. Dalzei. De Geschiedenis Van Dahomey.
1800. Sté de Géographie.
Tofa et sa cour
in Alexandre d'Albeca. op. cit.
Sté de Géographie.

───── PAGE 265 ─────

Dessin de Emile Bayard
Femme pilant du sorgho
Sté de Géographie.

Gravure anonyme
Audience du Roi
in A. Dalzei. op. cit. Sté de Géographie.

───── PAGE 266 ─────

Dessin de Labrousse
Ministre et nègre du Royaume du Bénin
(détail). Coll. part. D.R.

Amazone
Sté de Géographie.

Dessin de Emile Bayard
Sté de Géographie.

───── PAGE 267 ─────

Dessin de Emile Bayard
Jeune fille de l'Hamazène
Coll. part. D.R.

───── PAGE 268 ─────

Amazone
in Richard F. Burton. King of Dahomey.
1864. Sté de Géographie.

Gravure aquarellée de Lachaussée
Hommes et femme du Dahomey. 1805.
Coll. part. D.R.

───── PAGE 269 ─────

Gravure aquarellée de Laroque
Femme et enfants de Ouidah
Coll. part. D.R.

Modjadji I

───── PAGE 270 ─────

Gravure de Choubard
Jeune fille Houranko
d'après Massard. in Voyage en Afrique
Coll. part. D.R.

PAGE 272

Homme et femme Hottentot
Coll. part. D.R.

Gravure de CLARK
Ville de Mashow, vue de l'Ouest
in Jean CAMPBELL. op. cit.
Sté de Géographie.

Paysage. in Dr WANGEMAMM
Ein Reife. Tahrin. Sud Africa. 1868.
Sté de Géographie.

PAGE 273

Gravure aquatintée de FUMAGALI
Grands mamaques Hottentots
in Giulio FERRARIO. op. cit.
New-York, Schomburg Center/Edimédia.

PAGE 274

Jeune femme dansant
Sté de Géographie.

Danse Hottentot
Sté de Géographie.

PAGE 275

La faiseuse de pluie
in John CAMPBELL. op. cit.
Sté de Géographie.
Maisons et cours à Kurreechane.
Ibid.

PAGE 276

Village
Sté de Géographie.

Cérémonie religieuse des peuples de
Guinée pour la circoncision d'un enfant
Coll. part. D.R.

PAGE 277

Cérémonie pour faire tomber la pluie
Coll. part. D.R.

Gnou
Coll. part. D.R.

Lithographie de Paul PETIT
Antilope bubale
Coll. part. D.R.

PAGE 278

Dessin de Emile BAYARD d'après LIVINGSTONE
Danse des Baloudas au clair de lune
Sté de Géographie.

Gravure. 1879.
Coiffures de riverains du Zambèze
in Le Tour du Monde. Coll. part. D.R.

PAGE 279

Gravure. 1879.
Cérémonie du mariage chez les Zoulous. La
fiancée est amenée au Kraal de son époux
Coll. Viollet.

PAGE 280

Invocation à la pluie
Coll. part. D.R.

PAGE 281

Jeune roi des Marootze
in John CAMPBELL. op. cit.
Sté de Géographie.

Portrait
in Robert HARTMANN. op. cit.
Sté de Géographie.

Roi de Chumbiri
Sté de Géographie. Afrique du Sud. Hottentots
Sté de Géographie.

PAGE 282/283

Dessin de Émile BAYARD
Femmes Boshmènes faisant provision d'eau
dans des œufs d'autruche
in Dr LIVINGSTON. op. cit. Sté de Géographie.

Ranavalona I

PAGE 284

Gravure de H. LINTON
Coll. part. D.R.

PAGE 286

Ancien palais de la Reine à Tananarive
in Friedrich HAHN. Africa. 1901.
Coll. part/Agence Edimédia

PAGE 286/287

Une rue de Tananarive
in Le Petit Journal du 27/10/1895
Agence Edimédia.

PAGE 287

Danse guerrière des Sakalaves
in James SIBREE. Madagascar et ses habitants
Sté de Géographie.

PAGE 288

Femme et enfant
in Louis CATAT. Voyage à Madagascar.
1889/1890. Coll. part. D.R.

Imérina
Photo J. Millot/Musée de l'Homme.

PAGE 289

Binao, reine de Sakalaves
in Victor TISSOT. L'Afrique pittoresque. 1888.
Sté de Géographie.

Tananarive, le Palais de la reine
in James SIBREE. op. cit.
Sté de Géographie.

La maison du chef à Ambatomanga
Ibid.

PAGE 290

Photographie anonyme
Femme malgache avec ses enfants
1863. Sté de Géographie.

Photo IRRIBE
Jeunes femmes de Tananarive. vers 1880.
Sté de Géographie.

Groupe de femmes malgaches
in Louis CATAT. op. cit. Coll. part.

Photographie. Femmes de Madagascar
Sté de Géographie.

PAGE 291

Chasse aux bœufs sauvages
in James SIBREE. op. cit.
Sté de Géographie.

PAGE 292

Femme antimérina
in Louis CATAT. op. cit.
Sté de Géographie.

Incendie d'un village de Chahary
in G. LAFOND. Voyages autour du monde.
1844. Sté de Géographie.

Esclave vannant du riz
in Louis CATAT. op. cit. Coll. part.

Peinture de Henry PONTOY.
Village de Macenta. Guinée.
1947. 64 × 80 cm.
Paris, Musée des Arts Africains et Océaniens.

PAGE 294

Aquarelle de Jean LABORDE-HARRISSON
Coiffure malgache. 20 × 12,5 cm.
Droits Réservés.
Paris, Musée des Arts Africains et Océaniens.

Aquarelle de Jean LABORDE-HARRISSON
MAAO. 20 × 12,5 cm. Droits Réservés.
Paris, Musée des Arts Africains et Océaniens.

Peinture Jean LABORDE-HARRISSON
Brodeuse Hova. 20 × 12,5 cm.
Paris, Musée des Arts Africains et Océaniens.

Pastel de Willy WORMS
Jeune Hova. 1925. 31 × 22 cm
Paris, Musée des Arts Africains et Océaniens.

PAGE 295

Aquarelle de Jean LABORDE-HARRISSON
Coiffure malgache. 20 × 12,5 cm
Droits Réservés.
Paris, Musée des Arts Africains et Océaniens.

N'Daté Yalla

PAGE 296

Lithographie de LLANTA
Reine du Walo, Woloffe
in l'Abbé P.D. BOILAT, op. cit.
Sté de Géographie.

PAGE 298

Gravure de DESCAULTRE. Pont suspendu
Sté de Géographie.

Lithographie de Mauresque Braknas
in l'Abbé BOILAT. op. cit.
Sté de Géographie.

Convoi d'esclaves
Sté de Géographie.

Femme de St Louis
in Frédéric SHOBERL. op. cit.
Sté de Géographie.

PAGE 299
Lithographie de LLANTA
Signare. *in* l'Abbé BOILAT. *op. cit.*
Sté de Géographie.

PAGE 300
Lithographie de LLANTA
Thiédo. *in* l'Abbé BOILAT. *op. cit.*
Sté de Géographie.

Razzia maure sur le fleuve
in J.B.L. DURAND. *Atlas pour servir au voyage du Sénégal.* 1802. Sté de Géographie.

PAGE 301
Lithographie de LLANTA
Femmes Sérères
in l'Abbé BOILAT, *op. cit.* Sté de Géographie.

PAGE 302
L'île de Gorée
in Frédéric SHOBERL. *op. cit.*
Sté de Géographie.

Convoi d'esclaves
Ibid.

Vaisseau négrier
Sté de Géographie.

PAGE 303
Femme des environs de St Louis
in Anne RAFFENEL. *Voyage dans l'Afrique occidentale.* 1843-44. Sté de Géographie.

Maures attaquant un village
in Frédéric SHOBERL. *op. cit.*
Sté de Géographie.

PAGE 304
Femme mauresque
Coll. part. D.R.

Femme maure des bords du Sénégal
in Anne RAFFENEL. *op. cit.*
Sté de Géographie.

PAGE 305
Lithographie de LLANTA
Femme Bambara
in l'Abbé BOILAT. *op. cit.* Sté de Géographie.

PAGE 306
Gravure aquatintée
Vie quotidienne au Sénégal
in Guilio FERRARIO. *op. cit.*
New-York, Schomburg Center/Edimédia.

Lithographie de LLANTA
Mari de la Reine du Walo, Wolof
in l'Abbé BOILAT. *op. cit.* Sté de Géographie.

PAGE 307
Gravure anonyme. XIXe siècle.
Négresse pilant la farine pour faire le couscoussou. *in Le Monde Illustré.*
Coll. part.

Danses
in Anne RAFFENEL. *Nouveaux voyages dans le pays des nègres.* 1856.
Sté de Géographie.

Photographie de M. BONNEVIDE. 1885.
Femme Peule allaitant. Sté de Géographie.

Nongquwuse

PAGE 308
Gravure de CHOUBARD.
Femme du Cap de Bonne Espérance
in Voyage autour du Monde. Coll. part.

PAGE 310/311
Scène de vie quotidienne
in Gustave FRITSCH. *Die Zingeborenen Süd. Atlas.* 1872. Sté de Géographie.

PAGE 310
Urban
Sté de Géographie.

PAGE 311
Convoi de Boers
in John CAMPBELL. *op. cit.* Sté de Géographie.

PAGE 312
Dessin de A. de BAR
Musiciens du bord du Zambèze jouant du marimba. *in* David LIVINGSTONE.
Explorations du Zambèze. 1858/1864.
Sté de Géographie.

Gravure de MILBERT
Paysage. Coll. part. D.R.

Intérieur de case royale
in John CAMPBELL. *op. cit.*
Sté de Géographie.

Le gué de l'Orange
Coll. part. D.R.

PAGE 313
Gravure aquarellée
Lionnes de la cour du Roi Shinte
in Voyage du Dr LIVINGSTONE. Coll. part.

PAGE 314
Hottentot. Voyage de Burchell (1810/1815)
in Albert MONTEMONT. *op. cit.*
Sté de Géographie.

Scène de village
Sté de Géographie.

Scène de guerre
in Gustave FRITSCH. *op. cit.*
Sté de Géographie.

PAGE 315
Femme Hottentot avec son enfant.
Sté de Géographie.

Arrivée du Gouverneur Van Riebrek en 1652
in John NOBLE. *History, Productions And Ressources Of The Cape of Good Hope.* 1886.
Sté de Géographie.

PAGE 316
Damberger en Afrique du Sud
in C.F. DAMBERGER. *op. cit.* Sté de Géographie.

Yassakoua
Sté de Géographie.

PAGE 317
Femme Cafre
in Le magasin d'illustrations. 1859. Coll. part.

PAGE 318
Façon africaine de voyager
in W. ADAMS. *op. cit.*
New-York, Schomburg Center/Edimédia.

PAGE 319
Gravure aquarellée
Dessin de Emile BAYARD
Homme et femme du Manyéma
Coll. part. D.R.

Sarraounia

PAGE 320
Peinture de A. IACOVLEFF
Femme Haoussa (Zinder-Niger)
in A. IACOVLEFF. *op. cit.* Sté de Géographie.

PAGE 322
Les rives du Lac Tchad
in Henrich BARTH. *op. cit.* Sté de Géographie.

PAGE 323
Arrivée d'un prisonnier Mandjia
in C. MAISTRE. *A travers l'Afrique centrale du Congo au Niger.* 1892/1893.
Sté de Géographie.

Capitaine Voulet
Coll. part.

Lieutenant Chanoine
Coll. part.

PAGE 324
Touareg de la région Mourzouk
Voyage de Denham et Clapperton (1822)
in Albert MONTÉMONT. *op. cit.*
Sté de Géographie.

Peinture de A. IACOVLEFF
Magemma, Chei des cavaliers du Sultan Serky Mussa de Maradi. Territoire du Niger
in A. IACOVLEFF. *op. cit.* Sté de Géographie.

Cavaliers Djerna (Niamey - Niger)
ibid.

PAGE 325
Femme arabe Ouled Gopo avec son enfant (Fort Lamy). *Ibid.*

PAGE 326
Les photos des pages 326, 327, 329, 330, 331, 333 sont tirées du film de Melmed HONDO, *Sarraounia,* Production "Soleil Ô".

PAGE 327
Dessin de Emile BAYARD
Jeune fille Peule des environs de Ségou.
Coll. part. D.R.

PAGE 328
Carte postale
Niger. Zinder. Porte de Berny. vers 1900.
Sté de Géographie.

PAGE 330
Peinture de A. IACOVLEFF
Barma Mata, Sultan de Zinder
in A. IACOVLEFF.

Songhai. Niger. Amsäkai.
in Henrich Barth. *op. cit.* Sté de Géographie.

PAGE 332

Photo de Joseph Thomson
Sultanat de Sokoto (Nigéria). vers 1880.
Sté de Géographie.

Peinture de A. Iacovleff. Zinder.
in A. Iacovleff. *op. cit.* Sté de Géographie.

PAGE 334

Dessin de Emile Bayard
Griot de Nianttanso. Coll. Part.

PAGE 335

Photographie par Bernard et T. Monod
Femme du Niger. Mission Angérias. Draper.
1927/28 : Sahara algérien, Niger, Soudan et Sénégal. Sté de Géographie.

Photographie anonyme
Au bord du Tchad, femme Tébou et Kanembou. 1924. Sté de Géographie.

Peinture de A. Iacovleff
Fillette Bornou (Fort Lamy)
in A. Iacovleff. *op. cit.* Sté de Géographie.

The Story of Naga

PAGE 336

Dahoméens exhibés ou jardin d'acclimatation à Paris
in Le Petit Journal du 28/02/1891
Agence Edimédia.

PAGE 338/339

Béhanzin, Roi du Dahomey
Coll. René Dazy/Edimédia.

PAGE 339

Lithographie de Last. Paysage.
in J.S.G. Grambers. *Schetsen Van Africa's West Kust.* 1861. Sté de Géographie.

Les amazones à l'exercice
in Edouard Foa. *Le Dahomey.* 1895.
Sté de Géographie.

Béhanzin
in E. Chaudoin. *op. cit.*
Sté de Géographie.

Bivouac de la colonne Dodds sur la place d'Abomey. 1892.
in Alexandre L. d'Albeca. *op. cit.*
Sté de Géographie.

PAGE 340

Gravure aquatintée de Lancon
Habitants de l'île du Cap-Vert
in Giulio Ferrario. *op. cit.*
New-York, Schomburg Center/Edimédia.

PAGE 341

Gravure de Perrichon
Cour intérieur d'une habitation dahoméenne. *in* Edouard Foa. *op. cit.*
Sté de Géographie.

Fabrication de l'huile de Palme
in Alexandre L. d'Albeca. *op. cit.*
Sté de Géographie.

PAGE 342

Gravure de Fredillo
Amazones du Dahomey
in Petrus Durel. *La femme dans les colonies françaises.* 1848. Coll. Jean-Loup Charmet.

PAGE 343

Marché au Dahomey
in Edouard Foa. *op. cit.* Sté de Géographie.

Dahoméenne
in E. Chaudoin. *op. cit.* Sté de Géographie

Sur la place d'Abomey
Sté de Géographie.

Mitha, la plus illustre amazone du Roi Moleki. Sté de Géographie.

PAGE 344

Amazones
in E. Chaudoin. *op. cit.* Sté de Géographie.

PAGE 345

Prise de Kana au Dahomey
in Le Petit Journal du 19/11/1892
Agence Edimedia.

PAGE 346

Gravure de Tinavre
Bataille de Dogba. Sté de Géographie.

Retour à Whydah d'un cabécère venant de rendre hommage au Roi, à Abomey
in E. Chaudoin. *op. cit.* Sté de Géographie.

Le bombardement de la côte du Dahomey
Sté de Géographie.

Chef d'escorte
in E. Chaudoin. *op. cit.* Sté de Géographie.

PAGE 347

Amazones archères combattant
in E. Chaudoin. *op. cit.* Sté de Géographie.

PAGE 348

Gravure de Lachaussée
Amazone d'Afrique. Coll. part. D.R.

PAGE 349

Femme broyant du grain
in David et Charles Livingstone. *op. cit.*
Sté de Géographie.

Danse des féticheuses
in E. Chaudoin. *op. cit.* Sté de Géographie.

Femmes du Dahomey
in Henri Stanley. *A travers le continent mystérieux.* 1879. Sté de Géographie.

Manta Tisi

PAGE 350

Mahooto, reine de Lattakoo en tenue d'apparat. *in* John Campbell. *op. cit.*
Sté de Géographie.

PAGE 352

Lithographie de Paul Petit
Cannibale Béchuana. Coll. part.

Rassemblement de Béchuana
Sté de Géographie.

Guerrier Cafre.
Voyage de Cowper Rose (1828)
in Albert Montemont. *cp. cit.*
Sté de Géographie.

PAGE 353

Hottentote. Voyage de Burchelle (1810/15)
in Albert Montémont. *cp. cit.*
Sté de Géographie.

PAGE 354

Costume féminin pour a fête de la circoncision. *in* W. Adams. *op. cit.*
New-York, Schomburg Center/Edimédia.

PAGE 355

Plettenberg Bay. *in Three Months' Visitation* by the Bishop of Capetown. 1855.
Sté de Géographie.

Barque sur le fleuve Zcmbèze
in Livingstone. *op. cit.* Sté de Géographie.

PAGE 356

Le siège de Butha-Buthé
in Dr Wangermann. *op. cit.*
Sté de Géographie.

Cafres
Sté de Géographie.

Zoulou
Coll. Viollet.

PAGE 357

Femme Namaquoise
in F. Le Vaillant. *op. cit.* Sté de Géographie.

Convoi
Coll. Viollet.

PAGE 358

Guerrier Cafre
in Auguste Wahlen. *Mœurs, usages et costumes de tous les peuples du monde.* 1843.
Sté de Géographie.

Lithographie de Paul Petit
Cavalier. Coll. part. D.R.

Liqueling, régent de la Nation Marrotze
in John Campbell. *op. cit.* Sté de Géographie.

Gravure coloriée
Hottentots en voyage. Coll. part. D.R.

PAGE 359

Lithographie
Frontispice de l'Afrique. Coll. part. D.R.

PAGE 360/361

Gravure de Gallina
Types de Cafres appartenant aux Ngouis
in Giulio Ferrario. *op. cit.*
New-York, Schomburg Center.

Taitu Bethel

PAGE 362
Carte postale. 1900. Aquarellée.
Taytou, reine d'Éthiopie. Sté de Géographie.

PAGE 364
Photographie
Le fils du Négus Ménélik II. 1889.
Sté de Géographie.

Résidence de l'empereur à Gondar
Coll. part. D.R.

PAGE 365
Gravure de Eloevy
Woïzero Taytou. 1889.
in Jules Borelli. Éthiopie méridionale. 1878.
Sté de Géographie.

Carte postale. 1900
Ménélik II, empereur d'Éthiopie en 1889
in Jules Borelli. op. cit. Sté de Géographie.

PAGE 366
Jeune fille du Mindjar
Ibid.

Dessin de Emile Boyard
Femme broyant le grain. Coll. part. D.R.

PAGE 367
Femme de Djiren vêtue de peaux tannées
in Jules Borelli. op. cit. Sté de Géographie.

Lithographie de Hanhart
Costumes du Harar (détail)
in Richard F. Burton
East Africa and Exploration of Harar. 1856.
Sté de Géographie.

PAGE 368
Gravure anonyme
Vue d'ensemble du percement du canal de Suez (1859/1869)
Coll. part./Edimédia.

Lithographie de Vincent Brooks
Femmes du Shoa. in Lewis Krapf.
Travels in Eastern Africa. 1860.
Sté de Géographie.

Conférence internationale de Berlin.
Nov. 1884/Fév. 1885.
Paris, Arch. Nat./Edimédia.

PAGE 369
Coiffure de femme à Omo
in Jules Borelli. op. cit.
Sté de Géographie.

Dessin de M. Vierge
L'esclave à Zanzibar
in Le Monde Illustré. Coll. part.

PAGE 370
L'empereur Ménélik en costume de guerre
15 fév. 1896. Agence Edimédia.

Groupes de jeunes esclaves
in Le Monde illustré. Coll. part.

Dessin de Emile Bayard
Le negus Théodore II en tenue d'audience
Coll. part.

PAGE 371
Femme et enfant Danakil
in Jules Borelli. op. cit. Sté de Géographie.

PAGE 372
Peinture populaire éthiopienne
Coll. part. D.R.

PAGE 373
Ibid.

PAGE 374
Gravure aquarellée de Saunier. Abyssinie.
Coll. part.

PAGE 375
Mise en liberté de prisonniers italiens après la guerre d'Éthiopie
in Le Petit Journal du 29/11/1896
Agence Edimédia.

Arrivée à Djibouti d'un convoi de prisonniers italiens rendus par Ménélik. 1896.
Agence Edimédia.

Sceau de Ménélik II, Empereur d'Éthiopie (1889-1913). in Jules Borelli. op. cit.
Sté de Géographie.

PAGE 376
Lithographie de Vincent Brooks
La rivière Hawash. in Lewis Krapf. op. cit.
Sté de Géographie.

Lithographie de Hanhart
Vue de Harar
in Richard Burton. op. cit.
Sté de Géographie.

Photographie de M. Michel. 1897.
Famille galla du Harar
in Mission de Bouchamps à Djibouti et en Éthiopie. Sté de Géographie.

PAGE 377
Gravure de R. Lacker
Femme du Koullo. in Jules Borelli. op. cit.
Sté de Géographie.

Ranavalona III

PAGE 378
Gravure aquarellée
La reine Ranavalona Marijaka III
Sté de Géographie.

PAGE 380
Peinture de A. Iacovleff
Famille malgache (Tananarive) (détail)
in A. Iacovleff. op. cit. Sté de Géographie.

Le Roi Radama II
in James Sibree. op. cit. Sté de Géographie.

Photographie de Désiré Roblet, vers 1860.
Jeune fille Hova en deuil
Sté de Géographie.

PAGE 381
Le Palais de la Reine à Tananarive
in Le Petit Journal du 20/10/1897
Agence Edimédia.

Guerrier
in Bennet Burleigh. op. cit.
Sté de Géographie.

L'arbre des Voyageurs
in James Sibree. op. cit. Sté de Géographie.

PAGE 382
Photographie anonyme. Fin XIXe siècle
Femme Sakalave. Sté de Géographie.

PAGE 382/383
Femme Beninka
Sté de Géographie.

PAGE 383
Peinture de A. Iacovleff
Tananarive, vue du Palais de la Reine (Détail)
in A. Iacovleff. op. cit. Sté de Géographie.

PAGE 384
Couple
in Bennet Burleigh. op. cit.
Sté de Géographie.

Pont sur la rivière des fleurs jaunes
in Charles Buet. Madagascar. 1883.
Sté de Géographie.

Peinture de A. Iacovleff
Musiciens malgaches (Tananarive)
In A. Iacovleff. op. cit. Sté de Géographie.

PAGE 385
Palais Royal et Palais de Justice
in Bennet Burleigh. op. cit.
Sté de Géographie.

Photographie M. Macquet. vers 1880.
Ambohimanga, la ville sainte
Sté de Géographie.

PAGE 386/387
Expédition militaire française à Madagascar
Prise d'un camp Hova
in Le Petit Journal du 2/6/1895
Agence Edimédia.

PAGE 387
Défaite des Sakalaves
in Le Petit Journal du 3/4/1898
Agence Edimédia.

PAGE 388
Bœufs sauvages
Coll. part.

Le Filanzana. Manière malgache de voyager
in Etienne de Flacourt. L'histoire de Madagascar. 1658. Paris, Bibliothèque Nationale.

Photographie de Julien Laferrière
Porteurs de Filanzona. vers 1860.
Sté de Géographie.

PAGE 389
A Madagascar, les princesses royales prêchent la guerre Sainte contre les Français
in Le Petit Journal du 9/12/1894
Agence Edimédia.

PAGE 390
Carte postale. La Martinique. 1904
Le Roi Béhanzin, du Dahomey, et sa famille, en exil. Coll. part./Edimédia.

Fougère arborescente
in James SIBREE. *op. cit.* Sté de Géographie.

PAGE 391
Ranavalona III à Alger, en exil
in Le Petit Journal de 1899
Snark/Edimédia.

PAGE 392
Peinture de A. IACOVLEFF
Les hauts plateaux de Madagascar
in A. IACOVLEFF. *op. cit.* Sté de Géographie.

PAGE 393
Hovas
in James SIBREE. *op. cit.* Sté de Géographie.

Photographie de L.D.M. CATAT
Femme de la Côte Sud-Est et son bébé. 1891. Sté de Géographie.

Le bain
in Bennet BURLEIGH. *op. cit.*
Sté de Géographie.

Mamochisane

PAGE 394
Norman H. HARDY
Pondo girl. Droits Réservés. Coll. part.

PAGE 396
Photographie de G.T. FERNEYHOUGH
Groupe de femmes mariées. vers 1880.
Sté de Géographie.

Lithographie de LAST
in J.S.G. GRAMBERGS. *op. cit.*
Sté de Géographie.

Photographie de G.T. FERNEYHOUGH
Enfant hottentot. 1888.
Sté de Géographie.

PAGE 397
A. RIXENS
Couple. D.R. Coll. part.

PAGE 398
Guerrier hottentot
Coll. part.

Scène de chasse
in LIVINGSTONE. *op. cit.* Sté de Géographie.
Femme à la houe
Coll. part. D.R.

PAGE 399
Cafres
Coll. part. D.R.

Gravure anonyme.
Sté de Géographie.

Dessin de A. de BAR d'après LIVINGSTONE
Femme des bords du Zambèze défrichant à la houe. vers 1850.
in David et Charles LIVINGSTONE. *op. cit.*
Sté de Géographie.

PAGE 400
Gravure de Roberto FRESHI
Col. part.

Chute du Zambèze
Sté de Géographie.

Chute du Zambèze (détail)
Sté de Géographie.

PAGE 401
Dame de qualité
in W. ADAMS. *op. cit.*
New-York, Schomburg Center/Edimédia.

PAGE 402
Famille.
Sté de Géographie.

PAGE 403
Femmes et enfant
in J.S.G. GRAMBERS. *op. cit.*
Sté de Géographie.

Les photographies à la Société de Géographie ont été réalisées par Anne BRUEL et André BOULZE de l'Agence Edimédia. Celles du Schomburg Center ont été réalisées par Davoud BEY.

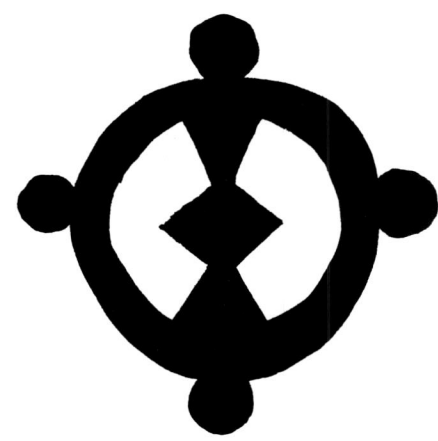

Once upon a time, between t
stretches of the high plateaus
under the sun, a tribe witho
born from the coming togethe
different directions who said t
North,…we are fleeing the Sou
and West: let us make one peo
Unfortunately, other tribes in
same way; and in vain did th
place, a mark on the ground,
they could put up borders and
Once upon a time, between t
stretches of the high plateaus
under the sun, a tribe witho